ENGLISH LANGUAGE CRITICISM ON THE FOREIGN NOVEL

ENGLISH LANGUAGE CRITICISM ON THE FOREIGN NOVEL: 1965-1975

COMPILED BY

HARRIET SEMMES ALEXANDER

SWALLOW PRESS/OHIO UNIVERSITY PRESS
ATHENS

Swallow Press/Ohio University Press books are printed on
acid-free paper. ∞

Library of Congress Cataloging-in-Publication Data

Alexander, Harriet Semmes, 1949–
    English language criticism on the foreign novel / compiled by
Harriet Semmes Alexander.
      p.   cm.
    Contents: [1] 1965–1975.
    Includes index.
    ISBN 0-8040-0907-4 (v. 1)
    1. Fiction—History and criticism—Bibliography.   I. Title.
Z5916.A39   1989
[PN3335]
016.8093—dc20   89-4430
                                         CIP

PREFACE

*E*nglish Language Criticism on the Foreign Novel is part of a two-volume work designed to list criticism written from 1965 to 1985 on foreign novels. The present volume lists criticism published between 1965 and 1975. The second volume will cover criticism written between 1976 and 1985.

'Foreign novel' in the sense used throughout the work includes novels and other longer works of fiction, such as novellas and novellen, produced in all countries other than the United States and the United Kingdom. Fictional works by authors living in Canada, Australia, New Zealand and the countries of Africa, the Middle East, Asia, Europe and Latin America are covered regardless of language of writing. Writers living in the United States and the United Kingdom are covered if they wrote in a foreign language (e.g., Samuel Beckett, Isaac Bashevis Singer) or wrote out of their experiences in a foreign country before emigrating from it (e.g., Doris Lessing, V. S. Naipaul.) Coverage ranges in time of writing from Apuleius' *Metamorphosis* (1st century, A. D.) and Murasaki's *Tale of Genji* (11th century) to Garcia Marquez' *100 Years of Solitude* (1967) and Margaret Atwood's *Surfacing* (1972).

The 277 journals indexed were chosen primarily because they are widely circulated. Some exceptions were made because of the specialized nature of some journals, as in the case of the *International Fiction Review*. Five hundred eighty-four books on foreign literatures and specifically on foreign authors were chosen for indexing. This volume contains approximately 13,000 bibliographic citations on 1500 authors.

Arrangement of the work is by author when known, and by the title when the author is unknown. Birth and death dates, country of origin, and the author's real name when a pseudonym is used, appear parenthetically after the author's name. A section of general criticism follows the author's name with criticism on individual novels arranged alphabetically thereafter. Titles are in English, if known, with the original title and date of original publication following parenthetically. Reviews of novels published between 1965 and 1975 are cited at the end, following the criticism.

I wish to thank the University of Illinois for allowing me unrestricted use of their superior journal collection. I also wish to thank Deborah Brackstone, the Interlibrary Loan Librarian here at Memphis State University, for her indefatigable efforts in obtaining the materials I needed. Lastly, I wish to thank my colleagues, editors, and publisher for their constant support and encouragement.

A

ABBAS, KHWAJA AHMAD (Indian, 1914–)
BOBBY

Reviews
RAO, SUSHEELA N. *World Literature Written In English,* 14 (1975), 425.

ABBS, AKOSUA
ASHANTI BOY

CARTEY, WILFRED. *Whispers From A Continent,* pp. 23–27.

ABE, KOBO (Japanese, 1924–)
GENERAL

HARDIN, NANCY S. "An Interview with Abe Kobo." *Contemporary Literature,* 15 (1974), 439–56.

KORGES, JAMES. "Abe and Ooka: Identity and Mind-Body." *Critique,* 10, No.2 (1968), 130–39.

THE FACE OF ANOTHER (Tanin no Kao, 1964)

Reviews
FITZSIMMONS, THOMAS. "Man Without an Image." *Saturday Review,* 10 September 1966, pp. 60–61.

INTER ICE AGE 4 (Daiyon Kampyoki, 1959)

Reviews
HIBBETT, HOWARD. *Saturday Review,* 26 September 1970, pp. 37–38.

THE RUINED MAP (Moetsukita chizu, 1967)

Reviews
MINER, EARL. *Saturday Review,* 11 October 1969, p. 40.

THE WOMAN IN THE DUNES (Suna no Onna, 1962)

KIMBALL, ARTHUR G. *Crisis And Identity And Contemporary Japanese Novels,* pp. 115–39.

KORGES, JAMES. "Abe and Ooka: Identity and Mind-Body." *Critique,* 10, No.2 (1968), 133–6.

RICHEY, CLARENCE W. "Abe's *The Woman In The Dunes.*" *Explicator,* 31 (1973), Item 77.

Reviews
TEELE, ROY E. *Literature East And West,* 9 (1965), 257–59.

ABRAMOWITZ, Shalom Jacob see MENDELE Mocher Seforim

ABRAHAMS, PETER (South African, 1919–)
GENERAL

HEYWOOD, CHRISTOPHER. "The Novels of Peter Abrahams," in *Perspectives On African Literature,* ed. Christopher Heywood, pp. 157–72.

MAES-JELINEK, HENA. "Race Relations and Identity in Peter Abraham's 'Pluralia.' " *English Studies,* 50 (1969), 106–12.

OGUNGBESAN, KOLAWOLE. "Peter Abrahams: A Selected Bibliography." *World Literature Written In English,* 13 (1974), 184–90.

WADE, MICHAEL. "The Novels of Peter Abrahams." *Critique,* 11, No.1 (1968), 82–95.

MINE BOY (1946)

LARSON, CHARLES R. "Characters and Modes of Characterization: Chinua Achebe, James Ngugi, and Peter Abrahams," in his *The Emergence Of African Fiction,* rev. ed., pp. 162–66.

A NIGHT OF THEIR OWN (1965)

CARTEY, WILFRED. *Whispers From A Continent,* pp. 186–89.

OGUNGBESAN, KOLAWOLE. "The Political Novels of Peter Abrahams." *Présence Africaine,* No.83 (1972), pp. 37–42.

Reviews
AMOSU, NUNASU. *Black Orpheus,* No.22 (1967), pp. 59–60.

THIS ISLAND NOW (1966)

OGUNGBESAN, KOLAWOLE. "The Political Novels of Peter Abrahams." *Présence Africaine,* No.83 (1972), pp. 42–48.

———. "The Politics of *This Island Now.*" *Journal of Commonwealth Literature,* 8, No.1 (1973), 33–41.

WILD CONQUEST (1950)

OGUNGBESAN, KOLAWOLE. "Peter Abraham's Wild Conquest: In the Beginning was Conflict." *Studies In Black Literature,* 4, No.2 (1973), 11–20.

A WREATH FOR UDOMO (1956)

CARTEY, WILFRED. *Whispers From A Continent,* pp. 195–203.

OGUNGBESAN, KOLAWOLE. "The Political Novels of Peter Abrahams." *Présence Africaine,* No.83 (1972), pp. 35–37.

WADE, MICHAEL. "The Novels of Peter Abrahams." *Critique,* 11, No.1 (1968), 90–93.

ACHEBE, CHINUA (Nigerian, 1930–)
GENERAL

EKO, EBELE. "Chinua Achebe and His Critics: Reception of His Novels in English and American Reviews." *Studies In Black Literature,* 6, No.3 (1975), 14–20.

HANNA, S. J. "Bibliography." *Studies In Black Literature,* 2, No.1 (1971), 20–21.

IRELE, ABIOLA. "Chinua Achebe: The Tragic Conflict in Achebe's Novels." *Black Orpheus,* No. 17 (1965), pp. 24–32; rpt. in *Introduction To African Literature,* ed. Ulli Beier, pp. 167–78.

LARSON, CHARLES R. "Characters and Modes of Characterization: Chinua Achebe, James Ngugi, and Peter Abrahams," in his *The Emergence Of African Fiction,* rev. ed., pp. 149–55.

LESLIE, OMALARA. "Nigeria, Alienation and The Novels of Achebe." *Présence Africaine,* No.84 (1972), 99–108.

LINDFORS, BERNTH. "The Blind Men and the Elephant." *African Literature Today,* 7 (1975), 59–64.

———. "Chinua Achebe: An Interview." *Studies In Black Literature,* 2, No.1 (1971), 1–8.

———. "The Palm Oil With Which Achebe's Words Are Eaten." *African Literature Today,* No.1 (1968), pp. 3–6.

McDANIEL, RICHARD BRYAN. "An Achebe Bibliography." *World Literature Written In English,* No.20 (1971), pp. 15–24.

McDOWELL, ROBERT. "Of What Is Past, Or Passing, or to Come." *Studies In Black Literature,* 2, No.1 (1971), 9–13.

MADUBUIKE, IHECHUKWU. "Chinua Achebe: His Ideas on African Literature." *Présence Africaine,* No.93 (1975), pp. 140–52.

OGUNGBESAN, KOLAWOLE. "Politics and the African Writer." *African Studies Review,* 17 (1974), 43–53.

PONNUTHURAI, CHARLES SARVAN. "The Pessimism of Chinua Achebe." *Critique,* 15, No.3 (1974), 95–109.

POVEY, JOHN. "The English Language of the Contemporary African Novel." *Critique,* 11, No.3 (1968/9), 92–5.

ROSCOE, ADRIAN A. *Mother Is Gold,* pp. 121–31.

SHELTON, AUSTIN J. "Failures and Individualism in Achebe's Stories." *Studies In Black Literature,* 2, No.1 (1971), 5–9.

SIBLEY, FRANCIS M. "Tragedy in the Novels of Chinua Achebe." *Southern Humanities Review,* 9 (1975), 359–73.

TURKINGTON, KATE. " 'This no be them country'—Chinua Achebe's Novels." *English Studies In Africa,* 14 (1971), 205–14.

WALSH, WILLIAM. *A Manifold Voice,* pp. 48–61.

ARROW OF GOD (1964)

CARROLL, DAVID. *Chinua Achebe,* pp. 89–118.

CARTEY, WILFRED. *Whispers From A Continent,* pp. 80–84.

DALE, JAMES. "Chinua Achebe, Nigerian Novelist." *Queen's Quarterly,* 75 (1968), 469–72.

GLEASON, JUDITH ILLSLEY. *This Africa,* pp. 87–93.

GRIFFITHS, GARETH. "Language and Action in the Novels of Chinua Achebe." *African Literature Today,* 5 (1971), 95–98.

IRELE, ABIOLA. "Chinua Achebe: The Tragic Conflict in Achebe's Novels." *Black Orpheus,* No.17 (1965), pp. 30–32; rpt. in *Introduction To African Literature,* ed. Ulli Beier, pp. 174–77.

JORDAN, JOHN O. "Culture Conflict and Social Change In Achebe's *Arrow of God.*" *Critique,* 13, No.1 (1970), 66–82.

KILLAM, G. D. "Chinua Achebe's Novels." *Sewanee Review,* 79 (1971), 534–39.

———. *The Novels of Chinua Achebe,* pp. 59–83.

LAURENCE, MARGARET. *Long Drums And Cannons,* pp. 111–17.

LINDFORS, BERNTH. *Folklore In Nigerian Literature,* pp. 84–88, 94–104.

———. "The Folktale as Paradigm in Chinua Achebe's *Arrow Of God.*" *Studies In Black Literature,* 1, No.1 (1970), 1–15.

———. "The Palm Oil With Which Achebe's Words Are Eaten." *African Literature Today,* No.1 (1968), pp. 12–15.

MELAMU, M. J. "The Quest for Power in Achebe's 'Arrow of God.' " *English Studies In Africa,* 14 (1971), 225–40.

POVEY, JOHN. "The Novels of Chinua Achebe," in *Introduction To Nigerian Literature,* ed. Bruce King, pp. 106–9.

RAVENSCROFT, ARTHUR. *Chinua Achebe,* pp. 24–31.

SHELTON, AUSTIN J. "The 'Palm-Oil' of Language: Proverbs in Chinua Achebe's Novels." *Modern Language Quarterly,* 30 (1969), 99–106.

SIBLEY, FRANCIS M. "Tragedy in the Novels of Chinua Achebe." *Southern Humanities Review,* 9 (1975), 367–70.

WALSH, WILLIAM. *A Manifold Voice,* pp. 55–61.

Reviews

BORT, BARRY D. *Literature East And West,* 12 (1968), 95–96.

JONES, ELDRED. "Achebe's Third Novel." *Journal Of Commonwealth Literature,* No.1 (1965), pp. 176–78.

MILLER, CHARLES. "Mixed Allegiances." *Saturday Review,* 6 January 1968, pp. 30–31.

A MAN OF THE PEOPLE (1966)

BROWN, LLOYD W. "Cultural Norms and Modes of Perception in Achebe's Fiction." *Research In African Literatures,* 3 (1972), 31–35.

CARROLL, DAVID. *Chinua Achebe,* pp. 119–45.

CARTEY, WILFRED. *Whispers From A Continent,* pp. 189–93.

DALE, JAMES. "Chinua Achebe, Nigerian Novelist." *Queen's Quarterly,* 75 (1968), 472–74.

GRIFFITHS, GARETH. "Language and Action in the Novels of Chinua Achebe." *African Literature Today,* 5 (1971), 98–104.

KILLAM, G. D. "Chinua Achebe's Novels." *Sewanee Review,* 79 (1971), 539–41.

———. *The Novels of Chinua Achebe,* pp. 84–96.

LAURENCE, MARGARET. *Long Drums And Cannons,* pp. 117–22.

LESLIE, OMALARA. "Nigeria, Alienation and The Novels of Achebe." *Présence Africaine,* No.84 (1972), pp. 105–8.

LINDFORS, BERNTH. "Achebe's African Parable." *Présence Africaine,* No.66 (1968), pp.130–36.

———. *Folklore In Nigerian Literature,* pp. 88–92.

———. "The Palm Oil With Which Achebe's Words Are Eaten." *African Literature Today,* No.1 (1968), pp. 15–18.

OKPAKU, JOSEPH O. "A Novel for the People." *Journal Of The New African Literature And The Arts,* No.2 (1966), pp. 76–80.

OLNEY, JAMES. "The African Novel in Transition: Chinua Achebe." *South Atlantic Quarterly,* 70 (1971), 313–16.

PALMER, EUSTACE. *An Introduction To The African Novel,* pp. 72–84.

———. "Social Comment in the West African Novel." *Studies In The Novel,* 4 (1972), 219–22.

PONNUTHURAI, CHARLES SARVAN. "The Pessimism of Chinua Achebe." *Critique,* 15, No.3 (1973/4), 101–5.

POVEY, JOHN. "The Novels of Chinua Achebe," in *Introduction To Nigerian Literature,* ed. Bruce King, pp. 109–12.

RAVENSCROFT, ARTHUR. "African Literature V: Novels of Disillusion." *Journal Of Commonwealth Literature,* No.6 (1969), pp. 120–23.

———. *Chinua Achebe,* pp. 31–37.

———. "Novels of Disillusion," in *Readings In Commonwealth Literature,* ed. William Walsh, pp. 187–90.

SHELTON, AUSTIN J. "The 'Palm-Oil' of Language: Proverbs in Chinua Achebe's Novels." *Modern Language Quarterly,* 30 (1969), 107–9.

WREN, ROBERT M. "Anticipations of Civil Conflict in Nigerian Novels: Aluko and Achebe." *Studies In Black Literature,* 1, No.2 (1970), 27–31.

Reviews

DATHORNE, O. R. *Black Orpheus,* No.21 (1967), p. 61.

JONES, ELDRED. "Locale and Universe—Three Nigerian Novels." *Journal Of Commonwealth Literature,* No.3 (1967), pp. 130-31.

NO LONGER AT EASE (1960)

BROWN, LLOYD W. "Cultural Norms and Modes of Perception in Achebe's Fiction." *Research In African Literatures,* 3 (1972), 25-31.

CARROLL, DAVID. *Chinua Achebe,* pp. 65-88.

CARTEY, WILFRED. *Whispers From A Continent,* pp. 173-77.

DALE, JAMES. "Chinua Achebe, Nigerian Novelist." *Queen's Quarterly,* 75 (1968), 465-69.

GLEASON, JUDITH ILLSLEY. *This Africa,* pp. 130-36.

GRIFFITHS, GARETH. "Language and Action in the Novels of Chinua Achebe." *African Literature Today,* 5 (1971), 92-95.

KILLAM, G. D. "Chinua Achebe's Novels." *Sewanee Review,* 79 (1971), 531-34.

———. *The Novels Of Chinua Achebe,* pp. 35-58.

LAURENCE, MARGARET. *Long Drums And Cannons,* pp. 107-11.

LINDFORS, BERNTH. *Folklore In Nigerian Literature,* pp. 81-84.

———. "The Palm Oil With Which Achebe's Words Are Eaten." *African Literature Today,* No.1 (1968), pp. 9-12.

NWOGA, DONATUS I. "Shadows of Christian Civilization." *Présence Africaine,* No.79 (1971), pp. 46-50.

OLNEY, JAMES. "The African Novel in Transition: Chinua Achebe." *South Atlantic Quarterly,* 70 (1971), 309-13.

PALMER, EUSTACE. *An Introduction To The African Novel,* pp. 63-72.

POVEY, JOHN. "The Novels of Chinua Achebe," in *Introduction To Nigerian Literature,* ed. Bruce King, pp. 103-6.

RAVENSCROFT, ARTHUR. *Chinua Achebe,* pp. 18-24.

RIDDY, FELICITY. "Language as a Theme in *No Longer At Ease.*" *Journal Of Commonwealth Literature,* No.9 (1970), pp. 38-47.

SHELTON, AUSTIN J. "The 'Palm-Oil' of Language: Proverbs in Chinua Achebe's Novels." *Modern Language Quarterly,* 30 (1969), 92-99.

TURKINGTON, KATE. "'This no be them country'—Chinua Achebe's Novels." *English Studies In Africa,* 14 (1971), 207-10.

WILSON, RODERICK. "Eliot and Achebe: An Analysis of Some Formal and Philosophical Qualities of 'No Longer at Ease.'" *English Studies In Africa,* 14 (1971), 215-23.

THINGS FALL APART (1958)

ACKLEY, DONALD G. "The Male-Female Motif in *Things Fall Apart.*" *Studies In Black Literature,* 5, No.1 (1974), 1-6.

CARROLL, DAVID. *Chinua Achebe,* pp. 36-64.

CARTEY, WILFRED. *Whispers From A Continent,* pp. 96-105.

DALE, JAMES. "Chinua Achebe, Nigerian Novelist." *Queen's Quarterly,* 75 (1968), 460-65.

FERGUSON, JOHN. "Nigerian Prose Literature in English." *English Studies In Africa,* 9 (1966), 49-52.

GLEASON, JUDITH ILLSLEY. *This Africa,* pp. 81-86.

GRIFFITHS, GARETH. "Language and Action in the Novels of Chinua Achebe." *African Literature Today,* 5 (1971), 88-92.

IRELE, ABIOLA. "Chinua Achebe: The Tragic Conflict in Achebe's Novels." *Black Orpheus,* No.17 (1965), pp. 24-28; rpt. in *Introduction To African Literature,* ed. Ulli Beier, pp. 167-72.

JABBI, BU-BUAKEI. "Fire and Transition in *Things Fall Apart.*" *Obsidian,* 1, No.3 (1975), 22-36.

JONES, ELDRED D. "Academic Problems and Critical Techniques," in *African Literature And The Universities,* ed. Gerald Moore, pp. 91-95.

KILLAM, G. D. "Chinua Achebe's Novels." *Sewanee Review,* 79 (1971), 514-30.

———. *The Novels of Chinua Achebe,* pp. 13-34.

KRONENFELD, J. Z. "The 'Communalistic' African and the 'Individualistic' Westerner: Some Comments on Misleading Generalizations in Western Criticism of Soyinka and Achebe." *Research In African Literatures,* 6 (1975), 215-24.

LARSON, CHARLES R. "Chinua Achebe's *Things Fall Apart:* The Archetypal African Novel," in his *The Emergence Of African Fiction,* pp. 27-65.

LAURENCE, MARGARET. *Long Drums And Cannons,* pp. 99-107.

LEACH, JOSEPHINE. "A Study of Chinua Achebe's *Things Fall Apart* in Mid-America." *English Journal,* 60 (1971), 1052-56.

LINDFORS, BERNTH O. *Folklore In Nigerian Literature,* pp. 77-80.

———. "Oral Tradition and the Individual Literary Talent." *Studies In The Novel,* 4 (1972), 213-16.

———. "The Palm Oil With Which Achebe's Words Are Eaten." *African Literature Today,* No.1 (1968), pp. 6-9.

MEYERS, JEFFREY. "Culture and History in *Things Fall Apart.*" *Critique,* 11, No.1 (1968), 25-32.

OLNEY, JAMES. "The African Novel in Transition: Chinua Achebe." *South Atlantic Quarterly,* 70 (1971), 302-9.

PALMER, EUSTACE. *An Introduction To The African Novel,* pp. 48-63.

RAVENSCROFT, ARTHUR. *Chinua Achebe,* pp. 8-18.

SCHEUB, HAROLD. "'When a Man Fails Alone.'" *Présence Africaine,* No.74 (1970), pp. 61-89.

POVEY, JOHN. "The Novels of Chinua Achebe," in *Introduction To Nigerian Literature,* ed. Bruce King, pp. 99-103.

SHELTON, AUSTIN J. "The 'Palm-Oil' of Language: Proverbs in Chinua Achebe's Novels." *Modern Language Quarterly,* 30 (1969), 88-92.

SIBLEY, FRANCIS M. "Tragedy in the Novels of Chinua Achebe." *Southern Humanities Review,* 9 (1975), 360-65.

STOCK, A. G. "Yeats and Achebe." *Journal Of Commonwealth Literature,* No.5 (1968), pp.105-11.

WALSH, WILLIAM. *A Manifold Voice,* pp. 50-53.

WEINSTOCK, DONALD J. "Achebe's Christ-Figure." *Journal Of The New African Literature And The Arts,* No.5/6 (1968), pp. 20-26.

———. "The Two Swarms of Locusts: Judgment by Indirection In *Things Fall Apart.*" *Studies In Black Literature,* 2, No.1 (1971), 14-19.

———and CATHY RAMADAN. "Symbolic Structure in *Things Fall Apart.*" *Critique,* 11, No.1 (1968), 33-41.

ACHILLES TATIUS (Greek, fl. 4th century A.D.)

LEUCIPPE AND CLITOPHON

BOORSCH, JEAN. "About Some Greek Romances." *Yale French Studies,* No.38 (1967), pp. 72-88.

ADAM, PAUL (French, 1862-1920)

GENERAL

DUNCAN, J. ANN. "The Early Novels of Paul Adam." *Modern Language Review,* 69 (1974), 534-40.

ADIGAL, ILANGO

SHILAPPADIKARAM

Reviews
Triveni, 35, No.3 (1966), 79–80.

AGARWAL, BHARAT BHUSHAN

LAHARON KI BANSURI

Reviews
SINGH, ATTAR. *Indian Literature,* 9, No.3 (1966), 100–2.

AGNON, SHMUEL YOSEF (Polish-born Israeli, 1888–1970)

GENERAL

AGNON, SHMUEL YOSEF. "Influences in My Writing." *Ariel: A Quarterly Review Of The Arts And Sciences In Israel,* No.17 (1966/7), pp. 5–6.

ALTER, ROBERT. "The Israeli Novel." *Daedalus,* 95 (1966), 974–9; rpt. in his *After The Tradition,* pp. 197–202.

————. "On Lea Goldberg & S. Y. Agnon." *Commentary,* 49, No.5 (1970), 83–4.

AMICHAI, YEHUDA. "Notes on Agnon." *Midstream Magazine,* 13, No.2 (1967), 12–15.

BAND, ARNOLD J. "The Evolving Masks of S. Y. Agnon." *Ariel: A Quarterly Review Of The Arts And Sciences In Israel,* No.17 (1966/7), pp. 55–71.

FELDMAN, EMANUEL. "A Man Touched by God." *Saturday Review,* 22 April 1967, pp. 94–97.

FISCH, HAROLD. "The Dreaming Narrator in S. Y. Agnon." *Novel,* 4 (1970), 49–68.

GOLDBERG, LEA. "The Author and his Hero." *Ariel: A Quarterly Review Of The Arts And Sciences In Israel,* No.17 (1966/7), pp. 37–54.

HOCHMAN, BARUCH. "Agnon's Quest." *Commentary,* 42, No.6 (1966), 45–51.

KURZWEIL, BARUCH. "Agnon's Jerusalem." *Ariel: A Quarterly Review Of The Arts And Sciences In Israel,* No.23 (1969), pp. 43–45.

————. "Religion in Agnon's Work." *Ariel: A Quarterly Review Of The Arts And Sciences in Israel,* No.17 (1966/7), pp. 7–30.

LEITER, SAMUEL. "The Vision of the Fallen House: The Art of S. Y. Agnon." *Midstream Magazine,* 13, No.2 (1967), 4–11.

PATTERSON, DAVID. "The Writer and the Legend." *Ariel: A Quarterly Review Of The Arts And Sciences In Israel,* No.11 (1965), pp. 22–25.

SCHOLEM, GERSHOM. "Reflections on S. Y. Agnon." *Commentary,* 44, No.6 (1967), 59–66.

WILSON, EDMUND. " 'A Man of Unquestionable Genius.' " *Ariel: A Quarterly Review Of The Arts And Sciences In Israel,* No.17 (1966/7), pp. 31–36.

BETROTHED (Shevu'ath Emunim, 1943)

BAND, ARNOLD J. *Nostalgia And Nightmare: A Study In The Fiction Of S. Y. Agnon,* pp. 367–82.

HOCHMAN, BARUCH. *The Fiction Of S. Y. Agnon,* pp. 177–84.

Reviews
FYTTON, FRANCIS. *London Magazine,* 6, No.10 (1967), 105–7.

THE BRIDAL CANOPY (Ha-Khnassath Kallah, 1931)

BAND, ARNOLD J. *Nostalgia And Nightmare: A Study In The Fiction Of S. Y. Agnon,* pp. 126–84.

HOCHMAN, BARUCH. *The Fiction Of S. Y. Agnon,* pp. 53–76.

ROSHWALD, MIRIAM. "Two Kinds of Belief: A Comparative Study of Two Jewish Literary Characters." *International Fiction Review,* No.2 (1975), pp. 35–42.

LEVIANT, CURT. "The Word and the World." *Saturday Review,* 22 April 1967, pp. 93–94.

RABINOVICH, ISAIAH. *Major Trends In Modern Hebrew Fiction,* pp. 178–92.

THE DAY BEFORE YESTERDAY see JUST YESTERDAY

EDO AND ENAM (Edo Ve'Enam, 1950)

BAND, ARNOLD J. *Nostalgia And Nightmare: A Study In The Fiction Of S. Y. Agnon,* pp. 382–96.

HOCHMAN, BARUCH. *The Fiction Of S. Y. Agnon,* pp. 177–84.

FISCH, HAROLD. "The Dreaming Narrator in S. Y. Agnon." *Novel,* 4 (1970), 49–52.

Reviews
FYTTON, FRANCIS. *London Magazine,* 6, No.10 (1967), 105–7.

FOREVERMORE

HOCHMAN, BARUCH. *The Fiction Of S. Y. Agnon,* pp. 177–84.

A GUEST FOR THE NIGHT (Ore'ah Nata Lalun, 1937)

ALTER, ROBERT. "Agnon's Last Word." *Commentary,* 51, No.6 (1971), 74–5.

BAND, ARNOLD J. *Nostalgia And Nightmare: A Study In The Fiction Of S. Y. Agnon,* pp. 283–327.

HOCHMAN, BARUCH. *The Fiction Of S. Y. Agnon,* pp. 112–33.

RABINOVICH, ISAIAH. *Major Trends In Modern Hebrew Fiction,* pp. 192–209.

Reviews
HALKIN, HILLEL. "A Regrettable Guest." *Midstream Magazine,* 14, No.6 (1968), 72–80.

LEVIANT, CURT. "The Search for a Secure Past." *Saturday Review,* 27 April 1968, pp. 38, 49.

JUST YESTERDAY (Tmol Shilshom)

ALTER, ROBERT. "The Israeli Novel." *Daedalus,* 95 (1966), 975–8; rpt. in his *After The Tradition,* pp. 197–202.

BAND, ARNOLD J. *Nostalgia And Nightmare: A Study In The Fiction Of S. Y. Agnon,* pp. 414–47.

BAR-ADON, AARON. "S. Y. Agnon and the Revival of Modern Hebrew." *Texas Studies In Literature And Language,* 14 (1972), 156–71.

HOCHMAN, BARUCH. *The Fiction Of S. Y. Agnon,* pp. 134–57.

RABINOVICH, ISAIAH. *Major Trends In Modern Hebrew Fiction,* pp. 218–32.

ONLY YESTERDAY see JUST YESTERDAY

SHIRA

ALTER, ROBERT. "Agnon's Last Word." *Commentary,* 51, No.6 (1971), 74–81.

BAND, ARNOLD J. "Agnon's Last Novel." *Ariel: A Quarterly Review Of Arts And Sciences In Israel,* No.29 (1971), pp. 84–87.

Reviews
HOCHMAN, BARUCH. "Agnon's Posthumous Novel." *Midstream Magazine,* 17, No.9 (1971), 68–75.

A SIMPLE TALE (Sippur Pashut, 1935)

BAND, ARNOLD J. *Nostalgia And Nightmare: A Study In The Fiction Of S. Y. Agnon,* pp. 239–54.

CUTTER, WILLIAM. "Setting as a Feature of Ambiguity in S. Y. Agnon's *Sippur Pashut.*" *Critique,* 15, No.3 (1974), 66–80.

FISCH, HAROLD. "Agnon's Simple Tale." *Modern Hebrew Literature,* 1, No.2 (1975), 9–16.

HOCHMAN, BARUCH. *The Fiction Of S. Y. Agnon,* pp. 94–111.

RAMRAS-RAUCH, GILA. "*Shira:* S. Y. Agnon's Posthumous Novel." *Books Abroad* 45 (1971), 636-8.

THUS FAR ('Ad Hena)

BAND, ARNOLD J. *Nostalgia And Nightmare: A Study In The Fiction Of S. Y. Agnon*, pp. 346-56.

HOCHMAN, BARUCH. *The Fiction Of S. Y. Agnon*, pp. 172-77.

VEHAYA HE'AKOV LEMISHOR

BAND, ARNOLD J. *Nostalgia And Nightmare: A Study In The Fiction Of S. Y. Agnon*, pp. 83-92.

WAYFARER FOR THE NIGHT see A GUEST FOR THE NIGHT

A WHOLE LOAF (Pat Shelema)

BAND, ARNOLD J. *Nostalgia And Nightmare: A Study In The Fiction Of S. Y. Agnon*, pp. 189-201.

YOUNG AND OLD TOGETHER (Bin' Arenu Uvizkenenu)

BAND, ARNOLD J. *Nostalgia And Nightmare: A Study In The Fiction Of S. Y. Agnon*, pp. 121-25.

HOCHMAN, BARUCH. *The Fiction Of S. Y. Agnon*, pp. 82-93.

AGUDIEZ, JUAN VENTURA (Chilean, emigrated to the United States, 1933-)

LAS TARDES DES THÉRÈZE LAMARCK (1964)

CLARKE, DOROTHY CLOTELLE. "Coconsciousness in Agudiez' *Las Tardes De Thérèze Lamarck.*" *Revista Hispanica Moderna,* 34 (1968), 586-95.

_____. "An Hispanic Variation on a French Theme: Mme. de Staël, Butor, Agudiez." *Symposium,* 22 (1968), 208-13.

AGUILERA-MALTA, DEMETRIO (Ecuadorian, 1909-)

LA CABALLERESA DEL SOL (1964)

DAVIS, J. CARY. "The 'Episodios Americanos' of Aguilera-Malta: First Installment." *USF Language Quarterly,* 9, No.1/2 (1970), 49-53.

DON GOYO (1933)

BRUSHWOOD, JOHN S. *The Spanish American Novel,* pp. 96-101.

EL QUIJOTE DE EL DORADO (1964)

DAVIS, J. CARY. "The 'Episodois Americanos' of Aguilera-Malta: Second Installment." *USF Language Quarterly,* 9, No. 3/4 (1971), 43-47.

EL SECUESTRO DEL GENERAL (1973)

Reviews
RABASSA, CLEMENTINE C. *Journal Of Spanish Studies,* 3 (1975), 85-86.

AGUIMANA DE VECA, TIRSO

UNA TEMPORADA EN EL MÁS BELLO DE LOS PLANETAS

DENDLE, BRIAN J. "A Romantic Voyage to Saturn: Tirso, Aguimana de Veca's *Una Temporada En El Más Bello De Los Planetas.*" *Studies in Romanticism,* 7 (1968), 243-47.

AGUSTIN, JOSÉ (Mexican, 1944-)

GENERAL

LANGFORD, WALTER M. *The Mexican Novel Comes Of Age,* pp. 200-3.

SE ESTÁ HACIENDO TARDE (1973)

Turner, John H. *Chasqui,* 3, No.3 (1974), 71-73.

AGYEYA (Indian, 1913-) pseudonym of S. H. Vatsyayan

GENERAL

AGYEYA. "Words, Silence, Existence: A Writer's Credo." *Indian Literature,* 9, No.3 (1966), 86-91.

MISRA, VIDYANIWAS. "Agyeya: The Man and the Writer." *Mahfil,* 2, No.1 (1964), 55-57.

"S. H. Vatsyayan: A Chronology." *Mahfil,* 2, No.1 (1964), 1-2

TO EACH HIS STRANGER (1967)

Reviews
DULAI, SURJIT SINGH. *Mahfil,* 5, No.1/2 (1968/9), 105-9.

AHLGREN, ERNST (Swedish, 1850-1888) pseudonym of Victoria Maria Benedictsson

GENERAL

BORLAND, HAROLD. "Ernst Ahlgren, Novelist in Theory and Practice." *Scandanavica,* 13 (1974), 97-106.

AHLIN, LARS (Swedish, 1915-)

GENERAL

LUNDELL, TORBORG. "Lars Ahlin's Concept of the Writer as Identifactor and Förbedjare." *Scandinavica,* 14 (1975), 27-35.

AHMAD, AZIZ

THE SHORE AND THE WAVE (Aisi Bulandi, Aisi Pasti)

Reviews
BANERJEE, SUMANTA. *Indian Literature,* 15, No.1 (1972), 76-81.

GHOSH, S. L. *Indian Horizons,* 21, No.1 (1972), 77-79.

AICHINGER, ILSE (Austrian, 1921-)

GENERAL

KOWAL, MICHAEL. "Ilse Aichinger as Storyteller." *American-German Review,* 33, No.2 (1966/7), 29.

HEROD'S CHILDREN (Die Grössere Hoffnung, 1948)

LANGER, LAWRENCE L. *The Holocaust And The Literary Imagination,* pp. 134-64.

AI HSÜAN

THE THUNDERING YANGTSE (Ta chiang feng lei)

HUANG, JOE C. *Heroes And Villains In Communist China,* pp. 117-29.

AI MING-CHIK

SEEDS OF FLAME (Huo chung)

HUANG, JOE C. *Heroes And Villains In Communist China,* pp. 214-19.

AI WU

STEELED AND TEMPERED (Pai lien ch'eng kang)

HUANG, JOE C. *Heroes And Villains In Communist China,* pp. 232-36.

AKSENOV, VASILY PAVLOVICH (Russian, 1932-)

GENERAL

BROWN, DEMING. "Vasili Aksenov at 33." *Triquarterly,* No.3 (1965), pp. 75–83.

MEYER, PRISCILLA. "Aksenov and Soviet Literature of the 1960s." *Russian Literature Triquarterly,* No.6 (1973), pp. 448–60.

———. "A Bibliography of Works By and About Vasilii Pavlovich Aksenov." *Russian Literature Triquarterly,* No.6 (1973), pp. 695–702.

———. "Interview with Vasily Pavlovich Aksenov." *Russian Literature Triquarterly,* No.6 (1973), 569–74.

AKUTAGAWA RYŪNOSUKE

A FOOL'S LIFE

Reviews

FITZSIMMONS, THOMAS. *Saturday Review,* 9 January 1971, pp. 32–33.

KAPPA

Reviews

TSURUTA, KINYA. *Monumenta Nipponica,* 27 (1972), 112–14.

ALAIN-FOURNIER, (HENRI) (French, 1886-1914)

THE WANDERER (Le Grand Meaulnes, 1913)

BOURAOUI, H. A. "A Structural Diptych in *Le Grand Meaulnes.*" *French Review,* 42 (1968), 233–47.

BROSMAN, CATHARINE SAVAGE. "Alain-Fournier's Domain: A New Look." *French Review,* 44 (1971), 499–507.

GIBSON, ROBERT. *The Land Without A Name: Alain-Fournier And His World,* pp. 168–304.

GOLDGAR, HARRY. "Alain-Fournier and the Initiation Archetype." *French Review,* 43, Special Issue No.1 (1970), 87–99.

JONES, LOUISA. "Window Imagery: Inner and Outer Worlds in Alain Fournier's *Le Grand Meaulnes.*" *Symposium,* 27 (1973), 333–51.

SAVAGE, CATHARINE H. "Nostalgia in Alain-Fournier and Proust." *French Review,* 38 (1964), 167–72.

SORRELL, MARTIN R. M. "Francois Seurel's Personal Adventure in 'Le Grand Meaulnes.' " *Modern Language Review,* 69 (1974), 79–87.

TURNELL, MARTIN. "Alain-Fournier and *Le Grand Meaulnes.*" *Southern Review,* NS, 2 (1966), 477–98.

WOODCOCK, GEORGE. "Alain-Fournier and the Lost Land." *Queen's Quarterly,* 81 (1974), 348–56.

ALARCÓN, PEDRO ANTONIO DE (Spanish, 1833-1891)

EL EXTRANJERO

SMIEJA, FLORIAN. "Pedro Antonio de Alarcón's *El Extranjero:* Some Aspects of the Historical Background." *Hispanic Review,* 37 (1969), 370–74.

THE SCANDAL (El escándolo, 1875)

HAFTER, MONROE Z. "Alarcón in *El Escandolo.*" *MLN,* 83 (1968), 212–25.

McCLENDON, BARNETT A. "Influences of *El Escándolo* on the Colombian Novel, *Ayer, Nada Más.*" *Romance Notes,* 14 (1972), 96–104.

POWERS, HARRIET B. "Allegory in *El Escándolo.*" *MLN,* 87 (1972), 324–29.

THE THREE CORNERED HAT (El sombrere tres picos, 1874)

MEDINA, JEREMY T. "Structural Techniques of Alarcón's *El Sombrero De Tres Picos.*" *Romance Notes,* 14 (1972), 83–85.

ALAS Y UREÑA, LEOPOLDO (Spanish, 1852-1901)

GENERAL

KRONIK, JOHN W. "The Function of Names in the Stories of Alas." *MLN,* 80 (1965), 260–65.

DOÑA BERTA

BORING, PHYLLIS Z. "Some Reflections on Clarín's *Doña Berta.*" *Romance Notes,* 11 (1969), 322–25.

LA REGENTA (1884-1885)

DURAND, FRANK. "Leopoldo Alas, 'Clarín': Consistency of Outlook as Critic and Novelist." *Romanic Review,* 56 (1965), 37–49.

IFE, BARRY W. "Idealism and Materialism in Clarin's *La Regenta:* Two Comparative Studies." *Revue De Littérature Comparée,* 44 (1970), 273–95.

JACKSON, ROBERT M. " 'Cervantismo' in the Creative Process of Clarin's *La Regenta.*" *MLN,* 84 (1969), 208–27.

MAZZEO, GUIDO E. "The Banquet Scene in *La Regenta,* a Case of Sacrilege." *Romance Notes,* 10 (1968), 68–72.

NIMETZ, MICHAEL. "*Eros* and *Ecclesia* in Clarín's Vetusta." *MLN,* 86 (1971), 242–53.

RUTHERFORD, JOHN. *Leopoldo Alas: La Regenta.*

SÁNCHEZ, ROBERTO G. "The Presence of the Theater and 'the Consciousness of the Theater' in Clarín's *La Regenta.*" *Hispanic Review,* 37 (1969), 491–509.

THOMPSON, CLIFFORD R. "Egoism and Alienation in the Works of Leopoldo Alas." *Romanische Forschungen,* 81 (1969), 198–203.

WEBER, FRANCES WYERS. "The Dynamics of Motif in Leopoldo Alas's *La Regenta.*" *Romanic Review,* 57 (1966), 188–99.

———. "Ideology and Religious Parody in the Novels of Leopoldo Alas." *Bulletin Of Hispanic Studies,* 43 (1966), 197–203.

SUPERCHERÍA

ROUND, NICHOLAS G. "The Fictional Integrity of Leopoldo Alas' *Superchería.*" *Bulletin Of Hispanic Studies,* 47 (1970), 97–116.

SU ÚNICO HIJO

WEBER, FRANCES WYERS. "Ideology and Religious Parody in the Novels of Leopoldo Alas." *Bulletin Of Hispanic Studies,* 43 (1966), 203–8.

ALBRECHT, JOHANN FRIEDRICH ERNST (German, 1752-1814)

DREYERLEI WIRKUNGEN

HADLEY, MICHAEL. *The German Novel In 1790,* pp. 140–46.

FACKLAND ODER SCHADEN MACHT KLUG

HADLEY, MICHAEL. *The German Novel In 1790,* pp. 97–100.

URANIE

HADLEY, MICHAEL. *The German Novel In 1790,* pp. 146–52.

ALCAYAGA, Lucila Godoy see MISTRAL, Gabriela

ALCORTA, GLORIA

LA PAREJA DE NÚÑEZ (1971)

Reviews

WALKER, JOHN. *Hispania,* 56 (1973), 508.

ALDÁNOV, Mark A. (pseudonym of Mark Aleksandrovich Landau, Russian, 1886-1957)

FOR THEE THE BEST (Mogila voina, 1940)

LEE, C. NICHOLAS. "The Philosophical Tales of M. A. Aldanov." *Slavic And East European Journal,* 15 (1971), 286-90.

PUNCH VODKA (Punševaja vodka, 1940)

LEE, C. NICHOLAS. "The Philosophical Tales of M. A. Aldanov." *Slavic And East European Journal,* 15 (1971), 281-86.

THE TENTH SYMPHONY (Desjataja simfonija, 1931)

LEE, C. NICHOLAS. "The Philosophical Tales of M. A. Aldanov." *Slavic And East European Journal,* 15 (1971), 276-81.

ALDECOA, IGNACIO (Spanish, 1925-1969)

GENERAL

DÍAZ, JANET WINECOFF. "The Novels of Ignacio Aldecoa." *Romance Notes,* 11 (1970), 475-81.

PARTE DE UNA HISTORIA

FIDDIAN, R. W. "Urban Man and the Pastoral Illusion: An Interpretation of Ignacio Aldecoa's *Parte De Una Historia.*" *Revista De Estudios Hispánicos,* 9 (1975), 371-89.

ALEGRÍA, CIRO (Peruvian, 1909-1967)

BROAD AND ALIEN IS THE WORLD (El mundo es ancho y ajeno)

ENDRES, VALERIE. "The Role of Animals in 'El Mundo Es Ancho y Ajeno.'" *Hispania,* 48 (1965), 67-69.

McGOURN, FRANCIS T. "The Priest in *El Mundo Es Ancho Y Ajeno.*" *Romance Notes,* 9 (1967), 224-30.

ALEGRIA, FERNANDO (Chilean, 1918-)

MY HORSE GONZÁLEZ (Gaballo de copas, 1957)

Reviews
KOLB, GLEN L. *Hispania,* 48 (1965), 187.

ALEICHEM, SHALOM (Yiddish, 1859-1916) pseudonym of Solomon Rabinowitz

GENERAL

RABINOVICH, ISAIAH. *Major Trends In Modern Hebrew Fiction,* pp. 14-24.

THE ADVENTURES OF MENACHEM-MENDL

KRESH, PAUL. "Even a One-Eyed Husband Is a Husband." *Saturday Review,* 26 April 1969, p. 44.

TUVIA THE MILKMAN

RABINOVICH, ISAIAH. *Major Trends In Modern Hebrew Fiction,* pp. 16-23.

ALEMÁN, MATEO (Spanish, 1547-1615)

BONIFACIO AND DOROTEA

McGRADY, DONALD. *Mateo Alemán,* pp. 164-67.

DON LUIS DE CASTRO

McGRADY, DONALD. *Mateo Alemán,* pp. 160-63.

DORIDO AND CLORINIA

McGRADY, DONALD. "*Dorido And Clorinia:* An Italianate *Novella* by Mateo Alemán." *Romance Notes,* 8 (1966), 91-95.

_____. *Mateo Alemán,* pp. 157-60.

GUZMÁN DE ALFARACHE (1599, 1602)

BJORNSON, RICHARD. "*Guzmán De Alfarache:* Apologia for a 'Converso.' " *Romanische Forschungen,* 85 (1973), 314-29.

DAVIS, BARBARA. "The Style of Mateo Alemán's *Guzman De Alfarache.*" *Romanic Review,* 66 (1975), 199-213.

FOLKENFLIK, VIVIAN. "Vision and Truth: Baroque Art Metaphors in *Guzmán De Alfarache.*" *MLN,* 88 (1973), 347-55.

JONES, J. A. "The Duality and Complexity of *Guzmán De Alfarache:* Some Thoughts on the Structure and Interpretation of Alemán's Novel," in *Knaves And Swindlers,* ed. Christine J. Whitbourn, pp. 25-47.

McGRADY, DONALD. "*Buena Ropa* in Torres Naharro, Lope de Vega, and Mateo Alemán." *Romance Philology,* 21 (1967), 183-5.

_____. "Heliodorus' Influence on Mateo Alemán." *Hispanic Review,* 34 (1966), 49-53.

_____. "Masuccio and Alemán: Italian Renaissance And Spanish Baroque." *Comparative Literature,* 18 (1966), 203-10.

_____. *Mateo Alemán,* pp. 44-167.

_____. "A Pirated Edition of *Guzmán De Alfarache:* More Light on Mateo Alemán's Life." *Hispanic Review,* 34 (1966), 326-28.

NORVAL, M. N. "Original Sin and the 'Conversion' in the *Guzmán De Alfarache.*" *Bulletin Of Hispanic Studies,* 51 (1974), 346-64.

OAKLEY, R. J. "The Problematic Unity of *Guzmán De Alfarache,*" in *Hispanic Studies In Honour Of Joseph Manson,* ed. Dorothy M. Atkinson and Anthony H. Clarke, pp. 185-206.

RICAPITO, JOSEPH V. "Comparatistica—Two Versions of Sin, Moral Transgression and Divine Will: *Guzmán De Alfarache* and *I Promessi Sposi.*" *Kentucky Romance Quarterly,* 16 (1969), 111-18.

_____. "From Boccaccio to Mateo Alemán: An Essay on Literary Sources and Adaptations." *Romanic Review,* 60 (1969), 83-95.

_____. "Love and Marriage in *Guzmán De Alfarache:* An Essay on Literary and Artistic Unity." *Kentucky Romance Quarterly,* 15 (1968), 123-38.

WHITBOURN, CHRISTINE J. "Moral Ambiguity in the Spanish Picaresque Tradition," in *Knaves And Swindlers,* ed. Christine J. Whitbourn, pp. 10-14.

OZMÍN AND DARAJA

McGRADY, DONALD. *Mateo Aléman,* pp. 147-57.

ALERAMO, SIBILLA (Italian, 1876-1960) pseudonym of Rina Faccio

A WOMAN AT BAY (Una Donna)

PACIFICI, SERGIO. *The Modern Italian Novel: From Capuana To Tozzi,* pp. 63-67.

ALFVEN, Hannes O. G. see JOHANNESON, Olaf

ALLFREY, P. SHAND (West Indian)

THE ORCHID HOUSE (1953)

RAMCHAND, KENNETH. "Terrified Consciousness." *Journal Of Commonwealth Literature,* No.7 (1969), pp. 9-12.

_____. *The West Indian Novel And Its Background,* pp. 225-28.

Reviews
DAVIES, BARRIE. "Neglected West Indian Writers." *World Literature Written In English,* 11, No.2 (1972), 81-83.

ALI, AHMED (Pakistani, 1910-)

GENERAL

ANDERSON, DAVID D. "Ahmed Ali and the Growth of Pakistan Literary Tradition in English." *World Literature Written In English,* 14 (1975), 436-49.

OCEAN OF NIGHT (1964)

BRANDER, LAURENCE. "Two Novels by Ahmed Ali." *Journal Of Commonweath Literature,* No.3 (1967), pp. 83-86.

TWILIGHT IN DELHI (1941)

ANDERSON, DAVID D. "Ahmed Ali and the Growth of a Pakistan Literary Tradition in English." *World Literature Written In English,* 14 (1975), 439-42.

—————. "Ahmed Ali and *Twilight in Dehli.*" *Mahfil,* 7, No.1/2 (1971), 81-86.

BRANDER, LAURENCE. "Two Novels by Ahmed Ali." *Journal Of Commonwealth Literature,* No.3 (1967), pp. 77-83.

ALMEIDA, MANOEL ANTONIO DE (Brazilian, 1831-1861)

MEMOIRS OF A MILITIA SERGEANT (Memórias de um Sargento de Milicias)

PARKER, JOHN M. "The Nature of Realism in *Memórias De Um Sargento De Milicias.*" *Bulletin Of Hispanic Studies,* 48 (1971), 128-50.

TAYLOR, A. CAREY. "Balzac and Manoel António de Almeida: The Beginnings of Realism in Brazil." *Revue De Littérature Comparée,* 41 (1967), 195-203.

ALMQVIST, C. J. L. (Swedish, 1793-1866)

GENERAL

BJÖRCK, STAFFAN. "C. J. L. Almqvist: Romantic Radical." *American Scandinavian Review,* 57 (1969), 24-31.

ALONSO, LUIS RICARDO (Spanish-born Cuban, 1929-)

EL CANDIDATO (1970)

Reviews
BORRÁS, A. A. *Hispania,* 54 (1971), 600-1.

ALUKO, TIMOTHY MOFOLORUNSO (Nigerian, 1918-)

GENERAL

LINDFORS, BERNTH. "T. M. Aluko: Nigerian Satirist." *African Literature Today,* 5 (1971), 41-53.

CHIEF THE HONOURABLE MINISTER (1970)

TAIWO, OLADELE. "T. M. Aluko: The Novelist and His Imagination." *Présence Africaine,* No.90 (1974), pp. 241-46.

Reviews
MBENG, ALLAAJI. *Présence Africaine,* No.86 (1973), pp. 195-96.

KINSMAN AND FOREMAN (1966)

STEGEMAN, BEATRICE. "The Courtroom Clash in T. M. Aluko's *Kinsman And Foreman.*" *Critique,* 17, No.2 (1975), 26-35.

NATIONAL AFFAIRS

TAIWO, OLADELE. "T. M. Aluko: The Novelist and His Imagination." *Présence Africaine,* No.90 (1974), pp. 236-41.

ONE MAN, ONE MATCHET (1964)

LAURENCE, MARGARET. *Long Drums And Cannons,* pp. 171-76.

NGUGI, JAMES. "Satire in Nigeria," in *Protest And Conflict In African Literature,* ed. Cosmo Pieterse and Donald Munro, pp. 59-62.

ONE MAN, ONE WIFE (1959)

LINDFORS, BERNTH. "T. M. Aluko: Nigerian Satirist." *African Literature Today,* 5 (1971), 42-45.

STEGEMAN, BEATRICE. "The Divorce Dilemma: The New Woman in Contemporary African Novels." *Critique,* 15, No.3 (1973/4), 85-86.

TAIWO, OLADELE. "T. M. Aluko: The Novelist and His Imagination." *Présence Africaine,* No.90 (1974), 231-36.

Reviews
AMOSU, NUNASU. *Black Orpheus,* No.19 (1966), p. 61.

ALVAREZ GARDEAZABAL, GUSTAVO

DABEIBA (1972)

Reviews
FRANZ, THOMAS R. *Hispania,* 57 (1974), 1020-21

ÁLVAREZ LLERAS, ANTONIO (Colombian, 1892-1956)

AYER, NADA MÁS

McCLENDON, BARNETT A. "Influences of *El Escándolo* on the Colombian Novel *Ayer Nada Más.*" *Romance Notes,* 14 (1972), 96-104.

ALVARO, CORRADO (Italian, 1896-1956)

L'UOMO NEL LABIRINTO (1926)

TERRIZZI, ANTHONY R. "Another Look at Alvaro's *L'uomo Nel Labirinto.*" *Forum Italicum,* 7 (1973), 23-29.

AMADI, ELECHI (Nigerian, 1934-)

THE CONCUBINE (1966)

FINCH, GEOFFREY. "Tragic design in the Novels of Elechi Amadi." *Critique,* 17, No.2 (1975), 5-16.

LAURENCE, MARGARET. *Long Drums And Cannons,* pp. 177-84.

SCHEUB, HAROLD. "Two African Women." *Revue Des Langues Vivantes,* 37 (1971). 545-58; 664-81.

Reviews
JONES, ELDRED. "Locale and Universe—Three Nigerian Novels." *Journal Of Commonwealth Literature,* No.3 (1967), 127-29.

PALMER, EUSTACE. *African Literature Today,* No. 1 (1968), pp. 56-58.

VINCENT, THEO. *Black Orpheus,* No.21 (1967), pp. 62-63.

THE GREAT PONDS (1969)

FINCH, GEOFFREY. "Tragic Design in the Novels of Elechi Amadi." *Critique,* 17, No.2 (1975), 5-16.

AMADO, JORGE (Brazilian, 1912-)

GENERAL

HAMILTON, RUSSELL G. "Afro-Brazilian Cults in the Novels of Jorge Amado." *Hispania,* 50 (1967), 242-52.

LOWE, ELIZABETH SCHLOMAN. "The 'New' Jorge Amado." *Luso-Brazilian Review,* 6, No.2 (1969), 73-82.

NUNES, MARIA LUISA. "The Preservation of African Culture in Brazilian Literature: The Novels of Jorge Amado." *Luso-Brazilian Review,* 10 (1973), 86-101.

DONA FLOR AND HER TWO HUSBANDS (Dona Flor e seus dois maridos, 1966)

SILVERMAN, MALCOLM. "Moral Dilemma in Jorge Amado's *Dona Flor E Seus Dois Maridos.*" *Romance Notes,* 13 (1971), 243-49.

Reviews

BRUSHWOOD, JOHN S. *Kansas City Star,* 14 September 1969; rpt. in *Review,* No. 2 (1969), pp. 11-13.

DOWLING, THOMAS. *Washington Star,* 19 October 1969; rpt. in *Review,* No. 2 (1969), pp. 13-14.

GALLAGHER, DAVID. *New York Times Book Review,* 17 August 1969; rpt. in *Review,* No.2 (1969), pp. 14-17.

GOODSELL, JAMES NELSON. *Christian Science Monitor,* 18 December 1969; rtp. in *Review,* No.2 (1969), pp. 17-18.

Time, 5 September 1969; rpt. in *Review,* No.2 (1969), pp. 18-19.

FILHO DE MASSU E. BENEDITAOU O COMPRADRE OGUN (1964)

NUNES, MARIA LUISA. "The Preservation of African Culture in Brazilian Literature: The Novels of Jorge Amado." *Luso-Brazilian Review,* 10 (1973), 96-98.

HOME IS THE SAILOR: THE WHOLE TRUTH CONCERNING THE REDOUBTABLE ADVENTURES OF CAPTAIN VASCO MOSCOSO DE ARÃGAO, MASTER MARINER (A completa verdad sobre as discuitidas aventuras do camandante Vasco Moscoso de Arãgao, Capitao longo curso)

BERNARD, JUDITII. "Narrative Focus in Jorge Amado's Story of Vasco Moscoso de Arãgao." *Romance Notes,* 8 (1966), 14-17.

Reviews

CALLAN, RICHARD J. *Hispania,* 48 (1965), 943-44.

JUBIABÁ (1935)

NUNES, MARIA LUISA. "The Preservation of African Culture in Brazilian Literature: The Novels of Jorge Amado." *Luso-Brazilian Review,* 10, (1973), 90-93.

SILVERMAN, MALCOLM. "Allegory in Two Works of Jorge Amado." *Romance Notes,* 13 (1971), 67-69.

SHEPHERDS OF THE NIGHT (Os Pastores da noite, 1964)

SILVERMAN, MALCOLM. "Allegory in Two Works of Jorge Amado." *Romance Notes,* 13 (1971), 69-70.

Reviews

HALES, DAVID. "The Peaceable Kingdom of Bahia." *Saturday Review,* 4, February 1967, p. 45.

TENT OF MIRACLES (Tenda dos Milagres, 1969)

BORING, PHILLIS Z. "Amado and Barroso: Two Novelists View Race Relations in Brazil." *College Language Association Journal,* 19 (1976), 412-15.

NUNES, MARIA LUISA. "The Preservation of African Culture in Brazilian Literature: The Novels of Jorge Amado." *Luso-Brazilian Review,* 10 (1973), 98-100.

Reviews

SILVERMAN, MALCOLM. *Hispania,* 54 (1971), 206.

YATES, DONALD A. *Saturday Review,* 28 August 1971, pp. 26-27.

TEREZA BATISTA, HOME FROM THE WARS (Tereza Batista cansada de guerra, 1972)

Reviews

SLATER, CANDACE. "A Ballad to Sing in the Streets." *Review,* No.16 (1975), pp. 82-84.

THE TWO DEATHS OF QUINCAS WATERYELL (A Morte e a morte de Quincas Berro da Agua, 1959)

Reviews

CAPOUYA, EMILE. "His Own Man at His Own Funeral." *Saturday Review,* 8 January 1966, pp. 86-87.

AMICHAI, YEHUDA (Israeli, 1924-)

GENERAL

GILLON, ADAM. "Contemporary Israeli Literature: A New Stance." *Books Abroad,* 46 (1972), 193-96.

NOT OF THIS TIME, NOT OF THIS PLACE (Lo me-' akhshav, lo mi-kan, 1968)

ALTER, ROBERT. "Confronting the Holocaust: Three Israeli Novels." *Commentary,* 41, No.3 (1966), 68-70; rpt. in his *After The Tradition,* pp. 166-70.

SHAKED, GERSHON. "Childhood Lost, Studies in the Holocaust Theme in Contemporary Israeli Fiction." *Literature East And West,* 14 (1970), 95-100.

Reviews

RORTY, AMELIE. "A Tale of Two Cities." *Midstream Magazine,* 14, No.9 (1968), 73-77.

ANAND, MULK RAJ (Indian, 1905-)

GENERAL

BERRY, MARGARET. *Mulk Raj Anand: The Man And The Novelist.*

COWASJEE, SAROS. "Anand's Literary Creed." *Journal Of Indian Writing In English,* 1, No.1 (1973), 66-71.

———. "Mulk Raj Anand: The Early Struggles of a Novelist." *Journal Of Commonwealth Literature,* 7, No.1 (1972), 49-56.

FISHER, MARLENE. "Interview with Mulk Raj Anand: May 19, 1973, Khandala." *World Literature Written In English,* 13 (1974), 109-22.

KAUSHIK, R. K. "From Potter's Wheel to Dragon's Teeth." *Mahfil,* 6, No.4 (1970), 17-31.

KURMANDHAM, K. "The Novels of Dr. Mulk Raj Anand." *Triveni,* 36, No.3 (1967), 50-57.

MUKHERJEE, MEENAKSHI. "The Tractor and the Plough: the Contrasted Vision of Sudhim Ghose and Mulk Raj Anand." *Indian Literature,* 13 (1970), 50-57.

MURTI, K. V. SURYANARAYANA. "The Theme of Salvation: Treatment by Mulk Raj Anand and R. K. Narayan." *Triveni,* 34, No.3 (1965), 50-59.

NAIK, M. K. "The Achievement of Mulk Raj Anand." *Journal Of Indian Writing In English,* 1, No.1 (1973), 41-50.

NIVEN, ALISTAIR. "The 'Lalu' Trilogy of Mulk Raj Anand," in *Readings In Commonwealth Literature,* ed. William Walsh, pp. 11-26.

RIEMENSCHNEIDER, D. "An Ideal of Man in Mulk Raj Anand's Novels." *Indian Literature,* 10, No.1 (1967), 29-51.

SINHA, KRISHNA NANDAN. *Mulk Raj Anand,* 105-35.

SRINIVASA IYENGAR, K. R. *Indian Writing in English,* pp. 331-57.

ACROSS THE BLACK WATERS (1940)

SINHA, KRISHNA NANDAN. *Mulk Raj Anand,* pp. 48-50.

THE BIG HEART (1945)

SINHA, KRISHNA NANDAN. *Mulk Raj Anand,* 54-58.

COOLIE (1936)

MURTI, K. V. SURYANARAYANA. "The Theme of Salvation: Treatment by Mulk Raj Anand and R. K. Narayan." *Triveni,* 34, No.3 (1965), 52-55.

SINHA, KRISHNA NANDAN. *Mulk Raj Anand,* pp. 31-35.

SRINIVASA IYENGAR, K. R. *Indian Writing In English,* pp. 339-43.

DEATH OF A HERO (1964)

SINHA, KRISHNA NANDAN. *Mulk Raj Anand,* pp. 76-80.

LAMENT ON THE DEATH OF A MASTER OF ARTS (1939)

BERRY, MARGARET. " 'Purpose' in Mulk Raj Anand's Fiction." *Mahfil,* 5, No.1/2 (1968), 85–90.

SINHA, KRISHNA NANDAN. *Mulk Raj Anand,* pp. 39–45.

MORNING FACE (1968)

Reviews

COWASJEE, SAROS. *Indian Literature,* 13, No.1 (1970), 147–49.

McDOWELL, JUDITH H. *World Literature Written In English,* No.18 (1970), pp. 42–43.

THE OLD WOMAN AND THE COW (1963)

RIEMENSCHNEIDER, D. "An Ideal of Man in Mulk Raj Anand's Novels." *Indian Literature,* 10, No.1 (1967), 44–47.

SINHA, KRISHNA NANDAN. *Mulk Raj Anand,* pp. 67–73.

PRIVATE LIFE OF AN INDIAN PRINCE (1953)

COWASJEE, SAROS. "Mulk Raj Anand: Princes and Proletarians." *Journal of Commonwealth Literature,* No.5 (1968), pp. 52–64.

DAVIES, M. BRYN. "British and Indian Images of India." *Ariel; A Review Of International English Literature,* 1, No.4 (1970), 52–55; rpt. in *Readings In Commonwealth Literature,* ed. William Walsh, pp. 7–10.

SINHA, KRISHNA NANDAN. *Mulk Raj Anand,* pp. 62–66.

THE ROAD (1962)

SINHA, KRISHNA NANDAN. *Mulk Raj Anand,* pp. 73–76.

Reviews

PANDIT, MANORMA. *World Literature Written In English,* 14 (1975), 419–20.

SEVEN SUMMERS (1951)

SINHA, KRISHNA NANDAN. *Mulk Raj Anand,* pp. 58–62.

THE SWORD AND THE SICKLE (1942)

COWASJEE, SAROS. "Mulk Raj Anand's *The Sword And The Sickle.*" *World Literature Written In English,* 14 (1975), 267–77.

SINHA, KRISHNA NANDAN. *Mulk Raj Anand,* pp. 50–53.

TWO LEAVES AND A BUD (1937)

COWASJEE, SAROS. "Anand's Two Leaves and a Bud." *Indian Literature,* 16, Nos.3/4 (1973), 134–47.

RIEMENSCHNEIDER, D. "An Ideal of Man in Mulk Raj Anand's Novels." *Indian Literature,* 10, No.1 (1967), 34–37.

SINHA, KRISHNA NANDAN. *Mulk Raj Anand,* pp. 35–38.

SCRINIVASA IYENGAR, K. R. *Indian Writing In English,* pp. 343–47.

UNTOUCHABLE (1935)

ANAND, MULK RAJ. "The Story of My Experiment with a White Lie." *Indian Literature,* 10, No.3 (1967), 28–43.

COWASJEE, SAROS. "Mulk Raj Anand's *Untouchable:* An Appraisal." *Literature East And West,* 17 (1973), 199–211.

ROBERTSON, R. T. "*Untouchable* as an Archetypal Novel." *World Literature Written In English,* 14 (1975), 339–46.

SINHA, KRISHNA NANDAN. *Mulk Raj Anand,* pp. 27–31.

SRINIVASA IYENGAR, K. R. *Indian Writing In English,* pp. 335–39.

THE VILLAGE (1939)

RIEMENSCHNEIDER, D. "An Ideal of Man in Mulk Raj Anand's Novels." *Indian Literature,* 10, No.1 (1967) 37–42.

ANANOU, DAVID (Togo)

LE FILS DU FÉTICHE

GLEASON, JUDITH ILLSLEY. *This Africa,* pp. 104–8.

ANDERMANN, FRANK

DAS GROSSE GESICHTE

KURZ, PAUL KONRAD. "The Contemporary Novel about Jesus," in his *On Modern German Literature,* Vol.4; 157–64.

ANDERSCH, ALFRED (German, 1914–)

GENERAL

GEORGE, E. F. "Paths of Escape in Alfred Andersch's Works." *Orbis Litterarum,* 29 (1974), 160–69.

EFRAIM'S BOOK (Efraim, 1967)

Reviews

CLEMENTS, ROBERT J. *Saturday Review,* 19 December 1970, p. 33.

EWART, GAVIN. "Rome-Berlin Axis." *London Magazine,* NS 12, No.4 (1972), 146–47.

OPITZ, KURT. *Mundus Artium,* 1, No.2 (1968), 100–3.

FLIGHT TO AFAR (Sansibar Oder de letze Grund, 1957)

Reviews

GEORGE, E. F. *German Life And Letters,* 19 (1965), 77–78.

THE REDHEAD (Die rote, 1960)

BANCE, A. F. "*Der Tod In Rom* and *Die Rote:* Two Italian Episodes." *Forum For Modern Language Studies,* 3 (1967), 126–34.

ANDERSEN, TRYGGVE (Norwegian, 1866–1920)

IN THE DAYS OF THE COUNCILLOR (1897)

Reviews

ARESTAD, SVERRE. *American Scandinavian Review,* 58 (1970), 415–16.

ANDERSON-IMBERT, ENRIQUE (Argentine, 1910–)

FUGUE (Fuga, 1962)

Reviews

SHAW, DONALD. *Novel,* 1 (1968), 293–94.

ANDREYEV, LEONID NIKOLYEVITCH (Russian, 1871–1919)

THE RED LAUGH (Krasnyi smelch, 1904)

DAVIES, RUTH. *The Great Books Of Russia,* pp. 351–54.

NEWCOMBE, JOSEPHINE M. *Leonid Andreyev,* pp. 50–54.

WOODWARD, JAMES B. *Leonid Andreyev: A Study,* pp. 98–107.

THE SEVEN THAT WERE HANGED (Razskaz o semi povieshennykh, 1908)

DAVIES, RUTH. *The Great Books Of Russia,* pp. 354–56.

NEWCOMBE, JOSEPHINE M. *Leonid Andreyev,* pp. 66–71.

WOODWARD, JAMES B. *Leonid Andreyev: A Study,* pp. 190–97.

ANDRÍC, IVO (Yugoslav, 1892–)

THE BRIDGE ON THE DRINA (Na Drini cuprija, 1945)

MORAVCEVICH, NICHOLAS. "Ivo Andric and the Quintessence of Time." *Slavic And East European Journal,* 16 (1972), 313–18.

DEVIL'S YARD (Prokleta avlija, 1954)

LOUD, JOHN. "Between Two Worlds: Andríc the Storyteller." *Review Of National Literatures,* 5, No.1 (1974), 121–24.

TRAVNIK CHRONICLE (Travnicka hronika, 1945)

FERGUSON, ALAN. "Public and Private Worlds in 'Travnik Chronicle.' " *Modern Language Review,* 70 (1975), 830–38.

THE WOMAN FROM SARAJEVO (Gospodjica, 1945)

Reviews
BARRETT, WILLIAM. *Atlantic Monthly,* 215, No.5 (1965), 148–49.

STILWELL, ROBERT L. "Death Was Not the End of Dying." *Saturday Review,* 17 April 1965, pp. 49–50.

ANDRZEJEWSKI, JERZY (Polish, 1909–)
GENERAL

NAJDER, ZDZISLAW. "Jerzy Andrzejewski: The Later Novels." *Triquarterly,* No.9 (1967), pp. 223–28.

ASHES AND DIAMONDS (Popiol i Diament, 1948)

IYENGAR, K. R. SRINVASA. "War and Peace in Contemporary Polish Fiction," *Indian Literature,* 17, No.1/2 (1974), 59–63.

HE COMETH LEAPING UPON THE MOUNTAINS see A SITTER FOR A SATYR

A SITTER FOR A SATYR (Idzie, skaczac po gorach, 1963)

Reviews
DARACK, ARTHUR. "Things Are Worse Than They Seem." *Saturday Review,* 3 July 1965, pp. 29–30.

ANTHONY, MICHAEL (Trinidadian, 1932–)
GENERAL

ANTHONY, MICHAEL. "Growing Up in Writing." *Journal Of Commonwealth Literature,* No.7 (1969), pp. 80–87.

McGUINNESS, FRANK. "West Indian Windfall." *London Magazine,* 7, No.1 (1967), 117–20.

GREEN DAYS BY THE RIVER (1967)

Reviews
SUBRAMANI. *World Literature Written In English,* No.19 (1971), pp. 84–85.

THE YEAR IN SAN FERNANDO (1965)

EDWARDS, PAUL AND KENNETH RAMCHAND. "The Art of Memory: Michael Anthony's *The Year In San Fernando.*" *Journal Of Commonwealth Literature,* No.7 (1969), pp. 59–72; rpt. in *Readings In Commonwealth Literature,* ed. William Walsh, pp. 298–313.

LUENGO, ANTHONY. "Growing Up in San Fernando: Change and Growth In Michael Anthony's The Year in San Fernando." *Ariel; A Review Of International English Literature,* 6, No.2 (1965), 81–95.

MOORE, GERALD. *The Chosen Tongue,* pp. 17–20.

RAMCHAND, KENNETH. *The West Indian Novel And Its Background,* pp. 205–22.

ANTILLANO, LAURA
LA MUERTE DEL MONSTRUO COME PIEDRA

Reviews
ADAMS, M. IAN. *Latin American Literary Review,* 2, No.4 (1974), 153–54.

ANTON-ULRICH VON BRAUNSCHWEIG-WOLFFENBUTTEL, HERZOG (German, 1633–1714)
DIE DURCHLEUCHTIGE SYRERINN ARAMENA (1669–1680)

SPAHR, BLAKE LEE. *Anton Ulrich And Aramena: The Genesis And Development Of A Baroque Novel.*

WAGENER, HANS. *The German Baroque Novel,* pp. 113–21.

DIE ROMISCHE OCTAVIA (1677)

WAGENER, HANS. *The German Baroque Novel,* pp. 113–21.

ANTUNES, DAVID
BRIGUELA

BOARINO, G. L. *Hispania,* 50 (1971), 394.

APULEIUS, LUCIUS (Africa Madaura, c. 125–175)
THE GOLDEN ASS (Metamorphosis)

DRAKE, GERTRUDE C. "Candidus: A Unifying Theme in Apuleius' *Metamorphoses.*" *Classical Journal,* 64 (1968), 102–9.

———. "Lucius's 'Business' in the *Metamorphoses* of Apuleius." *Papers On Language And Literature,* 5 (1969), 339–61.

DUST, PHILIP. "Apuleius, *Metamorphoses* 4.24.5." *Classical Journal,* 63 (1968), 266–67.

ENGLERT, JOHN AND TIMOTHY LONG. "Functions of Hair in Apuleius' *Metamorphoses.*" *Classical Review,* 68 (1973), 236–39.

HIJMANS, B. L. AND R. E. H. WESTENDORP BOERMA. "Apuleius *Met.* IV I (74,16): *Levigatos* or *Levatos?*" *Mnemosyne,* 4th ser., 26 (1973), 396–97.

NETHERCUT, WILLIAM R. "Apuleius' Literary Art: Resonance and Depth in the *Metamorphoses.*" *Classical Journal,* 64 (1968), 110–19.

PERRY, BEN EDWIN. *The Ancient Romances,* pp. 236–82.

———. "Who Was Lucius of Patrae?" *Classical Journal,* 64 (1968). 97–101.

REXROTH, KENNETH. "Classics Revisited—XXXI—Apuleius." *Saturday Review,* 2 July 1966, 15; rpt. in his *Classics Revisited,* pp. 116–20.

SANDY, GERALD. "The Isis Episode in Apuleius." *Classical Journal,* 68 (1973), 228–35.

SCHLAM, CARL C. "The Curiosity of the Golden Ass." *Classical Journal,* 64 (1968), 120–25.

SCOBIE, ALEXANDER. "The Confirmation of the Unbelievable in Apuleius' Metamorphoses," in his *More Essays On The Ancient Romance And Its Heritage,* pp. 35–46.

———. "The Dating of the Earliest Printed European Translations of Apuleius' Metamorphoses," in his *More Essays On The Ancient Romance And Its Heritage,* pp. 47–52.

———. "Juvenal XV and Apuleius' Metamorphoses," in his *More Essays On The Ancient Romance And Its Heritage,* pp. 53–63.

———. "The Structure and Unity of Apuleius' Metamorphoses," in his *More Essays On The Ancient Romance And Its Heritage,* pp. 64–83.

WALSH, P. G. *The Roman Novel: The 'Satyricon' Of Petronius And The 'Metamorphoses' Of Apuleius,* pp. 141–223.

AQUIN, HUBERT (Canadian, 1929–1977)
THE ANTIPHONARY (L'antiphonaire, 1969)

BEAUSANG, MICHAEL. "Music and Medicine." *Canadian Literature,* No.58 (1973), pp. 71–76.

PROCHAIN ÉPISODE (1965)

SUTHERLAND, RONALD. "The Fourth Separatism." *Canadian Literature,* No.45 (1970), pp. 9–11; rpt. in his *Second Image,* pp. 113–16.

Reviews

MOORE, C. H. "A Cry to be Heard." *Canadian Literature,* No.29 (1966), pp. 64–66.

ARAGON, LOUIS (French, 1897–1982)

GENERAL

ADERETH, M. *Commitment In Modern French Literature,* pp. 81–126.

BROWN, FREDERICK. "On Louis Aragon: Silence and History." *Southern Review,* NS, 3 (1967), 311–21.

THE EXECUTION (La Mise à Mort, 1965)

ADERETH, M. *Commitment In Modern French Literature,* pp. 81–126.

GUTERMUTH, MARY. "Triangular Schizophrenia and the *Execution* of Aragon." *Kentucky Romance Quarterly,* 14 (1967), 379–92.

NIGHTWALKER (Le paysan de paris, 1926)

FIRCHOW, PETER EDGERLY. "*Nadja* and *Le Paysan De Paris:* Two Surrealist 'Novels.'" *Wisconsin Studies In Contemporary Literature,* 6 (1965), 293–307.

ARAKI KAZUKUMA (Chinese)

THE SECRET SOCIETIES AND ORGANIZATIONS IN THE LOWER YANGTSE

HUANG, JOE C. *Heroes And Villains In Communist China,* pp. 129–34.

ARANHA, Jose Pereira de Graça see GRAÇA ARANHA, Jose Pereira de

ARBRUQUAH, J. W. (Ghanian)

GENERAL

MCDOWELL, ROBERT. "J. W. Arbruquah Talks About Ghana." *World Literature Written In English,* No.20 (1971), pp. 27–36.

ARENAS, REINALDO (Cuban, 1943–)

HALLUCINATIONS (El mundo alucinante, 1969)

GORDON, AMBROSE, JR. "Rippling Ribaldry and Pouncing Puns: the Two Lives of Friar Servando." *Review,* No.8 (1973), pp. 40–44.

ORTEGA, JULIO. "The Dazzling World of Friar Servando." Trans. Tom J. Lewis. *Review,* No.8 (1973), pp. 45–48.

VESTERMAN, WILLIAM. "Going No Place with Arenas." *Review,* No.8 (1973), pp. 49–51.

WALLER, CLAUDIA JOAN. "Reynaldo Arenas' *El Mundo Alucinante:* Aesthetic and Thematic Focal Points." *Kentucky Romance Quarterly,* 19 (1972), 41–50.

ARGÜEDAS, ALCIDES (Bolivian, 1879–1946)

RAZA DE BRONCE

BROTHERSTON, GORDON. "Alcides Argüedas a a 'Defender of Indians' in the First and Later Editions of *Raza De Bronce*." *Romance Notes,* 13 (1971), 41–47.

ARGUEDAS, JOSÉ MARÍA (Peruvian, 1911–69)

GENERAL

RODRÍGUEZ-PERALTA, PHYLLIS. "The Literary Progression of José María Arguedas." *Hispania,* 55 (1972), 225–33.

DEEP RIVERS (Los ríos profundos, 1959)

GOLD, PETER. "The *Indigenista* Fiction of José María Arguedas." *Bulletin of Hispanic Studies,* 50 (1973), 63–65.

TODAS LAS SANDRES (1964)

GOLD, PETER. "The *Indigenista* Fiction of José María Arguedas." *Bulletin Of Hispanic Studies,* 50 (1973), 65–70.

KLAREN, SARA CASTRO. "*Todas Las Sangres:* A Change of Skin." *Latin American Literary Review,* 1, No.2 (1973), 83–98.

YAWAR FIESTA (1941)

GOLD, PETER. "The *Indigenista* Fiction of Jose María Arguedas." *Bulletin of Hispanic Studies,* 50 (1973), 60–63.

ARGUETA, MANLIO (El Salvadorean, 1936–)

EL VALLE DE LAS HAMACAS (1970)

Reviews

SCHWARTZ, KESSEL. *Hispania,* 54 (1971), 974.

ARIAS, ABELARDO

DE TALES CUALES (1973)

Reviews

LEWALD, H. ERNEST. *Hispania,* 58 (1975), 403–4.

ARLT, ROBERTO (Argentine, 1900–1942)

GENERAL

LINDSTROM, NAOMI. "Madness in Arlt's Fiction." *Chasqui,* 4, No.3 (1975), 18–22.

ARMAH, AYI KWEI (Ghanian, 1939–)

THE BEAUTYFUL ONES ARE NOT YET BORN (1968)

COLLINS, HAROLD R. "The Ironic Imagery of Armah's *The Beautyful Ones Are Not Yet Born:* The Putrescent Vision." *World Literature Written In English,* No.20 (1971), pp. 37–50.

FOLARIN, MARGARET. "An Additional Comment on Ayi Kwei Armah's *The Beautyful Ones Are Not Yet Born.*" *African Literature Today,* 5 (1971), 116–29.

GRIFFITHS, GARETH. "Structure and Image in Kwei Armah's *The Beautyful Ones Are Not Born Yet.*" *Studies In Black Literature,* 2, No.2 (1971), 1–9.

LARSON, CHARLES R. "The Novel of the Future: Wole Soyinka and Ayi Kwei Armah," in his *The Emergence Of African Fiction,* rev. ed., pp. 258–68.

OGUNGBESAN, KOLAWOLE. "Symbol and Meaning in *The Beautyful Ones Are Not Yet Born.*" *World Literature Written In English,* 12, No.1 (1973), 4–25.

———. "Symbol and Meaning in *The Beautyful Ones Are Not Yet Born.*" *African Literature Today,* 7 (1975), 93–110.

PALMER, EUSTACE. "Social Comment in the West African Novel." *Studies In The Novel,* 4 (1972), 223–27.

Reviews

CASTAGNO, MARGARET. *Literature East And West,* 14 (1970), 577–58.

MILLER, CHARLES. "The Arts Of Venality." *Saturday Review,* 31 August 1968, pp. 24–25.

NOBLE, R. W. "A Beautiful Novel." *Journal Of Commonwealth Literature,* No.9 (1970), pp. 117–19.

FRAGMENTS (1970)

LARSON, CHARLES R. "The Novel of the Future: Wole Soyinka and Ayi Kwei Armah," in his *The Emergence Of African Fiction,* rev. ed., pp. 268–76.

Reviews

MAHOOD, M. M. *Saturday Review,* 17 January 1970, p. 40.

MOORE, GERALD. "Armah's Second Novel." *Journal Of Commonwealth Literature,* 9, No.1 (1974), 69-71.

WHY ARE WE SO BLEST? (1971)

Reviews

LARSON, CHARLES R. *Saturday Review,* 18 March 1972, pp. 73-74.

ARNIM, ACHIM VON (German, 1781-1831)

ISABELLA OF EGYPT (Isabella von AEgypten, 1812)

MORNIN, J. EDWARD W. "National Subjects in the Works of Achim von Arnim." *German Life And Letters,* 24 (1971), 323-25.

DIE KRONENWÄCHTER (1817)

HOLT, R. F. "Achim von Arnim and Sir Walter Scott." *German Life And Letters,* 26 (1973), 142-60.

ARTSYBASHEV, MIKHAIL (Russian, 1878-1927; died in Poland)

SANINE (Sanin, 1907)

PACHMUSS, TEMIRA. "Mikhail Artsybashev in the Criticism of Zinaida Gippius." *Slavonic And East European Review,* 44 (1966), 77-80.

ASTLEY, THEA (Australian, 1925-)

GENERAL

ASTLEY, THEA. "The Idiot Question." *Southerly,* 30 (1970), 3-8.

COUPER, J. M. "The Novels of Thea Astley." *Meanjin,* 26 (1967), 332-37.

MATTHEWS, BRIAN. "Life in the Eye of the Hurricane: The Novels of Thea Astley." *Southern Review: Literary And Interdisciplinary Essays,* 6 (1973), 148-73.

THE ACOLYTE (1972)

MATTHEWS, BRIAN. "Life in the Eye of the Hurricane: The Novels of Thea Astley." *Southern Review: Literary and Interdisciplinary Essays,* 6 (1973), 159-72.

Reviews

GILBEY, DAVID. *Southerly,* 33 (1973), 83-85.

THE SLOW NATIVES (1965)

MATTHEWS, BRIAN. "Life in the Eye of the Hurricane: The Novels of Thea Astley." *Southern Review: Literary And Interdisciplinary Essays,* 6 (1973), 155-59.

Reviews

ASHWORTH, ARTHUR. *Southerly,* 26 (1966), 62-66.

CUNEO, PAUL K. "Strains." *Saturday Review,* 4 November 1967, p. 34.

ASTURIAS, MIGUEL ÁNGEL (Guatemalan, 1899-1974)

GENERAL

CUSACK, DYMPHNA. "Miguel-Angel Asturias: Nobel Prize Winner, 1967." *Meanjin,* 27 (1968), 238-43.

DONOHUE, FRANCIS. "Commitment in the Spanish American Novel: Asturias." *Canadian Modern Language Review,* 27, No.4 (1971), 58-60.

HIMELBLAU, JACK. "Love, Self and Cosmos in the Early Works of Miguel Angel Asturias." *Kentucky Romance Quarterly,* 18 (1971), 243-64.

_____ . "Miguel Angel Asturias' Dawn of Creativity (1920-1930): The Minstrel of Merriment." *Latin American Literary Review,* 2, No.3 (1973), 85-104.

LEAL, LUIS. "Myth and Social Realism in Miguel Angel Asturias." *Comparative Literature Studies,* 5 (1968), 237-47.

LORENZ, GUNTER W. "An Interview with Asturias." Trans. Tom J. Lewis. *Review,* No.15 (1975), pp. 5-11.

LYON, THOMAS E. "Miguel Angel Asturias: Timeless Fantasy." *Books Abroad,* 42 (1968), 183-89.

"Miguel Angel Asturias: 1899-1974." *Review,* No.12 (1974), p. 52.

THE CYCLONE see STRONG WIND

THE EYES OF THE INTERRED (Los ojos de los enterrados, 1960)

CALLAN, RICHARD J. *Miguel Angel Asturias,* pp. 112-19.

THE GREEN POPE (El Papa verde, 1954)

CALLAN, RICHARD J. *Miguel Angel Asturias,* pp. 97-111.

MEN OF MAIZ (Hombres de Maíz, 1949)

BROTHERSTON, GORDON. "The Presence of Mayan Literature in 'Hombres de Maíz' and Other Works by Miguel Ángel Asturias." *Hispania,* 58 (1975), 68-74.

CALLAN, RICHARD J. *Miguel Angel Asturias,* pp. 53-84.

_____ . "The Quest Myth in Miguel Ángel Asturias' *Hombres de Maíz.*" *Hispanic Review,* 36 (1968), 249-61.

CHRIST, RONALD. "The Text as Translation." *Review,* No.15 (1975), pp. 28-33.

COLEMAN, ALEXANDER. "A Reader's Confession." *Review,* No.15 (1975), pp. 23-27.

DORFMAN, ARIEL. "Myth as Time and World." *Review,* No.15 (1975), pp. 12-22.

MARTIN, G. M. "Pattern for a Novel: An Analysis of the Opening of *Hombres de Maiz.*" *Revista De Estudios Hispánicos,* 5 (1971), 223-41.

_____ . "Theme and Structure in Asturias' *Hombres De Maiz.*" *Modern Language Quarterly,* 30 (1969), 582-602.

Reviews

CALLAN, RICHARD J. *Latin American Literary Review,* 4, No.8 (1976), 97-99.

MULATA (Mulata de tal, 1963)

MARTIN, GERALD. "*Mulata De Tal:* The Novel as Animated Cartoon." *Hispanic Review,* 41 (1973), 397-415.

Reviews

LASK, THOMAS. *New York Times,* 26 October 1967; rpt. in *Review,* No.1 (1968), 47-49.

MEAD, ROBERT G., JR. "A Myth for Mankind." *Saturday Review,* 4 November 1967, p. 32; rpt. in *Review,* No.1 (1968), 49-51.

THE MULATTA AND MR. FLY see MULATA

THE PRESIDENT (El Señor Presidente, 1946)

BRUSHWOOD, JOHN S. *The Spanish American Novel,* pp. 160-63.

CALLAN, RICHARD J. "Babylonian Mythology in 'El Señor Presidente.' " *Hispania,* 50 (1967), 417-24.

_____ . *Miguel Angel Asturias,* pp. 18-52.

GYURKO, LANIN A. "Modern Hispanic-American Fiction: Novel of Action and Narrative of Consciousness." *Symposium,* 25 (1971), 360-65.

HIMELBLAU, JACK. "*El Señor Presidente:* Antecedents, Sources, and Reality." *Hispanic Review,* 41 (1973), 43-78.

_____ . "The Theme of Love in *El Señor Presidente.*" *Romance Notes,* 15 (1974), 588-91.

IRVING, T. B. "The Hero in Asturias' Novel *The President.*" *University Of Toronto Quarterly,* 38 (1969), 192-206.

MARTIN, GERALD. "*El Señor Presidente* and How To Read It." *Bulletin of Hispanic Studies,* 47 (1970), 223-43.

WALKER, JOHN. "The Role of the Idiot in Asturias' *El Señor Presidente.*" *Romance Notes,* 12 (1970), 62-67.

STRONG WIND (Viento fuerte, 1950)

CALLAN, RICHARD J. *Miguel Angel Asturias,* pp. 85-96.

Reviews
CAPOUYA, EMILE. *Nation,* 17 February 1969; rpt. in *Review,* No.1 (1968), 51-53.

JOHNSON, HARVEY L. *Hispania,* 53 (1970), 162.

MEAD, ROBERT G., JR. "Nature's Cycle Slashed by Greed." *Saturday Review,* 25 January 1969, p. 30.

SCHECHNER, WILLIAM. "Capitalist Snakes in a Banana Garden." *Catholic World,* 209 (1969), 238.

WEEKS, EDWARD. *Atlantic Monthly,* 223, No.3 (1969), 144-46.

VIERNES DE DOLORES (1971)

Reviews
LYON, TED. *Chasqui,* 2, No.1 (1973), 65-66.

ATIYAH, EDWARD
GENERAL

RA'AD, BASEM ALEXI. "Edward Atiyah's Middle Eastern Fiction." *Literature East And West,* 15 (1971), 108-18.

LEBANON PARADISE

RA'AD, BASEM ALEXI. "Edward Atiyah's Middle Eastern Fiction." *Literature East And West,* 15 (1971), 112-16.

ATWOOD, MARGARET (Canadian, 1939-)
GENERAL

ROGERS, LINDA. "Margaret the Magician." *Canadian Literature,* No.60 (1974), pp. 83-85.

WOODCOCK, GEORGE. "Surfacing to Survive: Notes of the Recent Atwood." *Ariel: A Review Of International English Literature,* 4, No.3 (1973), 16-28.

THE EDIBLE WOMAN (1969)

Reviews
EASTON, ELIZABETH. *Saturday Review,* 3 October 1970, p. 40.

SURFACING (1972)

GAREBIAN, KEITH. "*Surfacing:* Apocalyptic Ghost Story." *Mosaic,* 9, No.3 (1976), 1-9.

McLAY, CATHERINE. "The Divided Self: Theme and Pattern in Margaret Atwood's *Surfacing.*" *Journal Of Canadian Fiction,* 4, No.1 (1975), 82-95.

SCHAEFFER, SUSAN FROMBERG. " 'It Is Time That Separates Us': Margaret Atwood's *Surfacing.*" *Centennial Review,* 18 (1974), 319-37.

WOODCOCK, GEORGE. "Surfacing to Survive: Notes of the Recent Atwood." *Ariel: A Review Of International English Literature,* 4, No.3 (1973), 23-28.

Reviews
DAVIS, FRANCES. *Dalhousie Review,* 52 (1972/3), 679-82.

DeMOTT, BENJAMIN. "Recycling Art." *Saturday Review,* 1 (April 1973), 85-86.

GROSSKURTH, PHYLLIS. "Victimization or Survival." *Canadian Literature,* No.55 (1973), pp. 108-10.

MORLEY, PATRICIA. "Multiple Surfaces." *Journal Of Canadian Fiction,* 1, No.4 (1972), 99-100.

AUCASSIN AND NICOLETTE (Author unknown, 13th Century)

BLAKEY, BRIAN. "*Aucassin Et Nicolette,* XXIV, 4." *French Studies,* 22 (1968), 97-98.

CH'EN, LI-LI. "*Pien-Wen* Chantefable and *Aucassin Et Nicolette.*" *Comparative Literature,* 23 (1971), 255-61.

CLEVENGER, DARNELL H. "Torelore in *Aucassin Et Nicolette.*" *Romance Notes,* 11 (1970), 656-65.

GRIFFIN, ROBERT. "*Aucassin Et Nicolette* and the Albigensian Crusade." *Modern Language Quarterly,* 26 (1965), 243-56.

HARDEN, ROBERT. "*Aucassin Et Nicolette* as Parody." *Studies In Philology,* 63 (1966), 1-9.

MARTIN, JUNE HALL. *Love's Fools: Aucassin, Troilus, Calisto And The Parody Of The Courtly Lover,* pp. 23-36, 135-43.

REA, JOHN A. "The Form of *Aucassin Et Nicolette.*" *Romance Notes,* 15 (1974), 504-8.

SARGENT, BARBARA NELSON. "Parody in *Aucassin Et Nicolette:* Some Further Considerations." *French Review,* 43 (1970), 597-605.

TRIEBEL, L. A. "Aucassin and Nicolette: A Neglected Medieval Masterpiece." *Canadian Modern Language Review,* 21, No.1 (1964), 17-19.

VANCE, EUGENE. "The Word at Heart: *Aucassin Et Nicolette* as a Medieval Comedy of Language." *Yale French Studies,* No.45 (1970), pp. 33-51.

WILLIAMSON, JOAN B. "Naming as a Source of Irony in 'Aucassin et Nicolette.' " *Studi Francesi,* 17 (1973), 401-9.

d'AULNOY, MARIE CATHERINE, BARONNE (French, c. 1650-1666)
GENERAL

PALMER, MELVIN D. "Madame d'Aulnoy In England." *Comparative Literature,* 27 (1975), 237-53.

HYPOLITUS EARL OF DOUGLAS (Histoire D'Hypolite, Comte De Duglas, 1690)

Reviews
MYERS, MITZI. *Mary Wollstonecraft Newsletter,* 2, No.2 (1973), 35-36. (review of facsimile edition)

AVELLANEDA, ALONSO FERNANDEZ DE (Spanish, 17th century)
SEGUNDO TOMO DEL INGENIOSO HIDALGO DON QUIJOTE (1614)

ABRAMS, FRED. "Aliaga, Avellaneda, and a Curious Passage in the *Quijote* (II, 61)." *Romance Notes,* 8 (1966), 86-90.

AVOTINA, DAINA
NENOGALINIET STIRNU

Reviews
EKMANIS, ROLFS. *Lituanus,* 19, No.4 (1973), 75-76.

AVRIL, NICOLE
LES GENS DE MISAR (1972)

JONES, LOUISA. *French Review,* 47 (1974), 651-52.

AWOONER, KOFI (Ghanian, 1935-)
THIS EARTH, MY BROTHER . . . (1971)

Reviews
HORNER, J. E. *World Literature Written In English,* 11, No.2 (1972), 99-100.

SNYDER, EMILE. *Saturday Review,* 19 June 1971, pp. 23-24.

AYALA, FRANCISCO (Spanish emigré, 1906-)
EL RAPTO

ELLIS, KEITH. "Cervantas and Ayala's *El Rapto:* The Art of Re-working a Story." *PMLA,* 84 (1969), 14-19.

AYALA, Ramón Pérez de see PÉREZ DE AYALA, Ramón

AZEVEDO, ALUÍZIO
O MULATO (1881)

MACNICOLL, MURRAY GRAEME. "O Mulato and Maranhão: The Socio-Historical Context." *Luso-Brazilian Review,* 12 (1975), 234-40.

AZORÍN (Spanish, 1873-1967) pseudonym of José Martínez Ruiz
GENERAL

BIERVLIET, M. D. VAN. José Martínez Ruiz's Obsession with Fame." *Forum For Modern Language Studies,* 8 (1972), 291-303.

CATSORIS, JOHN A. *Azorin And The Eighteenth Century.*

d'AMBROSIO SERVODIDIO, MIRELLA. "Azorín: A Changing Vision of Spain." *Revista De Estudios Hispánicos,* 5 (1971), 55-63.

FIDDIAN, ROBIN WILLIAM. "Azorín and Guyau: A Further Point of Comparison." *Romance Notes,* 16 (1975), 474-78.

GLENN, KATHLEEN M. *The Novelistic Technique Of Azorin (Jose Martinez Ruiz),* pp. 15-22, 57-68, 97-104, 119-22.

JOINER, LAWRENCE D. "Similarities in Proust's and Azorín's Theories of the Novel." *South Atlantic Bulletin,* 39, No.2 (1974), 43-50.

LIVINGSTONE, LEON. "Self-Creation and Alienation in the Novels of Azorín." *Journal Of Spanish Studies,* 1 (1973), 5-43.

————. "The Theme of Intelligence and Will in the Novels of Azorín." *Romanic Review,* 58 (1967), 83-94.

LOTT, ROBERT E. "Considerations on Azorín's Literary Techniques and the Other Arts." *Kentucky Romance Quarterly,* 18 (1971), 423-34.

NEWBERRY, WILMA. *The Pirandellian Mode In Spanish Literature From Cervantes To Sastre,* pp. 97-115.

ANTONIO AZORIN (1903)

GLENN, KATHLEEN M. *The Novelistic Technique Of Azorin (Jose Martinez Ruiz,)* pp. 23-36.

EL CABALLERO INACTUAL (1928)

JOINER, LAWRENCE D. "Proust and Azorín." *Romance Notes,* 13 (1972), 468-73.

DIARIO DE UN ENFERMO (1901)

LIVINGSTONE, LEON. "The 'Esthetic of Repose' in Azorín's *Diario De Un Enfermo.*" *Symposium,* 20 (1966), 241-53.

DOÑA INÉS (1925)

GLENN, KATHLEEN M. *The Novelistic Technique Of Azorin (Jose Martinez Ruiz),* pp. 69-94.

PALLEY, JULIAN. "Images of Time in 'Doña Inés.' " *Hispania,* 54 (1971), 250-55.

EL LIBRO DE LEVANTE (1929)

JOINER, LAWRENCE D. "Proust and Azorín." *Romance Notes,* 13 (1972), 468-73.

SALVADORA DE OLBENA (1944)

GLENN, KATHLEEN M. *The Novelistic Technique Of Azorin (Jose Martinez Ruiz),* pp. 105-18.

TOMAS RUEDA

GLENN, KATHLEEN M. "The Narrator's Changing Perspective in Azorín's *Tomas Rueda.*" *Revista De Estudios Hispánicos,* 9 (1975), 343-57.

————. *The Novelistic Technique Of Azorin (Jose Martinez Ruiz),* pp. 37-54.

LA VIDA ES SUEÑO

WEIGER, JOHN G. "Rebirth in *La Vida Es Sueño.*" *Romance Notes,* 10 (1968), 119-21.

AZUELA, ARTURO
EL TAMAÑO DEL INFIERNO

Reviews
McMURRAY, GEORGE R. *Chasqui,* 4, No.3 (1975), 77-78.

AZUELA, MARIANO (Mexican, 1873-1952)
GENERAL

LEAL, LUIS. "The Novelist's Craft," in his *Mariano Azuela,* pp. 95-122.

ANDRÉS PÉREZ, MADERISTA

LEAL, LUIS. *Mariano Azuela,* pp. 53-55.

LOS CACIQUES

LEAL LUIS. *Mariano Azuela,* pp. 55-57.

COMRADE PANTOJA

LEAL, LUIS. *Mariano Azuela,* pp. 74-77.

LOS FRACASADOS

LEAL, LUIS. *Mariano Azuela,* pp. 44-47.

THE FIREFLY (La luciérnaga)

LEAL, LUIS. *Mariano Azuela,* pp. 70-73.

LEVY, KURT L. "*La Luciérnaga:* Title, Leitmotif, and Structural Unity." *Philological Quarterly,* 51 (1972), 321-28.

MARTÍNEZ, ELIUD. "Mariano Azuela and 'The Height of the Times': A Study of *La Luciérnaga [The Firefly].*" *Latin American Literary Review,* 3, No.5 (1974), 113-30.

MULLEN, E. J. "Towards a Prototype of Mariano Azuela's *La Luciérnaga.*" *Romance Notes,* 11 (1970), 518-21.

MALA YERBA

LEAL, LUIS. *Mariano Azuela,* pp. 47-50.

LA MALHORA

LEAL, LUIS. *Mariano Azuela,* pp. 66-68.

MARÍA LUISA

LEAL, LUIS. *Mariano Azuela,* pp. 42-44.

SIN AMOR

LEAL, LUIS. *Mariano Azuela,* pp. 50-52.

THE TRIALS OF A RESPECTABLE FAMILY (Las Tribulaciones de una familia decente)

LANGFORD, WALTER M. *The Mexican Novel Comes Of Age,* pp. 24-26.

LEAL, LUIS. *Mariano Azuela,* pp. 62-65.

THE UNDERDOGS (Los de Abajo)

BRUSHWOOD, JOHN S. *The Spanish American Novel,* pp. 19–24.

JEROME, JUDSON. "On Mariano Azuela's *Los De Abajo (The Underdogs),*" in *Rediscoveries,* ed. David Madden, pp. 179–89.

LANGFORD, WALTER M. *The Mexican Novel Comes Of Age,* pp. 16–17, 19–23.

LEAL, LUIS. *Mariano Azuela,* pp. 57–60.

SOMMERS, JOSEPH. *After The Storm,* pp. 6–16.

B

BABEL, ISAAC (Russian, 1894–1941)
GENERAL

SHKLOVSKY, VICTOR. "Isaac Babel: A Critical Romance," in *Major Soviet Writers,* ed. Edward J. Brown, pp. 295-300.

STROUD NICHOLAS. "The Art of Mystification: The 'Prehistoric' Isaac Babel." *Russian Literature Triquarterly,* No.13 (1975), pp. 591-93.

VORONSKIJ, ALEKSANDR. "Isaac Babel," in *Twentieth-Century Russian Literary Criticism,* ed. Victor Erlich, pp. 182-97.

RED CAVALRY (Konarmiia, 1926)

CARDEN, PATRICIA. *The Art Of Isaac Babel,* pp. 86-151.

IRIBARNE, LOUIS. "Babel's *Red Cavalry* as a Baroque Novel." *Contemporary Literature,* 14 (1973), 58-77.

KLOTZ, MARTIN B. "Poetry of the Present: Isaak Babel's *Red Cavalry.*" *Slavic And East European Journal,* 18 (1974), 160-69.

LEE, ALICE. "Epiphany in Babel's *Red Cavalry.*" *Russian Literature Triquarterly,* No.2 (1972), pp. 249-60.

SINYAVSKY, ANDREY. "Isaac Babel," in *Major Soviet Writers,* ed. Edward J. Brown, pp. 301-9.

TERRAS, VICTOR. "Line and Color: The Structure of I. Babel's Short Stories in *Red Cavalry.*" *Studies In Short Fiction,* 3 (1966), 141-56.

VORONSKIJ, ALEKSANDR. "Isaac Babel," in *Twentieth-Century Russian Literary Criticism,* ed. Victor Erlich, pp. 189-96.

BACQUE, JAMES (Canadian, 1929–)
THE LONELY ONES (1969)

Reviews
SPETTIGUE, D. O. "Where to Go?" *Canadian Literature,* No. 45 (1970), pp. 74-75.

A MAN OF TALENT (1972)

Reviews
MCDONALD, LAWRENCE. "Native Sons." *Canadian Literature,* No.62 (1974), pp. 112-14.

MONKMAN, LESLIE. "Man on Fire." *Journal Of Canadian Fiction,* 2, No.4 (1973), 91-92.

BAHR, HERMANN (Austrian, 1863–1934)
GENERAL

WILLIAMS, CEDRIC E. *The Broken Eagle,* pp. 33-44.

BAHRDT, KARL FRIEDRICH (German, 1741–1792)

ALA LAMA ODER DER KONIG UNTER DEN SCHAFERN, AUCH EINGOLDENER SPIEGEL

HADLEY, MICHAEL. *The German Novel In 1790,* pp. 157-58.

GESCHICHTE DES PRINZEN YHAKANPOL

HADLEY, MICHAEL. *The German Novel In 1790,* pp. 159-60.

BAKIMCHANDRA
GENERAL

CHAUDHURI, NARAYAM. "Social Changes as Reflected in Bengali Literature." *Indian Literature,* 14, No.2 (1971), 41-44.

BAKIN, TAKIZAWA
SANTOMI AND THE EIGHT "DOGS"

ZOLBROD, LEON. "The Autumn of the Epic Romance in Japan: Theme and Motif in Takizawa Bakin's Historical Novels." *Literature East And West,* 14 (1970), 172-84.

———. *Takizawa Bakin,* pp. 107-20.

BALKA, MARIE (pseudonym of Marie Balkany) (Romanian, 1930–)
LA NUIT (1971)

Reviews
CAPRIO, ANTHONY. *French Review,* 46 (1972), 429-30.

BALKANY, Marie see BALKA, Marie

BALL, HUGO (Swiss, 1886–1927)
GENERAL

LAST, REX W. *German Dadaist Literature,* pp. 62-115.

FLAMMETTI ODER VOM DANDYSMUS DER ARMEN (1918)

LAST, REX W. *German Dadaist Literature,* pp. 106-13.

TENDERENDA DER PHANTAST

LAST, REX W. *German Dadaist Literature,* pp. 101-6.

PRAWER, SIEGBERT. "Hugo Ball's *Tenderenda Der Phantast,* in *The Discontinuous Tradition,* ed. P. F. Ganz, pp. 204-23.

BALLET, RENÉ
DÉRIVE (1972)

Reviews
GLASGOW, JANIS. *French Review,* 47 (1974), 652–54.

BALZAC, HONORÉ DE (French, 1799–1850)

GENERAL

ADAMSON, DONALD. "Stendhal and Balzac as Connoisseurs of Italian Art," in *Balzac And The Nineteenth Century,* pp. 123–41.

ANTONIADIS, ROXANDRA V. "Faulkner and Balzac: The Poetic Web." *Comparative Literature Studies,* 9 (1972), 303–25.

BART, B. F. "Hypercreativity in Stendhal and Balzac." *Nineteenth-Century Fiction Studies,* 3 (1974/5), 32–39.

BOLSTER, RICHARD. "Was Balzac a Revolutionary?" *French Studies,* 19 (1965), 29–33.

BROOKS, PETER. "Romantic Antipastoral and Urban Allegories." *Yale Review,* 64 (1974), 20–23.

———. "The Melodramatic Imagination." *Partisan Review,* 39 (1972), 195–212.

CHERRY, ADRIAN. "Honoré de Balzac and the Anti-Social Literature of the 19th Century." *USF Language Quarterly,* 4, No.3/4 (1966), 27–32.

———. "Vautrin." *USF Language Quarterly,* 3, No.3/4 (1965), 25–34; 4, No.1/2 (1965), 8–12.

CONNER, WAYNE. "Frame and Story in Balzac." *L'Esprit Créateur,* 7 (1967), 45–54.

DARGAN, E. P. "Balzac's General Method: An Analysis of His Realism," in his *Studies In Balzac's Realism,* pp. 1–32.

FRAPPIER-MAZUR, LUCIENNE. "Balzac and the Sex of Genius." *Renascence,* 27 (1974), 23–30.

FURBER, DONALD. "The Fate and Freedom of Balzac's Courtesans." *French Review,* 39 (1965), 346–53.

HAGGIS, D. R. "Beaumarchais and the Early Balzac," in *Studies In Eighteenth-Century French Literature,* ed. J. H. Fox, M. H. Waddicor, and D. A. Watts, pp. 87–96.

———. "Clotilde De Lusignan, Ivanhoe, and the Development of Scott's Influence on Balzac." *French Studies,* 28 (1974), 159–68.

HAYWARD, MARGARET. "Balzac's Metaphysics in His Early Writings." *Modern Language Review,* 69 (1974), 757–69.

HUNT, JOEL A. "Balzac and Dostoevsky: Some Elements of Scene." *Comparative Literature Studies,* 3 (1966), 439–43.

———. "Color Imagery in Dostoevskij and Balzac." *Slavic And East European Journal,* 10 (1966), 411–23.

KANES, MARTIN. "Balzac and the Problem of Expression." *Symposium,* 23 (1969), 284–93.

LEBOWITZ, NAOMI. "The Structure of Disappointment in Balzac and Dickens," in *Essays On European Literature,* ed. Peter Uwe Hohendahl, Herbert Lindenberger, and Egon Schwarz, pp. 53–60.

LOWRIE, JOYCE O. *The Violent Mystique,* pp. 41–62.

McVICKER, C. D. "Balzac and Otway." *Romance Notes,* 15 (1973), 248–54.

MEIN, MARGARET. *A Foretaste Of Proust: A Study Of Proust And His Precursors,* pp. 101–20.

PUGH, ANTHONY R. "Ten Years of Balzac Studies." *Modern Languages,* 46 (1965), 91–97.

RAPHAEL, SYLVIA. "Balzac and the Modern Reader," in *Balzac And The Nineteenth Century,* pp. 21–33.

RASER, GEORGE B. *The Heart Of Balzac's Paris.*

REES, GARNET. "Baudelaire and Balzac," in *Balzac And The Nineteenth Century,* pp. 165–76.

REXROTH, KENNETH. "Classics Revisited-LXX: Balzac." *Saturday Review,* 7 September 1968, pp. 12–13.

SHRODER, MAURICE Z. "Balzac's Theory of the Novel." *L'Esprit Créateur,* 7 (1967), 3–10.

TAYLOR, M. E. M. "Balzac's Reading," in his *The.Arriviste,* pp. 163–72.

———. "Characteristics of the Period After 1830 Favourable to the Emergence of the Balzacian 'Arriviste,' " in his *The Arriviste,* pp. 156–62.

———. "Traits in Balzac's Character Which Gave Him an Added Interest in the 'Arriviste,' " in his *The Arriviste,* pp. 173–82.

———. "The Two H. B.'s: The Letters Link: How the Stendhalian 'Arriviste' differs from the Balzacian 'Arriviste,' " in his *The Arriviste,* pp. 133–49.

WALL, STEPHEN. "Trollope, Balzac, and the Reappearing Character." *Essays In Criticism,* 25 (1975), 123–28.

ALBERT SAVARUS

HEMMINGS, F. W. J. *Balzac: An Interpretation Of La Comédie Humaine,* pp. 132–34.

MOORE, W. G. "The Changing Study of Balzac," in *Balzac And The Nineteenth Century,* pp. 187–92.

SMETHURST, COLIN. "Balzac and Stendhal: A Comparison of Electoral Scenes," in *Balzac And The Nineteenth Century,* pp. 111–21.

ANNETTE ET LE CRIMINEL

KANES, MARTIN. *Balzac's Comedy Of Words,* pp. 57–63.

A BACHELOR'S ESTABLISHMENT (La Rabouilleuse ou le menage de garcon, 1858)

TAYLOR, M. E. M. "The Balzacian 'Rogue-Arrivistes,' " in his *The Arriviste,* pp. 210–12.

BALTHAZAR; OR SCIENCE AND LOVE see THE QUEST OF THE ABSOLUTE

BEATRIX (Béatrix; ou, Les amours forcés, 1839)

HEMMINGS, F. W. J. *Balzac: In Interpretation Of La Comédie Humaine,* pp. 72–8, 152–55.

KANES, MARTIN. *Balzac's Comedy Of Words,* pp. 179–81.

LE CABINET DES ANTIQUES

SCHILLING, BERNARD N. *The Hero As Failure: Balzac And The Rumbempré Cycle,* pp. 75–81.

LE CENTENAIRE

KANES, MARTIN. *Balzac's Comedy Of Words,* pp. 50–56.

LE CHEF-D'OEUVRE INCONNU

GANS, ERIC. "Balzac's Unknowable Masterpiece and the Limits of the Classical Esthetic." *MLN,* 90 (1975), 504–16.

HEMMINGS, F. W. J. *Balzac: An Interpretation Of La Comédie Humaine,* pp. 10–13.

THE CHOUANS (Les chouans, 1834)

DARGAN, E. P. and W. L. CRAIN. "The First Monument: *Les Chouans,*" in *Studies In Balzac's Realism,* pp. 33–67.

HAGGIS, D. R. "Scott, Balzac, and the Historical Novel as Social and Political Analysis: 'Waverly' and 'Les Chouans.' " *Modern Language Review,* 68 (1973), 51–68.

HEMMINGS, F. W. J. "Balzac's *Les Chouans* and Stendhal's *De L'Amour,*" in *Balzac And The Nineteenth Century,* pp. 99–110.

CLOTILDE DE LUSIGNAN

HAGGIS, D. R. "Clotilde De Lusignan, Ivanhoe, and the Development of Scott's Influence on Balzac." *French Studies,* 28 (1974), 159–68.

LE COLONEL CHABERT

AFFRON, CHARLES. *Patterns Of Failure In La Comédie Humaine,* pp. 133-35.

DALE, R. C. "*Le Colonel Chabert* Between Gothicism and Naturalism." *L'Esprit Créateur,* 7 (1967), 11-16.

FISCHLER, ALEXANDER. "Fortune in *Le Colonel Chabert.*" *Studies In Romanticism,* 8 (1969), 65-77.

GOOD, GRAHAM. "*Le Colonel Chabert:* A Masquerade with Documents." *French Review,* 42 (1969), 846-56.

HEMMINGS, F. W. J. *Balzac: An Interpretation Of La Comédie Humaine,* pp. 135-39.

LA COMÉDIE HUMAINE

CRAMPTON, HOPE. "Melmoth in 'La Comédie Humaine.'" *Modern Language Review,* 61 (1966), 42-50.

KANES, MARTIN. "Balzac and the Problem of Expression." *Symposium,* 23 (1969), 284-90.

———. *Balzac's Comedy Of Words,* pp. 101-215.

LOCK, PETER W. "Hoarders and Spendthrifts in 'La Comédie humaine.'" *Modern Language Review,* 61 (1966), 29-41.

McVICKER, CECIL DON. "Narcotics and *Excitants* in the *Comédie Humaine.*" *Romance Notes,* 11 (1969), 291-301.

PRENDERGAST, CHRISTOPHER. "Balzac: Chance and Realism in the *Comédie Humaine.*" *Forum For Modern Language Studies,* 10 (1974), 109-20.

LA CONTRAT DE MARIAGE

AFFRON, CHARLES. *Patterns Of Failure In La Comédie Humaine,* pp. 54-56.

THE COUNTRY DOCTOR (Le Medécin de campagne, 1833)

SCHILLING, BERNARD N. *The Hero As Failure: Balzac And The Rubempré Cycle,* pp. 59-61.

TAYLOR, M. E. M. "The Balzacian 'Arrivistes,'" in his *The Arriviste,* pp. 185-87.

COUSIN BETTE (La Cousine Bette)

AFFRON, CHARLES. *Patterns Of Failure In La Comédie Humaine,* pp. 68-73, 83-85.

CHERRY, ADRIAN. "Balzac's Madame Marneffe: A Character Study of a Courtesan." *USF Language Quarterly,* 6, No.1/2 (1967), 2-12.

HAGGIS, D. R. "Fiction and Historical Change: *La Cousine Bette* and the Lesson of Walter Scott." *Forum For Modern Language Studies,* 10 (1974), 323-33.

HEMMINGS, F. W. J. *Balzac: An Interpretation Of La Comédie Humaine,* pp. 96-104.

JAMESON, FREDERIC. "*La Cousine Bette* and Allegorical Realism." *PMLA,* 86 (1971), 241-54.

ORTALI, HÉLÈNE. "Images of Women in Balzac's *La Cousine Bette.*" *Nineteenth-Century French Studies,* 4 (1976), 194-205.

PRENDERGAST, C. A. "Antithesis and Moral Ambiguity in 'La Cousine Bette.'" *Modern Language Review,* 68 (1973), 315-32.

TAYLOR, M. E. M. "The Balzacian 'Rogue-Arrivistes,'" in his *The Arriviste,* pp. 212-14.

LE COUSIN PONS

ADAMSON, DONALD. *The Genesis of Le Cousin Pons.*

HEMMINGS, F. W. J. *Balzac: An Interpretation Of La Comédie Humaine,* pp. 155-59.

ROSAIRE, FORREST. "A Slice of Somber Life: *Le Cousin Pons,*" in *Studies In Balzac's Realism,* pp. 191-213.

LE CURÉ DE TOURS see THE VICAR OF TOURS

DADDY GORIOT see OLD GORIOT

DEPUTE D'ARCIS

SMETHURST, COLIN. "Balzac and Stendhal: A Comparison of Electoral Scenes," in *Balzac And The Nineteenth Century,* pp. 111-21.

LA DERNIÈRE FÉE

KANES, MARTIN. *Balzac's Comedy Of Words,* pp. 57-62.

LES EMPLOYES

HEMMINGS, F. W. J. *Balzac: An Interpretation Of La Comédie Humaine,* pp. 126-28.

L'ENVERS DE L'HISTOIRE CONTEMPORAINE

HEMMINGS, F. W. J. *Balzac: An Interpretation Of La Comédie Humaine,* pp. 148-50.

EUGENIA GRANDET (EUGÉNIE GRANDET, 1837?)

GILES, ANTHONY E. "On a Supposed Inadvertence of Balzac in *Eugénie Grandet.*" *Romance Notes,* 9 (1967), 66-67.

GURKIN, JANET. "Romance Elements in *Eugénie Grandet.*" *L'Esprit Créateur,* 7 (1967), 17-24.

HEMMINGS, F. W. J. *Balzac: An Interpretation Of La Comédie Humaine,* pp. 87-96.

LUSH, ADALINE LINCOLN. "The House of the Miser: Eugénie Grandet," in *Studies In Balzac's Realism,* pp. 121-35.

WETHERILL, P. M. "A Reading of *Eugénie Grandet.*" *Modern Language,* 52 (1971), 166-76.

FALTHURNE

KANES, MARTIN. *Balzac's Comedy Of Words,* pp. 42-45.

LA FAUSSE MAÎTRESSE

HEMMINGS, F. W. J. *Balzac: An Interpretation Of La Comédie Humaine,* pp. 64-68.

UNE FILLE D'ÈVE

AFFRON, CHARLES. *Patterns Of Failure In La Comédie Humaine,* pp. 95-97.

HEMMINGS, F. W. J. *Balzac: An Interpretation Of La Comédie Humaine,* pp. 60-64.

TAYLOR, M. E. M. "The Balzacian 'Rogue-Arrivistes,'" in his *The Arriviste,* pp. 205-7.

TINTNER, ADELINE R. "Balzac's Two Maries and James's *The Ambassadors.*" *English Language Notes,* 9 (1972), 284-87.

WHITMORE, D. J. S. "Rita-Christina: A Reference to a Real Person in the *Comédie Humaine.*" *French Studies,* 21 (1967), 319-22.

LA FILLE AUX YEUX D'OR

HUNT, H. J. "Yes, and Back Again with Balzac." *French Studies,* 28 (1974), 36-38. <On the translation>

GAMBARA

AFFRON, CHARLES. *Patterns Of Failure In La Comédie Humaine,* pp. 124-28.

HEMMINGS, F. W. J. *Balzac: An Interpretation Of La Comédie Humaine,* pp. 3-7.

PUGH, ANTHONY R. "Balzac's Beethoven: A Note on *Gambara.*" *Romance Notes,* 8 (1966), 43-46.

GOBSECK

CHERRY, ADRIAN. "Balzac's 'Gobseck': A Character Study of a Usurer." *USF Language Quarterly,* 5, No.1/2 (1966), 5-14.

A HARLOT'S PROGRESS (SPLENDEURS ET MISÈRES DES COURTISANES, 1879)

AFFRON, CHARLES. *Patterns Of Failure In La Comédie Humaine,* pp. 106-11.

FANGER, DONALD. "Balzac: The Heightening of Substance," in

his *Dostoevsky And Romantic Realism: A Study Of Dostoevsky In Relation To Balzac, Dickens, And Gogol,* pp. 58–62.

PRENDERGAST, CHRISTOPHER. "Melodrama and Totality in *Splendeurs Et Misères Des Courtisanes.*" *Novel,* 6 (1973), 152–62.

SCHILLING, BERNARD N. *The Hero As Failure: Balzac And The Rubempré Cycle,* pp. 170–207.

L'HERITIERE DE BIRAGUE

KANES, MARTIN. *Balzac's Comedy Of Words,* pp. 48–55.

HONORINE (1844)

HEMMINGS, F. W. J. *Balzac: An Interpretation Of La Comédie Humaine,* pp. 55–60.

JEAN-LOUIS

HAGGIS, D. R. "Beaumarchais and the Early Balzac," in *Studies In Eighteenth Century French Literature,* ed. J. H. Fox, M. H. Waddicor, and D. A. Watts, pp. 89–92.

THE LILY IN THE VALLEY (Le Lys dans la vallée, 1836)

BERSANI, LEO. *Balzac To Beckett,* pp. 52–90.

BROOKS, PETER. "Virtue-Tripping: Notes on *Le Lys Dans La Vallée.*" *Yale French Studies,* No.50 (1974), pp. 150–62.

FLEURANT, KENNETH J. "Water and Desert in *Le Lys Dans La Vallée.*" *Romance Notes,* 12 (1970), 78–85.

HAIG, STIRLING. "Note on a Balzacian Character: Monsieur de Mortsauf." *Romance Notes,* 16 (1974), 95–98.

HEMMINGS, F. W. J. *Balzac: An Interpretation Of La Comédie Humaine,* pp. 79–83.

NIESS, ROBERT J. "Sainte-Beuve and Balzac: *Volupté* and *Le Lys Dans La Vallée.*" *Kentucky Romance Quarterly,* 20 (1973), 113–24.

RHODES, ENID H. "Concerning a Metaphor in *Le Lys Dans La Vallée.*" *Studi Francesi,* 13 (1969), 84.

LOST ILLUSIONS (Illusions perdues, 1842–48)

AFFRON, CHARLES. *Patterns Of Failure In La Comédie Humaine,* pp. 75–83, 85–89, 92–95, 97–106.

ALTER, ROBERT. *Partial Magic,* pp. 104–15.

BLACKBURN, BONNIE. "Master and Apprentice: A Realistic Relationship," in *Studies In Balzac's Realism,* pp. 174–82.

CHERRY, ADRIAN. "Vautrin." *USF Language Quarterly,* 4, No.1/2 (1965), 8–12.

HEMMINGS, F. W. J. *Balzac: An Interpretation Of La Comédie Humaine,* pp. 128–31.

KANES, MARTIN. *Balzac's Comedy Of Words,* pp. 219–59.

SCHILLING, BERNARD N. *The Hero As Failure: Balzac And The Rubempré Cycle,* pp. 82–86.

TAYLOR, M. E. M. "The Balzacian 'Arrivistes,'" in his *The Arriviste,* pp. 194–97.

LOUIS LAMBERT (Notice biographique sur Louis Lambert, 1832)

AFFRON, CHARLES. *Patterns Of Failure In La Comédie Humaine,* pp. 114–24.

HEMMINGS, F. W. J. *Balzac: An Interpretation Of La Comédie Humaine,* pp. 13–16.

KANES, MARTIN. *Balzac's Comedy Of Words,* pp. 67–70, 101–26.

LA MAISON DU CHAT-QUI PELOTE

BLACKBURN, BONNIE. "Master and Apprentice: A Realistic Relationship," in *Studies In Balzac's Realism,* pp. 158–66.

LA MAISON NUCINGEN

HEMMINGS, F. W. J. *Balzac: An Interpretation Of La Comédie Humaine,* pp. 116–18.

MASSIMILLA DONI

HEMMINGS, F. W. J. *Balzac: An Interpretation Of La Comédie Humaine,* pp. 7–10.

MÉMOIRES DE DEUX JEUNES MARIÉES

HEMMINGS, F. W. J. *Balzac: An Interpretation Of La Comédie Humaine,* pp. 44–46.

LA MUSE DU DEPARTEMENT

AFFRON, CHARLES. *Patterns Of Failure In La Comédie Humaine,* pp. 89–92.

FAIRLIE, ALISON. "Constant's *Adolphe* Read by Balzac and Nerval," in *Balzac And The Nineteenth Century,* pp. 209–20.

HEMMINGS, F. W. J. *Balzac: An Interpretation Of La Comédie Humaine,* pp. 68–72.

OLD GORIOT (Père Goriot, 1835)

ADAMSON, DONALD. "*Le Père Goriot:* Notes Towards a Reassessment." *Symposium,* 19 (1965), 101–14.

AFFRON, CHARLES. *Patterns Of Failure In La Comédie Humaine,* pp. 58–68.

ALLEN, ROBERT. "A Stylistic Study of the Adjectives of *Le Père Goriot.*" *Language And Style,* 4 (1971), 24–56.

BERMAN, RONALD. "Analogies and Realities in *Père Goriot.*" *Novel,* 3 (1969), 7–16.

BROOKS, PETER. "Balzac: Melodrama and Metaphor." *Hudson Review,* 22 (1969/70), 213–28.

DOWNING, GEORGE E. "A Famous Boarding-House: *Le Père Goriot,*' in *Studies In Balzac's Realism,* pp. 136–50.

FANGER, DONALD. "Balzac: The Heightening of Substance," in his *Dostoevsky And Romantic Realism: A Study of Dostoevsky In Relation To Balzac, Dickens, And Gogol,* pp. 38–56.

FISCHLER, ALEXANDER. "Rastignac-Télémaque: The Epic Scale in 'Le Père Goriot.'" *Modern Language Review,* 63 (1968), 840–48.

GOLATA, JOHN. "*Père Goriot* and *King Lear.*" *English Journal,* 56 (1967), 1288–89.

HEMMINGS, F. W. J. *Balzac: An Interpretation Of La Comédie Humaine,* pp. 104–16.

KEATES, LAURENCE W. "Mysterious Miraculous Mandarin: Origins, Literary Paternity, Implication in Ethics." *Revue De Littérature Comparée,* 40 (1966), 511–16.

PUGH, ANTHONY R. "The Complexity of *Le Père Goriot.*" *L'Esprit Créateur,* 7 (1967), 25–35.

SAVAGE, CATHERINE H. "The Romantic *Père Goriot.*" *Studies In Romanticism,* 5 (1966), 104–12.

SCHILLING, BERNARD N. *The Hero As Failure: Balzac And The Rubempré Cycle,* pp. 61–75.

TAYLOR, M. E. M. "The Balzacian 'Arrivistes,'" in his *The Arriviste,* pp. 187–92.

———. "The Balzacian 'Rouge-Arrivistes,'" in his *The Arriviste,* pp. 200–5.

WEINSTEIN, ANOLD L. *Vision And Response In Modern Fiction,* pp. 27–36.

WILLETT, MAURITA. "Henry James's Indebtedness to Balzac." *Revue De Littérature Comparée,* 41 (1967), 204–27.

THE PEASANTRY (Les Paysans, 1863)

BLACKBURN, BONNE. "Master and Apprentice: A Realistic Relationship," in *Studies In Balzac's Realism,* pp. 182–84.

HEMMINGS, F. W. J. *Balzac: An Interpretation Of La Comédie Humaine,* pp. 159–65.

PIERRETTE (1858)

WIRTZ, DOROTHY. "Animalism in Balzac's *Curé De Tours* and *Pierrette*." *Romance Notes*, 11 (1969), 61-67.

THE QUEST OF THE ABSOLUTE (Le Recherche de l'absolu, 1834)

HEMMINGS, F. W. J. *Balzac: An Interpretation Of La Comédie Humaine*, pp. 19-30.

THE RISE AND FALL OF CÉSAR BIROTTEAU (Histoire de la grandeur et la décadence de César Birotteau, parfumeur, 1838)

AFFRON, CHARLES. *Patterns Of Failure In La Comédie Humaine*, pp. 42-54.

BLACKBURN, BONNIE. "Master and Apprentice: A Realistic Relationship," in *Studies In Balzac's Realism*, pp. 166-74.

HEMMINGS, F. W. J. *Balzac: An Interpretation Of La Comédie Humaine*, pp. 118-23.

PUGH, ANTHONY R. "The Genesis of César Birotteau: Questions of Chronology." *French Studies*, 22 (1968), 9-25.

SARRASINE

PUGH, ANTHONY R. "B/Z and S/Z." *International Fiction Review*, 2 (1975), 173-77.

SPLENDEURS ET MISERÈS DES COURTISANES see A HARLOT'S PROGRESS

STÉNIE OU LES ERREURS PHILOSOPHIQUES

KANES, MARTIN. *Balzac's Comedy Of Words*, pp. 45-48.

UNE FILLE D'ÈVE

TINTNER, ADELINE R. "Balzac's Two Maries and James's *The Ambassadors*." *English Language Notes*, 9 (1971/2), 284-87.

WHITMORE, P. J. S. "Rita-Christina: A Reference to a Real Person in the *Comédie Humaine*." *French Studies*, 21 (1967), 319-22.

LE VICAIRE DES ARDENNES

KANES, MARTIN. *Balzac's Comedy Of Words*, pp. 50-55.

THE VICAR OF TOURS (Le Curé de Tours)

AFFRON, CHARLES. *Patterns Of Failure In La Comédie Humaine*, pp. 48-51.

HEMMINGS, F. W. J. *Balzac: An Interpretation Of La Comédie Humaine*, pp. 123-26.

LEEDS, FREDRIC M. "Balzac's *Le Curé De Tours*." *Explicator*, 34 (1975/6), Item 9.

MARHOFER, ESTHER. "Le Curé de Tours: A Study in Topography," in *Studies In Balzac's Realism*, pp. 91-120.

TINTNER, ADELINE R. " 'The Old Things': Balzac's *Le Curé De Tours* and James's *The Spoils Of Poynton*." *Nineteenth-Century Fiction*, 26 (1972), 436-55.

WIRTZ, DOROTHY. "Animalism in Balzac's *Curé De Tours* and *Pierrette*." *Romance Notes*, 11 (1969), 61-67.

WANN-CHLORE

KANES, MARTIN. *Balzac's Comedy Of Words*, pp. 57-61.

THE WILD ASS'S SKIN (La peau de chagrin, 1831)

ARAUJO, NORMAN. "Time and Rhythm in Balzac's *La Peau De Chagrin*." *French Review*, 44, Special Issue No.2 (1971), 59-68.

GREGG, RICHARD A. "Balzac and the Women in *The Queen Of Spades*." *Slavic And East European Journal*, 10 (1966), 279-82.

HAIG, STIRLING. "Dualistic Patterns in *La Peau De Chagrin*." *Nineteenth-Century French Studies*, 1 (1972/3), 211-18.

HEMMINGS, F. W. J. *Balzac: An Interpretation Of La Comédie Humaine*, pp. 168-77.

KANES, MARTIN. *Balzac's Comedy Of Words*, pp. 70-100.

————. "Logic and Language in 'La Peau de Chagrin." *Studi Francesi*, 14 (1970), 244-56.

MILLOTT, H. H. "La Peau de Chagrin: Method in Madness," in *Studies In Balzac's Realism*, pp. 68-90.

SCHILLING, BERNARD N. *The Hero As Failure: Balzac And The Rubempré Cycle*, pp. 56-59.

TAYLOR, M. E. M. "The Balzacian 'Arrivistes,' " in his *The Arriviste*, pp. 183-85.

A WOMAN OF THIRTY (La femme de trente ans, 1842)

HEMMINGS, F. W. J. *Balzac: An Interpretation Of La Comédie Humaine*, pp. 48-54.

KANES, MARTIN. *Balzac's Comedy Of Words*, pp. 212-15.

LOWRIE, JOYCE OLIVER. "Balzac and 'le doigt de Dieu.' " *L'Esprit Créateur*, 7 (1967), 36-44.

Z. MARCAS

AFFRON, CHARLES. *Patterns Of Failure In La Comédie Humaine*, pp. 128-31.

BANDELLO, MATTEO (Italian, 1485-1561)

GENERAL

CAVALCHINI, MARIELLA. "Bandello, Shakespeare, and the Tale of the Lovers from Verona." *Italian Quarterly*, 18, No.70 (1974), 37-48.

BANDOPADHYAYA, MANIK (Bengali, 1908-1956)

GENERAL

MUKHOPADHYAYA, ARUN KUMAR. "Manik Bandopadhyaya: A Novelist in Search of Life." *Indian Literature*, 16, Nos.1/2 (1973), 143-46.

PADMA RIVER BOATMAN (Padmā nadīr mājhi, 1936)

Reviews
GHOSH, S. L. *Indian Horizons*, 24, No.4 (1975), 101-4.

BANERJEE, TARASHANKAR (Bengali, 1898-)

GENERAL

DEVI, MAHASVETA. "Tarashankar Banerjee: His Achievement as a Novelist." *Indian Horizons*, 21, No.4 (1972), 76-86.

GANADEVATA

DEVI, MAHASVETA. "Tarashankar Banerjee: His Achievement as a Novelist." *Indian Horizons*, 21, No.4 (1972), 80-86.

PANCHAGRAAM

DEVI, MAHASVETA. "Tarashankar Banerjee: His Achievement as a Novelist." *Indian Horizons*, 21, No.4 (1972), 80-86.

BANERJI, BIBHUTIBHUSHAN (Indian, 1894-1950)

PATHER PANCHALI (1929)

Reviews
MUKHERJEE, PRITHWINDRA. *Indian Literature*, 14, No.1 (1971), 114-16. <On the Translation>

POULOS, STEVEN. *Mahfil*, 6, No.2/3 (1970), 133-34.

BANG, HERMAN (Danish, 1857-1912)

GENERAL

SIMONSEN, SOFUS E. "Herman Bang: Life and Theme." *Germanic Notes*, 3 (1972), 34-37.

BARBEY D'AUREVILLY, JULES AMÉDÉE (French, 1808-1889)

GENERAL

BIRKETT, JENNIFER. "Barbey d'Aurevilly and Leon Bloy: Love and Morality in the Catholic Novel." *Nottingham French Studies,* 14 (1975), 3-10.

McLENDON, WILL L. "Isolation and Ostracism in the Works of Barbey D'Aurevilly." *Forum,* 8, No.1 (1970), 23-29.

TERRY, BARBARA A. "The Influence of Casanova and Barbey d'Aurevilly on the *Sonatas* of Valle-Inclan." *Revista De Estudios Hispánicos,* 1 (1967), 61-88.

UN PRÊTRE MARIÉ (1865)

LOWRIE, JOYCE OLIVER. "Barbey's *Un Prêtre Marié*: Sources and Variations." *Renascence,* 20 (1967), 44-55.

———. *The Violent Mystique,* pp. 72-84.

THE SHE DEVILS (Les Diaboliques, 1874)

FREIMANIS, DZINTARS. "The Motif of the 'Dessous' in *Les Diaboliques.*" *Romance Notes,* 11 (1970), 553-56.

LOWRIE, JOYCE O. *The Violent Mystique,* pp. 64-72.

BARNARD, Marjorie see ELDERSHAW, M. Barnard

BAROJA, PÍO

GENERAL

BARROW, LEO L. *Negation In Baroja: A Key To His Novelistic Creativity.*

GLEAVES, EDWIN S. "Hemingway and Baroja: Studies in Spiritual Anarchism." *Revista De Estudios Hispánicos,* 5 (1971), 363-75.

ORTEGA Y GASSET, JOSÉ. "Thoughts on Pio Baroja." *Critical Inquiry,* 1 (1974), 415-46.

AGONÍAS DE NUESTRO TIEMPO

PRATT, BEATRICE P. *Pío Baroja,* pp. 147-51.

AVENTURAS, INVENTOS Y MIXTIFICACIONES DE SILVESTRE PARADOX

PRATT, BEATRICE P. *Pío Baroja,* pp. 84-88.

CAESAR OR NOTHING (César o nada, 1910)

PRATT, BEATRICE P. *Pío Baroja,* pp. 106-10.

CAMINO DE PERFECCIÓN (1902)

PRATT, BEATRICE P. *Pío Baroja,* pp. 88-94.

EL ESCUADRON DEL BRIGANTE

LOVETT, GABRIEL H. "Two Views of Guerilla Warfare: "Galdós' *Juan Martín El Empecinado* and Baroja's *El Escuadron Del Brigante.*" *Revista De Estudios Hispánicos,* 6 (1972), 335-44.

LA LUCHA POR LA VIDA

PRATT, BEATRICE P. *Pío Baroja,* pp. 94-97.

MEMORIAS DE UN HOMBRE DE ACCIÓN (1913-1935)

LONGHURST, C. A. "Pío Baroja and Aviraneta: Some Sources of the *Memorias De Un Hombre De Acción.*" *Bulletin Of Hispanic Studies,* 48 (1971), 328-45.

PRATT, BEATRICE P. *Pío Baroja,* pp. 125-34.

EL MUNDO ES ANSÍ (1912)

PRATT, BEATRICE P. *Pío Baroja,* pp. 125-34.

THE QUEST (La busca, 1904)

HOWITT, D. "Baroja's Preoccupation with Clocks and his Emphatic Treatment of Time in the Introduction to *La Busca,*" in *Hispanic Studies In Honour Of Joseph Manson,* ed. Dorothy M. Atkinson and Anthony H. Clarke, pp. 139-47.

LA SENSUALIDAD PERVERTIDA (1920)

PRATT, BEATRICE P. *Pío Baroja,* pp. 139-43.

THE TREE OF KNOWLEDGE (El árbol de la ciencia, 1911)

GLEAVES, EDWIN S. "Hemingway and Baroja: Studies in Spiritual Anarchism." *Revista De Estudios Hispánicos,* 5 (1971), 369-75.

MILLNER, CURTIS. "Structural Consistency and Artistic Economy in *El Árbol De La Ciencia.*" *Revista De Estudios Hispánicos,* 9 (1975), 99-105.

ORTEGA Y GASSET, JOSÉ. "Thoughts on Pio Baroja." *Critical Inquiry,* 1 (1974/5), 424-28.

PRATT, BEATRICE P. *Pío Baroja,* pp. 112-21.

Reviews
LUMSDEN, GEORGE. *Canadian Modern Language Review,* 29, No.3 (1973), 81-82.

LA VIDA FANTÁSTICA

ABRAMS, FRED. "Pío Baroja and Silvestre Paradox: An Onomastic Tour de Force." *Revista De Estudios Hispánicos,* 9 (1975), 259-62.

ZALACAIN EL AVENTURERO (1909)

JONES, R. J. "Urbia and Zaro: Birth and Burial of Zalacain." *Canadian Modern Language Review,* 22, No.3 (1966), 29-35.

BARONAS, ALOYZAS (Lithuanian, 1917-)

GENERAL

ŠILBAJORIS, RIMVYDAS. *Perfection Of Exile,* pp. 285-301.

FOOTBRIDGES AND ABYSSES

ŠILBAJORIS, RIMVYDAS. *Perfection Of Exile,* pp. 298-301.

Reviews
POTOKER, EDWARD M. "Starlings Over the Trenches." *Saturday Review,* 26 March 1966, pp. 34-35.

VASKAS, JOSEPH. "Man Between Fascism and Communism." *Lituanus,* 11, No.4 (1965), 79-80.

THE THIRD WOMAN

Reviews
ANGOFF, CHARLES. *Lituanus,* 15, No.1 (1969), 82-84.

UŽGESES SNIEGAS

ŠILBAJORIS, RIMVYDAS. *Perfection Of Exile,* pp. 289-92.

BARR, ROBERT

THE MEASURE OF THE RULE

Reviews
PARR, JOHN. "The Measure of Robert Barr." *Journal Of Canadian Fiction,* 3, No.2 (1974), 94-97.

BARRÈS, MAURICE (French, 1862-1923)

GENERAL

OUSTON, PHILIP. *The Imagination Of Maurice Barrès.*

SOUCY, ROBERT. "Barrès and Fascism." *French Historical Studies,* 5 (1967), 67-97.

———. *Fascism In France: The Case Of Maurice Barrès.*

COLETTE BAUDOCHE (1909)

FIELD, T. J. "A Note on Barrès's Documentation for *Colette Baudoche.*" *Romance Notes,* 16 (1974), 21–24.

BARRENECHEA Y ALBIS, JUAN DE (Chilean, d. 1707?)

RESTAURACIÓN DE LA IMPERIAL Y CONVERSIÓN DE ALMAS INFIELES

TOMANEK, THOMAS J. "Barrenechea's *Restauración De La Imperial Y Conversión De Almas Infieles*—The First Novel Written in Spanish America." *Revue Des Langues Vivantes,* 40 (1974), 257–68.

BARRETO, LIMA

RECORDAÇÕES DO ESCRIVÃO ISAÍSAS CAMINHA (1909)

HERRON, ROBERT. "Lima Barreto's *Isaias Caminha* As a Psychological Novel." *Luso-Brazilian Review,* 8, No.2 (1971), 26–38.

TRISTE FIM DE POLICARPO QUARESMA

KINNEAR, J. C. "The 'Sad End' of Lima Barreto's Policarpo Quaresma." *Bulletin Of Hispanic Studies,* 51 (1974), 60–75.

BARRIOS, EDUARDO (Chilean, 1884–1963)

GENERAL

BENBOW, JERRY L. "Grotesque Elements in Eduardo Barrios." *Hispania,* 51 (1968), 86–91.

DAVISON, NED. "Motifs and Methods: A Summing Up," in his *Eduardo Barrios,* pp. 124–43.

RAMÍREZ, MANUEL D. "Some Notes on the Prose Style of Eduardo Barrios." *Romance Notes,* 9 (1967), 40–48.

WALKER, JOHN. "Echoes of Pascal in the Works of Eduardo Barrios." *Romantic Review,* 61 (1970), 256–63.

BROTHER ASNO (El hermano Asno, 1922)

ANDERSON, ROBERT ROLAND. "The Doctrine of Quietism in 'El Hermano Asno.'" *Hispania,* 58 (1975), 874–83.

BROWN, JAMES W. "*El Hermano Asno* from *Fioretti* Through Freud." *Symposium,* 25 (1971), 321–32.

DAVISON, NED. *Eduardo Barrios,* pp. 61–82.

KELLY, JOHN R. "Name Symbolism in Barrios' *El Hermano Asno.*" *Romance Notes,* 13 (1971), 48–53.

GRAN SEÑOR Y RAJADIABLOS (1948)

DAVISON, NED. *Eduardo Barrios,* pp. 103–13.

WALKER, JOHN. "*Gran Señor Y Rajadiablos:* A Shift in Sensibility." *Bulletin Of Hispanic Studies,* 49 (1972), 279–88.

———. "The Theme of *Civilización Y Barbarie* in *Gran Señor Y Rajadiablos.*" *Hispanofila,* No.42 (1971), p. 57–67.

THE MEN IN MAN (Los homres de hombre, 1950)

DAVISON, NED. *Eduardo Barrios,* pp. 114–23.

HANCOCK, JOEL C. "The Purification of Eduardo Barrios' Sensorial Prose." *Hispania,* 56 (1973), 51–59.

UN PERDIDO (1917)

DAVISON, NED. *Eduardo Barrios,* pp. 46–60.

TAMARUGAL

DAVISON, NED. *Eduardo Barrios,* pp. 96–102.

WALKER, JOHN. "*Tamarugal*—Barrios' Neglected Link Novel." *Revista De Estudios Hispánicos,* 8 (1974), 345–55.

BARROSO, MARIA ALICE (Brazilian)

GENERAL

BORING, PHYLLIS Z. "Amado and Barroso: Two Novelists View Race Relations in Brazil." *College Language Association Journal,* 19 (1976), 415–17.

BARTOV, HANOCH (Israeli)

THE DISSEMBLER (1975)

Reviews
VARDI, DOV. *Modern Hebrew Literature,* 1 No.3–4 (1975), 75–77.

WOUNDS OF MATURITY

ALTER, ROBERT. "Confronting the Holocaust: Three Israeli Novels." *Commentary,* 41, No.6 (1966), 71–73; rpt. in his *After The Tradition,* pp. 175–80.

Reviews
DAVID, HILLEL. "Wounds of Maturity." *Midstream Magazine,* 14, No.1 (1968), 76–80.

BASSANI, GIORGIO (Italian, 1916–)

GENERAL

ESKIN, STANLEY G. "Sex and Jewishness in Giorgio Bassani." *Midstream Magazine,* 19 No.6 (1973), 71–75.

THE GARDEN OF THE FINZI-CONTINIS (Il giardino dei Finzi-Continis, 1962)

DOUGLAS RADCLIFF-UMSTEAD. "Transformation in Bassani's Garden." *Modern Fiction Studies,* 21 (1975/76), 521–33.

ESKIN, STANLEY G. "*The Garden Of The Finzi-Continis.*" *Literature/Film Quarterly,* 1 (1973), 171–75.

SCHNEIDER, MARILYN. "Mythical Dimensions of Micòl Finzi-Contini." *Italica,* 51 (1974), 43–67.

Reviews
FURBANK, P. N. "Opting Out." *Encounter,* 25, No.4 (1965), 83–84.

GREENBERG, MARTIN. "Past and Prologue." *Reporter,* 33, No.9 (1965), 51–53.

THE SMELL OF HAY

Reviews
RABINOWITZ, DOROTHY. *Saturday Review,* 20 September 1975, p. 39.

BASU (Bengali)

GENERAL

MUKHOPADHYAY, BHABANEE. "Manoje Basu." *Indian Literature,* 9, No.2 (1966), 61–66.

BATAILLE, MICHEL

LE CHAT SAUVAGE (1971)

Reviews
GOODRICH, NORMA L. *French Review,* 46 (1972), 430–31.

BATALOV, VLADIMIR

A TREE GROWS NEAR THE VILLAGE

Reviews
HEIMAN, LEO. "Nostalgia and Nihilism." *East Europe,* 15, No.8 (1966), 56.

BAUMONT, ELIE DE

LES LETTRES DU MARQUIS DE ROSELLE

MYLNE, VIVIENNE. *The Eighteenth-Century French Novel,* pp. 222–24.

BAYNTON, BARBARA (Australian, 1862–1929)

GENERAL

PHILLIPS, A. A. "Barbara Bayton and the Dissidence of the Nineties," in *The Australian Nationalists,* ed. Chris Wallace-Crabbe, pp. 149–58.

BAZÁN, Emilia Pardo see PARDO BAZÁN, Emilia

BAZIN, HERVÉ (pseudonym of Jean-Pierre Hervé-Bazin, French, 1911–)

GENERAL

CRANT, PHILLIP A. "Some Thoughts on the Literary Development of Hervé Bazin." *USF Language Quarterly,* 10, No.3/4 (1972), 31–34.

AU NOM DU FILS (1960)

Reviews
CHARLTON, DIANNE. *Canadian Modern Language Review,* 30, No.1 (1973), 72–73.

LES BIENHEUREUX DE LA DÉSOLATION (1970)

Reviews
CRANT, PHILLIP. *French Review,* 45 (1971), 187–88.

CRI DE LA CHOUETTE (1972)

Reviews
CRANT, PHILLIP A. *French Review,* 48 (1975), 951–52.

BEAULIEU, VICTOR LÉVY (Canadian, 1945–)

OH MIAMI MIAMI MIAMI

Reviews
POKORNY, AMY. "Déquébécoisé." *Journal of Canadian Fiction,* 3 No.2 (1974), 102–3.

UN RÊVE QUÉBÉCOIS (1972)

Reviews
POKORNY, AMY. "Le Cauchemar De La Vie." *Journal Of Canadian Fiction,* 2, No.1 (1973), 87.

BEAUVOIR, SIMONE DE (French, 1908–)

GENERAL

RADFORD, C. B. "The Authenticity of Simone de Beauvoir." *Nottingham French Studies,* 4 (1965), 91–104.

———. "Simone de Beauvoir: Feminism's Friend or Foe?" *Nottingham French Studies,* 6 (1967), 87–102; 7 (1968), 39–53.

RECK, RIMA DRELL. *Literature And Responsibility,* pp. 86–115.

ALL MEN ARE MORTAL (Tous les hommes sont mortels, 1946)

COTTRELL, ROBERT D. *Simone De Beauvoir,* pp. 68–78.

LES BELLES IMAGES (Les belles images, 1966)

COTTRELL, ROBERT D. *Simone De Beauvoir,* pp. 137–41.

PAGÈS, IRÈNE M. "Beauvoir's *Les Belles Images:*" 'Desubstantification' of Reality through a Narrative." *Forum For Modern Language Studies,* 11 (1975), 133–41.

Reviews
PAGONES, DORRIE. "Life as a Glossy Montage." *Saturday Review,* 24 February 1968, p. 44.

SMITH, A. M. SHERIDAN. *London Magazine,* NS, 8, No.1 (1968), 89–90.

THE MANDARINS (Les mandarins, 1954)

COTTRELL, ROBERT D. *Simone De Beauvoir,* pp. 107–21.

RECK, RIMA DRELL. *Literature And Responsibility,* pp. 105–14.

SHE CAME TO STAY (L'Invitée, 1943)

COTTRELL, ROBERT D. *Simone De Beauvoir,* pp. 29–42.

THE WOMAN DESTROYED (La Femme rompue, 1968)

Reviews
CULLIGAN, GLENDY. "Suffering Sisterhood." *Saturday Review,* 22 February 1969, pp. 45, 79.

SMITH, A. M. SHERIDAN. "Obsessions." *London Magazine,* NS, 9, No.1 (1969), 99–100.

BEAVER, BRUCE (Australian, 1928–)

YOU CAN'T COME BACK (1966)

Reviews
WHITELOCK, DEREK. *Southerly,* 26 (1966), 281–82.

BECKER, JILLIAN (South African, 1932–)

THE KEEP (1967)

Reviews
DETT, V. S. "New South African Literature—1967: A Critical Chronicle." *English Studies In Africa,* 11 (1968), 61–65.

BECKER, JÜRGEN (German, 1932–)

RÄNDER (1968)

Reviews
HOLTHUSEN, HANS EGON. TRANS. SANDRA SMITH. *Literature/Film Quarterly,* 2 No.1 (1968), 89–92.

BECKER, KNUTH (Danish, 1893–1917)

GENERAL

BIRKET-SMITH, KJELD. "Knuth Becker." *American Scandanavian Review,* 62 (1974), 285–90.

BECKETT, SAMUEL (Irish [wrote in French and English], 1906–)

GENERAL

ABBOTT, H. PORTER. "A Poetics of Radical Displacement: Samuel Beckett Coming up to Seventy." *Texas Studies In Literature And Language,* 17 (1975), 219–238.

BERSANI, LEO. "No Exit for Beckett." *Partisan Review,* 33 (1966), 261–67.

BISHOP, TOM. "Samuel Beckett." *Saturday Review,* 15 November 1969, pp. 26–27, 59.

BRÉE, GERMAINE. "The Strange World of Beckett's 'grands articulés,' " trans. Margaret Guiton, in *Samuel Beckett Now,* ed. Melvin J. Friedman, pp. 73–87.

BRUNS, GERALD. "The Storyteller and the Problem of Language in Samuel Beckett's Fiction." *Modern Language Quarterly,* 30 (1969), 265–81.

BRYER, ACKSON R. "Samuel Beckett: A Checklist of Criticism," in *Samuel Beckett Now,* ed. Melvin J. Friedman, pp. 219–59.

COE, RICHARD N. "God and Samuel Beckett." *Meanjin,* 24 (1965), 66–85; rpt. in *Twentieth Century Interpretations of Molloy, Malone Dies, The Unnamable: A Collection Of Critical Essays,* ed. J. D. O'Hara, pp. 91–113.

COHN, RUBY. "The Laughter of Sad Samuel Beckett," in *Samuel Beckett Now,* ed. Melvin J. Friedman, pp. 185–97.

CONLEY, JAMES. "Arcana: Molloy, Malone Dies, The Unnamable: A Brief Comparison of Forms." *Hartford Studies In Literature,* 4 (1972), 186–96.

CORNWELL, ETHEL F. "Samuel Beckett: The Flight from Self." *PMLA,* 88 (1973), 41–50.

DOBREZ, LIVIO. "Beckett and Heidegger: Existence, Being and Nothingness." *Southern Review: Literary and Interdisciplinary Essays,* 7 (1974), 140-53.

———. "Samuel Beckett's Irreducible." *Southern Review: Literary and Interdisciplinary Essays,* 6 (1973), 205-21.

ERICKSON, JOHN D. "Objects and Systems in the Novels of Samuel Beckett." *L'Esprit Créateur,* 7 (1967), 113-22.

FEDERMAN, RAYMOND. "Beckettian Paradox: Who Is Telling the Truth?" in *Samuel Beckett Now,* ed. Melvin J. Friedman, pp. 103-17.

———. "The Impossibility of Saying the Same Old Thing the Same Old Way—Samuel Beckett's Fiction Since *Comment C'est.*" *L'Esprit Créateur,* 11, No.3 (1971), 21-43.

FLETCHER, JOHN. "Samuel Beckett and The Philosophers." *Comparative Literature,* 17 (1965), 43-56.

———. "Beckett's Debt to Dante." *Nottingham French Studies,* 4 (1965), 41-52.

FRYE, NORTHROP. "The Nightmare Life in Death," in *Twentieth Century Interpretations of Molloy, Malone Dies, The Unnamable: A Collection Of Critical Essays,* ed. J. D. O'Hara, pp. 26-34.

GARZILLI, ENRICO. "The Other and Identity: The Couples of Samuel Beckett," in his *Circles Without Center,* pp. 28-38.

GREENE, NAOMI. "Creation and the Self: Artaud, Beckett, Michaux." *Criticism,* 13 (1971), 265-278.

HAMILTON, ALICE AND KENNETH. "The Guffaw of the Abderite: Samuel Beckett's Use of Democritus." *Mosaic,* 9, No.2 (1976), 1-13.

HARVEY, LAWRENCE E. "Samuel Beckett on Life, Art and Criticism." *MLN,* 80 (1965), 545-62.

HUGHES, CATHERINE. "The Paradox of Samuel Beckett." *Catholic World,* 211 (1970), 26-28.

ISER, WOLFGANG. "Subjectivity as the Autogenous Cancellation of Its Own Manifestations. S. Beckett: *Molloy, Malone Dies, The Unnamable,*" in his *The Implied Reader,* pp. 164-78.

———. "When Is the End Not the End? The Idea of Fiction in Beckett," in his *The Implied Reader,* pp. 257-73.

JANVIER, LUDOVIC. "Style in the Trilogy," in *Twentieth Century Interpretations Of Molloy, Malone Dies, The Unnamable: A Collection Of Critical Essays,* ed. J. D. O'Hara, pp. 82-90.

KERN, EDITH. "Black Humor: The Pockets of Lemuel Gulliver and Samuel Beckett," in *Samuel Beckett Now,* ed. Melvin J. Friedman, pp. 89-102.

———. "Ironic Structure in Beckett's Fiction." *L'Ésprit Créateur,* 11, No.3 (1971). 3-13.

KNAPP, ROBERT S. "Samuel Beckett's Allegory of the Uncreating Word." *Mosaic,* 6 No.2 (1973), 71-83.

KRAMER, HILTON. "The Anguish and the Comedy of Samuel Beckett." *Saturday Review,* 3 October 1970, pp. 27-30, 43.

LAMONT, ROSETTE. "Beckett's Metaphysics of Choiceless Awareness," in *Samuel Beckett Now,* ed. Melvin J. Friedman, pp. 199-217.

LEVENTHAL, A. J. "The Beckett Hero." *Critique,* 7, No.2 (1964/5), 18-35.

LORICH, BRUCE. "The Accommodating Form Of Samuel Beckett." *Southwest Review,* 55 (1970), 354-61.

MAYS, JAMES. "*Pons Asinorum:* Form and Value in Beckett's Writing, with some comments in Kafka and de Sade." *Irish University Review,* 4 (1974), 268-82.

MURRAY, PATRICK. "The Shandean Mode: Beckett and Sterne Compared." *Studies: An Irish Quarterly Review,* 60 (1971), 55-67.

O'BRIEN, JUSTIN. "Samuel Beckett and André Gide: An Hypothesis." *French Review,* 40 (1967), 485-86.

O'Hara, J. D. "Introduction," in *Twentieth Century Interpretations Of Molloy, Malone Dies, The Unnamable: A Collection Of Critical Essays,* ed. J. D. O'Hara, pp. 1-25.

O'NEILL, JOSEPH P. "The Absurd in Samuel Beckett." *Personalist,* 48 (1967), 56-76.

PARKIN, ANDREW. "Similarities in the plays of Yeats and Beckett." *Ariel: A Review Of International English Literature,* 1, No.3 (1970), 49-58.

RABINOVITZ, RUBIN. "Style and Obscurity in Samuel Beckett's Early Fiction." *Modern Fiction Studies,* 20 (1974), 399-406.

RIVA, RAYMOND T. "Beckett and Freud." *Criticism,* 12 (1970), 120-32.

"Samuel Beckett in Books Abroad 1955-1970." *Books Abroad,* 40 (1970), 250.

SELLIN, ERIC. "Samuel Beckett: The Apotheosis of Impotence." *Books Abroad,* 44 (1970), 244-50.

SOBOSAN, JEFFREY G. "Time and Absurdity in Samuel Beckett." *Thought,* 49 (1974), 187-95.

WHITE, PATRICIA O. "Existential Man in Beckett's Fiction." *Critique,* 12, No.2 (1970), 39-49.

ENOUGH

MOOD, JOHN J. " 'Silence Within': A Study of the *Residua* of Samuel Beckett." *Studies In Short Fiction,* 7 (1970), 385-90.

HOW IT IS (Comment c'est, 1961)

ABBOTT, H. PORTER. "Farewell to Incompetence: Beckett's *How It Is* and *Imagination Dead Imagine.*" *Contemporary Literature,* 11 (1970), 36-45.

FEDERMAN, RAYMOND. " 'How It Is': with Beckett's Fiction." *French Review,* 38 (1965), 459-68.

HASSAN, IHAB. *The Literature Of Silence,* pp. 168-73.

KENNER, HUGH. *A Reader's Guide To Samuel Beckett,* pp. 136-46.

KRANCE, CHARLES. "Alienation and Form in Beckett's How It Is." *Perspectives On Contemporary Literature,* 1, No.2 (1975), 85-103.

LEVY, ERIC P. "The Metaphysics of Ignorance: Time and Personality in *How It Is.*" *Renascence,* 28 (1975), 27-37.

ROBINSON, MICHAEL. *The Long Sonata Of The Dead: A Study Of Samuel Beckett,* pp. 213-25.

SCHWARTZ, PAUL J. "Life and Death in the Mud: A Study of Beckett's *Comment C'Est.*" *International Fiction Review,* 2 (1975), 43-48.

SHADOIAN, JACK. "The Achievement of *Comment C'Est.*" *Critique,* 12, No.2 (1969/70), 5-18.

IMAGINATION DEAD IMAGINE (Imagination morte imaginez, 1965)

ABBOTT, H. PORTER. "Farewell to Incompetence: Beckett's *How It Is* and *Imagination Dead Imagine.*" *Contemporary Literature,* 11 (1970), 45-47.

MOOD, JOHN J. " 'Silence Within': A Study of the *Residua* of Samuel Beckett." *Studies In Short Fiction,* 7 (1970), 390-93.

MALONE DIES (Malone Meurt, 1951)

BERSANI, LEO. *Balzac To Beckett,* pp. 309-28.

FLETCHER, JOHN. "Malone 'Given Birth To Into Death,'" in *Twentieth Century Interpretations Of Molloy, Malone Dies, The Unnamable: A Collection Of Critical Essays,* ed. J. D. O'Hara, pp. 58-61.

HASSAN, IHAB. *The Literature of Silence,* pp. 158-62.

HOFFMAN, FREDERICK J. "The Elusive Ego: Beckett's M's," in *Samuel Beckett Now,* ed. Melvin J. Friedman, pp. 50-54.

ISER, WOLFGANG. "Subjectivity as the Autogenous Cancellation of Its Own Manifestations. S. Beckett: *Molloy, Malone Dies, The Unnamable,*" in his *The Implied Reader,* pp. 167-70.

KENNER, HUGH. *A Reader's Guide To Samuel Beckett*, pp. 100–08.

O'HARA, J. D. "About Structure in *Malone Dies*," in *Twentieth Century Interpretations Of Molloy, Malone Dies, The Unnamable: A Collection Of Critical Essays*, ed. J. D. O'Hara, pp. 62–70.

ROBINSON, MICHAEL. *The Long Sonata Of The Dead: A Study Of Samuel Beckett*, pp. 170–90.

SELTZER, ALVIN J. *Chaos In The Novel: The Novel In Chaos*, pp. 194–210.

MOLLOY (1951)

BERSANI, LEO. *Balzac To Beckett*, pp. 309–28.

CHAMBERS, ROSS. "The Artist as Performing Dog." *Comparative Literature*, 23 (1971), 312–25.

FLETCHER, JOHN. "Interpreting *Molloy*," in *Samuel Beckett Now*, ed. Melvin J. Friedman, pp. 157–70.

FRIEDMAN, MELVIN J. "Molloy's 'Sacred' Stones." *Romance Notes*, 9 (1967), 8–11.

GEBHART, RICHARD C. "Technique of Alienation in Molloy." *Perspectives On Contemporary Literature*, 1, No.2 (1975), 74–84.

HASSAN, IHAB. *The Literature Of Silence*, pp. 151–58.

HAYMAN, DAVID. "*Molloy* or the Quest for Meaninglessness: A Global Interpretation," in *Samuel Beckett Now*, ed. Melvin J. Friedman, pp. 129–56.

HAYWARD, SUSAN. "Two Anti-Novels: *Molloy* and *Jacques Le Fataliste*," in *Studies In Eighteenth-Century French Literature*, ed. J. H. Fox, M. H. Waddicor, and D. A. Watts, pp. 97–107.

HOFFMAN, FREDERICK J. "The Elusive Ego: Beckett's M's," in *Samuel Beckett Now*, ed. Melvin J. Friedman, pp. 44–50.

ISER, WOLFGANG. "Subjectivity as the Autogenous Cancellation of Its Own Manifestations. S. Beckett: *Molloy, Malone Dies, The Unnamable*," in his *The Implied Reader*, pp. 164–67.

JANVIER, LUDOVIC. "*Molloy*," in *Twentieth Century Interpretations Of Molloy, Malone Dies, The Unnamable: A Collection Of Critical Essays*, ed. J. D. O'Hara, pp. 46–57.

KELLMAN, STEVEN G. "Beckett's Fatal Dual." *Romance Notes*, 16 (1975), 268–73.

KENNER, HUGH. *A Reader's Guide To Samuel Beckett*, pp. 92–100.

KERN, EDITH. "Moran-Molloy: The Hero as Author," in *Twentieth Century Interpretations Of Molloy, Malone Dies, The Unnamable: A Collection Of Critical Essays*, ed. J. D. O'Hara, pp. 35–45.

PEARCE, RICHARD. *Stages Of The Clown*, pp. 128–32.

ROBINSON, MICHAEL. *The Long Sonata Of The Dead: A Study Of Samuel Beckett*, pp. 140–69.

ROSE, GILBERT J. "On the Shores of Self: Samuel Beckett's 'Molloy'—Irredentism and the Creative Impulse." *Psychoanalytic Review*, 6 (1973/4), 587–604.

SCOTT, NATHAN A. *Craters Of The Spirit*, pp. 185–89.

SELTZER, ALVIN J. *Chaos In The Novel: The Novel In Chaos*, pp. 169–94.

SHAPIRO, BARBARA. "Toward a Psychoanalytic Reading of Beckett's Molloy, I." *Literature And Psychology*, 19, No.2 (1969), 71–86.

———. "Toward a Psychoanalytic Reading of Beckett's *Molloy*, II." *Literature and Psychology*, 19, No.3/4, (1969), 15–30.

SOLOMON, PHILIP HOWARD. "Samuel Beckett's *Molloy*: a Dog's Life." *French Review*, 41 (1967), 84–91.

MURPHY (1938)

COETZEE, J. M. "The Comedy of Point of View In Beckett's *Murphy*." *Critique*, 12, No.2 (1970), 19–27.

DOBREZ, LIVIO. "Samuel Beckett's Irreducible." *Southern Review: Literary And Interdisciplinary Essays*, 6 (1973), 207–11.

ERICKSON, JOHN D. "Alienation in Samuel Beckett: The Protago-

nist as Eiron." *Perspectives On Contemporary Literature*, 1, No.2 (1975). 62–73.

GARZILLI, ENRICO. *Circles Without Center*, pp. 18–27.

HARRISON, ROBERT. *Samuel Beckett's Murphy: A Critical Excursion*.

HASSAN, IHAB. *The Literature Of Silence*, pp. 140–45.

HOFFMAN, FREDERICK J. "The Elusive Ego: Beckett's M's," in *Samuel Beckett Now*, ed. Melvin J. Friedman, pp. 31–38.

KENNER, HUGH. *A Reader's Guide To Samuel Beckett*, pp. 57–71.

PARK, ERIC. "Fundamental Sounds: Music in Samuel Beckett's *Murphy* and *Watt*." *Modern Fiction Studies*, 21 (1975), 160–65.

ROBINSON, MICHAEL. *The Long Sonata Of The Dead: A Study Of Samuel Beckett*, pp. 82–99.

SELTZER, ALVIN J. *Chaos In The Novel: The Novel In Chaos*, pp. 156–62.

STEINBERG, S. C. "The External and Internal in <Murphy.>" *Twentieth Century Literature*, 18 (1972), 93–110.

PING (1966)

MOOD, JOHN J. " 'Silence Within': A Study of the *Residua* of Samuel Beckett." *Studies In Short Fiction*, 7 (1970), 393–401.

UNNAMABLE (L'Innommable, 1953)

BERSANI, LEO. *Balzac To Beckett*, pp. 309–28.

CHAMPIGNY, ROBERT. "Adventures of the First Person," in *Samuel Beckett Now*, ed. Melvin J. Friedman, pp. 119–28.

CORNWELL, ETHEL F. "Samuel Beckett: The Flight from Self." *PMLA*, 88 (1973), 45–48.

FANIZZA, FRANCO. "The Word and Silence in Samuel Beckett's *The Unnamable*," in *Twentieth Century Interpretations Of Molloy, Malone Dies, The Unnamable: A Collection Of Critical Essays*, ed. J. D. O'Hara, pp. 71–81.

GARZILLI, ENRICO. *Circles Without Center*, pp. 47–52.

HASSAN, IHAB. *The Literature Of Silence*, pp. 162–68.

HOFFMAN, FREDERICK J. "The Elusive Ego: Beckett's M's," in *Samuel Beckett Now*, ed. Melvin J. Friedman, pp. 54–58.

ISER, WOLFGANG. "Subjectivity as the Autogenous Cancellation of Its Own Manifestations. S. Beckett: *Molloy, Malone Dies, The Unnamable*," in his *The Implied Reader*, pp. 170–74.

KENNER, HUGH. *A Reader's Guide To Samuel Beckett*, pp. 108–15.

ROBINSON, MICHAEL. *The Long Sonata Of The Dead: A Study Of Samuel Beckett*, pp. 190–207.

ROSE, MARILYN GADDIS. "The Sterne Ways of Beckett and Jack B. Yeats." *Irish University Review*, 2 (1972), 164–71.

SELTZER, ALVIN J. *Chaos In The Novel: The Novel In Chaos*, pp. 211–35.

WATT (1953)

COETZEE, J. M. "The Manuscript Revisions of Beckett's *Watt*." *Journal Of Modern Literature*, 2 (1972), 472–80.

GREENBERG, ALVIN. "The Revolt of Objects: The Opposing World in the Modern Novel." *Centennial Review*, 13 (1969), 372–75.

HASSAN, IHAB. *The Literature Of Silence*, pp. 145–51.

HOFFMAN, FREDERICK J. "The Elusive Ego: Beckett's M's," in *Samuel Beckett Now*, ed. Melvin J. Friedman, pp. 38–43.

KENNER, HUGH. *A Reader's Guide To Samuel Beckett*, pp. 72–82.

MOOD, JOHN J. " 'The Personal System'—Samuel Beckett's *Watt*." *PMLA*, 86 (1971), 255–65.

PARK, ERIC. "Fundamental Sounds: Music in Samuel Beckett's *Murphy* and *Watt*." *Modern Fiction Studies*, 21 (1975), 165–71.

ROBINSON, MICHAEL. *The Long Sonata Of The Dead: A Study Of Samuel Beckett*, pp. 100–31.

SCOTT, NATHAN A. *Craters Of The Spirit*, pp. 180–85.

SELTZER, ALVIN J. *Chaos In The Novel: The Novel In Chaos,* pp. 162-69.

SKERL, JENNIE. "Fritz Mauthner's 'Critique of Language' in Samuel Beckett's *Watt.*" *Contemporary Literature,* 15 (1974), 474-87.

SMITH, FREDERIK N. "The Epistemology of Fictional Failure: Swift's *Tale Of A Tub* and Beckett's *Watt.*" *Texas Studies In Literature And Language,* 15 (1974), 649-72.

SOLOMON, PHILLIP HOWARD. "A Ladder Image in *Watt:* Samuel Beckett and Fritz Mauthner." *Papers On Language And Literature,* 7 (1971), 422-27.

SWANSON, ELEANOR. "Samuel Beckett's *Watt:* A Coming and A Going." *Modern Fiction Studies,* 17 (1971), 264-68.

TRIVISONNO, ANN M. "Meaning and Function of The Quest in Beckett's *Watt.*" *Critique,* 12, No.2 (1970), 28-38.

BEDI, RAJINDER SINGH (Urdu, 1915-)

I TAKE THIS WOMAN (1967)

Reviews
DULAI, SURJIT SINGH. *Mahfil,* 5, No.1/2 (1968/9), 110-15.

BEER, JOHANN (Austrian, 1655-1700)

GENERAL

HADLEY, MICHAEL L. "Johann Beer's Approach to the Novel." *Seminar,* 7 (1971), 31-41.

MENHENNET, A. "Narrative and Satire in Grimmelshausen and Beer." *Modern Language Review,* 70 (1975), 814-19.

BELLUM MUSICUM ODER MUSICALISCHER KRIEG (1701)

KNIGHT, K. G. "Johann Beer's *Bellum Musicum.*" *German Life And Letters,* 18 (1965), 291-94.

BEGGS, ALEXANDER (Canadian,)

DOT IT DOWN

HARRISON, DICK. "The Beginnings of Prairie Fiction." *Journal Of Canadian Fiction,* 4, No.1 (1975), 170.

BEHAR, SERGE

LA QUATRIEME SORTIE DE FERNANDO QUI (1972)

Reviews
KUHN, REINHARD. *French Review,* 47 (1974), 654-55.

BEKESSY, Jean see HABE, Hans

BELOV, VASILII

GENERAL

HOSKING, GEOFFREY A. "Vasilii Belov—Chronicler of the Soviet Village." *Russian Review,* 34 (1975), 165-85.

A COMMON AFFAIR (Privychnoe Delo)

DEDKOV, I. "Pages from Country Life." *Soviet Studies in Literature,* 5, No.3 (1969), 75-83.

HOSKING, GEOFFREY A. "Vasilii Belov—Chronicler of the Soviet Village." *Russian Review,* 34 (1975), 167-74.

KUZNETSOV, FELIKS. "The Fate of the Village in Prose and Criticism." *Soviet Studies In Fiction,* 10, No.2 (1974), 71-74.

PRIVYCHNOE DELO see A COMMON AFFAIR

BELS, ALBERTS (Latvian, 1938-)

GENERAL

KRATINS, OJARS. "Society and the Self in the Novels of Ilze Skipsna and Alberts Bels." *Books Abroad,* 47 (1973), 675-82.

BELTRAN, LUIS

EL FRUTO DE SU VIENTRE (1973)

Reviews
SCHWARTZ, KESSEL. *Hispania,* 58 (1975), 226-27.

BELY, ANDREI (Russian, 1880-1924) pseudonym of Bugaev, Boris Nikolayevich

GENERAL

BELY, ANDREI. "About Myself as a Writer." *Russian Literature Triquarterly,* No.13 (1975), pp. 561-66.

ELSWORTH, JOHN. "Andrei Bely's Theory of Symbolism." *Forum For Modern Language Studies,* 11 (1975), 305-33.

STAMMLER, HEINRICH A. "Belyj's Conflict with Vjačeslav Ivanov over War and Revolution." *Slavic And East European Journal,* 18 (1974), 259-70.

KOTIK LETAEV (1922)

CIORAN, SAMUEL. "The Eternal Return: Andrej Belyj's *Kotik Letaev.*" *Slavic And East European Journal,* 15 (1971), 22-37.

HART, PIERRE. "Psychological Primitivism in *Kotik Letaev.*" *Russian Literature Triquarterly,* No.4 (1972), pp. 319-30.

JANECEK, GERALD. "An Acoustico-Semantic Complex in Belyj's *Kotik Letaev.*" *Slavic And East European Journal,* 18 (1974), 153-59.

JANEČEK, GERALD. "Anthroposophy in Kotik Letaev." *Orbis Litterarum,* 29 (1974), 245-67.

ST. PETERSBURG (Peterburg, 1913)

MAGUIRE, ROBERT A. "Macrocosm or Microcosm? The Symbolists on Russia." *Review Of National Literatures,* 3, No.1 (1972), 144-47.

ZAPISKI CHUDAKA (1922)

CIORAN, SAMUEL D. "In the Imitation of Christ: A Study of Andrei Belyi's *Zapiski Chudaka.*" *Canadian Slavic Studies,* 4 (1970), 74-92.

BENEDETTI, MARIO (Uruguayan, 1920-)

THE TRUCE (Le tregua, 1960)

Reviews
CROW, JOHN A. *Saturday Review,* 10 January 1970, pp. 44-45, 98; rpt. in *Review,* No.2 (1969), pp. 21-23.

GOLD, ARTHUR. *New York Times Book Review,* 19 October 1969; rpt. in *Review,* No.2 (1969), pp. 23-25.

BENEDICTSSON, Victoria Maria see AHLGREN, Ernst

BENES, JAN (Czech, 1936-)

SECOND BREATH

Reviews
HITREC, JOSEPH. *Saturday Review,* 3 January 1970, p. 81.

BENET, JUAN (Spanish, 1927-)

LA OTRA CASA DE MAZÓN

Reviews
FRANZ, THOMAS R. *Journal Of Spanish Studies,* 2 (1974), 197–98.

BENITEZ, FERNANDO

THE POISONED WATER (El agua envenendada)

Reviews
ALLEN, BRUCE. *Review,* No.12 (1974), p. 75.
UDICK, BERENICE. *Hispania,* 52 (1969), 536.

BENN, GOTTFRIED (German, 1886–1956)

GENERAL

CASPER, M. KENT. "The Circle and the Centre: Symbols of Totality in Gottfried Benn." *German Life And Letters,* 26 (1973), 288–97.

BENNECKE, WILLIAM

REINHOLD LENZ

HARRIS, EDWARD P. "J. M. R. Lenz in German Literature: From Büchner to Bobrowski." *Colloquia Germanica,* 1973, pp. 222–24.

BENSON, MARY (South African, 1919–)

AT THE STILL POINT (1970)

Reviews
McGUINESS, FRANK. "Black and White Power." *London Magazine,* NS, 11, No.3 (1971), 146–47.

BERÁTIS, YIÁNNIS (Greek)

GENERAL

DOULIS, THOMAS. "Yiánnis Berátis: Objectivity in Freedom." *Forum For Modern Language Studies,* 8 (1972), 269–83.

THE WIDE RIVER

DOULIS, THOMAS. "Yiánnis Berátis: Objectivity in Freedom." *Forum For Modern Language Studies,* 8 (1972), 280–83.

BERDICHEVSKI, MIKHAH YOSEF (Russian, 1865-1921)

IN THE VALLEY

KAGAN, ZIPORA. "From Folktale to Novella: Literary Metamorphosis in a Work of M. Y. Berdichevski." Trans. Miriam Buzi. *Genre,* 7 (1974), 362–91.

BERESFORD-HOWE, CONSTANCE (Canadian, 1922–)

THE BOOK OF EVE (1973)

Reviews
THOMAS, AUDREY. "Closing Doors." *Canadian Literature,* No.61 (1974), pp. 79–80.

BERGENGRUEN, WERNER (German, 1892-1964)

GENERAL

AHLERS, HANS PETER. "Werner Bergengruen's Metaphysics of the Novelle." *Monatshefte,* 66 (1974), 387–400.

EICKHORST, WILLIAM. "The Idea of Tolerance as a Key to Werner Bergengruen's *Novellen.*" *USF Language Quarterly,* 8, No.1/2 (1969), 20–22.

JUNGFRÄULICHKEIT

ALEXANDER, MARY. "Virgo–Virago? Werner Bergengruen's Novelle *Jungfräulichkeit.*" *German Life And Letters,* 23 (1970), 206–16.

A MATTER OF CONSCIENCE (Der Grosstyrann und Das Gericht)

EICKHORST, WILLIAM. "Werner Bergengruen's *A Matter Of Conscience (Der Grosstyrann Und Das Gericht):* The Summit and Substance of Literary Crime Fiction." *Ball State University Forum,* 9, No.1 (1968), 13–16.

PASLICK, ROBERT H. "The Tempter: Bergengruen's *Grosstyrann* and the Hermetic Traditions." *Neophilologus,* 57 (1973), 66–73.

BERGONZO, JEAN LOUIS (French, 1939–)

THE SPANISH INN (L'Auberge espagnole, 1966)

Reviews
BISHOP, THOMAS. " 'Let (she said) Me Alone.' " *Saturday Review,* 26 October 1968, p. 40.

BERNANOS, GEORGES (French, 1888–1948)

GENERAL

BEAUMONT, ERNEST. "The Supernatural in Dostoyevsky and Bernanos: A Reply to Professor Sonnelfeld." *French Studies,* 23 (1969), 267–71.

CLARK, A. R. "Georges Bernanos and the French Revolution." *AUMLA,* No.38 (1972), pp. 177–96.

HEBBLETHWAITE, PETER. *Bernanos: An Introduction.*

NETTELBECK, C. W. "The Obsessional Dream World of Georges Bernanos." *AUMLA,* No.26 (1966), pp. 241–53.

RECK, RIMA DRELL. "George Bernanos: A Novelist and his Art." *French Review,* 38 (1965), 619–29.

SONNENFELD, ALBERT. "A Sharing of Darkness: Bernanos and Dostoevsky." *Renascence,* 17 (1964), 82–88.

SPEAIGHT, ROBERT. "Bernanos Redivivus." *The Month,* NS, 42 (1969), 187–93.

A CRIME (Un crime, 1935)

RECK, RIMA DRELL. "A Crime: Dostoevsky and Bernanos." *Forum,* 4, No.4 (1964), 10–13.

SPEAIGHT, ROBERT. *Georges Bernanos: A Study Of The Man And Writer,* pp. 135–38.

THE DIARY OF A COUNTRY PRIEST (Journal d'un Curé de Campagne, 1936)

BOURAOUI, H. A. "The Face in the Mirror: Bernanos' Hero as Artist in *Journal D'un Curé De Campagne.*" *Modern Fiction Studies,* 17 (1971), 181–92.

COR, LAURENCE W. "Mystical Perception in *Journal D'un Curé De Campagne.*" *Romance Notes,* 12 (1971), 244–50.

FLOWER, JOHN. "The *Comtesse* Episode in the *Journal D'un Curé De Campagne.*" *French Review,* 42 (1969), 673–82.

GUERS-VILLATE, YVONNE. "Revolt and Submission in Camus and Bernanos." *Renascence,* 24 (1972), 182–97.

KURZ, PAUL KONRAD. "The Priest in the Modern Novel," in his *On Modern German Literature,* Vol. 4: 136–41.

SISTER MARY SANDRA. "The Priest-Hero in Modern Fiction." *Personalist,* 46 (1965), 535–38.

O'SHARKEY, EITHNE M. "Portraits of Clergy in Bernanos' *Diary Of A Country Priest.*" *Dublin Review,* 239 (1965), 183–91.

SPEAIGHT, ROBERT. *Georges Bernanos: A Study Of The Man And Writer,* pp. 146–55.

L'IMPOSTURE (1927)

SPEAIGHT, ROBERT. *Georges Bernanos: A Study Of The Man And Writer,* pp. 91-97.

JOY (La joie, 1929)

SPEAIGHT, ROBERT. *Georges Bernanos: A Study Of The Man And Writer,* pp. 97-99.

MOUCHETTE (Nouvelle histoire de Mouchette, 1937)

NETTLEBECK, C. W. "The Obsessional Dream World of Georges Bernanos." *AUMLA,* No.26 (1966), pp. 246-53.

Reviews
FYTTON, FRANCIS. *London Magazine,* 6, No.6 (1966), 115-17.
MOORE, HARRY T. "Life Was a School for Despair." *Saturday Review,* 19 November 1966), pp. 44, 46.

NIGHT IS THE DARKEST (Un mauvais reve, 1951)

SPEAIGHT, ROBERT. *Georges Bernanos: A Study Of The Man And Writer,* pp. 142-46.

THE OPEN MIND (Monsieur Oine, 1943)

SPEAIGHT, ROBERT. *Georges Bernanos: A Study Of The Man And Writer,* pp. 215-26.

WEINSTEIN, ARNOLD L. "Bernanos' *Monsieur Ouine* and the Esthetic of Chaos." *Symposium,* 25 (1971), 392-407.

THE OTHER SIDE OF THE MOUNTAIN

Reviews
LESAGE, LAURENT. "Infernal Island." *Saturday Review,* 4 January 1969, p. 96.

THE STAR OF SATAN (Sous le soleil de satan, 1926)

SPEAIGHT, ROBERT. *Georges Bernanos: A Study Of The Man And Writer,* pp. 68-75.

BERNARD, Carlo see BERNARI, Carlo

BERNARDIN DE SAINT-PIERRE, JACQUES HENRI (French, 1737-1814)

PAUL ET VIRGINIE

CHERPACK, CLIFTON. "*Paul Et Virginie* and the Myths of Death." *PMLA,* 90 (1975), 247-55.

FRANCIS, R. A. "Bernardin de Saint-Pierre's 'Paul et Virginie' and the Failure of the Ideal State in the Eighteenth-Century French Novel." *Nottingham French Studies,* 13 (1974), 51-60.

LOWRIE, JOYCE O. "The Structural Significance of Sensual Imagery in *Paul Et Virginie.*" *Romance Notes,* 12 (1971), 351-56.

BERNARI, CARLO (Italian, 1909-) pseud. of Carlo Bernard

PROLOGO ALLE TENEBRE (1947)

CAPOZZI, ROCCO. "Time and Aesthetic Distance in Carlo Bernari's *Le Radiose Giornate.*" *International Fiction Review,* 2 (1975), 153-56.

LE RADIOSE GIRONATE (1969)

CAPOZZI, ROCCO. "Time and Aesthetic Distance in Carlo Bernari's *Le Radiose Giornate.*" *International Fiction Review,* 2 (1975), 153-56.

BERNHARD, THOMAS (Austrian, 1931-)

GENERAL

CRAIG, D. A. "The Novels of Thomas Bernhard—A Report." *German Life And Letters,* 25 (1972), 343-53.

GARGOYLES (Vestoerung, 1967)

Reviews
MAURER, ROBERT. *Saturday Review,* 31 October 1970, pp. 34-39.

BESSETTE, GÉRARD (French Canadian, 1920-)

GENERAL

SHEK, BEN-Z. "Gérard Bessette and Social Realism." *Canadian Modern Language Review,* 31 (1975), 292-300.

LA BAGARRE (1958)

SHEK, BEN-Z. "Gérard Bessette and Social Realism." *Canadian Modern Language Review,* 31 (1975), 292-94.

SUTHERLAND, RONALD. "Brawling with Gerard Bessette." *Ariel: A Review Of International English Literature,* 4, No.3 (1973), 29-37.

LE CYCLE (1971)

SUGDEN, LEONARD W. "The Unending Cycle." *Canadian Literature,* No.63 (1975), pp. 64-72.

INCUBATION (L'Incubation, 1965)

SUGDEN, LEONARD W. "Gerard Bessette's *L'Incubation.*" *Journal Of Canadian Fiction,* 3, No.2 (1974), 82-84.

Reviews
TOUGAS, GÉRARD. "Something or Nothing." *Canadian Literature,* No.36 (1968), pp. 62-67.

LE LIBRAIRE (1960)

SHEK, BEN-Z. "Gérard Bessette and Social Realism." *Canadian Modern Language Review,* 31 (1975), 295-98.

BESTUZHEV, Alexander Alexandrovich see MARLINSKY, Alexander

BÉSUS, ROGER

FRANCE DERIVÈRE

Reviews
ALFONSI, SANDRA R. *French Review,* 46 (1973), 848-49.

BETI, MONGO (Cameroons, France, 1932-) pseudonym of Alexandre Biyidi

GENERAL

CASSIRER, THOMAS. "The Dilemma of Leadership as Tragi-Comedy in the Novels of Mongo Beti." *L'Esprit Créateur,* 10 (1970), 223-33.

MACAULAY, JEANNETTE. "The Idea of Assimilation," in *Protest And Conflict In African Literature,* ed. Cosmo Pieterse and Donald Munro, pp. 86-92.

KING LAZARUS (Le Roi Miraculé; chronique des Essazam, 1958)

BRENCH, A. C. *The Novelists' Inheritance In French Africa,* pp. 68-74.

GLEASON, JUDITH ILLSLEY. *This Africa,* pp. 157-59.

MISSION TO KALA (Mission Terminée, 1957)

BRENCH, A. C. *The Novelists' Inheritance In French Africa,* pp. 63-68.

CARTEY, WILFRED. *Whispers From A Continent, pp. 32-38.*

CASSIRER, THOMAS. "The Dilemma of Leadership as Tragi-Comedy in the Novels of Mongo Beti." *L'Esprit Créateur,* 10 (1970), 228-31.

GLEASON, JUDITH ILLSLEY. *This Africa,* pp. 154-57.

PALMER, EUSTACE. *An Introduction To The African Novel,* pp. 143-54.

PERPETUA AND THE HABIT OF UNHAPPINESS (Perpétue ou l'habitude du malheur, 1974)

SMITH, ROBERT P. "Mongo Beti: The Novelist Looks at Independence and The Status of the African Woman." *College Language Association Journal,* 19 (1976), 301-11.

THE POOR CHRIST OF BOMBA (Le Pauvre Christ de Bomba, 1956)

CARTEY, WILFRED. *Whispers From A Continent,* pp. 70-77.

CASSIRER, THOMAS. "The Dilemma of Leadership as Tragi-Comedy in the Novels of Mongo Beti." *L'Esprit Créateur,* 10 (1970), 224-28.

GLEASON, JUDITH ILLSLEY. *This Africa,* pp. 152-54.

MOORE, GERALD. "The Debate on Existence in African Literature." *Présence Africaine,* No.81 (1972), pp. 28-32.

VILLE CRUELLE

GLEASON, JUDITH ILLSLEY. *This Africa,* pp. 149-51.

NOSS, PHILIP A. "The Cruel City." *Revue De Littérature Comparée,* 48 (1974), 462-70.

BEVILACQUA, ALBERTO (Italian, 1934-)

THE CALIFFA (La Califfa, 1964)

Reviews
HUGHES, SERGE. *Saturday Review,* 20 September 1969, p. 38.

BEYLE, Marie Henri see STENDHAL

BEYNON, FRANCIS

ALETA DAY

RICOU, LAURENCE. *Vertical Man/Horizontal World,* pp. 66-67.

BHANDARI, MANNU (1931-)

GENERAL

SINGH, R. S. "Mannu Bhandari." *Indian Literature,* 16, No.1/2 (1973), 133-42.

BHATTACHARYA, BHABANI (Indian, 1906-)

GENERAL

ARULANDRUM, H. G. S. "Tagore's Impact on Bhabani Bhattacharya." *Indian Literature,* 18, No.4 (1975), 27-31.

"BHABANI BHATTACHARYA." *Mahfil,* 5, No.1/2 (1968/9), 43-48.

FISHER, MARLENE. "Personal and Social Change in Bhattacharya's Novels." *World Literature Written In English,* 12, No.2 (1973), 288-96.

———. "The Women in Bhattacharya's Novels." *World Literature Written In English,* 11, No.1 (1972), 95-108.

GEMMILL, JANET P. "An Interview with Bhabani Bhattacharya." *World Literature Written In English,* 14 (1975), 300-9.

RAO, B. SYAMALA. "Dr. Bhabani Bhattacharya as a Novelist." *Triveni,* 40, No.1 (1971), 35-40.

RAY, LILA. "Bhabani Bhattacharya: A Profile." *Indian Literature,* 11, No.2 (1968), 73-76.

SRINIVASA IYENGAR, K. R. *Indian Writing In English,* pp. 412-23.

SHADOW FROM LADAKH (1966)

FISHER, MARLENE. "The Women in Bhattacharya's Novels." *World Literature Written In English,* 11, No.1 (1972), 103-6.

JAIN, JASBIR. "Coming to Terms with Gandhi: *Shadow From La-*

dakh." *Journal Of Indian Writing In English,* 3, No.2 (1975), 20-23.

SRINIVASA IYENGAR, K. R. *Indian Writing In English,* pp. 420-23.

Reviews
SHARPE, PATRICIA L. *Mahfil,* 5, No.1/2 (1968/9), 134-39.

SO MANY HUNGERS! (1947)

TARINAYYA, M. "Two Novels." *Indian Literature,* 13, No.1 (1970), 117-21.

THE VIRGIN FISH OF BABUGHAT

Reviews
SRINIVASAN, THAMBI. *Indian Literature,* 18, No.4 (1975), 111-13.

BIELER, MANFRED (German, 1934-)

THE SAILOR IN THE BOTTLE (Bonifaz oder der Matrose in der Flasche, 1963)

ANDREWS, R. C. "A Comic Novel from East Germany—Manfred Bieler: *Bonifaz Oder Der Matrose In Der Flasche.*" *German Life And Letters,* 20 (1967), 101-6.

Reviews
BAUKE, JOSEPH P. "Whisper of Evil in a Roar of Drums." *Saturday Review,* 22 January 1966, p. 42.

BIERBAUM, OTTO JULIUS (German, 1865-1910)

GENERAL

ACKERMAN, ROY L. "*Verbildung* in Bierbaum's Travel Novels." *Germanic Notes,* 4 (1973), 58-61.

BIOY CASARES, ADOLFO (Argentine, 1914-)

GENERAL

BIOY-CASARES, ADOLFO. "Chronology." Trans. Andrée Conrad. *Review,* No.15 (1975), pp. 35-39.

GALLAGHER, D. P. "The Novels and Short Stories of Adolfo Bioy Casares." *Bulletin Of Hispanic Studies,* 52 (1975), 247-66.

RODRIGUEZ MONEGAL, EMIR. "The Invention of Bioy-Casares." *Review,* No.15 (1975), pp. 41-44.

THE INVENTION OF MOREL (La invención de Morel, 1940)

GALLAGHER, D. P. "The Novels and Short Stories of Adolfo Bioy Casares." *Bulletin Of Hispanic Studies,* 52 (1975), 252-58.

PLAN FOR ESCAPE (Plan de evasión, 1945)

ADAMS, ROBERT M. "No Escaping Evasion." *Review,* No.15 (1975), pp. 50-54.

GALLAGHER, D. P. "The Novels and Short Stories of Adolfo Bioy Casares." *Bulletin Of Hispanic Studies,* 52 (1975), 249-52.

WEINBERGER, DEBORAH. "Problems in Perception." *Review,* No.15 (1975), pp. 45-49.

BIRD, WILL R. (Canadian, 1891-)

ANGEL COVE (1972)

Reviews
ZIMMER, ELIZABETH. "Desperation and Small Favours." *Journal Of Canadian Fiction,* 1, No.3 (1975), 85.

BIRNEY, EARLE (Canadian, 1904-)

DOWN THE LONG TABLE (1955)

DAVEY, FRANK. *Earle Birney,* pp. 38-43.

TURVEY, A MILITARY PICARESQUE (1949)

BIRNEY, EARLE. "Turvey and the Critics." *Canadian Literature,* No.30 (1966), pp. 21–25.

DAVEY, FRANK. *Earle Birney,* pp. 29–38.

BIYIDI, Alexandre see BETI, Mongo

BJØRNSØN, BJORNSTJERNE (Norwegian, 1832–1910)

GENERAL

TYSDAHL, B. J. "Joyce's Use of Norwegian Writers." *English Studies,* 50 (1969), 261–64.

ARNE (1858)

SEHMSDORF, HENNING K. "The Self in Isolation: A New Reading of Bjørnsøn's *Arne.*" *Scandinavian Studies,* 45 (1973), 310–23.

BLAIS, MARIE-CLAIRE (French Canadian, 1939–)

GENERAL

KEATING, L. CLARK. "Marie-Claire Blais, French-Canadian Naturalist." *Romance Notes,* 15 (1973), 10–17.

DAVID STERNE (1967)

Reviews
CAVANAGH, DAVID. "The Darkness at the Centre." *Journal Of Canadian Fiction,* 3, No.3 (1974), 105–6.

THE DAY IS DARK (Le Jour est noir, 1962)

Reviews
LeSAGE, LAURENT. "Journeys Into Night." *Saturday Review,* 29 April 1967, p. 29.

MAD SHADOWS (La Belle bête, 1959)

COLDWELL, JOAN. "*Mad Shadows* as Psychological Fiction." *Journal Of Canadian Fiction,* 2, No.4 (1973), 65–67.

PARKER, DOUGLAS H. "The Shattered Glass: Mirror and Illusion in *Mad Shadows.*" *Journal Of Canadian Fiction,* 2, No.4 (1973), 68–70.

THE MANUSCRIPTS OF PAULINE ARCHANGE (Les Manuscrits de Pauline Archange, 1968)

KRAFT, JAMES. "Fiction as Autobiography in Québec: Notes on Pierre Valliéres and Marie-Claire Blais." *Novel,* 6 (1972), 73–78.

Reviews
McPHERSON, HUGO. "Blais, Godbout, Roy: Love, Art, Time." *Tamarack Review,* No.57 (1971), pp. 85–86.

A SEASON IN THE LIFE OF EMMANUEL (Une Saison dans la vie D'Emmanuel, 1965)

Reviews
BUCKEYE, ROBERT. "Nouveau Roman Made Easy." *Canadian Literature,* No.31 (1967), pp. 67–69.

LeSAGE, LAURENT. "No Way Out of a Bleak House." *Saturday Review,* 25 June 1966, pp. 26–27.

THREE TRAVELERS (Le Voyageurs Sacres, 1967)

Reviews
LeSAGE, LAURENT. "Journeys Into Night." *Saturday Review,* 29 April 1967, p. 29

THE WOLF (1971)

DAVIS, FRANCES. *Dalhousie Review,* 54 (1974), 786–87.

SULLIVAN, ROSEMARY. "World of Two Faces." *Canadian Literature,* No.63 (1975), pp. 120–22.

BLAISE, CLARK (Canadian, 1940–)

GENERAL

METCALF, JOHN. "Interview: Clark Blaise." *Journal Of Canadian Fiction,* 2, No.4 (1973), 77–79.

BLANCHOT, MAURICE (French, 1907–)

THOMAS THE OBSCURE (Thomas l'obscur, 1941)

Reviews
GREENE, NAOMI. "Thomas, Come Back." *Novel,* 8 (1975), 175–77.

BLASCO IBÁÑEZ, VICENTE (Spanish, 1867–1928)

GENERAL

JUMP, J. R. "The Rehabilitation of Vicente Blasco Ibáñez." *Modern Languages,* 48 (1967), 109–10.

SMITH, PAUL. "Blasco Ibañez and the Theme of the Jews." *Hispania,* 56 (1973), 282–94.

LA ARAÑA NEGRA

DENDLE, BRIAN J. "Blasco Ibáñez and Coloma's *Pequeñeces.*" *Romance Notes,* 8 (1967), 200–3.

THE CABIN (La Barraca, 1898)

ROGERS, DOUGLASS. "The Descriptive Simile in Galdós and Blasco Ibáñez: A Study in Contrasts." *Hispania,* 53 (1970), 864–66.

THE MAYFLOWER (Flor de mayo, 1895)

SMITH, PAUL. "On Blasco Ibáñez's FLOR DE MAYO." *Symposium,* 24 (1970), 55–66.

BLICKER, SEYMOUR (French Canadian, 1940–)

SHMUCKS (1972)

Reviews
SHERMAN, JOSEPH. "Comic Confrontation." *Journal Of Canadian Fiction,* 2, No.2 (1973), 90–91.

TAUSKY, T. E. "Marshmallow Worlds." *Canadian Literature,* No.54 (1974), pp. 120–21.

BLICQ, ANTHONY (Canadian, 1926–)

THE RISE AND FALL OF MARRIED CHARLIE (1970)

Reviews
GROSSKURTH, PHYLLIS. "Crowded Space." *Canadian Literature,* No.48 (1971), pp. 83–84.

BLOCH-MICHEL, JEAN (French, 1912–)

DANIEL ET NOÉMI (1931)

Reviews
GOODRICH, NORMA L. *French Review,* 46 (1972), 201–2.

BLOY, LEON (French, 1846–1917)

GENERAL

BIRKETT, JENNIFER. "Barbey d'Aurevilly and Leon Bloy: Love and Morality in the Catholic Novel." *Nottingham French Studies,* 14 (1975), 3–10.

LE DÉSESPÉRÉ

BIRKETT, JENNIFER. "The Theme of Love in the Work of Leon Bloy" *Nottingham French Studies,* 14 (1975), 65–70.

THE WOMAN WHO WAS POOR (La Femme pauvre, 1897)

BIRKETT, JENNIFER. "The Theme of Love in the Work of Leon Bloy." *Nottingham French Studies,* 14 (1975), 70–76.

LOWRIE, JOYCE O. *The Violent Mystique,* pp. 94–101, 113–30.

REINHART, KURT F. *The Theological Novel Of Modern Europe,* pp. 78–89.

BOBROWSKI, JOHANNES (German, 1917–1965)

LEVIN'S MILL (Levins mühle, 1964)

BARNOUW, DAGMAR. "Bobrowski and Socialist Realism." *Germanic Review,* 48 (1973), 288–300.

LITAUISCHE CLAVIERE (1967)

BARNOUW, DAGMAR. "Bobrowski and Socialist Realism." *Germanic Review,* 48 (1973), 311–14.

BOCCACCIO, GIOVANNI (Italian, 1313–1375)

GENERAL

GATHERCOLE, PATRICIA M. "The French Translators of Boccaccio." *Italica,* 46 (1969), 300–9.

LAYMAN, B. J. "Boccaccio's Paradigm of the Artist and his Art." *Italian Quarterly,* 13, No.51 (1970), 19–36.

DECAMERON (1353)

BEIDLER, PETER G. "Chaucer's *Merchant's Tale* and the *Decameron.*" *Italica,* 50 (1973), 266–84.

BETTRIDGE, WILLIAM EDWIN and FRANCIS LEE UTLEY. "New Light on the Origin of the Griselda Story." *Texas Studies In Literature And Language,* 13 (1971), 153–208.

BONADEO, A. "Some Aspects of Love and Nobility in the Society of the *Decameron.*" *Philological Quarterly,* 47 (1968), 513–25.

BROWN, MARSHALL. "In The Valley of The Ladies." *Italian Quarterly,* 18, No.72 (1975), 33–52.

COLE, HOWARD C. "Dramatic Interplay in the *Decameron:* Boccaccio, Neifile and Giletta di Nerbona." *MLN,* 90 (1975), 38–57.

COPLAND, MURRAY. "*The Shipman's Tale:* Chaucer and Boccaccio." *Medium Aevum,* 35 (1966), 11–28.

COTTINO-JONES, MARGA. "Fabula vs. Figura: Another Interpretation of the Griselda Story." *Italica,* 50 (1973), 38–52.

———. "Magic and Superstition in Boccaccio's *Decameron.*" *Italian Quarterly,* 18, No.72 (1975), 5–32.

———. "The Mode and Structure of Tragedy in Boccaccio's *Decameron* (IV, 9)." *Italian Quarterly,* 11, No.43 (1967), 63–88.

———. "Observations on the Structure of the *Decameron* Novella." *Romance Notes,* 15 (1973), 378–87.

DELIGIORGIS, STAVROS. "Boccaccio and the Greek Romances." *Comparative Literature,* 19 (1967), 97–113.

DUTSCHKE, DENNIS. "Boccaccio: a Question of Love (A Comparative Study of *Filocolo* IV, 13 and *Decameron* X, 4.)" *Humanities Association Review,* 26 (1975), 300–12.

FERRANTE, JOAN M. "The Frame Characters of the *Decameron:* A Progression of Virtues." *Romance Philology,* 19 (1965), 212–26.

GREENE, THOMAS M. "Forms of Accommodation in the *Decameron.*" *Italica,* 45 (1968), 297–313.

KLEINHENZ, CHRISTOPHER. "Stylistic Gravity: Language and Prose Rhythms in *Decameron* I, 4." *Humanities Association Review,* 26 (1975), 289–99.

LAYMAN, B. J. "Eloquence of Pattern in Boccaccio's Tale of the Falcon." *Italica,* 46 (1969), 3–16.

LIMOLI, HOWARD. "Boccaccio's Masetto (*Decameron* III, 1) and Andreas Capellanus." *Romanische Forschungen,* 77 (1965), 281–92.

McWILLIAM, G. H. "On Translating the 'Decameron,' " in *Essays In Honour Of John Humphreys Whitfield,* pp. 71–83.

MARCUS, MILLICENT. "Ser Ciappelletto: A Reader's Guide to the *Decameron.*" *Humanities Association Review,* 26 (1975), 275–88.

MAZZOTTA, GIUSEPPE. "The *Decameron:* The Literal and the Allegorical." *Italian Quarterly,* 18, No.72 (1975), 53–73.

———. "The *Decameron:* The Marginality of Literature." *University Of Toronto Quarterly,* 42 (1972), 64–81.

McWILLIAM, G. H. "On Translating the 'Decameron,' " in *Essays In Honour Of John Humphreys Whitfield,* pp. 71–83.

MORAVIA, ALBERTO. "Boccaccio." *London Magazine,* 5, No.7 (1965), 26–42.

NORTON, GLYN P. "Laurent de Premierfait and the Fifteenth-Century French Assimilation of the *Decameron:* A Study in Tonal Transformation." *Comparative Literature Studies,* 9 (1972), 376–91.

PACE, ANTONIO. "Sage and Toad: A Boccaccion Motif (and a Misinterpretation by Musset)." *Italica,* 48 (1971), 187–99.

POTTER, JOY HAMBUECHEN. "Boccaccio as Illusionist: The Play of Frames in the *Decameron.*" *Humanities Association Review,* 26 (1975), 327–45.

RADCLIFF-UMSTEAD, DOUGLAS. "Boccaccio's Adaptation of Some Latin Sources for the *Decameron.*" *Italica,* 45 (1968), 171–94.

SCHILLING, BERNARD N. "The Fat Abbot," in his *The Comic Spirit: Boccaccio To Thomas Mann,* pp. 21–42.

STONE, DONALD. *From Tales To Truths,* pp. 21–29.

FIAMMETTA (1343?)

BAKER, M. J. "*Fiammetta* and the *Angoysses Douloureuses Qui Procedent Damours.*" *Symposium,* 27 (1973), 303–8.

GRIFFIN, ROBERT. "Boccaccio's *Fiammetta:* Pictures At An Exhibition." *Italian Quarterly,* 18, No.72 (1975), 75–94.

WALEY, PAMELA. "The Nurse in Boccaccio's Fiammetta: Source and Invention." *Neophilologus,* 56 (1972), 164–74.

FILOCOLO

KIRKHAM, VICTORIA. "Reckoning with Boccaccio's *Questioni D'Amore.*" *MLN,* 89 (1974), 47–59.

BODELSEN, ANDERS (Danish, 1937–)

THINK OF A NUMBER (Taenk på et tal, 1968)

Reviews
SPECTOR, ROBERT D. *American Scandinavian Review,* 58 (1970), 418.

BODSWORTH, FRED (Canadian, 1918–)

THE ATONEMENT OF ASHLEY MORDEN (1964)

Reviews
COLOMBO, JOHN ROBERT. "Guilt for the Wrong Reason." *Canadian Literature,* No.26 (1965), pp. 76–78.

BÖLL, HEINRICH (German, 1917–1985)

GENERAL

BRONSEN, DAVID. "Böll's Women: Patterns in Male-Female Relationships." *Monatshefte,* 57 (1965), 291–300.

CUNLIFF, W. G. "Heinrich Böll's Eccentric Rebels." *Humanities Association Review,* 25 (1974), 298–303; rpt. in *Modern Fiction Studies,* 21 (1975), 473–79.

KURZ, PAUL KONRAD. "Heinrich Böll: Not Reconciled," in his *On Modern German Literature,* vol. 4: 3–36.

LÖB, L. "The Novels of Heinrich Böll." *Modern Languages,* 49 (1968), 97–98.

NAHRGANG, W. LEE. "Heinrich Böll's War Books: A Study in Changing Literary Purpose." *MLN,* 88 (1973), 1011–19.

NELL, JUSTIN JAY. "Heinrich Böll: Nobel Prize Winning Author." *Rundschau*, 3, No.8 (1973), 3.

PICKETT, T. H. "Heinrich Boll's Plea for Civilization." *Southern Humanities Review*, 7 (1973), 1-9.

REID, JAMES HENDERSON. "Böll's Names." *Modern Language Review*, 69 (1974), 575-83.

_____. "Time in the Works of Heinrich Böll." *Modern Language Review*, 62 (1967) 476-85.

ABSENT WITHOUT LEAVE (Two novellas: Als der Krieg ausbrach and Als der Krieg zer Ende war, 1962)

Reviews
POTOKER, EDWARD MARTIN. "Last Haven in Limbo." *Saturday Review*, 11 September 1965, p. 42.

WILDING, MICHAEL. *London Magazine*, NS, 7, No.2 (1967), 87-88.

ADAM (Wo warst du, Adam?, 1951)

SOKEL, WALTER HERBERT. "Perspective and Dualism in the Novels of Boll," in *The Contemporary Novel In German: A Symposium*, ed. Robert R. Heitner, pp. 13-29.

Reviews
RIPPLEY, LA VERN J. *Saturday Review*, 12 September 1970, pp. 32-33.

BILLIARDS AT HALF-PAST NINE (Billard um Halb Zehn, 1959)

LANGER, LAWRENCE L. *The Holocaust And The Literary Imagination*, pp. 265-84.

SOKEL, WALTER HERBERT. "Perspective and Dualism in the Novels of Boll," in *The Contemporary Novel In German: A Symposium*, ed. Robert R. Heitner, pp. 22-31.

THOMAS, R. HINTON and WILFRIED VAN DER WILL. *The German Novel And The Affluent Society*, pp. 44-55.

DAS BROT DER FRÜHEN JAHRE

HANSON, W. P. "Heinrich Böll: *Das Brot Der Frühen Jahre*." *Modern Languages*, 48 (1967), 148-151.

THE CLOWN (Ansichten eines Clowns, 1963)

DUROCHE, LEONARD L. "Böll's *Ansichten Eines Clowns* in Existentialist Perspective." *Symposium*, 25 (1971), 347-58.

KLIENEBERGER, H. R. "Heinrich Böll in *Ansichten Eines Clowns*." *German Life And Letters*, 19 (1965), 34-9.

PASLICK, ROBERT H. "A Defense of Existence: Böll's *Ansichten Eines Clowns*." *German Quarterly*, 41 (1968), 698-710.

SOKEL, WALTER HERBERT. "Perspective and Dualism in the Novels of Boll," in *The Contemporary Novel In German: A Symposium*, ed. Robert R. Heitner, pp. 31-35.

THOMAS, R. HINTON and WILFRIED and VAN DER WILL. *The German Novel And The Affluent Society*, pp. 54-64.

Reviews
BAUKE, JOSEPH. "White Lies for Dark Lives." *Saturday Review*, 30 January 1965, p. 27.

FURBANK, P. N. "Opting Out." *Encounter*, 25, No.4 (1965), 82-83.

KIBEL, ALVIN C. "The New Nature of Events." *Midstream Magazine*, 11, No.2 (1965), 108-10.

STEINER, GEORGE. "Down and Out in Bonn." *Reporter*, 32, No.4 (1965), 53-54.

THE END OF A MISSION (Ende einer Dienstfahrt, 1966)

THOMAS, R. HINTON and WILFRIED VAN DER WILL. *The German Novel And The Affluent Society*, pp. 64-67.

Reviews
HOFFMEISTER, WERNER. *Novel*, 1 (1968), 291-92.

ZIOLKOWSKI, THEODORE. "Paradigms of the Recent German Novel." *Modern Language Journal*, 52 (1968), 29.

GROUP PORTRAIT WITH LADY (Gruppenbild mit Dame, 1971)

BAZAROV, KONSTANTIN. "Böll's 'Polished Shell.' " *The Month*, 2d n.s., 7 (1974), 549-52.

Reviews
STEWART, ROBERT SUSSMAN. "Group Portrait with Heinrich Böll." *Saturday Review*, 11 November 1972, pp. 66-67.

WAIDSON, H. M. "Heroine and Narrator in Heinrich Böll's *Gruppenbild Mit Dame*." *Forum For Modern Language Studies*, 9 (1973), 123-31.

THE UNGUARDED HOUSE (Haus ohne Huter)

SOKEL, WALTER HERBERT. "Perspective and Dualism in the Novels of Boll," in *The Contemporary Novel In German: A Symposium*, pp. 11-30.

BOETIE, DUGMORE (South African, c. 1920-1966)

FAMILIARITY IS THE KINGDOM OF THE LOST (1969)

Reviews
RABKIN, DAVID. "Reality in Fiction." *Journal Of Commonwealth Literature*, 7, No.1 (1972), 121-24.

BOGDANOV, A. A. (pseud. of Alexander Alexandrovich Malinovsky, Russian, 1873-1928)

RED STAR (Krasnia zvezda, 1907)

LEWIS, KATHLEEN and HARRY WEBER. "Zamyatin's *We*, The Proletarian Poets, and Bogdanov's *Red Star*." *Russian Literature Triquarterly*, No.12 (1975), 266-76.

BOLDREWOOD, ROLF (Australian, 1826-1915)
pseudonym of Thomas Alexander Browne

GENERAL

HAMER, CLIVE. "Boldrewood Reassessed." *Southerly*, 26 (1966), 263-78.

THE MINER'S RIGHT (1890)

WALKER, R. B. "History and Fiction in Rolf Boldrewood's *The Miner's Right*." *Australian Literary Studies*, 3 (1967), 28-40.

Reviews
WILDING, MICHAEL. "A New Colonialism?" *Southerly*, 35 (1975), 99-102.

ROBBERY UNDER ARMS (1888)

BRISSENDEN, ALAN. *Rolf Boldrewood*, pp. 32-42.

ROSENBERG, JEROME H. "Narrative Perspective and Cultural History in *Robbery Under Arms*." *Australian Literary Studies*, 6 (1973), 11-23.

BOLOMBA, G.

KAVWANGA

GLEASON, JUDITH ILLSLEY. *This Africa*, pp. 93-97.

BOMBAL, MARÍA LUISA (Chilean, 1910-)

HOUSE OF MIST (La última niebla, 1935)

ADAMS, M. IAN. *Three Authors Of Alienation: Bombal, Onetti, Carpentier*, pp. 15-35.

BONDAREV, YURI (Russian, 1924-)

SILENCE

Reviews
STERN, DANIEL. "Evidence Against Abstraction." *Saturday Review*, 19 February 1966, p. 48.

BOOKS, GLEANER

Reviews
COGSWELL, FRED. "Through Other Eyes." *Journal Of Canadian Fiction,* 2, No.2 (1973), 88.

BOREL, Joseph Pierre see BOREL, Pétrus

BOREL, PÉTRUS (French, 1809–59)
pseudonym of Joseph Pierre Borel
THE BOND

Reviews
BALAKIAN, ANNA. "Intimacies of Body and Mind." *Saturday Review,* 24 August 1968, p.46.

MADAME PUTIPHAR (1839)

BOMBERT, VICTOR. "Pétrus Borel, Prison Horrors, and the Gothic Tradition." *Novel,* 2 (1969), 143–52.

BORGEN, JOHAN (Norwegian, 1902–1979)
GENERAL

BIRN, RANDI MARIE. "The Quest for Authenticity in Three Novels by Johan Borgen." *Mosaic,* 4, No.2 (1971), 91–98.

LILLELORD TRILOGY (1955–57)

BIRN, RANDI MARIE. "The Quest for Authenticity in Three Novels by Johan Borgen." *Mosaic,* 4, No.2 (1971), 91–95.

BORGESE, GIUSEPPE (Italian, 1882–1952)
RUBÈ (1921)

PACIFICI, SERGIO. *The Modern Italian Novel: From Capuana To Tozzi,* pp. 80–85.

BOSCO, HENRI FERDINAND JOSEPH MARIUS (French, 1888–)
L'ANE CULOTTE (1937)

Reviews
CRANT, PHILLIP. *French Review,* 48 (1975), 657–58.

MALICROIX (1948)

PRINCE, JOHN. "New Light on the Origins and Symbolism of *Malicroix* by Henri Bosco." *French Review,* 47 (1974), 773–82.

BOSE, BUDDHADEVA (Indian, 1908–)
GENERAL

MUKHERJEE, DHURJATI. "The Art of Buddhadeva Bose." *Indian Literature,* 18, No.4 (1975), 8–11.

MOWLINATH

PEMPE, RUTA. "Buddhadeva's Portrait of an Artist." *Literature East And West,* 18 (1974), 216–32.

BOSQUET, ALAIN (Belgian, 1919–)
MONSIEUR VAUDEVILLE (1973)

Reviews
VINEBERG, ELSA. *French Review,* 48 (1975), 658–59.

BOUDJEDRA, RACHID (Algerian)
LA RÉPUDIATION (1969)

Reviews
SELLIN, ERIC. *French Review,* 45 (1971), 188–89.

BOUDOUT, PIERRE
LA MAL DE MINUIT (1972)

Reviews
ALFONSI, SANDRA R. *French Review,* 47 (1974), 655–56.

BOULANGER, DANIEL
GENERAL

HAMMOND, ROBERT. "The New Novel's Court Jester: Daniel Boulanger." *Symposium,* 20 (1966), 14–23.

BOULLE, PIERRE (French, 1912–)
GARDEN ON THE MOON (Le Jardin de Kanashima, 1964)

Reviews
LESAGE, LAURENT. "First Stop on the Way to a Star." *Saturday Review,* 13 March 1965, p. 127.

A NOBLE PROFESSION (Un métier de seigneur, 1960)

ROACH, J. O. *"Un Métier De Seigneur."* *Modern Languages,* 46 (1965), 31–32.

BOYD, MARTIN (Australian, 1893–1972)
GENERAL

BOYD, MARTIN. "Preoccupations and Intentions." *Southerly,* 28 (1968), 83–90.

BRADLEY, ANTHONY. "The Structure of Ideas Underlying Martin Boyd's Fiction." *Meanjin,* 28 (1969), 177–83.

MCFARLANE, BRIAN. "Martin Boyd's Langton Sequence." *Southerly,* 35 (1975), 69–87.

MCLAREN, JOHN. "Gentlefolk Errant—The Family Writings of Martin Boyd." *Australian Literary Studies,* 5 (1972), 339–51.

NASE, PAMELA. "Martin Boyd: A Checklist." *Australian Literary Studies,* 5 (1972), 404–14.

O'GRADY, DESMOND. "Those Marvellous Blue Skies: Martin Boyd's Seventeen Years in Rome." *Overland,* No.56 (1973), pp. 26–30.

THE CARDBOARD CROWN (1952)

MCFARLANE, BRIAN. "Martin Boyd's Langton Sequence." *Southerly,* 35 (1975), 72–76.

NIALL, BARBARA. *Martin Boyd,* pp. 27–30.

A DIFFICULT YOUNG MAN (1955)

KRAMER, LEONIE. "The Seriousness of Martin Boyd." *Southerly,* 28 (1968), 91–109.

NIALL, BARBARA. *Martin Boyd,* pp. 30–33.

LUCINDA BRAYFORD (1946)

GREEN, DOROTHY. " 'The Fragrance of Souls': A Study of *Lucinda Brayford.*" *Southerly,* 28 (1968), 110–26.

NIALL, BRENDA. *Martin Boyd,* pp. 19–25.

THE MONTFORTS

NIALL, BRENDA. *Martin Boyd,* pp. 8–13.

OUTBREAK OF LOVE (1957)

FRENCH, A. L. "Martin Boyd: An Appraisal." *Southerly,* 26 (1966), 219–34.

HERRING, THELMA. "Martin Boyd and the Critics: A Rejoinder to A. L. French." *Southerly,* 28 (1968), 127–40.

McFarlane, Brian. "Martin Boyd's Langton Sequence." *Southerly,* 35 (1975), 80–86.

Niall, Brenda. *Martin Boyd,* pp. 33–36.

WHEN BLACKBIRDS SING (1962)

Niall, Barbara. *Martin Boyd,* pp. 36–39.

BOYE, KARIN (Swedish, 1900–1941)

KALLOCAIN (1940)

Reviews

Spector, Robert. *American Scandinavian Review,* 55 (1967), 81–82.

BOYER, PHILIPPE

NON LIEU (1972)

Reviews

Knapp, Bettina L. *French Review,* 46 (1973), 657.

BOYLE, HARRY J. (Canadian, 1915–)

THE GREAT CANADIAN NOVEL (1972)

Reviews

McDonald, Lawrence. "Native Sons." *Canadian Literature,* No.62 (1974), pp. 112–14.

Sproxton, Birk. "Continentalism in a National Guise." *Journal Of Canadian Fiction,* 2, No.4 (1973), 87–88.

BRANCATI, VITALIANO (Italian, 1907–1954)

GENERAL

Huffman, C. Licari. "Vitaliano Brancati: A Reassessment." *Forum Italicum,* 6 (1972), 356–77.

ANTONIO, THE GREAT LOVER see BELL' ANTONIO

BELL'ANTONIO (Il Bell' Antonio, 1949)

Huffman, C. Licari. "Vitaliano Brancati: A Reassessment." *Forum Italicum,* 6 (1972), 367–71.

GLI ANNI PERDUTI (1941)

Huffman, C. Licari. "Vitaliano Brancati: A Reassessment." *Forum Italicum,* 6 (1972), 360–65.

PAOLO IL CALDO (1954)

Huffman, C. Licari. "Vitaliano Brancati: A Reassessment." *Forum Italicum,* 6 (1972), 371–76.

BRECHT, BERTHOLD (German, 1898–1956)

DIE BESTIE

Morley Michael. " 'Truth in Masquerade': Structure and Meaning in Brecht's *Die Bestie.*" MLN, 90 (1975), 687–95.

BREMER, FREDRIKA (Swedish, 1801–1865)

GENERAL

Asmundsson, Doris R. "Fredrika Bremer and her English Friends." *American Scandinavian Review,* 57 (1969), 159–68.

BREMOND, SEBASTIEN

L'AMOUREUX AFRICAIN

Grobe, Edwin P. "The Source of Mme. de Villedieu's 'Nouvelles Afriquaines.' " *Romance Notes,* 8 (1966), 70–74.

BRENNAN, ANTHONY

THE CARBON COPY

Reviews

Hunt, Russell A. "Carbon's Copy, Brennan's Book." *Journal Of Canadian Fiction,* 4, No.3 (1975), 176–79.

BRENNER, YOSEF HAIM (Russian-born Israeli, 1881–1921)

GENERAL

Patterson, David. "Yosef Haim Brenner." *Ariel: A Quarterly Review Of Arts And Sciences In Israel,* No.33/34 (1973), pp. 107–14.

AROUND THE POINT

Rabinovich, Isaiah. *Major Trends In Modern Hebrew Fiction,* pp. 81–98.

BRENTANO, CLEMENS MARIA (German, 1778–1842)

GODWI (1801-2)

Fetzer, John. "Clemens Brentano's *Godwi:* Variations on the Melos-Eros Theme." *Germanic Review,* 42 (1967), 108–23.

BRETON, ANDRÉ (French, 1896–1966)

GENERAL

Cardinal, Roger. "André Breton: The Surrealist Sensibility." *Mosaic,* 1 No.2 (1968), 112–26.

Matthews, J. H. "Surrealism in the Novel." *Books Abroad,* 43 (1969), 182–86.

NADJA (1928)

Cardinal, Roger. "*Nadja* and Breton." *University Of Toronto Quarterly,* 41 (1972), 185–99.

Firchow, Peter Edgerly. "*Nadja* and *Le Paysan De Paris:* Two Surrealist 'Novels.' " *Wisconsin Studies In Contemporary Literature,* 6 (1965), 293–307.

Hubert, Renée Riese. "The Coherence of Breton's *Nadja.*" *Contemporary Literature,* 10 (1969), 241–52.

Lynes, Carlos. "Surrealism and the Novel: Breton's *Nadja.*" *French Studies,* 20 (1966), 366–87.

Wylie, Harold. "Breton, Schizophrenia and *Nadja.*" *French Review,* 43, Special Issue No. 1 (1970), 100–6.

BREWSTER, ELIZABETH (Canadian, 1922–)

THE SISTERS (1974)

Reviews

Barclay, Pat. "Sticking to Lasts." *Canadian Literature,* No.65 (1975), pp. 110–11.

Kennedy, Alan. *Dalhousie Review,* 55 (1975), 371–73.

BRISSAC, ELVIRE DE

UN LONG MOIS DE SEPTEMBRE (1971)

Reviews

Schneider, Judith Morganroth. *French Review,* 46 (1972), 433–34.

BRITTING, GEORG

GENERAL

HEALD, D. "The Narrative Art of Georg Britting." *Modern Languages,* 51 (1970), 72-78.

BROCH, HERMANN (Austrian, 1886-1951)
GENERAL

HARDIN, JAMES N. "The Theme of Salvation in the Novels of Hermann Broch." *PMLA,* 85 (1970), 219-27.

HERD, ERIC. "The Guilt of the Hero in the Novels of Hermann Broch." *German Life And Letters,* 18 (1964), 30-39.

ZIOLKOWSKI, THEODORE. "Hermann Broch and Relatively in Fiction." *Wisconsin Studies In Contemporary Literature,* 8 (1967), 365-76.

THE DEATH OF VIRGIL (Der Tod des Vergil, 1945)

BAUMANN, WALTER. "Ezra Pound and Hermann Broch: A Comparison." *Seminar,* 4 (1968), 100-12.

_____ . "The Idea of Fate in Hermann Broch's *Tod Des Vergil.*" *Modern Language Quarterly,* 29 (1968), 196-206.

COHN, DORRIT. "Laughter at the Nadir: On a Theme in Hermann Broch's Novels." *Monatshefte,* 61 (1969), 113-2.

HERD, ERIC. "Myth Criticism: Limitations and Possibilities." *Mosaic,* 2, No.3 (1969), 73-77.

SCHLANT, ERNESTINE. "Hermann Broch's Theory of Symbols Exemplified in a Scene from *Der Tod Des Vergil.*" *Neophilologus,* 54 (1970), 53-64.

STRELKA, JOSEPH. "Hermann Broch: Comparatist and Humanist." *Comparative Literature Studies,* 12 (1975), 67-79.

WHITE, JOHN J. *Mythology In The Modern Novel,* pp. 156-66.

THE GUILTLESS (Die Schuldlosen, 1950)

WHITE, JOHN J. "Broch, Virgil, and the Cycle of History." *Germanic Review,* 41 (1966), 103-10.

_____ . *Mythology In The Modern Novel,* pp. 199-211.

THE SLEEPWALKERS (Die Schlafwandler, 1931/2)

COHN, DORRIT. "Laughter at the Nadir: On a Theme in Hermann Broch's Novels." *Monatshefte,* 61 (1969), 113-21.

HATFIELD, HENRY. *Crisis And Continuity In Modern German Fiction,* pp. 109-27.

KURZ, PAUL KONRAD. "Hermann Broch's Trilogy *Die Schlafwandler:* Contemporary Criticism and Novel of Redemption," in his *On Modern German Literature,* Vol. 1: 105-30.

OSTERLE, HEINZ D. "Hermann Broch, *Die Schlafwandler:* Revolution and Apocalypse." *PMLA,* 86 (1971), 946-58.

SCHLANT, ERNESTINE. "Herman Broch's *Sleepwalkers:* Dialectical Structure and Epistemological Unity." *Germanic Review,* 43 (1968), 201-14.

WATT, R. H. " 'Der Einbruch Von Unten': An Austrian Syndrome of the Inter-War Years?" *German Life And Letters,* 27 (1974), 316-18.

WHITE, JOHN J. "The Identity and Function of Bertrand in Hermann Broch's *Die Schlafwandler.*" *German Life And Letters,* 24 (1971), 135-44.

ZIOLKOWSKI, THEODORE. *Dimensions In The Modern Novel,* pp. 138-80.

BROOKE, FRANCES (Canadian, 1724-1789)
HISTORY OF EMILY MONTAGUE (1769)

PACEY, DESMOND. "The First Canadian Novel," in his *Essays In Canadian Literature, 1938-1968,* pp. 30-38.

BROWNE, Thomas Alexander see BOLDRE-WOOD, Rolf

BRÚ, HEDIN
FASTATØKUR

BRØNNER, HEDIN. *Three Faroese Novelists,* pp. 91-97.

FEDGAR Á FERD

BRØNNER, HEDIN. *Three Faroese Novelists,* pp. 101-8.

LEIKUM FAGURT . . .

BRØNNER, HEDIN. *Three Faroese Novelists,* pp. 97-101.

LOGNBRÁ

BRØNNER, HEDIN. *Three Faroese Novelists,* pp. 85-91.

BRULLER, Jean see VERCORS

BUCHEIM, LOTHAR-GÜNTHER (German, 1918-)
THE BOAT (Das Boot, 1973)

Reviews
TOBIN, RICHARD L. *Saturday Review,* 28 June 1975, p. 25.

BÜCHNER, GEORG (German, 1813-1837)
GENERAL

BENN, M. B. "Büchner and Gautier." *Seminar,* 9 (1973), 202-7.

COWEN, ROY C. "Identity and Conscience in Büchner's Works." *Germanic Review,* 43 (1968), 258-66.

LENZ

BELL, GERDA E. "Windows: A Study of a Symbol in Georg Büchner's Work." *Germanic Review,* 47 (1972), 103-5.

COWEN, ROY C. "Identity and Conscience in Büchner's Works." *Germanic Review,* 43 (1968), 258-62.

HARRIS, EDWARD P. "J. M. R. Lenz in German Literature: From Büchner to Bobrowski." *Colloquia Germanica,* 1973, pp. 217-20.

JANSEN, PETER K. "The Structural Function of the *Kunstgespräch* in Büchner's *Lenz.*" *Monatshefte,* 67 (1975), 145-56.

KING, JANET K. "*Lenz* Viewed Sane." *Germanic Review,* 49 (1974), 146-53.

PARKER, JOHN J. "Some Reflections on Georg Büchner's *Lenz* and Its Principal Source, the *Oberlin Record.*" *German Life And Letters,* 21 (1968), 103-11.

BUCHOLTZ, ANDREAS HEINRICH (German, 1607-1671)
HERKULES UND VALISKA

WAGENER, HANS. *The German Baroque Novel,* pp. 108-13.

HERKULISKUS UND HERKULADISLA

WAGENER, HANS. *The German Baroque Novel,* pp. 108-13.

BUCKLER, ERNEST (Canadian, 1908-1984)
THE CRUELEST MONTH (1963)

SPETTIGUE, D. O. "The Way It Was: Ernest Buckler." *Canadian Literature,* No.32 (1967), pp. 50-56.

THE MOUNTAIN AND THE VALLEY (1952)

KERTZER, J. M. "The Past Recaptured." *Canadian Literature,* No.65 (1975), pp. 74-85.

SPETTIGUE, D. O. "The Way It Was: Ernest Buckler." *Canadian Literature,* No.32 (1967), pp. 43-50.

YOUNG, ALAN R. "The Pastoral Vision of Ernest Buckler in *The Mountain And The Valley.*" *Dalhousie Review,* 53 (1973), 219-26.

BUCZKOWSKI, LEOPOLD (Ukrainian, 1905–)

BLACK TORRENT (Czarny potok, 1954)

Reviews
MIHAILOVICH, VASA D. *Saturday Review,* 20 June 1970, p. 43.

BUELL, JOHN (Canadian, 1927–)

GENERAL

DROLET, GILBERT. "A Conversation with John Buell, Canadian Novelist." *Journal Of Canadian Fiction,* 3, No.2 (1974), 60-71.

FOUR DAYS (1962)

CARGAS, HARRY J. "John Buell: Canada's Neglected Novelist." *Renascence,* 21, No.1 (1968), 28-31.

THE PYX (1959)

CARGAS, HARRY J. "John Buell: Canada's Neglected Novelist." *Renascence,* 21, No.1 (1968), 28-31.

THE SHREWSDALE EXIT

Reviews
ROSENGARTEN, HERBERT. "Survival of the Fittest." *Canadian Literature,* No.58 (1973), pp. 93-94.

BUGAEV, Boris Nikolayevich see BELY, Andrei

BUGNET, GEORGES (Canadian, 1879–)

GENERAL

CARPENTER, DAVE. "A Canadian Fête Mobile: Interview with Georges Bugnet." *Journal Of Canadian Fiction,* 2, No.2 (1973), 49-53.

LA FORET (1935)

CARPENTER, DAVID C. "Georges Bugnet: An Introduction." *Journal Of Canadian Fiction,* 1, No.4 (1972), 75-78.

NIPSYA (1924)

CARPENTER, DAVID C. "Georges Bugnet: An Introduction." *Journal Of Canadian Fiction,* 1, No.4 (1972), 72-75.

BULATOVIĆ, MIODRAY (Montenegrin, 1930–)

GENERAL

MIHAILOVICH, VASA D. "The Eerie World of Miodray Bulatović." *Slavic And East European Journal,* 12 (1968), 323-29.

THE HERO ON A DONKEY (Heroj na magarcu ili Vreme srama, 1964)

Reviews
HITREC, JOSEPH. *Saturday Review,* 14 March 1970, p. 40.

THE WAR WAS BETTER

Reviews
MIHAILOVICH, VASA D. *Saturday Review,* 13 May 1972, p. 84.

BULGAKOV, MIKHAIL (Russian, 1891–1940)

GENERAL

AL'TSHULER, ANATOLY. "Bulgakov as Prose Writer." *Soviet Studies In Literature,* 4, No.2 (1968), 60-71.

GLENNY, M. V. "Mikhail Bulgakov." *Survey: A Journal Of Soviet And East European Studies,* No.65 (1967), pp. 3-14.

MUCHNIC, HELEN. "Laughter in the Dark: Bulgakov," in her *Russian Writers,* pp. 299-306.

THOMPSON, EWA M. "The Artistic World of Michail Bulgakov." *Russian Literature,* No.5 (1973), pp. 54-64.

BLACK SNOW: A THEATRICAL NOVEL (Teatral' nyi Roman, 1965)

GLENNY, M. V. "Mikhail Bulgakov." *Survey: A Journal Of Soviet And East European Studies,* No.65 (1967), pp. 8-11.

Reviews
BISHOP, THOMAS. "Revenge for the Method." *Saturday Review,* 27 April 1968, p. 49.

THE MASTER AND MARGARITA (Master i Margarita, 1966-67)

AL'TSHULER, ANATOLY. "Bulgakov as Prose Writer." *Soviet Studies In Literature,* 4, No.2 (1968), 66-71.

BEAUJOUR, ELIZABETH KLOSTY. "The Uses of Witches in Fedin and Bulgakov." *Slavic Review,* 33 (1974), 695-707.

BOLEN, VAL. "Theme and Coherence in Bulgakov's *The Master And Margarita.*" *Slavic And East European Journal,* 16 (1972), 427-37.

DELANEY, JOAN. "*The Master And Margarita:* The Reach Exceeds the Grasp." *Slavic Review,* 31 (1972), 89-100.

ERICSON, EDWARD E. "The Satanic Incarnation: Parody in Bulgakov's *The Master And Margarita.*" *Russian Review,* 33 (1974), 20-36.

HABER, EDYTHE C. "The Mythic Structure of Bulgakov's *The Master And Margarita.*" *Russian Review,* 34 (1975), 382-409.

HART, PIERRE R. "*The Master And Margarita* as Creative Process." *Modern Fiction Studies,* 19 (1973), 169-78.

LAKSHIN, VLADIMIR. "M. Bulgakov's Novel *The Master And Margarita.*" *Soviet Studies In Literature,* 5, No.1 (1968/9), 3-65; rpt. in *Twentieth-Century Russian Literary Criticism,* ed. Victor Erlich, pp. 247-83.

MUCHNIC, HELEN. "The Master and Margarita," in her *Russian Writers,* pp. 307-33.

PROFFER, ELLENDEA. "Bulgakov's *The Master And Margarita:* Genre and Motif." *Canadian Slavic Studies,* 3 (1969), 615-28.

_____ . "The Master and Margarita," in *Major Soviet Writers,* ed. Edward J. Brown, pp. 388-411.

_____ . "On *The Master And Margarita.*" *Russian Literature Triquarterly,* No.6 (1973), pp. 533-64.

SEDURO, VLADIMIR. "The Great Testament Of the Master: The Novel of Mikhail Bulgakov, *The Master And Margarita.*" Trans. Sr. Mary Grace Swift. *New Orleans Review,* 2 (1970), 159-61.

SKORINO, L. "Characters Without Carnival Masks." *Soviet Studies In Literature,* 5, No.2 (1969), 20-45.

_____ . "Rejoinder." *Soviet Studies In Literature,* 5, No.2 (1969), 92-100.

STENBOCK-FERMOR, ELISABETH. "Bulgakov's *The Master And Margarita* and Goethe's *Faust.*" *Slavic And East European Journal,* 13 (1969), 309-25.

VINOGRADOV, I. "The Testament of a Master." *Soviet Studies In Literature,* 5, No.2 (1969), 46-91.

WRIGHT, A. C. "Satan in Moscow: An Approach to Bulgakov's *The Master And Margarita.*" *PMLA,* 88 (1973), 1162-72.

Reviews
LEHRMAN, EDGAR H. *Novel,* 5 (1971), 92-93.

PAWEL, ERNST. "The Devil in Moscow." *Commentary,* 45, No.3 (1968), 90-93.

SIMMONS, ERNEST J. "Out of the Drawer, Into the Light." *Saturday Review,* 11 November 1967, pp. 35-36.

STRUVE, GLEB. "The Re-Emergence of Mikhail Bulgakov." *Russian Review,* 27 (1968), 338-43.

WHITE GUARD (Belaia Gvardiia, 1927)

Reviews

FITZLYON, KYRIL. "Price Tags." *London Magazine*, NS, 11, No.1 (1971), 170-71.

SIMMONS, ERNEST J. *Saturday Review*, 24 July 1971, pp. 40-41,52.

BULGARIN, FADDEI (Russian, 1789-1859)

IVAN VYZHIGIN (1829)

ALKIRE, GILMAN H. "Gogol and Bulgarin's *Ivan Vyzhigin*." *Slavic Review*, 28 (1969), 289-96.

BULLER, HERMAN (Canadian, 1923-)

DAYS OF RAGE (1974)

Reviews

SPROXTON, BIRK. "An Underground Existence." *Journal Of Canadian Fiction*, 4, No.1 (1975), 203-5.

BULLOCK, MICHAEL (Canadian, 1918-)

RANDOLPH CRANSTONE AND THE PURSUING RIVER (1974)

Reviews

SMILEY, CALVIN L. "Arduous Games." *Canadian Literature*, No.66 (1975), pp. 109-10.

BURAČEK, S. A.

GEROI NAŠEGO VREMENI

HEIER, EDMUND. "The Second *Hero Of Our Time*." *Slavic And East European Journal*, 11 (1967), 35-43.

BURKE, JAMES

THE FIREFLY HUNT

Reviews

FRASER, KEATH. "Impetuous Iconoclasm." *Canadian Literature*, No.42 (1969), pp. 90-91.

BURKE, JAMES LESTER (Tasmanian)

GENERAL

HIENER, W. AND J. E. HEINER. "James Lester Burke, Author of *Martin Cash*." *Australian Literary Studies*, 2 (1965), 63-66.

BURLA, YEHUDA (Hebrew, 1886-1969)

IN DARKNESS STRIVING

Reviews

GOLDMAN, MARK. *Literature East And West*, 14 (1970), 131-34.

BUSSETT, JACQUES DE BOURBON

LE LION DE LA CAMPAGNE (1973)

Reviews

GERRARD, CHARLOTTE FRANKEL. *French Review*, 48 (1975), 1059-60.

BUTLER, JUAN (Canadian, 1942-)

CABBAGETOWN DIARY: A DOCUMENTARY (1969)

Reviews

EDWARDS, MARY JANE. "Two Torontos." *Canadian Literature*, No.51 (1972), pp. 91-92.

THE GARBAGE MAN (1972)

Reviews

WOLFE, MORRIS. "Gratuitous Action." *Canadian Literature*, No.66 (1975), pp. 120-21.

WOODCOCK, GEORGE. "Boredom, Distaste, Admiration." *Journal Of Canadian Fiction*, 1, No.4 (1972), 94.

BUTOR, MICHEL (French, 1926-)

GENERAL

GRANT, MARIAN. "The Function of Myth in the Novels of Michel Butor." *AUMLA*, No.32 (1969), pp. 214-22.

HOWITT, J. B. "Michel Butor and Manchester." *Nottingham French Studies*, 12 (1973), 74-85.

KOLBERT, JACK. "Points of View in Michel Butor's Criticism: Geometry and Optics." *Kentucky Romance Quarterly*, 18 (1971), 161-76.

LESAGE, LAURENT. "Michel Butor: Techniques of the Marvelous." *L'Esprit Créateur*, 6 (1966), 36-44.

McWILLIAMS, DEAN. "William Faulkner and Michel Butor's Novel of Awareness." *Kentucky Romance Quarterly*, 19 (1972), 387-402.

MERCIER, VIVIAN. "Michel Butor: The Schema and the Myth." *Mundus Artium*, 1, No.3 (1968), 16-27.

OTTEN, ANNA. "Butor Colloquium: A New Novelist Revisted." *Books Abroad*, 48 (1974), 46-51.

ROUDIEZ, L. S. "Problems of Point of View in the Early Fiction of Michel Butor." *Kentucky Romance Quarterly*, 18 (1971), 145-59.

SMOCK, ANN. "The Disclosure of Difference in Butor." *MLN*, 89 (1974), 654-58.

SPENCER, M. C. "Michel Butor: Literature in an Electronic Age." *Meanjin*, 28 (1969), 472-78.

STURROCK, JOHN. *The French New Novel*, pp. 104-69.

WALTERS, JENNIFER R. "Michel Butor and *The Thousand And One Nights*." *Neophilologus*, 59 (1975), 213-22.

A CHANGE OF HEART (La Modification, 1957)

CLARKE, DOROTHY CLOTELLE. "An Hispanic Variation on a French Theme: Mme de Staël, Butor, Agudiez." *Symposium*, 22 (1968), 208-13.

FROHOCK, W. M. *Style And Temper*, pp. 130-35.

LARSON, JEFFREY. "The Sibyl and the Iron Floor Heater in Michel Butor's *La Modification*." *Papers On Language And Literature*, 10 (1974), 403-14.

LEVITT, MORTON P. "Michel Butor: Polyphony, or the Voyage of Discovery." *Critique*, 14, No.1 (1971/2), 33-39.

LYDON, MARY. "Sibylline Imagery in Butor's 'La Modification.' " *Modern Language Review*, 67 (1972), 300-8.

MERCIER, VIVIAN. *The New Novel From Queneau To Pinget*, pp. 215-26.

MORRISSETTE, BRUCE. "Narrative 'You' in Contemporary Literature." *Comparative Literature Studies*, 2 (1965), 13-18.

PATAI, DAPHNE. "Temporal Structure as a Fictional Category in Michel Butor's *La Modification*." *French Review*, 46 (1973), 1117-28.

SIMON, JOHN K. "Perception and a Metaphor in the 'New Novel': Notes on Robbe-Grillet, Claude Simon and Butor." *Triquarterly*, No.4 (1965), pp. 173-79.

WARME, LARS G. "Reflection and Revelation in Michel Butor's *La Modification*." *International Fiction Review*, 1 (1974), 88-95.

DEGREES (Degrés, 1960)

LEVITT, MORTON P. "Michel Butor: Polyphony, or the Voyage of Discovery." *Critique*, 14, No.1 (1971/2), 39-45.

MERCIER, VIVIAN. "Michel Butor: The Schema and the Myth." *Mundus Artium,* 1, No.3 (1968), 23–27.

———— . *The New Novel From Queneau To Pinget,* pp. 250–64.

ROUDIEZ, LEON S. "Problems of Point of View in the Early Fiction of Michel Butor." *Kentucky Romance Quarterly,* 18 (1971), 155–59.

WALTERS, JENNIFER R. "Butor's Use of Literary Texts in *Degrès.*" *PMLA,* 88 (1973), 311–20.

INVENTORY

Reviews

MOORE, HARRY T. "Analogies in the Arts." *Saturday Review,* 3 May 1969, pp. 30–31.

MOBILE

BLOCK, ADÈLE. "Michel Butor and the Myth of Racial Supremacy." *Modern Fiction Studies,* 16 (1970), 57–65.

NIAGARA (6 810.000 litres d'eau par seconde, 1965)

Reviews

ROUDIEZ, LEON S. *French Review,* 39 (1966), 667–68.

OÙ

RICE, DONALD B. "The Exploration of Space in Butor's *Où,*" in *Twentieth Century French Fiction,* ed. George Stambolian, pp. 198–222.

PASSAGE DE MILAN (1954)

FIELD, TREVOR. "Imagery of Shafts and Tubes in Butor's 'Passage de Milan.' " *Modern Language Review,* 70 (1975), 760–63.

MERCIER, VIVIAN. *The New Novel From Queneau To Pinget,* pp. 226–39.

ROUDIEZ, LEON S. "Problems of Point of View in the Early Fiction of Michel Butor." *Kentucky Romance Quarterly,* 18 (1971), 147–52.

WALTERS, JENNIFER R. "Symbolism in *Passage De Milan.*" *French Review,* 42 (1968), 223–32.

PASSING TIME (L'Emploi du temps, 1956)

BLOCH, ADÈLE. "Michel Butor and the Myth of Racial Supremacy." *Modern Fiction Studies,* 16 (1970), 57–65.

GRANT, MARIAN. "The Function of Myth in the Novels of Michel Butor." *AUMLA,* No.32 (1969), pp. 215–18.

KUBINYI, LAURA R. "Defense of a Dialogue: Michel Butor's *Passing Time.*" *Boundary 2,* 4 (1976), 885–904.

LEVITT, MORTON P. "Michel Butor: Polyphony, or the Voyage of Discovery." *Critique,* 14, No.1 (1971/2), 27–33.

LYDON, MARY. "Sibylline Imagery in Butor's 'La Modification.' " *Modern Language Review,* 67 (1972), 300–8.

McWILLIAMS, DEAN. "The Novelist as Archaeologist: Butor's *L'Emploi Du Temps.*" *L'Esprit Créateur,* 15 (1975), 367–76.

MERCIER, VIVIAN. *The New Novel From Queneau To Pinget,* pp. 239–49.

O'NEILL, KATHLEEN. "On *Passing Time.*" *Mosaic,* 8, No.1 (1974), 29–37. [Includes Butor's response.]

WEINSTEIN, ARNOLD. "Order and Excess in Butor's *L'Emploi Du Temps.*" *Modern Fiction Studies,* 16 (1970), 41–55.

———— . *Vision And Response In Modern Fiction,* pp. 190–214.

WHITE, JOHN J. *Mythology In The Modern Novel,* pp. 211–18.

WITT, SUSAN C. "The Equivocal Truth." *Mosaic,* 8, No.1 (1974), 39–50. [Includes Butor's response.]

PORTRAIT OF THE ARTIST AS A YOUNG MONKEY (Portrait de L'Artiste en Jeune Singe: Capriccio)

O'DONNELL, THOMAS D. "Michel Butor and the Tradition of Alchemy." *International Fiction Review,* 2 (1975), 150–53.

WALTERS, JENNIFER. "Literary Alchemy." *Diacritics,* 1, No.2 (1971), 7–14.

SECOND THOUGHTS see CHANGE OF HEART

BUZZATI, DINO (Italian, 1906–1972)

UN AMORE (1940)

SCHNEIDER, MARILYN. "Beyond the Eroticism of Dino Buzzati's *Un Amore.*" *Italica,* 46 (1969), 292–99.

BUZZI, DAVID

MARIANA

MENTON, SEYMOUR. *Prose Fiction Of The Cuban Revolution,* pp. 77–80.

BYKOV, VASSILI (Russian, 1924–)

MERTVYM NYE BOLNO (1966)

Reviews

HEIMAN, LEO. "Nostalgia and Nihilism." *East Europe,* 15, No.8 (1966), 55–56.

C

CABALLERO CALDERÓN, EDUARDO (Colombian, 1910-)

EL BUEN SALVAJE (1966)

Reviews
LEVY, KURT L. *Hispania,* 51 (1968), 373-74.

EL NUEVO PRÍNCIPE

Reviews
DULSEY, BERNARD. *Hispania,* 54 (1971), 206-7.

CABRERA INFANTE, GUILLERMO (Cuban, 1929-)

GENERAL

CABRERA INFANTE, G. "(C)ave Attemptor! A Chronology of GCI (After Laurence Sterne's)." *Review,* No.4/5 (1971/2), pp. 5-9.

THREE TRAPPED TIGERS (Tres tristes tigres, 1965)

BRUSHWOOD, JOHN S. *The Spanish American Novel,* pp. 292-96.

CABRERA INFANTE, G. "Epilogue for Late(nt) Readers." *Review,* No.4/5 (1971/2), pp. 23-32.

FUENTES, CARLOS. "On *TTT.*" Trans. Susan Homar. *Review,* No.4/5 (1971/2), p. 22.

GALLAGHER, D. P. *Modern Latin American Literature,* pp. 164-85.

GUIBERT, RITA. "The Tongue-Twisted Tiger: an Interview with Cabrera Infante." *Review,* No.4/5 (1971/2), pp. 10-16.

HUSSEY, BARBARA L. "Mirror Images in *Three Trapped Tigers.*" *International Fiction Review,* 2 (1975), 165-68.

KADIR, DJELAL. "Nostalgia or Nihilism: Pop Art and the New Spanish American Novel." *Journal Of Spanish Studies,* 2 (1974), 127-35.

LEVINE, SUZANNE J. "Notes on Translation." *Review,* No.4/5 (1971/2), pp. 88-91.

_____ . "Writing as Translation: *Three Trapped Tigers* and a *Cobra.*" *MLN,* 90 (1975), 265-73.

ORTEGA, JULIO. "An Open Novel." Trans. Mary A. Kilmer. *Review,* No.4/5 (1971/2), pp. 17-21.

MENTON, SEYMOUR. *Prose Fiction Of The Cuban Revolution,* pp. 66-69.

RODRIGUEZ MONEGAL, EMIR. "Structure and Meanings of *Three Trapped Tigers.*" Trans. Susan Homer. *Latin American Literary Review,* 1, No.2 (1973), 19-35.

SARRIS, ANDREW. "Rerunning Puig and Cabrera Infante." *Review,* No.9 (1973), pp. 46-48.

SIEMENS, WILLIAM L. "The Devouring Female in Four Latin American Novels." *Essays In Literature,* 1 (1974), 123-28.

_____ . "*Heilgeschichte* and the Structure of *Tres Tristes Tigres.*" *Kentucky Romance Quarterly,* 22 (1975), 77-90.

_____ . "Women as Cosmic Phenomena in *Tres Tristes Tigres.*" *Journal Of Spanish Studies,* 3 (1975), 199-209.

CALAFERTE, LOUIS (Italian, 1928-)

PORTRAIT DE L'ENFANT (1969)

Reviews
GOODRICH, NORMA LORRE. *French Review,* 44 (1970), 171-72.

CALLADO, ANTONIO (Brazilian, 1917-)

QUARUP (1967)

Reviews
BASDEKIS, DEMETRIOS. *Saturday Review,* 8 August 1970, p. 38; rpt. in: *Review,* No.3 (1971), pp. 34-35.

CHRIST, RONALD. *Commonweal,* 9 October 1970; rpt. in: *Review,* No.3 (1971), pp. 36-37.

GALLAGHER, DAVID. *New York Times Book Review,* 14 June 1970; rpt. in: *Review,* No.3 (1971), pp. 37-39.

PAGE, JOSEPH A. *New Republic,* 4 July 1970; rpt. in: *Review,* No.3 (1971), pp. 40-41.

CALLAGHAN, MORLEY (Canadian, 1903-)

GENERAL

DAHLIE, HALLVARD. "Destructive Innocence in the Novel of Morley Callaghan." *Journal Of Canadian Fiction,* 1, No.3 (1972), 39-42.

SUTHERLAND, FRASER. "Hemmingway and Callaghan: Friends and Writers." *Canadian Literature,* No.53 (1972), pp. 8-17.

WALSH, WILLIAM. "Streets of Life: Novels of Morley Callaghan." *Ariel: A Review Of International English Literature,* 1, No.1 (1970), 31-42.

WARD, MARGARET JOAN. "The Gift of Grace." *Canadian Literature,* No.58 (1973), pp. 19-25.

WOODCOCK, GEORGE. "Callaghan's Toronto: The Persona of a City." *Journal Of Canadian Studies,* 7, No.3 (1972), 21-24.

_____ . "Lost Eurydice: The Novels of Callaghan," in *A Choice Of Critics,* ed. George Woodcock, pp. 185-202.

A FINE AND PRIVATE PLACE (1975)

Reviews
MONK, PATRICK. *Dalhousie Review,* 55 (1975), 590-91.

THE LOVED AND THE LOST (1951)

JONES, D. G. *Butterfly On Rock,* pp. 52-55.

WALSH, WILLIAM. *A Manifold Voice,* pp. 203-6.

———. "Streets of Life: Novels of Morley Callaghan." *Ariel: A Review Of International English Literature,* 1, No.1 (1970), 36-39.

THE MANY COLORED COAT (1960)

WALSH, WILLIAM. *A Manifold Voice,* pp. 206-12.

———. "Streets of Life: Novels of Morley Callaghan." *Ariel: A Review Of International English Literature,* 1, No.1 (1970), 39-42.

MORE JOY IN HEAVEN (1937)

WALSH, WILLIAM. *A Manifold Voice,* pp. 198-202.

SUCH IS MY BELOVED (1934)

WALSH, WILLIAM. *A Manifold Voice,* pp. 191-98.

———. "Streets of Life: Novels of Morley Callaghan." *Ariel: A Review Of International English Literature,* 1, No.1 (1970), 31-35.

CALVINO, ITALO (Italian, 1923-1985)

GENERAL

DE LAURETIS, TERESA. "Narrative Discourse in Calvino: Praxis or Poiesis?" *PMLA,* 90 (1975), 414-25.

GATT-RUTTER, JOHN. "Calvino Ludens: Literary Play and its Political Implications." *Journal Of European Studies,* 5 (1975), 319-40.

HEINEY, DONALD. "Calvino and Borges: Some Implications of Fantasy." *Mundus Artium,* 2, No.1 (1968), 66-76.

WOODHOUSE, J. R. "Italo Calvino and the Rediscovery of a Genre." *Italian Quarterly,* 12, No.45 (1968), 45-66.

THE BARON IN THE TREES (Il barone rampante, 1957)

WOODHOUSE, J. R. *Italo Calvino: A Reappraisal And An Appreciation Of The Trilogy.*

THE CLOVEN VISCOUNT (Il visconte dimezzato, 1952)

WOODHOUSE, J. R. *Italo Calvino: A Reappraisal And An Appreciation Of The Trilogy.*

THE NON-EXISTENT KNIGHT (Il cavaliere inesistente, 1957)

WOODHOUSE, J. R. *Italo Calvino: A Reappraisal And An Appreciation Of The Trilogy.*

THE PATH TO THE NEST OF SPIDERS (Il sentiero dei nidi di ragno, 1947)

DEMARA, NICHOLAS A. "Pathway to Calvino: Fantasy and Reality in *Il Sentiero Dei Nidi Di Ragno.*" *Italian Quarterly,* 14, No.55 (1971), 25-49.

ROSENGARTEN, FRANK. "The Italian Resistance Novel (1945-1962)," in *From Verismo To Experimentalism,* ed. Sergio Pacifici, pp. 224-26.

CAMBRIDGE, ADA

GENERAL

ROE, JILL. " 'The Scope of Women's Thought is Necessarily Less': The Case of Ada Cambridge." *Australian Literary Studies,* 5 (1972), 388-403.

CAMUS, ALBERT (French, 1913-1960)

GENERAL

ARCHAMBAULT, PAUL J. "Camus in Purgatory: Some Recent Scholarship." *Papers On Language And Literature,* 9 (1973), 95-110.

BATCHELOR, R. "Dostoevskii and Camus: Similarities and Contrasts." *Journal Of European Studies,* 5 (1975), 111-51.

CAMPIGNY, ROBERT. "Suffering and Death." *Symposium,* 24 (1970), 197-205.

CRANSTON, MAURICE. "Albert Camus." *Encounter,* 28, No.2 (1967), 43-54.

CURTIS, JERRY L. "Albert Camus as Anti-Existentialist." *Kentucky Romance Quarterly,* 22 (1975), 111-23.

———. "Camus' Vision of Greatness." *Orbis Litterarum,* 29 (1974), 338-54.

DAVISON, R. "Camus' Attitude to Dostoevsky's Kirilov and the Impact of the Engineer's Ideas on Camus' Early Work." *Orbis Litterarum,* 30 (1975), 225-40.

GARNHAM, B. G. "Albert Camus: Metaphysical Revolt and Historical Action." *Modern Language Review,* 62 (1967), 248-55.

GERSHMAN, HERBERT S. "The Structure of Revolt in Malraux, Camus, and Sartre." *Symposium,* 24 (1970), 27-35.

GROBE, EDWIN P. "Camus and the *Imparfait De Fixation.*" *Romance Notes,* 10 (1969), 213-17.

HENRY, PATRICK. "Camus on Capital Punishment." *Midwest Quarterly,* 16 (1975), 362-70.

KARPUSHIN, V. A. "The Concept of the Individual in the Work of Albert Camus." *Soviet Review,* 9, No.1, (1968), 47-55.

KOCKELMANS, JOSEPH J. "On Suicide: Reflections upon Camus' View of the Problem." *Psychoanalytic Review,* 54 (1967), 423-40.

MACKEY, JAMES P. "Christianity and Albert Camus." *Studies: An Irish Quarterly Review,* 55 (1966), 392-402.

MASON, HADYN T. "Voltaire and Camus." *Romanic Review,* 59 (1968), 198-212.

MATTHEWS, J. H. "In Which Albert Camus Makes His Leap: *Le Mythe De Sisyphe.*" *Symposium,* 24 (1970), 277-88.

MEAKIN, D. " 'Un Classicisme Créateur': Charles Péguy and Albert Camus." *Forum For Modern Language Studies,* 8 (1972), 184-93.

MURCHLAND, BERNARD. "Between Solitude and Solidarity." *Commonweal,* 93 (1970), 91-95.

NICHOLSON, GRAEME. "Camus and Heidegger: Anarchists." *University Of Toronto Quarterly,* 41 (1971), 14-23.

POHORYLES, BERNARD M. "The Influence of Albert Camus." *American Book Collector,* 19, No.8/9 (1969), 36-37.

RECK, RIMA DRELL. *Literature And Responsibility,* pp. 43-85.

SEFLER, GEORGE F. "The Existential vs. The Absurd: The Aesthetics of Nietzsche and Camus." *Journal Of Aesthetics And Art Criticism,* 32 (1974), 415-21.

SHARKEY, JAMES M. "Camus' Aesthetic of Rebellion." *South Atlantic Bulletin,* 38, No.4 (1973), 79-81.

STORZER, GERALD H. "The Concept of Dénouement in Camus's Prose Fiction," in *Twentieth Century French Fiction,* ed. George Stambolian, pp. 102-6.

STREM, GEORGE D. "The Theme of Rebellion in the Works of Camus and Dostoievsky." *Revue De Littérature Comparée,* 40 (1966), 246-57.

SUGDEN, LEONARD W. "Albert Camus: The Temptations of East and West." *Dalhousie Review,* 52 (1972), 436-48.

THE FALL (La Chute, 1956)

AMES, SANFORD. "*La Chute:* From Summitry to Speleology." *French Review,* 39 (1966), 559-66.

BRAUN, LEV. *Witness Of Decline,* pp. 208-12.

BREE, GERMAINE. *Camus,* pp. 101-11.

CURTIS, JERRY L. "Camus' Hero of Many Faces." *Studies In The Novel*, 6 (1974), 88–97.

DAVISON, RAY. "Clamence and Marmeladov: A Parallel." *Romance Notes*, 14 (1972), 226–29.

DERYCKE, ROBERT M. "La Chute: The Sterility of Guilt." *Romance Notes*, 10 (1969), 197–203.

EARL, A. J. "Albert Camus and the Christian Religion." *Modern Languages*, 54 (1973), 67–74.

JOHNSON, ROBERT B. "Camus' *La Chute*, or Montherlant s'éloigne." *French Review*, 44 (1971), 1026–32.

KEEFE, TERRY. "Camus's 'La Chute': Some Outstanding Problems of Interpretation Concerning Clamence's Past." *Modern Language Review*, 69 (1974), 541–55.

_____. "More on Clamence's Interlocutor in Albert Camus' *La Chute*." *Romance Notes*, 16 (1975), 552–58.

KIRK, IRINA. *Dostoevskij And Camus: The Themes Of Consciousness, Isolation, Freedom And Love.*

_____. "Dramatization of Consciousness in Camus and Dostoevsky." *Bucknell Review*, 16, No.1 (1968), 96–104.

LAKICH, JOHN J. "Tragedy and Satanism in Camus's *La Chute.*" *Symposium*, 24 (1970), 262–76.

LAZERE, DONALD. *The Unique Creation Of Albert Camus*, pp. 183–98.

LOCKE, F. W. "The Metamorphosis of Jean-Baptiste Clamence." *Symposium*, 21 (1967), 306–15.

MADDEN, DAVID. "Ambiguity in Albert Camus' *The Fall.*" *Modern Fiction Studies*, 12 (1966/7), 461–72.

MASTERS, BRIAN. *Camus: A Study*, pp. 117–27.

MEYERS, JEFFREY. "Camus' *The Fall* and Van Eyck's *The Adoration Of The Lamb.*" *Mosaic*, 7, No.3 (1974), 43–51.

_____. *Painting And The Novel*, pp. 148–56.

O'BRIEN, JUSTIN. "Camus and Conrad: An Hypothesis." *Romanic Review*, 58 (1967), 196–99; rpt. in his *Contemporary French Literature*, pp. 210–14.

PETRY, SANDY. "The Function of Christian Imagery in *La Chute.*" *Texas Studies In Literature And Language*, 11 (1970), 1445–54.

QUILLIOT, ROGER. *The Sea And Prisons: A Commentary On The Life And Thought Of Albert Camus*, pp. 239–51.

RECK, RIMA DRELL. *Literature And Responsibility*, pp. 80–85.

REDFERN, W. D. "Camus and Confusion." *Symposium*, 20 (1966), 329–42.

ROYCE, BARBARA C. "*La Chute* and *Saint-Genet:* The Question of Guilt." *French Review*, 39 (1966), 709–16.

RYSTEN, FELIX S. A. *False Prophets In The Fiction Of Camus, Dostoevsky, Melville, And Others*, pp. 52–70.

SCOTT, NATHAN A. *Craters Of The Spirit*, pp. 143–47.

SPERBER, MICHAEL A. "Camus' The Fall: The Icarus Complex." *American Imago*, 26 (1969), 269–80.

_____. "Symptoms and Structure of Borderline Personality Organization: Camus' *The Fall* and Dostoevsky's 'Notes from Underground.'" *Literature And Psychology*, 23 (1973), 102–13.

TRAHAN, ELIZABETH. "Clamence vs. Dostoevsky: An Approach to *La Chute.*" *Comparative Literature*, 18 (1966), 337–50.

WHARTENBY, H. ALLEN. "The Interlocutor in *La Chute:* A Key to Its Meaning." *PMLA*, 83 (1968), 1326–33.

THE PLAGUE (La Peste, 1947)

BATCHELOR, R. "Unity of Tone in Albert Camus' *La Peste.*" *Forum For Modern Language Studies*, 11 (1975), 234–51.

BERNARD, JACQUELINE. "The Background of *The Plague:* Albert Camus' Experience in the French Resistance." *Kentucky Romance Quarterly*, 14 (1967), 165–73.

BRAUN, LEV. *Witness Of Decline*, pp. 85–98.

BREE, GERMAINE. *Camus*, pp. 118–30.

CAMUS, ALBERT. *Lyrical And Critical Essays*, pp. 338–41.

FROHOCK, W. M. *Style And Temper*, pp. 115–17.

GARAPON, ROBERT. "Classical and Contemporary French Literature." *University Of Toronto Quarterly*, 36 (1967), 106–10.

GROBE, EDWIN P. "Camus and the Parable of the Perfect Sentence." *Symposium*, 24 (1970), 254–61.

_____. "Tarrou's Confession: the Ethical Force of the Past Definite." *French Review*, 39 (1966), 550–58.

GUERS-VILLATE, YVONNE. "A Few Notes Concering Rambert in *The Plague*." *Renascence*, 22 (1970), 218–22.

_____. "Revolt and Submission in Camus and Bernanos." *Renascence*, 24 (1972), 189–97.

HENNINGER, FRANCES J. "Plot-Theme Fusion in *The Plague.*" *Modern Fiction Studies*, 19 (1973), 216–21.

HERLAN, JAMES J. "A Note on Father Paneloux." *MLN*, 84 (1969), 675–76.

LANGER, LAWRENCE L. *The Holocaust And The Literary Imagination*, pp. 129–35.

LAZERE, DONALD. *The Unique Creation Of Albert Camus*, pp. 173–82.

MASTERS, BRIAN. *Camus: A Study*, pp. 60–97.

MERTON, THOMAS. *Albert Camus' The Plague: Introduction And Commentary.*

MOSES, EDWIN. "Functional Complexity: The Narrative Techniques of *The Plague.*" *Modern Fiction Studies*, 20 (1974), 419–29.

NELSON, ROY JAY. "Malraux and Camus: The Myth of the Beleaguered City." *Kentucky Foreign Language Quarterly*, 13 (1966), 86–94.

QUILLIOT, ROGER. *The Sea And Prisons: A Commentary On The Life And Thought Of Albert Camus*, pp. 136–57.

RECK, RIMA DRELL. *Literature And Responsibility*, pp. 77–80.

REINHARDT, KURT F. *The Theological Novel Of Modern Europe*, pp. 155–69.

SCOTT, NATHAN A. *Craters Of The Spirit*, pp. 121–28.

STORZER, GERALD H. "The Concept of Dénouement in Camus's Prose Fiction," in *Twentieth Century French Fiction*, ed. George Stambolian, pp. 111–15.

THE STRANGER (L'Étranger, 1942)

AMASH, PAUL J. "The Choice of an Arab in *L'Étranger*." *Romance Notes*, 9 (1967), 6–7.

ATKINS, ANSELM. "Fate and Freedom: Camus' *The Stranger.*" *Renascence*, 21, No.2 (1969), 64–75, 110.

BERSANI, LEO. *Balzac To Beckett*, pp. 247–72.

_____. "The Stranger's Secrets." *Novel*, 3 (1970), 212–24.

BRADY, PATRICK. "Manifestations of Eros and Thanatos In *L'Étranger.*" *Twentieth Century Literature*, 20 (1974), 183–88.

BRAUN, LEV. *Witness Of Decline*, pp. 56–72.

BREE, GERMAINE. *Camus*, pp. 112–17.

CAMUS, ALBERT. *Lyrical And Critical Essays*, pp. 335–37.

CURTIS, JERRY L. "Camus' Outsider: Or, the Games People Play." *Studies In Short Fiction*, 9 (1972), 379–86.

DEVI, K. LAKSHMI. "'The Stranger' by Albert Camus." *Triveni*, 39, No.4 (1971), 56–59.

DIBBLE, BRIAN. "Camus' *The Stranger*, Part Two, II." *Explicator*, 29 (1970), Item 29.

ELBRECHT, JOYCE. "The Stranger and Camus' Transcendental Existentialism." *Hartford Studies In Literature*, 4 (1972), 59–80.

FALK, EUGENE H. *Types Of Thematic Structure: The Nature And Function Of Motifs In Gide, Camus, And Sartre,* pp. 52–116.

FLETCHER, JOHN. "Interpreting *L'Étranger.*" *French Review,* 43, Special Issue No.1 (1970), 158–67.

———. "Meursault's Rhetoric." *Colorado Quarterly,* 13 (1971), 125–36.

FORDE, MARIANNA C. "Condemnation and Imprisonment in *L'Étranger* and *Le Dernier Jour D'Un Condamné.*" *Romance Notes,* 13 (1971), 211–16.

FRIEDMAN, NORMAN. *Form And Meaning In Fiction,* pp. 249–65.

FROHOCK, W. M. *Style And Temper,* pp. 103–15.

GALE, JOHN E. "Does America Know *The Stranger?* A Reappraisal of a Translation." *Modern Fiction Studies,* 20 (1974), 139–47.

———. "Meursault's Telegram." *Romance Notes,* 16 (1974), 29–32.

GIESE, FRANK S. "Camus and Algeria." *Colorado Quarterly,* 21 (1972), 203–12.

GUERARD, ALBERT J. "The Illuminating Distortion." *Novel,* 5 (1972) 106–07.

HACKEL, SERGEL. "Raskolnikov Through the Looking-Glass: Dostoevsky and Camus's *L'Étranger.*" *Contemporary Literature,* 9 (1968), 189–209.

HENRY, PATRICK. "Meursault as Antithesis of 'Homo Ludens' from J. Huizinga to Eric Berne." *Kentucky Romance Quarterly,* 21 (1974), 365–74.

JOHNSON, PATRICIA J. "Bergson's *Le Rire:* Game Plan for Camus' *L'Étranger?*" *French Review,* 47 (1973), 46–56.

———. "A Further Source for Camus' *L'Étranger.*" *Romance Notes,* 11 (1970), 465–68.

LANGER, LAWRENCE L. *Form And Meaning In Fiction,* pp. 249–65.

LAZERE, DONALD. *The Unique Creation Of Albert Camus,* pp. 151–72.

MADDEN, DAVID. "Camus' *The Stranger:* An Achievement in Simultaneity." *Renascence,* 20 (1968), 186–97.

MADDEN, DAVID. "James M. Cain's *The Postman Always Rings Twice* and Albert Camus's *L'Étranger.*" *Papers On Language And Literature,* 6 (1970), 407–19.

MARSON, ERIC. "Justice and the Obsessed Character In 'Michael Kohlhaas,' *Der Prozess* and *L'Étranger.*" *Seminar,* 2, No.2 (1966), 29–33.

MASTERS, BRIAN. *Camus: A Study,* pp. 19–34.

MATTHEWS, J. H. "From Naturalism to the Absurd: Edmond de Goncourt and Albert Camus." *Symposium,* 22 (1968), 241–55.

MORREALE, GERALD. "Meursault's Absurd Act." *French Review,* 40 (1967), 456–62.

NUTTALL, A. D. "Did Meursault Mean to Kill the Arab?—The International Fallacy Fallacy." *Colorado Quarterly,* 10 (1968), 95–106.

OTTEN, TERRY. " 'Mammam' in Camus' *The Stranger.*" *College Literature,* 2 (1975), 105–11.

PALMER, WILLIAM J. "Abelard's Fate: Sexual Politics in Stendhal, Faulkner and Camus." *Mosaic,* 7, No.3 (1974), 38–41.

PANTER, JAMES. "Remarks on a Phrase in Camus' *L'Étranger.*" *Romance Notes,* 16 (1974), 25–28.

PICKENS, RUPERT T. and JAMES D. TEDDER. "Liberation in Suicide: Meursault in the Light of Dante." *French Review,* 41 (1968), 524–31.

PURDY, STROTHER B. "*An American Tragedy* And *L'Étranger.*" *Comparative Literature,* 19 (1967), 252–68.

QUILLIOT, ROGER. *The Sea And Prisons: A Commentary On The Life And Thought Of Albert Camus,* pp. 69–83.

RECK, RIMA DRELL. *Literature And Responsibility,* pp. 70–77.

REDFERN, W. D. "The Prisoners of Stendhal and Camus." *French Review,* 41 (1968), 649–59.

ROSS, STEPHEN D. *Literature & Philosophy,* pp. 175–96.

ST. AUBYN, F. C. "A Note on Nietzsche and Camus." *Comparative Literature,* 20 (1968), 110–15.

SAVAGE, CATHARINE. "Tragic Values in *The Stranger* of Camus." *USF Language Quarterly,* 7, No.1/2 (1968), 11–16.

SCOTT, NATHAN A. *Craters Of The Spirit,* pp. 103–9.

SEBBA, HELEN. "Stuart Gilbert's Meursault: A Strange 'Stranger.' " *Contemporary Literature,* 13 (1972), 334–40.

SELLIN, ERIC. "Meursault and Myshkin on Executions: A Parallel." *Romance Notes,* 10 (1968), 11–14.

SLOCHOWER, HARRY. "Camus' *The Stranger:* The Silent Society and the Ecstasy of Rage." *American Imago,* 26 (1969), 291–94.

SMITH, ALBERT B. "Eden as Symbol in Camus' *L'Étranger.*" *Romance Notes,* 9 (1967), 1–5.

———. "Restriction and Consciousness in Camus' *L'Étranger.*" *Studies In Short Fiction,* 3 (1966), 451–53.

SOMERS, PAUL P. "Camus *Si,* Sartre *No.*" *French Review,* 42 (1969), 693–700.

STAMM, JULIAN L. "Camus' *Stranger:* His Act of Violence." *American Imago,* 26 (1969), 281–90.

STERLING, ELWYN F. "Camus' *L'Étranger.*" *Explicator,* 33 (1974), Item 28.

STORZER, GERALD H. "The Concept of Dénouement in Camus's Prose Fiction," in *Twentieth Century French Fiction,* ed. George Stambolian, pp. 106–10.

TANSELLE, G. THOMAS. "A Further Note on 'Whiteness' in Melville and Others." *PMLA,* 81 (1966), 604.

TUCKER, HARRY. "A Glance at 'Whiteness' in Melville and Camus." *PMLA,* 80 (1965), 605.

WAGNER, C. ROLAND. "The Silence of *The Stranger.*" *Modern Fiction Studies,* 16 (1970), 27–40.

WEITZ, MORRIS. "The Coinage of Man: 'King Lear' and Camus's 'L'Étranger.' " *Modern Language Review,* 66 (1971), 31–39.

CAMUS, J. P.

GENERAL

ALLOTT, T. J. D. "Poems by Bertaut in the Novels of J.P. Camus." *Forum For Modern Language Studies,* 4 (1968), 146–63.

CANETTI, ELIAS (Austrian emigrée from Bulgaria, 1905–)

AUTO DA FÉ (Die Blendung, 1935)

PARRY, IDRIS. "Elias Canetti's Novel *Die Blendung,*" in *Essays In German Literature*—I, ed. F. Norman, pp. 145–66.

RUSSELL, PETER. "The Vision of Man in Elias Canetti's *Die Blendung.*" *German Life And Letters,* 28 (1974), 24–35.

SACHAROFF, MARK. "Grotesque Comedy in Canetti's *Auto Da Fé.*" *Critique,* 14, No.1 (1972), 99–112.

THOMAS, EDWARD A. "Elias Canetti's *Die Blendung* and the Changing Image of Madness." *German Life And Letters,* 26 (1972), 38–47.

WATSON, IAN. "Elias Canetti: The One and the Many." *Chicago Review,* 20/1, No.4/1 (1968/9), 184–200.

CAPÉCIA, MAYOTTE

LA NÉGRESSE BLANCHE

CLARK, BEATRICE STITH. "The Works of Mayotte Capécia." *College Language Association Journal,* 16 (1973), 415–25.

ČAPEK, KAREL (Czechoslovakian, 1890–1938)

GENERAL

HAMAN, ALEŠ. "Man Against the Absolute: The Art of Karel Čapek." *Slavic And East European Journal,* 11 (1967), 168–84.

WAR WITH THE NEWTS (Válka s mloky, 1936)

TEST, GEORGE A. "Karel Capek's *War With The Newts:* A Neglected Modern Satire." *Studies In Contemporary Satire,* 1 (1974), 1–10.

CAPUANA, LUIGI (Italian, 1839–1915)

GENERAL

PACIFICI, SERGIO. *The Modern Italian Novel: From Capuana To Tozzi,* pp. 16–31.

WALKER, E. A. "Structural Techniques in Luigi Capuana's Novels." *Italica,* 42 (1965), 265–75.

GIACINTA (1879)

PACIFICI, SERGIO. *The Modern Italian Novel: From Capuana To Tozzi,* pp. 24–28.

WALKER, E. A. "Structural Techniques in Luigi Capuana's Novels." *Italica,* 42 (1965), 265–70.

IL MARCHESE DI ROCCAVERDINA (1901)

PACIFICI, SERGIO. *The Modern Italian Novel: From Capuana To Tozzi,* pp. 28–31.

CARBALLIDO, EMILO (Mexican, 1925–)

THE NORTHER (El Norte, 1968)

Reviews
BRUSHWOOD, JOHN S. *Kansas City Star,* 2 March 1969; rpt. in: *Review,* No.2 (1969), pp. 73–74.

CARCO, FRANCIS (pseudonym of François Carcopino-Tusoli, French, 1886–1958)

LES INNOCENTS

KING, RUSSELL S. "Francis Carco's *Les Innocents* and Katherine Mansfield's *Je Ne Parle Pas Français.*" *Revue De Littérature Comparée,* 47 (1973), 427–41.

CARCOPINO-TUSOLI, Francois see CARCO, Francis

CÁRDENAS, LÁZARO (Mexican, 1895–1970)

SUNBURST (El resplandor)

SOMMERS, JOSEPH. *After The Storm,* pp. 23–33.

CARETTE, Louis see MARCEAU, Félicién

CAROLATTI, PAUL

LA GUAPA (1973)

Reviews
GOODRICH, NORMA L. *French Review,* 48 (1975), 953–54.

CAROUTCH, YVONNE

LE GOUVERNEMENT DES EAUX (1971)

Reviews
STARY, SONJA G. *French Review,* 45 (1971), 192.

CARPENTIER, ALEJO (Cuban, 1904–)

EL AÑO 59

MENTON, SEYMOUR. *Prose Fiction Of The Cuban Revolution,* pp. 46–51.

ECUE-YAMBA-O (1933)

BRUSHWOOD, JOHN S. *The Spanish American Novel,* pp. 101–3.

EXPLOSION IN A CATHEDRAL (El Siglo des las luces, 1962)

MENTON, SEYMOUR. *Prose Fiction Of The Cuban Revolution,* pp. 44–46.

THE KINGDOM OF THIS WORLD (El reino de este Mundo, 1949)

BRUSHWOOD, JOHN S. *The Spanish American Novel,* pp. 170–73.

THE LOST STEPS (Los Pasos Perdidos, 1953)

ADAMS, M. IAN. *Three Authors Of Alienation: Bombal, Onetti, Carpentier,* pp. 81–105.

GLEAVES, ROBERT M. " 'Los Pasos Perdidos', 'Pedro Paramo', and the 'Classic' Novel in Spanish America." *USF Language Quarterly,* 8, No.1/2 (1969), 5–8.

GONZÁLEZ ECHEVARRÍA, R. "The Parting of the Waters." *Diacritics,* 4, No.4 (1974), 8–17.

PEAVLER, TERRY J. "The Source for the Archetype in *Los Pasos Perdidos.*" *Romance Notes,* 15 (1974), 581–87.

SÁNCHEZ, JOSÉ G. "Carpentier's *Los Pasos Perdidos:* A Middle Ground View." *Texas Quarterly,* 18, No.1 (1975), 32–48.

REASONS OF STATE (El Recurso del método, 1974)

PEAVLER, TERRY J. "A New Novel by Alejo Carpentier." *Latin American Literary Review,* 3, No.6 (1975), 31–36.

CARRANQUE DE RÍOS, ANDRÉS

CINEMATÓGRAFO

HENN, DAVID. "Social and Artistic Criticism in the Novels of Andrés Carranque de Ríos." *Hispanofila,* 54 (1975), 26–30.

UNO

HENN, DAVID. "Social and Artistic Criticism in the Novels of Andrés Carranque de Ríos." *Hispanofila,* 54 (1975), 18–23.

LA VIDA DIFÍCIL

HENN, DAVID. "Social and Artistic Criticism in the Novels of Andrés Carranque de Ríos." *Hispanofila,* 54 (1975), 23–26.

CARRIER, ROCH (French Canadian, 1937–)

GENERAL

HATHORN, RAMON. "The Imaginary World of Roch Carrier." *Canadian Modern Language Review,* 31 (1975), 196–202.

LE DEUX-MILLIÈME ÉTAGE

Reviews
POKORNY, AMY. "Demolition par Gratte-Ciel." *Journal Of Canadian Fiction,* 3, No.1 (1974), 97–98.

FLORALIE, WHERE ARE YOU? (Floralie, où es-tu?, 1969)

Reviews
SUTHERLAND, RONALD. "Crossing the Thin Line." *Canadian Literature,* No.44 (1970), pp. 88–89.

LA GUERRE, YES SIR! (1968)

BAILEY, NANCY I. "The Corriveau Wake: Carrier's Celebration of Life." *Journal Of Canadian Fiction,* 1, No.3 (1972), 43–47.

Reviews
BAILEY, DON. "Fishing for War." *Tamarack Review,* No.55 (1970), pp. 88–90.

GREEN, ROBERT J. "Québec's Two Enemies," *Journal Of Commonwealth Literature,* 7, No.1 (1972), 113-15.

SUTHERLAND, RONALD. "Faulknerian Quebec." *Canadian Literature,* No.40 (1969), pp. 86-87.

IL EST PARLA, LE SOLEIL

Reviews
SUTHERLAND, RONALD. "Uses of the Grotesque." *Canadian Literature,* No.50 (1971), pp. 87-88.

THEY WON'T DEMOLISH ME!

Reviews
ROSENGARTEN, H. J. "The Walking Ghosts of Empire." *Canadian Literature,* No.63 (1975), p. 96.

CARRIÈRE, JEAN

L'ÉPERVIER DE MATREUX (1972)

Reviews
MAY, GITA. *French Review,* 47 (1974), 1210-11.

CARS, GUY DES

UNE CERTAINE DAME (1971)

Reviews
O'CONNELL, DAVID. *French Review,* 46 (1972), 438-39.

LA VIPÈRE (1969)

Reviews
JOHNSON, PATRICIA J. *French Review,* 44 (1970), 172-73.

CARUNUNGAN, CELSO

LIKE A BIG BRAVE MAN

CASPER, LEONARD. *New Writing From The Philippines,* pp. 71-74.

CARVALHO, JOSÉ CÂNDIDO DE

O CORONEL E O LOBISOMEM

MURPHY, TERRANCE J. "Fact and Fantasy vs. the Coronel." *Kentucky Romance Quarterly,* 19 (1972), 515-24.

CASANOVA, EDUARDO

LOS CABALLOS DE LA CÓLERA

Reviews
LUCHTING, WOLFGANG. *Latin American Literary Review,* 2, No.4 (1974), 156-62.

CASSOLA, CARLO (Italian, 1917-)

GENERAL

O'NEILL, T. "Cassola on Realism." *Modern Language Review,* 65 (1970), 552-57.

FAUSTO AND ANNA (Fausto e Anna, 1952)

ROSENGARTEN, FRANK. "The Italian Resistance Novel (1945-1962)," in *From Verismo To Experimentalism,* ed. Sergio Pacifici, pp. 231-34.

CASTELLANOS, ROSARIO (Mexican, 1925-1974)

GENERAL

LANGFORD, WALTER M. *The Mexican Novel Comes of Age,* pp. 182-85.

CASTELLANOS VELASCO, FRANCISCO (Mexican, 1926-)

CUANDO LA CANA ES AMARGA

MENTON, SEYMOUR. *Prose Fiction Of The Cuban Revolution,* pp. 267-68.

CASTILLO PUCHE, JOSÊ LUIS (Spanish, 1919-)

ORO BLANCO (1963)

Reviews
SÁNCHEZ, JOSÉ. *Hispania,* 48 (1965), 182-83.

CASTRO, JOSUÉ DE

OF MEN AND CRABS

Reviews
MACEOIN, GARY. "Cycle in the Mud." *Catholic World,* 214 (1971), 42-43.

CAU, JEAN (French, 1925-)

LES ENTRAILLES DU TAUREAU (1971)

Reviews
TALBOT, EMILE J. *French Review,* 46 (1973), 1042-43.

CAULDER, Colline see NYNYCH, Stephanie J.

CAWTHORNE, W. A.

THE KANGAROO ISLANDERS

HEALY, J. J. "The Treatment of the Aborigine in Early Australian Fiction, 1840-70." *Australian Literary Studies,* 5 (1971/2), 244-45.

CAYROL, JEAN (French, 1911-)

HISTOIRE D'UN DÉSERT (1972)

Reviews
CARROLL, DAVID. *French Review,* 47 (1973), 217-18.

JE L'ENTENDS ENCORE (1968)

CARROLL, DAVID. "Jean Cayrol or the Fiction of the Writer." *MLN,* 88 (1973), 796-806.

JE VIVRAI L'AMOUR DES AUTRES

SAVAGE, CATHARINE. "The Trilogy of Jean Cayrol." *Thought,* 44 (1969), 513-30.

LE VENT DE LA MEMOIRE (1952)

CARROLL, DAVID. "Jean Cayrol or the Fiction of the Writer." *MLN,* 88 (1973), 789-96.

CECCHERINI, SILVANO

THE TRANSFER

Reviews
STILWELL, ROBERT L. "Return Passage to Prison." *Saturday Review,* 25 February 1967, pp. 54-55.

CELA, CAMILO JOSÉ (Spanish, 1916-)

GENERAL

DONAHUE, FRANCIS. "Cela and Spanish 'Tremendismo.' " *Western Humanities Review,* 20 (1966), 301-6.

_____ . "The Three Faces of Camilo José Cela." *Michigan Quarterly Review,* 8 (1969), 201-3.

"Interview/Camilo José Cela." *Diacritics,* 2, No.1 (1972), 42-45.

KIRSNER, ROBERT. "Cela's Quest for a Tragic Sense of Life." *Kentucky Romance Quarterly,* 17 (1970), 259-64.

SEATOR, LYNETTE HUBBARD. "The Antisocial Humanism of Cela and Hemingway." *Revista De Estudios Hispánicos,* 9 (1975), 425-39.

LA FAMILIA DEL HÉROE (1965)

FOSTER, DAVID WILLIAM. "Intrinsic and Extrinsic Pattern in Two New Novels by Camilo José Cela." *Papers On Language And Literature,* 5 (1969), 204-6.

FRANZ, THOMAS R. "Cela's *La Familia Del Héroe,* the *Nouveau Roman,* and the Creative Act." *MLN,* 88 (1973), 375-77.

THE FAMILY OF PASCUAL DUARTE (La Familia de Pascual Duarte)

BERNSTEIN, J. S. "Pascual Duarte and Orestes." *Symposium,* 22 (1968), 301-18.

BUSETTE, CEDRIC. "*La Familia De Pascual Duarte* and the Prominence of Fate." *Revista De Estudios Hispánicos,* 8 (1974), 61-67.

DONAHUE, FRANCIS. "Cela and Spanish 'Tremendismo.' " *Western Humanities Review,* 20 (1966), 301-4.

_____ . "The Three Faces of Camilo José Cela." *Michigan Quarterly Review,* 8 (1969), 201-2.

FOSTER, DAVID WILLIAM. "Social Criticism, Existentialism, and *Tremendismo* in Cela's *La Familia De Pascual Duarte.*" *Kentucky Foreign Language Quarterly,* 13, suppl. (1967), 25-33.

HUTMAN, NORMA LOUISE. "'Disproportionate Doom: Tragic Irony in the Spanish Post Civil War Novel." *Modern Fiction Studies,* 18 (1972), 199-206.

SPIRES, ROBERT C. "Systematic Doubt: The Moral Art of *La Familia De Pascual Duarte.*" *Hispanic Review,* 40 (1972), 283-302.

THE HIVE (La Colmena, 1951)

HENN, DAVID. "Cela's Portrayal of Martin Marco in 'La Colmena.' " *Neophilologus,* 55 (1971), 142-49.

_____ . "*La Colmena*—an Oversight on the Part of Cela." *Romance Notes,* 13 (1972), 414-18.

_____ . "Theme and Structure in *La Colmena.*" *Forum For Modern Language Studies,* 8 (1972), 304-19.

SPIRES, ROBERT C. "Cela's 'La colmena': The Creative Process as Message." *Hispania,* 55 (1972), 873-80.

MRS. CALDWELL SPEAKS TO HER SON (Mrs. Caldwell habla con su hijo, 1953)

Reviews
DONAHUE, FRANCIS. "Mad English Jocasta." *Saturday Review,* 22 June 1968, pp. 65-66.

SAN CAMILO (1969)

Reviews
SHEEHAN, ROBERT LOUIS. *Hispania,* 55 (1972), 386-87.

TOBOGAN DE HAMBRIENTOS

FOSTER, DAVID WILLIAM. "Intrinsic and Extrinsic Pattern in Two New Novels by Camilo José Cela." *Papers On Language And Literature,* 5 (1969), 206-8.

CÉLINE, LOUIS-FERDINAND (French, 1894-1961) pseudonym of Louis-Ferdinand Destouches

GENERAL

FROHOCK, W. M. *Style And Temper,* pp. 86-91.

HAMILTON, ALASTAIR. "Céline's Paris." *London Magazine,* 7, No.11 (1968), 41-52.

HINDUS, MILTON. "Céline: A Reappraisal." *Southern Review,* n.s., 1 (1965), 76-93.

_____ . "The Recent Revival of Céline: A Consideration." *Mosaic,* 6, No.3 (1973), 57-66.

HOKENSON, JAN. "Céline: Impressionist in Language." *L'Esprit Créateur,* 13 (1973), 329-39.

NETTELBECK, COLIN W. "Journey to the End of Art: The Evolution of the Novels of Louis-Ferdinand Céline." *PMLA,* 87 (1972), 80-89.

RECK, RIMA DRELL. *Literature And Responsibility,* pp. 190-215.

CASTLE TO CASTLE (D'un Chateau L'Autre, 1957)

BOSMAJIAN, HAMIDA. "Celine's *Castle To Castle:* Everyman on a Roundtrip." *Critique,* 14, No.1 (1972), 49-62.

Reviews
KRUPAT, ARNOLD. "Céline's Inferno." *Catholic World,* 209 (1969), pp. 142-43.

OSTROVSKY, ERIKA. "Buffoons of the Apocalypse." *Saturday Review,* 1 February 1969, pp. 31, 63.

WRIGHT, BARBARA. "A Dark Hatred." *Twentieth Century,* 177, No.2 (1969), 47-48.

DEATH ON THE INSTALLMENT PLAN (Mort à Crédit, 1936)

FRASER, JOHN. "The Darkest Journey: Céline's *Death On The Installment Plan.*" *Wisconsin Studies In Contemporary Literature,* 8 (1967), 96-110.

HAYMAN, DAVID. "The Broken Cranium—Headwounds in Zola, Rilke, Céline: A Study in Contrasting Modes." *Comparative Literature Studies,* 9 (1972), 221-33.

SOLOMON, PHILIP H. "Céline's *Death On The Installment Plan:* The Intoxications of Delirium." *Yale French Studies,* No.50 (1974), pp. 191-203.

GUIGNOL'S BAND (1944)

THIHER, ALLEN. "The Yet To Be Salvaged Céline: *Guignol's Band.*" *Modern Fiction Studies,* 16 (1970), 67-75.

JOURNEY TO THE END OF NIGHT (Voyage au bout de la nuit, 1932)

FORTIER, PAUL A. "Marxist Criticism of Céline's *Voyage Au Bout De La Nuit.*" *Modern Fiction Studies,* 17 (1971), 268-72.

GREENBERG, ALVIN. "Breakable Beginnings: The Fall into Reality in the Modern Novel." *Texas Studies In Literature And Language,* 10 (1968), 133-42.

_____ . "The Novel of Disintegration: Paradoxical Impossibility in Contemporary Fiction." *Wisconsin Studies In Contemporary Literature,* 7 (1966), 103-24.

NETTELBECK, COLIN W. "From Inside Destitution: Céline's Bardamu and Ellison's Invisible Man." *Southern Review: Literary And Interdisciplinary Studies,* 7 (1974), 246-53.

OWEN, CARYS T. "Networks of Symbol in *Voyage Au Bout De La Nuit.*" *Forum For Modern Language Studies,* 11 (1975), 46-58.

RECK, RIMA DRELL. *Literature And Responsibility,* pp. 207-12.

THIHER, ALLEN. "Céline and Sartre." *Philological Quarterly,* 50 (1971), 292-305.

WIDMER, KINGSLEY. "The Way Down to Wisdom of Louis-Ferdinand Céline." *Minnesota Review,* 8 (1968), 85-91.

NORTH (Nord, 1960)

Reviews
EWART, GAVIN. "Rome-Berlin Axis." *London Magazine,* NS, 12, No.4 (1972), 151.

SEAVER, RICHARD. "Céline: Swastika and Cross." *Saturday Review,* 5 February 1972, pp. 57-59.

CERVANTES SAAVEDRA, MIGUEL (Spanish, 1547-1616)

GENERAL

DAVISON, C. F. "Cervantes, Voiture and the Spirit of Chivalry in France." *Studi Francesi,* 18 (1974), 82–86.

EL SAFFAR, RUTH. "Development and Reorientation in the Works of Cervantes." *MLN,* 88 (1973), 203–14.

PILUSO, ROBERT V. "Honor in Valdívielso and Cervantes." *Kentucky Romance Quarterly,* 17 (1970), 72–81.

PREDMORE, RICHARD L. *Cervantes.*

ROTHBERG, IRVING P. "Two Similar Zeugmas in Cervantes and Lope." *Romance Notes,* 7 (1965), 51–53.

EL AMANTE LIBERAL

LOWE, JENNIFER. "A Note on Cervantes' *El Amante Liberal.*" *Romance Notes,* 12 (1971), 400–03.

EL CURIOSO IMPERTINENTE

NEUGAARD, EDWARD J. "The 'Curioso Impertinente' and its Relationship to the 'Quijote.' " *USF Language Quarterly,* 4, No.3/4 (1966), 2–6.

SIEBER, HARRY. "On Juan Huarte de San Juan and Anselmo's *Locura* in 'El Curioso Impertinente.' " *Revista Hispanica Moderna,* 36 (1970/1), 1–8.

DON QUIXOTE (El Ingenioso Hidalgo Don Quijote de la Mancha, 1605)

ABRAMS, FRED. "Aliaga, Avellaneda, and a Curious Passage in the *Quijote* (II, 61)." *Romance Notes,* 8 (1966), 86–90.

_____ . "Avellaneda and Tirso de Molina in Cervantes' Second Prologue to the *Quijote.*" *Romance Notes,* 11 (1969), 137–43.

_____ . "Pedro Noriz and Tirso de Molina in the Enchanted Head Episode of the *Quijote.*" *Romance Notes,* 10 (1968), 122–28.

_____ . "Tirso de Molina alias Sancho Panza and a New Cervantine Etymology for *Barataria.*" *Romance Notes,* 9 (1967), 281–86.

ALLEN, JOHN J. "Cide Hamete's English Translators." *Hispanic Review,* 35 (1967), 366–67.

_____ . "The Governorship of Sancho and Don Quijote's Chivalric Career." *Revista Hispanica Moderna,* 38 (1974/75), 141–52.

_____ . "Melisendra's Mishap in Maese Pedro's Puppet Show." *MLN,* 88 (1973), 330–35.

ALTER, ROBERT. "The Modernity of *Don Quixote* or, the Mirror of Knighthood and the World of Mirrors." *Southern Review,* NS, 9 (1973), 311–33.

_____ . *Partial Magic,* pp. 1–29.

BAKER, ARMAND F. "A New Look at the Structure of *Don Quijote.*" *Revista De Estudios Hispánicos,* 7 (1973), 3–21.

BARR, ALAN P. "Cervantes' Probing of Reality and Psychological Realism in 'Don Quixote.' " *Literature And Psychology,* 18 (1968), 111–22.

BARRICK, MAC E. "Sancho's Trip to El Toboso: A Possible Source." *MLN,* 81 (1966), 222–25.

BATES, MARGARET. "Cervantes and Martorell." *Hispanic Review,* 35 (1967), 365–66.

BAWCUTT, N. W. " 'Don Quixote,' Part I, and 'The Duchess of Malfi.' " *Modern Language Review,* 66 (1971), 488–91.

BELL, MICHAEL. "The Structure of *Don Quixote.*" *Essays In Criticism,* 18 (1968), 241–57.

BORING, PHYLLIS ZATLIN. "Women in the *Quixote,* Revisited." *Studies In The Humanities,* 4, No.1 (1974), 35–40.

BOURNE, MARJORIE A. "Don Quijote on the Boards in France." *Revista Estudios Hispánicos,* 5 (1971), 189–202.

BRANTLEY, FRANKLIN O. "Sancho's Ascent Into the Spheres." *Hispania,* 53 (1970), 37–45.

BRODY, ROBERT. "Don Quijote's Emotive Adventures: Fulling Hammers and Lions." *Neophilologus,* 59 (1975), 372–81.

CHAMBERLIN, VERNON A. and JACK WEINER. "Color Symbolism: A Key to a Possible New Interpretation of Cervantes' 'Caballero del Verde Gabán.' " *Romance Notes,* 10 (1969), 342–47.

CHAMBERS, LELAND H. "Irony in the Final Chapter of the *Quijote.*" *Romanic Review,* 61 (1970), 14–22.

_____ . "Structure and the Search for Truth in the *Quijote:* Notes Toward a Comprehensive View." *Hispanic Review,* 35 (1967), 309–26.

CLOSE, A. J. "*Don Quixote* and Unamuno's Philosophy of Art," in *Studies In Modern Spanish Literature And Art,* ed. Nigel Glendinning, pp. 25–44.

_____ . "Don Quixote's Love for Dulcinea: A Study of Cervantine Irony." *Bulletin of Hispanic Studies,* 50 (1973), 237–55.

_____ . "Sancho Panza: Wise Fool." *Modern Language Review,* 68 (1973), 344–57.

CLOSE, ANTHONY. "Don Quixote as a Burlesque Hero: A Reconstructed Eighteenth Century View." *Forum For Modern Language Studies,* 10 (1974), 365–78.

COSTA, RICHARD HAUER. "Intimations of *Don Quixote* in Sidney's *Defense Of Poetry.*" *Ball State University Forum,* 11, No.4 (1970), 60–63.

DIMLER, G. RICHARD. "Alienation in 'Don Quixote' and 'Simplicius Simplicissimus.' " *Thought,* 49 (1974), 72–74.

DRISKELL, LEON V. "Interpolated Tales in Joseph Andrews and Don Quixote: The Dramatic Method as Instruction." *South Atlantic Bulletin,* 33, No.3 (1968), 5–8.

DUDLEY, EDWARD. "Don Quixote as Magus: The Rhetoric of Interpolation." *Bulletin Of Hispanic Studies,* 49 (1972), 355–68.

EISENBERG, DANIEL. "*Don Quijote* and the Romances of Chivalry: The Need for a Reexamination." *Hispanic Review,* 41 (1973), 511–23.

_____ . "Pero Pérez the Priest and His Comment on *Tirant Lo Blanch.*" *MLN,* 88 (1973), 321–30.

EL SAFFAR, RUTH SNODGRASS. "Apropos of *Don Quixote:* Hero Or Fool?" *MLN,* 85 (1970), 269–73.

_____ . "The Function of the Fictional Narrator in *Don Quijote.*" *MLN,* 83 (1968), 164–77.

_____ . "Montesinos' Cave and the *Casamiento Engañoso* in the Development of Cervantes' Prose Fiction." *Kentucky Romance Quarterly,* 20 (1973), 451–67.

ELLIS, KEITH. "Cervantes and Ayala's *El Rapto:* The Art of Reworking a Story." *PMLA,* 84 (1969), 14–19.

FIRMAT, GUSTAVO PÉREZ. "*Don Quixote* in *Heart Of Darkness:* Two Notes." *Comparative Literature Studies,* 12 (1975), 374-83.

FLORES, R. M. "Sancho's Fabrications: A Mirror of the Development of His Imagination." *Hispanic Review,* 38 (1970), 174–82.

FORCIONE, ALBERT K. "Cervantes and the Freedom of the Artist." *Romanic Review,* 61 (1970), 243–55.

_____ . *Cervantes, Aristotle, And The [Persiles,]* pp. 91–166.

_____ . "Cervantes, Tasso, and the *Romanzi* Polemic." *Revue De Littérature Comparée,* 44 (1970), 433–43.

FRY, GLORIA M. "Symbolic Action in the Episode of the Cave of Montesinos from 'Don Quijote.' " *Hispania,* 48 (1965), 468–74.

GREENE, J. LEE. "Fielding's Gypsy Episode and Sancho Panza's Governorship." *South Atlantic Bulletin,* 39, No.2 (1974), 117–21.

GROSSVOGEL, DAVID I. *Limits Of The Novel,* pp. 74–107.

HAHN, JUERGEN. "*El Curioso Impertinente* and Don Quijote's Symbolic Struggle Against *Curiositas*." *Bulletin Of Hispanic Studies,* 49 (1972), 128-40.

HALEY, GEORGE. "The Narrator in *Don Quijote:* Maese Pedro's Puppet Show." *MLN,* 80 (1965), 145-65.

HALSEY, MARTHA T. "Buero's *Mito:* A Contemporary Vision of Don Quijote." *Revista De Estudios Hispánicos,* 6 (1972), 225-35.

HATZFELD, HELMUT A. "Why is *Don Quijote* Baroque?" *Philological Quarterly,* 51 (1972), 158-76.

HOLMES, THEODORE. "Don Quixote and Modern Man." *Sewanee Review,* 78 (1970), 40-59.

IVENTOSCH, HERMAN. "Cervantes and Courtly Love: The Grisóstomo-Marcela Episode of *Don Quixote.*" *PMLA,* 89 (1974), 64-76.

JOHNSON, CARROLL B. "A Second Look at Dulcinea's Ass: *Don Quijote,* II.10." *Hispanic Review,* 43 (1975), 191-98.

JONES, JOSEPH R. "Notes on the Diffusion and Influence of Avellaneda's 'Quixote.' " *Hispania,* 56 (1973), 229-37.

LOCKE, F. W. "El Sabio Encantador: The Author of *Don Quixote.*" *Symposium,* 23 (1969), 46-61.

McGAHA, MICHAEL D. "Oaths in *Don Quixote.*" *Romance Notes,* 14 (1973), 561-69.

McGRADY, DONALD. "The *Sospiros* of Sancho's Donkey." *MLN,* 88 (1973), 335-37.

MACKEY, MARY. "Rhetoric and Characterization in *Don Quijote.*" *Hispanic Review,* 42 (1974), 51-66.

MANCING, HOWARD. "Cervantes and the Tradition of Chivalric Parody." *Forum For Modern Language Studies,* 11 (1975), 177-87.

———. "Dulcinea's Ass: A Note on *Don Quixote,* Part II, Chapter 10." *Hispanic Review,* 40 (1972), 73-77.

MENDELOFF, HENRY. "The Maritornes Episodes (DQ: I, 16): A Cervantine Bedroom Farce." *Romance Notes,* 16 (1975), 753-59.

———. "The Pejorative Epithet in *Don Quijote.*" *Hispanofila,* 55 (1975), 47-55.

MEYER, HERMANN. *The Poetics Of Quotation In The European Novel,* pp. 55-71.

MOORE, JOHN A. "The Pastoral in the *Quixote* or Nuestro Gozo en el Pozo." *Romance Notes,* 13 (1972), 531-34.

MURILLO, L. A. "The Summer of Myth: *Don Quijote De La Mancha* and *Amadis De Gaula.*" *Philological Quarterly,* 5 (1972), 145-57.

NEUGAARD, EDWARD J. "The 'Curioso Impertinente' and its Relationship to the 'Quijote.' " *USF Language Quarterly,* 4, No.3/4 (1966), 2-6.

NEWBERRY, WILMA. *The Pirandellian Mode In Spanish Literature From Cervantes To Sastre,* pp. 3-13.

PALMER, DONALD D. "Unamuno, Freud and the Case of Alonso Quihano." *Hispania,* 54 (1971), 243-49.

PALOMO, DOLORES. "Chaucer, Cervantes, and the Birth of the Novel." *Mosaic,* 8, No.4 (1975), 61-72.

PENNER, A. R. "Fielding's Adaptation of Cervantes' Knight and Squire: The Character of Joseph." *Revue De Littérature Comparée,* 41 (1967), 508-14.

PÉREZ, LOUIS C. "The Theme of the Tapestry in Ariosto and Cervantes." *Revista De Estudios Hispánicos,* 7 (1973), 294-98.

———. "Wilder and Cervantes: In the Spirit of the Tapestry." *Symposium,* 25 (1971), 249-59.

PÉREZ FIRMAT, GUSTAVO. "*Don Quixote* in *Heart of Darkness:* Two Notes." *Comparative Literature Studies,* 12 (1975), 374-83.

PLANK, ROBERT. "Quixote's Mills: The Man-Machine Encounter in SF." *Science-Fiction Studies,* 1 (1973), 68-78.

PREDMORE, RICHARD L. *The World Of Don Quixote.*

PRITCHETT, V. S. *The Working Novelist,* pp. 166-71.

RAMÍREZ, ALEJANDRO. "The Concept of Ignorance in *Don Quixote.*" *Philological Quarterly,* 45 (1966), 474-79.

REXROTH, KENNETH. "Classics Revisited-VI: Don Quixote." *Saturday Review,* 15 May 1965, p. 19; rpt. in his *Classics Revisited,* pp. 172-77.

RILEY, E. C. "Three Versions of Don Quixote." *Modern Language Review,* 68 (1973), 807-19.

———. "Who's Who in *Don Quixote?* Or an Approach to the Problem of Identity." *MLN,* 81 (1966), 113-30.

RIVERS, ELIAS L. "Lope and Cervantes Once More." *Kentucky Romance Quarterly,* 14 (1967), 112-19.

ROTHBERG, IRVING P. "Two Similar Zeugmas in Cervantes and Lope." *Romance Notes,* 7 (1965), 51-53.

RUBIN, LOUIS D. "*Don Quixote* and Selected Progeny: Or, the Journeyman as Outsider." *Southern Review, NS,* 10 (1974), 31-58.

———. *The Teller In The Tale,* pp. 3-23.

RUSSELL, P. E. " 'Don Quixote' as a Funny Book." *Modern Language Review,* 64 (1969), 312-26.

SALINGAR, L. G. "*Don Quixote* as a Prose Epic." *Forum For Modern Language Studies,* 2 (1966), 53-68.

SELIG, KARL-LUDWIG. "The Battle of the Sheep (Don Quixote, I, xviii)." *Revista Hispanica Moderna,* 38 (1974/5), 64-72.

———. "Cervantes: 'En un lugar de. . .' " *MLN,* 86 (1971), 266-68.

———. "The Ricote Episode in *Don Quixote:* Observations on Literary Refractions." *Revista Hispanica Moderna,* 38 (1974/5), 73-77.

SERRANO-PLAJA, ARTURO. "*Magic*" *Realism In Cervantes:* <*Don Quixote*> *As Seen Through* <*Tom Sawyer*> *and* <*The Idiot.*>

SICILIANO, ERNEST A. "The Absent Hermit of the *Quijote.*" *Romance Notes,* 12 (1971), 400-6.

———. "The Use of Conscience in the Quijote." *Romance Notes,* 11 (1970), 607-10.

SIEBER, HARRY. "Literary Time in the 'Cueva de Montesinos.' " *MLN,* 86 (1971), 268-73.

SINNIGEN, JOHN. "Themes and Structures in the 'Bodas de Camacho.' " *MLN,* 84 (1969), 157-70.

SMITH, PAUL C. "Cervantes and Galdós: The Duques and Ido del Sagrario." *Romance Notes,* 8 (1966), 47-50.

SMOOT, JEAN J. "Alceste: The Incomplete Don Quixote." *Romance Notes,* 12 (1970), 169-73.

STAVES, SUSAN. "Don Quixote in Eighteenth-Century England." *Comparative Literature,* 24 (1972), 193-215.

STOUT, GARDNER D. "Some Borrowings in Sterne from Rabelais and Cervantes." *English Language Notes,* 3 (1965), 114-18.

THORBURN, DAVID. "Fiction and Imagination in Don Quixote." *Partisan Review,* 42 (1975), 431-43.

TURGENEV, IVAN. "*Hamlet* and *Don Quixote.*" Trans. Moshe Spiegel. *Chicago Review,* 17, No. 4 (1965), 92-109.

ULLMAN, PIERRE L. "The Surrogates of Baroque Marcela and Mannerist Leandra." *Revista De Estudios Hispánicos,* 5 (1971), 307-19.

WALKER, ROGER M. "Did Cervantes Know the *Cavallero Zifar?*" *Bulletin Of Hispanic Studies,* 49 (1972), 120-27.

WARDROPPER, BRUCE W. "Don Quixote: Story or History?" *Modern Philology,* 63 (1965), 1-11.

WELSH, ALEXANDER. "Waverley, Pickwick, and *Don Quixote.*" *Nineteenth-Century Fiction,* 22 (1967), 19-30.

WILLIS, RAYMOND S. "Sancho Panza: Prototype for the Modern Novel." *Hispanic Review,* 37 (1969), 207-27.

ZIOMEK, HENRYK. "Parallel Ingredients in *Don Quixote* and *Dom Casmurro.*" *Revista De Estudios Hispánicos,* 2 (1968), 229-40.

LA ESPAÑOLA INGLESA

DA COSTA FONTES, MANUEL. "Love as an Equalizer in *La Española Inglesa.*" *Romance Notes,* 16 (1975), 742-48.

HANRAHAN, THOMAS. "History in the *Española Inglesa.*" *MLN,* 83 (1968), 267-71.

LOWE, JENNIFER. "The Structure of Cervantes' *La Española Inglesa.*" *Romance Notes,* 9 (1967), 287-90.

LA FUERZA DE LA SANGRE

ALLEN, JOHN J. "*El Cristo De La Vega* and *La Fuerza De La Sangre.*" *MLN,* 83 (1968), 271-75.

SELIG, KARL-LUDWIG. "Some Observations on *La Fuerza De La Sangre.*" *MLN,* 87, No.6 (1972), 121-25.

LA GALATEA (1585)

KEIGHTLEY, R. G. "Narrative Perspectives in Spanish Pastoral Fiction." *AUMLA,* No.44 (1975), pp. 194-219.

LOWE, JENNIFER. "The *Cuestión De Amor* and the Structure of Cervantes' *Galatea.*" *Bulletin Of Hispanic Studies,* 43 (1966), 98-108.

STAGG, GEOFFREY. "A Matter of Masks: *La Galatea,*" in *Hispanic Studies In Honour Of Joseph Manson,* ed. Dorothy M. Atkinson and Anthony H. Clarke, pp. 255-67.

LA GITANILLA

FORCIONE, ALBAN K. *Cervantes, Aristotle, And The <Persiles,>* pp. 306-19.

THE GLASS LICENTIATE (El Licenciado Vidriera)

EDWARDS, GWYNNE. "Cervantes's 'El Licenciado Vidriera': Meaning and Structure." *Modern Language Review,* 68 (1973), 559-68.

ENGSTROM, ALFRED GARVIN. "The Man Who Thought Himself Made of Glass, and Certain Related Images." *Studies In Philology,* 67 (1970), 390-405.

FRIEDMAN, EDWARD H. "Conceptual Proportion in Cervantes' 'El licenciado Vidriera.' " *South Atlantic Bulletin,* 39, No.4 (1974), 51-59.

MESSICK, ALAN R. "Tomás Rodaja: A Clinical Case?" *Romance Notes,* 11 (1970), 623-28.

NOVELAS EXEMPLARES

SELIG, KARL-LUDWIG. "The Books in the Prologue to the *Novelas Exemplares.*" *MLN,* 85 (1970), 249.

SOONS, ALAN. "Three Novelas ejeplares of Cervantes. Diptych Pattern and Spiritual Intention." *Orbis Litterarum,* 26 (1971), 87-93.

PEDRO DE URDEMALAS

FORCIONE, ALBAN K. *Cervantes, Aristotle, And The <Persiles,>* pp. 319-37.

LOS TRABAJOS DE PERSILES Y SIGISMUNDA (1617)

ALLEN, KENNETH P. "Aspects of Time in *Los Trabajos De Persiles Y Sigismunda.*" *Revista Hispanica Moderna,* 36 (1970/1), 77-107.

BERINGER, ARTHUR A. "*Persiles* and the Time Labyrinth." *Hispanofila,* No.41 (1971), pp. 1-11.

FORCIONE, ALBAN K. *Cervantes, Aristotle, And The <Persiles,>* pp. 169-301.

———. *Cervantes' Christian Romance: A Study Of <Persiles Y Sigismunda.>*

LOWE, JENNIFER. "Themes and Structure in Cervantes' *Persiles Y Sigismunda.*" *Forum For Modern Language Studies,* 3 (1967), 334-51.

POPE, RANDOLPH D. "The Autobiographical Form in Persiles." *Anales Cervantinos,* 14 (1974/5), 93-106.

CÉSPEDES, AUGUSTO (Bolivian, 1904-)

REMORSE

Reviews
PAGONES, DORRIE. "Letters from Unbelievers." *Saturday Review,* 4 March 1967, p. 42.

CHAIB, Mohammed ben see MRABET, Mohammed

CHALLANS, Mary see RENAULT, Mary

CHALLE, ROBERT (French, 1659-1720?)

CONTINUATION DE L'HISTOIRE DE L'ADMIRABLE DON QUICHOTTE

SHOWALTER, ENGLISH. "Did Robert Challe Write a Sequel to *Don Quixote?*" *Romanic Review,* 62 (1971), 270-82.

LES ILLUSTRES FRANÇAISES

FORNO, LAWRENCE J. "Challe's Portrayal of Women." *French Review,* 47 (1974), 865-73.

———. "The Rebirth of a Novelist: Robert Challe in 1973." *French Review,* 46 (1973), 1138-47.

SHOWALTER, ENGLISH. "Robert Challe and *Don Quixote.*" *French Review,* 45 (1972), 1136-44.

CHAMBON, JACQUES

LE SENTINNELLE (1970)

Reviews
STOLTZFUS, BEN. *French Review,* 44 (1971), 637-38.

CHAMISSO, ADALBERT VON (Franco-German, 1781-1838) pseudonym of Chamisso de Boncourt, Louis Charles Adelaide

PETER SCHLEMIHL (Peter Schlemihlis wundersame geschichte, 1814)

FLORES, RALPH. "The Lost Shadow of Peter Schlemihl." *German Quarterly,* 47 (1974), 567-84.

NEUMARKT, PAUL. "Chamisso's Peter Schlemihl (A Literary Approach in Terms of Analytical Psychology.)" *Literature And Psychology,* 17 (1967), 120-26.

CHANDRA, JAGDISH

AADHA PUL

Reviews
KUMAR, SHARAT. *Indian Literature,* 16, No.1/2 (1973), 219-20.

CHANG, EILEEN (Chinese, 1921-)

GENERAL

HSIA, C. T. *A History Of Modern Chinese Fiction,* pp. 389-431.

LOVE IN REDLAND

HSIA, C. T. *A History Of Modern Chinese Fiction,* pp. 427-31.

THE RICE-SPROUT SONG (Yang-ko, 1954)

HALES, DELL R. "Social Criticism in Modern Chinese Essays and Novels." *Review Of National Literatures,* 6, No.1 (1975), 53-57.

HSIA, C. T. *A History Of Modern Chinese Fiction,* pp. 416-27.

THE ROUGE OF THE NORTH (1967)

Reviews
ARNOLD, SUSAN. *Literature East And West,* 12 (1968), 296–97.

CHANG T'IEN-I (Chinese, 1907–)

GENERAL

HSIA, C. T. *A History Of Modern Chinese Fiction,* pp. 212–36.

THE STRANGE KNIGHT OF SHANGHAI

HSIA, C. T. *A History Of Modern Chinese Fiction,* pp. 231–35.

CHAO SHU-LI (Chinese, 1906–1970)

THE CHANGES IN LI VILLAGE (Li-chia-chuang ti pien-ch'ien, 1945)

HSIA, C. T. *A History Of Modern Chinese Fiction,* pp. 483–87.

SAN-LI WAN VILLAGE (San-li-wan, 1955)

HSIA, C. T. *A History Of Modern Chinese Fiction,* pp. 491–94.

HUANG, JOE C. *Heroes And Villains In Communist China,* pp. 238–43, 278–80.

CHARITON OF APHRODISIAS (fl. 2d century A.D.)

CHEREAS AND CALLIRHOE

BOORSCH, JEAN. "About Some Greek Romances." *Yale French Studies,* No.38 (1967), pp. 72–88.

PERRY, BEN EDWIN. *The Ancient Romances,* pp. 96–148.

CHARLES-ROUX, EDMONDE (French, 1920–)

ELLE, ADRIENNE (1971)

Reviews
JONES, LOUISA. *French Review,* 45 (1972), 1175–76.

TO FORGET PALERMO (Oublier Palerme, 1966)

Reviews
EASTON, ELIZABETH. "The Good Old Days in the Old Country." *Saturday Review,* 8 June 1968, p. 51.

CHARRIERÈ, HENRI (French, 1906–1973)

PAPILLON (1969)

Reviews
FADIMAN, EDWIN, JR. *Saturday Review,* 24 October 1970, pp. 70–71.

CHATAIN, JACQUES

BLICHE OU L'HERBE RANCE (1970)

Reviews
GREENE, NAOMI. *French Review,* 45 (1971), 196–97.

CHATEAUBRIAND, FRANÇOIS RENÉ (French, 1768–1848)

GENERAL

MEIN, MARGARET. "Chateaubriand, a Precursor of Proust." *French Review,* 45 (1971), 388–400.

———. *A Foretaste Of Proust: A Study Of Proust And His Precursors,* pp. 35–47.

PORTER, CHARLES A. "Chateaubriand's Classicism." *Yale French Studies,* No.38 (1967), pp. 156–71.

ABEN-HAMET, THE LAST OF THE ABENCERAGES (Les aventures du dernier Abencerage, 1826)

STREET, JACK D. "A Statistical Study of the Vocabulary of Chateaubriand's *Les Aventures Du Dernier Abencerage.*" *French Review,* 43 (1969), 42–45.

ATALA (1801)

LOWRIE, JOYCE O. "Motifs of Kingdom and Exile in *Atala.*" *French Review,* 43 (1970), 755–64.

SPININGER, DENNIS J. "The Paradise Setting of Chateaubriand's *Atala.*" *PMLA,* 89 (1974), 530–36.

RENÉ (1805)

CHARLTON, D. G. "The Ambiguity of Chateaubriand's *René.*" *French Studies,* 23 (1969), 229–43.

GARBER, FREDERICK. "The Structure of Romantic Decadence." *Nineteenth-Century French Studies,* 1, (1973), 88–91.

HUNT, TONY. "Chateaubriand's *René* and Christian Apologetics." *Durham University Journal,* NS, 36 (1974), 68–78.

CHATEÂUBRIANT, ALPHONSE DE (French, 1882–1951)

GENERAL

MOORE-RINVOLUCRI, MINA J. "Alphonse de Chateâubriant: Novelist and Thinker." *Modern Languages,* 50 (1969), 14–18.

LA BRIÉRE

MOORE-RINVOLUCRI, MINA J. "Alphonse de Chateâubriant: Novelist and Thinker." *Modern Languages,* 50 (1969), 16–17.

CHATTERJEE, SARATCHANDRA (Indian, 1876–1938)

GENERAL

CHAUDHURI, NARAYAN. "Saratchandra: His Life and Literature." *Indian Literature,* 18, No.4 (1975), 86–93.

DAS, P. "Saratchandra Chattophadhya." *Indian Literature,* 18, No.4 (1975), 51–57.

CHEKHOV, ANTON PAVLOVITCH (Russian, 1860–1904)

GENERAL

BITSILLI, PËTR. "From Chekhonte to Chekhov," in *Twentieth-Century Russian Literary Criticism,* ed. Victor Erlich, pp. 212–18.

MOSS, HOWARD. "Notes on Fiction." *Wisconsin Studies In Contemporary Literature,* 7 (1966), 1–7.

MUCHNIC, HELEN. "Chekhov: A Biographical and Critical Study," in her *Russian Writers,* pp. 200–3.

NEWCOMBE, JOSEPHINE M. "Was Čexov a Tolstoyan?" *Slavic And East European Journal,* 18 (1974), 143–52.

RAHV, PHILIP. "The Education of Anton Chekhov," in his *Literature And The Sixth Sense,* pp. 216–21.

THE SHOOTING PARTY (Drama na okhote, 1885)

HAGAN, JOHN. "*The Shooting Party,* Čexov's Early Novel: Its Place in His Development." *Slavic And East European Journal,* 9 (1965), 123–40.

THREE YEARS

REEVE, F. D. *The Russian Novel,* pp. 274–301.

CHERNYSHEVSKY, NIKOLAY PAVRILOVICH (Russian, 1828–1889)

MY JUSTIFICATION (Moe opravdanie)

NIKOLAEV, M. P. "On the Highroad of Realistic Literature." *Soviet Studies In Literature,* 1, No.3 (1965), 18–29.

REFLECTED RADIANCE (Otbleski siiania)

NIKOLAEV, M. P. "On the Highroad of Realistic Literature." *Soviet Studies In Literature,* 1, No.3 (1965), 19–21.

THE STORY OF A GIRL (Istoriia odnoi devushki)

NIKOLAEV, M. P. "On the Highroad of Realistic Literature." *Soviet Studies In Literature,* 1, No.3 (1965), 14–18.

WHAT IS TO BE DONE? (Chto delat', 1863)

FRANK, JOSEPH. "N. G. Chernyshevsky: A Russian Utopia." *Southern Review,* NS, 3 (1967), 68–84.

FREEBORN, RICHARD. *The Rise Of The Russian Novel,* pp. 131–33.

RANDALL, FRANCIS B. *N. G. Chernyshevskii,* pp. 104–30.

CHIANG KUANG-TZ'U (Chinese, 1901–1931) pseudonym of Chiang Kuang-ch'ih

GENERAL

HSIA, C. T. *A History Of Modern Chinese Fiction,* pp. 257–62.

CHIANG KUEI (Taiwan, 1903–)

THE RIVAL SUNS (Ch'ung-yang, 1961)

HSIA, C. T. "The Continuing Obsession with China: Three Contemporary Writers." *Review Of National Literatures,* 6, No.1 (1975), 77–83.

CHIANG PING-CHIH see TING LING

CHIDZERO, BERNARD (Zimbabwian, 1927–)

NZVENGAMUTSWAIRO

FORTUNE, G. "Social Registers in Chidzero's '*Nzvengamutswairo.*'" *African Studies,* 32 (1973), 99–111.

KAHARI, G. P. "Tradition and Innovation in Shona Literature: Bernard Chidzero's *Nzvengamutswairo.*" *Revue Des Langues Vivantes,* 37 (1971), 75–80.

CH'IEN CHUNG-SHU (Chinese, 1910–)

GENERAL

HSIA, C. T. *A History Of Modern Chinese Fiction,* pp. 432–60.

BESIEGED FORTRESS (1947)

HSIA, C. T. *A History Of Modern Chinese Fiction,* pp. 441–60.

CHILD, PHILIP (Canadian, 1898–)

GENERAL

MAGEE, WILLIAM H. "Philip Child: A Re-appraisal." *Canadian Literature,* No.24 (1965), pp. 28–36.

CHINESE COURTSHIP (Author Unknown)

BLACKALL, ERIC A. "Goethe and the Chinese Novel," in *The Discontinuous Tradition,* ed. P. F. Ganz, pp. 30–35.

CHING-MAI, CHIN

SONG OF OUYANG HAI (Ou-yang Hai chih ko)

FOKKEMA, D. W. "Chinese Literature Under the Cultural Revolution." *Literature East And West,* 13 (1969), 347–58.

HUANG, JOE C. *Heroes And Villains Of Communist China,* pp. 292–319.

CHING P'ING MEI (Author Unknown)

HSIA, C. T. *The Classic Chinese Novel,* pp. 165–202.

CHIRICO, GIORGIO DE

HEBDOMEROS (1929)

MATTHEWS, J. H. *Surrealism And The Novel,* pp. 74–90.

CHITALE, VENU

IN TRANSIT (1956)

DARDINSKI, MADELYN. "India in Transition: A Politico-Literary View." *Mahfil,* 8, No.2/3 (1972), 215–22.

CHITTAL, YASHWANT

MURU DARIGALU (1964)

Reviews
AMUR, G. S. *Indian Writing Today,* 2, No.1 (1968), 26–28.

CHORELL, WALENTIN (Finnish, 1912–)

GENERAL

SALMINEN, JOHANNES. "Walentin Chorell: An Appreciation." *American Scandanavian Review,* 56 (1968), 137–39.

CHOU LI-PO (Chinese, 1908–1979)

GREAT CHANGES IN A MOUNTAIN VILLAGE (Shan-hsiang chü-pien, 1958)

HUANG, JOE C. *Heroes And Villains In Communist China,* pp. 238–43, 280–81.

HURRICANE (Pao-fen chou-yü, 1949)

HUANG, JOE C. *Heroes And Villains In Communist China,* pp. 195–211.

CHRAIBI, DRISS (Moroccan, 1926–)

LA CIVILISATION, MA MÉRE

Reviews
ROMEIKO, JOHN J. *Canadian Modern Language Review,* 29, No.3 (1973), 78–79.

THE SIMPLE PAST (Le passé simple, 1954)

YETIV, ISAAC. "The Crisis of Identity of the Native North African Writer," in *Twentieth Century French Fiction,* pp. 133–34.

CHUKOVSKAYA, LYDIA (Russian, 1907–)

THE DESERTED HOUSE (Opustelyi Dom)

MUCHNIC, HELEN. "Nightmares," in her *Russian Writers,* pp. 393–99.

CHULKOV, MIKHAIL DMITRIEVICH (Russian, 1743–1792)

GENERAL

GARRARD, J. G. "Narrative Technique in Chulkov's *Prigozhaia Povarikha.*" *Slavic Review,* 27 (1968), 554–63.

THE TALE OF THE ORIGIN OF THE TAFFETA BEAUTY PATCH (Skazka o rozhdenii taftianoi mushki)

TITUNIK, I. R. "Mikhail Chulkov's 'Double-Talk' Narrative." *Canadian-American Slavic Studies,* 9 (1975), 30–42.

CH'Ü PO

TRACKS IN THE SNOWY FOREST (Lin hai hsüeh yüan)

HUANG, JOE C. *Heroes And Villains In Communist China,* pp. 134–47.

CLAMAGES, NICHOLAS DE

FLORIDAN ET ÉLVIDE

FLEMING, JOHN V. "The Rustic Fête in *Floridan Et Élvide." Romance Notes,* 7 (1965), 68–70.

CLARKE, AUSTIN CHESTERFIELD (Barbadian, 1934–)

GENERAL

BROWN, LLOYD W. "Austin Clarke in Canadian Reviews," *Canadian Literature,* No.38 (1968), pp. 101–4.

_____ . "The West Indian Novel in North America: A Study of Austin Clarke." *Journal Of Commonwealth Literature,* No.9 (1970), pp. 89–103.

AMONG THISTLES AND THORNS (1965)

BROWN, LLOYD W. "The Crisis of Black Identity In the West Indian Novel." *Critique,* 11, No.3 (1968/9), 108.

THE MEETING POINT (1967)

BROWN, LLOYD W. "Beneath the North Star: The Canadian Image In Black Literature." *Dalhousie Review,* 50 (1970/1), 324–27.

_____ . "The West Indian Novel in North America: A Study of Austin Clarke." *Journal Of Commonwealth Literature,* No.9 (1970), pp. 95–103.

Reviews
WADDINGTON, MIRIAM. "No Meeting Points." *Canadian Literature,* No.35 (1968), pp. 74–78.

STORM OF FORTUNE (1973)

Reviews
BESSAI, DIANE. "West Indies: Here and There." *Canadian Literature,* No.61 (1974), pp. 106–8.

SHIRNIAN, LORNE. "West Indians in Toronto." *Journal Of Canadian Fiction,* 2, No.4 (1973), 96–97.

SURVIVORS OF THE CROSSING (1964)

Reviews
WATMOUGH, DAVID. "Humour in Affliction." *Canadian Literature,* No.23 (1965), pp. 74–76.

WHEN HE WAS FREE AND YOUNG AND HE USED TO WEAR SILKS (1971)

Reviews
JEFFERS, KEITH. "Clarke: Promise & Insight With Flaws." *Black Images,* 1, No.1 (1972), 14.

CLARKE, MARCUS HISLOP (Australian, 1846–1881)

CHIDIOCK TICHBOURNE

WILDING, MICHAEL. "Marcus Clarke's *Chidiock Tichbourne." Australian Literary Studies,* 6 (1974), 381–93.

FOR THE TERM OF HIS NATURAL LIFE (1874)

ARGYLE, BARRY. *An Introduction To The Australian Novel, 1830-1930,* pp. 118–47.

BOEHM, HAROLD J. "*His Natural Life* and its Sources." *Australian Literary Studies,* 5 (1971), 42–64.

_____ . "The Pattern of *His Natural Life:* Conflict, Imagery, and Theme as Elements of Structure." *Journal Of Commonwealth Literature,* 7, No.1 (1972), 57–71.

BURROWS, J. F. "*His Natural Life* and the Capacities of Melodrama." *Southern Review: Literary And Interdisciplinary Essays,* 34 (1974), 280–301.

DENHOLM, DECIE. "The Sources of *His Natural Life." Australian Literary Studies,* 4 (1969), 174–78.

HERGENHAN, L. T. "The Contemporary Reception of *His Natural Life." Southern Review: Literary And Interdisciplinary Essays,* 31 (1971), 50–63.

_____ . "The Corruption of Rufus Dawes." *Southern Review: Literary And Interdisciplinary Essays,* 29 (1969), 211–21.

_____ . "The Redemptive Theme in *His Natural Life." Australian Literary Studies,* 2 (1965), 32–49.

NESBITT, BRUCE. "Marcus Clarke, 'Damned Scamp.' " *Australian Literary Studies,* 5, (1971), 93–98.

PALMER, VANCE. "Marcus Clarke and His Critics," in *Twentieth Century Australian Literary Criticism,* ed. Clement Semmler, pp. 167–69.

POOLE, JOAN. " 'Damned Scamp': Marcus Clarke or James Erskine Calder?" *Australian Literary Studies,* 6 (1974), 423–28.

_____ . "Marcus Clarke: 'Christianity is Dead.' " *Australian Literary Studies,* 6 (1973), 128–42.

_____ . "Maurice Frere's Wife: Marcus Clarke's Revision of *His Natural Life." Australian Literary Studies,* 4(1970), 383–94.

ROBERTSON, R. T. "Form Into Shape: *His Natural Life* and *Capricornia* in a Commonwealth Context." *Journal of Canadian Fiction,* 3, No.4 (1975), 45–51.

STEWART, ANNETTE. "The Design of *For The Term Of His Natural Life." Australian Literary Studies,* 6 (1974), 394–403.

Reviews
POOLE, JOAN. "A Full Life." *Overland,* No.47 (1971), pp. 50–51.

HIS NATURAL LIFE see FOR THE TERM OF HIS NATURAL LIFE

LONG ODDS (1869)

STUART, LURLINE. "Marcus Clarke: *Long Odds* and the 1873 Melbourne Cup." *Australian Literary Studies,* 6 (1974), 422–23.

CLAVEL, BERNARD (French, 1923–)

THE FRUITS OF WINTER (Les fruits de l'hiver, 1968)

Reviews
LESAGE, LAURENT. *Saturday Review,* 29 November 1969, pp. 52–53.

COCCIOLI, CARLO (Italian, 1920–)

THE STRINGS OF THE HARP (Le corde dell' arpa, 1967)

FONDA, CARLO. "Narcissus' Complex: A Critico-psychological Interpretation of Carlo Coccioli's *The Strings Of The Harp." Italian Quarterly,* 15, No.58/9 (1971), 17–57.

THE WHITE STONE (Le Caillou blanc, 1958)

STALEY, THOMAS F. "A Novelist's Vision: Carlo Coccioli." *Commonweal,* 83 (1965), 95–98.

COCTEAU, JEAN (French, 1889–1963)

ENFANTS TERRIBLES (Les Enfants terribles, 1929)

ROUDLEZ, LEON S. "Cocteau's *Les Enfants Terribles* As a Blind Text." *Mosaic,* 5, No.3 (1972), 159–66.

LE POTOMAK (1919)

O'BRIEN, JUSTIN. " 'Paludes' and 'Le Potomak,' " in his *Contemporary French Literature,* pp. 245–64.

COFIÑO LÓPEZ, MANUEL
LA ÚLTIMA MUJER Y EL PRÓXIMO COMBATE (1971)

Reviews

NAVARRO, CARLOS. *Latin American Literary Review,* 1, No.1 (1972), 121–23.

SCHWARTZ, KESSEL. *Hispania,* 56 (1973), 182–83.

COHEN, LEONARD (Canadian, 1934–)
GENERAL

ALMANSI, G. "An Erotic Writer: the 'Minestrone' Novels of Leonard Cohen." *London Magazine,* NS, 15, No.3 (1975), 20–39.

DJWA, SANDRA. "Leonard Cohen: Black Romantic." *Canadian Literature,* No.34 (1967), pp. 39–42.

PURDY, A. W. "Leonard Cohen: A Personal Look." *Canadian Literature,* No.23 (1965), pp. 7–16.

BEAUTIFUL LOSERS (1966)

ALMANSI, G. "An Erotic Writer: The 'Minestrone' Novels of Leonard Cohen." *London Magazine,* 15 No.3 (1975), 28–39.

HUTCHEON, LINDA. "*Beautiful Losers:* All the Polarities." *Canadian Literature,* No.59 (1974), pp. 42–56.

JONES, D. G. *Butterfly On Rock,* pp. 77–82.

MACRI, F. M. "*Beautiful Losers* and the Canadian Experience." *Journal Of Commonwealth Literature,* 8, No.1 (1973), 88–96.

MONKMAN, LESLIE. "*Beautiful Losers:* Mohawk Myth and Jesuit Legend." *Journal Of Canadian Fiction,* 3, No.3 (1974), 57–59.

MORLEY, PATRICIA A. *The Immoralists: Hugh MacLennan And Leonard Cohen,* pp. 85–96.

PACEY, DESMOND. "The Phenomenon of Leonard Cohen." *Canadian Literature,* No.34 (1967), pp. 5–23; rpt. in his *Essays In Canadian Criticism, 1938–1968,* pp. 241–67.

SCOBIE, STEPHEN. "Magic, Not Magicians: 'Beautiful Losers' and 'Story of O.' " *Canadian Literature,* No.45 (1970), pp. 56–60.

Reviews

GOSE, E. B. "Of Beauty and Unmeaning." *Canadian Literature,* No.29 (1966), pp. 61–63.

THE DISINHERITED

Reviews

BAKER, JANET. *Dalhousie Review,* 54 (1974), 576–77.

MITCHELL, ADRIAN. "Getting the Voices Right." *Canadian Literature,* No.62 (1974), pp. 88–89.

PORTER, HELEN. "Cohen's Generations." *Journal Of Canadian Fiction,* 4, No.1 (1975), 187–89.

THE FAVOURITE GAME (1963)

MORLEY, PATRICIA A. *The Immoral Moralists: Hugh MacLennan And Leonard Cohen,* pp. 73–83.

————. " 'The Knowledge of Strangerhood': 'The Monuments' were *Made* of Worms." *Journal Of Canadian Fiction,* 3, No.3 (1972), 56–60.

PACEY, DESMOND. "The Phenomenon of Leonard Cohen." *Canadian Literature,* No.34 (1967), pp. 9–15; rpt. in his *Essays In Canadian Criticism, 1938–1968,* pp. 249–56.

JOHNNY CRACKLE SINGS

Reviews

ATHERTON, STAN. "Snap Crackle Pop." *Journal Of Canadian Fiction,* 1, No.1 (1972), 87–88.

COLE, ROBERT
KOSSOH TOWN BOY

CARTEY, WILFRED. *Whispers From A Continent,* pp. 20–23.

COLETTE, GABRIELLE CLAUDINE (French, 1873–1954), pseudonym of Colette, Sidonie Gabrielle
JULIE DE CARNEILHAN (1941)

SPRINGER, MARY DOYLE. *Forms Of The Modern Novella,* pp. 132–37.

THE PURE AND THE IMPURE (Le pur et l'impur, 1932)

Reviews

KOCH, STEPHEN. "Colette: Chronicler of the Erotic." *Saturday Review,* 20 September 1975, pp. 30–32.

RETREAT FROM LOVE (La retraite sentimentale, 1907)

Reviews

MARKHAM, CHARLES LAM. "Two Eves in Eden." *Saturday Review,* 13 July 1974, pp. 20–21.

RIPENING SEED (Le blé en herbe, 1923)

FISCHLER, ALEXANDER. "Unity in Colette's *Le Ble En Herbe.*" *Modern Language Quarterly,* 30 (1969), 248–64.

Reviews

KOCH, STEPHEN. "Colette: Chronicler of the Erotic." *Saturday Review,* 20 September 1975, pp. 30–32.

THE VAGABOND (La Vagabonde, 1910)

Reviews

KOCH, STEPHEN. "Colette: Chronicler of the Erotic." *Saturday Review,* 20 September 1975, pp. 30–32.

COLETTE, Sidonie Gabrielle see COLETTE, Gabrielle Claudine

CONNOR, RALPH (Canadian, 1860–1937), pseudonym of Charles William Gordan
THE FOREIGNER

STITCH, K. P. "Tom Brown and the Canadian West." *Journal Of Commonwealth Literature,* 10, No.1 (1975), 53–57.

GLENGARRY SCHOOLDAYS (1902)

BASSETT, ISABEL. "The Transformation of Imperialism: Connor to MacLennan." *Journal Of Canadian Fiction,* 2, No.1 (1973), 58–63.

MAJOR

BASSETT, ISABEL. "The Transformation of Imperialism: Connor to MacLennan." *Journal Of Canadian Fiction,* 2, No.1 (1973), 58–62.

THE MAN FROM GLENGARRY (1901)

DANIELLS, ROY. "Glengarry Revisited." *Canadian Literature,* No.31 (1967), pp. 45–33.

CONSTANT, BENJAMIN (French, 1767–1830)
GENERAL

COURTNEY, C. P. "Alexander Walker and Benjamin Constant: A Note on the English Translator of *Adolphe.*" *French Studies,* 29 (1975), 137–50.

ADOLPHE (1816)

AKMATOVA, ANNA. "Benjamin Constant's *Adolphe* in the Work of Pushkin." *Russian Literature Triquarterly,* No.10, pp. 157–79.

BAGULEY, DAVID. "The Role of Letters in Constant's *Adolphe.*" *Forum For Modern Language Studies,* 11 (1975), 29–35.

CALLEN, A. "L'Immoraliste as a Modern *Adolphe*." *Modern Language Quarterly*, 31 (1970), 450-60.

CASSILL, R. V. "On Benjamin Constant's *Adolpe*," in *Rediscoveries*, ed. David Madden, pp. 38-46.

FAIRLIE, ALISON. "The Art of Constant's *Adolphe*." *Forum For Modern Language Studies*, 2 (1966), 253-63.

———. "The Art of Constant's *Adolphe*: Structure and Style." *French Studies*, 20 (1966), 226-42.

———. "The Art of Constant's *Adolpe*: The Stylization of Experience." *Modern Language Review*, 62 (1967), 31-47.

———. "Constant's *Adolphe* read by Balzac and Nerval," in *Balzac And The Nineteenth Century*, pp. 209-24.

FRAUTSCHI, R. L. "Various Point of View in Benjamin Constant's *Adolphe*." *Kentucky Foreign Language Quarterly*, 12 (1965), 225-30.

GRESHOFF, C. J. "*Adolphe* and the Romantic Delusion." *Forum For Modern Language Studies*, 1 (1965), 30-36.

HOBSON, MARIAN. "Theme and Structure in 'Adolphe.'" *Modern Language Review*, 66 (1971), 306-14.

THOMAS, RUTH P. "The Ambiguous Narrator of *Adolphe*." *Romance Notes*, 14 (1973), 486-95.

TODOROV, TZVETAN. "The Discovery of Language: *Les Liaisons Dangereuses* and *Adolphe*." *Yale French Studies*, No.45 (1970), pp. 113-26.

CONSTANT, SAMUEL DE

MARI SENTIMENTAL OU LE MARIAGE COMME IL Y EN A QUELQUES-UNS

CLARKE, MARGARET. "Strindberg and Samuel de Constant: The Source of *The Father* and Strindbergian Sociology (1883-1887)." *Revue De Littérature Comparée*, 42 (1968), 583-96.

CONY, CARLOS HEITOR (Brazilian)

GENERAL

PARKER, JOHN M. "The Novels of Carlos Heitor Cony." *Luso-Brazilian Review*, 10 (1973), 163-86.

COONEY, TED

HOMAGE TO ANAIS

Reviews

RANA, FAROUK A. "From Disposable Diapers to Disposable Novel." *Journal Of Canadian Fiction*, 1, No.4 (1972), 97-98.

CORÇÃO, GUSTAVO

WHO IF I CRY OUT (Lições de Abismo, 1962)

WILSON, CLOTILDE. "Rilke and Corção." *Luso-Brazilian Review*, 7, No.1 (1970), 74-80.

CORTÁZAR, JULIO (Argentinian, 1914-1984)

GENERAL

ALONSO, J. M. "Cortázar, Borges and the Loss of Experience." *Review*, No.7 (1972), pp. 14-17.

CASTRO-KLAREN, SARA. "Cortázar, Surrealism, and 'Pataphysics.'" *Comparative Literature*, 27 (1975), 218-36.

GARFIELD, EVELYN PICON. "'The Exquisite Cadaver of Surrealism.'" *Review*, No.7 (1972), pp. 18-21.

HOLSTEN, KEN. "Three Characters and a Theme in Cortazar." *Revista De Estudios Hispánicos*, 9 (1975), 119-29.

"Interview/Julio Cortázar." *Diacritics*, 4, No.4 (1974), 35-40.

MACADAM, ALFRED J., comp. "Cortázar on Cortázar: A Literary Chronology." *Review*, No.7 (1972), pp. 35-41.

MÉRAS, PHYLLIS. "The Author." *Saturday Review*, 22 July 1967, p. 36.

CRONOPIOS AND FAMAS (Historias de cronopios y de famas, 1962)

Reviews

BISHOP, TOM. *Saturday Review*, 27 September 1969, pp. 26-27; rpt. in: *Review*, No.2 (1969), pp. 75-77.

BRYAN, C. D. B. *New York Times Book Review*, 15 June 1969; rpt. in: *Review*, No.2 (1969), pp. 77-80.

KLAIDMAN, STEPHEN. *International Herald Tribune*, 23 July 1969; rpt. in: *Review*, No.2 (1969), pp. 80-82.

MADDOCKS, MELVIN. *Atlantic Monthly*, June 1969; rpt. in: *Review*, No.2 (1969), pp. 82-86.

MILLAR, NEIL. *Christian Science Monitor*, 3 July 1969; rpt. in *Review*, No.2 (1969), pp. 86-88.

Time, 13 June 1969; rpt. in: *Review*, No.2 (1969), pp. 88-89.

WEST, PAUL. *Book World*, 17 August 1969; rpt. in: *Review*, No.2 (1969), pp. 89-90.

HOPSCOTCH (Rayuela, 1963)

BRODY, ROBERT. "Stream-of-Consciousness Techniques in Cortázar's *Rayuela*." *Symposium*, 29 (1975), 48-56.

BRUSHWOOD, JOHN S. *The Spanish American Novel*, pp. 249-53.

FOSTER, DAVID WILLIAM. *Currents In The Contemporary Argentine Novel*, pp. 99-127.

GARFIELD, EVELYN PICON. *Julio Cortázar*, pp. 90-115.

HOLSTEIN, KEN. "Three Characters and a Theme in Cortazar." *Revista De Estudios Hispánicos*, 9 (1975), 125-29.

IRBY, JAMES E. "Cortázar's Hopscotch and Other Games." *Novel*, 1, (1967), 64-70.

RODRIGUEZ, MONEGAL, EMIR. "The New Novelties." *Encounter*, 25, No.3 (1965), 100-2.

SERVODIDIO, MIRELLA D'AMBROSIO. "Facticity and Transcendence in Cortázar's *Rayuela*." *Journal Of Spanish Studies*, 2 (1974), 49-57.

TAYLOR, ANNA MARIE. "The 'Desdoblamiento' of Oliviera and Traveler in *Rayuela*." *Chasqui*, 1 No.3 (1972), 36-40.

Reviews

CAPOUYA, EMILE. "World Citizens Without a Country." *Saturday Review*, 9 April 1966, p. 34.

FUENTES, CARLOS. "A Demanding Novel." *Commentary*, 42, No.4 (1966), 142-43.

A MANUAL FOR MANUEL (Libro de Manuel, 1973)

FOSTER, DAVID WILLIAM. *Currents In The Contemporary Argentine Novel*, pp. 131-33.

GARFIELD, EVELYN PICON. *Julio Cortázar*, pp. 132-40.

VALENTINE, ROBERT Y. "The Artist's Quest for Freedom in *Libro De Manuel*." *Chasqui*, 3, No.2 (1974), 62-74.

Reviews

SCHWARTZ, KESSEL. *Hispania*, 58 (1975), 234-35.

62: A MODEL KIT (62: Modelo para armar, 1968)

BRYAN, C. D. B. "The Deluxe Model." *Review*, No.7 (1972), pp. 32-34.

GARFIELD, EVELYN PICON. *Julio Cortázar*, pp. 115-31.

GYURKO, LANIN A. "Identity and Fate in Cortázar's *62: Modelo Para Armar*." *Symposium*, 27 (1973), 214-34.

THE WINNERS (Los premios, 1960)

GARFIELD, EVELYN PICON. *Julis Cortázar*, pp. 80-89.

Reviews

CAPOUYA, EMILE. "Passenger List for Limbo." *Saturday Review*, 27 March 1965, p. 29.

COSSÍO WOODWARD, MIGUEL (Cuban, 1938-)

SACCHARIO (1970)

MENTON, SEYMOUR. *Prose Fiction Of The Cuban Revolution,* pp. 114-18.

Reviews
SCHWARTZ, KESSEL. *Hispania,* 55 (1972), 186.

COVIN, KELLY

MANY BROKEN HAMMERS

Reviews
BROWN, RUSSELL M. "Expatriate Variations." *Canadian Literature,* No.54 (1972), pp. 93-94.

COWAN, PETER (Australian, 1914-)

SEED (1966)

GREEN, DOROTHY. "Seed on Stony Ground: Peter Cowan's New Novel." *Meanjin,* 25 (1966), 480-84.

Reviews
WHITLOCK, DEREK. *Southern Review: Literary and Interdisciplinary Essays,* 26 (1966), 283-84.

COWASJEE, SAROS (Indian, 1931-)

GOODBYE TO ELSA (1974)

Reviews
MITCHELL, ADRIAN. "Getting the Voices Right." *Canadian Literature,* No.62 (1974), pp. 87-88.

MOORE, LILA. *Literature East And West,* 17 (1973), 450-54.

MURAD, ORLENE. *International Fiction Review,* 1 (1974), 151-52.

RUTHERFORD, ANNA. *World Literature Written In English,* 14 (1975), 427.

ZINKHAN, E. J. "The Tale of Tristan Elliott." *Journal Of Canadian Fiction,* 3, No.3 (1974), 97-98.

COWLEY, JOY (New Zealander, 1936-)

NEST IN A FALLING TREE (1967)

Reviews
EASTON, ELIZABETH. "Garden Made Eden." *Saturday Review,* 26 August 1967, p. 32.

CRÉBILLON, CLAUDE-PROSPER-JOLYOT (French, 1707-1777)

LES HEUREUX ORPHELINS

KENT, JOHN P. "Crebillon fils, Mrs. Eliza Haywood and *Les Heureux Orphelins:* A Problem of Authorship." *Romance Notes,* 11 (1969), 326-32.

MYLINE, VIVIENNE. *The Eighteenth Century French Novel,* pp. 140-43.

LETTERS FROM THE MARCHIONESS DE M*** TO THE COUNT DE R*** (Lettres de la Marquise de M *** au Comte de R***, 1732)

MYLNE, VIVIENNE. *The Eighteenth Century French Novel,* pp. 156-62.

LETTRES DE LA DUCHESSE DE *** AU DUC DE *** (1768)

MYLNE, VIVIENNE. *The Eighteenth Century French Novel,* pp. 162-65.

THE SOFA: A MORAL TALE (Le Sopha: Conte moral, 1740)

DOBRÉE, BONAMY. "Crébillon Fils: *The Sofa: A Moral Tale,"* in her *Milton To Ouida,* pp. 105-15.

THE WANDERINGS OF HEART AND MIND (Les egarements du coeur et de l'esprit)

BROOKS, PETER. *The Novel Of Worldliness,* pp. 11-35.

MYLNE, VIVIENNE. *The Eighteenth Century French Novel,* pp. 125-40.

CREVEL, RENÉ (French, 1900-1935)

BABYLONE (1927)

MATTHEWS, J. H. *Surrealism And The Novel,* pp. 61-67.

CRICK, DONALD HERBERT (Australian, 1916-)

PERIOD OF ADJUSTMENT (1966)

Reviews
WHITELOCK, DEREK. *Southern Review: Literary And Interdisciplinary Essays,* 26 (1966), 282-83.

CRUZ, JOSEFINA

EL VINETO SOBRE EL RÍO

TUCKER, SCOTTI MAE. "An Argentine 'Gone With The Wind.'" *Hispania,* 50 (1967), 69-73.

CONQUEIRO, ÁLVARO (Spanish, 1911-)

LAS MOCEDADES DE ULISES (1960)

Reviews
FLIGHTNER, JAMES A. *Hispania,* 54 (1971), 971-72.

UN HOMBRE QUE SE PARECÍA A ORESTES (1969)

Reviews
KRONIK, JOHN W. *Hispania,* 53 (1970), 152.

CUSACK, DYMPHNA (Australian, 1902-)

GENERAL

STIRLING, MONICA. "Dymphna Cusack: A Profile." *Meanjin,* 24 (1965), 317-25.

CUTT, W. TOWRIE (Canadian, 1898-)

MESSAGE FROM ARKMAE (1972)

Reviews
FRAZER, FRANCES. "Mermen and Hybrids." *Canadian Literature,* No.62 (1974), 118-19.

CYRANO DE BERGERAC, SAVINIEN (French, 1619-1655)

L'AUTRE MONDE

NEEFS, JACQUES. "Cyrano 'Des Miracles de Rivière.'" *Yale French Studies,* No.49 (1973), pp. 195-96.

VAN BAELEN, JACQUELINE. "Reality and Illusion in 'L'Autre Monde': The Narrative Voyage." *Yale French Studies,* No.49 (1973), pp. 178-84.

ETATS ET EMPIRES DE LA LUNE ET DU SOLEIL

LAUGAA, MAURICE. "Cyrano: Sound and Language." *Yale French Studies,* No.49 (1973), pp. 199-211.

D

DABROWSKA, MARIA (Polish, 1889–1965)
NIGHTS AND DAYS (1927–1934)

FOLEJEWSKI, ZBIGNIEW. *Maria Dabrowska*, pp. 37–78.

DADIÉ, BERNARD (Ivory Coast, 1916–)
CLIMBIE (1956)

GLEASON, JUDITH ILLSLEY. *This Africa*, pp. 17–22.

Reviews
JOYAUX, GEORGES J. *African Studies Review*, 15 (1972), 319–22.
PESHKIN, ALAN. *Conch Review Of Books*, 3, No.2–4 (1975), 87.

UN NÈGRE À PARIS (1956)

BRENCH, A. C. *The Novelists' Inheritance In French Africa*, pp. 86–91.

SHELTON, AUSTIN J. "Cultural Reversal as a Motif of Protest by Laye and Dadié." *L'Esprit Créateur*, 10 (1970), 217–22.

DAGERMAN, STIG (Swedish, 1923–1954)
VÅR NATTLIGA BADORT ___

THOMPSON, L. A. "Stig Dagerman's 'Vår nattliga badort': An Interpretation." *Scandinavica*, 13 (1974), 117–27.

DALAL, NERGIS (Indian, 1920–)
THE SISTERS (1973)

Reviews
POTTER, NANCY. *World Literature Written In English*, 14 (1975), 423.

DALVI, JAYAVANT
CAKRA

APTE, MAHADEO L. "Contemporary Marathi Fiction: Obscenity or Realism?" *Journal Of Asian Studies*, 29 (1969), 62–66.

DANDIN (Sanskrit, ca. 7th century A.D.)
GENERAL

SINGH, MAAN. "Dandin's Method of Narration." *Triveni*, 44, No.3 (1975), 34–39.

DANIEL, Stephanus Petrus see LEROUX, Étienne

D'ANNUNZIO, GABRIEL (Italian, 1863–1938)
GENERAL

MAIXNER, PAUL. "James on D'Annunzio—'A High Example of Exclusive Estheticism." *Criticism*, 13 (1971), 291–311.

THE CHILD OF PLEASURE (Il piacere, 1889)

GULLACE, GIOVANNI. *Gabriele D'Annunzio In France*, pp. 11–15.
JULLIAN, PHILIPE. *D'Annunzio*, pp. 60–67.

THE FLAME OF LIFE (Il fuoco, 1900)

GULLACE, GIOVANNI. *Gabriele D'Annunzio In France*, pp. 31–36.

FORSE CHE SÌ FORSE CHE NO (1910)

GULLACE, GIOVANNI. *Gabriele D'Annunzio In France*, pp. 38–40.

THE INTRUDER (L'innocente, 1892)

GULLACE, GIOVANNI. *Gabriele D'Annunzio In France*, pp. 1–8.

THE MAIDENS OF THE ROCKS (Vergini delle rocce, 1896)

GULLACE, GIOVANNI. *Gabriele D'Annunzio In France*, pp. 25–30.
JULLIAN, PHILIPPE. *D'Annunzio*, pp. 96–99.

THE TRIUMPH OF DEATH (Il trionfo della morte, 1894)

GULLACE, GIOVANNI. *Gabriele D'Annunzio In France*, pp. 16–18.

DARIEN, GEORGE
BIRIBI

REDFERN, W. D. "Exile and Exaggeration: George Darien's *Biribi*." *Mosaic*, No.3 (1975), 161–75.

DARÍO, RUBÉN (Nicaraguan, 1867–1916)
EMELINA (1887) with Eduardo Poirer

TILLES, SOLOMON H. "Ruben Dario's 'Emelina.' " *Hispania*, 49 (1966), 218–22.

DATHORNE, OSCAR RONALD (Guyanese, 1934–)
THE SCHOLAR MAN (1964)

Reviews
O. A. *Black Orpheus*, No.18 (1965), pp. 62–63.

DAUDET, ALPHONSE (French, 1840–1897)
GENERAL

POWERS, LYALL H. "James's Debt To Alphonse Daudet." *Comparative Literature*, 24 (1972), 150-62.

SACHS, MURRAY. "Alphonse Daudet's Tartarin Trilogy." *Modern Language Review*, 61 (1966), 209-17.

FROMONT THE YOUNGER AND RISLER THE ELDER (Fromont jeune et Risler aîné, 1874)

SACHS MURRAY. *The Career Of Alphonse Daudet*, pp. 83-96.

KINGS IN EXILE (Le rois en exil, 1879)

SACHS, MURRAY. *The Career Of Alphonse Daudet*, pp. 111-18.

THE LITTLE PARISH CHURCH (La petite paroisse, 1895)

SACHS MURRAY. *The Career Of Alphonse Daudet*, pp. 160-64.

MY BROTHER JACK (Le petit chose, 1868)

SACHS, MURRAY. *The Career Of Alphonse Daudet*, pp. 50-58.

THE NABOB (Le nabab, 1877)

SACHS, MURRAY. *The Career Of Alphonse Daudet*, pp. 103-13.

THE NEW DON QUIXOTE (Les aventures prodigieuses de Tartarin de Tarascon, 1872)

SACHS, MURRAY. "Alphonse Daudet's Tartarin Trilogy." *Modern Language Review*, 61 (1966), 209-13.

———. *The Career Of Alphonse Daudet*, pp. 65-72.

NUNA ROUMESTAN

SACHS, MURRAY. *The Career Of Alphonse Daudet*, pp. 119-21.

ONE OF THE "FORTY" (L'immortel, 1888)

SACHS, MURRAY. *The Career Of Alphonse Daudet*, pp. 143-47.

PORT TARASCON (Port-Tarascon, 1890)

SACHS, MURRAY. *The Career Of Alphonse Daudet*, pp. 148-52.

SAPPHO (Sapho, 1884)

SACHS, MURRAY. *The Career Of Alphonse Daudet*, pp. 130-35.

TARTARIN ON THE ALPS (Tartarin sur les Alpes, 1885)

SACHS, MURRAY. *The Career Of Alphonse Daudet*, pp. 136-40.

DAVIES, (WILLIAM) ROBERTSON (Canadian, 1913-)

GENERAL

McPHERSON, HUGO. "The Mask of Satire: "Character and Symbolic Pattern in Robertson Davies' Fiction," in *A Choice Of Critics*, ed. George Woodcock, pp. 233-47.

WARWICK, ELLEN D. "The Transformation of Robertson Davies." *Journal Of Canadian Fiction*, 3, No.3 (1974), 46-51.

FIFTH BUSINESS (1970)

BJERRING, NANCY E. "Deep in the Old Man's Puzzle." *Canadian Literature*, No.62 (1974), pp. 49-60.

CUDE, WILFRED. "Miracle and Art in Fifth Business or Who the Devil is Liselotte Vitzlipützli?" *Journal Of European Studies*, 9, No.4 (1974). 3-16.

ROPER, GORDON. "Robertson Davies' *Fifth Business* and 'That Old Fantastical Duke of Dark Corners', C. G. Jung." *Journal Of Canadian Fiction*, 1, No.1 (1972). 33-39.

WARWICK, ELLEN D. "The Transformation of Robertson Davies." *Journal Of Canadian Fiction*, 3, No.3 (1974), 46-50.

WEBSTER, DAVID. "Uncanny Correspondences: Synchronicity in *Fifth Business* and *The Manticore*." *Journal Of Canadian Fiction*, 3, No.3 (1974), 52-56.

Reviews

DOBBS, KILDARE. "Fifth Business." *Tamarack Review*, No.57 (1971), pp. 76-80.

HALL, W. F. "The Real and the Marvelous." *Canadian Literature*, No.49 (1971), pp. 80-81.

O'HARA, J. D. *Saturday Review*, 26 December 1970, pp. 25-26.

THE MANTICORE (1972)

WEBSTER, DAVID. "Uncanny Correspondences: Synchronicity in *Fifth Business* and *The Manticore*." *Journal Of Canadian Fiction*, 3, No.3 (1974), 52-56.

Reviews

BARCLAY, PAT. "Noble and Confused." *Canadian Literature*, No.56 (1973), pp. 113-14.

BEVAN, ALLAN. *Dalhousie Review*, 53 (1973), 163-65.

DYMENT, MARGARET. "Romantic Ore." *Journal Of Canadian Fiction*, 2, No.1 (1973), 83-84.

TEMPEST-TOST (1951)

McPHERSON, HUGO. "The Mask of Satire: Character and Symbolic Pattern in Robertson Davies' Fiction," in *A Choice Of Critics*, ed. George Woodcock, pp. 237-41.

DAVIS, JOHN GORDON

HOLD MY HAND, I'M DYING

Reviews

MILLER, CHARLES. "UDI-Past, Present and Future." *Saturday Review*. 19 October 1968. pp. 33, 53.

DAVISON, FRANK DALBY (Australian, 1893-1970)

GENERAL

HESELTINE, H. P. "The Fellowship of All Flesh: The Fiction of Frank Dalby Davison." *Meanjin*, 27 (1968), 275-90.

WEBSTER, OWEN. "The Crown Lands Ranger: Jack Cumming and Frank Dalby Davison." *Overland*, No.61 (1975), pp. 7-13.

THE WHITE THORNTREE

DAVISON, FRANK DALBY. "Testimony of a Veteran." *Southern Review: Literary And Interdisciplinary Essays*, 29 (1969), 83-92.

HESELTINE, H. P. "The Fellowship of All Flesh: The Fiction of Frank Dalby Davison." *Meanjin*, 27 (1968), 284-90.

Reviews

WEBSTER, OWEN. "Eros Malevolent." *Overland*, No.40 (1968), pp. 34-35.

WILKES, G. A. *Southern Review: Literary And Interdisciplinary Essays*, 29 (1969), 153-56.

DAWES, NEVILLE (Nigerian-born Ghanian, 1926-)

THE LAST ENCHANTMENT (1970)

MOORE, GERALD. *The Chosen Tongue*, pp. 46-48.

DAY, FRANK PARKER (Canadian)

ROCKBOUND

Reviews

HORWOOD, HAROLD. "Rockbound: Realism in Early Canadian Fiction." *Journal Of Canadian Fiction*, 3, No.4 (1975), 85-86.

DAYAN, YAEL (Israeli, 1939-)

DEATH HAD TWO SONS (1967)

KRESH, PAUL. "Fate's Choice." *Saturday Review,* 16 December 1967, pp. 31–32.

DAZAI OSAMU (Japanese, 1909–1948)
GENERAL

BRUDNOY, DAVID. "The Immutable Despair of Dazai Osamu." *Monumenta Nipponica,* 23 (1968), 457–74.

LYONS, PHYLLIS I. "Women in the Life and Art of Dazai Osamu." *Literature East and West,* 18 (1974), 44–57.

O'BRIEN, JAMES A. "Dazai Osamu: Comic Writer." *Critique,* 12, No.1 (1970), 79–86.

NO LONGER HUMAN (Ningen Shikkaku, 1948)

HIJIYA,, YUKIHITO. "A Religion of Humanity: A Study of Osamu Dazai's *No Longer Human.*" *Critique,* 15, No.3 (1974), 34–42.

O'BRIEN, JAMES A. *Dazai Osamu,* pp. 141–47.

THE SETTING SUN (Shayō, 1947)

LYONS, PHYLLIS I. "Women in the Life and Art of Dazai Osamu." *Literature East and West,* 18 (1974), 53–56.

MIYOSHI, MASAO. *Accomplices Of Silence,* pp. 131–39.

O'BRIEN, JAMES A. *Dazai Osamu,* pp. 134–41.

DEBOISSIÈRE, RALPH (Australian, 1907–)
GENERAL

BIRBALSINGH, F. M. "The Novels of Ralph DeBoissière." *Journal Of Commonwealth Literature,* No.9 (1970), pp. 104–8.

DE BOOS, CHARLES
FIFTY YEARS AGO

HEALY, J. J. "The Treatment of the Aborigine in Early Australian Fiction, 1840–70." *Australian Literary Studies,* 5 (1972), 246–53.

DE KERPELEY, THERESA
GENERAL

JUNKINS, DONALD. "The Novels of Theresa de Kerpely." *Critique,* 13, No.1 (1970), 48–58.

BLACK NIGHTSHADE

JUNKINS, DONALD. "The Novels of Theresa de Kerpely." *Critique,* 13, No.1 (1970), 53–57.

DE LA ROCHE, MAZO (Canadian, 1885–1961)
GENERAL

DAYMOND, DOUGLAS M. "Whiteoak Chronicles: A Reassessment." *Canadian Literature,* No.66 (1975), pp. 48–62.

LIVESAY, DOROTHY. "The Making of Jalna: A Reminiscence." *Canadian Literature,* No.23 (1965), pp. 25–30.

SNELL, J. G. "The United States at Jalna." *Canadian Literature,* No.66 (1975), pp. 31–40.

DELIGHT (1926)

HENDRICK, GEORGE. *Mazo De La Roche,* pp. 51–55.

GROWTH OF A MAN (1938)

DAYMOND, DOUGLAS M. "Mazo de la Roche's Forgotten Novel." *Journal Of Canadian Fiction,* 3, No.2 (1974), 55–59.

JALNA (1927)

HENDRICK, GEORGE. *Mazo De La Roche,* pp. 61–65.

LARK ASCENDING (1932)

HENDRICK, GEORGE. *Mazo De La Roche,* pp. 119–25.

MORNING AT JALNA (1960)

HENDRICK, GEORGE. *Mazo De La Roche,* pp. 71–74.

POSSESSION (1923)

DAYMOND, DOUGLAS M. "*Possession:* Realism in Mazo de la Roche's First Novel." *Journal Of Canadian Fiction,* 4, No.3 (1975), 87–94.

HENDRICK, GEORGE. *Mazo De La Roche,* pp. 46–49.

DE LASALE, ANTOINE
PETIT JEHAN DE SAINTRÉ

CHAMPAGNE, ROLAND. "Le Roman du Texte: A Response to Julia Kristeva's Reading of Antoine de LaSale's *Petit Jehan De Saintré.*" *Sub-Stance,* No.4 (1972), pp. 125–33.

SPEER, MARY B. "The Literary Fortune of the *Petit Jehan De Saintré.*" *Kentucky Romance Quarterly,* 22 (1975), 385–411.

DELBLANC, SVEN (Swedish, 1931–)
HOMUNCULUS (1965)

SJÖBERG, LEIF. "Delblanc's *Homunculus:* Some Magic Elements." *Germanic Review,* 49 (1974), 105–24.

VOWLES, RICHARD B. "Myth in Sweden: Sven Delblanc's *Homunculus.*" *Books Abroad,* 48 (1974), 20–25.

DELBO, CHARLOTTE
PHANTOMS, MY COMPANIONS

LAMONT, ROSETTE C. "Literature, the Exile's Agent of Survival: Alexander Solzhenitsyn and Charlotte Delbo." *Mosaic,* 9, No.1 (1975), 7–11.

DEL CABRAL, MANUEL (Dominican)
EL PRESIDENTE NEGRO

Reviews
ECHEVARRÍA, EVELLO. *Latin American Literary Review,* 3, No.5 (1974), 164–65.

DEL CASTILLO, MICHEL (Spanish-born, writes in French, 1933–)
THE SEMINARIAN

Reviews
CLEMENTS, ROBERT J. *Saturday Review,* 30 May 1970, pp. 30–31.

PEISSOW, HENRY. "Scorched Flesh." *Catholic World,* 212 (1971), 162.

DELEDDA, GRAZIA (Italian, 1875–1936)
GENERAL

GREGOR, D. B. "Polychrome in Grazia Deledda." *Modern Languages,* 51 (1970), 160–66.

PACIFICI, SERGIO. *The Modern Italian Novel: From Capuana To Tozzi,* pp. 86–97.

THE MOTHER (La Madre, 1920)

McCORMICK, E. ALLEN. "Grazia Deledda's *La Madre* and the Problem of Tragedy." *Symposium,* 22 (1968), 62–71.

DELIBES, MIGUEL (Spanish, 1920–)
GENERAL

DíAZ, JANET WINECOFF. "Miguel Delibes' Vision of Castilla." *South Atlantic Bulletin,* 36, No.3 (1971), 56–63.

HANDELSMAN, MICHAEL H. "Environmental Concerns in Miguel Delibes." *South Atlantic Bulletin,* 40, No.4 (1975), 61–66.

CINCO HORAS CON MARIO (1966)

Reviews
RIVAS, JOSEFA. *Hispania,* 51 (1968), 370.

PARÁBOLA DEL NÁUFRAGO (1969)

Reviews
DíAZ, JANET W. *Hispania,* 53 (1970), 1024.

EL PRINCIPE DESTRONADO (1973)

Reviews
DíAZ, JANET W. *Hispania,* 58 (1975), 401-2.

SMOKE ON THE GROUND (Las ratas, 1962)

EWING, DOROTHY. "The Religious Significance of Miguel Delibes' *Las Ratas.*" *Romance Notes,* 11 (1970), 492-97.

DEL PASO, FERNANDO

JOSÉ TRIGO

ORRANTIA, DAGOBERTO. "The Function of Myth in Fernando del Paso's *José Trigo,*" in *Tradition and Renewal,* ed. Merlin H. Forster, pp. 129-38.

DELICADO, FRANCISCO (Spanish, early 16th century)

LA LOZANA ANDALUZA

DAMIANI, BRUNO M. "Delicado and Aretino: Aspects of a Literary Profile." *Kentucky Romance Quarterly,* 17 (1970), 309-24.

PIKE, RUTH. "The *Conversos* in *La Lozana Andaluza.*" *MLN,* 84 (1969), 304-8.

Reviews
JONES, JOSEPH B. *Hispania,* 54 (1971), 968.

DELISSER, HERBERT G. (Jamaican, 1878-1944)

JANE'S CAREER (1913)

FIGUEROA, JOHN J. *"Jane's Career." World Literature Written In English,* 12, No.1 (1973), 97-105.

RAMCHAND, KENNETH. *The West Indian Novel And Its Background,* pp. 57-62.

Reviews
COOKE, MICHAEL G. "West Indian Picaresque." *Novel,* 7 (1973), 93-96.

DELMAS, CLAUDE

LE SCHOONER (1970)

Reviews
BAUER, GEORGE H. *French Review,* 46 (1972), 207-9.

DE MARCHI, EMILIO (Italian, 1851-1901)

GENERAL

PACIFICI, SERGIO. *The Modern Italian Novel: From Manzoni To Svevo,* pp. 73-78.

DEMÉLIER, JEAN

LE RÊVE DE JOB (1971)

Reviews
BROSMAN, CATHARINE SAVAGE. *French Review,* 46 (1973), 853-54.

DE MILLE, JAMES (Canadian, 1836-1880)

A STRANGE MANUSCRIPT FOUND IN A COPPER CYLINDER (1888)

KILIAN, CRAWFORD. "The Cheerful Inferno of James De Mille." *Journal Of Canadian Fiction,* 1, No.3 (1972), 61-67.

KIME, WAYNE R. "The American Antecedents of James De Mille's A Strange Manuscript Found in a Copper Cylinder." *Dalhousie Review,* 55 (1975), 280-306.

WOODCOCK, GEORGE. "De Mille and the Utopian Vision." *Journal Of Canadian Fiction,* 2, No.3 (1973), 174-79.

DER NISTER, (Yiddish, 1884-1950) pseudonym of Pinkhas Kahanovich

THE MASHBER FAMILY

REMINIK, HERSH. "Dostoevsky and Der Nister." *Soviet Studies In Literature,* 8 (1972), 410-19.

DE ROBERTO, FEDRICO (Italian, 1866-1927)

GENERAL

PACIFICI, SERGIO. *The Modern Italian Novel: From Manzoni To Svevo,* pp. 79-97.

THE VICEROYS (I Vicerè, 1894)

PACIFICI, SERGIO. *The Modern Italian Novel: From Manzoni To Svevo,* pp. 85-97.

DE ROUX, DOMINIQUE

MAISON JAUNE (1969)

Reviews
KNAPP, BETTINA L. *French Review,* 44 (1970), 422-23.

DÉRY, TIBOR (Hungarian, 1894-1977)

GENERAL

SANDERS, IVAN. "The Ironic Hungarian: Tibor Déry at Eighty." *Books Abroad,* 49 (1975), 12-18.

DESAI, ANITA (Indian, 1937-)

GENERAL

NARASIMHA, RAJ. "Desai Versus Desani: Norms of Appreciation." *Indian Literature,* 16, No.3/4 (1973), 180-84.

SRINIVASA IYENGAR, K. R. *Indian Writing In English,* pp. 464-70.

CRY, THE PEACOCK (1963)

SRINIVASA IYENGAR, K. R. *Indian Writing In English,* pp. 465-68.

DESANI, GOVINDAS VISHNOODAS (Indian, 1909-)

ALL ABOUT H. HATTERR (1951)

BANERJI, N. N. "G. V. Desani—The First Literary Beatnik of this Age." *Journal Of Indian Writing In English,* 1, No.2 (1973), 22-27.

BURJORJEE, D. M. "The Dialogue in G. V. Desani's *All About H. Hatterr.*" *World Literature Written In English,* 13 (1974), 191-224.

McCUTCHION, DAVID. "The Indian Novel in English." *Studies In The Novel,* 4 (1972), 315-19.

NARASIMHA, RAJ. "Desai Versus Desani: Norms of Appreciation." *Indian Literature,* 16, No.3/4 (1973), 180–84.

SRINIVASA IYENGAR, K. R. *Indian Writing In English,* pp. 489–93.

DESHUSSES, JÉRÔME

LA GRAND SOIR

Reviews
JOHNSON, PATRICIA J. *French Review,* 46 (1973), 1238–39.

DESNOES, EDMUNDO (Cuban, 1930–)

INCONSOLABLE MEMORIES (Memorias del subdesarrollo, 1965)

FERNANDEZ, HENRY, D. I. GROSSVOGEL and EMIR RODRIGUEZ MONEGAL. "3/ on 2: Desnoes, Gutiérrez Alea." *Diacritics,* 4, No.4 (1974), 51–64.

DESNOS, ROBERT (French, 1900–45)

GENERAL

CAWS, MARY ANN. "Robert Desnos and the Flasks of Night." *Yale French Studies,* No.50 (1974), pp. 108–19.

DEUIL POUR DEUIL (1924)

CAWS, MARY ANN. "Techniques of Alienation in the Early Novels of Robert Desnos." *Modern Language Quarterly,* 28 (1967), 473–77.

LA LIBERTÉ OU L'AMOUR! (1927)

CAWS, MARY ANN. "Techniques of Alienation in the Early Novels of Robert Desnoes." *Modern Language Quarterly,* 28 (1967), 473–77.

MATTHEWS, J. H. *Surrealism And The Novel,* pp. 67–73.

DESTOUCHES, Louis-Ferdinand see CÉLINE, Louis-Ferdinand

DEWDNEY, SELWYN (Canadian, 1909–)

WIND WITHOUT RAIN (1946)

Reviews
PARR, JOHN. "The Return of Selwyn Dewdney." *Journal Of Canadian Fiction,* 3, No.3 (1974), 102–4.

DHÔTEL, ANDRÉ (French, 1900–)

L'HONORABLE MONSIEUR JACQUES

Reviews
LEVINSKY, RUTH. *French Review,* 47 (1973), 224–25.

DÍAZ RODRÍGUEZ, MANUEL (Venezuelan, 1868–1927)

SANGRE PATRICIA (1902)

DEBICKI, ANDREW P. "Díaz Rodríguez's 'Sangre Patricia': A 'Point of View' Novel." *Hispania,* 53 (1970), 59–66.

FRANZ, THOMAS R. "Unamuno and Díaz Rodríguez's *Sangre Patricia:* The Case for a Mutual Influence." *Revista De Estudios Hispánicos,* 9 (1975), 217–29.

MATTESON, MARIANNA M. "Imagery in Díaz Rodríguez' 'Sangre Patricia.' " *Hispania,* 56 (1973), 1014–20.

WOODS, RICHARD D. "*Sangre Patricia* and *The Doors Of Perception.*" *Romance Notes,* 12 (1971), 302–6.

DÍAZ SÁNCHEZ, RAMÓN (Venezuelan, 1903–1968)

CUMBOTO (1950)

Reviews
JOHNSON, HARVEY L. *Hispania,* 53 (1970), 348–49.

ROSALDO, RENATO. *Arizona Quarterly,* 26 (1970), 90–92.

DIALLO, BAKARY (Senegalese, 1892–)

FORCE-BONTÉ (1926)

MICHELMAN, FREDERIC. "The Beginnings of French-African Fiction." *Research In African Literatures,* 2 (1971), 10–15.

DICK, WILLIAM (Canadian, 1933–)

A BUNCH OF RATBAGS

KENT, BILL. "A Bunch of Ratbags." *Overland,* No.33 (1965), pp. 48–49.

DIDEROT, DENIS (French, 1713–1784)

GENERAL

BAYM, MAX I. "The Mask of Things and the Desires of the Mind." *L'Esprit Créateur,* 8 (1968), 15–25.

BERRY, DAVID. "Diderot's Optics: An Aspect of his Philosophical and Literary Expression," in *Studies In Eighteenth-Century French Literature,* ed. J. H. Fox, M. H. Waddicor and D. A. Watts, pp. 15–28.

BONNEVILLE, DOUGLAS. "Diderot's Artist: Puppet and Poet," in *Literature And History In The Age Of Ideas,* ed. Charles G. S. Williams, pp. 245–52.

CARTWRIGHT, MICHAEL. "Diderot and the Idea of Performance and the Performer," in *Studies In Eighteenth-Century French Literature,* ed. J. H. Fox, M. H. Waddicor, and D. A. Watts, pp. 31–42.

DAEMMRICH, I. G. "Diderot and Schiller: Parallels in Literary Pictorialism." *Comparative Literature,* 19 (1967), 114–22.

DIECKMANN, JANE MARSH. " 'A Zerbina penserete': A Note on Diderot's Epigraph," in *Studies In Eighteenth-Century French Literature,* ed. J. H. Fox, M. H. Waddicor, and D. A. Watts, pp. 43–47.

McLAREN, JAMES C. "Diderot and the Paradox of Versatility." *L'Esprit Créateur,* 8 (1968), 26–33.

SINGH, CHRISTINE M. "The *Lettre Sur Les Aveugles:* Its Debt to Lucretius," in *Studies In Eighteenth-Century French Literature,* ed. J. H. Fox, M. H. Waddicor, and D. A. Watts, pp. 233–42.

STEEL, ERIC M. *Diderot's Imagery: A Study Of A Literary Personality.*

WADE, IRA O. "Organic Unity in Diderot." *L'Esprit Créateur,* 8 (1968), 3–14.

ZANTS, EMILY. "Dialogue, Diderot, and the New Novel in France." *Eighteenth-Century Studies,* 2 (1968), 172–81.

BIJOUX INDISCRÈTS

GREENBERG, IRWIN L. "The *Supplément Au Voyage De Bougainville* and Chapter XVIII of the *Bijoux Indiscrèts.*" *Kentucky Romance Quarterly,* 15, (1968), 231–36.

CECI N'EST PAS UN CONTE

FERGUSON, CHARLES. "Fiction Versus Fact in the Age of Reason: Diderot's *Ceci N'est Pas Un Conte.*" *Symposium,* 21 (1967), 231–40.

JACQUES THE FATALIST AND HIS MASTER (Jacques le fataliste et son maître, 1796)

ALTER, ROBERT. *Partial Magic,* pp. 57–83.

BONNEVILLE, DOUGLAS A. "Two Examples of Time-Technique in *Jacques Le Fataliste.*" *Romance Notes*, 8 (1967), 217-20.

BROGYANYI, GABRIEL JOHN. "The Functions of Narration in Diderot's *Jacques Le Fataliste.*" *MLN*, 89 (1974), 550-59.

FELLOWS, OTIS. "*Jacques Le Fataliste* Revisited." *L'Esprit Créateur*, 8 (1968), 42-52.

GREENBERG, IRWIN L. "Manipulation in Diderot's *Jacques Le Fataliste Et Son Maître.*" *Romance Notes*, 16 (1975), 605-10.

HAYWARD, SUSAN. "Two Anti-Novels: *Molloy* and *Jacques Le Fataliste,*" in *Studies In Eighteenth-Century French Literature*, ed. J. H. Fox, M. H. Waddicor, and D. A. Watts, pp. 97-107.

JENNINGS, C. WADE. "Diderot: A Suggested Source of the Jules-Phene Episode in *Pippa Passes.*" *English Language Notes*, 2 (1964), 32-36.

LEOV, NOLA M. "Jacques le Fataliste, Poème Parabolique." *AUMLA*, No. 23 (1965), pp. 24-48.

MYLNE, VIVIENNE. *The Eighteenth-Century French Novel*, pp. 214-20.

THOMAS, RUTH P. "*Le Roman Comique* and *Jacques Le Fataliste*: Some Parallels." *French Review*, 47 (1973), 13-24.

WILSON, ARTHUR M. *Diderot*, pp. 667-73.

THE NUN (La religieuse, 1796)

DUNKLEY, JOHN. "The Death of Madame Simonin." *Studi Francesi*, 17 (1973), 292-93.

FELLOWS, OTIS. "Diderot's *Supplément* as Pendant for *La Religieuse,*" in *Literature And History In The Age Of Ideas*, ed. Charles G. S. Williams, pp. 229-43.

MYLNE, VIVIENNE. *The Eighteenth Century French Novel*, pp. 198-214.

STEWART, PHILIP. "A Note on Chronology in *La Religieuse.*" *Romance Notes*, 12 (1970), 149-56.

WILSON, ARTHUR M. *Diderot*, pp. 382-91.

RAMEAU'S NEPHEW (Le Neveu de Rameau, 1823)

BRADY, PATRICK. "Structure and Sub-structure of *Le Neveu De Rameau.*" *L'Esprit Créateur*, 8 (1968), 34-41.

DEJEAN, JOAN. "Insertions and Interventions in *Le Neveu De Rameau.*" *Eighteenth-Century Studies*, 9 (1976), 511-22.

JOSEPHS, HERBERT. *Diderot's Dialogue Of Language And Gesture: Le Neveu De Rameau.*

MARSLAND, AMY L. "Identity and Theme in *Le Neveu De Rameau.*" *Romanic Review*, 60 (1969), 34-46.

O'GORMAN, DONAL. *Diderot The Satirist*, pp. 35-220.

PLOTKIN, FREDERICK. "Diderot's Nephew and the Mimics of Enlightenment." *Centennial Review*, 13 (1969), 409-23.

SHERMAN, CAROL. "The *Neveu De Rameau* and the Grotesque." *Romance Notes*, 16 (1974), 103-8.

SLUSSER, GEORGE EDGAR. "*Le Neveu De Rameau* and Hoffmann's Johannes Kreisler: Affinities and Influences." *Comparative Literature*, 27 (1975), 327-43.

STRUGNELL, A. R. "Diderot's *Neveu De Rameau*: Portrait of a Rogue in the French Enlightenment," in *Knaves And Swindlers*, ed. Christine J. Whitbourn, pp. 93-111.

THODY, P. M. W. "*Le Neveu De Rameau* and the Awareness of Mediocrity," in *Studies In Eighteenth-Century French Literature*, ed. J. H. Fox, M. H. Waddicor, and D. A. Watts, pp. 287-93.

WILSON, ARTHUR M. *Diderot*, pp. 415-23.

WILSON, W. D. "A Hidden Parable in the *Neveu De Rameau.*" *Romanische Forshungen*, 78 (1966), 115-18.

LE SUPPLÉMENT AU VOYAGE DE BOUGAINVILLE

FELLOWS, OTIS. "Diderot's *Supplément* as Pendant for *La Reli-

gieuse,*" in *Literature And History In The Age Of Ideas*, ed. Charles G. S. Williams, pp. 229-43.

DIEZ-CANSECO, Alfredo Paraja see PAREJA DIEZ-CANSECO, Alfredo

DIGGELMAN, WALTER MATTHIAS (Swiss, 1927-)

GENERAL

WAIDSON, H. M. "Childhood, Youth, and Autobiography in the Work of Walter Matthias Diggelmann." *Seminar*, 10 (1974), 213-25.

DIPOKO, MBELLA SONNE (Cameroon, 1936-)

A FEW NIGHTS AND DAYS (1965)

MOORE, GERALD. *The Chosen Tongue*, pp. 107-11.

DÖBLIN, ALFRED (German, 1878-1957)

GENERAL

RILEY, ANTHONY W. "The Professing Christian and the Ironic Humanist: A Comment on the Relationship of Alfred Döblin and Thomas Mann after 1933," in *Essays On German Literature in Honour Of G. Joyce Hallamore*, ed. Michael S. Batts and Marketa Goetz Stankiewicz, pp. 177-94.

ALEXANDERPLATZ, BERLIN (Berlin Alexanderplatz, 1929)

MCLEAN, ANDREW M. "Joyce's *Ulysses* and Döblin's *Alexanderplatz Berlin.*" *Comparative Literature*, 25 (1973), 97-113.

MITCHELL, BREON. "Joyce and Döblin: At the Crossroads of *Berlin Alexanderplatz.*" *Contemporary Literature*, 12 (1971), 173-87.

REID, JAMES H. "*Berlin Alexanderplatz*—A Political Novel." *German Life And Letters*, 21 (1968), 214-23.

TITCHE, LEON L. "Döblin and Dos Passos: Aspects of the City Novel." *Modern Fiction Studies*, 17 (1971), 125-35.

ZIOLKOWSKI, THEODORE. *Dimensions Of The Modern Novel*, pp. 99-137.

DODERER, HEIMITO VON (Austrian, 1896-1966)

GENERAL

BARKER, ANDREW. " 'Closely Observed Trains'—Some Thoughts on Heimito von Doderer's Use of the Railway Theme." *Forum For Modern Literature Studies*, 10 (1974), 357-64.

BOELCSKEVY, ANDREW. "Spatial Form and Moral Ambiguity: A Note on Heimito von Doderer's Narrative Technique." *German Quarterly*, 47 (1974), 55-59.

HABERL, FRANZ P. "Water Imagery in Doderer's Novels." *Books Abroad*, 42 (1968), 348-53.

IVASK, IVAR. "Heimito von Doderer, An Introduction." *Wisconsin Studies In Contemporary Literature*, 8 (1967), 528-47.

———. "Poet of the Vibrant Equilibrium: The Austrian Novelist Heimito von Doderer at 70." *Books Abroad*, 40 (1966), 415-18.

JONES, DAVID L. "Proust and Doderer as Historical Novelists." *Comparative Literature Studies*, 10 (1973), 9-24.

———. "A Quest for Tolerance." *Books Abroad*, 42 (1968), 357-59.

POLITZER, HEINZ. "An Aphorism by Heimito von Doderer." *Books Abroad*, 42 (1968), 366-68.

SWALES, MARTIN. "Doderer as a Realist." *Books Abroad,* 42 (1968), 371-75.

———. "The Narrator in the Novels of Heimito von Doderer." *Modern Language Review,* 61 (1966), 85-95.

WILLIAMS, CEDRIC E. *The Broken Eagle,* pp. 132-47.

WOLFF, HELEN. "Heimito von Doderer." *Books Abroad,* 42 (1968), 378-79.

THE DEMONS (Die Dämonen, 1956)

GUENTHER, PAUL F. "Heimito von Doderer's *Magnum Opus Austriacum.*" *Papers On Language And Literature,* 2 (1966), 81-90.

JONES, DAVID L. "Proust and Doderer as Historical Novelists." *Comparative Literature Studies,* 10 (1973), 16-23.

POLITZER, HEINZ. "Heimito von Doderer's *Demons* and the Modern Kakanian Novel," in *The Contemporary Novel In German: A Symposium,* ed. Robert R. Heitner, pp. 39-62.

WILLIAMS, CEDRIC E. *The Broken Eagle,* pp. 137-47.

EVERY MAN A MURDERER (Ein Mord den jeder begeht, 1938)

SHAW, MICHAEL. "An Interpretation of Heimito von Doderer's Novel *Ein Mord Den Jeder Begeht.*" *Symposium,* 19 (1965), 147-54.

DAS LETZTE ABENTEUR (1953)

WAIDSON, H. M. "Heimito von Doderer: *Das Letzte Abenteuer.*" *Books Abroad,* 42 (1968), 375-78.

DIE POSAUNEN VON JERICHO (1958)

SHAW, MICHAEL. "Doderer's *Posaunen Von Jericho.*" *Symposium,* 21 (1967), 141-54.

THE STRUDLHOF STAIRCASE (Die Strudlhofstiege, 1951)

GUENTHER, PAUL F. "Heimito von Doderer's *Magnum Opus Austriacum.*" *Papers On Language And Literature,* 2 (1966), 81-90.

———. "Heimito von Doderer's *Tangenten* and The Genesis of *Die Strudlhofstiege.*" *Papers On Language And Literature,* 11 (1975), 177-85.

HATFIELD, HENRY. *Crisis And Continuity In Modern German Fiction,* pp. 90-101.

THE WATERFALLS OF SLUNJ (Die Wasserfälle von Slunj, 1964)

HATFIELD, HENRY. *Crisis And Continuity In Modern German Fiction,* pp. 101-8.

———. "The Human Tragicomedy: Doderer's *Die Wasserfälle Von Slunj.*" *Books Abroad,* 42 (1968), 354-57.

Reviews
BAUKE, JOSEPH P. "Vienna Before the Holocaust." *Saturday Review,* 17 December 1966, pp. 38-39.

DONCHEV, ANTON (Bulgarian, 1930-)

TIME OF PARTING (1967)

Reviews
PRESCOTT, ORVILLE. "Forgotten Martyrs." *Saturday Review,* 4 May 1968, p. 37.

DONNADIEU, Marguerite see DURAS, Marguerite

DONOSO, JOSÉ (Chilean, 1924-)

GENERAL

DONOSO, JOSE. "Chronology." *Review,* No.9 (1973), pp. 12-19.

HASSETT, JOHN J., Charles M. Tatum, and Kirsten Nigro. "Biobibliography—Jose Donoso." *Chasqui,* 2, No.1 (1972), 15-30.

MCMURRAY, GEORGE R. "Jose Donoso: Bibliography—Addendum." *Chasqui,* 3, No.2 (1974), 23-44. <Updates that of Hassett, Tatum and Nigro.>

MARTÍNEZ, Z. NELLY. "José Donoso: A Short Study of His Works." *Books Abroad,* 49 (1975), 249-55.

NIGRO, KIRSTEN F. "From *Criollismo* to the Grotesque: Approaches to José Donoso," in *Tradition And Renewal,* ed. Merlin H. Forster, pp. 208-32.

TATUM, CHARLES M. "Los Medallones de Piedra: The Hermetic Beings of José Donoso's Fictional World." *USF Language Quarterly,* 13, No.1/2 (1974), 43-48.

CORONATION (Coronación, 1957)

Reviews
HICKS, GRANVILLE "Death Would Not Wait on Feeling." *Saturday Review,* 13 March 1965, pp. 27-28.

HELL HAS NO LIMITS (El lugar sin limites, 1966)

NIGRO, KIRSTEN F. "From *Criollismo* to the Grotesque: Approaches to José Donoso," in *Tradition And Renewal,* ed. Merlin H. Forster, pp. 222-31.

SARDUY, SEVERO. "Writing/Transvestism." Trans. Alfred MacAdam. *Review,* No.9 (1973), pp. 31-33.

THE OBSCENE BIRD OF NIGHT (Obsceno Pájaro de la Noche, 1970)

GERTEL, ZUNILDA. "Metamorphosis as a Metaphor of the World." *Review,* No.9 (1973), pp. 20-23.

HASSETT, JOHN J. "The Obscure Bird of Night." *Review,* No.9 (1973), pp. 27-30.

LIPSKI, JOHN M. "Donoso's *Obscene Bird:* Novel and Anti-Novel." *Latin American Literary Review,* 4, No.9 (1976), 39-47.

MCMURRAY, GEORGE R. "Jose Donoso's Tribute to Consciousness: *El Obsceno Pajaro De La Noche.*" *Chasqui,* 3, No.3 (1974), 40-48.

MARTÍNEZ, Z. NELLY. "José Donoso: A Short Study of His Works." *Books Abroad,* 49 (1975), 252-55.

OBERHELMAN, HARLEY D. "José Donoso and the 'Nueva Narrativa.' " *Revista De Estudios Hispánicos,* 9 (1975), 107-17.

RIVERA, FRANCISCO. "A Conflict of Themes." Trans. Deborah Davis. *Review,* No.9 (1973), pp. 24-26.

RODRIGUEZ MONEGAL, EMIR. "The Novel as Happening: an Interview with José Donoso." *Review,* No.9 (1973), pp. 34-39.

TATUM, CHARLES M. "*El Obsceno Pajaro De La Noche:* The Demise of a Feudal Society." *Latin American Literary Review,* 1, No.2 (1973), 99-105.

Reviews
FOSTER, DAVID WILLIAM. *Hispania,* 55 (1972), 392.

THIS SUNDAY (Este domingo, 1966)

TATUM, CHARLES M. "The Child Point of View in Donoso's Fiction." *Journal Of Spanish Studies,* 1 (1973), 187-91.

Reviews
KERSH, GERALD. "Study in Breaking Points." *Saturday Review,* 9 December 1967, p. 30.

DOSTOEVSKY, FYODOR (Russian, 1821-1881)

GENERAL

ARSENIEV, NICHOLAS. "The Central Inspiration of Dostoevsky," in *F. M. Dostoevsky: 1821-1881,* ed. Nicholas Arseniev and Constantine Belousow, pp. 7-16.

BARKSDALE, E. C. *The Dacha And The Duchess,* pp. 112-20.

BATCHELOR, R. "Dostoevskii and Camus: Similarities and Contrasts." *Journal Of European Studies,* 5 (1975), 111-51.

BEAUMONT, ERNEST. "The Supernatural in Dostoyevsky and Bernanos: A Reply to Professor Sonnenfeld." *French Studies,* 23 (1969), 264-67.

BELKNAP, ROBERT L. "Dostoevsky's Nationalist Ideology and Rhetoric." *Review Of National Literatures,* 3, No.1 (1972), 89-100.

———. "Recent Soviet Scholarship and Criticism on Dostoevskij: A Review Article." *Slavic And East European Journal,* 11 (1967), 75-86.

CAMPBELL, MAGDA. "Dostoevsky and Psychoanalysis," in *F. M. Dostoevsky: 1821-1881,* ed. Nicholas Arseniev and Constantine Belousow, pp. 18-27.

CHANCES, ELLEN. "Počvenničestvo—Evolution of an Ideology." *Modern Fiction Studies,* 20 (1974/5), 543-51.

DARRING, GERALD AND WALTER DARRING. "Dostoevsky's Prophetic *Notes.*" *Genre,* 6 (1973), 388-403.

DAVISON, R. "Camus' Attitude to Dostoevsky's Kirilov and the Impact of the Engineer's Ideas on Camus' Early Work." *Orbis Litterarum,* 30 (1975), 225-40.

DE JONGE, ALEX. *Dostoevsky And The Age Of Intensity.*

FANGER, DONALD. "The Most Fantastic City: Approaches to a Myth," in his *Dostoevsky And Romantic Realism: A Study Of Dostoevsky, Dickens, And Gogol,* pp. 129-51.

———. "Poetics of the City," in his *Dostoevsky And Romantic Realism: A Study Of Dostoevsky In Relation To Balzac, Dickens, And Gogol,* pp. 214-40.

FLOROVSKY, GEORGES. "Three Masters: The Quest for Religion in Nineteenth-Century Russian Literature." *Comparative Literature Studies,* 3 (1966), 128-33.

FRANK, JOSEPH. "Dostoevsky and the Socialists." *Partisan Review,* 32 (1965), 409-22.

GOODHEART, EUGENE. "Dostoevsky and the Hubris of the Immoralist," in his *The Cult Of The Ego,* pp. 90-113.

HUNT, JOEL A. "Balzac and Dostoevsky: Some Elements of Scene." *Comparatiave Literature Studies,* 3 (1966), 439-43.

———. "Color Imagery in Dostoevskij and Balzac." *Slavic And East European Review,* 10 (1966), 411-23.

JACKSON, ROBERT LOUIS. "The Root and the Flower: Dostoevsky and Turgenev: A Comparative Aesthetic." *Yale Review,* 63 (1973), 228-50.

———. "The Testament of F. M. Dostoevskij." *Russian Literature,* No.4 (1973), pp. 87-99.

JONES, MALCOLM V. "Dostoevsky and an Aspect of Schiller's Psychology." *Slavonic And East European Review,* 52 (1974), 337-54.

———. "Dostoevsky's Conception of the Idea." *Renaissance And Modern Studies,* 13 (1969), 106-31.

———. "Some Echoes of Hegel in Dostoyevsky." *Slavonic And East European Review,* 49 (1971), 500-20.

KIRILLOFF, ARIAN. "The 'Outsider' Figure in Dostoievsky's Works." *Renaissance And Modern Studies,* 18 (1974), 126-40.

MASLENIKOV, OLEG A. "The Ludicrous Man-of-the-Family: A Recurrent Type in Dostoevskij." *California Slavic Studies,* 6 (1971), 29-36.

MILOSZ, CZESLAW. "Dostoevsky and Swedenborg." *Slavic Review,* 34 (1975), 302-18.

MORAVCEVICH, NICHOLAS. "Humor in Dostoevsky." *Bucknell Review,* 14, No.3 (1966), 59-77.

MOSSMAN, ELLIOTT D. "Dostoevskij's Early Works: The More than Rational Distortion." *Slavic And East European Journal,* 10 (1966), 268-78.

MUCHNIC, HELEN. "Common Sense in Dostoevsky," in her *Russian Writers,* pp. 158-62.

———. "Dostoevsky Abroad," in her *Russian Writers,* pp. 169-76.

———. "Dostoevsky's Journalism," in her *Russian Writers,* pp. 163-68.

NATOV, NADINE. "Some Plot Invariants in the Works of F. M. Dostoevsky as a Means of Expression of His Ideas," in *F. M. Dostoevsky: 1821-1881,* ed. Nicholas Arseniev and Constantine Belousow, pp. 79-92.

NEUHÄUSER, RUDOLF. "Recent Dostoevskii Studies and Trends in Dostoevskii Research." *Journal Of European Studies,* 2 (1972), 355-73.

PACHMUSS, TEMIRA. "Dostoevsky and Hermann Hesse: Analogies and Congruences." *Orbis Litterarum,* 30 (1975), 210-24.

———. "Dostoevsky, Werfel, and Virginia Woolf: Influences and Confluences." *Comparative Literature Studies,* 9 (1972), 416-28.

POULAKIDAS, ANDREAS K. "Dostoevsky, Kanzantzakis' Unacknowledged Mentor." *Comparative Literature,* 21 (1969), 307-18.

PURDY, S. B. "Poe and Dostoevsky." *Studies In Short Fiction,* 4 (1967), 169-71.

ROODKOWSKY, NIKITA D. "Dostoevsky: Seer of Modern Totalitarianism." *Thought,* 47 (1972), 587-98.

ROWE, WILLIAM WOODIN. *Dostoevsky: Child And Man In His Works.*

RUDICINA, ALEXANDRA F. "Crime and Myth: The Archetypal Pattern of Rebirth in Three Novels of Dostoevsky." *PMLA,* 87 (1972), 1065-74.

SEDURO, VLADIMIR. "The Controversy Over Dostoevsky in the 1960s in Soviet Dostoevsky Studies," in *F. M. Dostoevsky: 1821-1881,* ed. Nicholas Arseniev and Contantine Belousow, pp. 125-79.

———. *Dostoevski's Image In Russia Today.*

SEIDEN, MELVIN. "Nabokov and Dostoevsky." *Contemporary Literature,* 13 (1972), 423-44.

SHNEIDMAN, N. N. "Soviet Theory of Literature and the Struggle Around Dostoevsky in Recent Soviet Scholarship." *Slavic Review,* 34 (1975), 523-38.

SHESTOV, LEV. "Dostoevsky and Nietzsche: The Philosophy of Tragedy," in *Essays In Russian Literature,* ed. Spence E. Roberts, pp. 3-99.

SIMMONS, ERNEST J. "Dostoevsky—'A Realist in the Higher Sense.'" in his *Introduction To Russian Realism,* pp. 91-134.

SIMONS, JOHN D. "The Myth of Progress in Schiller and Dostoevsky." *Comparative Literature,* 24 (1972), 328-37.

SOLOVEV, VLADIMIR. "In Memory of Dostoevsky," in *Literature And National Identity,* ed. Paul Debreczeny and Jesse Zeldin, pp. 169-79.

SONNENFELD, ALBERT. "A Sharing of Darkness: Bernanos and Dostoevsky." *Renascence,* 17 (1964), 82-88.

STREM, GEORGE G. "The Theme of Rebellion in the Works of Camus and Dostoievsky." *Revue De Littérature Comparée,* 40 (1966), 246-57.

STRUC, ROMAN S. "'Petty Demons' and Beauty: Gogol, Dostoevsky, Sologub," in *Essays On European Literature,* ed. Peter Uwe Hohendahl, Herbert Lindenberger, and Egon Schwarz, pp. 69-76.

WASIOLEK, EDWARD. "Dostoevsky: A Revolutionary Conservative." *Modern Age,* 9 (1964/5), 62-68.

BELYYE NOCHI

LEATHERBARROW, W. J. "Dostoevsky's Treatment of the Theme

of Romantic Dreaming in 'Khozyayka' and 'Belyye nochi.' " *Modern Language Review,* 69 (1974), 592-95.

THE BROTHERS KARAMAZOV (Brat'ya Karamazovy, 1880)

BANERJEE, MARIA. "Rozanov on Dostoevskij." *Slavic And East European Journal,* 15 (1971), 411-24.

BELKNAP, ROBERT L. *The Structure Of <The Brothers Karamazov.>*

BRAUN, MAXIMILIAN. "*The Brothers Karamazov* as a Expository Novel." *Canadian-American Slavic Studies,* 6 (1972), 199-208.

CHAITIN, GILBERT D. "Religion as Defense: The Structure of *The Brothers Karamazov.*" *Literature And Psychology,* 22 (1972), 69-87.

COX, ROGER L. *Between Earth And Heaven: Shakespeare, Dostoevsky, And The Meaning Of Christian Tragedy,* pp. 192-214.

DAVIES, RUTH. *The Great Books Of Russia,* pp. 215-33.

ENG, JAN VAN DER. "A Note on Comic Relief in 'The Brothers Karamazov.' " in *The Brothers Karamazov By F. M. Dostoevskij,* pp. 149-62.

FREEBORN, R. H. "Realism in Russia, to the Death of Dostoevsky," in *The Age Of Realism,* ed. F. W. J. Hemmings, pp. 134-39.

FRIEDMAN, MAURICE. "Martin Buber's *For The Sake Of Heaven* and F. M. Dostoevsky's *The Brothers Karamazov.*" *Comparative Literature Studies,* 3 (1966), 155-67.

GIBSON, A. BOYLE. *The Religion Of Dostoevsky,* pp. 169-208.

GOLDSTEIN, MARTIN. "The Debate in *The Brothers Karamazov.*" *Slavic And East European Journal,* 14 (1970), 326-40.

The Grand Inquisitor. Ed. Jerry S. Wasserman.

GRANT, JOHN E. "The Revelation of the Grand Inquisitor." *Southern Review: Literary And Interdisciplinary Essays,* 2 (1967), 240-60.

GROSSMAN, LEONID. *Dostoevsky: A Biography,* pp. 569-93.

GUERARD, ALBERT J. *The Triumph Of The Novel: Dickens, Dostoevsky, Faulkner,* pp. 63-66, 94-103, 185-91.

HALL, VERNON. "Dostoevsky's Use of French as a Symbolic Devise in *The Brothers Karamazov.*" *Comparative Literature Studies,* 2 (1965), 171-74.

JACKSON, ROBERT L. "Dmitrij Karamazov and the 'Legend.' " *Slavic And East European Journal,* 9 (1965), 257-67.

KENT, LEONARD J. *The Subconscious In Gogol And Dostoevskij And Its Antecedents,* pp. 148-57.

KIRILLOFF, ARIAN. "The 'Outsider' Figure in Dostoievsky's Works." *Renaissance And Modern Studies,* 18 (1974), 131-35.

KOLENDA, KONSTANTIN. "Two Analyses of Dostoevsky: Alyosha's Answer to Alienation . . ." *Forum,* 4, No.4 (1964), 4-9.

KOPRINCE, RALPH. "Background Characters and *The Brothers Karamazov.*" *Russian Literature Triquarterly,* No.10 (1974), pp. 343-50.

LANGER, LAWRENCE L. *The Holocaust And The Literary Imagination,* pp. 125-33.

LARY, N. M. *Dostoevsky And Dickens,* pp. 139-48.

LAVRIN, JANKO. "A Note on Nietzsche and Dostoevsky." *Russian Review,* 28 (1969), 160-70.

LEBOWITZ, NAOMI. *Humanism And The Absurd In The Modern Novel,* pp. 85-102.

MACEINA, ANTANAS. " 'The Metaphysical Meaning of the Legend' from *The Grand Inquisitor.*" *Lituanus,* 15, No.2 (1969), 14-26.

MEIJER, JAN M. "The Author of 'Brat'ja Karamazovy,' " in *The Brothers Karamazov By F. M. Dostoevskij,* pp. 7-46.

——— . "A Note on Time in 'Brat'ja Karamazovy,' " in *The Brothers Karamazov By F. M. Dostoevskij,* pp. 47-62.

——— . "Some Notes on Dostoevskij and Russian Realism." *Russian Literature,* No.4 (1973), pp. 5-17.

MERRILL, REED B. "Ivan Karamazov and Harry Haller: The Consolation of Philosophy." *Comparative Literature Studies,* 8 (1971), 58-69, 75-77.

MINDESS, HARVEY. "Freud on Dostoevsky." *American Scholar,* 36 (1967), 446-52.

MOCHULSKY, KONSTANTIN. *Dostoevsky: His Life And Work,* pp. 565-636.

OATES, JOYCE CAROL. "The Double Vision of *The Brothers Karamazov.*" *Journal Of Aesthetics And Art Criticism,* 27 (1968), 203-13.

PEACE, RICHARD. *Dostoevsky: An Examination Of The Major Novels,* pp. 218-96.

REXROTH, KENNETH. "Classics Revisited—XXXIX—'The Brothers Karamazov.' " *Saturday Review,* 3 December 1966, p. 24; rpt. in his *Classics Revisited,* pp. 253-57.

ROSEN, NATHAN. "Style and Structure in *The Brothers Karamazov* (The Grand Inquisitor and The Russian Monk.)" *Russian Literature Triquarterly,* No.1/2 (1971), 352-65.

——— . "Why Dmitrii Karamazov Did Not Kill His Father." *Canadian-American Slavic Studies,* 6 (1972), 209-24.

ROSS, ROCHELLE H. "Who Is Ivan Karamazov?" *Forum,* 8, No.2 (1970), 39-43.

ROSS, STEPHEN D. *Literature & Philosophy,* pp. 137-74.

ROWE, WILLIAM W. "*Crime And Punishment* and *The Brothers Karamazov:* Some Comparative Observations." *Russian Literature Triquarterly,* No.10 (1974), pp. 331-42.

ROZANOV, VASILY. *Dostoevsky And The Legend Of The Grand Inquisitor.*

RUDICINA, ALEXANDRA F. "Crime and Myth: The Archetypal Pattern of Rebirth in Three Novels of Dostoevsky." *PMLA,* 87 (1972), 1069-72.

SANDOZ, ELLIS. *Political Apocalypse: A Study Of Dostoevsky's Grand Inquisitor.*

SCOTT, NATHAN A. *Craters Of The Spirit,* pp. 39-43.

SIMMONS, ERNEST J. "Dostoevsky—'A Realist in the Higher Sense,' " in his *Introduction To Russian Realism,* pp. 129-34.

——— . *Feodor Dostoevsky,* pp. 41-45.

SPILKA, MARK. "Human Worth in *The Brothers Karamazov.*" *Minnesota Review,* 5 (1965), 38-49.

TERRAS, VICTOR. "Turgenev and the Devil in *The Brothers Karamazov.*" *Canadian-American Slavic Studies,* 6 (1972), 265-71.

VIVAS, ELISEO. "Dostoevsky, 'Poet' in Spite of Himself." *Southern Review,* n.s., 10 (1974), 307-28.

YARMOLINSKY, AVRAHAM. *Dostoevsky: Works And Days,* pp. 384-410.

CRIME AND PUNISHMENT (Prestuplenye i nakazanye, 1866)

ALDEN, DOUGLAS W. "Quinette, Landru, and Raskolnikoff." *French Review,* 43 (1969), 215-26.

BUSCH, ROBERT L. "Humor in Dostoevskii's *Crime And Punishment.*" *Canadian-American Slavic Studies,* 9 (1975), 54-68.

CHANCES, ELLEN. "Počvenničestvo—Evolution of an Ideology." *Modern Fiction Studies,* 20 (1974/5), 543-51.

CHURCH, MARGARET. "Dostoevsky's 'Crime and Punishment' and Kafka's 'The Trial.' " *Literature And Psychology,* 19, No.3/4, 1969, 47-55.

COX, ROGER L. *Between Earth And Heaven: Shakespeare, Dostoevsky, And The Meaning Of Christian Tragedy,* pp. 140-63.

CURTIS, JAMES M. "Spatial Form as the Intrinsic Genre of Dostoevsky's Novels." *Modern Fiction Studies,* 18 (1972), 135-54.

DAVIES, RUTH. *The Great Books Of Russia,* pp. 166-80.

FANGER, DONALD. "Apogee: Crime and Punishment," in his *Dostoevsky And Romantic Realism: A Study Of Dostoevsky In Relation To Balzac, Dickens, And Gogol*, pp. 184-213.

———. "Poetics of the City," in his *Dostoevsky And Romantic Realism: A Study Of Dostoevsky In Relation To Balzac, Dickens, And Gogol*, pp. 214-40.

FRANK, JOSEPH. "The World of Raskolnikov." *Encounter*, 26, No.6 (1966), 30-35.

FREEBORN, RICHARD. *The Rise Of The Russian Novel*, pp. 157-207.

GIBSON, A. BOYLE. *The Religion Of Dostoevsky*, pp. 88-103.

GROSSMAN, LEONID. *Dostoevsky: A Biography*, pp. 342-70.

GUERARD, ALBERT J. *The Triumph Of The Novel: Dickens, Dostoevsky, Faulkner*, pp. 94-96, 175-81.

HACKEL, SERGEI. "Raskolnikov Through the Looking-Glass: Dostoevsky and Camus's *L'Étranger.*" *Contemporary Literature*, 9 (1968), 189-209.

HAIG, STIRLING. "The Epilogue of *Crime And Punishment* and Camus' La 'Femme adultère.' " *Comparative Literature Studies*, 3 (1966), 445-49.

HALLIE, PHILIP PAUL. "Raskolnikov, the *Scholar,* and Fresh Air." *American Scholar*, 40 (1971), 579-82.

HART, PIERRE R. "Looking Over Raskol'nikov's Shoulder: The Narrator in 'Crime and Punishment.' " *Criticism*, 13 (1971), 166-79.

HAUGH, RICHARD. "Dostoevsky and Hawthorne?" in *F. M. Dostoevsky: 1821-1881*, ed. Nicholas Arseniev and Constantine Belousow, pp. 38-59.

JONES, MALCOLM V. "Raskol'nikov's Humanitarianism." *Canadian-American Slavic Studies*, 8 (1974), 370-80.

KENT, LEONARD J. *The Subconscious In Gogol And Dostoevskij And Its Antecedents*, pp. 112-22.

KIRILLOFF, ARIAN. "The 'Outsider' Figure in Dostoievsky's Works." *Renaissance And Modern Studies*, 18 (1974), 129-32.

KUHN, ALFRED. "A Note on Raskol'nikov's Hats." *Slavic And East European Journal*, 15 (1971), 425-32.

LEATHERBARROW, W. J. "Raskolnikov and the 'Enigma of His Personality.' " *Forum For Modern Language Studies*, 9 (1973), 153-65.

McDONALD, WALTER R. "Coincidence in the Novel: a Necessary Technique." *College English*, 29 (1968), 377-80.

MILOSZ, CZELAW. "Dostoevsky and Swedenborg." *Slavic Review*, 34 (1975), 306-11.

MOCHULSKY, KONSTANTIN. *Dostoevsky: His Life And Work*, pp. 270-313.

MUCHNIC, HELEN. "Clues to the Crime: *The Notebooks For Crime And Punishment,*" in her *Russian Writers*, pp. 177-84.

NAUMANN, MARINA TURKEVICH. "Raskol'nikov's Shadow: Porfirij Petrovič." *Slavic And East European Journal*, 16 (1972), 42-54.

NILSSON, NILS ÅKE. "Rhyming as a Stylistic Device in *Crime And Punishment.*" *Russian Literature*, No.4 (1973), pp. 65-71.

PEACE, RICHARD. *Dostoevsky: An Examination Of The Major Novels*, pp. 19-58.

RECK, RIMA DRELL. "A Crime: Dostoevsky and Bernanos." *Forum*, 4, No.4 (1964), 10-13.

REEVE, F. D. *The Russian Novel*, pp. 159-204.

ROSENSHIELD, GARY. "First- versus Third-Person Narration in *Crime And Punishment.*" *Slavic And East European Journal*, 17 (1973), 399-407.

ROWE, WILLIAM W. "*Crime And Punishment* and *The Brothers Karamazov*: Some Comparative Observations." *Russian Literature Triquarterly*, No.10 (1974), pp. 331-42.

———. "Dostoevskian Patterned Antinomy and Its Function in *Crime And Punishment.*" *Slavic And East European Journal*, 16 (1972), 287-96.

SANTANGELO, GENNARO. "The Five Motives of Raskolnikov." *Dalhousie Review*, 54 (1974), 710-19.

SHAW, J. THOMAS. "Raskol'nikov's Dreams." *Slavic And East European Journal*, 17 (1973), 131-45.

SHESTOV, LEV. "Dostoevsky and Nietzsche: The Philosophy of Tragedy," in *Essays In Russian Literature*, ed. Spencer E. Roberts, pp. 72-87.

SIMMONS, ERNEST J. "Dostoevsky—'A Realist in the Higher Sense,' " in his *Introduction To Russian Realism*, pp. 117-21.

———. *Feodor Dostoevsky*, pp. 25-28.

SMITH, RAYMOND. "A Note on Dostoevsky's Dr. Zossimov." *College Language Association Journal*, 10 (1966), 162-64.

SPIVACK, CHARLOTTE K. "The Journey to Hell: Satan, the Shadow, and the Self." *Centennial Review*, 9 (1965), 434-36.

Twentieth Century Interpretations Of Crime And Punishment: A Collection Of Critical Essays. Ed. Robert Louis Jackson.

WASIOLECK, EDWARD. "Dostoevsky's *Notebooks For Crime And Punishment.*" *Psychoanalytic Review*, 55 (1968), 349-59.

———. "Raskolnikov's Motives: Love and Murder." *American Imago*, 31 (1974), 252-69.

WEISGERBER, JEAN. "Faulkner's Monomanics: Their Indebtedness to Raskolnikov." *Comparative Literature Studies*, 5 (1968), 181-93.

WERGE, THOMAS. "The Word as Deed in *Crime And Punishment.*" *Renascence*, 27 (1975), 207-19.

YARMOLINSKY, AVRAHAM. *Dostoevsky: Works And Days*, pp. 210-22.

THE DEVILS see THE POSSESSED

THE DOUBLE (Dvoynik, 1846)

ANDERSON, ROGER B. "Dostoevsky's Hero in *The Double*: A Re-examination of the Divided Self." *Symposium*, 26 (1972), 101-13.

FANGER, DONALD. "Evolution of the Myth: From Poor Folk to Notes from Underground," in his *Dostoevsky And Romantic Realism: A Study Of Dostoevsky In Relation To Balzac, Dickens, And Gogol*, pp. 159-62.

GROSSMAN, LEONID. *Dostoevsky: A Biography*, pp. 70-76.

GUERARD, ALBERT J. *The Triumph Of The Novel: Dickens, Dostoevsky, Faulkner*, pp. 33-36, 162-66.

KENT, LEONARD J. *The Subconscious In Gogol And Dostoevskij And Its Antecedents*, pp. 90-94.

LEATHERBARROW, W. J. "The Rag with Ambition: The Problem of Self-will in Dostoevsky's 'Bednyye lyudi' and 'Dvoynik.' " *Modern Language Review*, 68 (1973), 610-18.

MOCHULSKY, KONSTANTIN. *Dostoevsky: His Life And Work*, pp. 46-52.

ROGERS, ROBERT. *A Psychoanalytic Study Of The Double In Literature*, pp. 34-39.

SHERRY, CHARLES. "Folie à Deux: Gogol and Dostoevsky." *Texas Studies In Literature And Language*, 17 (1975), 257-67.

THE DREAM OF A RIDICULOUS MAN

GIBSON, A. BOYLE. *The Religion Of Dostoevsky*, pp. 161-68.

KENT, LEONARD J. *The Subconscious In Gogol And Dostoevskij And Its Antecedents*, pp. 144-48.

PHILLIPS, ROGER W. "Dostoevsky's 'Dream of a Ridiculous Man': A Study in Ambiguity." *Criticism*, 17 (1975), 355-63.

THE ETERNAL HUSBAND

GUERARD, ALBERT J. "The Illuminating Distortion." *Novel*, 5 (1972), 117-20.

———. *The Triumph Of The Novel: Dickens, Dostoevsky, Faulkner*, pp. 181-85.

KENT, LEONARD J. *The Subconscious In Gogol And Dostoevskij And Its Antecedents,* pp. 131–37.

MOCHULSKY, KONSTANTIN. *Dostoevsky: His Life And Work,* pp. 382–94.

PRATT, BRANWEN E. B. "The Role of the Unconscious in *The Eternal Husband.*" *Literature And Psychology,* 21 (1971), 29–40. Reprinted in: *Literature And Psychology,* 22 (1972), 13–25.

RAHV, PHILIP. "Dostoevsky: Two Short Novels," in his *Literature And The Sixth Sense,* pp. 277–79.

THE GAMBLER

GROSSMAN, LEONID. *Dostoevsky: A Biography,* pp. 292–304.

MOCHULSKY, KONSTANTIN. *Dostoesvsky: His Life And Work,* pp. 314–21.

VINOGRADE, ANN G. "*The Gambler:* Prokf'ev's Libretto and Dostoevskij's Novel." *Slavic And East European Journal,* 16 (1972), 414–18.

THE HOUSE OF THE DEAD (Zapiski iz myortvogo doma, 1862)

FRANK, JOSEPH. "Dostoevsky: The House of the Dead." *Sewanee Review,* 74 (1966), 779–803.

THE IDIOT (Idiot, 1869)

COX, ROGER L. *Between Earth And Heaven: Shakespeare, Dostoevsky, And The Meaning Of Christian Tragedy,* pp. 164–91.

DAVIES, RUTH. *The Great Books Of Russia,* pp. 180–88.

FRANK, JOSEPH. "A Reading of *The Idiot.*" *Southern Review,* NS, 5 (1969), 303–31.

FRIEDMAN, MELVIN. "The Cracked Vase." *Romance Notes,* 7 (1966), 128.

GIBSON, A. BOYLE. *The Religion Of Dostoevsky,* pp. 104–24.

GROSSMAN, LEONID. *Dostoevsky: A Biography,* pp. 435–51.

GROSSVOGEL, DAVID I. *Limits Of The Novel,* pp. 310–19.

GUERARD, ALBERT J. "On the Composition of Dostoevsky's *The Idiot.*" *Mosaic,* 8, No.1 (1974), 201–15.

———. *The Triumph Of The Novel: Dickens, Dostoevsky, Faulkner,* pp. 61–63, 193–203.

HOLLANDER, ROBERT. "The Apocalyptic Framework of Dostoevsky's *The Idiot.*" *Mosaic,* 7, No.2 (1974), 123–39.

KENT, LEONARD J. *The Subconscious In Gogol And Dostoevskij And Its Antecedents,* pp. 122–31.

LARY, N. M. *Dostoevsky And Dickens,* pp. 51–104.

LESSER, SIMON O. AND RICHARD W. NOLAND. "Saint and Sinner— Dostoevsky's 'Idiot'—1958, 1975." *Modern Fiction Studies,* 21 (1975), 387–404.

LORD, R. "A Reconsideration of Dostoyevsky's Novel, *The Idiot.*" *Slavonic And East European Review,* 45 (1967), 30–45.

LOURIA, YVETTE. "Dostoevskii and Goncharov." *MLN,* 88 (1973), 1325–28.

MEYERS, JEFFREY. *Painting And The Novel,* pp. 136–47.

MOCHULSKY, KONSTANTIN. *Dostoevsky: His Life And Work,* pp. 334–81.

MUCHNIC, HELEN. "The Leap and the Vision: A Note on the Pattern of Dostoevsky's Novels," in her *Russian Writers,* pp. 139–57.

NEBOLSINE, ARCADI. "Simultaneity of Good and Evil: The Case of Lebedev," in *F. M. Dostoevsky: 1821–1881,* ed. Nicholas Arseniev and Constantine Belousow, pp. 93–104.

PEACE, RICHARD. *Dostoevsky: An Examination Of The Major Novels,* pp. 59–139.

PEARCE, RICHARD. *Stages Of The Clown,* pp. 6–19.

SIMMONS, ERNEST J. "Dostoevsky—'A Realist in the Higher Sense.,'" in his *Introduction To Russian Realism,* pp. 121–25.

———. *Feodor Dostoevsky,* pp. 30–33.

YARMOLINSKY, AVRAHAM. *Dostoevsky: Works And Days,* pp. 260–69.

THE INSULTED AND INJURED (Ynizhenyei i oskorblenye, 1861)

FANGER, DONALD. "Evolution of the Myth: From Poor Folk to Notes from Underground," in his *Dostoevsky And Romantic Realism: A Study Of Dostoevsky In Relation To Balzac, Dickens, And Gogol,* pp. 171–77.

FRANK, JOSEPH. "Dostoevsky's Discovery of 'Fantastic Realism.'" *Russian Review,* 27 (1968), 286–95.

GROSSMAN, LEONID. *Dostoevsky: A Biography,* pp. 248–51.

GUERARD, ALBERT J. *The Triumph Of The Novel: Dickens, Dostoevsky, Faulkner,* pp. 103–8.

LARY, N. M. *Dostoevsky And Dickens,* pp. 46–49.

MOCHULSKY, KONSTANTIN. *Dostoevsky: His Life And Work,* pp. 198–218.

NEUHÄUSER, RUDOLF. "Romanticism in the Post-Romantic Age: A Typological Study of Antecedents of Dostoevskii's Man from Underground." *Canadian-American Slavic Studies,* 8 (1974), 353–57.

SEELEY, FRANK FRIEDEBERG. "Aglaja Epančina." *Slavic And East European Journal,* 18 (1974), 1–10.

SELLIN, ERIC. "Meursault and Myshkin on Executions: A Parallel." *Romance Notes,* 10 (1968), 11–14.

KHOZYAYKA

LEATHERBARROW, W. J. "Dostoevsky's Treatment of the Theme of Romantic Dreaming in 'Khozyayka' and 'Belyye nochi.'" *Modern Language Review,* 69 (1974), 584–92.

THE LANDLADY

GROSSMAN, LEONID. *Dostoevsky: A Biography,* pp. 98–102.

MOCHULSKY, KONSTANTIN. *Dostoevsky: His Life And Work,* pp. 73–82.

THE MANOR OF STEPANCHIKOVO

TYNJANOV, JURIJ. "Dostoevsky and Gogol," in *Twentieth-Century Russian Literary Criticism,* ed. Victor Erlich, pp. 102–16.

NETOCHKA NEZVANOVA

GROSSMAN, LEONID. *Dostoevsky: A Biography,* pp. 126–32.

GUERARD, ALBERT J. *The Triumph Of The Novel: Dickens, Dostoevsky, And Faulkner,* pp. 173–75.

JONES, MALCOLM V. "An Aspect of Romanticism in Dostoevsky: 'Netochka Nezvanova' and Eugène Sue's 'Mathilde.'" *Renaissance And Modern Studies,* 17 (1973), 38–61.

KENT, LEONARD J. *The Subconscious In Gogol And Dostoeveskij And Its Antecedents,* pp. 106–9.

LARY, N. M. *Dostoevsky And Dickens,* pp. 43–46.

MOCHULSKY, KONSTANTIN. *Dostoevsky: His Life And Work,* pp. 99–113.

Reviews
ROWE, W. WOODIN. *Saturday Review,* 21 November 1970, p. 43–44.

NOTES FROM THE HOUSE OF THE DEAD (Zapiski iz mertrogo doma, 1861)

MOCHULSKY, KONSTANTIN. *Dostoevsky: His Life And Work,* pp. 182–97.

NOTES FROM THE UNDERGROUND (Zapiski iz podpol'ia, 1864)

CARDACI, PAUL F. "Dostoevsky's Underground as Allusion and Symbol." *Symposium,* 28 (1974), 248–58.

CASH, EARL A. "The Narrators in *Invisible Man* and *Notes From*

Underground: Brothers in the Spirit." *College Language Association Journal,* 16 (1973), 505-7.

DAVIES, RUTH. *The Great Books Of Russia,* pp. 161-64.

FANGER, DONALD. "Evolution of the Myth: From Poor Folk to Notes from Underground," in his *Dostoevsky And Romantic Realism: A Study Of Dostoevsky In Relation To Balzac, Dickens, And Gogol,* pp. 177-83.

GIBSON, A. BOYLE. *The Religion Of Dostoevsky,* pp. 78-87.

GREGG, RICHARD. "Apollo Underground: His Master's Still, Small Voice." *Russian Review,* 32 (1973), 64-71.

_____. "Two Adams and Eve in the Crystal Palace: Dostoevsky, the Bible, and *We,*" in *Major Soviet Writers,* ed. Edward J. Brown, pp. 202-8.

GROSSMAN, LEONID. *Dostoevsky: A Biography,* pp. 255-59, 310-17.

GUERARD, ALBERT J. *The Triumph Of The Novel: Dickens, Dostoevsky, Faulkner,* pp. 166-71.

HALTRESHT, MICHAEL. "Symbolism of Rats and Mice in Dostoevsky's 'Notes from Underground.' " *South Atlantic Bulletin,* 39, No.4 (1974), 60-62.

HOLQUIST, JAMES M. "Plot and Counter-Plot in *Notes From Underground.*" *Canadian-American Slavic Studies,* 6 (1972), 225-38.

HOLZAPFEL, TAMARA. "Dostoevsky's 'Notes from the Underground' and Sábato's 'El Túnel.' " *Hispania,* 51 (1968), 440-46.

KAVANAGH, THOMAS M. "Dostoevsky's *Notes From Underground:* The Form of The Fiction." *Texas Studies In Literature And Language,* 14 (1972), 491-507.

KIRK, IRINA. *Dostoevskij And Camus: The Themes Of Consciousness, Isolation, Freedom And Love.*

_____. "Dramatization of Consciousness In Camus and Dostoevsky." *Bucknell Review,* 16, No.1 (1968), 96-104.

LETHCOE, JAMES. "Self-Deception in Dostoevskij's *Notes From The Underground.*" *Slavic And East European Journal,* 10 (1966), 9-21.

McCORQUODALE, MARJORIE K. "The Desperate Man—Today's Hero." *Forum,* 4, No.8 (1965), 4-7.

MERRILL, REED. "The Mistaken Endeavor: Dostoevsky's *Notes From Underground.*" *Modern Fiction Studies,* 18 (1972/73), 505-16.

MOCHULSKY, KONSTANTIN. *Dostoevsky: His Life And Work,* pp. 242-60.

NEUHÄUSER, RUDOLPH. "Observations on the Structure of *Notes From Underground* with Reference to the Main Themes of Part II." *Canadian-American Slavic Studies,* 6 (1972), 239-55.

_____. "Romanticism in the Post-Romantic Age: A Typological Study of Antecedents of Dostoevskii's Man from Underground." *Canadian-American Slavic Studies,* 8 (1974), 333-58.

PARIS, BERNARD J. "*Notes From Underground:* A Horneyan Analysis." *PMLA,* 88 (1973), 511-22.

_____. *A Psychological Approach To Fiction,* pp. 190-214.

PEACE, RICHARD. *Dostoevsky: An Examination Of The Major Novels,* pp. 5-18.

RICE, MARTIN P. "Dostoevskii's *Notes From Underground* and Hegel's 'Master and Slave.' " *Canadian-American Slavic Studies,* 8 (1974), 359-69.

SCOTT, NATHAN A. *Craters Of The Spirit,* pp. 29-34.

SIMMONS, ERNEST J. "Dostoevsky—'A Realist in the Higher Sense,' " in his *Introduction To Russian Realism,* pp. 114-17.

SMALLEY, BARBARA. "The Compulsive Patterns of Dostoyevsky's Underground Man." *Studies In Short Fiction,* 10 (1973), 389-96.

SPERBER, MICHAEL A. "Symptoms and Structure of Borderline Personality Organization: Camus' *The Fall* and Dostoevsky's

'Notes from Underground.' " *Literature And Psychology,* 23 (1973, 102-13.

TRASCHEN, ISADORE. "Existential Ambiguities in *Notes From Underground.*" *South Atlantic Quarterly,* 13 (1974), 363-76.

WEISBERG, RICHARD. "An Example Not to Follow: *Ressentiment* and the Underground Man." *Modern Fiction Studies,* 21 (1975/6), 553-63.

YARMOLINSKY, AVRAHAM. *Dostoevsky: Works And Days,* pp. 190-97.

POOR FOLK (Bednye lyudi, 1846)

DUNLOP, JOHN. "Dostoevsky's Poor Folk Reconsidered," in *F. M. Dostoevsky: 1821-1881,* ed. Nicholas Arseniev and Constantine Belousow, pp. 29-37.

FANGER, DONALD. "Evolution of the Myth: From Poor Folk to Notes from Underground," in his *Dostoevsky And Romantic Realism: A Study Of Dostoevsky In Relation To Balzac, Dickens, And Gogol,* pp. 152-59.

GROSSMAN, LEONID. *Dostoevsky: A Biography,* pp. 51-66.

LARY, N. M. *Dostoevsky And Dickens,* pp. 21-34.

LEATHERBARROW, W. J. "The Rag with Ambition: The Problem of Self-will in Dostoevsky's 'Bednyye lyudi' and 'Dvoynik.' " *Modern Language Review,* 68 (1973), 607-10.

MOCHULSKY, KONSTANTIN. *Dostoevsky: His Life And Work,* pp. 24-39.

THE POSSESSED (Besy, 1872)

BAUMGARTEN, MURRAY. "The Extraordinary Events of *The Devils.*" *Western Humanities Review,* 22 (1968), 23-33.

DAVIES, RUTH. *The Great Books Of Russia,* pp. 189-207.

DAVISON, R. "Camus' Attitude to Dostoevsky's Kirilov and the Impact of The Engineer's Ideas on Camus' Early Work." *Orbis Litterarum,* 30 (1975), 225-40.

EGAN, MICHAEL and DAVID CRAIG. "Dostoevsky's Realism?" *Encounter,* 41, No.3 (1973), 85-87.

FRANK, JOSEPH. "Dostoevsky's Realism." *Encounter,* 40, No.3 (1973), 31-38.

_____. "The Masks of Stavrogin." *Sewanee Review,* 77 (1969), 660-91.

_____. "A Reply." *Encounter,* 41, No.3 (1973), 87.

FREEBORN, R. H. "Realism in Russia, to the Death of Dostoevsky," in *The Age Of Realism,* ed. F. W. J. Hemmings, pp. 132-34.

GIBSON, A. BOYLE. *The Religion Of Dostoevsky,* pp. 125-53.

GROSSMAN, LEONID. *Dostoevsky: A Biography,* pp. 464-86.

GUERARD, ALBERT J. *The Triumph Of The Novel: Dickens, Dostoevsky, Faulkner,* pp. 45-47, 261-301.

KENT, LEONARD J. *The Subconscious In Gogol And Dostoevskij And Its Antecedents,* pp. 137-43.

LANGBAUM, ROBERT. "Thoughts for Our Time: Three Novels on Anarchism." *American Scholar,* 42 (1973), 243-50.

LARY, N. M. *Dostoevsky And Dickens,* pp. 106-37.

MOCHULSKY, KONSTANTIN. *Dostoevsky: His Life And Work,* pp. 404-69.

MUCHNIC, HELEN. "The Leap and the Vision: A Note on the Pattern of Dostoevsky's Novels," in her *Russian Writers,* pp. 139-57.

PEACE, RICHARD. *Dostoevsky: An Examination Of The Major Novels,* pp. 140-217.

PETERSON, DALE E. "Dostoevsky's Mock Apocalypse." *Centennial Review,* 18 (1974), 76-90.

REID, STEPHEN. "Dostoevski's Kirilov and Freedom of the Will." *Hartford Studies In Literature,* 3 (1971), 197-208.

REINHARDT, KURT F. *The Theological Novel Of Modern Europe,* pp. 48–73.

RYSTEN, FELIX S. A. *False Prophets In The Fiction Of Camus, Dostoevsky, Melville, And Others,* pp. 71–91.

SCOTT, NATHAN A. *Craters Of The Spirit,* pp. 35–39.

SEDURO, VLADIMIR. "The Fate of Stavrogin's Confession." *Russian Review,* 25 (1966), 397–404.

SIMMONS, ERNEST J. "Dostoevsky—'A Realist in the Higher Sense,' " in his *Introduction To Russian Realism,* pp. 125–29.

YARMOLINSKY, AVRAHAM. *Dostoevsky: Works And Days,* pp. 294–310.

THE RAW YOUTH (Podrostok, 1876)

GIBSON, A. BOYLE. *The Religion Of Dostoevsky,* pp. 154–61.

GROSSMAN, LEONID. *Dostoevsky: A Biography,* pp. 507–27.

JONES, MALCOLM V. "Dostoevsky and an Aspect of Schiller's Psychology." *Slavonic And East European Review,* 52 (1974), 346–54.

MOCHULSKY, KONSTANTIN. *Dostoevsky: His Life And Work,* pp. 488–534.

SIMMONS, ERNEST J. *Fëodor Dostoevsky,* pp. 38–41.

YARMOLINSKY, AVRAHAM. *Dostoevsky: Works And Days,* pp. 331–41.

VECHNYI MUZH

WOODWARD, JAMES B. " 'Transferred Speech' in Dostoevskii's *Vechnyi Muzh.*" *Canadian-American Slavic Studies,* 8 (1974), 398–407.

THE VILLAGE OF STEPANČIKOVO

MOCHULSKY, KONSTANTIN. *Dostoevsky: His Life And Work,* pp. 172–80.

MONTER, BARBARA HELD. "The Quality of Dostoevskij's Humor: *The Village Of Stepančikovo.*" *Slavic And East European Journal,* 17 (1973), 33–41.

RAHV, PHILLIP. "Dostoevsky: Two Short Novels," in his *Literature And The Sixth Sense,* pp. 273–77.

DOURADO, AUTRAN (Brazilian, 1926–)

A HIDDEN LIFE (Uma Vida em Segredo, 1969)

Reviews

BARROW, LEO L. *Book World,* 13 April 1969; rpt. in *Review,* No.2 (1969), p. 91.

YATES, DONALD A. "Biela's Small Crises." *Saturday Review,* 29 March 1969, p. 28; rpt. in *Review,* No.2 (1969), pp. 91-92.

ÓPERA DOS MORTOS (1967)

POLLOCK–CHAGAS, JEREMY E. "Rosalina and Amelia: A Structural Approach to Narrative." *Luso-Brazilian Review,* 12 (1975), 263–72.

DOWNES, IAN

THE STOLEN LAND

GRIFFIN, JAMES. "Two Novels from Niugini." *Meanjin,* 30 (1971), 457–59.

WILSON, R. KENT. "A Comment on 'The Stolen Land.' " *Overland,* No.47 (1971), pp. 43–44.

Reviews

MCCONCHIE, BELINDA. "Handbook for Rebels." *Overland,* No.47 (1971), pp. 42–43.

DOYON, JACQUES (Canadian, 1931–)

YOB (1971)

Reviews

GREENE NAOMI. *French Review* (1972), 691–92.

DRIEU LA ROCHELLE, PIERRE (French, 1893–1945)

GENERAL

SOUCY, ROBERT. "Romanticism and Realism in the Fascism of Drieu La Rochelle." *Journal Of The History Of Ideas,* 31 (1970), 69–90.

THE FIRE WITHIN (Le Feu Follet, 1931)

THIHER, ALLEN. *"Le Feu Follet:* The Drug Addict as a Tragic Hero." *PMLA,* 88 (1973), 34–40.

GILLES

LEAL, R. B. "Drieu la Rochelle as Social Critic." *AUMLA,* No. 33 (1970), pp. 25–38.

DRIVER, CHARLES JONATHAN (South African, 1939–)

GENERAL

SMITH, ROWLAND. "The Plot beneath the Skin: The Novels of C. J. Driver." *Journal Of Commonwealth Literature,* 10, No.1 (1975), 58–68.

ELEGY FOR A REVOLUTIONARY (1969)

SMITH, ROWLAND. "The Plot beneath the Skin: The Novels of C. J. Driver." *Journal Of Commonwealth Literature,* 10, No.1 (1975), 59–65.

DROSTE-HÜLSHOFF, ANNETTE VON (German, 1797–1848)

THE JEW'S BEECH TREE (Die Judenbuche, 1842)

BELCHAMBER, N. P. "A Case of Identity: A New Look at *Die Judenbuche* by Annette von Droste-Hülshoff." *Modern Languages,* 55 (1974), 80–82.

BERND, CLIFFORD ALBRECHT. "Clarity and Obscurity in Annette von Droste-Hülshoff's *Judenbuche*" in *Studies In German Literature Of The Nineteenth And Twentieth Centuries,* ed. Siegfried Mews, pp. 64–77.

CHICK, EDSON. "Voices in Discord: Some Observations on *Die Judenbuche.*" *German Quarterly,* 42 (1969), 147–57.

COTTRELL, ALAN P. "The Significance of the Name 'Johannes' in *Die Judenbuche.*" *Seminar,* 6 (1970), 207–15.

KING, JANET K. "Conscience and Conviction in 'Die Judenbuche.' " *Monatshefte,* 64 (1972), 349–55.

MARE, MARGARET. *Annette Von Droste-Hülshoff,* pp. 253–66.

THOMAS, L. H. C. " 'Die Judenbuche' and English Literature." *Modern Language Review,* 64 (1969), 351–54.

WEBER, BETTY NANCE. "Droste's *Judenbuche:* Westphalia in International Context." *Germanic Review,* 50 (1975), 203–12.

DROT, JEAN-MARIE

LES TEMPS DES DÉSILLUSIONS OU LE RETOUR D'ULYSSE MANCHOT (1971)

Reviews

JONES, LOUISA. *French Review,* 46 (1972), 211–12.

DU MESNIL, ARMAND

VALDIEU

WRIGHT, BARBARA. " 'Valdieu': A Forgotten Precursor of Fromentin's 'Dominique.' " *Modern Language Review,* 60 (1965), 520–28.

DUCASSE, ISADORE LUCIEN see LAUTRÉAMONT, LE COMTE DE

DUCHARME, RÉJEAN (Canadian, 1941–)
GENERAL

BOND, D. J. "The Search for Identity in the Novels of Réjean Ducharme." *Mosaic,* 9, No.2 (1976), 31–44.

THE SWALLOW SWALLOWED (L'avalée des avalés, 1966)

SUTHERLAND, RONALD. "Children of the Changing Wind," in his *Second Image,* pp. 89–107.

DUCLOS, CHARLES PINOT (French, 1704–1772)
THE PLEASURES OF RETIREMENT (Les confessions du Comte de ***, 1742)

BROOKS, PETER. *The Novel Of Worldliness,* pp. 37–40.

DUDEVANT, MME. see SAND, GEORGE

DUHAMEL, GEORGES (French, 1884–1966)
GENERAL

THODY, PHILIP. "The Politics of the Family Novel: Is Conservatism Inevitable?" *Mosaic,* 3, No. 1 (1969), 87–101.

CONFESSION AT MIDNIGHT (Confession de minuit, 1920)

KEATING, L. CLARK. *Critic Of Civilization: Georges Duhamel And His Writings,* pp. 54–61.

DEUX HOMMES (1924)

KEATING, L. CLARK. *Critic Of Civilization: Georges Duhamel And His Writings,* pp. 61–64.

THE FIGHT AGAINST THE SHADOWS (Le combat contre les ombres, 1939)

KEATING, L CLARK. *Critic Of Civilization: Georges Duhamel And His Writings,* pp. 114–17.

THE LYONNAIS CLUB (Le club des Lyonnais, 1929)

KEATING, L. CLARK. *Critic Of Civilization: Georges Duhamel And His Writings,* pp. 68–71.

NEWS FROM HAVRE (Le notaire du Havre, 1933)

KEATING, L. CLARK. *Critic Of Civilization: Georges Duhamel And His Writings,* pp. 87–102.

SALAVIN'S JOURNAL (Journal de Salavin, 1927)

KEATING, L. CLARK. *Critic Of Civilization: Georges Duhamel And His Writings,* pp. 64–68.

THE SIGHT OF THE PROMISED LAND (Vue de la terre promise, 1934)

KEATING, L. CLARK. *Critic Of Civilization: Georges Duhamel And His Writings,* pp. 105–107.

SUZANNE AND THE YOUNG MEN (Suzanne et les jeunes hommes, 1941)

KEATING, L. CLARK. *Critic Of Civilization: Georges Duhamel And His Writings,* pp. 117–19.

YOUNG PASQUIER (Le jardin des bêtes sauvages, 1934)

KEATING, L. CLARK. *Critic Of Civilization: Georges Duhamel And His Writings,* pp. 102–105.

DUITS, CHARLES
PTAH HOTEP (1971)

Reviews
GUGLI, WILLIAM V. *French Review,* 46 (1972), 440–41.

DUJARDIN, ÉDOUARD (French, 1861–1949)
WE'LL TO THE WOODS NO MORE (Les Lauriers son coupés)

ALEXANDER, THEODOR W. and BEATRICE W. "Schnitzler's 'Leutnant Gustl' and Dujardin's 'Les Lauriers sont coupés.' " *Modern Austrian Literature,* 2, No.2 (1969), 7–15.

HANDLER, PHILIP. "The Case for Édouard Dujardin." *Romanic Review,* 56 (1965), 195–202.

DUMAS, ALEXANDRE, fils (French, 1824–1895)
LA DAME AUX CAMÉLIAS

FINN, MICHAEL R. "Proust and Dumas fils: Odette and *La Dame Aux Camélias*." *French Review,* 47 (1974), 528–42.

DUMITRIU, PETRU (Romanian, 1924–)
THE EXTREME OCCIDENT (1966)

Reviews
STILWELL, ROBERT L. "Ideological Framework for Fiction." *Saturday Review,* 10 September 1966, pp. 61–63.

DUNCAN, SARA JEANETTE (Canadian, 1862–1922)
GENERAL

NAGARAJAN, S. "The Anglo-Indian Novels of Sara Jeanette Duncan." *Journal Of Canadian Fiction,* 3, No.4 (1974), 74–84.

ROSS, M. E. "Sara Jeannette Duncan: Personal Glimpses." *Canadian Literature,* No.27 (1966), pp. 15–19.

AN AMERICAN GIRL IN LONDON (1893)

TAUSKY, THOMAS E. "The American Girls of William Dean Howells and Sara Jeanette Duncan." *Journal Of Canadian Fiction,* 4, No.1 (1975), 146–53.

COUSIN CINDERELLA (1908)

TAUSKY, THOMAS E. "The American Girls of William Dean Howells and Sara Jeanette Duncan." *Journal Of Canadian Fiction,* 4, No.1 (1975), 153–57.

A DAUGHTER OF TODAY

CLOUTIER, PIERRE. "The First Exile." *Canadian Literature,* No.59 (1974), pp. 30–37.

THE IMPERIALIST (1904)

BAILEY, ALFRED G. "The Historical Setting of Sara Duncan's *The Imperialist*." *Journal Of Canadian Fiction,* 2, No.3 (1973), 205–10.

GERSON, CAROLE. "Duncan's Web." *Canadian Literature,* No.63 (1975), pp. 73–80.

McKENNA, ISOBEL. "Women in Canadian Literature," *Canadian Literature,* No.62 (1974), pp. 71–72.

THOMAS, CLARA. "Happily Every After: Canadian Women in Fiction and Fact." *Canadian Literature,* No.34 (1967), pp. 43–44.

DUODU, CAMERON (Ghanian, 1937-)
THE GAB BOYS (1967)

STEWART, DANÌELE. "Ghanian Writing in Prose: A Critical Survey." *Présence Africaine,* No.91 (1974), pp. 92–95.

DUPIN, AMATINE AURORE LUCILLE see SAND, GEORGE

DURÁN, MANUEL (Spanish, 1925-)
TRÍPTICO MEXICANO (1973)

Reviews
REEVE, RICHARD M. *Hispania,* 58 (1975), 235.

DURANDEAUX, JACQUES (French, 1926-)
QU'ELLE: ROMAN (1972)

Reviews
SULEIMAN, SUSAN. *French Review,* 48 (1975), 661–62.

DURAS, MARGUERITE (French, 1914-)
pseudonym of Marguerite Donnadieu
GENERAL

BRÉE, GERMAINE. "An Interview with Marguerite Duras." *Contemporary Literature,* 13 (1972), 401–22.

CISMARU, ALFRED. "Marguerite Duras and the New Novel." *Dalhousie Review,* 47 (1967), 203–12.

CRAIG, GEORGE. "Duras Country." *London Magazine,* NS 8, No.7 (1968), 100–4.

EISINGER, ERICA M. "Crime and Detection in the Novels of Marguerite Duras." *Contemporary Literature,* 15 (1974), 503–20.

THE AFTERNOON OF MONSIEUR ANDESMAS (L'après-midi de Monsieur Andesmas, 1962)

CISMARU, ALFRED. *Marguerite Duras,* pp. 100–8.

SAVAGE, CATHARINE. "A Stylistic Analysis of *L'Après-Midi De Monsieur Andesmas* by Marguerite Duras." *Language And Style,* 2 (1969), 51–62.

L'AMANTE ANGLAISE (1967)

EISINGER, ERICA M. "Crime and Detection in the Novels of Marguerite Duras." *Contemporary Literature,* 15 (1974), 515–20.

Reviews
BALAKIAN, ANNA. "Do-It-Yourself Detective Story." *Saturday Review,* 23 November 1968, p. 67.

DESTROY, SHE SAID (Détruire, dit-elle, 1969)

MCWILLIAMS, DEAN. "The Novelist as Filmmaker: Marguerite Duras' *Destroy, She Said.*" *Literature/Film Quarterly,* 3 (1975), 264–69.

LES IMPUDENTS (1943)

CISMARU, ALFRED. *Marguerite Duras,* pp. 20–28.

THE LITTLE HORSES OF TARQUINIA (Les petits chevaux de Tarquinia, 1953)

CISMARU, ALFRED. *Marguerite Duras,* pp. 55–63.

MODERATO CANTABILE (1958)

CHAMPAGNE, ROLAND A. "An Incantation of the Sirens: The Structure of *Moderato Cantabile.*" *French Review,* 48 (1975), 981–89.

CISMARU, ALFRED. *Marguerite Duras,* pp. 88–95.

EISINGER, ERICA. "Crime and Detection in the Novels of Marguerite Duras." *Contemporary Literature,* 15 (1974), 508–12.

WEISS, VICTORIA L. "Form and Meaning in Marguerite Duras' *Moderato Cantabile.*" *Critique,* 16, No.1 (1974), 79–87.

THE RAVISHING OF LOL STEIN (Le ravissement de Lol V. Stein, 1964)

CISMARU, ALFRED. *Marguerite Duras,* pp. 108–12.

SHOUKRI, DORIS ENRIGHT—CLARK. "The Nature of Being in Woolf and Duras." *Contemporary Literature,* 12 (1971), 317–28.

THE SAILOR FROM GIBRALTAR (Le Marin de Gilbraltar, 1952)

CISMARU, ALFRED. *Marguerite Duras,* pp. 46–53.

Reviews
PAGONES, DORRIE. "Blue-eyed Tar with Scar." *Saturday Review,* 22 July 1967, pp. 37–38.

THE SEA WALL (Un barrage contre le Pacifique, 1950)

CISMARU, ALFRED. *Marguerite Duras,* pp. 34–46.

THE SQUARE (Le square, 1955)

CISMARU, ALFRED. *Marguerite Duras,* pp. 82–88.

TEN-THIRTY ON A SUMMER NIGHT (Dix heures et demie du soir en été, 1962)

CISMARU, ALFRED. *Marguerite Duras,* pp. 95–100.

EISINGER, ERICA M. "Crime and Detection in the Novels of Marguerite Duras." *Contemporary Literature,* 15 (1974), 512–15.

HECK, FRANCIS S. "*Dix Heures Et Demie Du Soir En Été:* The Heroine as Artist, a New Dimension." *Romance Notes,* 16 (1975), 249–53.

THE VICE-CONSUL (Le Vice-consul, 1966)

CISMARU, ALFRED. *Marguerite Duras,* pp. 112–16.

LA VIE TRANQUILLE (1944)

CISMARU, ALFRED. *Marguerite Duras,* pp. 28–34.

DURAS, MME DE
OURIKA

SWITZER, RICHARD. "Mme de Staël, Mme de Duras and the Question of Race." *Kentucky Romance Quarterly,* 20 (1973), 309–16.

DÜRRENMATT, FRIEDRICH (Swiss, 1921-)
GENERAL

DILLER, EDWARD. "Friedrich Dürrenmatt's Theological Concept of History." *German Quarterly,* 40 (1967), 363–71.

GONTRUM, PETER B. "*Ritter, Tod Und Teufel:* Protagonists and Antagonists in the Prose Works of Friedrich Dürrenmatt." *Seminar,* 1 (1965), 88–98.

KURZ, PAUL KONRAD. "The Fool and Doubt: On One Aspect of the Work of Friedrich Dürrenmatt," in his *On The Modern German Literature,* Vol.4: 37–58.

———. "Wolves and Lambs: Friedrich Dürrenmatt's Dramaturgy of Politics," in his *On Modern German Literature,* Vol.4: 59–72.

LEAH, GORDON N. "Dürrenmatt's Detective Stories." *Modern Languages,* 48 (1968), 65–69.

MAYER, HANS. "Friedrich Dürrenmatt: The Worst Possible Turn of Events," in his *Steppenwolf And Everyman,* pp. 163–80.

PFEIFFER, JOHN R. "Windows, Detectives, and Justice in Dürrenmatt's Detective Stories." *Revue Des Langues Vivantes,* 33 (1967), 451–60.

USMIANI, RENATE. "Justice and the Monstruous Meal in the

70

Work of Friedrich Dürrenmatt." *Humanities Association Bulletin,* 20, No.2 (1969), 8-14.

THE JUDGE AND HIS HANGMAN (Der Richter und sein Henker, 1952)

ARNOLD, ARMIN. *Friedrich Dürrenmatt,* pp. 48-51.

ONCE A GREEK . . . (Grieche sucht Griechin, 1955)

USMIANI, RENATE. "Friedrich Dürrenmatt, Escape Artist: A Look at the Novels." *Mosaic,* 5, No.3 (1972), 27-38.

Reviews
DARACK, ARTHUR. "An Accident of Life." *Saturday Review,* 17 July 1965, p. 36.

THE PLEDGE (Das Versprechen, 1958)

ARMIN, ARNOLD. *Friedrich Dürrenmatt,* pp. 55-57.

DAVIAU, DONALD G. "The Role of *Zufall* in the Writings of Friedrich Dürrenmatt." *Germanic Review,* 47 (1972), 291-92.

LEAH, GORDON N. "Dürrenmatt's Detective Stories." *Modern Languages,* 48 (1967), 65-69.

RAMSEY, ROGER. "Parody and Mystery in Dürrenmatt's *The Pledge.*" *Modern Fiction Studies,* 17 (1971/2), 525-32.

THE PROMISE

USMIANI, RENATE. "Friedrich Dürrenmatt, Escape Artist: A Look at the Novels." *Mosaic,* 5, No.3 (1972), 38-40.

THE QUARRY (Der Verdacht, 1953)

ARNOLD, ARMIN. *Friedrich Dürrenmatt,* pp. 51-55.

GONTRUM, PETER B. "*Ritter, Tod Und Teufel:* Protagonists and Antagonists in the Prose Works of Friedrich Dürrenmatt." *Seminar,* 1 (1965), 88-92.

TRAPS (Die Panne, 1960)

ARNOLD, ARMIN. *Friedrich Dürrenmatt,* pp. 57-59.

DUTOURD, JEAN (French, 1920-)

THE HORRORS OF LOVE (Les Horreurs de l'amour, 1963)

Reviews
PEYRE, HENRI. "Trysts with a Typist." *Saturday Review,* 27 May 1967, p. 30.

DUTT, ROMESH CHUNDER (Bengali, 1848-1909)

GENERAL

SRINIVASA IYENGAR, K. R. *Indian Writing In English,* pp. 74-82.

DUUN, OLAV (Norwegian, 1876-1939)

GENERAL

BIRKELAND, BJARTE. "Olav Duun." *Scandinavica,* 10 (1971), 112-21.

DUVIGNAUD, JEAN

L'EMPIRE DU MILIEU (1971)

Reviews
GOODRICH, NORMA L. *French Review,* 46 (1972), 441-42.

DWIVEDI, HAZARI PRASAD (1907-)

GENERAL

BHANOT, S. D. "Lofty Humanism of Hazari Prasad Dwivedi." *Indian Literature,* 11, No.3 (1968), 53-61.

E

EASMON, R. SARIF (Sierra Leone, ca. 1930–)

THE BURNT-OUT MARRIAGE (1967)

MOORE, JACK B. "*The Burnt-Out Marriage* and Burned-Up Reviewers." *African Literature Today,* 5 (1971), 66–87.

STEGEMAN, BEATRICE. "The Divorce Dilemma: The New Woman in Contemporary African Novels." *Critique,* 15, No.3 (1973/4), 82–85.

EÇA DE QUEIRÓS, JOSÉ MARIA DE (Portuguese, 1845–1900)

GENERAL

ANDREWS, NORWOOD H. "The Artist and the Servant Problem: Example, Eça de Queiroz." *Luso-Brazilian Review,* 2, No.1 (1965), 43–55.

BROWN, TIMOTHY. "Pessimism in the Novels of Eça de Queiroz: All's Well That Ends Well?" *Kentucky Romance Quarterly,* 21 (1974), 343–51.

DEMETZ, PETER. "Eça de Queiróz As a Literary Critic." *Comparative Literature,* 19 (1967), 289–307.

FORSTER, MERLIN H. "The Returning Traveler and Portuguese Reality in Eça de Querioz." *Luso-Brazilian Review,* 9, No.1 (1972), 28–35.

NUNN, FREDERICK M. "Eça de Queiroz, *Francesismo,* and Plagiarism." *Luso-Brazilian Review,* 5, No.1 (1968), 101-105.

ALVES E CIA

BROWN, TIMOTHY. "Alves e Cia. as Comedy." *Kentucky Romance Quarterly,* 16 (1969), 135–41.

THE CITY AND THE MOUNTAINS (A Cidade e as Serras, 1901)

DE COSTA, RENÉ. "The Mythic Quest Theme in *A Cicade E As Serras," Luso-Brazilian Review,* 5, No.2 (1968), 71–79.

REISING, ROBERT W. "Huysman's 'Against Nature' and Eça de Queroz's 'The City and the Mountains': A Comparative Study." *USF Language Quarterly,* 9, No.1/2 (1970), 37–40.

Reviews
CLEMENTS, ROBERT J. "He Loved Gadgets and Good Earth." *Saturday Review,* 9 September 1967, p. 34.

COUSIN BASILIO (O primo Basilio, 1878)

ANDREWS, NORWOOD H. "The Artist and the Servant Problem: Example, Eça de Queiroz." *Luso-Brazilian Review,* 2, No.1 (1965), 43–52.

CLARKE, SHIRLEY. "A Study of Valle-Incań's Translations of Three Novels by Eça de Queiroz," in *Hispanic Studies In Hon-our Of Joseph Manson,* ed. Dorothy M. Atkinson and Anthony H. Clarke, pp. 75–83.

FEDORCHEK, ROBERT M. "Luísa's Dream Worlds in *O Primo Basílio." Romance Notes,* 15 (1974), 532–35.

STEVENS, JAMES R. "Eça and Flaubert." *Luso-Brazilian Review,* 3, No.1 (1966), 47–61.

O CRIME DO PADRE AMARO (1875)

CLARKE, SHIRLEY. "A Study of Valle-Inclán's Translations of Three Novels by Eça de Queiroz," in *Hispanic Studies In Honour Of Joseph Manson,* ed. Dorothy M. Atkinson and Anthony H. Clarke, pp. 60-70.

WHITMORE, DON. "Music in *O Crime Do Padre Amaro." Luso-Brazilian Review,* 10 (1973), 247–55.

THE ILLUSTRIOUS HOUSE OF RAMIRES (A Ilustre Casa de Ramires, 1900)

BROWN, TIMOTHY. "The Love Triangle in *A Ilustre Casa De Ramires." Romance Notes,* 12 (1971), 312–17.

———. "The Individual and Society: An Interpretation of *A Ilustre Casa De Ramires." Revista De Estudios Hispánicos,* 8 (1974), 381–92.

———. "Marriage and the Relucant Hero in Eça de Queiroz." *Romance Notes,* 14 (1972), 304–8.

THE MAIAS (Os Maias, 1888)

Reviews
ELLIOT, GEORGE P. "A Great Provincial." *Hudson Review,* 19 (1966), 515–17.

HANDLIN, OSCAR. *Atlantic Monthly,* 216, No.5 (1965), 193.

O MANDARIM (1880)

KEATES, LAURENCE W. "Mysterious Miraculous Mandarin: Origins, Literary Paternity, Implication in Ethics." *Revue De Littérature Comparée,* 40 (1966), 520–23.

THE RELIC (A relíquia, 1887)

CLARKE, SHIRLEY. "A Study of Valle-Inclán's Translations of Three Novels by Eça de Queiroz," in *Hispanic Studies In Honour Of Joseph Manson,* ed. Dorothy M. Atkinson and Anthony H. Clarke, pp. 70-75.

EDWARDS BELLO, JOAQUÍN (Chilean, 1887–1968)

EL ROTO (1920)

BRUSHWOOD, JOHN S. *The Spanish American Novel,* pp. 39-42.

EGBUNA, OBI (Nigerian, 1938-)
WIND VERSUS POLYGAMY (1964)

Reviews
DATHORNE, O. R. *Black Orpheus,* No.17 (1965), p. 59.

ÉHRENBURG, ILYA (Russian, 1891-1967)
GENERAL

OULANOFF, HONGOR. "Motives of Pessimism in Érenburg's Early Works." *Slavic And East European Journal,* 11 (1967), 266-77.

THE EXTRAORDINARY ADVENTURES OF JULIO JURENITO AND HIS DISCIPLES (Neobyknovennye pokhozhdenia Khulio Khurenito, 1922)

AUSTIN, PAUL M. "Further Surgery of Érenburg's *Xulio Xurenito:* A Review Article." *Slavic And East European Journal,* 11 (1967), 204-8.

EISCHENDORFF, JOSEPH VON (German, 1788-1857)
GENERAL

BLACKALL, ERIC A. "Moonlight and Moonshine: A Disquisition on Eichendorff's Novels." *Seminar,* 6 (1970), 111-27.

EKWENSI, CYPRIAN (Nigerian, 1921-)
GENERAL

KILLAM, DOUGLAS. "Cyprian Ekwensi," in *Introduction To Nigerian Literature,* ed. Bruce King, pp. 77-96.

LINDFORS, BERNTH, "The Blind Men and the Elephant." *African Literature Today,* 7 (1975), 55-59.

———. *Folklore In Nigerian Literature,* pp. 116-29.

———. "Interview with Cyprian Ekwensi." *World Literature Written In English,* 13 (1974), 141-54.

OBIECHINA, E. N. "Ekwensi As Novelist." *Présence Africaine,* No. 86 (1973), pp. 152-64.

POVEY, JOHN. "The English Language of the Contemporary African Novel." *Critique,* 11, No.3 (1968/9), 87-89.

ROSCOE, ADRIAN A. *Mother Is Gold,* pp. 88-94.

BEAUTIFUL FEATHERS

CARTEY, WILFRED. *Whispers From A Continent,* pp. 193-95.

OBIECHINA, E. N. "Ekwensi As Novelist." *Présence Africaine,* No.86 (1973), pp. 160-64.

POVEY, JOHN F. "Cyprian Ekwensi and *Beautiful Feathers.*" *Critique,* 8, No.1 (1965), 63-69.

ISKA

LAURENCE, MARGARET. *Long Drums And Cannons,* pp. 162-68.

JAGUA NANA (1961)

KILLAM, DOUGLAS. "Cyprian Ekwensi," in *Introduction To Nigerian Literature,* ed. Bruce King, pp. 86-91.

LARSON, CHARLES R. "*Pamela* in Africa: Onitsha Market Literature," in his *The Emergence Of African Fiction,* rev. ed., pp. 87-91.

LAURENCE, MARGARET. *Long Drums And Cannons,* pp. 152-57.

OBIECHINA, E. N. "Ekwensi As Novelist." *Présence Africaine,* No.86 (1973), pp. 155-59.

PEOPLE OF THE CITY (1954)

CARTEY, WILFRED. *Whispers From A Continent,* pp. 167-70.

GLEASON, JUDITH ILLSLEY. *This Africa,* pp. 126-30.

KILLAM, DOUGLAS. "Cyprian Ekwensi," in *Introduction To Nigerian Literature,* ed. Bruce King, pp. 80-86.

LAURENCE, MARGARET. *Long Drums And Cannons,* pp. 149-52.

OBIECHINA, E. N. "Ekwensi As Novelist." *Présence Africaine,* No.86 (1973), pp. 152-55.

WHEN LOVE WHISPERS (1947)

LARSON, CHARLES R. "*Pamela* in Africa: Onitsha Market Literature," in his *The Emergence Of African Fiction,* rev. ed., pp. 82-87.

ELDERSHAW, FLORA see ELDERSHAW, M. BARNARD

ELDERSHAW, M. BARNARD
THE GLASSHOUSE

RORABACKER, LOUISE E. *Marjorie Barnard And M. Barnard Eldershaw,* pp. 49-56.

GREEN MEMORY

RORABACKER, LOUISE E. *Marjorie Barnard And M. Barnard Eldershaw,* pp. 41-48.

A HOUSE IS BUILT

RORABACKER, LOUISE E. *Marjorie Barnard And M. Barnard Eldershaw,* pp. 32-41.

PLAQUE WITH LAUREL

RORABACKER, LOUISE E. *Marjorie Barnard And M. Barnard Eldershaw,* pp. 56-64.

TOMORROW AND TOMORROW (1947)

BARNARD, MARJORIE. "How 'Tomorrow and Tomorrow' Came to be Written." *Meanjin,* 29 (1970), 328-30.

BURNS, ROBERT. "Flux and Fixity: M. Barnard Eldershaw's 'Tomorrow and Tomorrow.' " *Meanjin,* 29 (1970), 320-27.

RORABACKER, LOUISE E. *Marjorie Barnard And M. Barnard Eldershaw,* pp. 64-76.

ELIZONDO, SALVADOR (Mexican, 1932-)
FARABEUF O LA CRÓNICA DE UN INSTANTE (1965)

McMURRAY, GEORGE R. "Salvador Elizondo's 'Farabeuf.' " *Hispania,* 50 (1967), 596-601.

EL HIPOGEO SECRETO (1968)

McMURRAY, GEORGE M. "Salvador Elizondo's 'El Hipogeo Secreto' and Wittgenstein's Philosophy." *Hispania,* 53 (1970), 330-34.

ELKHADEM, SAAD (Egyptian)
AJINHA MIN RASAS (1972)

MOUSSA-MAHMOUD, FATMA. "A New Oriental Bird with Leaden Wings: On Saad Elkhadem's *Ajniha Min Rasas.*" *International Fiction Review,* 2 (1975), 69-70.

ELWIN, VERRIER (1902-1964)
GENERAL

MISRA, BHABAGRAHI. "Folklore in Verrier Elwin's Novels." *Indian Literature,* 13, No.1 (1970), 132-38.

ENDO, SHUSAKU (Japanese, 1923-)
GENERAL

MATHY, FRANCIS. "Endo Shusaku: White Man, Yellow Man." *Comparative Literature,* 19 (1967), 58–74.

KIIROI HITO

MATHY, FRANCIS. "Shusaku Endo: Japanese Catholic Novelist." *Thought,* 42 (1967), 597–600.

NANJI MO MATA

MATHY, FRANCIS. "Shusaku Endo: Japanese Catholic Novelist." *Thought,* 42 (1967), 600–3.

THE SILENCE (Chinmoku, 1966)

GALLAGHER, MICHAEL. "Exploring a Dark and Cruel Period: A Japanese-Catholic Novel." *Commonweal,* 85 (1966), 136–8.

MATHY, FRANCIS. "Shusaku Endo: Japanese Catholic Novelist." *Thought,* 42 (1967), 585–614.

ENGEL, MARIAN (Canadian, 1933–)

THE HONEYMAN FESTIVAL (1970)

PARKER, DOUGLAS H. " 'Memories of My Own Patterns': Levels of Reality in *The Honeyman Festival.*" *Journal Of Canadian Fiction,* 4, No.3 (1975), 111–16.

MONODROMOS (1973)

Reviews
THOMAS, AUDREY. "Closing Doors." *Canadian Literature,* No.61 (1974), pp. 80–81.

ENTENZA, PEDRO

NO HAY ACERAS

WOODS, RICHARD D. "The Cuban Revolution Interpreted Through the Novel *No Hay Aceras.*" *Romance Notes,* 13 (1971), 234–38.

Reviews
SCHWARTZ, KESSEL. *Hispania,* 53 (1970), 346.

EPPS, BERNARD

PILGARIC THE DEATH

Reviews
HALL, WILLIAM F. "Banks and Drifts." *Canadian Literature,* No.37 (1968), pp. 94–96.

ERASMUS, DESIDERIUS (Dutch, 1469–1536)

GENERAL

MOORE, JOHN A. "A Note on Erasmus and Fray Luis de Granada." *Romance Notes,* 9 (1967), 314–19.

NUGENT, DONALD. "The Erasmus Renaissance." *The Month,* 1, 2nd N.S. (1970), 36–45.

THE PRAISE OF FOLLY (Moriae Encomium, 1509)

CHRISTIAN, LYNDA GREGORIAN. "The Metamorphoses of Erasmus' 'Folly.' " *Journal Of The History Of Ideas,* 32 (1971), 289–94.

GAVIN, J. AUSTIN and THOMAS M. WALSH. "The *Praise Of Folly* in Context: The Commentary of Girardus Listrius." *Renaissance Quarterly,* 24 (1971), 193–209.

GREENFIELD, THELMA N. "*A Midsummer Night's Dream* and *The Praise Of Folly.*" *Comparative Literature,* 20 (1968), 236–44.

KRISTELLER, PAUL OSKAR. "Erasmus from an Italian Perspective." *Renaissance Quarterly,* 23 (1970), 11–13.

MILLER, CLARENCE H. "Current English Translations of *The Praise Of Folly:* Some Corrections." *Philological Quarterly,* 45 (1966), 718–33.

———. "Some Medieval Elements and Structural Unity in Erasmus' *The Praise Of Folly.*" *Renaissance Quarterly,* 27 (1974), 499–511.

REBHORN, WAYNE A. "The Metamorphoses of Moria: Structure and Meaning in *The Praise Of Folly.*" *PMLA,* 89 (1974), 463–76.

ROTHSCHILD, HERBERT B. "Blind and Purblind: A Reading of *The Praise Of Folly.*" *Neophilologus,* 54 (1970), 223–34.

TRUMAN, R. W. "*Lazarillo De Tormes,* Petrarch's *De Remediis Adversae Fortunae,* and Erasmus's *Praise Of Folly.*" *Bulletin Of Hispanic Studies,* 52 (1975), 33–53.

ERI, VINCENT

THE CROCODILE (1970)

GRIFFIN, JAMES. "Two Novels from Niugini." *Meanjin,* 30 (1971), 454–57.

Reviews
KOLL, MICHAEL. "New Nation, New Literature: Niugini." *Journal Of Commonwealth Literature,* 9, No.1 (1974), 66–69.

MCLAREN, JOHN. "Through Native Eyes." *Overland,* No. 47 (1971), p. 44.

ERIC, SPEEDY

MABEL THE SWEET HONEY

LARSON, CHARLES R. "*Pamela* in Africa: Onitsha Market Literature," in his *The Emergence Of African Fiction,* rev. ed., pp. 75–82.

ESFANDIARY, F. M. (Iranian, 1930–)

GENERAL

MULLER, GILBERT H. "The Fiction of F. M. Esfandiary." *Literature East And West,* 15 (1971), 119–26.

THE BEGGAR (1965)

KRIEGEL, LEONARD. "The Novels of F. M. Esfandiary." *Literature East And West,* 11 (1967), 192–93.

THE DAY OF SACRIFICE (1959)

KRIEGEL, LEONARD. "The Novels of F. M. Esfandiary." *Literature East And West,* 11 (1967), 191–92.

IDENTITY CARD (1966)

KRIEGEL, LEONARD. "The Novels of F. M. Esfandiary." *Literature East And West,* 11 (1967), 193–4.

ESPINEL, VINCENTE (Spanish, 1550–1624)

MARCOS DE OBREGÓN (1618)

BJORNSON, RICHARD. "Social Conformity and Justice in *Marcos De Obregon.*" *Revista De Estudios Hispánicos,* 9 (1975), 285–307.

ESTRADA, Ezequel Martinez see MARTÍNEZ ESTRADA, Ezequiel

ETCHERELLI, CLAIRE

ELISE, OR THE REAL LIFE

Reviews
PAGONES, DORRIE. *Saturday Review,* 30 August 1969, pp. 26–27.

ÉTIEMBLE, JEANNINE

GENERAL

PESCHEL, ENID RHODES. "Étiemeble: The Novelist As Healer." *USF Language Quarterly,* 12, No.1/2 (1973), 35–42.

F

FABRE, JACQUELINE

LA DOUVE (1971)

Reviews
TEDESCHI, RICHARD. *French Review,* 47 (1973), 226–27.

FADEYEV, ALEXANDER (Russian, 1901–1956)

GENERAL

SSACHNO, HELEN VON. "Two Russian Writers: Fadeyev & Tvardovsky." *Encounter,* 44, No.2 (1975), 56–58.

THE NINETEEN see THE ROUT

THE ROUT (Razgrom, 1927)

RZHEVSKY, NICOLAES. "Idea and Heritage in Soviet Literature." *Comparative Literature Studies,* 6 (1969), 419–34.

THE YOUNG GUARD (Molodaia Gvardiia, 1945)

PREOBRAZHENSKY, S. "The Lofty Romanticism of Bolshevik Traditions." *Soviet Studies In Literature,* 6 (1970), 365–76.

FAECKE, PETER

THE FIREBUGS

Reviews
BAUKE, JOSEPH P. "Whisper of Evil in a Roar of Drums." *Saturday Review,* 22 January 1966, p. 42.

FAFOURNOUX, LOUIS

L'ABBAYE DE GRAND VENT (1971)

Reviews
BUCKNALL, BARBARA J. *French Review,* 46 (1972), 444–45.

FAGUNWA, DANIEL OLORUNFEMI (Nigerian, ca. 1910–1963)

GENERAL

BEIER, ULLI. "Fagunwa: A Yoruba Novelist." *Black Orpheus,* No.17 (1965), pp. 51–56; rpt. in *Introduction To African Literature,* ed. Ulli Beier, pp. 188–95.

LINDFORS, BERNTH. "Amos Tutuola and D. O. Fagunwa." *Journal Of Commonwealth Literature,* No.9 (1970), pp. 57–65.

ROSCOE, ADRIAN A. *Mother Is Gold,* pp. 95–98.

FALKBERGET, JOHAN (Norwegian, 1879–1967)

GENERAL

RAASTAD, OTTAR. "Johan Falkberget: An Appreciation." *American Scandinavian Review,* 58 (1970), 153–56.

THE FOURTH NIGHT WATCH (Den fjerde na Hevakt, 1923)

Reviews
SPECTOR, ROBERT D. *American Scandinavian Review,* 57 (1969), 197.

FALLANA, SAMUEL

LA FEMME DE BAVE (1971)

Reviews
ABEL, ADELINE. *French Review,* 45 (1972), 1044–45.

FARAGGI, CLAUDE

LA SIGNE DE LA BÊTE

Reviews
JOHNSON, PATRICIA J. *French Review,* 48 (1975), 662–63.

FARMILOE, DOROTHY (Canadian, 1920–)

AND SOME IN FIRE (1974)

Reviews
BARCLAY, PAT. "Sticking to Lasts." *Canadian Literature,* No.65 (1975), pp. 111–12.

FAUCHER, Claire see MARTIN, Claire

FEDIN, KONSTANTIN ALEKSANDROVICH (Russian, 1892–)

CITIES AND YEARS (Goroda i gody, 1924)

BEAUJOUR, ELIZABETH KLOSTY. "Some Problems of Construction in Fedin's *Cities And Years.*" *Slavic And East European Journal,* 16 (1972), 1–18.

———. "The Uses of Witches in Fedin and Bulgakov." *Slavic Review,* 33 (1974), 695–707.

FEDUCHY, MANIN M.

LA BRUJAROJA

Reviews
HULSE, LLOYD K. *Chasqui,* No.1 (1974), 82–84.

FEJES, ENDRE (Hungarian, 1923–)

GENERATION OF RUST (Rozsdatemeto, 1962)

Reviews
MAURER, ROBERT. *Saturday Review,* 13 June 1970, pp. 43–44.

FENELON, FRANCOIS DE SALIGNAC DE LA MOTHE (1651–1715)

LES AVENTURES DE TELEMAQUE (1699)

KNAPP, LEWIS M. "Smollett's Translation of Fenelon's *Telemaque.*" *Philological Quarterly,* 44 (1965), 405–7.

FENG, MÊNG-LUNG (Chinese, 1574–1646)

P'ING YAO CHUAN (ca. 1620)

HANAN, PATRICK. "The Composition of the *P'ing Yao Chuan.*" *Harvard Journal Of Asiatic Studies,* 31 (1971), 201–19.

FENOGLIO, BEPPE (Italian, 1922–1963)

CARTELLA 2 (Unpublished)

MERRY, BRUCE. "More on Fenoglio: An Unpublished Novel in English and an English Source." *Italica,* 49 (1972), 3–17.

FERNÁNDEZ, PABLO ARMANDO (Cuban, 1930–)

LOS NIÑOS SE DESPIDAN (1968)

Reviews
MENTON, SEYMOUR. *Hispania,* 52 (1969), 972.

FERNÁNDEZ DE LIZARDI, JOSÉ JOAQUÍN (Mexican, 1776–1827)

DON CATRIN DE LA FACHENDA Y NOCHES TRISTES Y DÍA ALEGRE (1818)

BANCROFT, ROBERT L. "*El Periquillo Sarniento* and *Don Catrin De La Fachenda:* Which Is the Masterpiece?" *Revista Hispanica Moderna,* 34 (1968), 533–38.

PAWLOWSKI, JOHN. " 'Periquillo' and 'Catrín': Comparison and Contrast." *Hispania,* 58 (1975), 830–42.

EL PERIQUILLO SARNIENTO (1930–31)

BANCROFT, ROBERT L. "*El Periquillo Sarniento* and *Don Catrin De La Fachenda:* Which Is the Masterpiece?" *Revista Hispanica Moderna,* 34 (1968), 533–38.

FOX, HUGH B. "The Uses of Satire in Latin America." *Arizona Quarterly,* 24 (1968), 67–70.

LANGFORD, WALTER M. *The Mexican Novel Comes Of Age,* pp. 4–7.

PAWLOWSKI, JOHN. " 'Periquillo' and 'Catrín': Comparison and Contrast." *Hispania,* 58 (1975), 830–42.

FERNÁNDEZ FLÓREZ, WENCESLAO (Spanish, 1884–1964)

GENERAL

ZAETTA, ROBERT. "The *Burla* in the Novels of Wenceslao Fernández Flórez." *Revista De Estudios Hispánicos,* 6 (1972), 283–92.

———. "Wenceslao Fernández Flórez: The Evolution of His Technique in His Novels." *Kentucky Romance Quarterly,* 17 (1970), 127–37.

EL HOMBRE QUE COMPRÓ UN AUTOMÓVIL (1932)

ZAETTA, ROBERT. "Wenceslao Fernández Flórez: The Evolution of His Technique in His Novels." *Kentucky Romance Quarterly,* 17 (1970), 133–36.

EL SISTEM PELEGRÍN

ZAETTA, ROBERT. "Wenceslao Fernández Flóez' Comic Technique in *El Sistema Pelegrín*" *Romance Notes,* 15 (1973), 234–37.

FERNÁNDEZ NICHOLÁS, SEVERIANO (Spanish, 1919–)

DESPUÉS DE LA TORMENTA (1964)

Reviews
FABIAN, DONALD L. *Hispania,* 48 (1965), 388–89.

FERNANDEZ SANTOS, JESÚS (Spanish, 1926–)

EL HOMBRE DE LOS SANTOS (1969)

Reviews
DÍAZ, JANET W. *Hispania,* 53 (1970), 340–41.

FERREIRA DE CASTRO, JOSÉ MARIA (Portuguese, 1898–1974)

A LÃ E A NEVE

MEGENNEY, WILLIAM W. "Descriptive Sensationism in Ferreira de Castro." *Romance Notes,* 13 (1971), 61–66.

FERRES, ANTONIO (Spanish, 1925–)

EN EL SEGUNDO HEMISFERIO (1970)

Reviews
FRANZ, THOMAS R. *Hispania,* 56 (1973), 736.

FERRON, JACQUES (Canadian, 1921–)

DR. COTNOIR (Cotnoir, 1962)

Reviews
GODARD, BARBARA. "Ferron's Magical Ark." *Journal Of Canadian Fiction,* 3, No.2 (1974), 107–8.

THE JUNEBERRY TREE

Reviews
DUNLOP, DONNA. "Four from Ferron." *Tamarack Review,* No.68 (1976), pp. 91–92.

FESSLER, IGNAZ AURELIUS

MARC-AUREL

HADLEY, MICHAEL. *The German Novel In 1790,* pp. 214–18.

FEUCHTWANGER, LION (German, 1884–1958)

GENERAL

BERENDSOHN, WALTER A. "Lion Feuchtwanger and Judaism," in *Lion Feuchtwanger: The Man, His Ideas, His Work,* ed. John M. Spalek, pp. 25–32.

FAULHABER, UWE KARL. "Lion Feuchtwanger's Theory of the Historical Novel," in *Lion Feuchtwanger: The Man, His Ideas, His Work,* ed. John M. Spalek, pp. 67–81.

FUEGI, JOHN. "Feuchtwanger, Brecht and the 'Epic' Media: The Novel and the Film," in *Lion Feuchtwanger: The Man, His Ideas, His Work,* ed. John M. Spalek, pp. 307–22.

HOFE, HAROLD VON. "Lion Feuchtwanger and America," in *Lion Feuchtwanger: The Man, His Ideas, His Work,* ed. John M. Spalek, pp. 33–50.

JAHN, WERNER. "The Meaning of 'Progress' in the Work of Lion Feuchtwanger," in *Lion Feuchtwanger: The Man, His Ideas, His Work,* ed. John M. Spalek, pp. 51-65.

KAHN, LOTHAR. *Insight And Action: The Life And Work Of Lion Feuchtwanger.*

KEUNE, MANFRED. "*Das Haus Der Desdemona:* Lion Feuchtwanger's Apologia for a Mimesis of History," in *Lion Feuchtwanger: The Man, His Ideas, His Work,* ed. John M. Spalek, pp. 83-98.

MUELLER, DENNIS. "Characterization of Types in Feuchtwanger's Novels," in *Lion Feuchtwanger: The Man, His Ideas, His Work,* ed. John M. Spalek, pp. 99-111.

SCHNAUBER, CORNELIUS. "Feuchtwanger as a Theater Critic," in *Lion Feuchtwanger: The Man, His Ideas, His Work,* ed. John M. Spalek, pp. 265-76.

WALDO, HILDE. "Lion Feuchtwanger: A Biography," in *Lion Feuchtwanger: The Man, His Ideas, His Work,* ed. John M. Spalek, pp. 1-24.

WEISSENBERGER, KLAUS. "Flavius Josephus—A Jewish Archetype," in *Lion Feuchtwanger: The Man, His Ideas, His Work,* ed. John M. Spalek, pp. 187-99.

JEPHTA AND HIS DAUGHTER (Jefta und seine tochter, 1957)

JESPERSEN, ROBERT C. "*Jefta Und Seine Tochter:* The Problem of Credibility," in *Lion Feuchtwanger: The Man, His Ideas, His Work,* ed. John M. Spalek, pp. 245-63.

JEW SÜSS see POWER

DIE JÜDIN VON TOLEDO

WAGENER, HANS. "Lion Feuchtwanger's *Die Jüdin Von Toledo,*" in *Lion Feuchtwanger: The Man, His Ideas, His Work,* ed. John M. Spalek, pp. 231-44.

THE OPERMANNS (Die geschwister Oppermann, 1933)

BERNDT, WOLFGANG. "The Trilogy *Der Wartesaal,*" in *Lion Feuchtwanger: The Man, His Ideas, His Work,* ed. John M. Spalek, pp. 141-47.

PARIS GAZETTE (Exil, 1939)

BERNDT, WOLFGANG. "The Trilogy *Der Wartesaal,*" in *Lion Feuchtwanger: The Man, His Ideas, His Work,* ed. John M. Spalek, pp. 147-55.

POWER (Jud Süss, 1925)

YUILL, W. E. "*Jud Süss:* Anatomy of a Best-Seller," in *Lion Feuchtwanger: The Man, His Ideas, His Work,* ed. John M. Spalek, pp. 113-29.

SUCCESS: A NOVEL (Erfolg, 1930)

BERNDT, WOLFGANG. "The Trilogy *Der Wartesaal,*" in *Lion Feuchtwanger: The Man, His Ideas, His Work,* ed. John M. Spalek, pp. 131-41.

WEISSTEIN, ULRICH. "Clio the Muse: An Analysis of Lion Feuchtwanger's *Erfolg,*" in *Lion Feuchtwanger: The Man, His Ideas, His Work,* ed. John M. Spalek, pp. 157-86.

THIS IS THE HOUR (Goya oder der arge weg der erkenntnis, 1951)

KAHN, LOTHAR. "*Der Arge Weg Der Erkenntnis,*" in *Lion Feuchtwanger: The Man, His Ideas, His Work,* ed. John M. Spalek, pp. 201-16.

'TIS FOLLY TO BE WISE (Narrenweisheit oder tod und verklärung des Jean-Jacques Rousseau, 1952)

MOELLER, HANS-BERNHARD. "Feuchtwanger's *Rousseau:* Springboard of Dialecticism and Revolution," in *Lion Feuchtwanger: The Man, His Ideas, His Work,* ed. John M. Spalek, pp. 217-30.

FEUILLET, OCATAVE (French, 1821-1890)
LA PETITE COMTESSE

TINTNER, ADELINE R. "Octave Feuillet, *La Petite Comtesse* and Henry James." *Revue De Littérature Comparée,* 48 (1974), 218-32.

FICHTE, HUBERT (German, 1935-)
DIE PALETTE (1968)

Reviews
SAMMONS, JEFFREY L. "Hamburg Dropouts." *Novel,* 2 (1969), 280-81.

FICKELSON, MAURICE
UNE SOIRÉE CHEZ AZERBACH (1971)

Reviews
GREENE, NAOMI. *French Review,* 46 (1972), 212-13.

FIELDEN, CHARLOTTE
CRYING AS SHE RAN

Reviews
BENAZON, MICHAEL. *Dalhousie Review,* 51 (1971), 297-301.

THOMAS, AUDREY. "Heeeeelllp!" *Canadian Literature,* No.48 (1971), pp. 84-85.

FIELDING, JOY (Canadian, 1945-)
THE BEST OF FRIENDS (1972)

Reviews
ROSENGARTEN, HERBERT. "Survival of the Fittest." *Canadian Literature,* No.58 (1973), pp. 94-95.

FILHO, ADONIAS
CORPO VIVO (1962)

FOSTER, DAVID WILLIAM. "An Introduction to Adonias Filho's *Corpo Vivo.*" *Latin American Literary Review,* 1, No.2 (1973), 43-50.

MEMORIES OF LAZARUS (1969)

Reviews
NEISWENDER, ROSEMARY. *Library Journal,* 1 October 1969; rpt. in *Review,* No.2 (1969), p. 93.

FLAKE, OTTO (German, 1880-1963)
GENERAL

BOESCHENSTEIN, HERMANN. "Observations on Otto Flake," in *Essays On German Literature In Honour Of G. Joyce Hallamore,* ed. Michael S. Batts and Marketa Goetz Stankiewicz, pp. 236-55.

FORTUNAT (1946)

BOESCHENSTEIN, HERMANN. "Observations on Otto Flake," in *Essays On German Literature In Honour Of G. Joyce Hallamore,* ed. Michael S. Batts and Marketa Goetz Stankiewicz, pp. 247-51.

FLAUBERT, GUSTAVE (French, 1821-1880)
GENERAL

ADAMOWSKI, T. H. "The Condemned of Rouen: Sartre's Flauberts." *Novel,* 6 (1972), 79-83.

BART, B. F. "Flaubert's Concept of the Novel." *PMLA,* 80 (1965), 84–89.

BERSANI, LEO. "Flaubert: The Politics of Mystical Realism." *Massachusetts Review,* 11 (1970), 35–50.

CHARNEY, HANNA. "Images of Absence in Flaubert and Some Contemporary Films." *Style,* 9 (1975), 488–501.

COOK, DAVID A. "James and Flaubert: The Evolution of Perception." *Comparative Literature,* 25 (1973), 289–307.

DONATO, E. " 'A Mere Labyrinth of Letters'/Flaubert and the Quest for Fiction/A Montage." *MLN,* 89 (1974), 885–910.

FAIRLIE, ALISON. "Flaubert and the Authors of the French Renaissance, in *The French Renaissance And Its Heritage,* pp. 43–62.

FLETCHER, JOHN. *A Critical Commentary On Flaubert's 'Trois Contes,'* pp. 9–37.

GRAY, EUGENE F. "Flaubert's Esthetics and the Problem of Knowledge." *Nineteenth-Century French Studies,* 4 (1976), 295–302.

HAINSWORTH, G. "Schopenhauer, Flaubert, Maupassant: Conceptual Thought and Artistic 'Truth,' " in *Currents Of Thought In French Literature,* pp. 165–90.

HUNTLEY, H. ROBERT. "Flaubert and Ford: The Fallacy of *'Le Mot Juste.'* " *English Language Notes,* 4 (1967), 283–87.

PRENDERGAST, CHRISTOPHER. "Flaubert: Writing and Negativity." *Novel,* 8 (1975), 197–213.

PURDY, STROTHER B. "Henry James, Gustave Flaubert, and the Ideal Style." *Language And Style,* 3 (1970), 163–84.

REDFERN, WALTER D. "People and Things in Flaubert." *French Review,* 44, Special issue No.2 (1971), 79–88.

SACHS, MURRAY. "Flaubert's Laughter." *Nineteenth-Century French Studies,* 3 (1974/5), 112–23.

———. "Flaubert's Trois Contes: The Reconquest of Art." *L'Esprit Créateur,* 10 (1970), 62–74.

SARRAUTE, NATHALIE. "Flaubert." *Partisan Review,* 33 (1966), 193–208.

SPIEGEL, ALAN. "Flaubert to Joyce: Evolution of a Cinematographic Form." *Novel,* 6 (1973), 229–33.

WEST, CONSTANCE B. "Ten Years of Flaubert Studies." *Modern Languages,* 49 (1968), 99–107.

WETHERILL, PETER M. "Montaigne and Flaubert." *Studi Francesi,* 18 (1974), 416–28.

BOUVARD AND PÉCUCHET (Bouvard et Pécuchet, 1881)

BERNHEIMER, CHARLES. "Linguistic Realism in Flaubert's *Bouvard Et Pécuchet." Novel,* 7 (1974), 143–58.

BUCK, STRATTON. *Gustave Flaubert,* pp. 113–23.

CROSS, RICHARD K. *Flaubert And Joyce: The Rite Of Fiction,* pp. 153–73.

HAINSWORTH, G. "Schopenhauer, Flaubert, Maupassant: Conceptual Thought and Artistic 'Truth,' " in *Currents Of Thought In French Literature,* pp. 177–81.

NADEAU, MAURICE. "Bouvard et Pécuchet." *London Magazine,* NS 10, No.4 (1970), 42–55.

———. *The Greatness Of Flaubert,* pp. 261–79.

STARKIE, ENID. *Flaubert The Master: A Critical And Biographical Study (1856-1880),* pp. 307–35.

HÉRODIAS (1877)

CORTLAND, PETER. *A Reader's Guide To Flaubert,* pp. 155–68.

FLETCHER, JOHN. *A Critical Commentary On Flaubert's 'Trois Contes,'* pp. 66–73.

NADEAU, MAURICE. *The Greatness Of Flaubert,* pp. 254–56.

STARKIE, ENID. *Flaubert The Master: A Critical And Biographical Study (1856-1880),* pp. 264–74.

TILLET, MARGARET G. "An Approach to *Herodias." French Studies,* 21 (1967), 24–31.

WAKE, C. H. "Symbolism in Flaubert's *Hérodias:* An Interpretation." *Forum For Modern Language Studies,* 4 (1968), 322–29.

THE LEGEND OF SAINT JULIAN THE HOSPITALIER
(La Légende de Saint Julien L'Hospitalier, 1877)

BANCROFT, W. JANE. "Flaubert's *Légende De Saint Julien:* The Duality of the Artist-Saint." *L'Esprit Créateur,* 10 (1970), 75–84.

BART, BENJAMIN F. "Flaubert and Hunting: *La Légende De St. Julien L'Hospitalier." Nineteenth-Century French Studies,* 4 (1975/6), 31–52.

———. "Psyche into Myth: Humanity and Animality in Flaubert's *Saint-Julien." Kentucky Romance Quarterly,* 20 (1973), 317–42.

BART, HEIDI CULBERTSON AND BENJAMIN F. BART. "Space, Time, and Reality in Flaubert's *Saint Julien." Romanic Review,* 59 (1968), 30–39.

BERSANI, LEO. "The Anxious Imagination." *Partisan Review,* 35 (1968), 49–52.

BROMBERT, VICTOR. "Flaubert's *Saint Julien:* The Sin of Existing." *PMLA,* 81 (1966), 297–302.

BUCK, STRATTON. *Gustave Flaubert,* pp. 108–10.

CORTLAND, PETER. *A Reader's Guide To Flaubert,* pp. 146–55.

DUCKWORTH, COLIN. "Flaubert and the Legend of St. Julian: A Non-Exclusive View of Sources." *French Studies,* 22 (1968), 107–13.

FLETCHER, JOHN. *A Critical Commentary On Flaubert's 'Trois Contes,'* pp. 54–66.

McCRADY, JAMES WARING. "The Saint Julien Window at Rouen as a Source for Flaubert's *Légende De Saint Julien L'Hospitalier." Romance Notes,* 10 (1969), 268–76.

NADEAU, MAURICE. *The Greatness Of Flaubert,* pp. 250–52.

PILKINGTON, A. E. "Point of View in Flaubert's *La Legende De Saint Julien." French Studies,* 29 (1975), 266–79.

RAITT, A. W. "The Composition of Flaubert's *Saint Julien L'Hospitalier." French Studies,* 19 (1965), 358–72.

SACHS, MURRAY. "Flaubert's Trois Contes: The Reconquest of Art." *L'Esprit Créateur,* 10 (1970), 63–71.

SHERZER, DINA. "Narrative Figures in *La Légende De Saint Julien L'Hospitalier." Genre,* 7 (1974), 54–70.

STARKIE, ENID. *Flaubert The Master: A Critical And Biographical Study (1856-1880),* pp. 244–56.

MADAME BOVARY (1856)

ARTINIAN, ROBERT WILLARD. "Flaubert's *Madame Bovary." Explicator,* 30 (1971), Item 34.

BABCOCK-ABRAHAMS, BARBARA. "The Novel and the Carnival World: An Essay in Memory of Joe Doherty." *MLN,* 89 (1974), 930–34.

BENTLEY, CHRISTOPHER. "Wilfred Owen and Gustave Flaubert." *Notes & Queries,* n.s., 17 (1970), 456–57.

BERSANI, LEO. "The Anxious Imagination." *Partisan Review,* 35 (1968), 49–66.

———. *Balzac To Beckett,* pp. 154–91.

———. "Flaubert and Emma Bovary: The Hazards of Literary Fusion." *Novel,* 8 (1974), 16–28.

BESTON, JOHN R. "The Influence of *Madame Bovary* on *The Tree Of Man." Revue De Littérature Comparée,* 46 (1972), 555–68.

BUCK, STRATTON. *Gustave Flaubert,* pp. 63–86.

CHURCH, MARGARET. "A Triad of Images: Nature in *Madame Bovary.*" *Mosaic,* 5, No.3 (1972), 203-13.

CORTLAND, PETER. *A Reader's Guide To Flaubert,* pp. 17-82.

CROSS, RICHARD K. *Flaubert And Joyce: The Rite Of Fiction,* pp. 71-121.

EVANS, WILLIAM M. "The Question of Emma's Eyes." *Romance Notes,* 16 (1975), 274-77.

GALE, JOHN E. "Sainte-Beuve and Baudelaire on *Madame Bovary.*" *French Review,* 41 (1967), 30-37.

GILL, RICHARD. "The Soundtrack of *Madame Bovary:* Flaubert's Orchestration of Aural Imagery."*Literature/Film Quarterly,* 1 (1973), 206-17.

GOODHEART, EUGENE. "Flaubert and the Powerlessness of Art." *Centennial Review,* 19 (1975), 157-71.

GRANT, RICHARD B. "The Role of Minerva in *Madame Bovary.*" *Romance Notes,* 6 (1965), 113-15.

HAGAN, JOHN. "Une Ruse de Style: A Pattern of Allusion in *Madame Bovary.*" *Studies In The Novel,* 1 (1969), 6-16.

HAIG, STIRLING. "The *Madame Bovary* Blues." *Romanic Review,* 61 (1970), 27-34.

HEMMINGS, F. W. J. "Emma and the 'Maw of Wifedom.' " *L'Esprit Créateur,* 10 (1970), 13-23.

————. "The Realist and Naturalist Movements in France," in *The Age Of Realism.* ed. F. W. J. Hemmings, pp. 153-62.

HYSLOP, LOIS BOE. "Baudelaire: 'Madame Bovary, C'est moi'?" *Kentucky Romance Quarterly,* 20 (1973), 343-58.

KAPLAN, HAROLD. *The Passive Voice,* pp. 23-41.

KIRTON, W. J. S. "Flaubert's Use of Sound in *Madame Bovary.*" *Forum For Modern Language Studies,* 11 (1975), 36-45.

LOWE, A. M. "Emma Bovary, A Modern Arachne." *French Studies,* 26 (1972), 30-41.

McCARTHY, MARY. "On *Madame Bovary,*" in her *The Writing On The Wall And Other Literary Essays,* pp. 72-94.

McCONNELL, FRANK D. "Félicité, Passion, Ivresse; The Lexicography of *Madame Bovary.*" *Novel,* 3 (1970), 153-66.

Madame Bovary And The Critics: A Collection Of Essays, Ed. B. F. Bart.

MEIN, MARGARET. *A Foretaste Of Proust: A Study Of Proust And His Precursors,* pp. 161-81.

MUIR, EDWIN. "Emma Bovary and Becky Sharp," in his *Essays On Literature And Society,* rev. ed., pp. 182-94.

NADEAU, MAURICE. *The Greatness Of Flaubert,* pp. 107-43.

PALMER, MELVIN D. "The Literary Ancestry of Flaubert's Hippolyte." *Studies In The Novel,* 3 (1971), 97-98.

REDFERN, WALTER D. "People and Things in Flaubert." *French Review,* 44, Special Issue No.2 (1971), 80-82.

SABISTON, ELIZABETH. "The Prison of Womanhood." *Comparative Literature,* 25 (1973), 336-51.

SACHS, MURRAY. "The Role of the Blind Begger in *Madame Bovary.*" *Symposium,* 22 (1968), 72-80.

ST. AUBYN, F. C. "Madame Bovary Outside the Window." *Nineteenth-Century French Studies,* 1 (1973), 105-11.

SHERRINGTON, R. J. *Three Novels By Flaubert: A Study Of Techniques,* pp. 79-152.

SHRIVER, M. "*Madame Bovary* versus *The Woman Of Rome.*" *Nineteenth-Century French Studies,* 1 (1973), 197-209.

SLOCHOWER, HARRY. "Suicides in Literature: Their Ego Function." *American Imago,* 32 (1975), 397-99.

STARKIE, ENID. *Flaubert: The Making Of The Master,* pp. 223-333.

STEIN, WILLIAM BYSSHE. "*Madame Bovary* and Cupid Unmasked." *Sewanee Review,* 73 (1965), 197-209.

STEPHENS, DORIS. "A Focus on Fingernails in *Madame Bovary.*" *Romance Notes,* 12 (1970), 74-77.

STEVENS, JAMES R. "Eça and Flaubert." *Luso-Brazilian Review,* 3, No.1 (1966), 47-61.

VIRTANEN, REINO. "A Possible Source for a Passage of *Madame Bovary.*" *Romance Notes,* 11 (1969), 302-4.

WATT, IAN. "*Almayer's Folly:* Memories and Models." *Mosaic,* 8, No.1 (1974), 175-77.

WEINBERG, HENRY H. "The Function of Italics in *Madame Bovary.*" *Nineteenth-Century French Studies,* 3 (1974/5), 97-111.

WETHERILL, P. M. "*Madame Bovary's* Blind Man: Symbolism in Flaubert." *Romanic Review,* 61 (1970), 35-42.

WILLIAMS, D. A. *Psychological Determinism In <Madame Bovary.>*

LES MEMORIES D'UN FOU

DIAMOND, MARIE J. *Flaubert: The Problem Of Aesthetic Discontinuity,* pp. 18-46.

NOVEMBER (Novembre)

DIAMOND, MARIE J. *Flaubert: The Problem of Aesthetic Discontinuity,* pp. 47-75.

STARKIE, ENID. *Flaubert: The Making of the Master,* pp. 73-89.

SALAMMBÔ (1862)

BART, B. F. "Louis Bouilhet and the Redaction of *Salammbô.*" *Symposium,* 27 (1973), 197-213.

BUCK, STRATTON. *Gustave Flaubert,* pp. 87 99.

JAY, BRUCE LOUIS. "Anti-History and the Method of *Salammbô.*" *Romanic Review,* 63 (1972), 20-33.

LEAL, R. B. "*Salammbô:* An Aspect of Structure." *French Studies,* 27 (1973), 16-29.

NADEAU, MAURICE. *The Greatness of Flaubert,* pp. 159-74.

PORTER, DENNIS. "Aestheticism versus the Novel: The Example of *Salammbô.*" *Novel,* 4 (1971), 101-6.

————. "*Salammbô:* A Rebuttal." *Novel,* 6 (1972), 70-72.

ROSE, MARILYN GADDIS. "Decadent Prose: The Example of *Salammbô.*" *Nineteenth-Century French Studies,* 3 (1975), 213-23.

————. "*Salammbô:* A Meaningful Novel." *Novel,* 6 (1972), 66-69.

SHERRINGTON, R. J. *Three Novels by Flaubert: A Study of Techniques,* pp. 153-231.

SHRODER, MAURICE Z. "On Reading *Salammbô.*" *L'Esprit Crèateur,* 10 (1970), 24-35.

STARKIE, ENID. *Flaubert the Master: A Critical and Biographical Study (1856-1880),* pp. 55-85.

STRONG, ISABELLE. "Flaubert's Controversy with Froehner: The Manuscript Tradition." *Romance Notes,* 16 (1975), 283-99.

SENTIMENTAL EDUCATION (L'Éducation sentimentale, 1869)

BROMBERT, VICTOR. "Flaubert and the Impossible Artist-Hero." *Southern Review,* NS, 5 (1969), 976-86.

BUCK, STRATTON. *Gustave Flaubert,* pp. 124-42.

COATES, CARROL F. "Daumier and Flaubert: Examples of Graphic and Literary Caricature." *Nineteenth-Century French Studies,* 4 (1976), 303-11.

CORTLAND, PETER. "Homecoming: The Fate of the Flaubertian Hero." *Ball State University Forum,* 9, No.2 (1968), 10-18.

————. *A Reader's Guide To Flaubert,* pp. 83-126.

————. *Sentiment In Flaubert's <Éducation Sentimentale.>*

————. *The Sentimental Adventure: An Examination Of Flaubert's <Éducation Sentimentale.>*

Cross, Richard K. *Flaubert And Joyce: The Rite Of Fiction,* pp. 35–67.

Danahy, Michael. "The Esthetics of Documentation: The Case of *L'Éducation Sentimentale.*" *Romance Notes,* 14 (1972), 61–65.

———. "Narrative Timing and the Structures of *L'Éducation Sentimentale.*" *Romanic Review,* 66 (1975), 32–46.

Denommé, Robert T. "The Theme of Disintegration in Flaubert's *Education Sentimentale.*" *Kentucky Romance Quarterly,* 20 (1973), 163–71.

Diamond, Marie J. *Flaubert: The Problem Of Aesthetic Discontinuity,* pp. 76–104.

Gans, Eric. "Éducation Sentimentale: The Hero as Storyteller." *MLN,* 89 (1974), 614–25.

Gerhardi, Gerhard C. "Romantic Love and the Prostitution of Politics: On the Structural Unity in *L'Éducation Sentimentale.*" *Studies In The Novel,* 4 (1972), 402–15.

Grover, P. R. "Two Modes of Possessing—Conquest and Appreciation: 'The Princess Casamassima' and 'L'Éducation Sentimentale.'" *Modern Language Review,* 66 (1971), 760–71.

Hemmings, F. W. J. "The Realist and Naturalist Movements in France," in *The Age Of Realism,* ed. F. W. J. Hemmings, pp. 173–79.

Lebowitz, Naomi. *Humanism And The Absurd In The Modern Novel,* pp. 23–42.

Miller, Marcia K. "A Note on Structure and Theme in *L'Éducation Sentimentale.*" *Studies In Romanticism,* 10 (1971), 130–36.

Moon, H. Kay. "Description: Flaubert's 'External World' in *L'Éducation Sentimentale.*" *French Review,* 39 (1966), 501–12.

Nadeau, Maurice. *The Greatness Of Flaubert,* pp. 49–61, 175–95.

Rexroth, Kenneth. "Classics Revisted-XLI: 'Sentimental Education.'" *Saturday Review,* 31 December 1966, p. 41; rpt. in his *Classics Revisited,* pp. 258–62.

Seaton, Beverly. "Mirror Imagery and Related Concepts in *L'Éducation Sentimentale.*" *Romance Notes,* 11 (1969), 46–50.

Sherrington, R. J. "Louise Roque and *L'Éducation Sentimentale.*" *French Studies,* 25 (1971), 427–36.

———. *Three Novels By Flaubert: A Study Of Techniques,* pp. 232–333.

Starkie, Enid. *Flaubert: The Making Of The Master,* pp. 103–19.

———. *Flaubert The Master: A Critical And Biographical Study (1856-1880),* pp. 140–78.

Thiher, Roberta Joyce. "Dehumanization through Style." *Romance Notes,* 10 (1969), 265–67.

Reviews

Brady, Patrick. *French Review,* 46 (1973), 1052–53.

A SIMPLE HEART (Un Coeur Simple, 1877)

Beck, William J. "Félicité and the Bull in Flaubert's *Un Coeur Simple.*" *Xavier University Studies,* 10, No.1 (1971), 16–26.

———. "Flaubert's 'Un Coeur Simple:' The Path to Sainthood?" *Xavier University Studies,* 7, No.2 (1968), 59–67.

Buck, Stratton. *Gustave Flaubert,* pp. 104–8.

Chamberlain, John S. "Ibsen's 'Vildanden' in Relation to George Brandes's 'Gustave Flaubert' and Flaubert's 'Un Coeur Simple.'" *Scandinavica,* 14 (1975), 37–43.

Cortland, Peter. *A Reader's Guide To Flaubert,* pp. 128–46.

Cross, Richard K. *Flaubert And Joyce: The Rite Of Fiction,* pp. 17–25.

Denommé, Robert T. "Félicité's View of Reality and the Nature of Flaubert's Irony in 'Un Coeur Simple.'" *Studies In Short Fiction,* 7 (1970), 573–81.

Dobray-Rifelj, Carol de. "Doors, Walls, and Barriers in Flaubert's 'Un Coeur Simple." *Studies In Short Fiction,* 11 (1974), 291–95.

Fletcher, John. *A Critical Commentary On Flaubert's 'Trois Contes,'* pp. 39–54.

Nadeau, Maurice. *The Greatness Of Flaubert,* pp. 252–54.

Showalter, English. "*Un Coeur Simple* as an Ironic Reply to Bernardin de Saint-Pierre.." *French Review,* 40 (1966), 47–55.

Starkie, Enid. *Flaubert The Master: A Critical And Biographical Study (1856-1880),* pp. 256–64.

Wake, C. H. "Flaubert's Search for Identity: Some Reflections on *Un Coeur Simple.*" *French Review,* 44, Special issue No.2 (1971), 89–96.

THE TEMPTATION OF SAINT ANTHONY (Tentation de Saint Antoine, 1874)

Buck, Stratton. *Gustave Flaubert,* pp. 50–61.

Cross, Richard K. *Flaubert And Joyce: The Rite Of Fiction,* pp. 125–49.

Diamond, Marie J. *Flaubert: The Problem Of Aesthetic Discontinuity,* pp. 105–31.

Nadeau, Maurice. The Greatness of Flaubert, pp. 62–73, 238–48.

Porter, Laurence M. "A Fourth Version of Flaubert's *Tentation De Saint Antoine* (1869)." *Nineteenth-Century French Studies,* 4 (1975/6), 53–66.

Reff, Theodore. "The Influence of Flaubert's Queen of Sheba on Later Nineteenth Century Literature." *Romanic Review,* 65 (1974), 249–65.

Sachs, Murray. "Flaubert's *Trois Contes:* The Reconquest of Art." *L'Esprit Créateur,* 10 (1970), 63–71.

Sherrington, R. J. "Illusion and Reality in 'La Tentation de Saint Antoine.'" *AUMLA,* No.24 (1965), pp. 272–89.

Starkie, Enid. *Flaubert: The Making Of The Master,* pp. 159–66.

———. *Flaubert The Master: A Critical And Biographical Study (1856-1880),* pp. 213–28.

FLORES, JUAN DE (Spanish, late 15th century)
BREVE TRACTADO DE GRIMALTE Y GRADISSA

Waley, Pamela. "Love and Honour in the *Novelas Sentimentales* of Diego de San Pedro and Juan de Flores." *Bulletin Of Hispanic Studies,* 43 (1966), 267–75.

HISTORIA DE GRISEL Y MIRABELLA

Waley, Pamela. "*Cárcel De Amor* and *Grisel Y Mirabella* A Question of Priority." *Bulletin Of Hispanic Studies,* 50 (1973), 340–56.

———. "Love and Honour in the *Novelas Sentimentales* of Diego de San Pedro and Juan de Flores." *Bulletin Of Hispanic Studies,* 43 (1966), 263–67.

FOCK, GORCH (GERMAN, 1880–1916) pseudonym of Johann Kinau
GENERAL

Kurz, Edmund. "Gorch Fock and the Regional Novel." *Revue Des Langues Vivantes,* 32 (1966), 42–47.

FOGAZZARO, ANTONIO (Italian, 1842–1911)
GENERAL

Hall, Robert A., Jr. "Fogazzaro's Maironi Tetralogy." *Italica,* 42 (1965), 248–59.

Pacifici, Sergio. *The Modern Italian Novel: From Manzoni To Svevo,* pp. 138–48.

LEILA (1911)

HALL, ROBERT A., JR., "Fogazzaro's Maironi Tetralogy." *Italica*, 42 (1965), 255-58.

THE LITTLE WORLD OF THE PAST (Piccolo mondo antico, 1895)

PACIFICI, SERGIO. *The Modern Italian Novel: From Manzoni To Svevo*, pp. 144-48.

IL SANTO (1905)

HALL, ROBERT A., JR. "Fogazzaro's *Il Santo* and Hochhuth's *Der Stellvertreter*." *Italian Quarterly*, 10, No.36-37 (1965), 22-33.

FONTANE, THEODOR (German, 1819-1898)
GENERAL

KLEINEBERGER, H. R. "Social Conformity and Non-Conformity in the Novels of Fontane." *Forum For Modern Language Studies*, 4 (1968), 387-95.

KOESTER, RUDOLF. "Death by Miscalculation: Some Notes on Suicide in Fontane's Prose." *German Life And Letters*, 20 (1966), 34-42.

SASSE, H.-C. "The Unknown Fontane: Sketches, Fragments, Plans." *German Life And Letters*, 20 (1966), 25-33.

SUBIOTTO, FRANCES M. "Aspects of the Theatre in Fontane's Novels." *Forum For Modern Language Studies*, 6 (1970), 149-68.

L'ADULTERA (1882)

MEYER, HERMANN. *The Poetics Of Quotation In The European Novel*, pp. 169-91.

BEYOND RECALL (Unwiederbringlich)

SUBIOTTO, FRANCES M. "The Function of Letters in Fontane's 'Unwiederbringlich.' " *Modern Language Review*, 65 (1970), 306-18.

EFFI BRIEST (1895)

HATFIELD, HENRY. *Crisis And Continuity In Modern German Fiction*, pp. 18-27.

RIECHEL, DONALD C. "*Effi Briest* and the Calendar of Fate." *Germanic Review*, 48 (1973), 189-211.

RITCHIE, J. M. "Realism in Germany, from the Death of Goethe," in *The Age Of Realism*, ed. F. W. J. Hemmings, pp. 250-53.

THANNER, JOSEF. "Symbol and Function of the Symbol in Theodor Fontane's 'Effi Briest.' " *Monatshefte*, 57 (1965), 187-92.

FRAU JENNY TREIBEL (1892)

BRUFORD, W. H. *The German Tradition Of Self-Cultivation*, pp. 190-205.

HATFIELD, HENRY. *Crisis And Continuity In Modern German Fiction*, pp. 14-18.

TURNER, DAVID. "Coffee or Milk?—That is the Question: On an Incident from Fontane's *Frau Jenny Treibel*." *German Life And Letters*, 21 (1968), 330-35.

———. "Fontane's *Frau Jenny Treibel*: A Study in Ironic Discrepancy." *Forum For Modern Language Studies*, 8 (1972), 132-47.

MATHILDE MÖHRING

BANCE, A. F. "Fontane's 'Mathilde Möhring.' " *Modern Language Review*, 69 (1974), 121-33.

DER STECHLIN (1898)

GEORGE, E. F. "The Symbol of the Lake and Related Themes in Fontane's *Der Stechlin*." *Forum For Modern Language Studies*, 9 (1973), 143-52.

HATFIELD, HENRY. *Crisis And Continuity In Modern German Fiction*, pp. 28-34.

MEYER, HERMANN. *The Poetics Of Quotation In The European Novel*, pp. 191-203.

UNTERM BIRNBAUM

THOMAS, LIONEL. "Fontane's *Unterm Birnbaum*." *German Life And Letters*, 23 (1970), 193-205.

FONTES, AMANDO (Brazilian, 1899-1967)
OS CORUMBAS (1933)

TOOP, WALTER R. "Amando Fontes: Time and Chronology." *Luso-Brazilian Review*, 6, No.1 (1969), 60-84.

RUA DO SIRIRI (1937)

TOOP, WALTER R. "Amando Fontes: Time and Chronology." *Luso-Brazilian Review*, 6, No.1 (1969), 60-84.

FORER, MORT (Canadian, 1922-)
THE HUMBACK (1970)

Reviews
LAURENCE, MARGARET. "Stubborn Pride." *Tamarack Review*, No.55 (1970), pp. 77-79.

WIEBE, RUBY. "Pushed Back to the Ridge." *Canadian Review*, No.48 (1971), pp. 86-87.

FORRESTER, VIVIANE
LE GRAND FESTIN (1971)

Reviews
STARY, SONJA G. *French Review*, 45 (1972), 1176-77.

FORTUNATUS (Author Unknown)

ROHRMANN, P. "The Central Role of Money in the Chapbook *Fortunatus*." *Neophilologus*, 59 (1975), 262-72.

FOUGÈRES, MICHEL
CHO' QUA'N (1971)

Reviews
TALBOT, EMILE J. *French Review*, 46 (1972), 213-15.

FOUGERET DE MONBRON, JEAN-LOUIS
MARGOT LA RAVAUDEUSE

PIZZORUSSO, ARNALDO. "Situations and Environment in *Margot La Ravaudeuse*." *Yale French Studies*, No.40 (1968), pp. 142-55.

FOUQUÉ, FRIEDRICH, BARON DE LA MOTTE (German, 1777-1843)
GENERAL

MORNIN, EDWARD. "Some Patriotic Novels and Tales by La Motte Fouqué." *Seminar*, 11 (1975), 141-56.

UNDINE (1811)

LILLYMAN, W. J. "Fouqué's *Undine*." *Studies In Romanticism*, 10 (1971), 94-104.

MCHANEY, THOMAS L. "Fouqué's *Undine* and Edith Wharton's *Custom Of The Country*." *Revue De Littérature Comparée*, 45 (1971), 180-86.

POLLIN, BURTON R. "*Undine* in the Works of Poe." *Studies In Romanticism*, 14 (1975), 59-74.

FOURNEL, PAUL

L'ÉQUILATÈRE (1972)

Reviews
SCHNEIDER, JUDITH MORGANROTH. *French Review,* 47 (1973), 227-28.

FOURNIER, Pierre see GASCAR, Pierre

FOURRÉ, MAURICE

TÊTE-DE-NÈGRE (1960)

MATTHEWS, J. H. *Surrealism And The Novel,* pp. 141-57.

FRAME, JANET (New Zealander, 1924–)

GENERAL

DELBAERE-GARANT, JEANNE. "Daphne's Metamorphosis in Janet Frame's Early Novels." *Ariel: A Review Of International English Literature,* 6, No.2 (1975), 23-37.

EVANS, PATRICK. "Alienation and the Imagery of Death: The Novels of Janet Frame." *Meanjin,* 32 (1973), 294-303.

ROBERTSON, ROBERT T. "Bird, Hawk, Bogie: Janet Frame, 1952-62." *Studies In The Novel,* 4 (1972), 186-99.

RUTHERFORD, ANNA. "Janet Frame's Divided and Distinguished Worlds." *World Literature Written In English,* 14 (1975), 51-68.

THE EDGE OF THE ALPHABET (1962)

DELBAERE-GARANT, JEANNE. "Daphne's Metamorphosis in Janet Frame's Early Novels." *Ariel: A Review Of International English Literature,* 6, No.2 (1975), 26-29.

INTENSIVE CARE (1970)

Reviews
EASTON, ELIZABETH. *Saturday Review,* 1 August 1970, pp. 29, 37.

SCENTED GARDENS FOR THE BLIND (1963)

DELBAERE-GARENT, JEANNE. "Daphne's Metamorphosis in Janet Frame's Early Novels." *Ariel: A Review Of International English Literature,* 6, No.2 (1975), 29-34.

YELLOW FLOWERS IN THE ANTIPODEAN ROOM (1969)

Reviews
HAYNES, MURIEL. "Nature as Status." *Saturday Review,* 19 April 1969, pp. 41-42.

FRANCE, ANATOLE pseudonym of Jacques-Anatole-François Thibault (French, 1844–1924)

GENERAL

BRESKY, DUSHAN. *The Art Of Anatole France.*

HERVOUET, YVES. "Conrad and Anatole France." *Ariel: A Review Of International English Literature,* 1, No.1 (1970), 84-99.

THE ASPIRATIONS OF JEAN SERVIEN (Les désirs de Jean Servien, 1882)

VIRTANEN, REINO. *Anatole France,* pp. 51-54.

AT THE SIGN OF THE REINE PÉDAUQUE (La rôtisserie de la Reine Pédauque, 1893)

VIRTANEN, REINO. *Anatole France,* pp. 88-93.

THE CRIME OF SYLVESTER BONNARD (Le crime de Sylvestre Bonnard, 1881)

VIRTANEN, REINO. *Anatole France,* pp. 47-51.

THE ELM TREE ON THE MALL (L'orme du mail, 1897)

VIRTANEN, REINO. *Anatole France,* pp. 104-8.

THE GODS ARE ATHIRST (Les dieux ont soif, 1912)

VIRTANEN, REINO. *Anatole France,* pp. 135-50.

MONSIEUR BERGERET IN PARIS (Monsieur Bergeret à Paris, 1901)

VIRTANEN, REINO. *Anatole France,* pp. 111-15.

A MUMMER'S TALE (Histoire comique, 1903)

VIRTANEN, REINO. *Anatole France,* pp. 116-19.

PENGUIN ISLAND (L'île des pingouins, 1907)

VIRTANEN, REINO. *Anatole France,* pp. 126-34.

THE RED LILY (Le lys rouge, 1894)

VIRTANEN, REINO. *Anatole France,* pp. 94-98.

THE REVOLT OF THE ANGELS (La révolte des anges, 1914)

VIRTANEN, REINO. *Anatole France,* pp. 150-56.

THAÏS (1890)

VIRTANEN, REINO. *Anatole France,* pp. 54-60.

THE WHITE STONE (Sur la pierre blanche, 1905)

VIRTANEN, REINO. *Anatole France,* pp. 121-25.

FRANK, BRUNO (German, 1887–1945)

THE LOST HERITAGE (Der reisepass, 1937)

KAMLA, THOMAS A. "Bruno Frank's *Der Reisepass:* The Exile as an Aristocrat of Humanity." *Monatshefte,* 67 (1975), 37-47.

FRANK, CHRISTOPHER

LA NUIT AMÉRICAINE

Reviews
LUETHANS, TOD N. *French Review,* 47 (1974), 1212-14.

FRANKLIN, STEPHEN

KNOWLEDGE PARK

Reviews
SORFLEET, JOHN ROBERT. "Knowledge Park: Year One—A Challenge to Canadians." *Journal Of Canadian Fiction,* 1, No.4 (1972), 106.

FRASER, RAYMOND (Canadian, 1941–)

THE STRUGGLE OUTSIDE (1975)

Reviews
ATHERTON, STAN. *International Fiction Review,* 2 (1975), 183-84.

FRASER, SYLVIA (Canadian, 1935–)

THE CANDY FACTORY (1975)

Reviews
MACDONALD, RAE MCCARTHY. *Dalhousie Review,* 55 (1975), 558-60.

PANDORA (1973)

Reviews
BARCLAY, PAT. "Rationality in Mind." *Canadian Literature,* No.60 (1974), pp. 109-10.

MCCARTHY, RAE. *Dalhousie Review,* 52 (1972/3), 701-4.

PORTER, HELEN. "When I Was Just a Little Child." *Journal Of Canadian Fiction,* 1, No.4 (1972), 92-93.

FREIBERG, JOHANNES VON
DAS RÄDLEIN

WAILES, STEPHEN L. "The Title of *Das Rädlein* by Johannes von Freiberg." *German Quarterly,* 47 (1974), 52-54.

FREYRE, GILBERTO (Brazilian, 1900-)
GENERAL

LOOS, DOROTHY SCOTT. "Gilberto Freyre as a Literary Figure: An Introductory Study." *Revista Hispanica Moderna,* 34 (1968), 714-20.

MOTHER AND SON: A BRAZILIAN TALE (1967)

Reviews
GROSSMAN, WILLIAM L. "Dona and Water Madona." *Saturday Review,* 13 May 1967, p. 40

FREYTAG, GUSTAV
DEBIT AND CREDIT (Soll und haben, 1855)

CARTER, T. E. "Freytag's *Soll Und Haben:* A Liberal National Manifesto as a Best-seller." *German Life And Letters,* 21 (1968), 320-29.

SAMMONS, JEFFREY L. "The Evaluation of Freytag's *Soll Und Haben.*" *German Life And Letters,* 22 (1969), 315-24.

FRÍAS, IIERIBERTO (Mexican, 1870-1925)
GENERAL

BROWN, JAMES W. "Heriberto Frías, a Mexican Zola." *Hispanica,* 50 (1967), 467-71.

¿ ÁGUILA O SOL? (1923)

BROWN, JAMES W. "Heriberto Frías, a Mexican Zola." *Hispanica,* 50 (1967), 468-71.

FRISCH, MAX (RUDOLF) (Swiss, 1911-)
GENERAL

BARLOW, D. " 'Ordnung' and 'das wirliche Leben' in the Work of Max Frisch." *German Life And Letters,* 19 (1965), 52-60.

COCK, MARY E. " 'Countries of the Mind': Max Frisch's Narrative Technique." *Modern Language Review,* 65 (1970), 820-28.

CUNLIFFE, W. G. "Existentialist Elements in Frisch's Works." *Monatshefte,* 62 (1970), 113-22.

KIESER, ROLF. "Man as his own Novel: Max Frisch and the Literary Diary." *Germanic Review,* 47 (1972), 109-17.

————, Trans. "An Interview with Max Frisch." *Contemporary Literature,* 13 (1972), 1-14.

KURZ, PAUL KONRAD. "Identity and Society: The World of Max Frisch," in his *On Modern German Literature,* pp. 104-54.

LIVINGSTONE, R. S. "The World-View of Max Frisch." *Southern Review: Literary And Interdisciplinary Essays,* 1, No.3 (1965), 32-45.

MUSGRAVE, MARIAN E. "The Evolution of the Black Character in the Works of Max Frisch." *Monatshefte,* 66 (1974), 117-32.

PALMER, PETER R. "Max Frisch and the Crucifixion of Sex." *Delta: The Cambridge Literary Magazine,* No.39 (1966), 34-39.

ANTWORT AUS DER STILLE (1937)

WEISSTEIN, ULRICH. *Max Frisch,* pp. 37-42.

BIN, OR THE JOURNEY TO PEKING (Bin oder die reise nach Peking, 1945)

PETERSON, CAROL. *Max Frisch,* pp. 27-30.

WEISSTEIN, ULRICH. *Max Frisch,* pp. 42-47.

THE DIFFICULT ONES (Die Schwierigen: order, J'adore ce qui me brûle, 1943)

PETERSON, CAROL. *Max Frisch,* pp. 22-25

WEISSTEIN, ULRICH. *Max Frisch,* pp. 24-37.

HOMO FABER: A REPORT (Homo Faber, 1957)

BRADLEY, BRIGITTE L. "Max Frisch's *Homo Faber:* Theme and Structural Devices." *Germanic Review,* 41 (1966), 279-90.

HOFFMAN, CHARLES W. "The Search for Self, Inner Freedom, and Relatedness in the Novels of Max Frisch," in *The Contemporary Novel In German: A Symposium,* ed. Robert R. Heitner, pp. 94-110.

PETERSON, CAROL. *Max Frisch,* pp. 83-88.

WEISSTEIN, ULICH. *Max Frisch,* pp. 64-77.

I'M NOT STILLER (Stiller, 1954)

BARLOW, D. " 'Ordnung' and 'das Wirliche Leben' in the Work of Max Frisch." *German Life And Letters,* 19 (1965), 57-60.

HELMETAG, CHARLES H. "The Image of the Automobile in Max Frisch's *Stiller.*" *Germanic Review,* 47 (1972), 118-26.

HOFFMANN, CHARLES W. "The Search for Self, Inner Freedom, and Relatedness in the Novels of Max Frisch," in *The Contemporary Novel In German: A Symposium,* ed. Robert R. Heitner, pp. 103-6.

KURZ, PAUL KONRAD. "Identity and Society: The World of Max Frisch," in his *On Modern German Literature,* pp. 132-41.

LIVINGSTONE, R. S. "The World-View of Max Frisch." *Southern Review: Literary And Interdisciplinary Essays,* 1, No.3 (1965), 37-41.

MANGER, PHILIP. "Kierkegaard in Max Frisch's Novel *Stiller.*" German *Life And Letters,* 20 (1967), 119-31.

MUSGRAVE, MARIAN E. "The Evolution of the Black Character in the Works of Max Frisch." *Monatshefte,* 66 (1974), 120-24.

PETERSON, CAROL. *Max Frisch,* pp. 77-83.

WEISSTEIN, ULRICH. *Max Frisch,* pp. 48-63.

JURG REINHART (1934)

WEISSTEIN, ULRICH. *Max Frisch,* pp. 24-31.

A WILDERNESS OF MIRRORS (Mein Name Sei Gantenbein, 1964)

HOFFMANN, CHARLES W. "The Search for Self, Inner Freedom, and Relatedness in the Novels of Max Frisch," in *The Contemporary Novel In German: A Symposium,* ed. Robert R. Heitner, pp. 93-113.

PETERSON, CAROL. *Max Frisch,* pp. 100-6.

WEISSTEIN, ULRICH. *Max Frisch,* pp. 78-89.

Reviews
CAPOUYA, EMILE. "To Be But Not to See." *Saturday Review,* 26 February 1966, p. 38.

FRIZZLE, NORMAN
THE RAPE OF MOZART

Reviews
BAILEY, NANCY. "A Dead Man in Life." *Journal Of Canadian Fiction,* 3, No.1 (1974), 107.

FROMENTIN, EUGÉNE SAMUEL AUGUSTE (French, 1820-1876)
DOMINIQUE (1863)

BREMNER, GEOFFREY. "Ambivalence in *Dominique.*" *Forum For Modern Language Studies,* 5 (1969), 323-30.

GRANT, RICHARD B. and NELLY H. SEVERIN. "Weaving Imagery in

Fromentin's *Dominique.*" *Nineteenth-Century French Studies,* 1 (1973), 155–61.

HUBERT, RENEÉ RIESE. "Fromentin's *Dominique:* The Confession of a Man Who Judges Himself." *PMLA,* 82 (1967), 634–39.

LATIOLAIS, F. M. " 'Not Quite a Masterpiece'—Fromentin's *Dominique* Reconsidered." *Mosaic,* 4, No.1 (1970), 35–48.

MAGOWAN, ROBIN. "*Dominique:* The Genesis of a Pastoral." *L'Esprit Créateur,* 13 (1973), 340–50.

MEIN, MARGARET. *A Foretaste Of Proust: A Study Of Proust And His Precursors,* pp. 143–60.

WRIGHT, BARBARA. " 'Valdieu': A Forgotten Precursor of Fromentin's 'Dominique.' " *Modern Language Review,* 60 (1965), 520–28.

FRY, ALAN (Canadian, 1931–)

COME A LONG JOURNEY (1971)

Reviews
ATHERTON, STAN. "Northern Miscellany." *Journal Of Canadian Fiction,* 1, No.2 (1972), 82–83.

HOW A PEOPLE DIE (1970)

Reviews
BARCLAY, PAT. "Indian Seesaw." *Canadian Literature,* No.50 (1971), pp. 94–95.

FUCHS, ANTON (Austrian, 1920–)

VOM MORGEN IN DIE NACHT (1968)

Reviews
WEYR, THOMAS. "Vom Morgen in die Nacht." *American-German Review,* 35, No.3 (1969), 33–34.

FUENTES, CARLOS (Mexican, 1928–)

GENERAL

DEGUZMAN, DANIEL. *Carlos Fuentes,* pp. 13–71.

DWYER, JOHN P. "Conversation with a Blue Novelist." *Review,* No.12 (1974), pp. 54–58.

HALL, LINDA B. "The Cipactli Monster: Woman as Destroyer in Carlos Fuentes." *Southwest Review,* 60 (1975), 246–55.

HELLERMAN, M. KASEY. "The Coatlicue-Malinche Conflict: A Mother and Son Identity Crisis in the Writings of Carlos Fuentes." *Hispania,* 57 (1974), 868–75.

REEVE, RICHARD. "An Annotated Bibliography on Carlos Fuentes: 1949–69." *Hispania,* 53 (1970), 597–652.

AURA (1962)

CALLAN, RICHARD J. "The Jungian Basis of Carlos Fuentes' *Aura.*" *Kentucky Romance Quarterly,* 18 (1971), 65–75.

DEGUZMAN, DANIEL. *Carlos Fuentes,* pp. 118–25.

LANDEIRA, RICARDO LÓPEZ. " 'Aura,' 'The Aspern Papers,' 'A Rose for Emily': A Literary Relationship." *Journal Of Spanish Studies,* 3 (1975), 125–43.

PETERSEN, GERALD W. "A Literary Parallel: 'La Cena' by Alfonso Reyes and *Aura* by Carlos Fuentes." *Romance Notes,* 12 (1970), 41–44.

SOMMERS, JOSEPH. *After The Storm,* pp. 178–81.

Reviews
REEVE, RICHARD M. *Hispania,* 49 (1966), 355.

A CHANGE OF SKIN (Cambio de piel, 1967)

BRUSHWOOD, JOHN S. *The Spanish American Novel,* pp. 296–99.

DEGUZMAN, DANIEL. *Carlos Fuentes,* pp. 126–30.

DOEZEMA, HERMAN P. "An Interview with Carlos Fuentes." *Modern Fiction Studies,* 18 (1972/3), 491–98.

GROSSMAN, EDITH. "Myth and Madness in Carlos Fuentes' *A Change Of Skin.*" *Latin American Literary Review,* 3, No.5 (1974), 99–112.

GYURKO, LANIN A. "Women in Mexican Society: Fuentes' Portrayal of Oppression." *Revista Hispanica Moderna,* 38 (1974/5), 213–29.

HALL, LINDA B. "The Cipactli Monster: Woman as Destroyer in Carlos Fuentes." *Southwest Review,* 60 (1975), 252–55.

KNIGHT, THOMAS J. and FLORA M. WERNER. " 'Timeliness' in Carlos Fuentes' *Cambio De Piel.*" *Latin American Literary Review,* 4, No.7 (1975), 23–30.

LANGFORD, WALTER M. *The Mexican Novel Comes Of Age,* pp. 141–43.

Reviews
CLEMENTS, ROBERT J. "A Riddle of Life and the Good Love." *Saturday Review,* 27 January 1968, pp. 27–28.

HJORTSBERG, WILLIAM. "An Accidental Pilgrimage." *Catholic Review,* 207 (1968), 140, 142.

KENNEDY, WILLIAM. *National Observer,* 26 February 1968; rpt. in *Review,* No.1 (1968), pp. 71–73.

McMURRAY, GEORGE R. " 'Cambio de piel,' An Existentialist Novel of Protest." *Hispania,* 52 (1969), 150–54.

Time, 26 January 1968; rpt. in *Review,* No.1 (1968), pp. 76–77.

WEST, ANTHONY. *New Yorker,* 8 June 1968; rpt. in *Review,* No.1 (1968), pp. 73–75.

CUMPLEAÑOS (1969)

DURAN, GLORIA. "Carlos Fuentes *Cumpleaños [Birthday]:* A Mythological Interpretation of an Ambiguous Novel." *Latin American Literary Review,* 2, No.4 (1974), 75–86.

Reviews
REEVE, RICHARD M. *Hispania,* 54 (1971), 212–13.

THE DEATH OF ARTEMIO CRUZ (La Muerte de Artemio Cruz, 1964)

BOTSFORD, KEITH. "My Friend Fuentes." *Commentary,* 39, No.2 (1965), 64–67.

DEGUZMAN, DANIEL. *Carlos Fuentes,* pp. 108–18.

GYURKO, LANIN A. "Modern Hispanic-American Fiction: Novel of Action and Narrative of Consciousness." *Symposium,* 25 (1971), 368–72.

——— . "Self, Double, and Mask in Fuentes' *La Muerte De Artemio Cruz.*" *Texas Studies In Literature And Language,* 16 (1974), 363–84.

——— . "Women in Mexican Society: Fuentes' Portrayal of Oppression." *Revista Hispanica Moderna,* 38 (1974/5), 206–13.

LANGFORD, WALTER M. *The Mexican Novel Comes Of Age,* pp. 135–39.

MOODY, MICHAEL W. "Existentialism, Mexico and Artemio Cruz." *Romance Notes,* 10 (1968), 27–31.

SOMMERS, JOSEPH. *After The Storm,* pp. 153–64.

THE GOOD CONSCIENCE (Las buenas conciencias, 1959)

DEGUZMAN, DANIEL. *Carlos Fuentes,* pp. 100–8.

HOLY PLACE (Zona sagrada, 1967)

CALLAN, RICHARD J. "The Function of Myth and Analytical Psychology in *Zona Sagrada.*" *Kentucky Romance Quarterly,* 21 (1974), 261–74.

GYURKO, LANIN A. "The Myths of Ulysses in Fuentes's 'Zona sagrada.' " *Modern Language Review,* 69 (1974), 316–24.

——— . "The Pseudo-Liberated Woman in Fuentes' *Zona Sagrada.*" *Journal Of Spanish Studies,* 3 (1975), 17–43.

——— . "The Sacred and the Profane in Fuentes' *Zona Sagrada.*" *Revista Hispanica Moderna,* 37 (1972/3), 188–209.

Reviews

MICHAELS, LEONARD. "Truth in Triple Masquerade." *Review,* No.6 (1972), pp. 57-60.

WHERE THE AIR IS CLEAR (La región más transparente, 1958)

CRISPIN, RUTH KATZ. "The Artistic Unity of *La Región Más Transparente.*" *Kentucky Romance Quarterly,* 16 (1969), 277-87.

DEGUZMAN, DANIEL. *Carlos Fuentes,* pp. 93-100.

FOSTER, DAVID WILLIAM. " 'La Región más Transparente' and the Limits of Prophetic Art." *Hispania,* 56 (1973), 35-42.

LANGFORD, WALTER M. *The Mexican Novel Comes Of Age,* pp. 131-34.

REEVE, RICHARD M. "Octavio Paz And Hiperión In *La Región Más Transparente:* Plagiarism, Caricature Or . . . ?" *Chasqui,* 3, No.3 (1974), 13-25.

SOMMERS, JOSEPH. *After The Storm,* pp. 97-152.

FÜHMANN, FRANZ (German, 1922-)
BÖHMEN AM MEER

HUTCHINSON, PETER. "Franz Fühmann's 'Böhmen am Meer': A Socialist Version of 'The Winter's Tale.' " *Modern Language Review,* 67 (1972), 579-89.

FUKS, LADISLAV (Czech, 1923-)
MR. THEODORE MUNDSTOCK (Pan Theodor Mundstock, 1963)

LANGER, LAWRENCE L. *The Holocaust And The Literary Imagination,* pp. 94-123.

FUMIKO, ENCHI
THE WAITING YEARS (Onnazaka)

Reviews

MATHY, FRANCIS. *Monumenta Nipponica,* 27 (1972), 462-63.

FURETIÉRE, ANTOINE (French, 1619-1688)
LE ROMAN BOURGEOIS (1666)

KAHLER, ERICH. *The Inward Turn Of Narrative,* pp. 41-43.

THIHER, ROBERTA J. "The Depersonalized World of the *Roman Bourgeois.*" *Romance Notes,* 11 (1969), 127-29.

FURPHY, JOSEPH (Australian, 1843-1912)
GENERAL

LEBEDEWA, NINA. "Furphy Criticism Since 1955: A Checklist." *Australian Literary Studies,* 3 (1967), 149-50.

MCKENZIE, K. A. "Joseph Furphy, Jacobean." *Australian Literary Studies,* 2 (1966), 266-77.

SUCH IS LIFE (1903)

ARGYLE, BARRY. *An Introduction To The Australian Novel, 1830-1930,* pp. 178-207.

BARNES, JOHN. "The Structure of Joseph Furphy's *Such Is Life,*" in *The Australian Nationalists,* ed. Chris Wallace-Crabbe, pp. 114-33.

HOPE, A. D. "Review of Miles Franklin's *Joseph Furphy,*" in *The Australian Nationalists,* ed. Chris Wallace-Crabbe, pp. 108-13.

KIERNAN, BRYAN. "Society and Nature in *Such Is Life,*" in *The Australian Nationalists,* ed. Chris Wallace-Crabbe, pp. 134-48.

KNIGHT, NINA. "Furphy and Romance: *Such Is Life* Reconsidered." *Southerly,* 29 (1969), 243-55.

MITCHELL, A. G. "*Such Is Life:* The Title and the Structure of the Book," in *Twentieth Century Australian Literary Criticism,* ed. Clement Semmler, pp. 149-66.

RODRIGUEZ, JUDITH. "The Original Nosey Alf." *Australian Literary Studies,* 7 (1975), 176-84.

WALLACE-CRABBE, CHRIS. "Furphy's 'Masculine Strength,' " in *An Introduction To Australian Literature,* ed. C. D. Narasimhaiah, pp. 83-92.

FUTABATEI SHIMEI (Japanese, 1864-1909)
pseudonym of Hasegawa Tatsunosuke
UKIGUMO (1887-89)

MIYOSHI, MASAO. *Accomplices Of Silence,* pp. 17-37.

G

GADDA, CARLO EMILIO (Italian, 1893–1973)
GENERAL

BIASIN, GIAN-PAOLO. "Literary Diseases: From Pathology to Ontology." *MLN,* 82 (1967), 97–101.

ACQUAINTED WITH GRIEF (La cognizione del dolore, 1963)

PUCCI, PIETRO. "The Obscure Sickness." Trans. Ann H. Hallock. *Italian Quarterly,* 11, No.42 (1967), 43–62.

Reviews
CLEMENTS, ROBERT J. "Demons in Graustark." *Saturday Review,* 19 April 1969, pp. 40–41.

THAT AWFUL MESS ON VIA MERULANA (Quer Pasticciaccio Brutto de Via Merulana, 1957)

BONGIORNO, ROBERT. "Prose Texture as Content in *Quer Pasticciaccio Brutto De Via Merulana.*" *Romance Notes,* 14 (1972), 49–55.

DOMBROSKI, ROBERT S. "Some Observations on the Revision of *Quer Pasticciaccio.*" *MLN,* 86 (1971), 61–72.

RAGUSA, OLGA. "Gadda, Pasolini, and Experimentalism: Form or Ideology?" in *From Verismo To Experimentalism,* ed, Sergio Pacifici, pp. 246–53.

Reviews
WINTERS, WARRINGTON. "The Dark Unconscious Causes." *Saturday Review,* 4 September 1965, pp. 25–26.

GAISER, GERD (German, 1908–)
GENERAL

BATTS, MICHAEL. "The Shadow-Line: The Grenze-Motif in the Works of Gaiser, Kasack and Nossack." *Humanities Association Review,* 22, No.3 (1971), 41–44.

THOMAS, R. HINTON and WILFRIED VAN DER WILL. *The German Novel And The Affluent Society,* pp. 1–19.

GALDÓS, Benito Peréz see PERÉZ GALDÓS, Benito

GALINDO, SERGIO (Mexican, 1926–)
GENERAL

BRUSHWOOD, JOHN S. "The Novels of Sergio Galindo: Planes of Human Relationship." *Hispania,* 51 (1968), 812–16.

LA COMPARSA

Reviews
SOMMERS, JOSEPH. *Hispania,* 48 (1965), 621–22.

THE PRECIPICE (El bordo)

LANGFORD, WALTER M. *The Mexican Novel Comes Of Age,* pp. 173–76.

GALLANT, MAVIS (Canadian, 1922–)
GENERAL

STEVENS, PETER. "Perils of Compassion." *Canadian Literature,* No.56 (1973), pp. 61–70.

ITS IMAGE IN THE MIRROR

STEVENS, PETER. "Perils of Compassion." *Canadian Literature,* No.56 (1973), pp. 64–68.

GALLEGOS, RÓMULO (Venezuelan, 1884–1969)
GENERAL

ZIOMEK, HENRYK. "Rómulo Gallegos: Some Observations on Folkloric Elements in His Novels." *Revista De Estudios Hispánicos,* 8 (1974), 23–42.

DOÑA BÁRBARA (1931)

BRUSHWOOD, JOHN S. *The Spanish American Novel,* pp. 68–72.

LEAVITT, STURGIS E. "Sex vs. Symbolism in *Doña Barbara.*" *Revista De Estudios Hispánicos,* 1 (1967), 117–20.

SHAW, DONALD. "Gallegos' Revision of *Doña Bárbara* 1929–1930." *Hispanic Review,* 42 (1974), 265–78.

GALLO, MAX (French, 1932–)
LE CORTÈGE DES VAINQUEURS (1972)

Reviews
CROSBY, VIRGINIA. *French Review,* 48 (1975), 664–65.

GANGULI, SUNIL
ATMA PRAKASH (1966)

Reviews
SINHA, MIHIR. "The Private Inferno of a Poet." *Indian Writing Today,* No.1 (1967), pp. 19–23.

GANIVET, ANGEL (Spanish, 1865–1898)
LA CONQUISTA DEL REINO DE MAYA (1897)

FRANCO, JEAN. "Ganivet and the Technique of Satire in *La Conquista Del Reino De Maya.*" *Bulletin Of Hispanic Studies,* 42 (1965), 34–44.

GARCÍA MÁRQUEZ, GABRIEL (Colombian, 1928-)

GENERAL

"Chronology." *Books Abroad,* 47 (1973), 501-4.

"Gabriel García Márquez in *Books Abroad* 1963-1973." *Books Abroad,* 47 (1973), 505.

IVASK, IVAR. "Allegro Barbaro, or Gabriel García Márquez in Oklahoma." *Books Abroad,* 47 (1973), 439-40.

LUCHTING, WOLFGANG A. "Gabriel García Márquez: The Boom and Whimper." *Books Abroad,* 44 (1970), 26-30.

OBERHELMAN, HARLEY D. "García Márquez and the American South." *Chasqui,* 5, No.1 (1975), 29-38.

RABASSA, GREGORY. "Beyond Magic Realism: Thoughts on the Art of Gabriel García Marquez." *Books Abroad,* 47 (1973), 444-50.

THE AUTUMN OF THE PATRIARCH (El otoño del patriarca, 1975)

Reviews
McMURRAY, GEORGE R. *Chasqui,* 5, No.1 (1975), 50-53.

WILLIAMS, RAYMOND L. *Journal Of Spanish Studies,* 3 (1975), 215-17.

IN EVIL HOUR (La mala hora, 1962)

LUCHTING, WOLFGANG A. "Lampooning Literature: *La Mala Hora." Books Abroad,* 47 (1973), 471-78.

NO ONE WRITES TO THE COLONEL (El coronel no tiene quien le escriba, 1961)

PONTIERO, GIOVANNI. "Art and Commitment in Gabriel García Márquez's *El Coronel No Tiene Quien Le Escriba." Kentucky Romance Quarterly,* 22 (1975), 443-57.

WOODS, RICHARD D. "Time and Futility in the Novel *El Coronel No Tiene Quien Le Escriba." Kentucky Romance Quarterly,* 17 (1970), 287-95.

ONE HUNDRED YEARS OF SOLITUDE (Cien años de soledad, 1967)

ALAZRAKI, JAIME. "Borges and the New Latin-American Novel." *Triquarterly,* No.25 (1972), pp. 385-89.

ARENAS, REINALDO. "In the Town of Mirages." *Review,* No.3 (1971), pp. 101-8.

BRUSHWOOD, JOHN S. *The Spanish American Novel,* pp. 287-92.

CIPLIJAUSKAITÉ, BIRUTÉ. "Foreshadowing as Technique and Theme in *One Hundred Years Of Solitude." Books Abroad,* 47 (1973), 479-84.

DURÁN, ARMANDO. "Conversations with Gabriel García Marquez." *Review,* No.3 (1971), pp. 109-18.

FUENTES, CARLOS. "Macondo, Seat of Time." *Review,* No.3 (1971), pp. 119-21.

GALLAGHER, D. P. *Modern Latin American Literature,* pp. 144-63.

GONZÁLEZ ECHEVARRÍA, ROBERTO. "Big Mama's Wake." *Diacritics,* 4, No.2 (1974), 55-57.

GULLON, RICARDO. "Gabriel Garcia Marquez & the Lost Art of Storytelling." *Diacritics,* 1, No.1 (1971), 27-32.

HALL, LINDA B. "Labyrinthine Solitude: The Impact of Garcia Marquez." *Southwest Review,* 58 (1973), 253-63.

LAWRENCE, GREGORY. "Marx in Macondo." *Latin American Literary Review,* 2, No.4 (1974), 49-57.

LEVINE, SUZANNE JILL. "*One Hundred Years Of Solitude* and *Pedro Paramo:* A Parallel." *Books Abroad,* 47 (1973), 490-95.

LUCHTING, WOLFGANG A. "Gabriel García Márquez: The Boom and Whimper." *Books Abroad,* 44 (1970), 26-30.

MERREL, FLOYD. "Jose Arcadio Buendia's Scientific Paradigms:

Man in Search of Himself." *Latin American Literary Review,* 2, No.4 (1974), 59-70.

OLLIVIER, LOUIS L. "*One Hundred Years Of Solitude:* Existence is the Word." *Latin American Literary Review,* 4, No.7 (1975), 9-14.

RODRÍGUEZ MONEGAL, EMIR. "*One Hundred Years Of Solitude:* The Last Three Pages." *Books Abroad,* 47 (1973), 485-89.

_____. "A Writer's Feat." *Review,* No.3 (1971), pp. 122-28.

SILVA-CÁCERES, RAÚL. "The Narrative Intensification in One Hundred Years of Solitude." *Review,* No.3 (1971), pp. 143-48.

TOBIN, PATRICIA. "Garcia Márquez and the Genealogical Imperative." *Diacritics,* 4 No.2 (1974), 52-55.

_____. "Garcia Marquez and the Subversion of the Line." *Latin American Literary Review,* 2, No.4 (1974), 39-48.

VARGAS LLOSA, MARIO. "Garcia Marquez: From Aracataca to Macondo." *Review,* No.3 (1971), pp. 129-42.

WOOD, MICHAEL. "I've Been Reading: Latin American Mirages." *Columbia Forum,* 13, No.2 (1970), 28-29.

Reviews
AUDEJEAN, CHRISTIAN. *Review,* No.3 (1971), pp. 166-68.

CARRILLO, GERMAN D. "Lyrical Solitudes." *Novel,* 4 (1971), 187-89.

CHRIST, RONALD. *Commonweal,* 6 March 1970; rpt. in *Review,* No.3 (1971), pp. 149-51.

DE LA CUESTA, BARBARA. *New Orleans Review,* 3 (1973), 197-98.

DWYER, DAVID J. "Creeping Green World." *Catholic World,* 212 (1971), 105.

GILLES, SERGE. *Review,* No.3 (1971), pp. 168-71.

HAHNL, HANS HEINZ. *Review,* No.3 (1971), p. 183.

LEONARD, JOHN. *New York Times Book Review,* 3 March 1970; Rpt. in *Review,* No.3 (1971), pp. 151-52.

LORENZ, GUNTHER W. *Review,* No.3 (1971), pp. 183-86.

MEAD, ROBERT G., JR. *Saturday Review,* 7 March 1970, pp. 34-35.

PUCCINI, DARIO. *Review,* No.3 (1971), pp. 190-91.

RICHARDSON, JACK. *New York Review Of Books,* 26 March 1970; rpt. *Review,* No.3 (1971), 153-57.

SANT'ANNA, SÉRGIO. *Review,* No.3 (1971), pp. 178-82.

SARDUY, SEVERO. *Review,* No.3 (1971), pp. 171-74.

SCHMITT, HANS-JÜRGEN. *Review,* No.3 (1971), pp. 186-89.

SHORRIS, EARL. *Harper's Magazine,* February 1972; rpt. in *Review,* No.4/5 (1971/2), pp. 98-103.

SORIN, RAPHAEL. *Review,* No.3 (1971), pp. 174-77.

WEST, PAUL. *Book World,* 22 February 1970, rpt. *Review,* No.3 (1971), pp 158-60.

WOOD, MICHAEL. "I've Been Reading: Latin American Mirages." *Columbia Forum,* 13, No.2 (1970), 27-29; rpt. *Review,* No.3 (1971), pp. 160-65.

GARCÍA PAVÓN, FRANCISCO (Spanish, 1919-)

GENERAL

O'CONNOR, PATRICIA W. "Francisco García Pavón's Sexual Politics in the Plinio Novels." *Journal Of Spanish Studies,* 1 (1973), 65-81.

_____. "A Spanish Sleuth at Last: Francisco García Pavón's Plinio." *Hispanofila,* No.48 (1973), pp. 47-68.

VANCE, BIRGITTA. "The Great Clash: Feminist Criticism Meets Up with Spanish Reality." *Journal Of Spanish Studies,* 2 (1974), 109-14.

LAS HERMANAS COLORADAS: PLINIO EN MADRID (1970)

Reviews
GUINAZZO, LEONORA. *Hispania,* 54 (1971), 394–95.

EL RAPTO DE LA SABINAS (1969)

Reviews
MACÍAS, MANUEL JATO. *Hispania,* 54 (1971), 395.

GARCÍA PONCE, JUAN (Mexican, 1932–)

GENERAL

BRUCE-NOVOA. "The Encounters of Juan García Ponce." *Latin American Literary Review,* 3, No.6 (1975), 49–52.

UNIÓN (1964)

Reviews
BRUCE-NOVOA. *Latin American Literary Review,* 3, No.6 (1975), pp. 104–5.

GARIBALDI, GIUSEPPI

GENERAL

GRIFFITHS, C. E. J. "The Novels of Garibaldi." *Italian Studies,* 30 (1975), 86–98.

GARNER, HUGH (Canadian, 1913–)

GENERAL

ANDERSON, ALLAN. "An Interview with Hugh Garner." *Tamarack Review,* No.52 (1969), pp. 19–34.

MOSS, JOHN G. "A Conversation with Hugh Garner." *Journal Of Canadian Fiction,* 1, No.2 (1972), 50–55.

CABBAGETOWN (1968)

ANDERSON, ALLAN. "An Interview with Hugh Garner." *Tamarack Review,* No.52 (1969), pp. 23–29.

A NICE PLACE TO VISIT (1970)

Reviews
WADDINGTON, MIRIAM. "Garner's Good Ear." *Canadian Literature,* No.50 (1971), pp. 72–75.

THE SILENCE ON THE SHORE (1962)

Reviews
HALL, W. F. "New Interest in Reality." *Canadian Literature,* No.40 (1969), pp. 66–68.

STORM BELOW (1968)

Reviews
HALL, W. F. "New Interest in Reality." *Canadian Literature,* No.40 (1969), pp. 66–68.

GARRO, ELENA (1920–)

RECOLLECTIONS OF THINGS TO COME (1969)

Reviews
BRUSHWOOD, JOHN S. *Kansas City Star,* 16 November 1969; rpt. *Review,* No.2 (1969), pp. 93–94.

HUNTER, SAM. *Fort Worth Press,* 2 November 1966; rpt. *Review,* No.2 (1969), p. 95.

GASCAR, PIERRE (French, 1916–) pseudonym of Pierre Fournier

THE BEST YEARS (Le Meilleur de la vie, 1964)

Reviews
LESAGE, LAURENT. "Autumn Came Too Soon." *Saturday Review,* 11 February 1967, pp. 54–55.

THE SEASON OF THE DEAD

LANGER, LAWRENCE L. *The Holocaust And The Literary Imagination,* pp. 59–72.

GASPÉ, PHILLIPPE AUBERT DE (French Canadian, 1786–1871)

GENERAL

MACRI, F. M. "Phillipe Aubert de Gaspé, Son and Father." *Journal Of Canadian Fiction,* 2, No.3 (1973), 49–55.

LES ANCIENNES CANADIENS (1863)

WATERSTON, ELIZABETH. "The Politics of Conquest in Canadian Historical Fiction." *Mosaic,* 3, No.1 (1969/70), 116–24.

GAUTIER, THÉOPHILE (French, 1811–1872)

GENERAL

BENN, M. B. "Büchner and Gautier." *Seminar,* 9 (1973), 202–7.

COCKERHAM, HARRY. "Gautier: From Hallucination to Supernatural Vision." *Yale French Studies,* No.50 (1974), pp. 42–53.

DRISCOLL, IRENE JOAN. "Visual Allusion in the Work of Théophile Gautier." *French Studies,* 27 (1973), 418–28.

EPSTEIN, EDNA SELAN. "The Entanglement of Sexuality and Aesthetics in Gautier and Mallarmé." *Nineteenth-Century French Studies,* 1 (1972), 5–16.

GIRAUD, RAYMOND. "Winckelmann's Part in Gautier's Perception of Classical Beauty." *Yale French Studies,* No.38 (1967), pp. 172–82.

NELSON, HILDA. "Théophile Gautier: The Invisible and Impalpable World: *A Demi-Conviction." French Review,* 45 (1972), 819–30.

ARIA MARCELLA (1852)

SMITH, ALBERT B. "The Changing Ideal in Two of Gautier's Fictional Narratives." *Romanic Review,* 60 (1969), 168–73.

————. "Gautier and Mallarmé: An Unnoticed Parallel." *Romance Notes,* 10 (1969), 249–52.

CAPTAIN FRACASSE (Le capitaine Fracasse, 1863)

GRANT, RICHARD B. *Théophile Gautier,* pp. 146–57.

ROSSITER, ANDREW. "Metamorphoses and the Second Self in Gautier's *Le capitaine Fracasse." Forum For Modern Language Studies,* 11 (1975), 213–26.

SMITH, ALBERT B. *Ideal And Reality In The Fictional Narratives Of Théophile Gautier,* pp. 146–57.

JETTATURA (1857)

SMITH, ALBERT B. *Ideal And Reality In The Fictional Narratives Of Théophile Gautier,* pp. 30–32.

MADEMOISELLE DE MAUPIN (1835–36)

CHAMBERS, ROSS. "Two Theatrical Microcosms: *Die Prinzessin Brambilla* and *Mademoiselle De Maupin." Comparative Literature,* 27 (1975), 40–46.

GRANT, RICHARD B. *Théophile Gautier,* pp. 34–42.

SMITH, ALBERT B. "Gutier's *Mademoiselle De Maupin:* The Quest for Happiness." *Modern Language Quarterly,* 32 (1971), 168–74.

————. *Ideal And Reality In The Fictional Narratives Of Théophile Gautier,* pp. 16–20.

LA MORTE AMOUREUSE

> SMITH, ALBERT B. "The Changing Ideal in Two of Gautier's Fictional Narratives." *Romanic Review,* 60 (1969), 168-73.

LE PIED DE MOMIE

> SMITH, ALBERT B. *Ideal And Reality In The Fictional Narratives Of Théophile Gautier,* pp. 24-26.

THE ROMANCE OF A MUMMY (La roman de momie, 1858)

> SMITH, ALBERT B. *Ideal And Reality In The Fictional Narratives Of Théophile Gautier,* pp. 24-26.

SPIRITE (1866)

> LOWIN, JOSEPH G. "Two 'Inédits' of Théophile Gautier: Letters to Carlotta Grisi à propos of his novel *Spirite.*" *Romance Notes,* 16 (1974), 54-56.

> SMITH, ALBERT B. *Ideal And Reality In The Fictional Narratives Of Théophile Gautier,* pp. 26-30.

GEIGER, CARL IGNAZ (1756-1791)

REISE EINES ERDBEWOHNERS IN DEN MARS

> HADLEY, MICHAEL. *The German Novel In 1790,* pp. 152-57.

GELLERT, C. F. (German, 1715-1769)

LEBEN DER SCHWEDISCHEN GRÄFIN VON G. . . (1746)

> VAN ABBÉ, D. M. "Some Unspoken Assumptions in Gellert's 'Schwedische Gräfin.' " *Orbis Litterarum,* 28 (1973), 113-23.

GENET, JEAN (French, 1910-1986)

GENERAL

> BARISH, JONAS A. "The Veritable Saint Genet." *Wisconsin Studies In Contemporary Literature,* 6 (1965), 267-85.

> CISMARU, ALFRED. "The Antitheism of Jean Genet." *Antioch Review,* 24 (1964), 387-401.

> COE, RICHARD M. *The Vision Of Jean Genet,* pp. 3-28.

> THODY, PHILIP. "Problems and Themes," in his *Jean Genet: A Study Of His Novels And Plays,* pp. 25-54.

> YEAGER, HENRY J. "The Uncompromising Morality of Jean Genet." *French Review,* 39 (1965), 214-19.

FUNERAL RITES (Pompes funebres, ca. 1947)

> COE, RICHARD N. *The Vision Of Jean Genet,* pp. 135-69.

> DRIVER, TOM F. *Jean Genet,* pp. 16-19.

> KNAPP, BETTINA LIEBOWITZ. *Jean Genet,* pp. 57-69.

> THODY, PHILLIP. *Jean Genet: A Study Of His Novels And Plays,* pp. 105-18.

> **Reviews**
> BISHOP, TOM. *Saturday Review,* 12 July 1969, pp. 36-37.

MIRACLE OF THE ROSE (Miracle de la rose)

> COE, RICHARD N. *The Vision Of Jean Genet,* pp. 66-98.

> DRIVER, TOM F. *Jean Genet,* pp. 13-16.

> GERBER, BARBARA L. "Genet's *Miracle De La Rose:* An Alchemical Vision." *Sub-Stance,* No.3 (1972), pp. 101-7.

> KNAPP, BETTINA LIEBOWITZ. *Jean Genet,* pp. 40-56.

> SELTZER, ALBIN J. *Chaos In The Novel: The Novel In Chaos,* pp. 236-73.

> THODY, PHILIP. *Jean Genet: A Study Of His Novels And Plays,* pp. 80-104.

> **Reviews**
> DRIVER, TOM F. "An Exaltation of Evil." *Saturday Review,* 11 March 1967, pp. 36-37.

OUR LADY OF THE FLOWERS (Notre-Dame-des-fleurs, 1942)

> COE, RICHARD N. *The Vision Of Jean Genet,* pp. 31-65.

> DRIVER, TOM F. *Jean Genet,* pp. 7-13.

> GERBER, BARBARA L. "Ambiguity and Redemption in the Prose Fiction of Jean Genet," in *Twentieth Century French Fiction,* ed. George Stambolian, pp. 89-93.

> KNAPP, BETTINA LIEBOWITZ. *Jean Genet,* pp. 23-39.

> THODY, PHILIP. *Jean Genet: A Study Of His Novels And Plays,* pp. 55-59.

QUERELLE OF BREST (Querelle de Brest, 1947)

> COE, RICHARD N. *The Vision Of Jean Genet,* pp. 170-209.

> DRIVER, TOM F. *Jean Genet,* pp. 19-23.

> GERBER, BARBARA L. "Ambiguity and Redemption in the Prose Fiction of Jean Genet," in *Twentieth Century French Fiction,* ed. George Stambolian, pp. 95-99.

> KNAPP, BETTINA LIEBOWITZ. *Jean Genet,* pp. 70-85.

> THODY, PHILLIP. *Jean Genet: A Study Of His Novels And Plays,* pp. 119-40.

> **Reviews**
> McGUINNESS, FRANK. *London Magazine,* 6, No.12 (1967), 111-13.

THE THIEF'S JOURNAL (Journal du voleur, 1949)

> COE, RICHARD N. *The Vision Of Jean Genet,* pp. 99-134.

> THODY, PHILIP. *Jean Genet: A Study Of His Novels And Plays,* pp. 141-54.

GENEVOIX, MAURICE (French, 1890-1980)

RABOLIOT (1925)

> WALLING, J. J. "*Raboliot:* A Major French Regional Novel." *Modern Languages,* 55 (1974), 182-88.

GHEORGHIU, CONSTANTIN VIRGIL (Rumanian, 1916-)

GENERAL

> ROSE, MARILYN GADDIS. "C. V. Gheorghiu—After 'The Twenty-Fifth Hour.' " *Books Abroad,* 41 (1967), 166-68.

GHOSE, SUDHIN N. (Indian, 1899-)

GENERAL

> MUKHERJEE, MEENAKSHI. "The Tractor and the Plough: The Contrasted Visions of Sudhim Ghose and Mulk Raj Anand." *Indian Literature,* 13, No.1 (1970), 88-101.

CRADLE OF THE CLOUDS (1951)

> MUKHERJEE, MEENAKSHI. "The Tractor and the Plough: The Contrasted Visions of Sudhim Ghose and Mulk Raj Anand." *Indian Literature,* 13, No.1 (1970), 91-95.

THE FLAME OF THE FOREST (1955)

> SRINIVASA IYENGAR, K. R. *Indian Writing In English,* pp. 483-86.

GHOSE, ZULFIKAR (Pakistani, 1935-)

THE MURDER OF AZIZ KHAN (1967)

> **Reviews**
> CHAFFEE, PAUL. *World Literature Written In English,* No.18 (1970), pp. 40-41.

GIBSON, GRAEME (Canadian, 1914-)

FIVE LEGS (1969)

Reviews

GEDDES, GARY. "The Muse Acclimatized." *Canadian Literature,* No.42 (1969), pp. 93–96.

MACKENZIE, NORMAN. *Dalhousie Review,* 49 (1969), 436–39.

GIDE, ANDRÉ (French, 1869–1951)
GENERAL

ABEL, ROBERT H. "Gide and Henry James: Suffering, Death, and Responsibility." *Midwest Quarterly,* 9 (1968), 403–15.

BLANCHOT, MAURICE. "Gide and the Concept of Literature as Adventure," in *Gide: A Collection Of Critical Essays,* ed. David Littlejohn, pp. 49–62.

BULGIN, KATHLEEN. "Swamp Imagery and the Moral-Esthetic Problem in Gide's Early Works." *French Review,* 45 (1972), 813–18.

CAMUS, ALBERT. *Lyrical And Critical Essays,* pp. 248–53.

CHAMBERS, LELAND H. "Gide's Fictional Journals." *Criticism,* 10 (1968), 300–12.

DELAY, JEAN. "The Consultation," in *Gide: A Collection Of Critical Essays,* ed. David Littlejohn, pp. 129–51.

GIRARD, ALAIN. "The Role of the *Journal* in Gide's Work," in *Gide: A Collection Of Critical Essays,* ed. David Littlejohn, pp. 152–63.

HOLDHEIM, W. WOLFGANG. "Art and the Theory of the Novel," in his *Theory And Practice Of The Novel: A Study on André Gide,* pp. 123–46.

––––––. "Gide and the Novel," in his *Theory And Practice Of The Novel: A Study On André Gide,* pp. 82–101.

––––––. "Gide's Narrative Genres," in his *Theory And Practice Of The Novel: A Study On André Gide,* pp. 149–70.

––––––. "Gide's Vitalistic Theory of the Novel," in his *Theory And Practice Of The Novel: A Study On André Gide,* pp. 102–22.

IRELAND, G. W. "Prolegomena to a Study of Inspiration in Gide," in *Currents Of Thought In French Literature,* pp. 191–208.

JOINER, LAWRENCE D. and ELIZABETH G. "Gide and Green: Rencontres." USF *Language Quarterly,* 13, No.3/4 (1975), 10–12, 52.

LINDSAY, MARSHALL. "Time in Gide's Early Fiction." *Symposium,* 26 (1972), 39–56.

LITTLEJOHN, DAVID. "Introduction," in *Gide: A Collection Of Critical Essays,* ed. David Littlejohn, pp. 1–14.

McLENDON, WILL L. "The Last Time Gide Left Paris." *Forum,* 4, No.5 (1964), 34–36.

MAURIAC, FRANCOIS. "The Death of André Gide," in *Gide: A Collection Of Critical Essays,* ed. David Littlejohn, pp. 19–29.

O'BRIEN, JUSTIN. "Additions to the Gide Bibliography," in his *Contemporary French Literature,* pp. 173–209.

––––––. "André Gide and Music," in his *Contemporary French Literature,* pp. 169–72.

––––––. "Gide and Antigyde," in his *Contemporary French Literature,* pp. 229–32.

––––––. "Samuel Beckett and André Gide: An Hypothesis." *French Review,* 40 (1967), 485–86; rpt. in his *Contemporary French Literature,* pp. 5–6.

O'NEILL, KEVIN. "Gide Today." *AUMLA,* No.32 (1969), pp. 190–205.

PASCO, A. H. and WILFRID J. ROLLMAN. "The Artistry of Gide's Onomastics." *MLN,* 86 (1971), 523–31.

SARTRE, JEAN-PAUL. "The Living Gide," in *Gide: A Collection Of Critical Essays,* ed. David Littlejohn, pp. 15–18.

SHEPARD, LESLIE A. "The Development of Gide's Concept of Personality." *Bucknell Review,* 17, No.2 (1969), 47–66.

Supreme Sacred Congregation of the Holy Office. "Condemnation of the Works of André Gide," in *Gide: A Collection Of Critical Essays,* ed. David Littlejohn, pp. 30–35.

TOLTON, C. D. E. "Image-Conveying Abstractions in the Works of André Gide," in *Image And Theme,* ed. W. M. Frohock, pp. 99–123.

WHARTENBY, H. ALLEN. "Precursors of the Gidian *Récit.*" *Romanic Review,* 60 (1969), 104–14.

THE COUNTERFEITERS (Les Faux-Monnayeurs, 1926)

BARRY, CATHERINE A. "Some Transpositions of Dostoevsky in *Les Faux-Monnayeurs.*" *French Review,* 45 (1972), 580–87.

BRACHFELD, GEORGES I. "The Novel of Ideas," in *Approaches To The Twentieth-Century Novel,* ed. John Unterecker, pp. 153–81.

BRÉE, GERMAINE. "*The Counterfeiters,*" in *Gide: A Collection Of Critical Essays,* ed. David Littlejohn, pp. 112–28.

BROSMAN, CATHARINE SAVAGE. "The Relativization of Character in 'Les Faux-Monnayeurs.' " *Modern Language Review,* 69 (1974), 770–78.

CIHOLAS, KARIN NORDENHAUG. *Gide's Art Of The Fugue: A Thematic Study Of "Les Faux-Monnayeurs."*

CORDLE, THOMAS. *André Gide,* pp. 120–38.

DERÔME, R. F. "Some Reflections on Gide's *Les Faux-Monnayeurs.* An Attempt at a 'Mise au Point.' " *Modern Languages,* 56 (1975), 185–88.

FOWLIE, WALLACE. *André Gide: His Life And Art,* pp. 85–97.

FROHOCK, W. M. *Style And Temper,* pp. 7–10.

GARZILLI, ENRICO. *Circles Without Center,* pp. 118–27.

HABERSTITCH, DAVID. "Gide and the Fantasts: The Nature of Reality and Freedom." *Criticism,* 11 (1969), 140–50.

HILL, CHARLES G. "André Gide and Blake's *Marriage Of Heaven And Hell.*" *Comparative Literature Studies,* 3 (1966), 21–32.

HOLDHEIM, W. WOLFGANG. *Theory And Practice Of The Novel: A Study On André Gide,* pp. 235–65.

IRELAND, G. W. *André Gide: A Study Of His Creative Writings,* pp. 340–76.

LANDY, MARCIA. "Gide's Pastoralism and Critics of the New Novel." *French Review,* 47 (1973), 356–59.

RIEDER, DOLLY S. "*Les Faux-Monnayeurs:* Gide's Essay on Bad Faith." *Romanic Review,* 62 (1971), 87–98.

ROSSI, VINIO. *André Gide,* pp. 29–36.

STOLTZFUS, BEN. *Gide's Eagles,* pp. 126–38.

TASJIAN, DICKRAN L. "The Counterfeiters by André Gide: The Esthetic Ontology of Dada." *Minnesota Review,* 6 (1966), 50–57.

THE FRUITS OF THE EARTH (Les nourritures terrestres, 1897)

CORDLE, THOMAS. *André Gide,* pp. 67–74.

FOWLIE, WALLACE. *André Gide: His Life And Art,* pp. 34–45.

HOLDHEIM, W. WOLFGANG. *Theory And Practice Of The Novel: A Study On André Gide,* pp. 90–97.

IRELAND, G. W. *André Gide: A Study Of His Creative Writings,* pp. 120–42.

LINDSAY, MARSHALL. "Time in Gide's Early Fiction." *Symposium,* 26 (1972), 47–56.

O'BRIEN, JUSTIN. "Gide's 'Nourritures terrestres' and Vergil's 'Bucolics,' " in his *Contemporary French Literature,* pp. 14–27.

––––––. "A Rapprochement: M. André Gide and Lautréamont," in his *Contemporary French Literature,* pp. 7–13.

PERRY, KENNETH I. *The Religious Symbolism Of André Gide,* pp. 64–76.

ROSSI, VINIO. *André Gide,* pp. 38–42.

STOLTZFUS, BEN. *Gide's Eagles,* pp. 51-57.

GENEVIEVE

CORDLE, THOMAS. *André Gide,* pp. 146-50.

IRELAND, G. W. *André Gide: A Study Of His Creative Writings,* pp. 377-92.

EL HADJ

CORDLE, THOMAS. *André Gide,* pp. 46-50.

IRELAND, G. W. *André Gide: A Study Of His Creative Writings,* pp. 171-77.

THE IMMORALIST (L'Immoraliste, 1902)

BRENNAN, JOSEPH GERARD. "Three Novels of *Dépaysement.*" *Comparative Literature,* 22 (1970), 223-36.

BROWN, FRIEDA S. "*L'Immoraliste:* Prelude to the Gidian Problem of the Individual and Society." *French Review,* 43, Special Issue No. 1 (1970), 65-76.

CALLEN, A. "*L'Immoraliste* as a Modern *Adolphe.*" *Modern Language Quarterly,* 31 (1970), 450-60.

CORDLE, THOMAS. *André Gide,* pp. 84-92.

FOWLIE, WALLACE. *André Gide: His Life And Art,* pp. 46-56.

GOODHAND, ROBERT. "Locale as Thematic Expression in *L'Immoraliste.*" *French Review,* 43, Special Issue No.1 (1970), 77-86.

————. "The Religious Leitmotif in *L'Immoraliste.*" *Romanic Review,* 57 (1966), 263-76.

GUERARD, ALBERT J. "The Illuminating Distortion." *Novel,* 5 (1972), 102, 111-12.

HYTIER, JEAN. "The *Récits,*" in *Gide: A Collection Of Critical Essays,* ed. David Littlejohn, pp. 73-92.

IRELAND, G. W. *André Gide: A Study Of His Creative Writings,* pp. 178-98.

KORGES, JAMES. "Gide and Mishima: Homosexuality as Metaphor." *Critique,* 12, No.1 (1970), 127-37.

LANDY, MARCIA. "Gide's Pastoralism and Critics of the New Novel." *French Review,* 47 (1973), 348-56.

MCCONNELL, FRANK D. "Toward a Syntax of Fiction." *College English,* 36 (1974/5), 153-54.

O'REILLY, ROBERT F. "Ritual, Myth, and Symbol in Gide's *L'Immoraliste.*" *Symposium,* 28 (1974), 346-55.

PASCO, ALLAN H. "Irony and Art in Gide's *L'Immoraliste: In Memoriam: Edward Glaser.*" *Romanic Review,* 64 (1973), 184-203.

PERRY, KENNETH I. *The Religious Symbolism Of André Gide,* pp. 77-85.

SAVAGE, CATHERINE H. " 'L'Immoraliste': Psychology and Rhetoric." *Xavier University Studies,* 6 (1967), 43-62.

STOLTZFUS, BEN. *Gide's Eagles,* pp. 24-27.

ISABELLE (1911)

HYTIER, JEAN. "The *Récits,*" in *Gide: A Collection Of Critical Essays,* ed. David Littlejohn, pp. 73-92.

IRELAND, G. W. *André Gide: A Study Of His Creative Writings,* pp. 237-48.

LAFCADIO'S ADVENTURES (Les Caves du Vatican, 1914)

ALTER, ROBERT. *Partial Magic,* pp. 161-78.

ATKINSON, JOHN KEITH. "*Les Caves Du Vatican* and Bergson's *Le Rire.*" *PMLA,* 84 (1969), 328-35.

BETTINSON, CHRISTOPHER D. *Gide: Les Caves Du Vatican.*

CORDLE, THOMAS. *André Gide,* pp. 108-15.

FOWLIE, WALLACE. *André Gide: His Life And Art,* pp. 68-75.

FROHOCK, W. M. *Style And Temper,* pp. 3-7.

GÉRACHT, MAURICE ARON. "A Guide Through the Vatican Caves: A Study of the Structure of *Les Caves Du Vatican.*" *Wisconsin Studies In Contemporary Literature,* 6 (1965), 330-45.

HOLDHEIM, W. WOLFGANG. *Theory And Practice Of The Novel: A Study On André Gide,* pp. 213-34.

IRELAND, G. W. *André Gide: A Study Of His Creative Writings,* pp. 249-73.

MCCLELLAND, JOHN. "The Lexicon of *Les Caves Du Vatican.*" *PMLA,* 89 (1974), 256-67.

O'BRIEN, JUSTIN. "Lafcadio and Barnabooth: A Supposition," in his *Contemporary French Literature,* pp. 233-44.

ROSSI, VINIO. *André Gide,* pp. 16-20.

STEEL, D. A. " 'Lafcadio Ludens': Ideas of Play and Levity in 'Les Caves du Vatican.' " *Modern Language Review,* 66 (1971), 554-64.

MARSHLANDS (Paludes, 1895)

CORDLE, THOMAS. *André Gide,* pp. 50-55.

FOWLIE, WALLACE. *André Gide: His Life And Art,* pp. 24-26.

HOLDHEIM, W. WOLFGANG. *Theory And Practice Of The Novel: A Study On André Gide,* pp. 171-89.

IRELAND, G. W. *André Gide: A Study Of His Creative Writing,* pp. 103-19.

LINDSAY, MARSHALL. "Time in Gide's Early Fiction." *Symposium,* 26 (1972), 44-47.

O'BRIEN, JUSTIN. " 'Paludes' and 'Le Potomak,' " in his *Contemporary French Literature,* pp. 245-64.

O'REILLY, ROBERT F. "The Emergence of Gide's Art Form in *Paludes.*" *Symposium,* 19 (1965), 236-48.

ROSSI, VINIO. *André Gide: The Evolution Of An Aesthetic,* pp. 87-98, 124-43.

SPININGER, DENNIS J. "The Complex Generic Mode of André Gide's *Paludes,*" in *Twentieth Century French Fiction,* ed. George Stambolian, pp. 3-26.

THE NOTEBOOKS OF ANDRÉ WALTER (Les Cahiers d'André Walter, 1891)

CORDLE, THOMAS. *André Gide,* pp. 36-41.

IRELAND G. W. *André Gide: A Study Of His Creative Writings,* pp. 24-48.

PERRY, KENNETH I. *The Religious Symbolism Of André Gide,* pp. 26-35.

ROSSI, VINIO. *André Gide: The Evolution Of An Aesthetic,* pp. 17-62.

STORZER, GERALD H. "*Les Cahiers D'André Walter:* Idea, Emotion, and Dream in the Gidian Novel." *Philological Quarterly,* 54 (1975), 647-62.

THE PASTORAL SYMPHONY (La symphonie pastorale, 1919)

CORDLE, THOMAS. *André Gide,* pp. 100-7.

FALK, EUGENE H. *Types Of Thematic Structure: The Nature And Function Of Motifs In Gide, Camus, And Sartre,* pp. 30-51.

FOWLIE, WALLACE. *André Gide: His Life And Art,* pp. 76-84.

GROBE, EDWIN P. "Estrangement as Verbal Aspect in *La Symphonie Pastorale.*" *French Review,* 43, Special Issue No.1 (1970), 56-64.

HYTIER, JEAN. "The *Récits,*" in *Gide: A Collection Of Critical Essays,* ed. David Littlejohn, pp. 73-92.

IRELAND, G. W. *André Gide: A Study Of His Creative Writings,* pp. 283-308.

PERRY, KENNETH I. *The Religious Symbolism Of André Gide,* pp. 117-27.

ROSSI, VINIO. *André Gide,* pp. 25-29.

STOLTZFUS, BEN. *Gide's Eagles,* pp. 38-50.

PROMETHEUS MISBOUND (Le prométhée mal enchaîné, 1899)

CORDLE, THOMAS. *André Gide*, pp. 55–59.

HOLDHEIM, W. WOLFGANG. *Theory And Practice Of The Novel: A Study On André Gide*, pp. 190–212.

IRELAND, G. W. *André Gide: A Study Of His Creative Writings*, pp. 257–60.

ROSSI, VINIO. *André Gide*, pp. 12–16.

———. *André Gide: The Evolution Of An Aesthetic*, pp. 147–49.

WATSON-WILLIAMS, HELEN. *André Gide And The Greek Myth: A Critical Study*, pp. 40–57.

WEINBERG, KURT. *On Gide's <Prométhée>: Private Myth And Public Mystification.*

LE RETOUR DE L'ENFANT PRODIGUE

IRELAND, G. W. *André Gide: A Study Of His Creative Writings*, pp. 222–36.

PERRY, KENNETH I. *The Religious Symbolism of André Gide*, pp. 98–116.

TURNER, ALISON M. "An Interpretation of André Gide's *Le Retour De L'Enfant Prodigue* in the Light of its Dual Inspiration." *Kentucky Romance Quarterly*, 21 (1974), 183–94.

ROBERT

CORDLE, THOMAS. *André Gide*, pp. 144–46.

IRELAND, G. W. *André Gide: A Study Of His Creative Writings*, pp. 377–92.

THE SCHOOL FOR WIVES (L'école des femmes, 1929)

CORDLE, THOMAS. *André Gide*, pp. 138–44.

IRELAND, G. W. *André Gide: A Study Of His Creative Writings*, pp. 377–92.

STRAIT IS THE GATE (La porte étroite, 1909)

BROWN, FRIEDA S. "Montaigne and Gide's *La Porte Étroite*." *PMLA*, 82 (1967), 136–41.

CANCALON, ELAINE D. "Symbols of Motion and Immobility in Gide's Twin 'Récits.' " *Modern Language Review*, 66 (1971), 798–801.

CORDLE, THOMAS. *André Gide*, pp. 92–100.

FOWLIE, WALLACE. *André Gide: His Life And Art*, pp. 61–67.

HOOKS, Z. and M. C. VOS. "Who Caused Alissa's Death? Gide's 'Straight is the Gate' Reconsidered." *USF Language Quarterly*, 11, No.3/4 (1973), 48–50.

HYTIER, JEAN. "The *Récits*," in *Gide: A Collection Of Critical Essays*, ed. David Littlejohn, pp. 73–92.

IRELAND, G. W. *André Gide: A Study Of His Creative Writings*, pp. 199–221.

KNECHT, LORING D. "A New Reading of Gide's *La Porte Étroite*." *PMLA*, 82 (1967), 640–48; rpt. in *Gide: A Collection Of Critical Essays*, ed. David Littlejohn, pp. 93–111.

PERRY, KENNETH I. *The Religious Symbolism Of André Gide*, pp. 85–97.

ROSSI, VINIO. *André Gide*, pp. 22–25.

ROWLAND, MICHAEL L. "Gide's *La Porte Étroite*." *Explicator*, 31 (1973), Item 68.

SONNENFELD, ALBERT. "*Strait Is The Gate*: Byroads in Gide's Labyrinth." *Novel*, 1 (1968), 118–32.

STOLTZFUS, BEN. *Gide's Eagles*, pp. 24–37.

LA TENTATIVE AMOUREUSE

IRELAND, G. W. *André Gide: A Study Of His Creative Writings*, pp. 70–77.

PERRY, KENNETH I. *The Religious Symbolism of André Gide*, pp. 48–53.

ROSSI, VINIO. *André Gide: The Evolution Of An Aesthetic*, pp. 82–87.

THESEUS (Thésée, 1946)

CORDLE, THOMAS. *André Gide*, pp. 157–61.

FOWLIE, WALLACE. *André Gide: His Life And Art*, pp. 111–20.

GARZILLI, ENRICO. *Circles Without Center*, pp. 92–100.

IRELAND, G. W. *André Gide: A Study Of His Creative Writings*, pp. 408–21.

PICON, GAËTAN. "The Presence of André Gide," in *Gide: A Collection Of Critical Essays*, ed. David Littlejohn, pp. 36–48.

POLLARD, PATRICK. "Gide's *Thésée*: The Diary of a Moralist." *French Studies*, 26 (1972), 166–77.

———. "The Sources of André Gide's 'Thésée.' " *Modern Language Review*, 65 (1970), 290–97.

ROSSI, VINIO. *André Gide*, pp. 42–45.

STOLTZFUS, BEN. *Gide's Eagles*, pp. 150–58.

WATSON-WILLIAMS, HELEN. *André Gide And The Greek Myth: A Critical Study*, pp. 126–46.

URIEN'S VOYAGE (Le voyage d'Urien, 1893)

CORDLE, THOMAS. *André Gide*, pp. 41–46.

GUERARD, ALBERT J. "*Le Voyage D'Urien*," in *Gide: A Collection Of Critical Essays*, ed. David Littlejohn, pp. 63–72.

IRELAND, G. W. *André Gide: A Study Of His Creative Writings*, pp. 78–90.

PERRY, KENNETH I. *The Religious Symbolism Of André Gide*, pp. 36–48.

ROSSI, VINIO. *André Gide: The Evolution Of An Aesthetic*, pp. 63–81.

THE VATICAN SWINDLE see LAFCADIO'S ADVENTURES

GIGUERE, DIANE (Canadian, 1937–)

WHIRLPOOL (L'Eau est profonde, 1965)

Reviews

GOSE, E. B. "Universe Before Creation." *Canadian Literature*, No.33 (1967), pp. 79–80.

GIL POLO, GASPAR

DIANA ENAMORADA

KEIGHTLEY, R. G. "Narrative Perspectives in Spanish Pastoral Fiction." *AUMLA*, No.44 (1975), pp. 194–219.

GILL, RAJ

THE RAPE (1974)

Reviews

NEBEL, E. JOYCE. *World Literature Written In English*, 14 (1975), 417–18.

GINZBURG, NATALIA (Italian, 1916–)

GENERAL

BOWE, CLOTILDE SOAVE. "The Narrative Strategy of Natalia Ginzburg." *Modern Language Review*, 68 (1973), 788–95.

GIONO, JEAN (French, 1895–1970)

GENERAL

LAWRENCE, DEREK W. "The Ideological Writings of Jean Giono (1937–1946)." *French Review*, 45 (1972), 588–95.

———. "The Transitional Works of Jean Giono (1937-1946)." *French Review,* Special Issue No.1 (1970), 126-34.

MADDEN, MARILYN I. "Imagery in Giono's Novels, with Special Consideration of *La Naissance De L'Odyssée.*" *French Review,* 46 (1973), 522-34.

REDFERN, W. D. "A Postwar World," in his *The Private World Of Jean Giono,* pp. 143-90.

———. "A World Of Words," in his *The Private World Of Jean Giono,* pp. 119-42.

SCOTT, MALCOLM. "Giono's Song of the World: The Theme of Language and Its Associations in Giono's Pre-War Writings." *French Studies,* 26 (1972), 289-304.

LES AMES FORTES (1949)

SMITH, MAXWELL. *Jean Giono,* pp. 136-39.

ANGELO (1958)

REDFERN, W. D. *The Private World Of Jean Giono,* pp. 174-81.

SMITH, MAXWELL A. *Jean Giono,* pp. 147-49.

BATAILLES DANS LA MONTAGNE (1937)

REDFERN, W. D. *The Private World Of Jean Giono,* pp. 107-18.

SMITH, MAXWELL A. *Jean Giono,* pp. 84-87.

BLUE BOY (Jean le bleu, 1932)

REDFERN, W. D. *The Private World Of Jean Giono,* pp. 59-61.

SMITH, MAXWELL A. *Jean Giono,* pp. 65-67.

COLLINE (1929)

REDFERN, W. D. *The Private World Of Jean Giono,* pp. 20-28.

SMITH, MAXWELL A. *Jean Giono,* pp. 49-52.

L'ECOSSAIS

SMITH, MAXWELL A. *Jean Giono,* pp. 145-47.

LES GRANDS CHEMINS (1951)

SMITH, MAXWELL A. *Jean Giono,* pp. 139-41.

HARVEST (Regain, 1930)

REDFERN, W. D. *The Private World Of Jean Giono,* pp. 33-40.

SMITH, MAXWELL A. *Jean Giono,* pp. 55-57.

THE HORSEMAN ON THE ROOF see THE HUSSAR ON THE ROOF

THE HUSSAR ON THE ROOF (Le Hussard sur le toit)

ELLIOTT, GEORGE P. "On Ramón Sender's *A Man's Place* and Jean Giono's *The Horseman On the Roof,*" in *Rediscoveries,* ed. David Madden, pp. 104-14.

GOODRICH, NORMA L. "Further Investigations Concerning Jean Giono's *Hussard Sur Le Toit.*" *Romanic Review,* 59 (1968), 267-77.

REDFERN, W. D. *The Private World Of Jean Giono,* pp. 174-81.

SMITH, MAXWELL A. *Jean Giono,* pp. 149-52.

LOVERS ARE NEVER LOSERS (Un de baumugnes, 1929)

FROHOCK, W. M. *Style And Temper,* pp. 91-94.

REDFERN, W. D. *The Private World Of Jean Giono,* pp. 28-33.

SMITH, MAXWELL A. *Jean Giono,* pp. 52-55.

THE MALEDICTION (Le Moulin de Pologne, 1952)

GOODRICH, NORMA LORRE. "*Le Moulin De Pologne* and its Narrator." *French Review,* 40 (1966), 65-76.

———. "*Le Moulin De Pologne:* Modern Novel and Elizabethan Tragedy." *Revue De Littérature Comparée,* 41 (1967), 88-97.

SMITH, MAXWELL A. *Jean Giono,* pp. 141-43.

MORT D'UN PERSONNAGE (1949)

REDFERN, W. D. *The Private World Of Jean Giono,* pp. 174-81.

SMITH, MAXWELL A. *Jean Giono,* pp. 156-59.

LA NAISSANCE DE L'ODYSSÉE (1930)

MADDEN, MARILYN I. "Imagery in Giono's Novels, with Special Consideration of *La Naissance De L'Odyssée.*" *French Review,* 46 (1973), 522-34.

REDFERN, W. D. *The Private World Of Jean Giono,* pp. 11-19.

RYSTEIN, FELIX. "Jean Giono's *Naissance De L'Odyssée.*" *French Review,* 45 (1971), 378-87.

SMITH, MAXWELL A. *Jean Giono,* pp. 42-48.

NOE

SMITH, MAXWELL A. *Jean Giono,* pp. 134-36.

LE POIDS DU CIEL (1938)

REDFERN, W. D. *The Private World Of Jean Giono,* pp. 99-107.

SMITH, MAXWELL A. *Jean Giono,* pp. 97-99.

QUE MA JOIE DEMEURE (1935)

REDFERN, W. D. *The Private World Of Jean Giono,* pp. 72-82, 129-30.

SMITH, MAXWELL A. *Jean Giono,* pp. 80-84.

UN ROI SANS DIVERTISSEMENT (1947)

ASPINWALL, DOROTHY B. "Giono's *Un Roi Sans Divertissement.*" *Explicator,* 29 (1971), Item 54.

SMITH, MAXWELL A. *Jean Giono,* pp. 131-34.

THE SONG OF THE WORLD (Le chant du monde, 1934)

REDFERN, W. D. *The Private World Of Jean Giono,* pp. 40-47.

SMITH, MAXWELL A. *Jean Giono,* pp. 76-80.

THE STRAW MAN (Le Bonheur fou, 1957)

REDFERN, W. D. *The Private World Of Jean Giono,* pp. 174-83.

SMITH, MAXWELL A. *Jean Giono,* pp. 152-55.

TO THE SLAUGHTERHOUSE (Le Grand troupeau, 1931)

REDFERN, W. D. *The Private World Of Jean Giono,* pp. 63-68.

SMITH, MAXWELL A. *Jean Giono,* pp. 63-65.

TWO RIDERS OF THE STORM (Deux cavaliers de l'orage, 1965)

POMERAI, ODILE DE. "An Unknown Giono: *Deux Cavaliers De L'Orage.*" *French Review,* 39 (1965), 78-84.

LES VRAIES RICHESSES (1936)

SMITH, MAXWELL A. *Jean Giono,* pp. 94-97.

GIOVENE, ANDREA (Italian, 1904–)

THE BOOK OF SAN SEVERO (L'autobiographia di Giuliano di Sanservero, v. 2)

Reviews

HUGHES, SERGE. *Saturday Review,* 21 November 1970, pp. 42-43.

GIRAUDOUX, JOSÉ MARÍA (Spanish, 1917–)

LES ADVENTURES DE JÉRÔME BARDINI (1930)

LEMAITRE, GEORGES. *Jean Giraudoux: The Writer And His Work,* pp. 76-79.

LEWIS, ROY. "Giraudoux's Dark Night of the Soul: A Study of *Les Adventures De Jérôme Bardini.*" *French Studies,* 28 (1974), 421-34.

BELLA

> LEMAITRE, GEORGES. *Jean Giraudoux: The Writer And His Work,* pp. 67-72.

CHOIX DES ELUES (1939)

> LEMAITRE, GEORGES. *Jean Giraudoux: The Writer And His Work,* pp. 84-91.

COMBAT AVEC L'ANGE (1934)

> LEMAITRE, GEORGES. *Jean Giraudoux: The Writer And His Work,* pp. 79-81.

EGLANTINE (1927)

> GOODHAND, ROBERT. "Psychological Development in Jean Giraudoux's 'Eglantine.' " *French Review,* 38 (1964), 173-79.

LYING WOMAN

> **Reviews**
> BISHOP, TOM. *Saturday Review,* 5 February 1972, pp. 59-60.

LA MENTEUSE

> LEMAITRE, GEORGES. *Jean Giraudoux: The Writer And His Work,* pp. 81-84.

MY FRIEND FROM LIMOUSIN (Siegfried et le Limousin, 1922)

> LEMAITRE, GEORGES. *Jean Giraudoux: The Writer And His Work,* pp. 62-67.

SIMON LE PATHETIQUE (1918)

> LEMAITRE, GEORGES. *Jean Giraudoux: The Writer And His Work,* pp. 56-58.

SUZANNE ET LE PACIFIQUE (1921)

> LEMAITRE, GEORGES. *Jean Giraudoux: The Writer And His Work,* pp. 58-60.

GIRONELLA, JOSÉ MARÍA (Spanish, 1917-)

GENERAL

> DIAL, JOHN E. "Gironella's Chronicles Revisited: A Panorama of Fratricide." *Papers On Language And Literature,* 10 (1974), 98-110.

THE CYPRESSES BELIEVE IN GOD (Los Cipreses creen en dios, 1953)

> ILIE, PAUL. "Fictive History in Gironella." *Journal Of Spanish Studies,* 2 (1974), 77-94.

> SCHWARTZ, RONALD. *José María Gironella,* pp. 47-48, 51-69.

LA MAREA (1949)

> SCHWARTZ, RONALD. *José María Gironella,* pp. 41-44, 46-47.

MUJER, LEVANTATE Y ANDA (1962)

> SCHWARTZ, RONALD. *José María Gironella,* pp. 48-50, 106-12.

ONE MILLION DEAD (Un Millón de muertos, 1961)

> ILIE, PAUL. "Fictive History in Gironella." *Journal Of Spanish Studies,* 2 (1974), 77-94.

> SCHWARTZ, RONALD. *José María Gironella,* pp. 70-85.

PEACE AFTER WAR (Ha estallado la paz, 1966)

> SCHWARTZ, RONALD. *José María Gironella,* pp. 150-56.

> **Reviews**
> PAYNE, ROBERT. "The Victors, Spoiled." *Saturday Review,* 17 May 1969, p. 49.

WHERE THE SOIL WAS SHALLOW (Um Hombre, 1946)

> SCHWARTZ, RONALD. *José María Gironella,* pp. 38-41, 44-46.

GLADWIN, PETER

THE LONG BEAT HOME

> VINTNER, MAURICE. "Peter Gladwin." *Overland,* No.49 (1971), pp. 37-38.

GLISSANT, ÉDOUARD (Martinican, 1928-)

GENERAL

> ORMEROD, BEVERLEY. "Beyond *Négritude:* Some Aspects of the Work of Édouard Glissant." *Contemporary Literature,* 15 (1974), 360-69.

GLOWACKI, ALEXANDER see PRUS, BOLESLAW

GNESSIN, URI-NISSAN (Hebrew, 1879-1913)

ASIDE

> RABINOVICH, ISAIAH. *Major Trends In Modern Hebrew Fiction,* pp. 57-63.

BEFOREHAND

> RABINOVICH, ISAIAH. *Major Trends In Modern Hebrew Fiction,* pp. 65-74.

THERE

> RABINOVICH, ISAIAH. *Major Trends In Modern Hebrew Fiction,* pp. 75-79.

GOCHHAUSEN, ERNST AUGUST

EIN BUCHLEIN ZUR BEFORDERUNG EINFALTIGER LEBENSWEISHEIT UNTER VERSTANDIGEN EHRLICHEN BURGERN UND LANDLEUTEN

> HADLEY, MICHAEL. *The German Novel In 1790,* pp. 197-200.

GODBOUT, JACQUES (Canadian, 1933-)

D'AMOUR, P. Q.

> **Reviews**
> PIVATO, JOSEPH. "Antinovel and Journal." *Canadian Literature,* No.62 (1974), pp. 114-15.

LE COUTEAU SUR LA TABLE (1965)

> PRIVATO, JOSEPH. "Nouveau Roman Canadien." *Canadian Literature,* No.58 (1973), pp. 51-60.

HAIL GALARNEAU! (Salut Galarneau!, 1967)

> **Reviews**
> McPHERSON, HUGO. "Blais, Godbout, Roy: Love, Art, Time." *Tamarack Review,* No.57 (1971), pp. 86-87.

> WARWICK, JACK. "Vecrire." *Canadian Literature,* No.49 (1971), pp. 87-88.

GODDEN, JON (Indian-born Englishman, 1906-)

GENERAL

> HARTLEY, LOIS. "The Indian Novels of Jon Godden." *Mahfil,* 4, No.1 (1967), 39-43.

GODDEN, RUMER (Indian-born Englishwoman,)

GENERAL

> HARTLEY, LOIS. "The Indian Novels of Rumer Godden." *Mahfil,* 3, No.2/3 (1966), 65-75.

THIS FAR AND NO FURTHER (1946)

> HARTLEY, LOIS. "The Indian Novels of Rumer Godden." *Mahfil*, 3, No.2/3 (1966), 65–68.

GODFREY, DAVE (Canadian, 1938-)

THE NEW ANCESTORS (1970)

> MARGESON, ROBERT W. "A Preliminary Interpretation of *The New Ancestors*." *Journal Of Canadian Fiction*, 4, No.1 (1975), 96–110.

Reviews

> THOMAS, AUDREY. "The Smell of Recognition." *Canadian Literature*, No.49 (1971), pp. 78–80.

NO ENGLISHMAN NEED APPLY

Reviews

> CREIGH, GEOFFREY. "Campus Caricatures." *Canadian Literature*, No.31 (1967), pp. 75–76.

GOETHE, JOHANN WOLFGANG VON (German, 1749-1832)

GENERAL

> BLACKALL, ERIC A. "Goethe and the Chinese Novel," in *The Discontinuous Tradition*, ed. P. F. Ganz, pp. 29–53.

> HERZFELD, MARIANNE VON. "Goethe's Images of Children." *German Life And Letters*, 25 (1972), 219–31.

> KELLING, H. W. "Goethe the 'Dichterprophet': Thoughts on Interpreting Goethe's Religion." *German Life And Letters*, 26 (1973), 112–19.

> O'BRIEN JOHN CONWAY. "Goethe and Schweitzer: The Hunger for Perfection." *USF Language Quarterly*, 12, No.1/2 (1973), 2–8.

> PARRY, IDRIS. "Goethe, Dada, and Zen." *German Life And Letters*, 22 (1969), 111–20.

> PERLOFF, MARJORIE. "Yeats and Goethe." *Comparative Literature*, 23 (1971), 125–40.

> TERRAS, RITA. "Goethe's Use of the Mirror Image." *Monatshefte*, 67 (1975), 387–402.

ELECTIVE AFFINITIES (Die Wahlverwandtschaften, 1809)

> BARNES, H. G. *Goethe's <Die Wahlverwandtschaften:> A Literary Interpretation.*

> DICKSON, KEITH. "Spatial Concentration and Themes in *Die Wahlverwandtschaften*." *Forum For Modern Language Studies*, 1 (1965), 159–74.

> ———. "The Temporal Structure of *Die Wahlverwandtschaften*." *Germanic Review*, 41 (1966), 170–85.

> ELLIS, J. M. "Names in *Faust* and *Die Wahlverwandtschaften*." *Seminar*, 1 (1965), 25–30.

> GOULD, ROBERT. "The Critical Reception of *Die Wahlverwandtschaften* in the French Press: An Unknown Review of *Ottilia, Ou Le Pourvoir De La Sympathie*." *Seminar*, 9 (1973), 28–35.

> GRAY, RONALD. *Goethe: A Critical Introduction*, pp. 216–25.

> HUNTLEY, H. ROBERT. "*The Good Soldier* and *Die Wahlverwandtschaften*." *Comparative Literature*, 19 (1967), 133–41.

> LANGE, VICTOR. "Goethe's Craft of Fiction," in *Goethe: A Collection Of Critical Essays*, ed Victor Lange, pp. 79–81.

> LEU, PAUL. "Time and Transcendence in Goethe's 'Wahlverwandtschaften.'" *Monatshefte*, 60 (1968), 369–78.

> MACEY, SAMUEL L. "On the Relationship between Eduard and Ottilie in Goethe's *Wahlverwandtschaften*." *Seminar*, 7 (1971), 79–84.

> McLAREN, NEIL. "Goethe's 'Elective Affinities.'" *Delta: The Cambridge Literary Magazine*, No.42 (1968), pp. 28–33.

> MARAHRENS, GERWIN. "Narrator and Narrative in Goethe's *Die Wahlverwandtschaften*," in *Essays on German Literature In Honour Of G. Joyce Hallamore*, ed. Michael S. Batts and Marketa Goetz Stankiewicz, pp. 94–127.

> MILFULL, JOHN. "The Function of the Novelle 'Die Wunderlichen Nachbarskinder' in Goethe's *Die Wahlverwandtschaften*." *German Life And Letters*, 25 (1971), 1–5.

> ———. "The 'Idea' of Goethe's *Wahlverwandtschaften*." *Germanic Review*, 47 (1972), 83–94.

> NISBET, H. B. "'Die Wahlverwandtschaften': Explanation and its Limits." *Deutsche Vierteljahresschrift Fur Literaturwissenschaft Und Geistegeschichte*, 43 (1969), 458–86.

> REISS, HANS. *Goethe's Novels*, pp. 145–221.

> ROBERTS, DAVID. "'Die Wahlverwandtschaften': A Note on the Symbolism of the Seasons and the Time Structure of *Die Wahlverwandtschaften* with Reference to *Werther*." *AUMLA*, No.38 (1972), pp. 197–203.

> SNYDER, CAROLINE. "The Helmsman-Rescue Motif in Goethe's 'Die Wahlverwandtschaften.'" *Monatshefte*, 63 (1971), 41–47.

> STOCK, IRVIN. "Goethe's Tragedy: A View of *Elective Affinities*." *Mosaic*, 7, No.3 (1974), 17–27.

> VAN ABBÉ, DEREK. *Goethe: New Perspectives On A Writer And His Time*, pp. 133–36, 150–54.

THE SORROWS OF YOUNG WERTHER (Die Leiden des jungen Werthers, 1774)

> DUKAS, VYTAS and RICHARD H. LAWSON. "*Werther* and *Diary Of A Superfluous Man*." *Comparative Literature*, 21 (1969), 146–54.

> DYE, ROBERT ELLIS. "Man and God in Goethe's *Werther*." *Symposium*, 29 (1975), 314–29.

> FABER, M. D. "The Suicide of Young Werther." *Psychoanalytic Review*, 60 (1973), 239–76.

> FETZER, JOHN. "Schatten ohne Frau: Marginalia on a *Werther* Motif." *Germanic Review*, 46 (1971), 87–94.

> GISH, THEODORE G. "The Evolution of the Goethean Theme of the 'Wanderer' and the 'Cottage.'" *Seminar*, 9 (1973), 19–21.

> GOODHEART, EUGENE. "Goethe, Carlyle, and 'The Sorrows of Werther,'" in his *The Cult Of The Ego*, pp. 61–89.

> GRAY, RONALD. *Goethe: A Critical Introduction*, pp. 48–55.

> HATCH, MARY GIES. "Werther and Student Protest." *South Atlantic Bulletin*, 39, No.2 (1974), 107–11.

> LANGE, VICTOR. "Fact in Fiction." *Comparative Literature Studies*, 6 (1969), 253–61.

> ———. "Goethe's Craft of Fiction," in *Goethe: A Collection Of Critical Essays*, ed. Victor Lange, pp. 65–73.

> LUKÁCS, GEORG. *Goethe And His Age*, pp. 35–49.

> MOLNAR, GÉZA VON. "Confinement or Containment: Goethe's *Werther* and the Concept of Limitation." *German Life And Letters*, 23 (1970), 226–34.

> OSBORNE, JOHN. "Exhibitionism and Criticism: J. M. R. Lenz's *Briefe Übert Die Moralität Der Leiden Des Jungen Werthers*." *Seminar*, 10 (1974), 199–212.

> REISS, HANS. *Goethe's Novels*, pp. 10–67.

> SALM, PETER. "Werther and the Sensibility of Estrangement." *German Quarterly*, 46 (1973), 47–55.

> SCHULZ, GERHARD. "The Lonely Hero, or: The Germans and the Novel." *AUMLA*, No.43 (1975), pp. 7–11.

> SPANN, MENO. "*Werther* Revisited: Two Hundred Years of a Masterpiece." *Mosaic*, 5, No.3 (1972), 73–83.

> STEINHAUER, HARRY. "Goethe's *Werther* after Two Centuries." *University Of Toronto Quarterly*, 44 (1974), 1–13.

> VAN ABBÉ, DEREK. *Goethe: New Perspectives On A Writer And His Time*, pp. 48–57.

VIËTOR, KARL. "La Maladie du Siècle," in *Goethe: A Collection Of Critical Essays,* ed. Victor Lange, pp. 26–32.

WILSON, JAMES D. "Goethe's *Werther:* A Keatsian Quest for Self-Annihilation." *Mosaic,* 9, No.1 (1975), 93–109.

WILHELM MEISTER'S APPRENTICESHIP (Wilhelm Meisters Lehrjahre, 1795–96)

ATKINS, STUART. "Wilhelm Meisters Lehrjahre: Novel or Romance?" in *Essays On European Literature,* ed. Peter Uwe Hohendahl, Herbert Lindenberger, and Egon Schwarz, pp. 45–52.

BRUFORD, W. H. *The German Tradition Of Self-Cultivation,* pp. 29–57.

CASEY, PAUL F. "Carlyle as Translator: '*Wilhelm Meisters Lehrjahre*'." *Neuphilologische Mitteilungen,* 76 (1975), 488–94.

CITATI, PIETRO. *Goethe,* pp. 3–139.

DUNCAN, BRUCE. "The Marchese's Story in *Wilhelm Meisters Lehrjahre.*" *Seminar,* 8 (1972), 169–80.

FARRELLY, DANIEL J. *Goethe And Inner Harmony: A Study Of The 'Schöne Seele' In The <Apprenticeship Of Wilhem Meister.>*

FLEISCHER, STEFAN. " 'Bekenntnisse einer schönen Seele': Figural Representation in *Wilhelm Meisters Lehrjahre.*" *MLN,* 83 (1968), 807–20.

GRAY, RONALD. *Goethe: A Critical Introduction,* pp. 186–96.

KAHN, ROBERT L. "Tieck's *Franz Sternbalds Wanderungen* and Novalis' *Heinrich Von Ofterdingen.*" *Studies In Romanticism,* 7 (1967), 40–47.

LANGE, VICTOR. "Goethe's Craft of Fiction," in *Goethe: A Collection Of Critical Essays,* ed. Victor Lange, pp. 73–77.

LUKÁCS, GEORG. *Goethe And His Age,* pp. 50–67.

––––––. "*Wilhelm Meisters Lehrjahre,*" in *Goethe: A Collection Of Critical Essays,* ed. Victor Lange, pp. 86–98.

MILES, DAVID H. "The Picaro's Journey to the Confessional: The Changing Image of the Hero in the German Bildungsroman." *PMLA,* 89 (1974), 981–84.

REISS, HANS. *Goethe's Novels,* pp. 68–144.

SAINE, THOMAS P. "Wilhelm Meister's Homecoming." *Journal Of English And Germanic Philology,* 69 (1970), 450–69.

STEER, A. G. "The Wound and the Physician in Goethe's *Wilhelm Meister,*" in *Studies In German Literature Of The Nineteenth And Twentieth Centuries,* ed. Siegfried Mews, pp. 11–23.

STEIN, JACK M. "Musical Settings of the Songs from *Wilhelm Meister.*" *Comparative Literature,* 22 (1970), 125–46.

TEMMER, MARK J. "Rousseau's *La Nouvelle Héloïse* and Goethe's *Wilhelm Meisters Lehrjahre.*" *Studies In Romanticism,* 10 (1971), 309–39.

VAN ABBÉ, DEREK. *Goethe: New Perspectives On A Writer And His Time,* pp. 156–61.

WILKINSON, ELIZABETH M. and L. A. WILLOUGHBY. "Having and Being, or Bourgeois Mobility: Notes for a Chapter on Social and Cultural History or for a Commentary on *Wilhelm Meister.*" *German Life And Letters,* 22 (1968), 101–5.

ZIPSER, RICHARD A. "Bulwer-Lytton and Goethe's Mignon." *MLN,* 89 (1974), 465–68.

WILHELM MEISTER'S TRAVELS (Wilhelm Meisters wanderjahre, 1821)

BAHR, EHRHARD. "Goethe's *Wanderjahre* as an Experimental Novel." *Mosaic,* 5, No.3 (1972), 61–71.

BLACKALL, ERIC A. "Wilhelm Meister's Pious Pilgrimage." *German Life And Letters,* 18 (1965), 246–51.

BRUFORD, W. H. *The German Tradition Of Self-Cultivation,* pp. 88–112.

GISH, THEODORE G. "The Evolution of the Goethean Theme of the 'Wanderer' and the 'Cottage.' " *Seminar,* 9 (1973), 15–27.

GRAY, RONALD. *Goethe: A Critical Introduction,* pp. 196–200.

LANGE, VICTOR. "Goethe's Craft of Fiction," in *Goethe: A Collection Of Critical Essays,* ed. Victor Lange, pp. 82–84.

REISS, HANS. *Goethe's Novels,* pp. 222–68.

STEER, A. G. "The Wound and the Physician in Goethe's *Wilhelm Meister,*" in *Studies In German Literature Of The Nineteenth And Twentieth Centuries,* ed. Siegfried Mews, pp. 11–23.

GÖRLING, LARS (Swedish, 1931–1966)

491 (1962)

Reviews
SAMUELS, GERTRUDE. "A Finite Forgiveness." *Saturday Review,* 23 July 1966, p. 54.

GOGOL, NICOLAI VASILIEVICH (Russian, 1809–1905)

GENERAL

ALKIRE, GILMAN H. "Gogol and Bulgarin's *Ivan Vyzhigin.*" *Slavic Review,* 28 (1969), 289–96.

BARKSDALE, E. C. *The Dacha And The Duchess,* pp. 105–12.

BELY, ANDREI. "Gogol." Trans. Elizabeth Trahan. *Russian Literature Triquarterly,* No.4 (1972), pp. 131–44; rpt. in *Twentieth-Century Russian Literary Criticism,* ed. Victor Erlich, pp. 33–50.

BRYUSOV, VALERY. "Burnt to Ashes." Trans. Robert A. Maguire. *Russian Literature Triquarterly,* No.3 (1972), pp. 106–16; rpt. in *Gogol From The Twentieth Century: Eleven Essays,* ed. Robert A. Maguire, pp. 105–31.

FLOROVSKY, GEORGES. "Three Masters: The Quest for Religion in Nineteenth-Century Russian Literature." *Comparative Literature Studies,* 3 (1966), 122–28.

HALLETT, R. W. "The Laughter of Gogol." *Russian Review,* 30 (1971), 373–84.

HOLQUIST, JAMES M. "The Burden of Prophecy: Gogol's Conception of Russia." *Review Of National Literatures,* 3, No.1 (1972), 39–55.

KARLINSKY, SIMON. "Portrait of Gogol as a Word Glutton: With Rabelais, Sterne, and Gertrude Stein as Background Figures." *California Slavic Studies,* 5 (1970), 169–86.

KARST, ROMAN. "The Reality of the Absurd and the Absurdity of the Real: Kafka and Gogol." *Mosaic,* 9, No.1 (1975), 67–81.

KEEFER, LUBOV. "Gogol' and Music." *Slavic And East European Journal,* 14 (1970), 160–81.

KOLB-SELETSKI, NATALIA M. "Gastronomy, Gogol, and His Fiction." *Slavic Review,* 29 (1970), 35–57.

LITTLE, EDMUND. "Some Observations on the Biography and Work of Lewis Carroll and Nikolai Gogol.' " *Forum For Modern Language Studies,* 11 (1975), 74–92.

MUCHNIC, HELEN. "The Unhappy Consciousness: Gogol, Poe, Baudelaire," in her *Russian Writers,* pp. 22–46.

OBOLENSKY, ALEXANDER P. "Nicholas Gogol and Hieronimous Bosch." *Russian Review,* 32 (1973), 158–72.

PEREVERZEV, VALERIAN. "The Evolution of Gogol's Art," in *Gogol From The Twentieth Century,* ed. Robert A. Maguire, pp. 134–54.

RAHV, PHILIP. "Gogol as a Modern Instance," in his *Literature And The Sixth Sense,* pp. 196–201.

ROWE, WILLIAM. "Gogolesque Perception-Expanding Reversals in Nabokov." *Slavic Review,* 30 (1971), 110–20.

ROZANOV, VASILY. "Pushkin and Gogol," in *Essays In Russian Literature,* ed. Spencer E. Roberts, 357–68.

SHERRY, CHARLES. "Folie à Deux: Gogol and Dostoevsky." *Texas Studies In Literature And Language,* 17 (1975), 257–73.

SIMMONS, ERNEST J. "Gogol—Live or Dead Souls," in his *Introduction To Russian Realism*, pp. 44-65.

SLONIMSKY, ALEXANDER. "The Technique of the Comic in Gogol," in *Gogol From The Twentieth Century: Eleven Essays*, ed. Robert A. Maguire, pp. 324-73.

STRUC, ROMAN S. " 'Petty Demons' and Beauty: Gogol, Dostoevsky, Sologub," in *Essays On European Literature*, ed. Peter Uwe Hohendahl, Herbert Lindenberger, and Egon Schwarz, pp. 61-69.

TYNJANOV, JURIJ. "Dostoevsky and Gogol," in *Twentieth-Century Russian Literary Criticism*, ed. Victor Erlich, pp. 102-16.

VROON, RONALD. "Gogol in Oblomovka." *Russian Literature Triquarterly*, No.3 (1972), pp. 282-96.

DEAD SOULS (Mertuye Duši, 1842)

ANNENSKIJ, INNOKENTIJ. "The Aesthetics of Gogol's *Dead Souls* and Its Legacy," in *Twentieth-Century Russian Literary Criticism*, ed. Victor Erlich, pp. 51-60.

BOYD, ALEXANDER F. *Aspects Of The Russian Novel*, pp. 46-67.

DAVIES, RUTH. *The Great Books Of Russia*, pp. 36-49.

ERLICH, VICTOR. *Gogol*, pp. 112-41, 170-208.

FREEBORN, RICHARD. "*Dead Souls:* a Study." *Slavonic And East European Review*, 49 (1971), 18-44.

———. "Realism in Russia, to the Death of Dostoevsky," in *The Age Of Realism*, ed. F. W. J. Hemmings, pp. 87-91.

———. *The Rise Of The Russian Novel*, pp. 74-114.

LITTLE, T. E. "*Dead Souls*," in *Knaves And Swindlers*, ed. Christine J. Whitbourn, pp. 112-38.

MEREZHKOVSKY, DMITRY. "Gogol and the Devil," in *Gogol From The Twentieth Century: Eleven Essays*, ed. Robert A. Maguire, pp. 76-97.

PROFFER, CARL R. *The Simile And Gogol's <Dead Souls.>*

REEVE, F. D. *The Russian Novel*, pp. 64-102.

ROWE, W. WOODIN. "Observations on Black Humor in Gogol' and Nabokov." *Slavic And East European Journal*, 18 (1974), 392-99.

ROZANOV, VASILY. "Pushkin and Gogol," in *Essays In Russian Literature*, ed. Spencer E. Roberts, pp. 357-68.

SEELEY, FRANK FRIEDEBERG. "Gogol's *Dead Souls*." *Forum For Modern Language Studies*, 4 (1968), 33-44.

SHEVYREV, STEPAN. "The Adventures of Chichikov, or Dead Souls a Narrative Poem by N. Gogol," in *Literature And National Identity*, ed. Paul Debreczeny and Jesse Zeldin, pp. 17-64.

SIMMONS, ERNEST J. "Gogol—Live or Dead Souls," in his *Introduction To Russian Realism*, pp. 65-99.

SMITH, RAOUL N. "The Stylistic Use of Syntactic Features in Some Russian Novels." *Language And Style*, 6 (1973), 127-34.

SMITH, THOMAS A. "Gogol's Hollow Men." *English Journal*, 61 (1972), 32-35.

STILMAN, LEON. "The 'All-Seeing Eye' in Gogol," in *Gogol From The Twentieth Century: Eleven Essays*, ed. Robert A. Maguire, pp. 376-89.

TIMMER, CHARLES B. "*Dead Souls* Speaking." *Slavonic And East European Review*, 45 (1967), 273-91.

TROYAT, HENRI. *Divided Soul: The Life Of Gogol*, pp. 267-92.

OLD WORLD LANDOWNERS

PEACE, R. A. "Gogol's *Old World Landowners*." *Slavonic And East European Review*, 53 (1975), 504-20.

ROME (Rim)

VOGEL, LUCY. "Gogol's *Rome*." *Slavic And East European Journal*, 11 (1967), 145-58.

TARAS BULBA (1835)

KENT, LEONARD J. *The Subconscious In Gogol And Dostoevskij And Its Antecedents*, pp. 70-73.

PROFFER, CARL R. "Gogol's *Taras Bulba* and the *Iliad*." *Comparative Literature*, 17 (1965), 142-50.

STROMECKY, O. *The How Of Gogol: A Study Of The Methods And Sources Of Gogol*, pp. 27-65.

TROYAT, HENRI. *Divided Soul: The Life Of Gogol*, pp. 125-27.

GOKAK, PADMA SRI V. K.

NARAHARI: PROPHET OF NEW INDIA

KALLAPUR, S. T. "*Narahari*: A Study." *Journal Of Indian Writing In English*, 1, No.1 (1973), 52-57.

Reviews

TYABJI, ADIL. *Indian Horizons*, 22, No.1 (1973), 105-7.

GOŁUBIEW, ANTONI (Polish, 1907-)

BOLESLAW CHROBRY

GASIOROWSKA, XENIA. "Bolesław the Brave by A. Golubiew: A Modern Polish Epic." *California Slavic Studies*, 4 (1967), 119-44.

GOMBROWICZ, WITOLD (Polish, 1904-1969)

GENERAL

PETERKIEWICZ, JERZY. "The Fork & the Fear: Remembering Gombrowicz." *Encounter*, 36, No.3 (1971), 57-60.

COSMOS (Kosmos, 1965)

Reviews

MIHAILOVICH, VASA D. *Saturday Review*, 28 February 1970, p. 43.

FERDYDURKE (1937)

BOYERS, ROBERT. "Gombrowicz and *Ferdydurke:* The Tyranny of Form." *Centennial Review*, 14 (1970), 284-312.

Jelenski, K. A. "Witold Gombrowicz." *Triquarterly*, No.9 (1967), pp. 37-42.

MEYER, HANS. "The Views of Witold Gombrowicz," in his *Steppenwolf And Everyman*, pp. 241-47.

Reviews

SEGEL, HAROLD B. "Tyranny of Form That Deforms." *Saturday Review*, 15 July 1967, pp. 33-34.

PORNOGRAFIA (1960)

MAYER, HANS. "The Views of Witold Gombrowicz," in his *Steppenwolf And Everyman*, pp. 247-51.

GÓMEZ DE LA SERNA, RAMÓN (Spanish, 1891-1963)

GENERAL

HOYLE, ALAN. "The Politics of a Hatless Revolutionary, Ramón Gómez de la Serna," in *Studies In Modern Spanish Literature And Art*, ed. Nigel Glendinning, pp. 79-96.

JACKSON, RICHARD L. "The Surrealist Image in the *Greguería* of Ramón Gómez de la Serna." *Romance Notes*, 8 (1966), 11-13.

MAZZETTI, RITA. "The Use of Imagery in the Works of Ramón Gómez de la Serna." *Hispania*, 54 (1971), 80-90.

GONCHAROV, IVAN (Russian, 1812-1891)

GENERAL

BARKSDALE, E. C. *The Dacha And The Duchess,* pp. 49–56.

EHRE, MILTON. "Ivan Goncharov on Art, Literature, and the Novel." *Slavic Review,* 29 (1970), 203–18.

LYNGSTAD, ALEXANDRA and SVERRE LYNGSTAD. "The Art of Goncharov," in their *Ivan Goncharov,* pp. 149–66.

A COMMON STORY see AN ORDINARY STORY

OBLOMOV (1859)

BARKSDALE, E. C. *The Dacha And The Duchess,* pp. 56–75.

DAVIES, RUTH. *The Great Books Of Russia,* pp. 50–63.

EHRE, MILTON. *Oblomov And His Creator: The Life And Art Of Ivan Goncharov,* pp. 154–232.

FREEBORN, RICHARD. *The Rise Of The Russian Novel,* pp. 145–55.

KUHN, ALFRED. "Dobroliubov's Critique of *Oblomov:* Polemics and Psychology." *Slavic Review,* 30 (1971), 93–109.

LOURIA, YVETTE. "Dostoevskii and Goncharov." *MLN,* 88 (1973), 1325–28.

———— and MORTON I. SEIDEN. "Ivan Goncharov's *Oblomov:* The Anti-Faust As Christian Hero." *Canadian Slavic Studies,* 3 (1969), 39–68.

LYNGSTAD, ALEXANDRA and SVERRE LYNGSTAD. *Ivan Goncharov,* pp. 72–114.

MAYS, MILTON A. "Oblomov as Anti-Faust." *Western Humanities Review,* 21 (1967), 141–52.

REEVE, F. D. *The Russian Novel,* pp. 103–18.

SETCHKAREV, VSEVOLOD. *Ivan Goncharov: His Life And His Works,* pp. 127–61.

VROON, RONALD. "Gogol in Oblomovka." *Russian Literature Triquarterly,* No.3 (1972), pp. 282–96.

AN ORDINARY STORY (Obyknovennaja Istorija, 1847)

EHRE, MILTON. *Oblomov And His Creator: The Life And Art Of Ivan Goncharov,* pp. 114–41.

FREEBORN, RICHARD. *The Rise Of The Russian Novel,* pp. 142–45.

LYNGSTAD, ALEXANDRA and SVERRE LYNGSTAD. *Ivan Goncharov,* pp. 41–71.

SETCHKAREV, VSEVOLOD. *Ivan Goncharov: His Life And His Works,* pp. 41–72.

THE PRECIPICE (Oibryv, 1869)

EHRE, MILTON. *Oblomov And His Creator: The Life And Art Of Ivan Goncharov,* pp. 233–63.

LYNGSTAD, ALEXANDRA and SVERRE LYNGSTAD. *Ivan Goncharov,* pp. 115–48.

SETCHKAREV, VSEVOLOD. *Ivan Goncharov: His Life And Works,* pp. 203–39.

RAVINE see THE PRECIPICE

GONCOURT, EDMOND LOUIS ANTOINE HUOT DE (French, 1822–1896)

GENERAL

GRANT, RICHARD B. *The Goncourt Brothers,* pp. 13–31.

————. "Illusion and Reality in the Goncourts' Novels." *South Atlantic Bulletin,* 35, No.3 (1970), 3–10.

CHARLES DEMAILLY (Les Hommes de lettres, 1860)

GRANT, RICHARD B. *The Goncourt Brothers,* pp. 33–43.

CHERIE (1884)

GRANT, RICHARD B. *The Goncourt Brothers,* pp. 136–39.

ELISA (La fille Élisa, 1877)

GRANT, RICHARD B. *The Goncourt Brothers,* pp. 108–18.

MATTHEWS, J. H. "From Naturalism to the Absurd: Edmond de Goncourt and Albert Camus." *Symposium,* 22 (1968), 241–55.

MICHOT-DIETRICH, HELA. "Blindness to 'Goodness': The Critics' Chauvinism? An Analysis of Four Novels by Zola and the Goncourts." *Modern Fiction Studies,* 21 (1975), 218–19.

LA FAUSTIN (1882)

GRANT, RICHARD B. *The Goncourt Brothers,* pp. 131–36.

GERMINIE LACERTEUX (1864)

GRANT, RICHARD B. *The Goncourt Brothers,* pp. 62–72.

MICHOT-DIETRICH, HELA. "Blindness to 'Goodness': The Critics' Chauvinism? An Analysis of Four Novels by Zola and the Goncourts." *Modern Fiction Studies,* 21 (1975), 216–18.

MADAME GERVAISAIS (1969)

GRANT, RICHARD B. *The Goncourt Brothers,* pp. 97–102.

MANETTE SALOMON (1867)

GRANT, RICHARD B. *The Goncourt Brothers,* pp. 85–96.

RENEE MAUPERIN (1864)

GRANT, RICHARD B. *The Goncourt Brothers,* pp. 55–62.

SISTER PHILOMENE (Soeur Philomène, 1861)

GRANT, RICHARD B. *The Goncourt Brothers,* pp. 44–52.

THE ZEMGANNO BROTHERS (Les Frères Zemganno, 1879)

GRANT, RICHARD B. *The Goncourt Brothers,* pp. 119–30.

GONCOURT, JULES ALFRED HUOT DE (French, 1830–1870) see GONCOURT, EDMOND

GONZALEZ, NESTOR VICENTE MADALI (Philippine, 1915–)

THE BAMBOO DANCERS (1959)

CASPER, LEONARD. *New Writing From The Philippines,* pp. 49–55.

GOR, GENNADII

GENERAL

URBAN, A. "Science Fiction: Fantasy or Philosophy?" *Soviet Studies In Literature,* 3, No.1 (1966/7), 59–63.

GORDAN, Charles William see CONNOR, Ralph

GORDIMER, NADINE (South African, 1923–)

GENERAL

BURROWS, E. G. "An Interview with Nadine Gordimer." *Michigan Quarterly Review,* 9 (1970), 231–34.

CRONIN, JOHN F. "Writer versus Situation: Three South African Novelists." *Studies: An Irish Quarterly Review,* 56 (1967), 81–84.

GORDIMER, NADINE AND ALAN ROSS. "A Writer in South Africa." *London Magazine,* 5, No.2 (1965), 21–28. (Interview)

HOPE, CHRISTOPHER. "Out of the Picture: The Novels of Nadine Gordimer." *London Magazine,* NS 15, No.1 (1975), 49–55.

LAREDO, URSULA. "African Mosaic: The Novels of Nadine Gordimer." *Journal Of Commonwealth Literature,* 8, No.1 (1973), 42–53.

McGuiness, Frank. "The Novels of Nadine Gordimer." *London Magazine,* NS 5, No.3 (1965), 97-102.

THE CONSERVATIONIST (1974)

O'Sheel, P. "Nadine Gordimer's *The Conservationist.*" *World Literature Written In English,* 14 (1975), 514-19.

Reviews

Bellette, A. F. *Ariel: A Review Of International English Literature,* 6, No.3 (1975), 106-8.

Geismar, Maxwell. "Black Man's Burden." *Saturday Review,* 8 March 1975, pp. 24-25.

Ravenscroft, Arthur. "Nadine Gordimer's New Assurance." *Journal Of Commonwealth Literature,* 10, No.1 (1975), 80-81.

Weeks, Edward. *Atlantic Monthly,* 235, No.4 (1975), 98.

A GUEST OF HONOUR (1970)

Reviews

Haynes, Muriel. *Saturday Review,* 24 October 1970, pp. 34-36.

McGuiness, Frank. "Black and White Power." *London Magazine,* NS, 11, No.3 (1971), 143-46.

Weeks, Edward. *Atlantic Monthly,* 227, No.2 (1971), 126-27.

THE LATE BOURGEOIS WORLD (1966)

Reviews

McCabe, Bernard. "A Code for the Pale." *Saturday Review,* 20 August 1966, p. 32.

Weeks, Edward. *Atlantic Monthly,* 218, No.2 (1966), 116.

GORKI, MAXIM (Russian, 1868-1936)

GENERAL

Struve, Gleb. "Gorky in the Soviet Period," in *Major Soviet Writers,* ed. Edward J. Brown, pp. 197-201.

THE LIFE OF A USELESS MAN (1917)

Reviews

Wasiolek, Edward. *Saturday Review,* 16 October 1971, pp. 59-60.

MOTHER (Mat, 1906)

Davies, Ruth. *The Great Books Of Russia,* pp. 382-87.

GOTLIEB, PHYLLIS (Canadian, 1926-)

SUNBURST (1964)

Barbour, Douglas. "Phyllis Gotlieb's Children of the Future: *Sunburst* and *Ordinary, Moving.*" *Journal Of Canadian Fiction,* 3, No.2 (1974), 72-76.

WHY SHOULD I HAVE ALL THE GRIEF? (1969)

Reviews

Purdy, A. W. "Betrayed by the Evening Star." *Canadian Literature,* No. 44 (1970), pp. 84-85.

Rapoport, Janis. "The Grief Is Shared." *Tamarack Review,* No.54 (1970), pp. 87-89.

GOTTLIEB, PAUL (Hungarian-born Canadian, 1936-)

AGENCY (1974)

Reviews

Williamson, David. "Back to the Drawing Board? *Journal Of Canadian Fiction,* 3, No.4 (1975), 99-100.

GOURI, HAIM (Israeli, 1923-)

THE CHOCOLATE DEAL (Iskat Ha-Shokolad, 1964)

Alter, Robert. "Confronting the Holocaust," in his *After The Tradition,* pp. 171-75.

Reviews

Cohen, Arthur A. "The Metaphysics of Survival." *Midstream Magazine,* 14, No.9 (1968), 77-79.

Leviant, Curt. "Collage of the Genocide's Aftermath." *Saturday Review,* 11 May 1968, pp. 78-79.

GOYTISOLO, JUAN (Spanish, 1931-)

GENERAL

Ortega, Julio. "An Interview with Juan Goytisolo." *Texas Quarterly,* 18, No.1 (1975), 56-77.

Schwartz, Kessel. "Juan Goytisolo—Ambivalent Artist in Search of His Soul." *Journal of Spanish Studies,* 3 (1975), 187-97.

_____ . "Language and Literature: Ricardo Palma and Juan Goytisolo." *International Fiction Review,* 2 (1975), 138-42.

_____ . "Literary Backgrounds and Structural Experimentation," in his *Juan Goytisolo,* pp. 19-37.

_____ . "The United States in the Novels of Juan Goytisolo." *Romance Notes,* 6 (1965), 122-25.

CHILDREN OF CHAOS (Duelo en el Paraíso, 1955)

Glenn, Kathleen. "Duelo en el Paraíso: A Study of the Spanish Civil War." *Canadian Modern Language Review,* 30, No.1 (1973), 62-66.

Schwartz, Kessel. *Juan Goytisolo,* pp. 49-59.

EL CIRCO (1957)

Schwartz, Kessel. *Juan Goytisolo,* pp. 60-66.

COUNT JULIAN (Reivindicacion del conde Don Julian, 1970)

Reviews

Schwartz, Kessel. "Juan Goytisolo, Cultural Constraints and the Historical Vindication of Count Julian." *Hispania,* 54 (1971), 960-66.

FIESTAS (1958)

Busette, Cedric. "Goytisolo's *Fiesta:* A Search for Meaning." *Romance Notes,* 12 (1971), 270-73.

Peden, Margaret Sayers. "Juan Goytisolo's 'Fiestas,' an Analysis and Commentary." *Hispania,* 50 (1967), 461-66.

Schwartz, Kessel. *Juan Goytisolo,* pp. 67-73.

FIN DE FIESTA

Newberry, Wilma. "The Baptist Betrayed: Juan Goytisolo's *La Resaca* and *Fin De Fiesta.*" *Revista De Estudios Hispánicos,* 9 (1975), 57-63.

ISLAND OF WOMEN (La Isla, 1961)

Schwartz, Kessel. *Juan Goytisolo,* pp. 86-91.

MARKS OF IDENTITY (Señas de identidad, 1966)

Bieder, Maryellen. "A Case of Altered Identity: Two Editions of Juan Goytisolo's *Señas De Identidad.*" *MLN,* 89 (1974), 298-310.

Schwartz, Kessel. *Juan Goytisolo,* pp. 95-107.

Reviews

Clements, Robert J. *Saturday Review,* 28 June 1969, pp. 37, 40.

LA RESACA (1958)

Newberry, Wilma. "The Baptist Betrayed: Juan Goytisolo's *La Resaca* and *Fin De Fiesta.*" *Revista De Estudios Hispánicos,* 9 (1975), 47-57.

Schwartz, Kessel. *Juan Goytisolo,* pp. 77-85.

THE YOUNG ASSASSINS (Juegos de manos, 1954)

GILES, MARY E. "Juan Goytisolo's 'Juegos de Manos': An Archetypal Interpretation." *Hispania,* 56 (1973), 1021–29.

SCHWARTZ, KESSEL. *Juan Goytisolo,* pp. 38–48.

GRAÇA ARANHA, JOSE PEREIRA DE (Brazilian, 1868–1931)

GENERAL

AIEX, ANOAR. "Graça Aranha and Brazilian Modernism," in *Tradition And Renewal,* ed. Merlin H. Forster, pp. 51–57.

GRACQ, JULIEN (French, 1910–)

GENERAL

BROOME, PETER. "Julien Gracq's Surrealist Hero." *Forum For Modern Language Studies,* 5 (1969), 50–67.

MOORE-RINVOLUCRI, MINA J. "Julien Gracq, Homme de Lettres." *Modern Languages,* 51 (1970), 156–59.

A BALCONY IN THE FOREST (Un balcon en forêt, 1958)

BROOME, PETER. "Julien Gracq's Surrealist Hero." *Forum For Modern Language Studies,* 5 (1969), 64–67.

DOBBS, ANNIE-CLAUDE. "Reality and Dream in Julien Gracq: A Stylistic Study," in *Twentieth Century French Fiction,* ed. George Stambolian, pp. 158–64.

THE CASTLE OF ARGOL (Au Château d'Argol, 1938)

DOBBS, ANNIE-CLAUDE. "Reality and Dream in Julien Gracq: A Stylistic Study," in *Twentieth Century French Fiction,* ed. George Stambolian, pp. 142–46.

MATTHEWS, J. H. *Surrealism And The Novel,* pp. 91–106.

OSGOOD, EUGENIA V. "A Surrealist Synthesis of History: *Au Château D'Argol.*" *L'Esprit Créateur,* 15 (1975), 319–31.

A DARK STRANGER (Un beau ténébreux, 1945)

DOBBS, ANNIE-CLAUDE. "Reality and Dream in Julien Gracq: A Stylistic Study," in *Twentieth Century French Fiction,* pp. 146–50.

LE RIVAGE DES SYRTES (1951)

BROOME, PETER. "Julien Gracq's Surrealist Hero." *Forum For Modern Language Studies,* 5 (1969), 58–64.

DOBBS, ANNIE-CLAUDE. "Reality and Dream in Julien Gracq: A Stylistic Study," in *Twentieth Century French Fiction,* ed. George Stambolian, pp. 150–57.

LE ROI PÊCHEUR (1948)

MATTHEWS, J. H. "Julien Gracq and the Theme of the Grail in Surrealism." *Romanic Review,* 58 (1967), 95–108.

GRADE, CHAIM (Yiddish, 1910–)

GENERAL

LEVIANT, CURT. "The Prose of Chaim Grade." *Midstream Magazine,* 20, No.9 (1974), 60–64.

GRAINVILLE, PATRICK

LA TOISON (1972)

Reviews

LAWRENCE, DEREK W. *French Review,* 47 (1974), 658–59.

GRAMONT, SANCHE DE

LE JOURS SANS (1972)

Reviews

ROSMARIN, LEONARD. *French Review,* 48 (1974), 240–41.

GRANATA, MARÍA

LOS TUMULTOS (1972)

Reviews

BEARSE, GRACE M. *Latin American Literary Review,* 4, No.7 (1975), 83–84.

LOS VIERNES DE LA ETERNIDAD (1972)

Reviews

BEARSE, GRACE M. *Latin American Literary Review,* 4, No.7 (1975), 84–86.

GRASS, GÜNTER (German, 1927–)

GENERAL

CUNLIFFE, W. G. "Grass and the Denial of Drama," in *A Günter Grass Symposium,* ed. A. Leslie Willson, pp. 60–65.

FORSTER, LEONARD. "Günter Grass." *University Of Toronto Quarterly,* 38 (1968), 1–16.

"Grass and Johnson in New York." *American-German Review,* 31, No.5 (1965), 35–37.

IDRIS, PARRY. "Aspects of Günter Grass's Narrative Technique." *Forum For Modern Language Studies,* 3 (1967), 99–114.

MASON, ANN L. "Günter Grass and the Artist in History." *Contemporary Literature,* 14 (1973), 347–62.

ROLOFF, MICHAEL. "Günter Grass." *Atlantic Monthly,* 215, No.6 (1965), 94–97.

"Two Interviews/Günter Grass." *Encounter,* 35, No.3 (1970), 26–29.

MACAINSH, NOEL. "Cooking Up a Good Democracy." *Overland,* No.62 (1975), pp. 65–67.

CAT AND MOUSE (Katz und Maus, 1961)

BRUCE, JAMES C. "The Equivocating Narrator in Günter Grass's 'Katz und Maus.' " *Monatschefte,* 58 (1966), 139–49.

COFT, HELEN. "Günter Grass's *Katz Und Maus.*" *Seminar,* 9 (1973), 253–64.

CUNLIFFE, W. G. *Günter Grass,* pp. 87–97.

———. "Gunter Grass: *Katz Und Maus.*" *Studies In Short Fiction,* 3 (1966), 174–85.

EZERGAILIS, INTA M. "Günter Grass's 'Fearful Symmetry': Dialectic, Mock and Real, in *Katz Und Maus* and *Die Blechtrommel.*" *Texas Studies In Literature And Language,* 16 (1974), 221–28.

FICKERT, KURT J. "The Use of Ambiguity in *Cat And Mouse.*" *German Quarterly,* 44 (1971), 372–78.

FRIEDRICHSMEYER, ERHARD M. "Aspects of Myth, Parody, and Obscenity in Grass' *Die Blechtrommel* and *Katz Und Maus.*" *Germanic Review,* 40 (1965), 245–49.

FULTON, EDYTHE KING. "Günter Grass's Cat and Mouse—Obsession and Life." *Forum,* 7, No.2 (1969), 26–31.

HATFIELD, HENRY. *Crisis And Continuity In Modern German Fiction,* pp. 138–41.

———. "Günter Grass: The Artist as Satirist," in *The Contemporary Novel In German: A Symposium,* ed. Robert R. Heitner, pp. 125–28.

KUNKEL, FRANCIS L. "Clowns and Saviors: Two Contemporary Novels." *Renascence,* 18, No.1 (1965), 40–44.

MILES, KEITH. *Günter Grass,* pp. 84–107.

PFEIFFER, JOHN R. "*Katz Und Maus:* Grass's Debt to Augustine." *Papers On Language And Literature,* 7 (1971), 279–92.

PICKAR, GERTRUD BAUER. "The Aspect of Colour in Günter

Grass's *Katz Und Maus.*" *German Life And Letters,* 23 (1970), 304-9.

———. "Intentional Ambiguity in Günter Grass' 'Katz und Maus.' " *Orbis Litterarum,* 26 (1971), 232-45.

REDDICK, JOHN. *The 'Danzig Trilogy' Of Günter Grass: A Study Of The Tin Drum, Cat And Mouse And Dog Years,* pp. 89-169.

RUHLEDER, KARL H. "A Pattern of Messianic Thought in Günter Grass' *Cat And Mouse.*" *German Quarterly,* 39 (1966), 599-612.

SPAETHLING, ROBERT H. "Günter Grass: 'Cat and Mouse.' " *Monatschefte,* 62 (1970), 141-53.

TANK, KURT LOTHAR. *Günter Grass,* pp. 86-91.

THOMAS, N. L. "An Analysis of Günter Grass' *Katz Und Maus* with Particular Reference to Religious Themes." *German Life And Letters,* 26 (1973), 227-38.

YATES, NORRIS W. *Günter Grass: A Critical Essay,* pp. 28-34.

DOG YEARS (Hundejahre, 1963)

ALTER, MARIA P. "Gunter Grass: Man as a Scarecrow." *Perspectives On Contemporary Literature,* 1, No.2 (1975), 20-30.

BLOMSTER, WESLEY V. "The Demonic in History: Thomas Mann and Günter Grass." *Contemporary Literature,* 10 (1969), 75-84.

———. "The Documentation of a Novel: Otto Weininger and 'Hundejahre' by Günter Grass." *Monatshefte,* 61 (1969), 122-38.

CUNLIFFE, W. G. "Aspects of the Absurd in Günter Grass." *Wisconsin Studies In Contemporary Literature,* 7 (1966), 311-27.

———. *Günter Grass,* pp. 13-26, 98-123.

FORSTER, LEONARD. "Günter Grass." *University Of Toronto Quarterly,* 38 (1968), 9-13.

HATFIELD, HENRY. *Crisis And Continuity In Modern German Fiction,* pp. 142-49.

———. "Günter Grass: The Artist as Satirist," in *The Contemporary Novel In German: A Symposium,* ed. Robert R. Heitner, pp. 128-34.

KURZ, PAUL KONRAD. "*Hundejahre:* Some Remarks about a Novel of Contemporary Criticism," in his *On Modern German Literature,* Vol.1: 131-48.

MASON, ANN L. *The Skeptical Muse: A Study Of Günter Grass' Conception Of The Artist,* pp. 17-74.

MILES, KEITH. *Günter Grass,* pp. 108-41.

MITCHELL, BREON. "The Demonic Comedy: Dante and Grass's *Hundejahre.*" *Papers On Language And Literature,* 9 (1973), 65-77.

REDDICK, JOHN. *The 'Danzig Trilogy' of Günter Grass: A Study Of The Tin Drum, Cat And Mouse And Dog Years,* pp. 173-270.

ŠLIAŽAS, RIMVYDAS. "Elements of Old Prussian Mythology in Günter Grass' 'Dog Years.' " *Lituanus,* 19, No.1 (1973), 39-48.

STEINER, GEORGE. "A Note on Günter Grass," in his *Language And Silence,* pp. 110-17.

TANK, KURT LOTHAR. *Günter Grass,* pp. 94-101.

YATES, NORRIS W. *Günter Grass: A Critical Essay,* pp. 34-42.

Reviews

KLEIN, MARCUS. "The Thirty-two Tiers of Hell." *Reporter,* 33, No.3 (1965), 51-54.

LEVAY, Z. JOHN. "The Pathological Muse." *Modern Age,* 10 (1965/6), 87-91.

McGUINNESS, FRANK. *London Magazine,* NS, 5, No.11 (1966), 83-85.

PETERS, H. F. "Creator of Superior Scarecrows." *Saturday Review,* 29 May 1965, pp. 25-26.

LOCAL ANAESTHETIC (Örtlich Betäubt, 1969)

BRUCE, JAMES C. "The Motif of Failure and the Act of Narrating in Günter Grass's *Örtlich Betäubt.*" *Modern Fiction Studies,* 17 (1971), 45-60.

FRIEDRICHSMEYER, ERHARD. "The Dogmatism of Pain: *Local Anaesthetic,*" in *A Günter Grass Symposium,* ed. A. Leslie Willson, pp. 32-45.

GRAVES, PETER J. "Günter Grass's *Die Blechtrommel* and *Örtlich Betäubt:* The Pain of Polarities." *Forum For Modern Language Studies,* 9 (1973), 138-42.

KURZ, PAUL KONRAD. "The Insecure Heraldic Animal: On Günter Grass's *Uptight* and *Local Anaesthetic,*" in his *On Modern German Literature,* Vol.4: 87-95.

MASON, ANN L. *The Skeptical Muse: A Study Of Günter Grass' Conception Of The Artist,* pp. 86-92, 122-28.

MILES, KEITH. *Günter Grass,* pp. 172-98.

REDDICK, JOHN. "Action and Impotence: Günter Grass's 'Örtlich Betäubt.' " *Modern Language Review,* 67 (1972), 563-78.

Reviews

MANHEIM, RALPH. *Saturday Review,* 4 April 1970, p. 34.

THE TIN DRUM (Die Blechtrommel, 1959)

BANCE, A. F. "The Enigma of Oskar in Grass's *Blechtrommel.*" *Seminar,* 3 (1967), 147-56.

BLOMSTER, WESLEY V. "Oskar at the *Zoppoter Waldoper.*" *MLN,* 84 (1969), 467-72.

BUCKEYE, ROBERT. "The Anatomy of the Psychic Novel." *Critique,* 9, No.2 (1967), 38-43.

CUNLIFFE, W. G. "Aspects of the Absurd in Günter Grass." *Wisconsin Studies In Contemporary Literature,* 7 (1966), 311-27.

———. *Günter Grass,* pp. 13-26, 52-86.

DILLER, EDWARD. *A Mythic Journey: Günter Grass's Tin Drum.*

EZERGAILIS, INTA M. "Günter Grass's 'Fearful Symmetry': Dialectic, Mock and Real, in *Katz Und Maus* and *Die Blechtrommel.*" *Texas Studies In Literature And Language,* 16 (1974), 228-35.

FREEDMAN, RALPH. "The Poet's Dilemma: The Narrative Worlds of Günter Grass," in *A Günter Grass Symposium,* ed. A Leslie Willson, pp. 46-59.

FRIEDRICHSMEYER, ERHARD M. "Aspects of Myth, Parody, and Obscenity in Grass' *Die Blechtrommel* and *Katz Und Maus.*" *Germanic Review,* 40 (1965), 240-45, 249-50.

GELLEY, ALEXANDER. "Art and Reality in *Die Blechtrommel.*" *Forum For Modern Language Studies,* 3 (1967), 115-25.

GRAVES, PETER J. "Günter Grass's *Die Blechtrommel* and *Örtlich Betäubt:* The Pain of Polarities." *Forum For Modern Language Studies,* 9 (1973), 132-38.

HATFIELD, HENRY. "Günter Grass: The Artist as Satirist," In *The Contemporary Novel In German: A Symposium,* ed. Robert R. Heitner, pp. 117-25.

MASON, ANN L. *The Skeptical Muse: A Study Of Günter Grass' Conception Of The Artist,* p. 17-86.

MAURER, ROBERT. "The End of Innocence: Gunter Grass' *The Tin Drum.*" *Bucknell Review,* 16, No.2 (1968), 45-65.

MAYER, HANS. "Günter Grass and Thomas Mann: Aspects of the Novel," in his *Steppenwolf and Everyman,* pp. 181-99.

MILES, DAVID H. "Kafka's Hapless Pilgrims and Grass's Scurrilous Dwarf: Notes on Representative Figures in the Anti-Bildungsroman." *Monatshefte,* 65 (1973), 344-46.

MILES, KEITH. *Günter Grass,* pp. 48-83.

O'NAN, MARTHA. *The Role Of Mind In Hugo, Faulkner, Beckett And Grass,* pp. 36-48.

O'NEILL, PATRICK. "Musical Form and the Pauline Message in a Key Chapter of Grass's *Blechtrommel.*" *Seminar,* 10 (1974), 298-307.

PEARCE, RICHARD. *Stages Of The Clown,* pp. 123–28.

REDDICK, JOHN. *The 'Danzig Trilogy' Of Günter Grass: A Study Of The Tin Drum, Cat And Mouse And Dog Years,* pp. 3–86.

SHARFMAN, WILLIAM L. "The Organization of Experience in The Tin Drum." *Minnesota Review,* 6 (1966), 59–65.

SOSNOSKI, M. K. "Oskar's Hungry Witch." *Modern Fiction Studies,* 17 (1971), 61–77.

STEIG, MICHAEL. "The Grotesque and the Aesthetic Response in Shakespeare, Dickens, and Günter Grass." *Comparative Literature Studies,* 6, (1969), 177–80.

TANK, KURT LOTHAR. *Günter Grass,* pp. 2–11, 68–84.

THOMAS, R. HINTON and WILFRIED VAN DER WILL. *The German Novel And The Affluent Society,* pp. 68–85.

VAN ABBÉ, DEREK. "Metamorphoses of 'Unbewältigte Vergangenheit' in *Die Blechtrommel.*" *German Life And Letters,* 23 (1970), 152–60.

WILLSON, A. LESLIE. "The Grotesque Everyman in Günter Grass's 'Die Blechtrommel.' " *Monatshefte,* 58 (1966), 131–38.

YATES, NORRIS W. *Günter Grass: A Critical Essay,* pp. 19–28.

GREEN, ANNE

LA PORTE DES SONGES (1969)

Reviews
GUGLI, WILLIAM V. *French Review,* 44 (1970), 416–17.

GREEN, JULIEN (French, 1900–)

GENERAL

BURNE, GLENN S. *Julian Green,* pp. 11–36.

JOINER, LAWRENCE D. and ELIZABETH G. "Gide and Green: *Recontres.*" *USF Language Quarterly,* 13, No.3/4 (1975), 10–12, 52.

RECK, RIMA DRELL. *Literature And Responsibility,* pp. 142–61.

ROSE, MARILYN GADDIS. *Julian Green: Gallic-American Novelist,* pp. 109–23.

L'AUTRE SOMMEIL (1931)

KOSTIS, NICHOLAS. *The Exorcism Of Sex And Death In Julien Green's Novels,* pp. 50–57.

ROSE, MARILYN GADDIS. *Julian Green: Gallic-American Novelist,* pp. 62–65.

AVARICE HOUSE (Mont-Cinere, 1926)

BURNE, GLENN S. *Julian Green,* pp. 53–58.

KOSTIS, NICHOLAS. *The Exorcism Of Sex And Death in Julien Green's Novels,* pp. 18–26.

ROSE, MARILYN GADDIS. *Julian Green: Gallic-American Novelist,* pp. 51–53.

LES CLEFS DE LA MORT (1928)

BURNE, GLENN S. *Julian Green,* pp. 48–52.

THE CLOSED GARDEN (Adrienne Mesurat, 1927)

BURNE, GLENN S. *Julian Green,* pp. 58–65.

KOSTIS, NICHOLAS. *The Exorcism Of Sex And Death In Julien Green's Novels,* pp. 26–34.

ROSE, MARILYN GADDIS. *Julian Green: Gallic-American Novelist,* pp. 53–57.

THE DARK JOURNEY (Leviathan, 1929)

BURNE, GLENN S. *Julian Green,* pp. 65–68.

KOSTIS, NICHOLAS. *The Exorcism Of Sex And Death In Julien Green's Novels,* pp. 43–49.

ROSE, MARILYN GADDIS. *Julian Green: Gallic-American Novelist,* pp. 59–62.

THE DREAMER (Le Visionnaire, 1934)

BURNE, GLENN S. *Julian Green,* pp. 82–97.

KOSTIS, NICHOLAS. *The Exorcism Of Sex And Death In Julien Green's Novels,* pp. 65–75.

ROSE, MARILYN GADDIS. *Julian Green: Gallic-American Novelist,* pp. 67–73.

EACH IN HIS DARKNESS (Chaque homme dans sa nuit, 1960)

BURNE, GLENN S. *Julian Green,* pp. 130–34.

KOSTIS, NICHOLAS. *The Exorcism Of Sex And Death In Julien Green's Novels,* pp. 90–106.

ROSE, MARILYN GADDIS. *Julian Green: Gallic-American Novelist,* pp. 91–98.

IF I WERE YOU (Si j'etais vous, 1947)

BURNE, GLENN S. *Julian Green,* pp. 102–10.

MIDNIGHT (Minuit, 1936)

BURNE, GLENN S. *Julian Green,* pp. 97–102.

KOSTIS, NICHOLAS. *The Exorcism Of Sex And Death In Julien Green's Novels,* pp. 76–89.

ROSE, MARILYN GADDIS. *Julian Green: Gallic-American Novelist,* pp. 67–73.

MOIRA (1950)

BURNE, GLENN S. *Julian Green,* pp. 125–30.

JOSLIN, MARY COKER. "A Nature Lover's View of *Moira* by Julien Green." *Romance Notes,* 13 (1971), 8–11.

KOSTIS, NICHOLAS. *The Exorcism Of Sex And Death In Julien Green's Novels,* pp. 90–106.

ROSE, MARILYN GADDIS. *Julian Green: Gallic-American Novelist,* pp. 91–98.

THE OTHER ONE (L'Autre, 1971)

Reviews
ROSE, MARILYN GADDIS. "Green's Otherness." *Novel,* 5 (1972), 177–80.

WEEKS, EDWARD. *Atlantic Monthly,* 231, No.6 (1973), 120–22.

THE PILGRIM ON THE EARTH (Voyageur sur la terre, 1927)

BURNE, GLENN S. *Julian Green,* pp. 43–48.

KOSTIS, NICHOLAS. *The Exorcism Of Sex And Death In Julien Green's Novels,* pp. 35–42.

THE STRANGE RIVER (Epaves, 1932)

ALTER, JEAN. "Julien Green: Structure of the Catholic Imagination," in *The Vision Obscured,* ed. Melvin J. Friedman, pp. 151–85.

BURNE, GLENN S. *Julian Green,* pp. 68–80.

FIELD, TREVOR. "Reflections of a Novelist: Mirror Imagery in Julien Green's *Epaves.*" *Symposium,* 29 (1975), 103–16.

KOSTIS, NICHOLAS. *The Exorcism Of Sex And Death In Julien Green's Novels,* pp. 58–64.

THEN SHALL THE DUST RETURN (Varouna, 1940)

BURNE, GLENN S. *Julian Green,* pp. 102–10.

ROSE, MARILYN GADDIS. *Julian Green: Gallic-American Novelist,* pp. 76–78.

THE TRANSGRESSOR (Le Malfaiteur, 1955)

BURNE, GLENN S. *Julian Green,* pp. 114–17.

KOSTIS, NICHOLAS. *The Exorcism Of Sex And Death In Julien Green's Novels,* pp. 90–106.

ROSE, MARILYN GADDIS. *Julian Green: Gallic-American Novelist,* pp. 79–81.

GRENIER, JEAN

LES ÎLES

CAMUS, ALBERT. *Lyrical And Critical Essays,* pp. 326-31.

GRIEG, NORDAHL (Norwegian, 1902-1943)

THE SHIP SAILS ON (Skibet går videre, 1924)

DAHLIE, HALLVARD. "On Nordahl Grieg's *The Ship Sails On.*" *International Fiction Review,* 2 (1975), 49-53.

GRILLPARZER, FRANZ (Austrian, 1791-1872)

THE POOR FIDDLER (Der arme spielmann, 1848)

ELLIS, JOHN M. "Grillparzer's *Der Arme Spielmann.*" *German Quarterly,* 45 (1972), 662-83.

———. *Narration In The German Novelle,* pp. 113-35.

HODGE, JAMES L. "Symmetry and Tension in 'Der arme Spielmann.' " *German Quarterly,* 47 (1974), 262-64.

LIEDKE, OTTO K. "Considerations on the Structure of Grillparzer's *Der Arme Spielmann.*" *Modern Austrian Literature,* 3, No.3 (1970), 7-12.

SWALES, M. W. "The Narrative Perspective in Grillparzer's *Der Arme Spielmann.*" *German Life And Letters,* 20 (1967), 107-16.

YATES, W. E. *Grillparzer: A Critical Introduction,* pp. 76-83.

DAS KLOSTER BEI SENDOMIR

LAWSON, RICHARD H. "The Starost's Daughter: Elga in Grillparzer's Kloster bei Sendomir." *Modern Austrian Literature,* 1, No.3 (1968), 31-37.

GRIMMELSHAUSEN, HANS JAKOB CHRISTOFFEL VON (German, 1622-1676)

GENERAL

JACOBSON, JOHN W. "The Culpable Male: Grimmelshausen on Women." *German Quarterly,* 39 (1966), 149-61.

MENHENNET, A. "Narrative and Satire in Grimmelshausen and Beer." *Modern Language Review,* 70 (1975), 808-14.

THE ADVENTURES OF A SIMPLETON (Der Abenteuerlich Simplissimus, 1669)

ASHCROFT, JEFFREY. "Ad Astra Volandum: Emblems and Imagery in Grimmelshausen's 'Simplicissimus.' " *Modern Language Review,* 68 (1973), 843-62.

DIMLER, G. RICHARD. "Alienation in 'Don Quixote' and 'Simplicius Simplicissimus.' " *Thought,* 49 (1974), 72-80.

GILBERT, MARY E. "Simplex and the Battle of Wittstock." *German Life And Letters,* 18 (1965), 264-9.

HECKMAN, JOHN. "Emblematic Structures in *Simplicissimus Teutsch.*" *MLN,* 84 (1969), 876-90.

MANDEL, SIEGFRIED. "From the Mummelsee to the Moon: Refractions of Science in Seventeenth-Century Literature." *Comparative Literature Studies,* 9 (1972), 411-14.

RITCHIE, J. M. "Grimmelshausen's *Simplicissimus* and *The Runagate Courage,*" in *Knaves And Swindlers,* ed. Christine J. Whitbourn, pp. 48-74.

SHEPPARD, RICHARD. "The Narrative Structure of Grimmelshausen's *Simpliccissimus.*" *Forum For Modern Language Studies,* 8 (1972), 15-26.

WEGENER, HANS. *The German Baroque Novel,* pp. 41-67.

THE RUNAGATE COURAGE (Courasche, 1669)

JACOBSON, JOHN W. "A Defense of Grimmelshausen's Courasche." *German Quarterly,* 41 (1968), 42-54.

RITCHIE, J. M. "Grimmelshausen's *Simplicissimus* and *The Run-*

agate Courage," in *Knaves And Swindlers,* ed. Christine J. Whitbourn, pp. 48-74.

DES VOTREFFLICH KEUSCHEN JOSEPHS IN EGYPTEN LEBENSBESCHREIBUNG

WEGENER, HANS. *The German Baroque Novel,* pp. 134-42.

GRIN, ALEXANDER (Russian, 1880-1932) pseudonym of Alexander Stepanovich Grinevsky

GENERAL

LUKER, NICHOLAS J. L. "Alexander Grin: A Survey." *Russian Literature Triquarterly,* No.8 (1974), pp. 341-61.

GRINEVSKY, Alexander Stepanovich see GRIN, Alexander

GROSSMAN, EDITH SEARLE

THE HEART OF THE BUSH (1910)

HANKIN, CHERRY. "New Zealand Women Novelists: Their Attitudes Towards Life in a Developing Society." *World Literature Written In English,* 14 (1975), 146-49.

GROULX, LIONEL-ADOLPHE (French Canadian, 1878-1967)

L'APPEL DE LA RACE (1922)

SUTHERLAND, RONALD. "The Body-Odour of Race." *Canadian Literature,* No.37 (1968), pp. 54-57; rpt. in his *Second Image,* pp. 40-46.

GROVE, FREDERICK PHILLIP (Canadian, 1879-1948)

GENERAL

BIRBALSINGH, FRANK. "Grove and Existentialism." *Canadian Literature,* No.43 (1970), pp. 67-76.

DEWAR, KENNETH C. "Technology and the Pastoral Ideal in Frederick Philip Grove." *Journal Of Canadian Studies,* 8, No.1 (1973), 19-28.

MCMULLIN, STANLEY E. "Grove and the Promised Land." *Canadian Literature,* No.49 (1971), pp. 10-19.

PACEY, DESMOND. "Frederick Philip Grove," in his *Essays In Canadian Literature, 1938-1968,* pp. 5-21.

———. "In Search of Grove in Sweden: A Progress Report." *Journal Of Canadian Fiction,* 1, No.1 (1972), 69-73.

SPETTIGUE, DOUGLAS O. " 'Frederick Philip Grove.' " *Queen's Quarterly,* 78 (1971), 614-15.

———. "Frederick Philip Grove in Manitoba." *Mosaic,* 3, No.3 (1970), 19-33.

———. "The Grove Enigma Resolved." *Queen's Quarterly,* 79 (1972), 1-2.

STOBIE, MARGARET R. " 'Frederick Philip Grove' And The Canadian Movement." *Studies In The Novel,* 4 (1972), 173-85.

WEBBER, BERNARD. "Grove in Politics." *Canadian Literature,* No.63 (1975), pp. 126-27.

CONSIDER HER WAYS (1947)

HIND-SMITH, JOAN. *Three Voices: The Lives Of Margaret Laurence, Gabrielle Roy, Frederick Philip Grove,* pp. 190-93.

STOBIE, MARGARET R. *Frederick Philip Grove,* pp. 162-67, 184-87.

SUTHERLAND, RONALD. *Frederick Philip Grove,* pp. 33-35.

FRUITS OF THE EARTH (1933)

HIND-SMITH, JOAN. *Three Voices: The Lives Of Margaret Laurence, Gabrielle Roy, Frederick Philip Grove,* pp. 171–73.

RICOU, LAURENCE. *Vertical Man/Horizontal World,* pp. 58–63.

STOBIE, MARGARET R. *Frederick Philip Grove,* pp. 128–31.

———. " 'Frederick Philip Grove' And the Canadian Movement." *Studies In The Novel,* 4 (1972), 180–83.

SUTHERLAND, RONALD. *Frederick Philip Grove,* pp. 41–46.

JANE ATKINSON

STOBIE, MARGARET R. *Frederick Philip Grove,* pp. 107–10.

THE MASTER OF THE MILL (1944)

HIND-SMITH, JOAN. *Three Voices: The Lives Of Margaret Laurence, Gabrielle Roy, Frederick Philip Grove,* pp. 180–83.

JONES, D. G. *Butterfly On Rock,* pp. 72–77.

KEITH, W. J. "F. P. Grove's 'Difficult' Novel: The Master of the Mill." *Ariel: A Review Of International Literature,* 4, No.2 (1973), 34–48.

MACDONALD, R. D. "The Power of F. P. Grove's *The Master Of The Mill.*" *Mosaic,* 7, No.2 (1974), 89–100.

MITCHELL, BEVERLY. "The 'Message' and the 'Inevitable Form' in *The Master Of The Mill.*" *Journal Of Canadian Fiction,* 3, No.3 (1974), 74–79.

STOBIE, MARGARET R. *Frederick Philip Grove,* pp. 170–75.

SUTHERLAND, RONALD. *Frederick Philip Grove,* p. 36–39, 42–46.

OUR DAILY BREAD (1928)

HIND-SMITH, JOAN. *Three Voices: The Lives Of Margaret Laurence, Gabrielle Roy, Frederick Philip Grove,* pp. 180–83.

RICOU, LAURENCE. *Vertical Man/ Horizontal World,* pp. 55–58.

STOBIE, MARGARET R. *Frederick Philip Grove,* pp. 101–4.

SUTHERLAND, RONALD. *Frederick Philip Grove,* pp. 40–46.

A SEARCH FOR AMERICA (1927)

HIND-SMITH, JOAN. *Three Voices: The Lives Of Margaret Laurence, Gabrielle Roy, Frederick Philip Grove,* pp. 156–60.

KEITH, W. J. "Grove's Search for America." *Canadian Literature,* No.59 (1974), pp. 57–66.

STOBIE, MARGARET R. *Frederick Philip Grove,* pp. 59–69.

SETTLERS OF THE MARSH (1925)

HIND-SMITH, JOAN. *Three Voices: The Lives Of Margaret Laurence, Gabrielle Roy, Frederick Philip Grove,* pp. 147–54.

KEITH, W. J. "The Art of Frederick Philip Grove: Settlers of the Marsh as an Example." *Journal Of European Studies,* 9, No.3 (1974), 26–36.

SPETTIGUE, DOUGLAS. "Frederick Philip Grove in Manitoba." *Mosaic,* 3, No.3 (1969/70), 24–27.

STOBIE, MARGARET R. *Frederick Philip Grove,* pp. 77–84.

SUTHERLAND, RONALD. *Frederick Philip Grove,* pp. 47–51.

THOMPSON, J. LEE. "In Search of Order: The Structure of Grove's *Settlers Of The Marsh.*" *Journal Of Canadian Fiction,* 3, No.3 (1974), 65–73.

TWO GENERATIONS (1939)

HIND-SMITH, JOAN. *Three Voices: The Lives Of Margaret Laurence, Gabrielle Roy, Frederick Philip Grove,* pp. 176–78.

STOBIE, MARGARET R. *Frederick Philip Grove,* pp. 167–70.

SUTHERLAND, RONALD. *Frederick Philip Grove,* pp. 42–46.

THE WEATHERHEAD FORTUNES

STOBIE, MARGARET R. *Frederick Philip Grove,* p. 104–7.

THE YOKE OF LIFE (1930)

HIND-SMITH, JOAN. *Three Voices: The Lives Of Margaret Laurence, Gabrielle Roy, Frederick Philip Grove,* pp. 167–69.

RICOU, LAURENCE. *Vertical Man/ Horizontal World,* pp. 50–54.

STOBIE, MARGARET R. *Frederick Philip Grove,* pp. 84–88.

SUTHERLAND, RONALD. *Frederick Philip Grove,* pp. 52–55.

GRÜN, MAX VON DER (German, 1926–)

STELLENWEIS GLATTEIS (1973)

Reviews
ELKHADEM, S. *International Fiction Review,* 2 (1975), 83–85.

GUERRAZZI, F. D.

GENERAL

CONSTABLE, MADELEINE. "Anti-Heroic and Mock-Heroic Elements in the Later Novels of F. D. Guerrazzi." *Forum Italicum,* 3 (1969), 213–31.

PASQUALE PAOLI (1860)

CONSTABLE, M. V. "F. D. Guerrazzi's Corsican Novel *Pasquale Paoli:* A Contribution to the Regional Novel of the *Verismo* Period." *Forum Italicum,* 5 (1971), 187–203.

IL SECOLO CHE MUORE

ROY, MARILYN PICCINI. "Social Inquiry in F. D. Guerrazzi's *Il Secolo Che Muore.*" *Forum Italicum,* 7, No.4/8, No.1 (1973/4), 56–69.

GUEVREMONT, GERMAINE (Canadian, 1900–)

LE SURVENANT (1945)

MOLLICA, ANTHONY. "Imagery and Internal Monologue in *Le Survenant.*" *Canadian Modern Language Review,* 25, No.1 (1968), 5–11.

GUIDO, BEATRIZ (Argentine)

END OF A DAY

Reviews
YATES, DONALD A. "A Gift of Adversity." *Saturday Review,* 4 June 1966, p. 53.

GUILLOUX, LOUIS (French, 1899–)

GENERAL

KING, J. H. "Louis Guilloux's Working Class Novels: Some Problems of Social Realism." *Modern Language Review,* 68 (1973), 69–76.

BITTER VICTORY (Le sang noir, 1935)

GREENE, FRANCIS J. "Louis Guilloux's *Le Sang Noir:* A Prefiguration of Sartre's *La Nausée.*" *French Review,* 43 (1969), 205–14.

KING, J. H. "Louis Guilloux's Ambiguous Epic *Le Sang Noir.*" *Forum For Modern Language Studies,* 8 (1972), 1–14.

LA MAISON DU PEUPLE (1927)

REDFERN, W. D. "Political Novel and Art of Simplicity: Louis Guilloux." *Journal Of European Studies,* 1 (1971), 115–27.

GUIMÃRAES, BERNARDO JOAQUIM DA SILVA (Brazilian, 1825–1884)

GENERAL

ANDREWS, NORWOOD. "A Modern Classification of Bernardo

Guimãraes' Prose Narratives." *Luso-Brazilian Review*, 3, No.2 (1966), 59–82.

_____. "Some Notes on the Mythography of Bernardo Guimãraes: Brazilian Nineteenth-Century Historical Fiction as an Expression of National Identity." *Hispania*, 56 (1973), 371–78.

A FILHA DO FAZENDEIRO

ANDREWS, NORWOOD. "Early Anticipations of Naturalism in Brazil: The Dramatic Novels of Bernardo Guimãraes." *Papers On Language And Literature*, 8 (1972), 396–403.

O SEMINARISTA

ANDREWS, NORWOOD. "Early Anticipations of Naturalism in Brazil: The Dramatic Novels of Bernardo Guimãraes." *Papers On Language And Literature*, 8 (1972), 403–14.

GÜIRALDES, RICARDO (Argentinian, 1886–1927)

GENERAL

BEARDSELL, P. R. "The Dichotomy in Güiraldes's Aesthetic Principles." *Modern Language Review*, 66 (1971), 322–27.

DON SEGUNDO SOMBRA: SHADOWS ON THE PAMPAS (1926)

BRUSHWOOD, JOHN S. *The Spanish American Novel*, pp. 45–49.

SAZ, SARA M. "Güiraldes and Kipling—A Possible Influence." *Neophilologus*, 55 (1971), 274–79.

Reviews
ALLEN, MARCUS. *College Language Association Journal*, 15 (1971), 96 98.

RAUCHO (1927)

BRUSHWOOD, JOHN S. *The Spanish American Novel*, pp. 34–36.

XAIMACA (1923)

SAZ, SARA M. "Güiraldes and Kipling—A Possible Influence." *Neophilologus*, 55 (1971), 270–74.

GULYASHKI, ANDREI (Bulgarian, 1914–)

AVAKOUM ZAHOV CONTRA 07

Reviews
BLUMENFELD, YORICK. "Zahov vs. Agent 07." *East Europe*, 16, No.6 (1967), 47–48.

GUNNARSSON, GUNNAR (Icelandic, 1889–1975)

GENERAL

BECK, RICHARD. "Gunnar Gunnarsson: Some Observations," in *Scandinavian Studies*, ed. Carl F. Bayerschmidt and Erik J. Friis, pp. 293–301.

THE BLACK CLIFFS (Svartfugl, 1939)

Reviews
SPECTOR, ROBERT D. *American Scandinavian Review*, 56 (1968), 416, 418.

GUPTA, PADMINI SEN

RED HIBISCUS (1962)

Reviews
BEGUM, NOORUSAUBAH. *Indian Literature*, 14, No.1 (1971), pp. 116-19.

GURYIKAR, RAMCANDRA BHIKAJI

MOCANGAD

RAESIDE, IAN. "Early Prose Fiction in Marathi, 1828-1885." *Journal Of Asian Studies*, 27 (1967/8), 804-6.

GUTZKOW, KARL FERDINAND (German, 1811–1818)

WALLY, A DOUBTING GIRL (Wally, Die Zweiflerin, 1835)

FLAVELL, M. KAY. "Women and Individualism: A Re-examination of Schlegel's 'Lucinde' and Gutzkow's 'Wally die Zweiflerin.' " *Modern Language Review*, 70 (1975), 562-66.

JOERES, RUTH-ELLEN B. "The Gutzkow-Menzel Tracts: A Critical Response to a Novel and an Era." *MLN*, 88 (1973), 988-1010.

SAMMONS, JEFFREY L. *Six Essays On The Young German Novel*, pp. 30-51.

GUYOTAT, PIERRE (French)

GENERAL

ST. AUBYN, F. C. "Piere Guyotat: Sex and Revolution or Alienation and Censorship." *International Fiction Review*, 2 (1975), 54-57.

GUZMÁN, AUGUSTO (1903–)

BELLACOS Y PALADINES (1964)

Reviews
BARB, ARTHUR L. *Latin American Literary Review*, 1, No.1 (1972), 109-11.

GUZMÁN, JORGE

JOB-BOJ

DOUDOROFF, MICHAEL J. "Coordinate Design in a Chilean Nueva Novela: *Job-Boj* by Jorge Guzmán." *Latin American Literary Review*, 3, No.6 (1975), 23-29.

GUZMÁN, MARTÍN LUIS (Mexican, 1887–1976)

SHADOW OF THE TYRANT (La sombra del caudillo, 1929)

SOMMERS, JOSEPH. *After The Storm*, pp. 16-23.

GYLLENSTEN, LARS (Swedish, 1921–)

GENERAL

SJÖBERG, LEIF. "Lars Gyllensten: Master of Arts of Science." *American Scandinavian Review*, 55 (1967), 158-62.

H

HABE, HANS (German, 1911–1977)
pseudonym of Jean Bekessy

CHRISTOPHER AND HIS FATHER (Chistoph und sein Vater, 1966)

Reviews
BAUKE, J. P. "German Generation Gap." *Saturday Review,* 18 November 1967, p. 44.

THE MISSION (Die Mission, 1965)

Reviews
HALPERIN, IRVING. "A Price Tag on Humanity." *Saturday Review,* 4 June 1966, pp. 51–52.

HAIKAL, MUHAMMAD HUSAIN (Egyptian, 1888–)

ZAINAB (1914)

KILPATRICK, HILARY. *The Modern Egyptian Novel,* pp. 20–26, 200–1.

HAILEY, ARTHUR (Canadian, 1920–)

HOTEL (1965)

Reviews
CAMERON, D. A. "Enough! Cried the Duchess." *Canadian Literature,* No.25 (1965), pp. 77–79.

HAKIM, TAUFIQ AL- (Egyptian, ca.1898–)

AWDAT AL RUH (1933)

KILPATRICK, HILARY. *The Modern Egyptian Novel,* pp. 41–44, 205–6.

SFEIR, GEORGE N. "The Contemporary Arabic Novel." *Daedalus,* 95 (1966), 944–46.

BIRD OF THE EAST ('Usfūr min al-sharq, 1938)

KILPATRICK, HILARY. *The Modern Egyptian Novel,* pp. 47–49.

Reviews
BEZIRGAN, N. A. *Literature East And West,* 14 (1970), 578–80.

AL-RIBAT AL-MUQADDAS

KILPATRICK, HILARY. *The Modern Egyptian Novel,* pp. 49–50, 207–8.

THE MAZE OF JUSTICE (Yaumiyyāt nā'ib fī al-aryāf, 1937)

KILPATRICK, HILARY. *The Modern Egyptian Novel,* pp. 44–47, 206–7.

HAKSAR, URMILA

THE FUTURE THAT WAS (1973)

Reviews
PANDIT, MANORMA. *World Literature Written In English,* 14 (1975), 421.

HALLS, GERALDINE (Australian, 1919–)

THE CATS OF BENARES (1967)

Reviews
CARR, SHERWYN. *Mahfil,* 8, No.2/3 (1972), 247–50.

HAMSUN, KNUT (Norwegian 1859–1952)

GENERAL

KNAPLUND, PAUL. "Knut Hamsun: Triumph and Tragedy." *Modern Age,* 9 (1965), 165–74.

NAESS, HARALD. "Knut Hamsun and America." *Scandinavian Studies,* 39 (1967), 305–28.

———. "Knut Hamsun and Rasmus Anderson," in *Scandinavian Studies,* ed. Carl F. Bayerschmidt and Erik J. Friis, pp. 269–77.

POPPERWELL, RONALD G. "Critical Attitudes to Knut Hamsun, 1890–1969." *Scandinavica,* 9 (1970), 1–23.

CHAPTER THE LAST (Siste Kaptel, 1923)

VAN MARKEN, AMY. "One of Knut Hamsun's Female Main Characters, Julie d'Espard." *Scandinavica,* 13 (1974), 107–15.

GROWTH OF THE SOIL (Markens grøde, 1917)

FORD, JESSE HILL. "On Knut Hamsun's *Growth Of The Soil,*" in *Rediscoveries,* ed. David Madden, pp. 165–78.

HUNGER (Sult, 1890)

BOLCKMANS, ALEX. "Henry Miller's 'Tropic of Cancer' and Knut Hamsun's 'Sult.' " *Scandinavica,* 14 (1975), 115–26.

MYSTERIES (Mysterier, 1892)

POPPERWELL, RONALD G. "Interrelatedness in Hamsun's *Mysterier.*" *Scandinavian Studies,* 38 (1966), 295–301.

Reviews
ROSENTHAL, RONALD. *Saturday Review,* 28 August 1971, p. 26.

THE RING IS CLOSED (Ringen sluttet, 1936)

NAESS, HARALD. "Knut Hamsun and America." *Scandinavian Studies,* 39 (1967), 323–27.

HANDKE, PETER (Austrian, 1942-)

THE GOALIE'S ANXIETY AT THE PENALTY KICK (Die angst des tormanns beim elfmeter, 1970)

WHITE, J. J. "Signs of Disturbance: The Semiological Import of Some Recent Fiction by Michel Tournier and Peter Handke." *Journal Of European Studies,* 4 (1974), 242-49.

Reviews
SEAVER, RICHARD. *Saturday Review,* 10 June 1972, pp. 64, 66.

SHORT LETTER, LONG FAREWELL (Der kurze brief zum langen abschied, 1972)

WHITE, J. J. "Signs of Disturbance: The Semiological Import of Some Recent Fiction by Michel Tournier and Peter Handke." *Journal Of European Studies,* 4 (1974), 249-54.

A SORROW BEYOND DREAMS (Wunschloses Unglück, 1972)

Reviews
RABINOWITZ, DOROTHY. *Saturday Review,* 22 March 1975, pp. 27-28.

HANSEN, MARTIN A. (Danish, 1909-1955)

THE LIAR (Løgneren, 1950)

SCHOW, H. WAYNE. "Kierkegaardian Perspectives in Martin A. Hansen's *The Liar.*" *Critique* 15, No.3 (1974), 53-65.

Reviews
JØRGENSEN, AAGE. *American Scandinavian Review,* 58 (1970), 306-7.

HAO JAN

BRIGHT SUNNY DAYS (Yen yang t'ien)

HUANG, JOE C. *Heroes And Villains In Communist China,* pp. 253-62, 284-91.

HARCOURT, J. M.

UPSURGE (1934)

HARCOURT, J. M. "The Banning of 'Upsurge.' " *Overland,* No.46 (1970/1), pp. 30-33.

HARDENBERG, Friedrich Leopold see NOVALIS

HARKER, HERBERT (Canadian)

GOLDENROD (1972)

Reviews
THOMPSON, ERIC. "Stampeder's Luck." *Journal Of Canadian Fiction,* 1, No.4 (1972), 103-4.

HARLOW, ROBERT (Canadian)

A GIFT OF ECHOES (1965)

Reviews
STOBIE, MARGARET. "Skeletal Novel." *Canadian Literature,* No.28 (1966), pp. 72-74.

SCANN (1972)

Reviews
THOMAS, AUDREY. "Almost. . ." *Canadian Literature,* No.56 (1973), pp. 114-15.

HARRIS, WILSON (Guyanese, 1921-)

GENERAL

HEARNE, JOHN. "The Fugitive in the Forest: A Study of Four Novels by Wilson Harris." *Journal Of Commonwealth Literature,* No.4 (1967), pp. 99-112; rpt. in *The Islands In Between,* ed Louis James, pp. 140-53.

MOSS, JOHN G. "William Blake and Wilson Harris: The Objective Vision." *Journal Of Commonwealth Literature,* 9, No.3 (1975), 29-40.

VAN SERTIMA, IVAN. "Introducing Wilson Harris." *Review,* No.11 (1974), pp. 60-62.

BLACK MARSDEN (1972)

Reviews
GILKES, MICHAEL. "Magical Reality." *Journal Of Commonwealth Literature,* 9, No.1 (1974), 77-79.

GUIANA QUARTET

HOWARD, W. J. "Wilson Harris's 'Guiana Quartet' from Personal Myth to National Identity." *Ariel: A Review Of International English Literature,* 1, No.1 (1970), 46-60.

HEARTLAND (1964)

RAMCHAND, KENNETH. *The West Indian Novel And Its Background,* pp. 169-73.

Reviews
DATHORNE, O. R. *Black Orpheus,* No.17 (1965), pp. 59-60.

PALACE OF THE PEACOCK (1960)

BOXILL, ANTHONY. "Wilson Harris' *Palace Of The Peacock:* A New Dimension in West Indian Fiction." *College Language Association Journal,* 14 (1971), 380-86.

HEARNE, JOHN. "The Fugitive in the Forest: A Study of Four Novels by Wilson Harris." *Journal Of Commonwealth Literature,* No.4 (1967), pp. 99-107; rpt. in *The Islands In Between,* ed. Louis James, pp. 141-48.

HOWARD, W. J. "Wilson Harris's 'Guiana Quartet' from Personal Myth to National Identity." *Ariel: A Review Of International English Literature,* 1, No.1 (1970), 46-54; rpt. in *Readings In Commonwealth Literature,* ed. William Walsh, pp. 314-22.

MOORE, GERALD. *The Chosen Tongue,* pp. 75-82.

RAMCHAND, KENNETH. *The West Indian Novel And Its Background,* pp. 165-68.

THE SECRET LADDER (1964)

HOWARD, W. J. "Wilson Harris's 'Guiana Quartet' from Personal Myth to National Identity." *Ariel: A Review Of International English Literature,* 1, No.1 (1970), 56-60; rpt. in *Readings In Commonwealth Literature,* ed. William Walsh, pp. 324-28.

TUMATUMARI (1968)

ADLER, JOYCE. "*Tumatumari* and the Imagination of Wilson Harris." *Journal Of Commonwealth Literature,* No.7 (1969), pp. 20-31.

RUSSELL, D. W. "The Dislocating Act of Memory: An Analysis of Wilson Harris' *Tumatumari.*" *World Literature Written In English,* 13 (1974), 237-49.

THE WHOLE ARMOUR (1962)

MOORE, GERALD. *The Chosen Tongue,* pp. 65-72.

HARRISON, SUSAN FRANCES

THE FOREST OF BOURG-MARIE

COGSWELL, FRED. "*The Forest Of Bourg-Marie:* An Ancestor of *Maria Chapdelaine* and *Trente Arpents.*" *Journal Of Canadian Fiction,* 2, No.3 (1973), 199-200.

HARROWER, ELIZABETH (Australian, 1928–)

THE CATHERINE WHEEL (1960)

GEERING, R. G. "Elizabeth Harrower's Novels: A Survey." *Southerly,* 30 (1970), 137–42.

DOWN IN THE CITY (1957)

GEERING, R. G. "Elizabeth Harrower's Novels: A Survey." *Southerly,* 30 (1970), 131–34.

THE LONG PROSPECT (1958)

GEERING, R. G. "Elizabeth Harrower's Novels: A Survey." *Southerly,* 30 (1970), 134–37.

THE WATCH TOWER (1966)

GEERING, R. G. "Elizabeth Harrower's Novels: A Survey." *Southerly,* 30 (1970), 142–47.

Reviews
KEESING, NANCY. *Southerly,* 27 (1967), 139–41.

HARUKI SHIMAZAKI see TŌSAN, Shimazaki

HAŠEK, JAROSLAV (Czech, 1882–1923)

THE GOOD SOLDIER SCHEWIK (Osudy dobrého vojáka Švejka za světové války, 1921–23)

STERN, J. P. "On the Integrity of the Good Soldier Schweik." *Forum For Modern Language Studies,* 2 (1966), 14–25.

———. "War and the Comic Muse: *The Good Soldier Schweik* and *Catch-22.*" *Comparative Literature,* 20 (1968), 193–216.

HAU KIOU CHOANN (Author Unknown)

BLACKALL, ERIC A. "Goethe and the Chinese Novel," in *The Discontinuous Tradition,* ed. P. F. Ganz, pp. 36–42.

HAUPTMANN, GERHART

BAHNWÄRTER THIEL

DRIVER, BEVERLY and WLATER K. FRANCKE. "The Symbolism of Deer and Squirrel in Hauptmann's 'Bahnwarter Thiel.' " *South Atlantic Bulletin,* 37, No.2 (1972), 47–51.

ELLIS, JOHN M. *Narration In The German Novelle,* pp. 169–87.

HODGE, JAMES L. "The Dramaturgy of *Bahnwärter Thiel.*" *Mosaic,* 9, No.3 (1976), 97–116.

THE FOOL IN CHRIST, EMANUEL QUINT (Der narr in Christo Emanuel Quint, 1910)

RILEY, GRAHAM A. "An Examination of the Autobiographical Elements in Gerhart Hauptmann's Novel: *Der Narr In Christo Emanuel Quint.*" *Forum For Modern Language Studies,* 6 (1970), 169–72.

HAY, WILLIAM (Australian, 1875–1945)

GENERAL

MUECKE, I. D. "William Hay and History: A Comment on Aims, Sources and Method." *Australian Literary Studies,* 2 (1965), 117–37.

THE ESCAPE OF THE NOTORIOUS SIR WILLIAM HEANS (1918)

ARGYLE, BARRY. *An Introduction To The Australian Novel, 1830-1930,* pp. 208–28.

HERGENHAN, L. T. "The Strange World of Sir William Heans (and The Mystery of William Hay)." *Southerly,* 27 (1967), 118–37.

HERRING, THELMA. "The Escape of Sir William Heans: Hay's

Debt to Hawthorne and Meredith." *Southerly,* 26 (1966), 75–92.

HAZAZ, HAYYIM (Ukrainian born Israeli, 1898–)

GENERAL

RABINOVICH, ISAIAH. *Major Trends In Modern Hebrew Fiction,* pp. 169–77.

SPICEHANDLER, EZRA. "Hayyim Hazaz." *Ariel: A Quarterly Review Of The Arts And Sciences In Israel,* No.20 (1967), pp. 33–35.

HAZOUME, PAUL (Dahomey, 1890–)

DOGUICIMI (1938)

GLEASON, JUDITH ILLSLEY. *This Africa,* pp. 48–54.

HAZZARD, SHIRLEY (Australian, 1931–)

GENERAL

COLMER, JOHN. "Patterns and Preoccupations of Love: The Novels of Shirley Hazzard." *Meanjin,* 29 (1970), 461–67.

HEAD, BESSIE (South African, 1937–)

WHEN RAIN CLOUDS GATHER (1969)

Reviews
MCDOWELL, ROBERT E. *World Literature Written In English,* No.20 (1971), pp. 113–15.

HEARNE, JOHN (Jamaican, 1926–)

GENERAL

CARTEY, WILFRED. "The Novels of John Hearne." *Journal Of Commonwealth Literature,* No.7 (1969), pp. 45–58.

DAVIES, BARRIE. "The Seekers: The Novels of John Hearne," in *The Islands In Between,* ed. Louis James, pp. 109–20.

THE FACES OF LOVE (1957)

RAMCHAND, KENNETH. *The West Indian Novel And Its Background,* pp. 45–50.

LAND OF THE LIVING (1961)

DAVIES, BARRIE. "The Seekers: The Novels of John Hearne," in *The Islands In Between,* ed. Louis James, pp. 117–20.

HEAVYSEGE, CHARLES (Canadian, 1816–1870)

THE ADVOCATE (1864)

HUGHES, KENNETH J. "Heavysege's *The Advocate:* The Art of Failure." *Journal Of Canadian Fiction,* 2, No.3 (1973), 95–98.

HÉBERT, ANNE (Canadian, 1916–)

KAMOURASKA (1970)

Reviews
JONES, LOUISA. *French Review,* 44 (1971), 961–62.

THE SILENT ROOMS (Les chambres de bois, 1958)

Reviews
GROSSKURTH, PHYLLIS. "Vapour from a Jewelled Casket." *Canadian Literature,* No.65 (1975), pp. 117–18.

RASPA, ANTHONY. "Les Chambres de Bois." *Journal Of Canadian Fiction,* 4, No.3 (1975), 173–75.

HEDAYAT, DASHIELL
LE LIVRE DES MORTS-VIVANTS (1972)

Reviews
FESTA-MCCORMICK, DIANA. *French Review,* 47 (1974), 1018-19.

HEGRAD, FRIEDRICH
FELIX MIT DER LIEBESGEIGE

HADLEY, MICHAEL. *The German Novel In 1790,* pp. 103-5.

HEINESEN, WILLIAM (Faroese, 1900-)
GENERAL

BRØNNER, HEDIN. "William Heinesen: Faroese Voice—Danish Pen." *American Scandanavian Review,* 61 (1973), 142-54.

BLAESENDE GRY (1934)

BRØNNER, HEDIN. *Three Faroese Novelists,* pp. 42-48.

DE FORTABTE SPILLEMAEND (1950)

BRØNNER, HEDIN. *Three Faroese Novelists,* pp. 58-64.

DET GODE HÅB (1964)

BRØNNER, HEDIN. *Three Faroese Novelists,* pp. 72-78.

THE LOST MUSICIANS

Reviews
RIES, PAUL. *American Scandanavian Review,* 61 (1973), 83.

MODER SYVSTJERNE

BRØNNER, HEDIN. *Three Faroese Novelists,* pp. 64-67.

NIELS PETER (Noatun, 1938)

BRONNER, HEDIN. *Three Faroese Novelists,* pp. 48-53.

JONES, W. GLYN. "Noatun and the Collective Novel." *Scandanavian Studies,* 41 (1969), 217-30.

DEN SORTE GRYDE (1949)

BRØNNER, HEDIN. *Three Faroese Novelists,* pp. 53-57.

HEINRICH UND HENRIETTE ODER DIE TRAURIGEN FOLGEN EINES RASCHEN ENTSCHLUSSES EINE ROBINSONADE (Author Unknown)
HADLEY, MICHAEL. *The German Novel In 1790,* pp. 82-84.

HEINSE, GOTTLOB HEINRICH
HEINRICH DER EISERNE, GRAF VON HOLLSTEIN

HADLEY, MICHAEL. *The German Novel In 1790,* pp. 114-21.

HELIODORUS (Greek, fl. 3rd Century A. D.)
ROMANCE OF THEAGENES AND CHARICLEIA

BOORSCH, JEAN. "About Some Greek Romances." *Yale French Studies,* No.38 (1967), pp. 72-88.

HÉLISENNE DE GRENNE
LES ANGOYSSES DOULOUREUSES QUI PROCÉDENT DAMOURS

BAKER, M. J. "*Fiametta* and the *Angoysses Douloureuses Qui Procédent Damours.*" *Symposium,* 27 (1973), 303-8.

_____ . "France's First Sentimental Novel and Novels of Chivalry." *Bibiliotheque D'Humanisme Et Renaissance,* 36 (1974), 33-45.

CONLEY, TOM. "Feminism, *Écriture,* and the Closed Room: The *Angoysses Douloureuses Qui Procédent Damours.*" *Symposium,* 27 (1973), 322-32.

STONE, DONALD. *From Tales To Truths,* pp. 12-21.

HELLER, WILHELM FRIEDRICH
SOKRATES

HADLEY, MICHAEL. *The German Novel In 1790,* pp. 209-14.

HELOISE AND ABELARD (Author Unknown)
ARCHAMBAULT, PAUL. "The Silencing of Cornelia: Heloïse, Abelard, and Their Classics." *Papers On Language And Literature,* 6 (1970), 3-17.

HÉMON, LOUIS (French Canadian, 1880-1913)
MARIA CHAPDELAINE (1913)

RASPORICH, BEVERLY. "Sacrifice and Death in French-Canadian Fiction: An English Reading." *Dalhousie Review,* 55 (1975), 451-55.

HERBURGER, GÜNTER
JESUS IN OSAKA

KURZ, PAUL KONARD. "The Contemporary Novel about Jesus," in his *On Modern German Literature,* Vol.4. 164-72.

HERBERT, XAVIER (Australian, 1901-1984)
GENERAL

HERBERT, XAVIER. "The Agony and the Joy." *Overland,* No.50 (1972), pp. 65-68.

CAPRICORNIA (1937)

CLANCY, LAURIE. "The Design of 'Capricornia.'" *Meanjin,* 34 (1975), 150-56.

HERBERT, XAVIER. "The Writing of *Capricornia.*" *Australian Literary Studies,* 4 (1970), 207-14.

KIERNAN, BRIAN. "Xavier Herbert: *Capricornia.*" *Australian Literary Studies,* 4 (1970), 360-70.

ROBERTSON, R. T. "Form Into Shape: *His Natural Life* and *Capricornia* in a Commonwealth Context." *Journal Of Canadian Fiction,* 3, No.4 (1975), 45-51.

POOR FELLOW MY COUNTRY (1975)

HESELTINE, H. P. "Xavier Herbert's Magnum Opus." *Meanjin,* 34 (1975), 133-36.

Reviews
KYNASTON, EDWARD. "Flawed Achievement." *Overland,* No.62 (1975), pp. 76-78.

HERHAUS, ERNST
A CITIZEN'S NOVEL

Reviews
BAUKE, JOSEPH P. *Saturday Review,* 27 November 1971, p. 57.

HERLIN, HANS (German, 1925-)
COMMEMORATIONS (Freunde, 1974)

Reviews
ALLEN, BRUCE. *Saturday Review,* 6 September 1975, pp. 31-32.

HERMANS, WILLEM FREDERIK (Dutch 1921-)

GENERAL

WEVERBERGH. "The Complete Writer: Willem Frederik Hermans." *Delta,* 9, No.3 (1966), 29–30.

WOLF, MANFRED. "The Dark World of Willem F. Hermans: Some Themes in the Major Novels." *Books Abroad,* 41 (1967), 274–78.

HERNÁNDEZ, JOSÉ (Argentine, 1834–1886)

THE GAUCHO MARTIN FIERRO (El gaucho Martin Fierro, 1872)

KAYE, FRANCES W. "Cooper, Sarmiento, Wister, and Hernández: The Search for a New World Literary Hero." *College Language Association Journal,* 19 (1975/6), 408–11.

HERNÁNDEZ, JUAN JOSÉ (Argentine)

LA CIUDAD DE LOS SUEÑOS (1971)

CORVALÁN, OCTAVIO. "Juan José Hernández and his City of Dreams." *International Fiction Review,* 1 (1974), 138–40.

HERNANDEZ, LUISA JOSEFINA (Mexican, 1928-)

GENERAL

LANGFORD, WALTER M. *The Mexican Novel Comes Of Age,* pp. 188–90.

HERVÉ-BAZIN, Jean-Pierre see BAZIN, Hervé

HERZEN, ALEXANDER (Russian, 1812–1870)

HELENA

PARTRIDGE, MONICA. "Herzen's Changing Concept of Reality and its Reflection in his Literary Works." *Slavonic And East European Review,* 46 (1968), 407–10.

WHO IS GUILTY? (Kto Vinovat? 1846–47)

FREEBORN, RICHARD. *The Rise Of The Russian Novel,* pp. 120–22.

PARTRIDGE, MONICA. "Herzen's Changing Concept of Reality and its Reflection in his Literary Works." *Slavonic And East European Review,* 46 (1968), 414–18.

HESSE, HERMANN (German, 1877–1962)

GENERAL

BOULBY, MARK. "The Reputation of Hermann Hesse." *Rundschau,* 2, No.3 (1972), 2–3.

BUBER, MARTIN. "Hermann Hesse in the Service of the Spirit," in *Hesse: A Collection Of Critical Essays,* ed. Theodore Ziolkowski, pp. 25–33.

BUTLER, COLIN. "The Defective Art of Hermann Hesse." *Journal Of European Studies,* 5 (1975), 41–54.

COLBY, THOMAS E. "The Impenitent Prodigal: Hermann Hesse's Hero." *German Quarterly,* 40 (1967), 14–23.

CURTIUS, ERNST ROBERT. "Hermann Hesse," in *Hesse: A Collection Of Critical Essays,* ed. Theodore Ziolkowski, pp. 34–50.

DEVERT, KRYSTYNA. "Hermann Hesse: Apostle of the Apolitical 'Revolution.' " *Triquarterly,* No.23/4 (1972), pp. 302–17.

FIELD, G. W. "Hermann Hesse: Polarities and Symbols of Synthesis." *Queen's Quarterly,* 81 (1974), 87–101.

FORD, RICHARD J. "Hermann Hesse: Prophet of the Pot Generation." *Catholic World,* 212 (1971), 15–19.

GIDE, ANDRÉ. "Preface to *The Journey To The East,*" in *Hesse: A Collection Of Critical Essays,* ed. Theodore Ziolkowski, pp. 21–24.

GROPPER, ESTHER C. "The Disenchanted Turn to Hesse." *English Journal,* 61 (1972), 979–84.

——— . "Literature for the Restive: Hermann Hesse's Books." *English Journal,* 59 (1970), 122–28.

KOESTER, RUDOLF. "The Portrayal of Age in Hesse's Narrative Prose." *Germanic Review,* 41 (1966), 111–19.

——— . "Self-Realization: Hesse's Reflections on Youth." *Monatshefte,* 57 (1965), 181–86.

MANN, THOMAS. "Introduction to *Demian,*" in *Hesse: A Collection Of Critical Essays,* ed. Theodore Ziolkowski, pp. 15–20.

MAYER, HANS. "Hermann Hesse and the 'Age of the Feuilleton,'" in *Hesse: A Collection Of Critical Essays,* ed. Theodore Ziolkowski, pp. 76–93.

MILECK, JOSEPH. "Hermann Hesse as an Editor," in *Studies In German Literature Of The Nineteenth And Twentieth Centuries,* ed. Siegfried Mews, pp. 210–22.

NORTON, ROGER C. "Hermann Hesse's Criticism of Technology." *Germanic Review,* 43 (1968), 267–73.

OLSEN, GARY R. "To Castalia and Beyond: The Function of Time and History in the Later Works of Hermann Hesse." *Arizona Quarterly,* 30 (1974), 343–54.

PACHMUSS, TEMIRA. "Dostoevsky and Hermann Hesse: Analogies and Congruences." *Orbis Litterarum,* 30 (1975), 210–14.

REICHERT, HERBERT W. "Discussion of Herbert W. Reichert: 'Nietzsche's Impact on the Prose Writings of Hermann Hesse.' " *Symposium,* 28 (1974), 52–57.

——— . "The Impact of Nietzsche on Hermann Hesse," in his *Friedrich Nietzsche's Impact On Modern German Literature,* pp. 88–116.

SAMMONS, JEFFREY L. "Hermann Hesse and the Over-Thirty Germanist," in *Hesse: A Collection Of Critical Essays,* ed. Theodore Ziolkowski, pp. 112–33.

SEIDLIN, OSKAR. "Hermann Hesse: The Exorcism of the Demon," in *Hesse: A Collection Of Critical Essays,* ed. Theodore Ziolkowski, pp. 51–75.

SORELL, WALTER. *Hermann Hesse: The Man Who Sought And Found Himself,* pp. 83–136.

SPIVEY, TED R. "The Reintegration of Modern Man: An Essay on James Joyce and Hermann Hesse." *Studies In The Literary Imagination,* 3, No.2 (1970), 49–64.

TIMPE, EUGENE F. "Hermann Hesse in the United States." *Symposium,* 23 (1969), 73–79.

ZELLER, BERNHARD. "Herman Hesse: Steppenwolf & Montagnola." *London Magazine,* 12, No.2 (1972/3), 85–106.

ZIOLKOWSKI, THEODORE. *The Novels Of Hermann Hesse: A Study In Theme And Structure,* pp. 3–84.

BENEATH THE WHEEL (Unterm rad, 1906)

BOULBY, MARK. *Hermann Hesse: His Mind And Art,* pp. 39–69.

FIELD, GEORGE WALLIS. *Hermann Hesse,* pp. 25–31.

Reviews

POTOKER, EDWARD M. "Narrow Path in Swabia." *Saturday Review,* 28 September 1968, pp. 40–41.

DEMIAN (1919)

BOULBY, MARK. *Hermann Hesse: His Mind And Art,* pp. 81–120.

BRINK, A. W. "Hermann Hesse and the Oedipal Quest." *Literature And Psychology,* 24 (1974), 66–72.

BUTLER, COLIN. "Literary Malpractice in Some Work of Hermann Hesse." *University Of Toronto Quarterly,* 40 (1971), 168–71.

FIELD, GEORGE WALLIS. *Hermann Hesse,* pp. 44–61.

NORTON, ROGER C. *Hermann Hesse's Future Idealism: <The Glass Bead Game> And Its Predecessors*, pp. 37-42.

REICHERT, HERBERT W. "The Impact of Nietzsche on Hermann Hesse," in his *Friedrich Nietzsche's Impact On Modern German Literature*, pp. 97-100.

ZIOLKOWSKI, THEODORE. *The Novels Of Hermann Hesse: A Study In Theme And Structure*, pp. 87-145.

———. "The Quest for the Grail in Hesse's *Demian*." *Germanic Review*, 49 (1974), 44-59; rpt. in *Hesse: A Collection Of Critical Essays*, ed. Theodore Ziolkowski, pp. 134-52.

Reviews
BAUKE, JOSEPH P. "Learning to Live with Chaos." *Saturday Review*, 19 June 1965, p. 38.

GERTRUDE (Gertrud, 1910)

FIELD, GEORGE WALLIS. *Hermann Hesse*, pp. 33-36.

Reviews
POTOKER, EDWARD M. "Connoisseur of Chaos." *Saturday Review*, 5 April 1969, p. 39.

THE GLASS BEAD GAME (Das Glasperlenspiel, 1943)

BANDY, STEPHEN C. "Hermann Hesse's *Das Glasperlenspiel*: In Search of Josef Knecht." *Modern Language Quarterly*, 33 (1972), 299-311.

BAUMER, FRANZ. *Hermann Hesse*, pp. 84-88.

BOULBY, MARK. *Hermann Hesse: His Mind And Art*, pp. 261-321.

———. " 'Der Vierte Lebenslauf' as a Key to 'Das Glasperlenspiel.' " *Modern Language Review*, 61 (1966), 635-46.

BRINK, A. W. "Hermann Hesse and the Oedipal Quest." *Literature And Psychology*, 24 (1974), 76-78.

BUTLER, COLIN. "Literary Malpractice in Some Works of Hermann Hesse." *University Of Toronto Quarterly*, 40 (1971), 177-80.

CURTIUS, ERNST ROBERT. "Hermann Hesse," in *Hesse: A Collection Of Critical Essays*, ed. Theodore Ziolkowski, pp. 46-50.

FIELD, G. W. "Goethe and *Das Glasperlenspiel*: Reflections on 'Alterswerke.' " *German Life And Letters*, 23 (1969), 93-101.

———. *Hermann Hesse*, pp. 148-72.

———. "Hermann Hesse: Polarities and Symbols of Synthesis." *Queen's Quarterly*, 81 (1974), 96-100.

———. "Music and Morality in Thomas Mann and Hermann Hesse," in *Hesse: A Collection Of Critical Essays*, ed. Theodore Ziolkowski, pp. 101-11.

———. "On the Genesis of the *Glasperlenspiel*." *German Quarterly*, 41 (1968), 673-88.

FRIEDRICHSMEYER, ERHARD. "The Bertram Episode in Hesse's *Glass Bead Game*." *Germanic Review*, 49 (1974), 284-97.

GOLDGAR, HARRY. "Hesse's *Glasperlenspiel* and the Game of Go." *German Life And Letters*, 20 (1967), 132-37.

KLAWITER, RANDOLPH J. "The Artist-Intellectual, in or versus Society? A Dilemma," in *Studies In German Literature Of The Nineteenth And Twentieth Centuries*, ed. Siegfried Mews, pp. 239-43.

KOESTER, RUDOLF. "Hesse's Music Master: In Search of a Prototype." *Forum For Modern Language Studies*, 3 (1967), 135-41.

MAYER, HANS. "Hermann Hesse and the 'Age of Feuilleton,' " in *Hesse: A Collection Of Critical Essays*, ed. Theodore Ziolkowski, pp. 76-93.

MILECK, JOSEPH. "*Das Glasperlenspiel*: Genesis, Manuscripts, and History of Publication." *German Quarterly*, 43 (1970), 55-83.

NORTON, ROGER C. "Hermann Hesse's Criticism of Technology." *Germanic Review*, 43 (1968), 270-73.

———. *Hermann Hesse's Future Idealism: <The Glass Bead Game> And Its Predecessors*, pp. 73-122.

———. "Variant Endings of Hesse's *Glasperlenspiel*.' " *Monatshefte*, 60 (1968), 141-46.

OLSEN, GARY R. "To Castalia and Beyond: The Function of Time and History in the Later Works of Hermann Hesse." *Arizona Quarterly*, 30 (1974), 351-54.

REICHERT, HERBERT W. "The Impact of Nietzsche on Hermann Hesse," in his *Friedrich Nietzsche's Impact On Modern German Literature*, pp. 111-15.

RESNIK, HENRY S. "How Hermann Hesse Speaks to the College Generation." *Saturday Review*, 18 October 1969, pp. 35-37.

RILEY, ANTHONY W. " 'Das Glasperlenspiel' in English Translation (with an Unpublished Letter of Hermann Hesse's)." *Monatshefte*, 59 (1967), 344-50.

ROSS, STEPHEN D. *Literature & Philosophy*, pp. 65-107.

SORELL, WALTER. *Hermann Hesse: The Man Who Sought And Found Himself*, pp. 51-53, 91-92.

ZELLER, BERNHARD. *Portrait Of Hesse: An Illustrated Biography*, pp. 141-53.

ZIOLKOWSKI, THEODORE. "Hermann Hesse: Der Vierte Lebenslauf." *Germanic Review*, 42 (1967), 124-43.

———. *The Novels Of Hermann Hesse: A Study In Theme And Structure*, pp. 283-338.

Reviews
FALLOWELL, DUNCAN. "Mountain Climbing." *London Magazine*, NS, 10, No.9 (1970), 96-98.

JOURNEY TO THE EAST (Die Morganlandfahrt, 1932)

BOULBY, MARK. *Hermann Hesse: His Mind And Art*, pp. 245-61.

CRENSHAW, KAREN O. and RICHARD H. LAWSON. "Technique and Function of Time in Hesse's *Morgenlandfahrt*: A Culmination." *Mosaic*, 5, No.3 (1972), 53-59.

DERRENBERGER, JOHN. "Who is Leo?: Astrology in Hermann Hesse's *Die Morgenlandfahrt*." *Monatshefte*, 67 (1975), 167-72.

FIELD, GEORGE WALLIS. *Hermann Hesse*, pp. 142-48.

HALLAMORE, JOYCE. "Paul Klee, H. H. and *Die Morgenlandfahrt*." *Seminar*, 1 (1965), 17-24.

NORTON, ROGER C. *Hermann Hesse's Future Idealism: <The Glass Bead Game> And Its Predecessors*, pp. 63-69.

SORELL, WALTER. *Hermann Hesse: The Man Who Sought And Found Himself*, pp. 49-51, 90-91.

ZELLER, BERNHARD. *Portrait Of Hesse: An Illustrated Biography*, pp. 134-37.

ZIOLKOWSKI, THEODORE. *The Novels Of Hermann Hesse: A Study In Theme And Structure*, pp. 253-82.

Reviews
BAUKE, JOSEPH. "Into the Id and Youth of the Soul." *Saturday Review*, 4 May 1968, pp. 32.

KLEIN UND WAGNER

FICKERT, KURT J. "The Portrait of the Artist in Hesse's 'Klein und Wagner.' " *Hartford Studies In Literature*, 6 (1974), 180-87.

FIELD, GEORGE WALLIS. *Hermann Hesse*, pp. 64-66.

KLINGSOR'S LAST SUMMER (Klingsors Letzter Sommer)

FIELD, GEORGE WALLIS. *Hermann Hesse*, pp. 66-70.

ZELLER, BERNHARD. *Portrait Of Hesse: An Illustrated Biography*, pp. 91-94.

Reviews
FORD, RICHARD J. "Renoir of Print." *Catholic World*, 213 (1971), 109-10.

MAGISTER LUDI see THE GLASS BEAD GAME

NARCISSUS AND GOLDMUND (Narziss und Goldmund, 1930)

BOULBY, MARK. *Hermann Hesse: His Mind And Art*, pp. 207-43.

FIELD, GEORGE WALLIS. *Hermann Hesse*, pp. 109-20.

NEUSWANGER, RUSSELL. "Names as Glass Beads in Hesse's *Narziss Und Goldmund.*" *Monatshefte*, 67 (1975), 48-58.

ZELLER, BERNHARD. *Portrait Of Hesse: An Illustrated Biography*, pp. 114-17.

ZIOLKOWSKI, THEODORE. *The Novels Of Hermann Hesse: A Study In Theme And Structure*, pp. 229-52.

Reviews

BAUKE, JOSEPH. "Into the Id and Youth of the Soul." *Saturday Review*, 4 May 1968, pp. 32, 37.

WALLENSTEIN, BARRY. "No Guide for Hippies." *Catholic World*, 208 (1969), pp. 92-93.

PETER CAMENZIND (1904)

BOULBY, MARK. *Hermann Hesse: His Mind And Art*, pp. 1-37.

FIELD, GEORGE WALLIS. *Hermann Hesse*, pp. 22-25.

RESORT GUEST (Kurgast, 1924)

MAURER, WARREN R. "Some Aspects of the Jean Paul-Hermann Hesse Relationship with Special Reference to *Katzenberger* and *Kurgast.*" *Seminar*, 4 (1968), 113-28.

ROSSHALDE (1914)

FIELD, GEORGE WALLIS. *Hermann Hesse*, pp. 36-40.

SIDDHARTHA (1923)

BOULBY, MARK. *Hermann Hesse: His Mind And Art*, pp. 121-57.

BRESTENSKY, DENNIS F. "*Siddhartha*: A Casebook on Teaching Methods." *English Journal*, 62 (1973), 279-82.

BUTLER, COLIN. "Hermann Hesse's 'Siddhartha': Some Critical Objections." *Monatshefte*, 63 (1971), 117-24.

———. "Literary Malpractice in Some Works of Hermann Hesse." *University Of Toronto Quarterly*, 40 (1971), 171-74.

CONRAD, ROBERT C. "Hermann Hesse's *Siddhartha, Eine Indische Dichtung*, as a Western Archetype." *German Quarterly*, 48 (1975), 358-69.

FIELD, GEORGE WALLIS. *Hermann Hesse*, pp. 71-85.

HUGHES, KENNETH. "Hesse's Use of *Gilgamesh*—Motifs in the Humanization of Siddhartha and Harry Haller." *Seminar*, 5 (1969), 129-40.

KASSIM, HUSAIN. "Toward a Mahayana Buddhist Interpretation of Hermann Hesse's Siddhartha." *Literature East And West*, 18 (1974), 233-43.

MISRA, BHABAGRAHI. "An Analysis of Indic Tradition in Hermann Hesse's Siddhartha." *Indian Literature*, 11, No.2 (1968), 111-23.

NORTON, ROGER C. *Hermann Hesse's Future Idealism: <The Glass Bead Game> And Its Predecessors*, pp. 45-53.

PASLICK, ROBERT H. "Dialectic and Non-Attachment: The Structure of Hermann Hesse's *Siddhartha.*" *Symposium*, 27 (1973), 64-75.

SCHLUDERMANN, BRIGITTE AND ROSEMARIE FINLAY. "Mythical Reflections of the East in Hermann Hesse." *Mosaic*, 2, No.3 (1969), 100-05.

TIMPE, EUGENE F. "Hesse's *Siddhartha* and the *Bhagavad Gita.*" *Comparative Literature*, 22 (1970), 346-57.

ZIOLKOWSKI, THEODORE. *The Novels Of Hermann Hesse: A Study In Theme And Structure*, pp. 146-77.

STEPPENWOLF (Der Steppenwolf, 1929)

ABOOD, EDWARD. "Jung's Concept of Individuation in Hesse's *Steppenwolf.*" *Southern Humanities Review*, 3 (1969), 1-13.

ARTISS, DAVID. "Key Symbols in Hesse's *Steppenwolf.*" *Seminar*, 7 (1971), 85-101.

BAUMER, FRANZ. *Hermann Hesse*, pp. 75-78.

BOULBY, MARK. *Hermann Hesse: His Mind And Art*, pp. 159-205.

BRINK, A. W. "Hermann Hesse and the Oedipal Quest." *Literature And Psychology*, 24 (1974), 72-76.

BUTLER, COLIN. "Literary Malpractice in Some Works of Hermann Hesse." *University Of Toronto Quarterly*, 40 (1971), 174-77.

COHN, DORRIT. "Narration of Consciousness in *Der Steppenwolf.*" *Germanic Review*, 44 (1969), 121-31.

DHORITY, LYNN. "Who Wrote the *Tractat Vom Steppenwolf?*" *German Life And Letters*, 27 (1973), 59-66.

FIELD, GEORGE WALLIS. *Hermann Hesse*, pp. 86-108.

———. "Hermann Hesse: Polarities and Symbols of Synthesis." *Queen's Quarterly*, 81 (1974), 91-94.

———. "Music and Morality in Thomas Mann and Hermann Hesse," in *Hesse: A Collection Of Critical Essays*, ed. Theodore Ziolkowski, pp. 99-101.

FREEDMAN, RALPH. "*Person* and *Persona:* The Magic Mirrors of *Steppenwolf*," in *Hesse: A Collection Of Critical Essays*, ed. Theodore Ziolkowski, pp. 153-79.

HUGHES, KENNETH. "Hesse's Use of *Gilgamesh*—Motifs in the Humanization of Siddhartha and Harry Haller." *Seminar*, 5 (1969), 129-40.

HATFIELD, HENRY. *Crisis And Continuity In Modern German Fiction*, pp. 63-77.

MAYER, HANS. "Hermann Hesse's Steppenwolf," in his *Steppenwolf And Everyman*, pp. 1-13.

MERRILL, REED B. "Ivan Karamazov and Harry Haller: The Consolation of Philosophy." *Comparative Literature Studies*, 8 (1971), 69-77.

NORTON, ROGER C. *Hermann Hesse's Future Idealism: <The Glass Bead Game> And Its Predecessors*, pp. 53-61.

OLSEN, GARY R. "To Castalia and Beyond: The Function of Time and History in the Later Works of Hermann Hesse." *Arizona Quarterly*, 30 (1974), 346-50.

REICHERT, HERBERT W. "The Impact of Nietzsche on Hermann Hesse," in his *Friedrich Nietzsche's Impact On Modern German Literature*, pp. 104-8.

ROGERS, ROBERT. *A Psychoanalytic Study Of The Double In Literature*, pp. 94-98.

STANEK, LOU WILLETT. "Hesse and Moffett Team Teach the Theory of Discourse." *English Journal*, 61 (1972), 985-93.

STELZMANN, RAINULF A. "Kafka's *The Trial* and Hesse's *Steppenwolf:* Two Views of Reality and Transcendence." *Xavier University Studies*, 5 (1966), 165-72.

WEBB, EUGENE. "Hermine and the Problem of Harry's Failure in Hesse's *Steppenwolf.*" *Modern Fiction Studies*, 17 (1971), 115-24.

ZELLER, BERNHARD. *Portrait Of Hesse: An Illustrated Biography*, pp. 111-14.

ZIOLKOWSKI, THEODORE. *The Novels Of Hermann Hesse: A Study In Theme And Structure*, pp. 178-228.

HEYM, GEORG (German, 1887-1912)

DER IRRE

BLUNDEN, ALLAN. "Notes on Georg Heym's Novelle *Der Irre.*" *German Life and Letters*, 28 (1975), 107-19.

HIRAOKA, Kimitake see MISHIMA YUKIO

HOFFMANN, ERNST THEODOR AMADEUS (German, 1776-1822)

GENERAL

DAEMMRICH, HORST S. "Hoffmann's Tragic Heroes." *Germanic Review,* 45 (1970), 94-104.

PETERS, DIANA STONE. "E. T. A. Hoffmann: The Conciliatory Satirist." *Monatshefte,* 66 (1974), 55-73.

THE DEVIL'S ELIXIRS (Die Elixiere des Teufels, 1815-16)

DAEMMRICH, HORST S. "*The Devil's Elixirs:* Precursor of the Modern Psychological Novel." *Papers On Language And Literature,* 6 (1970), 374-86.

————. "Hoffmann's Tragic Heroes." *Germanic Review,* 45 (1970), 96-99.

THE EDUCATED CAT see THE LIFE AND OPINIONS OF KATER MURR

DAS FRÄULEIN VON SCUDERI

ELLIS, J. M. "E. T. A. Hoffmann's 'Das Fräulein von Scuderi.' " *Modern Language Review,* 64 (1969), 340-50.

DER GOLDNE TOPF

McGLATHERY, JAMES M. "The Suicide Motif in E. T. A. Hoffmann's 'Der Goldne Topf.' " *Monatshefte,* 58 (1966), 115-23.

TATAR, MARIA M. "Mesmerism, Madness, and Death in E. T. A. Hoffmann's *Der Goldne Topf.*" *Studies In Romanticism,* 14 (1975), 365-89.

LIFE AND OPINIONS OF KATER MURR (Lebensansichten des Katers Murr nebst Fragmentarischer Biographie des Kapell meisters Johannes Kreisler in Zufälligen Makulaturblättern)

DAEMMRICH, HORST S. "Hoffmann's Tragic Heroes." *Germanic Review,* 45 (1970), 99-102.

FRYE, LAWRENCE O. "The Language of Romantic High Feeling: A Case of Dialogue Technique in Hoffmann's *Kater Murr* and Novalis' *Heinrich Von Ofterdingen.*" *Deutsche Vierteljahresschrift Fur Literaturwissenschaft Und Geistegeschichte,* 49 (1975), 520-29.

GROVES, PETER J. "E. T. A. Hoffmann's Johannes Kreisler 'Verruckter Musikus.'?" *Modern Language Quarterly,* 30 (1969), 222-33.

MEYER, HERMANN. *The Poetics Of Quotation In The European Novel,* pp. 125-47.

MASTER FLEA (Meister floh, 1822)

PETERS, DIANA STONE. "E. T. A. Hoffmann: The Conciliatory Satirist." *Monatshefte,* 66 (1974), 67-71.

PRINCESS BRAMBILLA (Prinzessin Brambilla, 1821)

CHAMBERS, ROSS. "Two Theatrical Microcosms: *Die Prinzessin Brambilla* and *Mademoiselle De Maupin.*" *Comparative Literature,* 27 (1975), 37-40.

DUNN, HOUGH-LEWIS. "The Circle of Love in Hoffmann and Shakespeare." *Studies In Romanticism,* 11 (1972), 113-37.

SLESSAREV, HELGA. "E. T. A. Hoffmann's *Prinzessin Brambilla:* A Romanticist's Contribution to the Aesthetic Education of Man." *Studies In Romanticism,* 9 (1970), 147-60.

RAT KRESPEL

ELLIS, JOHN M. *Narration In The German Novelle,* pp. 94-112.

HABERLAND, PAUL M. "Number Symbolism: The Father-Daughter Relationship in E. T. A. Hoffmann's 'Rat Krespel.' " *USF Language Quarterly,* 13, No.3/4 (1975), 39-52.

RIPPLEY, LA VERN J. "The House as Metaphor in E. T. A. Hoffmann's *Rat Krespel.*" *Papers On Language And Literature,* 7 (1971), 52-60.

THE SANDMAN (Der Sandmann)

LAWSON, URSULA D. "Pathological Time in E. T. A. Hoffmann's 'Der Sandmann.' " *Monatshefte,* 60 (1968), 51-61.

MAHLENDORF, URSULA. "E. T. A. Hoffmann's *The Sandman:* The fictional Psycho-Biography of a Romantic Poet." *American Imago,* 32 (1975), 217-39.

MASSEY, IRVING. "Narcissism in 'The Sandman': Nathanael vs. E. T. A. Hoffmann." *Genre,* 6 (1973), 114-20.

PRAWER, S. S. "Hoffmann's Uncanny Guest: A Reading of *Der Sandmann.*" *German Life And Letters,* 18 (1965), 297-308.

HOFFMANNSTHAL, HUGO VON (Austrian, 1874-1929)

GENERAL

NORTON, ROGER C. "The Significance of Deeds in Hofmannsthal's Works." *Modern Austrian Literature,* 2, No.3 (1969), 21-23.

WILLIAMS, CEDRIC E. *The Broken Eagle,* pp. 1-32.

ANDREAS (Andreas oder Die Vereinigten, 1932)

MILES, DAVID H. *Hofmannsthal's Novel Andreas: Memory And Self,* pp. 101-210.

CAVALRY PATROL (Reitergeschichte, 1908)

DONOP, WILLIAM R. "Archetypal Vision in Hofmannsthal's *Reitergeschichte.*" *German Life And Letters,* 22 (1969), 126-34.

LAKIN, MICHAEL. "Hofmannsthal's Reitergeschichte and Kafka's Ein Landarzt." *Modern Austrian Literature,* 3, No.1 (1970), 39-50.

DAS GESPRÄCH ÜBER GEDICHTE

REID, J. H. " 'Draussen Sind Wir Zu Finden. . .'—The Development of a Hofmannsthal Symbol." *German Life And Letters,* 27 (1973), 35-51.

HOLMES, ABRAHAM S. (Canadian)

BELINDA: OR, THE RIVALS (1843)

DAVIS, MARILYN I. "Anglo-Boston Bamboozled on the Canadian Thames: Holmes's *Belinda: Or, The Rivals.*" *Journal Of Canadian Fiction,* 2, No.3 (1973), 56-61.

HOLMES, JOHN (Canadian)

ON TARGET

Reviews
ORANGE, JOHN. "Near Miss." *Journal Of Canadian Fiction,* 3, No.2 (1974), 100-2.

HOMÄIS, REINE DE TUNIS (Author Unknown)

GROBE, EDWIN P. "The Anonymous Tunisian Novels of Sébastien Brémond." *Romance Notes,* 6 (1965), 148-52.

HOOD, HUGH (Canadian, 1928-)

GENERAL

CLOUTIER, PIERRE. "An Interview with Hugh Hood." *Journal Of Canadian Fiction,* 2, No.1 (1973), 49-52.

HALE, VICTORIA G., ed. "An Interview with Hugh Hood." *World Literature Written In English,* 11, No.1 (1972), 35-41.

HOOD, HUGH. "Sober Colouring: The Ontology of Super-Realism." *Canadian Literature,* No.49 (1971), pp. 28-34.

THOMPSON, KENT. "Hugh Hood and His Expanding Universe." *Journal Of Canadian Fiction,* 3, No.1 (1974), 55-59.

THE CAMERA ALWAYS LIES (1967)

DUFFY, DENNIS. "Grace: The Novels of Hugh Hood." *Canadian Literature*, No.47 (1971), pp. 12–17.

A GAME OF TOUCH (1970)

DUFFY, DENNIS. "Grace: The Novels of Hugh Hood." *Canadian Literature*, No.47 (1971), pp. 20–25.

THE SWING IN THE GARDEN (1975)

FULFORD, ROBERT. "An Interview with Hugh Hood." *Tamarack Review*, No.66 (1975), pp. 65–77.

WHITE FIGURE, WHITE GROUND (1964)

CLOUTIER, PIERRE. "Space, Time and the Creative Imagination: Hugh Hood's *White Figure, White Ground*." *Journal Of Canadian Fiction*, 3, No.1 (1974), 60–63.

DUFFY, DENNIS. "Grace: The Novels of Hugh Hood." *Canadian Literature*, No.47 (1971), pp. 17–20.

Reviews

WARREN, MICHAEL. "Artist's Passion." *Canadian Literature*, No.25 (1965), pp. 76–77.

WATT, F. W. *University Of Toronto Quarterly*, 34 (1965), 376–77.

YOU CAN'T GET THERE FROM HERE (1972)

MOSS, JOHN G. "Man Divided Amongst Himself: Hood's Leofrica." *Journal Of Canadian Fiction*, 3, No.1 (1974), 64–69.

Reviews

LEITOLD, RON. *Dalhousie Review*, 53 (1973), 169–71.

SMITH, ROWLAND. "Telegrams and Anger." *Canadian Literature*, No.58 (1973), pp. 101–2.

HORNMAN, WIN (Dutch, 1920–)

THE GUERILLA PRIEST (Der Guerilla-Priester)

KURZ, PAUL KONRAD. "The Priest in the Modern Novel," in his *On Modern German Literature*, Vol.4: 129–36.

HORVÁTH, ÖDÖN VON (Hungarian, 1901-1938)

GENERAL

LORAM, IAN C. "Ödön von Horváth: An Appraisal." *Monatshefte*, 59 (1967), 19–34.

HORWOOD, HAROLD (Canadian, 1923–)

WHITE ESKIMO (1972)

Reviews

GODARD, BARBARA. "A Novel With a Message." *Journal Of Canadian Fiction*, 2, No.1 (1973), 98–99.

ROSENGARTEN, HERBERT. "Survival of the Fittest." *Canadian Literature*, No.58 (1973), pp. 92–93.

HOSAIN, ATTIA (Indian, 1913–)

GENERAL

SRINIVASA IYENGAR, K. R. *Indian Writing In English*, pp. 461–64.

HOWARD, BLANCHE (Canadian, 1923–)

THE MANIPULATOR (1972)

Reviews

JEWISON, DON. "Picturesque and Moralistic." *Canadian Literature*, No.60 (1974), 122–23.

POTTS, MAUREEN. *World Literature Written In English*, 13 (1974), pp. 103–5.

HSIAO CHÜN (Chinese, 1908–) pseudonym of T'ien Chün

GENERAL

HSIA, C. T. *A History Of Modern Chinese Fiction*, pp. 273–79.

HUGO, VICTOR (French, 1802–1885)

GENERAL

BANDY, W. T. "Hugo's View of Poe." *Revue De Littérature Comparée*, 49 (1975), 480–83.

POLLIN, BURTON R. "Victor Hugo and Poe." *Revue De Littérature Comparée*, 42 (1968), 494–519.

WARD, PATRICIA A. "Nodier, Hugo, and the Concept of the Type Character." *French Review*, 45 (1972), 944–53.

———. "The Political Evolution of Victor Hugo's Gothic Vision." *Modern Language Quarterly*, 34 (1973), 272–82.

BUG—JARGAL (1826)

GRANT, RICHARD B. *The Perilous Quest: Image, Myth, And Prophecy In The Narratives Of Victor Hugo*, pp. 18–27.

HAN D'ISLANDE (1823)

GRANT, RICHARD B. *The Perilous Quest: Image, Myth, And Prophecy In The Narratives Of Victor Hugo*, pp. 3–18.

L'HOMME QUI RIT (1869)

FORDE, MARIANNA C. "The Pessimism of an Idealist: Hugo's *L'Homme Qui Rit*." *French Review*, 41 (1968), 641–48.

GRANT, RICHARD B. *The Perilous Quest: Image, Myth, And Prophecy In The Narratives Of Victor Hugo*, pp. 199–221.

THE HUNCHBACK OF NOTRE DAME (Notre-Dame de Paris, 1831)

GRANT, RICHARD B. *The Perilous Quest: Image, Myth, And Prophecy In The Narratives Of Victor Hugo*, pp. 46–72.

O'NAN, MARTHA. *The Role Of Mind In Hugo, Faulkner, Beckett And Grass*, pp. 3–12.

POLLIN, BURTON R. "*Notre-Dame De Paris* in Two of Poe's Tales." *Revue Des Langues Vivantes*, 34 (1968), 354–65.

PRITCHETT, V. S. *The Working Novelist*, pp. 103–8.

WARD, PATRICIA A. *The Medievalism Of Victor Hugo*, pp. 34–52.

LAST DAY OF A MAN CONDEMNED TO DEATH (Le Dernier Jour d'un Condamné, 1829)

FORDE, MARIANNA C. "Condemnation and Imprisonment in *L'Étranger* and *Le Dernier Jour D'Un Condamné*." *Romance Notes*, 13 (1971), 211–16.

WHARTENBY, H. ALLEN. "Precursors of the Gidian *Récit*." *Romanic Review*, 60 (1969), 110–12.

LES MISÉRABLES (1862)

DENOMMÉ, ROBERT T. "Lamartine's Criticism of Les Misérables." *Orbis Litterarum*, 26 (1971), 211–19.

GRANT, RICHARD B. *The Perilous Quest: Image, Myth, and Prophecy In The Narratives Of Victor Hugo*, pp. 154–76.

HYSLOP, LOIS BOE. "Baudelaire on *Les Misérables*." *French Review*, 41 (1967), 23–29.

PRITCHETT, V. S. *The Working Novelist*, pp. 103–8.

QUATREVINGT-TREIZE (1874)

EDWARDS, SAMUEL. *Victor Hugo: A Tumultuous Life*, pp. 289–96.

GRANT, RICHARD B. *The Perilous Quest: Image, Myth, And Prophecy In The Narratives Of Victor Hugo*, pp. 222–38.

THE SEVEN WONDERS OF THE WORLD (La Légende des Siècles, 1877)

GUGELBERGER, G. M. " 'Tentative Vers l'Ideal: "Genero-periodicism and Victor Hugo's *La Légende Des Siècles* (A Reconsideration of the Term 'Romantic' Through Genology.)" *Genre,* 7 (1974), 322–41.

SCHOR, NAOMI. "Superposition of Models in *La Légende Des Siècles.*" *Romanic Review,* 65 (1974), 42–51.

LES TRAVAILLEURS DE LA MER (1866)

GRANT, RICHARD B. *The Perilous Quest: Image, Myth, And Prophecy In The Narratives Of Victor Hugo,* pp. 177–98.

HUNOLD, CHRISTIAN FRIEDRICH (German, 1680-1721)

DIE LIEBENSWURDIGE ADALIE (1702)

WAGENER, HANS. *The German Baroque Novel,* pp. 150–58.

HUNTER, ROBERT (Canadian)

EREBUS (1968)

RICOU, LAURENCE R. "Empty as Nightmare: Man and Landscape in Recent Canadian Prairie Fiction." *Mosaic,* 6, No.2 (1972/3), 155–56.

Reviews

NEW, WILLIAM H. "Cock and Bull Stories." *Canadian Literature,* No.39 (1969), pp. 84–85.

SMITH, RONALD F. "A Dark World." *Journal Of Commonwealth Literature,* 7, No.1 (1972), 107–8.

HUTCHINSON, ALFRED (Nigerian, 1924-1972)

ROAD TO GHANA (1960)

CARTEY, WILFRED. *Whispers From A Continent,* pp. 133–37.

HUYSMANS, JORIS-KARL (French, 1848-1907)

GENERAL

ROSSMANN, EDWARD. "The Conflict Over Food in the Work of J.-K. Huysmans." *Nineteenth-Century French Fiction,* 2 (1973/4), 61–67.

AGAINST THE GRAIN (A Rebours, 1884)

CEVASCO, G. A. "Des Esseinte's Library." *American Book Collector,* 21, No.7 (1970), 7–11.

———. "A Dose of Opium: J. K. Huysman's 'A Rebours.' " *American Book Collector,* 17, No.8 (1967), 13–16.

———. "*A Rebours* and Poe's Reputation in France." *Romance Notes,* 13 (1971), 255–61.

———. "Satirical and Parodical Interpretations of J.-K. Huysmans' *A Rebours.*" *Romance Notes,* 16 (1975), 278–82.

FURST, LILLIAN R. "The Structure of Romantic Agony." *Comparative Literature Studies,* 10 (1973), 125–38.

MEYERS, JEFFREY. *Painting And The Novel,* pp. 84–95.

NUCCITELLI, ANGELA. "*A Rebours*'s Symbol of the 'Femme-Fleur': A Key to Des Esseintes's Obsession." *Symposium,* 28 (1974), 336–45.

RIDGE, GEORGE ROSS. *Joris-Karl Huysmans,* pp. 60–66.

TAYLOR, JOHN. "John-Karl Huysmans as Impressionist in Prose." *Papers On Language And Literature,* 8 (1972), 67–75.

WEST, THOMAS G. "Schopenhauer, Huysmans and French Naturalism." *Journal Of European Studies,* 1 (1971), 313–24.

UN DILEMME

RIDGE, GEORGE ROSS. *Joris-Karl Huysmans,* pp. 69–72.

DOWN THERE (Là-Bas, 1891)

ERICKSON, JOHN D. "Huysmans' *Là-Bas:* A Metaphor of Search." *French Review,* 43 (1970), 418–25.

LOWRIE, JOYCE O. *The Violent Mystique,* pp. 132–37.

RIDGE, GEORGE ROSS. *Joris-Karl Huysmans,* pp. 77–80.

TAYLOR, JOHN. "Joris-Karl Huysmans as Impressionist in Prose." *Papers On Language And Literature,* 8 (1972), 75–78.

DOWNSTREAM (A Vau-l'eau, 1882)

RIDGE, GEORGE ROSS. *Joris-Karl Huysmans,* pp. 57–59.

WINNER, ANTHONY. "The Indigestible Reality: J.-K. Huysmans' 'Down Stream.' " *Virginia Quarterly Review,* 50 (1974), 39–50.

EN RADE (1887)

MATTHEWS, J. H. *Surrealism And The Novel,* pp. 28–40.

RIDGE, GEORGE ROSS. *Joris-Karl Huysmans,* pp. 66–68.

WADE, CLAIRE. "The Contributions of Color and Light to Differing Levels of Reality in the Novels of Joris-Karl Huysmans." *Symposium,* 28 (1974), 371–76.

EN ROUTE (1895)

LOWRIE, JOYCE O. *The Violent Mystique,* pp. 137–55.

RIDGE, GEORGE ROSS. *Joris-Karl Huysmans,* pp. 81–86.

WADE, CLAIRE. "The Contributions of Color and Light to Differing Levels of Reality in the Novels of Joris-Karl Huysmans." *Symposium,* 28 (1974), 376–79.

LIVING TOGETHER (En menage, 1881)

HEMMINGS, F. W. J. "The Realist and Naturalist Movements in France," in *The Age of Realism,* ed. F. W. J. Hemmings, pp. 204–6.

RIDGE, GEORGE ROSS. *Joris-Karl Huysmans,* pp. 52–57.

MARTHE (Marthe, l'histoire d'une fille, 1876)

RIDGE, GEORGE ROSS. *Joris-Karl Huysmans,* pp. 41–45.

WADE, CLAIRE. "The Contributions of Color and Light to Differing Levels of Reality in the Novels of Joris-Karl Huysmans." *Symposium,* 28 (1974), 366–70.

THE OBLATE (L'Oblat, 1903)

RIDGE, GEORGE ROSS. *Joris-Karl Huysmans,* pp. 95–98.

LES SOEURS VATARD (1879)

RIDGE, GEORGE ROSS. *Joris-Karl Huysmans,* pp. 45–48.

HYDE, ROBIN (New Zealander, 1906-1939) pseudonym of Iris Guiver Wilkinson

THE GODWITS FLY (1938)

HANKIN, CHERRY. "New Zealand Women Novelists: Their Attitudes Towards Life in a Developing Society." *World Literature Written In English,* 14 (1975), 155–58.

I

IBARRA, VICENTE
EL ÚLTIMO MES

Reviews
GONZÁLEZ ECHEVARRÍA, ROBERTO. *Latin American Literary Review,* 3, No.5 (1974), 162-63.

IBUSE MASUJI (Japanese, 1898–)
BLACK RAIN (Kuroi ame, 1966)

KIMBALL, ARTHUR G. *Crisis In Identity And Contemporary Japanese Novels,* pp. 43-59.

ICAZA, JORGE (Ecuadorian, 1906–1978)
LOS ATRAPADOS (1972)

Reviews
SACKETT, THEODORE A. *Chasqui,* 2, No.3 (1973), 62-65.

HUAIRAPAMUSHCAS (1948)

VETRANO, ANTHONY J. "Imagery in Two of Jorge Icaza's Novels: *Huasipungo* and *Huairapamushcas.*" *Revista De Estudios Hispánicos,* 6 (1972), 293-301.

THE VILLAGERS (Huasipungo, 1934)

JOHNSON, DAVID D. "*Huasipungo* for Children?" *Romance Notes,* 14 (1972), 41-43.

VETRANO, ANTHONY J. "Imagery in Two of Jorge Icaza's Novels: *Huasipungo* and *Huairapamushcas.*" *Revista De Estudios Hispánicos,* 6 (1972), 293-301.

IDĪS, YŪSUF (Egyptian, 1927–)
AL-'AYB (1962)

KILPATRICK, HILARY. *The Modern Egyptian Novel,* pp. 122-26, 238-39.

AL-BAYDĀ (1970)

KILPATRICK, HILARY. *The Modern Egyptian Novel,* pp. 113-18, 235-36.

AL-HARAM (1959)

KILPATRICK, HILARY. *The Modern Egyptian Novel,* pp. 118-22, 236-38.

IBARA, SAIKAKU (Japancsc, 1642–1693)
THE LIFE OF AN AMOROUS MAN

Reviews
TEELE, ROY E. *Literature East And West,* 9 (1965), 260-63.

IHIMAERA, WITI (New Zealander, 1944–)
GENERAL

IHIMAERA, WITI. "Why I Write." *World Literature Written In English,* 14 (1975), 117-19.

WYNN, GRAEME. "Tradition and Change in Recent Maori Fiction: The Writing of Witi Ihimaera." *International Fiction Review,* 2 (1975), 127-31.

TOADS FOR SUPPER (1965)

Reviews
DATHORNE, O. R. *Black Orpheus,* No.20 (1966), pp. 61-62.

IKOR, ROGER (French, 1912–)
LES FILS D'AVROM

ROSE, MARILYN GADDIS. "Roger Ikor's Moral Metaphor." *French Review,* 39 (1965), 220-29.

IMMERMANN, KARL (German, 1796–1840)
THE LATE-COMERS (Die epigonen)

SAMMONS, JEFFREY L. *Six Essays On The Young German Novel,* pp. 129-39.

MÜNCHHAUSEN, EINE GESCHICHTE IN ARABESKEN (1841)

MCCLAIN, WILLIAM. "Karl Lebrecht Immermann's Portrait of a Folk-Hero in *Münchhausen,* in *Studies In German Literature Of The Nineteenth And Twentieth Centuries,* ed. Siegfried Mews, pp. 55-63.

MEYER, HERMANN. *The Poetics Of Quotation In The European Novel,* pp. 148-68.

SAMMONS, JEFFREY. *Six Essays On The Young German Novel,* pp. 139-46.

DER OBERHOF (1863)

SAMMONS, JEFFREY L. *Six Essays On The Young German Novel,* pp. 141-46.

INOUÉ, YASUSHI (Japanese, 1907–)
TEMPYŌ

ARAKI, JAMES T. "Yasushi Inoué and His 'Tempyō.' " *Books Abroad,* 44 (1970), 55-59.

IRELAND, DAVID (Australian, 1927–)

GENERAL

MITCHELL, ADRIAN. "Paradigms of Purpose: David Ireland's Fiction." *Meanjin,* 34 (1975), 189–97.

THE FLESHEATERS (1972)

Reviews

O'HEARN, D. J. "Humanising the World." *Overland,* No.56 (1973), p. 60.

IRISH, LOLA

TIME OF THE DOLPHINS (1972)

Reviews

GILBEY, DAVID. *Southerly,* 33 (1973), 85–86.

ISAKSSON, ULLA (Swedish, 1916–1963)

THE BLESSED ONES

Reviews

SPECTOR, ROBERT D. *American Scandinavian Review,* 59 (1971), 427.

ISLA (Y ROJO), JOSÉ FRANCISCO DE (Spanish, 1703–1781)

FRAY GERUNDIO DE CAMPANZAS (1758)

PALMER, JOE L. "Elements of Social Satire in Padre Isla's *Fray Gerundio De Campazas.*" *Kentucky Romance Quarterly,* 18 (1971), 195–205.

ISRAEL, CHARLES E. (Canadian, 1920–)

THE HOSTAGES (1966)

Reviews

NEW, W. H. "Clichés and Roaring Words." *Canadian Literature,* No.31 (1967), pp. 64–65.

SHADOWS ON A WALL (1965)

Reviews

HARLOW, ROBERT. "A Concoction Called Fufu." *Canadian Literature,* No.25 (1965), pp. 74–76.

ISVARAN, MANJERI (Indian, ?–1967)

GENERAL

PARAMESWARAN, UMA. "An Indo-English Minstrel: A Study of Manjeri Isvaran's Fiction." *Literature East And West,* 13 (1969), 43–67.

IU-KIAO-LI (Author Unknown)

BLACKALL, ERIC A. "Goethe and the Chinese Novel," in *The Discontinuous Tradition,* ed. P. F. Ganz, pp. 42–50.

J

JACKSON, JAMES (Canadian)

TO THE EDGE OF MORNING

DOOLEY, D. J. "Flight from Liberation." *Canadian Literature,* No.36 (1968), pp. 34–39.

JACOBSEN, JØRGEN-FRANTZ (Faroese, 1900–1938)

BARBARA

BRØNNER, HEDIN. "Jorgen-Frantz Jacobsen and *Barbara.*" *American Scandanavian Review,* 61 (1973), 39–45.

———. *Three Faroese Novelists,* pp. 25–37.

JACOBSEN, JENS PETER (Danish, 1847–1885)

NIELS LYHNE (1880)

ARESTAD, SVERRE. "J. P. Jacobsen's *Niels Lyhne,*" in *Scandanavian Studies,* ed. Carl F. Bayerschmidt and Erik J. Friis, pp. 202–12.

MADSEN, BØRGE GEDSØ. "George Brandes' Criticism of *Niels Lyhne.*" *Scandinavian Studies,* 38 (1966), 98–102.

JACOBSON, DAN (South African)

GENERAL

CRONIN, JOHN F. "Writer versus Situation: Three South African Novelists." *Studies: An Irish Quarterly Review,* 56 (1967), 78–81.

WADE, MICHAEL. "Apollo, Dionysus and Other Performers in Dan Jacobson's South African Circus." *World Literature Written In English,* 13 (1974), 39–82.

THE BEGINNERS

WADE, MICHAEL. "Apollo, Dionysus and Other Performers in Dan Jacobson's South African Circus." *World Literature Written In English,* 13 (1974), 74–79.

A DANCE IN THE SUN

WADE, MICHAEL. "Apollo, Dionysus and Other Performers in Dan Jacobson's South African Circus." *World Literature Written In English,* 13 (1974), 49–58.

THE EVIDENCE OF LOVE

WADE, MICHAEL. "Apollo, Dionysus and Other Performers in Dan Jacobson's South African Circus." *World Literature Written In English,* 13 (1974), 63–74.

THE PRICE OF DIAMONDS

WADE, MICHAEL. "Apollo, Dionysus and Other Performers in Dan Jacobson's South African Circus." *World Literature Written In English,* 13 (1974), 58–63.

THE RAPE OF TAMAR

Reviews
PINSKER, SANFORD. *Saturday Review,* 29 August 1970, p. 25.

THE TRAP

WADE, MICHAEL. "Apollo, Dionysus and Other Performers in Dan Jacobson's South African Circus." *World Literature Written In English,* 13 (1974), 40–49.

JAEGER, HENRY

THE FORTRESS

Reviews
PLANT, RICHARD. "Slump from Nowhere to Nowhere." *Saturday Review,* 18 March 1967, p. 34.

JAHNN, HANS HENNY (German, 1894–1954)

GENERAL

BROWN, RUSSELL E. "On Classifying the Setting of the Novel (Hans Henny Jahnn's *Fluss Ohne Ufer.*" *Neophilologus,* 51 (1967), 395–401.

DETSCH, RICHARD. "The Theme of the Black Race in the Works of Hans Henny Jahnn." *Mosaic,* 7, No.2 (1974), 165–87.

JENKINSON, D. E. "The Rôle of Vitalism in the Novels of Hans Henny Jahnn." *German Life And Letters,* 25 (1972), 359–68.

DIE NIEDERSCHRIFT DES GUSTAV ANIAS HORN (1949–50)

DETSCH, RICHARD. "The Theme of the Black Race in the Works of Hans Henny Jahnn." *Mosaic,* 7, No.2 (1974), 181–84.

JENKINSON, D. E. "The Rôle of Vitalism in the Novels of Hans Henny Jahnn." *German Life And Letters,* 25 (1972), 362–68.

PERRUDJA (1929)

FREEMAN, THOMAS. "The Lotus and the Tigress: Symbols of Mediation of Hans Henny Jahnn's *Perrudja.*" *Genre,* 7 (1974), 91–111.

JANES, PERCY (Canadian, 1922–)

HOUSE OF HATE (1970)

HESSE, M. G. "Vipers' Tangles: A Comparative Study of Claire Martin's *Dans Un Gant De Fer* and *La Joue Droite* and Percy

Janes' *House Of Hate.*" *Journal Of Canadian Fiction,* 3, No.2 (1974), 77–81.

JANSSON, TOVE (Finnish, 1914–)

THE SUMMER BOOK (Sommarboken, 1972)

Reviews

CAMERINI, INGRID. *Scandanavian Review,* 63, No.3 (1975), 75–76.

JAVELLANA, STEVAN

WITHOUT SEEING THE DAWN (1947)

CASPER, LEONARD. *New Writing From The Philippines,* pp. 82–85.

JEFFERIS, BARBARA (Australian, 1917–)

ONE BLACK SUMMER (1967)

Reviews

KEESING, NANCY. *Southerly,* 29 (1969), 77–78.

JENSEN, WILHELM (German, 1837–1911)

GRADIVA

HAMILTON, JAMES W. "Jensen's *Gradiva:* A Further Interpretation." *American Imago,* 30 (1973), 380–412.

JHA, UPENDRANATH (Maithili) Popularly known as Vyasaji

DU PATRA (1969)

Reviews

JHA, RAMANATH. *Indian Literature,* 13, No.3 (1970), 97–99.

JHABVALA, RUTH PRAWER (German-born Indian, 1927–)

GENERAL

AGARWAL, RAMLAL. "Forster, Jhabvala and Readers." *Journal Of Indian Writing In English,* 3, No.2 (1975), 25–27.

ASNANI, SHYAM. "Jhabvala's Novels—A Thematic Study." *Journal Of Indian Writing In English,* 2, No.1 (1974), 38–47.

HARTLEY, LOIS. "R. Prawer Jhabvala, Novelist of Urban India." *Literature East And West,* 9 (1965), 265–73.

SRINIVASA IYENGAR, K. R. *Indian Writing In English,* pp. 450–61.

WILLIAMS, HAYDN MOORE. "English Writing in Free India (1947–67)." *Twentieth Century Literature,* 16 (1970), 9–11.

———. "R. K. Narayan and R. Prawer Jhabvala: Two Interpreters of Modern India." *Literature East And West,* 16 (1972), 1136–54.

———. "Strangers in a Backward Place: Modern India in the Fiction of Ruth Prawer Jhabvala." *Journal Of Commonwealth Literature,* 6, No.1 (1971), 53–64.

———. "The Yogi and the Babbitt: Themes and Characters of the New India in the Novels of R. Prawer Jhabvala." *Twentieth Century Literature,* 15 (1969), 81–90.

WINEGARTEN, RENEE. "Ruth Prawer Jhabvala: A Jewish Passage to India." *Midstream Magazine,* 20, No.3 (1974), 72–79.

A BACKWARD PLACE (1965)

Reviews

BENNETT, CARL D. *Literature East And West,* 10 (1966), 164–67.

KARNANI, CHETAN. "Satirical Indian Novel." *Journal Of Commonwealth Literature,* No.3 (1967), pp. 132–33.

THE NATURE OF PASSION (1956)

WILLIAMS, H. MOORE. "The Yogi and the Babbitt: Themes and

Characters of the New India in the Novels of R. Prawer Jhabvala." *Twentieth Century Literature,* 15 (1969), 81–84.

A NEW DOMINION (1973)

Reviews

KAPLAN, JOHANNA. "Between Two Worlds." *Commentary,* 56, No.6 (1973), 80–84.

TRAVELERS see A NEW DOMINION

JOHANNESON, OLAF (Swedish, 1908–) pseudonym of Hannes O. G. Alfven

THE TALE OF THE BIG COMPUTER: A VISION (Sagan om den stora datamaskinen, 1966)

Reviews

SPECTOR, ROBERT D. *American Scandinavian Review,* 57 (1969), 87.

JOHNSON, COLIN

WILD CAT FALLING

Reviews

KING, ALEC. *Westerly,* 1, No.1 (1965), 70–71.

JOHNSON, EYVIND (Swedish, 1900–1976)

GENERAL

ORTON, GAVIN. "Eyvind Johnson—An Introduction." *Scandinavica,* 5 (1966), 111–23.

SJOBERG, LEIF. "Eyvind Johnson." *American Scandinavian Review,* 56 (1968), 369–78.

———. "The 1974 Nobel Prize in Literature: Eyvind Johnson and Harry Martinson." *Books Abroad,* 49 (1975), 415–18.

THE DAYS OF HIS GRACE (Hans nådes tid, 1960)

"An Interview with Eyvind Johnson." *Contemporary Literature,* 12 (1971), 301–4.

Reviews

SPECTOR, ROBERT D. *American Scandinavian Review,* 59 (1971), 312.

JOHNSON, JOSEPH

WOMB TO LET

Reviews

WEBSTER, OWEN. "Three Womb Universe." *Overland,* No.56 (1973), pp. 57–59.

JOHNSON, UWE (German, 1934–)

GENERAL

BOULBY, MARK. "Surmises on Love and Family Life in the Work of Uwe Johnson." *Seminar,* 10 (1974), 131–41.

CUNLIFFE, W. G. "Uwe Johnson's Anti-Liberalism." *Mosaic,* 5, No.3 (1972), 19–25.

DETWEILER, ROBERT. "The Achievement of Uwe Johnson." *South Atlantic Bulletin,* 33, No.4 (1968), 22–24.

FLETCHER, JOHN. "The Themes of Alienation and Mutual Incomprehension in the Novels of Uwe Johnson." *International Fiction Review,* 1 (1974), 81–87.

ANNIVERSARIES: FROM THE LIFE OF GESINE CRESSPAHL (Jahrestage, 1970–73)

BOULBY, MARK. *Uwe Johnson,* pp. 96–126.

KURZ, PAUL KONRAD. "German Lesson in New York: Uwe Johnson's Novel *Days Of The Year,*" in his *On Modern German Literature,* Vol.4: 96–108.

MILLER, LESLIE L. "Uwe Johnson's *Jahrestage:* The Choice of Alternatives." *Seminar,* 10 (1974), 50-70.

Reviews
HOWARD, RICHARD. "City Spirals." *Saturday Review,* 22 February 1975, pp. 38-40.

KARSCH, UND ANDERE PROSA (1964)

DILLER, EDWARD. "Uwe Johnson's Karsch: Language as a Reflection of the Two Germanies." *Monatshefte,* 60 (1968), 35-39.

SPECULATIONS ABOUT JACOB (Mutmassungen über Jakob, 1959)

BOULBY, MARK. *Uwe Johnson,* pp. 8-36.

COCK, MARY E. "Uwe Johnson: An Interpretation of Two Novels." *Modern Language Review,* 69 (1974), 348-53.

CUNLIFFE, W. G. "Uwe Johnson's Anti-Liberalism." *Mosaic,* 5, No.3 (1971/2), 19-23.

DETWEILER, ROBERT. " 'Speculations about Jakob': The Truth of Ambiguity." *Monatshefte,* 58 (1966), 25-32.

FRIEDRICHSMEYER, ERHARD. "Quest by Supposition: Johnson's *Mutmassungen Über Jakob.*" *Germanic Review,* 42 (1967), 215-26.

GOOD, COLIN H. "Uwe Johnson's Treatment of the Narrative in *Mutmassungen Über Jakob.*" *German Life And Letters,* 24 (1971), 358-70.

JACKIW, SHARON EDWARDS "The Manifold Difficulties of Uwe Johnson's 'Mutmassungen über Jakob.' " *Monatshefte,* 65 (1973), 126-43.

THOMAS, R. HINTON and WILFRIED VAN DER WILL. *The German Novel And The Affluent Society,* pp. 112-16.

THE THIRD BOOK ABOUT ACHIM (Das Dritte Buch Über Achim, 1961)

ABBÉ, DEREK VAN. "From Proust to Johnson: Some Notes After *Das Dritte Buch Über Achim.*" *Modern Languages,* 55 (1974), 73-79.

BOULBY, MARK. *Uwe Johnson,* pp. 38-65.

COCK, MARY E. "Uwe Johnson: An Interpretation of Two Novels." *Modern Language Review,* 69 (1974), 353-58.

THOMAS, R. HINTON and WILFRIED VAN DER WILL. *The German Novel And The Affluent Society,* pp. 116-33.

Reviews
POTOKER, EDWARD M. "The World's Two Camps." *Saturday Review,* 20 May 1967, p. 42.

SMITH, A. M. SHERIDAN. *London Magazine,* NS, 8, No.1 (1968), 87-88.

TWO VIEWS (Zwei Ansichten, 1965)

BOULBY, MARK. *Uwe Johnson,* pp. 68-93.

CUNLIFFE, W. G. "Uwe Johnson's Anti-Liberalism." *Mosaic,* 5, No.3 (1971/2), 24.

HATFIELD, HENRY. *Crisis And Continuity In Modern German Fiction,* pp. 150-65.

Reviews
HANDLIN, OSCAR. *Atlantic Monthly,* 219, No.1 (1967), 117-18.

SMITH, A. M. SHERIDAN. *London Magazine,* NS, 7, No.7 (1967), 101-3.

JOHNSTON, GEORGE (Australian)

A CARTLOAD OF CLAY

GOODWIN, A. E. "Voyage and Kaleidoscope in George Johnston's Trilogy." *Australian Literary Studies,* 6 (1973), 143-51.

CLEAN STRAW FOR NOTHING

GOODWIN, A. E. "Voyage and Kaleidoscope in George Johnston's Trilogy." *Australian Literary Studies,* 6 (1973), 143-51.

Reviews
CASTLE, EDGAR. "The Meaning of Ithacas." *Overland,* No.43 (1969-70), pp. 53-54.

WEBSTER, OWEN. "The Success and Failure of George Johnston." *Southerly,* 29 (1969), 315-17.

MY BROTHER JACK

DAY, MARTIN S. "Australian Fiction Scrutinizes National Life." *Forum,* 9, No.3 (1972), 7.

GOODWIN, A. E. "Voyage and Kaleidoscope in George Johnston's Trilogy." *Australian Literary Studies,* 6 (1973), 143-51.

THURLEY, GEOFFREY. "My Brother Jack: an Australian Masterpiece?" *Ariel: A Review Of International English Literature,* 5, No.3 (1974), 61-80.

JONES, SUZANNE HOLLY

HARRY'S CHILD

Reviews
McLAREN, JOHN. "New Novels." *Overland,* No.32 (1965), 43-44.

JOSHI, ARUN (Indian, 1939-)

THE APPRENTICE (1974)

Reviews
HEGDE, NARAYAN. *World Literature Written In English,* 14 (1975), 408-9.

THE FOREIGNER (1968)

BHATNAGAR, O. P. "Arun Joshi's *The Foreigner:* A Critique of East & West." *Journal Of Indian Writing In English,* No.2 (1973), 9-14.

JOTWANI, MOTILAL

NARANGI TRAFFIC LIGHT

Reviews
KOMAL, LAXMAN. *Indian Literature,* 18, No.2 (1975), 104-5.

JOUDRY, PATRICIA (Canadian, 1921-)

THE DWELLER ON THE THRESHOLD (1973)

Reviews
O'DONNELL, KATHLEEN. "On the Thresholds." *Journal Of Canadian Fiction,* 3, No.2 (1974), 106-7.

JOUFFROY, ALAIN

UN RÊVE PLUS LONG QUE LA NUIT (1963)

MATTHEWS, J. H. *Surrealism And The Novel,* pp. 158-73.

JÜNGER, ERNST (German, 1895-)

ON THE MARBLE CLIFFS (Auf den Marmorklippen, 1939)

STEINER, GEORGE. "The Zero at the Bone: On Ernst Jünger." *Encounter,* 35, No.1 (1970), 72-76.

JUNST—ERBAWETE SCHAFFEREY, ODER KEUSCHE LIEBES-BESCHRIEBUNG, VON DER VERLIEBIEN NIMFEN AMOENA, UND DEM LOBWURDIGEN SCHAFFER AMANDUS (Author Unknown)

WAGENER, HANS. *The German Baroque Novel,* pp. 19-21.

K

KABAK, AHARON A.
THE NARROW PATH, THE MAN OF NAZARETH

Reviews
ARNON, MIRA. *Literature East And West,* 14 (1970), 129-31.

KABALE UND LIEBE, EINE HOFBEGENBEN-HEIT VON EINEM UNGENANNTEN (Author Unknown)
HADLEY, MICHAEL. *The German Novel In 1790,* pp. 91-94.

KACHINGWE, AUBREY (Malawi, 1926-)
NO EASY TASK (1966)

Reviews
FYTTON, FRANCIS. "Delinquincy and Desperation." *London Magazine,* NS, 5, No.12 (1966), 102-3.

KAFKA, FRANZ (Czech-born Austrian, 1883-1924)
GENERAL

ANDERS, GÜNTHER. "Reflections of My Book *Kafka—Pro Und Contra.*" *Mosaic,* 3, No.4 (1970), 59-72.

AUDEN, W. H. "The I Without a Self," in *Franz Kafka: A Collection Of Criticism,* ed. Leo Hamalian, pp. 39-44.

BAHR, E. "Kafka and the Prague Spring." *Mosaic,* 3, No.4 (1970), 15-29.

BARTHES, ROLAND. "Kafka's Answer," in *Franz Kafka: A Collection Of Criticism,* ed. Leo Hamalian, pp. 140-43.

BAUMER, FRANZ. *Franz Kafka.*

BAXANDALL, LEE. "Kafka and Radical Perspective." *Mosaic,* 3, No.4 (1970), 73-79.

BECK, EVELYN TORTON. "Franz Kafka and Else Lasker-Schüler: Alienation and Exile—A Psychocultural Comparison." *Perspectives On Contemporary Literature,* 1, No.2 (1975), 31-47.

BORGES, JORGE LUIS. "Kafka and His Precursors," in *Franz Kafka: A Collection Of Criticism,* ed. Leo Hamalian, pp. 18-20.

BRIDGWATER, PATRICK. *Kafka And Nietzsche,* pp. 9-59.

BROD, MAX. "Frank Kafka." *Ariel: A Quarterly Review Of The Arts And Sciences In Israel,* No.11 (1965), pp. 12-14.

CARROUGES, MICHEL. "The Struggle Against the Father," in *Franz Kafka: A Collection Of Criticism,* ed. Leo Hamalian, pp. 27-38.

COHN, DORRIT. "Castles and Anti-Castles, or Kafka and Robbe-Grillet." *Novel,* 5 (1971), 19-31.

COLLINS, R. G. "Kafka's Special Methods of Thinking." *Mosaic,* 3, No.4 (1969/70), 43-57.

DE MALLAC, GUY. "Kafka in Russia." *Russian Review,* 31 (1972), 64-73.

EDWARDS, BRIAN F. M. "Kafka and Kierkegaard: A Reassessment." *German Life And Letters,* 20 (1967), 218-25.

ERLICH, STANISLAW. "Franz Kafka, Doctor of Laws." Trans. by I. Zaleski. *Queen's Quarterly,* 81 (1974), 576-85.

FOULKES, A. P. "Dream Pictures in Kafka's Writings." *Germanic Review,* 40 (1965), 17-30.

———. "Kafka's Cage Image." *MLN,* 82 (1967), 462-71.

FURST, LILIAN R. "Kafka and the Romantic Imagination." *Mosaic,* 3, No.4 (1970), 81-89.

GAIER, ULRICH. " 'Chorus of Lies'—On Interpreting Kafka." *German Life And Letters,* 22 (1969), 283-96.

GLASER, FREDERICK B. "The Case of Franz Kafka." *Psychoanalytic Review,* 51 (1964), 99-121.

GRAY, RONALD. "Religious Ideas," in his *Franz Kafka,* pp. 187-99.

GREENBERG, MARTIN. "Art and Dreams," in his *The Terror Of Art: Kafka And Modern Literature,* pp. 3-27.

HALL, CALVIN S. and RICHARD E. LIND. *Dreams, Life, And Literature: A Study Of Franz Kafka.*

HELLER, PETER. *Dialectics And Nihilism: Essays On Lessing, Nietzsche, Mann And Kafka,* pp. 229-306.

———. "On Not Understanding Kafka." *German Quarterly,* 47 (1974), 373-93.

KARST, ROMAN. "Franz Kafka: Word-Space-Time." *Mosaic,* 3, No.4 (1970), 1-13.

———. "The Reality of the Absurd and the Absurdity of the Real: Kafka and Gogol." *Mosaic,* 9, No.1 (1975), 67-81.

KIRSHNER, SUMNER. "Kafka's Gnostic Imagery." *Germanic Notes,* 4 (1973), 42-46.

KUNA, FRANZ. *Kafka: Literature As Corrective Punishment,* pp. 13-48.

LIEHM, A. J. "Kafka and His Communist Critics." *Partisan Review,* 42 (1975), 406-15.

KURZ, PAUL KONRAD. "Perspectives in Kafka Interpretation," in his *On Modern German Literature,* Vol.1: 30-55.

LIVERMORE, ANN LAPRAIK. "Kafka and Stendhal's *De L'Amour.*" *Revue De Littérature Comparée,* 43 (1969), 173-218.

LYONS, NATHAN. "Kafka and Poe—and Hope." *Minnesota Review,* 5 (1965), 158-68.

MAGNY, CLAUDE-EDMONDE. "The Objective Depiction of Absurdity." Trans. by Angel Flores. *Quarterly Review Of Literature,* 20 (1975), 40-56.

MAYS, JAMES. "*Pons Asinorum:* Form and Value in Beckett's Writing, with Some Comments on Kafka and de Sade." *Irish University Review,* 4 (1974), 268–82.

NICHEL-MICHOT P. "Franz Kafka and William Sansom Reconsidered." *Revue Des Langues Vivantes,* 37 (1971), 712–18.

MILES, DAVID H. "Kafka's Hapless Pilgrims and Grass's Scurrilous Dwarf: Notes on Representative Figures in the Anti-Bildungsroman." *Monatshefte,* 65 (1973), 341–50.

MUIR, EDWIN. "Franz Kafka," in his *Essays On Literature And Society,* rev. ed., pp. 120–24.

NEUMEYER, PETER F. "Franz Kafka and Friedrich Wilhelm Foerster." *Germanic Notes,* 6, No.3 (1975), 41–42.

———. "Franz Kafka and Jonathan Swift: A Symbiosis." *Dalhousie Review,* 45 (1965), 60–65.

———. "Franz Kafka and William Sansom." *Wisconsin Studies In Contemporary Literature,* 7 (1966), 76–84.

———. "Franz Kafka, Sugar Baron." *Modern Fiction Studies,* 17 (1971), 5–19.

OATES, JOYCE CAROL. "Kafka's Paradise." *Hudson Review,* 26 (1973/4), 623–46.

PLATZER, HILDEGARD. "Sex, Marriage, and Guilt: The Dilemma of Mating in Kafka." *Mosaic,* 3, No.4 (1970), 119–30.

POLITZER, H. "Kafka Returns to Czechoslovakia." *Survey: A Journal Of Soviet And East European Studies,* No.57 (1965), pp. 86–97.

PREISNER, RIO. "Franz Kafka and the Czechs." *Mosaic,* 3, No.4 (1969/70), 131–41.

RAHV, PHILIP. "An Introduction to Kafka," in his *Literature And The Sixth Sense,* pp. 183–95.

RAO, ILA. "Franz Kafka." *Triveni,* 41, No.3 (1972), 53–60.

REISS, HANS. "Kafka on the Writer's Task." *Modern Language Review,* 66 (1971), 113–24.

RHEIN, PHILLIP H. "Two Examples of Twentieth-Century Art: Giorgio di Chirico and Franz Kafka," in *Studies In German Literature Of The Nineteenth And Twentieth Centuries,* ed. Siegfried Mews, pp. 201–9.

SANDBANK, S. "Structures of Paradox in Kafka." *Modern Language Quarterly,* 28 (1967), 462–72.

STEINER, GEORGE. "K," in his *Language And Silence,* pp. 118–26.

STERN, J. P. "Franz Kafka: The Labyrinth of Guilt." *Critical Quarterly,* 7 (1965), 35–47.

STRUC, ROMAN S. "Franz Kafka in the Soviet Union: A Report." *Monatshefte,* 57 (1965), 193–97.

SUCHKOV, B. "Kafka: His Fate and Work (Part 1)." *Soviet Studies In Literature,* 2, No.2 (1966), 10–46.

———. "Kafka, His Fate and Work (Part 2)." *Soviet Studies In Literature,* 2, No.3 (1966), 58–93.

SVITAK, IVAN. "Kafka as Philosopher." *Survey: A Journal Of Soviet And East European Studies,* No.59 (1966), pp. 36–40.

TOMANEK, THOMAS J. "The Estranged Man: Kafka's Influence on Arreola." *Revue Des Langues Vivantes,* 37 (1971), 305–8.

URZIDIL, JOHANNES. "Kafka's Prague," in *Franz Kafka: A Collection Of Criticism,* ed. Leo Hamalian, pp. 21–26.

———. *There Goes Kafka.*

WEINSTEIN, ARNOLD L. *Vision And Response In Modern Fiction,* pp. 157–67.

AMERICA (Amerika, 1927)

ALBÉRÈS, R. M. and PIERRE DE BOISDEFFRE. *Kafka: The Torment Of Man,* pp. 30–32.

GRAY, RONALD. *Franz Kafka,* pp. 67–82.

GREENBERG, MARTIN. *The Terror Of Art: Kafka And Modern Literature,* pp. 92–104.

HALL, CALVIN S. and RICHARD E. LIND. *Dreams, Life, And Literature: A Study Of Franz Kafka,* pp. 63–65, 68–70.

HIBBERD, JOHN. *Kafka In Context,* pp. 50–58.

KUNA, FRANZ. *Kafka: Literature As Corrective Punishment,* pp. 64–98.

LIVERMORE, ANN LAPRAIK. "Kafka and Stendhal's *De L'Amour.*" *Revue De Littérature Comparée,* 43 (1969), 205–18.

MALMSHEIMER, RICHARD R. "Kafka's 'Nature Theatre of Oklahoma': The End of Karl Rossman's Journey to Maturity." *Modern Fiction Studies,* 13 (1967/8), 493–501.

MANN, KLAUS. "Preface to *Amerika,*" in *Franz Kafka: A Collection Of Criticism,* ed. Leo Hamalian, pp. 133–39.

ROLLESTON, JAMES. *Kafka's Narrative Theater,* pp. 18–31.

SCHLANT, ERNESTINE. "Kafka's 'Amerika': The Trial of Karl Rossmann." *Criticism,* 12 (1970), 213–25.

TAUBER, HERBERT. *Franz Kafka: An Interpretation Of His Works,* pp. 27–57.

THE CASTLE (Das Schloss, 1926)

ALBÉRÈS, R. M. and PIERRE DE BOISDEFFRE. *Kafka: The Torment Of Man,* pp. 83–89.

BECK, EVELYN TORTON. *Kafka And The Yiddish Theater: Its Impact On His Work,* pp. 194–200.

BRAYBROOKE, NEVILLE. "The Two Castles: St. Theresa and Franz Kafka." *The Month,* 42, NS (1969), 266–72.

BRIDGWATER, PATRICK. *Kafka And Nietzsche,* pp. 90–103.

FRIEDERICH, REINHARD H. "K.'s 'Bitteres Kraut' and *Exodus.*" *German Quarterly,* 48 (1975), 355–57.

GRAY, RONALD. *Franz Kafka,* pp. 140–72.

GREENBERG, MARTIN. *The Terror Of Art: Kafka And Modern Literature,* pp. 154–220.

GRIMES, MARGARET. "Kafka's Use of Cue-Names: Its Importance for an Interpretation of *The Castle.*" *Centennial Review,* 18 (1974), 221–30.

GUERARD, ALBERT J. "The Illuminating Distortion." *Novel,* 5 (1972), 105–06.

HALL, CALVIN S. and RICHARD E. LIND. *Dreams, Life, And Literature: A Study Of Franz Kafka,* pp. 57–63, 68–70.

HELLER, ERICH. *Franz Kafka,* pp. 98–130.

HIBBERD, JOHN. *Kafka In Context,* pp. 120–29.

KUDSZUS, WINFRIED. "Between Past and Future: Kafka's Later Novels." *Mosaic,* 3, No.4 (1970), 107–18.

KUNA, FRANZ. *Kafka: Literature As Corrective Punishment,* pp. 136–82.

LIVERMORE, ANN LAPRAIK. "Kafka and Stendhal's *De L'Amour.*" *Revue De Littérature Comparée,* 43 (1969), 173–95.

MAGNY, CLAUDE-EDMONDE. "The Objective Depiction of Absurdity." Trans. by Angel Flores. *Quarterly Review Of Literature,* 20 (1975), 40–56.

OATES, JOYCE CAROL. "Kafka's Paradise." *Hudson Review,* 26 (1973/74), 639–46.

POLITZER, HEINZ. "The Alienated Self—A Key to Franz Kafka's *Castle.?*" *Michigan Quarterly Review,* 14 (1975), 398–414.

ROLLESTON, JAMES. *Kafka's Narrative Theater,* pp. 112–29.

SANDBANK, S. "Action as Self-Mirror: On Kafka's Plots." *Modern Fiction Studies,* 17 (1971), 21–29.

SCOTT, NATHAN A. *Craters Of The Spirit,* pp. 77–86.

SEBALD, W. G. "The Undiscover'd Country: The Death Motif in Kafka's *Castle.*" *Journal Of European Studies,* 2 (1972), 22–34.

SHEPPARD, RICHARD. *On Kafka's Castle: A Study.*

SOKEL, WALTER H. *Franz Kafka,* pp. 39–44.

STEINBERG, ERWIN R. "K. of *The Castle:* Ostensible Land-

Surveyor." *College English,* 27 (1965), 185-89; rpt. in *Franz Kafka: A Collection Of Criticism,* ed. Leo Hamalian, pp. 126-32.

SUCHKOV, B. "Kafka, His Fate and Work (Part 2)." *Soviet Studies In Literature,* 2, No.3 (1966), 72-78.

TATE, ELEANOR. "Kafka's *The Castle:* Another Dickens Novel?" *Southern Review: Literary And Interdisciplinary Essays,* 7 (1974), 157-68.

TAUBER, HERBERT. *Franz Kafka: An Interpretation Of His Works,* pp. 131-85.

THORLBY, ANTHONY. *Kafka: A Study,* pp. 68-83.

Twentieth Century Interpretations Of< The Castle>: A Collection Of Critical Essays. Ed. Peter F. Neumeyer.

WEST, REBECCA. "Kafka and the Mystery of Bureaucracy," in *Franz Kafka: A Collection Of Criticism,* ed. Leo Hamalian, pp. 109-17.

WINKELMAN, JOHN. "An Interpretation of Kafka's 'Das Schloss.' " *Monatshefte,* 64 (1972), 115-31.

LOST WITHOUT TRACE

SUCHKOV, B. "Kafka, His Fate and Work (Part 2)." *Soviet Studies In Literature,* 2, No.3 (1966), 58-93.

METAMORPHOSIS (Der Verwandlung, 1915)

ALBÉRÈS, R. M. AND PIERRE DE BOISDEFFRE. *Kafka: The Torment Of Man,* pp. 50-52.

ANGRESS, R. K. "Kafka and Sacher-Masoch: A Note on *The Metamorphosis.*" *MLN,* 85 (1970), 745-46.

BECK, EVELYN TORTON. *Kafka And The Yiddish Theater: Its Impact On His Work,* pp. 135-46.

CORNGOLD, STANLEY. *The Commentators' Despair: The Interpretation Of Kafka's <Metamorphosis.>*

———. "Kafka's *Die Verwandlung:* Metamorphosis of the Metaphor." *Mosaic,* 3, No.4 (1970), 91-106.

GILMAN, SANDER L. "A View of Kafka's Treatment of Actuality in *Die Verwandlung.*" *Germanic Notes,* 2 (1971), 26-30.

GRAY, RONALD. *Franz Kafka,* pp. 83-92.

GREENBERG, MARTIN. "Gregor Samsa and Modern Spirituality," in *Franz Kafka: A Collection Of Criticism,* ed. Leo Hamalian, pp. 50-64.

———. "Kafka's 'Metamorphosis' and Modern Spirituality." *Triquarterly,* No.6 (1966), pp. 5-20.

———. *The Terror Of Art: Kafka And Modern Literature,* pp. 69-91.

HIBBERD, JOHN. *Kafka In Context,* pp. 47-50.

KUNA, F. M. "Art as Direct Vision: Kafka and Sacher-Masoch." *Journal Of European Studies,* 2 (1972), 237-46.

———. *Kafka: Literature As Corrective Punishment,* pp. 49-63.

LANDSBERG, PAUL L. "Kafka and *The Metamorphosis.*" Trans. by Caroline Muhlenberg. *Quarterly Review Of Literature,* 20 (1975), 57-65.

MACANDREW, M. ELIZABETH. "A Splacknuck and a Dung-Beetle: Realism and Probability in Swift and Kafka." *College English,* 31 (1970), 385-91.

MOSS, LEONARD. "A Key to the Door Image in 'The Metamorphosis.' " *Modern Fiction Studies,* 17 (1971), 37-42.

PEARCE, RICHARD. *Stages Of The Clown,* pp. 19-25.

ROLLESTON, JAMES. *Kafka's Narrative Theater,* pp. 52-68.

SOKEL, WALTER H. *Franz Kafka,* pp. 16-25.

SPARKS, KIMBERLY. "Kafka's *Metamorphosis:* On Banishing the Lodgers." *Journal Of European Studies,* 3 (1973), 230-40.

SPRINGER, MARY DOYLE. *Forms Of The Modern Novella,* pp. 105-09.

TAUBER, HERBERT. *Franz Kafka: An Interpretation Of His Works,* pp. 18-26.

TAYLOR, ALEXANDER. "The Waking: The Theme of Kafka's *Metamorphosis.*" *Studies In Short Fiction,* 2 (1965), 337-42.

THORLBY, ANTHONY. *Kafka: A Study,* pp. 34-40.

WITT, MARY ANN. "Confinement in *Die Verwandlung* and *Les Séquestrés D'Altona.*" *Comparative Literature,* 23 (1971), 32-44.

WOLKENFELD, SUZANNE. "Christian Symbolism in Kafka's 'The Metamorphosis.' " *Studies In Short Fiction,* 10 (1973), 205-07.

THE TRIAL (Der Prozess, 1925)

ALBÉRÈS, R. M. and PIERRE DE BOISDEFFRE. *Kafka: The Torment Of Man,* pp. 83-89.

BECK, EVELYN TORTON. *Kafka And The Yiddish Theater: Its Impact On His Work,* pp. 154-71.

BORN, JÜRGEN. "Kafka's Parable *Before The Law:* Reflections Towards A Positive Interpretation." *Mosaic,* No.4 (1970), 153-62.

BRIDGWATER, PATRICK. *Kafka And Nietzsche,* pp. 67-90.

BRYANT, JERRY H. "The Delusion of Hope: Franz Kafka's *The Trial.*" *Symposium,* 23 (1969), 116-20.

CHURCH, MARGARET. "Dostoevsky's 'Crime and Punishment' and Kafka's 'The Trial.' " *Literature And Psychology,* 19, No.3-4, (1969), 47-55.

COLLINS, R. G. "Kafka's Special Methods of Thinking." *Mosaic,* 3, No.4 (1970), 43-57.

DILLER, EDWARD. " 'Heteronomy' Versus 'Autonomy': A Retrial of *The Trial* by Franz Kafka." *College Language Association Journal,* 12 (1969), 214-22.

———. " 'Theonomous' Homiletics *Vor Dem Gesetz:* Franz Kafka and Paul Tillich." *Revue Des Langues Vivantes,* 36 (1970), 289-94.

FEUERLICHT, IGNACE. "Kafka's Chaplain." *German Quarterly,* 39 (1966), 208-20.

———. "Kafka's Josef K.—A Man with Qualities." *Seminar,* 3 (1967), 103-16.

———. "Omissions and Contradictions in Kafka's *Trial.*" *German Quarterly,* 40 (1967), 339-49.

FICKERT, KURT J. "The Window Metaphor in Kafka's 'Trial.' " *Monatshefte,* 58 (1966), 345-52.

GRAY, RONALD. *Franz Kafka,* pp. 103-25.

GREENBERG, MARTIN. *The Terror Of Art: Kafka And Modern Literature,* pp. 113-53.

GROSSVOGEL, DAVID I. *Limits Of The Novel,* pp. 160-88.

HALL, CALVIN S. and RICHARD E. LIND. *Dreams, Life, And Literature: A Study Of Franz Kafka,* pp. 65-66, 68-70.

HANDLER, GARY. "A Note on the Structure of Kafka's *Der Prozess.*" *MLN,* 84 (1969), 798-99.

HELLER, ERICH. *Franz Kafka,* pp. 71-97.

HIBBERD, JOHN. *Kafka In Context,* pp. 65-74.

JAFFE, ADRIAN. *The Process Of Kafka's <Trial.>*

KAVANAGH, THOMAS. "Kafka's *The Trial:* The Semiotics of the Absurd." *Novel,* 5 (1972), 242-53.

KUDSZUS, WINFRIED. "Between Past and Future: Kafka's Later Novels." *Mosaic,* 3, No.4 (1970), 107-18.

KUEPPER, KARL J. "Gesture and Posture as Elemental Symbolism in Kafka's *The Trial.*" *Mosaic,* 3, No.4 (1970), 143-52.

KUHN, IRA. "The Metamorphosis of *The Trial.*" *Symposium,* 26 (1972), 226-41.

KUNA, FRANZ. *Kafka: Literature As Corrective Punishment,* pp. 99-135.

LIVERMORE, ANN LAPRAIK. "Kafka and Stendhal's *De L'Amour.*" *Revue De Littérature Comparée,* 43 (1969), 195–205.

MARSON, ERIC. "Justice and the Obsessed Character in 'Michael Kohlhaas,' *Der Prozess* and *L'Etranger.*" *Seminar,* 2, No.2 (1966), 25–29.

MAYS, JAMES. "*Pons Asinorum:* Form and Value in Beckett's Writing, with Some Comments on Kafka and de Sade." *Irish University Review,* 4 (1974), 272–75.

MELLEN, JOAN. "Joseph K. and the Law." *Texas Studies In Literature And Language,* 12 (1970), 295–302.

PASLEY, MALCOLM. "Two Literary Sources of Kafka's *Der Prozess.*" *Forum For Modern Language Studies,* 3 (1967), 142–47.

PEARCE, RICHARD. *Stages Of The Clown,* pp. 38–46.

PONDROM, CYRENA NORMAN. "Kafka and Phenomenology: Josef K.'s Search for Information." *Wisconsin Studies In Contemporary Literature,* 8 (1967), 78–95.

PURDY, STROTHER B. "Religion and Death in Kafka's *Der Prozess.*" *Papers On Language And Literature,* 5 (1969), 170–82.

––––––. "A Talmudic Analogy to Kafka's Parable *Vor Dem Gesetz.*" *Papers On Language And Literature,* 4 (1968), 420–27.

RAHV, PHILIP. "The Death of Ivan Ilyich and Joseph K.," in his *Literature And The Sixth Sense,* pp. 38–54.

ROLLESTON, JAMES. *Kafka's Narrative Theater,* pp. 69–87.

ROSS, STEPHEN D. *Literature & Philosophy,* pp. 109–36.

SELTZER, ALVIN J. *Chaos In The Novel: The Novel In Chaos,* pp. 141–52.

SINGER, CARL S. "The Examined Life," in *Approaches To The Twentieth-Century Novel,* ed. John Unterecker, pp. 182–217.

SOKEL, WALTER H. *Franz Kafka,* pp. 27–36.

SPIRO, SOLOMON J. "Verdict—Guilty! A Study of *The Trial.*" *Twentieth Century Literature,* 17 (1971), 169–79.

STELZMANN, RAINULF A. "Kafka's *The Trial* and Hesse's *Steppenwolf:* Two Views of Reality and Transcendence." *Xavier University Studies,* 5 (1966), 165–72.

STERN, J. P. "Franz Kafka: The Labyrinth of Guilt." *Critical Quarterly,* 7 (1965), 42–46.

SUCHKOV, B. "Kafka, His Fate and Work (Part 2)." *Soviet Studies In Literature,* 2, No.3 (1966), 63–72.

TAUBER, HERBERT. *Franz Kafka: An Interpretation Of His Works,* pp. 77–120.

THORLBY, ANTHONY. *Kafka: A Study,* pp. 53–68.

USMIANI, RENATE. "Twentieth-Century Man, the Guilt-Ridden Animal." *Mosaic,* 3, No.4 (1970), 163–78.

WEBSTER, PETER DOW. " 'Dies Irae' in the Unconscious, or the Significance of Franz Kafka," in *Franz Kafka: A Collection Of Criticism,* ed. Leo Hamalian, pp. 118–25.

WEST, REBECCA. "Kafka and the Mystery of Bureaucracy," in *Franz Kafka: A Collection of Criticism,* ed. Leo Hamalian, pp. 109–17.

WILDMAN, EUGENE. "The Signal in the Flames: Ordeal as Game." *Triquarterly,* No.11 (1968), pp. 145–62.

ZIOLKOWSKI, THEODORE. *Dimensions Of The Modern Novel,* pp. 37–67.

KAHANOVICH, Pinkhas see DER NISTER

KAMIL, 'ADIL (Egyptian, 1916–)
MILLIM AL-AKBAR

KILPATRICK, HILARY. *The Modern Egyptian Novel,* pp. 60–65, 209–11.

KANE, CHEIKH HAMIDOU (Senegalese, 1928–)
AMBIGUOUS ADVENTURE (L'Aventure ambiguë, 1962)

BRENCH, A. C. *The Novelists' Inheritance In French Africa,* pp. 99–109.

CALIN, WILLIAM. "Between Two Worlds: The Quest for Death and Life in Cheikh Hamidou Kane's *L'Aventure Ambiguë.*" *Kentucky Romance Quarterly,* 19 (1972), 183–97.

CARTEY, WILFRED. *Whispers From A Continent,* pp. 9–13.

GLEASON, JUDITH ILLSLEY. *This Africa,* pp. 112–14.

GORE, JEANNE-LYDIC. "The Solitude of Cheikh Kane: Solitude as the Theme of 'Aventure Ambiguë' by Cheikh Hamidou Kane," in *African Literature And The Universities,* ed. Gerald Moore, pp. 27–40.

MAKOUTA-MBOUKOU, J. P. *Black African Literature,* pp. 77–84.

MOORE, GERALD. "The Debate on Existence in African Literature." *Présence Africaine,* No.81 (1972), pp. 18–25.

KANGRO, BERNARD (Estonian, 1910–)
GENERAL

LEHISTE, ILSE. "Three Estonian Writers and the Experience of Exile." *Lituanus,* 18, No.1 (1972), 23–27.

KANIUK, YORAM (Israeli, ca. 1930–)
ADAM RESURRECTED

Reviews
FISCH, HAROLD. "Unique and Universal." *Commentary,* 54, No.2 (1972), 75.

MILCH, ROBERT J. *Saturday Review,* 14 August 1971, p. 28.

HIMMO: KING OF JERUSALEM

Reviews
BELLMAN, SAMUEL I. "Macabre Union." *Saturday Review,* 15 February 1969, p. 45.

THE STORY OF BIG AUNT SHLOMZION (1975)

Reviews
FEINBERG, ANAT. *Modern Hebrew Literature,* 1, No.3-4 (1975), 73–75.

KANSUKE, NAKA
THE SILVER SPOON (Gin no saji)

Reviews
MORITA, JAMES R. *Literature East And West,* 19 (1975), 261–62.

KANT, HERMANN (German, 1926–)
DIE AULA (1965)

GERBER, MARGY. "Confrontations with Reality in Hermann Kant's *Die Aula.*" *Monatshefte,* 67 (1975), 173–84.

LANGENBRUCH, THEODOR. *Dialectical Humor In Hermann Kant's Novel 'Die Aula.'*

VAN ABBÉ, DEREK. "Autobiography of an Extrovert Generation." *German Life And Letters,* 26 (1972), 50–58.

KAO YUN-LAN (Chinese)

ANNALS OF A PROVINCIAL TOWN

HUANG, JOE C. *Heroes And Villains In Communist China*, pp. 58-73.

KARINTHY, FERENC

GENERAL

MOREAU, JEAN-LUC. "Strangers in Confrontation in the Work of Ferenc Karinthy." Trans. Wendell E. McClendon. *Books Abroad*, 47 (1973), 260-65.

KASACK, HERMANN (German, 1896-1966)

GENERAL

BATTS, MICHAEL. "The Shadow-Line: The Grenze-Motif in the Works of Gaiser, Kasack and Nossack." *Humanities Association Bulletin*, 22, No.3 (1971), 44-46.

SCHUTZ, H. "The Theme of Anonimity in the Work of Hermann Kasack." *Revue Des Langues Vivantes*, 37 (1971), 400-13.

FÄLSCHUNGEN

REINHARDT, GEORGE W. "The Ordeal of Art: Hermann Kasack's 'Falschungen.' " *Studies In Short Fiction*, 9 (1972), 365-72.

DAS GROSSE NETZ (1952)

SCHÜTZ, HERBERT. *Hermann Kasack: The Role Of The Critical Intellect In The Creative Writer's Work.*

DIE STADT HINTER DEM STROM (1947)

GUTMANN, HELMUT. "A Clash of Symbols: Historical and Universal Dimensions in *Die Stadt Hinter Der Strom.*" *Germanic Review*, 46 (1971), 182-97.

SCHUELER, H. J. "Initiatory Patterns and Symbols in Alfred Döblin's *Manas* and Hermann Kasacks's *Die Stadt Hinter Dem Strom.*" *German Life And Letters*, 24 (1971), 182-92.

SCHÜTZ, HERBERT. *Hermann Kasack: The Role Of The Critical Intellect In The Creative Writer's Work.*

KATEV, VALENTIN PETROVICH (Russian, 1897-)

GENERAL

RUSSELL, R. "The Problem of Self-Expression in the Later Works of Valentin Katev." *Forum For Modern Language Studies*, 11 (1975), 366-79.

THE HOLY WELL (Svyatoi kolodets, 1966)

Reviews
CARDEN, PATRICIA. "A Surviving Russian Modernist." *Novel*, 4 (1971), 273-74.

KATAI, TAYAMA

GENERAL

RICHTER, FREDERICK. "Tayama Katai and Two Narrative Modes of Japanese Literary Naturalism." *Literature East And West*, 15 (1971), 773-90.

JUEMON NO SAIGO

RICHTER, FREDERICK. "Tayama Katai and Two Narrative Modes of Japanese Literary Naturalism." *Literature East And West*, 15 (1971), 774-80.

KATILISKIS, ALBINAS MARIUS

GENERAL

ŠILBAJORIS, RIMVYDAS. *Perfection Of Exile*, pp. 252-70.

IŠEJUSIEMS NEGRIŽTI

ŠILBAJORIS, RIMVYDAS. *Perfection Of Exile*, pp. 267-70.

MIŠKAIS ATEINA RUDUO

ŠILBAJORIS, RIMVYDAS. *Perfection Of Exile*, pp. 262-67.

UŽUOVEJA

ŠILBAJORIS, RIMVYDAS. *Perfection Of Exile*, pp. 259-62.

KAVERIN, VENIAMIN K. (Russian, 1902-)

GENERAL

OULANOFF, HONGOR. "V. Kaverin's Novels of Development and Adventure." *Canadian Slavic Studies*, 2 (1968), 464-85.

THE UNKNOWN ARTIST (Xudožnik Neizvesten, 1931)

OULANOFF, HONGOR. "Kaverin's *Xudožnik Neizvesten:* Structure and Motivation." *Slavic And East European Journal*, 10 (1966), 389-99.

KAWABATA YASUNARI (Japanese, 1899-1972)

GENERAL

ARAKI, JAMES T. "Kawabata: Achievements of the Novel Laureate." *Books Abroad*, 43 (1969), 319-23.

BOARDMAN, GWENN, R. "Kawabata Yasunari: A Critical Introduction." *Journal Of Modern Literature*, 2 (1971), 86-104.

HIBBERT, HOWARD. "Tradition and Trauma in the Contemporary Japanese Novel." *Daedalus*, 95 (1966), 936-40.

MATHY, FRANCIS. "Kawabata Yasunari: Bridge-Builder to the West." *Monumenta Nipponica*, 24 (1969), 211-17.

MORRIS, IVAN. "Kawabata and the Japanese Tradition." *London Magazine*, NS, 9, No.2 (1969), 58-63.

HOUSE OF THE SLEEPING BEAUTIES (Nemureru bijo, 1961)

KIMBALL, ARTHUR G. *Crisis In Identity And Contemporary Japanese Novels*, pp. 94-109.

———— . "Last Extremity: Kawabata's *House Of The Sleeping Beauties.*" *Critique*, 13, No.1 (1970), 19-30.

SCHLIEMAN, DOROTHY S. "Yasunari Kawabata's 'Narrow Bridge of Art.' " *Literature East And West*, 15 (1971), 899-903.

Reviews
BAYES, RONALD H. *Arizona Quarterly*, 27 (1971), 287-88.

FITZSIMMONS, THOMAS R. *Saturday Review*, 14 June 1969, pp. 34-35.

THE LAKE (Mizuumi, 1954)

Reviews
SWANN, THOMAS E. *Literature East And West*, 18 (1974), 383-84.

THE MASTER OF GO (Meijin, 1954)

IWAMOTO, YOSHIO and DICK WAGENAAR. "The Last Sad Sigh: Time and Kawabata's The Master of Go." *Literature East And West*, 18 (1974), 330-45.

SNOW COUNTRY (Yukigumi, 1935-48)

ARAKI, JAMES T. "Kawabata and His *Snow Country.*" *Centennial Review*, 13 (1969), 331-49.

BOARDMAN, GWENN R. "Kawabata Yasunari: Snow in the Mirror." *Critique*, 11, No.2 (1969), 5-15.

HIBBERT, HOWARD. "Tradition and Trauma in the Contemporary Japanese Novel." *Daedalus,* 95 (1966), 936-40.

LIMAN, ANTHONY. "Kawabata's Lyrical Mode in *Snow Country.*" *Monumenta Nipponica,* 26 (1971), 267-85.

MIYOSHI, MASAO. *Accomplices Of Silence,* pp. 102-12.

SCHLIEMAN, DOROTHY S. "Yasunari Kawabata's 'Narrow Bridge of Art.' " *Literature East And West,* 15, (1971), 891-96.

TSURUTA, KINYA. "The Flow-Dynamics in Kawabata Yasunari's *Snow Country.*" *Monumenta Nipponica,* 26 (1971), 253-65.

SOUND OF THE MOUNTAIN (Yama no Oto, 1954)

BOARDMAN, GWENN R. "Kawabata Yasunari: A Critical Introduction." *Journal Of Modern Literature,* 2 (1971), 100-3.

MIYOSHI, MASAO. *Accomplices Of Silence,* pp. 112-20.

Reviews
HIBBERTT, HOWARD. *Saturday Review,* 6 June 1970, pp. 38-39.

A THOUSAND CRANES (Sembazuru, 1952)

HARRINGTON, DAVID V. "The Quality of Feeling in Kawabata's *Thousand Cranes.*" *Bucknell Review,* 18, No.1 (1970), 81-91.

SCHLIEMAN, DOROTHY S. "Yasunari Kawabata's 'Narrow Bridge of Art.' " *Literature East And West,* 15, (1971), 896-99.

KAYIRA, LEGSON

THE LOOMING SHADOW

Reviews
MOORE, GERALD. "Rubadiri & Kayira." *African Literature Today,* No.2 (1969), pp. 51-52.

KAZANTZAKIS, NIKOS (Greek, 1883-1957)

GENERAL

ALDRIDGE, A. OWEN. "The Modern Spirit: Kazantzakis and Some of His Contemporaries." *Journal Of Modern Literature,* 2 (1971/2), 303-13.

BIEN, PETER. *Kazantzakis And The Linguistic Revolution In Greek Literature,* pp. 240-61.

———. "Kazantzakis' Nietzchianism." *Journal Of Modern Literature,* 2 (1971/2), 245-66.

BLENKINSOPP, JOSEPH. "My Entire Soul Is a Cry: The Religious Passion of Nikos Kazantzakis." *Commonweal,* 93 (1971), 514-18.

BLOCH, ADÈLE. "The Dual Masks of Nikos Kazantzakis." *Journal Of Modern Literature,* 2 (1971/2), 189-98.

FALCONIO, DONALD. "Critics of Kazantzakis: Selected Checklist of Writings in English." *Journal Of Modern Literature,* 2 (1971/2), 314-26.

FRIAR, KIMON. "Nikos Kazantzakis in the United States." *Literary Review,* 18 (1975), 381-97.

GREEN, ROGER. "Kazantzakis in Iraklion." *Cornhill,* 176, No.1053 (1967), 189-216.

POULAKIDAS, ANDREAS K. "Dostoevsky, Kazantzakis' Unacknowledged Mentor." *Comparative Literature,* 21 (1969), 307-18.

———. "Kazantzakis and Bergson: Metaphysic Aestheticians." *Journal Of Modern Literature,* 2 (1971/2), 267-83.

———. "Kazantzakis' Recurrent Victim: Woman." *Southern Humanities Review,* 6 (1972), 177-89.

RAIZIS, M. BYRON. "Nikos Kazantzakis and Chaucer." *Comparative Literature Studies,* 6 (1969), 141-47.

RICHARDS, LEWIS A. "Christianity in the Novels of Kazantzakis." *Western Humanities Review,* 21 (1967), 49-55.

SAVVAS, MINAS. "Kazantzakis and Marxism." *Journal Of Modern Literature,* 2 (1971/2), 284-92.

STAVROU, C. N. "The Limits of the Possible: Nikos Kazantzakis's Arduous Odyssey." *Southwest Review,* 56 (1972), 54-65.

WILSON, COLIN. "The Greatness of Nikos Kazantzakis." *Minnesota Review,* 8 (1968), 159-80.

CAPTAIN MICHAELIS see FREEDOM OR DEATH

THE FRATRICIDES (I adherfofadhes, 1963)

RAIZIS, M. BYRON. "Nikos Kazantzakis and Chaucer." *Comparative Literature Studies,* 6 (1969), 141-47.

Reviews
BIEN, PETER. "Freedom to Walk on the Fire." *Saturday Review,* 6 February 1965, p. 37.

SCOTT-KILVERT, IAN. *London Magazine,* NS, 8, No.1 (1968), 84-86.

FREEDOM OR DEATH (O Kapetan Mihalis, 1953)

LEVITT, MORTON P. "The Cretan Glance: The World and Art of Nikos Kazantzakis." *Journal Of Modern Literature,* 2 (1971/2), 163-88.

POULAKIDAS, ANDREAS K. "Kazantzakis and Bergson: Metaphysic Aestheticians." *Journal Of Modern Literature,* 2 (1971/2), 267-83.

THE GREEK PASSION (O Hristos xanastavronete, 1954)

RAIZIS, M. BYRON. "Symbolism and Meaning in Kazantzakis' *The Greek Passion.*" *Ball State University Forum,* 11, No.3 (1970), 57-66.

THE LAST TEMPTATION OF CHRIST (O telefteos pirasmos, 1955)

BLOCH, ADÈLE. "Kazantzakis and the Image of Christ." *Literature And Psychology,* 15 (1965), 2-11.

CHILSON, RICHARD W. "The Christ of Nikos Kazantzakis." *Thought,* 47 (1972), 69-89.

LEVITT, MORTON P. "The Modernist Kazantzakis and *The Last Temptation Of Christ.*" *Mosaic,* 6 No.2 (1973), 103-24.

REPORT TO GRECO (Ana fora son Greko, 1961)

Reviews
FRIAR, KIMON. "The Kazantzakis Report." *Saturday Review,* 14 August 1965, p. 34.

McGUINNESS, FRANK. *London Magazine,* NS, 5, No.12 (1966), 97-98.

ZORBA THE GREEK (Vios kai politia toy Alexi Zorba, 1946)

BIEN, PETER. "The Mellowed Nationalism of Kazantzakis' 'Zorba the Greek.' " *Review Of National Literatures,* 5, No.2 (1974), 113-36.

———. *Nikos Kazantzakis,* pp. 38-40.

———. "*Zorba The Greek,* Nietzsche, and the Perennial Greek Predicament." *Antioch Review,* 25 (1965), 147-63.

MERRILL, REED B. "*Zorba The Greek* and Nietzschean Nihilism." *Mosaic,* 8, No.2 (1975), 99-113.

POULAKIDAS, ANDREAS K. "Kazantzakis' *Zorba The Greek* and Nietzsche's *Thus Spake Zarathustra.*" *Philological Quarterly,* 49 (1970), 234-44.

KELLER, GOTTFRIED (Swiss, 1819-1890)

GENERAL

LECKIE, R. WILLIAM. "Gottfried Keller's *Das Sinngedicht* as Novella Cycle." *Germanic Review,* 40 (1965), 96-115.

RADANDT, FRIEDHELM. "Transitional Time in Keller's *Züricher Novellen.*" *PMLA,* 89 (1974), 77–84.

SHAW, MICHAEL. "The Mirror and Its Uses: A Study of a Pattern in Gottfried Keller's Prose." *Symposium,* 22 (1968), 358–83.

DIETEGEN

LINDSAY, J. M. *Gottfried Keller: Life And Works,* pp. 165–68.

DIE DREI GERECHTEN KAMMACHER

ELLIS, JOHN M. *Narration In The German Novelle,* pp. 136–54.

LINDSAY, J. M. *Gottfried Keller: Life And Works,* pp. 154–57.

THOMAS, BARRY G. "Paradise Lost: The Search for Order in Three Tales by Gottfried Keller." *Germanic Review,* 46 (1971), 67–71.

DAS FÄHNLEIN DER SIEBEN AUFRECHTEN

LINDSAY, J. M. *Gottfried Keller: Life And Works,* pp. 201–5.

FRAU REGEL AMRAIN UND IHR JUNGSTER

LINDSAY, J. M. *Gottfried Keller: Life And Works,* pp. 151–54.

GREEN HENRY (Der Grüne Heinrich, 1880)

LINDSAY, J. M. *Gottfried Keller: Life And Works,* pp. 109–43.

SHAW, MICHAEL. "The Mirror and Its Uses: A Study of a Pattern in Gottfried Keller's Prose." *Symposium,* 22 (1968), 375–78.

STOPP, FREDERICK. "Keller's *Der Grüne Heinrich:* the Pattern of the Labyrinth," in *The Discontinuous Tradition,* ed. P. F. Ganz, pp. 129–45.

TEMMER, MARK J. "Jean-Jacques Rousseau's *Confessions* and Gottfried Keller's *Der Grüne Heinrich.*" *Revue De Littérature Comparée,* 44 (1970), 155–83.

HADLAUB

LINDSAY, J. M. *Gottfried Keller: Life And Works,* pp. 191–93.

KLEIDER MACHEN LEUTE

LINDSAY, J. M. *Gottfried Keller: Life And Works,* pp. 159–61.

SHAW, MICHAEL. "The Mirror and Its Uses: A Study of a Pattern in Gottfried Keller's Prose." *Symposium,* 22 (1968), 363–69.

DER LANDVOGT VON GREIFENSEE

LINDSAY, J. M. *Gottfried Keller: Life And Works,* pp. 196–201.

MARTIN SALANDER (1886)

LINDSAY, J. M. *Gottfried Keller: Life And Works,* pp. 229–39.

RITCHIE, J. M. "Realism in Germany, From the Death of Goethe," in *The Age Of Realism,* ed. F. W. J. Hemmings, pp. 254–56.

DIE MISSBRAUCHTEN LIEBESBRIEFE

LOB, LADISLAUS. " 'Die Missbrauchten Liebesbriefe': A Story of Human Vocation." *German Life And Letters,* 20 (1966), 13–24.

DER NARR AUF MANEGG

LINDSAY, J. M. *Gottfried Keller: Life And Works,* pp. 193–96.

PANKRAZ DER SCHMOLLER

LINDSAY, J. M. *Gottfried Keller: Life And Works,* pp. 145–48.

SHAW, MICHAEL. "The Mirror and Its Uses: A Study of a Pattern in Gottfried Keller's Prose." *Symposium,* 22 (1968), 358–63.

DER SCHMIED SEINES GLUCKES

THOMAS, BARRY G. "Paradise Lost: The Search for Order in Three Tales by Gottfried Keller." *Germanic Review,* 46 (1971), 65–67.

DAS SINNGEDICHT (1881)

LECKIE, R. WILLIAM. "Gottfried Keller's *Das Sinngedicht* as a Novella Cycle." *Germanic Review,* 40 (1965), 96–115.

LINDSAY, J. M. *Gottfried Keller: Life And Works,* pp. 211–28.

REICHERT, HERBERT W. "Symbolism in Gottfried Keller's *Sinngedicht,*" in *Studies In German Literature Of The Nineteenth And Twentieth Centuries,* ed. Siegfried Mews, pp. 111–25.

SPIEGEL DAS KATZCHEN

LINDSAY, J. M. *Gottfried Keller: Life And Works,* pp. 157–59.

URSULA

LINDSAY, J. M. *Gottfried Keller: Life And Works,* pp. 205–10.

DAS VERLORENE LACHEN

LINDSAY, J. M. *Gottfried Keller: Life And Works,* pp. 168–71.

A VILLAGE ROMEO AND JULIET (Romeo und Julia auf dem Dorfe, 1914)

COOKE, A. T. "Gottfried Keller's 'Romeo und Julia auf dem Dorfe.' " *German Life And Letters,* 24 (1971), 235–43.

LINDSAY, J. M. *Gottfried Keller: Life And Works,* pp. 148–51.

PUKNAT, E. M. and S. B. "Edith Wharton and Gottfried Keller." *Comparative Literature,* 21 (1969), 245–54.

RITCHIE, J. M. "Realism in Germany, From the Death of Goethe," in *The Age Of Realism,* Ed. F. W. J. Hemmings, pp. 239–41.

THOMAS, BARRY G. "Paradise Lost: The Search for Order in Three Tales by Gottfried Keller." *Germanic Review,* 46 (1971), 71–76.

THOMAS, LIONEL. "An Approach to Keller's *Romeo Und Julia Auf Dem Dorfe.*" *Modern Languages,* 54 (1973), 131–38.

TUCKER, HARRY. "Post-Traumatic Psychosis in *Romeo Und Julia Auf Dem Dorfe.*" *German Life And Letters,* 24 (1971), 234–43.

KELLNER, GEORG CHRISTOPH (German, ?–1809)

FAMILIENGESCHICHTE DER ROSENBUSCHE, AUS AUTHENTISCHEN QUELLEN

HADLEY, MICHAEL. *The German Novel In 1790,* pp. 84–88.

KLINGSTEIN

HADLEY, MICHAEL. *The German Novel In 1790,* pp. 218–23.

MOLLY AND URANIA

HADLEY, MICHAEL. *The German Novel In 1790,* pp. 89–91.

KEMAL, YASHAR (Turkish, 1923–)

THE WIND FROM THE PLAIN (Ortadirek, 1960)

Reviews

WINDER, R. B. *Literature East And West,* 15 (1971), 173–75.

KEMPOWSKI, WALTER

GENERAL

KANE, B. M. "Scenes From Family Life: The Novels of Walter Kempowski." *German Life And Letters,* 28 (1975), 418–26.

KENDALL, HENRY

GENERAL

CLARKE, DONOVAN. "New Light on Henry Kendall." *Australian Literary Studies,* 2 (1966), 211–13.

KENEALLY, THOMAS (Australian, 1935-)
GENERAL

BESTON, JOHN B., ed. "An Interview with Thomas Keneally." *World Literature Written In English*, 12, No.1 (1973), 48–56.

BURNS, ROBERT. "Out of Context: A Study of Thomas Keneally's Novels." *Australian Literary Studies*, 4 (1969), 31–48.

CLANCY, L. J. "Conscience and Corruption: Thomas Keneally's Three Novels." *Meanjin*, 27 (1968), 33–41.

KIERNAN, BRIAN. "Fable or Novel? The Development of Thomas Keneally." *Meanjin*, 31 (1972), 489–93.

BRING LARKS AND HEROES (1967)

BESTON, JOHN B. "The Hero's 'Fear of Freedom' in Keneally." *Australian Literary Studies*, 5 (1972), 374–87.

CANTRELL, KERIN. "Perspective on Thomas Keneally." *Southerly*, 28 (1968), 57–63.

DAY, MARTIN S. "Australian Fiction Scrutinizes National Life." *Forum*, 9, No.3 (1972), 3–4.

KIERNAN, BRIAN. "Thomas Keneally and the Australian Novel: a Study of *Bring Larks And Heroes*." *Southerly*, 28 (1968), 189–99.

Reviews
McLAREN, JOHN. "New Novels." *Overland*, No.38 (1968), pp. 41–42.

THE CHANT OF JIMMIE BLACKSMITH (1972)

STURM, TERRY. "Thomas Keneally and Australian Racism: *The Chant Of Jimmie Blacksmith*." *Southerly*, 33 (1973), 261–74.

Reviews
BESTON, JOHN B. "Keneally's Violence." *Journal Of Commonwealth Literature*, 9, No.1 (1974), 71–73.

McLAREN, JOHN. "New Novels." *Overland*, No.51 (1972), pp. 52–53.

A DUTIFUL DAUGHTER (1971)

Reviews
BESTON, JOHN B. "Obsession with Dependence." *Journal Of Commonwealth Literature*, 7, No.2 (1972), 154–55.

HAYNES, MURIEL. *Saturday Review*, 24 July 1971, p. 53.

THE FEAR (1965)

CANTRELL, KERIN. "Perspective on Thomas Keneally." *Southerly*, 28 (1968), 63–67.

Reviews
McLAREN, JOHN. "New Novels." *Overland*, No.33 (1965), p. 44.

WILDING, MICHAEL. *Southerly*, 26 (1966), 60–61.

THE PLACE AT WHITTON (1964)

CANTRELL, KERIN. "Perspective on Thomas Keneally." *Southerly*, 28 (1968), 54–57.

THE SURVIVOR

Reviews
McLAREN, JOHN. "Doubtful Survivor." *Overland*, No.43 (1969/70), pp. 50–51.

THREE CHEERS FOR THE PARACLETE (1968)

BESTON, JOHN B. "The Hero's 'Fear of Freedom' in Keneally." *Australian Literary Studies*, 5 (1972), 374–87.

BURNS, ROBERT. "Out of Context: A Study of Thomas Keneally's Novels." *Australian Literary Studies*, 4 (1969), 31–48.

WILDING, MICHAEL. "Two Cheers for Keneally." *Southerly*, 29 (1969), 131–38.

Reviews

CUNEO, PAUL. "Low-down on Clergy Down Under." *Saturday Review*, 12 April 1969, p. 94.

KESHAVDEV, P.
AEENA

Reviews
RAINA, A. N. *Indian Literature*, 18, No.1 (1974), 130–31.

KESSEL, JOSEPH (French, 1898–1979)
THE HORSEMEN (Les Cavaliers, 1967)

Reviews
WRIGHT, GLEN. "For the Need of a Father's Love." *Saturday Review*, 1 June 1968, pp. 34–35.

KEYSERLING, EDUARD VON (German, 1855–1918)
GENERAL

WONDERLY, A. WAYNE. "Keyserling and Feminism." *South Atlantic Bulletin*, 39, No.2 (1974), 17–21.

DER BERUF

WONDERLEY, A. WAYNE. "A 'New' Novella by Keyserling." *MLN*, 87 (1972), 777–80.

DUMALA (1907)

McCORMICK, E. ALLEN. "Inner and Outer Landscape in Eduard von Keyserling's *Dumala*," in *Studies In German Literature Of The Nineteenth And Twentieth Centuries*, ed. Siegfried Mews, pp. 126–36.

LANDPARTIE

WONDERLEY, WAYNE. "Keyserling's *Landpartie*," in *Studies In German Literature Of The Nineteenth And Twentieth Centuries*, ed. Siegfried Mews, pp. 137–48.

KHANDEKAR, VISHNU SAKHARAM (Indian, 1898–1976)
GENERAL

SARDESAI, GARGI. "V. S. Khandekar: A Social Humanist." *Indian Literature*, 11, No.1 (1968), 92–97.

KIERKEGAARD, SOREN (Danish, 1813–1855)
REPETITION (Gjentagelsen, 1843)

PEDERSEN, BERTEL. "Fictionality and Authority: A Point of View for Kierkegaard's Work as an Author." *MLN*, 89 (1974), 938–56.

KIM, RICHARD E. (Korean, 1932-)
THE INNOCENT (1968)

Reviews
SIMPSON, HASSELL A. "A Bitter Lesson of Brutal Passion." *Saturday Review*, 23 November 1968, pp. 66–67.

KINAU, Johann see FOCK, Gorch

KINGSLEY, HENRY (Australian, 1830–1876)

GENERAL

BARNES, JOHN. " 'A Young Man Called Kingsley.' " *Meanjin,* 30 (1971), 72-84.

BAXTER, ROSILYN. "Henry Kingsley and the Australian Landscape." *Australian Literary Studies,* 4 (1970). 395-98.

HAMER, CLIVE. "Henry Kingsley's Australian Novels." *Southerly,* 26 (1966), 40-57.

THE HARVEYS

SCHEUERLE, WILLIAM H. *The Neglected Brother: A Study Of Henry Kingsley,* pp. 143-46.

THE HILLYARS AND THE BURTONS (1865)

BARNES, JOHN. *Henry Kingsley And Colonial Fiction,* pp. 27-31.

SCHEUERLE, WILLIAM H. *The Neglected Brother: A Study Of Henry Kingsley,* pp. 100-05.

Reviews
WILDING, MICHAEL. "A New Colonialism?" *Southerly,* 35 (1975), 97-99.

LEIGHTON COURT

SCHEUERLE, WILLAM H. *The Neglected Brother: A Study Of Henry Kingsley,* pp. 124-27.

MADEMOISELLE MATHILDE

SCHEUERLE, WILLIAM H. *The Neglected Brother: A Study Of Henry Kingsley,* pp. 113-21.

OAKSHOTT CASTLE

SCHEUERLE, WILLIAM H. *The Neglected Brother: A Study Of Henry Kingsley,* pp. 146-55.

RAVENSHOE (1861)

SCHEUERLE, WILLIAM H. *The Neglected Brother: A Study Of Henry Kingsley,* pp. 60-87.

WELLINGS, N. G. "Henry Kingsley: *Ravenshoe.*" *Australian Literary Studies,* 4 (1969), 115-29.

THE RECOLLECTIONS OF GEOFFREY HAMLYN (1859)

ANDERSON, HUGH. "The Composition of *Geoffry Hamlyn:* A Comment." *Australian Literary Studies,* 4 (1969), 79-80.

ARGYLE, BARRY. *An Introduction To The Australian Novel, 1830-1930,* pp. 84-117.

BARNES, JOHN. *Henry Kingsley And Colonial Fiction,* pp. 18-25.

CROFT, JULIAN. "Is *Geoffry Hamlyn* a Creole Novel?" *Australian Literary Studies,* 6 (1974), 269-76.

ELLIOTT, BRIAN. "The Composition of *Geoffry Hamlyn:* The Legend and the Facts." *Australian Literary Studies,* 3 (1968), 271-89.

HERGENHAN, L. T. "*Geoffry Hamlyn* Through Contemporary Eyes." *Australian Literary Studies,* 2 (1966), 289-95.

SCHEUERLE, WILLIAM H. *The Neglected Brother: A Study Of Henry Kingsley,* pp. 27-52.

———. "Romantic Attitudes in *Geoffry Hamlyn.*" *Australian Literary Studies,* 2 (1965), 79-91.

WILKES, G. A. "Kingsley's *Geoffry Hamlyn:* A Study in Literary Survival." *Southerly,* 32 (1972), 243-54.

SILCOTE OF SILCOTES

SCHEUERLE, WILLIAM H. *The Neglected Brother: A Study Of Henry Kingsley,* pp. 105-11.

STRETTON

SCHEUERLE, WILLIAM H. *The Neglected Brother: A Study Of Henry Kingsley,* pp. 121-24.

KINNOSUKE NATSUME see NATSUME SŌSEKI

KINOSHITA, NAOE

PILLAR OF FIRE (Hi no Hashira)

Reviews
O'BRIEN, JAMES A. *Literature East And West,* 16 (1972), 1253-54.

TAKAYA, TED T. *Journal Of The American Oriental Society,* 94 (1974), 517-18.

KIRBY, WILLIAM (Canadian, 1817-1906)

THE GOLDEN DOG (1877)

SORFLEET, JOHN ROBERT. "Fiction and the Fall of New France: William Kirby vs. Gilbert Parker." *Journal Of Canadian Fiction,* 2, No.3 (1973), 142-46.

KIRST, HANS HELMUT (German, 1914-)

BROTHERS IN ARMS (Kameraden, 1961)

Reviews
BAUKE, J. P. "Fraternity of Rapists." *Saturday Review,* 3 June 1967, p. 36.

LAST STOP CAMP SEVEN (Letzte Station Camp 7, 1966)

Reviews
DWYER, DAVID J. "War the Waster." *Catholic World,* 210 (1970), 235-36.

ZOHN, HARRY. *Saturday Review,* 2 August 1969, pp. 27-28.

THE NIGHT OF THE GENERALS (Die Nacht der Generale, 1962)

Reviews
PLANT, RICHARD. "Cattle-rustling Brown Shirts." *Saturday Review,* 20 July 1968, pp. 25-26.

WHAT BECAME OF GUNNER ASCH (Null-acht fuenfzehn heute, 1963)

Reviews
HILL, CLAUDE. "Minds Like Machine Guns." *Saturday Review,* 27 February 1965, p. 32.

KITEREZA, ANICETTI (Tanzanian, ca. 1900-)

GENERAL

HARTWIG, CHARLOTTE M. and GERALD W. "Aniceti Kitereza: A Kerebe Novelist." *Research In African Literatures,* 3 (1972), 162-66.

BWANA MYOMBEKERE NA BIBI BUGONOKA NA NTULANALWO NA BULIHWALI

HARTWIG, CHARLOTTE M. and GERALD W. "Aniceti Kitereza: A Kerebe Novelist." *Research In African Literatures,* 3 (1972), 165-70.

KIYOHIKO NOJIRI see OSARAGI, Jíro

KJELLGREN, JOSEF (Swedish, 1907-1948)

MÄNNISKOR KRING EN BRO

GRAVES, PETER. "The Collective Novel in Sweden." *Scandinavica,* 12 (1973), 121-24.

KLEIN, ABRAHAM MOSES (Canadian, 1909-1972)

GENERAL

MATTHEWS, JOHN. "Abraham Klein and the Problem of Synthesis," in *Readings In Commonwealth Literature,* ed. William Walsh, pp. 267-82.

THE SECOND SCROLL (1951)

FISHER, G. K. *In Search Of Jerusalem: Religion And Ethics In The Writings Of A. M. Klein,* pp. 161-210.

MATTHEWS, JOHN. "Abraham Klein and the Problem of Synthesis." *Journal Of Commonwealth Literature,* No.1 (1965), pp. 149-63.

MIDDLEBRO', TOM. "Yet Another Gloss on A. M. Klein's *The Second Scroll.*" *Journal Of Canadian Fiction,* 4, No.3 (1975), 117-22.

WADDINGTON, MIRIAM. "Signs on a White Field: Klein's *Second Scroll,*" in *A Choice Of Critics,* ed. George Woodcock, pp. 142-55.

KLEIST, HEINRICH VON (German, 1777-1811)

GENERAL

HARDY, SWANA L. "Heinrich von Kleist: Portrait of a Mannerist." *Studies In Romanticism,* 6 (1967), 203-13.

LINDSAY, J. M. "Figures of Authority in the Works of Heinrich von Kleist." *Forum For Modern Language Studies,* 8 (1972), 107-19.

THE DUEL

HELBLING, ROBERT E. *The Major Works Of Heinrich Von Kleist,* pp. 152-58.

THE EARTHQUAKE IN CHILI (Das Erdbeben in Chili)

ELLIS, JOHN M. *Narration In The German Novelle,* pp. 46-76.

GEAREY, JOHN. *Heinrich Von Kleist: A Study In Tragedy And Anxiety,* pp. 43-48.

HELBLING, ROBERT E. *The Major Works Of Heinrich Von Kleist,* pp. 106-12.

OSSAR, MICHAEL. "Kleist's *Das Erdbeben In Chili* and *Die Marquise Von O. . . .*" *Revue Des Langues Vivantes,* 34 (1968), 151-61.

THE ENGAGEMENT IN SANTO DOMINGO (Die Verlobung in St. Domingo)

GEAREY, JOHN. *Heinrich Von Kleist: A Study In Tragedy And Anxiety,* pp. 70-76.

GILMAN, SANDER L. "The Aesthetics of Blackness in Heinrich von Kleist's 'Die Verlobung in St. Domingo.' " *MLN,* 90 (1975), 661-72.

HELBLING, ROBERT E. *The Major Works Of Heinrich Von Kleist,* pp. 100-5.

THE FOUNDLING (Der Findling)

GEAREY, JOHN. *Heinrich Von Kleist: A Study In Tragedy And Anxiety,* pp. 76-79.

HELBLING, ROBERT E. *The Major Works Of Heinrich Von Kleist,* pp. 114-17.

DIE HEILIGE CACILIE

GEAREY, JOHN. *Heinrich Von Kleist: A Study In Tragedy And Anxiety,* pp. 56-58.

DIE MARQUISE VON O . . .

COHN, DORRIT. "Kleist's 'Marquise von O . . .': The Problem of Knowledge." *Monatshefte,* 67 (1975), 129-44.

CROSTY, DONALD H. "Psychological Realism in the Works of Kleist: 'Penthesilea' and 'Die Marquise von O. . . .' " *Literature And Psychology,* 19, No.1 (1969), 9-15.

GEAREY, JOHN. *Heinrich Von Kleist: A Study In Tragedy And Anxiety,* pp. 60-70.

HELBLING, ROBERT E. *The Major Works Of Heinrich Von Kleist,* pp. 145-50.

OSSAR, MICHAEL. "Kleist's *Das Erdbeben In Chili* and *Die Marquise Von O. . . .*" *Revue Des Langues Vivantes,* 34 (1968), 161-68.

SOKEL, WALTER H. "Kleist's Marquise of O., Kierkegaard's Abraham and Musil's Tonka: Three Stages of the Absurd as the Touchstone of Faith." *Wisconsin Studies In Contemporary Literature,* 8 (1967), 505-16.

MICHAEL KOHLHAAS (1811)

CARY, JOHN R. "A Reading of Kleist's *Michael Kohlhaas.*" *PMLA,* 85 (1970), 212-18.

DYER, D. G. "Junker Wenzel von Tronka." *German Life And Letters,* 18 (1965), 252-57.

ELLIS, J. M. "Der Herr Lässt Regnen über Gerechte und Ungerechte: Kleist's 'Michael Kohlhaas.' " *Monatshefte,* 59 (1967), 35-40.

GEAREY, JOHN. *Heinrich Von Kleist: A Study In Tragedy And Anxiety,* pp. 102-19.

HELBLING, ROBERT E. *The Major Works Of Heinrich Von Kleist,* pp. 193-209.

LUCAS, R. S. "Studies in Kleist, 'Michael Kohlhaas.' " *Deutsche Vierteljahresschrift Fur Literaturwissenschaft Und Geistegeschichte,* 44 (1970), 120-45.

MARSON, ERIC. "Justice and the Obsessed Character in 'Michael Kohlhaas.' *Der Prozess* and L'*Etranger.*" *Seminar,* 2, No.2 (1966), 21-24.

DER ZWEIKAMPF

ELLIS, JOHN M. "Kleist's 'Der Zweikampf.' " *Monatshefte,* 65 (1973), 48-60.

GEAREY, JOHN. *Heinrich Von Kleist: A Study In Tragedy And Anxiety,* pp. 48-56.

KLIMA, IVAN (Czech, 1931-)

A SHIP NAMED HOPE (Lodjmenem nadeje, 1969)

Reviews

VANSITTART, PETER. "Horse-Riding." *London Magazine,* NS, 10, No.11 (1971), 95.

KLOSSOWSKI, PIERRE

ROBERTE CE SOIR

RICE, DONALD. "Theological Pornography: A 'Non-reading' of Klossowski's *Roberte Ce Soir.*" *Sub-Stance,* No.10 (1974), pp. 39-45.

KLUGE, ALEXANDER (German, 1932-)

THE BATTLE (Schlachbeschreibung, 1962)

Reviews

BAUKE, J. P. "Defeat on the Volga." *Saturday Review,* 30 September 1967, pp. 43, 57.

KNIGGE, ADOLF FRANZ FRIEDRICH, FREIHERR VON (German, 1752–1796)

DAS ZAUBERSCHLOSS ODER GESCHICHTE DES GRAFEN TUNGER

HADLEY, MICHAEL. *The German Novel In 1790*, pp. 177–79.

KNIGHT, DAVID

FARQUHARSON'S PHYSIQUE AND WHAT IT DID TO HIS MIND

Reviews

LAURENCE, MARGARET. "African Experience." *Journal Of Canadian Fiction*, 1, No.1 (1972), 77–78.

WOLFE, MORRIS. "Uncertain Experience." *Canadian Literature*, No.53 (1972), pp. 105–7.

KNOX, ALEXANDER (Canadian, 1907–)

NIGHT OF THE WHITE BEAR (1971)

Reviews

BROWN, RUSSELL M. "Expatriate Variations." *Canadian Literature*, No.54 (1972), pp. 96–97.

KNUDSEN, JAKOB CHRISTIAN LINDBERG (Danish, 1858–1917)

FREMSKRIDT

JONES, W. GLYN. "*Det Forjaettede Land* and *Fremskridt* as Social Novels: A Comparison." *Scandanavian Studies*, 37 (1965), 77–90.

KOCH, CHRISTOPHER

ACROSS THE SEA WALL

Reviews

MCLAREN, JOHN. "New Novels." *Overland*, No.32 (1965), p. 44.

MCPHERSON, NEIL. "Writers for a 'No' Generation." *Westerly*, 2, No.1 (1966), 59–60.

KOCHETOV, VSEVOLOD (Russian, 1912–1973)

WHAT DO YOU WANT?

HOOD, STUART. "Comrade Bulatov's Italian Journey." *Survey: A Journal Of Soviet And East European Studies*, No.74/5, (1970), 175–84.

KOEPPEN, WOLFGANG (German, 1906–)

GENERAL

THOMAS, R. HINTON and WILFRIED VAN DER WILL. *The German Novel And The Affluent Society*, pp. 20–39.

THE BONN PARLIAMENT (Das Treibhaus, 1953)

CRAVEN, STANLEY. "Two Novels by Wolfgang Koeppen—*Tauben Im Gras* and *Das Treibhaus*." *Modern Languages*, 51 (1970), 169–72.

THOMAS, R. HINTON and WILFRIED VAN DER WILL. *The German Novel And The Affluent Society*, pp. 26–36.

DEATH IN ROME (Der tod in Rom, 1954)

BANCE, A. F. "*Der Tod In Rom* and *Die Rote*: Two Italian Episodes." *Forum For Modern Language Studies*, 3 (1967), 126–34.

TAUBEN IM GRAS (1951)

CRAVEN, STANLEY. "Two Novels by Wolfgang Koeppen—*Tauben Im Gras* and *Das Treibhaus*." *Modern Languages*, 51 (1970), 168–69.

KOMAROV, MATVEJ (Russian, 18th Century)

VAN'KA KAIN (1779)

TITUNIK, I. R. "Matvej Komarov's *Van'ka Kain* and Eighteenth-Century Prose Fiction." *Slavic And East European Journal*, 18 (1974), 351–66.

KOMPERT, LEOPOLD

GENERAL

IGGERS, WILMA A. "Leopold Kompert, Romancier of the Bohemian Ghetto." *Modern Austrian Literature*, 6, No.3/4 (1973), 117–38.

KONRAD, GEORGE (Hungarian, 1933–)

THE CASE WORKER (A latogato, 1969)

Reviews

CHERNUSH, AKOSH. "The Madness File." *Canadian Forum*, NS, 3, No.2 (1974), 40–42.

KONWICKI, TADEUSZ (Polish, 1926–)

GENERAL

KRZYZANOWSKI, JERZY R. "The Haunted World of Tadeusz Konwicki." *Books Abroad*, 48 (1974), 485–90.

A DREAMBOOK FOR OUR TIME (Sennik wspólczesny, 1963)

IYENGAR, K. R. SRINAVASA. "War and Peace in Contemporary Polish Fiction." *Indian Literature*, 17, No.1/2 (1974), 63–67.

Reviews

MIHAILOVICH, VASA D. *Saturday Review*, 20 June 1970, pp. 43–44.

KOŠ, ERIH (Yugoslav, 1913–)

NAMES (1966)

Reviews

LENSKI, BRANKO. "A Nominal Nightmare." *Saturday Review*, 19 November 1966, p. 44.

KOSENKO, PAVEL

THE HEART REMAINS THE SAME (Serdtse Ostaetsia Odno)

GURAL'NIK, U. "Don't Simplify: It's Dostoevsky!" *Soviet Studies In Literature*, 7 (1970/1), 53–60.

KOTZEBUE, AUGUST FRIEDRICH FERDINAND VON (German, 1761–1819)

DIE GEFÄHRLICHE WETTE

HADLEY, MICHAEL. *The German Novel In 1790*, pp. 160–63.

KOUROUMA, AHMADOU (Mali)

LES SOLEILS DES INDÉPENDANCES (1971)

Reviews

SELLIN, ERIC. *French Review*, 44 (1971), 641–42.

KRATTER, FRANZ
DAS SCHLEIFERMADCHEN AUS SCHWABEN

HADLEY, MICHAEL. *The German Novel in 1790,* pp. 75–82.

KREISEL, HENRY (Canadian, 1922–)
THE BETRAYAL (1964)

RICOU, LAURENCE. *Vertical Man/ Horizontal World,* pp. 126–28.

Reviews
ROBERTSON, GEORGE. "Guilt and Counter-Guilt." *Canadian Literature,* No.23 (1965), pp. 72–74.

WATT, F. W. *University Of Toronto Quarterly,* 34 (1965), 377–79.

KRĖVĖ, VINCAS (Lithuanian, 1882–1954)
GENERAL

VAŠKELIS, BRONIUS. "Vincas Krėvė, the Lithuanian Classic." *Lituanus,* 11, No.3 (1965), 5–17.

THE SONS OF HEAVEN AND EARTH (Dangaus ir žemės Sūnus, 1949)

MACIŪNAS, VINCAS. "From Native Lithuania to the Distant Orient: A Survey of the Literary Heritage of Vincas Krėve." *Lituanus,* 11, No.3 (1965), 35–62.

KRISHNAN, SRIMATI RAJAM
AMUTHAMAAGI VARUGA

Reviews
KALYANASUNDARAM, M. S. *Indian Writing Today,* 2, No.4 (1968), 50–51.

KRISTENSEN, TOM (Danish, 1893–1974)
HAVOC (Hoevoerk, 1930)

Reviews
SPECTOR, ROBERT D. *American Scandanavian Review,* 57 (1969), 86–87.

KROETSCH, ROBERT (Canadian, 1927–)
GENERAL

CAMERON, DONALD. "Robert Kroetsch: The American Experience and The Canadian Voice." *Journal Of Canadian Fiction,* 1, No.3 (1972), 48–52.

HARRISON, DICK. "The American Adam and the Canadian Christ." *Twentieth Century Literature,* 16 (1970), 166–67.

THOMAS, PETER. "Keeping Mum: Kroetsch's 'Alberta.' " *Journal Of Canadian Fiction,* 2, No.2 (1973), 54–56.

———. "Priapus in the Danse Macabre." *Canadian Literature,* No.61 (1974), pp. 54–64.

GONE INDIAN (1973)

Reviews
BROWN, RUSSELL M. "Freedom to Depart." *Canadian Literature,* No.61 (1974), pp. 103–4.

STOW, GLENYS. "The Trickster Reborn." *Journal Of Canadian Fiction,* 3, No.1 (1974), 93–95.

THE STUDHORSE MAN (1970)

NEW, WILLIAM H. "The Studhorse Quests," in his *Articulating West,* pp. 179–86.

RICOU, LAURENCE R. "Empty as Nightmare: Man and Landscape in Recent Canadian Prairie Fiction." *Mosaic,* 6, No.2 (1972/3), 158–60.

THOMAS, PETER. "Priapus in the Danse Macabre." *Canadian Literature,* No.61 (1974), 60–64.

Reviews
BROWN, RUSSELL M. "Odyssean Journey." *Canadian Literature,* No.45 (1970), pp. 88–90.

THE WORDS OF MY ROARING (1966)

HARRISON, DICK. "The American Adam and the Canadian Christ." *Twentieth Century Literature,* 16 (1970), 166.

RICOU, LAURENCE R. "Empty as Nightmare: Man and Landscape in Recent Canadian Prairie Fiction." *Mosaic,* 6, No.2 (1972/3), 157–58.

THOMAS, PETER. "Priapus in the Danse Macabre." Canadian Literature, No.61 (1974), pp. 57–60.

Reviews
NEW, W. H. "Clichés and Roaring Words." *Canadian Literature,* No.31 (1967), pp. 66–67.

KÜHNE, FERDINAND GUSTAV (German, 1806–1888)
EINE QUARANTÄNE IM IRRENHAUSE (1835)

SAMMONS, JEFFREY L. *Six Essays On The Young German Novel,* pp. 81–103.

KŪKAI (Japanese, 774–835)
INDICATIONS TO THE THREE TEACHINGS (Sangō-shīki)

HAKEDA, Y. S. "The Religious Novel of Kūkai." *Monumenta Nipponica,* 20 (1965), 283–97.

KUMAR, JAINENDRA
ANANTARA

KULSHRESTHA, CHIRANTAN. "In Defense of Jainendra Kumar." *Indian Literature,* 14, No.2 (1971), 63–73.

THE RESIGNATION (Tyāgpatra, 1950)

ORMAN, STANLEY. "The Resignation: A Fully Indian Novel." *Mahfil,* 6, No.4 (1970), 61–72.

KUNDERA, MILAN (Czechoslovak, 1929-)
THE JOKE (Zert, 1967)

Reviews
MIHAILOVICH, VASA D. *Saturday Review,* 20 December 1969, pp. 31–32.

IM NAMEN DER HUTE

SCHLANT, ERNESTINE. "Fiction in the German Democratic Republic During the Past Decade." *Modern Fiction Studies,* 21 (1975), 147.

KURAHASHI YUMIKO (Japanese, 1935-)
GENERAL

MORI, JŌJI. "Drag the Doctors into the Area of Metaphysics: An Introduction to Kurahashi Yumiko." *Literature East And West,* 18 (1974), 76–89.

THE ADVENTURE OF SUMIYAKIST Q.

MORI, JŌJI. "Drag the Doctors into the Area of Metaphysics: An Introduction to Kurahashi Yumiko." *Literature East And West*, 18 (1974), 79–83.

NAGAI YUME

MORI, JŌJO. "Drag the Doctors into the Area of Metaphysics: An Introduction to Kurahashi Yumiko." *Literature East And West*, 18 (1974), 85–89.

KUZMIN, MIKHAIL (Russian, 1872–1936)

WINGS (Krilya, 1906)

GRANOIEN, NEIL. "Wings and 'The World of Art.' " *Russian Literature Triquarterly*, No.11 (1975), pp. 393–405.

KUZNETSOV, ANATOLY (Russian, 1929–1979)

BABI YAR: A DOCUMENTARY NOVEL

Reviews

FITZLYON, KYRIL. "Bitter Fruit." *London Magazine*, NS, 10, No.11 (1971), 84–88.

KALB, MARVIN. "Russian Record of Nazi Terror." *Saturday Review*, 11 March 1967, pp. 37, 112.

SOLOTAROFF, THEODORE. "Reality and Socialist Realism." *Saturday Review*, 23 January 1971, pp. 59–62.

KYUCHOUKOV, Prodan see PETROV, Ivalyo

L

LABRUNIE, Gérard see NERVAL, Gérard.

LACLOS, PIERRE AMBROISE FRANÇOIS CHODERLOS DE (French, 1741-1803)

DANGEROUS CONNECTIONS (Les Liaisons dangereuses, 1782)

ALSTAD, DIANNE. "*Les Liaisons Dangereuses:* Hustlers and Hypocrites." *Yale French Studies,* No.40 (1968), pp. 156-67.

BLUM, CAROL. "A Hint from the Author of *Les Liaisons Dangereuses?*" *MLN,* 84 (1969), 662-67.

———— . "Styles of Cognition as Moral Options in *La Nouvelle Héloïse* and *Les Liaisons Dangereuses*" *PMLA,* 88 (1973), 289-98.

BROOKS, PETER. *The Novel Of Worldliness,* pp. 172-216.

CHAMPAGNE, ROLAND A. "The Spiralling *Discours:* Todorov's Model for Narratology in *Les Liaisons Dangereuses.*" *L'Esprit Créateur,* 14 (1974), 342-52.

COWARD, D. A. "Laclos and the *Dénouement* of the *Liaisons Dangereuses.*" *Eighteenth-Century Studies,* 5 (1972), 431-49.

GREENE, MILDRED S. "*Les Liaisons Dangereuses* and *The Golden Bowl:* Maggie's 'Loving Reason.' " *Modern Fiction Studies,* 19 (1973/4), 531-40.

HEMMINGS, F. W. J. "Realism and the Novel: The Eighteenth-Century Beginnings," in *The Age Of Realism,* ed. F. W. J. Hemmings, pp. 29-30.

HILL, EMITA B. "Man and Mask: The Art of the Actor in the *Liaisons Dangereuses.*" *Romanic Review,* 63 (1972), 111-24.

KATZ, EVE. "Ambiguity in *Les Liaisons Dangereuses.*" *Forum For Modern Language Studies,* 10 (1974), 121-29.

KRONENBERGER, LOUIS. "Sinuous Arts and Sophisticated Games: *Les Liaisons Dangereuses.*" *Michigan Quarterly Review,* 8 (1969), 181-88.

LEE, VERA. "Decoding Letter 50 in *Les Liaisons Dangereuses.*" *Romance Notes,* 10 (1969), 305-10.

MILLER, NANCY K. *The Heroine's Text,* pp. 116-48.

MYLNE, VIVIENNE. *The Eighteenth Century French Novel,* pp. 233-44.

PRESTON, JOHN. "*Les Liaisons Dangereuses:* Epistolary Narrative and Moral Discovery." *French Studies,* 24 (1970), 23-36.

REXROTH, KENNETH. "Classics Revisited—LXIX: 'Les Liaisons Dangereuses.' " *Saturday Review,* 24 August 1968, pp. 8-9.

THODY, PHILIP. *Laclos: Les Liaisons Dangereuses.*

———— . " 'Les Liaisons Dangereuses': Some Problems of Interpretation." *Modern Language Review,* 63 (1968), 832-39.

———— . "The Twentyman Lecture: *Manon Lescaut* and *Les Liaisons Dangereuses:* The Problems of Morality in Literature." *Modern Languages,* 56 (1975), 61-72.

TODOROV, TZVETAN. "The Discovery of Language: *Les Liaisons Dangereuses* and *Adolphe.*" *Yale French Studies,* No.45 (1970), pp. 113-26.

TOPLAK, MARIE. "Homo Ludens et Homo Belligerens." *Modern Language Quarterly,* 28 (1967), 167-76.

LACRETELLE, JACQUES DE (French, 1888-)

GENERAL

MOORE-RINVOLUCRI, MINA J. "Jacques de Lacretelle: Novelist." *Modern Languages,* 47 (1966), 92-98.

LACROSIL, MICHÈLE (West Indian)

GENERAL

SMITH, ROBERT P. "Michèle Lacrosil: Novelist with a Color Complex." *French Review,* 47 (1974), 783-90.

LADOO, HAROLD S. (Trinidad-born Canadian)

NO PAIN LIKE THIS BODY (1972)

Reviews

BESSAI, DIANE. "West Indies: Here and There." *Canadian Literature,* No.61 (1974), pp. 108-9.

YESTERDAYS

Reviews

ROSENGARTEN, H. J. "The Walking Ghosts of Empire." *Canadian Literature,* No.63 (1975), pp. 96-98.

LAFAYETTE, (MME DE) MARIE MADELEINE PIOCHE DE LA VERGNE, COMTESSE DE (French, 1634-1693)

LA COMTESSE DE TENDE (1724)

HAIG, STIRLING. "*La Comtesse De Tende:* A Singular Heroine." *Romance Notes,* 10 (1969), 311-16.

———— . *Madame De Lafayette,* pp. 135-40.

LA PRINCESSE DE CLÈVES (1678)

ALLENTUCH, HARRIET RAY. "Pauline and the Princesse de Cleves." *Modern Language Quarterly,* 30 (1969), 171-82.

———— . "The Will to Refuse in the *Princesse De Clèves.*" *University Of Toronto Quarterly,* 44 (1975), 185-98.

BIDWELL, JEAN S. "*La Princesse De Clèves* and *Le Roman*

Comique—*Two Different Worlds.*" *USF Language Quarterly,* 11, No.3/4 (1973), 43-47.

BRODY, JULES. "*La Princesse De Clèves* and the Myth of Courtly Love." *University Of Toronto Quarterly,* 38 (1969), 105-35.

BROOKS, PETER. *The Novel Of Worldliness,* pp. 68-77.

DE JAGER WERMAN, MARJOLIJN R. "A Linking Image in *La Princesse De Clèves.*" *Romance Notes,* 13 (1971), 130-31.

GOODE, WILLIAM O. "A Mother's Goals in *La Princesse De Clèves:* Worldly and Spiritual Distinction." *Neophilologus,* 56 (1972), 398-406.

GREENE, MILDRED S. "Isolation and Integrity: Madame de Lafayette's Princesse de Clèves and George Eliot's Dorothea Brooke." *Revue De Littérature Comparée,* 44 (1970), 145-54.

GROSSVOGEL, DAVID I. *Limits Of The Novel,* pp. 108-35.

HAIG, STIRLING. *Madame De Lafayette,* pp. 105-34.

———. "*La Princesse De Clèves* and Saint-Réal's *Dom Carlos.*" *French Studies,* 22 (1968), 201-5.

———. "La Rochefoucauld's 'Mémoires' and an Episode of 'La Princesse de Clèves.'" *Studi Francesi,* 12 (1968), 477-79.

HYMAN, RICHARD J. "The Virtuous 'Princesse de Clèves.'" *French Review,* 38 (1964), 15-22.

KAHLER, ERICH. *The Inward Turn Of Narrative,* pp. 22-34.

KAPS, HELEN KAREN. *Moral Perspective In 'La Princesse De Clèves.'*

LAWRENCE, FRANCIS L. "*La Princesse De Clèves* Reconsidered." *French Review,* 39 (1965), 15-21.

LEOV, NOLA M. "Sincerity and Order in the 'Princesse de Clèves." *AUMLA,* No.30 (1968), pp. 133-50.

NICOLICH, ROBERT N. "The Language of Vision in *La Princesse De Clèves:* The Baroque Principle of Control and Release." *Language And Style,* 4 (1971), 279-96.

RAITT, JANET. *Madame De Lafayette And 'La Princesse De Clèves.'*

SCANLAN, TIMOTHY M. "Maternal Mask and Literary Craft in *La Princesse De Clèves.*" *Revue Du Pacifique,* 2 (1976), 23-32.

SIMON, JOHN KENNETH. "A Study of Classical Gesture: Henry James and Madame de Lafayette." *Comparative Literature Studies,* 3 (1966), 273-83.

SINGERMAN, ALAN J. "History as Metaphor in Mme de Lafayette's *La Princesse De Clèves.*" *Modern Language Quarterly,* 36 (1975), 261-71.

TIEFENBRUN, SUSAN W. "The Art of Repetition in 'La Princesse de Clèves.'" *Modern Language Review,* 68 (1973), 40-50.

WOSHINSKY, BARBARA R. "The Art of Persuasion in the 'Princesse de Clèves.'" *USF Language Quarterly,* 12, No.3/4 (1974), 34-38, 42.

LA PRINCESSE DE MONPENSIER (1662)

HAIG, STIRLING. *Madame De Lafayette,* pp. 73-90.

KESTNER, JOSEPH A. "Defoe and Madame de La Fayette: *Roxana* and *La Princesse De Monpensier.*" *Papers On Language And Literature,* 8 (1972), 297-301.

ZÄIDE (1670)

HAIG, STIRLING. *Madame De Lafayette,* pp. 91-104.

LA FONTAINE, JEAN DE (French, 1621-1695)

LES AMOURS DE PSYCHÉ ET DE CUPIDON (1669)

GROSS, NATHAN. "Functions of the Framework in La Fontaine's *Psyché.*" *PMLA,* 84 (1969), 577-86.

LAFORET, CARMEN (Spanish, 1929-)

LA ISLA Y LOS DEMONIOS (1952)

ULLMAN, PIERRE L. "The Moral Structure of Carmen Laforet's Novels," in *The Vision Obscured,* ed. Melvin J. Friedman, pp. 205-10.

NADA (1945)

EL SAFFAR, RUTH. "Structural and Thematic Tactics of Suppression in Carmen Laforet's *Nada.*" *Symposium,* 28 (1974), 119-29.

ULLMAN, PIERRE L. "The Moral Structure of Carmen Laforet's Novels," in *The Vision Obscured,* pp. 202-7.

LA NUEVA MUJER (1955)

ULLMAN, PIERRE L. "The Moral Structure of Carmen Laforet's Novels," in *The Vision Obscured,* ed. Melvin J. Friedman, pp. 216-19.

LAFOURCADE, ENRIQUE (Chilean, 1919-)

LA FIESTA DEL REY ACAB (1959)

LICHTBLAU, MYRON I. "The Dictator Theme as Irony in Lafourcade's *La Fiesta Del Rey Acab [King Ahab's Feast.]*" *Latin American Literary Review,* 2, No.3 (1973), 75-83.

LAGERKVIST, PÄR (Swedish, 1891-1974)

GENERAL

ELLESTAD, EVERETT M. "Lagerkvist and Cubism: A Study of Theory and Practice." *Scandinavian Studies,* 45 (1973), 38-53.

KEHL, D. G. "The Chiaroscuro World of Pär Lagerkvist." *Modern Fiction Studies,* 15 (1969), 241-50.

RYBERG, ANDERS. "A Note on Pär Lagerkvist in Translation." *Minnesota Review,* 6 (1966), 312-15.

SLOMAN, JUDITH. "Existentialism in Pär Lagerkvist and Isaac Bashevis Singer." *Minnesota Review,* 5 (1965), 206-12.

SPECTOR, ROBERT DONALD. "Pär Lagerkvist's Dialogue of the Soul," in *Scandinavian Studies,* ed. Carl F. Bayerschmidt and Erik J. Friis, pp. 302-10.

SWANSON, ROY ARTHUR. "Evil and Love in Lagerkvist's Crucifixion Cycle." *Scandinavian Studies,* 38 (1966), 302-17.

WEATHERS, WINSTON. "Lazarus as Hero: The Novels of Lagerkvist." *Commonweal,* 81 (1965), 688-91.

BARABBAS (1950)

SPECTOR, ROBERT DONALD. *Pär Lagerkvist,* pp. 64-81.

WEATHERS, WINSTON. *Pär Lagerkvist: A Critical Essay,* pp.31-37.

THE DEATH OF AHASUERUS (Ahasuerus Död, 1950)

SPECTOR, ROBERT DONALD. *Pär Lagerkvist,* pp. 100-12.

THE DWARF (Dvärgen, 1944)

RAMSEY, ROGER. "Par Lagerkvist: *The Dwarf* and Dogma." *Mosaic,* 5, No.3 (1972), 97-106.

SPECTOR, ROBERT DONALD. *Pär Lagerkvist,* pp. 45-63.

WEATHERS, WINSTON. *Pär Lagerkvist: A Critical Essay,* pp. 16-18.

THE ETERNAL SMILE (Det Eviga Leendet)

KEHL, D. G. "The Chiaroscuro World of Pär Lagerkvist." *Modern Fiction Studies,* 15 (1969), 241-50.

LINNÉR, SVEN. "Pär Lagerkvist's *The Eternal Smile* and *The Sibyl.*" *Scandinavian Studies,* 37 (1965), 160-67.

SPECTOR, ROBERT DONALD. *Pär Lagerkvist,* pp. 37-39.

EVENING LAND (Aftonland, 1953)

Reviews
ROVINSKY, ROBERT T. *Scandinavian Review,* 63, No.4 (1975), 76-78.

GUEST OF REALITY (Gäst hos verkligheten, 1925)

SPECTOR, ROBERT DONALD. *Pär Lagerkvist,* pp. 34–37.

THE HANGMAN (Brödeln, 1933)

ELLESTAD, EVERETT M. "Lagerkvist and Cubism: A Study of Theory and Practice." *Scandinavian Studies,* 45 (1973), 41–45.

SPECTOR, ROBERT DONALD. *Pär Lagerkvist,* pp. 41–44.

HEROD AND MARIAMNE (Mariamne, 1967)

SCOBBIE, IRENE. "An Interpretation of Lagerkvist's *Mariamne.*" *Scandinavian Studies,* 45 (1973), 120–34.

SPECTOR, ROBERT DONALD. *Pär Lagerkvist,* pp. 127–36.

Reviews
SPECTOR, ROBERT D. *American Scandinavian Review,* 57 (1969), 198.

SWANSON, ROY ARTHUR. *Novel,* 2 (1969), 168–71.

THE HOLY LAND (Det Heliga Landet, 1964)

SPECTOR, ROBERT DONALD. *Pär Lagerkvist,* pp. 118–26.

WEATHERS, WINSTON. *Pär Lagerkvist: A Critical Essay,* pp. 38–45.

Reviews
Minnesota Review, 6 (1966), 371–72.

SPECTOR, ROBERT D. *American Scandinavian Review,* 54 (1966), 308.

PILGRIM AT SEA (Pilgrim på Havet, 1964)

SPECTOR, ROBERT DONALD. *Pär Lagerkvist,* pp. 112–18.

WEATHERS, WINSTON. *Pär Lagerkvist: A Critical Essay,* pp. 38–45.

THE SIBYL (Sibyllan, 1956)

LINNÉR, SVEN. "Pär Lagerkvist's *The Eternal Smile* and *The Sibyl.*" *Scandinavian Studies,* 37 (1965), 160–67.

SPECTOR, ROBERT DONALD. *Pär Lagerkvist,* pp. 82–98.

SJARLARNAS MASKERAD

SPECTOR, ROBERT DONALD. *Pär Lagerkvist,* pp. 39–41.

LAGERLÖF, SELMA (Swedish, 1858–1940)
GENERAL

LAGERROTH, ULLA-BRITTA. "The Troll in Man—A Lagerlöf Motif." *Scandinavian Studies,* 40 (1968), 51–60.

LA GUMA, ALEX (South African, 1925–)
GENERAL

COETZEE, J. M. "Man's Fate in the Novels of Alex La Guma." *Studies In Black Literature,* 5, No.1 (1974), 16–23.

LINDFORS, BERNTH. "Form and Technique in the Novels of Richard Rive and Alex La Guma." *Journal Of The New African Literature And The Arts,* No.2 (1966), pp. 10–15.

RABKIN, DAVID. "La Guma and Reality in South Africa." *Journal Of Commonwealth Literature,* 8, No.1 (1973), 54–62.

AND A THREEFOLD CORD (1964)

CARTEY, WILFRED. *Whispers From A Continent,* pp. 125–33.

A WALK IN THE NIGHT (1962)

CARTEY, WILFRED. *Whispers From A Continent,* pp. 125–33.

COETZEE, J. M. "Alex La Guma and the Responsibilities of the South African Writer." *Journal Of The New African Literature And The Arts,* No.9/10 (1971), pp. 5–11.

JULY, ROBERT W. "The African Personality in the African Novel," in *Introduction To African Literature,* ed. Ulli Beier, pp. 218–21.

LINDFORS, BERNTH. "Form and Technique in the Novels of Richard Rive and Alex La Guma." *Journal Of The New African Literature And The Arts,* No.2 (1966), pp. 12–14.

LAINÉ, PASCAL
L'IRRÉVOLUTION (1971)

Reviews
KUHN, REINHARD. *French Review,* 46 (1972), 218–19.

LAINEZ, MANUEL MUJICA see MUJICA LAINEZ, Manuel

LAMBERT, ERIC
GENERAL

MULLET, JACK. "Eric Lambert." *Overland,* No.34 (1966), pp. 19–20.

LAMMING, GEORGE (Barbadian, 1927–)
GENERAL

GÜNTHER, HELMUT. "George Lamming," in *Introduction To African Literature,* ed. Ulli Beier, pp. 205–10.

MORRIS, MERVYN. "The Poet as Novelist: The Novels of George Lamming," in *The Islands In Between,* ed. Louis James, pp. 73–85.

THE EMIGRANTS (1954)

MOORE, GERALD. *The Chosen Tongue,* pp. 37–42.

IN THE CASTLE OF MY SKIN (1953)

MOORE, GERALD. *The Chosen Tongue,* pp. 12–17.

MUNRO, IAN H. "The Theme of Exile in George Lamming's *In The Castle Of My Skin.*" *World Literature Written in English,* No.20 (1971), pp. 51–60.

NATIVES OF MY PERSON (1972)

POUCHET-PAQUET, SANDRA. "The Politics of George Lamming's *Natives Of My Person.*" *College Language Association Journal* 17 (1973), 109–16.

Reviews
CASH, EARL A. *College Language Association Journal,* 15 (1972), 381–82.

OF AGE AND INNOCENCE (1958)

MOORE, GERALD. *The Chosen Tongue,* pp. 49–57.

MORRIS, MERVYN. "The Poet as Novelist: The Novels of George Lamming," in *The Islands In Between,* ed. Louis James, pp. 77–80.

SEASON OF ADVENTURE (1960)

RAMCHAND, KENNETH. *The West Indian Novel And Its Background,* pp. 135–49.

LAMPEDUSA, GIUSEPPE TOMASI DI (Italian, 1896–1957)
THE LEOPARD (Il Gattopardo, 1958)

GILBERT, JOHN. "The Metamorphosis of the Gods in *Il Gattopardo.*" *MLN,* 81 (1966), 22–32.

MEYERS, JEFFREY. "Greuze and Lampedusa's 'Il Gattopardo.'" *Modern Language Review,* 69 (1974), 308–15.

———. "The Influence of *La Chartreuse De Parme* on *Il Gattopardo.*" *Italica,* 44 (1967), 314–25.

———. *Painting And The Novel,* pp. 124–34.

_____ . "Symbol and Structure in *The Leopard.*" *Italian Quarterly,* 9, No.34/5 (1965), 50–70.

NOLAN, DAVID. "Lampedusa's *The Leopard.*" *Studies: An Irish Quarterly Review,* 55 (1966), 403–14.

O'NEILL, T. "Lampedusa and De Roberto." *Italica,* 47 (1970), 170–82.

PALLOTTA, A. "*Il Gattopardo:* A Theme-Structure Analysis." *Italica,* 43 (1966), 57–65.

RAGUSA, OLGA. "Stendhal, Tomasi di Lampedusa, and the Novel." *Comparative Literature Studies,* 10 (1973), 195–228.

LANDAU, Mark Aleksandrovich see ALDÁNOV, Mark A.

LANDSBERGIS, ALGIRDAS (Lithuanian, 1924–)

GENERAL

ŠILBAJORIS, RIMVYDAS. *Perfection Of Exile,* pp. 135–60.

THE JOURNEY (Kelione, 1954)

ŠILBAJORIS, RIMVYDAS. *Perfection Of Exile,* pp. 137–42.

LANDWIRTH, HEINZ see LIND, JAKOV

LANGEVIN, ANDRÉ (French Canadian, 1927–)

DUST OVER THE CITY (Poussière sur la ville, 1953)

Reviews
MOORE, ROGER. *International Fiction Review,* 2 (1975), 85–86.

LANGFORD, CAMERON (Canadian)

THE WINTER OF THE FISHER

Reviews
BARCLAY, PAT. "Hope for a Happy Ending." *Canadian Literature,* No. 53 (1972), p. 110.

LANGGÄSSER, ELISABETH MARIA (German, 1899–1950)

THE INDELIBLE SEAL (Das unauslöschliche Siegel, 1946)

ANGRESS, R. K. "The Christian Surrealism of Elisabeth Langgässer," in *The Vision Obscured,* ed. Melvin J. Friedman, pp. 189–95.

RILEY, ANTHONY W. "Elisabeth Langgässer and Juan Donoso Cortés: A Source of the 'Turm-Kapitel' in *Das Unauslöschliche Siegel.*" *PMLA,* 83 (1968), 357–67.

THE QUEST (Märkische Argonautenfahrt, 1950)

ANGRESS, R. K. "The Christian Surrealism of Elisabeth Langgässer," in *The Vision Obscured,* ed. Melvin J. Friedman, pp. 195–99.

LANOUX, ARMAND (French, 1913–1983)

QUAND LA MER SE RETIRE (1963)

Reviews
NIESS, ROBERT J. *French Review,* 38 (1964), 133–34.

LAO SHE (Chinese, 1899–1966) pseudonym of Shu Ch'ing-ch'un

GENERAL

HSIA, C. T. *A History Of Modern Chinese Fiction,* pp. 165–88, 366–75.

CAMEL XIANGZI (Lo-t'o hsiang-tsu, 1938)

HALES, DELL R. "Social Criticism in Modern Chinese Essays and Novels." *Review Of National Literatures,* 6, No. 1 (1975), 49–52.

HSIA, C. T. *A History Of Modern Chinese Fiction,* pp. 181–88.

CHAO TZU—YÜEH (1927)

HSIA, C. T. *A History Of Modern Chinese Fiction,* pp. 167–71.

DIVORCE

HSIA, C. T. *A History Of Modern Chinese Fiction,* pp. 176–79.

FOUR GENERATIONS UNDER ONE ROOF

HSIA, C. T. *A History Of Modern Chinese Fiction,* pp. 369–75.

NOTES ON THE CITY OF CATS

TISHKOV, A. " 'Great Leaps' in the Arts of China Today." *Soviet Studies In Literature,* 7 (1971), 146–49.

RICKSHAW see CAMEL XIANGZI

THE TWO MAS

HSIA, C. T. *A History Of Modern Chinese Fiction,* pp. 171–76.

LARBAUD, VALERY (French, 1881–1957)

A. O. BARNABOOTH (1913)

O'BRIEN, JUSTIN, "Lafcadio and Barnabooth: A Supposition," in his *Contemporary French Literature,* pp. 233–44.

FERMINA MÁRQUEZ (1911)

SIMON, JOHN KENNETH. "Valery Larbaud's *Fermina.*" *MLN,* 83 (1968), 543–64.

LA ROQUE, GILBERT

APRES LA BOUE

Reviews
POKORNY, AMY E. "L'Evolution des Quebecoises," *Journal Of Canadian Fiction,* 2, No. 2 (1973), 89.

LARRETA, ENRIQUE RODRÍGUEZ (Argentine, 1875–1961)

THE GLORY OF DON RAMIRO (La Gloria de don ramiro, 1908)

FOSTER, DAVID WILLIAM. *Currents In The Contemporary Argentine Novel,* pp. 12–14.

_____ . "Toward an Interpretation of the 'Epilogo' of La Gloria de Don Ramiro." *Chasqui,* 2, No.2 (1973), 33–35.

LARTÉGUY, JEAN (1920–)

GENERAL

O'CONNELL, DAVID. "Jean Lartéguy: A Popular Phenomenon." *French Review,* 45 (1972), 1087–97.

THE BRONZE DRUM

Reviews
HAAS, JOSEPH. "Undercover Agent in Laos." *Saturday Review,* 4 November 1967, p. 34.

ENQUÊTE SUR UN CRUCIFIÉ (1973)

Reviews
O'CONNELL, DAVID. *French Review,* 48 (1975), 1066–67.

THE HOUNDS OF HELL

Reviews
DUPREY, RICHARD A. *Catholic World,* 204 (1966), p. 126.

LA SALE, ANTOINE DE (French, ca. 1386–ca. 1460)

PETIT JEHAN DE SAINTRÉ (1459)

> CHOLAKIAN, PATRICIA FRANCIS. "The Two Narrative Styles of A. de la Sale." *Romance Notes,* 10 (1969), 362–72.

LASHIN, MAHMAU TAHIR (Egyptian, 1894–)

HAUWA BILA ADAM (1934)

> KILPATRICK, HILARY. *The Modern Egyptian Novel,* pp. 51–54, 208–9.

LASO, JAIME

BLACK Y BLANC

> BOYD, ANTONIO OLLIZ. "Latin American Literature and the Subject of Racism." *College Language Association Journal,* 19 (1976), 570–73.

LATORRE, MARIANO (Chilean, 1886–1955)

GENERAL

> LANDIS, ALBERT E. "The Interaction of Character and Environment in the Fiction of Mariano Latorre," *Kentucky Foreign Language Quarterly,* 12 (1965), 83–89.

LAUBE, HEINRICH (German, 1806–1884)

DIE BURGER (1837)

> SAMMONS, JEFFREY L. *Six Essays On The Young German Novel,* pp. 111–13.

DIE KRIEGER (1837)

> SAMMONS, JEFFREY L. *Six Essays On The Young German Novel,* pp. 104–23.

LAURENCE, MARGARET (Canadian, 1926–)

GENERAL

> "A Conversation About Literature: An Interview With Margaret Laurence and Irving Layton." *Journal Of Canadian Fiction,* 1, No.1 (1972), 65–69.

> DJWA, SANDRA. "False Gods and the True Covenant: Thematic Continuity Between Margaret Laurence and Sinclair Ross." *Journal Of Canadian Fiction,* 1, No.4 (1972), 43–50.

> FORMAN, DENYSE and UMA PARAMESWARAN. "Echoes and Refrains in the Canadian Novels of Margaret Laurence." *Centennial Review,* 16 (1972), 233–53.

> GOM, LEONA M. "Margaret Laurence and The First Person." *Dalhousie Review,* 55 (1975), 236–51.

> LAURENCE, MARGARET. "Sources." *Mosaic,* 3, No.3 (1970), 80–84.

> ———. "Ten Years' Sentences." *Canadian Literature,* No.41 (1969), pp. 10–16.

> PESANDO, FRANK. "In a Nameless Land: The Use of Apocalyptic Mythology in the Writings of Margaret Laurence." *Journal Of Canadian Fiction,* 2, No.1 (1973), 53–58.

> READ, S. E. "The Maze of Life: The Work of Margaret Laurence." *Canadian Literature,* No.27 (1966), pp. 5–14.

> RICOU, LAURENCE R. "Empty as Nightmare: Man and Landscape in Recent Canadian Prairie Fiction." *Mosaic,* 6, No.2 (1972/3), 146–48.

> THOMAS, CLARA. "The Novels of Margaret Laurence." *Studies In The Novel,* 4 (1972), 154–64.

A BIRD IN THE HOUSE (1970)

Reviews

> WEEKS, EDWARD. *Atlantic Monthly,* 225, No.3 (1970), 144.

THE DIVINERS (1974)

> ATHERTON, STAN. "Margaret Laurence's Progress." *International Fiction Review,* 2 (1975), 61–64.

> HIND-SMITH, JOAN. *Three Voices: The Lives Of Margaret Laurence, Gabrielle Roy, Frederick Philip Grove,* pp. 56–60.

Reviews

> BEVAN, ALLAN. *Dalhousie Review,* 54 (1974), 360–63.

> LEVER, BERNICE. "Manawaka Magic." *Journal Of Canadian Fiction,* 3, No.3 (1974), 93–96.

> THOMAS, AUDREY. "A Broken Wand?" *Canadian Literature,* No.62 (1974), pp. 89–91.

> WEEKS, EDWARD. *Atlantic Monthly,* 233, No.6 (1974), 108–9.

THE FIRE-DWELLERS (1969)

> HIND-SMITH, JOAN. *Three Voices: The Lives Of Margaret Laurence, Gabrielle Roy, Frederick Philip Grove,* pp. 42–46.

Reviews

> GROSSKURTH, PHYLLIS. "Wise and Gentle." *Canadian Literature,* No.43 (1970), pp. 91–92.

> WEEKS, EDWARD. *Atlantic Monthly,* 223, No.6 (1969), 112–13.

JASON'S QUEST (1970)

Reviews

> THOMAS, CLARA. "Bashing On." *Canadian Literature,* No.50 (1971), pp. 88–90.

A JEST OF GOD (1966)

> BOWERING, GEORGE. "That Fool of a Fear: Notes on 'A Jest of God.'" *Canadian Literature,* No.50 (1971), pp. 41–56.

> DJWA, SANDRA. "False Gods and the True Covenant: Thematic Continuity Between Margaret Laurence and Sinclair Ross." *Journal Of Canadian Fiction,* 1, No.4 (1972), 47–50.

> HIND-SMITH, JOAN. *Three Voices: The Lives Of Margaret Laurence, Gabrielle Roy, Frederick Philip Grove,* pp. 37–40.

> McLAY, C. M. "Every Man Is an Island: Isolation in 'A Jest of God.'" *Canadian Literature,* No.50 (1971), pp. 41–56.

> ROSENGARTEN, H. J. "Inescapable Bonds." *Canadian Literature,* No.35 (1968), pp. 99–100.

> THOMAS, CLARA. *Margaret Laurence,* pp. 45–54.

Reviews

> CAMERON, DONALD. "Of Tyranny and Growth." *Journal Of Commonwealth Literature,* No.5 (1968), pp. 133–35.

> HALL, JOAN JOFFE. "Prison of the Self." *Saturday Review,* 27 August 1966, p. 29.

> HARLOW, ROBERT. "Lack of Distance." *Canadian Literature,* No.31 (1967), pp. 71–75.

> ROSENGARTEN, H. J. "Inescapable Bonds." *Canadian Literature,* No.35 (1968), 99–100.

THE STONE ANGEL (1964)

> HIND-SMITH, JOAN. *Three Voices: The Lives Of Margaret Laurence, Gabrielle Roy, Frederick Philip Grove,* pp. 31–35.

> KERTZER, J. M. "*The Stone Angel:* Time and Responsibility." *Dalhousie Review,* 54 (1974), 499–509.

> NEW, WILLIAM H. "Life and Time: Laurence's *The Stone Angel,*" in his *Articulating West,* pp. 207–15.

> RICOU, LAURENCE. *Vertical Man/ Horizontal World,* pp. 116–18.

> THOMAS, CLARA. *Margaret Laurence,* pp. 35–44.

> THOMPSON, ANNE. "The Wilderness of Pride: Form and Image in

The Stone Angel." Journal Of Canadian Fiction, 4, No.3 (1975), 95-110.

Reviews
WATT, F. W. *University Of Toronto Quarterly,* 34 (1965), 373-75.

THIS SIDE JORDAN (1960)

THOMAS, CLARA. *Margaret Laurence,* pp. 28-34.

LAWSON, HENRY (Australian, 1867-1922)

GENERAL

FOX, LEN. "Henry Lawson and Ragnar Redbeard." *Overland,* No.38 (1968), pp. 31-34.

HOPE, A. D. "Steele Rudd and Henry Lawson," in *The Australian Nationalists,* ed. Chris Wallace-Crabbe, pp. 58-68.

O'GRADY, DESMOND. "Henry Lawson," in *The Australian Nationalists,* ed. Chris Wallace-Crabbe, pp. 69-84.

PHILLIPS, A. A. "Henry Lawson as Craftsman," in *Twentieth Century Australian Literary Criticism,* ed. Clement Semmler, pp. 181-93.

———. "Lawson Revisited," in *The Australian Nationalists,* ed. Chris Wallace-Crabbe, pp. 85-99.

JOE WILSON

WALLACE-CRABBE, CHRIS. "Lawson's *Joe Wilson:* A Skeletal Novel," in *The Australian Nationalists,* ed. Chris Wallace-Crabbe, pp. 100-7.

LAXNESS, HALLDÓR KILJAN (Icelandic, 1902-)

THE ATOM STATION (Atómstöin, 1948)

HALLBERG, PETER. *Halldór Laxness,* pp., 156-64.

THE FISH CAN SING (Brekkukotsannáll, 1957)

HALLBERG, PETER. *Halldór Laxness,* pp. 191-95.

Reviews
JACOBS, BARRY. "Back Home to a Stern Heritage." *Saturday Review,* 27 May 1967, p. 37.

McGREW, JULIA H. *American Scandanavian Review,* 56 (1968), 307-8.

THE HAPPY WARRIORS (Gerpla, 1952)

HALLBERG, PETER. *Halldór Laxness,* pp. 165-79.

HUS SKALDSINS

HALLBERG, PETER. *Halldór Laxness,* pp. 120-22.

INDEPENDENT PEOPLE (Sjálfstaett fólk, 1934-35)

HALLBERG, PETER. *Halldór Laxness,* pp. 93-116.

ÍSLANDSKLUKKAN (1943-46)

HALLBERG, PETER. *Halldór Laxness,* pp. 144-55.

KRISTNIHALD UNDER JÖKLI (1968)

Reviews
RINGLER, RICHARD N. "Christianity on the Slopes of the Glacier." *Books Abroad,* 44 (1970), 54-55.

LJOS HEIM SINS

HALLBERG, PETER. *Halldór Laxness,* pp. 117-19.

PARADISE RECLAIMED (Paradisarheimt, 1960)

HALLBERG, PETER. *Halldór Laxness,* pp. 186-90.

SALKA VALKA (1931-32)

HALLBERG, PETER. *Halldór Laxness,* pp. 68-92.

VEPARINN MIKLI FRA KASMIR (1927)

HALLBERG, PETER. *Halldór Laxness,* pp. 36-51.

WORLD LIGHT (Heimsljós, 1937-40)

HALLBERG, PETER. *Halldór Laxness,* pp. 117-43.

Reviews
SPECTOR, ROBERT D. *American Scandanavian Review,* 57 (1969), 420-21.

LAYA, JUAN

THIS BARANGAY (1950)

CASPER, LEONARD. *New Writing From The Philippines,* pp. 74-77.

LAYE, CAMARA (Guinean, 1928-1980)

GENERAL

MACAULAY, JEANNETTE. "The Idea of Assimilation," in *Protest And Conflict In African Literature,* ed. Cosmo Pieterse and Donald Munro, pp. 81-92.

THE AFRICAN CHILD (L'Enfant noir)

BRENCH, A. C. "Idealist & Mystic: Camara Laye." *African Literature Today,* No.2 (1969), pp. 11-16.

———. *The Novelists' Inheritance In French Africa,* pp. 37-46.

CARROLL, DAVID. "Camara Laye's *The African Child:* A Reply." *African Literature Today,* 5 (1971), 129-36.

CARTEY, WILFRED. *Whispers From A Continent,* pp. 3-8.

GLEASON, JUDITH ILLSLEY. *This Africa,* pp. 109-12.

MAKOUTA-MBOUKOU, J. P. *Black African Literature,* pp. 69-75.

PALMER, EUSTACE. *An Introduction To The African Novel,* pp. 85-95.

VAN LENT, PETER C. "*Hantu* and The Theme of Self-Realization in Camara Laye's *L'Enfant Noir.*" *College Language Association Journal,* 18 (1975), 532-41.

THE DARK CHILD see THE AFRICAN CHILD

A DREAM OF AFRICA (Dramouss, 1966)

BRENCH, A. C. "Idealist & Mystic: Camara Laye." *African Literature Today,* No.2 (1969), pp. 27-31.

LARSON, CHARLES R. "Laye's Unfulfilled African Dream." *Books Abroad,* 43 (1969), 209-11.

Reviews
GREEN, ROBERT J. "Laye Disillusioned." *Journal Of Commonwealth Literature,* No.9 (1970), pp. 122-26.

THE RADIANCE OF THE KING (Le Regard du Roi, 1954)

BRENCH, A. C. "Idealist & Mystic: Camara Laye." *African Literature Today,* No.2 (1969), pp. 16-23.

———. *The Novelists' Inheritance In French Africa,* pp. 120-27.

COOK, DAVID. "The Relevance of the King in Camara Laye's *Le Regard Du Roi,*" in *Perspectives On African Literature,* ed. Christopher Heywood, pp. 138-47.

JAHN, JANHEINZ. "Camara Laye: Another Interpretation," in *Introduction To African Literature,* ed. Ulli Beier, pp. 200-3.

LARSON, CHARLES R. "Assimilated Négritude: Camara Laye's *Le Regard Du Roi,*" in his *The Emergence Of African Fiction,* rev. ed., pp. 167-226.

PALMER, EUSTACE. *An Introduction To The African Novel,* pp. 95-116.

RAMSARAN, J. A. "Camara Laye's Symbolism: An Interpretation of: 'The Radiance of the King,' " in *Introduction To African Literature,* ed. Ulli Beier, pp. 196-99, 203-4.

SHELTON, AUSTIN J. "Cultural Reversal as a Motif of Protest by Laye and Dadié." *L'Esprit Créateur*, 10 (1970), 213-17.

LAZARILLO DE TORMES (Author Unknown, 1554)

ABRAMS, FRED. "Hurtado de Mendoza's Concealed Signatures in the *Lazarillo De Tormes*." *Romance Notes*, 15 (1973), 341-45.

———. "A Note on the Mercedarian Friar in the *Lazarillo De Tormes*." *Romance Notes*, 11 (1969), 444-46.

———. "To Whom Was the Anonymous *Lazarillo De Tormes* Dedicated?" *Romance Notes*, 8 (1967), 273-77.

BELL, A. "The Rhetoric of Self-defence of 'Lázaro de Tormes.' " *Modern Language Review*, 68 (1973), 84-93.

CAREY, DOUGLAS M. "Asides and Interiority in *Lazarillo De Tormes:* A Study in Psychological Realism." *Studies In Philology*, 66 (1969), 119-34.

COLLARD, ANDREE. "The Unity of *Lazarillo De Tormes*." *MLN*, 83 (1968), 262-67.

DEYERMOND, A. D. "The Corrupted Vision: Further Thoughts on *Lazarillo De Tormes*." *Forum For Modern Language Studies*, 1 (1965), 246-49.

———. *<Lazarillo De Tormes:> A Critical Guide*.

———. "Lazarus and Lazarillo." *Studies In Short Fiction*, 2 (1965), 351-57.

DURAND, FRANK. "The Author and Lazaro: Levels of Comic Meaning." *Bulletin Of Hispanic Studies*, 45 (1968), 89-101.

GILMAN, STEPHEN. "The Death of Lazarillo de Tormes." *PMLA*, 81 (1966), 149-66.

HESSE, EVERETT W. "The *Lazarillo De Tormes* and The Playing of a Role." *Kentucky Romance Quarterly*, 22 (1975), 61-76.

HITCHCOCK, RICHARD. "Lazarillo and 'Vuestra Merced.' " *MLN*, 86 (1971), 264-66.

HOLZINGER, WALTER. "The Breadly Paradise Revisited: *Lazarillo De Tormes*, Segundo Tratado." *Revista Hispanica Moderna*, 37 (1972/3), 229-36.

KEARFUL, FRANK J. "Spanish Rogues and English Foundlings: On the Disintegration of Picaresque." *Genre*, 4 (1971), 379-82.

McGRADY, DONALD. "Social Irony in *Lazarillo De Tormes* and its Implications for Authorship." *Romance Philology*, 23 (1970), 557-67.

MANCING, HOWARD. "The Deceptiveness of *Lazarillo De Tormes*." *PMLA*, 90 (1975), 426-32.

PERRY, T. ANTHONY. "Biblical Symbolism in the *Lazarillo De Tormes*." *Studies In Philology*, 67 (1970), 139-46.

RICAPITO, JOSEPH V. "*Lazarillo De Tormes* (Chap. V) and Masuccio's Fourth Novella." *Romance Philology*, 23 (1970), 305-11.

———. "*Lazarillo De Tormes* and Machiavelli: Two Facets of Renaissance Perspective." *Romanische Forschungen*, 83 (1971), 151-72.

SCHWARTZ, KESSEL. "A Statistical Note on the Authorship of *Lazarillo De Tormes*." *Romance Notes*, 9 (1967), 118-19.

SPIVAKOVSKY, ERIKA. "New Arguments in Favor of Mendoza's Authorship of the *Lazarillo De Tormes*." *Symposium*, 24 (1970), 67-80.

TRUMAN, R. W. "*Lazarillo De Tormes*, Petrarch's *De Remediis Adversae Fortunae*, and Erasmus's *Praise Of Folly*." *Bulletin Of Hispanic Studies*, 52 (1975), 33-53.

———. "Lázaro de Tormes and The 'Homo Novus' Tradition." *Modern Language Review*, 64 (1969), 62-67.

———. "Parody and Irony in the Self-Portrayal of Lázaro de Tormes." *Modern Language Review*, 63 (1968), 600-5.

WAGENER, HANS. *The German Baroque Novel*, pp. 37-41.

WHITBOURN, CHRISTINE J. "Moral Ambiguity in the Spanish Picaresque Tradition," in *Knaves And Swindlers*, ed. Christine J. Whitbourn, pp. 7-10.

WILTROUT, ANN. "The *Lazarillo De Tormes* and Erasmus' 'Opulentia Sordida.' " *Romanische Forschungen*, 81 (1969), 550-64.

WOODWARD, L. J. "Author-Reader Relationship in the *Lazarillo De Tormes*." *Forum For Modern Language Studies*, 1 (1965), 43-53.

LE FORT, GERTRUDE BARONESS VON (German, 1876-1971)

THE SONG OF THE SCAFFOLD (Die Letzte am Schafott, 1931)

FALK, EUGENE H. "The Leap to Faith: Two Paths to the Scaffold." *Symposium*, 21 (1967), 241-54.

REINHARDT, KURT F. *The Theological Novel Of Modern Europe*, pp. 225-34.

LEACOCK, STEPHEN (Canadian, 1869-1944)

GENERAL

BERGER, CARL. "The Other Mr. Leacock." *Canadian Literature*, No.55 (1973), pp. 23-40.

BISSELL, CLAUDE T. "Haliburton, Leacock and the American Humorous Tradition." *Canadian Literature*, No.39 (1969), 5-19.

CAMERON, DONALD A. "Stephen Leacock: The Boy Behind the Arras." *Journal Of Commonwealth Literature*, No.3 (1967), pp. 3-18.

LEGATE, DAVID M. *Stephen Leacock: A Biography*.

MAGEE, W. H. "Stephen Leacock: Local Colourist." *Canadian Literature*, No.39 (1969), pp. 34-42.

PACEY, DESMOND. "Leacock as a Satirist," in his *Essays In Canadian Literature, 1938-1968*, pp. 67-76.

ARCADIAN ADVENTURES WITH THE IDLE RICH (1914)

BISSELL, CLAUDE T. "Haliburton, Leacock and the American Humorous Tradition." *Canadian Literature*, No.39 (1969), 14-19.

CAMERON, D. A. "Stephen Leacock: The Novelist Who Never Was." *Dalhousie Review*, 46 (1966), 15-28.

MAGEE, W. H. "Stephen Leacock: Local Colourist." *Canadian Literature*, No.39 (1969), pp. 41-42.

SUNSHINE SKETCHES OF A LITTLE TOWN (1912)

CAMERON, D. A. "The Enchanted Houses: Leacock's Irony." *Canadian Literature*, No.23 (1965), pp. 31-44.

———. "Stephen Leacock: The Novelist Who Never Was." *Dalhousie Review*, 46 (1966), 15-28.

DAVIES, ROBERTSON. *Stephen Leacock*, pp. 23-29.

MAGEE, W. H. "Stephen Leacock: Local Colourist." *Canadian Literature*, No.39 (1969), pp. 37-41.

SAVAGE, DAVID. "Leacock on Survival: Sunshine Sketches Sixty Years After." *Journal Of Canadian Fiction*, 1, No.4 (1972), 64-67.

SHARMAN, VINCENT. "The Satire of Stephen Leacock's 'Sunshine Sketches.' " *Queen's Quarterly*, 78 (1971), 261-67.

LEAKEY, CAROLINE

THE BROAD ARROW (1859)

POOLE, JOAN E. "The Broad Arrow—A Re-appraisal." *Southerly*, 26 (1966), 117-24.

LEBON, JEAN

LA COURONNE CRUESE (1972)

Reviews
NELSON, HILDA. *French Review,* 48 (1974), 241-43.

LE CLÉZIO, JEAN MARIE GUSTAVE (French, 1940-)

THE BOOK OF FLIGHTS (Le livre des fuits, 1969)

CAGNON, MAURICE. "J. M. G. Le Clezio: The Genesis of Writing." *Language And Style,* 5 (1972), 221-27.

Reviews
CAGNON, MAURICE. *French Review,* 44 (1971), 644-45.

THE FLOOD (Le déluge, 1968)

Reviews
LESAGE, LAURENT. "A Special Kind of Horror." *Saturday Review,* 27 January 1968, pp. 28-29.

SZANTO, GEORGE H. "One Spectator Among Many." *Catholic World,* 207 (1968), 235-36.

THE GIANTS (Les géants, 1973)

Reviews
KUHN, REINHARD. *French Review,* 48 (1975), 799-800.

TERRA AMATA (1968)

Reviews
SMITH, A. M. SHERIDAN. "Obsessions." *London Magazine,* NS, 9, No.1 (1969), 100-2.

WAR (La guerre, 1970)

Reviews
CAGNON, MAURICE. *French Review,* 44 (1971), 1122-23.

LEDUC, VIOLETTE (French, 1901-1972)

LA BÂTARDE (1964)

Reviews
PEYRE, HENRI. "Passions of a Gallic Sappho." *Saturday Review,* 30 October 1965, pp. 46-47.

MAD IN PURSUIT (La folie en tête, 1970)

Reviews
BALAKIAN, ANNA. *Saturday Review,* 18 September 1971, p. 47.

RAVAGES (1955)

Reviews
SMITH, A. M. SHERIDAN. *London Magazine,* NS, 8, No.1 (1968), 88-89.

THÉRÈSE AND ISABELLE (1966)

Reviews
PEYRE, HENRI. "Rapture in Little Girls' Room." *Saturday Review,* 15 July 1967, p. 36.

LEIRIS, MICHEL (French, 1901-)

AURORA (1946)

HUBERT, RENÉE RIESE. "*Aurora:* Adventure in Word and Image." *Sub-stance,* No.11/2 (1975), pp. 74-87.

MATTHEWS, J. H. *Surrealism And The Novel,* pp. 107-23.

LEM, STANISLAW (Polish, 1921-)

GENERAL

KANDEL, MICHAEL. "Stanislaw Lem on Men and Robots." *Extrapolation,* 14 (1972), 13-24.

THE INVESTIGATION see SOLARIS

SOLARIS (Sledztwo, 1959)

BALCERZAN, EDWARD. "Seeking Only Man: Language and Ethics in *Solaris.*" *Science-Fiction Studies,* 2 (1975), 152-56.

KETTERER, DAVID. "*Solaris* and the Illegitimate Suns of Science Fiction." *Extrapolation,* 14 (1972), 73-89.

LEÑERO, VINCENTE (Mexican, 1933-)

GENERAL

MCMURRAY, GEORGE R. "The Novels of Vicente Leñero." *Critique,* 8, No.3 (1965/6), 55-61.

LOS ALBANILES (1964)

LANGFORD, WALTER M. *The Mexican Novel Comes Of Age,* pp. 156-59.

Reviews
SOMMERS, JOSEPH. *Hispania,* 49 (1966), 172-73.

ESTUDIO Q (1965)

LANGFORD, WALTER M. *The Mexican Novel Comes Of Age,* pp. 159-61.

MCMURRAY, GEORGE R. "The Novels of Vicente Leñero." *Critique,* 8, No.3 (1965/6), 57-61.

EL GARABATO (1967)

LANGFORD, WALTER M. *The Mexican Novel Comes Of Age,* pp. 161-64.

LA VOZ ADOLORIDA (1961)

LANGFORD, WALTER M. *The Mexican Novel Comes Of Age,* pp. 154-56.

LENGYEL, JÓZSEF (Hungarian, 1896-1975)

GENERAL

GÖMÖRI, GEORGE. "József Lengyel: Chronicler of Cruel Years." *Books Abroad,* 49 (1975), 471-74.

LENZ, (J.M.R.) JAKOB MICHAEL REINHOLD (German, 1751-1792)

GENERAL

DIFFEY, NORMAN R. "Lenz, Rousseau, and the Problem of Striving." *Seminar,* 10 (1974), 165-80.

OSBORNE, JOHN. "Exhibitionism and Criticism: J. M. R. Lenz's *Briefe Über Die Moralität Der Leiden Des Jungen Werthers.*" *Seminar,* 10 (1974), 199-212.

DER LANDPREDIGER

OSBORNE, JOHN. "The Postponed Idyll: Two Moral Tales by J. M. R. Lenz." *Neophilologus,* 59 (1975), 73-81.

ZERBIN ODER DIE NEUERE PHILOSOPHIE

OSBORNE, JOHN. "The Postponed Idyll: Two Moral Tales by J. M. R. Lenz." *Neophilologus,* 59 (1975), 68-73.

LENZ, SIEGFRIED (German, 1926-)

THE GERMAN LESSON (Deutschstunde, 1968)

PASLICK, ROBERT H. "Narrowing the Distance: Siegfried Lenz's *Deutschstunde.*" *German Quarterly,* 46 (1973), 210-18.

RUSSELL, PETER. "Siegfried Lenz's *Deutschestunde:* A North German Novel." *German Life And Letters,* 28 (1975), 405-18.

ZIPES, JACK D. "Growing Pains in the Contemporary German Novel—East and West." *Mosaic,* 5, No.3 (1971/2), 8-9.

Reviews
BERNSTEIN, JOSEPH M. "Deutschstunde." *American-German Review,* 35, No.6 (1969), 24-25.

EWART, GAVIN. "Rome-Berlin Axis." *London Magazine,* NS, 12, No.4 (1972), 147-48.

HAMBURGER, MICHAEL. "A Third Reich with No Demons." *Saturday Review,* 18 March 1972, pp. 71–73.

THE SURVIVOR (Stadtgespräch, 1963)

Reviews
LEDERER, HERBERT. *Novel,* 1 (1967), 95–96.

LEONOV, LEONID (Russian, 1899–)
GENERAL

THOMSON, R. D. B. "Leonid Leonov." *Forum For Modern Language Studies,* 2 (1966), 264–73.

THE BADGERS (Barsuki, 1924)

PLANK, D. L. "Unconscious Motifs in Leonid Leonov's *The Badgers.*" *Slavic And East European Journal,* 16 (1972), 19–35.

THE ROAD TO THE OCEAN (Doroga na okean, 1935)

MATHEWSON, RUFUS. "Four Novels," in *Major Soviet Writers,* ed. Edward J. Brown, pp. 336–41.

THE THIEF (Vor, 1927)

THOMSON, R. D. B. "Leonid Leonov." *Forum For Modern Language Studies,* 2 (1966), 264–68.

LE PAN, DOUGLAS (Canadian, 1914–)
THE DESERTER (1964)

JONES, D. G. *Butterfly On Rock,* pp. 153–57.

PRIESTMAN, DONALD G. "Man in the Maze." *Canadian Literature,* No.64 (1975), pp. 60–65.

Reviews
GOSE, ELLIOTT. "Bright But Powdery." *Canadian Literature,* No.24 (1965), pp. 70–73.

KIRKWOOD, HILDA. *Canadian Forum,* 45 (1965), 44–45.

WATT, F. W. *University Of Toronto Quarterly,* 34 (1965), 370–73.

LEPROHON, ROSANNA ELANOR MULLINS (Canadian, 1832–1879)
ANTOINETTE DE MIRECOURT (1864)

EDWARDS, MARY JANE. "Essentially Canadian." *Canadian Literature,* No.52 (1972), pp. 17–20.

LERA, ANGEL MARIA DE (Spanish, 1912–)
SE VENDE UN HOMBRE

Reviews
FRANZ, THOMAS R. *Journal Of Spanish Studies,* 3 (1975), 217–18.

LERMONTOV, MIKHAIL YURYEVICH (Russian, 1814–1841)
GENERAL

GRONICKA, ANDRÉ VON. "Lermontov's Debt to Goethe: A Reappraisal." *Revue De Littérature Comparée,* 40 (1966), 567–84.

HALPERT, EUGENE. "Lermontov and the Wolf Man." *American Imago,* 32 (1975), 315–28.

IVANOVA, T. A. "Lermontov and Washington Irving: A Creative Encounter." *Soviet Studies In Literature,* 1, No.3 (1965), 25–41.

MICHAILOFF, HELEN. "The Death of Lermontov (The Poet and the Tsar.)" *Russian Literature Triquarterly,* No.10 (1974), pp. 279–97.

A HERO OF OUR TIME (Geroy Nashego Vremeni, 1840)

ARIAN, I. "Some Aspects of Lermontov's *A Hero Of Our Time.*" *Forum For Modern Language Studies,* 4 (1968), 22–32.

BOYD, ALEXANDER F. *Aspects Of The Russian Novel,* pp. 24–45.

EAGLE, HERBERT. "Lermontov's 'Play' with Romantic Genre Expectations in *A Hero Of Our Time.*" *Russian Literature Triquarterly,* No.10 (1974), pp. 299–315.

FREEBORN, R. H. "Realism in Russia, to the Death of Dostoevsky," in *The Age Of Realism,* ed. F. W. J. Hemmings, pp. 84–87.

———. *The Rise Of The Russian Novel,* pp. 38–73.

GRONICKA, ANDRÉ VON. "Lermontov's Debt To Goethe: A Reappraisal." *Revue De Littérature Comparée,* 40 (1966), 579–83.

PEACE, R. A. "The Role of *Tamán* in Lermontov's *Geroy Nashego Vremeni.*" *Slavonic And East European Review,* 45 (1967), 12–29.

REEVE, F. D. *The Russian Novel,* pp. 45–63.

ULPH, OWEN. "Unmasking the Masked Guardsman: A Case-Study of the Moral Man in the Immoral Society." *Russian Literature Triquarterly,* No.3 (1972), pp. 269–80.

SHTOSS

IVANOVA, T. A. "Lermontov and Washington Irving: A Creative Encounter." *Soviet Studies In Literature,* 1, No.3 (1965), 31–36.

LEROUX, ÉTIENNE (Afrikaans, 1922–) pseudonym of Stephanus Petrus Daniel Le Roux
18/44

BERNER, ROBERT L. "Etienne Leroux: A Jungian Introduction." *Books Abroad,* 49 (1975), 255–62.

ONE FOR THE DEVIL

Reviews
LARSON, CHARLES R. "Bleached Society Stained by Blood." *Saturday Review,* 4 May 1968, pp. 37–38.

THE THIRD EYE

Reviews
LARSON, CHARLES R. *Saturday Review,* 7 June 1969, p. 34.

LE SAGE, ALAIN RENÉ (French, 1668–1747)
GIL BLAS DE SANTILLANE (1715–1735)

GROVES, MARGARET. "An Early Version of Villiers de l'Isle Adam's *La Maison Du Bonheur.*" *Romance Notes,* 10 (1969), 238–44.

LONGHURST, JENNIFER. "Le Sage and the Spanish Tradition: *Gil Blas* as a Picaresque Novel," in *Studies In Eighteenth-Century French Literature,* ed. J. H. Fox, M. H. Waddicor, and D. A. Watts, pp. 123–37.

MYLNE, VIVIENNE. *The Eighteenth Century French Novel,* pp. 49–72.

LESKOV, NIKOLAI SEMYONOVICH (Russian, 1831–1895)
GENERAL

EIKHENBAUM, B. M. "Leskov and Contemporary Prose." Trans. Martin P. Rice. *Russian Literature Triquarterly,* No.11 (1975), 211–24.

McLEAN, HUGH. "Theodore the Christian Looks at Abraham the Hebrew: Leskov and the Jews." *California Slavic Studies,* 7 (1973), 65–98.

THE CATHEDRAL CLERGY (Soboryane, 1872)

REEVE, F. D. *The Russian Novel,* pp. 205–35.

THE ENCHANTED WANDERER (Ocharovanni Strannik)

BRIDGMAN, RICHARD. "Leskov under the Bushel of Translation." *Texas Quarterly,* 9, No.3 (1966), 82–84.

LÉSOUALC'H, THÉO
PHOSPHÈNES

Reviews
GUGLI, WILLIAM V. *French Review,* 47 (1974), 1215–16.

LESSING, DORIS (Zimbabwe, emmigrated to England, 1919–)
GENERAL

BROWN, LLOYD W. "The Shape of Things: Sexual Images and the Sense of Form in Doris Lessing's Fiction." *World Literature Written In English,* 14 (1975), 176–86.

BURKOM, SELMA R. "A Doris Lessing Checklist." *Critique,* 11, No.1 (1968), 69–81.

———. " 'Only Connect': Form and Content in the Works of Doris Lessing." *Critique,* 11 (1968), 51–68.

HARDIN, NANCY SHIELDS. "Doris Lessing and the Sufi Way." *Contemporary Literature,* 14 (1973), 565–81.

HOWE, FLORENCE. "A Conversation with Doris Lessing (1966)." *Contemporary Literature,* 14 (1973), 418–36; rpt. in *Doris Lessing: Critical Studies,* ed. Annis Pratt and L. S. Dembo, pp. 1–19.

KAPLAN, SYDNEY JANET. "The Limits of Consciousness in the Novels of Doris Lessing." *Contemporary Literature,* 14 (1973), 536–49.

McDOWELL, FREDERICK P. W. "The Fiction of Doris Lessing: An Interim View." *Arizona Quarterly,* 21 (1965), 315–45.

MARKOW, ALICE BRADLEY. "The Pathology of Feminine Failure in the Fiction of Doris Lessing." *Critique,* 16, No.1 (1974), 88–99.

OATES, JOYCE CAROL. "A Visit with Doris Lessing." *Southern Review,* NS, 9 (1973), 873–82.

RUBENSTEIN, ROBERTA. "Outer Space, Inner Space: Doris Lessing's Metaphor of Science Fiction." *World Literature Written In English,* 14 (1975), 187–97.

SELIGMAN, DEE. "The Sufi Quest." *World Literature Written In English,* 12, No.2 (1973), 190–206.

SPILKA, MARK. "Lessing and Lawrence: The Battle of the Sexes." *Contemporary Literature,* 16 (1975), 218–40.

SUKENICK, LYNN. "Feeling and Reason in Doris Lessing's Fiction." *Contemporary Literature,* 14 (1973), 515–35.

BRIEFING FOR A DESCENT INTO HELL (1970)

BOLLING, DOUGLASS. "Structure and Theme in *Briefing For A Descent Into Hell.*" *Contemporary Literature,* 14 (1973), 550–64.

DeMOTT, BENJAMIN. "Toward a More Human World." *Saturday Review,* 13 March 1971, pp. 25–27, 86–87.

RYF, ROBERT S. "Beyond Ideology: Doris Lessing's Mature Vision." *Modern Fiction Studies,* 21 (1975), 193–201.

SCHLUETER, PAUL. *The Novels Of Doris Lessing,* pp. 119–24.

SELIGMAN, DEE. "The Sufi Quest." *World Literature Written In English,* 12, No.2 (1973), 202–05.

Reviews
THORPE, MICHAEL. "Doris Lessing's Risky Inner World." *Journal Of Commonwealth Literature,* 7, No.1 (1972), 133–35.

CHILDREN OF VIOLENCE (1952-1965)

McDOWELL, FREDRICK P. W. "The Fiction of Doris Lessing: An Interim View." *Arizona Quarterly,* 21 (1965), 330–45.

MARCHINO, LOIS A. "The Search for Self in the Novels of Doris Lessing." *Studies In The Novel,* 4 (1972), 252–61.

PORTER, NANCY. "Silenced History—*Children Of Violence* and

The Golden Notebook." *World Literature Written In English,* 12, No.2 (1973), 161–79.

PRATT, ANNIS. "Women and Nature in Modern Fiction." *Contemporary Literature,* 13 (1972), 487–88.

SCHLUETER, PAUL. *The Novels Of Doris Lessing,* pp. 23–76.

Reviews
DALTON, ELIZABETH. *Kenyon Review,* 27 (1965), 572–73.

HICKS, GRANVILLE. "All About a Modern Eve." *Saturday Review,* 2 April 1966, 31–32.

THE FOUR-GATED CITY (1969)

BARNOUW, DAGMAR. "Disorderly Company: From *The Golden Notebook* to *The Four-Gated City.*" *Contemporary Literature,* 14 (1973), 500–14.

KARL, FREDERICK R. "Doris Lessing in the Sixties: The New Anatomy of Melancholy." *Contemporary Literature,* 13 (1972), 23–33.

O'FALLON, KATHLEEN. "Quest for a New Vision." *World Literature Written In English,* 12, No.2 (1973), 183–88.

RAPPING, ELAYNE ANTLER. "Unfree Women: Feminism in Doris Lessing's Novels." *Women's Studies,* 3 (1975), 29–44.

ROSE, ELLEN CRONAN. "The Eriksonian Bildungsroman: An Approach Through Doris Lessing." *Hartford Studies In Literature,* 7 (1975), 1–17.

RUBENSTEIN, ROBERTA. "Outer Space, Inner Space: Doris Lessing's Metaphor of Science Fiction." *World Literature Written In English,* 14 (1975), 187–93.

SCHLUETER, PAUL. *The Novels Of Doris Lessing,* pp. 64–76.

SELIGMAN, DEE. "The Sufi Quest." *World Literature Written In English,* 12, No.2 (1973), 199–202.

SUDRANN, JEAN. "Hearth and Horizon: Changing Concepts of the 'Domestic' Life of the Heroine." *Massachusetts Review,* 14 (1973), 238–50.

Reviews
DALTON, ELIZABETH. "Quest's End." *Commentary,* 49, No.1 (1970), 85–87.

OATES, JOYCE CAROL. "Last Children of Violence." *Saturday Review,* 17 May 1969, p. 48.

THORPE, MICHAEL. "Real and Ideal Cities." *Journal Of Commonwealth Literature,* No.9 (1970), pp. 119–22.

THE GOLDEN NOTEBOOK (1962)

BARNOUW, DAGMAR. "Disorderly Company: From *The Golden Notebook* to *The Four-Gated City.*" Contemporary Literature, 14 (1973), 491–500.

BROOKS, ELLEN W. "The Image of Woman in Lessing's *The Golden Notebook.*" *Critique,* 15, No.1 (1973), 101–9.

BROWN, LLOYD W. "The Shape of Things: Sexual Images and the Sense of Form in Doris Lessing's Fiction." *World Literature Written In English,* 14 (1975), 181–84.

CAREY, JOHN L. "Art and Reality in *The Golden Notebook.*" *Contemporary Literature,* 14 (1973), 437–56; rpt. in *Doris Lessing: Critical Essays,* ed. Annis Pratt and L. S. Dembo, pp. 20–39.

HINZ, EVELYN J. and JOHN J. TEUNISSEN. "The Pietà as Icon in *The Golden Notebook.*" *Contemporary Literature,* 14 (1973), 457–70; rpt. in *Doris Lessing: Critical Studies,* ed. Annis Pratt and L. S. Dembo, pp. 40–53.

KARL, FREDERICK R. "Doris Lessing in the Sixties: The New Anatomy of Melancholy." *Contemporary Literature,* 13 (1972), 15–23.

LEBOWITZ, NAOMI. *Humanism And The Absurd In The Modern Novel,* pp. 130–36.

LESSING, DORIS. "On The Golden Notebook." *Partisan Review,* 40 (1973), 14–30.

LIGHTFOOT, MARJORIE J. "Breakthrough in *The Golden Note-book*." *Studies In The Novel*, 7 (1975), 277–84.

MARCHINO, LOIS A. "The Search for Self in the Novels of Doris Lessing." *Studies In The Novel*, 4 (1972), 252–61.

MARKOW, ALICE BRADLEY. "The Pathology of Feminine Failure in the Fiction of Doris Lessing." *Critique*, 16, No.1 (1974), 91–93.

MORGAN, ELLEN. "Alienation of the Woman Writer in *The Golden Notebook*." *Contemporary Literature*, 14 (1973), 471–80; rpt. in *Doris Lessing: Critical Studies*, ed. Annis Pratt and L. S. Dembo, pp. 54–63.

MULKEEN, ANNE M. "Twentieth-Century Realism: The 'Grid' Structure of *The Golden Notebook*." *Studies In The Novel*, 4 (1972), 262–74.

O'FALLON, KATHLEEN. "Quest for a New Vision." *World Literature Written In English*, 12, No.2 (1973), 180–83.

PORTER, DENNIS. "Realism and Failure in *The Golden Notebook*." *Modern Language Quarterly*, 35 (1974), 56–65.

PORTER, NANCY. "Silenced History—*Children Of Violence* and *The Golden Notebook*." *World Literature Written In English*, 12, No.2 (1973), 169–73.

PRATT, ANNIS. "The Contrary Structure of Doris Lessing's *The Golden Notebook*." *World Literature Written In English*, 12, No.2 (1973), 150–60.

RAPPING, ELAYNE ANTLER. "Unfree Women: Feminism in Doris Lessing's Novels." *Women's Studies*, 3 (1975), 29–44.

RUBENSTEIN, ROBERTA. "Doris Lessing's *The Golden Notebook*: The Meaning of its Shape." *American Imago*, 32 (1975), 40–58.

SCHLUETER, PAUL. *The Novels Of Doris Lessing*, pp. 77–116.

SPENCER, SHARON. " 'Femininity' and the Woman Writer: Doris Lessing's *The Golden Notebook* and the *Diary* of Anais Nin." *Women's Studies*, 1 (1973), 247–57.

THE GRASS IS SINGING (1950)

SCHLUETER, PAUL. *The Novels Of Doris Lessing*, pp. 7–22.

ZAK, MICHELE WENDER. "*The Grass Is Singing*: A Little Novel About the Emotions." *Contemporary Literature*, 14 (1973), 481–90; rpt. in *Doris Lessing: Critical Studies*, pp. 64–73.

Reviews

PHILCOX, RICHARD. *Présence Africaine*, No.87 (1973), pp. 14–16.

LANDLOCKED (1965)

SELIGMAN, DEE. "The Sufi Quest." *World Literature Written In English*, 12, No.2 (1973), 193–99.

Reviews

GOULD, TONY. "All at Sea with 'Landlocked.' " *Twentieth Century*, 174, No.1028 (1966), 73.

MARTHA QUEST (1952)

Reviews

OWEN, ROGER. "A Good Man Is Hard to Find." *Commentary*, 39, No.4 (1965), 79–82.

MEMOIRS OF A SURVIVOR (1974)

Reviews

COWLEY, MALCOLM. "Future Notebook." *Saturday Review*, 28 June 1975, pp. 23–24.

A PROPER MARRIAGE (1954)

Reviews

OWEN, ROGER. "A Good Man Is Hard to Find." *Commentary*, 39, No.4 (1965), 79–82.

RETREAT TO INNOCENCE (1956)

SCHLUETER, PAUL. *The Novels Of Doris Lessing*, pp. 117–19.

THE SUMMER BEFORE THE DARK (1973)

LEFCOWITZ, BARBARA F. "Dream and Action in Lessing's *The Summer Before The Dark*." *Critique*, 17, No.2 (1975), 107–20.

Reviews

LIBBY, MARION VLASTOS. *Ohio Review*, 15, No.1 (1973), 93–95.

WIDMAN, R. L. "Lessing's *The Summer Before The Dark*." *Contemporary Literature*, 14 (1973), 582–85.

LEVINE, NORMAN (Canadian, 1925–)
GENERAL

COX, JOHN D. "Norman Levine: An Interview." *Canadian Literature*, No.45 (1970), pp. 61–67.

LEZAMA LIMA, JOSÉ (Cuban, 1910–)
PARADISO (1960)

ALONSO, J. M. "A Sentimental Realism." *Review*, No.12 (1974), pp. 46–47.

CONRAD, ANDREE. "An Expanding Imagination." *Review*, No.12 (1974), pp. 48–51.

CORTAZAR, JULIO. "An Approach to Lezama Lima." Trans. Paula Speck. *Review*, No.12 (1974), pp. 20–25.

CORTAZAR, MERCEDES. "Entering Paradise." *Review*, No.12 (1974), pp. 17–19.

LEZAMA LIMA, JOSE. "Confluences." Trans. Andrée Conrad. *Review*, No.12 (1974), pp. 6–16.

MENTON, SEYMOUR. *Prose Fiction Of The Cuban Revolution*, pp. 52–54.

MÜLLER-BERGH, KLAUS. "José Lezama Lima and *Paradiso*." *Books Abroad*, 44 (1970), 36–40.

ORTEGA, JULIO. "Language as Hero." *Review*, No.12 (1974), pp. 35–42.

RODRIGUEZ MONEGAL, EMIR. "The Text in Its Context." Trans. Enrico-Mario Santí and the author. *Review*, No.12 (1974), pp. 30–34.

SARDUY, SEVERO. "A Cuban Proust." Trans. Enrico-Mario Santí. *Review*, No.12 (1974), pp. 43–45.

VARGAS LLOSA, MARIO. "Attempting the Impossible." Trans. Susan Jean Pels. *Review*, No.12 (1974), pp. 26–29.

WALLER, CLAUDIA JOAN. "José Lezama Lima's 'Paradiso': The Theme of Light and the Resurrection." *Hispania*, 56 (1973), 275–82.

LIANG PIN
KEEP THE RED FLAG FLYING

HUANG, JOE C. *Heroes And Villains In Communist China*, pp. 27–54.

LIBERTELLA, HÉCTOR
EL CAMINO DE LOS HIPERBÓREOS

Reviews

SCHWARTZ, KESSEL. *Hispania*, 54 (1971), 972.

LIBRO DE CAVALLERO ZIFAR (Author Unknown, 14th Century)

BURKE, JAMES. "The Meaning of the Islas Dotadas Episode in the *Libro Del Cavallero Cifar*." *Hispanic Review*, 38 (1970), 56–68.

———. "Names and the Significance of Etymology in the *Libro Del Cavallero Cifar*." *Romanic Review*, 59 (1968), 161–73.

———. "Symbolic Allegory in the Portus Salutaris Episode in the *Libro Del Cavallero Cifar*." *Kentucky Romance Quarterly*, 15 (1968), 69–84.

MULLEN, EDWARD J. "The Role of the Supernatural in *El Libro Del Cavallero Zifar*." *Revista De Estudios Hispánicos*, 5 (1971), 257-68.

WALKER, ROGER M. "Did Cervantes Know the *Cavallero Zifar?*" *Bulletin Of Hispanic Studies*, 49 (1972), 120-27.

———. "The Genesis of 'El Libro del Cavallero Zifar.' " *Modern Language Review*, 62 (1967), 61-69.

———. "Juan Ruiz's Defence of Love." *MLN*, 84 (1969), 292-97.

———. "The Unit of *El Libro Del Cavallero Zifar*." *Bulletin Of Hispanic Studies*, 42 (1965), 149-59.

LIDCHI, MAGGI

MAN OF EARTH

Reviews

RUBIN, DAVID. *Literature East And West*, 14 (1970), 293-94.

LIDMAN, SARA (Swedish, 1923-)

GENERAL

BORLAND, HAROLD H. "Sara Lidman's Progress: A Critical Survey of Six Novels." *Scandanavian Studies*, 39 (1967), 97-114.

JAG OCH MIN SON (1961)

BORLAND, HAROLD H. "Sara Lidman's Progress: A Critical Survey of Six Novels." *Scandanavian Studies*, 39 (1967), 107-11.

MED FEM DIAMANTER (1964)

BORLAND, HAROLD H. "Sara Lidman's Progress: A Critical Survey of Six Novels." *Scandanavian Studies*, 39 (1967), 111-14.

THE RAIN BIRD (Regnspiran, 1958)

"An Interview with Sara Lidman." *Contemporary Literature*, 12 (1971), 252-57.

TJÄRDALEN (1953)

BORLAND, HAROLD H. "Sara Lidman's Progress: A Critical Survey of Six Novels." *Scandanavian Studies*, 39 (1967), 97-100.

LIE, JONAS (Norwegian, 1833-1908)

GENERAL

TYSDAHL, B. J. "Joyce's Use of Norwegian Writers." *English Studies*, 50 (1969), 261-73.

LI FEI-KAN see PA CHIN

LIKHONOSOV, V.

FOR REMEMBRANCE (Na Doguiu Pamiat')

CHUDAKOVA, M. "Notes on the Language of Contemporary Prose." *Soviet Studies In Literature*, 9, No.1 (1972/3), 59-73.

LIND, JAKOV (Austrian, 1927-)

GENERAL

ROSENFELD, STELLA P. "Jakov Lind: Writer at the Crossroads." *Modern Austrian Literature*, 4, No.4 (1971), 42-46.

ERGO (Eine bessere Welt, 1966)

LANGER, LAWRENCE L. *The Holocaust And The Literary Imagination*, pp. 240-49.

POTOKER, EDWARD M. "A Distillation of Horror." *Saturday Review*, 21 October 1967, pp. 35-36.

Reviews

WEIMAR, KARL S. *Novel*, (1969), 172-73.

LANDSCAPE IN CONCRETE (Landscaft in Beton, 1962)

LANGER, LAWRENCE L. *The Holocaust And The Literary Imagination*, pp. 222-40.

Reviews

DENEAU, DANIEL P. "Jakov Lind's *Landscape In Concrete*." *Critique*, 9, No.2 (1967) 89-92.

ROSENTHAL, RAYMOND. "Exploring the Abyss." *Midstream Magazine*, 12, No.9 (1966), 76-78.

STERN, DANIEL. "A Contemporary Nightmare." *Saturday Review*, 25 June 1966, pp. 25-26.

WEIMAR, KARL S. *Novel*, 2 (1969), 171-72.

WOLFE, PETER. "End of the World Gestapo Style." *Prairie Schooner*, 40 (1966), 371-372.

LINDSAY, NORMAN (Australian, ca. 1919-1980)

GENERAL

BURNS, D. R. "Of Sex and Other Eruptions: The Novels of Norman Lindsay." *Meanjin*, 32 (1973), 67-72.

LINDSAY, JACK. "Norman Lindsay: Problems of his Life and Work." *Meanjin*, 29 (1970), 39-48.

LINS DO RÊGO, JOSÉ (Brazilian, 1901-1957)

GENERAL

KELLY, JOHN R. "An Annotated Bibliography of the Early Writings of José Lins do Rêgo." *Luso-Brazilian Review*, 9, No.1 (1972), 72-85.

O MOLEQUE RICARDO

PRETO-RODAS, RICHARD A. "The Black Presence and Two Brazilian Modernists: Jorge de Lima and José Lins do Rêgo," in *Tradition And Renewal*, ed. Merlin H. Forster, pp. 94-101.

PLANTATION BOY (1932-34)

Reviews

HANDLIN, OSCAR. *Atlantic Monthly*, 218, No.1 (1966), 139.

YATES, DONALD A. "Blue Mood from Brazil." *Saturday Review*, 9 July 1966, pp. 31, 34.

LISPECTOR, CLARICE (Brazilian, 1925-1977)

GENERAL

MONEGAL, E. R. "The Contemporary Brazilian Novel." *Daedalus*, 95 (1966), 998-1001.

THE APPLE IN THE DARK (A maça no escuro, 1961)

Reviews

GOLDMAN, RICHARD FRANKO. "Deeds in the Mind." *Saturday Review*, 19 August 1967, pp. 33, 48.

LIU CH'ING

THE BUILDERS (Ch'uang yeh shih)

HUANG, JOE C. *Heroes And Villians In Communist China*, pp. 244-52, 273-78.

LI YING-JU

IN AN OLD CITY

HUANG, JOE C. *Heroes And Villains In Communist China*, pp. 73-86.

LI YU

THE TWELVE TOWERS

Reviews

MARNEY, JOHN. *Literature East And West,* 19 (1975), 237–38.

LOBA, AKE (Ivory Coast, 1927–)

KOCOUMBO, L'ÉTUDIANT NOIR (1960)

BRENCH, A. C. *The Novelists' Inheritance Is French Africa,* pp. 91–98.

LOBATO, José Bento Monteiro see MONTEIRO LOBATO, José Bento

LOHENSTEIN, DANIEL CASPER VON (German, 1635–1683)

ARMINIUS AND THUSNELDA (1689–90)

WAGENER, HANS. *The German Baroque Novel,* pp. 121–26.

LO-JOHANNSSON, IVAR (Swedish, 1901–)

GENERAL

PAULSSON, JAN-ANDERS. "Ivar Lo-Johansson: Crusader for Social Justice." *American Scandinavian Review,* 59 (1971), 21–31.

TRAKTORN (1943)

GRAVES, PETER. "The Collective Novel in Sweden." *Scandinavica,* 12 (1973), 118–21.

LO KUANG-PIN

RED CRAG (Hung yen)

HUANG, JOE C. *Heroes And Villains In Communist China,* pp. 87–113.

LONDEIX, GEORGES

FOOTBALL

Reviews

CAPRIO, ANTHONY and DANA CARTON-CAPRIO. *French Review,* 47 (1974), 663–64.

LONGARES ALONSO, MANUEL

EL ENFERMO (1964)

Reviews

TRIFILO, S. SAMUEL. *Hispania,* 48 (1965), 616.

LONGUS (Greek, ca. 3rd century B.C.)

DAPHNIS AND CHLOE

TURNER, PAUL. "Novels, Ancient and Modern." *Novel,* 2 (1968), 15–20.

LOPES, MOACIR C.

A OSTRA E O VENTO

BARROW, LEO L. "Symbol in *A Ostra E O Vento.*" *Luso-Brazilian Review,* 4, No.1 (1967), 61–67.

LOPEZ-NUSSA, LEONEL (Cuban, 1916–)

RECUERDOS DEL 36

MENTON, SEYMOUR. *Prose Fiction Of The Cuban Revolution,* pp. 70–73.

LOPEZ PACHECO, JESUS

CENTRAL ELECTRICA (1970)

JIMENEZ-FAJARDO, SALVADOR. "Lopez Pacheco's *Central Electrica.*'" *Critique,* 14, No.1 (1972), 5–15.

LO TAN

DAWN IN WIND AND RAIN (Feng-yü ti li-ming)

HUANG, JOE C. *Heroes And Villains In Communist China,* pp. 219–31.

LOVEIRA Y CHIRINO, CARLOS (Cuban, 1882-1898)

LOS INMORALES (1919)

OWRE, J. RIIS. "Carlos Loveira's 'Los Inmorales.'" *Revista De Estudios Hispánicos,* 5 (1971), 321–32.

LOVELACE, EARL (Trinidad, 1935–)

THE SCHOOLMASTER (1968)

MOORE, GERALD. "The Debate on Existence in African Literature." *Présence Africaine,* No.81 (1972), pp. 33–38.

Reviews

BRATHWAITE, EDWARD. "Priest and Peasant." *Journal Of Commonwealth Literature,* No.7 (1969), pp. 117–22.

LOWRY, MALCOLM (Canadian, 1909–1957)

GENERAL

AUSTIN, PAUL W. "Russian Views of Lowry." *Canadian Literature,* No.62 (1974), pp. 126–28.

COSTA, RICHARD HAUER. "The Northern Paradise: Malcolm Lowry in Canada." *Studies In The Novel,* 4 (1972), 165–72.

CAREY, MAURICE J. "Life with Malcolm Lowry," in *Malcolm Lowry: The Man And His Work,* ed. George Woodcock, pp. 163–70.

CROSS, RICHARD K. "Malcolm Lowry and the Columbian Eden." *Contemporary Literature,* 14 (1973), 19–30.

EPSTEIN, PERLE. "Swinging the Maelstrom: Malcolm Lowry and Jazz." *Canadian Literature,* No.44 (1970), pp. 57–66; rpt. in *Malcolm Lowry: The Man And His Work,* ed. George Woodcock, pp. 144–53.

KIRK, DOWNIE. "More Than Music: The Critic as Correspondent," in *Malcolm Lowry: The Man And His Work,* ed. George Woodcock, pp. 117–24.

McCONNELL, WILLIAM. "Recollections of Malcolm Lowry," in *Malcolm Lowry: The Man And His Work,* ed. George Woodcock, pp. 154–62.

NEW, W. H. "Lowry's Reading: An Introductory Essay." *Canadian Literature,* No.44 (1970), pp. 5–12; rpt. in *Malcolm Lowry: The Man And His Work,* ed. George Woodcock, pp. 125–32.

STERN, JAMES. "Malcolm Lowry: A First Impression." *Encounter,* 29, No.3 (1967), 58–68.

TIESSEN, PAUL G. "Malcolm Lowry and the Cinema," in *Malcolm Lowry: The Man And His Work,* ed. George Woodcock, pp. 133–43.

DARK AS THE GRAVE WHERIN MY FRIEND IS LAID (1968)

COSTA, RICHARD HAUER. *Malcolm Lowry,* pp. 115–23.

CROSS, RICHARD K. *Malcolm Lowry: A Preface To His Fiction,* pp. 68–75.

WAIN, JOHN. "Another Room in Hell." *Atlantic Monthly,* 222, No.2 (1968), 84–86.

WOODCOCK, GEORGE. "Art as the Writer's Mirror: Literary Solipsism in 'Dark as the Grave,' " in *Malcolm Lowry: The Man And His Work,* ed. George Woodcock, pp. 66-70.

Reviews

HICKS, GRANVILLE. "Fragments from Beyond." *Saturday Review,* 6 July 1968, pp. 19-20.

KILGALLIN, TONY. "Lowry Posthumous." *Canadian Literature,* No.39 (1969), pp. 81-83.

SUMMERS, EILEEN. "Journey to Self-Discovery." *Catholic World,* 208 (1969), p. 140.

THE FOREST PATH TO THE SPRING (1961)

COSTA, RICHARD HAUER. "Lowry's Forest Path: Echoes of Walden." *Canadian Literature,* No.62 (1974), pp. 61-68.

LUNAR CAUSTIC (1968)

BENHAM, DAVID. "Lowry's Purgatory: Versions of 'Lunar Caustic.' " *Canadian Literature,* No.44 (1970), pp. 28-37; rpt. in *Malcolm Lowry: The Man And His Work,* ed. George Woodcock, pp. 56-65.

Reviews

KILGALLIN, TONY. "Lowry Posthumous." *Canadian Literature,* No.39 (1969), 80-81.

OCTOBER FERRY TO GABRIOLA (1970)

BAREHAM, TERENCE. "After the Volcano: An Assessment of Malcolm Lowry's Posthumous Fiction." *Studies In The Novel,* 6 (1974), 349-62.

BRADBROOK, M. C. *Malcolm Lowry: His Art And Early Life,* pp. 85-106.

CORRIGAN, MATTHEW. "The Writer as Consciousness: A View of 'October Ferry to Gabriola,' " in *Malcolm Lowry; The Man And His Work,* ed. George Woodcock, pp. 71-77.

COSTA, RICHARD HAUER. *Malcolm Lowry,* pp. 146-54.

———. "The Northern Paradise: Malcolm Lowry in Canada." *Studies In The Novel,* 4 (1972), 170-71.

CROSS, RICHARD K. *Malcolm Lowry: A Preface to His Fiction,* pp. 75-84.

DAY, DOUGLAS. *Malcolm Lowry: A Biography,* pp. 435-44.

KILGALLIN, ANTHONY R. "The Long Voyage Home: *October Ferry To Gabriola,*" in *Malcolm Lowry: The Man And His Work,* ed. George Woodcock, pp. 78-87.

NEW, WILLIAM H. "Gabriola: Malcolm Lowry's Floating Island," in his *Articulating West,* pp. 196-206.

Reviews

CORRIGAN, MATTHEW. "Lowry's Last Novel." *Canadian Literature,* No.48 (1971), pp. 74-80.

FIELD, J. C. "The Literary Scene: 1971." *Revue des Langues Vivantes,* 39 (1973), 83-84.

ULTRAMARINE (1933)

BINNS, RONALD. "Lowry's Anatomy of Melancholy." *Canadian Literature,* No.64 (1975), pp. 8-23.

BRADBROOK, M. C. *Malcolm Lowry: His Art And Early Life,* pp. 40-53.

COSTA, RICHARD HAUER. *Malcolm Lowry,* pp. 37-40.

CROSS, RICHARD K. *Malcolm Lowry: A Preface To His Fiction,* pp. 3-13.

DAHLIE, HALLVARD. "Lowry's Debt to Nordahl Grieg." *Canadian Literature,* No.64 (1975), pp. 41-51.

———. "Malcolm Lowry's *Ultramarine.*" *Journal Of Canadian Fiction,* 3, No.4 (1975), 65-68.

DAY, DOUGLAS. *Malcolm Lowry: A Biography,* pp. 161-68.

DURRANT, GEOFFREY. "Aiken and Lowry." *Canadian Literature,* No.64 (1975), pp. 24-40.

UNDER THE VOLCANO (1947)

BARNES, JIM. "The Myth of Sisyphus in *Under The Volcano.*" *Prairie Schooner,* 42 (1968/9), 341-48.

BRADBROOK, M. C. *Malcolm Lowry: His Art And Early Life,* pp. 54-68.

SISTER CHRISTELLA MARIE. "*Under the Volcano:* A Consideration of the Novel by Malcolm Lowry." *Xavier University Studies,* 4 (1965), 13-27.

COSTA, RICHARD HAUER. *Malcolm Lowry,* pp. 61-85.

———. "*Pietà, Pelado,* and 'The Ratification of Death': The Ten-Year Evolvement of Malcolm Lowry's *Volcano.*" *Journal Of Modern Literature,* 2 (1971), 3-18.

———. "*Ulysses,* Lowry's *Volcano,* and the *Voyage* Between: A Study of an Unacknowledged Literary Kinship." *University Of Toronto Quarterly,* 36 (1967), 335-52.

CROSS, RICHARD K. *Malcolm Lowry: A Preface To His Fiction,* pp. 26-64.

———. "Malcolm Lowry and the Columbian Eden." *Contemporary Literature,* 14 (1973), 19-24.

———. "Moby-Dick and *Under The Volcano:* Poetry From The Abyss." *Modern Fiction Studies,* 20 (1974), 149-56.

DAY, DOUGLAS. *Malcolm Lowry: A Biography,* pp. 258-73, 316-50.

DOYEN, VICTOR. "Elements Towards a Spatial Reading of Malcolm Lowry's *Under The Volcano.*" *English Studies,* 50 (1969), 65-74.

EPSTEIN, PERLE. *The Private Labyrinth Of Malcolm Lowry: <Under The Volcano> And The Cabbala.*

———. "Swinging the Maelstrom: Malcolm Lowry and Jazz." *Canadian Literature,* No.44 (1970), pp. 63-66.

GRACE, SHERRILL E. "Under the Volcano: Narrative Mode and Technique." *Journal Of Canadian Fiction,* 2, No.2 (1973), 57-61.

HEILMAN, ROBERT B. "The Possessed Artist and the Ailing Soul," in *Malcolm Lowry: The Man And His Work,* ed. George Woodcock, pp. 16-25.

HILL, ART. "The Alcoholic on Alcoholism." *Canadian Literature,* No.62 (1974), pp. 33-48.

KILGALLIN, ANTHONY R. "Faust and Under the Volcano." *Canadian Literature,* No.26 (1965), pp. 43-54; rpt. in *Malcolm Lowry: The Man And His Work,* ed. George Woodcock, pp. 26-37.

LOWRY, MALCOLM. "Preface to a Novel," in *Malcolm Lowry: The Man And His Work,* ed. George Woodcock, pp. 9-15.

NEW, WILLIAM H. "Lowry, the Cabbala and Charles Jones," in his *Articulating West,* pp. 189-95.

TIESSEN, PAUL G. "Malcolm Lowry and the Cinema." *Canadian Literature,* No.44 (1970), pp. 38-49.

WRIGHT, TERENCE. " 'Under the Volcano'; The Static Art of Malcolm Lowry." *Ariel: A Review Of International English Literature,* 1, No.4 (1970), 67-76.

Reviews

BROOKE-ROSE, CHRISTINE. "Mescalusions." *London Magazine,* NS, 7, No.1 (1967), 100-5.

HICKS, GRANVILLE. "One Great Statement." *Saturday Review,* 4 December 1965, pp. 39-40.

LUBEGA, BONNIE

THE OUTCASTS

Reviews

OHAEGBU, ALOYS U. *Présence Africaine,* No.88 (1973), pp. 233-35.

LUCIAN (Greek, ca. 120 A. D.)

METAMORPHOSES

PERRY, BEN EDWIN. *The Ancient Romans,* pp. 211-35.

LUDWIG, JACK (Canadian, 1922-)

ABOVE GROUND (1968)

Reviews

NEW, WILLIAM H. "Cock and Bull Stories." *Canadian Literature,* No.39 (1969), pp. 83-84.

CONFUSIONS (1963)

JAMES, ESTHER. "Ludwig's 'Confusions.' " *Canadian Literature,* No.40 (1969), pp. 49-53.

STONEHEWER, LILA. "Anatomy of Confusion: Jack Ludwig's Evolution." *Canadian Literature,* No.29 (1966), pp. 37-42.

A WOMAN OF HER AGE (1973)

Reviews

GROSSKURTH, PHYLLIS. "The Sound of Nemesis." *Canadian Literature,* No.61 (1974), pp. 123-24.

MANSBRIDGE, FRANCIS. *Dalhousie Review,* 54 (1974), 365-67.

LUDWIG, OTTO (German, 1813-1865)

GENERAL

KOLISKO, GERTRUDE. "Syntactic Anomalies and Pronomial Ambiguity in Otto Ludwig's Narrative Prose." *Modern Language Review,* 60 (1965), 65-72.

AUS DEM REGEN IN DIE TRAUFE

TURNER, DAVID. *Roles And Relationships In Otto Ludwig's Narrative Fiction,* pp. 40-47.

BETWEEN HEAVEN AND EARTH (Zwischen Himmel und Erde, 1856)

DICKSON, KEITH A. " 'Die Moral von der Geschicht': Art and Artifice in 'Zwischen Himmel und Erde.' " *Modern Language Review,* 68 (1973), 115-28.

LILLYMAN, W. J. "The Function of the Leitmotifs in Otto Ludwig's 'Zwischen Himmel und Erde.' " *Monatshefte,* 57 (1965), 60-68.

_____ . "The Interior Monologue In James Joyce and Otto Ludwig." *Comparative Literature,* 23 (1971), 45-54.

McCLAIN, WILLIAM H. "Otto Ludwig and the Problem of *Spannung* in Fiction." *MLN,* 80 (1965), 639-47.

TURNER, DAVID. *Roles And Relationships In Otto Ludwig's Narrative Fiction,* pp. 48-64.

WASHINGTON, IDA H. and CAROL E. WASHINGTON. "*Zwischen Himmel Und Erde:* a Problem Without a Solution." *Germanic Notes,* 1, (1970), 46-48.

DIE HEITERETEI (1853)

TURNER, DAVID. *Roles And Relationships In Otto Ludwig's Narrative Fiction,* pp. 29-39.

MARIA

TURNER, DAVID. *Roles And Relationships In Otto Ludwig's Narrative Fiction,* pp. 15-28.

LUSTIG, ARNOST (Czechoslovak, 1926-)

A PRAYER FOR KATERINA HOROVITZOVA (Mod litba pro Kateřinu Horovitzovou, 1964)

Reviews

EVANIER, DAVID. "The Burning Subject." *Midstream Magazine,* 19, No.10 (1973), 89-91.

LYNCH, BENITO (Argentine, 1885-1951)

LOS CARANCHOS DE LA FLORIDA (1916)

BRUSHWOOD, JOHN S. *The Spanish American Novel,* pp. 25-28.

LYNCH, MARTA (1930-)

EL CRUCE DEL RÍO

Reviews

DULSEY, BERNARD. *Hispania,* 57 (1974), 605-6.

M

MCCLENAGHAN, JACK

MOVING TARGET

Reviews

FYTTON, FRANCIS. *London Magazine,* NS 6, No.6 (1966), 117-19.

MCCOMBIE, THOMAS

ARABIN

ARGYLE, BARRY. *An Introduction To The Australian Novel,* 1830-1930, pp. 54-59.

MCCOURT, EDWARD ALEXANDER (Canadian, 1907-)

THE ETTINGER AFFAIR see THE FASTING FRIAR

THE FASTING FRIAR (1963)

RICOU, LAURENCE R. "Empty as Nightmare: Man and Landscape in Recent Canadian Prairie Fiction." *Mosiac,* 6, No.2 (1972/3), 153-55.

———. *Vertical Man/ Horizontal World,* pp. 129-31.

HOME IS THE STRANGER (1950)

RICOU, LAURENCE. *Vertical Man/ Horizontal World,* pp. 113-15.

THE WOODEN SWORD (1956)

RICOU, LAURENCE R. "Empty as Nightmare: Man and Landscape in Recent Canadian Prairie Fiction," *Mosaic,* 6, No.2 (1972/3), 152-53.

MACDERMOT, THOMAS HENRY (Jamaican, 1870-1933) wrote under pseudonym Tom Redcam

GENERAL

RAMCHAND, KENNETH. *The West Indian Novel And Its Background,* pp. 51-55.

MCDOUGALL, COLIN (Canadian, 1917-)

EXECUTION

SUTHERLAND, RONALD. "The Vital Pretense: *McDougall's Execution.*" *Canadian Literature,* No.27 (1966), pp. 20-31.

MACEWEN, GWENDOLYN (Canadian, 1941-)

KING OF EGYPT, KING OF DREAMS

Reviews

RINGROSE, CHRISTOPHER XERXES. "Vision Enveloped in Night." *Canadian Literature,* No.53 (1972), pp. 102-4.

WATERSTON, ELIZABETH. "Akhenaton in Art." *Journal Of Canadian Fiction,* 1, No.3 (1972), 76-77.

MACHADO DE ASSÍS, JOAQUIN MARIA (Brazilian, 1839-1908)

GENERAL

BAGBY, ALBERTO I., JR. "Machado de Assis and Foreign Languages." *Luso-Brazilian Review,* 12 (1975), 225-33.

BARROW, LEO L. "Ingratitude in the Works of Machado de Assis." *Hispania,* 49 (1966), 211-17.

COLEMAN, ALEXANDER. "A New World Is Not a Home." *Review,* No.16 (1975), pp. 51-54.

———. Comp. "The Essential Machado de Assis." *Review,* No.16 (1975), pp. 39-42.

HAMILTON, RUSSELL G., Comp. "Chronology." *Review,* No.16 (1975), pp. 36-38.

SISTER KATHARINE ELAINE. "Man in the Landscape of Antonio Machado," in *Spanish Thought And Letters In The Twentieth Century,* ed. Germán Bleiberg and E. Inman Fox, pp. 271-86.

MACADAM, ALFRED J. "Machado de Assis: An Introduction to Latin American Satire." *Revista Hispanica Moderna,* 37 (1972/3), 180-87.

MERQUIOR, JOSE GUILHERME. "A Problematic Vision." Trans. Peter Lownds, *Review,* No.16 (1975), pp. 45-51.

NUNES, MARIA LUISA. "Machado de Assis' Theory of the Novel," *Latin American Literary Review,* 4, No.7 (1975), 57-66.

PARAM, CHARLES. "Jealousy in the Novels of Machado de Assis." *Hispania,* 53 (1970), 198-206.

———. "Machado de Asssis and Dostoevsky." *Hispania,* 49 (1966), 81-87.

———. "Politics in the Novels of Machado de Assis." *Hispania,* 56 (1973), 557-68.

RODRIGUEZ MONEGAL, EMIR. "Revisiting Catate." *Review,* No.16 (1975), pp. 43-45.

TANNER, TONY. "Machado de Assis." *London Magazine,* NS 6, No.1 (1966), 41-57.

COUNSELOR AYRE'S MEMORIAL (Memorial de Ayres, 1908)

CALDWELL, HELEN. *Machado De Assis: The Brazilian Master And His Novels,* pp. 182-96.

DOM CASMURRO (1899)

CALDWELL, HELEN. *Machado De Assis: The Brazilian Master And His Novels,* pp. 142–49.

ELLIS, KEITH. "Ambiguity and Point of View in Some Novelistic Representations of Jealousy." *MLN,* 86 (1971), 899–909.

MACADAM, ALFRED J. "Machado de Assis: An Introduction to Latin American Satire." *Revista Hispanica Moderna,* 37 (1972/73), 183–86.

MARTINS, WILSON. "Pro or Contra in Casmurro." *Review,* No.16 (1975), pp. 60–62.

MAZZARA, RICHARD A. "*Dom Casmurro* and *A Flor E O Fructo,*" *Chasqui,* 1, No.4 (1972), 52–53.

TANNER, TONY. "Machado de Assis," *London Magazine,* NS 6, No.1 (1966), 51–54.

ZIOMEK, HENRYK. "Parallel Ingredients in *Don Quixote* and *Dom Casmurro,*" *Revista De Estudios Hispánicos,* 2 (1968), 229–40.

EPITAPH OF A SMALL WINTER (Memórias pósthumas de Braz Cubas, 1881)

CALDWELL, HELEN. *Machado De Assis: The Brazilian Master And His Novels,* pp. 73–126.

TANNER, TONY. "Machado de Assis." *London Magazine,* NS 6, No.1 (1966), 42–46.

WILLIAMS, LORNA V. "Perspective in the *Memorias Posthumas De Braz Cubas* by Machado de Assis." *College Language Association Journal,* 18 (1975), 501–6.

ESAU AND JACOB (Esaú e Jacob, 1904)

CALDWELL, HELEN. *Machado De Assis: The Brazilian Master And His Novels,* pp. 153–81.

TANNER, TONY. "Machado de Assis," *London Magazine,* NS 6, No.1 (1966), 54–57.

Reviews
CAPOUYA, EMILE. "Resentment Was Their Birthright," *Saturday Review,* 7 August 1965, p. 27.

THE HAND AND THE GLOVE (A mão e a luva, 1874)

BARROW, LEO L. "Ingratitude in the Works of Machado de Assis," *Hispania,* 49 (1966), 212–13.

CALDWELL, HELEN. *Machado De Assis: The Brazilian Master And His Novels,* pp. 44–48.

Reviews
BROOKS, ZELDA. *Luso-Brazilian Review,* 11 (1974), 136–38.

RABASSA, GREGORY. *New York Times Book Review,* 22 November 1970; rpt. in *Review,* No.3 (1971), pp. 51–53.

HELENA (1876)

CALDWELL, HELEN. *Machado De Assis: The Brazilian Master And His Novels,* pp. 49–61.

THE HERITAGE OF QUINCAS BORBA see PHILOSOPHER OR DOG?

PHILOSOPHER OR DOG? (Quincas Borba, 1891)

CALDWELL, HELEN. *Machado De Assis: The Brazilian Master And His Novels,* pp. 129–41.

PARAM, CHARLES. "The Case for 'Quincas Borba' as Confession," *Hispania,* 50 (1967), 430–41.

RESURRECTION (Ressurreicão) (1872)

CALDWELL, HELEN. *Machado De Assis: The Brazilian Master And His Novels,* pp. 40–43.

MACADAM, ALFRED J. "Rereading *Ressurreição,*" *Luso-Brazilian Review,* 9, No.2 (1972), 47–57.

YAYÁ GARCIA (1878)

CALDWELL, HELEN. *Machado De Assis: The Brazilian Master And His Novels,* pp. 62–69.

MCINTOSH, JOHN (South African, 1930–1970)

COME TO MY HOUSE (1968)

Reviews
WAGNER, CONSTANCE. "Eclipse of Innocence," *Saturday Review,* 9 November 1968, p. 44.

THE THORN TREES (1967)

DETT, V. S. "New South African Literature—1967: A Critical Chronicle," *English Studies In Africa,* 11 (1968), 65–67.

McKAY, CLAUDE (Jamaican, 1889–1948)

BANANA BOTTOM (1933)

RAMCHAND, KENNETH. *The West Indian Novel and Its Background,* pp. 259–73.

BANJO (1929)

MOORE, GERALD. *The Chosen Tongue.* pp. 99–100.

RAMCHAND, KENNETH. *The West Indian Novel and Its Background,* pp. 255–59.

HOME TO HARLEM (1928)

RAMCHAND, KENNETH. *The West Indian Novel and Its Background,* pp. 247–55.

MACKENZIE, KENNETH IVO "SEAFORTH" (Australian, 1913–54)

GENERAL

CLARKE, DONOVAN. "Seaforth Mackenzie: Novelist of Alienation." *Southerly,* 25 (1965), 75–90.

COWAN, PETER. "Seaforth Mackenzie's Novels." *Meanjin,* 24 (1965), 298–307.

DAVIS, DIANA. "A Checklist of Kenneth Mackenzie's Works: Including Manuscript Material." *Australian Literary Studies,* 4 (1970), 398–404.

———. "The Genesis of a Writer: The Early Years of Kenneth Mackenzie." *Australian Literary Studies,* 3 (1968), 254–70.

GEERING, R. G. "Seaforth Mackenzie's Fiction: Another View." *Southerly,* 26 (1966), 25–39.

CHOSEN PEOPLE (1938)

CLARKE, DONOVAN. "Seaforth Mackenzie: Novelist of Alienation." *Southerly,* 25 (1965), 80–83.

DEAD MEN RISING (1951)

CLARKE, DONOVAN. "Seaforth Mackenzie: Novelist of Alienation." *Southerly,* 25 (1965), 83–86.

COWAN, PETER. "Seaforth Mackenzie's Novels." *Meanjin,* 24 (1965), 301–4.

THE REFUGE (1954)

CLARKE, DONOVAN. "Seaforth Mackenzie: Novelist of Alienation." *Southerly,* 25 (1965), 86–89.

COWAN, PETER. "Seaforth Mackenzie's Novels." *Meanjin,* 24 (1965), 304–7.

GEERING, R. G. "Seaforth Mackenzie's Fiction: Another View." *Southerly,* 26 (1966), 35–38.

THE YOUNG DESIRE IT (1937)

CLARKE, DONOVAN. "Seaforth Mackenzie: Novelist of Alienation." *Southerly,* 25 (1965), 77–80.

GEERING, R. G. "Seaforth Mackenzie's Fiction: Another View." *Southerly,* 26 (1966), 25–33.

MACLENNAN, HUGH (Canadian, 1907–)
GENERAL

CAMERON, DONALD. "Hugh MacLennan: The Tennis Racket is an Antelope Bone." *Journal Of Canadian Fiction,* 1, No.1 (1972), 40–47.

CHAMBERS, ROBERT D. "The Novels of Hugh MacLennan." *Journal Of Canadian Studies,* 2, No.3 (1967), 3–11.

DAHLIE, HALLVARD. "Self-Conscious Canadians." *Canadian Literature,* No.62 (1974), pp. 6–10.

HYMAN, ROGER LESLIE. "Hugh MacLennan: His Art, His Society and His Critics." *Queen's Quarterly,* 82 (1975), 515–27.

MACLENNAN, HUGH. "Reflections on Two Decades." *Canadian Literature,* No.41 (1969), pp. 28–39.

WOODCOCK, GEORGE. "A Nation's Odyssey: The Novels of Hugh MacLennan," in *A Choice Of Critics,* ed. George Woodcock, pp. 79–92.

BAROMETER RISING (1941)

ARNASON, DAVID. "Canadian Nationalism in Search of a Form: Hugh MacLennan's Barometer Rising." *Journal Of Canadian Fiction,* 1 No.4 (1972), 68–71.

BASSETT, ISABEL. "The Transformation of Imperialism: Connor to MacLennan." *Journal Of Canadian Fiction,* 2, No.1 (1973), 58–62.

NEW, WILLIAM H. "The Storm and After: Imagery and Symbolism in Hugh MacLennan's 'Barometer Rising.'" *Queen's Quarterly,* 74 (1967), 302–13: rpt. in his *Articulating West,* pp. 95–107.

WOODCOCK, GEORGE. "A Nation's Odyssey: The Novels of Hugh MacLennan," in *A Choice of Critics,* ed. George Woodcock, pp. 79–84.

EACH MAN'S SON (1951)

DAVIS, MARILYN J. "Fathers and Sons." *Canadian Literature,* No.58 (1973), pp. 41–46.

JONES, D. G. *Butterfly on Rock.* pp. 62–65.

MORLEY, PATRICIA A. *The Immoral Moralists: Hugh MacLennan and Leonard Cohen,* pp. 63–72.

TALLMAN, WARREN. "Wolf in the Snow," in *A Choice of Critics,* ed. George Woodcock, pp. 64–67.

THE RETURN OF THE SPHINX (1967)

DAVIS, MARILYN J. "Fathers and Sons." *Canadian Literature,* No.58 (1973), pp. 46–49.

HYMAN, ROGER. "Return to *Return Of The Sphinx.*" *English Studies In Canada,* 1 (1975), 450–65.

MORLEY, PATRICIA A. *The Immoral Moralists: Hugh MacLennan And Leonard Cohen,* pp. 110–25.

NEW, WILLIAM H. "Winter and the Night-People." *Canadian Literature,* No.36 (1968), pp. 26–33; rpt. in his *Articulating West,* pp. 128–38.

SUTHERLAND, RONALD. "The Fourth Separatism." *Canadian Literature,* No.45 (1970), pp. 15–21; rpt. in his *Second Image,* pp. 126–32.

ZEZULKA, JOSEPH. "MacLennan's Defeated Pilgrim: A Perspective on *Return Of The Sphinx.*" *Journal Of Canadian Fiction,* 4, No.1 (1975), 121–31.

Reviews

COCKBURN, ROBERT H. *Dalhousie Review,* 47 (1967), 435–39.

GARDNER, PAUL. "Canadian Father and Son." *Catholic World,* 206 (1967), 95.

MAUER, ROBERT. "Canadian Eye-Opener." *Saturday Review,* 7 October 1967, pp. 44–45.

TWO SOLITUDES (1945)

ARNASON, DAVID. "Canadian Nationalism in Search of a Form: Hugh MacLennan's Barometer Rising." *Journal Of Canadian Fiction,* 1, No.4 (1972), 68.

KELLY, SISTER CATHERINE. "The Unity of Two Solitudes." *Ariel: A Review Of International English Literature,* 6, No.2 (1975), 38–61.

THE WATCH THAT ENDS THE NIGHT (1959)

FARMILOE, DOROTHY. "Hugh MacLennan and the Canadian Myth." *Mosaic,* 2, No.3 (1969), 1–9.

JONES, D. G. *Butterfly On Rock,* pp. 157–62.

MORLEY, PATRICIA. *The Immoral Moralists: Hugh MacLennan and Leonard Cohen,* pp. 98–109.

NEW, WILLIAM H. "The Apprenticeship of Discovery." *Canadian Literature,* No.29 (1966), pp. 24–33; rpt. in his *Articulating West,* pp. 108–27.

THORNE, W. B. "The Relation of Structure to Theme in The Watch That Ends the Night." *Humanities Association Bulletin,* 20, No.2 (1969), 42–45.

MCMENEMY, NICKIE (South African, 1925–)
ASSEGAI! (1973)

OGUNBESAN, KOLAWOLE. "A King for All Seasons: Chaka in African Literature." *Présence Africaine,* No.88 (1973), pp. 212–16.

———. "A King for All Seasons: Chaka in African Literature." *Black Orpheus,* 3, No.2/3 (1974/5), 91–94.

MACSKIMMING, ROY (Canadian)
FORMENTERA (1972)

Reviews

MOSS, JOHN G. "In the Midst of Transition." *Journal Of Canadian Fiction,* 2, No.1 (1973), 101.

SUTHERLAND, FRASER. "Love Disguised." *Canadian Literature,* No.59 (1974), pp. 121–22.

MADARASZ, GEORGES
MICHIGAN TRANSIT

Reviews

KRANCE, CHARLES. *French Review,* 47 (1973), 664–65.

MADDY, YULISSA AMADU
NO PAST, NO PRESENT, NO FUTURE

PALMER, EUSTACE. "Yulissa Amadu Maddy: *No Past, No Present, No Future.*" *African Literature Today,* 7 (1975), 163–66.

Reviews

PALMER, EUSTACE. *African Literature Today,* 7 (1975), 163–66.

MADGULKAR, VYANKATESH (Indian, 1927–)
THE WINDS OF FIRE (1974)

Reviews

KRISHNAN, A. R. *Journal Of Indian Writing In English,* 3, No.2 (1975), 48.

MADHAVIAH, A.
PADMAVATI

BANGARUSWAMI, R. "Early Classics of Tamil Fiction." *Indian Literature*, 11, No.2 (1968), 50–52.

MAGIERA, KURTMARTIN

LIDDL, EICHHORN UND ANDERE

KURZ, PAUL KONRAD. "The Priest in the Modern Novel," in his *On Modern German Literature*, Vol.4:146–50.

MAHFOUZ, NAGIB (Egyptian, 1912–)

GENERAL

SFEIR, GEORGE N. "The Contemporary Arabic Novel." *Daedalus*, 95 (1966), 947–53.

BIDAYA WA NIHAYA (ca. 1951)

KILPATRICK, HILARY. *The Modern Egyptian Novel*, pp. 83–85, 218–19.

AL-KARNAK (1974)

Reviews
ELKHADEM, S. *International Fiction Review*, 2 (1975), 81.

KHAN AL-KHALILI (1946)

KILPATRICK. HILARY. *The Modern Egyptian Novel*, pp. 75–79, 214–15.

THE KIDS OF THE NEIGHBORHOOD (Awlad Haritna)

KILPATRICK, HILARY. *The Modern Egyptian Novel*, pp. 95–98, 224–28.

AL-LISS WAL-KILĀB (1961)

KILPATRICK, HILARY. *The Modern Egyptian Novel*, pp. 98–100, 228–29.

MIDAQ ALLEY (Zuqaq al-Midaq, 1947)

KILPATRICK, HILARY. *The Modern Egyptian Novel*, pp. 79–81, 215–16.

MĪRĀMĀR (1966)

KILPATRICK, HILARY. *The Modern Egyptian Novel*, pp. 109–12, 233–34.

AL-QĀHIRA AL-JADĪDA (1946)

KILPATRICK, HILARY. *The Modern Egyptian Novel*, pp. 73–75, 213–14.

AL-SARĀB (1948)

KILPATRICK, HILARY. *The Modern Egyptian Novel*, pp. 81–83, 216–18.

AL-SHAHHĀDH (1965)

KILPATRICK, HILARY. *The Modern Egyptian Novel*, pp. 104–6, 231–32.

AL-SUMMĀN WAL-KHARĪF (1962)

KILPATRICK, HILARY. *The Modern Egyptian Novel*, pp. 100–2, 229–30.

AL-TARĪQ (1964)

KILPATRICK, HILARY. *The Modern Egyptian Novel*, pp. 102–4, 230–31.

THARTHARA FAUQ AL-NĪL (1966)

KILPATRICK, HILARY. *The Modern Egyptian Novel*, pp. 106–9, 232–33.

AL-THULĀTHIYA (1956–57)

KILPATRICK, HILARY. *The Modern Egyptian Novel*, pp. 85–87, 219–23.

MAIS, ROGER (Jamaican, 1905–1955)

GENERAL

CREARY, JEAN. "A Prophet Armed: The Novels of Roger Mais," in *The Islands In Between*, ed. Louis James, pp. 50–63.

DAVIES, BARRIE. "The Novels of Roger Mais." *International Fiction Review*, 1 (1974), 140–43.

DATHORNE, OSCAR R. "Roger Mais: The Man on the Cross." *Studies In The Novel*, 4 (1972), 275–83.

LACOVIA, R. M. "Roger Mais: An Approach to Suffering and Freedom." *Black Images*, 1, No.2 (1972), 7–11.

WILLIAMSON, KARINA. "Roger Mais: West Indian Novelists." *Journal Of Commonwealth Literature*, No.2 (1966), pp. 138–47.

BLACK LIGHTNING (1955)

HARRIS, WILSON. "Black Lightning." *Journal Of Canadian Fiction*, 3, No.4 (1975), 41–44.

RAMCHAND, KENNETH. *The West Indian Novel And Its Background* pp. 185–88.

BROTHER MAN (1954)

CREARY, JEAN. "A Prophet Armed: The Novels of Roger Mais," in *The Islands In Between*, ed. Louis James, pp. 55–58.

MOORE, GERALD. *The Chosen Tongue*, pp. 90–92.

RAMCHAND, KENNETH. *The West Indian Novel And Its Background*, pp. 182–85.

THE HILLS WERE JOYFUL TOGETHER (1953)

CREARY, JEAN. "A Prophet Armed: The Novels of Roger Mais," in *The Islands In Between*, ed. Louis James, pp. 52–55.

MOORE, GERALD. *The Chosen Tongue*, pp. 86–90.

MAJOR, ANDRÉ

L'ÉPOUVANTAIL

Reviews
MACRI, F. M. "A Scarecrow in a Field of Corn." *Journal Of Canadian Fiction*, 3, No.4 (1975), 95–96.

MAKAROV, IVAN

STARI TOVARISH

Reviews
HEIMAN, LEO. "Cloak-and-Dagger Literature Behind the Iron Curtain." *East Europe*, 14, No.1 (1965), 56.

MALERBA, LUIGI (Italian, 1927–)

THE SERPENT (Il serpente, 1966)

Reviews
BERGIN, THOMAS G. "Mental Music in Rome." *Saturday Review*, 18 May 1968, p. 60.

MALGONKAR, MANOHAR (Indian, 1913–)

GENERAL

DAYANANDA, Y. J. "Interview with Manohar Malgonkar." *World Literature Written In English*, 12, No.2 (1973), 260–87.

PARAMESWARAN, UMA. "Manohar Malgonkar as a Historical Novelist." *World Literature Written In English*, 14 (1975), 329–38.

SINGH, RAM SEWAK. "Manohar Malgonkar the Novelist." *Indian Literature*, 13, No.1 (1970), 122–31.

SRINIVASA IYENGAR, K. R. *Indian Writing In English,* pp. 423–34.

A BEND IN THE GANGES (1964)

AMUR, G. S. *Manohar Malgonkar,* pp. 103–22.

BATRA, SHAKTI. "Two Partition Novels." *Indian Literature,* 18, No.3 (1975), 83–103.

JAIAN, JASBIR. "Vishnu and Shiva: Symbols of Duality in *A Bend In The Ganges.*" *Journal Of Indian Writing In English,* 3, No.1 (1975), 21–23.

SRINIVASA IYENGAR, K. R. *Indian Writing In English,* pp. 431–34.

Reviews
NATWAR-SINGH, K. "Divided Conscience, Common Cause." *Saturday Review,* 6 March 1965, p. 42.

WENDT, ALLAN. *Literature East And West,* 9 (1965), 145–48.

COMBAT OF SHADOWS (1962)

AMUR, G. S. *Manohar Malgonkar,* pp. 60–77.

SRINIVASA IYENGAR, K. R. *Indian Writing In English,* pp. 425–28.

THE DEVIL'S WIND (1972)

AMUR, G. S. *Manohar Malgonkar,* pp. 123–39.

DAYANANDA, Y. J. "Interview with Manohar Malgonkar." *World Literature Written In English,* 12, No.2 (1973), 268–71.

_____. "The Novelist as Historian." *Journal Of South Asian Literature,* 10, No.1 (1974), 55–67.

Reviews
DAYANANDA, Y. J. *Literature East And West,* 15 (1971), 523–25.

_____. *World Literature Written In English,* 11, No.2 (1972), 112–15.

DISTANT DRUM (1960)

AMUR, G. S. *Manohar Malgonkar,* pp. 46–59.

THE PRINCES (1963)

AMUR, G. S. *Manohar Malgonkar,* pp. 78–102.

DAYANANDA, Y. J. "Initiatory Motifs in Manohar Malgonkar's *The Princes.*" *Mahfil,* 8, No.2/3 (1972), 223–35.

_____. "Manohar Malgonkar on His Novel *The Princes:* An Interview." *Journal Of Commonwealth Literature,* 9, No.3 (1975), 21–28.

_____. "Rhythm in M. Malgonkar's *The Princes.*" *Literature East And West,* 15 (1971), 55–73.

SRINIVASA IYENGAR, K. R. *Indian Writing In English,* pp. 428–31.

MALINOVSKY, Alexander Alexandrovich see BOGDANOV, A. A.

MALLE, LOUIS (French, 1932–)

LE SOUFFLE AU COEUR (1971)

Reviews
KAY, BURF. *French Review,* 46 (1972) 219–20.

MALLEA, EDUARDO (Argentine, 1903–ca. 1982)

GENERAL

DURAN, MANUEL. "Argentine and Universal." *New York Times Book Review,* 10 July 1966, p. 4.

EDWARDS, ALICIA BETSY. "Eduardo Mallea: Man as Child." *Latin American Literary Review,* 2, No.3 (1973), 31–34.

FLINT, J. M. "The Expression of Isolation: Notes on Mallea's Stylistic Technique." *Bulletin Of Hispanic Studies,* 44 (1967), 203–9.

ALL GREEN SHALL PERISH (Todo Verdor Perecera)

BRUSHWOOD, JOHN S. *The Spanish American Novel,* pp. 130–34.

HAYDEN, ROSE LEE. *An Existential Focus On Some Novels Of The River Plate.*

THE BAY OF SILENCE (La Bahía de Silencio, 1940)

FOSTER, DAVID WILLIAM. *Currents In The Contemporary Argentine Novel,* pp. 48–69.

HAYDEN, ROSE LEE. *An Existential Focus On Some Novels Of The River Plate.*

SHAW, DONALD L. "Narrative Technique in Malleau's *La Bahía De Silencio.*" *Symposium,* 20 (1966), 50–55.

CHAVES (1953)

HAYDEN, ROSE LEE. *An Existential Focus On Some Novels Of The River Plate.*

EN LA CRECIENTE OSCURIDAD (1972)

Reviews
LICHTBLAU, MYRON I. *Hispania,* 58 (1975), 232.

FIESTA IN NOVEMBER (Fiesta en Noviembre, 1938)

BRUSHWOOD, JOHN S. *The Spanish American Novel,* pp. 126–29.

MILETICH, JOHN S. "Biblical Allusions in Mallea's *Fiesta En Noviembre.*" *Romance Notes,* 16 (1975), 731–33.

HISTORIA DE UN PASION ARGENTINA (1937)

HAYDEN, ROSE LEE. *An Existential Focus On Some Novels Of The River Plate.*

TRISTE PIEL DEL UNIVERSO (1971)

Reviews
LICHTBLAU, MYRON I. *Hispania,* 56 (1973), 739–40.

MALLET-JORIS, FRANÇOIS (French, 1930–)

THE PAPER HOUSE (La maison de papier, 1970)

Reviews
LOTTMAN, EILEEN. *Saturday Review,* 5 June 1971, p. 34.

SIGNS AND WONDERS (Les Signes et les prodiges, 1966)

JANEWAY, ELIZABETH. "One Summer in the South of France." *New York Times Book Review,* 6 August 1967, pp. 4–5.

Reviews
LESAGE, LAURENT. "Life is a Cruel Absurdity." *Saturday Review,* 29 July 1967, pp. 30–31.

THE UNCOMPROMISING HEART (Marie Mancini, 1964)

Reviews
PLUMB, J. H. "In Love with Louis XIV." *Saturday Review,* 30 April 1966, pp. 31–32.

MALONGA, JEAN (Congo, 1907–)

COEUR D'ARYENNE (1954)

BRENCH, A. C. *The Novelists' Inheritance In French Africa,* pp. 75–83.

MALRAUX, ANDRÉ (French, 1901–1976)

GENERAL

BAUMGARTNER, PAUL. "Solitude and Involvement: Two Aspects of Tragedy in Malraux's Novels." *French Review,* 38 (1965), 766–76.

BEVAN, DAVID. "Malraux's Renunciation of the Novel." *Nottingham French Studies,* 12 (1973), 49–62.

BORNSTEIN, STEPHEN E. "Myth, Man and Memoirs: The Case of André Malraux." *American Scholar,* 41 (1972), 444–59.

COLLINS, LARRY and DOMINIQUE LAPIERRE. "The Remarkable Life of André Malraux." *Saturday Review,* 27 April 1968, pp. 20–23, 59–61.

GAUTHIER, JOSEPH D. "The Religious Dimension in the *Anti-mémoires.*" *Kentucky Romance Quarterly,* 16 (1969), 221–30.

GERSHMAN, HERBERT S. "The Structure of Revolt in Malraux, Camus, and Sartre." *Symposium,* 24 (1970), 27–35.

HARRAULT, JEANNINE. "André Malraux's Political Philosophy." *Triveni,* 43, No.1 (1974), 9–12.

———. "Explaining André Malraux." *Triveni,* 41, No.3 (1972), 18–22.

HEALY, CATHLEEN M. "Malraux and His Legend: An Incident in the Resistance." *French Studies,* 26 (1972), 305–12.

LANGLOIS, WALTER G. "André Malraux: Spokesman for an Alienated Generation." *Perspectives On Contemporary Literature,* 1, No.2 (1975), 48–61.

———. "The Novelist Malraux and History." *L'Esprit Créateur,* 15 (1975), 345–66.

———. "Young Malraux and the Values of the Communist Metaphysic." *Southern Review,* NS, 4 (1968), 884–93.

RECK, RIMA DRELL. "The *Antimémoires:* Malraux's Ultimate Form." *Kentucky Romance Quarterly,* 16 (1969), 155–62.

———. *Literature And Responsibility,* pp. 257–301.

———. "Malraux and the Duality of Western Man." *Personalist,* 48 (1967), 345–60.

SAYRE, ROBERT. "Solitude and Solidarity: The Case of André Malraux." *Mosaic,* 9, No.1 (1975), 53–66.

SOBEL, MARGARET. "Malraux the Romantic." *Studies In Romanticism,* 12 (1973), 551–58.

STOKES, SAMUEL E., JR. "Malraux and Pascal." *Wisconsin Studies In Contemporary Literature,* 6 (1965), 286–92.

TARICA, RALPH. "Ironic Figures in Malraux's Novels," in *Image And Theme,* ed. W. M. Frohock, pp. 38–73.

TURNELL, MARTIN. "Novelist as Picaresque Hero: Malraux's Fate." *Commonweal,* 82 (1965), 410–13.

"Two Interviews: André Malraux." *Encounter,* 35, No.3 (1970), 23–26.

WINEGARTEN, RENEE. "Malraux's Fate." *Commentary,* 2, No.5 (1971), 69–74.

THE CONQUERORS (Les conquérants, 1928)

BOAK, DENNIS. *André Malraux,* pp. 44–62.

BRITWUM, KWABENA. "Garine, the Self and the Tragic Theme in 'Les Conquérants.'" *Modern Language Review,* 69 (1974), 779–84.

GREENLEE, JAMES W. *Malraux's Heroes And History,* pp. 33–45.

HORVATH, VIOLET M. *André Malraux:* <*The Human Adventure*> pp. 163–77.

JENKINS, CECIL. *André Malraux,* pp. 51–55.

PAYNE, ROBERT. *A Portrait Of André Malraux,* pp. 129–39.

DAYS OF HOPE see MAN'S HOPE

DAYS OF WRATH (Le Temps du mepris, 1935)

BOAK, DENNIS. *André Malraux,* pp. 96–105.

GREENLEE, JAMES W. *Malraux's Heroes And History,* pp. 87–100.

HORVATH, VIOLET M. *André Malraux:* <*The Human Adventure,*> pp. 217–27.

JENKINS, CECIL. *André Malraux,* pp. 81–84.

PAYNE, ROBERT. *A Portrait Of André Malraux,* pp. 220–30.

MAN'S ESTATE see MAN'S FATE

MAN'S FATE (La Condition Humaine, 1933)

BOAK, DENNIS. *André Malraux,* pp. 63–95.

FRIEDMAN, MELVIN J. "Some Notes on the Technique of *Man's Fate,*' in *The Shaken Realist,* ed. Melvin Friedman and John B. Vickery, pp. 128–43.

GREENLEE, JAMES W. *Malraux's Heroes And History,* pp. 59–85.

GROVES, MARGARET. "Malraux's Lyricism and the Death of Kyo." *Modern Language Review,* 64 (1969), 53–61.

HIDDLESTON, J. A. *Malraux: La Condition Humaine.*

HORVATH, VIOLET M. *André Malraux:* <*The Human Adventure,*> pp. 195–216.

JENKINS, CECIL. *André Malraux,* pp. 61–77.

LANGLOIS, WALTER G. "*The Dream Of The Red Chamber, The Good Earth,* and *Man's Fate:* Chronicles of Social Change in China." *Literature East And West,* 11 (1967), 6–9.

NELSON, ROY JAY. "Malraux and Camus: The Myth of the Beleaguered City." *Kentucky Foreign Language Quarterly,* 13 (1966), 86–94.

PAYNE, ROBERT. *A Portrait Of André Malraux,* pp. 165–78.

SAVAGE, CATHARINE. *Malraux, Sartre, And Aragon As Political Novelists,* pp. 6–16.

SILVERSTEIN, NORMAN. "Institutional and Individual Reformers: The Existentialist Element in *Man's Fate.*" *Ball State University Forum,* 6, No.1 (1965), 37–44.

MAN'S HOPE (L'Espoir, 1937)

BATCHELOR, R. "The Role of Manuel in André Malraux's *L'Espoir.*" *Neophilologus,* 59 (1975), 512–21.

BOAK, DENNIS. *André Malraux,* pp. 106–38.

CHUA, C. L. "Nature and Art in the Aesthetics of Malraux's L'Espoir." *Symposium,* 26 (1972), 114–27.

GREENLEE, JAMES W. *Malraux's Heroes And History,* pp. 101–31.

HORVATH, VIOLET M. *André Malraux:* <*The Human Adventure,*> pp. 229–43.

JENKINS, CECIL. *André Malraux,* pp. 87–101.

PAYNE, ROBERT. *A Portrait Of André Malraux,* pp. 247–61.

ROMEISER, JOHN BEALS. *Critical Reception Of André Malraux's* <*L'Espoir*> *In The French Press: December 1937–June 1940.*

THE ROYAL WAY (La Voie Royale, 1930)

BAUMGARTNER, PAUL. "Solitude and Involvement: Two Aspects of Tragedy in Malraux's Novels." *French Review,* 38 (1965), 768–70.

BOAK, DENNIS. *André Malraux,* pp. 29–43.

———. "Malraux's *La Voie Royale.*" *French Studies,* 19 (1965), 42–50.

DALE, JONATHAN. "Sartre and Malraux: *La Nausée* and *La Voie Royale.*" *Forum For Modern Language Studies,* 4 (1968), 335–46.

GREENLEE, JAMES W. *Malraux's Heroes And History,* pp. 45–58.

HORVATH, VIOLET M. *André Malraux:* <*The Human Adventure,*> pp. 179–93.

JENKINS, CECIL. *André Malraux,* pp. 47–51.

PAYNE, ROBERT. *A Portrait Of André Malraux,* pp. 151–65.

STORM IN SHANGHAI see MAN'S FATE

THE TEMPTATION OF THE ORIENT (La Tentation de l'Occident, 1926)

BOAK, DENNIS. *André Malraux,* pp. 22–28.

GREENLEE, JAMES W. *Malraux's Heroes And History,* pp. 13–31.

HORVATH, VIOLET M. *André Malraux:* <*The Human Adventure*> pp. 147–62.

PAYNE, ROBERT. *A Portrait Of André Malraux,* pp. 118-26.

THE WALNUT TREES OF ALTENBURG (Les Noyers de l'Altenburg, 1943)

BOAK, DENNIS. *André Malraux,* pp. 139-76.

BOND, DAVID J. "Malraux's *Les Noyers De L'Altenburg.*" *Explicator,* 33 (1975), Item 62.

CHUA, C. L. 'André Malraux's Unfinished Novel, *Les Noyers De L'Altenburg:* A *Caveat* for Critics." *Neophilologus,* 53 (1969), 10-13.

FROHOCK, W. M. *Style and Temper,* pp. 62-77.

GREENLEE, JAMES W. *Malraux's Heroes And History,* pp. 139-68.

HORVATH, VIOLET M. *André Malraux: <The Human Adventure,>* pp. 249-83.

JENKINS, CECIL. *André Malraux,* pp. 103-15.

PAYNE, ROBERT. *A Portrait Of André Malraux,* pp. 303-15.

RECK, RIMA DRELL. *Literature And Responsibility,* pp. 298-301.

MAMMERI, MOULOUD (Algerian, 1917-)
THE SLEEP OF THE JUST (Le sommeil du juste, 1955)

YETIV, ISAAC. "The Crisis of Identity of the Native North African Writer," in *Twentieth Century French Fiction,* ed. George Stambolian, pp. 134-36.

MANDEL, ARNOLD
LE PÉRIPLE (1973)

Reviews
WEINBERG, HENRY H. *French Review,* 47 (1974), 1216-17.

MANDER, JANE (New Zealander)
ALLEN ADAIR

Reviews
EAGLE, CHESTER. "New Zealand Rediscoveries—." *Overland,* No.51 (1972), pp. 57-58.

MANDIARGUES, ANDRÉ PIEYRE DE (French, 1909-)
GENERAL

BOND, DAVID J. "Recurring Patterns of Fantasy in the Fiction of André Pieyre de Mandiargues." *Symposium,* 29 (1975), 30-47.

THE MARGIN (La Marge, 1967)
Reviews
BISHOP, THOMAS. *Saturday Review,* 31 May 1969, pp. 27, 30.

THE MOTORCYCLE (La Motocyclette, 1963)
Reviews
BRÉE, GERMAINE. *Kenyon Review,* 27 (1965), 575-76.
HAKALA, WILLIAM. "Have On, Black Devil." *Minnesota Review,* 7 (1967), 245-47.

MANET, EDUARDO (French Cuban, 1927-)
UN CRI SUR LE RIVAGE

MENTON, SEYMOUR. *Prose Fiction Of The Cuban Revolution,* pp. 31-33.

MANN, HEINRICH
DER ATEM (1949)

LINN, ROLF N. *Heinrich Mann,* pp. 119-24.

DIE BRANZILLA
LINN, ROLF N. *Heinrich Mann,* pp. 53-58.

DIANA (Die Göttinnen, 1903)
LINN, ROLF N. *Heinrich Mann,* pp. 24-35.

DIE GROSSE SACHE (1930)
LINN, ROLF N. *Heinrich Mann,* pp. 93-96.

IN THE LAND OF COCKAIGNE (Im Schlaraffenland, 1900)
LINN, ROLF N. *Heinrich Mann,* pp. 21-24.

KOBES (1925)
LINN, ROLF N. *Heinrich Mann,* pp. 83-86.

DER KOPF
LINN, ROLF N. *Heinrich Mann,* pp. 86-88.

THE LITTLE TOWN (Die Kleine Stadt, 1909)
LINN, ROLF N. *Heinrich Mann,* pp. 58-65.
ROBERTS, DAVID. *Artistic Consciousness And Political Conscience: The Novels Of Heinrich Mann 1900-1938,* pp. 52-83.

THE PATRIOTEER (Der Untertan, 1918)
LINN, ROLF N. *Heinrich Mann,* pp. 67-73.
ROBERTS, DAVID. *Artistic Consciousness And Political Conscience: The Novels Of Heinrich Mann 1900-1938,* pp. 84-124.

THE ROYAL WOMAN (Eugenie oder die Bürgerzeit, 1928)
LINN, ROLF N. *Heinrich Mann,* pp. 89-93.

SMALL TOWN TYRANT (Professor Unrat, 1905)
LINN, ROLF N. *Heinrich Mann,* pp. 40-46.

DER TYRANN
LINN, ROLF N. *Heinrich Mann,* pp. 51-53.

YOUNG HENRY OF NAVARRE (Die Jugen des Königs Henri Quatre, 1935)
LINN, ROLF N. *Heinrich Mann,* pp. 105-12.
ROBERTS, DAVID. *Artistic Consciousness And Political Conscience: The Novels Of Heinrich Mann 1900-1938,* pp. 190-242.

ZWISCHEN DEN RASSEN (1907)
LINN, ROLF N. *Heinrich Mann,* pp. 47-51.

MANN, LEONARD (Australian, 1895-)
GENERAL

MANN, LEONARD. "A Double Life." *Southerly,* 29 (1969), 163-74.

A MURDER IN SYDNEY (1937)

VINTNER, MAURICE. "Rediscovery-1: Leonard Mann's 'A Murder in Sydney.' " *Overland,* No.44 (1970), pp. 39-40.

MANN, THOMAS (German, 1875-1955)
GENERAL

BEHLER, DIANA. "Thomas Mann as a Theoretician of the Novel." *Colloquia Germanica,* No.1/2 (1974), pp. 52-88.

BLOMSTER, WESLEY V. "Thomas Mann and the Munich Manifesto." *German Life And Letters,* 22 (1969), 134-46.

BRUFORD, W. H. *The German Tradition Of Self-Cultivation,* pp. 226-63.

CONVERSI, LEONARD. "Mann, Yeats, and the Truth of Art." *Yale Review,* 56 (1967), 506-23.

DAEMMRICH, HORST S. "Mann's Portrait of the Artist: Archetypal Patterns." *Bucknell Review,* 14, No.3 (1966), 27–43.

EXNER, RICHARD. "Reading Thomas Mann: An Appreciation." *Books Abroad,* 49 (1975), 480–83.

EZERGAILIS, INTA MISKE. "Male and Female Principles: Thomas Mann's Image of Schiller and Goethe." *Mosaic,* 6, No.2 (1973), 37–53.

———. "Thomas Mann's Resort." *MLN,* 90 (1975), 345–62.

HUNT, JOEL A. "Thomas Mann and Faulkner: Portrait of a Magician." *Wisconsin Studies In Contemporary Literature,* 8 (1967), 431–36.

JONAS, KLAUS W. and D. L. ASHLIMAN. "Thomas Mann and Caroline Newton." *Modern Austrian Literature,* 6, No.3/4 (1973), 107–16.

KAMENETSKY, CHRISTA. "*Dichter* vs. *Literat:* Thomas Mann's Ironic View of the Literary Man." *College Language Association Journal,* 14 (1971), 420–31.

KELLEN, KONRAD. "Reminiscences of Thomas Mann." *Yale Review,* 54 (1965), 383–91.

KURZ, PAUL KONRAD. "Thomas Mann and Irony," in his *On Modern German Literature,* Vol. 2: 3–21.

MOTYLEVA, T. "Thomas Mann and His Novels." *Soviet Studies In Literature,* 1, No.1 (1964/5), 23–49.

MYERS, DAVID. "Sexual Love and *Caritas* in Thomas Mann." *Journal Of English And Germanic Philology,* 68 (1969), 593–604.

NEUBAUER, JOHN. "The Artist as Citizen: On Georg Lukác's View of Thomas Mann." *German Life And Letters,* 26 (1973), 202–8.

REED, T.J. "Thomas Mann and Tradition: Some Clarifications," in *The Discontinuous Tradition,* ed. P. F. Ganz, pp. 158–81.

RILEY, ANTHONY W. "Notes on Thomas Mann and English and American Literature." *Comparative Literature,* 17 (1965), 57–72.

———. "The Professing Christian and the Ironic Humanist: A Comment on the Relationship of Alfred Döblin and Thomas Mann after 1933," in *Essays On German Literature In Honour Of G. Joyce Hallamore,* ed. Michael S. Batts and Marketa Goetz Stankiewicz, pp. 177–94.

SCHMIDT, WILLA. "The 'Wiedersehen' Motif in the Works of Thomas Mann." *Monatshefte,* 65 (1973), 144–60.

STEINBERG, MICHAEL. "Mann's Fate." *Atlantic Monthly,* 235, No.6 (1975), 62–66.

WIRTZ, ERIKA. "Thomas Mann, Humorist and Educator." *Modern Languages,* 47 (1966), 145–51.

ZIOLKOWSKI, THEODORE. "Hermann Weigand and a Letter from Thomas Mann: The Critical Dialogue." *Yale Review,* 56 (1967), 537–49.

THE BELOVED RETURNS (Lotte in Weimar, 1939)

EZERGAILIS, INTA MISKE. "Male and Female Principles: Thomas Mann's Image of Schiller and Goethe." *Mosaic,* 6, No.2 (1972/3), 50–53.

FEUERLICHT, IGNACE. *Thomas Mann,* pp. 59–66.

HOLLINGDALE, R. J. *Thomas Mann: A Critical Study,* pp. 117–24.

MEYER, HERMANN. *The Poetics Of Quotation In The European Novel,* pp. 253–74.

SCHMIDT, WILLIAM. "The 'Wiedersehen' Motif in the Works of Thomas Mann." *Monatshefte,* 65 (1973), 149–53.

THE BLACK SWAN (Die betrogene, 1953)

FEUERLICHT, IGNACE. *Thomas Mann,* pp. 146–49.

McWILLIAMS, JAMES R. "Thomas Mann's *Die Betrogene*—A Study in Ambivalence." *College Language Association Journal,* 10 (1966), 56–63.

RAHV, PHILIP. "Thomas Mann at Eighty," in his *Literature And The Sixth Sense,* pp. 369–72.

BUDDENBROOKS (1901)

BLOCK, HASKELL M. *Naturalistic Triptych,* pp. 32–53.

FEUERLICHT, IGNACE. *Thomas Mann,* pp. 13–21.

GRAY, RONALD. *The German Tradition In Literature: 1871–1945,* pp. 105–36.

HOLLINGDALE, R. J. *Thomas Mann: A Critical Study,* pp. 24–28, 56–62.

JOLLES, CHARLOTTE. "Sesemi Weichbrodt: Observations on a Minor Character of Thomas Mann's Fictional World." *German Life And Letters,* 22 (1968), 32–38.

MOLONEY, BRIAN. "Italo Svevo and Thomas Mann's *Buddenbrooks,*" in *Essays In Honour Of John Humphreys Whitfield,* pp. 258–67.

NACHMAN, LARRY DAVID and ALBERT S. BRAVERMAN. "Thomas Mann's *Buddenbrooks:* Bourgeois Society and the Inner Life." *Germanic Review,* 45 (1970), 201–25.

RIDLEY, HUGH. "Nature and Society in 'Buddenbrooks.' " *Orbis Litterarum,* 28 (1973), 138–47.

SCHILLING, BERNARD N. "Hanno, Kai, and the 'Oil of Sorrow,' " in his *The Comic Spirit: Boccaccio To Thomas Mann,* pp. 217–36.

———. " 'Tränen-Trieschke . . . Grünlich . . . Permaneder,' " in his *The Comic Spirit: Boccaccio To Thomas Mann,* pp. 194–216.

THE CONFESSIONS OF FELIX KRULL (Bekentnisse des hochstaplers Felix Krull, 1922)

FEUERLICHT, IGNACE. *Thomas Mann,* pp. 92–107.

HEILMAN, ROBERT B. "Felix Krull: Variations on Picaresque," in *Perspectives On Fiction,* ed. James L. Calderwood and Harold E. Toliver, pp. 101–25.

HOLLINGDALE, R. J. *Thomas Mann: A Critical Study,* pp. 102–5, 136–39.

KEARFUL, FRANK J. "The Role of Hermes in the *Confessions Of Felix Krull.*" *Modern Fiction Studies,* 17 (1971), 91–108.

MAYER, HANS. "Günter Grass and Thomas Mann: Aspects of the Novel," in his *Steppenwolf And Everyman,* pp. 188–99.

NELSON, DONALD F. "Felix Krull or: 'All the World's a Stage.' " *Germanic Review,* 45 (1970), 41–51.

RILEY, ANTHONY W. "Three Cryptic Quotations in Thomas Mann's *Felix Krull.*" *Journal Of English And Germanic Philology,* 65 (1966), 99–106.

STEINER, GEORGE. "Thomas Mann's *Felix Krull,*" in his *Language And Silence,* pp. 269–79.

ZIPES, JACK D. "Growing Pains in the Contemporary German Novel—East and West." *Mosaic,* 5, No.3 (1971/2), 4–5.

DEATH IN VENICE (Der Tod in Venedig, 1913)

BANCE, A. F. "*Der Tod In Venedig* and the Triadic Structure." *Forum For Modern Language Studies,* 8 (1972), 148–61.

BARON, FRANK. "Sensuality and Morality in Thomas Mann's *Tod In Venedig.*" *Germanic Review,* 45 (1970), 115–25.

BRAVERMAN, ALBERT and LARRY DAVID NACHMAN. "The Dialectic of Decadence: An Analysis of Thomas Mann's *Death In Venice.*" *Germanic Review,* 45 (1970), 289–98.

COX, CATHERINE. "Pater's 'Apollo in Picardy' and Mann's *Death In Venice.*" *Anglia,* 86 (1968), 143–54.

DYSON, A. E. "The Stranger God: 'Death in Venice.' " *Critical Quarterly,* 13 (1971), 5–20.

FEUERLICHT, IGNACE. *Thomas Mann,* pp. 117–26.

GOOD, GRAHAM. "The Death of Language in *Death In Venice.*" *Mosaic,* 5, No.3 (1972), 43–52.

GRAY, RONALD. *The German Tradition In Literature: 1871–1945,* pp. 145–56.

GREENBERG, ALVIN. "A Sense of Place in Modern Fiction: The

Novelist's World and the Allegorist's Heaven." *Genre,* 5 (1972), 356-59.

GROSSVOGEL, DAVID I. "Visconti and the Too, Too Solid Flesh." *Diacritics,* 1, No.2 (1971), 52-55.

HAYES, JAMES A. "The Translator and the Form-Content Dilemma in Literary Translation." *MLN,* 90 (1975), 838-48.

HOLLINGDALE, R. J. *Thomas Mann: A Critical Study,* pp. 90-94.

HUTCHINSON, ALEXANDER. "Luchino Visconti's *Death In Venice.*" *Literature/Film Quarterly,* 2 (1974), 31-43. [on the motion picture]

KIRCHBERGER, LIDA. " 'Death in Venice' and the Eighteenth Century." *Monatshefte,* 58 (1966), 321-34.

LEHNERT, HERBERT. "Note on Mann's *Der Tod In Venedig* and the *Odyssey.*" *PMLA,* 80 (1965), 306-7.

LEPPMANN, WOLFGANG. "Time and Place in *Death In Venice.*" *German Quarterly,* 48 (1975), 66-75.

McINTYRE, ALLAN J. "Psychology and Symbol: Correspondences Between *Heart Of Darkness* and *Death In Venice.*" *Hartford Studies In Literature,* 7 (1975), 216-35.

McWILLIAMS, J. R. "The Failure of a Repression: Thomas Mann's *Tod In Venedig.*" *German Life And Letters,* 20 (1967), 233-41.

PLANK, ROBERT. "Death in Venice: Tragedy or Mishap?" *Hartford Studies In Literature,* 4 (1972), 95-103.

SLOWCHOWER, HARRY. "Thomas Mann's *Death In Venice.*" *American Imago,* 26 (1969), 99-122.

SPRINGER, MARY DOYLE. *Forms Of The Modern Novella,* pp. 102-05.

TARBOX, RAYMOND. "*Death In Venice:* The Aesthetic Object as Dream Guide." *American Imago,* 26 (1969), 123-44.

TRASCHEN, ISADORE. "The Uses of Myth in 'Death in Venice.' " *Modern Fiction Studies,* 11 (1965), 165-79.

WOLF, ERNEST M. "A Case of Slightly Mistaken Identity: Gustave Mahler and Gustave Aschenbach." *Twentieth Century Literature,* 19 (1973), 40-52.

WOODWARD, ANTHONY. "The Figure of the Artist in Thomas Mann's *Tonio Kröger* and *Death In Venice.*" *English Studies In Africa,* 9 (1966), 158-67.

DOCTOR FAUSTUS (Doktor Faustus, 1947)

APTER, T. E. "Thomas Mann's *Doktor Faustus:* Nihilism or Humanism?" *Forum For Modern Language Studies,* 11 (1975), 59-73.

BLOMSTER, WESLEY V. "The Demonic in History: Thomas Mann and Gunter Grass." *Contemporary Literature,* 10 (1969), 75-84.

———. "A Pietà in Mann's *Faustus?*" *MLN,* 90 (1975), 336-44.

FASS, BARBARA F. "The Little Mermaid and the Artist's Quest for a Soul." *Comparative Literature Studies,* 9 (1972), 291-302.

FEUERLICHT, IGNACE. *Thomas Mann,* pp. 67-84.

FICKERT, KURT J. "Mann's *Doctor Faustus.*" *Explicator,* 31 (1973), Item 58.

FIELD, G. W. "Music and Morality in Thomas Mann and Hermann Hesse," in *Hesse: A Collection Of Critical Essays,* ed. Theodore Ziolkowski, pp. 94-111.

GANDELMAN, CLAUDE. "The 'Inferno Astratto' of Thomas Mann." *Revue De Littérature Comparée,* 47 (1973), 611-19.

GRAY, RONALD. *The German Tradition In Literature: 1871-1945,* pp. 208-23.

HANNUM, HILDEGARDE DREXL. "Self Sacrifice in *Doktor Faustus:* Thomas Mann's Contribution to the Faust Legend." *Modern Language Quarterly,* 35 (1974), 289-301.

HATFIELD, HENRY. *Crisis And Continuity In Modern German Fiction,* pp. 166-76.

HOLLINGDALE, R. J. *Thomas Mann: A Critical Study,* pp. 44-50.

HONSA, WILLIAM M., JR., "Parody and Narrator in Thomas Mann's 'Dr. Faustus' and 'The Holy Sinner.' " *Orbis Litterarum,* 29 (1974), 61-76.

KLAWITER, RANDOLPH J. "The Artist-Intellectual, in or versus Society? A Dilemma," in *Studies In German Literature Of The Nineteenth And Twentieth Centuries,* ed. Siegfried Mews, pp. 243-47.

MAGLIOLA, ROBERT. "The Magic Square: Polar Unity in Thomas Mann's *Doctor Faustus.*" *Hartford Studies In Literature,* 6 (1974), 55-71.

MEYERS, JEFFREY. *Painting And The Novel,* pp. 157-74.

———. "Shakespeare and Mann's *Doctor Faustus.*" *Modern Fiction Studies,* 19 (1973/4), 541-45.

MILLER, LESLIE L. "Reflections On Thomas Mann's *Doktor Faustus,*" in *Essays On German Literature In Honour Of G. Joyce Hallamore,* ed. Michael S. Batts and Marketa Goetz Stankiewicz, pp. 195-217.

MOTYLEVA, T. "Thomas Mann and His Novels." *Soviet Studies In Literature,* 1, No.1 (1964/5), 41-46.

NIXON, LIANA DE BONA. "The Concept of Barbarism in Thomas Mann's *Doctor Faustus.*" *Midwest Quarterly,* 16 (1975), 438-52.

OATES, JOYCE CAROL. " 'Art at the Edge of Impossibility': Mann's *Dr. Faustus.*" *Southern Review,* NS, 5 (1969), 375-97.

OSTERLE, HEINZ D. "The Other Germany: Resistance to the Third Reich in German Literature." *German Quarterly,* 41 (1968), 17-20.

ROSE, MARILYN GADDIS. "More on the Musical Composition of *Doktor Faustus.*" *Modern Fiction Studies,* 17 (1971), 81-89.

SCHER, STEVEN PAUL. "Thomas Mann's 'Verbal Score': Adrian Leverkuhn's Symbolic Confession." *MLN,* 82 (1967), 403-20.

STERN, J. P. "Thomas Mann's Last Period." *Critical Quarterly,* 8 (1966), 244-54.

TUSKA, JON. "The Vision of Doktor Faustus." *Germanic Review,* 40 (1965), 277-309.

VISWANATHAN, JACQUELINE. "Point of View and Unrealiability in Bontë's >>Wuthering Heights<<, Conrad's >>Under Western Eyes<<, and Mann's >>Doktor Faustus.<<" *Orbis Litterarum,* 29 (1974), 42-60.

WHITE, JOHN H. *Mythology In The Modern Novel,* pp. 149-56.

THE HOLY SINNER (Der Erwählte, 1951)

FEUERLICHT, IGNACE. *Thomas Mann,* pp. 85-91.

HONSA, WILLIAM M., JR. "Parody and Narrator in Thomas Mann's 'Dr. Faustus' and 'The Holy Sinner.' " *Orbis Litterarum,* 29 (1974), 61-76.

WASHINGTON, IDA H. "A Source for Mann's Penitent Gregorius." *Germanic Notes,* 6, No.3 (1975), 38-41.

JOSEPH AND HIS BROTHERS (Joseph und seine Bruder, 1933-42)

DAEMMRICH, HORST S. "Fertility-Sterility: A Sequence of Motifs in Thomas Mann's *Joseph* Novels." *Modern Language Quarterly,* 31 (1970), 461-73.

DASSIN, JOAN. "The Dialectics of Recurrence: The Relation of the Individual to Myth and Legend in Thomas Mann's *Joseph And His Brothers.*" *Centennial Review,* 15 (1971), 362-90.

FEUERLICHT, IGNACE. *Thomas Mann,* pp. 43-58.

GRAY, RONALD. *The German Tradition In Literature: 1871-1945,* pp. 185-207.

HATFIELD, HENRY. *Crisis And Continuity In Modern German Fiction,* pp. 78-89.

HELLER, PETER. *Dialectics And Nihilism: Essays On Lessing, Nietzsche, Mann And Kafka,* pp. 151-226.

HELTAY, HILARY. "Der Mann auf dem Felde: Virtuousity in Thomas Mann's Later Narrative Technique." *German Life And Letters,* 24 (1971), 192-204.

HOLLINGDALE, R. J. *Thomas Mann: A Critical Study*, pp. 113–17.

HUGHES, KENNETH. "Theme and Structure in Thomas Mann's 'Die Geschichten Jaakobs.' " *Monatshefte*, 62 (1970), 24–36.

SLADE, JOSEPH W. "The Functions of Eternal Recurrence in Thomas Mann's *Joseph And His Brothers*." *Symposium*, 25 (1971), 180–97.

JOSEPH THE PROVIDER (Joseph, der Ernährer, 1943)

HUGHES, KENNETH. "The Sources and Function of Serach's Song in Thomas Mann's *Joseph, Der Ernährer*." *Germanic Review*, 45 (1970), 126–33.

SCHMIDT, WILLA. "The 'Wiedersehen' Motif in the Works of Thomas Mann." *Monatshefte*, 65 (1973), 153–59.

SPININGER, DENNIS J. "The 'Thamar' Section of 'Joseph und sein Brüder': A Formal Analysis." *Monatshefte*, 61 (1969), 157–72.

THE MAGIC MOUNTAIN (Der Zauberberg, 1924)

BASILIUS, HAROLD A. "Mann's Naphta-Settembrini and the Battle of the Books." *Modern Fiction Studies*, 14 (1968/9), 415–21.

BRAUN, FRANK X. "A Lesson in Articulation in Thomas Mann's 'Zauberberg.' " *Monatshefte*, 58 (1966), 124–30.

BRENNAN, JOSEPH GERARD. "Fifty Years of *The Magic Mountain*." *Columbia Forum*, 3, No.3 (1974), 31–39.

———. "Heard and Unheard Speech in *The Magic Mountain*." *Novel*, 3 (1970), 129–38.

———. "Three Novels of *Dépaysement*." *Comparative Literature*, 22 (1970), 223–36.

BRUFORD, W. H. *The German Tradition Of Self-Cultivation*, pp. 206–25.

FEUERLICHT, IGNACE. *Thomas Mann*, pp. 28–42.

FURST, LILIAN R. "Italo Svevo's *La Coscienza Di Zeno* and Thomas Mann's *Der Zauberberg*." *Contemporary Literature*, 9 (1978), 492–506.

GAERTNER, JOHANNES A. "Dialectic Thought in Thomas Mann's *The Magic Mountain*." *German Quarterly*, 38 (1965), 605–18.

GRAY, RONALD. *The German Tradition In Literature: 1871–1945*, pp. 157–72.

HATFIELD, HENRY. "The Journey and the Mountain." *MLN*, 90 (1975), 363–70.

HOLLINGDALE, R. J. *Thomas Mann: A Critical Study*, pp. 28–40.

HUNT, JOEL A. "Thomas Mann and André Spire: The *Walpurgisnacht* Chapter." *MLN*, 87 (1972), 502–5.

KAMENETSKY, CHRISTA. "*Dichter* vs. *Literat*: Thomas Mann's Ironic View of the Literary Man." *College Language Association Journal*, 14 (1971), 426–31.

LATTA, ALAN D. "The Mystery of Life: A Theme in *Der Zauberberg*." *Monatshefte*, 66 (1974), 19–32.

———. "Symbolic Structure: Toward an Understanding of the Structure of Thomas Mann's *Zauberberg*." *Germanic Review*, 50 (1975), 34–54.

LOOSE, GERHARD. "Ludovico Settembrini and 'Soziologie der Leiden' Notes on Thomas Mann's *Zauberberg*." *MLN*, 83 (1968), 420–29.

MEYER, HERMANN. *The Poetics Of Quotation In The European Novel*, pp. 230–53.

MUELLER, WILLIAM R. "Thomas Mann's 'The Magic Mountain.' " *Thought*, 49 (1974), 419–35.

PRUSOK, RUDI. "Science in Mann's *Zauberberg*: The Concept of Space." *PMLA*, 88 (1973), 52–61.

ROTH, MARIA C. "Mynheer Peeperkorn in the Light of Schopenhauer's Philosophy." *Monatshefte*, 58 (1966), 335–44.

SEIDLIN, OSKAR. "The Lofty Game of Numbers: The Mynheer Peeperkorn Episode in Thomas Mann's *Der Zauberberg*." *PMLA*, 86 (1971), 924–39.

SWALES, MARTIN. "The Story and the Hero: A Study of Thomas Mann's 'Der Zauberberg.' " *Deutsche Vjerteljahresschrift Fur Literaturwissenschaft Und Geistegeschichte*, 46 (1972), 359–76.

THAYER, TERENCE K. "Hans Castorp's Hermetic Adventures." *Germanic Review*, 46 (1971), 299–312.

WILLIAMS, C. E. "Not an Inn, But an Hospital. *The Magic Mountain* and *Cancer Ward*." *Forum For Modern Language Studies*, 9 (1973), 311–32.

ZIOLKOWSKI, THEODORE. *Dimensions Of The Modern Novel*, pp. 68–98.

MARIO AND THE MAGICIAN (Mario und der zauberer, 1930)

FEUERLICHT, IGNACE. *Thomas Mann*, pp. 126–29.

GRAY, RONALD. *The German Tradition In Literature: 1871–1945*, pp. 173–84.

HOLLINGDALE, R. J. *Thomas Mann: A Critical Study*, pp. 40–44.

HUNT, JOEL A. "Thomas Mann and Faulkner: Portrait of a Magician." *Wisconsin Studies In Contemporary Literature*, 8 (1967), 431–36.

WAGENER, HANS. "Mann's Cipolla and Earlier Prototypes of the Magician." *MLN*, 84 (1969), 800–2.

ROYAL HIGHNESS (Königliche hoheit, 1909)

FEUERLICHT, IGNACE. *Thomas Mann*, pp. 22–27.

FREY, ERICH A. "An American Prototype in Thomas Mann's *Königliche Hoheit*." *Kentucky Foreign Language Quarterly*, 13 (1966), 125–29.

SCHWERE STUNDE

DAEMMRICH, HORST S. "Thomas Mann's *Schwere Stunde* Reconsidered." *Papers On Language And Literature*, 3 (1967), 34–41.

THE TALES OF JACOB (Die Geschichten Jaakobs, 1933)

HUGHES, KENNETH. "Theme and Structure in Thomas Mann's 'Die Geschichten Jaakobs.' " *Monatshefte*, 62 (1970), 24–36.

TONIO KRÖGER (1903)

FEUERLICHT, IGNACE. *Thomas Mann*, pp. 109–14.

GRAY, RONALD. *The German Tradition In Literature: 1871–1945*, pp. 137–45.

HOLLINGDALE, R. J. *Thomas Mann: A Critical Study*, pp. 62–65.

KIRCHBERGER, LIDA. "Popularity as a Technique: Notes on 'Tonio Kröger.' " *Monatshefte*, 63 (1971), 321–34.

McWILLIAMS, J. R. "Conflict and Compromise—Tonio Kröger's Paradox." *Revue Des Langues Vivantes*, 32 (1966), 376–83.

PEMPE, RUTA. "Buddhadeva's Portrait of an Artist." *Literature East And West*, 18 (1974), 216–32.

SPRINGER, MARY DOYLE. *Forms Of The Modern Novella*, pp. 148–57.

SWALES, M. W. "Punctuation and the Narrative Mode: Some Remarks on *Tonio Kröger*." *Forum For Modern Language Studies*, 6 (1970), 235–42.

WETZEL, HEINZ. "The Seer in the Spring: On *Tonio Kröger* and *The Wasteland*." *Revue De Littérature Comparée*, 44 (1970), 322–32.

WITTHOFT, BRUCIA. " 'Tonio Kröger' and Muybridge's 'Animals in Motion.' " *Modern Language Review*, 62 (1967), 459–61.

TRISTAN (1903)

EZERGAILIS, INTA. "Spinell's Letter: An Approach to Thomas Mann's *Tristan*." *German Life And Letters*, 25 (1972), 377–82.

FEUERLICHT, IGNACE. *Thomas Mann*, pp. 114–17.

NORTHCOTE-BADE, JAMES. "Thomas Mann's Use of Wagner's 'Sehnsuchtsmotiv' in *Tristan*." *Seminar*, 8 (1972), 55–60.

SCHNITMAN, SOPHIA. "Musical Motives in Thomas Mann's *Tristan*." *MLN*, 86 (1971), 399–414.

SONNENFELD, ALBERT. "*Tristan* for Pianoforte: Thomas Mann and Marcel Proust." *Southern Review*, NS, 5 (1969), 1004–18.

MANNING, FREDERIC (Australian, 1887–1935)

HER PRIVATES WE (1930)

KLEIN, H. M. "The Structure of Frederic Manning's War Novel *Her Privates We*." *Australian Literary Studies*, 6 (1974), 404–17.

MANSOUR, JOYCE

LES GISANTS SATISFAITS (1958)

MATTHEWS, J. H. *Surrealism And The Novel*, pp. 124–40.

MANZONI, ALESSANDRO FRANCISCO TOMMASO ANTONIO (Italian, 1785–1873)

GENERAL

BRANCA, VITTORE. "Manzoni and Venice." Trans. Donna Beckage. *Italian Quarterly*, 17, No.67 (1973), 63–78.

CASERTA, ERNESTO G. "Manzoni's Aesthetic Theory." *Comparative Literature Studies*, 10 (1973), 229–51.

CHANDLER, S. B. "Passion, Reason and Evil in theWorks of Alessandro Manzoni." *Italica*, 50 (1973), 551–65.

FOSTER, KENELM. "Alessandro Manzoni (1785–1873)." *Italian Quarterly*, 17, No.67 (1973), 7–23.

MONTANO, ROCCO. "Manzoni, Today." *Italian Quarterly*, 17, No.67 (1973), 25–54.

PACIFICI, SERGIO. *The Modern Italian Novel: From Manzoni To Svevo*, pp. 26–56.

PEER, LARRY H. "Manzoni's Use of the Term 'Romanticismo.'" *Italian Quarterly*, 17, No.67 (1973), 55–62.

———. "Schlegel, Christianity, and History: Manzoni's Theory of the Novel." *Comparative Literature Studies*, 9 (1972), 266–82.

THE BETROTHED (I Promessi sposi, 1825–27)

BARRICELLI, JEAN-PIERRE. "Structure and Symbol in Manzoni's *I Promessi Sposi*." *PMLA*, 87 (1972), 499–507.

CHANDLER, S. BERNARD. "Point of View in the Descriptions of *I Promessi Sposi*." *Italica*, 43 (1966), 386–403.

———. "The Portrait of Federigo Borromeo in *I Promessi Sposi*." *Philological Quarterly*, 44 (1965), 519–26.

PACIFICI, SERGIO. *The Modern Italian Novel: From Manzoni To Svevo*, pp. 31–56.

PALLOTTA, AUGUSTUS. "British and American Translations of *I Promessi Sposi*." *Italica*, 50 (1973), 483–523.

PEER, LARRY H. "Schlegel, Christianity, and History: Manzoni's Theory of the Novel." *Comparative Literature Studies*, 9 (1972), 266–82.

PURDY, STROTHER B. "Manzoni, Stendhal, and the Murder of Prina: A Counterpart of Literature and History." *Studies In Romanticism*, 7 (1968), 140–58.

RICAPITO, J. V. "Camparatistica—Two Versions of Sin, Moral Transgression and Divine Will: *Guzmán de Alfarache* and *I Promessi Sposi*." *Kentucky Romance Quarterly*, 16 (1969), 111–18.

MAO TUN (Chinese, 1896–1981) pseudonym of Shen Yin-ping

GENERAL

HSIA, C. T. *A History Of Modern Chinese Fiction*, pp. 140–64, 350–59.

HUNG (1930)

HSIA, C. T. *A History Of Modern Chinese Fiction*, pp. 148–55.

MIDNIGHT (Tzu-yeh, 1932)

YANG, RICHARD. "'Midnight': Mao Tun's Political Novel." *Review Of National Literature*, 6, No.1 (1975), 60–75.

TUNG-YAO (1930)

HSIA, C. T. *A History Of Modern Chinese Fiction*, pp. 143–46.

THE TWILIGHT

HSIA, C. T. *A History Of Modern Chinese Fiction*, pp. 155–60.

MARAN, RENÉ (Martinican, 1887–1960)

BATOUALA (1921)

CARTEY, WILFRED. *Whispers From A Continent*, pp. 84–88.

IKONNÉ, CHIDI. "René Maran, 1887–1960: A Black Francophone Writer Between Two Worlds." *Research In African Literatures*, 5 (1974), 5–22.

JAMES, CHARLES L. "*Batouala*: Rene Maran and the Art of Objectivity." *Studies in Black Literature*, 4, No.3 (1973), 19–23.

Reviews
ALLEN, BRUCE. *Review*, No. 9 (1973), pp. 71–72.

CONDE, MARYSE. *Présence Africaine*, No.87 (1973), pp. 212–13.

LE LIVRE DE LA BROUSSE (1934)

GLEASON, JUDITH ILLSLEY. *This Africa*, pp. 76–79.

MARCEAU, FÉLICIEN (French, 1913–) pseudonym of Louis Carette

CREEZY (1969)

Reviews
LESAGE, LAURENT. *Saturday Review*, 21 February 1970, p. 48.

MARDOR, MUNYA M. (Israeli, 1913–)

STRICTLY ILLEGAL (Haganah, 1964)

Reviews
LEHRMAN, HAL. "Underground to Independence." *Saturday Review*, 26 March 1966, 32–33.

MARECHAL, LEOPOLDO (Argentine, 1900–1970)

ADAN BUENOSAYRES (1948)

BRUSHWOOD, JOHN S. *The Spanish American Novel*, pp. 167–70.

THE BANQUET OF SEVERO ARCANGELO (El banquete de Severo Arcangelo, 1965)

FOSTER, DAVID WILLIAM. *Currents In The Contemporary Argentine Novel*, pp. 134–37.

MARGUERITE D'ANGOULÉME, QUEEN OF NAVARRE (French, 1492–1549)

L'HEPTAMÉRON

BAKER, M. J. "Didacticism and the *Heptaméron*: The Misinterpretation of the Tenth Tale as an Exemplum." *French Review*, 45, Special Issue No. 3 (1971), 84–90.

KRAILSHEIMER, A. J. "The *Heptaméron* Reconsidered," in *The French Renaissance And Its Heritage*, pp. 75–92.

STONE, DONALD. *From Tales to Truths*, pp. 21–29.

_____ ."Narrative Technique in 'L'Heptaméron.' " *Studi Francesi,* 11 (1967), 473-76.

MARÍN, JUAN (Chilean, 1900-1963)

UN AVION VOLABA (1935)

SWAIN, JAMES O. *Juan Marín—Chilean: The Man And His Writings,* pp. 83-86.

ORESTES Y YO (1938)

SWAIN, JAMES O. *Juan Marín—Chilean: The Man And His Writings,* pp. 94-97.

PARALELO 53 SUR (1936)

SWAIN, JAMES O. *Juan Marín—Chilean: The Man And His Writings,* pp. 86-90.

VIENTO NEGRO (1944)

SWAIN, JAMES O. *Juan Marín—Chilean: The Man And His Writings,* pp. 97-100.

MARIVAUX, PIERRE CARLET DE (French, 1688-1763)

GENERAL

CISMARU, ALFRED. "Molière's *Le Tartuffe* in Marivaux's Work." *Kentucky Foreign Language Quarterly,* 12 (1965), 142-54.

HAAC, OSCAR A. "The Art of Marivaux," in his *Marivaux,* pp. 124-50.

MUNRO, JAMES S. "Richardson, Marivaux, and the French Romance Tradition," *Modern Language Review,* 70 (1975), 752-59.

THOMAS, RUTH P. "The Art of the Portrait in the Novels of Marivaux." *French Review,* 42 (1968), 23-31.

TRAPNELL, WILLIAM H. "Marivaux's Unfinished Narratives." *French Studies,* 24 (1970), 237-53.

LES EFFETS SURPRENANTS DE LA SYMPATHIE, OU LES AVENTURES DE * * *

ROSBOTTOM, RONALD C. *Marivaux's Novels,* pp. 57-62.

PHARSAMON

HARTWIG, ROBERT J. "*Pharsamon* and *Joseph Andrews.*" *Texas Studies In Literature and Language,* 14 (1972), 45-52.

ROSBOTTOM, RONALD C. *Marivaux's Novels,* pp. 62-65.

LE TÉLÉMAQUE TRAVESTI

ROSBOTTOM, RONALD C. *Marivaux's Novels,* pp. 65-70.

THE UPSTART PEASANT (Le Paysan Parvenu, 1735-36)

CISMARU, ALFRED. "Molière's *Le Tartuffe* in Marivaux's Work." *Kentucky Foreign Language Quarterly,* 12 (1965), 147-52.

HAAC, OSCAR A. *Marivaux,* pp. 83-86.

MYLNE, VIVIENNE. *The Eighteenth Century French Novel,* pp. 121-24.

ROSBOTTOM, RONALD C. *Marivaux's Novels,* pp. 171-222.

THOMAS, RUTH P. "The Critical Narrators of Marivaux's Unfinished Novels." *Forum For Modern Language Studies,* 9 (1973), 363-66.

_____ . "The Role of the Narrator in the Comic Tone of *Le Paysan Parvenu.*" *Romance Notes,* 12 (1970), 134-41.

TRAPNELL, WILLIAM H. "Marivaux's Unfinished Narratives." *French Studies,* 24 (1970), 247-51.

THE VIRTUOUS ORPIIAN (La Vie de Marianne ou les Aventures de Madame la comtesse de * * *, 1731-41)

BRADY, PATRICK. "Other-Portrayal and Self-Betrayal in *Manon Lescaut* and *La Vie De Marianne.*" *Romanic Review,* 64 (1973), 99-110.

_____ . "Rococo Style in the Novel: 'La Vie de Marianne.' " *Studi Francesi,* 19 (1975), 225-43.

BROOKS, PETER. *The Novel Of Worldliness,* pp. 96-141.

CISMARU, ALFRED. "Molière's *Le Tartuffe* in Marivaux's Work." *Kentucky Foreign Language Quarterly,* 12 (1965), 143-47.

HAAC, OSCAR. *Marivaux,* pp. 69-75.

_____ . "Violence in Marivaux." *Kentucky Romance Quarterly,* 14 (1967), 191-99.

HECKMAN, JOHN. "*Marianne:* The Making of an Author." *MLN,* 86 (1971), 509-22.

KAHLER, ERICH. *The Inward Turn of Narrative,* pp. 145-48.

LARSON, JEFFRY. " 'La Vie de Marianne Pajot': A Real-Live Source of Marivaux's Heroine." *MLN,* 83 (1968), 598-609.

MYLNE, VIVIENNE. *The Eighteenth Century French Novel,* pp. 104-24.

ROBBINS, ARTHUR. "Marianne and Moral Expediency." *Revue Des Langues Vivantes,* 36 (1970), 258-65.

ROSBOTTOM, RONALD C. "Marivaux and the Possibilities of the Memoir-Novel." *Neophilologus,* 56 (1972), 43-49.

_____ . *Marivaux's Novels,* pp. 93-170.

SHOWALTER, ENGLISH. "Symbolic Space and Fictional Forms in the Eighteenth-Century French Novel." *Novel,* 8 (1975), 218-22.

THOMAS, RUTH P. "The Critical Narrators of Marivaux's Unfinished Novels." *Forum For Modern Language Studies,* 9 (1973), 366-69.

TRAPNELL, WILLIAM H. "Marivaux's Unfinished Narratives." *French Studies,* 24 (1970), 242-47.

LA VOITURE EMBOURBÉE

HAAC, OSCAR A. *Marivaux,* pp. 25-28.

ROSBOTTOM, RONALD C. *Marivaux's Novels, pp. 70-75.*

MARKANDAYA, KAMALA (Indian, 1924-)

GENERAL

ADKINS, JOAN F. "Kamala Markandaya: Indo-Anglian Conflict as Unity." *Journal of South Asian Literature,* 10, No.1 (1974), 89-101.

HARREX, S. C. "A Sense of Identity: The Novels of Kamala Markandaya." *Journal Of Commonwealth Literature,* 6, No.1 (1971), 65-78.

JAIN, JASBIR. "The Novels of Kamala Markandaya." *Indian Literature,* 18, No.2 (1975), 36-43.

KUMAR, SHIV K. "Tradition and Change in the Novels of Kamala Markandaya." *Books Abroad,* 43 (1969), 508-13.

PARMESWARAN, UNA. "India for the Western Reader: A Study of Kamala Markandaya's Novels." *Texas Quarterly,* 11, No.2 (1968), 231-47.

RAO, K. S. NARAYANA. "The Novels of Kamala Markandaya: A Contemporary Indo-Anglican Novelist." *Literature East And West,* 15 (1971), 209-18.

_____ . "Some Notes on the Plots of Kamala Markandaya's Novels." *Indian Literature,* 13, No.1 (1970), 102-12.

SHIMER, DOROTHY BLAIR. "Sociological Imagery in the Novels of Kamala Markandaya." *World Literature Written In English,* 14 (1975), 357-70.

SRINIVASA IYENGAR, K. R. *Indian Writing In English,* pp. 438-50.

THE COFFER DAMS (1969)

Reviews

CHAFFEE, PAUL. *World Literature Written In English,* No.18 (1970), pp. 41-42.

GONDAL, YOGESH CHANDRA. "Relationships and Dams." *Journal Of Commonwealth Literature,* 8, No.1 (1973), 134-35.

HESS, LINDA. *Saturday Review,* 14 June 1969, p. 35.

A HANDFUL OF RICE (1966)

FRACHT, SYLVIA. "A Study of Kamala Markandaya's *A Handful Of Rice.*" *English Journal,* 57 (1968), 1143-46.

Reviews

McGUINNESS, FRANK. *London Magazine,* NS 6, No.2 (1966), 106-8.

PARTON, MARGARET. "Cursed with Conscience." *Saturday Review,* 27 August 1966, p. 34.

POWERS, JANET M. *Mahfil,* 4, No.1 (1967), 58-60.

WENDT, ALLAN. *Literature East And West,* 11 (1967), 206-9.

NECTAR IN A SIEVE (1954)

ADKINS, JOAN F. "Kamala Markandaya: Indo-Anglian Conflict as Unity." *Journal Of South Asian Literature,* 10, No.1 (1974), 92-95.

ARGYLE, BARRY. 'Kamala Markandaya's *Nectar In A Sieve.*" *Ariel: A Review Of International English Literature,* 4 (1973), 35-45.

PARMESWARAN, UNA. "India for the Western Reader: A Study of Kamala Markandaya's Novels." *Texas Quarterly,* 11, No.2 (1968), 231-36.

POSSESSION (1963)

ADKINS, JOAN F. "Kamala Markandaya: Indo-Anglian Conflict as Unity." *Journal Of South Asian Literature,* 10, No.1 (1974), 99-101.

HARREX, S. C. "A Sense of Identity: the Novels of Kamala Markandaya." *Journal Of Commonwealth Literature,* 6, No.1 (1971), 69-72.

PARMESWARAN, UNA. "India for the Western Reader: A Study of Kamala Markandaya's Novels." *Texas Quarterly,* 11, No.2 (1968), 238-41.

SOME INNER FURY (1956)

ADKINS, JOAN. "Kamala Markandaya: Indo-Anglian Conflict as Unity." *Journal Of South Asian Literature,* 10, No.1 (1974), 95-99.

HARREX, S. C. "A Sense of Identity: The Novels of Kamala Markandaya." *Journal Of Commonwealth Literature,* 6, No.1 (1971), 75-78.

PARMESWARAN, UNA. "India for the Western Reader: A Study of Kamala Markandaya's Novels." *Texas Quarterly,* 11, No.2 (1968), 242-45.

TWO VIRGINS (1973)

RUBENSTEIN, ROBERTA. "Kamala Markandaya. *Two Virgins.*" *World Literature Written In English,* 13 (1974), 225-30.

Reviews

FLETCHER, JOHN. *International Fiction Review,* 2 (1975), 80-81.

MARKOOSIE (Canadian, 1942) pseudonym of Markoosie Patsauq

HARPOON OF THE HUNTER (1970)

Reviews

NOBLE, R. W. "The Way to the True North." *Journal Of Commonwealth Literature,* 9, No.3 (1975), 79-81.

MARLINSKY, ALEXANDER (Russian, 1797-1837) pseudonym of Alexander Alexandrovich Bestuzhev

GENERAL

LEIGHTON, LAUREN G. "Marlinsky." *Russian Literature Triquarterly,* No.3 (1972), pp. 249-68.

MARQUET, GABRIELLE

LA BOÎTE À BOUTONS (1973)

Reviews

BULGIN, KATHLEEN. *French Review,* 48 (1974), 487-88.

MÁRQUEZ, Gabriel Garcia see GARCÍA MÁRQUEZ, Gabriel

MARSÉ, JUAN (Spanish, 1933-)

ULTIMAS TARDES CON TERESA (1966)

NICHOLS, GERALDINE CLEARY. "Dialectical Realism and Beyond: *Últimas Tardes Con Teresa.*" *Journal Of Spanish Studies,* 3 (1975), 163-74.

MARTEAU, ROBERT

PENTECÔTE (1973)

Reviews

MANKIN, PAUL A. *French Review,* 48 (1974), 488-89.

MARTELLI, JUAN CARLOS

LOS TIGRES DE LA MEMORIA (1973)

Reviews

DAUSTER, FRANK. *Hispania,* 58 (1975), 578-79.

MARTIN, CLAIRE (Canadian, 1914-) pseudonym of Mme. Claire Faucher

DANS UN GANT DE FER (1965)

HESSE, M. G. "Vipers' Tangles: A Comparative Study of Claire Martin's *Dans Un Gant De Fer* and *La Joue Droite* and Percy Janes' *House Of Hate.*" *Journal Of Canadian Fiction,* 3, No.2 (1974), 77-81.

IN AN IRON GLOVE (Translation of Dans un gant de fer and La joue droite, 1968)

Reviews

OWEN, PATRICIA. "All Is Forgiven?" *Tamarack Review,* No.52 (1969), pp. 80-82.

LA JOUE DROITE (1966)

HESSE, M. G. "Vipers' Tangles: A Comparative Study of Claire Martin's *Dans Un Gant De Fer* and *La Joue Droite* and Percy Janes' *House Of Hate.*" *Journal Of Canadian Fiction,* 3, No.2 (1974), 77-81.

MARTIN, DAVID (Australian, 1915-)

GENERAL

MARTIN, DAVID. "David Martin on David Martin." *Southerly,* 31 (1971), 163-69.

THE HERO OF TOO (1965)

Reviews

McLAREN, JOHN. "New Novels." *Overland,* 33 (1965), 43-44.

WILDING, MICHAEL. *Southerly,* 26 (1966), 58-59.

MARTIN DU GARD, ROGER (French, 1881-1958)

GENERAL

BARBERET, GENE J. "Roger Martin du Gard: Recent Criticism." *French Review*, 41 (1967), 60-69.

CAMUS, ALBERT. *Lyrical And Critical Essays*, pp. 254-87.

McMURRAY, GEORGE R. "The Role of History in the Works of Roger Martin du Gard." *Xavier University Studies*, 5 (1966), 27-36.

LA BELLE SAISON (part of Les Thibault, 1923)

SAVAGE, CATHARINE. *Roger Martin Du Gard*, pp. 88-97.

SCHALK, DAVID L. *Roger Martin Du Gard: The Novelist And History*, pp. 77-83.

LA CAHIER GRIS (part of Les Thibault, 1922)

SAVAGE, CATHARINE. *Roger Martin Du Gard*, pp. 74-81.

SCHALK, DAVID L. *Roger Martin Du Gard: The Novelist And History*, pp. 69-73.

LA CONSULTATION (part of Les Thibault, 1928)

SAVAGE, CATHARINE. *Roger Martin Du Gard*, pp. 97-103.

SCHALK, DAVID L. *Roger Martin Du Gard: The Novelist And History*, pp. 83-88.

DEVENIR! (1909)

SAVAGE, CATHARINE. *Roger Martin Du Gard*, pp. 35-40.

SPURDLE, SONIA. "Some Sources of Roger Martin du Gard's Inspiration in *Devenir!*" *Neophilologus*, 55 (1971), 261-69.

EPILOGUE (part of Les Thibault, 1940)

SAVAGE, CATHARINE. *Roger Martin Du Gard*, pp. 142-51.

SCHALK, DAVID L. *Roger Martin Du Gard: The Novelist And History*, pp. 157-75.

L'ÉTÉ, 1914 (part of Les Thibault, 1936)

SAVAGE, CATHARINE. *Roger Martin Du Gard*, pp. 116-41.

SCHALK, DAVID L. *Roger Martin Du Gard: The Novelist And History*, pp. 124-56.

JEAN BAROIS (1913)

FIELD, TREVOR. "The Internal Chronology of 'Jean Barois.'" *Studi Francesi*, 17 (1973), 300-3.

SAVAGE, CATHARINE. *Roger Martin Du Gard*, pp. 41-64.

SCHALK, DAVID L. *Roger Martin Du Gard: The Novelist And History*, pp. 18-54.

WILSON, W. D. "The Theme of Abdication in the Novels of Roger Martin du Gard." *Neophilologus*, 59 (1975), 194-98.

LE JOURNAL DU COLONEL DE MAUMORT

SCHALK, DAVID L. *Roger Martin Du Gard: The Novelist And History*, pp. 214-25.

LA MORT DU PÈRE (part of Les Thibault, 1929)

SAVAGE, CATHARINE. *Roger Martin Du Gard*, pp. 110-15.

SCHALK, DAVID L. *Roger Martin Du Gard: The Novelist And History*, pp. 90-96.

LE PÉNITENCIER (part of Les Thibault, 1922)

SAVAGE, CATHARINE. *Roger Martin Du Gard*, pp. 81-87.

SCHALK, DAVID L. *Roger Martin Du Gard: The Novelist And History*, pp. 73-77.

THE POSTMAN (Vieille France, 1933)

SCHALK, DAVID L. *Roger Martin Du Gard: The Novelist And History*, pp. 191-97.

LA SORELLINA (part of Les Thibault, 1928)

SCHALK, DAVID L. *Roger Martin Du Gard: The Novelist And History*, pp. 88-90.

LES THIBAULT (1922-1940)

CAMUS, ALBERT. *Lyrical And Critical Essays*, pp. 270-87.

DEJONGH, WILLIAM F. J. "Unnatural Death in *Les Thibault*." *Romance Notes*, 9 (1967), 190-94.

GILBERT, JOHN. "Symbols of Continuity and the Unity of *Les Thibault*," in *Image And Theme*, ed. W. M. Frohock, pp. 124-48.

SAVAGE, CATHARINE. *Roger Martin Du Gard*, pp. 65-151.

SCHALK, DAVID L. *Rogert Martin Du Gard: The Novelist And History*, pp. 65-175.

SPURDLE, SONIA. "Roger Martin du Gard's Debt to Ibsen in 'L'Une de nous . . .' and 'Les Thibault.'" *Modern Language Review*, 6 (1970), 59-64.

———. "Tolstoy and Martin Du Gard's *Les Thibault*." *Comparative Literature*, 23 (1971), 325-45.

THODY, PHILIP. "The Politics of the Family Novel: Is Conservatism Inevitable?" *Mosaic*, 3, No.1 (1969), 87-101.

WILSON, W. D. "The Theme of Abdication in the Novels of Roger Martin du Gard." *Neophilologus*, 59 (1975), 190-94.

L'UNE DE NOUS . . . (1910)

SAVAGE, CATHARINE. *Roger Martin Du Gard*, pp. 33-35.

SPURDLE, SONIA M. "Roger Martin du Gard's Debt to Ibsen in 'L'Une de nous . . .' and 'Les Thibault.'" *Modern Language Review*, 65 (1970), 54-59.

MARTÍN-SANTOS, LUIS (Spanish, 1924-1964)

TIME OF SILENCE (Tiempo de silencio, 1962)

DIAZ, JANET WINECOFF. "Luis Martin Santos and the Contemporary Spanish Novel." *Hispania*, 51 (1968), 232-38.

HOLZINGER, WALTER. "*Tiempo De Silencio*: An Analysis." *Revista Hispanica Moderna*, 37 (1972/73), 73-90.

PALLEY, JULIAN. "The Periplus of Don Pedro: *Tiempo De Silencio*." *Bulletin Of Hispanic Studies*, 48 (1971), 239-54.

SEALE, MARY L. "Hangman and Victim: An Analysis of Martin-Santos' *Tiempo De Silencio*." *Hispanofila*, No.44 (1972), pp. 45-52.

MARTINERIE, ANDRÉE

SECOND SPRING

Reviews
RIESE, LAURE. "Old Themes Renewed." *Canadian Forum*, 45 (1965), 69-70.

MARTÍNEZ, ALFONSO

EL CORBACHO

SIMS, EDNA N. "The Antifeminist Element in the Works of Alfonso Martínez and Juan Luis Vives." *College Language Association Journal*, 18 (1974), 54-61.

MARTÍNEZ, TOMÁS ELOY

SAGRADO (1969)

Reviews
McMURRAY, GEORGE R. *Hispania*, 54 (1971), 205-6.

MARTÍNEZ ESTRADA, EZEQUIEL (Argentine, 1895-1964)

GENERAL

FEUSTLE, JOSEPH A., JR. "Sarmiento and Martínez Estrada: A Concept of Argentine History." *Hispania,* 55 (1972), 446-55.

LA CABEZA DE GOLIAT (1940)

EARLE, PETER G. *Prophet In The Wilderness: The Works Of Ezequiel Martínez Estrada,* pp. 144-58.

DEATH AND TRANSFIGURATION OF MARTÍN FIERRO
(Muerte y transfiguración de Martín Fierro, 1948)

EARLE, PETER G. *Prophet In The Wilderness: The Works Of Ezequiel Martínez Estrada,* p. 106-43.

SARMIENTO (1946)

EARLE, PETER G. *Prophet In The Wilderness: The Works Of Ezequiel Martínez Estrada,* p. 106-43.

X-RAY OF THE PAMPA (Radiografía de la pampa, 1933)

EARLE, PETER G. *Prophet In The Wilderness: The Works Of Ezequiel Martínez Estrada,* pp. 66-105.

Reviews
COLEMAN, ALEXANDER. "Positive Signs from a Negative Prophet." *Review,* No.8 (1973), pp. 62-65.

MARTINI, VIRGILIO (Italian, 1903-)

THE WORLD WITHOUT WOMEN (Il mondo senza donne, 1936)

Reviews
MARKMANN, CHARLES LAM. *Saturday Review,* 7 August 1971, p. 24

MARTINSON, HARRY (Swedish 1904-1978)

GENERAL

SJÖBERG, LEIF. "Harry Martinson: From Vagabond to Space Explorer." *Books Abroad,* 48 (1974), 476-85.

MASSIAN, MICHEL

LA DOUZIÈME ANEÉ (1971)

Reviews
DUNAWAY, JOHN M. *French Review,* 46 (1973), 862-63.

MATA, GONZALO HUMBERTO (Ecuardorian, 1904-)

SAL

GOLD, PETER J. "The Development of the Novelistic Technique of G. Humberto Mata." *Kentucky Romance Quarterly,* 21 (1974), 283-91.

SANAGUIN

GOLD, PETER J. "The Development of the Novelistic Technique of G. Humberto Mata." *Kentucky Romance Quarterly,* 21 (1974), 279-83.

SUMAG ALLPA (1940)

GOLD, PETER. "The Development of the Novelistic Technique of G. Humberto Mata." *Kentucky Romance Quarterly,* 21 (1974), 275-79.

MATHERS, PETER (Australian, 1931-)

GENERAL

COLLINSON, LAURENCE. "Seeing Mathers Subjectively." *Overland,* No.35 (1966), pp. 11-12.

MATHERS, PETER. "Extractions." *Southerly,* 31 (1971), 210-15.

TRAP (1966)

BUCKLEY, VINCENT. "Peter Mathers' Trap." *Ariel: A Review Of International English Literature,* 5, No.3 (1974), 115-27.

BURNS, ROBERT. "The Underdog-Outsider: The Achievement of Mathers' *Trap.*" *Meanjin,* 29 (1970), 95-105.

CLANCY, L. J. "Peter Mathers' Words." *Meanjin,* 33 (1974), 272-77.

———. "Trap for Young Players: Peter Mathers' Novel." *Meanjin,* 25 (1966), 485-88.

Reviews
BARBOUR, JUDY. *Southerly,* 26 (1966), 279-80.

MCLAREN, JOHN. "Recent Novels." *Overland,* No.34 (1966), p. 50.

THE WORT PAPERS (1972)

CLANCY, L. J. "Peter Mathers' Words." *Meanjin,* 33 (1974), 272-77.

Reviews
KEESING, NANCY. "Mathers and the Worts." *Southerly,* 33 (1973), 345-46.

WEBSTER, OWEN. "Comic Genius." *Overland,* No.55 (1973), pp. 56-58.

MATIGNON, BERNARD

LES SOLDATS DE BOIS (1972)

Reviews
WAELTI-WALTERS, JENNIFER R. *French Review,* 47 (1973), 499-500.

MATTEI, EDOUARD

L'AUTOPORTRAIT (1972)

Reviews
BRADY, PATRICK. *French Review,* 47 (1973), 400-1.

MATUTE, ANA MARÍA (Spanish, 1925-)

GENERAL

DÍAZ, JANET WINECOFF. "The Autobiographical Element in the Works of Ana María Matute." *Kentucky Romance Quarterly,* 15 (1968), 139-48.

JONES, MARGARET E. W. "Antipathetic Fallacy: The Hostile World of Ana Maria Matute's Novels." *Kentucky Foreign Language Quarterly,* 13, suppl. (1967), 5-16.

———. *The Literary World Of Ana María Matute.*

———. "Religious Motifs and Biblical Allusions in the Works of Ana María Matute." *Hispania,* 51 (1968),

———. "Temporal Patterns in the Works of Ana Maria Matute." *Romance Notes,* 12 (1971), 282-88.

WINECOFF, JANET. "Style and Solitude in the Works of Ana María Matute." *Hispania,* 49 (1966), 61-69.

WYTHE, GEORGE. "The World of Ana María Matute." *Books Abroad,* 40 (1966), 17-28.

LOS ABEL (1948)

DÍAZ, JANET. *Ana María Matute,* pp. 45-50.

AWAKENING see SCHOOL OF THE SUN

EN ESTA TIERRA (1955)

DÍAZ, JANET. *Ana María Matute,* pp. 62-70.

FIESTA AL NOROESTE (1953)

DÍAZ, JANET. *Ana María Matute,* pp. 102-8.

WINECOFF, JANET. "Style and Solitude in the Works of Ana Maria Matute." *Hispania,* 49 (1966), 62-65.

THE LOST CHILDREN (Los hijos muertos, 1958)

DÍAZ, JANET. *Ana María Matute*, pp. 122–29.

JONES, MARGARET W. "Antipathetic Fallacy: The Hostile World of Ana Maria Matute's Novels." *Kentucky Foreign Language Quarterly*, 13, suppl. (1967), 9–12.

LAS LUCIÉRNAGAS

DÍAZ, JANET. *Ana María Matute*, pp. 62–70.

PEQUEÑO TEATRO (1954)

DÍAZ, JANET. *Ana María Matute*, pp. 54–61.

SCHOOL OF THE SUN (Primera memoria, 1959)

BURNS, ADELAIDE. "The Anguish of Ana María Matute in *Los Mercaderes*," in *Hispanic Studies In Honour Of Joseph Manson*, ed. Dorothy M. Atkinson and Anthony H. Clarke, pp. 21–27.

DÍAZ, JANET. *Ana María Matute*, pp. 132–35.

JONES, MARGARET W. "Antipathetic Fallacy: The Hostile World of Ana Maria Matute's Novels." *Kentucky Foreign Language Quarterly*, 13, suppl. (1967), 12–15.

STEVENS, JAMES R. "Myth and Memory: Ana María Matute's *Primera Memoria*." *Symposium*, 25 (1971), 198–203.

LOS SOLDADOS LLORAN DE NOCHE (1964)

BURNS, ADELAIDE. "The Anguish of Ana María Matute in *Los Mercaderes*," in *Hispanic Studies In Honour Of Joseph Manson*, ed. Dorothy M. Atkinson and Anthony H. Clarke, pp. 27–33.

DÍAZ, JANET. *Ana María Matute*, pp. 135–37.

Reviews

WINECOFF, JANET. *Hispania*, 48 (1965), 942.

LA TORRE VIGÍA (1971)

Reviews

DÍAZ, JANET W. *Hispania*, 55 (1972), 593–94.

LA TRAMPA (1969)

BURNS, ADELAIDE. "The Anguish of Ana María Matute in *Los Mercaderes*," in *Hispanic Studies In Honour Of Joseph Manson*, ed. Dorothy M. Atkinson and Anthony H. Clarke, pp. 33–42.

DÍAZ, JANET. *Ana María Matute*, pp. 137–43.

Reviews

JONES, MARGARET E. W. *Hispania*, 53 (1970), 339–40.

MAUPASSANT, GUY DE (French, 1850–1893)

GENERAL

HAINSWORTH, G. "Schopenhauer, Flaubert, Maupassant: Conceptual Thought and Artistic 'Thought,' " in *Currents Of Thought In French Literature*, pp. 183–90.

KILKER, JAMES A. "Maupassant: Patriot and Pacifist." *Canadian Modern Language Review*, 24, No.4 (1968), 8–21.

WALLACE, A. H. *Guy De Maupassant.*

BEL-AMI (1885)

DUGAN, JOHN RAYMOND. *Illusion And Reality: A Study Of Descriptive Techniques In The Works Of Guy De Maupassant*, pp. 38–42.

LERNER, MICHAEL G. *Maupassant*, pp. 201–6.

MONT-ORIOL (1887)

DUGAN, JOHN RAYMOND. *Illusion And Reality: A Study Of Descriptive Techniques In The Works Of Guy De Maupassant*, pp. 42–45.

NOTRE COEUR (1890)

LERNER, MICHAEL G. *Maupassant*, pp. 254–62.

PIERRE ET JEAN (1888)

ARTINIAN, ROBERT WILLARD. " 'Then, Venom, To Thy Work': Pathological Representation in *Pierre Et Jean*." *Modern Fiction Studies*, 18 (1972), 225–29.

DUGAN, JOHN RAYMOND. *Illusion And Reality: A Study Of Descriptive Techniques In The Works Of Guy De Maupassant*, pp. 45–49.

FREIMANIS, DZINTARS. "More on the Meaning of 'Pierre et Jean.' " *French Review*, 38 (1965), 326–31.

HEMMINGS, F. W. J. "The Realist and Naturalist Movements in France," in *The Age Of Realism*, ed. F. W. J. Hemmings, pp. 212–14.

LERNER, MICHAEL G. *Maupassant*, pp. 235–38.

STRONG AS DEATH (Fort comme la mort, 1889)

DUGAN, JOHN RAYMOND. *Illusion And Reality: A Study Of Descriptive Techniques In The Works Of Guy De Maupassant*, pp. 49–54.

A WOMAN'S LIFE (Une vie, 1924)

DeCOSTER, CYRUS C. "Maupassant's 'Une Vie' and Pardo Bazán's 'Los Pazos de Ulloa.' " *Hispania*, 56 (1973), 587–92.

DUGAN, JOHN RAYMOND. *Illusion And Reality: A Study Of Descriptive Techniques In The Works Of Guy De Maupassant*, pp. 35–38.

LERNER, MICHAEL G. *Maupassant*, pp. 149–50, 166–70.

WALLACE, A. H. *Guy De Maupassant*, pp. 59–63.

YVETTE

ALEXANDER, THEODOR W. and BEATRICE W. "Maupassant's *Yvette* and Schnitzler's *Fräulein Else*." *Modern Austrian Literature*, 4, No.3 (1971), 44–55.

MAURIAC, CLAUDE (French, 1914–)

GENERAL

JOHNSTON, STUART L. "Structure in the Novels of Claude Mauriac." *French Review*, 38 (1965), 451–58.

L'AGRANDISSEMENT (1963)

JOHNSTON, STUART L. "Structure in the Novels of Claude Mauriac." *French Review*, 38 (1964/5), 455–58.

MERCIER, VIVIAN. *The New Novel From Queneau To Pinget*, pp. 345–52.

ALL WOMEN ARE FATAL (Toutes les femmes sont fatales, 1957)

MERCIER, VIVIAN. *The New Novel From Queneau To Pinget*, pp. 317–27.

Reviews

MAYHEW, ALICE. "All Things At Once." *Commonweal*, 81 (1964), 20–21.

THE DINNER PARTY (Le dîner en ville, 1959)

MERCIER, VIVIAN. *The New Novel From Queneau To Pinget*, pp. 327–36.

THE MARQUISE WENT OUT AT FIVE (La Marquise sortit à cinq heures, 1961)

ALTER, ROBERT. *Partial Magic*, pp. 238–43.

———. "The Self-Conscious Moment: Reflections on the Aftermath of Modernism." *Triquarterly*, No.33 (1975), pp. 225–29.

MERCIER, VIVIAN. *The New Novel From Queneau To Pinget*, pp. 336–45.

L'OUBLI (1966)

> MERCIER, VIVIAN. *The New Novel From Queneau To Pinget*, pp. 352-59.

MAURIAC, FRANÇOIS (French, 1885-1970)
GENERAL

> ALLEN, TREVOR. "The Mauriac Novels." *Contemporary Review*, 208 (1966), 211-15.

> BRÉE, GERMAINE. "The Novels of François Mauriac," in *The Vision Obscured*, ed. Melvin J. Friedman, pp. 141-50.

> EUSTIS, ALVIN. "Youth in Mauriac: An Assessment." *French Review*, 39 (1966), 536-41.

> FLOWER, J. E. *Intention And Achievement: An Essay On The Novels Of Francois Mauriac.*

> ———. "The Role of the Natural World in the Novels of François Mauriac." *Modern Languages*, 49 (1968), 55-61.

> JEROME, SISTER M. "Human and Divine Love In Dante and Mauriac." *Renascence*, 18, No.4 (1966), 176-84.

> MELLARD, JAMES M. "Violence and Belief in Mauriac and O'Connor." *Renascence*, 26 (1974), 158-68.

> O'FLAHERTY, KATHLEEN. "François Mauriac, 1885-1970: An Effort at Assessment." *Studies: An Irish Quarterly Review*, 60 (1971), 33-42.

> RECK, RIMA DRELL. *Literature And Responsibility*, pp. 162-89.

> RUBIN, LOUIS D. "Francois Mauriac and the Freedom of the Religious Novelist." *Southern Review*, NS, 2 (1966), 17-39.

> SMITH, MAXWELL A. "Pascal and François Mauriac," in *Renaissance And Other Studies In Honor Of William Leon Wiley*, ed. George Bernard Daniel, pp. 229-40.

> SPEAIGHT, ROBERT. "François Mauriac: The Making of a Novelist." *Thought*, 50 (1975), 289-300.

> TURNELL, MARTIN. "François Mauriac." *Encounter*, 36, No.2 (1971), 46-48.

> WILDGEN, KATHRYN E. "Dieu et Maman: Women in the Novels of Francois Mauriac." *Renascence*, 27 (1974), 15-22.

THE BLACK ANGELS (Les anges noirs, 1936)

> FLOWER, J. E. "Form and Unity in Mauriac's *The Black Angels*." *Renascence*, 19 (1967), 79-87.

> SMITH, MAXWELL A. *François Mauriac*, pp. 65-70.

THE DESERT OF LOVE (Le Desert de amour, 1925)

> JENKINS, CECIL. *Mauriac*, pp. 64-73.

> McCULLAGH, JAMES C. "The Psychology of Love in Francois Mauriac's *The Desert Of Love*." *Studies In The Humanities*, 4, No.2 (1975), 43-48.

> MAY, JOHN R. "The Apprenticeship of a Catholic Writer: Mauriac." *Renascence*, 24 (1972), 181-88.

> RUBIN, LOUIS D. *The Teller In The Tale*, pp. 204-6.

> SMITH, MAXWELL A. *François Mauriac*, pp. 91-96.

DESTINIES (Destins, 1928)

> SMITH, MAXWELL A. *François Mauriac*, pp. 54-59.

THE END OF NIGHT (La Fin de la nuit, 1935)

> JENKINS, CECIL. *Mauriac*, pp. 93-96.

> SMITH, MAXWELL A. *François Mauriac*, pp. 104-15.

THE FRONTENAC MYSTERY (Le Mystère Frontenac, 1933)

> JENKINS, CECIL. *Mauriac*, pp. 87-90.

GENITRIX (1923)

> JENKINS, CECIL. *Mauriac*, pp. 57-61.

> McNAB, JAMES P. "The Mother in François Mauriac's *Genitrix*." *Hartford Studies In Literature*, 2 (1970), 207-13.

> RUBIN, LOUIS D. *The Teller In The Tale*, pp. 193-95.

> SMITH, MAXWELL A. *François Mauriac*, pp. 86-91.

A KISS FOR THE LEPER (Le Baiser au Lepreux, 1922)

> MELLARD, JAMES M. "The Constructed Reality: Mauriac's *A Kiss For The Leper*." *Renascence*, 25 (1972), 24-34.

> RUBIN, LOUIS D. *The Teller In The Tale*, pp. 190-93.

> SMITH, MAXWELL A. *François Mauriac*, pp. 82-86.

THE KNOT OF VIPERS see VIPER'S TANGLE

THE LAMB (L'Agneau, 1954)

> SMITH, MAXWELL A. *François Mauriac*, pp. 77-81.

THE LOVED AND THE UNLOVED (Galigai, 1952)

> MAURIAC, FRANCOIS. "My Work and My Critics." *Renascence*, 25 (1973), 177-81.

> SMITH, MAXWELL A. *François Mauriac*, pp. 74-77.

MALTAVERNE (Un Adolescent d'autre fois, 1955)

> **Reviews**
> BALAKIAN, ANNA. *Saturday Review*, 18 July 1970, p. 31.

> FORBES, ROBERT ELLIOTT. "L'envoi." *Catholic World*, 212 (1971), 157.

LE NOEUD DE VIPERES see THE VIPERS' TANGLE

SUSPICION (Ce qui était perdu, 1930)

> SMITH, MAXWELL A. *François Mauriac*, pp. 59-65.

THAT WHICH WAS LOST see SUSPICION

THERESE (Thérèse Desqueyroux, 1927)

> FARRELL, C. FREDERICK and EDITH R. FARRELL. "The Animal Imagery of Therese Desqueyroux." *Kentucky Romance Quarterly*, 21 (1974), 429-45.

> ———. "The Multiple Murders of Therese Desqueyroux." *Hartford Studies In Literature*, 2 (1970), 195-206.

> HUNT, TONY. "Fatality and the Novel: *Tristran, Manon Lescaut* and *Thérèse Desqueyroux*." *Durham University Journal*, NS, 37 (1976), 191-95.

> JENKINS, CECIL. *Mauriac*, pp. 73-78.

> RECK, RIMA DRELL. *Literature And Responsibility*, pp. 184-87.

> RUBIN, LOUIS D. *The Teller In The Tale*, pp. 197-204.

> SMITH, MAXWELL A. *François Mauriac*, pp. 96-104.

THE VIPERS' TANGLE (Le Noeud de Vipères, 1932)

> BATCHELOR, R. "Art and Theology in Mauriac's 'Le Noeud de Vipères.' " *Nottingham French Studies*, 12 (1973), 33-43.

> DENOMMÉ, ROBERT T. "*The Viper's Tangle:* Relative and Absolute Values." *Renascence*, 18, No.1 (1965), 32-39.

> FLOWER, JOHN. *A Critical Commentary On Mauriac's 'Le Noeud De Vipères.'*

> JENKINS, CECIL. *Mauriac*, pp. 81-86.

> RECK, RIMA DRELL. *Literature And Responsibility*, pp. 187-89.

> REINHARDT, KURT F. *The Theological Novel Of Modern Europe*, pp. 148-53.

> RUBIN, LOUIS D. *The Teller In The Tale*, pp. 183-88.

> SONNENFELD, ALBERT. "The Catholic Novelist and the Supernatural." *French Studies*, 22 (1968), 314-15.

> TARTELLA, VINCENT P. "Thematic Imagery in Mauriac's *Vipers' Tangle*." *Renascence*, 17, No.4 (1965), 195-200.

> WENTERSDORF, KARL P. "The Chronology of Mauriac's *Le Noeud*

De Vipères." Kentucky Foreign Language Quarterly, 13, suppl. (1967), 89–100.

WOMEN OF THE PHARISEES (La Pharisienne, 1941)

SMITH, MAXWELL A. *François Mauriac,* pp. 115–20.

THE YOUNG MAN IN CHAINS (L'enfant chargé de chaînes, 1913)

FLOWER, J. E. "François Mauriac and Social Catholicism: An Episode in 'L'Enfant chargé de chaînes.' " *French Studies,* 21 (1967), 125–38.

MAURO DE VASCONCELAS, JOSÉ

GENERAL

"The Fictional World of José Mauro de Vasconcelos." *Kentucky Romance Quarterly,* 22 (1975), 169–91.

CHUVA CRIOULA (1972)

Reviews
SILVERMAN, MALCOLM. *Hispania,* 56 (1973), 1122–23.

MAUROIS, MICHELLE

LE CARILLON DE FÉNELON (1972)

Reviews
KOLBERT, JACK. *French Review,* 47 (1974), 665–66.

MAX MÜLLER, FRIEDRICH (German, 1823–1900)

GERMAN LOVE (Deutsche Liebe)

CASTEN, C. "The Influence of F. Max Müller's *German Love* on Meredith's *Modern Love." English Language Notes,* 10 (1972/73), 282–86.

MAXIMOV, VLADIMIR (Russian, 1930–)

THE SEVEN DAYS OF CREATION (Sem' Dnei Tvoreniya)

HOSKING, GEOFFREY. "The Search for an Image of Man in Contemporary Soviet Fiction." *Forum For Modern Language Studies,* 11 (1975), 360–63.

Reviews
JACOBY, SUSAN. "War, Peace, and Dissent." *Saturday Review,* 25 January 1975, pp. 40–41.

AL-MĀZINĪ, IBRĀHĪM 'ABD AL-QĀDIR (Egyptian, 1890–1949)

IBRĀHĪM AL-KĀTIB (1931)

KILPATRICK, HILARY. *The Modern Egyptian Novel,* pp. 26–30, 201–2.

IBRĀHĪM AL-THĀNĪ (1943)

KILPATRICK, HILARY. *The Modern Egyptian Novel,* pp. 28–30, 202.

MAZZANTI, CARLOS

EL SUSTITUTO

HAYDEN, ROSE LEE. *An Existential Focus On Some Novels Of The River Plate.*

MEDIO, DELORES

GENERAL

DIAZ, JANET WINECOFF. "Three New Works of Dolores Medio." *Romance Notes,* 11 (1969), 246.

WINECOFF, JANET. "Fictionalized Autobiography in the Novels of Dolores Medio." *Kentucky Foreign Language Quarterly,* 13 (1966), 170–78.

EL DIARIO DE UNA MAESTRA

PENUEL, ARNOLD M. "The Influence of Galdós' *El Amigo Manso* on Dolores Medio's *El Diario De Una Maestra." Revista De Estudios Hispánicos,* 7 (1973), 91–96.

FUNCIONARIO PÚBLICO

HUTMAN, NORMA LOUISE. "Disproportionate Doom: Tragic Irony in the Spanish Post Civil War Novel." *Modern Fiction Studies,* 18 (1972), 199–206.

EL SEÑOR GARCÍA

DIAZ, JANET WINECOFF. "Three New Works of Dolores Medio." *Romance Notes,* 11 (1969), 246.

MEGGED, AHARON (Israeli, 1920–)

GENERAL

SHIFRA, SHIN. "An Interview with Aharon Megged: Literature as an Act of Love." *Ariel: A Quarterly Review Of The Arts And Sciences In Israel,* No.33/4 (1973), pp. 33–42.

HAHAYIM HAKETSARIM (1971)

Reviews
ARAD, MIRIAM. "New Novels." *Ariel: A Quarterly Review Of The Arts And Sciences In Israel,* No.31 (1972), pp. 110–11.

THE LIVING ON THE DEAD (ha-Hai 'al ha-met, 1965)

Reviews
FISCH, HAROLD. "Unique and Universal." *Commentary,* 54, No.2 (1972), 74–75.

MEHTA, VED (Indian, 1934–)

DADDYJI (1972)

Reviews
RAJAN, P. K. SUNDARA. *Saturday Review,* 20 May 1972, pp. 72–73.

DELINQUENT CHACHA (1967)

Reviews
HARTLEY, LOIS. *Literature East And West,* 11 (1967), 329–30.

MEJÍA VALLEJO, MANUEL (Colombian, 1923–)

EL DÍA SEÑALADO (1964)

DEUEL, PAULINE B. "Sound and Rhythm in 'El Día Señalado.' " *Hispania,* 52 (1969), 198–202.

MEMMI, ALBERT (Tunisian, 1920–)

GENERAL

YETIV, ISAAC. "Albert Memmi: The Syndrome of Self-exile." *International Fiction Review,* 1 (1974), 125–34.

THE PILLAR OF SALT (La statue de sel, 1953)

YETIV, ISAAC. "The Crisis of Identity of the Native North African Writer," in *Twentieth Century French Fiction,* ed. George Stambolian, pp. 136–38.

LE SCORPION (1969)

Reviews
CAPOUYA, EMILE. "Suicidal Stings of Truth." *Saturday Review,* 26 June 1971, pp. 19–21.

MENDELE MOKHER SEFARIM (Yiddish, 1836-1917) pseudonym of Shalom Jacob Abramowitz

GENERAL

RABINOVICH, ISAIAH. *Major Trends In Modern Hebrew Fiction*, pp. 7-14.

MÉNDEZ, MIGUEL

PEREGRINOS DE AZTLÁN

Reviews
GONZÁLES-BERRY, ERLINDA. *Chasqui*, 5, No.2 (1976), 86-87.

MENDOZA, MARÍA LUISA

DE AUSENCIA

Reviews
TATUM, CHARLES. *Chasqui*, 5, No.1 (1975), 54-55.

MENG YAO

GENERAL

LANCASHIRE, EDEL MARIE. "The Novels of Meng Yao." *AUMLA*, No.34 (1970), pp. 212-40.

FU-YÜN PAI-JIH

LANCASHIRE, EDEL MARIE. "The Novels of Meng Yao." *AUMLA*, No.34 (1970), pp. 226-31.

LI-MING CH'IEN

LANCASHIRE, EDEL MARIE. "The Novels of Meng Yao." *AUMLA*, No.34 (1970), pp. 231-36.

LUAN-LI JEN

LANCASHIRE, EDEL MARIE. "The Novels of Meng Yao." *AUMLA*, No.34 (1970), pp. 220-24.

MENON, O. CHANDU

INDULEKA

Reviews
ANJANEYULU, D. *Triveni*, 35, No.3 (1966), 77-79.

MERCIER, LOUIS-SÉBASTIEN (French, 1740-1814)

GENERAL

MAJEWSKI, HENRY F. "Genius and Poetry in the Pre-Romantic Imagination of L.-S. Mercier." *Romanic Review*, 57 (1966), 177-87.

L'HOMME SAUVAGE

ANNANDALE, E. T. "Johann Gottlob Benjamin Pfeil and Louis-Sébastien Mercier." *Revue De Littérature Comparée*, 44 (1970), 444-59.

MERI, VEIJO (Finnish, 1928-)

GENERAL

STORMBOM, N.-B. "Veijo Meri and the New Finnish Novel." *American Scandinavian Review*, 55 (1967), 264-69.

THE MANILA ROPE (Manilla köysi, 1957)

Reviews
SCHOOLFIELD, GEORGE C. *American Scandinavian Review*, 58 (1970), 80, 82.

MÉRIMÉE, PROSPER (French, 1803-1870)

GENERAL

GOBERT, D. L. "Mérimée Revisited." *Symposium*, 26 (1972), 128-46.

STEINER, GEORGE. "Mérimée," in his *Language And Silence*, pp. 261-68.

CARMEN (1845)

RAITT, A. W. *Prosper Mérimée*, pp. 191-96.

COLOMBA (1841)

GOBERT, D. L. "Mérimée Revisited." *Symposium*, 26 (1972), 131-35.

GROVER, PHILIP. "Characters & Milieux in the Stories of Prosper Merimee." *Delta: The Cambridge Literary Magazine*, No.48 (1971), pp. 13-16.

RAITT, A. W. *Prosper Mérimée*, pp. 187-91.

1572: A CHRONICLE OF THE TIMES OF CHARLES THE NINTH (La Chronique du règne de Charles IX, 1829)

GROVER, PHILIP. "Characters & Milieux in the Stories of Prosper Merimee." *Delta: The Cambridge Literary Magazine*, No.48 (1971), pp. 5-10.

MICKEL, EMMANUEL J. "Some Sources for Mérimée's CHARLES IX." *Modern Language Quarterly*, 29 (1968), 190-95.

RAITT, A. W. *Prosper Mérimée*, pp. 88-97.

MERKUR, DAN

AROUND AND ABOUT SALLY'S SHACK

Reviews
SHIRINIAN, LORNE. "Not Without a Warning." *Journal Of Canadian Fiction*, 3, No.1 (1974), 102-3.

MERLE, ROBERT (French, 1908-)

MALEVIL (1972)

Reviews
CAPRIO, A. and D. *French Review*, 47 (1973), 232-33.

METCALF, JOHN (Canadian, 1938-)

GOING DOWN SLOW (1972)

Reviews
JEWISON, DON. "Up Against the System." *Journal Of Canadian Fiction*, 2, No.1 (1973), 91-92.

LEITOLD, J. R. *Dalhousie Review*, 53 (1973), 367-68.

MORLEY, PATRICIA. "Poisoned by the System." *Canadian Literature*, No.58 (1973), pp. 102-4.

MEYER, CONRAD FERDINAND (Swiss, 1825-1898)

GENERAL

JACKSON, D. "Recent Meyer Criticism: New Avenues or Cul-de-Sac?" *Revue Des Langues Vivantes*, 34 (1968), 620-35.

REINHARDT, GEORGE W. "The Political Views of the Young Conrad Ferdinand Meyer. With a Note on *Das Amulett*." *German Quarterly*, 45 (1972), 270-94.

DAS AMULETT (1873)

SCHIMMELPFENNIG, PAUL. "C. F. Meyer's Religion of the Heart: A Reevaluation of *Das Amulett*." *Germanic Review*, 47 (1972), 181-202.

THE CHANCELLOR'S SECRET see THOMAS BECKETT THE SAINT

DAS LEIDEN EINES KNABEN (1883)

REINHARDT, GEORGE W. "Two Romance Wordplays in C. F. Meyer's *Novellen.*" *Germanic Review,* 46 (1971), 51–62.

THE MONK'S WEDDING (Die Hochzelt des Mönchs, 1884)

JACKSON, D. A. "Dante the Dupe in C. F. Meyer's *Die Hochzeit Des Mönchs.*" *German Life and Letters,* 25 (1971), 5–15.

PLATER, EDWARD M. V. "The Figure of Dante in *Die Hochzeit des Mönchs.*" *MLN,* 90 (1975), 678–86.

REINHARDT, GEORGE W. "Two Romance Wordplays in C. F. Meyer's *Novellen.*" *Germanic Review,* 46 (1971), 44–51.

THE SAINT see THOMAS BECKETT THE SAINT

DER SCHUSS VON DER KANZEL (1878)

JENNINGS, LEE B. "The Ambiguous Explosion: C. F. Meyer's *Der Schuss Von Der Kanzel.*" *German Quarterly,* 43 (1970), 210–22.

THE TEMPTING OF PESCARA (Die Versuchung des Pescara, 1887)

PLATER, EDWARD M. V. "The Banquet of Life: Conrad Ferdinand Meyer's *Die Versuchung Des Pescara.*" *Seminar,* 8 (1972), 88–98.

THOMAS BECKETT THE SAINT (Der heilige, 1880)

TUSKEN, LEWIS W. "C. F. Meyer's *Der Heilige:* The Problem of Beckett's Conversion." *Seminar,* 7 (1971), 201–15.

WALKER, COLIN. "Unbelief and Martyrdom in C. F. Meyer's *Der Heilige.*" *German Life and Letters,* 21 (1968), 111–22.

MICHEL, GEORGES (French, 1926–)

THE TIMID ADVENTURES OF A WINDOW WASHER (Les timides aventures d'un laveur de carreaux, 1966)

Reviews
LESAGE, LAURENT. *Saturday Review,* 5 July 1969, p. 33.

MIRÓ, GABRIEL (Spanish, 1879–1930)

GENERAL

COOPE, MARIAN G. R. "Gabriel Miró's Image of the Garden as 'Hortus Conslusus' and 'Paraíso Terrenal.' " *Modern Language Review,* 68 (1973), 94–104.

O'SULLIVAN, SUSAN. "Watches, Lemons and Spectacles: Recurrent Images in the Works of Gabriel Miró." *Bulletin Of Hispanic Studies,* 44 (1967), 107–21.

NUESTRO PADRE SAN DANIEL (1921)

BROWN, G. G. "The Biblical Allusions in Gabriel Miró's Oleza Novels." *Modern Language Review,* 70 (1975), 786–91.

COOPE, M. G. R. "The Critics' View of *Nuestro Padre San Daniel* and *El Obispo Leproso* by Gabriel Miró," in *University Of British Columbia Hispanic Studies,* ed. Harold Livermore, pp. 51–60.

EL OBISPO LEPROSO (1926)

BROWN, G. G. "The Biblical Allusions in Gabriel Miró's Oleza Novels." *Modern Language Review,* 70 (1975), 791–94.

COOPE, M. G. R. "The Critics' View of *Nuestro Padre San Daniel* and *El Obispo Leproso* by Gabriel Miró," in *University Of British Columbia Hispanic Studies,* ed. Harold Livermore, pp. 51–60.

MILLS, JOHN (Canadian)

THE LAND OF IS

Reviews
TAUSKY, T. E. "Marshmallow Worlds." *Canadian Literature,* No. 59 (1974), pp. 119–20.

THE OCTOBER MEN

Reviews
FOSTER, MALCOLM. "The October Incident Revisited." *Journal Of Canadian Fiction,* 3, No. 2 (1974), 97–98.

MISHIMA YUKIO (Japanese, 1925–1970) pseudonym of Hiraoka Kimitake

GENERAL

BOARDMAN, GWENN R. "Greek Hero and Japanese Samurai: Mishima's New Aesthetic." *Critique,* 12, No.1 (1970), 103–15.

ENRIGHT, D. J. "Mishima's Way." *Encounter,* 36, No.2 (1971), 57–61.

SCOTT STOKES, HENRY. *The Life And Death Of Yukio Mishima.*

SEIDENSTICKER, EDWARD. "Mishima Yukio." *Hudson Review,* 24 (1971), 272–82.

WAGENAAR, DICK and YOSHIO IWAMOTO. "Yukio Mishima: Dialectics of Mind and Body." *Contemporary Literature,* 16 (1975), 41–60.

CONFESSIONS OF A MASK (Kamen no kokuhaku, 1948)

BOARDMAN, GWEN R. "Greek Hero and Japanese Samurai: Mishima's New Aesthetic." *Critique,* 12, No.1 (1970), 104–8.

DANA, ROBERT. "The Stuffer of Eternity: A Study of the Themes of Isolation and Meaninglessness in Three Novels by Yukio Mishima." *Critique,* 12, No.1 (1970), 87–92.

KORGES, JAMES. "Gide and Mishima: Homosexuality as Metaphor." *Critique,* 12, No.1 (1970), 127–37.

MIYOSHI, MASAO. *Accomplices Of Silence,* pp. 146–57.

THE DECAY OF THE ANGEL (Tennin gosui, 1971) see SEA OF FERTILITY

FORBIDDEN COLORS (Kinjiki, 1951-53)

Reviews
FITZSIMMONS, THOMAS. "For 500,000 Yen He Avenged His Yens." *Saturday Review,* 1 June 1968, pp. 35, 42.

REES, DAVID. "The Way It Was." *Encounter,* 32, No.1 (1969), 85–86.

RUNAWAY HORSES (Homba, 1969)

See also SEA OF FERTILITY

Reviews
MELLORS, JOHN. "Afro-Asiatica." *London Magazine,* NS 14, No.1 (1974), 136–37.

THE SAILOR WHO FELL FROM GRACE WITH THE SEA (Gogo no eikō, 1963)

DANA, ROBERT. "The Stuffer of Eternity: A Study of the Themes of Isolation and Meaninglessness in Three Novels by Yukio Mishima." *Critique,* 12, No.1 (1970), 97–102.

GOLDSTEIN, BERNICE and SANFORD. "Observations on *The Sailor Who Fell From Grace With The Sea.*" *Critique,* 12, No.1 (1970), 116–26.

Reviews
STRYK, LUCIEN. *Literature East And West,* 11 (1967), 76.

THE SEA OF FERTILITY (Hōjō no umi, 1969-71)

MIYOSHI, MASAO. *Accomplices Of Silence,* pp. 171–74.

WAGENAAR, DICK and YUSHIO IWAMOTO. "Yukio Mishima: Dialectics of Mind and Body." *Contemporary Literature,* 16 (1975), 55–60.

Reviews

RYAN, MARLEIGH. "The Mishima Tetralogy." *Journal Of Japanese Studies,* 1 (1974), 165-73.

SPRING SNOW (Haro no yuki, 1969)

See also SEA OF FERTILITY

Reviews

KEENE, DONALD. "Mishima's Monument to Distant Japan." *Saturday Review,* 10 June 1972, pp. 57-59.

SCRUTON, ROGER. "Love, Madness, & Other Anxieties." *Encounter,* 40, No.1 (1973), 85.

SUN AND STEEL (Taiyō to tetsu, 1968)

Reviews

WALSTEN, DAVID M. *Saturday Review,* 12 December 1970, p. 38.

THE TEMPLE OF DAWN (Akatsuki no tera, 1970) see SEA OF FERTILITY

THE TEMPLE OF THE GOLDEN PAVILION (Kinkakuji, 1956)

DANA, ROBERT. "The Stuffer of Eternity: A Study of the Themes of Isolation and Meaninglessness in Three Novels by Yukio Mishima." *Critique,* 12, No.1 (1970), 92-96.

DUUS, LOUISE. "The Novel as Koan: Mishima Yukio's *The Temple Of The Golden Pavilion.*" *Critique,* 10, No.2 (1968), 120-29.

KIMBALL, ARTHUR. *Crisis And Identity And Contemporary Japanese Novels,* pp. 75-93.

MIYOSHI, MASAO. *Accomplices Of Silence,* pp. 159-69.

SWANN, THOMAS E. "What Happens in *Kinkakuji.*" *Monumenta Nipponica,* 27 (1972), 399-414.

Reviews

SINGH, KIRANPAL. *Indian Horizons,* 24, No.1 (1975), 74-78.

MISTRAL, GABRIELA (Chilean, 1889-1957) pseudonym of Lucila Godoy Alcayaga

CRICKETS AND FROGS: A FABLE

Reviews

BALDUCCI, CAROLYN. "Not for Children." *Review,* No.9 (1973), p. 60.

MITCHELL, KEN (Canadian, 1940-)

WANDERING RAFFERTY (1972)

Reviews

JEWISON, DON. "Picturesque and Moralistic." *Canadian Literature,* No.60 (1974), pp. 122-23.

MITCHELL, WILLIAM ORMOND (Canadian, 1914-)

THE KITE

CARPENTER, DAVID C. "Alberta in Fiction: The Emergence of a Provincial Consciousness." *Journal Of European Studies,* 10, No.4 (1975), 14-17.

McLAY, CATHERINE. "W. O. Mitchell's *The Kite:* A Study in Immortality." *Journal Of Canadian Fiction,* 2, No.2 (1973), 43-48.

NEW, WILLIAM H. "A Feeling of Completion: Aspects of W. O. Mitchell," in his *Articulating West,* pp. 50-59.

RICOU, LAURENCE. *Vertical Man/Horizontal World,* pp. 106-8.

THE VANISHING POINT (1973)

Reviews

GUTTERIDGE, DON. "Surviving Paradise." *Journal Of Canadian Fiction,* 3, No.1 (1974), 95-97.

ROSENGARTEN, HERBERT. "Preferable Paradise." *Canadian Literature,* No.61 (1974), pp. 109-11.

WHO HAS SEEN THE WIND (1947)

NEW, WILLIAM H. "A Feeling of Completion: Aspects of W. O. Mitchell," in his *Articulating West,* pp. 45-50.

RICOU, LAURENCE. *Vertical Man/Horizontal World,* pp. 96-106.

SUTHERLAND, RONALD. "Children of the Changing Wind," in his *Second Image,* pp. 89-107.

MITRA, PREMENDRA (Bengali, 1904-)

GENERAL

CHAKRAVORTY, JAGANNATH. "Premendra Mitra, Bengali Poet and Novelist." *Indian Literature,* 12, No.4 (1969), 16-23.

MITTELHOLZER, EDGAR (Guyanese, 1909-1965)

GENERAL

BIRBALSINGH, F. M. "Edgar Mittelholzer: Moralist or Pornographer?" *Journal Of Commonwealth Literature,* No.7 (1969), pp. 88-106.

A MORNING AT THE OFFICE (1950)

GILKES, MICHAEL. "The Spirit in the Bottle—A Reading of Mittleholzer's *A Morning At The Office.*" *World Literature Written In English,* 14 (1975), 237-52.

JAMES, LOUIS. "Introduction," in *The Islands In Between,* ed. Louis James, pp. 36-39.

MOORE, GERALD. *The Chosen Tongue,* pp. 9-12.

MIXAILOVIĆ, DRAGOSLAV (Yugoslavian)

WHEN THE PUMPKINS WERE BLOSSOMING (Kad su Svetale Tikve)

Matejić, Mateja. "On the Contemporary Yugoslav Novel." *Canadian Slavic Studies,* 5 (1971), 368-71.

MŇAČKO, LADISLAV (Czechoslovak, 1919-)

THE TASTE OF POWER (Ako chuti moc, 1968)

Reviews

STILWELL, ROBERT L. "Victim of His Own Might." *Saturday Review,* 19 August 1967, p. 33.

TIKOS, LASZLO M. "The Distaste of Power." *East Europe,* 16, No.8 (1967), 54-55.

MOBERG, VILHELM (Swedish, 1898-1973)

GENERAL

ALEXIS, GERHARD T. "Moberg's Immigrant Trilogy: A Dubious Conclusion." *Scandinavian Studies,* 38 (1966), 20-25.

THE LAST LETTER HOME (Sista brevet till Sverige, 1959)

ALEXIS, GERHARD T. "Moberg's Immigrant Trilogy: A Dubious Conclusion." *Scandinavian Studies,* 38 (1966), 20-25.

A TIME ON EARTH (Din stund på jorden, 1961)

ALEXIS, GERHARD T. "Wilhelm Moberg: You Can Go Home Again." *Scandinavian Studies,* 40 (1968), 230-32.

Reviews

SPECTOR, ROBERT DONALD. *American Scandinavian Review,* 53 (1965), 428, 430.

WHEN I WAS A CHILD (Soldat med brutet gevär, 1944)

ALEXIS, GERHARD T. "Wilhelm Moberg: You Can Go Home Again."*Scandinavian Studies,* 40 (1968), 227–28.

MODISANE, BLOKE (South African, 1923–)

BLAME ME ON HISTORY (1963)

CARTEY, WILFRED. *Whispers from a Continent,* pp. 137–41.

MÖRIKE, EDUARD (German, 1804–1875)

MOZART AUF DER REISE NACH PRAGUE (1855)

WOODS, JEAN M. "Memory and Inspiration in Mörike's *Mozart Auf Der Reise Nach Prag.*" *Revue Des Langues Vivantes,* 41 (1975), 6–14.

MOFOLO, THOMAS (Lesotho, 1948–)

GENERAL

KUNENE, DANIEL P. "Towards an Aesthetic of Sesotho Prose." *Dalhousie Review,* 53 (1973/4), 701–9.

CHAKA (1925)

OGUNGBESAN, KOLAWOLE. "A King for All Seasons: Chaka in African Literature." *Présence Africaine,* No.88 (1973), pp. 198–204.

MOHANTY, SURENDRA (Indian)

NEELA SHAILA (1969)

Reviews
JOTWANI, MOTILAL. *Indian Literature,* 13, No.3 (1970), 102–4.

MOIX, TERENCI

OLAS SOBRE UNA ROCA DESIERTA

Reviews
SHEEHAN, ROBERT LOUIS. *Hispania,* 54 (1971), 600.

MONESI, IRENE

UN PEUPLE DE COLOMBES

Reviews
KAY, BURF. *French Review,* 45 (1971), 479–80.

MONTALBÁN, Manuel Vázquez see VÁZQUEZ MONTALBÁN, Manuel

MONTANER, CARLOS ALBERTO (Cuban, 1943–)

PERROMUNDO (1972)

MENTON, SEYMOUR. *Prose Fiction Of The Cuban Revolution,* pp. 230–34.

Reviews
SCHWARTZ, KESSEL. *Hispania,* 57 (1974), 188–89.

MONTEIRO, LUIS DE STTAU (Portuguese, 1926–)

A MAN OF MEANS (Anguistis para o jantar, 1961)

Reviews
LESAGE, LAURENT. "First Stop on the Way to a Star." *Saturday Review,* 13 March 1965, pp. 127–28.

THE RULES OF THE GAME see A MAN OF MEANS

MONTEIRO LOBATO, JOSÉ BENTO (Brazilian, 1882–1948)

O PRESIDENTE NEGRO (O choque das raças)

BROWN, TIMOTHY. "Monteiro Lobato As a Novelist." *Luso-Brazilian Review,* 2, No.1 (1965), 99–104.

MONTEL, JEAN-CLAUDE

LE CARNAVAL

Reviews
GREENE, NAOMI. *French Review,* 44 (1970), 418–19.

MONTEMAYOR, JORGE DE (Spanish, 1519–1561)

LOS SIETE LIBROS DE LA DIANA (ca. 1559)

EL SAFFAR, RUTH. "Structural and Thematic Discontinuity in Montemayor's *Diana.*" *MLN,* 86 (1971), 182–98.

HOFFMEISTER, GERHART. "Courtly Decorum: Kuffstein and the Spanish *Diana.*" *Comparative Literature Studies,* 8 (1971), 214–23.

JOHNSON, CARROLL B. "Montemayor's *Diana:* A Novel Pastoral." *Bulletin of Hispanic Studies,* 48 (1971), 20–35.

JONES, JOSEPH R. " 'Human Time' in *La Diana.*" *Romance Notes,* 10 (1968), 140–46.

KEIGHTLEY, R. G. "Narrative Perspectives in Spanish Pastoral Fiction." *AUMLA,* No. 44 (1975), pp. 194–219.

REYNOLDS, JOHN J. "Ananio or Montano: A note on Montemayor's *Diana.*" *MLN,* 87 (1972), 315–17.

MONTES HUIDOBRO, MATIAS (Cuban, 1931–)

DESTERRADOS AL FUEGO (1975)

Reviews
FREYRE, MIREYA JAIMES. *Latin American Literary Review,* 4, No.9 (1976), 96–98.

MONTHERLANT, HENRY DE (French, 1895–1972)

GENERAL

ARTHOS, JOHN. "The Montherlant Manner." *French Review,* 43, special issue No.1 (1970), 135–43.

BECKER, LUCILLE, *Henry De Montherlant: A Critical Biography.*

HAFT, CYNTHIA J. "A Thematic Study of the Novels of Montherlant." *International Fiction Review,* 2 (1975), 121–26.

KOPS, HENRI. "Montherlant, A Memoir." *Books Abroad,* 48 (1974), 42–46.

NEVILLE, DANIEL E. *Henry De Montherlant: A Contemporary Master.*

PRICE, JONATHAN REEVE. "Montherlant: the Jansenist Libertine." *Renascence,* 19 (1967), 208–16.

UN ASSASSIN EST MON MAÎTRE (1971)

Reviews
ROSENBERG, MERRILL. *French Review,* 45 (1972), 1182–83.

THE BACHELORS see LAMENT FOR THE DEATH OF AN UPPER CLASS

CHAOS AND NIGHT (La Chaos et la nuit, 1963)

JOHNSON, ROBERT B. *Henry De Montherlant,* pp. 75–80.

THE DEMON OF GOOD (Le Demon du bien, 1937)

JOHNSON, ROBERT B. *Henry De Montherlant,* pp. 69–73.

DESERT LOVE (L'Histoire D'amour de la rose de sable, 1954)

PRITCHETT, V. S. *The Working Novelist,* pp. 79–84.

THE DREAM (Le Songe, 1922)

JOHNSON, ROBERT B. *Henry De Montherlant,* pp. 36–40.

LAMENT FOR THE DEATH OF AN UPPER CLASS (Les Célibataires, 1934)

JOHNSON, ROBERT B. *Henry De Montherlant,* pp. 51–55.

THE MATADOR (Les Bestiaires, 1926)

FROHOCK, W. M. *Style and Temper,* pp. 12–21, 21–29.
JOHNSON, ROBERT B. *Henry De Montherlant,* pp. 41–45.

PERISH IN THEIR PRIDE see LAMENT FOR THE DEATH OF AN UPPER CLASS

LA PETITE INFANTE DE CASTILLE (1929)

JOHNSON, ROBERT B. *Henry De Montherlant,* pp. 45–48.

PITY FOR WOMEN (Pitie pour les femmes, 1936)

JOHNSON, ROBERT B. *Henry De Montherlant,* pp. 62–69.

YOUNG GIRLS (Les Jeunes Filles, 1936)

JOHNSON, ROBERT B. *Henry De Montherlant,* pp. 55–62.

MONTREUX, NICHOLAS DE

OEUVRE DE LA CHASTETE

STONE, DONALD. *From Tales to Truths,* pp. 36–41.

MOORE, BRIAN (Canadian, 1921-)

GENERAL

FOSTER, JOHN WILSON. "Passage Through Limbo: Brian Moore's North American Novels." *Critique,* 13, No.1 (1970), 5–18.

CATHOLICS (1972)

Reviews
SMITH, ROWLAND. "Telegrams and Anger." *Canadian Literature,* No.58 (1973), pp. 100–1.

THE EMPEROR OF ICE-CREAM (1965)

DAHLIE, HALLVARD. "Brian Moore's Broader Vision: *The Emperor of Ice-Cream.*" *Critique,* 9, No.1 (1966), 43–50.

Reviews
BUCKEYE, ROBERT. *Dalhousie Review,* 46 (1966), 135–39.
SMITH, MARION B. "Existential Morality?" *Canadian Literature,* No.28 (1966), pp. 68–70.
STEDMOND, JOHN. "Poem and Book." *Canadian Forum,* 45 (1965), 263.

FERGUS (1970)

Reviews
WOODCOCK, GEORGE. "A Matter of Loyalty." *Canadian Literature,* No.49 (1971), pp. 81–83.

THE GREAT VICTORIAN COLLECTION (1975)

Reviews
DAHLIE, HALLVARD. "The Minor Marvel." *Canadian Literature,* No.66 (1975), pp. 101–4.
RABINOWITZ, DOROTHY. *Saturday Review,* 26 July 1975, p. 30.

I AM MARY DUNNE (1968)

FOSTER, JOHN WILSON. "Passage Through Limbo: Brian Moore's North American Novels." *Critique,* 13, No.1 (1970), 13–17.

Reviews
DAHLIE, HALLVARD. "Moore's New Perspective." *Canadian Literature,* No.38 (1968), pp. 81–84.

MOPELI-PAULUS, ATTWELL SIDWELL AND MIRIAM BASNER (Lesotho, 1913-)

TURN TO THE DARK

GLEASON, JUDITH ILLSLEY. *This Africa,* pp. 97–103.

MORALES-PINO, AUGUSTO

CIELO Y ASFALTO (1966)

Reviews
LEVY, KURT L. *Hispania,* 51 (1968), 374.

RÉQUIEM POR UND CORAZÓN: PRIMERA NOVELA SOBRE UN TRANSPLANTE DE CORÁZON (1970)

Reviews
WADE, GERALD E. *Hispania,* 54 (1971), 974–75.

MORANTE, ELSA (Italian, 1918-)

LA STORIA (1974)

FERRERI, DENISE VALTZ. "Elsa Morante's *La Storia.*" *Books Abroad,* 50 (1976), 85–86.

MORAVIA, ALBERTO (Italian, 1907-)
pseudonym of Alberto Pincherle

GENERAL

"Alberto Moravia: The Successor of Pirandello." *Contemporary Review,* 212 (1968), 295–99, 301.
HEINEY, DONALD. *Three Italian Novelists,* pp. 1–23.
KIBLER, LOUIS. "The Reality and Realism of Alberto Moravia." *Italian Quarterly,* 17, No.65 (1973), 3–25.
LANCASTER, CHARLES MAXWELL. "Fantasy in Moravia's Social and Political Satire." *Forum Italicum,* 2 (1968), 3–12.
REBAY, LUCIANO. *Alberto Moravia.*
RIMANELLI, GIOSE. "Moravia and the Philosophy of Personal Existence." *Italian Quarterly,* 11, No.41 (1967), 39–68.

AGOSTINO (1945)

COTTRELL, JANE E. *Alberto Moravia,* pp. 54–59.
RIMANELLI, GIOSE. "Moravia and the Philosophy of Personal Existence." *Italian Quarterly,* 11, No.41 (1967), 40–54.

THE CONFORMIST (Il conformista, 1951)

COTTRELL, JANE E. *Alberto Moravia,* pp. 87–91.
CULBERTSON, DIANA and JOHN A. VALLEY. "Alberto Moravia's Melancholy Murderer: The Conformist as Personality Type." *Literature And Psychology,* 25 (1975), 79–85.
HEINEY, DONALD. *Three Italian Novelists,* pp. 46–51.
ROSS, JOAN and DONALD FREED. *The Existentialism Of Alberto Moravia,* pp. 92–95.

CONJUGAL LOVE (L'Amore Coniugale, 1949)

COTTRELL, JANE E. *Alberto Moravia,* pp. 80–83.
LEWIS, R. W. B. "Alberto Moravia: Eros and Existence," in *From Verismo To Experimentalism,* ed. Sergio Pacifici, pp. 153–54.
ROSS, JOAN and DONALD FREED. *The Existentialism Of Alberto Moravia,* pp. 108–14.

CONTEMPT see A GHOST AT NOON

DISOBEDIENCE (La disubbidienza, 1948)

COTTRELL, JANE E. *Alberto Moravia,* pp. 59-64.

RIMANELLI, GIOSE. "Moravia and the Philosophy of Personal Existence." *Italian Quarterly,* 11, No.41 (1967), 40-54.

THE EMPTY CANVAS (La Noia, 1960)

COTTRELL, JANE E. *Alberto Moravia,* pp. 94-101.

HEINEY, DONALD. *Three Italian Novelists,* pp. 65-73.

ROSS, JOAN and DONALD FREED. *The Existentialism Of Alberto Moravia,* pp. 48-51.

THE FANCY DRESS PARTY (La mascherata, 1941)

COTTRELL, JANE E. *Alberto Moravia,* pp. 48-51.

HEINEY, DONALD. *Three Italian Novelists,* pp. 32-36.

A GHOST AT NOON (Il Disprezzo, 1954)

COTTRELL, JANE E. *Alberto Moravia,* pp. 83-87.

HEINEY, DONALD. *Three Italian Novelists,* pp. 51-58.

KORTE, WALTER. "Godard's Adaptation of Moravia's *Contempt.*" *Literature/Film Quarterly,* 2 (1974), 284-89.

ROSS, JOAN and DONALD FREED. *The Existentialism Of Alberto Moravia,* pp. 116-19.

WHITE, JOHN J. *Mythology In The Modern Novel,* pp. 166-75.

THE INDIFFERENT ONES see THE TIME OF INDIFFERENCE

THE LIE (L'attenzione, 1965)

BALDANZA, FRANK. "Mature Moravia." *Contemporary Literature,* 9 (1968), 510-21.

COTTRELL, JANE E. *Alberto Moravia,* pp. 101-5.

HEINEY, DONALD. *Three Italian Novelists,* pp. 73-82.

RAGUSA, OLGA. "Alberto Moravia: Voyeurism and Storytelling." *Southern Review,* NS, 4 (1968), 129-32.

ROSS, JOAN and DONALD FREED. *The Existentialism Of Alberto Moravia,* pp. 56-59.

Reviews

CAPOUYA, EMILE. "Ailments of the Spirit." *Saturday Review,* 13 August 1966, pp. 30-31, 34.

RAVEN, SIMON. *London Magazine,* NS, 6 No.7 (1966), 110-12.

MISTAKEN AMBITIONS see THE WHEEL OF FORTUNE

THE TIME OF INDIFFERENCE (Gli indifferenti, 1929)

BUCKINGHAM, MARILYN, "A Comment on 'Imagery as Expression:' Moravia's *Gli Indifferenti.*" *Italica,* 50 (1973), 299-300.

COTTRELL, JANE E. *Alberto Moravia,* pp. 36-44.

HEINEY, DONALD. *Three Italian Novelists,* pp. 23-28.

KIBLER, LOUIS. "Imagery as Expression: Moravia's *Gli Indifferenti.*" *Italica,* 49 (1972), 315-34.

———. "Response to Ms. Buckingham's Comment." *Italica,* 50 (1973), 300-2.

ROSS, JOAN and DONALD FREED. *The Existentialism Of Alberto Moravia,* pp. 37-41.

TWO: A PHALLIC NOVEL (Io et Lui, 1971)

COTTRELL, JANE E. *Alberto Moravia,* pp. 108-12.

Reviews

EWART, GAVIN. "Rome-Berlin Axis." *London Magazine,* NS 12, No.4 (1972), 149-50.

WOOD, PETER. *Saturday Review,* 29 April 1972, p. 76.

TWO WOMEN (La ciociara, 1957)

COTTRELL, JANE E. *Alberto Moravia,* pp. 72-77.

HEINEY, DONALD. *Three Italian Novelists,* pp. 58-65.

LEWIS, R. W. B. "Alberto Moravia: Eros and Existence," in *From Verismo To Experimentalism,* ed. Sergio Pacifici, pp. 156-58.

ROSS, JOAN and DONALD FREED. *The Existentialism Of Alberto Moravia,* pp. 37-41.

THE WHEEL OF FORTUNE (Le ambizioni sbagliate, 1935)

COTTRELL, JANE E. *Alberto Moravia,* pp. 44-48.

HEINEY, DONALD. *Three Italian Novelists,* pp. 29-32.

THE WOMAN OF ROME (La Romana, 1947)

COTTRELL, JANE E. *Alberto Moravia,* pp. 66-72.

HEINEY, DONALD. *Three Italian Novelists,* pp. 36-46.

ROSS, JOAN and DONALD FREED. *The Existentialism Of Alberto Moravia,* pp. 66-68.

MORETTI, MARINO (Italian, ca. 1885-1979)

GENERAL

PACIFICI, SERGIO. *The Modern Italian Novel: From Capuana To Tozzi,* pp. 97-107.

MORI ŌGAI (Japanese, 1862-1922) pseudonym of Rintaro M

GENERAL

BRAZELL, KAREN. "Mori Ōgai in Germany." *Monumenta Nipponica,* 26 (1971), 77-100.

HOPPER, HELEN M. "Mori Ōgai's Response to Suppression of Intellectual Freedom, 1909-12." *Monumenta Nipponica,* 29 (1974), 381-413.

VITA SEXUALIS (1909)

HOPPER, HELEN M. "Mori Ōgai's Response to Suppression of Intellectual Freedom, 1909-12." *Monumenta Nipponica,* 29 (1974), 385-88.

Reviews

DILWORTH, DAVID A. *Monumenta Nipponica,* 28 (1973), 101-3.

JOHNSON, ERIC W. *Literature East And West,* 18 (1974), 379-82.

THE WILD GEESE (Gan, 1913)

MIYOSHI, MASAO. *Accomplices Of Silence,* pp. 38-54.

MORITZ, KARL PHILIPP (German, 1757-1793)

ANTON REISER (1785-1790)

BOULBY, MARK. "The Gates of Brunswick: Some Aspects of Symbol, Structure and Theme in Karl Philipp Moritz's 'Anton Reiser.'" *Modern Language Review,* 68 (1973), 105-14.

MORIYA, TADASHI

NO REQUIEM

KIMBALL, ARTHUR G. *Crisis In Identity And Contemporary Japanese Novels,* pp. 27-30.

MORPHETT, TONY

DYNASTY

Reviews

McLAREN, JOHN. "New Novels." *Overland,* No.38 (1968), p. 42.

MOURGUE, GERARD

BLEU MARINE (1973)

Reviews
WEINBERG, HENRY H. *French Review,* 48 (1975), 801-2.

MOURTHÉ, CLAUDE

AMOUR NOIR

Reviews
HENKELS, ROBERT M., JR. *French Review,* 46 (1973), 1060-61.

L'ENLÈVEMENT (1971)

Reviews
BULGIN, KATHLEEN. *French Review,* 47 (1974), 1020-21.

MOUSTIERS, PIERRE (French, 1924-)

L'HIVER D'UN GENTILHOMME (1971)

Reviews
CRANT, PHILLIP A. *French Review,* 47 (1973), 233-34.

MOYANO, DANIEL (Argentine, 1930-)

THE DARK ONE (El Oscuro, 1961)

FOSTER, DAVID WILLIAM. *Currents In The Contemporary Argentine Novel,* pp. 139-41.

MPHAHLELE, EZEKIEL (South African, 1919-)

GENERAL

MUNRO, IAN, RICHARD PRIEBE, REINHARD SANDER. "An Interview With: Ezekiel Mphahlele." *Studies In Black Literature,* 2, No.3 (1971), 6-8.

DOWN SECOND AVENUE (1959)

CARTEY, WILFRED. *Whispers From A Continent,* pp. 27-32.

THE WANDERERS (1971)

Reviews
JARRETT-KERR, MARTIN. "Novel of Exile." *Journal Of Commonwealth Literature,* 8, No.1 (1973), 112-16.
POVEY, JOHN. "Search for a Homeland." *African Studies Review,* 14 (1971), 494-97.
SNYDER, EMILE. *Saturday Review,* 19 June 1971, p. 24.
TUCKER, MARTIN. *World Literature Written In English,* No.20 (1971), pp. 130-31.

MRABET, MOHAMMED (Moroccan, 1940-) pseudonym of Mahammed ben Chaib el Hajjam

LOVE WITH A FEW HAIRS (1967)

Reviews
STERN, JEROME H. "Moroccan Viewpoint." *Saturday Review,* 6 April 1968, pp. 30-31, 40.

MÜLLER, F. M.

GERMAN LOVE

CASTEN, C. "The Influence of F. Max Müller's *German Love* on Meredith's *Modern Love.*" *English Language Notes,* 10 (1973), 282-86.

MÜLLER, JOHANN CHRISTIAN WILHELM

FRAGMENTE AUS DEM LEBEN UND WANDEL EINES PHYSIOGNOMISTEN

HADLEY, MICHAEL. *The German Novel in 1790,* pp. 179-86.

MÜLLER, JOHANN GOTTWERTH (German, 1743-1828)

HERR THOMAS

HADLEY, MICHAEL. *The German Novel In 1790,* pp. 163-69.

MUJICA LAINEZ, MANUEL (Argentine, 1910-)

BOMARZO (1962)

HENNEBERG, JOSEPHINE VON. "Bomarzo: The Extravagant Garden Pier Francesco Orsini." *Italian Quarterly,* 11, No.42 (1967), 3-19.

Reviews
HUME, PAUL. *Washington Post,* 31 December 1969; rpt. in *Review,* No.2 (1969), 95-97.
SULLIVAN, SHIRLEY. *Houston Texas Post,* 28 December 1969; rpt. in *Review,* No.2 (1969), 97-98.
Time, 12 December 1969; rpt. in *Review,* No.2 (1969), 98-100.

CECIL (1972)

Reviews
SCHWARTZ, KESSEL. *Hispania,* 57 (1974), 186-87.

DE MILAGROS Y DE MELANCOLÍAS (1968)

SCHANZER, GEORGE O. "The Four Hundred Years of Myths and Melancholies of Mujica Lainez." *Latin American Literary Review,* 1, No.2 (1973), 65-71.

EL LABERINTO (1974)

Reviews
SCHANZER, GEORGE O. *Latin American Literary Review,* 4, No.7 (1975), 92-94.

MUKHERJEE, BHARATI (Indian, 1940-)

WIFE (1975)

Reviews
MANI, LAKSHMI. *World Literature Written In English,* 14 (1975), 415.

THE TIGER'S DAUGHTER (1972)

Reviews
HITREC, JOSEPH. *Saturday Review,* 11 March 1972, pp. 76-77.

MUNDT, THEODOR (German, 1808-1861)

MADONNA (1835)

SAMMONS, JEFFREY L. *Six Essays On The Young German Novel,* pp. 71-80.

MUNRO, ALICE

GENERAL

METCALF, JOHN. "A Conversation with Alice Munro." *Journal Of Canadian Fiction,* 1, No.4 (1972), 54-62.

LIVES OF GIRLS AND WOMEN (1971)

Reviews
POLK, JAMES. "Deep Caves and Kitchen Linoleum." *Canadian Literature,* No.54 (1972), pp. 102-4.
THOMAS, CLARA. "Woman Invincible." *Journal Of Canadian Fiction,* 1, No.4 (1972), 95-96.

MURARI, TIMERI (Indian, 1941-)

THE MARRIAGE (1973)

Reviews

RUSTOMJI, ROSHNI. *World Literature Written In English*, 14 (1975), 426.

MURASAKI SHIKIBU (Japanese, ca. 978–ca. 1031)

THE TALE OF GENJI (Genji monogatari)

McLEOD, DAN. "Some Approaches to The Tale of Genji." *Literature East And West*, 18 (1974), 301–13.

PUTZAR, EDWARD D. "Japanese Literature: Theoretically Speaking." *Literature East And West*, 11 (1967), 23–35.

REXROTH, KENNETH. "Classics Revisited—XIX." *Saturday Review*, 11 December 1965, p. 27; rpt. in *Classics Revisited*, pp. 136–40.

URY, MARIAN. "The Imaginary Kingdom and the Translator's Art: Notes on Re-reading Waley's *Genji*." *Journal Of Japanese Studies*, 2 (1976), 267–94.

WILSON, WILLIAM R. "The 'Bell-Crickets' Chapter of *The Tale Of Genji*." *Literature East And West*, 16 (1972), 1196–1201.

MURENA, HÉCTOR A. (Argentine, 1923–)

GENERAL

STABB, MARTIN S. "The New Murena and the New Novel." *Kentucky Romance Quarterly*, 22 (1975), 139–57.

EPITALÁMICA (1969)

Reviews

McMURRAY, GEORGE R. *Hispania*, 53 (1970), 581.

LA FATALIDAD DE LOS CUERPOS (1955)

BRUSHWOOD, JOHN S. *The Spanish American Novel*, pp. 207–9.

LOS HEREDEROS DE LA PROMESA (1965)

Reviews

LEWALD, H. ERNEST. *Hispania*, 50 (1967), 191.

LAWS OF THE NIGHT (Las leyes de la noche, 1958)

Reviews

Kirkus Service, 1 June 1970; rpt. *Review*, No.3 (1971), p. 54.

Publishers Weekly, 15 June 1970; rpt. *Review*, No.3 (1971), p. 55.

POLISPUERCÓN

Reviews

LYON, THOMAS E. *Hispania*, 55 (1972), 596–97.

MUSCHG, ADOLF (Swiss, 1934–)

GENERAL

WAIDSON, H. M. "The Near and the Far: The Writings of Adolf Muschg." *German Life And Letters*, 28 (1975), 426–37.

MUSIL, ROBERT (Austrian, 1880–1942)

GENERAL

KERMODE, FRANK. "Robert Musil." *Kenyon Review*, 28 (1966), 224–30.

MAYER, HANS. "Robert Musil: A Remembrance of Things Past," in his *Steppenwolf And Everyman*, pp. 14–34.

TANNER, TONY. "Robert Musil." *London Magazine*, NS 5, No.3 (1965), 43–56.

VON NARDROFF, ELLEN. "Robert Musil's Concept of the Poet and Writer." *Modern Austrian Literature*, 4, No.1 (1971), 23–29.

WILLIAMS, CEDRIC E. *The Broken Eagle*, pp. 146–86.

THE CONFUSIONS OF YOUNG TORLESS (Die Verwirrungen des Zoglings Törless, 1906)

BRAUN, WILHELM. "The Confusions of Toerless." *Germanic Review*, 40 (1965), 116–31.

GOLDGAR, HARRY. "The Square Root of Minus One: Freud and Robert Musil's *Törless*." *Comparative Literature*, 17 (1965), 117–32.

HATFIELD, HENRY. *Crisis And Continuity In Modern German Fiction*, pp. 35–48.

ROSE, MARILYN GADDIS. "Musil's Use of Simile in 'Törless.' " *Studies In Short Fiction*, 8 (1971), 295–300.

STOPP, ELISABETH. "Musil's 'Törless': Content and Form." *Modern Language Review*, 63 (1968), 94–118.

TANNER, TONY. "Robert Musil." *London Magazine*, 5, No.3 (1965), 43–46.

TURNER, DAVID. "The Evasions of the Aesthete Törless." *Forum For Modern Language Studies*, 10 (1974), 19–44.

WHITE, JOHN J. "Mathematical Imagery in Musil's *Young Törless* and Zamyatin's *We*." *Comparative Literature*, 18 (1966), 71–78.

DREI FRAUEN (1925)

APPIGNANESI, LISA. *Femininity & The Creative Imagination*, pp. 105–16.

BOA, ELIZABETH J. "Austrian Ironies in Musil's 'Drei Frauen.' " *Modern Language Review*, 63 (1968), 119–31.

GRIGIA (1925)

BOA, ELIZABETH J. "Austrian Ironies in Musil's 'Drei Frauen.' " *Modern Language Review*, 63 (1968), 119–23.

THE MAN WITHOUT QUALITIES (Der Mann ohne Eigenschaften, 1930–43)

APPIGNANESI, LISA. *Femininity & The Creative Imagination*, pp. 124–56.

CHARNEY, HANNA. "Monsieur Teste and der Mann ohne Eigenschaften: *Homo Possibilis* in Fiction." *Comparative Literature*, 27 (1975), 1–7.

HEALD, DAVID. " 'All the World's a Stave'—A Central Motif in Musil's 'Mann ohne Eigenschaften.' " *German Life And Letters*, 27 (1973), 51–59.

HOLMES, F. A. "Some Comic Elements in Musil's *Der Mann Ohne Eigenschaften*." *German Life And Letters*, 18 (1964), 25–29.

KLAWITER, RANDOLPH J. "The Artist-Intellectual, in or versus Society? A Dilemma," in *Studies In German Literature Of The Nineteenth And Twentieth Centuries*, ed. Siegfried Mews, pp. 236–39.

NOBLE, C. A. M. "Musil's Novel Without Qualities." *Revue Des Langues Vivantes*, 39 (1973), 28–38.

PRITCHETT, V. S. *The Working Novelist*, pp. 154–65.

REICHERT, HERBERT W. "Nietzchean Influence in Musil's *Der Mann Ohne Eigenschaften*." *German Quarterly*, 39 (1966), 12–28; rpt. in his *Friedrich Nietzsche's Impact On Modern German Literature*, pp. 73–87.

TANNER, TONY. "Robert Musil." *London Magazine*, 5, No.3 (1965), 53–56.

TITCHE, LEON L. "The Concept of the Hermaphrodite: Agathe and Ulrich in Musil's Novel *Der Mann Ohne Eigenschaften*." *German Life And Letters*, 23 (1970), 160–68.

WILKINS, EITHNE. "Musil's 'Affair of the Major's Wife' With an Unpublished Text." *Modern Language Review*, 63 (1968), 74–93.

WILLIAMS, CEDRIC E. *The Broken Eagle*, pp. 171–86.

DIE PORTUGIESIN (1925)

> BOA, ELIZABETH J. "Austrian Ironies in Musil's 'Drei Frauen.' " *Modern Language Review,* 63 (1968), 123-26.

DIE SCHWÄRMER (1921)

> BRAUN, WILHELM. "Musil's Anselm and 'The Motivated Life.' " *Wisconsin Studies In Contemporary Literature,* 8 (1967), 517-27.

TONKA (1925)

> BOA, ELIZABETH J. "Austrian Ironies in Musil's 'Drei Frauen,' " *Modern Language Review,* 63 (1968), 126-31.

> STELZMANN, RAINULF A. "Kantian Faith in Musil's *Tonka.*" *Germanic Review,* 50 (1975), 294-304.

MUSSET, ALFRED DE (French, 1810-1857)

CONFESSION OF A CHILD OF THE CENTURY (Confession d'un enfant du Siècle)

> GRIMSLEY, RONALD. "Romantic Emotion in Musset's *Confession D'un Enfant Du Siècle.*" *Studies In Romanticism,* 9 (1970), 125-42.

> KING, RUSSELL S. "Romanticism and Musset's 'Confession d'un Enfant du Siècle." *Nottingham French Studies,* 11 (1972), 3-13.

MYERS, MARTIN (Canadian, 1927-)

THE ASSIGNMENT (1970)

> **Reviews**
> DUFFY, DENNIS. "Mod Model." *Canadian Literature,* No. 54 (1972), pp. 107-9.

MYKLE, AGNAR (Norwegian, 1915-)

RUBICON (Roman, 1965)

> **Reviews**
> MITCHELL, P. M. "Angst on the Autobahn." *Saturday Review,* 22 April 1967, p. 97.

> SPECTOR, ROBERT D. *American Scandinavian Review,* 56 (1968), 308.

MYKOLAITIS, Vincas see PUTINAS, Vincas Mykolaitis

MYRDAL, JAN (Swedish, 1927-)

CONFESSIONS OF A DISLOYAL EUROPEAN

> **Reviews**
> SPECTOR, ROBERT D. *American Scandinavian Review,* 57 (1969), 198.

N

NABOKOV, VLADIMIR (Russian, emmigrated to the United States, 1899–)

GENERAL

ADAMOVICH, GEORGI. "Vladimir Nabokov." in *Twentieth-Century Russian Literary Criticism,* ed. Victor Erlich, pp. 219–31.

APPEL, ALFRED. "Backgrounds of *Lolita.'* " *Triquarterly,* No. 17 (1970), pp. 17–40.

———. "Conversations With Nabokov." *Novel,*4 (1971), 209–22.

———. "An Interview with Vladimir Nabokov." *Wisconsin Studies In Contemporary Literature,* 8 (1967), 127–52.

———. "An Interview with Vladimir Nabokov," in *Nabokov: The Man And His Work,* ed. L. S. Dembo, pp. 19–44.

———. "Nabokov: A Portrait." *Atlantic Monthly,* 228, No. (1971), 77–92.

———. "Nabokov's Dark Cinema: A Diptych." *Triquarterly,* No. 27 (1973), pp. 196–273.

BERBEROVA, NINA. "Nabokov in the Thirties," in *Nabokov: Criticism, Reminiscences, Translations And Tributes,* ed. Alfred Appel Jr. and Charles Newman, pp. 220–33.

BISHOP, MORRIS. "Nabokov at Cornell," in *Nabokov: Criticism, Reminiscences, Translations And Tributes,* ed. Alfred Appel Jr. and Charles Newman, pp. 234–39.

BITSILLI, P. M. "The Revival of Allegory," in *Nabokov: Criticism, Reminiscences, Translations And Tributes,* ed. Alfred Appel Jr. and Charles Newman, pp. 102–18.

BROWN, CLARENCE. "Nabokov's Pushkin and Nabokov's Nabokov." *Wisconsin Studies In Contemporary Literature,* 8 (1967), 280–93; rpt. in *Nabokov: The Man And His Work,* ed. L. S. Dembo, pp. 195–208.

BRYER, JACKSON R. and THOMAS J. BERGIN, JR. "Vladimir Nabokov's Critical Reputation in English: A Note and a Checklist," *Wisconsin Studies In Contemporary Literature,* 8 (1967), 312–64; rpt. in *Nabokov: The Man And His Work,* ed. L. S. Dembo, pp. 225–76.

CHERNYSHEV, A. and V. PRONIN. "Vladimir Nabokov, in the Second Place and in the First Place. . . " *Soviet Studies In Literature,* 7 (1971), 345–54.

DEMBO, L. S. "Vladimir Nabokov, an Introduction." *Wisconsin Studies In Contemporary Literature,* 8 (1967), 111–26; rpt. in *Nabokov: The Man And His Work,* ed. L. S. Dembo, pp. 3–18.

ELKIN, STANLEY. "Three Meetings," in *Nabokov: Criticism, Reminiscences, Translations And Tributes,* ed. Alfred Appel Jr. and Charles Newman, pp. 261–65.

FIELD, ANDREW. "The Artist as Failure in Nabokov's Early Prose." *Wisconsin Studies In Contemporary Literature,* 8 (1967), 165–73.

FLEISCHAUER, JOHN F. "Simultaneity in Nabokov's Prose Style." *Style,* 5 (1971), 57–69.

FOSTER, LUDMILA A. "Nabokov in Russian Emigre Criticism." *Russian Literature Triquarterly,* No.3 (1972), pp. 330–41.

GROSSHANS, HENRY. "Vladimir Nabokov and the Dream of Old Russia." *Texas Studies In Literature And Language,* 7 (1966), 401–9.

HICKS, GRANVILLE. "A Man of Many Words," *Saturday Review,* 28 January 1967, pp. 31–32.

JOHNSON, D. BARTON. "Synesthesia, Polychromatism, and Nabokov." *Russian Literature Triquarterly,* No. 3 (1972), pp. 378–97.

KARLINSKY, SIMON. "Anya in Wonderland: Nabokov's Russified Lewis Carroll," in *Nabokov: Criticism, Reminiscences, Translations And Tributes,* ed. Alfred Appel Jr. and Charles Newman, pp. 310–15.

———. "Illusion, Reality, and Parody in Nabokov's Plays," in *Nabokov: The Man And His Work,* ed. L. S. Dembo, pp. 183–94.

———. "Nabokov and Chekhov: The Lesser Russian Tradition," in *Nabokov: Criticism, Reminiscence, Translations And Tributes,* ed. Alfred Appel Jr. and Charles Newman, pp. 7–16.

KHODASEVICH, VLADISLAV. "On Sirin," *Triquarterly,* No. 17 (1970), pp. 96–101; rpt. in *Nabokov: Criticism, Reminiscences, Translations And Tributes,* ed. Alfred Appel Jr. and Charles Newman, pp. 96–101.

LOURIA, YVETTE. "Nabokov and Proust: The Challenge of Time." *Books Abroad,* 48 (1974), 469–76.

LUBIN, PETER. "Kickshaws and Motley." *Triquarterly,* No. 17 (1970), pp. 187–208; rpt. in *Nabokov: Criticism, Reminiscences, Translations And Tributes,* ed. Alfred Appel Jr. and Charles Newman, pp. 187–208.

MERIVALE, PATRICIA. "The Flaunting of Artifice in Vladimir Nabokov and Jorge Luis Borges." *Wisconsin Studies In Contemporary Literature,* 8 (1967), 294–309; rpt. in *Nabokov: The Man And His Work,* ed. L. S. Dembo, pp. 209–24.

MOYNAHAN, JULLIAN. "*Lolita* and Related Memories," in *Nabokov: Criticism, Reminiscences, Translations And Tributes,* ed. Alfred Appel Jr. and Charles Newman, pp. 247–52.

———. "A Russian Preface for Nabokov's *Beheading.*" *Novel,* 1 (1967), 12–18.

NABOKOV, VLADIMIR. "Inspiration." *Saturday Review,* January 1973, pp. 30–32.

NOEL, LUCIE LÉON. "Playback," in *Nabokov: Criticism, Reminiscences, Translations And Tributes,* ed. Alfred Appel Jr. and Charles Newman, pp. 209–19.

PARRY, ALBERT. "Introducing Nabokov to America." *Texas Quarterly,* 14, No. 1 (1971), 16–26.

PROFFER, ELLENDEA. "Nabokov's Russian Readers," in *Nabokov: Criticism, Reminiscences, Translations And Tributes,* ed. Alfred Appel Jr. and Charles Newman, pp. 253-60.

PURDY, STROTHER B. "Solus Rex: Nabokov and the Chess Novel." *Modern Fiction Studies,* 14 (1968/69), 379-95.

ROWE, WILLIAM. "Gogolesque Perception-Expanding Reversals in Nabokov." *Slavic Review,* 30 (1971), 110-20.

SCOTT, W. B. "The Cypress Veil," in *Nabokov: Criticism, Reminiscences, Translations And Tributes,* ed. Alfred Appel Jr. and Charles Newman, pp. 316-31.

"Selected Bibliography of Nabokov's Work." *Wisconsin Studies In Contemporary Literature,* 8 (1967), 310-11.

STEINER, GEORGE. "Extraterritorial." *Triquarterly,* No. 17 (1970), pp. 119-27; rpt. in *Nabokov: Criticism, Reminiscences, Translations And Tributes,* ed. Alfred Appel Jr. and Charles Newman, pp. 119-27.

STRUVE, GLEB. "Notes on Nabokov as a Russian Writer" *Wisconsin Studies In Contemporary Literture,* 8 (1967), 153-64; rpt. in *Nabokov: The Man And His Work,* ed. L. S. Dembo, pp. 45-56.

WEIL, IRWIN. "Odyssey of a Translator." *Triquarterly,* No. 17 (1970), pp. 266-83; rpt. in *Nabokov: Criticism, Reminiscences, Translations And Tributes,* ed. Alfred Appel Jr. and Charles Newman, pp. 266-83.

WESTZSTEON, ROSS. "Nabokov as Teacher," in *Nabokov: Criticism, Reminiscences, Translations And Tributes,* ed. Alfred Appel Jr. and Charles Newman, pp. 240-46.

WHITE, EDMUND. "The Esthetics of Bliss." *Saturday Review,* 1 (January 1973), pp. 33-34.

WILLIAMS, CAROL T. "Nabokov's Dialectical Structure." *Wisconsin Studies In Contemporary Literature,* 8 (1967), 250-67; rpt. in *Nabokov: The Man And His Work,* ed. L. S. Dembo, pp. 165-82.

WILLIAMS, ROBERT C. "Memory's Defense: The Real Life of Vladimir Nabokov's Berlin." *Yale Review,* 60 (1970), 241-50.

ADA; OR, ARDOR: A FAMILY CHRONICLE (1969)

APPEL, ALFRED. "*Ada* Described." *Triquarterly,* No. 17 (1970), pp. 160-86; rpt. in *Nabokov: Criticism, Reminiscences, Translations And Tributes,* ed. Alfred Appel Jr. and Charles Newman, pp. 160-86.

BOK, SISSELA. "Redemption Through Art in Nabokov's *Ada.*" *Critique,* 12, No. 3 (1970), 110-20.

FOWLER, DOUGLAS. *Reading Nabokov,* pp. 176-201.

LEONARD, JEFFREY. "In Place of Lost Time: *Ada.*" *Triquarterly,* No. 17 (1970), pp. 136-46; rpt. in *Nabokov: Criticism, Reminiscences, Translations And Tributes,* ed. Alfred Appel Jr. and Charles Newman, pp. 136-46.

MORTON, DONALD E. *Vladimir Nabokov,* pp. 130-42.

PROFFER, CARL R. "*Ada* as Wonderland: A Glossary of Allusions to Russian Literature." *Russian Literature Triquarterly,* No. 3 (1972), pp. 399-430.

SWANSON, ROY ARTHUR. "Nabokov's *Ada* as Science Fiction." *Science-Fiction Studies,* 2 (1975), 76-88.

Reviews
ADAMS, ROBERT MARTIN. "Passion Among the Polyglots." *Hudson Review,* 22 (1969/70), 717-24.

ALTER, ROBERT. "Nabokov's Ardor." *Commentary,* 48, No. 2 (1969), 47-50.

KAZIN, ALFRED. "In the Mind of Nabokov." *Saturday Review,* 10 May 1969, pp. 27-29, 35.

BEND SINISTER (1947)

FOWLER, DOUGLAS. *Reading Nabokov,* pp. 21-61.

GOVE, ANTONINA FILONOV. "Multilingualism and Ranges of Tone in Nabokov's *Bend Sinister.*" *Slavic Review,* 32 (1973), 79-90.

HYMAN, STANLEY EDGAR. "The Handle: *Invitation To A Beheading* and *Bend Sinister.*" *Triquarterly,* No. 17 (1970), pp. 60-71; rpt. in *Nabokov: Criticism, Reminiscences, Translations And Tributes,* ed. Alfred Appel Jr. and Charles Newman, pp. 64-71.

LEE, L. L. "*Bend Sinister:* Nabokov's Political Dream." *Wisconsin Studies In Contemporary Literature,* 8 (1967), 193-203; rpt. in *Nabokov: The Man And His Work,* ed. L. S. Dembo, pp. 95-105.

MORTON, DONALD E. *Vladimir Nabokov,* pp. 53-61.

SCHAEFFER, SUSAN FROMBERG. "*Bend Sinister* and the Novelist as Anthropomorphic Deity." *Centennial Review,* 17 (1973), 115-51.

STEGNER, PAGE. *Escape Into Aesthetics: The Art Of Vladimir Nabokov,* pp. 76-89.

Reviews
GROSSMAN, EDWARD. "Butterflies, Chessboards, and Anagrams." *Saturday Review,* 23 October 1973, p. 59.

THE DEFENSE (Zaščita Lužina, 1930)

Reviews
FURBANK, P. N. "Chess and Jigsaw." *Encounter,* 24, No. 1 (1965), 83-86.

PETERSON, VIRGILIA. "Understudy for Humbert." *Reporter,* 34, No. 11 (1966), 42-44.

DESPAIR (Otchaianie, 1934)

BITSILLI, P. M. "The Revival of Allegory." *Triquarterly,* No. 17 (1970), pp. 102-18; rpt. in *Nabokov: Criticism, Reminiscences, Translations And Tributes,* ed. Alfred Appel Jr. and Charles Newman, pp. 102-18.

PROFFER, CARL R. "From *Otchaianie* to *Despair.*" *Slavic Review,* 27 (1968), 258-67.

ROGERS, ROBERT. *A Psychoanalytic Study Of The Double In Literature,* pp. 164-67.

ROSENFIELD, CLAIRE. "*Despair* and the Lust for Immortality." *Wisconsin Studies In Contemporary Literature,* 8 (1967), 174-92; rpt. in *Nabokov: The Man And His Work,* ed. L. S. Dembo, pp. 66-84.

Reviews
DARACK, ARTHUR. "Trouble with Doubles." *Saturday Review,* 21 May 1966, pp. 33-34.

THE EYE (Soglyadatay, 1938)

FIELD, ANDREW. "The Artist as Failure in Nabokov's Early Prose." *Wisconsin Studies In Contemporary Literature,* 8 (1967), 165-73; rpt. in *Nabokov: The Man And His Work,* ed. L. S. Dembo, pp. 57-65.

Reviews
FYTTON, FRANCIS. *London Magazine,* NS 6, No. 6 (1966), 117.

INVITATION TO A BEHEADING (Prigašenie na kazn', 1938)

ALTER, ROBERT. "*Invitation To A Beheading:* Nabokov and the Art of Politics." *Triquarterly,* No. 17 (1970), pp. 41-59; rpt. in *Nabokov: Criticism, Reminiscences, Translations And Tributes,* ed. Alfred Appel Jr. and Charles Newman, pp. 41-59.

BITSILLI, P. M. "The Revival of Allegory." *Triquarterly,* No. 17 (1970), pp. 102-18; rpt. in *Nabokov: Criticism: Reminiscencs, Translations And Tributes,* ed. Alfred Appel Jr. and Charles Newman, pp. 102-18.

HUGHES, ROBERT P. "Notes on the Translation of *Invitation To A Beheading.*" *Triquarterly,* No. 17 (1970), pp. 284-92; rpt. in *Nabokov: Criticism, Reminiscences, Translations And Tributes,* ed. Alfred Appel Jr. and Charles Newman, pp. 284-92.

HYMAN, STANLEY EDGAR. "The Handle: *Invitation To a Beheading* and *Bend Sinister.*" *Triquarterly,* No. 17 (1970), pp. 60-71; rpt. in *Nabokov: Criticism, Reminiscences, Translations And Tributes,* ed. Alfred Appel Jr. and Charles Newman, pp. 60-71.

SCHUMAN, SAMUEL. "Vladimir Nabokov's *Invitation To A Beheading* and Robert Heinlein's 'They.' " *Twentieth Century Literature,* 19 (1973), 99–106.

KING, QUEEN, KNAVE (Korol', Dama, Valet, 1928)

PROFFER, CARL R. "A New Deck for Nabokov's Knaves." *Triquarterly,* No.17 (1970), pp. 293–309; rpt. in *Nabokov: Criticism, Reminiscences, Translations And Tributes,* ed. Alfred Appel Jr. and Charles Newman, pp. 293–309.

Reviews
HJORTSBERG, WILLIAM J. "Nabokov's Contempt." *Catholic World,* 207 (1968), 236.

NICOLE, CHARLES. "Nabokov's Card Tricks." *Atlantic Monthly,* 221, No.6 (1968), 107–14.

STEGNER, PAGE. "Games Cards Play." *Saturday Review,* 18 May 1968, p. 39.

LAUGHTER IN THE DARK (Kamera obskura, 1932)

STUART, DABNEY. "*Laughter In The Dark:* Dimensions of Parody." *Triquarterly,* No.17 (1970), pp. 72–95; rpt. in *Nabokov: Criticism, Reminiscences, Translations And Tributes,* ed. Alfred Appel Jr. and Charles Newman, pp. 72–95.

WILLIAMS, CAROL T. "Nabokov's Dialectical Structure." *Wisconsin Studies In Contemporary Literature,* 8 (1967), 258–61; rpt. in *Nabokov: The Man And His Work,* ed. L. S. Dembo, pp. 173–76.

LOLITA (1967)

APPEL, ALFRED, JR. "Backgrounds of *Lolita.*" *Triquarterly,* No.17 (1970), pp. 17–40; rpt. in *Nabokov: Criticism, Reminiscences, Translations And Tributes,* ed. Alfred Appel Jr. and Charles Newman, pp. 17–40.

——— . "*Lolita:* The Springboard of Parody." *Wisconsin Studies In Contemporary Literature,* 8 (1967), 204–41; rpt. in *Nabokov: The Man And His Work,* ed. L. S. Dembo, pp. 106–43.

——— . "The Road to *Lolita,* or the Americanization of an Émigré." *Journal Of Modern Literature,* 4 (1974), 3–31.

——— . "Tristram in Movielove: *Lolita* at the Movies." *Russian Literature Triquarterly,* No.7 (1973), 343–88.

BELL, MICHAEL. "*Lolita* and Pure Art." *Essays In Criticism,* 24 (1974), 169–84.

BRENT, HAROLD. "*Lolita:* Nabokov's Critique of Aloofness." *Papers On Language And Literature,* 11 (1975), 71–82.

FOWLER, DOUGLAS. *Reading Nabokov,* pp. 147–75.

GREEN, MARTIN. "The Morality of *Lolita.*" *Kenyon Review,* 28 (1966), 352–77.

HIATT, L. R. "Nabokov's *Lolita:* A 'Freudian' Cryptic Crossword." *American Imago,* 24 (1967), 360–70.

JONES, DAVID L. " 'Dolorès Disparue.' " *Symposium,* 20 (1966), 135–40.

JOYCE, JAMES. "Lolita in Humberland." *Studies In The Novel,* 6 (1974), 339–48.

MCDONALD, JAMES L. "John Ray, Jr., Critic and Artist: The Foreward to *Lolita.*" *Studies In The Novel,* 5 (1973), 352–57.

MORTON, DONALD E. *Vladimir Nabokov,* pp. 64–81.

PEARCE, RICHARD. *Stages Of The Clown,* pp. 94–101.

PRIOLEAU, ELIZABETH. "Humbert Humbert *Through The Looking Glass.*" *Twentieth Century Literature,* 21 (1975), 428–37.

PROFFITT, EDWARD. "A Clue to John Ray, Jr." *Modern Fiction Studies,* 20 (1974/5), 551–52.

PURDY, STROTHER B. "Solus Rex: Nabokov and the Chess Novel." *Modern Fiction Studies,* 14 (1968/9), 391–95.

ROTH, PHYLLIS A. "In Search of Aesthetic Bliss: A Rereading of *Lolita.*" *College Literature,* 2 (1975), 28–49.

ROWE, W. WOODIN. "Observations on Black Humor in Gogol and Nabokov." *Slavic And East European Journal,* 18 (1974), 392–99.

RUBINSTEIN, E. "Approaching *Lolita.*" *Minnesota Review,* 6 (1966), 361–67.

RUBMAN, LOUIS H. "Creatures and Creators in *Lolita* and 'Death and the Compass.' " *Modern Fiction Studies,* 19 (1973), 433–52.

SEIDEN, MELVIN. "Nabokov and Dostoevsky." *Contemporary Literature,* 13 (1972), 423–44.

STEGNER, PAGE. *Escape Into Aesthetics: The Art Of Vladimir Nabokov,* pp. 102–15.

TWITCHELL, JAMES. "*Lolita* as Bildungsroman." *Genre,* 7 (1974), 272–78.

UPHAUS, ROBERT W. "Nabokov's Kunstler-Roman: Portrait of the Artist as a Dying Man." *Twentieth Century Literature,* 13 (1967), 104–10.

WILLIAMS, CAROL T. "Nabokov's Dialectical Structure." *Wisconsin Studies In Contemporary Literature,* 8 (1967), 261–67; rpt. in *Nabokov: The Man And His Work,* ed. L. S. Dembo, pp. 176–82.

WINSTON, MATHEW. "*Lolita* and the Dangers of Fiction." *Twentieth Century Literature,* 21 (1975), 421–27.

Reviews
ALVAREZ, A. " 'A Tale of a Tub' for Our Time." *Saturday Review,* 13 June 1970, pp. 27–29, 45.

LOOK AT THE HARLEQUINS! (1974)

Reviews
RABAN, JONATHAN. "Exiles: New Fiction." *Encounter,* 44, No.6 (1975), 79–81.

MARY (Mashenka, 1926)

Reviews
HULTQUIST, MARIANNE K. "Early Nabokov." *Prairie Schooner,* 45 (1971), 276–77.

MELANCON, MICHAEL S. *New Orleans Review,* 3 (1973), 198–99.

O'HARA, J. D. *Saturday Review,* 28 November 1970, pp. 37, 47.

PALE FIRE (1962)

ALTER, ROBERT. *Partial Magic,* pp. 183–217.

BERBEROVA, NINA. "The Mechanics of *Pale Fire.*" *Triquarterly,* No.17 (1970), pp. 147–59; rpt. in *Nabokov: Criticism, Reminiscences, Translations And Tributes,* ed. Alfred Appel Jr. and Charles Newman, pp. 147–59.

FIELD, ANDREW. "Pale Fire: The Labyrinth of a Great Novel." *Triquarterly,* No.8 (1967), pp. 13–36.

FLOWER, TIMOTHY F. "The Scientific Art of Nabokov's 'Pale Fire.' " *Criticism,* 17 (1975), 223–33.

FOWLER, DOUGLAS. *Reading Nabokov,* pp. 91–121.

LYONS, JOHN O. "*Pale Fire* and the Fine Art of Annotation." *Wisconsin Studies In Contemporary Literature,* 8 (1967), 242–49; rpt. in *Nabokov: The Man And His Work,* ed. L. S. Dembo, pp. 157–64.

MCCARTHY, MARY. "A Bolt from the Blue," in her *The Writing On The Wall And Other Literary Essays,* pp. 15–34.

MORTON, DONALD E. *Vladimir Nabokov,* pp. 104–27.

PILON, KEVIN. "A Chronology of *Pale Fire.*" *Russian Literature Triquarterly,* No.3 (1972), pp. 370–77.

ROTH, PHYLLIS A. "The Psychology of the Double in Nabokov's *Pale Fire.*" *Essays In Literature,* 2 (1975), 209–29.

STARK, JOHN. "'Borges' 'Tlön, Uqbar, Orbis Tertius' and Nabokov's *Pale Fire:* Literature of Exhaustion." *Texas Studies In Literature And Language,* 14 (1972), 139–45.

STEGNER, PAGE. *Escape Into Aesthetics: The Art Of Vladimir Nabokov,* pp. 116–32.

PNIN (1957)

FOWLER, DOUGLAS. *Reading Nabokov,* pp. 122-46.

GORDON, AMBROSE, JR. "The Double Pnin," in *Nabokov: The Man And His Work,* ed. L. S. Dembo, pp. 144-56.

GRAMS, PAUL. "*Pnin:* The Biographer as Meddler." *Russian Literature Triquarterly,* No.3 (1972), pp. 360-69.

MIZENER, ARTHUR. "The Seriousness of Vladimir Nabokov." *Sewanee Review,* 76 (1968), 655-64.

MORTON, DONALD E. *Vladimir Nabokov,* pp. 84-101.

NICOL, CHARLES. "Pnin's History." *Novel,* 4 (1971), 197-200.

STEGNER, PAGE. *Escape Into Aesthetics: The Art Of Vladimir Nabokov,* pp. 90-101.

WEIL, IRWIN. "Odyssey of a Translator," in *Nabokov: Criticism, Reminiscences, Translations And Tributes,* ed. Alfred Appel Jr. and Charles Newman, pp. 272-75.

THE REAL LIFE OF SEBASTIAN KNIGHT (1941)

BRUFFEE, K. A. "Form and Meaning in Nabokov's *Real Life Of Sebastian Knight:* An Example of Elegaic Romance." *Modern Language Quarterly,* 34 (1973), 180-90.

FROMBERG, SUSAN. "The Unwritten Chapters in *The Real Life Of Sebastian Knight.*" *Modern Fiction Studies,* 13 (1967/8), 427-42.

MORTON, DONALD E. *Vladimir Nabokov,* pp. 42-53.

NICOL, CHARLES. "The Mirrors of Sebastian Knight," in *Nabokov: The Man And His Work,* ed. L. S. Dembo, pp. 85-94.

OLCOTT, ANTHONY. "The Author's Special Intention: A Study of *The Real Life Of Sebastian Knight.*" *Russian Literature Triquarterly,* No.3 (1972), pp. 342-59.

PURDY, STROTHER B. "Solus Rex: Nabokov and the Chess Novel." *Modern Fiction Studies,* 14 (1968/9), 384-87.

STEGNER, S. PAGE. *Escape Into Aesthetics: The Art Of Vladimir Nabokov,* pp. 63-75.

––––––. "The Immortality of Art—Vladimir Nabokov's *The Real Life Of Sebastian Knight.*" *Southern Review,* NS, 2 (1966), 286-96.

STUART, DABNEY. "*The Real Life Of Sebastian Knight:* Angles of Perception." *Modern Language Quarterly,* 29 (1968), 312-28.

TRANSPARENT THINGS (1972)

MORTON, DONALD E. *Vladimir Nabokov,* pp. 142-46.

Reviews

ALTER, ROBERT. "Mirrors for Immortality." *Saturday Review,* 11 November 1972, pp. 72-74, 76.

KARLINSKY, SIMON. "Russian Transparencies." *Saturday Review,* January 1973, pp. 44-45.

LEVINE, JUNE PERRY. "States of Being." *Prairie Schooner,* 48 (1974), 85-87.

RABAN, JONATHAN. "Transparent Likenesses: New Novels." *Encounter,* 41, No.3 (1973), 74-76.

WEEKS, EDWARD. *Atlantic Monthly,* 230, No.6 (1972), 141-42.

DIE NACHTWACHEN DES BONAVENTURA (Author Unknown, 1804)

GILLESPIE, GERALD. "Bonaventura's Romantic Agony: Prevision of an Art of Existential Despair." *MLN,* 85 (1970), 697-726.

NĀGAR, AMRTLĀL (Hindi, 1916-)

AMRIT AUR VISH (1965)

WAJAHAT, ASGHAR. *Mahfil,* 5, No.1/2 (1968/9), 121-24.

NAIPAUL, SHIVA (Trinidad, 1945-)

FIREFLIES (1970)

NIVEN, ALASTAIR. "A Sophisticated Talent." *Journal Of Commonwealth Literature,* 8, No.1 (1973), 131-33.

Reviews

GATHORNE-HARDY, J. "Snow, Flak and Sunshine." *London Magazine,* NS 10, No.11 (1971), 98-100.

HESS, LINDA. *Saturday Review,* 20 March 1971, p. 37; rpt: *Review,* No.4/5 (1971/2), pp. 97-98.

THORPE, MICHAEL. "Laws of Life." *Encounter,* 38, No.6 (1972), 71-72.

NAIPAUL, VIDIADHAR SURAJPRASAD (West Indian, 1932-)

GENERAL

BOXILL, ANTHONY. "V. S. Naipaul's Starting Point." *Journal Of Commonwealth Literature,* 10, No.1 (1975), 1-9.

DERRICK, A. C. "Naipaul's Technique as a Novelist." *Journal Of Commonwealth Literature,* No.7 (1969), pp. 32-44.

GAREBIAN, KEITH. "V. S. Naipaul's Negative Sense of Place." *Journal Of Commonwealth Literature,* 10, No.1 (1975), 23-35.

HAMMNER, ROBERT D. "V. S. Naipaul: A Selected Bibliography." *Journal Of Commonwealth Literature,* 10, No.1 (1975), 36-44.

LACOVIA, R. M. "The Medium Is the Divide: An Examination of V. S. Naipaul's Early Works." *Black Images,* 1, No.2 (1972), 3-6.

MACDONALD, BRUCE F. "Symbolic Action in Three of V.S. Naipaul's Novels." *Journal Of Commonwealth Literature,* 9, No.3 (1975), 41-52.

MAES-JELINEK, HENA. "V. S. Naipaul: A Commonwealth Writer?" *Revue Des Langues Vivantes,* 33 (1967), 499-513.

MELLORS, JOHN. "Mimics into Puppets: The Fiction of V. S. Naipaul." *London Magazine,* NS 15, No.6 (1976), 117-21.

NARASIMHAIAH, C. D. " 'Somewhere Something has Snapped.' " *Indian Horizons,* 21, No.4 (1972), 37-50.

ORMEROD, DAVID. "In a Derelict Land: The Novels of V. S. Naipaul." *Contemporary Literature,* 9 (1968), 74-90.

ROHLEHR, GORDON. "The Ironic Approach: The Novels of V. S. Naipaul," in *The Islands In Between,* ed. Louis James, pp. 121-39.

THEROUX, PAUL. *V. S. Naipaul: An Introduction To His Work.*

THIEME, JOHN. "V. S. Naipaul's Third World: A Not So Free State." *Journal Of Commonwealth Literature,* 10, No.1 (1975), 10-22.

WALSH, WILLIAM. *A Manifold Voice,* pp. 62-85.

GUERILLAS (1975)

MELLORS, JOHN. "Mimics into Puppets: The Fiction of V. S. Naipaul." *London Magazine,* 15, No.6 (1976), 119-21.

Reviews

DEMOTT, BENJAMIN. "Lost Words, Lost Heroes." *Saturday Review,* 15 November 1975, pp. 23-24.

SPURLING, JOHN. "The Novelist as Dictator: New Fiction." *Encounter,* 45, No.6 (1975), 73-76.

A HOUSE FOR MR BISWAS (1961)

BLODGETT, HARRIET. "Beyond Trinidad: Five Novels by V. S. Naipaul." *South Atlantic Quarterly,* 73 (1974), 395-98.

DAVIS, BARRIE. "The Personal Sense of a Society-Minority View: Aspects of the 'East Indian' Novel in the West Indies." *Studies In The Novel,* 4 (1972), 291-95.

FIDO, MARTIN. "Mr Biswas and Mr. Polly." *Ariel: A Review Of International English Literature,* 5, No.4 (1974), 30-37.

MACDONALD, BRUCE F. "Symbolic Action in Three of V. S. Naipaul's Novels." *Journal Of Commonwealth Literature,* 9, No.3 (1975), 43-47.

ORMEROD, DAVID. "Theme and Image in V. S. Naipaul's *A House For Mr. Biswas.*" *Texas Studies In Literature And Language,* 8 (1967), 589–602.

RAMCHAND, KENNETH. *The West Indian Novel And Its Background,* pp. 189–204.

ROHLEHR, GORDON. "The Ironic Approach: The Novels of V. S. Naipaul," in *The Islands In Between,* ed. Louis James, pp. 132–38.

WALSH, WILLIAM. *A Manifold Voice,* pp. 70–77.

THE MIMIC MEN (1967)

BLODGETT, HARRIET. "Beyond Trinidad: Five Novels by V. S. Naipaul." *South Atlantic Quarterly,* 73 (1974), 400–3.

MACDONALD, BRUCE F. "Symbolic Action in Three of V. S. Naipaul's Novels." *Journal Of Commonwealth Literature,* 9 No.3 (1975), 47–52.

WALSH, WILLIAM. *A Manifold Voice,* pp. 78–85.

Reviews

BELOFF, MAX. "Verandahs of Impotence." *Encounter,* 29, No.4 (1967), 87–90.

FIELD, J. C. "The Literary Scene: 1968–1970." *Revue Des Langues Vivantes,* 36 (1970), 660–62.

MCALEER, JOHN H. *Literature East And West,* 14 (1970), 292.

MILLER, KARL. "V. S. Naipaul and the New Order." *Kenyon Review,* 29 (1967), 685–98.

PLANT, RICHARD. "Caribbean Seesaw." *Saturday Review,* 23 December 1967, pp. 32–33.

PRYCE-JONES, DAVID. *London Magazine,* NS 7, No.2 (1967), 82–84.

MR. STONE AND THE KNIGHTS COMPANION (1964)

BLODGETT, HARRIET. "Beyond Trinidad: Five Novels by V. S. Naipaul." *South Atlantic Quarterly,* 73 (1974), 398–400.

BOXILL, ANTHONY. "The Concept of Spring in V. S. Naipaul's Mr. Stone and the Knights Companion." *Ariel: A Review Of International English Literature,* 5, No.4 (1974), 21–28.

THE MYSTIC NASSEUR (1957)

BLODGETT, HARRIET. "Beyond Trinidad: Five Novels by V. S. Naipaul." *South Atlantic Quarterly,* 73 (1974), 392–95.

BOXILL, ANTHONY. "The Physical and Historical Environment of V. S. Naipaul's *The Mystic Masseur* and *The Suffrage Of Elvira.*" *Journal Of Canadian Fiction,* 3, No.4 (1975), 52–53.

THE SUFFRAGE OF ELVIRA (1958)

BLODGETT, HARRIET. "Beyond Trinidad: Five Novels by V. S. Naipaul." *South Atlantic Quarterly,* 73 (1974), 390–92.

BOXILL, ANTHONY. "The Physical and Historical Environment of V. S. Naipaul'ls *The Mystic Masseur* and *The Suffrage Of Elvira.*" *Journal Of Canadian Fiction,* 3, No.4 (1975), 53–55.

NANDI, MOTI (Bengali)

NAYAKER PRABESH O PRASTHAN (1969)

Reviews

MUKHERJEE, SUJIT. *Indian Literature,* 13, No.2 (1970), 125–29.

MUKHERJEE, SUJIT. *Mahfil,* 6, No.2/3 (1970), 139–43.

NARAYAN, RASIPURAM KRISHNASWAMY (Indian, 1906–)

GENERAL

CHEW, SHIRLEY. "A Proper Detachment: The Novels of R. K. Narayan." *Southern Review: Literary And Interdisciplinary Essays,* 5 (1972), 147–59; rpt. in *Readings In Commonwealth Literature,* ed. William Walsh, pp. 58–74.

GAREBIAN, KEITH. " 'The Spirit of Place' in R. K. Narayan." *World Literature Written In English,* 14 (1975), 291–99.

———. "Strategy and Theme in the Art of R. K. Narayan." *Ariel: A Review Of International English Literature,* 5, No.4 (1974), 70–81.

GHAI, T. C. "Pattern and Significance in R. K. Narayan's Novels." *Indian Literature,* 18, No.3 (1975), 33–58.

HARREX, S. C. "R. K. Narayan and the Temple of Indian Fiction." *Meanjin,* 31 (1972), 397–407.

HARTLEY, LOIS. "In 'Malgudi' with R. K. Narayan." *Literature East And West,* 9 (1965), 87–90.

MCCUTCHION, DAVID. "The Indian Novel in English." *Studies In The Novel,* 4 (1972), 307–12.

MUKHERJEE, MEENAKSHI. "The Storyteller of Malgudi." *Indian Horizons,* 21, No.1 (1972), 44–49.

NAZARETH, PETER. "R. K. Narayan: Novelist." *English Studies In Africa,* 8 (1965), 121–34.

PARAMESWARAN, UMA. "On the Theme of Paternal Love in the Novels of R. K. Narayan." *International Fiction Review,* 1 (1974), 146–48.

PARAMESWARAN, UMA. "Rogues in R. K. Narayan's Fiction." *Literature East And West,* 18 (1974), 203–15.

RAO, V. PANDURANGA. "The Art of R. K. Narayan." *Journal Of Commonwealth Literature,* No.5 (1968), pp. 29–40.

SRINIVASA IYENGAR, K. R. *Indian Writing In English,* pp. 358–85.

VENKATACHARI, K. "R. K. Narayan's Novels: Acceptance of Life." *Indian Literature,* 13, No.1 (1970), 73–87.

WILLIAMS, HAYDN MOORE. "R. K. Narayan and R. Prawer Jhabvala: Two Interpreters of Modern India." *Literature East And West,* 16 (1972), 1136–54.

THE BACHELOR OF ARTS (1937)

NAZARETH, PETER. "R. K. Narayan: Novelist." *English Studies In Africa,* 8 (1965), 121–34.

THE ENGLISH TEACHER (1945)

VENKATACHARI, K. "R. K. Narayan's Novels: Acceptance of Life." *Indian Literature,* 13, No.1 (1970), 76–79.

THE GUIDE (1958)

GHAI, T. C. "Pattern and Significance in R. K. Narayan's Novels." *Indian Literature,* 18, No.3 (1975), 47–50.

HARREX, S. C. "R. K. Narayan and the Temple of Indian Fiction." *Meanjin,* 31 (1972), 404–06.

MUKHERJEE, MEENAKSHI. "The Storyteller of Malgudi." *Indian Horizons,* 21, No.1 (1972), 46–48.

MURTI, K. V. SURYANARAYANA. "The Theme of Salvation: Treatment by Mulk Raj Anand And R. K. Narayan." *Triveni,* 34, No.3 (1965), 55–58.

PARAMESWARAN, UMA. "Rogues in R. K. Narayan's Fiction." *Literature East And West,* 18 (1974), 207–14.

RAO, S. SUBBA. " 'The Guide': A Glimpse of Narayan's Attitude and Achievement." *Triveni,* 36, No.2 (1967), 65–67.

THE MAN-EATER OF MALGUDI (1961)

GEROW, EDWIN. "The Quintessential Narayan." *Literature East And West,* 10 (1966), 1–18.

NAIK, M. K. "Theme and Form in R. K. Narayan's *The Man-Eater Of Malgudi.*" *Journal Of Commonwealth Literature,* 10, No.3 (1975), 65–72.

WALSH, WILLIAM. *A Manifold Voice,* pp. 13–20.

MR. SAMPATH (1949)

HARREX, S. C. "R. K. Narayan's The Printer of Malgudi." *Literature East And West,* 13 (1969), 68–82.

PARAMESWARAN, UMA. "Rogues in R. K. Narayan's Fiction." *Literature East and East,* 18 (1974), 203-5.

THE PRINTER OF MALGUDI see MR. SAMPATH

THE SWEET-VENDOR see THE VENDOR OF SWEETS

THE VENDOR OF SWEETS (1969)

ARGYLE, BARRY. "Narayan's *The Sweet Vendor.*" *Journal Of Commonwealth Literature,* 7, No.1 (1972), 35-44.

GHAI, T. C. "Pattern and Significance in R. K. Narayan's Novels." *Indian Literature,* 18, No.3 (1975), 53-56.

RAO, CH. SAMBASIVA. "R. K. Narayan's 'The Vendor of Sweets'— A Study." *Triveni,* 39, No.4 (1971), 60-64.

RAO, S. SUBBA RAO. "R. K. Narayan's Art and 'The Vendor of Sweets.' " *Triveni,* 37, No.4 (1969), 37-42.

WALSH, WILLIAM. *A Manifold Voice,* pp. 20-22.

Reviews
SAMSTAG, NICHOLAS. "Pandemonium in the Candy Store." *Saturday Review,* 3 June 1967, p. 35.

WALSH, WILLIAM. "The Spiritual and the Practical." *Journal Of Commonwealth Literature,* No.5 (1968), pp. 121-23.

WAITING FOR THE MAHATMA (1955)

BATRA, SHAKTI. "Impact of Gandhi on Indian Writing." *Indian Literature,* 17, No.3 (1974), 38-51.

NATHANSEN, HENRI (Danish, 1868-1944)

AF HUGO DAVIDS LIV (1917)

BREDSDORFF, ELIAS. "George Brandes as a Fictional Character in Some Danish Novels and Plays." *Scandinavian Studies,* 45 (1973), 13-18.

NATSUME SŌSEKI (Japanese, 1867-1916)
pseudonym of Kinnosuke Natsume

GENERAL

BIDDLE, WARD WILLIAM. "The Authenticity of Natsume Sōseki." *Monumenta Nipponica,* 28 (1973), 391-418.

ETŌ, JUN. "Natsume Sōseki: A Japanese Meiji Intellectual." *American Scholar,* 34 (1965), 603-19.

MCCLELLAN, EDWIN. "The Impressionistic Tendency in Some Modern Japanese Writers." *Chicago Review,* 17, No.4 (1965), 48-52.

————. *Two Japanese Novelists: Sōseki And Tōson,* pp. 3-15.

MATSUI, SAKUKO. "East and West in Natsume Sōseki: The Formation of a Modern Japanese Novelist." *Meanjin,* 26 (1967), 282-94.

AND THEN—(Sorekara, 1910)

MCCLELLAN, EDWIN. *Two Japanese Novelists: Sōseki And Tōson,* pp. 34-41.

YU, BEONGCHEON. *Natsume Soseki,* pp. 80-88.

AUTUMN WIND

MCCLELLAN, EDWIN. *Two Japanese Novelists: Sōseki And Tōson,* pp. 26-31.

BOTCHAN see LITTLE MASTER

THE GATE (Mon, 1911)

MCCLELLAN, EDWIN. *Two Japanese Novelists: Sōseki And Tōson,* pp. 42-45.

YU, BEONGCHEON. *Natsume Soseki,* pp. 91-98.

Reviews
SIBLEY, WILLIAM F. *Monumenta Nipponica,* 27 (1972), 455-57.

GRASS ON THE WAYSIDE (Michikusa, 1915)

BIDDLE, WARD WILLIAM. "The Authenticity of Natusume Sōseki." *Monumenta Nipponica,* 28 (1973), 415-18.

MCCLELLAN, EDWIN. *Two Japanese Novelists: Sōseki And Tōson,* pp. 59-69.

MIYOSHI, MASAO. *Accomplices Of Silence,* pp. 62-72.

YU, BEONGCHEON. *Natsume Soseki,* pp. 139-46.

Reviews
MATHY, FRANCIS. *Monumenta Nipponica,* 26 (1971), 240-42.

RYAN, MARLEIGH. *Journal Of The American Oriental Society,* 93 (1973), 91.

YOSHIO IWAMOTO. *Harvard Journal Of Asiatic Studies,* 30 (1970), 258-63.

THE HEART

MCCLELLAN, EDWIN. *Two Japanese Novelists: Sōseki And Tōson,* pp. 52-58.

I AM A CAT (Wagahai wa Neko de Aru, 1905-7)

MCCLELLAN, EDWIN. *Two Japanese Novelists: Sōseki And Tōson,* pp. 15-19.

YU, BEONGCHEON. *Natsume Soseki,* pp. 39-44.

KOKORO

ETŌ, JUN. "Natsume Sōseki: A Japanese Meiji Intellectual." *American Scholar,* 34 (1965), 609-19.

YU, BEONGCHEON. *Natsume Soseki,* pp. 123-34.

LIGHT AND DARKNESS (Meian)

BIDDLE, WARD WILLIAM. "The Authenticity of Natsume Sōseki." *Monumenta Nipponica,* 28 (1973), 418-23.

MIYOSHI, MASAO. *Accomplices Of Silence,* pp. 72-92.

YU, BEONGCHEON. *Natsume Soseki,* pp. 146-62.

Reviews
NAFF, WILLIAM E. *Monumenta Nipponica,* 27 (1972), 114-17.

RIMER, THOMAS. *Literature East And West,* 17 (1973), 145-47.

RUBIN, JAY. *Journal Of The American Oriental Society,* 93 (1973), 627-28.

LITTLE MASTER (Botchan)

MCCLELLAN, EDWIN. *Two Japanese Novelists: Sōseki And Tōson,* pp. 19-22.

YU, BEONGCHEON. *Natsume Soseki,* pp. 46-48.

LOITERING see GRASS ON THE WAYSIDE

MICHIKUSA see GRASS ON THE WAYSIDE

THE MINER (Kofu)

YU, BEONGCHEON. *Natsume Soseki,* pp. 64-69.

MON see THE GATE

PILLOW OF GRASS

MCCLELLAN, EDWIN. *Two Japanese Novelists: Sōseki And Tōson,* pp. 23-26.

THE POPPY (Gubinjinso, 1908)

YU, BEONGCHEON. *Natsume Soseki,* pp. 60-64.

SANSHIRŌ (1908)

MCCLELLAN, EDWIN. *Two Japanese Novelists: Sōseki And Tōson,* pp. 31-34.

YU, BEONGCHEON. *Natsume Soseki,* pp. 72-78.

THE THREE-CORNERED WORLD (Kasamakura, 1906)

Reviews
MATHY, FRANCIS. *Monumenta Nipponica,* 22 (1967), 235–37.

UNTIL AFTER THE SPRING EQUINOX (Higan Sugi Made, 1912)

YU, BEONGCHEON. *Natsume Soseki,* pp. 107–14.

THE WANDERER (Kōjin, 1914)

McCLELLAN, EDWIN. *Two Japanese Novelists: Sōseki And Tōson,* pp. 45–51.

YU, BEONGCHEON. *Natsume Soseki,* pp. 114–23.

Reviews
McCLELLAN, EDWIN. *Journal Of The American Oriental Society,* 90 (1970), 383–84.

PUTZAR, ED. *Arizona Quarterly,* 24 (1968), 85–86.

NAUBERT, CHRISTIANE BENEDICTE (German, 1756–1819)

ALF VON DULMEN

HADLEY, MICHAEL. *The German Novel In 1790,* pp. 132–35.

BARBARA BLOMBERG

HADLEY, MICHAEL. *The German Novel In 1790,* pp. 128–32.

BRUNILDE

HADLEY, MICHAEL. *The German Novel In 1790,* pp. 123–25.

MERKWURDIGE BEGEBENHEITEN DER GRAFLICHEN FAMILIE VON WALLIS

HADLEY, MICHAEL. *The German Novel In 1790,* pp. 206–209.

WERNER, GRAF VON BERBURG

HADLEY, MICHAEL. *The German Novel In 1790,* pp. 125–28.

NAVARRE, YVES

LADY BLACK (1971)

Reviews
O'CONNELL, DAVID. *French Review,* 46 (1972), 446–47.

NAVARRETE, RAÚL

LUZ QUE SE DUERME (1969)

Reviews
HOLDSWORTH, CAROLE A. *Hispania,* 54 (1971), 209.

NAVARRO, NOEL (Cuban, 1931–)

EL PLANO INCLINADO

MENTON, SEYMOUR. *Prose Fiction Of The Cuban Revolution,* pp. 92–94.

NEERA

GENERAL

PACIFICI, SERGIO. *The Modern Italian Novel: From Capuana To Tozzi,* pp. 54–60.

LYDIA

PACIFICI, SERGIO. *The Modern Italian Novel: From Capuana To Tozzi,* pp. 58–60.

NEKRASOV, VIKTOR (Russian, 1911–)

GENERAL

CARMEL, HERMAN. "Viktor Nekrasov: Pioneer of Renaissance in Post-Stalin Russian Prose." *Books Abroad,* (1966), 381–85.

NÉMETH, LÁSZLÓ (Hungarian, 1901–1975)

REVULSION (Iszony, 1947)

Reviews
STILWELL, ROBERT L. "Grounds for Despair." *Saturday Review,* 12 March 1966, p. 36.

NERVO, AMADO (Mexican, 1870–1919)

GENERAL

BRATSAS, DOROTHY. "The Problem of Ideal Love in Nervo's Novels." *Romance Notes,* 9 (1967), 244–48.

NEUTSCH, ERIK (German, 1931–)

SPUR DER STEINE

PARKES, K. S. "Criticism of East German Society in Some Incidents in Erik Neutsch's Novel 'Spur der Steine.' " *German Life And Letters,* 25 (1971/2), 261–69.

SCHLANT, ERNESTINE. "Fiction in the German Democratic Republic During the Past Decade." *Modern Fiction Studies,* 21 (1975), 148–49.

NGUBIAH, STEPHEN

A CURSE FROM GOD

Reviews
TEJANI, BAHADUR. "*A Curse From God* By Stephen Ngubiah." *African Literature Today,* 5 (1971), 148–50.

NGUGI WA THIONG 'O, JAMES (Kenyan, 1938–)

GENERAL

LARSON, CHARLES R. "Characters and Modes of Characterization: Chinua Achebe, James Ngugi, and Peter Abrahams," in his *The Emergence Of African Fiction,* rev. ed., pp. 155–60.

REED, JOHN. "James Ngugi and the African Novel." *Journal Of Commonwealth Literature,* No.1 (1965), 117–21.

A GRAIN OF WHEAT (1967)

GORDIMER, NADINE. "Modern African Writing." *Michigan Quarterly Review,* 9 (1970), 226.

IKIDDEH, IME. "James Ngugi as Novelist." *African Literature Today,* No.2 (1969), pp. 8–10.

LARSON, CHARLES R. "The 'Situational' Novel: The Novels of James Ngugi," in his *The Emergence Of African Fiction,* rev. ed., pp. 138–46.

MONKMAN, LESLIE. "Kenya and the New Jerusalem in *A Grain Of Wheat.*" *African Literature Today,* 7 (1975), 111–16.

PALMER, EUSTACE. *An Introduction To The African Novel,* pp. 24–47.

Reviews
ELDERS, DEREK. *African Literature Today,* No.1 (1968), pp. 51–53.

REED, JOHN. "Ngugi's New Strength." *Journal Of Commonwealth Literature,* No.5 (1968), pp. 135–36.

THE RIVER BETWEEN (1965)

CARTEY, WILFRED. *Whispers From a Continent,* pp. 88–93.

GORDIMER, NADINE. "Modern African Writing." *Michigan Quarterly Review,* 9 (1970), 225–26.

GURR, ANDREW. "Engagement is not Marriage: Perspectives on Cultural Conflict in East Africa." *Mosaic,* 5, No.2 (1971/2), 76–77.

KNIPP, THOMAS R. "Two Novels from Kenya: J. Ngugi." *Books Abroad,* 41 (1967), 393–97.

LARSON, CHARLES R. "The 'Situational' Novel: The Novels of Jame Ngugi," in his *The Emergence Of African Fiction,* rev. ed., pp. 135–38.

PALMER, EUSTACE. *An Introduction To The African Novel,* pp. 11–24.

WILLIAMS, LLOYD. "Religion and Life in James Ngugi's *The River Between.*" *African Literature Today,* 5 (1971), 54–65.

Reviews
AMOSU, MARGARET. *Black Orpheus,* No.20 (1966), pp. 62–63.

WEEP NOT, CHILD (1964)

CARTEY, WILFRED. *Whispers From a Continent,* pp. 13–20.

IKIDDEH, IME. "James Ngugi as Novelist." *African Literature Today,* No.2 (1969), pp. 3–8.

KNIPP, THOMAS R. "Two Novels from Kenya: J. Ngugi." *Books Abroad,* 41 (1967), 393–97.

LARSON, CHARLES R. "Characters and Modes of Characterization: Chinua Achebe, James Ngugi, and Peter Abrahams," in his *The Emergence Of African Fiction,* rev. ed., pp. 155–58.

———. "The 'Situational' Novel: The Novels of James Ngugi," in his *The Emergence Of African Fiction,* rev. ed., pp. 121–35.

———. "Things Fall Further Apart—New African Novels." *College Language Association Journal,* 10 (1966/7), 64–65.

PALMER, EUSTACE. *An Introduction To The African Novel,* pp. 1–10.

NGUYEN-DU

KIM-VAN-KIEU

APROBERTS, RUTH. "Vietnamese Classic." *Literature East And West,* 13 (1969), 395–403.

NIANE, DJIBRIL TAMSIR (Mali, ca. 1920–)

SUDIATA (Soundjata, 1960)

GLEASON, JUDITH ILLSLEY. *This Africa,* pp. 44–48.

NIEVO, IPPOLITO (Italian, 1831–1861)

THE CASTLE OF FRATTA (Le Confessioni di un Italiano, 1858)

PACIFICI, SERGIO. *The Modern Italian Novel: From Manzoni To Svevo,* pp. 58–72.

NINUS (Author Unknown)

PERRY, BEN EDWIN. *The Ancient Romances,* pp. 153–66.

NIVEN, FREDERICK JOHN (Canadian, 1878–1944)

GENERAL

NEW, WILLIAM H. "A Life and Four Landscapes: Frederick John Niven." *Canadian Literature,* No.32 (1967), pp. 15–28; rpt. in his *Articulating West,* pp. 3–19.

THE FLYING YEARS (1935)

GROSS, KONRAD. "Looking Back in Anger? Frederick Niven, W. O. Mitchell, and Robert Kroetsch on the History of the Canadian West." *Journal Of Canadian Fiction,* 3, No.2 (1974), 49–51.

NIZAN, PAUL (French, 1905–1940)

ANTOINE BLOYÉ (1933)

ELMAN, RICHARD. "About 'Antoine Bloy.' " *Columbia Forum,* NS, 1, No.4 (1972), 40–42.

LA CONSPIRATION (1938)

REDFERN, W. D. "A Vigorous Corpse: Paul Nizan and La Conspiration." *Romanic Review,* 59 (1968), 278–95.

NODIER, CHARLES (French, 1780–1844)

GENERAL

DIJKSTRA, BRAM. "The Androgyne In Nineteenth-Century Art and Literature." *Comparative Literature,* 26 (1974), 62–73.

PORTER, LAURENCE M. "Charles Nodier and Pierre-Simon Ballanche." *Orbis Litterarum,* 27 (1972), 229–36.

SWITZER, RICHARD. "Charles Nodier and the Introduction of Illyrian Literature into France.' *Mosaic,* 6, No.4 (1973), 223–35.

LA FÉE AUX MIETTES

MAPLES, ROBERT J. B. "Individuation in Nodier's *La Fée Aux Miettes.*" *Studies In Romanticism,* 8 (1968), 43–64.

L'HISTOIRE DU ROI DE BOHÈME

PORTER, LAURENCE M. "The Stylistic Debate of Charles Nodier's *Histoire Du Roi De Bohème.*" *Nineteenth-Century French Studies,* 1 (1972), 21–32.

LYDIE OU LA RESURRECTION

BELL, SARAH F. "Charles Nodier, Imitator of Dante." *Romance Notes,* 11 (1970), 544–48.

SMARRA OU LES DÉMONS DE LA NUIT (1821)

PORTER, LAURENCE M. "The Forbidden City: A Psychoanalytical Interpretation of Nodier's *Smarra.*" *Symposium,* 26 (1972), 331–48.

TRILBY OU LE LUTIN D'ARGAIL (1822)

PORTER, LAURENCE M. "Towards a Prehistory of Depth Psychology in French Romanticism: Temptation and Repression in Nodier's *Trilby.*" *Nineteenth-Century French Studies,* 2 (1974), 97–110.

NOLL, DIETER (German)

DIE ABENTEUER DES WERNER HOLT

ZIPES, JACK D. "Growing Pains in the Contemporary German Novel—East and West." *Mosaic,* 5, No.3 (1971/2), 10–11.

NOSSACK, HANS ERICH (German, 1901–1977)

GENERAL

BATTS, MICHAEL. "The Shadow-Line: the Grenze-Motif in the Works of Gaiser, Kasack, and Nossack." *Humanities Association Bulletin,* 22, No.3 (1971), 46–49.

PROCHNIK, PETER. "Controlling Thoughts in the Work of Hans Erich Nossack." *German Life And Letters,* 19 (1965), 68–74.

THE D'ARTHEZ CASE (Der Fall d'Arthez, 1968)

Reviews
ZOHN, HARRY. *Saturday Review,* 30 October 1971, pp. 50, 52–53.

THE IMPOSSIBLE PROOF (Unmögliche Beweisaufnahme, 1959)

Reviews
POTOKER, EDWARD M. "Desperation as His Judge and Jury." *Saturday Review,* 30 March 1968, pp. 28–29.

INTERVIEW MIT DEM TODE (1948)

WHITE, JOHN J. *Mythology In The Modern Novel,* pp. 182–86.

NEKYIA: BERICHT EINES ÜBERLEBENDEN (1947)

WHITE, JOHN J. *Mythology In The Modern Novel,* pp. 218–28.

WAIT FOR NOVEMBER (Spatestens im November, 1955)

BATTS, MICHAEL S. "Tristan and Isolde in Modern Literature: L'éternal Retour." *Seminar,* 5 (1969), 79-91.

NOVAK, SLOBODAN (Croatian, 1924-)
ODORS, GOLD AND INCENSE (Mirisi, Zlato i Tamjan, 1957)

MATEJIĆ, MATEJA. "On the Contemporary Yugoslav Novel." *Canadian Slavic Studies,* 5 (1971), 367-68.

NOVALIS (German, 1772-1801) pseudonym of Friedrich Leopold Hardenberg
GENERAL

DAUER, DOROTHEA W. "Early Romanticism and India as Seen by Herder and Novalis." *Kentucky Foreign Language Quarterly,* 12 (1965), 218-24.

MEIN, MARGARET. *A Foretaste Of Proust: A Study Of Proust And His Precursors,* pp. 85-100.

WESSELL, LEONARD P. "Novalis' Revolutionary Religion of Death." *Studies In Romanticism,* 14 (1975), 425-52.

HENRY VON OFTERDINGEN (Heinrich von Ofterdingen, 1799-1800)

BARRACK, CHARLES M. "Conscience in *Heinrich Von Ofterdingen:* Novalis' Metaphysic of the Poet." *Germanic Review,* 46 (1971), 257-84.

FRYE, LAWRENCE O. "The Language of Romantic High Feeling, A Case of Dialog Technique in Hoffmann's *Kater Murr* and Novalis' *Heinrich Von Ofterdingen.*" *Deutsche Vierteljahresschrift Fur Literaturwissenschaft Und Geistegeschichte,* 49 (1975), 529-45.

FURST, LILIAN R. "The Structure of Romantic Agony." *Comparative Literature Studies,* 10 (1973), 125-38.

KAHN, ROBERT L. "Tieck's *Franz Sternbalds Wanderungen* and Novalis' *Heinrich Von Ofterdingen.*" *Studies In Romanticism,* 7 (1967), 49-64.

STOPP, ELISABETH. " 'Übergang vom Roman zur Mythologie': Formal Aspects of the Opening Chapter of Hardenberg's *Heinrich Von Ofterdingen, Part II.*" *Deutsche Vierteljahresschrift Fur Literaturwissenschaft Und Geistegeschichte,* 48 (1974), 318-41.

NOWLAN, ALDEN (Canadian, 1933-)
VARIOUS PERSONS NAMED KEVIN O'BRIEN (1973)

Reviews
CAVANAGH, DAVID. "Time Past, Time Present." *Journal Of Canadian Fiction,* 2, No.4 (1973), 111-12.

McGREGOR, GRANT. *Ariel: A Review Of International English Literature,* 4, No.3 (1973), 112-13.

SUTHERLAND, FRASER. "A Lurking Devil." *Canadian Literature,* No.60 (1974), pp. 119-20.

NÚÑEZ, NICHOLÁS
CÁRCEL DE AMOR

WHINNOM, KEITH. "Nicholas Núñez's Continuation of the *Cárcel De Amor* (Burgos, 1496)," in *Studies In Spanish Literature Of The Golden Age,* ed. R. O. Jones, pp. 357-66.

NWANA, PETER
OMENUKO (1933)

EMENYONU, ERNEST. "Early Fiction in Igbo." *Research In African Literatures,* 4 (1973), 7-20.

NWANKWO, NKEM (Nigerian, 1936-)
DANDA (1964)

MOORE, GERALD. *The Chosen Tongue,* pp. 191-93.

POVEY, JOHN. "The English Language of the Contemporary African Novel." *Critique,* 11, No.3 (1968/9), 89-90.

TAIWO, OLADELE. "*Danda* Revisited: A Reassessment of Nwankwo's Jester." *World Literature Written In English,* 13 (1974), 7-16.

Reviews
DATHORNE, O. R. *Black Orpheus,* No.18 (1965), pp. 59-60.

NWAPA, FLORA (Nigerian, 1931-)
EFURU (1966)

CONDE, MARYSE. "Three Female Writers in Modern Africa: Flora Nwapa, Ama Ata Aidoo and Grace Ogot." *Présence Africaine,* No.82 (1972), 132-43.

LAURENCE, MARGARET. *Long Drums And Cannons,* pp. 187-91.

SCHEUB, HAROLD. "Two African Women." *Revue Des Langues Vivantes,* 37 (1971), 545-58; 664-81.

Reviews
JONES, ELDRED. "Locale and Universe—Three Nigerian Novels." *Journal Of Commonwealth Literature,* No.3 (1967), pp. 129-30.

PALMER, EUSTACE. *African Literature Today,* No.1 (1968), pp. 57-58.

IDU (1970)

EMENYONU, ERNEST N. "Who does Flora Nwapa write for?" *African Literature Today,* 7 (1975), 28-33.

Reviews
JAMES, ADEOLA A. *African Literature Today,* 5 (1971), 150-53.

NYNYCH, STEPHANIE J. (Canadian, 1945-) pseudonym of Colline Caulder
Reviews
COGSWELL, FRED. "Through Other Eyes." *Journal Of Canadian Fiction,* 2, No.2 (1973), 88.

NZEKWU, ONUORA (Nigerian, 1928-)
BLADE AMONG THE BOYS (1962)

GLEASON, JUDITH ILLSLEY. *This Africa,* pp. 172-75.

JULY, ROBERT W. "The African Personality in the African Novel," in *Introduction To African Literature,* ed. Ulli Beier, pp. 223-26.

KILLAM, G. D. "The Novels of Onuora Nzekwu." *African Literature Today,* 5 (1971), 30-35.

POVEY, JOHN. "The Novels of Onuora Nzekwu." *Literature East And West,* 12 (1968), 77-80.

HIGHLIFE FOR LIZARDS (1965)

KILLAM, G. D. "The Novels of Onuora Nzekwu." *African Literature Today,* 5 (1971), 35-40.

LINDFORS, BERNTH. *Folklore In Nigerian Literature,* pp. 42-47.

POVEY, JOHN. "The Novels of Onuora Nzekwu." *Literature East And West,* 12 (1968), 81-83.

WAND OF NOBLE WOOD (1961)

GLEASON, JUDITH ILLSLEY. *This Africa,* pp. 169-72.

KILLAM, G. D. "The Novels of Onuora Nzekwu." *African Literature Today,* 5 (1971), 23-30.

POVEY, JOHN. "The Novels of Onuora Nzekwu." *Literature East And West,* 12 (1968), 68-77.

O

OCANTOS, CARLOS MARIA (Argentine, 1860-1949)

GENERAL

TAYLOR, A. CAREY. "Balzac and the Latin-American Novel," in *Balzac And The Nineteenth Century,* pp. 184–85.

OCHIKUBO MONOGATARI (10th Century) Anon.

Reviews
MISAKO, IIIMURO. *Monumenta Nipponica,* 21 (1966), 420–21.

OE KENZABURO (Japanese, 1935-)

A PERSONAL MATTER (Kojinteki na taiken, 1964)

FALKE, WAYNE. "Japanese Tradition in Kenzaburo Oe's *A Personal Matter.*" *Critique,* 15, No.3 (1974), 43–52.

KIMBALL, ARTHUR G. *Crisis In Identity And Contemporary Japanese Novels,* pp. 140–56.

Reviews
HAAS, ROBERT and TOMI. "Confused Young Man Hung Up in Tokyo." *Saturday Review,* 15 June 1968, p. 31.

HEARSUM, JOHN. "Random times Nine." *London Magazine,* NS 9, No.3 (1969), 101–2.

OERTEL, FRIEDRICH VON

KILBUR, EIN BEITRAG ZUR GESCHICHTE DES SITTLICHEN GANGS MENSCHLICHER NATUR

HADLEY, MICHAEL. *The German Novel In 1790,* pp. 223–30.

O'HAGAN, HOWARD (Canadian, 1902-)

TAY JOHN (1960)

JONES, D. G. *Butterfly On Rock,* pp. 66–68, 70–71.

ONDAATJE, MICHAEL. "O'Hagan's Rough-Edged Chronicle." *Canadian Literature,* No.61 (1974), pp. 24–31.

OKAGAMI (Author Unknown)

Reviews
BERNSTEIN, GAIL. *Literature East And West,* 13 (1969), 198–99.

OKARA, GABRIEL (Nigerian, 1921-)

GENERAL

LINDFORS, BERNTH. "Interview with Gabriel Okara." *World Literature Written In English,* 12, No.2 (1973), 133–41.

THE VOICE (1964)

ANOZIE, SUNDAY O. "The Theme of Alienation And Commitment in Okara's 'The Voice.' " *Association For African Literature In English Bulletin,* No.3 (1965), pp. 54–67.

GOODLEY, NANCY C. "Two Levels of Meaning in Gabriel Okara's *The Voice.*" *College Language Association Journal,* 19 (1976), 312–17.

LAURENCE, MARGARET. *Long Drums And Cannons,* pp. 193–98.

LINDFORS, BERNTH. "Interview with Gabriel Okara." *World Literature Written In English,* 12, No.2 (1973), 135–38.

McDOWELL, ROBERT E. "Three Nigerian Storytellers: Okara, Tutuola, and Ekwensi." *Ball State University Forum,* 10, No.3 (1969), 67–69.

PALMER, EUSTACE. *An Introduction To The African Novel,* pp. 155–67.

———. "Social Comment in the West African Novel." *Studies In The Novel,* 4 (1972), 227–30.

POVEY, JOHN. "The English Language of the Contemporary African Novel." *Critique,* 11, No.3 (1968/9), 91–92.

RAVENSCROFT, ARTHUR. "African Literature V: Novels of Disillusion." *Journal Of Commonwealth Literature,* No.6 (1969), 129–35; rpt. in *Readings In Commonwealth Literature,* ed. William Walsh, pp. 197–203.

ROSCOE, ADRIAN A. *Mother Is Gold,* pp. 113–21.

Reviews
BEIER, ULLI. *Black Orpheus,* No.17 (1965), pp. 60–61.

OKIGBO, CHRISTOPHER (Nigerian, 1932-1967)

GENERAL

PURCELL, JAMES MARK. "Christopher Okigbo (1932–67): Preliminary Checklist of His Books." *Studies In Black Literature,* 4, No.2 (1973), 8–10.

OKLIANSKY, IL'IA GRIGOR'EVICH

GENERAL

EHRENBURG, ILYA. "The Gift of Empathy." *Soviet Studies In Literature,* 3, No.2 (1967), 6–8.

OLBRACT, IVAN (Czechoslovak, 1882-1952) pseudonym of Kamil Zeman

THE BITTER AND THE SWEET

Reviews

LEVIANT, CURT. "A Universal Village." *Saturday Review,* 3 June 1967, pp. 34–35.

OLDENBOURG, ZOÉ (French, 1916–)

THE HEIRS OF THE KINGDOM

Reviews

BORGIN, THOMAS G. *Saturday Review,* 26 June 1971, p. 28.

WEEKS, EDWARD. *Atlantic Monthly,* 228, No.1 (1971), 102.

OLESHA, YURY (Russian, 1899–1960)

GENERAL

NILSSON, NILS ÅKE. "Through the Wrong End of the Binoculars: An Introduction to Jurij Oleša," in *Major Soviet Writers,* ed. Edward J. Brown, pp. 254–79.

SHKLOVSKII, VIKTOR. " 'A Chord Resounds in the Mist.' " *Soviet Studies In Literature,* 11, No.4 (1975), 75–102.

ENVY (Zavist', 1927)

BEAUJOUR, ELIZABETH KLOSTY. *The Invisible Land: A Study Of The Artistic Imagination Of Iurii Olesha,* pp. 38–58.

BERCZYNSKI, T. S. "Kavalerov's Monologue in *Envy:* A Baroque Soliloquy." *Russian Literature Triquarterly,* Nos.1/2 (1971), 375–85.

HARKINS, WILLIAM E. "The Theme of Sterility in Olesha's *Envy.*" *Slavic Review,* 25 (1966), 443–57; rpt. in *Major Soviet Writers,* ed. Edward J. Brown, pp. 280–94.

PIPER, D. G. B. "Yuriy Olesha's *Zavist':* an Interpretation." *Slavic And East European Journal,* 48 (1970), 27–43.

REEVE, F. D. *The Russian Novel,* pp. 346–59.

WILSON, WAYNE P. "The Objective of Jurij Oleša's *Envy.*" *Slavic And East European Journal,* 18 (1974), 31–40.

OLLER, NARCÍS (Spanish, 1846–1930)

LA FEBRE D'OR (1890)

YATES, ALAN. "The Creation of Narcís Oller's *La Febre D'Or.*" *Bulletin Of Hispanic Studies,* 52 (1975), 55–77.

OLSSON, HAGAR (Finnish, 1893–)

CHITAMBO (1933)

SCHOOLFIELD, GEORGE C. "Hagar Olsson's *Chitambo:* Anniversary Thoughts on Names and Structure." *Scandinavian Studies,* 45 (1973), 223–62.

THE WOODCARVER AND DEATH

Reviews

SPECTOR, ROBERT D. *American Scandinavian Review,* 54 (1966), 410–11.

ONETTI, JUAN CARLOS (Uruguayan, 1909–)

GENERAL

AINSA, FERNANDO. "Onetti's Devices." Trans. by Cedric Busette." *Latin American Literary Review,* 3, No.5 (1974), 81–97.

KADIR, DJELAL, Comp. "Chronology." *Review,* No.16 (1975), pp. 6–8.

A BRIEF LIFE (La vida breve, 1950)

ADAMS, M. IAN. *Three Authors Of Alienation: Bombal, Onetti, Carpentier,* pp. 72–77.

DEREDITA, JOHN. "Dream and Spatial Form." *Review,* No.16 (1975), pp. 19–23.

GERTEL, ZUNILDA. "The Fragment as Disintegrated Unit." Trans. Andrée Conrad. *Review,* No.16 (1975), pp. 24–30.

HAYDEN, ROSE LEE. *An Existential Focus On Some Novels Of The River Plate.*

LEVINE, GEORGE. "Anguish of the Ordinary." *Review,* No.16 (1975), pp. 30–33.

RODRIGUEZ MONEGAL, EMIR. "Liberation through Creation." Trans. Gregory Kolovakos. *Review,* No.16 (1975), pp. 9–12.

VERANI, HUGO J. "The Novel as Self-Creation." *Review,* No.16 (1975), pp. 13–18.

LOS ADIOSES (1954)

HANCOCK, JOEL C. "Psychopathic Point of View: Juan Carlos Onetti's *Los Adioses [The Goodbyes].*" *Latin American Literary Review,* 2, No.3 (1973), 19–29.

EL POZO (1939)

ADAMS, M. IAN. *Three Authors Of Alienation: Bombal, Onetti, Carpentier,* pp. 37–55.

HAYDEN, ROSE LEE. *An Existential Focus On Some Novels Of The River Plate.*

THE SHIPYARD (El astillero, 1961)

ADAMS, M. IAN. *Three Authors Of Alienation: Bombal, Onetti, Carpentier,* pp. 77–80.

GIBBS, BEVERLY J. "Ambiguity in Onetti's 'El astillero.' " *Hispania,* 56 (1973), 260–69.

Reviews

BRUSHWOOD, JOHN S. *Kansas City Star,* 9 June 1968; rpt. *Review,* No.1 (1968), 60–61.

GALLAGHER, DAVID. *New York Times Book Review,* 16 June 1968; rpt. *Review,* No.1 (1968), pp. 58–60.

TAN TRISTE COMO ELLA (1963)

ADAMS, M. IAN. *Three Authors Of Alienation: Bombal, Onetti, Carpentier,* pp. 56–72.

TIERRA DE NADIE (1941)

BRUSHWOOD, JOHN S. *The Spanish American Novel,* pp. 134–36.

HAYDEN, ROSE LEE. *An Existential Focus On Some Novels Of The River Plate.*

ŌOKA, SHŌHEI (Japanese, 1909–)

FIRES ON THE PLAIN (Nobi, 1951)

KIMBALL, ARTHUR G. *Crisis In Identity And Contemporary Japanese Novels,* pp. 30–36.

KORGES, JAMES. "Abe and Ooka: Identity and Mind-Body." *Critique,* 10, No.2 (1968), 139–48.

OPITZ VON BOBERFELD, MARTIN (German, 1597–1639)

SCHAFFEREY VON DER NIMFEN HERCINIE (1630)

WAGENER, HANS. *The German Baroque Novel,* pp. 15–18.

ORGAMBIDE, PEDRO (1929–)

THE WASTELAND (El paramo)

FOSTER, DAVID WILLIAM. *Currents In The Contemporary Argentine Novel,* pp. 142–44.

ORTEGA, JULIO (Peruvian, 1942–)

MEDIODÍA

Reviews

DULSEY, BERNARD. *Hispania,* 55 (1972), 394.

OSARAGI, JIRO (Japanese, 1897-1973), pseudonym of Kiyohiko Nojiri

HOMECOMING (Kikyo, 1949)

KIMBALL, ARTHUR G. *Crisis In Identity And Contemporary Japanese Novels*, pp. 60-74.

SCHMITT, LORRAINE. "Character Development from *Homecoming* to *The Journey*." *Literature East And West*, 11 (1967), 416-20.

THE JOURNEY (Tabiji, 1953)

SCHMITT, LORRAINE. "Character Development from *Homecoming* to *The Journey*." *Literature East And West*, 11 (1967), 416-20.

OSTROVSKY, NIKOLAY ALEXEEVICH (Russian, 1904-1936)

HOW THE STEEL WAS TEMPERED see THE MAKING OF A HERO

THE MAKING OF A HERO (Kak zakalyalas stal, 1935)

MATHEWSON, RUFUS. "Four Novels," in *Major Soviet Writers*, ed. Edward J. Brown, pp. 345-47.

OTERO, LISANDRO

EN CIUDAD SEMEJANTE

MENTON, SEYMOUR. *Prose Fiction Of The Cuban Revolution*, pp. 61-65.

LA SITUACIÓN (1963)

MARBÁN, JORGE A. "Socialist Realism in a Cuban Novel: *La Situación* by Lisandro Otero." *International Fiction Review*, 2 (1975), 58-61.

OTERO SILVA, MIGUEL (Venezuelan, 1908-)

CASAS MUERTAS (1955)

BRUSHWOOD, JOHN S. *The Spanish American Novel*, pp. 205-7.

OTTIERI, OTTIERO (Italian, 1924-)

GENERAL

FANTAZZI, CHARLES. "Otiero Ottieri: Involvement Italian Style." *Symposium*, 25 (1971), 236-48.

OTTLIK, GÉZA (Hungarian, 1912-)

GENERAL

TABORI, PAUL. "The Solitary Mr. Ottlik." *Contemporary Review*, 213 (1968), 146-50.

OUOLOGUEM, YAMBO (Malian, 1940-)

BOUND TO VIOLENCE (Le Devoir de violence, 1968)

"An Interview with Yambo Ouologuem." *Journal Of The New African Literature And The Arts*, No.9/10 (1971), pp. 134-38.

MOORE, GERALD. "The Debate on Existence in African Literature." *Présence Africaine*, No.81 (1972), pp. 25-28.

MPIKU, J. MBELOLU YA. "From One Mystification to Another: 'Negritude' and 'Négraille' in 'Le Devoir de violence.' " *Review Of National Literatures*, 2, No.2 (1975), 124-47; rpt. in *Black Africa*, ed. Albert S. Gerard, pp. 124-47.

SELLIN, ERIC. "Ouologuem's Blueprint for *Le Devoir De Violence*." *Research In African Literatures*, 2 (1971), 117-20.

Reviews

DELANEY, J. DENNIS. "Conceptualizing the African Past." *African Studies Review*, 14 (1971), 145-47.

OKORE, ODE. *Journal Of The New African Literature And The Arts*, No.9/10 (1971), pp. 128-31.

SNYDER, EMILE. *Saturday Review*, 19 June 1971, p. 23.

OU-YANG SHAN

THREE FAMILY LANE

HUANG, JOE C. *Heroes And Villains In Communist China*, pp. 1-24.

OYONO, FERDINAND (Cameroons, 1929-)

BOY! see HOUSEBOY

CHEMIN DE L'EUROPE

GLEASON, JUDITH ILLSLEY. *This Africa*, pp. 164-68.

HOUSEBOY (Une Vie de boy, 1956)

BRENCH, A. C. *The Novelists' Inheritance In French Africa*, pp. 50-55.

CARTEY, WILFRED. *Whispers From A Continent*, pp. 62-65.

MAKOUTA-MBOUKOU, J. P. *Black African Literature*, pp. 59-68.

NNOLIM, CHARLES E. "Jungian Archetypes and the Main Characters in Oyono's *Une Vie De Boy*." *African Literature Today*, 7 (1975), 117-22.

Reviews

JONES, ELDRED D. *Association For African Literature In English Bulletin*, No.4 (1966), pp. 42-43.

THE OLD MAN AND THE MEDAL (Le vieux negre et la medaille, 1956)

BRENCH, A. C. *The Novelists' Inheritance In French Africa*, pp. 56-63.

CARTEY, WILFRED. *Whispers From A Continent*, pp. 65-70.

GLEASON, JUDITH ILLSLEY. *This Africa*, pp. 160-64.

Reviews

CASTAGNO, MARGARET. *Literature East And West*, 14 (1970), 575-76.

OZ, AMOS (Israeli, 1939-)

GENERAL

ALTER, ROBERT. "New Israeli Fiction." *Commentary*, 47, No.6 (1969), 59-66.

HOCHMAN, BARUCH. "Amos Oz—Where the Jackals Howled." *Midstream Magazine*, 18, No.9 (1972), 63-72.

ELSEWHERE, PERHAPS (Makom acher, 1966)

Reviews

STERN, DAVID. "Morality Tale." *Commentary*, 58, No.1 (1974), 100-1.

Times Literary Supplement. *Ariel: A Quarterly Review Of The Arts And Sciences In Israel*, No.36 (1974), pp. 118-19.

MY MICHAEL (Michael Sheli, 1968)

HOCHMAN, BARUCH. "Amos Oz—Where the Jackals Howled." *Midstream Magazine*, 18, No.9 (1972), 68-70.

Reviews

ALTER, ROBERT. *Ariel: A Quarterly Review Of The Arts And Sciences In Israel*, No.32 (1973), pp. 210-11.

RUGOFF, MILTON. *Saturday Review*, 24 June 1972, p. 60.

TOUCH THE WATER, TOUCH THE WIND (Laga'at Bamayim, Laga'at Baruah, 1973)

Reviews

ARAD, MIRIAM. *Ariel: A Quarterly Review Of The Arts And Sciences In Israel*, No.36 (1974), pp. 96-97.

P

PA CHIN (Chinese, 1904–) pseudonym of Li Fei-kan
GENERAL

HSIA, C. T. *A History Of Modern Chinese Fiction*, pp. 237–56, 375–88.

AI-CH'ING TI SAN-PU-CH'Ü (1931–33)

LANG, OLGA. *Pa Chin And His Writings*, pp. 171–86.

CHI-LIU (1931–39)

LANG, OLGA. *Pa Chin And His Writings*, pp. 70–84.

COLD NIGHTS (Han yeh, 1947)

HSIA, C. T. *A History Of Modern Chinese Fiction*, pp. 381–87.

HUO (1938–43)

LANG, OLGA. *Pa Chin And His Writings*, pp. 198–204, 206–11.

MEIH-WANG (1929)

LANG, OLGA. *Pa Chin And His Writings*, pp. 108–11.

SSU-CH'Ü TI T'AI-YANG, (1930)

LANG, OLGA. *Pa Chin And His Writings*, pp. 105–8.

PACKER, JOY (South African, 1905–1977)
VERONICA (1970)

Reviews

MOSS, JOHN G. *World Literature Written In English*, No.20 (1971), pp. 118–19.

PĀDHYE, BHĀŪ
VĀSŪNĀKĀ

APTE, MAHADEO L. "Contemporary Marathi Fiction: Obscenity or Realism?" *Journal Of Asian Studies*, 29 (1969), 59–66.

PALACIO VALDÉS, ARMANDO (Spanish, 1853–1938)
LA NOVELA DE UN NOVELISTA (1921)

JONES, R. J. "The Setting of 'La Novela de un Novelista.' " *Canadian Modern Language Review*, 24, No.? (1968), 35–51.

PALANGYO, PETER K. (Tanzanian, 1939–)
DYING IN THE SUN (1968)

MILLER, MARY MARGARET. "*Dying In The Sun:* Existentialism

and Beyond." *World Literature Written In English*, 11, No.2 (1972), 93–97.

Reviews

DYSON, DIANNE E. *Journal Of The New African Literature And The Arts*, No.9/10 (1971), pp. 120–22.

PALAZZESCHI, ALDO (Italian, 1885–1974)
GENERAL

BERGIN, THOMAS G. "The Enjoyable Horrendous World of Aldo Palazzeschi." *Books Abroad*, 46 (1972), 55–60.

ALLEGORIA DI NOVEMBRE

SINGH, G. "Aldo Palazzeschi: A Survey," in *From Verismo To Experimentalism*, ed. Sergio Pacifici, pp. 84–87.

THE SISTERS MATERASSI (Sorelle Materassi, 1934)

SINGH, G. "Aldo Palazzeschi: A Survey," in *From Verismo To Experimentalism*, ed. Sergio Pacifici, pp. 90–99.

PALMER, VANCE (Australian, 1885–1959)
GENERAL

BURNS, D. R. "Vance Palmer and the Unguarded Awareness." *Australian Literary Studies*, 6 (1974), 259–68.

SMITH, VIVIAN. "Vance and Nettie Palmer: The Literary Journalism." *Australian Literary Studies*, 6 (1973), 115–27.

THE BIG FELLOW (1960)

HESELTINE, HARRY. *Vance Palmer*, pp. 134–39.

DAYBREAK

BURNS, D. R. "Vance Palmer and the Unguarded Awareness." *Australian Literary Studies*, 6 (1973/4), 264–68.

HESELTINE, HARRY. *Vance Palmer*, pp. 94–102.

GOLCONDA (1948)

HESELTINE, HARRY. *Vance Palmer*, pp. 125–29.

LEGEND FOR SANDERSON

HESELTINE, HARRY. *Vance Palmer*, pp. 110–16.

THE MAN HAMILTON

HESELTINE, HARRY. *Vance Palmer*, pp. 69–75.

MEN ARE HUMAN

HESELTINE, HARRY. *Vance Palmer*, pp. 75–79.

THE PASSAGE

HESELTINE, HARRY. *Vance Palmer*, pp. 79-91.

SEEDTIME (1957)

HESELTINE, HARRY. *Vance Palmer*, pp. 129-34.

THE SWAYNE FAMILY

HESELTINE, HARRY. *Vance Palmer*, pp. 102-10.

PANAEVA, AVDOTYA (Russian, 1819/20?-1893)

GENERAL

LEDKOVSKY, MARINA. "Avdotya Panaeva: Her Salon and Her Life." *Russian Literature Triquarterly*, No. 9 (1974), pp. 423-32.

PANDURO, LEIF (Danish, 1923-1977)

ONE OF OUR MILLIONAIRES IS MISSING (Vejen til Jylland, 1966)

Reviews
SPECTOR, ROBERT D. *American Scandinavian Review*, 58 (1970), 86.

PANNETON, PHILLIPPE (French Canadian, 1895-1960)

THIRTY ACRES (Trente arpents, 1938)

RASPORICH, BEVERLY. "Sacrifice and Death In French-Canadian Fiction: An English Reading." *Dalhousie Review*, 55 (1975), 455-58.

PANOVA, VERA (Russian, 1905-1973)

THE TRAIN (Sputniki, 1946)

PANOVA, VERA. "What Prompted Me to Write *The Train*." *Soviet Studies In Literature*, 3, No.1 (1966/7), 3-16.

PANZINI, ALFREDO (Italian, 1863-1939)

GENERAL

PACIFICI, SERGIO. *The Modern Italian Novel: From Capuana To Tozzi*, pp. 68-77.

LA MADONNA DI MAMA

PACIFICI, SERGIO. *The Modern Italian Novel: From Capuana To Tozzi*, pp. 74-77.

PAPINI, GIOVANNI (Italian, 1881-1956)

THE LETTERS OF POPE CELESTINE VI TO ALL MANKIND (Lettere agli uomini di Papa Celestino Sesto)

SESSIONS, WILLIAM A. "Giovanni Papini, or the Probabilities of Christian Egoism," in *The Vision Obscured*, ed. Melvin J. Friedman, pp. 234-36.

PARDO BAZÁN, EMILIA (Spanish, 1852-1921)

GENERAL

DAVIS, GIFFORD. "The Literary Relations of Clarín and Emilia Pardo Bazán." *Hispanic Review*, 39 (1971), 378-94.

GILES, MARY E. "Color Adjectives in Pardo Bazan's Novels." *Romance Notes*, 10 (1968), 54-58.

———. "Pardo Bazán's Two Styles." *Hispania*, 48 (1965), 456-62.

SÁNCHEZ, PORFIRIO. "How and Why Emilia Pardo Bazán Went from the Novel to the Short Story." *Romance Notes*, 11 (1969), 309-14.

UNA CRISTIANA (1890)

DENDLE, BRIAN J. "The Racial Theories of Emilia Pardo Bazán." *Hispanic Review*, 38 (1970), 24-29.

INSOLACIÓN (1889)

DECOSTER, CYRUS C. "Pardo Bazán's *Insolación:* A Naturalistic Novel?" *Romance Notes*, 13 (1971), 87-91.

SCHMIDT, RUTH A. "Woman's Place in the Sun: Feminism in *Insolación*." *Revista De Estudios Hispánicos*, 8 (1974), 69-81.

LOS PAZOS DE ULLOA (1886)

DECOSTER, CYRUS C. "Maupassant's 'Une Vie' and Pardo Bazán's 'Los Pazos de Ulloa.'" *Hispania*, 56 (1973), 587-92.

LOTT, ROBERT E. "Observations on the Narrative Method, the Psychology, and the Style of 'Los Pazos de Ulloa.'" *Hispania*, 52 (1969), 3-12.

LA PRUEBA

DENDLE, BRIAN J. "The Racial Theories of Emilia Pardo Bazán." *Hispanic Review*, 38 (1970), 24-29.

LA SIRENA NEGRA (1908)

GILES, MARY E. "Symbolic Imagery in *La Sirena Negra*." *Papers On Language and Literature*, 4 (1968), 182-91.

HEMINGWAY M. J. D. "The Religious Content of Pardo Bazán's *La Sirena Negra*." *Bulletin Of Hispanic Studies*, 49 (1972), 369-82.

PAREJA DIEZ-CANSECO, ALFREDO (Ecuadorian, 1908-)

LA MUELLE (1933)

BRUSHWOOD, JOHN S. *The Spanish American Novel*, pp. 104-6.

LAS PEQUEÑAS ESTATURAS (1970)

Reviews
DULSEY, BERNARD. *Hispania*, 54 (1971), 975-76.

PARGAONKAR, V. S.

KALA CHAKRA (1967)

Reviews
BEDEKAR, D. K. *Indian Writing Today*, No. 1 (1967), pp. 54-55.

PARISE, GOFFREDO (Italian, 1929-)

THE BOSS

Reviews
SMITH, A. M. SHERIDAN. *London Magazine*, NS 7, No.7 (1967), 99-101.

WINTERS, WARRINGTON. "Struggle for Identity." *Saturday Review*, 24 September 1966, p. 43.

PARKER, GILBERT (Canadian, 1862-1932)

THE SEATS OF THE MIGHTY (1896)

SORFLEET, JOHN ROBERT. "Fiction and the Fall of New France: William Kirby vs. Gilbert Parker." *Journal of Canadian Fiction*, 2 No.3 (1973), 132-46.

WATERSTON, ELIZABETH. "The Politics of Conquest in Canadian Historical Fiction." *Mosaic*, 3, No.1 (1969), 116-24.

Reviews
KLINCK CARL F. "The Temple and the Cave." *Journal of Canadian Fiction*, 1, No.1 (1972), 81-83.

PARMELIN, HÉLÈNE

LA MANIÈRE NOIRE (1970)

Reviews
KAY, BURF. *French Review*, 44 (1971), 965–66.

PASINETTI, PIER MARIA (Italian, 1913–)

THE SMILE ON THE FACE OF THE LION (La Confusione, 1964)

HOUSTON, M. T. and S. N. ROSENBERG. "The Onomastics of Pasinetti." *Italian Quarterly*, 10, No.38 (1966), 41–44.

Reviews
PACIFICI, SERGIO. "The Dream of Finding Reality." *Saturday Review*, 13 February 1965, p. 49.

VENETIAN RED (Rosso Veneziano, 1959)

HOUSTON, M. T. and S. N. ROSENBERG. "The Onomastics of Pasinetti." *Italian Quarterly*, 10, No.38 (1966), 33–44.

PASOLINI, PIER PAOLO (Italian, 1922–1975)

GENERAL

O'NEILL, THOMAS. "A Problem of Character Development in Pasolini's Trilogy." *Forum For Modern Language Studies*, 5 (1969), 80–84.

STACK, OSWALD. *Pasolini On Pasolini.*

BICICLETTONE

O'NEILL, T. "Pier Paolo Pasolini: *Biciclettone.*" *Modern Languages*, 50 (1969), 11–13.

THE RAGAZZI (Ragazzi di vita, 1955)

RAGUSA, OLGA. "Gadda, Pasolini, and Experimentalism: Form or Ideology?" in *From Verismo To Experimentalism*, ed. Sergio Pacifici, pp. 256–62.

A VIOLENT LIFE (Una vita violenta, 1959)

RAGUSA, OLGA. "Gadda, Pasolini, and Experimentalism: Form or Ideology?" in *From Verismo To Experimentalism*, ed. Sergio Pacifici, pp. 262–64.

PASTERNAK, BORIS (Russian, 1890–1960)

GENERAL

BARNES, CHRISTOPHER J. "Boris Pasternak's Revolutionary Year." *Forum For Modern Language Studies*, 11 (1975), 334–48.

"Boris Pasternak in *Books Abroad* 1935–70." *Books Abroad*, 44 (1970), 243.

DE MALLAC, GUY. "Pasternak and Religion." *Russian Review*, 32 (1973), 360–75.

———. "Pasternak's Critical-Esthetic Views." *Russian Literature Triquarterly*, No.6 (1973), pp. 503–32.

DYCK, J. W. *Boris Pasternak*, pp. 17–105.

HARRIS, JANE GARY. "Pasternak's Vision of Life: The History of a Feminine Image." *Russian Literature Triquarterly*, No.9 (1974), pp. 389–421.

JAKOBSON, ROMAN. "Marginal Notes on the Prose of the Poet Pasternak (1935)," in *Pasternak: Modern Judgements*, ed. Donald Davie and Angela Livingstone, pp. 135–51.

"Judgement on Pasternak: The All-Moscow Meeting of Writers 31 October 1958." *Survey: A Journal Of Soviet And East European Studies*, No.60 (1966), pp. 134–63.

MAGIDOFF, ROBERT. "The Life, Times and Art of Boris Pasternak." *Thought*, 42 (1967), 327–57.

MOSSMAN, ELLIOTT. "Pasternak's Prose Style: Some Observations." *Russian Literature Triquarterly*, Nos.1/2 (1971), pp. 386–98.

———. "Pasternak's Short Fiction." *Russian Literature Triquarterly*, No.2 (1972), pp. 279–302.

MUCHNIC, HELEN. "Pasternak in His Letters," in her *Russian Writers*, pp. 334–42.

POMORSKA, KRYSTYNA. "Ochrannaja Gramota." *Russian Literature*, No.3 (1972), pp. 40–46.

ŠILBAJORIS, RIMVYDAS. "The Conception of Life in the Art of Pasternak." *Books Abroad*, 44 (1970), 209–14.

SINJAVSKIJ, ANDREJ. "On Boris Pasternak," in *Twentieth-Century Russian Literature Criticism*, ed. Victor Erlich, pp. 235–46.

———. "The Poetry of Pasternak," in *Major Soviet Writers*, ed. Edward J. Brown, pp. 100–37.

TAUBMAN, JANE ANDELMAN. "Marina Tsvetaeva and Boris Pasternak: Toward the History of a Friendship." *Russian Literature Triquarterly*, No.2 (1972), pp. 304–21.

WEIDLE, WLADIMIR. "The Poetry and Prose of Boris Pasternak (1928)," in *Pasternak: Modern Judgements*, ed. Donald Davie and Angela Livingstone, pp. 108–25.

DR. ZHIVAGO (1957)

BOWMAN, HERBERT E. "Postscript on Pasternak," in *Major Soviet Writers*, ed. Edward J. Brown, pp. 138–45.

BOYD, ALEXANDER F. *Aspects Of The Russian Novel*, pp. 109–30.

CHIAROMONTE, NICOLA. "Pasternak's Message (1958)," in *Pasternak: Modern Judgements*, ed. Donald Davie and Angela Livingstone, pp. 231–39.

COSTELLO, D. P. "*Zhivago* Reconsidered." *Forum For Modern Language Studies*, 4 (1968), 70–80.

DE MALLAC, GUY. "Zhivago versus Prometheus." *Books Abroad*, 44 (1970), 227–31.

DEUTSCHER, ISAAC. "Pasternak and the Calendar of the Revolution (1959)," in *Pasternak: Modern Judgements*, ed. Donald Davie and Angela Livingstone, pp. 240–58.

DYCK, J. W. *Boris Pasternak*, pp. 106–60.

FORTIN, RENÉ E. "Home and the Uses of Creative Nostalgia in *Doctor Zhivago*." *Modern Fiction Studies*, 20 (1974), 203–9.

HARRIS, JANE GARY. "Pasternak's Vision of Life: The History of A Feminine Image." *Russian Literature Triquarterly*, No.9 (1974), 410–21.

HOWE, IRVING. "Freedom and the Ashcan of History (1959)," in *Pasternak: Modern Judgements*, ed. Donald Davie and Angela Livingstone, pp. 259–68.

IVASK, GEORGE. "A Note on the Real Zhivagos." *Russian Review*, 25 (1966), 405–8.

KAYDEN, EUGENE M. "On Re-Reading the Poems of Doctor Zhivago." *Colorado Quarterly*, 23 (1975), 395–401.

MAYER, HANS. *Steppenwolf And Everyman*, pp. 256–80.

MIŁOSZ, CZESŁAW. "On Pasternak Soberly." *Books Abroad*, 44 (1970), 205–9.

MOREAU, JEAN-LUC. "The Passion According to Zhivago." *Books Abroad*, 44 (1970), 237–42.

PASTERNAK, JOSEPHINE. "*Patior*." *Russian Literature Triquarterly*, No.9 (1974), pp. 371–88.

REEVE, F. D. *The Russian Novel*, pp. 360–78.

ROGERS, THOMAS F. "The Implications of Christ's Passion in *Doktor Živago*." *Slavic And East European Journal*, 18 (1974), 384–91.

ROWLAND, MARY F. AND PAUL ROWLAND. *Pasternak's 'Doctor Zhivago.'*

ŠILBAJORIS, RIMVYDAS. "Pasternak and Tolstoj: Some Comparisons." *Slavic And East European Journal*, 11 (1967), 23–34.

———. "The Poetic Texture of *Doktor Zhivago*." *Slavic And East European Journal*, 9 (1965), 19–28.

STRUVE, GLEB. "The Hippodrome of Life: The Problem of Coincidences in *Doctor Zhivago.*" *Books Abroad,* 44 (1970), 231-36.

TIERNAN, KATHERINE. "Pasternak's *Hamlet* (from *Dr. Zhivago*)." *Explicator,* 24 (1966), Item 45.

WAIN, JOHN. "The Meaning of *Dr. Zhivago.*" *Critical Quarterly,* 10 (1968), 113-37; rpt. in his *A House For The Truth,* pp. 128-60.

ZASLOVE, JERALD. "*Dr. Zhivago* and the Obliterated Man: The Novel and Literary Criticism." *Journal Of Aesthetics And Art Criticism,* 26 (1967), 65-80.

THE HISTORY OF A CONTRAOCTAVE (1913)

MOSSMAN, ELLIOTT. "Pasternak's Short Fiction." *Russian Literature Triquarterly,* No.2 (1972), pp. 281-88.

TALE (1929)

AUCOUTURIER, MICHEL. "The Metonymous Hero or the Beginnings of Pasternak the Novelist." *Books Abroad,* 44 (1970), 222-27.

PATON, ALAN (South African, 1903-1988)

GENERAL

CRONIN, JOHN F. "Writer versus Situation: Three South African Novelists." *Studies: An Irish Quarterly Review,* 56 (1967), 74-77.

CRY THE BELOVED COUNTRY (1948)

CALLAN, EDWARD. *Alan Paton,* pp. 49-66.

TOO LATE THE PHALAROPE (1953)

CALLAN, EDWARD. *Alan Paton,* pp. 67-84.

PATSAUQ, Markoosie see MARKOOSIE

PAUL, JEAN

GENERAL

SMEED, J. W. "Jean Paul's Dreams," in *Essays In German Literature*-I, ed. F. Norman, pp. 92-116.

KATZENBERGER

MAURER, WARREN R. "Some Aspects of the Jean Paul—Hermann Hesse Relationship with Special Reference to *Katzenberger* and *Kurgast.*" *Seminar,* 4 (1968), 113-28.

LEVANA

BENHAM, G. F. "Jean Paul's *Levana,* in Contextual Perspective." *German Life And Letters,* 27 (1974), 197-98.

TITAN

SWEDIUK-CHEYNE, HELEN. " 'Einkräftigkeit,' Jean Paul's Term for Self-Destruction." *German Life And Letters,* 26 (1973), 136-42.

PAULUS, MOPELI

TURN TO THE DARK

CARTEY, WILFRED. *Whispers From A Continent,* pp. 77-80.

PAUSEWANG, GUDRUN

BOLIVIAN WEDDING

Reviews
BERGIN, THOMAS G. *Saturday Review,* 16 January 1971, p. 34.

PAUSTOVSKY, KONSTANTIN (Russian, 1892-1968)

GENERAL

PAUSTOVSKII, K. AND IU. OLESHA. "A Dialogue about the Novella." *Soviet Studies In Literature,* 9, No.3 (1973), 12-18.

SHKLOVSKII, VIKTOR. "On a Master of Sailing Directions—The Writer Konstantin Paustovskii." *Soviet Studies In Literature,* 10, No.1 (1973/4), 109-17.

PAVESE, CESARE (Italian, 1908-1950)

GENERAL

BIASIN, GIAN-PAOLO. "Diacritics for Pavese." *Italica,* 50 (1973), 83-94.

————. "The Smile of the Gods." *Italian Quarterly,* 10, No.38 (1966), 3-32.

HEINEY, DONALD. *Three Italian Novelists,* pp. 83-94.

HUTCHEON, LINDA. "Pavese's Intellectual Rhythm." *Italian Quarterly,* 15 No.60/61, (1972), 5-26.

RIMANELLI, GIOSE. "Myth and De-Mythification of Pavese's Art." *Italian Quarterly,* 13, No.49 (1969), 3-39.

AMONG WOMEN ONLY (Tra donne sole, 1949)

BIASIN, GIAN-PAOLO. *The Smile Of The Gods: A Thematic Study Of Cesare Pavese's Works,* pp. 153-62.

HEINEY, DONALD. *Three Italian Novelists,* pp. 115-18.

THE BEACH (La spiaggia, 1942)

BIASIN, GIAN-PAOLO. *The Smile Of The Gods: A Thematic Study Of Cesare Pavese's Works,* pp. 133-38.

HEINEY, DONALD. *Three Italian Novelists,* pp. 118-23.

THE BEAUTIFUL SUMMER (La bella estate, 1949)

BIASIN, GIAN-PAOLO. *The Smile Of The Gods: A Thematic Study Of Cesare Pavese's Works,* pp. 87-99.

HEINEY, DONALD. *Three Italian Novelists,* pp. 109-15.

THE COMRADE (Il compagno, 1947)

BIASIN, GIAN-PAOLO. *The Smile Of The Gods: A Thematic Study Of Cesare Pavese's Works,* pp. 165-73.

HEINEY, DONALD. *Three Italian Novelists,* pp. 128-33.

THE DEVIL IN THE HILLS (Il diavolo sulle colline, 1949)

BIASIN, GIAN-PAOLO. *The Smile Of The Gods: A Thematic Study Of Cesare Pavese's Works,* pp. 138-53, 290-94.

HEINEY, DONALD. *Three Italian Novelists,* pp. 123-28.

MONTANO, ROCCO. "The Wrong Religious Search: Pavese as Poli." *Italian Quarterly,* 18, No.70 (1974), 63-69.

SCHNEIDER, FRANZ K. "Quest, Romance and Myth in Pavese's *The Devil In The Hills.*" *Italica,* 49 (1972), 393-425.

THE HARVESTERS (Paesi tuoi, 1941)

BIASIN, GIAN-PAOLO. *The Smile Of The Gods: A Thematic Study Of Cesare Pavese's Works,* pp. 62-77.

HEINEY, DONALD. *Three Italian Novelists,* pp. 101-9.

THE HOUSE ON THE HILL (La casa in collina, 1949)

ANSORGE, PETER. "Pavese's Civil War." *London Magazine,* NS 9, No.11 (1970), 83-88.

BIASIN, GIAN-PAOLO. *The Smile Of The Gods: A Thematic Study Of Cesare Pavese's Works,* pp. 178-88.

HEINEY, DONALD. *Three Italian Novelists,* pp. 133-36.

THE MOON AND THE BONFIRES (La luna e i falò, 1950)

BIASIN, GIAN-PAOLO. "Myth and Death in Cesare Pavese's *The*

Moon And The Bonfires," in *From Verismo To Experimentalism*, ed. Sergio Pacifici, pp. 184–211.

———. *The Smile Of The Gods: A Thematic Study Of Cesare Pavese's Works*, pp. 215–52, 316–25.

HEINEY, DONALD. "Pavese: The Geography of the Moon." *Contemporary Literature*, 9 (1968), 522–37.

———. *Three Italian Novelists*, pp. 136–46.

MERRY, BRUCE. "Artifice and Structure in *La Luna E I Falò*." *Forum Italicum*, 5 (1971), 351–58.

THE POLITICAL PRISONER (El carcere, 1949)

BIASIN, GIAN-PAOLO. *The Smile Of The Gods: A Thematic Study Of Cesare Pavese's Works*, pp. 36–51, 273–76.

HEINEY, DONALD. *Three Italian Novelists*, pp. 96–101.

ROOPNARAINE, R. RUPERT. "Structures of Self and Art in Pavese's *Il Carcere*." *Italian Quarterly*, 17, No.66 (1973), 25–46.

PAVLOVA, KAROLINA (Russian emigrée to Germany, 1807–1894)

GENERAL

MONTER, BARBARA HELDT. "From an Introduction to Pavlova's *A Double Life*." *Russian Literature Triquarterly*, No.9 (1974), pp. 337–53.

A DOUBLE LIFE

MONTER, BARBARA HELDT. "From an Introduction to Pavlova's *A Double Life*." *Russian Literature Triquarterly*, No.9 (1974), pp. 348–52.

PAVÓN, Francisco García see GARCÍA PAVÓN, Francisco

PAYERLE, GEORGE (Canadian, 1945–)

THE AFTERPEOPLE

Reviews
ROSENGARTEN, HERBERT. "Novel No Story." *Canadian Literature*, No.54 (1972), pp. 109–10.

PEKIĆ, BORISLAV (Yugoslavian, 1930–)

HODOČAŠĆE ARSENIJA NEGOVANA (1970)

MATEJIĆ, MATEJA. "On the Contemporary Yugoslav Novel." *Canadian Slavic Studies*, 5 (1971), 377–78.

P'ENG KUNG AU (Author Unknown)

CH'EN, JEROME. "Rebels Between Rebellions—Secret Societies in the Novel, *P'Eng Kung Au*." *Journal Of Asian Studies*, 29 (1970), 807–22.

PEREC, GEORGES

LES CHOSES: A STORY OF THE SIXTIES

Reviews
EASTON, ELIZABETH. "All or Nothing." *Saturday Review*, 13 April 1968, pp. 46–47.

UN HOMME QUI DORT

Reviews
GILBERT, JOHN. *Novel*, 2 (1968), 94–96.

PEREDA, JOSÉ MARÍA DE (Spanish, 1833–1906)

DE TAL PALO, TAL ASTILLA (1880)

KLIBBE, LAWRENCE H. *Jose Maria De Pereda*, pp. 75–85.

DON GONZALO GONZALEZ DE LA GONZALERA (1879)

KLIBBE, LAWRENCE H. *Jose Maria De Pereda*, pp. 68–75.

THE MOUNTAINS OF SANTANDER

KLIBBE, LAWRENCE H. *Jose Maria De Pereda*, pp. 130–43.

PEDRO SÁNCHEZ (1883)

KLIBBE, LAWRENCE H. *Jose Maria De Pereda*, pp. 93–104.

EL SABOR DE LA TIERRUCA

KLIBBE, LAWRENCE H. *Jose Maria De Pereda*, pp. 86–93.

SOTILEZA (1885)

KLIBBE, LAWRENCE H. *Jose Maria De Pereda*, pp. 105–29.

PEREIRA, ANTONIO OLAVO

MARCORÉ (1957)

Reviews
BOISSE, JOSEPH A. *Library Journal*, 15 June 1970; rpt. *Review*, No.3 (1971), p. 66.

DANIEL, MARY L. *Modern Language Journal*, 54 (1970); rpt. *Review*, No.3 (1971), p. 67.

GANIM, JOHN M. *Times Of The Americas*, 17 June 1970; rpt. *Review*, No.3 (1971), pp. 68–69.

PÉREZ DE AYALA, RAMÓN (Spanish, 1880–1962)

GENERAL

CAMPBELL, BRENTON. "The Esthetic Theories of Ramón Pérez de Ayala." *Hispania*, 50 (1967), 447–53.

FEENY, THOMAS P. " 'El Hombre de Acción' as Hero in Pérez de Ayala's *Bajo El Signo De Artemisa*." *Revista De Estudios Hispánicos*, 9 (1975), 231–40.

ZAMORA, CARLOS. "*Homo Impotens* and the Vanity of Human Striving: Two Related Themes in the Novels of Ramon Perez de Ayala." *Revista De Estudios Hispánicos*, 5 (1971), 413–26.

A. M. D. G. (1910)

RAND, MARGUERITE C. *Ramón Pérez De Ayala*, pp. 65–68.

BELARMINO Y APOLONIO (1927)

RAND, MARGUERITE C. *Ramón Pérez De Ayala*, pp. 95–108.

EL CURANDERO DE SU HONRA (1926)

RAND, MARGUERITE C. *Ramón Pérez De Ayala*, pp. 118–24.

THE FALL OF THE HOUSE OF LIMÓN (La caída de los Limones, 1916)

RAND, MARGUERITE C. *Ramón Pérez De Ayala*, pp. 87–91.

THE FOX'S PAW (La pata de la raposa, 1912)

RAND, MARGUERITE C. *Ramón Pérez De Ayala*, pp. 69–74.

LUNA DE MIEL, LUNA DE HIEL (1923)

RAND, MARGUERITE C. *Ramón Pérez De Ayala*, pp. 108–12.

EL OMBLIGO DEL MUNDO (1924)

RAND, MARGUERITE C. *Ramón Pérez De Ayala*, pp. 91–93.

PROMETHEUS (Prometeo, 1916)

RAND, MARGUERITE C. *Ramón Pérez De Ayala*, pp. 81–84.

SUNDAY SUNLIGHT (Luz de domingo, 1916)

> RAND, MARGUERITE C. *Ramón Pérez De Ayala,* pp. 84–87.

TIGER JUAN (Tigre Juan, 1926)

> CARGILL, MARUXA SALGUÉS and JULIÁN PALLEY. "Myth and Anti-Myth in *Tigre Juan.*" *Revista De Estudios Hispánicos,* 7 (1973), 399–416.

> RAND, MARGUERITE C. *Ramón Pérez De Ayala,* pp. 116–18.

TINIEBLAS EN LAS CUMBRES (1907)

> RAND, MARGUERITE C. *Ramón Pérez De Ayala,* pp. 61–65.

LOS TRABAJOS DE URBANO Y SIMONA (1923)

> RAND, MARGUERITE C. *Ramón Pérez De Ayala,* pp. 112–16.

TROTERAS Y DANZADERAS (1913)

> RAND, MARGUERITE C. *Ramón Pérez De Ayala,* pp. 74–78.

PÉREZ GALDÓS, BENITO (Spanish, 1843–1920)

GENERAL

> CARDWELL, R. A. "Galdós' Early Novels and the *Segunda Manera:* A Case for the Total View." *Renaissance And Modern Studies,* 15 (1971), 44–62.

> CHAMBERLIN, VERNON A. "Galdós and Galdosistas in the United States: On the Fiftieth Anniversary of the Author's Death." *Hispania,* 53 (1970), 819–27.

> FOLLEY, T. "Clothes and the Man: An Aspect of Benito Peréz Galdós' Method of Literary Characterization." *Bulletin Of Hispanic Studies,* 49 (1972), 30–39.

> GILLESPIE, GERALD. "Galdós and the Unlocking of the Psyche." *Hispania,* 53 (1970), 852–56.

> GOODALE, HOPE K. "Allusions to Shakespeare in Galdós." *Hispanic Review,* 39 (1971), 249–60.

> NEWBERRY, WILMA. *The Pirandellian Mode In Spanish Literature From Cervantes To Sastre,* pp. 24–27.

> NIMETZ, MICHAEL. *Humor In Galdós: A Study Of The <Novelas Contemporáneas.>*

> PAOLINI, GILBERTO. "The Benefactor in the Novels of Galdos." *Revista De Estudios Hispánicos,* 2 (1968), 241–49.

> PATTISON, WALTER T. "The Prehistory of the 'Episodios Nacionales.'" *Hispania,* 53 (1970), 857–63.

> PENUEL, ARNOLD M. *Charity In The Novels Of Galdós.*

> ———. "Galdós, Freud, and Humanistic Psychology." *Hispania,* 55 (1972), 66–75.

> RODRÍGUEZ, ALFRED. *An Introduction To The Episodios Nacionales Of Galdós.*

> SANTALÓ, JOAQUÍN. *The Tragic Import In The Novels Of Pérez Galdós.*

> VAREY, J. E. "Torquemada and *La Lógica,*" in *Studies In Modern Spanish Literature And Art,* ed. Nigel Glendinning, pp. 207–21.

> WOODBRIDGE, HENSLEY C. "Benito Pérez Galdós: A Selected Annotated Bibliography." *Hispania,* 53 (1970), 899–971.

AITA TETTAUEN (1905)

> COHEN, SARA E. "Christians, Jews, and Moors: Galdós' Search for Values in *Aita Tettauen* and *Carlos VII, En La Rapita.*" *Symposium,* 29 (1975), 84–102.

> COLIN, VERA. "Tolstoy and Galdós' Santuiste: Their Ideology on War and Their Spiritual Conversion." *Hispania,* 53 (1970), 836–41.

EL AMIGO MANSO (1881)

> NEWTON, NANCY A. "*El Amigo Manso* and the Relativity of Reality." *Revista De Estudios Hispánicos,* 7 (1973), 113–25.

> PENUEL, ARNOLD M. "The Influence of Galdós' *El Amigo Manso* on Dolores Medio's *El Diario De Una Maestra.*" *Revista De Estudios Hispánicos,* 7 (1973), 91–96.

> PRICE, R. M. "The Five *Padrotes* in Pérez Galdós' *El Amigo Manso.*" *Philological Quarterly,* 48 (1969), 234–46.

ÁNGEL GUERRA (1890–91)

> FEDORCHEK, ROBERT M. "The Ideal of Christian Poverty in Galdós' Novels." *Romance Notes,* 11 (1969), 76–78.

> PATTISON, WALTER THOMAS. *Benito Pérez Galdós,* pp. 117–24.

CARLOS VII EN LA RAPITA (1905)

> COHEN, SARA E. "Christians, Jews, and Moors: Galdós' Search for Values in *Aita Tettauen* and *Carlos VII, En La Rapita.*" *Symposium,* 29 (1975), 84–102.

COMPASSION (Misericordia, 1897)

> PATTISON, WALTER THOMAS. *Benito Pérez Galdós,* pp. 134–37.

> PENUEL, ARNOLD M. "Galdós, Freud, and Humanistic Psychology." *Hispania,* 55 (1972), 69–74.

THE DISINHERITED LADY (La descheredada, 1881)

> DURAND, FRANK. "The Reality of Illusion: *La Desheredada.*" *MLN,* 89 (1974), 191–201.

> FEDORCHEK, ROBERT M. "Social Representation in *La Desheredada.*" *Revista De Estudios Hispánicos,* 8 (1974), 43–59.

> PATTISON, WALTER THOMAS. *Benito Pérez Galdós,* pp. 65–67.

> ROGERS, EAMONN. "Galdós' *La Desheredada* and Naturalism." *Bulletin Of Hispanic Studies,* 45 (1968), 285–98.

> WRIGHT, CHAD S. "The Representation Qualities of Isidora Rufete's House and Her Son Riquin in Benito Perez Galdos' Novel *La Desheredada.*" *Romanische Forschungen,* 83 (1971), 230–45.

DOÑA PERFECTA (1876)

> CHAMBERLIN, VERNON A. and JACK WEINER. "Galdos' *Doña Perfecta* and Turgenev's *Fathers And Sons:* Two Interpretations of the Conflict between Generations." *PMLA,* 86 (1971), 19–24.

> SÁNCHEZ, ROBERTO G. "*Doña Perfecta* and the Histrionic Projection of Character." *Revista De Estudios Hispánicos,* 3 (1969), 175–90.

> VAREY, J. E. *Perez Galdos: Dona Perfecta.*

EL DR. CENTENO (1883)

> PATTISON, WALTER THOMAS. *Benito Pérez Galdós,* pp. 71–74.

LA FONTANA DE ORO (1870)

> PATTISON, WALTER THOMAS. *Benito Pérez Galdós,* pp. 37–40.

> SMIEJA, FLORIAN. "An Alternative Ending of 'La Fontana de Oro.'" *Modern Language Review,* 61 (1966), 426–33.

> WELLINGTON, MARIE A. "The Awakening of Galdós' Lázaro." *Hispania,* 55 (1972), 463–70.

FORTUNATA AND JACINTA (Fortunata y Jacinta, 1886–87)

> BACARISSE, S. "The Realism of Galdós: Some Reflections on Language and the Preception of Reality." *Bulletin Of Hispanic Studies,* 42 (1965), 239–50.

> BRAUN, LUCILLE V. "Galdós' Re-creation of Ernestina Manuel de Villena as Guillermina Pacheo." *Hispanic Review,* 38 (1970), 32–55.

> ENGLER, KAY. "Notes on the Narrative Structure of *Fortunata Y Jacinta.*" *Symposium,* 24 (1970), 111–27.

PATTISON, WALTER THOMAS. *Benito Pérez Galdós,* pp. 90–106.

RANDOLPH, E. DALE A. "A Source for Maxi Rubín in 'Fortunata y Jacinta.' " *Hispania,* 51 (1968), 49–56.

ROGERS, DOUGLASS. "The Descriptive Simile in Galdós and Blasco Ibáñez: A Study in Contrasts." *Hispania,* 53 (1970), 866–69.

SMITH, PAUL C. "Cervantes and Galdós: The Duque and Ido del Sagrario" *Romance Notes,* 8 (1966), 47–50.

STERN, J. P. "Reflections on Realism." *Journal Of European Studies,* 1 (1971), 19–24.

ZAHAREAS, ANTHONY. "The Tragic Sense in *Fortunata Y Jacinta.*" *Symposium,* 19 (1965), 38–49.

GLORIA (1876–77)

PATTISON, WALTER THOMAS. *Benito Pérez Galdós,* pp. 55–57.

LA INCÓGNITA (1888–89)

PATTISON, WALTER THOMAS. *Benito Pérez Galdós,* pp. 111–15.

PENUEL, ARNOLD M. "The Ambiguity of Orozco's Virtue in Galdós' 'La Incógnita' and 'Realidad.' " *Hispania,* 53 (1970), 411–18.

JUAN MARTÍN EL EMPECINADO (1874)

LOVETT, GABRIEL H. "Some Observations on Galdós' *Juan Martín El Empecinado.*" *MLN,* 84 (1969), 196–207.

———. "Two Views of Guerrilla Warfare: Galdós' *Juan Martin El Empecinado* and Baroja's *El Escuadron Del Brigante.*" *Revista De Estudios Hispánicos,* 6 (1972), 335–44.

LEON ROCH: A ROMANCE (La familia de León Roch, 1878–79)

PATTISON, WALTER THOMAS. *Benito Pérez Galdós,* pp. 58–61.

MARIANELLA (1878)

BLANCO, LOUISE S. "Origin and History of the Plot of 'Marianella.' " *Hispania,* 48 (1965), 463–67.

MIAU (1888)

PATTISON, WALTER THOMAS. *Benito Pérez Galdós,* pp. 106–10.

NAZARÍN (1895)

FEDORCHEK, ROBERT M. "The Ideal of Christian Poverty in Galdós' Novels." *Romance Notes,* 11 (1969), 78–81.

PATTISON, WALTER THOMAS. *Benito Pérez Galdós,* pp. 130–32.

LO PROHIBIDO (1884–85)

PATTISON, WALTER THOMAS. *Benito Pérez Galdós,* pp. 81–87.

REALIDAD (1889)

PATTISON, WALTER THOMAS. *Benito Pérez Galdós,* pp. 111–15.

PENUEL, ARNOLD M. "The Ambiguity of Orozco's Virtue in Galdós' 'La Incógnita' and 'Realidad.' " *Hispania,* 53 (1970), 411–18.

THE SHADOW (La sombra, 1870)

PATTISON, WALTER THOMAS. *Benito Pérez Galdós,* pp. 34–37.

THE SPENDTHRIFTS (La de bringas, 1884)

BLY, P. A. "The Use of Distance in Galdós's 'La de Bringas.' " *Modern Language Review,* 69 (1974), 88–97.

LOWE, JENNIFER. "Galdós' Presentation of Rosalia in *La De Bringas.*" *Hispanofila,* No.50 (1974), pp. 49–65.

PATTISON, WALTER THOMAS. *Benito Pérez Galdós,* pp. 78–81.

TORMENT (Tormento, 1884)

PATTISON, WALTER THOMAS. *Benito Pérez Galdós,* pp. 74–78.

RODGERS, EAMONN. "The Appearance-Reality Contrast in Galdós' *Tormento.*" *Forum For Modern Language Studies,* 6 (1970), 382–98.

TORQUEMADA EN LA CRUZ (1893)

VAREY, J. E. "Torquemada and *La Lógica,*" in *Studies In Modern Spanish Literature And Art,* ed. Nigel Glendinning, pp. 209–16.

TORQUEMADA EN LA HOGUERA (1889)

BAUML, B. J. ZEIDNER. "The Mundane Demon: The Bourgeois Grotesque in Galdós, *Torquemada En La Hoguera.*" *Symposium,* (1970), 158–65.

ULLMAN, PIERRE L. "The Exordium of *Torquemada En La Hoguera.*" *MLN,* 80 (1965), 258–60.

TORQUEMADA Y SAN PEDRO (1895)

VAREY, J. E. "Torquemada and *La Lógica,*" in *Studies In Modern Spanish Literature And Art,* ed. Nigel Glendinning, pp. 216–21.

WEBER, ROBERT J. "Gladós Preliminary Sketches for *Torquemada Y San Pedro.*" *Bulletin Of Hispanic Studies,* 44 (1967), 16–27.

TRISTANA DISMEMBERED

GROSSVOGEL, DAVID I. "Buñuel's Obsessed Camera: *Tristana Dismembered.*" *Diacritics,* 2, No.1 (1972), 51–56.

PERREAULT, E. G.

THE KINGDOM CARVER (1968)

Reviews
READ, S. E. "A Western Realm." *Canadian Literature,* No.40 (1969), pp. 92–94.

THE TWELFTH MILE

Reviews
READ, S. E. "Spies and Tempests." *Canadian Literature,* No.58 (1973), pp. 106–8.

SCOTT, ANDREW. "Captain Westholme's Last Ride." *Journal Of Canadian Fiction,* 1, No.3 (1972), 88–89.

PETER, JOHN (South African, 1921–)

ALONG THAT COAST (1964)

Reviews
KILLAM, DOUGLAS. "Apartheid Novel from Canada." *Journal Of Commonwealth Literature,* No.2 (1966), pp. 175–76.

TAKE HANDS AT WINTER (1967)

RICOU, LAURENCE R. "Empty as Nightmare: Man and Landscape in Recent Canadian Prairie Fiction." *Mosaic,* 6, No.2 (1972/3), 155.

Reviews
DJWA, SANDRA. "Canadian Cod." *Canadian Literature,* No.33 (1967), pp. 80–82.

PETERS, LENRIE (Gambian, 1932–)

THE SECOND ROUND (1965)

LARSON, CHARLES R. "Lenrie Peters' *The Second Round:* West African Gothic," in his *The Emergence Of African Fiction,* rev. ed., pp. 227–41.

Reviews
DATHORNE, O. R. *Black Orpheus,* No.19 (1966), pp. 55–56.

PETRONIUS (Roman, d. 66 A.D.)

THE SATYRICON

PERRY, BEN EDWIN. *The Ancient Romances,* pp. 186–210.

REXROTH, KENNETH. "Classics Revisited—VIII: The Satyricon." *Saturday Review,* 5 June 1965, p. 15; rpt. in his *Classics Revisited,* pp. 99-103.

WALSH, P. G. *The Roman Novel: The 'Satyricon' Of Petronius And The 'Metamorphoses' Of Apuleius,* pp. 67-140.

PETROV, IVALYO (Bulgarian, 1923–) pseudonym of Prodan Kyuchoukov

SENECHKA

DEDKOV, I. "Pages from Country Life." *Soviet Studies In Literature,* 5, No.3 (1969), 68-74.

PEYRE, MARC

THE CAPTIVE OF ZOUR

Reviews
SMITH, A. M. SHERIDAN. *London Magazine,* NS 6, No.3 (1966), 108-9.

PEYROU, MANUEL (Argentinian, 1902–)

THUNDER OF THE ROSES (El estruendo de las rosas, 1948)

Reviews
NAGLE, JOHN. "Oedipus in Argentina." *Review,* No.6 (1972), 69-70.

PIETRI, Arturo Uslar see USLAR PIETRI, Arturo

PIEYRE DE MANDIAGUES, André see MANDIARGUES, André Pieyre de

PIGAULT-LEBRUN, CHARLES-ANTOINE-GUILLAUME PIGAULT DE L'ÉPINOY (French, 1753-1835)

GENERAL

LUDLOW, GREGORY. "Pigault-Lebrun: A Popular French Novelist of the Post-Revolutionary Period." *French Review,* 46 (1973), 946-50.

——— . "Pigault-Lebrun and the Satire of the Novel after *Jacques Le Fataliste.*" *French Studies,* 27 (1973), 9-15.

PILAR, YURI

LUDI OSTAYUTSA LUDMI

Reviews
HEIMAN, LEO. "Prison Camp Literature." *East Europe,* 14, No.7 (1965), 55.

PILHES, RENÉ-VICTOR

LA RHUBARBE

Reviews
BISHOP, THOMAS. "Two Wrongs for Right." *Saturday Review,* 1 March 1969, p. 33.

PILNYAK, BORIS (Russian, 1894-1938)

GENERAL

MAGUIRE, ROBERT A. "The Pioneers: Pil'nyak and Ivanov," in *Major Soviet Writers,* ed. Edward J. Brown, pp. 221-41.

MALONEY, PHILIP. "Anarchism and Bolshevism in the Works of Boris Pilnyak." *Russian Review,* 32 (1973), 43-53.

A CHINESE TALE (Kitayskaya povest, 1927)

BROSTROM, KENNETH. "Boris Pil'njak's *A Chinese Tale:* Exile as Allegory," *Mosaic,* 9, No.3 (1976), 11-25.

MACHINES AND WOLVES (Mashiny i volki, 1924)

TULLOCH, A. R. "The 'Man vs. Machine' Theme in Pilnyak's *Machines And Wolves,*" *Russian Literature Triquarterly,* No.8 (1974), pp. 329-91.

MATERIALS FOR A NOVEL (Materialy k romanu, 1924)

MAGUIRE, ROBERT A. "The Pioneers: Pil'nyak and Ivanov," in *Major Soviet Writers,* ed. Edward J. Brown, pp. 228-38.

THE VOLGA FALLS TO THE CASPIAN SEA (Volga vpadaet v kaspyskoe more, 1930)

BROSTROM, KENNETH N. "The Enigma of Pil'njak's *The Volga Falls To The Caspian Sea.*" *Slavic And East European Journal,* 18 (1974), 271-98.

SWADOS, HARVEY. "On Boris Pilnyak's *The Volga Falls To The Caspian Sea,*" in *Rediscoveries,* ed. David Madden, pp. 147-64.

PINCHERLE, Alberto see MORAVIA, Alberto

PINGAUD, BERNARD

LA VOIX DE SON MAÎTRE (1973)

Reviews
SOLOMON, PHILIP H. *French Review,* 48 (1974), 490-91.

PINGET, ROBERT (French, 1913–)

GENERAL

KELLMAN, STEVEN G. " 'Quelqu'un' in Robert Pinget's Fiction." *Mosaic,* 5, No.3 (1972), 137-44.

BAGA (1958)

MERCIER, VIVIAN. *The New Novel From Queneau To Pinget,* pp. 387-91.

Reviews
SMITH, A. M. SHERIDAN. *London Magazine,* NS 7, No.7 (1967), 98-99.

CLOPE AU DOSSIER (1961)

MERCIER, VIVIAN. *The New Novel From Queneau To Pinget,* pp. 397-402.

FABLE (1971)

Reviews
HENKELS, ROBERT M., Jr. *French Review,* 46 (1972), 232-33.

GRAAL FLIBUSTE (1956)

MERCIER, VIVIAN. *The New Novel From Queneau To Pinget,* pp. 383-87.

THE INQUISITORY (L'inquisitoire, 1962)

HENKELS, ROBERT M. "The House Metaphor in Pinget's *The Inquisitory.*" *Critique,* 14, No.3 (1973), 100-8.

MERCIER, VIVIAN. *The New Novel From Queneau To Pinget,* pp. 363-76.

STEISEL, MARIE-GEORGETTE. "Pinget's Method in *L'Inquisitoire.*" *Books Abroad,* 40 (1966), 267-71.

Reviews
BISHOP, THOMAS. "Life in the Labyrinth." *Saturday Review,* 11 February 1967, pp. 41, 54.

HENKELS, ROBERT, Jr. *French Review,* 45 (1972), 707-9.

THE LIBERA ME DOMINE (Le libera, 1968)

MERCIER, VIVIAN. *The New Novel From Queneau To Pinget,* pp. 410–15.

Reviews
HENKELS, ROBERT. "French Voices." *Novel,* 3 (1969), 89–90.

MAHU: OR, THE MATERIAL (Mahu ou le matériau, 1952)

MERCER, VIVIAN. *The New Novel From Queneau To Pinget,* pp. 376–79.

MONSIEUR LEVERT (Le fiston, 1959)

MERCIER, VIVIAN. *The New Novel From Queneau To Pinget,* pp. 391–97.

QUELQU'UN (1965)

KELLMAN, STEVEN G. " 'Quelqu'un' in Robert Pinget's Fiction." *Mosaic,* 5, No.3 (1972), 137–44.

MERCIER, VIVIAN. *The New Novel From Queneau To Pinget,* pp. 403–10.

ROSE, MARILYN GADDIS. "Robert Pinget's Agapa Land." *Forum,* 8, No. 1 (1970), 68–70.

Reviews
BANN, STEPHEN. *London Magazine,* NS 6, No.2 (1966), 94–97.
KUHN, REINHARD. *Novel,* 1 (1967), 93–95.

RECURRENT MELODY (Passacaille, 1969)

BROOME, PETER. "A New Mode of Reading: Pinget's 'Passacaille.' " *Nottingham French Studies,* 12 (1973), 86–99.

———. "Robert Pinget's *Passacaille.*" *International Fiction Review,* 1 (1974), 135–38.

Reviews
HENKELS, ROBERT. "The New Novel: Self-Analysis." *Novel,* 5 (1972), 274–77.

LE RENARD ET LA BOUSSOLE (1955)

MERCIER, VIVIAN. *The New Novel From Queneau To Pinget,* pp. 379–83.

PINSENT, GORDON (Canadian, 1930–)

JOHN AND THE MISSUS (1974)

BRENNAN, ANTHONY. "Gordon Pinsent: "A True Newfoundlander." *International Fiction Review,* 2 (1975), 73–74.

THE ROWDYMAN (1973)

Reviews
BRENNAN, ANTHONY. International Fiction Review, 1 (1974), 152–53.
SCOTT, ANDREW. "He's the Bye." *Journal Of Canadian Fiction,* 3, No.4 (1975), 98–99.

PINILLA, RAMIRO

EN EL TIEMPO DE LOS TALLOS VERDES (1969)

Reviews
DÍAZ, JANET W. *Hispania,* 54 (1971), 395–96.

PIRANDELLO, LUIGI (Italian, 1867–1936)

GENERAL

BÜDEL, OSCAR. *Pirandello.*

"Luigi Pirandello: An Autobiographical Sketch." *Forum Italicum,* 1 (1967), 241–42.

MCCORMICK, E. ALLEN. "Luigi Pirandello: Major Writer, Minor Novelist," in *From Verismo To Experimentalism,* ed. Sergio Pacifici, pp. 61–80.

PACIFICI, SERGIO. *The Modern Italian Novel: From Capuana To Tozzi,* pp. 108–35.

RAGUSA, OLGA. *Luigi Pirandello.*

THE LATE MATTIA PASCAL (Il fu Mattia Pascal, 1904)

CASTRIS, A. L. DE. "The Experimental Novelist," in *Pirandello: A Collection Of Critical Essays,* ed. Glauco Cambon, pp. 91–95.

MCCORMICK, E. ALLEN. "Luigi Pirandello: Major Writer, Minor Novelist," in *From Verismo To Experimentalism,* pp. 65–68.

PACIFICI, SERGIO. *The Modern Italian Novel: From Capuana To Tozzi,* pp. 122–28.

STARKIE, WALTER. *Luigi Pirandello: 1867–1936,* pp. 96–104.

THE MERRY-GO-ROUND OF LOVE (Il turno, 1902)

MCCORMICK, E. ALLEN. "Luigi Pirandello: Major Writer, Minor Novelist," in *From Verismo To Experimentalism,* ed. Sergio Pacifici, pp. 63–65.

THE OLD AND THE YOUNG (I vecchi e i Giovani, 1913)

STARKIE, WALTER. *Luigi Pirandello: 1867–1936,* pp. 88–93.

ONE, NONE AND AN HUNDRED (Uno, nessuno e centomila, 1926)

MCCORMICK, E. ALLEN. "Luigi Pirandello: Major Writer, Minor Novelist," in *From Verismo To Experimentalism,* ed. Sergio Pacifici, pp. 69–71.

PACIFICI, SERGIO. *The Modern Italian Novel: From Capuana To Tozzi,* pp. 128–33.

STARKIE, WALTER. *Luigi Pirandello: 1867–1936,* pp. 109–12.

THE OUTCAST (L'Esclusa, 1908)

PACIFICI, SERGIO. *The Modern Italian Novel: From Capuana To Tozzi,* pp. 119–22.

STARKIE, WALTER. *Luigi Pirandello: 1867–1936,* pp. 65–68.

SHOOT (Si gira, 1916)

CASTRIS, A. L. DE. "The Experimental Novelist," in *Pirandello: A Collection Of Critical Essays,* ed. Glauco Cambon, pp. 95–102.

STARKIE, WALTER. *Luigi Pirandello: 1867–1936,* pp. 105–9.

PIROUÉ, GEORGES

LA VIE SUPPOSÉE DE THÉODORE NÈFLE (1972)

Reviews
SUTHER, JUDITH D. *French Review,* 48 (1974), 492–93.

PISEMSKY, ALEXEY FEOFILAKTOVICH (Russian, 1820–1881)

GENERAL

STEUSSY, R. E. "The Bitter Fate of A. F. Pisemsky." *Russian Review,* 25 (1966), 170–83.

THE BOURGEOIS

MOSER, CHARLES A. *Pisemsky: A Provincial Realist,* pp. 175–79.

IN THE WHIRLPOOL

MOSER, CHARLES A. *Pisemsky: A Provincial Realist,* pp. 155–58.

THE MASONS

MOSER, CHARLES A. *Pisemsky: A Provincial Realist,* pp. 181–83.

MEN OF THE 1840'S

MOSER, CHARLES A. *Pisemsky: A Provincial Realist,* pp. 147–52.

A THOUSAND SOULS (1858)

FREEBORN, RICHARD. *The Rise Of The Russian Novel,* pp. 127–30.
MOSER, CHARLES A. *Pisemsky: A Provincial Realist,* pp. 82–91.

TROUBLED SEAS

MOSER, CHARLES A. *Pisemsky: A Provincial Realist,* pp. 123-30.

PITOL, SERGIO (1933-)

EL TAÑIDO DE UNA FLAUTA (1972)

Reviews
MASSEY, KENNETH W. *Chasqui,* 2, No.1 (1972), 59-60.

PIVIDAL, RAFAËL

TENTATIVE DE VISITE À UNE BASE ÉTRANGÈRE

Reviews
JOHNSON, PATRICIA J. *French Review,* 44 (1971), 1125.

PLAATJE, SOL (South African, 1878-1932)

MHUDI (1930)

COUZENS, T. J. "The Dark Side of the World: Sol Plaatje's 'Mhudi.' " *English Studies In Africa,* 14 (1971), 187-203.

————. "Sol Plaatje's *Mhudi." Journal Of Commonwealth Literature,* 8, No.1 (1973), 1-19.

PLACOLY, VINCENT

LA VIE ET LA MORT DE MARCEL GONSTRAN (1971)

Reviews
CAPRIO, ANTHONY. *French Review,* 46 (1973), 1065-66.

PLOMER, WILLIAM (South African, 1903-1973)

TURBOTT WOLFE (1925)

PIETERSE, COSMO. "Conflict in the Germ," in *Protest And Conflict In African Literature,* ed. Cosmo Pieterse and Donald Munro, pp. 1-18.

WADE, MICHAEL. "William Plomer, English Liberalism, and the South African Novel." *Journal Of Commonwealth Literature,* 8, No.1 (1973), 20-32.

Reviews
GORDIMER, NADINE. "A Wilder Fowl." *London Magazine,* NS 5, No.3 (1965), 90-92.

POIROT-DELPECH, BERTRAND

LA FOLLE DE LITUANIE (1970)

Reviews
GOODRICH, NORMA L. *French Review,* 45 (1971), 482-83.

POLOTAN-TUVERA, KERIMA (Filipino, 1925-) pseudonym of Patricia S. Torre

THE HAND OF THE ENEMY (1961)

CASPER, LEONARD. *New Writing From The Philippines,* pp. 99-102.

PONCE, Juan Garcia see GARCÍA PONCE, Juan

PONTOPPIDAN, HENRIK (Danish, 1857-1943)

DE FORJAETTEDE LAND (1891-95)

JONES, W. GLYN. "*Det Forjaettede Land* and *Fremskridt* as Social Novels: A Comparison." *Scandinavian Studies,* 37 (1965), 77-90.

MADSEN BØRGE GEDSØ. "Henrik Pontoppidan's Emanuel Han-

sted and Per Sidenius," in *Scandinavian Studies,* ed. Carl F. Bayerschmidt and Erik J. Friis, pp. 227-33.

LYKKE-PER (1898-1904)

BREDSDORFF, ELIAS. "George Brandes as a Fictional Character in Some Danish Novels and Plays." *Scandinavian Studies,* 45 (1973), 18-24.

MADSEN, BORGE GEDSO. "Henrik Pontoppidan's Emanuel Hansted and Per Sidenius," in *Scandinavian Studies,* ed. Carl F. Bayerschmidt and Erik J. Friis, pp. 233-35.

PORTAL, ELLIS (Canadian, 1925-) pseudonym of Bruce Powe

KILLING GROUND (1968)

Reviews
SUTHERLAND, RONALD. "It Could Happen." *Canadian Literature,* No.38 (1968), pp. 89-91.

PORTER, HAL (Australian, 1911-)

GENERAL

BURNS, ROBERT. "A Sort of Triumph Over Time: Hal Porter's Prose Narratives." *Meanjin,* 28 (1969), 19-28.

DUNCAN, R. A. "Hal Porter's Writing and the Impact of the Absurd." *Meanjin,* 29 (1970), 468-73.

GEERING R. G. "Hal Porter: The Controls of Melodrama." *Southerly,* 33 (1973), 18-33.

LORD, MARY, "A Contribution to the Bibliography of Hal Porter." *Australian Literary Studies,* 4 (1970), 405-9.

PORTER, HAL. "Answers to the Funny, Kind Man." *Southerly,* 29 (1969), 3-14.

THE PAPER CHASE (1966)

GEERING, R. G. "Two Aspects of Hal Porter." *Southerly,* 27 (1967), 180-85.

THE RIGHT THING (1971)

GEERING, R. G. "Hal Porter: The Controls of Melodrama." *Southerly,* 33 (1973), 26-33.

MITCHELL, ADRIAN. "The Many Mansions: Recent Australian Fiction." *Ariel: A Review Of International English Literature,* 5, No.3 (1974), 6-9.

PORTER, HAL. "Gavin's Diary: An Unused Last Chapter of *The Right Thing." Southerly,* 33 (1973), 355-63.

THE TILTED CROSS (1961)

HERGENHAN, L. T. "*The Tilted Cross:* the 'Duties of Innocence.' " *Southerly,* 34 (1974), 157-67.

PORTNER, PAUL (1925-)

TOBIAS IMMERGRUN

Reviews
HERD, E. W. *German Life And Letters,* 19 (1965), 81-82.

POSADA, JOSÉ

VIDA CORRIENTE (1964)

Reviews
FABIAN, DONALD L. *Hispania,* 48 (1965), 389.

POSTL, Karl Anton See SEALSFIELD, Charles

POWE, Bruce see PORTAL, Ellis

PRADO, PEDRO (Chilean, 1886-1952)

COUNTRY JUDGE (Un juez rural, 1924)

Reviews
YATES, DONALD A. *Hispania,* 52 (1969), 163-64.

PRATOLINI, VASCO (Italian, 1913-)

BRUNO SANTINI (La costanza della ragione, 1963)

Reviews
FURBANK, P. N. "Manning, Pratolini." *Encounter,* 25, No.6 (1965), 78-79.

WINTERS, WARRINGTON. "The Saving Surrender to Reality." *Saturday Review,* 6 March 1965, pp. 28-29.

THE GIRLS OF SAN FREDIANO (Le ragazze di San Frediano, 1952)

ROSENGARTEN, FRANK. *Vasco Pratolini: The Development Of A Social Novelist,* pp. 81-85.

A HERO OF OUR TIME (Un eroe del nostro tempo, 1949)

ROSENGARTEN, FRANK. *Vasco Pratolini: The Development Of A Social Novelist,* pp. 75-81.

METELLO (1955)

ROSENGARTEN, FRANK. *Vasco Pratolini: The Development Of A Social Novelist,* pp. 96-107.

Reviews
CLEMENTS, ROBERT J. "Villains, Victims, and a Happy Ending." *Saturday Review,* 13 July 1968, pp. 31-32.

THE NAKED STREETS (Il quartiere, 1944)

ROSENGARTEN, FRANK. *Vasco Pratolini: The Development Of A Social Novelist,* pp. 53-61.

LO SCIALO (1960)

ROSENGARTEN, FRANK. *Vasco Pratolini: The Development Of A Social Novelist,* pp. 107-26.

A TALE OF POOR LOVERS (Cronache di poveri amanti, 1947)

ROSENGARTEN, FRANK. "The Italian Resistance Novel (1945-1962)," in *From Verismo To Experimentalism,* ed. Sergio Pacifici, pp. 221-24.

——. *Vasco Pratolini: The Development Of A Social Novelist,* pp. 64-75.

VIA DE' MAGAZZINI (1942)

ROSENGARTEN, FRANK. *Vasco Pratolini: The Development Of A Social Novelist,* pp. 35-42

PREMCHAND (Indian, 1880-1936) pseudonym of Dhanpat Rai Srivastav

GENERAL

ASNANI, SHYAM M. "An Indian Gorki." *Indian Literature,* 18, No.2 (1975), 62-72.

COPPOLA, CARLO. "A Bibliography of English Sources for the Study of Prem Chand." *Mahfil,* 1, No.2 (1963), 21-24.

THE GIFT OF A COW (Godan, A Novel of Peasant Indian, 1936)

CARNIE, DANIEL. "The Modern Middle Class: In Premchand and in Forster." *Indian Literature,* 17, Nos.1/2 (1974), 25-32.

SPIVAK, GAYATRI C. "Versions of a Colossus: A Review of Gordon C. Roadarmel's Translation of Premchand's *Godan.*" *Mahfil,* 6, No.2/3 (1970), 31-37.

Reviews
GEMMILL, JANET. P. *Literature East And West,* 14 (1970), 288-89.

ROCHER, LUDO. *Journal Of Asian Studies,* 29 (1969), 196-97.

SWAN, ROBERT O. *Journal Of Asian Studies,* 30 (1970), 218-20.

RANGABHUMI (1925)

JAIN, PRATIBHA. "Prem Chand's Rangabhumi—A Historical Evaluation." *Indian Literature,* 16, No.1/2 (1973), 28-35.

PRÉVOST, (ABBÉ) ANTOINE FRANÇOIS (French, 1697-1763)

GENERAL

CHERPACK, CLIFTON. "Prospects of, and Prospects for, the Fiction of Prévost." *L'Esprit Créateur,* 12 (1972), 75-81.

WINANDY, RITA. "Prévost and Morality of Sentiment." *L'Esprit Créateur,* 12 (1972), 94-102.

THE DEAL OF COLERAINE (Le doyen de Killérine, 1735-40)

MEAD, WILLIAM. "The Puzzle of Prévost: *Le Doyen De Killerine.*" *L'Esprit Créateur,* 12 (1972), 82-93.

MYLNE, VIVIENNE. *The Eighteenth Century French Novel,* pp. 83-90.

HISTORY OF A FAIR GREEK (Histoire d'un Greque moderne, 1740)

SINGERMAN, ALAN J. "The Abbé Prévost's 'Grecque Moderne': A Witness for the Defense." *French Review,* 46 (1973), 938-45.

HISTORY OF THE CHEVALIER DES GRIEUX AND OF MANON LESCAUT (Histoire du Chevalier des Grieux et de Manon Lescaut, 1753)

BRADY, PATRICK. "Other-Portrayal and Self-Betrayal in *Manon Lescaut* and *La Vie De Marianne.*" *Romanic Review,* 64 (1973), 99-110.

DONOHOE, JOSEPH I. "The Death of Manon: A Literary Inquest." *L'Esprit Créateur,* 12 (1972), 129-46.

FAMBROUGH, PRESTON. *"L'Âme Généreuse* in Prévost's Romantic Hero." *Romance Notes,* 14 (1972), 112-15.

FRAUTSCHI, RICHARD L. WITH DIANA APOSTOLIDES. "Narrative Voice in *Manon Lescaut:* Some Quantitative Observations." *L'Esprit Créateur,* 12 (1972), 103-17.

GOSSMAN, LIONEL. "Prévost's *Manon:* Love in the New World." *Yale French Studies,* No.40 (1968), pp. 91-102.

GRESHOFF, C. J. "A Note on the Ambiguity of *Manon Lescaut.*" *Forum For Modern Language Studies,* 3 (1967), 166-71.

HIGGINS, I. R. W. "The Ambiguity of *Manon Lescaut:* A Reply to C. J. Greshoff." *Forum For Modern Language Studies,* 4 (1968), 192-98.

HUNT, TONY. "Fatality and the Novel: *Tristran, Manon Lescaut* and *Thérèse Desqueyroux.*" *Durham University Journal,* NS, 37 (1976), 185-91.

JOSEPHS, HERBERT. "*Manon Lescaut:* A Rhetoric of Intellectual Evasion." *Romanic Review,* 59 (1968), 185-97.

MEAD, WILLIAM. "Manon Lescaut, c'est moi?" *L'Esprit Créateur,* 6 (1966), 85-96.

MYLINE, VIVIENNE. *The Eighteenth Century French Novel,* pp. 90-103.

——. *Prévost: Manon Lescaut.*

NICHOLS, STEPHEN G. "The Double Register of Time and Character in *Manon Lescaut.*" *Romance Notes,* 7 (1966), 149-54.

O'REILLY, ROBERT F. "New Considerations on Point of View in *Manon Lescaut.*" *Romance Notes,* 13 (1971), 107-12.

PUGH, ANTHONY R. "The *Manon* Debate—A Post-Script." *Forum For Modern Language Studies,* 5 (1969), 347-49.

SINGERMAN, ALAN J. "A *Fille De Plaisir* and Her *Greluchon:* Society and the Perspective of Manon Lescaut." *L'Esprit Créateur,* 12 (1972), 118-28.

THODY, P. M. W. "The Twentyman Lecture: *Manon Lescaut* and

Les Liaisons Dangereuses: The Problems of Morality in Literature." *Modern Languages,* 56 (1975), 61–72.

THE LIFE AND ENTERTAINING ADVENTURES OF MR. CLEVELAND (Le philosophe anglais, 1738)

CHERPACK, CLIFTON. "Literature and Belief: The Example of Prévost's *Cleveland.*" *Eighteenth-Century Studies,* 6 (1972/3), 186–202.

———. "Reply to Philip Stewart." *Eighteenth-Century Studies,* 7 (1973/4), 210–12.

STEWART, PHILIP. "Prévost's English Philosopher." *Eighteenth-Century Studies,* 7 (1973/4), 207–10.

PRICHARD, KATHARINE S. (Australian, 1883–)

GENERAL

HEWETT, DOROTHY. "Excess of Love: The Irreconcilable in Katharine Susannah Prichard." *Overland,* No.43 (1969/70), pp. 27–31.

"Katharine Susannah Prichard: 'Excess of Love'? Some Comments." *Overland,* No.44 (1970), pp. 25–28.

PRICHARD, KATHARINE, SUSANNAH. "Some Perceptions and Aspirations." *Southerly,* 28 (1968), 235–44.

ROLAND, BETTY. "Requiem for K. S. P." *Overland,* No.44 (1970), pp. 29–31.

PRIETO, JENARO (Chilean, 1889–1946)

GENERAL

MEEHAN, THOMAS C. "Jenaro Prieto: The Man and His Work," in *Tradition And Renewal,* ed. Merlin H. Forster, pp. 157–207.

PRISCO, MICHELE (Italian, 1920–)

A SPIRAL OF MIST (Una spirale di nebbia, 1966)

Reviews
FANTAZZI, CHARLES. *Saturday Review,* 6 September 1969, p. 36.

PRITAM, AMRITA (1919–)

TWO FACES OF EVE

LAL, P. N. "Tragic Contents in Amrita Pritam's *Two Faces Of Eve.*" *Journal Of Indian Writing In English,* 1, No.2 (1973), 43–50.

PROU, SUZANNE (French, 1920–)

THE PAPERHANGER (Mérchamment les oiseaux, 1971)

Reviews
KNAPP, BETTINA, L. *French Review,* 46 (1972), 449.

PROUST, MARCEL (French, 1871–1922)

GENERAL

BALAKIAN, ANNA. "Proust Fifty Years Later." *Comparative Literature Studies,* 10 (1973), 93–111.

BANCROFT, W. JANE. "Realist or Decadent? Proust in the U. S. S. R." *Mosaic,* No.2 (1973), 1–18.

COHN, ROBERT G. "Proust and Mallarmé." *French Studies,* 24 (1970), 262–75.

HOUSTON, JOHN PORTER. "Literature and Psychology: The Case of Proust." *L'Esprit Créateur,* 5 (1965), 3–13.

JACOBS, CAROL. "Walter Benjamin: Image of Proust." *MLN,* 86 (1971), 910–32.

JOINER, LAWRENCE O. "Proust and Azorín." *Romance Notes,* 13 (1972), 468–73.

———. "Similarities in Proust's and Azorin's Theories of the Novel." *South Atlantic Bulletin,* 39, No.2 (1974), 43–50.

KASELL, WALTER. "Proust the Pilgrim: His Idolatrous Reading of Ruskin." *Revue De Littérature Comparée,* 49 (1975), 547–60.

KOPP, RICHARD L. *Marcel Proust As A Social Critic.*

LERNER, MICHAEL G. "Édouard Rod and Marcel Proust." *French Studies,* 25 (1971), 162–68.

LOURIA, YVETTE. "Nabokov and Proust: The Challenge of Time." *Books Abroad,* 48 (1974), 469–76.

MEIN, MARGARET. "Chateaubriand, a Precursor of Proust." *French Review,* 45 (1971), 388–400.

———. *A Foretaste Of Proust: A Study Of Proust And His Precursors.*

———. "Nerval: A Precursor of Proust." *Romanic Review,* 62 (1971), 99–112.

———. "Novalis a Precursor of Proust." *Comparative Literature,* 23 (1971), 217–32.

———. "Proust and Pascal." *L'Esprit Créateur,* 11, No.1 (1971), 74–93.

MURRAY, JACK. "Mind and Reality in Proust and Robbe-Grillet." *Wisconsin Studies In Contemporary Literature,* 8 (1967), 407–20.

———. "Proust's Views on Perception as a Metaphoric Framework." *French Review,* 42 (1969), 380–94.

NAUGHTON, HELEN THOMAS. "A Contemporary Views Proust." *L'Esprit Créateur,* 5 (1965), 48–55.

O'BRIEN, JUSTIN. "Involuntary Memory Before Marcel Proust," in his *Contemporary French Literature,* pp. 28–47.

———. "Proust Confirmed by Neurosurgery." *PMLA,* 85 (1970), 295–97; rpt. in his *Contemporary French Literature,* pp. 265–71.

PEYRE, HENRI. *Marcel Proust.*

REVEL, JEAN-FRANÇOIS. "Proust & the Snobs." *Encounter,* 38, No.4 (1972), 27–33.

RIVA, RAYMOND T. "Marcel Proust: An Immodest Proposal." *Criticism,* 10 (1968), 217–24.

SANSOM, WILLIAM. *Proust And His World.*

SOUCY, ROBERT. "Bad Readers in the World of Proust" *French Review,* 44 (1971), 677–86.

STOLTZFUS, BEN. "Proust and Robbe-Grillet." *Romance Notes,* 12 (1971), 251–58.

URMAN, DOROTHY FULDHEIM. "Konstantin Paustovskii, Marcel Proust and the Golden Rose of Memory." *Canadian Slavic Studies,* 2 (1968), 311–26.

THE CAPTIVE (La prisonnierre, 1929)

MEYERS, JEFFREY. *Painting And The Novel,* pp. 112–23.

SONNENFELD, ALBERT. "*Tristan* for Pianoforte: Thomas Mann and Marcel Proust." *Southern Review,* NS, 5 (1969), 1004–18.

COMBRAY

TAYLOR, ROSALIE. "The Adult World and Childhood in *Combray.*" *French Studies,* 22 (1968), 26–36.

JEAN SANTEUIL (1952)

ALDEN, DOUGLAS W. "The Break with Realism," in *Marcel Proust: A Critical Panorama,* ed. Larkin B. Price, pp. 24–48.

BRÉE, GERMAINE. "*Jean Santeuil:* An Appraisal." *L'Esprit Créateur,* 5 (1965), 14–25.

CATTAUI, GEORGES. *Marcel Proust,* pp. 22–41.

FINN, MICHAEL R. "*Jean Santeuil* and *A La Recherche Du Temps*

Perdu: Instinct and Intellect." *Forum For Modern Language Studies,* 11 (1975), 122-28.

JEPHCOTT, E. F. N. *Proust And Rilke: The Literature Of Expanded Consciousness,* pp. 82-94.

MCMAHON, JOSEPH H. "From Things to Themes." *Yale French Studies,* No.34 (1965), pp. 5-12.

O'BRIEN, JUSTIN. "The Wisdom of the Young Proust," in his *Contemporary French Literature,* pp. 60-84.

PRICE, LARKIN B. "Marcel Proust's 'Dieu Déguisé: The Artist-Myth in *Jean Santeuil.*" *L'Esprit Créateur,* 11, No.1 (1971), 61-73.

ROGERS, B. G. *Proust's Narrative Techniques,* pp. 43-61.

SLATER, MAYA. " 'L'Inconnu': A Fragment of 'Jean Santeuil.' " *Modern Language Review,* 56 (1970), 778-84.

ULLMAN, STEPHEN. "Images of Time and Memory in 'Jean Santeuil,' " in *Currents Of Thought In French Literature,* pp. 209-26.

LA MORT DE BALDASSARE SILVANDE

ZIMMERMAN, EUGENIA N. "Death and Transfiguration in Proust and Tolstoy." *Mosaic,* 6, No.2 (1973), 161-72.

REMEMBRANCE OF THINGS PAST (A la recherche du temps perdu, 1913-1927)

APPIGNANESI, LISA. *Femininity & The Creative Imagination,* pp. 157-215.

BALAKIAN, ANNA. "Proust Fifty Years Later." *Comparative Literature Studies,* 10 (1973), 93-111.

BALES, RICHARD. *Proust And The Middle Ages,* pp. 117-38.

BERSANI, LEO. *Balzac To Beckett,* pp. 192-239.

———. *Marcel Proust: The Fictions Of Life And Art.*

BEYNON, SUSAN E. "Life, Time and Art in Proust's 'Le Temps retrouve.' " *Nottingham French Studies,* 14 (1975), 86-93.

BEZNOS, MAURICE J. "Aspects of Time according to the Theories of Relativity in Marcel Proust's *A La Recherche Du Temps Perdu:* A Study of the Similitudes in Conceptual Limits." *Ohio University Review,* 10 (1968), 74-102.

BIRN, RANDI MARIE. "Love and Communication: An Interpretation of Proust's Albertine." *French Review,* 40 (1966), 221-28.

———. "The Theoretical Background for Proust's Personages 'Préparés.' " *L'Esprit Créateur,* 11, No.1 (1971), 42-51.

BONDANELLA, PETER E. and J. E. RIVERS. "Sacripant and Sacripante: A Note on Proust and Ariosto." *Romance Notes,* 11 (1969), 4-7.

BRÉE, GERMAINE. *Marcel Proust And Deliverance From Time.*

———. "Proust's Dormant Gods." *Yale French Studies,* No.38 (1967), pp. 83-94.

BUCKNALL, BARBARA J. "From Material to Spiritual Food in *A La Recherche Du Temps Perdu.*" *L'Esprit Créateur,* 11, No.1 (1971), 52-60.

———. *The Religion Of Art In Proust.*

BYCHOWSKI, GUSTAV. "Marcel Proust and His Mother." *American Imago,* 30 (1973), 8-25.

———. "Marcel Proust as Poet of Psychoanalysis." *American Imago,* 30 (1973), 26-32.

CATTAUI, GEORGES. *Marcel Proust,* pp. 42-90.

COCKING, J. M. "The Coherence of *Le Temps Retrouvé,*" in *Marcel Proust: A Critical Panorama,* ed. Larkin B. Price, pp. 82-101.

COHEN, ALAIN. "Proust and President Schreber: A Theory of Primal Quotation or For a *Psychoanalytics Of (Desire-In) Philosophy.*" *Yale French Studies,* No.52 (1975), pp. 13-17.

COLLIN, P. H. "Food and Drink in *A La Recherche Du Temps Perdu.*" *Neophilologus,* 54 (1970), 244-57.

CONROY, PETER V. "The Hôtel de Balbec as a Church and Theater," in *Marcel Proust: A Critical Panorama,* ed. Larkin B. Price, pp. 206-25.

CRUICKSHANK, JOHN. "The Shifting World of Proust." *Critical Quarterly,* 8 (1966), 220-28.

CULBERTSON, DIANA. "A la Recherche de Vermeer: Proust and the 'Sphinx of Delft.' " *Southern Humanities Review,* 9 (1975), 77-87.

DELEUZE, GILLES. *Proust And Signs.*

DE LEY, HERBERT. " 'L'Hôpital sans style vaut le glorieux portail': Salon Painters in *A La Recherche Du Temps Perdu.*" *L'Esprit Créateur,* 11, No.1 (1971), 32-41.

DOUBROVSKY, SERGE. "The Place of the Madeleine: Writing and Phantasy in Proust." *Boundary* 2, 4 (1975), 107-34.

DUNCAN, J. ANN. "Imaginary Artists in 'A la recherche du temps perdu.' " *Modern Language Review,* 64 (1969), 555-64.

ERICKSON, JOHN D. "The Proust-Einstein Relation: A Study in Relative Point of View," in *Marcel Proust: A Critical Panorama,* ed. Larkin B. Price, pp. 247-76.

FINN, MICHAEL R. " *Jean Santeuil* and *A La Recherche Du Temps Perdu:* Instinct and Intellect." *Forum For Modern Language Studies,* 11 (1975), 128-32.

FISHER, CLARICE. "Character as a Way of Knowing in *A La Recherche Du Temps Perdu:* The Baron de Charlus." *Modern Fiction Studies,* 20 (1974), 407-18.

FOWLIE, WALLACE. *A Reading Of Proust.*

GRAHAM, VICTOR E. *The Imagery Of Proust.*

———. "Proust's Alchemy." *Modern Language Review,* 60 (1965), 197-206.

———. "Proust's Etymologies." *French Studies,* 29 (1975), 300-12.

GRAY, STANLEY E. "Phenomenology, Structuralism and Marcel Proust." *L'Esprit Créateur,* 8 (1968), 58-74.

GROSS, BEVERLY. "Narrative Time and the Open-ended Novel." *Criticism,* 8 (1966), 362-67.

GROSSVOGEL, DAVID I. *Limits Of The Novel,* pp. 189-225.

GUTWIRTH, MARCEL. "Swann and the Duchess." *French Review,* 38 (1964), 143-51.

HEMMINGS, F. W. J. " 'Le moi oeuvrant': The Enigma of a Proustian theme." *Forum For Modern Language Studies,* 8 (1972), 215-36.

HEWITT, JAMES ROBERT. *Marcel Proust.*

HOLDRIDGE, DAVID. "Suspended Structures in Proust's *A La Recherche Du Temps Perdu.*" *Modern Languages,* 52 (1971), 112-18.

HOUSTON, JOHN PORTER. "Theme and Structure in *A La Recherche Du Temps Perdu.*" *Kentucky Romance Quarterly,* 17 (1970), 209-21.

———. "Thought, Style, and Shape in Proust's Novel." *Southern Review,* NS, 5 (1969), 987-1003.

HYDE, JOHN K. "Proust, His Jews and His Jewishness." *French Review,* 39 (1966), 837-48.

JACKSON, ELIZABETH R. "The Crystallization of *A La Recherche Du Temps Perdu* 1908-1909." *French Review,* 38 (1964), 157-66.

JEFFERSON, LOUISE M. "Proust and Racine." *Yale French Studies,* No.34 (1965), pp. 99-105.

JEPHCOTT, E. F. N. *Proust And Rilke: The Literature Of Expanded Consciousness,* pp. 251-93.

JOHNSON, J. THEODORE. "From Artistic Celibacy to Artistic Contemplation." *Yale French Studies,* No.34 (1965), pp. 81-89.

———. " 'La Lanterne Magique': Proust's Metaphorical Toy." *L'Esprit Créateur,* 11, No.1 (1971), 17-31.

_____. "Proust and Giotto: Foundations for an Allegorical Interpretation of *A La Recherche Du Temps Perdu.*" in *Marcel Proust: A Critical Panorama,* ed. Larkin B. Price, pp. 168-205.

_____. "Proust's 'Impressionism' Reconsidered in the Light of the Visual Arts of the Twentieth Century," in *Twentieth Century French Fiction,* ed. George Stambolian, pp. 27-56.

JOINER, LAWRENCE P. "Proust and Azorín." *Romance Notes,* 13 (1972), 468-73.

JONES, DAVID L. " 'Dolorès Disparue.' " *Symposium,* 20 (1966), 135-40.

_____. "Proust and Doderer as Historical Novelists." *Comparative Literature Studies,* 10 (1973), 9-16.

JONES, EDWARD T. "Summer of 1900: *A La Récherche* of *The Go-Between.*" *Literature/Film Quarterly,* 1 (1973), 154-60.

JONES, PETER. "Knowledge and Illusion in *A La Recherche Du Temps Perdu.*" *Forum For Modern Language Studies,* 5 (1969), 303-22.

JOSIPOVICI, GABRIEL. "Proust: A Voice in Search of Itself." *Critical Quarterly,* 13 (1971), 105-23.

_____. "Structures of Truth: The Premises of the French New Criticism." *Critical Quarterly,* 10 (1968), 73-78.

KAMBER, GERALD and RICHARD MACKSEY. " 'Negative Metaphor' and Proust's Rhetoric of Absence." *MLN,* 85 (1970), 858-83.

KOLB, PHILIP. "The Birth of Elstir and Vinteuil," in *Marcel Proust: A Critical Panorama,* ed. Larkin B. Price, pp. 147-67.

_____. "Proust's Protagonist as a 'Beacon.' " *L'Esprit Créateur,* 5 (1965), 38-47.

KOSTIS, NICHOLAS. "Albertine: Characterization Through Image and Symbol." *PMLA,* 84 (1969), 125-35.

LABAT, ALVIN. "Proust's Mme de Sévigné." *L'Esprit Créateur,* 15 (1975), 271-85.

LANGUTH, WILLIAM. "The World and Life of the Dream." *Yale French Studies,* No.34 (1965), pp. 117-30.

LEWIS, PHILIP E. "Idealism and Reality." *Yale French Studies,* No.34 (1965), pp. 24-28.

LOURIA, YVETTE. "Nabokov and Proust: The Challenge of Time." *Books Abroad,* 48 (1974), 469-76.

LYNN, THÉRÈSE B. "The Narrator, Not Marcel: Manuscript Proofs." *Romance Notes,* 16 (1975), 258-61.

MCMAHON, JOSEPH H. "From Things to Themes." *Yale French Studies,* No.34 (1965), pp. 13-17.

MARCH, HAROLD. "The Imprisoned." *Yale French Studies,* No.34 (1965), pp. 43-54.

MARKS, JONATHAN E. "The Verdurins and their Cult." *Yale French Studies,* No.34 (1965), pp. 73-80.

MORACEVICH, NICHOLAS. "Ivo Andrić and the Quintessence of Time." *Slavic And East European Journal,* 16 (1972), 313-18.

MURRAY, JACK. "The Mystery of Others." *Yale French Studies,* No.34 (1965), pp. 65-72.

_____. "Proust, Montesquiou, Balzac." *Texas Studies In Literature And Language,* 15 (1973), 177-87.

_____. "Proust's Robert de Saint-Loup and the Diagnostic Eye." *Texas Studies In Literature And Language,* 6 (1964), 68-75.

NAUGHTON, HELEN THOMAS. "A Contemporary Views Proust." *L'Esprit Créateur,* 5 (1965), 48-55.

O'BRIEN, JUSTIN. "Albertine the Ambiguous: Notes on Proust's Transposition of Sexes," in his *Contemporary French Literature,* pp. 85-114.

_____. "An Aspect of Proust's Baron de Charlus," in his *Contemporary French Literature,* pp. 115-21.

_____. "Fall and redemption in Proust," in his *Contemporary French Literature,* pp. 145-47.

_____. "Marcel Proust as a 'moraliste,' " in his *Contemporary French Literature,* pp. 48-59.

_____. "Proust and 'le joli language.' " *PMLA,* 80 (1965), 259-63; rpt. in his *Contemporary French Literature,* pp. 122-44.

_____. "Proust's Use of Syllepsis," in his *Contemporary French Literature,* pp. 148-68.

PASCO, ALLAN H. "Blue and the Ideal of *A La Recherche Du Temps Perdu.*" *Romanische Forschungen,* 85 (1973), 119-38.

_____. "Marcel, Albertine and Balbec in Proust's Allusive Complex." *Romanic Review,* 62 (1971), 113-26.

PHILIP, MICHEL. "The Hidden Onlooker." *Yale French Studies,* No.34 (1965), pp. 37-42.

PORTER, AGNES R. "Proust's Final Montesquiou Pastiche," in *Marcel Proust: A Critical Panorama,* ed. Larkin B. Price, pp. 124-46.

PRICE, LARKIN B. "Bird Imagery Surrounding Proust's Albertine." *Symposium,* 26 (1972), 242-60.

REDDICK, BRYAN. "Proust: The 'La Berma' Passages." *French Review,* 42 (1969), 683-92.

REVEL, JEAN-FRANÇOIS. *On Proust.*

ROBERTSON, JANE. "The Relationship between the Hero and François in *A La Recherche Du Temps Perdu.*" *French Studies,* 25 (1971), 437-41.

RODITI, EDOUARD. "Proust Recaptured." *Kenyon Review,* 30 (1968), 23-39.

ROGERS, BRIAN G. "Narrative Tones and Perspectives in Proust's Novel." *Modern Language Review,* 60 (1965), 207-11.

_____. "Proust and the Mémoires of the Comtesse de Boigne." *English Studies In Africa,* 18 (1975), 49-62.

_____. *Proust's Narrative Techniques,* pp. 94-201.

ROWLAND, MICHAEL. "*Contre Sainte-Beuve* and Character-Presentation in *A La Recherche Du Temps Perdu.*" *Romance Notes,* 8 (1967), 183-87.

RUBIN, LOUIS D. *The Teller In The Tale,* pp. 103-40.

SAVAGE, CATHARINE H. "Death in A La Recherche Du Temps Perdu." *Forum,* 4, No.1 (1963), 7-11.

_____. "Nostalgia in Alain-Fournier and Proust." *French Review,* 38 (1964), 167-72.

SAYCE, R. A. "The Goncourt Pastiche in *Le Temps Retrouvé,*" in *Marcel Proust: A Critical Panorama,* ed. Larkin B. Price, pp. 102-23.

SEIDEN, MELVIN. "Proust's Marcel and Saint-Loup: Inversion Reconsidered." *Contemporary Literature,* 10 (1969), 220-40.

SHATTUCK, ROGER. *Marcel Proust.*

_____. "Proust's Stilts." *Yale French Studies,* No.34 (1965), pp. 91-98.

SLATER, MAYA. "Some Recurrent Comparisons in 'A la recherche du temps perdu.' " *Modern Language Review,* 62 (1967), 629-32.

SMITH, A. M. SHERIDAN. "Madeleine and the Proust: A Recent Discovery." *London Magazine,* 7, No.1 (1967), 66-74.

SOUCY, ROBERT. "Proust's Aesthetic of Reading." *French Review,* 41 (1967), 48-59.

STAMBOLIAN, GEORGE. *Marcel Proust And The Creative Encounter.*

STICCA, SANDRO. "Anticipation as a Literary Technique in Proust's *A La Recherche Du Temps Perdu.*" *Symposium,* 20 (1966), 254-62.

STRAUSS, WALTER A. "Nonrecognition and Recognition in Proust." *Nineteenth-Century French Studies,* 4 (1975/6), 105-23.

SULLIVAN, DENNIS G. "On Theatricality in Proust: Desire and the Actress." *MLN,* 86 (1971), 532-54.

———. "On Vision in Proust: The Icon and the *Voyeur.*" *MLN,* 84 (1969), 646-61.

SUTTON, HOWARD. "Two Poets of Childhood: Marcel Proust and Marie Nöel." *Books Abroad,* 41 (1967), 261-66.

THIBAUDEAU, BARBARA. "Condemned to Lie." *Yale French Studies,* No.34 (1965), pp. 55-63.

TOLMACHEV, M. V. "Impressionist-Classicist Tensions." *Yale French Studies,* No.34 (1965), pp. 29-35.

TUKEY, ANN. "Notes on Involuntary Memory in Proust." *French Review,* 42 (1969), 395-402.

VINEBERG, ELSA. "Marcel Proust, Nathalie Sarraute, and the Psychological Novel." *MLN,* 90 (1975), 575-83.

VIRTANEN, REINO. "Differing Essences: Santayana and Proust," in *Marcel Proust: A Critical Panorama,* ed. Larkin B. Price, pp. 277-88.

WEBER, SAMUEL M. "The Madrepore." *MLN,* 87 (1972), 915-61.

WEINSTEIN, ARNOLD L. *Vision And Response In Modern Fiction,* pp. 216-24.

WILSON, STEPHEN. "Proust's 'À la Recherche du Temps Perdu' as a Document of Social History." *Journal Of European Studies,* 1 (1971), 213-43.

WOLITZ, SETH L. *The Proustian Community.*

ZANTS, EMILY. "Proust and the New Novel in France." *PMLA,* 88 (1973), 25-33.

———. "Proust's Magic Lantern." *Modern Fiction Studies,* 19 (1973), 211-16.

ZIMMERMAN, EUGENIA NOIK. "The Metamorphosis of Adam: Names and Things in Sartre and Proust," in *Twentieth Century French Fiction,* ed. George Stambolian, pp. 57-71.

SWANN IN LOVE (Un Amour de Swann)

BELL, WILLIAM S. "Proust's 'Un Amour de Swann': A Voyage to Cytherea." *L'Esprit Créateur,* 5 (1965), 26-37.

CHUA, C. L. "Proust's *Un Amour De Swann.*" *Explicator,* 26 (1968), Item 69.

FINN, MICHAEL R. "Proust and Dumas fils: Odette and *La Dame Aux Camélias.*" *French Review,* 47 (1974), 528-42.

HICKS, ERIC C. "Swann's Dream and the World of Sleep." *Yale French Studies,* No.34 (1965), pp. 106-16.

JONES. LOUISA. "Swann and the *Tables Tournantes.*" *French Review,* 48 (1975), 711-21.

LAPP, JOHN C. "The Jealous Window-Watcher in Zola and Proust." *French Studies,* 29 (1975), 165-76.

ZIMMERMANN, ELÉONORE M. "Proust's Novel in a Novel: 'Un Amour de Swann.'" *Modern Language Review,* 68 (1973), 551-58.

SWANN'S WAY (Du Côté de Chez Swann, 1913)

CUNNINGHAM, WILLIAM. "Giorgione Transfigured—A Note on Proust's Method." *Romance Notes,* 9 (1967), 11-15.

HALL, VERNON. "Proust's *Du Côté De Chez Swann.*" *Explicator,* 30 (1972), Item 52.

JOHNSON, J. THEODORE. "Proust's 'Impressionism' Reconsidered, in the Light of the Visual Arts of the Twentieth Century," in *Twentieth Century French Fiction,* ed. George Stambolian, pp. 27-56.

MEYERS, JEFFREY. *Painting And The Novel,* pp. 96-111.

———. "Proust's Aesthetic Analogies: Character and Painting in *Swann's Way.*" *Journal Of Aesthetics And Art Criticism,* 30 (1972), 337-88.

MINOGUE, VALERIE. *Proust: Du Côté De Chez Swann.*

NITZBERG, HOWARD. " 'Du côté de chez Swann': The Orpheus

and Euridice Theme." *USF Language Quarterly,* 14, No.1/2 (1975), 15, 26.

PARDEE, W. HEARNE. "The Images of Vision." *Yale French Studies,* No.34 (1965), pp. 19-23.

PSICHARI, ERNEST (French, 1883-1914)
GENERAL

MOYLAN, PAUL A. "Ernest Psichari's Mystical Heroism." *Renascence,* 21, No.2 (1969), 103-9.

PUIG, MANUEL (Argentine, 1932-)
GENERAL

PUIG, MANUEL. "Growing up at the Movies: a Chronology." *Review,* No.4/5 (1971/2), pp. 49-51.

BETRAYED BY RITA HAYWORTH (La tración de Rita Hayworth, 1968)

BRUSHWOOD, JOHN S. *The Spanish American Novel,* pp. 305-8.

CHRIST, RONALD. "Fact and Fiction." *Review,* No.9 (1973), pp. 49-54.

FOSTER, DAVID WILLIAM. *Currents In The Contemporary Argentine Novel,* pp. 144-47.

FROSCH, MARTA MORELLO. "The New Art of Narrating Films." Trans. Mary A. Kilmer. *Review,* No.4/5 (1971/2), pp. 52-55.

KADIR, DJELAL. "Nostalgia or Nihilism: Pop Art and the New Spanish American Novel." *Journal Of Spanish Studies,* 2 (1974), 127-35.

LEVINE, SUZANNE JILL. "Notes on Translation." *Review,* No.4/5 (1971/2), pp. 91-94.

MACADAM, ALFRED J. "Manuel Puig's Chronicles of Provincial Life." *Revista Hispanica Moderna,* 36 (1970/1) 50-60.

RODRIGUEZ MONEGAL, EMIR. "A Literary Myth Exploded." Trans. Mary A. Kilmer. *Review,* No.4/5 (1971/2), pp. 56-64.

SARRIS, ANDREW. "Rerunning Puig and Cabrera Infante." *Review,* No.9 (1973), pp. 46-48.

THE BUENOS AIRES AFFAIR (1973)

Reviews
CHEUSE, ALAN. "Puig's Last Picture Show." *Review,* No.16 (1975), pp. 79-81.

FOSTER, DAVID WILLIAM. *Latin American Literary Review,* 2, No.4 (1974), 149-50.

LEWALD, H. ERNEST. *Journal Of Spanish Studies,* 3 (1975), 220-22.

HEARTBREAK TANGO (Boquitas pintadas, 1969)

CHRIST, RONALD. "Fact and Fiction." *Review,* No.9 (1973), pp. 49-54.

FOSTER, DAVID WILLIAM. "Manuel Puig and the Uses of Nostalgia." *Latin American Literary Review,* 1, No.1 (1972), 79-81.

HAZERA, LYDIA D. "Narrative Technique in Manuel Puig's *Boquitas Pintadas [Painted Little Mouths.]*" *Latin American Literary Review,* 2, No.3 (1973), 45-53.

MACADAM, ALFRED J. "Manuel Puig's Chronicles of Provincial Life." *Revista Hispanica Moderna,* 36 (1970/1), 61-65.

WEISS, JUDITH A. "Dynamic Correlations in *Heartbreak Tango.*" *Latin American Literary Review,* 3, No.5 (1974), 137-41.

PUSHKIN, ALEXANDER (Russian, 1799-1837)
GENERAL

AKMATOVA, ANNA. "Benjamin Constant's *Adolphe,* in the Work of Pushkin." *Russian Literature Triquarterly,* No.10, (1974) pp. 157-79.

BRIGGS, A. D. "Alexander Pushkin: A Possible Influence on Henry James." *Forum For Modern Language Studies,* 8 (1972), 52-60.

CROSS, ANTHONY. "Pushkin's Bawdy: Or, Notes from the Literary Underground." *Russian Literature Triquarterly,* No.10 (1974), pp. 203-36.

DEBRECZENY, PAUL. "The Reception of Pushkin's Poetic Works in the 1820s: A Study of the Critic's Role." *Slavic Review,* 28 (1969), 394-415.

EIKHENBAUM, BORIS. "Pushkin's Path to Prose," in *Twentieth-Century Russian Literary Criticism,* ed. Victor Erlich, pp. 86-96.

GREENE, MILITSA. "Pushkin and Sir Walter Scott." *Forum for Modern Language Studies,* 1 (1965), 207-15.

GROSSMAN, I. P. " 'The Art of the Anecdote in Pushkin.' " *Russian Literature Triquarterly,* No.10 (1974), pp. 129-48.

IEZUITOVA, R. "The Twentieth Pushkin Conference." *Soviet Studies In Literature,* 8 (1971/2), 81-94.

JOCELYN, MICHAEL. "Pushkin and Barclay de Tolly." *Russian Literature Triquarterly,* No.10 (1974), pp. 237-43.

JOHNSON, C. A. "Pushkin: A Personal View." *Contemporary Review,* 207 (1965), 254-60.

MEILAKH, B. "The Great Innovator." *Soviet Studies In Literature,* 11, No.1 (1974/5), 16-39.

MUCHNIC, HELEN. "Grand Master: Pushkin," in her *Russian Writers,* pp. 3-10.

SIMMONS, ERNEST J. "Pushkin—The Poet as Novelist," in his *Introduction To Russian Realism,* pp. 23-43.

VICKERY, WALTER N. "Recent Soviet Research on the Events Leading to Pushkin's Death." *Slavic And East European Journal,* 14 (1970), 489-502.

THE CAPTAIN'S DAUGHTER (Kapitanskaja dočka, 1836)

BAYLEY, JOHN. *Pushkin: A Comparative Commentary,* pp. 331-54.

MEILAKH, B. "The Great Innovator." *Soviet Studies In Literature,* 11, No.1 (1974/5), 31-33.

MIKKELSON, GERALD E. "The Mythopoetic Element in Pushkin's Historical Novel *The Captain's Daughter." Canadian-American Slavic Studies,* 7 (1973), 296-313.

EUGENE ONEGIN (Yevgeny Onegin, 1833)

ALEKSANDROV, A. " 'Pushkin Is Broad and Generous': Sergei Iursky." *Soviet Studies In Literature,* 8 (1971/2), 52-58.

BAYLEY, JOHN. *Pushkin: A Comparative Commentary,* pp. 236-305.

_____ . "Pushkin's Secret of Distance." *Oxford Slavonic Papers,* 1 NS (1968), 74-82.

BOYD, ALEXANDER F. *Aspects Of The Russian Novel,* pp. 1-23.

CLAYTON, J. DOUGLAS. "The Epigraph of *Eugene Onegin:* A Hypothesis." *Canadian Slavic Studies,* 5 (1971), 226-33.

EIDEN'MAN, N. *Evengenii Onegin:* The Mystery of the Tenth Chapter." *Soviet Studies in Literature,* 11, No.1 (1974/5), 8-15.

FORSYTH, J. "Pisarev, Belinsky and *Yevgeniy Onegin." Slavonic And East European Review,* 48 (1970), 163-80.

FREEBORN, R. H. "Realism in Russia, to the Death of Dostoevsky," in *The Age Of Realism,* ed. F. W. J. Hemmings, pp. 81-84.

_____ . *The Rise Of The Russian Novel,* pp. 10-37.

GREGG, RICHARD A. "Tat'yana's Two Dreams: The Unwanted Spouse and the Demonic Lover." *Slavonic And East European Review,* 48 (1970), 492-505.

HOISINGTON, SONA STEPHAN. "*Eugene Onegin:* An Inverted Byronic Poem." *Comparative Literature,* 27 (1975) 136-52.

LEIGHTON, LAUREN G. "Marlinskij's 'Ispytanie': A Romantic Rejoinder to *Evgenij Onegin." Slavic And East European Journal,* 13 (1969), 200-16.

MCLEAN, HUGH. "The Tone(s) of *Evgenij Onegin." California Slavic Studies,* 6 (1971), 3-15.

MIKKELSON, GERALD E. "The Mythopoetic Element in Pushkin's Historical Novel *The Captain's Daughter." Canadian-American Slavic Studies,* 7 (1973), 296-313.

MITCHELL, STANLEY. "The Digressions of *Yevgeny Onegin:* Apropos of Some Essays by Ettore Lo Gatto." *Slavonic And East European Review,* 44 (1966), 51-65.

_____ . "Tatiana's Reading." *Forum For Modern Language Studies,* 4 (1968), 1-21.

PEER, LARRY H. "Pushkin and Goethe Again: Lensky's Character." *Papers On Language And Literature,* 5 (1969), 267-72.

REEVE, F. D. *The Russian Novel,* pp. 14-44.

SCOTT, W. B. "The Cypress Veil." *Triquarterly,* No.17 (1970), pp. 316-31.

_____ . "The Cypress Veil: Reflections on Recent Translations of Eugene Onegin." *Triquarterly,* No.2 (1965), pp. 94-103.

SHAW, J. THOMAS. "Translations of 'Onegin.' " *Russian Review,* 24 (1965), 111-27.

SHKLOVSKIJ, VIKTOR. "Pushkin and Sterne: *Eugene Onegin,*" in *Twentieth-Century Russian Literary Criticism,* ed. Victor Erlich, pp. 63-80.

SIMMONS, ERNEST J. "Pushkin—The Poet as Novelist," in his *Introduction To Russian Realism,* pp. 28-37.

VICKERY, WALTER N. *Alexander Pushkin,* pp. 102-29.

WEIL, IRWIN. "Onegin's Echo." *Russian Literature Triquarterly,* No.10 (1974), pp. 260-73.

A JOURNEY TO ARZRUM (Puteshestvie v Arzrum)

OLCOTT, ANTHONY. "Parody as Realism: The *Journey To Arzrum." Russian Literature Triquarterly,* No.10 (1974), pp. 245-59.

THE MOOR OF PETER THE GREAT (Arap Petra Velikogo, 1837)

DEBRECZENY, PAUL. "*The Blackamoor Of Peter The Great:* Puškin's Experiment with a Detached Mode of Narration." *Slavic And East European Journal,* 18 (1974), 119-31.

THE QUEEN OF SPADES (Pikovaya dama, 1834)

BAYLEY, JOHN. *Pushkin: A Comparative Commentary,* pp. 316-22.

GREGG, RICHARD A. "Balzac and the Women in *The Queen Of Spades." Slavic And East European Journal,* 10 (1966), 279-82.

ROSEN, NATHAN. "The Magic Cards in *The Queen Of Spades." Slavic And East European Journal,* 19 (1975), 255-75.

SCHWARTZ, MURRAY M. and ALBERT SCHWARTZ. "*The Queen Of Spades:* a Psychoanalytic Interpretation." *Texas Studies In Literature And Language,* 17 (1975), 275-88.

PUTINAS, VINCAS MYKOLAITIS (Lithuanian, 1893-1967) pseudonym of Vincas Mykolaitis

GENERAL

SIETYNAS, ANDRIUS. "The Condition of a Free Prisoner: Poetry and Prose of Vincas Mykolaitis-Putinas." *Lituanus,* 11, No.1 (1965), 48-63.

IN THE SHADOW OF ALTARS (Altoriu šešėly, 1933)

SIETYNAS, ANDRIUS. "The Condition of a Free Prisoner: Poetry and Prose of Vincas Mykolaitis-Putinas." *Lituanus,* 11, No.1 (1965), 55-59.

QASIM, 'ABD AL-HAKIM (Egyptian, 1935–)

AIYAN AL-INSAN AL-SAB'A

KILPATRICK, HILARY. *The Modern Egyptian Novel,* pp. 140–47, 246–47.

QUEIROZ, RACHEL DE (Brazilian, 1910–)

THE THREE MARIAS (As Três Marias, 1939)

Reviews
MOSER, GERALD M. *Hispania,* 48 (1965), 189–90.

QUENEAU, RAYMOND (French, 1903–1976)

GENERAL

MAYNE, RICHARD. "The Queneau Country." *Encounter,* 24, No.6 (1965), 64–71.

MERCIER, VIVIAN. *The New Novel From Queneau To Pinget,* pp. 43–103.

———. "Raymond Queneau: The First New Novelist?" *L'Esprit Créateur,* 7 (1967), 102–12.

SWIGGER, RONALD T. "Fictional Encyclopedism and the Cognitive Value of Literature." *Comparative Literature Studies,* 12 (1975), 360–64.

———. "Reflections on Language in Queneau's Novels." *Contemporary Literature,* 13 (1972), 491–506.

WARSHOW, PAUL. "An Undiscovered Master." *Commentary,* 45, No.3 (1968), 61–68.

THE BARK-TREE (Le Chiendent, 1933)

ALTER, ROBERT. "The Self-Conscious Moment: Reflections on the Aftermath of Modernism." *Triquarterly,* No.33 (1975), pp. 221–22.

MAYNE, RICHARD. "The Queneau Country." *Encounter,* 24, No.6 (1965), 64–68.

MERCIER, VIVIAN. *The New Novel From Queneau To Pinget,* pp. 54–66.

SWIGGER, RONALD T. "Reflections on Language in Queneau's Novels." *Contemporary Literature,* 13 (1972), 493–96.

Reviews
BISHOP, TOM. *Saturday Review,* 7 August 1971, p. 25.

BETWEEN BLUE AND BLUE

Reviews
FYTTON, FRANCIS. *London Magazine,* NS 6, No.12 (1967), 116–18.

BLUE FLOWERS (Les fleurs bleues, 1965)

SWIGGER, RONALD T. "Reflections on Language in Queneau's Novels." *Contemporary Literature,* 13 (1972), 500–6.

CHÊNE ET CHIEN (1937)

MERCIER, VIVIAN. *The New Novel From Queneau To Pinget,* pp. 77–81.

LE DIMANCHE DE LA VIE (1952)

MERCIER, VIVIAN. *The New Novel From Queneau To Pinget,* pp. 95–98.

LES ENFANTS DU LIMON (1938)

MERCIER, VIVIAN. *The New Novel From Queneau To Pinget,* pp. 81–87.

EXERCISES IN STYLE (Exercices de style, 1947)

ALTER, ROBERT. "The Self-Conscious Moment: Reflections on the Aftermath of Modernism." *Triquarterly,* No.33 (1975), pp. 211–12.

THE FLIGHT OF ICARUS (Le vol d'Icare, 1968)

Reviews
JONES, LOUISA. *French Review,* 44 (1970), 185.

SAINT GLINGLIN (1948)

MERCIER, VIVIAN. *The New Novel From Queneau To Pinget,* pp. 67–77.

QUESENEY LANGLOIS, VALERIO

CALICÓ

Reviews
STAIS, JAMES. *Hispania,* 50 (1967), 395–96.

QUEVEDO (y Villegas), FRANCISCO GÓMEZ DE (Spanish, 1580–1645)

EL CUENTO DE CUENTOS (1626)

BAUM, DORIS L. "Quevedo's Satiric Prologues." *Revista De Estudios Hispánicos,* 7 (1973), 233–53.

SOONS, ALAN. " 'El cuento de cuentos:' Quevedo's Anticipation of a Genre." *Orbis Litterarum,* 30 (1975), 187–91.

LA HORA DE TODOS Y FORTUNA CON SESO

PRICE, R. M. "Fiction and False Testimony in *La Hora De Todos.*" *Romanic Review,* 66 (1975), 113–22.

SUEÑO DE JUICIO FINAL

HALEY, GEORGE. "The Earliest Dated Manuscript of Quevedo's *Sueño Del Juicio Final.*" *Modern Philology,* 67 (1970), 238-58.

SUEÑO DE LAS CALAVERAS

SHEPARD, SANFORD. "Talmudic and Koranic Parallels to a Passage in Quevedo's *Sueño De Las Calaveras.*" *Philological Quarterly,* 52 (1973), 306-7.

LA VIDA DEL BUSCÓN (1626)

BAGBY, ALBERT I. "The Conventional Golden Age *Pícaro* and Quevedo's Criminal *Pícaro.*" *Kentucky Romance Quarterly,* 14 (1967), 311-19.

HESSE, EVERETT W. "The Protean Changes in Quevedo's *Buscón.*" *Kentucky Romance Quarterly,* 16 (1969), 243-59.

MAY, T. E. "A Narrative Conceit in 'La Vida del Buscón." *Modern Language Review,* 64 (1969), 327-33.

PRICE, R. M. "On Religious Parody in the *Buscón.*" *MLN,* 86 (1971), 273-79.

ROSE, CONSTANCE HUBBARD. "Pablo's *Damnosa Heritas.*" *Romanische Forschungen,* 82 (1970), 94-101.

SIEBER, HARRY. "Apostrophes in the *Buscon:* An Approach to Quevedo's Narrative Technique." *MLN,* 83 (1968), 178-211.

QUOIREZ, FRANÇOIS see SAGAN, FRANÇOIS

R

RAABE, WILHELM KARL (German, 1831–1910)

GENERAL

HANSON, WILLIAM P. "Some Basic Themes in Raabe." *German Life And Letters,* 21 (1968), 122–30.

STANKIEWICZ, MARKETA GOETZ. "The Tailor and the Sweeper: A New Look at Wilhelm Raabe," in *Essays On German Literature In Honour Of G. Joyce Hallamore,* ed. Michael S. Batts and Marketa Goetz Stankiewicz, pp. 152–76.

DIE AKTEN DES VOGELSANGS (1896)

STANKIEWICZ, MARKETA GOETZ. "The Tailor and the Sweeper: A New Look at Wilhelm Raabe," in *Essays On German Literature In Honour Of G. Joyce Hallamore,* ed. Michael S. Batts and Marketa Goetz Stankiewicz, pp. 170–76.

ELSE VON DER TANNE

KING, JANET K. "Raabe's *Else Von Der Tanne.*" *German Quarterly,* 40 (1967), 653–63.

RADCLIFFE, STANLEY. "Wilhelm Raabe, The Thirty Years War and the Novelle." *German Life And Letters,* 22 (1969), 220–29.

HASTENBECK (1899)

MEYER, HERMANN. *The Poetics Of Quotation In The European Novel,* pp. 204–29.

RABELAIS, FRANÇOIS (French, ca. 1494–ca.1553)

GENERAL

BOWEN, BARBARA. "Rabelais and the Comedy of the Spoken Word." *Modern Language Review,* 63 (1968), 575–80.

COLEMAN, DOROTHY. "Rabelais and 'The Water-Babies.' " *Modern Language Review,* 66 (1971), 511–21.

ELDRIDGE, PAUL. *François Rabelais: The Great Story Teller.*

GREENE, THOMAS M. *Rabelais: A Study In Comic Courage,* pp. 1–19.

GRIFFIN, ROBERT. "The Devil and Panurge." *Studi Francesi,* 16 (1972), 329–36.

HORNIK, HENRY. "Rabelais and Idealism." *Studi Francesi,* 13 (1969), 16–25.

KARLINSKY, SIMON. "Portrait of Gogol as a Word Glutton: With Rabelais, Sterne, and Gertrude Stein as Background Figures." *California Slavic Studies,* 5 (1970), 169–86.

KELLER, ABRAHAM C. "Absurd and Absurdity in Rabelais." *Kentucky Romance Quarterly,* 19 (1972), 149–57.

_____ . "Stage and Theater in Rabelais." *French Review,* 41 (1968), 479–84.

KLEIS, CHARLOTTE COSTA. "Structural Parallels and Thematic Unity in Rabelais." *Modern Language Quarterly,* 31 (1970), 403–23.

LA CHARITÉ, RAYMOND C. "An Aspect of Obscenity in Rabelais," in *Renaissance And Other Studies In Honor Of William Leon Wiley,* ed. George Bernard Daniel, pp. 167–89.

LEBÈGUE, RAYMOND. "Rabelais, the Last of the French Erasmians," in *Rabelais,* ed. August Buck, pp. 136–51.

MASTERS, G. MALLARY. *Rabelaisian Dialectic And The Platonic-Hermetic Tradition.*

WINANDY, ANDRE. "Rabelais' Barrel." *Yale French Studies,* No.50 (1974), pp. 8–25.

WORTLEY, W. VICTOR. "François Rabelais' Contrasting Descriptive Devices." *USF Language Quarterly,* 4, No.3/4 (1966), 11–14.

GARGANTUA AND PANTAGRUEL (1532–1564)

BABCOCK-ABRAHAMS, BARBARA. "The Novel and the Carnival World: An Essay in Memory of Joe Doherty." *MLN,* 89 (1974), 921–30.

BAKHTIN, MIKHAIL M. *Rabelais And His World.*

_____ . "The Role of Games in Rabelais." *Yale French Studies,* No.41 (1968), pp. 124–32.

BEAUJOUR, MICHEL. "The Unicorn in the Carpet." *Yale French Studies,* No.45 (1970), pp. 52–63.

BERRY, ALICE FIOLA. "Apollo versus Bacchus: The Dynamics of Inspiration (Rabelais's Prologues to *Gargantua* and to the *Tiers Livre.*)" *PMLA,* 90 (1975), 88–93.

BOWEN, BARBARA C. *The Age Of Bluff: Paradox And Ambiguity In Rabelais And Montaigne,* pp. 38–102.

BRAULT, GERALD J. "The Comic Design of Rabelais' *Pantagruel.*" *Studies In Philology,* 65 (1968), 140–46.

_____ . "A Neglected Aspect of Rabelaisian Pedagogy: Associating with Men of Letters." *Romance Notes,* 14 (1972), 151–53.

_____ . "The Significance of Eudémon's Praise of Gargantua (Rabelais, I, 15)." *Kentucky Romance Quarterly,* 18 (1971), 307–17.

BRENT, STEVEN T. "Concerning the Resurrection of Epistémon." *Romance Notes,* 12 (1971), 392–96.

CHOLAKLAN, R. "A Re-examination of the Tempest Scene in the *Quart Livre.*" *French Studies,* 21 (1967), 104–10.

COLEMAN, DOROTHY. "The Prologues of Rabelais." *Modern Language Review,* 62 (1967), 407–19.

_____ . *Rabelais: A Critical Study In Prose Fiction.*

_____. "Rabelais: Menippean Satirist or Comic Novelist?" in *The French Renaissance And Its Heritage*, pp. 29-42.

_____. "Rabelais: Two Versions of the 'Storm at Sea' Episode." *French Studies*, 23 (1969), 113-30.

FRAME, DONALD M. "The Impact of Frerè Jean on Panurge in Rabelais's *Tiers Livre*," in *Renaissance And Other Studies In Honor Of William Leon Wiley*, ed. George Bernard Daniel, pp. 83-91.

_____. "Interaction of Characters in Rabelais." *MLN*, 87, No.6 (1972), 12-23.

GAUNA, S. M. "De Genio Pantagruelis: An Examination of Rabelaisian Demonology." *Bibliotheque D'Humanisme Et Renaissance*, 33 (1971), 557-70.

GRAY, FLOYD. "Ambiguity and Point of View in the Prologue to *Gargantua*." *Romanic Review*, 56 (1965), 12-21; rpt. in *Rabelais*, ed. August Buck, pp. 397-410.

GREENE, THOMAS M. *Rabelais: A Study In Comic Courage*, pp. 20-112.

HUNT, JOEL A. "William Faulkner and Rabelais: The Dog Story." *Contemporary Literature*, 10 (1969), 383-88.

IANZITI, GARY. "Rabelais and Machiavelli." *Romance Notes*, 16 (1975), 460-73.

KALWIES, HOWARD H. "Hugues Salel and François Rabelais." *Romance Notes*, 14 (1972), 341-46.

KELLER, ABRAHAM C. "The Geophysics of Rabelais' Frozen Words," in *Renaissance And Other Studies In Honor Of William Leon Wiley*, ed. George Bernard Daniel, pp. 151-65.

_____. "Pace and Timing in Rabelais's Stories," in *Rabelais*, ed. August Buck, pp. 356-76.

KIRSTEIN, BONI H.-J. "Could the Lion-Fox Episode in Chapter XV of *Pantagruel* Be A Fable?" *Romance Notes*, 12 (1970), 180-85.

KLEIS, CHARLOTTE COSTA. "Structural Parallels and Thematic Unity in Rabelais." *Modern Language Quarterly*, 31 (1970), 406-23.

LA CHARITÉ, RAYMOND C. "The Drum and the Owl: Functional Symbolism in Panurge's Quest." *Symposium*, 20 (1974), 154-65.

_____. "Panurge's Heartbeat: An Interpretation of *Mitaine* (*Tiers Livre*, Ch.XI)." *Romance Notes*, 15 (1974), 479-85.

_____. "The Unity of Rabelais's *Pantagruel*." *French Studies*, 26 (1972), 257-65.

LONIGAN, PAUL R. "Rabelais' Pantagruélion." *Studi Francesi*, 12 (1968), 73-79.

LOSSE, DEBORAH. "Thematic and Structural Unity in the Symposium of Rabelais's *Tiers Livre*." *Romance Notes*, 16 (1975), 390-405.

MASTERS, GEORGE MALLARY. "The Hermetic and Platonic Traditions in Rabelais' Dive Bouteille." *Studi Francesi*, 10 (1966), 15-29; rpt. in *Rabelais*, ed. August Buck, pp. 446-72.

MASTERS, G. MALLARY. "Panurge at the Crossroads: A Mythopoetic Study of the Pythagorean Y in Rabelais's Satirical Romance (QL/33-34)." *Romance Notes*, 15 (1973), 134-54.

MEYER, HERMANN. *The Poetics Of Quotation In The European Novel*, pp. 25-54.

MUIR, EDWIN. "Panurge and Falstaff," in his *Essays On Literature And Society*, rev. ed. pp. 166-81.

MULHAUSER, RUTH. "Rabelais and the Fictional World of Alcofribas Nasier." *Romanic Review*, 64 (1973), 175-83.

OLIVER, RAYMOND. "Urquhart's *Rabelais*." *Southern Humanities Review*, 8 (1974), 317-28.

PRICE, ROBERT H. "*Pantagruel* and *Le Petit Prince*." *Symposium*, 21 (1967), 264-70.

RAWSON, C. J. "Rabelais and Horace: A Contact in *Tiers Livre* Ch. III." *French Studies*, 19 (1965), 373-78.

REGOSIN, RICHARD L. "The Artist and the *Abbaye*." *Studies In Philology*, 68 (1971), 121-29.

REXROTH, KENNETH. "Classics Revisited—XIII: Gargantua and Pantagruel." *Saturday Review*, 28 August 1965, p. 20; rpt. in his *Classics Revisited*, pp. 146-50.

RUSSELL, DANIEL. "Some Observations on Rabelais's Choice of Names: Nazdecabre." *Romance Notes*, 12 (1970), 186-88.

SCHWARTZ, JEROME. "Gargantua's Device and the Abbey of Theleme: A Study in Rabelais' Iconography." *Yale French Studies*, No.47 (1971), 232-42.

SCREECH, M. A. "The Sense of Rabelais's *Énigme En Prophétie (Gargantua LVII)*," in *Rabelais*, ed. August Buck, pp. 213-28.

STONE, DONALD. "A Word About the Prologue to *Gargantua*." *Romance Notes*, 13 (1972), 511-14.

STOUT, GARDNER D. "Some Borrowings in Sterne from Rabelais and Cervantes." *English Language Notes*, 3 (1965), 111-14.

TETEL, MARCEL. "The Function and Meaning of the Mock Epic Framework in Rabelais." *Neophilologus*, 59 (1975), 157-64.

_____. *Rabelais*, pp. 17-81.

THOMPSON, PAUL L. "Thematic Consistency in *Tiers Livre*, Chapter 28." *Romance Notes*, 14 (1973), 577-82.

WEINBERG, FLORENCE M. "Francesco Colonna and Rabelais's Tribute to Guillaume du Bellay." *Romance Notes*, 16 (1974), 178-82.

_____. *The Wine And The Will: Rabelais's Bacchic Christianity*.

WINTER, JOHN F. "Visual Variety and Spatial Grandeur in Rabelais." *Romance Review*, 56 (1965), 81-91.

WORTLEY, W. VICTOR. "From *Pantagruel* to *Gargantua*: The Development of an Action Scene." *Romance Notes*, 10 (1968), 129-38.

RABINOWITZ, Solomon see ALEICHEM. Shalom

RADDALL, THOMAS HEAD (Canadian, 1903-)

GENERAL

HAWKINS, W. J. "Thomas H. Raddall: The Man and His Work." *Queen's Quarterly*, 75 (1968), 137-46.

SORFLEET, JOHN ROBERT. "Thomas Raddall: I Was Always a Rebel Underneath." *Journal Of Canadian Fiction*, 2, No.4 (1973), 45-64.

HIS MAJESTY'S YANKEES (1942)

CAMERON, DONALD. "Thomas Raddall: The Art of Historical Fiction." *Dalhousie Review*, 49 (1969/70), 540-48.

RADIGUET, RAYMOND (French, 1903-1923)

GENERAL

TURNELL, MARTIN. "Raymond Radiguet." *Southern Review*, NS 11 (1975), 553-76.

THE DEVIL IN THE FLESH (Le diable au corps, 1923)

BOURAOUI, H. A. "Radiguet's *Le Diable Au Corps*: Beneath the Glass Cage of Form." *Modern Language Quarterly*, 34 (1973), 64-77.

RAJAMIER, B. R.

KAMALAMBAL

BANGARUSWAMI, R. "Early Classics of Tamil Fiction." *Indian Literature*, 11, No.2 (1968), 48-50.

RAJAN, BALACHANDRA (Burman-born Canadian, 1920-)

THE DARK DANCER (1958)

HARREX, S. C. "Dancing in the Dark: Balachandra Rajan and T. S. Eliot." *World Literature Written In English,* 14 (1975), 310–21.

SRINIVASA IYENGAR, K. R. *Indian Writing In English,* pp. 506–10.

RAMBAUD, JEAN

LA CIRQUE À JULES (1972)

Reviews

CHURCH, D. M. *French Review,* 48 (1975), 803–4.

RAMOS, GRACILIANO (Brazilian, 1892–1953)

GENERAL

MAZZARA, RICHARD A. "New Perspectives on Graciliano Ramos." *Luso-Brazilian Review,* 5, No.1 (1968), 93–100.

SOVEREIGN, MARIE F. "Pessimism in Graciliano Ramos." *Luso-Brazilian Review,* 7, No.1 (1970), 57–63.

BARREN LIVES (Vidas sêcas, 1938)

ATKINSON, DOROTHY M. "The Language of *Vidas Sêcas,*" in *Hispanic Studies In Honour Of Joseph Manson,* ed. Dorothy M. Atkinson and Anthony H. Clarke, pp. 9–20.

HAMILTON, RUSSELL G. "Character and Idea in Ramos' *Vidas Sêcas.*" *Luso-Brazilian Review,* 5, No.1 (1968), 86–92.

RANGANAYAKAMMA, MUPPALA (Teluga, 1939-)

GENERAL

SJOBERG, ANDRÉE F. "The Individual Versus Tradition: The Novels of Muppala Ranganayakamma." *Books Abroad,* 43 (1969), 530–34.

RAO, RAJA (Indian, 1909-)

GENERAL

ALI, AHMED. "Illusion and Reality: The Art and Philosophy of Raja Rao." *Journal Of Commonwealth Literature,* No.5 (1968), pp. 16–28.

MUKHERJEE, MEENAKSHI. "Raja Rao's Shorter Fiction." *Indian Literature,* 10, No.3 (1967), 66–76.

NAIK, M. K. "Heir to Two Worlds: Influences on Raja Rao." *Triveni,* 41, No.1 (1972), 68–76.

RAY, ROBERT J. "The Novels of Raja Rao." *Books Abroad,* 40 (1966), 411–14.

THE CAT AND SHAKESPEARE (1965)

GEMMILL, JANET POWERS. "Rhythm in The Cat and Shakespeare." *Literature East And West,* 13 (1969), 27–42.

MUKHERJEE, MEENAKSHI. "Raja Rao's Shorter Fiction." *Indian Literature,* 10, No.3 (1967), 70–76.

PARAMESWARAN, UMA. "*Karma* at Work: The Allegory in Raja Rao's *The Cat And Shakespeare.*" *Journal Of Commonwealth Literature,* No.7 (1969), pp. 107–15.

SHAHANE, VASANT A. "Raja Rao's *The Cat And Shakespeare:* A Study in the Form of Fiction." *Journal Of Indian Writing In English,* 3, No.1 (1975), 7–11.

SHEPHERD, R. "Raja Rao: Symbolism in *The Cat And Shakespeare.*" *World Literature Written In English,* 14 (1975), 347–56.

SRINIVASA IYENGAR, K. R. *Indian Writing In English,* pp. 406–10.

Reviews

DIMOCK, EDWARD C., JR. "The Garden Wall Between Worlds." *Saturday Review,* 16 January 1965, pp. 27–28.

RAY, ROBERT J. *Mahfil,* 2, No.3 (1965), 47–50.

KANTHAPURA (1938)

FISKE, ADELE M. "Karma in Five Indian Novels." *Literature East And West,* 10 (1966), 98–111.

GEMMILL, JANET. "The Transcreation of Spoken Kannada in Raja Rao's Kanthapura." *Literature East And West,* 18 (1974), 191–202.

RAO, N. MADHAVA. " 'Kanthapura'—An Appreciation." *Triveni,* 44, No.3 (1975), 55–59.

SASTRY, L. S. R. KRISHNA. "Raja Rao." *Triveni,* 36, No.4 (1968), 19–26.

SRINIVASA IYENGAR, K. R. *Indian Writing In English,* pp. 390–96.

THE SERPENT AND THE ROPE (1960)

ALI, AHMED. "Illusion and Reality: The Art and Philosophy of Raja Rao." *Journal Of Commonwealth Literature,* No.5 (1968), pp. 16–28.

BHALLA, BRIJ M. "Quest for Identity in Raja Rao's The Serpent and the Rope." *Ariel: A Review Of International English Literature,* 4, No.4 (1973), 95–105.

GEMMILL, JANET P. "Dualities and Non-Duality in Raja Rao's *The Serpent And The Rope.*" *World Literature Written In English,* 12, No.2 (1973), 247–59.

GURUPRASAD, THAKUR. "Reflections on Rama: India as Depicted in *The Serpent And The Rope.*" *Journal Of Indian Writing In English,* 1, No.1 (1973), 19–28.

NAGARAJAN, S. "A Note on Myth and Ritual in *The Serpent And The Rope.*" *Journal Of Commonwealth Literature,* 7, No.1 (1972), 45–48.

NARASIMHAIAH, C. D. "Indian Writing in English." *Journal Of Canadian Fiction,* 9, No.1 (1974), 41–45.

———. "Raja Rao: The Metaphysical Novel (*The Serpent And The Rope*) and Its Significance for Our Age," in *Readings In Commonwealth Literature,* ed. William Walsh, pp. 39–50.

SASTRY, L. S. R. KRISHNA. "Rajo Rao." *Triveni,* 36, No.4 (1968), 26–30.

SHEPHERD, RON. "Symbolic Organization in *The Serpent And The Rope.*" *Southern Review: Literary And Interdisciplinary Essays,* 6 (1973), 93–107.

SRINIVASA IYENGAR, K. R. *Indian Writing In English,* pp. 397–406.

WESTBROOK, PERRY D. "Theme and Inaction in Raja Rao's *The Serpent And The Rope.*" *World Literature Written In English,* 14 (1975), 385–98.

YOK, CHOI KIM. "The Concept of Love in Raja Rao's 'The Serpent and the Rope.' " *Triveni,* 44, No.4 (1976), 39–47.

RASPUTIN, VALENTIN (1937-)

THE LAST DAYS

CHUDAKOVA, M. "Notes on the Language of Contemporary Prose." *Soviet Studies In Literature,* 9, No.1 (1972/3), 81–89.

RÉAGE, PAULINE

STORY OF O

COSMAN, CAROL. "Story of O." *Women's Studies,* 2 (1974), 25–36.

FRASER, JOHN. "A Dangerous Book?—*The Story Of O.*" *Western Humanities Review,* 20 (1966), 51–65.

GORDON, JAN B. "*The Story Of O* and the Strategy of Pornography: Cosmos and Nothingness." *Western Humanities Review,* 25 (1971), 27–43.

SCOBIE, STEPHEN. "Magic, Not Magicians: 'Beautiful Losers' and 'Story Of O.'" *Canadian Literature,* No.45 (1970), pp. 56–60.

REANEY, JAMES (Canadian, 1926–)

THE BOY WITH AN R IN HIS HAND (1965)

Reviews
FRAZER, FRANCES. "A Push from the Author." *Canadian Literature,* No.27 (1966), pp. 79–80.

REDCAM, TOM see MACDERMOT, Thomas Henry

REDOL, ALES

THE MAN WITH SEVEN NAMES

KORGES, JAMES. "A Masterpiece from Portugal: Ales Redol's *The Man With Seven Names.*" *Critique,* 8, No.1 (1965), 7–20.

REHKOPF, HEINRICH

FRANZ WALL ODER DER PHILOSOPH AUD DEM SCHAFOT

HADLEY, MICHAEL. *The German Novel In 1790,* pp. 94–97.

REID, JOHN (Canadian)

THE FAITHLESS MIRROR

Reviews
ROSENGARTEN, HERBERT. "Admirable Purpose." *Canadian Literature,* No.65 (1975), pp. 115–17.

HORSES WITH BLINDFOLDS (1968)

Reviews
GROSSKURTH, PHYLLIS. "A Disturbing Vitality." *Canadian Literature,* No.38 (1968), pp. 88–89.

REID, VICTOR STAFFORD (Jamaican, 1913–)

THE LEOPARD (1958)

JAMES, LOUIS. "Of Redcoats and Leopards: Two Novels by V. S. Reid," in *The Islands In Between,* ed. Louis James, pp. 67–72.
RAMCHAND, KENNETH. *The West Indian Novel And Its Background,* pp. 154–59.

NEW DAY (1947)

JAMES, LOUIS. "Of Redcoats and Leopards: Two Novels by V. S. Reid," in *The Islands In Between,* ed. Louis James, pp. 64–66.
MOORE, GERALD. *The Chosen Tongue,* pp. 3–6.

RELIQUET, PHILIPPE

L'OUTRAGE

Reviews
CAGNON, MAURICE. *French Review,* 48 (1975), 668–69.

REMARQUE, ERICH MARIA (German, 1897–1970)

ALL QUIET ON THE WESTERN FRONT (Im Westen Nichts Neues, 1929)

LIEDLOFF, HELMUT. "Two War Novels: A Critical Comparison." *Revue De Littérature Comparée,* 42 (1968), 390–406.

SHADOWS IN PARADISE (Schatten im Paradies, 1971)

Reviews
EWART, GAVIN. "Rome-Berlin Axis." *London Magazine,* NS 12, No.4 (1972), 150–51.

McCULLOUGH, DAVID W. *Saturday Review,* 26 February 1972, p. 78.

REMIZOV, ALEKSEY (Russian, 1877–1957)

THE FIFTH PESTILENCE (Pjataja jazva, 1912)

BIALY, RENATE S. "Parody in Remizov's *Pjataja Jazva.*" *Slavic And East European Journal,* 19 (1975), 403–10.

PRUD (1908)

SHANE, ALEX M. "Remizov's *Prud:* From Symbolism to Neo-Realism." *California Slavic Studies,* 6 (1971), 71–82.

REMY, YVES AND ADA

LE GRAND MIDI (1971)

Reviews
STARY, SONJA G. *French Review,* 45 (1972), 709–10.

RENAULT, MARY (South African, 1905–) pseudonym of Mary Challans

FIRE FROM HEAVEN (1969)

Reviews
CASSON, LIONEL. "Alexander's Ascent to Greatness on a Ladder of Gore." *Saturday Review,* 29 November 1969, pp. 27–29, 61–62.
DWYER, DAVID J. "Colossus as Tad." *Catholic World,* 211 (1970), 279–80.

REQUENA, JOSÉ MARÍA

EL CUAJARÓN (1972)

Reviews
SHEEHAN, ROBERT LOUIS. *Hispania,* 58 (1975), 227.

RESTIF DE LA BRETONNE, NICHOLAS EDMÉ (French, 1734–1806)

GENERAL

PORTER, CHARLES A. "Life in Restif Country." *Yale Fiction Studies,* No.40 (1968), pp. 103–17.
STRINGER, PATRICIA. "Restif de la Bretonne and the Subject of Evil." *Romance Notes,* 16 (1975), 592–98.

PAYSAN PERVERTI

MYLNE, VIVIENNE. *The Eighteenth Century French Novel,* pp. 225–33.

REUTER, CHRISTIAN (German, 1665–c.1712)

SCHELMUFFSKY (Schelmuffskys wahrhafftige kuriöse und sehr gefährliche Reisebeschreibung zu wasser und lande, 1696)

WAGENER, HANS. *The German Baroque Novel,* pp. 78–86.

REVOL, ENRIQUE LUIS

MUTACIONES BRUSCAS (1971)

Reviews
McMURRAY, GEORGE R. *Hispania,* 56 (1973), 1122.

REYMONT, WLADYSLAW STANISLAW (Polish, 1867–1925)

THE COMEDIENNE (Komediantka, 1896)

KRZYZANOWSKI, JERZY R. *Wladyslaw Stanislaw Reymont,* pp. 27–31.

THE DREAMER (Marzyciel, 1910)

KRZYZANOWSKI, JERZY R. *Wladyslaw Stanislaw Reymont,* pp. 119–24.

FERMENTY (1897)

KRZYZANOWSKI, JERZY R. *Wladyslaw Stanislaw Reymont,* pp. 31–39.

THE INSURRECTION

KRZYZANOWSKI, JERZY R. *Wladyslaw Stanislaw Reymont,* pp. 113–18.

THE LAST DIET

KRZYZANOWSKI, JERZY R. *Wladyslaw Stanislaw Reymont,* pp. 97–107.

NIL DESPERANDUM

KRZYZANOWSKI, JERZY R. *Wladyslaw Stanislaw Reymont,* pp. 107–13.

THE PEASANTS (Chlopi, 1904–9)

KRZYZANOWSKI, JERZY R. *Wladyslaw Stanislaw Reymont,* pp. 73–93.

THE PROMISED LAND (Ziemia obiecana, 1899)

KRZYZANOWSKI, JERZY R. *Wladyslaw Stanislaw Reymont,* pp. 44–63.

THE VAMPIRE (Wampir, 1911)

KRZYZANOWSKI, JERZY R. *Wladyslaw Stanislaw Reymont,* pp. 124–27.

REYNOSO, OSWALDO (Peruvian, 1932–)

EN OCTUBRE NO HAY MILAGROS (1965)

Reviews
LUCHTING, WOLFGANG A. *Hispania,* 49 (1966), 546–47.

REZVANI

COMA

Reviews
CAGNON, MAURICE. *French Review,* 45 (1971), 211–12.

RICARDOU, JEAN (French, 1932–)

LA PRISE DE CONSTANTINOPLE (1965)

JONES, TOBIN H. "In Quest of a Newer New Novel: Ricardou's *La Prise De Constantinople.*" *Contemporary Literature,* 14 (1973), 296–309.

RICE, DONALD B. "The Ex-centricities of Jean Ricardou's *La Prise/Prose De Constantinople.*" *International Fiction Review,* 2 (1975), 106–12.

RICHARD, JEAN-JULES (Canadian, 1911–)

EXOVIDE LOUIS RIEL (1972)

Reviews
SILVERSIDES, MARY. "Ils Ont Pendu Louis riel." *Journal Of Canadian Fiction,* 2, No.2 (1973), 93–94.

RICHARDS, DAVID ADAMS (Canadian, 1950–)

THE COMING OF WINTER (1974)

Reviews
GIBBS, ROBERT. "A Book's True Music." *Journal Of Canadian Fiction,* 4, No.3 (1975), 166–68.

KENNEDY, ALAN. *Dalhousie Review,* 55 (1975), 373–74.

RICHARDSON, HENRY HANDEL (Australian, 1870–1946) pseudonym of Ethel Florence Richardson Robertson

GENERAL

CLUTTON-BROCK, M. A. "Mrs. Lins: Sister to Henry Handel Richardson." *Southerly,* 27 (1967), 46–59.

ELLIOTT, WILLIAM D. "H. H. Richardson: The Education of an Australian Realist." *Studies In The Novel,* 4 (1972), 141–53.

PALMER, NETTIE. "Henry Handel Richardson: The Writer," in *Twentieth Century Australian Literary Criticism,* ed. Clement Semmler, pp. 170–80.

THE FORTUNES OF RICHARD MAHONY (1917–1929)

ARGYLE, BARRY. *An Introduction To The Australian Novel, 1830–1930,* pp. 229–54.

DAY, MARTIN S. "Australian Fiction Scrutinizes National Life." *Forum,* 9, No.3 (1972), 5–7.

FOSTER, I. M. " 'Richard Mahony's Tragedy.' " *Australian Literary Studies,* 4 (1970), 279–80.

GREEN, DOROTHY. "Henry Handel Richardson Minus Ned Kelly." *Meanjin,* 31 (1972), 162–66.

———. "The Pilgrim Soul: The Philosophical Structure of 'The Fortunes of Richard Mahony.' " *Meanjin,* 28 (1969), 328–37.

JEFFARES, A. NORMAN. "Richard Mahony, Exile." *Journal Of Commonwealth Literature,* No.6 (1969), pp. 106–19; rpt. in *Readings In Commonwealth Literature,* ed. William Walsh, pp. 404–19.

KIERNAN, BRIAN. "The Fortunes of Richard Mahony." *Southerly,* 29 (1969), 199–209.

LODER, ELIZABETH. "The Fortunes of Richard Mahoney: Dream and Nightmare." *Southerly,* 25 (1965), 251–63.

STEWART, KENNETH. "Dr Richardson and Dr Mahony." *Southerly,* 33 (1973), 74–79.

———. "The Prototype of Richard Mahony." *Australian Literary Studies,* 4 (1970), 227–40.

———. "Their Road to Life: A Note on Richard Mahony and Walter Richardson." *Meanjin,* 29 (1970), 505–8.

STOLLER, ALAN AND R. H. EMMERSON. "The Fortunes of Walter Lindesy Richardson." *Meanjin,* 29 (1970), 21–33.

THOMSON, A. K. "Henry Handel Richardson's 'The Fortunes of Richard Mahony.' " *Meanjin,* 26 (1967), 423–34.

THE GETTING OF WISDOM (1910)

MCFARLANE, BRIAN. "*The Getting Of Wisdom:* Not 'Merry' at All." *Australian Literary Studies,* 8 (1977), 51–63.

MAURICE GUEST (1908)

HOPE, A. D. "Henry Handel Richardson's *Maurice Guest,*" in *Twentieth Century Australian Literary Criticism,* ed. Clement Semmler, pp. 295–309.

KIERNAN, BRIAN. "Romantic Conventions and *Maurice Guest.*" *Southerly,* 28 (1968), 286–94.

LODER, ELIZABETH. "Maurice Guest: Some Nineteenth-Century Progenitors." *Southerly,* 26 (1966), 94–105.

PALMER, ANTHONY J. "A Link with Late Nineteenth-Century Decadence in *Maurice Guest.*" *Australian Literary Studies,* 5 (1972), 366–73.

STEWART, KEN. "*Maurice Guest* and the Siren Voices." *Australian Literary Studies,* 5 (1972), 352–65.

RICHARDSON, JOHN (Canadian)

GENERAL

PACEY, DESMOND. "A Colonial Romantic: Major John Richardson, Soldier and Novelist," in his *Essays In Canadian Criticism, 1938-1968,* pp. 151-71.

FRASCATI'S

SINCLAIR, DAVID. "*John Richardson's Frascati's; Or, Scenes In Paris:* A Little Known Novel the Manner of Ecarte." *Journal Of Canadian Fiction,* 2, No.3 (1973), 31-35.

WACOUSTA

MOSS, JOHN G. "Canadian Frontiers: Sexuality and Violence from Richardson to Kroetsch." *Journal Of Canadian Fiction,* 2, No.3 (1973), 38-41.

WESTBROOK THE OUTLAW

Reviews
MORLEY, F. E. "Richardson's *Westbrook:* Where Fact and Fiction Meet." *Journal Of Canadian Fiction,* 2, No.3 (1973), 112-14.

RICHLER, MORDECAI (Canadian, 1931-)
GENERAL

BIRBALSINGH, F. M. "Mordecai Richler and the Jewish-Canadian Novel." *Journal Of Commonwealth Literature,* 7, No.1 (1972), 72-82.

METCALF, JOHN. "Black Humour: An Interview: Mordecai Richler." *Journal Of Canadian Fiction,* 3, No.1 (1974), 73-76.

MYERS, DAVID. "Mordecai Richler as Satirist." *Ariel: A Review Of International English Literature,* 4 (1973), 47-61.

RICHLER, MORDECAI. "The Uncertain World." *Canadian Literature,* No.41 (1969), pp. 23-27.

THE ACROBATS

BOWERING, GEORGE. "And the Sun Goes Down: Richler's First Novel." *Canadian Literature,* No.29 (1966), pp. 7-17.

THE APPRENTICESHIP OF DUDDY KRAVITZ (1959)

FERNS, JOHN. "Sympathy and Judgement in Mordecai Richler's *The Apprenticeship Of Duddy Kravitz.*" *Journal Of Canadian Fiction,* 3, No.1 (1974), 77-82.

NEW, WILLIAM H. "The Apprenticeship of Discovery." *Canadian Literature,* No.29 (1966), pp. 18-25; rpt. in his *Articulating West,* pp. 108-27.

TALLMAN, WARREN. "Wolf in the Snow," in *A Choice Of Critics,* ed. George Woodcock, pp. 72-76.

A CHOICE OF ENEMIES

CLOUTIER, PIERRE. "Mordecai Richler's Exiles: *A Choice Of Enemies.*" *Journal Of Canadian Fiction,* 1, No.2 (1972), 43-49.

COCKSURE (1968)

MYERS, DAVID. "Mordecai Richler as Satirist." *Ariel: A Review Of International English Literature,* 4 (1973), 51-56.

NEW, WILLIAM H. "Cock and Bull Stories." *Canadian Literature,* No.39 (1969), pp. 85-86.

TOYNBEE, PHILIP. *London Magazine,* NS, No.2 (1968), 77-79.

Reviews
CAMERON, DONALD. "Expatriate's Dilemma." *Journal Of Commonwealth Literature,* No.8 (1969), pp. 150-52.

ST. URBAIN'S HORSEMAN (1971)

MYERS, DAVID. "Mordecai Richler as Satirist." *Ariel: A Review Of International English Literature,* 4 (1973), 56-60.

SHEPS, G. DAVID. "Waiting for Joey: The Theme of the Vicarious in *St. Urbain's Horseman.*" *Journal Of Canadian Fiction,* 3, No.1 (1974), 83-92.

TALLMAN, WARREN. "Need for Laughter." *Canadian Literature,* No.56 (1973), pp. 71-83.

Reviews
FELD, MICHAEL. "Cocks of the Walk." *London Magazine,* NS 11, No.5 (1971), 163-64.

FRASER, KEATH. "Richler's Larger Jewishness." *Journal Of Commonwealth Literature,* 7, No.1 (1972), 115-17.

THOMAS, AUDREY. "An Offwhite Horse." *Canadian Literature,* No.51 (1972), pp. 83-84.

WOODCOCK, GEORGE. "The Wheel of Exile." *Tamarack Review,* No.58 (1971), pp. 65-72.

SON OF A SMALLER HERO (1955)

Reviews
TALLMAN, WARREN. "Politics Neglected." *Canadian Literature,* No.30 (1966), pp. 77-79.

THE STREET

Reviews
PURDY, A. W. "Betrayed by the Evening Star." *Canadian Literature,* No.44 (1970), pp. 85-86.

DES RIEUX, VIRGINIE
LA SATYRE

Reviews
LeSAGE, LAURENT. "Baronial Bestiary." *Saturday Review,* 26 August 1967, p. 33.

RIFBJERG, KLAUS (Danish, 1931-)
GENERAL

GRAY, CHARLOTTE SCHIANDER. "Klaus Rifbjerg: A Contemporary Danish Writer." *Books Abroad,* 49 (1975), 25-28.

RILKE, RAINER MARIA (Austrian, 1875-1926)
THE NOTEBOOKS OF MALTE LAURIDS BRIGGE (Die Aufzeichnungen des Malte Laurids Brigge, 1910)

BETHKE, FREDERICK J. "Rilke's *Malte Laurids Brigge* as Prose Poetry." *Kentucky Foreign Language Quarterly,* 12 (1965), 73-82.

GRAY, RONALD. *The German Tradition In Literature: 1871-1945,* pp. 263-72.

HAYMAN, DAVID. "The Broken Cranium—Headwounds in Zola, Rilke, Céline: A Study in Contrasting Modes." *Comparative Literature Studies,* 9 (1972), 215-21.

HERD, E. W. "An Interpretation of *Die Aufzeichnungen Des Malte Laurids Brigge* Based on an Analysis of the Structure." *Seminar,* 9 (1973), 208-28.

JEPHCOTT, E. F. N. *Proust And Rilke: The Literature Of Expanded Consciousness,* pp. 155-75.

MILES, DAVID H. "The Picaro's Journey to the Confessional: The Changing Image of the Hero in the German Bildungsroman." *PMLA,* 89 (1974), 986-89.

ZIOLKOWSKI, THEODORE. *Dimensions Of The Modern Novel,* pp. 3-36.

RIMANELLI, GIOSE (Canadian)
GENERAL

RICCIARDELLI, MICHAEL. "Development of Giose Rimanelli's Fiction." *Books Abroad,* 40 (1966), 386-91.

RINADLI, ANGELO
LA MAISON DES ATLANTES (1971)

Reviews
ZANTS, EMILY. *French Review,* 46 (1973), 865-66.

RISTIKIVI, KARL (Estonian, 1912-1977)
GENERAL

> LEHISTE, ILSE. "Three Estonian Writers and the Experience of Exile." *Lituanus,* 18, No.1 (1972), 16-23.

THE TEETH OF THE DRAGON

> LEHISTE, ILSE. "Three Estonian Writers and the Experience of Exile." *Lituanus,* 18, No.1 (1972), 20-23.

RIVE, RICHARD (South African, 1931-)
GENERAL

> LINDFORS, BERNTH. "Form and Technique in the Novels of Richard Rive and Alex la Guma." *Journal Of The New African Literature And The Arts,* No.2 (1966), pp. 10-15.

EMERGENCY (1964)

> CARTEY, WILFRED. *Whispers From A Continent,* pp. 182-86.

> LARSON, CHARLES R. "Things Fall Further Apart—New African Novels." *College Language Association Journal,* 10 (1966/7), 65-66.

> **Reviews**
> STEVENSON, W. *Black Orpheus,* No.19 (1966), p. 58.

RIVERA, JOSÉ EUSTASIO (Colombian, 1888-1928)
THE VORTEX (La vorágine, 1924)

> BRUSHWOOD, JOHN S. *The Spanish American Novel,* pp. 42-44.

> CALLAN, RICHARD J. "The Archetype of Psychic Renewal in 'La Vorágine.' " *Hispania,* 54 (1971), 470-76.

RIVIÈRE, JACQUES (French, 1886-1926)
AIMÉE (1922)

> NAUGHTON, HELEN THOMAS. "The Critic's Cure: Rivière's *Aimée.*" *Renascence,* 17 (1965), 201-6.

RIZAL, JOSE (Philippine, 1861-1896)
GENERAL

> CASPER, LEONARD. *New Writing From The Philippines,* pp. 28-33.

ROA BASTOS, AUGUSTO (Paraguayan, 1917-)
GENERAL

> FOSTER, DAVID WILLIAM. "*La Pensée Sauvage* in A. Roa Bastos' Recent Fiction." *Chasqui,* 4, No.2 (1975), 29-34.

YO EL SUPREMO (1974)

> FOSTER, DAVID WILLIAM. "Augusto Roa Bastos' *I, The Supreme:* The Image of a Dictator." *Latin American Literary Review,* 4, No.7 (1975), 31-35.

ROBBE-GRILLET, ALAIN (French, 1922-)
GENERAL

> CHAPSAL, MADELEINE. "Who Is Robbe-Grillet?" *Reporter,* 35, No.1 (1966), 54-57.

> COHN, DORRIT. "Castles and Anti-Castles, or Kafka and Robbe-Grillet." *Novel,* 5 (1971), 19-31.

> CONNERTON, PAUL. "Alain Robbe-Grillet: A Question of Self-Deception?" *Forum For Modern Language Studies,* 4 (1968), 347-59.

> GERHART, MARY JANE. "The Purpose of Meaninglessness in Robbe-Grillet." *Renascence,* 23 (1971), 79-97.

> HAYMAN, DAVID. "An Interview with Alain Robbe-Grillet." *Contemporary Literature,* 16 (1975), 273-85.

> HEATH, STEPHEN. *The Nouveau Roman,* pp. 67-136.

> MISTACCO, VICKI. "Interview: Alain Robbe-Grillet." *Diacritics,* 6, No.4 (1976), 35-43.

> MORRISSETTE, BRUCE. "The Evolution of Narrative Viewpoint in Robbe-Grillet." *Novel,* 1 (1967), 24-33.

> ———. "Games and Game Structures in Robbe-Grillet." *Yale French Studies,* No.41 (1968), pp. 159-67.

> ———. "Topology and the French *Nouveau Roman.*" *Boundary 2,* 1 (1972/3), 45-57.

> MURRAY, JACK. "Mind and Reality in Proust and Robbe-Grillet." *Wisconsin Studies In Contemporary Literature,* 8 (1967), 407-20.

> PORTER, DENNIS. "Sartre, Robbe-Grillet and the Psychotic Hero." *Modern Fiction Studies,* 16 (1970), 22-25.

> SELTZER, ALVIN J. *Chaos In The Novel: The Novel In Chaos,* pp. 274-95.

> STOLTZFUS, BEN. "Proust and Robbe-Grillet." *Romance Notes,* 12 (1971), 251-58.

> STURROCK, JOHN. *The French New Novel,* pp. 170-235.

> SZANTO, GEORGE H. "The Internalized Reality of Robbe-Grillet." *Critique,* 12, No.1 (1970), 28-42.

> WYLIE, HAROLD A. "Alain Robbe-Grillet: Scientific Humanist." *Bucknell Review,* 15, No.2 (1967), 1-9.

> ———. "The Reality-Game of Robbe-Grillet." *French Review,* 40 (1967), 774-80.

THE ERASERS (Les Gommes, 1953)

> GERHART, MARY JANE. "The Purpose of Meaninglessness in Robbe-Grillet." *Renascence,* 23 (1971), 80-83.

> GROSSVOGEL, DAVID I. *Limits Of The Novel,* pp. 283-91.

> MERCIER, VIVIAN. *The New Novel From Queneau To Pinget,* pp. 185-89.

> MINOGUE, VALERIE. "The Workings of Fiction in 'Les Gommes.' " *Modern Language Review,* 62 (1967), 430-42.

> MORRISETTE, BRUCE. *The Novels of Robbe-Grillet,* pp. 38-74.

> **Reviews**
> McDONNELL, THOMAS P. "Recording Camera." *Commonweal,* 81 (1964), 430-31.

THE HOUSE OF ASSIGNATION (La maison des rendez-vous, 1965)

> GOODSTEIN, JACK. "Pattern and Structure in Robbe-Grillet's *La Maison De Rendez-vous.*" *Critique,* 14, No.1 (1972), 91-97.

> MERCIER, VIVIAN. *The New Novel From Queneau to Pinget,* pp. 206-14.

> MORRISETTE, BRUCE. *The Novels Of Robbe-Grillet,* pp. 237-61.

> **Reviews**
> BANN, STEPHEN. *London Magazine,* NS 6, No.2 (1966), 97-98.

> BISHOP, THOMAS. "Dragon Lady's Palace of Pleasure." *Saturday Review,* 3 December 1966, pp. 60-61.

> MORRISETTE, BRUCE. *French Review,* 39 (1966), 821-22.

IN THE LABYRINTH (Dans le labyrinthe, 1959)

> BROOKE-ROSE, CHRISTINE. "The Baroque Imagination of Robbe-Grillet." *Modern Fiction Studies,* 11 (1965/6), 405-23.

> GARZILLI, ENRICO. *Circles Without Center,* pp. 109-12.

> HEATH, STEPHEN. *The Nouveau Roman,* pp. 137-52.

> LETHCOE, JAMES. "The Structure of Robbe-Grillet's Labyrinth." *French Review,* 38 (1965), 497-507.

MERCIER, VIVIAN. *The New Novel From Queneau To Pinget*, pp. 194-98.

MORRISETTE, BRUCE. *The Novels Of Robbe-Grillet*, pp. 153-84.

RAHV, BETTY T. *From Sartre To The New Novel*, pp. 101-48.

RAHV, E. T. "Robbe-Grillet's Uses of the Past in 'Dans le Labyrinthe.'" *Modern Language Review*, 66 (1971), 76-84.

SELTZER, ALVIN J. *Chaos In The Novel: The Novel In Chaos*, pp. 315-29.

WEINSTEIN, ARNOLD L. *Vision And Response In Modern Fiction*, pp. 246-56.

JEALOUSY (La jalousie, 1957)

BERSANI, LEO. *Balzac To Beckett*, pp. 272-99.

CARRABINO, VICTOR. "Robbe-Grillet's *La Jalousie* and the Phenomenological *Epoché*." *Kentucky Romance Quarterly*, 22 (1975), 159-67.

DENEAU, DANIEL P. "Crouching Natives in Robbe-Grillet's *Jealousy*." *Modern Fiction Studies*, 20 (1974), 429-36.

ELLIS, ZILPHA. "Robbe-Grillet's Use of Pun and Related Figures in *La Jalousie*." *International Fiction Review*, 2 (1975), 9-17.

GROSSVOGEL, DAVID I. *Limits Of The Novel*, pp. 295-97.

LECUYER, MAURICE A. "Robbe-Grillet's *La Jalousie* and a Parallel in the Graphic Arts." *Hartford Studies In Literature*, 3 (1971), 19-38.

MERCIER, VIVIAN. *The New Novel From Queneau To Pinget*, pp. 165-84.

MOELLER, HANS-BERNHARD. "Literature in the Vicinity of the Film: On German and *Nouveau Roman* Authors." *Symposium*, 28 (1974), 323-28.

MORRISETTE, BRUCE. *The Novels Of Robbe-Grillet*, pp. 112-52.

PENOT, DOMINIQUE. "Psychology of the Characters in Robbe-Grillet's *La Jalousie*." *Books Abroad*, 40 (1966), 5-16.

SAVAGE, CATHERINE. "Alain Robbe-Grillet, The Novelist Behind the Venetian Blinds." *New Orleans Review*, 1 (1969), 213-17.

SELTZER, ALVIN J. *Chaos In The Novel: The Novel In Chaos*, pp. 302-15.

SIMON, JOHN K. "Perception and Metaphor in the 'New Novel': Notes on Robbe-Grillet, Claude Simon and Butor." *Triquarterly*, No.4 (1965), pp. 155-64.

PROJECT FOR A REVOLUTION IN NEW YORK (Projet pour une révolution à New York, 1970)

MORISSETTE, BRUCE. *The Novels Of Robbe-Grillet*, pp. 262-87.

———. "Topology and the French *Nouveau Roman*." *Boundary 2* 1, (1972), 50-56.

O'DONNELL, THOMAS D. "Thematic Generation in Robbe-Grillet's *Projet Pour Une Révolution A New York*," in *Twentieth Century French Fiction*, ed. George Stambolian, pp. 184-97.

PUGH, ANTHONY R. "Robbe-Grillet in New York." *International Fiction Review*, 1 (1974), 120-24.

Reviews

STOLTZFUS, BEN. *French Review*, 45 (1971), 213-14.

THE VOYEUR (Le Voyeur, 1955)

GARZILLI, ENRICO. *Circles Without Center*, pp. 112-17.

GERHART, MARY JANE. "The Purpose of Meaninglessness in Robbe-Grillet." *Renascence*, 23 (1971), 83-86.

GROSSVOGEL, DAVID I. *Limits Of The Novel*, pp. 291-95.

MERCIER, VIVIAN. *The New Novel From Queneau To Pinget*, pp. 189-94.

MORRISETTE, BRUCE. *The Novels Of Robbe-Grillet*, pp. 75-111.

SELTZER, ALVIN J. *Chaos In The Novel: The Novel In Chaos*, pp. 295-302.

ROBERT, MARIKA (Czechoslovakian)

A STRANGER AND AFRAID (1964)

Reviews

BRAYBROOKE, DAVID. *Dalhousie Review*, 44 (1964), 371-72.

ROBERTS, CHARLES GEORGE DOUGLAS (Canadian, 1860-1943)

GENERAL

MATHEWS, ROBIN. "Charles G. D. Roberts and the Destruction of Canadian Imagination." *Journal Of Canadian Fiction*, 1, No.1 (1972), 47-56.

PACEY, DESMOND. "Sir Charles G. D. Roberts," in his *Essays In Canadian Criticism, 1938-1968*, pp. 172-98.

THE HEART OF THE ANCIENT WOOD (1900)

Reviews

MURRAY, TIM. "In the Ancient Wood." *Journal Of Canadian Fiction*, 4, No.3 (1975), 158-60.

ROBERTSON, Ethel Florence Richardson see RICHARDSON, Henry Handel

ROCHE, MAURICE

CIRCUS

Reviews

CAGNON, MAURICE. *French Review*, 47 (1973), 504-5.

COMPACT

LEIGH, JAMES. "Reading *Compact*." *Modern Fiction Studies*, 20 (1974), 437-46.

ROCHE, MANUELLE

SISMOS (1971)

Reviews

CRANT, PHILLIP A. *French Review*, 46 (1973), 868-69.

ROCHÉ, PIERRE-HENRI

GENERAL

GROSSVOGEL, DAVID I. "Truffaut & Roché: Diverse Voices of the Novel & Film." *Diacritics*, 3, No.1 (1973), 47-52.

ROD, ÉDOUARD (Swiss, 1857-1910)

GENERAL

LERNER, MICHAEL G. "Edouard Rod and Emile Zola, II: From 'La Course a la Mort' to Dreyfus." *Nottingham French Studies*, 8 (1969), 28-39.

———. "Édouard Rod and Marcel Proust." *French Studies*, 25 (1971), 162-68.

———. "Edouard Rod and the Russian Novelists in France." *Nottingham French Studies*, 9 (1970), 31-43.

———. "Edouard Rod and the Naturistes." *Nottingham French Studies*, 10 (1971), 67-73.

———. "Edouard Rod's Last Novel: 'La Vie.'" *Nottingham French Studies*, 9 (1970), 71-80.

———. "A Literary Age in Evolution: 'Les Idées Morales du Temps Present' of Edouard Rod." *Nottingham French Studies*, 11 (1972), 27-38.

RODRIGUÉ, EMILIO (Argentine)

HEROÍNA

Reviews
McMurray, George R. *Hispania,* 54 (1971), 205.

RODRÍGUEZ DE LA CAMÁRA, JUAN (Spanish, 15th century)

EL SIERVO LIBRE DE AMOR

Dudley, Edward. "Court and Country: The Fusion of Two Images of Love in Juan Rodríguez's *El Siervo Libre De Amor.*" *PMLA,* 82 (1967), 117–20.

RÖLVAAG, OLE EDVART (Norwegian, 1876–1931)

THE BOAT OF LONGING (Loengselens baat, 1921)

Reigstad, Paul. *Rölvaag: His Life And Art,* pp. 75–95.

GIANTS IN THE EARTH (1927)

Reigstad, Paul. *Rölvaag: His Life And Art,* pp. 97–125.

LETTERS FROM AMERICA (Amerika-Breve, 1912)

Reigstad, Paul. *Rölvaag: His Life And Art,* pp. 45–49.

ON FORGOTTEN PATHS (Paa Glemte Veie, 1914)

Reigstad, Paul. *Rölvaag: His Life And Art,* pp. 49–59.

PEDER VICTORIOUS (Peder Seier, 1928)

Reigstad, Paul. *Rölvaag: His Life And Art,* pp. 127–36.

PURE GOLD (To Tullinger: Et Billede fra Idag, 1920)

Reigstad, Paul. *Rölvaag: His Life And Art,* pp. 61–75.

THEIR FATHER'S GOD (Den signede dag, 1931)

Reigstad, Paul. *Rölvaag: His Life And Art,* pp. 136–48.

ROHMER, RICHARD (Canadian, 1924–)

ULTIMATUM (1973)

Reviews
Angus, Terry. "Let Them Take Gas." *Journal Of Canadian Fiction,* 3, No.3 (1974), 114–15.

ROJAS, CARLOS (Spanish, 1928–)

AQUELLARE (1970)

Reviews
Lott, Robert E. *Hispania,* 56 (1973), 505–6.

LA TERNURA DEL HOMBRE INVISIBLE (1963)

Reviews
Seay, Hugh N., Jr. *Hispania,* 48 (1965), 183.

ROJAS, FERNANDO DE (Spanish, d. 1541?)

GENERAL

Gilman, Stephen and Ramón Gonzálvez. "The Family of Fernando de Rojas." *Romanische Forschungen,* 78 (1966), 1–26.

LA CELESTINA (1499)

Abrams, Fred. "The Name 'Celestina': Why Did Fernando de Rojas Choose It?" *Romance Notes,* 14 (1972), 165–67.

Baldwin, Spurgeon W. " 'En tan pocas palabras' (*La Celestina,* Auto IV)." *Romance Notes,* 9 (1967), 120–25.

Barbera, Raymond E. "A Harlot, A Heroine." *Hispania,* 48 (1965), 790–99.

Brault, Gerard J. "Textual Filiation of the Early Editions of the *Celestina* and the First French Translation (1527)." *Hispanic Review,* 36 (1968), 95–109.

Carroll, William and Albert Bagby, Jr. "A Note on Shakespeare and *The Celestina.*" *Revista De Estudios Hispánicos,* 5 (1971), 79–93.

De Armas, F. A. "*La Celestina:* An Example of Love Melancholy." *Romanic Review,* 66 (1975), 288–95.

Foster, David William. "Some Attitudes Towards Love in the 'Celestina.' " *Hispania,* 48 (1965), 484–92.

Fraker, Charles F. "The Importance of Pleberio's Soliloquy." *Romanische Forschungen,* 78 (1966), 515–29.

Gilman, Steve. *The Spain Of Fernando De Rojas: The Intellectual And Social Landscape of <La Celestina.>*

Goldman, Peter B. "A New Interpretation of '*Comedor De Huevos Asados' Las Celestina, Act I.*" *Romanische Forschungen,* 77 (1965), 363–67.

Green, Otis H. "The Artistic Originality of 'La Celestina.' " *Hispanic Review,* 33 (1965), 15–31.

Herriott, J. Homer. "Notes on Selectivity of Language in the *Celestina.*" *Hispanic Review,* 37 (1969), 77–101.

Martin, June Hall. *Love's Fools: Aucassin, Troilus, Calisto And The Parody Of The Courtly Lover,* pp. 71–143.

Mendeloff, Henry. "On Translating 'La Celestina' into French and Italian." *Hispania,* 51 (1968), 111–15.

Nepaulsingh, Colbert. "The Rhetorical Structure of the Prologues to the *Libro De Buen Amor* and the *Celestina.*" *Bulletin Of Hispanic Studies,* 51 (1974), 330–34.

———. "The Passive Voice in *La Celestina.*" *Romance Philology,* 18 (1964), 41–46.

Olson, Paul R. "An Ovidian Conceit in Petrarch and Rojas." *MLN,* 81 (1966), 217–21.

Purcell, H. D. "The *Celestina* and the *Interlude Of Calisto And Melebea.*" *Bulletin Of Hispanic Studies,* 44 (1967), 1–15.

Ruggerio, M. J. "*La Celestina:* Didacticism Once More." *Romanische Forschungen,* 82 (1970), 56–64.

Shipley, George A. "'¿Qual dolor puede ser tal . . . ?': A Rhetorical Strategy for Containing Pain in *La Celestina.*" *MLN,* 90 (1975), 143–53.

Truesdell, William D. "Pármeno's Triple Temptation: 'Celestina,' Act I." *Hispania,* 58 (1975), 267–76.

Weinberg, F. M. "Aspects of Symbolism in *La Celestina.*" *MLN,* 86 (1971), 136–53.

ROJAS, MANUEL (Chilean, 1896–1973)

BORN GUILTY (Hijo de ladron, 1951)

Lichtblau, Myron I. "Ironic Devices in Manuel Rojas' *Hijo De Ladron.*" *Symposium,* 19 (1965), 214–25.

LANCHAS EN LA BAHÍA (1932)

Pontiero, Giovanni. "The Two Versions of *Lanchas En La Bahía:* Some Observations on Rojas' Approach to Style." *Bulletin Of Hispanic Studies,* 45 (1968), 123–32.

ROLFE, PATRICIA

NO LOVE LOST (1965)

Reviews
Wilding, Michael. *Southerly,* 26 (1966), 59–60.

ROLIN, DOMINIQUE (Belgian, 1913–)

LES ÉCLAIRS

Reviews
Marks, Elaine. *French Review,* 46 (1972), 233–35.

ROLLAND, ROMAIN (French, 1866–1944)
GENERAL

FRANCIS, R. A. "Romain Rolland and Jean-Jacques Rousseau." *Nottingham French Studies,* 8 (1969), 40–53.

JEAN-CHRISTOPHE (1904–1912)

ALDEN, DOUGLAS W. "Proustian Configuration in *Jean-Christophe.*" *French Review,* 41 (1967), 262–71.

MURTI, V. V. RAMANA. "Romain Rolland's Jean-Christophe." *Triveni,* 37, No.4 (1969), 53–62.

SICE, DAVID. "*Jean-Christophe* as a 'Musical' Novel." *French Review,* 39 (1966), 862–74.

THE SOUL ENCHANTED (L'âme enchantée, 1922–33)

ALDEN, DOUGLAS W. "Léon Blum as a Source for *L'âme Enchantée.*" *Kentucky Romance Quarterly,* 17 (1970), 9–18.

ROMAINS, JULES (French, 1885–1972)
THE DEATH OF A NOBODY (Mort de quelqu'un, 1911)

WILSON, CLOTILDE. "Sartre's Graveyard of Chimeras: 'La Nausée' and 'Mort de Quelqu'un.'" *French Review,* 38 (1965), 744–53.

MEN OF GOOD WILL (Les hommes de bonne volonté, 1932–46)

ALDEN, DOUGLAS W. "The News on October 6." *Romance Notes,* 12 (1971), 235–43.

———. "Quinette, Landru, and Raskolnikoff." *French Review,* 43 (1969), 215–26.

FRANÇON, MARCEL. "On October 6." *Romance Notes,* 14 (1972), 17–18.

ROMANCE OF THE THREE KINGDOMS (San kuo Chih Yen I)

MARNEY, JOHN. "The 'Other World' in Chinese Literature." *Literature East And West,* 18 (1974), 158–65.

ROMERO, Anselmo Suarez see SUAREZ Y ROMERO, Anselmo

ROMERO, JOSÉ RUBÉN (Mexican, 1890–1952)
THE FUTILE LIFE OF PITO PÉREZ (La vida inutil de Pito Perez, 1938)

Reviews
CROW, JOHN A. "Man Trapped by Tension." *Saturday Review,* 27 May 1967, p. 33.

HOBART, LOIS. "Wandering Rogue." *New York Times Book Review,* 29 January 1967, pp. 4, 40.

MI CABALLO, MI PERRO Y MI RIFLE (1936)

GULSTAD, DANIEL E. "Antithesis in a Novel by Rubén Romero." *Hispania,* 56 (1973), 237–44.

ROSA, JOÃO GUIMARÃES (Brazilian, 1908–1967)
GENERAL

RABASSA, GREGORY. "João Guimarães Rosa: The Third Bank of The River." *Books Abroad,* 44 (1970), 30–36.

THE DEVIL TO PAY IN THE BACKLANDS (Grande Sertão: Veredas, 1956)

BORING, PHYLLIS ZATLIN. "The Brazilian Novel in the 1960s." *Papers On Language And Literature,* 11 (1975), 97–100.

DANIEL, MARY L. "Word Formation and Deformation in *Grande Sertao: Veredas.*" *Luso-Brazilian Review,* 2, No.1 (1965), 81–97.

DAVIS, WILLIAM MYRON. "Japanese Elements in *Grand Sertão: Veredas.*" *Romance Philology,* 29 (1966), 409–34.

MARTINS, WILSON. "Tradition and Ambition in Brazilian Literature." *Hispanic Review,* 40 (1972), 141–43.

MONEGAL, E. R. "The Contemporary Brazilian Novel." *Daedalus,* 95 (1966), 993–98.

RODRIGUEZ MONEGAL, EMIR. "In Praise of Guimaraes Rosa." *Commentary,* 41, No.1 (1966), 65–67.

VALENZUELA, VICTOR M. *Contemporary Latin American Writers,* pp. 101–10.

ROSNY, AÎNÉ
GENERAL

VERNIER, J.-P. "The SF of J. H. Rosny the Elder." *Science-Fiction Studies,* 2 (1975), 156–63.

ROSS, ELLEN (Canadian)
GENERAL

WOLLOCK, JEFFREY L. "Ellen Ross (1816?–1892): 'Violet Keith and All That Sort of Thing.'" *Journal Of Canadian Fiction,* 3, No.3 (1974), 80–88.

ROSS, SINCLAIR (Canadian, 1908–)
GENERAL

DJWA, SANDRA. "False Gods and the True Covenant: Thematic Continuity Between Margaret Laurence and Sinclair Ross." *Journal Of Canadian Fiction,* 1, No.4 (1972), 43–50.

AS FOR ME AND MY HOUSE (1941)

CUDE, WILFRED. "Beyond Mrs. Bentley: a Study of As For Me and My House." *Journal Of Canadian Studies,* 8, No.1 (1973), 3–18.

DJWA, SANDRA. "No Other Way: Sinclair Ross's Stories and Novels." *Canadian Literature,* No.47 (1971), pp. 53–65.

JONES, D. G. *Butterfly On Rock,* pp. 38–42.

NEW, WILLIAM H. "Sinclair Ross's Ambivalent World." *Canadian Literature,* No.40 (1969), pp. 26–32; rpt. in his *Articulating West,* pp. 60–67.

RICOU, LAURENCE. *Vertical Man/Horizontal World,* pp. 82–90.

STEPHENS, DONALD. "Wind, Sun and Dust." *Canadian Literature,* No.23 (1965), pp. 17–24.

STOUCK, DAVID. "The Mirror and the Lamp in Sinclair Ross's *As For Me And My House.*" *Mosaic,* 7, No.2 (1974), 141–50.

TALLMAN, WARREN. "Wolf in the Snow," in *A Choice Of Critics,* ed. George Woodcock, pp. 60–64.

SAWBONES MEMORIAL (1974)

Reviews
MUNTON, ANN. *Dalhousie Review,* 55 (1975), 573–75.

WHIR OF GOLD (1970)

Reviews
STEPHENS, DONALD. "Fluid Time." *Canadian Literature,* No.48 (1971), pp. 92–94.

ROTH, JOSEPH (Austrian, 1894–1939)
GENERAL

SANGER, CURT. "The Figure of the Non-Hero in the Austrian Novels of Joseph Roth." *Modern Austrian Literature,* 2, No.4 (1969), 35–37.

WILLIAMS, CEDRIC E. *The Broken Eagle,* pp. 91–112.

RADETZKY MARCH (Radetzkymarsch, 1932)

WILLIAMS, CEDRIC E. *The Broken Eagle,* pp. 103–8.

SEINE K. UND K. APOSTOLISCHE MAJESTÄT

MARGETTS, JOHN. "Joseph Roth's *Seine K. Und K. Apostolische Majestät:* 'Die Zwiespältige Trauer' and 'Der Traurige Zwiespalt.' " *German Life And Letters,* 25 (1972), 236–46.

THE SILENT PROPHET (Der stumme Prophet, 1966)

Reviews
ZIOLKOWSKI, THEODORE. "Paradigms of the Recent German Novel." *Modern Language Journal,* 52 (1968), 28–29.

ROUMAIN, JACQUES (Haitian)

MASTERS OF THE DEW (Gouverneurs de la rosée, 1944)

BLOCH, ADÈLE. "The Mythological Themes In The Fictional Works Of Jacques Roumain." *International Fiction Review,* 2 (1975), 132–37.

FOWLER, CAROLYN. "Motif Symbolism in Jacques Roumain's *Gouverneurs De La Rosée.*" *College Language Association Journal,* 18 (1974), 44–51.

MAKOUTA-MBOUKOU, J. P. *Black African Literature,* pp. 85–92.

LA MONTAGNE ENSORCELÉE (1931)

BLOCH, ADÈLE. "The Mythological Themes In The Fictional Works Of Jacques Roumain." *International Fiction Review,* 2 (1975), 132–37.

ROUSSEAU, JEAN-JACQUES (French, 1712-1778)

GENERAL

BROOKS, PETER. "Romantic Antipastoral and Urban Allegories." *Yale Review,* 64 (1974), 14–20.

DIFFEY, NORMAN R. "Lenz, Rousseau, and the Problem of Striving." *Seminar,* 10 (1974), 165–80.

FRANCIS, R. A. "Romain Rolland and Jean-Jacques Rousseau." *Nottingham French Studies,* 8 (1969), 40–53.

GOODHEART, EUGENE. "The Antinomianism of Jean-Jacques Rousseau," in his *The Cult Of The Ego,* pp. 9–35.

GRIMSLEY, RONALD. "Rousseau and Allan Ramsay, or Psychology versus Art." *Revue Du Pacifique,* 1 (1975), 54–61.

KELLY, G. D. "Godwin, Wollstonecraft, and Rousseau." *Women & Literature,* 3, No.2 (1975), 21–26.

LEIGH, R. A. "Rousseau's English Pension," in *Studies In Eighteenth-Century French Literature,* ed. J. H. Fox, M. H. Waddicor, and D. A. Watts, pp. 109–22.

MEYER, PAUL H. "Rousseau and the French Language." *L'Esprit Créateur,* 9 (1969), 187–97.

ROSENBERG, AUBREY. "The Temperamental Affinities of Rousseau and Lévi-Strauss." *Queen's Quarterly,* 82 (1975), 543–55.

SHELL, MARC. "The Lie of the Fox: Rousseau's Theory of Verbal, Monetary and Political Representations." *Sub-Stance,* No.10 (1974), pp. 111–23.

TATE, ROBERT S., JR. "Rousseau and Voltaire as Deists: A Comparison." *L'Esprit Créateur,* 9 (1969), 175–86.

TOPAZIO, VIRGIL W. "A Reevaluation of Rousseau's Political Doctrine," in *Literature And History In the Age of Ideas,* ed. Charles G. S. Williams, pp. 179–92.

———. "Rousseau: Humanism and Humanitarianism." *Kentucky Romance Quarterly,* 20 (1973), 403–13.

JULIE, OR, THE NEW ELOISE (La Nouvelle Héloïs, 1761)

ANDERSON, DAVID L. "Edouard and Jean-Jacques in Retrospect." *L'Esprit Créateur,* 9 (1969), 219–26.

BLUM, CAROL. "*La Nouvelle Héloise:* An Act in the Life of Jean-Jacques Rousseau." *L'Esprit Créateur,* 9 (1969), 198–206.

———. "Styles of Cognition as Moral Options in *La Nouvelle Héloise* and *Les Liaisons Dangereuses.*" *PMLA,* 88 (1973), 289–98.

BRADY, PATRICK. "Structural Affiliations of *La Nouvelle Héloïse.*" *L'Esprit Créateur,* 9 (1969), 207–18.

BROOKS, PETER. *The Novel Of Worldliness,* pp. 147–63.

DAVIS, JAMES HERBERT. "Montherlant, *La Nouvelle Héloïse,* and the *Argument De Renfort.*" *Romance Notes,* 13 (1972), 297–401.

GRIMSLEY, RONALD. "Rousseau and the Ideal of Self-Sufficiency." *Studies In Romanticism,* 10 (1971), 288–91.

MILLER, NANCY K. *The Heroine's Text,* pp. 96–115.

MYLNE, VIVIENNE. *The Eighteenth Century French Novel,* pp. 167–91.

SCANLAN, TIMOTHY M. "The Notion of 'Paradis sur la terre' in Rousseau's 'La Nouvelle Heloise.' " *Nottingham French Studies,* 13 (1974), 12–22.

TEMMER, MARK J. "Rousseau's *La Nouvelle Héloïse* and Goethe's *Wilhelm Meisters Lehrjahre.*" *Studies In Romanticism,* 10 (1971), 309–39.

TOPAZIO, VIRGIL W. "J. J. Rousseau: The Real Riddle Within the Enigma." *Forum,* 8, No.1 (1970), 11–14.

ULMER, GREGORY L. "*Clarissa* and *La Nouvelle Heloise.*" *Comparative Literature,* 24 (1972), 289–308.

VANCE, CHRISTIE. "*La Nouvelle Héloïse:* The Language of Paris." *Yale French Studies,* (1970), pp. 127–36.

VARTANIAN, ARAM. "The Death of Julie: A Psychological Post-mortem." *L'Esprit Créateur,* 6 (1966), 77–84.

WEBB, DONALD P. "Did Rousseau Bungle the *Nuit D'Amour?*" *Kentucky Romance Quarterly,* 17 (1970), 3–8.

———. "Julie d'Étange and the Lac(s) D'Amour." *Romance Notes,* 12 (1971), 343–45.

———. "Rousseau's *La Nouvelle Héloïse.*" *Explicator,* 30 (1972), Item 73.

WEIGHTMAN, JOHN. "The Conflict of Values in *La Nouvelle Héloïse.*" *Forum For Modern Language Studies,* 4 (1968), 309–21.

ROUSSEL, RAYMOND (French, 1877-1933)

IMPRESSIONS OF AFRICA (Impressions d'Afrique, 1910)

MATTHEWS, J. H. *Surrealism And The Novel,* pp. 41–55.

ROWCROFT, CHARLES (Australian)

GENERAL

HADGRAFT, CECIL. "Charles Rowcroft, for Example." *Australian Literary Studies,* 2 (1966), 171–78.

SHIPLEY, JOHN B. "Charles Rowcroft: An Unpublished Memoir." *Australian Literary Studies,* 3 (1967), 116–25.

THE BUSHRANGERS OF VAN DIEMEN'S LAND

ARGYLE, BARRY. *An Introduction To The Australian Novel, 1830-1930,* pp. 39–53.

HEALY, J. J. "The Treatment of the Aborigine in Early Australian Fiction, 1840–70." *Australian Literary Studies,* 5 (1972), 239–44.

TALES OF THE COLONIES

ARGYLE, BARRY. *An Introduction To The Australian Novel, 1830-1930,* pp. 27–39.

ROY, GABRIELLE (French Canadian, 1909-1983)

GENERAL

GROSSKURTH, PHYLLIS. "Gabrielle Roy and the Silken Noose." *Canadian Literature,* No.42 (1969), pp. 6-13.

HAYNE, DAVID M. "Gabrielle Roy." *Canadian Modern Language Review,* 21, No.1 (1964), 20-26.

MCPHERSON, HUGO. "The Garden and the Cage: The Achievement of Gabrielle Roy," in *A Choice Of Critics,* ed. George Woodcock, pp. 110-22.

MITCHAM, ALLISON. "The Northern Innocent in the Fiction of Gabrielle Roy." *Humanities Association Review,* 24 (1973), 25-31.

SOCKEN, PAUL. "Gabrielle Roy as Journalist." *Canadian Modern Language Review,* 30 (1974), 96-100.

URBAS, JEANNETTE. "Equations and Flutes." *Journal Of Canadian Fiction,* 1, No.2 (1972), 69-73.

THE CASHIER (Alexandre Chenevert, Caissier, 1954)

HIND-SMITH, JOAN. *Three Voices: The Lives Of Margaret Laurence, Gabrielle Roy, Frederick Philip Grove,* pp. 99-101.

MURPHY, JOHN J. "Alexandre Chenevert: Gabrielle Roy's Crucified Canadian." *Queen's Quarterly,* 72 (1965), 334-46.

THE HIDDEN MOUNTAIN (La Montagne secrète, 1961)

HIND-SMITH, JOAN. *Three Voices: The Lives Of Margaret Laurence, Gabrielle Roy, Frederick Philip Grove,* pp. 106-10.

JONES, D. G. *Butterfly On Rock,* pp. 145-47.

THE ROAD PAST ALTAMONT (La route d'Altamont, 1966)

HIND-SMITH, JOAN. *Three Voices: The Lives Of Margaret Laurence, Gabrielle Roy, Frederick Philip Grove,* pp. 111-15.

Reviews
LESAGE, LAURENT. *Saturday Review,* 3 September 1966, p. 37.

MCPHERSON, HUGO. "First and Last Things." *Canadian Literature,* No.32 (1967), pp. 59-60.

THE TIN FLUTE (Bonheur-d'occasion, 1945)

HIND-SMITH, JOAN. *Three Voices: The Lives Of Margaret Laurence, Gabrielle Roy, Frederick Philip Grove,* pp. 84-88.

THOMAS, CLARA. "Crusoe and the Precious Kingdom: Fables of our Literature." *Journal Of Canadian Fiction,* 1, No.2 (1972), 62-64.

THORNE, W. B. "Poverty and Wrath: A Study of The Tin Flute." *Journal Of Canadian Studies,* 3, No.3 (1968), 3-10.

WHERE NESTS THE WATER HEN (La Petite Poule d'Eau, 1950)

HIND-SMITH, JOAN. *Three Voices: The Lives Of Margaret Laurence, Gabrielle Roy, Frederick Philip Grove,* pp. 93-98.

WINDFLOWER (La rivière sans repos, 1970)

HIND-SMITH, JOAN. *Three Voices: The Lives Of Margaret Laurence, Gabrielle Roy, Frederick Philip Grove,* pp. 120-22.

Reviews
GROSSKURTH, PHYLLIS. "Gentle Quebec." *Canadian Literature,* No.49 (1971), pp. 83-85.

MCPHERSON, HUGO. "Blais, Godbout, Roy: Love, Art, Time." *Tamarack Review,* No.57 (1971), pp. 87-88.

ROY, JULES (French, 1907-)

LES ÂMES INTERDITES (1972)

Reviews
O'CONNELL, DAVID. *French Review,* 47 (1974), 1219-20.

THE HAPPY VALLEY (La Vallée heureuse, 1946)

CAMUS, ALBERT. *Lyrical And Critical Essays,* pp. 242-47.

ROY, NAMBA

BLACK ALBINO (1961)

RAMCHAND, KENNETH. *The West Indian Novel And Its Background,* pp. 149-54.

RUBADIRI, DAVID (Tanzanian, 1930-)

NO BRIDE PRICE (1967)

Reviews
MOORE, GERALD. "Rubadiri & Kayira." *African Literature Today,* No.2 (1969), pp. 51-52.

RUBÍN, RAMÓN

GENERAL

RINGWALD, ELEANOR MEYER. "Imagery in the Works of Ramón Rubín." *Hispania,* 53 (1970), 225-29.

RUIZ, José Martínez see AZORÍN

RULE, JANE (Canadian, 1931-)

AGAINST THE SEASON (1971)

Reviews
NEWTON, ELAINE. "The Persisting Possibility of Love." *Journal Of Canadian Fiction,* 1, No.2 (1972), 87-88.

THIS IS NOT FOR YOU (1970)

Reviews
FRASER, KEATH. "The Paradox of Life." *Canadian Literature,* No.47 (1971), pp. 104-5.

RULFO, JUAN (Mexican, 1918-)

LA CORDILLERA

GORDON, DONALD K. "Juan Rulfo's Elusive Novel: 'La Cordillera.' " *Hispania,* 56 (1973), 1040-41.

PEDRO PÁRAMO (1955)

BELL, ALAN S. "Rulfo's *Pedro Páramo:* A Vision of Hope." *MLN,* 81 (1966), 238-45.

BRUSHWOOD, JOHN S. *The Spanish American Novel,* pp. 195-200.

BURTON, JULIANNE. "Sexuality and the Mythic Dimension in Juan Rulfo's *Pedro Páramo.*" *Symposium,* 28 (1974), 228-47.

GLEAVES, ROBERT M. " 'Los pasos Perdidos', 'Pedro Paramo', and the 'Classic' Novel in Spanish America." *USF Language Quarterly,* 8, No.1/2 (1969), 5-8.

GYURKO, LANIN A. "Modern Hispanic-American Fiction: Novel of Action and Narrative of Consciousness." *Symposium,* 25 (1971), 365-68.

———. "Rulfo's Aesthetic Nihilism: Narrative Antecedents of *Pedro Páramo.*" *Hispanic Review,* 40 (1972), 451-66.

LANGFORD, WALTER M. *The Mexican Novel Comes Of Age,* pp. 93-101.

LEVINE, SUZANNE JILL. "*One Hundred Years of Solitude* and *Pedro Páramo:* A Parallel." *Books Abroad,* 47 (1973), 490-95.

SOMMER, JOSEPH. *After The Storm,* pp. 69-94.

RUŅĢIS, AIVARS

GENERAL

NOLLENDORFS, VALTERS. "The Lonesome Patriot in the Prose of Latvian Writer Aivars Ruņgis." *Lituanus,* 20, No.3 (1974), 13–16, 19–21, 25.

RYGA, GEORGE

GENERAL

CARSON, NEIL. "George Ryga and the Lost Country." *Canadian Literature,* No.45 (1970), pp. 33–40.

BALLAD OF A STONE-PICKER (1966)

RICOU, LAURENCE R. "Empty as Nightmare: Man and Landscape in Recent Canadian Prairie Fiction." *Mosaic,* 6, No.2 (1972/3), 150–51.

_____ . *Vertical Man/ Horizontal World,* pp. 122–24.

Reviews

FLAMENGO, MARYA. "Epic Miseries." *Canadian Literature,* No.34 (1967), pp. 76–78.

HUNGRY HILLS (1963)

RICOU, LAURENCE R. "Empty as Nightmare: Man and Landscape in Recent Canadian Prairie Fiction." *Mosaic,* 6, No.2 (1972/3), 149–50.

S

SAAR, FERDINAND VON

SCHLOSS KOSTENITZ

VON NARDROFF, ERNEST H. "Ferdinand von Saar's *Schloss Kostenitz:* A Prelude to Schnitzler?" *Modern Austrian Literature,* 4, No. 4 (1971), 21-36.

SÁBATO, ERNESTO (Argentine, 1911-)

GENERAL

BROWER, GARY L. "Sábato, Martínez Estrada, Mumford: Attack on the Megalopolis." *Chasqui,* 3, No.1 (1973), 7-16.

ON HEROES AND TOMBS (Sobre Héroes y tumbas, 1961)

ALAZRAKI, JAIME. "Borges and the New Latin-American Novel." *Triquarterly,* No.25 (1972), pp. 380-83.

CALLAN, RICHARD J. "Sábato's Fiction: A Jungian Interpretation." *Bulletin Of Hispanic Studies,* 51 (1974), 52-59.

FOSTER, DAVID WILLIAM. *Currents In The Contemporary Argentine Novel,* pp. 72-97.

————. "The Integral Role of 'El Informe Sobre Ciegos' in Sábato's *Sobre Héroes Y Tumbas.*" *Romance Notes,* 14 (1972), 44-48.

HAYDEN, ROSE LEE. *An Existential Focus On Some Novels Of The River Plate.*

HOLZAPFEL, TAMARA. "Metaphysical Revolt in Ernst Sábato's 'Sobre Héroes y Tumbas.' " *Hispania,* 52 (1969), 857-63.

OBERHELMAN, HARLEY D. *Ernesto Sábato,* pp. 139-50.

SOUZA, RAYMOND D. "Fernando as Hero in Sábato's 'Sobre Héroes y tumbas.' " *Hispania,* 55 (1972), 241-46.

THE OUTSIDER (El túnel, 1948)

CALLAN, RICHARD J. "Sábato's Fiction: A Jungian Interpretation." *Bulletin Of Hispanic Studies,* 51 (1974), 49-52.

GIBBS, BEVERLY J. " 'El Túnel': Portrayal of Isolation." *Hispania,* 48 (1965), 429-36.

HAYDEN, ROSE LEE. *An Existential Focus On Some Novels Of The River Plate.*

HOLZAPFEL, TAMARA "Dostoevsky's 'Notes from the Underground' and Sábato's 'El Túnel.' " *Hispania,* 51 (1968), 440-46.

LYDAY, LEON F. " 'Maternidad' in Sábato's *El Túnel.*" *Romance Notes,* 10 (1968), 20-26.

MEEHAN, THOMAS C. "Ernesto Sábato's Sexual Metaphysics: Theme and Form in *El Túnel.*" *MLN,* 83 (1968), 226-52.

OBERHELMAN, HARLEY D. *Ernest Sábato,* pp. 49-64.

PETERSEN, FRED. "Sábato's 'El Túnel': More Freud Than Sartre." *Hispania,* 50 (1967), 271-76.

SÁ-CARNEIRO, MÁRIO DE (Portuguese, 1890-1916)

GENERAL

BACARISSE, PAMELA. "Sá-Carneiro and the Conte Fantastique." *Luso-Brazilian Review,* 12 (1975), 65-79.

SADE, DONATIEN ALPHONSE, COMTE, CALLED MARQUIS DE (French, 1740-1814)

GENERAL

BENTLEY, JOSEPH. "Satire and the Rhetoric of Sadism." *Centennial Review,* 11 (1967), 387-404.

BERMAN, LORNA. "The Marquis de Sade and his Critics." *Mosaic,* 1, No.2 (1968), 57-73.

BLANCHOT, MAURICE. "The Main Impropriety (Excerpts)." Trans. June Guicharnaud. *Yale French Studies,* No.39 (1967), pp. 50-63.

COREY, LEWIS. "Marquis de Sade—The Cult of Despotism." *Antioch Review,* 26 (1966), 17-31.

FINK, BEATRICE C. "Food as Object, Activity and Symbol in Sade." *Romanic Review,* 65 (1974), 96-102.

————. "Sade and Cannibalism." *L'Esprit Créateur,* 15 (1975), 403-12.

HARARI, JOSUÉ V. "De Sade's Narrative Ill-Logical or Illogical." Trans. Hélène Pellegrin. *Genre,* 7 (1974), 112-31.

HASSAN, IHAB. "Sade: Prisoner of Consciousness." *Triquarterly,* No.15 (1969), pp. 23-41.

KLOSSOWSKI, PIERRE. "A Destructive Philosophy." *Yale French Studies,* No.35 (1965), pp. 61-79.

MATTHEWS, J. H. "The Right Person for Surrealism." *Yale French Studies,* No.35 (1965), pp. 89-95.

MAY, GEORGES. "Novel Reader, Fiction Writer." *Yale French Studies,* No.35 (1965), pp. 5-11.

MITCHELL, JEREMY. "Swinburne—The Disappointed Protagonist." *Yale French Studies,* No.35 (1965), pp. 81-88.

PASTOUREAU, HENRI. "Sado-Masochism and the Philosophies of Ambivalence." *Yale French Studies,* No.35 (1965), pp. 48-60.

SADE, D. A. F. "Notes on the Novel." *Yale French Studies,* No.35 (1965), pp. 12-19.

SZOGYI, ALEX. "A Full Measure of Madness." *New York Times Book Review,* 25 July 1965, pp. 4-5, 22.

TEMMER, MARK J. "Style and Rhetoric." *Yale French Studies,* No.35 (1965), pp. 20-28.

DIALOGUE BETWEEN A PRIEST AND A DYING MAN (Dialogue entre un prêtre et un moribund, 1926)

HASSAN, IHAB. "Sade: Prisoner of Consciousness." *Triquarterly,* No. 15 (1969), pp. 29–30.

JUSTINE: OR, GOOD CONDUCT WELL CHASTISED (Justine, ou les malheurs de la vertu, 1791)

GIRAUD, RAYMOND. "The First *Justine." Yale French Studies,* No. 35 (1965), pp. 39–47.

LENNIG, WALTER. *Portrait Of De Sade: An Illustrated Biography,* pp. 139–43.

THE 120 DAYS OF SODOM (Les 120 journées de Sodome, 1904)

MAYS, JAMES. "*Pons Asinorum:* Form and Value in Beckett's Writing, with some comments on Kafka and de Sade." *Irish University Review,* 4 (1974), 277–82.

THE STORY OF JULIETTE (Juliette, ou les prospérités du vice, 1797)

FINK, BEATRICE C. "Sade and Cannibalism." *L'Esprit Créateur,* 15 (1975), 409–12.

GUICHARNAUD, JACQUES. "The Wreathed Columns of St. Peter's." *Yale French Studies,* No.35 (1965), pp. 29–38.

LENNIG, WALTER. *Portrait Of De Sade: An Illustrated Biography,* pp. 143–54.

MILLER, NANCY K. "*Juliette* and the Posterity of Prosperity." *L'Esprit Créateur,* 15 (1975), 413–24.

SADEEK, SHEIK (Guyanese)

GENERAL

McDOWELL, ROBERT E. "Interview with Sheik Sadeek—A Guyanese Popular Writer." *World Literature Written In English,* 14 (1975), 525–35.

SADEH, PINHAS (Polish, 1929–)

THE DEATH OF ABIMELECH AND HIS ASCENT TO HEAVEN IN HIS MOTHER'S ARMS (Mot abimelech va'aliyato hashamaymah bizro'ot imo, 1969)

RAMRAS-RAUCH, GILA. "An Existential Treatment of a Biblical Theme: Pinhas Sadeh's 'The Death of Abimelech.' " *Books Abroad,* 45 (1971), 50–53.

SADJI, ABDOULAYE (Senegalese, 1910–1961)

MAIMOUNA (1953)

BRENCH, A. C. *The Novelists' Inheritance In French Africa,* pp. 24–31.

GLEASON, JUDITH ILLSLEY. *This Africa,* pp. 136–40.

NINI, MULATRESSE DU SENEGAL (1947–48)

BRENCH, A. C. *The Novelists' Inheritance In French Africa,* pp. 31–36.

SADOVEANU, MIHAIL (Romanian, 1880–1961)

THE HATCHET (Baltagul, 1930)

SIMMS, NORMAN. "From Stasis To Freedom, In Mihail Sadoveanu's *The Hatchet." Mosaic,* 7, No.2 (1974), 45–56.

SAGAN, FRANÇOISE (French, 1935–)
pseudonym of Francois Quoirez

LA CHAMADE (1965)

Reviews
LUMSDEN, GEORGE. *Canadian Modern Language Review,* 27, No.2 (1971), 101–2.

PAGONES, DORRIE. "Bonsoir Tristisse." *Saturday Review,* 12 November 1966, p. 63.

SAHANI, BHISMA

TAMAS

Reviews
SHUKLA, PRAYAQ. *Indian Literature,* 16, Nos.3/4 (1973), 220–22.

SAHGAL, NAYANTRA (Indian, 1927–)

THE DAY IN THE SHADOW (1971)

ASNANI, SHYAM M. "The Novels of Nayantara Sahgal." *Indian Literature,* 16, Nos. 1/2 (1973), 60–68.

STORM IN CHANDIGARH (1969)

ASNANI, SHYAM M. "The Novels of Nayantara Sahgal." *Indian Literature,* 16, Nos. 1/2 (1973), 49–60.

Reviews
ZUCKERMAN, RUTH VAN HORN. *Mahfil,* 6, No.4 (1970), 86–87.

THIS TIME OF MORNING (1965)

ASNANI, SHYAM M. "The Novels of Nayantara Sahgal." *Indian Literature,* 16, Nos. 1/2 (1973), 43–49.

Reviews
HARTLEY, LOIS. *Literature East And West,* 10 (1966), 168.
ZUCKERMAN, RUTH VAN HORN. *Mahfil,* 6, No.4 (1970), 84–86.

A TIME TO BE HAPPY (1958)

ASNANI, SHYAM M. "The Novels of Nayantara Sahgal." *Indian Literature,* 16, Nos. 1/2 (1973), 39–43.

SAHNI, BALRAJ

GENERAL

KUMAR, SHARAT. "Balraj Sahni: In Remembrance." *Indian Literature,* 16, Nos. 1/2 (1973), 211–15.

SAID, KURBAN

ALI & NINO

Reviews
HITREC, JOSEPH. *Saturday Review,* 21 August 1971, pp. 28–29.

SAINT-EXUPÉRY, ANTOINE DE (French, 1900–1944)

GENERAL

KESTNER, JOSEPH. "Pindar and Saint-Exupéry: The Heroic Form of Space." *Modern Fiction Studies,* 19 (1973/4), 507–16.

McKEON, JOSEPH T. "Saint-Exupéry, The Myth of the Pilot." *PMLA,* 89 (1974), 1084–89.

THE LITTLE PRINCE (Le Petit Prince, 1943)

PRICE, ROBERT H. "*Pantagruel* and *Le Petit Prince." Symposium,* 21 (1967), 264–70.

NIGHT FLIGHT (Vol de nuit, 1931)

COR, LAURENCE W. "*Vol De Nuit:* The World of Light and Darkness." *Romance Notes,* 15 (1973), 7–9.

FROHOCK, W. H. *Style And Temper,* pp. 34–39.

YOUNG, MICHAEL T. *Saint-Exupéry: Vol De Nuit.*

SOUTHERN MAIL (Courrier sud, 1929)

PARRY, M. "A Symbolic Interpretation of 'Courrier Sud.' " *Modern Language Review,* 69 (1974), 297–307.

WIND, SAND AND STARS (Terre des hommes, 1939)

FROHOCK, W. H. *Style And Temper,* pp. 39-43.

ST. OMER, GARTH (West Indian)
GENERAL

KAYE, JACQUELINE. "Anonymity and Subjectivism in the Novels of Garth St. Omer." *Journal Of Commonwealth Literature,* 10, No.1 (1975), 45-52.

SAINT-PIERRE, BERNARDIN DE (French, 1737-1814)
PAUL ET VIRGINIE (1787)

MYLNE, VIVIENNE. *The Eighteenth Century French Novel,* pp. 245-62.

SAINT-RÉAL
DON CARLOS

BREMNER, GEOFFEY. "The Lesson of Saint-Réal." *French Studies,* 24 (1970), 356-67.

HAIG, STIRLING. "*La Princesse De Clèves* and Saint-Réal's *Don Carlos.*" *French Studies,* 22 (1968), 201-5.

SAINT ROBERT, PHILIPPE DE
LA MÊME DOULEUR DÉMENTE (1973)

Reviews
ALFONSI, SANDRA R. *French Review,* 48 (1975), 1071-72.

SAINTE-BEAUVE, CHARLES AUGUSTIN (French, 1804-1869)
GENERAL

CHADBOURNE, RICHARD M. "Criticism as Creation in Sainte Beuve." *L'Esprit Créateur,* 14 (1974), 44-54.

MARKS, EMERSON R. "Sainte-Beuve's Literary Portraiture." *L'Esprit Créateur,* 14 (1974), 24-34.

MULHAUSER, RUTH. "A Legacy of Sainte-Beuve." *L'Esprit Créateur,* 14 (1974), 55-63.

———. *Sainte-Beuve And Greco-Roman Antiquity.*

VOLUPTÉ (1834)

NIESS, ROBERT J. "Sainte-Beuve and Balzac: *Volupté* and *Le Lys Dans La Vallée.*" *Kentucky Romance Quarterly,* 20 (1973), 113-24.

SÁINZ, GUSTAVO (Mexican, 1940-)
GAZAPO (1965)

GYURKO, LANIN A. "Reality and Fantasy in *Gazapo.*" *Revista De Estudios Hispánicos,* 8 (1974), 117-46.

Reviews
BRUSHWOOD, JOHN S. *Kansas City Star,* 14 July 1968; rpt. in *Review,* No.1 (1968), 79-80.

GELLER, STEPHEN. *New York Times Book Review,* 21 July 1968; rpt. in *Review,* No.1 (1968), pp. 78-79.

LEONARD, IRVING A. "Kin to Children of Sanchez." *Saturday Review,* 3 August 1968, p. 24; rpt in *Review,* No.1 (1968), pp. 77-78.

SAUNDERS, JOHN F. *Hispania,* 51 (1968), 378.

SALAZAR BONDY, SEBASTIÁN (Peruvian, 1924-1964)
ALFÉREZ ARCE, TENIENTE ARCE, CAPITÁN ARCE . . .

LUCHTING, WOLFGANG A. "Sebastián Salazar Bondy's Last Novel." *Journal Of Spanish Studies,* 1 (1973), 45-63.

SALTYKOV-SCHEDRIN, MIKHAIL YEVGRA-FOVICH (Russian, 1826-1849)
THE GOLOVLOVS (Gospoda Golovyovi)

FOOTE, I. P. "M. E. Saltykov-Shchedrin: *The Golovlyov Family.*" *Forum For Modern Language Studies,* 4 (1968), 53-63.

KRAMER, KARL D. "Satiric Form in Saltykov's *Gospoda Golovlevy.*" *Slavic And East European Journal,* 14 (1970), 453-64.

THE HISTORY OF A TOWN (1869)

FOOTE, I. P. "Reaction or Revolution? The Ending of Saltykov's *The History Of A Town.*" *Oxford Slavonic Papers,* NS 1 (1968), 105-25.

SALZMANN, CHRISTIAN GOTTHILF
SEBASTIAN KLUGE

HADLEY, MICHAEL. *The German Novel In 1790,* pp. 203-6.

SAMARKIS, ANDONIS (Greek, 1919-)
GENERAL

JAHIEL, EDWIN. "Antonis Samarkis: Fiction as Scenario." *Books Abroad,* 42 (1968), 531-34.

THE FLAW (Io lathos, 1965)

Reviews
FRIAR, KIMON. *Saturday Review,* 3 January 1970, p. 82.

SAMKANGE, STANLAKE (Zimbabwean, 1922-)
ON TRIAL FOR MY COUNTRY (1966)

GORDIMER, NADINE. "The Interpreters: Some Themes and Directions in African Literature." *Kenyon Review,* 32 (1970), 22-24.

SAND, GEORGE (French, 1804-1876), pseudonym of Amantine Aurore Lucille Dupin, Mme Dudevant
GENERAL

BRÉE, GERMAINE. "George Sand: The Fictions of Autobiography." *Nineteenth-Century French Studies,* 4 (1976), 438-49.

DENOMMÉ, ROBERT T. "A Note Concerning the Death of George Sand." *Romance Notes,* 10 (1969), 261-64.

LEEMING, DAVID ADAMS. "Henry James and George Sand." *Revue De Littérature Comparée,* 43 (1969), 47-55.

THOMSON, PATRICIA. "George Sand and English Reviewers: The First Twenty Years." *Modern Language Review,* 67 (1972), 501-16.

MAUPRAT

ARNOLD, J. V. "George Sand's *Mauprat* and Emily Brontë's *Wuthering Heights.*" *Revue De Littérature Comparée,* 46 (1972), 209-18.

SANDEL, CORA (Norwegian, 1880-) pseudonym of Sara Margarethe Fabricius
ALBERTA ALONE (Bare Alberte, 1939)

Reviews
PAGONES, DORRIE. "Growing Up in Paris." *Saturday Review,* 7 May 1966, pp. 94-95.

KRANE'S CAFÉ (Kranes konditori, 1945)

Reviews
BAYERSCHMIDT, CARL F. *American Scandinavian Review,* 58 (1970), 85.

SANDEMOSE, AKSEL (Norwegian, 1899–1965)

GENERAL

NIELSEN, ERLING. "Aksel Sandemose: Investigator of the Mystery of Human Nature." *Scandinavica,* 8 (1969), 1–18.

THE WEREWOLF (Varulven, 1958)

Reviews
MITCHELL, P. M. "The Hidden Enemy in the Self." *Saturday Review,* 11 June 1966, pp. 58–59.

SPECTOR, ROBERT D. *American Scandinavian Review,* 55 (1967), 196–97.

SANGUINETI, EDUARDO (Italian, 1930–)

IL GIOCO DELL'OCA (1967)

RAGUSA, OLGA. "Gadda, Pasolini, and Experimentalism: Form or Ideology?" in *From Verismo To Experimentalism,* ed. Sergio Pacifici, pp. 264–66.

SÁINTOMAS DE ÉXODO (1969)

Reviews
KRONIK, JOHN W. *Hispania,* 54 (1971), 397.

SANKAR

GENERAL

BAUMER, RACHEL VAN M. "Sankar: Twentieth-Century *Kathak.*" *Books Abroad,* 43 (1969), 487–98.

CĀRANGĪ

BAUMER, RACHEL VAN M. "Sankar: Twentieth-Century *Kathak.*" *Books Abroad,* 43 (1969), 489–94.

KATA AJĀNĀRE

BAUMER, RACHEL VAN M. "Sankar: Twentieth-Century *Kathak.*" *Books Abroad,* 43 (1969), 489–96.

SAN PEDRO, DIEGO DE (fl. late 15th Century)

LA CÁRCEL DE AMOR

WALEY, PAMELA. "*Cárcel De Amor* and *Grisel Y Mirabella*: A Question of Priority." *Bulletin Of Hispanic Studies,* 50 (1973), 340–56.

————. "Love and Honour in the *Novelas Sentimentales* of Diego de San Pedro and Juan de Flores." *Bulletin Of Hispanic Studies,* 43 (1966), 249–73.

WHINNOM, KEITH. "Nicolás Núñez's Continuation of the *Cárcel De Amor* (Burgos, 1496)," in *Studies In Spanish Literature Of The Golden Age,* ed. R. O. Jones, pp. 357–66.

SANSOVINO, FRANCESCO

CENTO NOVELLE SCELTE

LEE, PHILIP A., Jr. "Sansovino's *Cento Novelle Scelte* in the *Motif-Index Of The Italian Novella In Prose.*" *Romance Notes,* 9 (1967), 295–98.

SANTOS, BIENVENIDO N. (Philippine, 1911–)

GENERAL

CASPER, LEONARD. *New Writing From The Philippines,* pp. 125–33.

SANTUCCI, LUIGI

ORFEO IN PARADISE

Reviews
BERGIN, THOMAS G. "Return to Mom in Old Milan." *Saturday Review,* 12 April 1969, p. 94.

SARAT CHANDRA

GENERAL

SARKER, SUBHAS CHANDRA. "Sarat Chandra as a Man." *Indian Literature,* 16, Nos. 3/4 (1973), 11–25.

SARDUY, SEVERO (Cuban, 1937–)

GENERAL

FOSSEY, JEAN-MICHEL. "From Boom to Big Bang." Trans. Edith Grossman. *Review,* No.13 (1974), pp. 6–12.

LEVINE, SUZANNE JILL. "Jorge Luis Borges and Severo Sarduy: Two Writers of the Neo-Baroque." *Latin American Literary Review,* 2, No.4 (1974), 25–37.

SARDUY, SEVERO. "Chronology." Trans. Suzanne Jill Levine. *Review,* No.6 (1972), pp. 24–27.

COBRA (1972)

ADAMS, ROBERT M. "A Shrill Chill." *Review,* No.13 (1974), pp. 23–25.

CIXOUS, HELENE. "O C,O,B,R,A,B,A,R,O,C,O: A Text-Twister." Trans. Keith Cohen. *Review,* No.13 (1974), pp. 26–31.

GONZALEZ ECHEVARRIA, ROBERTO. "Rehearsal for Cobra." Trans. Paula Speck. *Review,* No.13 (1974), pp. 38–44.

LEVINE, SUZANNE JILL. "Discourse as Bricolage." *Review,* No.13 (1974), pp. 32–37.

————. "Writing as Translation: *Three Trapped Tigers* and a *Cobra.*" *MLN,* 90 (1975), 265–77.

RODRIGUEZ MONEGAL, EMIR. "Metamorphoses of the Text." Trans. Enrique Sacerio Gari. *Review,* No.13 (1974), pp. 16–22.

SOLLERS, PHILIPPE. "La Boca Obra." Trans. E. Rubinstein. *Review,* No.13 (1974), pp. 13–15.

Reviews
SKINNER, EUGENE R. *Hispania,* 57 (1974), 606–7.

FROM CUBA WITH A SONG (De donde son las cantantes, 1967)

BARTHES, ROLAND. "The Baroque Face." Trans. Susan Homar. *Review,* No.6 (1972), pp. 31–32.

CHRIST, RONALD. "Emergency Essay." *Review,* No.6 (1972), pp. 33–36.

ECHEVARRÍA, ROBERTO GONZÁLEZ. "In Search of the Lost Center." *Review,* No.6 (1972), 28–31.

JOHNDROW, DONALD RAY. " 'Total' Reality in Severo Sarduy's Search for *Lo Cubano.*" *Romance Notes,* 13 (1972), 448–52.

MENTON, SEYMOUR. *Prose Fiction Of The Cuban Revolution,* pp. 54–59.

GESTOS (1963)

JOHNDROW, DONALD RAY. " 'Total' Reality in Severo Sarduy's Search for *Lo Cubano.*" *Romance Notes,* 13 (1972), 446–48.

MENTON, SEYMOUR. *Prose Fiction Of The Cuban Revolution,* pp. 86–88.

SARGESON, FRANK (New Zealander, 1903–1982)

I SAW IN MY DREAM (1949)

NEW, W. H. "Enclosures: Frank Sargeson's *I Saw In My*

Dream." *World Literature Written In English,* 14 (1975), 15–22.

SARMIENTO, DOMINGO FAUSTINO (Argentine, 1811–1888)

GENERAL

FEUSTLE, JOSEPH A., Jr. "Sarmiento and Martinez Estrada: A Concept of Argentine History." *Hispania,* 55 (1972), 446–55.

FACUNDO O CIVILIZACIÓN Y BARBARIE (1845)

FOSTER, DAVID WILLIAM. *Currents In The Contemporary Argentine Novel,* pp. 3–5.

_____. "Noé Jitrik, Facundo, and the Uses of Literary Stylistics." *Chasqui,* 5, No.1 (1975), 15–27.

KAYE, FRANCES W. "Cooper, Sarmiento, Wister, and Hernández: The Search for a New World Literary Hero." *College Language Association Journal,* 19 (1976), 405–8.

VIVIAN, DOROTHY SHERMAN. "The Protagonist in the Works of Sarmiento and Cooper." *Hispania,* 48 (1965), 806–10.

SARRAUTE, NATHALIE (French, 1900-)

GENERAL

BRÉE, GERMAINE. "Interviews with Two French Novelists." *Contemporary Literature,* 14 (1973), 137–46.

FLEMING, JOHN A. "The Imagery of Tropism in the Novels of Nathalie Sarraute," in *Image And Theme,* ed. W. M. Frohock, pp. 74–98.

HEATH, STEPHEN. "Nathalie Sarraute and the Practice of Writing." *Novel,* 3 (1970), 101–18.

_____. *The Nouveau Roman,* pp. 44–66.

McGOWAN, MARGARET. "Nathalie Sarraute: The Failure of an Experiment?" *Studi Francesi,* 11 (1967), 442–48.

VINEBERG, ELSA. "Marcel Proust, Nathalie Sarraute, and the Psychological Novel." *MLN,* 90 (1975), 575–83.

WHITING, CHARLES G. "Nathalie Sarraute: *Moraliste.*" *French Review,* 43, Special Issue No.1 (1970), 168–74.

BETWEEN LIFE AND DEATH (Entre la vie et la mort, 1968)

HEATH, STEPHEN. "Nathalie Sarraute and the Practice of Writing." *Novel,* 3 (1970), 101–8.

_____. *The Nouveau Roman,* pp. 58–65.

McCARTHY, MARY. "Hanging by a Thread," in her *The Writing On The Wall And Other Literary Essays,* pp. 172–88.

MERCIER, VIVIAN. *The New Novel From Queneau To Pinget,* pp. 157–64.

Reviews
SCHOLES, ROBERT J. *Saturday Review,* 24 May 1969, p. 52.

DO YOU HEAR THEM ? (Vous les entendez?,1972)
Reviews
CAGNON, MAURICE. *French Review,* 46 (1973), 1070–71.

THE GOLDEN FRUITS (Les fruits d'or, 1963)

MERCIER, VIVIAN. *The New Novel From Queneau To Pinget,* pp. 148–57.

MARTEREAU (1953)

GROBE, EDWIN P. "Symbolic Sound Patterns in Nathalie Sarraute's *Martereau.*" *French Review,* 40 (1966), 84–91.

HEATH, STEPHEN. *The Nouveau Roman,* pp. 51–53.

MERCIER, VIVIAN. *The New Novel From Queneau To Pinget,* pp. 127–34.

THE PLANETARIUM (Le planétarium, 1959)

MERCIER, VIVIAN. *The New Novel From Queneau To Pinget,* pp. 140–48.

MINOGUE, VALERIE. "Nathalie Sarraute's *Le Planétarium:* The Narrator Narrated." *Forum For Modern Language Studies,* 9 (1973), 217–34.

PORTRAIT OF A MAN UNKNOWN (Le portrait d'un inconnu, 1948)

BOURAOUI, H. A. "Sarraute's Narrative Portraiture: the Artist in Search of a Voice." *Critique,* 14, No.1 (1972), 77–89.

MERCIER, VIVIAN. *The New Novel From Queneau To Pinget,* pp. 117–27.

MINOGUE, VALERIE. "The Imagery of Childhood in Nathalie Sarraute's *Portrait D'un Inconnu.*" *French Studies,* 27 (1973), 177–86.

ST. AUBYN, F. C. "Rilke, Sartre, and Sarraute: The Role of the Third." *Revue De Littérature Comparée,* 41 (1967), 275–84.

WOOD, MARGERY. "Norman Mailer and Nathalie Sarraute: A Comparison of Existential Novels." *Minnesota Review,* 6 (1966), 67–72.

TROPISMS (Tropismes, 1939)

MERCIER, VIVIAN. *The New Novel From Queneau To Pinget,* pp. 110–17.

SARTRE, JEAN-PAUL (French, 1905–1980)

GENERAL

ADERETH, M. *Commitment In Modern French Literature,* pp. 127–71.

BUKALA, C. R. "Sartre's Dramatic Philosophical Quest." *Thought,* 48 (1973), 79–106.

DUNCAN, ELMER H. "Something About Sartre." *Forum,* 6, No.1 (1968), 22–24.

GERSHMAN, HERBERT S. "The Structure of Revolt in Malraux, Camus, and Sartre." *Symposium,* 24 (1970), 32–34.

GRIMSLEY, RONALD. "Two Philosophical Views of the Literary Imagination: Sartre and Bachelard." *Comparative Literature Studies,* 8 (1971), 42–57.

MARANTZ, ENID. "The Theme of Alienation in the Literary Works of Jean-Paul Sartre." *Mosaic,* 2, No.1 (1968), 29–44.

MASTERS, BRIAN. *Sartre: A Study.*

_____. *A Student's Guide To Sartre.*

RECK, RIMA DRELL. *Literature And Responsibility,* pp. 3–42.

THE AGE OF REASON (L'age de raison, 1945)

RECK, RIMA DRELL. *Literature And Responsibility,* pp. 36–38.

SAVAGE, CATHARINE. *Malraux, Sartre, And Aragon As Political Novelists,* pp. 23–27.

L'ENFANCE D'UN CHEF

RAHV, BETTY T. *From Sartre To The New Novel,* pp. 37–55.

NAUSEA (La Nausée, 1938)

ARNOLD, A. JAMES. "*La Nausée* Revisited." *French Review,* 39 (1965), 199–213.

BAUER, GEORGE HOWARD. *Sartre And The Artist,* pp. 13–44.

BARNES, HAZEL E. *Sartre,* pp. 36–47.

CAMUS, ALBERT. *Lyrical And Critical Essays,* pp. 199–202.

CURTIS, JERRY L. "A Camus Commentary: Sartre's Debt to Husserl." *South Atlantic Bulletin,* 40, No.4 (1975), 3–6.

DALE, JONATHAN. "Sartre and Malraux: *La Nausée* and *La Voie Royale.*" *Forum For Modern Language Studies,* 4 (1968), 335–46.

DAVIS, JOHN F. "'La Nausée: Imagery and Use of the Diary Form." *Nottingham French Studies,* 10 (1971), 33–46.

FALK, EUGENE H. *Types Of Thematic Structure: The Nature And Function Of Motifs In Gide, Camus, And Sartre,* pp. 117–76.

FLETCHER, DENNIS J. "The Use of Colour in 'La Nausée.'" *Modern Language Review,* 63 (1968), 370–80.

————. "Sartre and Barrès: Some Notes on *La Nausée.*" *Forum For Modern Language Studies,* 4 (1968), 330–34.

FROHOCK, W. M. *Style And Temper,* pp. 94–103.

GOLDTHORPE, RHIANNON. "The Presentation of Consciousness in Sartre's *La Nausée* and Its Theoretical Basis: Reflection and Facticity." *French Studies,* 22 (1968), 114–32.

————. "The Presentation of Consciousness in Sartre's *La Nausée* and Its Theoretical Basis: 2. Transcendence and Intentionality." *French Studies,* 25 (1971), 32–46.

GREENE, FRANCIS J. "Louis Guilloux's *Le Sang Noir:* A Prefiguration of Sartre's *La Nausée.*" *French Review,* 43 (1969), 205–14.

GROSSVOGEL, DAVID I. *Limits Of The Novel,* pp. 226–55.

JOHNSON, PATRICIA J. "Empty Gesture: Descriptive Technique in Sartre's *La Nausée.*" *Romance Notes,* 14 (1973), 421–24.

KELLMAN, STEVEN G. "Sartre's *La Nausée* as Self-Begetting Novel." *Symposium,* 28 (1974), 303–14.

MORACEVICH, JUNE. "*La Nausée* and *Les Mots:* Vision and Revision." *Studies In Philology,* 70 (1973), 222–32.

NUTTALL, A. D. *A Common Sky: Philosophy And The Literary Imagination,* pp. 163–99.

PORTER, DENNIS. "Sartre, Robbe-Grillet and the Psychotic Hero." *Modern Fiction Studies,* 16 (1970), 13–25.

RECK, RIMA DRELL. *Literature And Responsibility,* pp. 32–36.

SOMERS, PAUL P. "Camus *Si,* Sartre *No.*" *French Review,* 42 (1969), 693–700.

THIHER, ALLEN. "Céline and Sartre." *Philological Quarterly,* 50 (1971), 292–305.

WILSON, CLOTILDE. "Sartre's Graveyard of Chimeras: 'La Nausée' and 'Mort de quelqu'un.' *French Review,* 38 (1964), 744–53.

ZIMMERMAN, EUGENIA NOIK. "The Metamorphosis of Adam: Names and Things in Sartre and Proust," in *Twentieth Century French Fiction,* ed. George Stambolian, pp. 57–71.

————. "*La Nausée* and the Avators of Being." *Mosaic,* 5, No.3 (1972), 151–57.

THE REPRIEVE (Le sursis, 1945)

SAVAGE, CATHARINE. *Malraux, Sartre, And Aragon As Political Novelists,* pp. 27–31.

THE ROADS TO FREEDOM (Les chemins de la liberté, 1945–1949)

ADERETH, M. *Commitment In Modern French Literature: Politics And Society In Péguy, Aragon, And Sartre* pp. 151–56.

BAUER, GEORGE HOWARD. *Sartre And The Artist,* pp. 65–91.

RECK, RIMA DRELL. *Literature And Responsibility,* pp. 36–40.

SAVAGE, CATHARINE. *Malraux, Sartre, And Aragon As Political Novelists,* pp. 18–42.

TROUBLED SLEEP (La mort dans l'ame, 1949)

BAUER, GEORGE. "Sartre and the 'Sugars' of History." *L'Esprit Créateur,* 15 (1975), 377–86.

RECK, RIMA DRELL. *Literature And Responsibility,* pp. 39–40.

SAVAGE, CATHARINE. *Malraux, Sartre, And Aragon As Political Novelists,* pp. 31–35.

SATCHELL, WILLIAM (New Zealander, 1860–1942)

THE LAND OF THE LOST (1902)

Reviews

EAGLE, CHESTER. "New Zealand Re-discoveries—." *Overland,* No.51 (1972), p. 57.

SATYÁNÁRAYANA, VIŚWANÁTHA (Telugu, 1895–)

GENERAL

RAMAN, A. S. "Literary Rapport: Dr. Viswanatha Satyanarayana." *Triveni,* 40, No.3 (1971), 13–18.

SAVERY, HENRY

QUINTUS SERVINTON

ARGYLE, BARRY. *An Introduction To The Australian Novel, 1830–1930,* pp. 10–26.

SCARRON, PAUL (French, 1610–1660)

LE ROMAN COMIQUE

BIDWELL, JEAN S. "*La Princesse De Clèves* and *Le Roman Comique*—Two Different Worlds." *USF Language Quarterly,* 11, No.3/4 (1973), 43–47.

CARTER, NANCY G. "The Theme of Sleep in *Le Roman Comique.*" *Romance Notes,* 11 (1969), 362–67.

THOMAS, RUTH P. "*Le Roman Comique* and *Jacques Le Fataliste:* Some Parallels." *French Review,* 47 (1973), 13–24.

SCHACK, HANS EGEDE (Danish, 1820–1859)

PHANTASTERNE (1857)

JØRGENSEN, AAGE. "Hans Egede Schack's *Phantasterne.*" *Forum For Modern Language Studies,* 6 (1970), 173–77.

————. "On 'Phantasterne', the Novel by Hans Egede Schack." *Scandinavica,* 5 (1966), 50–53.

SCHAPER, EDZARD (German, 1908–)

GENERAL

JEPSON, J. E. "Edzard Schaper's Image of Man and Society in the *Gesammelte Erzählungen.*" *German Life And Letters,* 23 (1967), 323–31.

SCHECHTMAN, ELYA

EREV

Reviews

LEVIANT, CURT. "Hebrew Clan in the Ukraine." *Saturday Review,* 8 July 1967, pp. 24–25.

SCHLEGEL, DOROTHEA (German, 1763–1839)

FLORENTIN (1801)

THORNTON, KARIN STUEBBEN. "Enlightenment and Romanticism in the Work of Dorothea Schlegel." *German Quarterly,* 39 (1966), 163–71.

SCHLEGEL, FRIEDRICH VON (1772–1829)

LUCINDE

FLAVELL, M. KAY. "Women and Individualism: A Re-examination of Schlegel's 'Lucinde' and Gutzkow's 'Wally die Zweiflerin.'" *Modern Language Review,* 70 (1975), 550–60.

SCHMIDT, ARNO (German, 1914–1979)

ZETTEL'S TRAUM (1970)

MOELLER, HANS-BERNHARD. "Perception, Word-Play, and the Printed Page: Arno Schmidt and his Poe Novel." *Books Abroad*, 45 (1971), 25–30.

PRAWER, SIEGBERT. " 'Bless Thee, Bottom! Bless Thee! Thou Art Translated:' Typographical Parallelism, Word-Play and Literary Allusion in Arno Schmidt's *Zettel's Traum*," in *Essays In German And Dutch Literature*, ed. W. D. Robson-Scott, pp. 156–91.

SCHMITZ, Ettore see SVEVO, Italo

SCHNEIDER, MARCEL
LE LIEUTENANT PERDU

Reviews
ALBERT, WALTER. *French Review,* 47 (1974), 838–39.

SCHNITZLER, ARTHUR (Austrian, 1862–1931)
GENERAL

ALTER, MARIA P. "Schnitzler's Physician: An Existential Character." *Modern Austrian Literature,* 4, No. 3 (1971), 7–23.

BERLIN, JEFFREY B. "Arthur Schnitzler: A Bibliography." *Modern Austrian Literature,* 6, No.1/2 (1973), 81–122.

_____. "Arthur Schnitzler: A Bibliography of Criticism, 1965-1971." *Modern Austrian Literature,* 4, No. 4 (1971), 7–20.

_____. "Some Images of the Betrayer in Arthur Schnitzler's Work." *German Life And Letters,* 26 (1972), 20–24.

KANN, ROBERT A. "Arthur Schnitzler: Reflections on the Evolution of His Image." *Wisconsin Studies In Contemporary Literature,* 8 (1967), 548–55.

LO CICERO, VINCENT. "A Study of the Persona in Selected Works of Arthur Schnitzler." *Modern Austrian Literature,* 2, No. 4 (1969), 7–29.

REICHERT, HERBERT W. "Nietzsche's *Geniemoral* and Schnitzler's Ethics," in his *Friedrich Nietzsche's Impact On Modern German Literature,* pp. 4–28.

STAMON, PEGGY AND RICHARD H. LAWSON. "Love-Death Structures in the Works of Arthur Schnitzler." *Modern Austrian Literature,* 8, No. 3/4 (1975), 266–81.

VIERECK, GEORGE S. "The World of Arthur Schnitzler." *Modern Austrian Literature,* 5, No. 3/4 (1972), 7–17.

WEISS, ROBERT O. "The Human Element in Schnitzler's Social Criticism." *Modern Austrian Literature,* 5, No.1/2 (1972), 30–44.

_____. "The Psychoses in the Works of Arthur Schnitzler." *German Quarterly,* 41 (1968), 377–400.

WILLIAMS, CEDRIC E. *The Broken Eagle,* pp. 45–59.

BERTHA GARLAN (Frau Berta Garlan, 1901)

DRIVER, BEVERLEY R. "Arthur Schnitzler's *Frau Berta Garlan:* A Study in Form." *Germanic Review,* 46 (1971), 285–98.

DER BLINDE GERONIMO UND SEIN BRUDER (1900)

COOK, WILLIAM K. "Arthur Schnitzler's *Der Blinde Geronimo Und Sein Bruder:* A Critical Discussion." *Modern Austrian Literature,* 5, No. 3/4 (1972), 120–37.

DOCTOR GRAESLER (Doktor Gräsler, Badearzt, 1917)

NARDROFF, ERNEST H. VON. "*Doktor Gräsler, Badearzt:* Weather as an Aspect of Schnitzler's Symbolism." *Germanic Review,* 43 (1968), 109–19.

DYING (Sterben, 1894)

BERLIN, JEFFREY B. "The Element of 'Hope' in Arthur Schnitzler's *Sterben*." *Seminar,* 10 (1974), 38–49.

DIE FRAU DES RICHTERS

DICKERSON, HAROLD D. "Arthur Schnitzler's *Die Frau Des Richters:* A Statement of Futility." *German Quarterly,* 43 (1970), 223–36.

FRÄULEIN ELSE (1924)

ALEXANDER, THEODOR W. AND BEATRICE W. "Maupassant's *Yvette* and Schnitzler's *Fräulein Else*." *Modern Austrian Literature,* 4, No.3 (1971), 44–55.

BAREIKIS, ROBERT. "Arthur Schnitzler's 'Fraulein Else:' a Freudian Novella?" *Literature And Psychology,* 19, No.1 (1969), 19–32.

DIE HIRTENFLÖTE

REID, MAJA D. "Die Hirtenflöte." *Modern Austrian Literature,* 4, No.2 (1971), 18–27.

LEUTNANT GUSTL

ALEXANDER, THEODOR W. AND BEATRICE W. "Schnitzler's 'Leutnant Gustl' and Dujardin's 'Les Lauriers sont coupés.' " *Modern Austrian Literature,* 2, No.2 (1969), 7–15.

DIE TOTEN SCHWEIGEN

COOK, WILLIAM K. "Isolation, Flight, and Resolution in Arthur Schnitzler's *Die Toten Schweigen*." *Germanic Review,* 50 (1975), 213–26.

DER WEG INS FREIE (1908)

REICHERT, HERBERT W. "Nietzsche's *Geniemoral* and Schnitzler's Ethics," in his *Friedrich Nietzsche's Impact On Modern German Literature,* pp. 14–19.

SWALES, MARTIN. "Nürnberger's Novel: A Study of Arthur Schnitzler's 'Der Weg ins Freie.' " *Modern Language Review,* 70 (1975), 567–75.

SCHREINER, OLIVE (South African, 1855–1920)
GENERAL

BEETON, RIDLEY. "In Search of Olive Schreiner in Texas." *Texas Quarterly,* 17, No.3 (1974), 105–54.

JACOBSON, DAN. "Olive Schreiner: A South African Writer." *London Magazine,* NS 10, 11 (1970–71), 5–21.

LAREDO, URSULA. "Olive Schreiner." *Journal Of Commonwealth Literature,* No.8 (1969), p. 107–24.

RIVE, RICHARD M. "Olive Schreiner: A Critical Study and a Checklist." *Studies In The Novel,* 4 (1972), 231–51.

THE STORY OF AN AFRICAN FARM (1883)

JACOBSON, DAN. "Olive Schreiner: A South African Writer." *London Magazine,* NS 10, No.11 (1970–71), 5–21.

LAREDO, URSULA. "Olive Schreiner." *Journal Of Commonwealth Literature,* No. 8 (1969), pp. 120–24.

VAN ZYL, JOHN. "The Liberal Dilemma: Uncle Otto in '*The Story Of An African Farm*.' " *Association For African Literature In English Bulletin,* No.3 (1965), pp. 48–53.

WALSH, WILLIAM. *A Manifold Voice,* pp. 36–48.

WILSON, ELAINE. "Pervasive Symbolism in 'The Story of an African Farm.' " *English Studies In Africa,* 14 (1971), 179–86.

SCHUHL, JEAN-JACQUES
ROSE POUSSIÈRE (1972)

Reviews
ZANTS, EMILY. *French Review,* 47 (1973), 238–39.

SCHULZ, MAX WALTER
WIR SIND NICHT STAUB IM WIND

ZIPES, JACK D. "Growing Pains in the Contemporary German Novel—East and West." *Mosaic,* 5, No.3 (1971/2), 11–12.

SCHWARZ–BART, ANDRÉ (French, 1928–)
GENERAL

SALOMON, MICHEL. "Jewishness and Negritude: An Interview with André Schwarz-Bart." *Midstream Magazine,* 13, No.3 (1967), 3–12.

THE LAST OF THE JUST (Le Dernier des justes, 1959)

LANGER, LAWRENCE L. *The Holocaust And The Literary Imagination,* pp. 252–65.

A WOMAN NAMED SOLITUDE (La Mulâtresse Solitude, 1972)

Reviews
ALTER, ROBERT. "History's Victims." *Commentary,* 55, No.5 (1973), 94–96.

HINDUS, MILTON. "Across Different Cultures." *Midstream Magazine,* 19, No.3 (1973), 75–79.

SPENCER, JACK. "Still Life in Guadeloupe." *Saturday Review,* February 1973, p. 66.

WEEKS, EDWARD. *Atlantic Monthly,* 231, No.3 (1973), 105.

WEINBERG, HENRY H. *French Review,* 46 (1973), 1071–72.

SCHWARZ–BART, SIMONE (West Indian, 1938–)

THE BRIDGE OF BEYOND (Pluie et vent sur télumée miracle, 1972)

Reviews
TALBOT, EMILE J. *French Review,* 47 (1974), 669–70.

SCHWARZMANN, Lev Isaakovich see SHESTOV, Lev

SCUDERY, MADELEINE DE (1607–1701)

LE GRAND CYRUS (1649–53)

BROOKS, PETER. *The Novel Of Worldliness,* pp. 48–52.

SEALSFIELD, CHARLES (Austrian, 1793–1864) pseudonym of Karl Anton Postl
GENERAL

FRIESEN, GERHARD. "Charles Sealsfield and the German Panoramic Novel of the 19th Century." *MLN,* 84 (1969), 734–75.

DAS CAJÜTENBUCH ODER NATIONALE CHARAKTERISTIKEN (1842)

ROBBINS, WALTER L. "A Hoffmann Influence on Sealsfield's *Die Prairie Am Jacinto.*" *Germanic Notes,* 6, No.1 (1975), 5.

SEARS, DENNIS T. PATRICK

THE LARK IN THE CLEAR AIR

Reviews
MITCHELL, ADRIAN. "Getting the Voices Right." *Canadian Literature,* No.62 (1974), pp. 86–87.

POKORNY, AMY. "Flamboyant Entities." *Journal Of Canadian Fiction,* 3, No.4 (1975), 90–91.

SEGHERS, ANNA (German, 1900–1983)
THE SEVENTH CROSS (Das Siebte Kreuz, 1942)

JENKINSON, D. E. "Three East German Novels." *Modern Languages,* 53 (1972), 117–19.

TRANSIT VISA (Transit, 1944)

SZÉPE, HELENA. "The Problem of Identity in Anna Seghers' 'Transit.'" *Orbis Litterarum,* 27 (1972), 145–52.

ÜBERFAHRT (1971)

THOMANECK, JÜRGEN. "The Iceberg in Anna Segher's Novel *Überfahrt.*" *German Life And Letters,* 28 (1974), 36–45.

ŠEINIUS, IGNAS
REJUVENATION OF SIEGFRIED IMMERSELBE

Reviews
MATULIS, ANATOLE C. "Šeinius Novel in English Translation." *Lituanus,* 12, No.2 (1966), 79–80.

SELENIĆ, SLOBODAN
THE MEMOIRS OF PETER THE CRIPPLE (Memoari Pere Bogalja)

MATEJIĆ, MATEJA. "On the Contemporary Yugoslav Novel." *Canadian Slavic Studies,* 5 (1971), 371–77.

SELIMOVIĆ, MEŠA (Yugoslav, 1910–)
THE DERVISH AND DEATH (Derviš i smrt, 1966)

BUTLER, THOMAS J. "Literary Style and Poetic Function in Meša Selimović's *The Dervish And Death.*" *Slavonic And East European Review,* 52 (1974), 533–47.

SELORMEY, FRANCIS (Ghanian, 1927–)
THE NARROW PATH: AN AFRICAN CHILDHOOD (1966)

Reviews
CASTAGNO, MARGARET. *Literature East And West,* 11 (1967), 335.

SELVON, SAMUEL (West Indian, 1923–1963)
A BRIGHTER SUN (1952)

DAVIS, BARRIE. "The Personal Sense of a Society—Minority View: Aspects of the 'East Indian' Novel in the West Indies." *Studies In The Novel,* 4 (1972), 288–90.

THE LONELY LONDONERS (1956)

MOORE, GERALD. *The Chosen Tongue,* pp. 101–5.

THE PLAINS OF CARONI (1970)

Reviews
SCOTT, ANDREW P. *World Literature Written In English,* No.19 (1971), pp. 92–93.

SEMBÈNE OUSMANE (Senegalese, 1923–)
GENERAL

LEE, SONIA. "The Awakening of the Self in the Heroines of Sembène Ousmane." *Critique,* 17, No.2 (1975), 17–25.

GOD'S BITS OF WOOD (Les bouts de bois de dieu, 1960)

BRENCH, A. C. *The Novelist's Inheritance In French Africa,* pp. 109–19.

CARTEY, WILFRED. *Whispers From A Continent,* pp. 177–82.

THE MONEY ORDER (Le Mandat, 1965)

OHAEGBU, A. U. "Literature For The People: Two Novels by Sembène Ousmane." *Présence Africaine,* No.91 (1974), pp. 117–23.

XALA

OHAEGBU, A. U. "Literature For the People: Two Novels by Sembène Ousmane." *Présence Africaine,* No.91 (1974), 123-31.

SEMIN, LEONID
ODIN NA ODIN

Reviews
HEIMAN, LEO. "Prison Camp Literature." *East Europe,* 14, No.7 (1965), 54-55.

SEMPRUN, JORGE (Spanish, ca. 1920-)
THE LONG VOYAGE (1964)

LANGER, LAWRENCE L. *The Holocaust And The Literary Imagination,* pp. 285-96.

SÉNANCOUR, ÉTIENNE PIVERT DE (French, 1770-1846)
OBERMANN (1804)

GRIMSLEY, RONALD. "Reflection and Irony in *Obermann.*" *French Studies,* 25 (1971), 411-26.

SENDER, RAMÓN J. (Spanish, 1902-1982)
GENERAL

KING, CHARLES L. "Ramón J. Sender: Don Quixote Rides Again." *American Book Collector,* 20, No.6 (1970), 17-22.

LA ANTESALA (1971)

Reviews
PEDEN, MARGARET. *Hispania,* 57 (1974), 602-3.

EL BANDIDO ADOLESCENTE (1965)

Reviews
KING, CHARLES L. *Hispania,* 50 (1967), 389.

CRÓNICA DEL ALBA (1966)

Reviews
KING, CHARLES L. *Hispania,* 52 (1969), 161.
OLSTAD, CHARLES. *Hispania,* 48 (1965), 179-80.

DARK WEDDING (Epitalamio del prieto Trinidad, 1942)

JONES, MARGARET E. W. " 'A Positive Geometry': Structural Patterns and Symbols in Sender's *Epitalamio Del Prieto Trinidad.*" *Symposium,* 29 (1975), 117-30.

EL FUGITIVO (1972)

O'BRIEN, MARY EIDE. "Fantasy in 'El fugitivo.' " *Journal Of Spanish Studies,* 2 (1974), 95-108.

THE KING AND THE QUEEN (El rey y la reina, 1949)

KING, CHARLES L. "Surrealism in Two Novels by Sender." *Hispania,* 51 (1968), 247-50.

Reviews
PEDEN, MARGARET. *Hispania,* 55 (1972), 386.

A MAN'S PLACE (El lugar de un hombre, 1939)

KING, CHARLES L. "The Role of Sabino in Sender's 'El lugar de un hombre.' " *Hispania,* 50 (1967), 95-98.

MOSÉN MILLÁN see REQUIEM FOR A SPANISH PEASANT

REQUIEM FOR A SPANISH PEASANT (Réquiem por un campesino español, 1953)

BUSETTE, CEDRIC. "Religious Symbolism in Sender's *Mosén Millán.*" *Romance Notes,* 11 (1970), 482-86.

HENN, DAVID. "The Priest in Sender's *Réquiem Por Un Campesino Español.*" *International Fiction Review,* 1 (1974), 106-11.

THE SPHERE (La esfera, 1947)

KING, CHARLES L. "Surrealism in Two Novels by Sender." *Hispania,* 51 (1968), 244-47.
PALLEY, JULIAN. "*The Sphere* Revisited." *Symposium,* 25 (1971), 171-79.

TÚPAC AMARU (1973)

Reviews
ESPADAS, ELIZABETH. *Journal Of Spanish Studies,* 2 (1974), 204-5.

SERAO, MATILDE (Italian, 1856-1927)
GENERAL

GISOLFI, ANTHONY M. "The Dramatic Element in Matilde Serao's Little Masterpieces." *Italica,* 44 (1967), 433-45.
HOWARD, JUDITH JEFFREY. "The Feminine Vision of Matilde Serao." *Italian Quarterly,* 18, No.71 (1975), 55-77.
PACIFICI, SERGIO. *The Modern Italian Novel: From Manzoni To Svevo,* pp. 129-37.

SERCAMBI, GIOVANNI (Italian, 1348-1424)
NOVELLE

VIVARELLI, ANN WEST. "Giovanni Sercambi's *Novelle* and the Legacy of Boccaccio." *MLN,* 90 (1975), 109-27.

SERGE, VICTOR (Russian, 1890-1947)
GENERAL

GREEMAN, RICHARD. "Victor Serge and the Tradition of Revolutionary Literature." *Triquarterly,* No.8 (1967), pp. 39-60.

BIRTH OF OUR POWER

GREEMAN, RICHARD. " 'The Laws are Burning'—Literary and Revolutionary Realism in Victor Serge." *Yale French Studies,* No.39 (1967), pp. 146-59.

———. "Victor Serge and the Tradition of Revolutionary Literature." *Triquarterly,* No.8 (1967), pp. 53-56.

SERGUINE, JACQUES
LES ABOIS (1971)

Reviews
CAGNON, MAURICE. *French Review,* 47 (1974), 1022-23.

SERNA, Ramón Gómez de la see GÓMEZ DE LA SERNA, Ramón

SERVICE, ROBERT (Canadian, 1874-1958)
GENERAL

ATHERTON, STANLEY S. "The Klondike Muse." *Canadian Literature,* No.47 (1971), pp. 67-72.

SEUREN, GUNTER
LEBECK

Reviews
ZIOLKOWSKI, THEODORE. "Paradigms of the Recent German Novel." *Modern Language Journal,* 52 (1968), 30.

SHAHAR, DAVID (Israeli, 1926-)
GENERAL

BE'ER, HAYIM. "Shattered Vessels: An Interview with David Shahar." *Ariel: A Quarterly Review Of The Arts And Sciences In Israel,* No.30 (1972), pp. 15–18.

SHALOM, SHIN (Israeli, 1904–)
STORM OVER GALILEE (1967)

Reviews
GOLDMAN, MARK. *Literature East And West,* 14 (1970), 131–34.

SHARQAWI, ABD AL RAHMAN AL- (Egyptian, 1920–)
AL-ARD

KILPATRICK, HILARY. *The Modern Egyptian Novel,* pp. 127–33, 239–42.

EMPTY HEARTS (Qūlub Khāliya)

KILPATRICK, HILARY. *The Modern Egyptian Novel,* pp. 133–36, 242–44.

AL-FALLAH

KILPATRICK, HILARY. *The Modern Egyptian Novel,* pp. 137–39, 244–45.

SHE, LAO
CAT COUNTRY

Reviews
CHIN-TANG WANG, PETER. *Literature East And West,* 15 (1971), 155–57.

SHELDON, MICHAEL (Canadian, 1918–)
THE DEATH OF A LEADER (1971)

Reviews
SUTHERLAND, RONALD. "Suspenseful Separatism." *Canadian Literature,* No.58 (1973), pp. 111–12.

THE UNMELTING POT (1965)

Reviews
ROBERTSON, GEORGE. "Middle of the Way." *Canadian Literature,* No.31 (1967), pp. 70–71.

SHEN TS'UNG-WEN (Chinese, 1903–)
THE LONG RIVER

HSIA, C. T. *A History Of Modern Chinese Fiction,* pp. 359–66.

SHEN YIN-PING see MAO TUN

SHERMAN, D. R. (Indian, 1934–)
OLD MALI AND THE BOY (1964)

Reviews
WENDT, ALLAN. *Literature East And West,* 9 (1965), 154–56.

SHESTOV, LEV (Russian, 1866–1938) pseudonym of Lev Isaakovich Schwarzmann
ATHENS AND JERUSALEM

Reviews
SAVAN, DAVID. "A Russian Existentialist." *University Of Toronto Quarterly,* 37 (1967), 102–5.

SHEVTSOV, IVAN
PLANT-LOUSE

SINYAVSKY, ANDREI. "Pamphlet or Lampoon?" in his *For Freedom Of Imagination,* pp. 78–91.

SHIH NAI-AN (Chinese, fl. before 1400)
THE WATER MARGIN (Shui-hu Chuan)

HSIA, C. T. *The Classic Chinese Novel,* pp. 75–114.

SHIH T'O (Chinese, ca. 1908–) pseudonym of Wang Ch'ang-chien
GENERAL

HSIA, C. T. *A History Of Modern Chinese Fiction,* pp. 461–68.

MARRIAGE (Chieh-hun, 1947)

HSIA, C. T. *A History Of Modern Chinese Fiction,* pp. 464–68.

SHIMAKI KENSAKU (Japanese, 1903–45)
GENERAL

KEENE, DONALD. "Japanese Literature and Politics in the 1930s." *Journal Of Japanese Studies,* 2 (1976), 228–36.

SHINTARO, ISHIHARA
SEASON OF VIOLENCE

Reviews
TEELE, ROY E. *Literature East And West,* 11 (1967), 337–38.

SHOLOKHOV, MIKHAIL (Russian, 1905–)
GENERAL

MUKERJEE, GUNDADA. "Mikhail Sholokov." *Indian Literature,* 9, No.1 (1966), 71–77.

STEWART, D. H. *Mikhail Sholokov: A Critical Introduction,* pp. 1–42, 163–202.

WERTH, ALEXANDER. "Sholokhov and His Enemies." *London Magazine,* 7, No.1 (1967), 91–96.

AND QUIET FLOWS THE DON (Tikhiy Don, 1928–40)

ERMOLAEV, HERMAN. "Riddles of *The Quiet Don:* A Review Article." *Slavic And East European Journal,* 18 (1974), 299–310.

————. "The Role of Nature in *The Quiet Don.*" *California Slavic Studies,* 6 (1971), 97–111.

HALLETT, DON. "Soviet Criticism of *Tikhiy Don* 1928–1940." *Slavonic And East European Review,* 46 (1968), 60–74.

MATHEWSON, RUFUS. "Four Novels," in *Major Soviet Writers,* ed. Edward J. Brown, pp. 333–36.

SIMMONS, ERNEST J. "Sholokhov—Literary Artist and Socialist Realist," in his *Introduction To Russian Realism,* pp. 233–47.

STEWART, D. H. *Mikhail Sholokov: A Critical Introduction,* pp. 43–131, 203–218.

DESTINY OF A MAN

WADDINGTON, PATRICK. " 'Attack or defend. . . .'—Sholokhov Examined." *Survey: A Journal Of Soviet And East European Studies,* No.69 (1968), 99–106.

FATE OF A MAN see DESTINY OF A MAN

PODNJATAJA CELINA

MOREL, JEAN PIERRE. "A 'Revolutionary' Poetics?" *Yale French Studies,* No.39 (1967), pp. 174–77.

SCHAARSCHMIDT, GUNTER. "Interior Monologue in Šoloxov's *Podnjataja Celina.*" *Slavic And East European Journal,* 11 (1967), 257–65.

THE QUIET DON See AND QUIET FLOWS THE DON

THE SILENT DON see AND QUIET FLOWS THE DON

VIRGIN SOIL UPTURNED

SIMMONS, ERNEST J. "Sholokhov—Literary Artist and Socialist Realist," in his *Introduction To Russian Realism*, pp. 248-53.

STEWART, D. H. *Mikhail Sholokhov: A Critical Introduction*, pp. 132-62.

SHOURI

HALADI MEENU (1966)

Reviews

AMUR, G. S. *Indian Writing Today*, 2, No.1 (1968), 25-26.

SHU CH'ING-CH'UN see LAO SHE

SHUSAKU, ENDO

CHINMOKU

MATHY, FRANCIS. "Endo Shusaku: White Man, Yellow Man." *Comparative Literature*, 19 (1967), 70-71.

KIIROI HITO

MATHY, FRANCIS. "Endo Shusaku: White Man, Yellow Man." *Comparative Literature*, 19 (1967), 65-66.

NANJI MO MATA

MATHY, FRANCIS. "Endo Shusaku: White Man, Yellow Man." *Comparative Literature*, 19 (1967), 66-69.

OGON NO KUNI

MATHY, FRANCIS. "Endo Shusaku: White Man, Yellow Man." *Comparative Literature*, 19 (1967), 71-72.

SIENKIEWICZ, HENRYK (Polish, 1846-1916)

GENERAL

WELSH, D. J. "Sienkiewicz as Narrator." *Slavonic And East European Review*, 43 (1965), 371-83.

CHILDREN OF THE SOIL (Rodzina Połanieckich, 1894)

GIERGIELEWICZ, MIECZYSLAW. *Henryk Sienkiewicz*, pp. 115-21.

WELSH, DAVID. "Two Contemporary Novels of Henryk Sienkiewicz: A Reappraisal." *Slavic And East European Journal*, 16 (1972), 309-11.

THE DELUGE (Potop, 1886)

GIERGIELEWICZ, MIECZYSLAW. *Henryk Sienkiewicz*, pp. 75-109.

IN DESERT AND WILDERNESS (W pustyni i puszczy, 1912)

GIERGIELEWICZ, MIECZYSLAW. *Henryk Sienkiewicz*, pp. 158-62.

THE KNIGHTS OF THE CROSS (Krzyzacy, 1897-1900)

GIERGIELEWICZ, MIECZYSLAW. *Henryk Sienkiewicz*, pp. 147-56.

PAN MICHAEL (Pan Wolodyjowski 1887-1888)

GIERGIELEWICZ, MIECZYSLAW. *Henryk Sienkiewicz*, pp. 75-109.

QUO VADIS? A TALE OF THE TIME OF NERO (1896)

GIERGIELEWICZ, MIECZYSLAW. *Henryk Sienkiewicz*, pp. 127-46.

THE WHIRLPOOLS (Wiry, 1910)

GIERGIELEWICZ, MIECZYSLAW. *Henryk Sienkiewicz*, pp. 122-26.

WITH FIRE AND SWORD (Ogniem i Mieczem)

GIERGIELEWICZ, MIECZYSLAW. *Henryk Sienkiewicz*, pp. 75-109.

WITHOUT DOGMA (Bez dogmatu, 1889)

GIERGIELEWICZ, MIECZYSLAW. *Henryk Sienkiewicz*, pp. 109-15.

WELSH, DAVID. "Two Contemporary Novels of Henryk Sienkiewicz: A Reappraisal." *Slavic And East European Journal*, 16 (1972), 307-9.

SILLANPÄÄ, FRANZ EMIL (Finnish, 1888-1964)

GENERAL

LAURILA, AARNE. "F. E. Sillanpää: An Appreciation." *American Scandinavian Review*, 53 (1965), 284-87.

PEOPLE IN THE SUMMER NIGHT (Ihmiset suviyössä, 1934)

Reviews

SPECTOR, ROBERT D. *American Scandinavian Review*, 55 (1967), 197-98.

WUORINEN, JOHN H. "Evening for Insights." *Saturday Review*, 11 June 1966, p. 74.

SILONE, IGNAZIO (Italian, 1900-1978) pseudonym of Secondo Tranquilli

GENERAL

CASERTA, ERNESTO G. "The Meaning of Christianity in the Novels of Silone." *Italian Quarterly*, 16, No.62/63 (1972), 19-39.

NYCE, BENJAMIN M. "Ignazio Silone's Political Trilogy." *New Orleans Review*, 1 (1969), 152-55.

ORIGO, IRIS. "Ignazio Silone: A Study in Integrity." *Atlantic Monthly*, 219, No.3 (1967), 86-93.

———. "Ignazio Silone: A Study in Integrity." *Cornhill*, 175, No. 1050 (1966/67), 385-401.

RESZLER, ANDRE. "Fiction and Ideology: The Case of Ignazio Silone." *Clio*, 3 (1974), 247-56.

WHYTE, JEAN. "The Evolution of Silone's Central Theme." *Italian Studies*, 25 (1970), 49-62.

THE ADVENTURE OF A POOR CHRISTIAN (L'Avventura d'un Povero Cristiano, 1968)

GAFFNEY, JAMES. "Refusing the Machinery of Power: Silone and the Pope." *Commonweal*, 89 (1968), 112-15.

Reviews

CAPOUYA, EMILE. *Saturday Review*, 24 April 1971, pp. 31, 41.

FITZLYON, KYRIL. "The Same Silone." *London Magazine*, NS 9, No.3 (1969), 94-98.

BREAD AND WINE (Vino e pane, 1937)

CAMUS, ALBERT. *Lyrical And Critical Essays*, pp. 207-9.

HOWE, IRVING. "Ignazio Silone: Politics and the Novel," in *From Verismo To Experimentalism*, ed. Sergio Pacifici, pp. 126-30.

RADCLIFF-UMSTEAD, DOUGLAS. "Animal Symbolism in Silone's *Vino E Pane*." *Italica*, 49 (1972), 18-29.

SCHNEIDER, FRANZ. "Scriptural Symbolism in Silone's *Bread And Wine*." *Italica*, 44 (1967), 387-99.

FONTANMARA (1930)

HOWE, IRVING. "Ignazio Silone: Poltics and the Novel," in *From Verismo To Experimentalism*, ed. Sergio Pacifici, pp. 124-26.

A HANDFUL OF BLACKBERRIES (Una manciata di more, 1952)

HOWE, IRVING. "Ignazio Silone: Politics and the Novel," in *From Verismo To Experimentalism*, ed. Sergio Pacifici, pp. 131-33.

THE STORY OF A HUMBLE CHRISTIAN see THE ADVENTURE OF A POOR CHRISTIAN

SIM, GEORGE see SIMENON, Georges Joseph Christian

SIMENON, GEORGES JOSEPH CHRISTIAN (Belgian, 1903–) pseudonym of George Sim

GENERAL

BODE, ELROY. "The World on Its Own Terms: A Brief for Steinbeck, Miller, and Simenon." *Southwest Review,* 53 (1968), 409–12.

DRYSDALE, DENNIS H. "Simenon and Social Justice." *Nottingham French Studies,* 13 (1974), 85–97.

GALLIGAN, EDWARD L. "Simenon's Mosaic of Small Novels." *South Atlantic Quarterly,* 66 (1967), 534–43.

JACOBS, JAY. "Simenon's Mosaic." *Reporter,* 32, No.1 (1965), 38–40.

ABOARD THE AQUITAINE (45° à l'ombre, 1936)

RAYMOND, JOHN. *Simenon In Court,* pp. 94–100.

L'AÎNÉ DES FERCHAUX

RAYMOND, JOHN. *Simenon In Court,* pp. 142–45.

LES ANNEAUX DE BICÊTRE

RAYMOND, JOHN. *Simenon In Court,* pp. 24–28.

AU BOUT DU ROULEAU

RAYMOND, JOHN. *Simenon In Court,* pp. 100–106.

BIG BOB (Le grand bob, 1954)

RAYMOND, JOHN. *Simenon In Court,* pp. 148–52.

LE BLANC À LUNETTES

RAYMOND, JOHN. *Simenon In Court,* pp. 124–27.

THE CAT (Le chat, 1967)

Reviews
MOORE, HARRY T. "Marital Blight." *Saturday Review,* 9 December 1967, pp. 31, 55.

CHEZ KRULL (1939)

RAYMOND, JOHN. *Simenon In Court,* pp. 87–91.

THE CONFESSIONAL

Reviews
MOORE, HARRY T. "Bleating at the Milk-Shake Bar." *Saturday Review,* 4 May 1968, p. 48.

COUR D'ASSISES

RAYMOND, JOHN. *Simenon In Court,* pp. 108–12.

LA FUITE DE MONSIEUR MONDE

RAYMOND, JOHN. *Simenon In Court,* pp. 128–32.

LES INCONNUS DANS LA MAISON

RAYMOND, JOHN. *Simenon In Court,* pp. 114–19.

LETTRE À MON JUGE

RAYMOND, JOHN. *Simenon In Court,* pp. 133–36.

THE LITTLE MAN FROM ARCHANGEL (Le petit homme d'Arkhangelsk, 1956)

Reviews
MACMANUS, PATRICIA. "The Irony of Murder." *Saturday Review,* 5 November 1966, p. 42.

THE LITTLE SAINT (Le petit saint, 1965)

RAYMOND, JOHN. *Simenon In Court,* pp. 168–71.

Reviews
MOORE, HARRY T. "One Who Was Saved." *Saturday Review,* 30 October 1965, p. 48.

LA NEIGE ETAIT SALE

RAYMOND, JOHN. *Simenon In Court,* pp. 136–42.

PEDIGREE (1948)

RAYMOND, JOHN. *Simenon In Court,* pp. 34–44.

THE PREMIER (Le président, 1958)

RAYMOND, JOHN. *Simenon In Court,* pp. 19–24.

Reviews
SAMSTAG, NICHOLAS. "A Great Man Dies, a Dull Man Tries." *Saturday Review,* 4 June 1966, p. 52.

SUNDAY (Dimanche, 1958)

Reviews
MACMANUS, PATRICIA. "The Irony of Murder." *Saturday Review,* 5 November 1966, p. 42.

TEDDY BEAR (L'ours en peluche, 1960)

Reviews
CATINELLA, JOSEPH. *Saturday Review,* 26 February 1972, p. 78.

TOURISTE DE BANANES

RAYMOND, JOHN. *Simenon In Court,* pp. 61–66.

THE TRAIN (Le train, 1961)

Reviews
SAMSTAG, NICHOLAS. "A Great Man Dies, A Dull Man Tries." *Saturday Review,* 4 June 1966, p. 52.

LE VOYAGEUR DE LA TOUSSAINT

RAYMOND, JOHN. *Simenon In Court,* pp. 145–48.

SIMON, CLAUDE (French, 1913–)

GENERAL

FROHOCK, W. M. *Style And Temper,* pp. 122–28.

HEATH, STEPHEN. *The Nouveau Roman,* pp. 153–78.

STURROCK, JOHN. *The French New Novel,* pp. 43–103.

SYKES, STUART W. "*Mise En Abyme* in the Novels of Claude Simon." *Forum For Modern Language Studies,* 9 (1973), 333–45.

THE BATTLE OF PHARSALUS (La bataille de Pharsale, 1969)

Reviews
BERGIN, THOMAS G. *Saturday Review,* 17 April 1971, p. 36.

THE FLANDERS ROAD (La Route des Flandres, 1960)

BROSMAN, CATHARINE SAVAGE. "Man's Animal Condition in Claude Simon's *La Route Des Flandres.*" *Symposium,* 29 (1975), 57–68.

HEATH, STEPHEN. *The Nouveau Roman,* pp. 161–78.

LEVITT, MORTON P. "*Disillusionment And Epiphany:* The Novels of Claude Simon." *Critique,* 12, No.1 (1970), 54–59.

MERCIER, VIVIAN. "Claude Simon: Order and Disorder." *Shenandoah,* 17, No.4 (1966), 79–92.

———. *The New Novel From Queneau To Pinget,* pp. 268–79.

WEINSTEIN, ARNOLD. *Vision And Response In Modern Fiction,* pp. 232–44.

THE GRASS (L'Herbe, 1959)

LEVITT, MORTON P. "*Disillusionment And Epiphany:* The Novels of Claude Simon." *Critique,* 12, No.1 (1970), 50–54.

MERCIER, VIVIAN. *The New Novel From Queneau To Pinget,* pp. 294-300.

SIMON, JOHN K. "Perception and Metaphor in the 'New Novel': Notes on Robbe-Grillet, Claude Simon and Butor." *Triquarterly,* No.4 (1965), pp. 164-73.

GULLIVER (1952)

MERCIER, VIVIAN. *The New Novel From Queneau To Pinget,* pp. 280-85.

HISTOIRE (1967)

LEVITT, MORTON P. "*Disillusionment And Epiphany:* The Novels of Claude Simon." *Critique,* 12, No.1 (1970), 63-70.

MERCIER, VIVIAN. *The New Novel From Queneau To Pinget,* pp. 305-14.

Reviews

BISHOP, THOMAS. "Fusion of Then and Now." *Saturday Review,* 30 March 1968, p. 28.

LEVITT, MORTON P. "The Burden of History." *Kenyon Review,* 31 (1969), 128-34.

THE PALACE (Le Palace, 1962)

LEVITT, MORTON P. "*Disillusionment And Epiphany:* The Novels of Claude Simon." *Critique,* 12, No.1 (1970), 59-63.

LOUBÉRE, J. A. E. "Claude Simon's *Le Palace:* A Paradigm of Otherness." *Symposium,* 27 (1973), 46-63.

MERCIER, VIVIAN. *The New Novel From Queneau To Pinget,* pp. 300-5.

SOLOMON, PHILIP H. "Flights of Time Lost: Bird Imagery in Claude Simon's *Le Palace,*" in *Twentieth Century French Fiction,* ed. George Stambolian, pp. 166-83.

LE SACRE DE PRINTEMPS (1954)

MERCIER, VIVIAN. *The New Novel From Queneau To Pinget,* pp. 285-88.

THE WIND (Le Vent, 1957)

DUNCAN, ALISTAIR B. "Claude Simon and William Faulkner." *Forum For Modern Language Studies,* 9 (1973), 235-52.

LEVITT, MORTON P. "*Disillusionment and Epiphany:* The Novels of Claude Simon." *Critique,* 12, No.1 (1970), 46-50.

MERCIER, VIVIAN. *The New Novel From Queneau To Pinget,* pp. 288-94.

SYKES, STUART W. "*Mise En Abyme* in the Novels of Claude Simon." *Forum For Modern Language Studies,* 9 (1973), 333-36.

SIMONOV, KONSTANTIN (Russian, 1915-1979)

COMRADES IN ARMS (Tovarish chi po oruzhiyu, 1952)

LAZAREV, L. "The War Novels of Konstantin Simonov." *Soviet Studies In Literature,* 1, No.3 (1965), 45-48.

THE LIVING AND THE DEAD (Zivye i Mertvye, 1960)

LAZAREV, L. "The War Novels of Konstantin Simonov." *Soviet Studies In Literature,* 1, No.3 (1965), 48-62.

NO ONE IS BORN A SOLDIER

LAZAREV, L. "The War Novels of Konstantin Simonov." *Soviet Studies In Literature,* 1, No.3 (1965), 62-72.

SIMPSON, LEO (Canadian, 1934-)

GENERAL

McMULLEN, LORRAINE. "A Conversation With Leo Simpson." *Journal Of Canadian Fiction,* 4, No.1 (1975), 111-20.

ARKWRIGHT (1971)

Reviews

BROWN, RUSSELL M. "Expatriate Variations." *Canadian Literature,* No.54 (1972), pp. 94-97.

RICOU, LAURENCE. "A Place of Refuge." *Journal Of Canadian Fiction,* 1, No.2 (1972), 90-91.

THE PEACOCK PAPERS (1973)

Reviews

PEIRCE, JANET BAKER. *Dalhousie Review,* 54 (1974), 192-93.

RICOU, LAURENCE. "A Precious Madness." *Journal Of Canadian Fiction,* 3, No.3 (1974), 100-1.

SINGER, CHRISTIANE

NOTES OF A HYPOCRITE

Reviews

LESAGE, LAURENT. "Memories and Fantasies." *Saturday Review,* 14 January 1967, p. 87.

SINGER, ISAAC BASHEVIS (Yiddish, 1904-)

GENERAL

ANDERSEN, DAVID M. "Isaac Bashevis Singer: Conversations in California." *Modern Fiction Studies,* 16 (1970/1), 423-39.

BEZANKER, ABRAHAM. "I. B. Singer's Crises of Identity." *Critique,* 14, No.2 (1972), 70-88.

BUCHEN, IRVING H. "Isaac Bashevis Singer and the Eternal Past." *Critique,* 8, No.3 (1966), 5-17.

GASS, WILLIAM H. "The Shut-In," in *The Achievement Of Isaac Bashevis Singer,* ed. Marcia Allentuck, pp. 1-13.

GOLDEN, MORRIS. "Dr. Fischelson's Miracle: Duality and Vision in Singer's Fiction," in *The Achievement Of Isaac Bashevis Singer,* ed. Marcia Allentuck, pp. 26-43.

HOCHMAN, BARUCH. "I.B. Singer's Vision of Good and Evil." *Midstream Magazine,* 13, No.3 (1967), 66-73.

"Interview/Isaac Bashevis Singer." *Diacritics,* 4, No.1 (1974), 30-33.

JACOBSON, DAN. "The Problem of Isaac Bashevis Singer." *Commentary,* 39, No.2 (1965), 48-52.

KATZ, ELI. "Isaac Bashevis Singer and Classical Yiddish Tradition," in *The Achievement Of Isaac Bashevis Singer,* ed. Marcia Allentuck, pp. 14-25.

MUCKE, EDITH. "Isaac B. Singer and Hassidic Philosophy." *Minnesota Review,* 7 (1967), 214-21.

NEWMAN, RICHARD A. "Isaac Bashevis Singer." *Hibbert Journal,* 65 (1966), 27-28.

NOVAK, MAXIMILLIAN E. "Moral Grotesque and Decorative Grotesque in Singer's Fiction," in *The Achievement Of Isaac Bashevis Singer,* ed. Marcia Allentuck, pp. 44-63.

PINSKER, SANFORD. "The Fictive Worlds of Isaac Bashevis Singer." *Critique,* 11, No.2 (1969), 26-39.

———. "Isaac Bashevis Singer: An Interview." *Critique,* 11, No.2 (1969), 16-25.

———. "Isaac Bashevis Singer and Joyce Carol Oates: Some Versions of Gothic." *Southern Review,* NS 9 (1973), 895-908.

PONDROM, CYRENA. "Isaac Bashevis Singer: An Interview and a Biographical Sketch." *Contemporary Literature,* 10 (1969), 1-38.

SCHULZ, MAX F. "Isaac Bashevis Singer, Radical Sophistication, and the Jewish American Novel." *Southern Humanities Review,* 3 (1969), 60-66.

SINGER, ISAAC BASHEVIS AND IRVING HOWE. "Yiddish Tradition vs. Jewish Tradition: A Dialogue." *Midstream Magazine,* 19, No.6 (1973), 33-38.

SLOMAN, JUDITH. "Existentialism in Pär Lagerkvist and Isaac Bashevis Singer." *Minnesota Review,* 5 (1965), 206–12.

ENEMIES: A LOVE STORY (1972)

Reviews

LEVIANT, CURT. "I. B. Singer in the USA." *Midstream Magazine,* 19, No.3 (1973), 74–75.

WOLFF, GEOFFREY. *Saturday Review,* 22 July 1972, pp. 54, 57.

THE ESTATE (1969)

Reviews

ALTER, ROBERT. *Saturday Review,* 1 November 1969, pp. 38–39.

RABINOWITZ, DOROTHY. "Sequels." *Commentary,* 49, No.5 (1970), 104–6.

THE FAMILY MOSKAT (1950)

BEZANKER, ABRAHAM. "I. B. Singer's Crises of Identity." *Critique,* 14, No.2 (1972), 74–77.

JACOBSON, DAN. "The Problem of Isaac Bashevis Singer." *Commentary,* 39, No.2 (1965), 51–52.

SCHULZ, MAX F. "The Family Chronicle as Paradigm of History: The Brothers Ashkenazi and The Family Moskat," in *The Achievement Of Isaac Bashevis Singer,* ed. Marcia Allentuck, pp. 81–92.

Reviews

POPKIN, HENRY. "A Waste of Dreams." *Saturday Review,* 15 May 1965, pp. 31, 53.

THE MAGICIAN OF LUBLIN

BUCHEN, IRVING H. "Isaac Bashevis Singer and the Eternal Past." *Critique,* 8, No.3 (1966), 9–17.

NOVAK, MAXIMILLIAN E. "Moral Grotesque and Decorative Grotesque in Singer's Fiction," in *The Achievement Of Isaac Bashevis Singer,* ed. Marcia Allentuck, pp. 52–55.

PINSKER, SANFORD. "The Fictive Worlds of Isaac Bashevis Singer." *Critique,* 11, No.2 (1969), 34–39.

PONDROM, CYRENA N. "Conjuring Reality: I. B. Singer's *The Magician Of Lublin,*" in *The Achievement Of Isaac Bashevis Singer,* ed. Marcia Allentuck, pp. 93–111.

THE MANOR (1967)

ELLMANN, MARY. "The Piety of Things in *The Manor,*" in *The Achievement Of Isaac Bashevis Singer,* ed. Marcia Allentuck, pp. 124–44.

NOVAK, MAXIMILLIAN E. "Moral Grotesque and Decorative Grotesque in Singer's Fiction," in *The Achievement Of Isaac Bashevis Singer,* ed. Marcia Allentuck, pp. 55–57.

Reviews

ALTER, ROBERT. "Down to Lilith's Domain." *Saturday Review,* 4 November 1967, p. 33.

RABINOWITZ, DOROTHY. "Sequels." *Commentary,* 49, No.5 (1970), 104–6.

SZANTO, GEORGE H. "A Man in a Changing World." *Catholic World,* 207 (1968), 94–96.

MAZEL AND SCHLIMAZEL

WOLF, H. R. "Singer's Children's Stories and *In My Father's Court:* Universalism in the Rankian Hero," in *The Achievement Of Isaac Bashevis Singer,* ed. Marcia Allentuck, pp. 145–58.

SATAN IN GORAY (Shoten an Goray, 1935)

BUCHEN, IRVING H. "Isaac Bashevis Singer and the Revival of Satan." *Texas Studies In Literature And Language,* 9 (1967), 129–42.

GITTLEMAN, EDWIN. "Singer's Apocalyptic Town: *Satan In Go-*

ray," in *The Achievement Of Isaac Bashevis Singer,* ed. Marcia Allentuck, pp. 64–76.

NOVAK, MAXIMILLIAN E. "Moral Grotesque and Decorative Grotesque in Singer's Fiction," in *The Achievement Of Isaac Bashevis Singer,* ed. Marcia Allentuck, pp. 58–63.

THE SLAVE (1962)

KARL, FREDERICK R. "Jacob Reborn, Zion Regained: I. B. Singer's *The Slave,*" in *The Achievement Of Isaac Bashevis Singer,* ed. Marcia Allentuck, pp. 112–23.

SINGER, ISRAEL JOSHUA (Yiddish, 1893–1944)

THE BROTHERS ASHKENAZI (Di brider Ashkenazi, 1936)

SCHULZ, MAX F. "The Family Chronicle as Paradigm of History: *The Brothers Ashkenazi* and *The Family Moskat,*" in *The Achievement Of Isaac Bashevis Singer,* ed. Marcia Allentuck, pp. 77–81.

THE FAMILY CARNOVSKY (Di mishopkhe Karnovsky, 1943)

Reviews

BAUKE, JOSEPH. "'Our Crowd' in Berlin." *Saturday Review,* 22 March 1969, p. 66.

RABINOWITZ, DOROTHY. "Old-Fashioned Virtues." *Commentary,* 49, No.2 (1970), 85–87.

STEEL AND IRON

Reviews

PINSKER, SANFORD. *Saturday Review,* 1 November 1969, pp. 39–40.

YOSHE KALB (1932)

Reviews

CAPOUYA, EMILE. "The Prodigal Son-in-Law." *Saturday Review,* 9 October 1965, pp. 55–56.

SINGH, KHUSHWANT (Indian, 1915–)

GENERAL

FISHER, MARLENE AND ROBERT MCDOWELL, eds. "Kushwant Singh on Language and Literature." *World Literature Written In English,* No.18 (1970), pp. 27–32.

"Kushwant Singh." *Mahfil,* 5, No.1/2 (1968/9), 27–42.

TRAIN TO PAKISTAN

ADKINS, JOAN F. "History as Art Form: Khushwant Singh's *Train To Pakistan.*" *Journal Of Indian Writing In English,* 2, No.2 (1974), 1–12.

BATRA, SHAKTI. "Two Partition Novels." *Indian Literature,* 18, No.3 (1975), 83–103.

RAY, R. J. "Khushwant Singh's *Mano Majra:* A Study in Structure, Symbol, and Style." *Ball State University Forum,* 6, No.1 (1965), 25–29.

SRINIVASA IYENGAR, K. R. *Indian Writing In English,* pp. 498–502.

TARINAYYA, M. "Two Novels." *Indian Literature,* 13, No.1 (1970), 113–17.

SINYAVSKY, Abraham see TERTZ, Abraham

SINYAVKSY, ANDREY (Russian, 1925–)

GENERAL

BROWN, DEMING. "The Art of Andrei Siniavsky," in *Major Soviet Writers,* ed. Edward J. Brown, pp. 367–87.

FRAYN, MICHAEL. "Writers on Trial: Thoughts on the Sinyavsky-Daniel Case." *Encounter,* 30, No.1 (1968), 80–88.

SIONIL JOSE, FRANCISCO (Philippine, 1924–)
THE PRETENDERS (1962)

CASPER, LEONARD. *New Writing From The Philippines*, pp. 96–99.

SIVSANKARA PILLAI THAKAZHI (Indian, 1914–)
GENERAL

VERGHESE, C. PAUL. "Thakazhi Sivasankara Pillai—An Assessment." *Indian Literature*, 13, No.2 (1970), 119–24.

SJÖGREN, PEDER (Swedish, 1905–)
GENERAL

VOWLES, RICHARD B. "The Art of Peder Sjögren," in *Scandinavian Studies*, ed. Carl F. Bayerschmidt and Erik J. Friis, pp. 320–30.

ŠKĖMA, ANTANAS
GENERAL

ŠILBAJORIS, RIMVYDAS. *Perfection Of Exile*, pp. 94–111.

———. "The Tragedy of Creative Consciousness, Literary Heritage of Antanas Škėma." *Lituanus*, 12, No.4 (1966), 5–23.

THE WHITE SHROUD (Balta drobule, 1958)
ŠILBAJORIS, RIMVYDAS. *Perfection Of Exile*, pp. 107–111.

ŠKIPSNA, ILZE (Latvian, 1928–)
GENERAL

KRATINS, OJARS. "Society and the Self in the Novels of Ilze Skipsna and Alberts Bels." *Books Abroad*, 47 (1973), 675–82.

SLATER, PATRICK (Canadian, 1882–1951) pseudonym of John Mitchell
THE YELLOW BRIAR (1933)

Reviews
NEW, W. H. "John Mitchell's Roses." *Canadian Literature*, No.45 (1970), pp. 100–1.

SLAUERHOFF, JAN JACOB (Dutch, 1898–1936)
HET VERBODEN RIJK (1932)

BULHOF, F. "Slauerhoff's Camões Novel *Het Verboden Rijk*." *Texas Quarterly*, 15, No.4 (1972), 39–46.

SMITH, PAULINE (South African)
GENERAL

HARESNAPE, GEOFFREY. "A Note on Pauline Smith's Presentation of Country Life." *English Studies In Africa*, 9 (1966), 83–86.

SMITH, RAY (Canadian, 1941–)
LORD NELSON TAVERN (1974)

Reviews
ESCHE, SANDRA. "Smith & Others." *Tamarack Review*, No.64 (1974), 87–88.

SCOBIE, STEPHEN. *Dalhousie Review*, 54 (1974), 372–73.

SCOTT, ANDREW. "A Ray of Fantasy." *Journal Of Canadian Fiction*, 4, No.1 (1975), 197–99.

SUTHERLAND, FRASER. "The Nellie." *Canadian Literature*, No.63 (1975), pp. 116–17.

SOCE, OUSMANE DIOP (Senegalese, 1911–)
KARIM (1935)

GLEASON, JUDITH ILLSLEY. *This Africa*, pp. 120–26.

SOLDATI, MARIO (Italian, 1906–)
THE MALACCA CANE (Le due città, 1964)

Reviews
EWART, GAVIN. "Rome-Berlin Axis." *London Magazine*, NS 12, No.4 (1972), 148–49.

THE ORANGE ENVELOPE (La busta aracione, 1966)
Reviews
FANTAZZI, CHARLES. *Saturday Review*, 31 May 1969, p. 30.

SOLER PUIG, JOSE
EL ANO DE ENERO

MENTON, SEYMOUR. *Prose Fiction Of The Cuban Revolution*, pp. 26–28.

SOLLERS, PHILIPPE (French, 1936–)
GENERAL

HEATH, STEPHEN. *The Nouveau Roman*, pp. 179–42.

DRAME (1965)
HEATH, STEPHEN. *The Nouveau Roman*, pp. 228–42.

LOIS (1972)
Reviews
CAGNON, MAURICE. *French Review*, 47 (1974), 670–71.

NOMBRES (1968)
CHAMPAGNE, ROLAND A. "Un Déclenchement: The Revolutionary Implications of Philippe Sollers' *Nombres* for a Logocentric Western Culture." *Sub-Stance*, No.7 (1973), pp. 101–11.

HEATH, STEPHEN. *The Nouveau Roman*, pp. 239–42.

THE PARK (Le parc, 1961)
Reviews
BISHOP, TOM. *Saturday Review*, 25 July 1970, p. 30.

GREET, ANNE HYDE. *French Review*, 46 (1973), 1252–1253.

SOLOGUB, FËDOR (Russian, 1863–1927) pseudonym of Fëdor Kuz'nich Teternikov
THE PETTY DEMON (Melky bes, 1907)

GIPPIUS, ZINAIDA. "Peredonov's Little Tear (What Sologub Doesn't Know)." Trans. Sharon Leiter. *Russian Literature Triquarterly*, No.4 (1972), pp. 145–49.

REEVE, F. D. *The Russian Novel*, pp. 302–24.

STRUC, ROMAN S. " 'Petty Demons' and Beauty: Gogol, Dostoevsky, Sologub," in *Essays On European Literature*, ed. Peter Uwe Hohendahl, Herbert Lindenberger, and Egon Schwarz, pp. 76–80.

Reviews
ROSS, ROCHELLE H. *New Orleans Review*, 4 (1975), 371–72.

SOLÓRZANO, CARLOS (Guatemalan, 1922–)
LOS FALSOS DEMONIOS (1966)

Reviews
CARLISLE, JOHN E. *Hispania*, 51 (1968), 376–77.

SOLZHENITSYN, ALEXANDER (Russian, 1918-)

GENERAL

ATKINSON, DOROTHY G. "Solzhenitsyn's Heroes as Russian Historical Types." *Russian Review,* 30 (1971), 1–16.

BÖLL, HEINRICH. "Heinrich Böll on Solzhenitsyn," in *Aleksandr Solzhenitsyn: Critical Essays And Documentary Materials,* ed. John B. Dunlop, Richard Haugh, and Alexis Klimoff, pp. 13–15.

————. "Solzhenitsyn and New Realism," in *Aleksandr Solzhenitsyn: Critical Essays And Documentary Materials,* ed. John B. Dunlop, Richard Haugh, and Alexis Klimoff, pp. 185–87.

BROWN, EDWARD J. "Solzhentisyn's Cast of Characters," in *Major Soviet Writers,* ed. Edward J. Brown, pp. 351–66.

BURG, DAVID AND GEORGE FEIFER. *Solzhenitsyn.*

CALLAGHAN, MORLEY. "Solzhenitsyn." *Tamarack Review,* No.55 (1970), 71–76.

CARPOVICH, VERA. "Lexical Peculiarities of Solzhenitsyn's Language," in *Aleksandr Solzhenitsyn: Critical Essays And Documentary Materials,* ed. John B. Dunlop, Richard Haugh, and Alexis Klimoff, pp. 188–94.

CHRISTESEN, NINA. "Alexander Solzhenitsyn's Dialogue with Tolstoy." *Meanjin,* 28 (1969), 351–58.

CLARDY, J. V. "Alexander Solzhenitsyn's Concept of the Artist's Relationship to Society." *Slavonic And East European Review,* 52 (1974), 1–9.

DES PRES, TERENCE. "The Heroism of Survival," in *Aleksandr Solzhenitsyn: Critical Essays And Documentary Materials,* ed. John B. Dunlop, Richard Haugh, Alexis Klimoff, pp. 45–62.

ERLICH, VICTOR. "The Writer as Witness: The Achievement of Aleksandr Solzhenitsyn," in *Aleksandr Solzhenitsyn: Critical Essays And Documentary Materials,* ed. John B. Dunlop, Richard Haugh, and Alexis Klimoff, pp. 16–27.

FANGER, DONALD. "Solzhenitsyn: Art and Foreign Matter," in *Aleksandr Solzhenitsyn: Critical Essays And Documentary Materials,* ed. John B. Dunlop, Richard Haugh, and Alexis Klimoff, pp. 156–67.

FEUER, KATHRYN B. "Solženicyn and the Legacy of Tolstoy." *California Slavic Studies,* 6 (1971), 113–28; rpt. in *Aleksandr Solzhenitsyn: Critical Essays And Documentary Materials,* ed. John B. Dunlop, Richard Haugh, and Alexis Klimoff, pp. 129–46..

GARRARD, J. G. "The 'Inner Freedom' of Alexander Solzhenitsyn." *Books Abroad,* 45 (1971), 7–18.

GASIOROWSKA, XENIA. "Solzhenitsyn's Women," in *Aleksandr Solzhenitsyn: Critical Essays And Documentary Materials,* ed. John B. Dunlop, Richard Haugh, and Alexis Klimoff, pp. 117–28.

GLASKOW, WASILI G. "Visit With Solzhenitsyn." *East Europe,* 24, No.3 (1975), 2–3.

HAUGH, RICHARD. "The Philosophical Foundations of Solzhenitsyn's Vision of Art," in *Aleksandr Solzhenitsyn: Critical Essays And Documentary Materials,* ed. John B. Dunlop, Richard Haugh, and Alexis Klimoff, pp. 168–84.

HOWE, IRVING. "Lukacs and Solzhenitsyn," in *Aleksandr Solzhenitsyn: Critical Essays And Documentary Materials,* ed. John B. Dunlop, Richard Haugh, and Alexis Klimoff, pp. 147–55.

JACOBSON, DAN. "The Example of Solzhenitsyn." *Commentary,* 47, No.5 (1969), 81–84.

LABER, JERI. "The Real Solzhenitsyn." *Commentary,* 57, No.5 (1974), 32–35.

LAMONT, ROSETTE C. "Solzhenitsyn's 'Maimed Oak.'" *Review Of National Literatures,* 3, No.1 (1972), 153–82.

————. "Solzhenitsyn's Nationalism," in *Aleksandr Solzhenitsyn: Critical Essays And Documentary Materials,* ed. John B. Dunlop, Richard Haugh, and Alexis Klimoff, pp. 94–116.

LINDSAY, JACK. "Alexander Solzhenitsyn: The Question of a Socialist Ethic." *Meanjin,* 30 (1971), 389–401.

MCLAREN, JOHN. "The Faces of Tyranny: Alexander Solzhenitsyn's Moral Vision." *Overland,* No. 60 (1975), pp. 20–27.

————. "Tribute to Alexander Solzhenitsyn." *Overland,* No.46 (1970/1), p. 34.

MARK, ELISABETH. "Solzhenitsyn in the Context of Soviet Literature." *Mosaic,* 5, No.4 (1972), 135–48.

MAYNE, MELBA. "A Look at Solzhenitsyn." *English Journal,* 60 (1971), 205–7.

MILOSZ, CZESLAW. "Questions," in *Aleksandr Solzhenitsyn: Critical Essays And Documentary Materials,* ed. John B. Dunlop, Richard Haugh, and Alexis Klimoff, pp. 447–55.

MOODY, CHRISTOPHER. "Biography," in his *Solzhenitsyn,* rev. ed., pp. 1–27.

————. "Language and Style," in his *Solzhenitsyn,* rev. ed., pp. 50–68.

MUCHNIC, HELEN. "Aleksandr Solzhenitsyn," in her *Russian Writers,* pp. 400–50.

NICHOLSON, MICHAEL. "Solzhenitsyn and *Samizdat,*" in *Aleksandr Solzhenitsyn: Critical Essays And Documentary Materials,* ed. John B. Dunlop, Richard Haugh, and Alexis Klimoff, pp. 63–93.

PORTER, R. "Literature, Politics and the Solzhenitsyn Affair." *Modern Languages,* 53 (1972), 177–83.

ROSS, ROCHELLE. "Alexander Solzhenitsyn: Freedom of Conscience." *New Orleans Review,* 3 (1972), 58–61.

ROTHBERG, ABRAHAM. "The Writer's Life," in his *Alexander Solzhenitsyn: The Major Novels,* pp. 1–18.

SAPIETS, JANIS. "The Urge to Seek the Truth: Alexander Solzhenitsyn." *The Month,* 2d Ser., 7 (1974), 708–10.

SCHMEMANN, ALEXANDER. "On Solzhenitsyn," in *Aleksandr Solzhenitsyn: Critical Essays And Documentary Materials,* ed. John B. Dunlop, Richard Haugh, and Alexis Klimoff, pp. 28–44.

SCHWARTZ, HARRY. "Solzhenitsyn Without Stereotype." *Saturday Review,* 20 April 1974, p. 24.

SOLOV'EV, I. "The Path of Treason." *Soviet Studies In Literature,* 10, No.3 (1974), 4–9.

WILLIAMS, RAYMOND. "On Solzhenitsyn." *Triquarterly,* No.23/4 (1972), pp. 318–31.

ZAMOYSKA, HÉLÈNE. "Solzhenitsyn and the Grand Tradition," in *Aleksandr Solzhenitsyn: Critical Essays And Documentary Materials,* ed. John B. Dunlop, Richard Haugh, and Alexis Klimoff, pp. 201–18.

AUGUST 1914 (August Četyrnadcatuyo, 1971)

ATKINSON, DOROTHY. "*August 1914:* Historical Novel or Novel History," in *Aleksandr Solzhenitsyn: Critical Essays And Documentary Materials,* ed. John B. Dunlop, Richard Haugh, and Alexis Klimoff, pp. 408–29.

———— AND NICHOLAS S. PASHIN. "'August 1914': Art and History." *Russian Review,* 31 (1972), 1–10.

CHRISTESEN, NINA. "August 1914. Alexander Solzhenitsyn." *AUMLA,* No. 36 (1971), pp. 153–56.

DJILAS, MILOVAN. "Indomitable Faith," in *Aleksandr Solzhenitsyn: Critical Essays And Documentary Materials,* ed. John B. Dunlop, Richard Haugh, and Alexis Klimoff, pp. 328–31.

DOWLER, WAYNE. "Echoes of *Pochvennichestvo* in Solzhenitsyn's *August 1914.*" *Slavic Review,* 34 (1975), 109–22.

EHRE, MILTON. "On *August 1914,*" in *Aleksandr Solzhenitsyn: Critical Essays And Documentary Materials,* ed. John B. Dunlop, Richard Haugh, and Alexis Klimoff, pp. 365–71.

ERLICH, VICTOR. "Solzhenitsyn's Quest," in *Aleksandr Solzhenitsyn: Critical Essays And Documentary Materials,* ed. John B. Dunlop, Richard Haugh, and Alexis Klimoff, pp. 351–55.

FEUER, KATHRYN B. "*August 1914:* Solzhenitsyn and Tolstoy," in *Aleksandr Solzhenitsyn: Critical Essays And Documentary Materials,* ed. John B. Dunlop, Richard Haugh, and Alexis Klimoff, pp. 372–81.

GARRARD, J. G. "Alexander Solzhenitsyn's *August 1914.*" *Books Abroad,* 46 (1972), 409–11.

JAKOBSON, ROMAN. "Note on *August 1914,*" in *Aleksandr Solzhenitsyn: Critical Essays And Documentary Materials,* ed. John B. Dunlop, Richard Haugh, and Alexis Klimoff, pp. 326–27.

LAMONT, ROSETTE C. "Solzhenitsyn's Nationalism," in *Aleksandr Solzhenitsyn: Critical Essays And Documentary Materials,* ed. John B. Dunlop, Richard Haugh, and Alexis Klimoff, pp. 94–100.

McCARTHY, MARY. "The Tolstoy Connection," in *Aleksandr Solzhenitsyn: Critical Essays And Documentary Materials,* ed. John B. Dunlop, Richard Haugh, and Alexis Klimoff, pp. 332–50.

MOODY, CHRISTOPHER. *Solzhenitsyn,* rev. ed., pp. 162–79.

RAHV, PHILIP. "In Dubious Battle," in *Aleksandr Solzhenitsyn: Critical Essays And Documentary Materials,* ed. John B. Dunlop, Richard Haugh, and Alexis Klimoff, pp. 356–64.

ROMANOWSKI, JERZY. "Aleksandr Solzhenitsyn's *August 1914,* or the Truth about Book and Myth." *Soviet Studies In Literature,* 8 (1972), 315–40.

———. "Aleksandr Solzhenitsyn's *August 1914,* or the Truth about Book and Myth." *Soviet Review,* 14, No.1 (1973), 36–61.

SCHMEMANN, ALEXANDER. "A Lucid Love," in *Aleksandr Solzhenitsyn: Critical Essays And Documentary Materials,* ed. John B. Dunlop, Richard Haugh, and Alexis Klimoff, pp. 382–92.

STRUVE, GLEB. "Behind the Front Lines: On Some Neglected Chapters in *August 1914,*" in *Aleksandr Solzhenitsyn: Critical Essays And Documentary Materials,* ed. John B. Dunlop, Richard Haugh, and Alexis Klimoff, pp. 430–46.

STRUVE, NIKITA. "The Debate Over *August 1914,*" in *Aleksandr Solzhenitsyn: Critical Essays And Documentary Materials,* ed. John B. Dunlop, Richard Haugh, and Alexis Klimoff, pp. 393–407.

WINDLE, KEVIN. "The Theme of Fate in Solzhenitsyn's *August 1914.*" *Slavic Review,* 31 (1972), 399–411.

Reviews

CONQUEST, ROBERT. "Liberalism of the Catacombs." *Commentary,* 55, No.1 (1973), 92–96.

FITZLYON, KYRIL. "Russian Knots." *London Magazine,* NS 11, No.5 (1971), 139–43.

McCARTHY, MARY. "The Tolstoy Connection." *Saturday Review,* 16 September 1972, pp. 79–82, 88, 90–92, 96.

McNASPY, C. J. *New Orleans Review,* 3 (1973), 201–2.

PAWEL, ERNST. "War Without Peace." *Midstream Magazine,* 17, No.10 (1971), 68–71.

CANCER WARD (Rakovy korpus, 1968)

BELINKOV, A. V. "A. V. Belinkov's Defense of Solzhenitsyn's *The Cancer Ward* at a Special Meeting of the Writer's Union, November 1917, 1966." *Russian Review,* 28 (1969), 453–58.

BRADLEY, THOMPSON. "Aleksandr Solzhenitsyn's *Cancer Ward:* The Failure of Defiant Stoicism," in *Aleksandr Solzhenitsyn: Critical Essays And Documentary Materials,* ed. John B. Dunlop, Richard Haugh, and Alexis Klimoff, pp. 295–302.

BROWN, DEMING. "*Cancer Ward* and *The First Circle.*" *Slavic Review,* 28 (1969), 304–13.

BROWN, EDWARD J. "Solžencyn's Cast of Characters." *Slavic And East European Journal,* 15 (1971), 153–66.

HARARI, MANYA. "Solzhenitsyn's 'Cancer Ward'—Part II." *Survey: A Journal Of Soviet And East European Studies,* No.69 (1968), 145–49.

KERN, GARY. "The Case of Kostoglotov." *Russian Literature Triquarterly,* No.11 (1975), 407–34.

KOEHLER, LUDMILA. "Eternal Themes in Solzhenitsyn's 'The Cancer Ward.' " *Russian Review,* 28 (1969), 53–65.

KORG, JACOB. "Solzhenitsyn's Metaphors." *Centennial Review,* 17 (1973), 80–90.

LUKÁCS, GEORG. *Solzhenitsyn,* pp. 65–75.

MOODY, CHRISTOPHER. *Solzhenitsyn,* rev. ed., pp. 135–61.

MUCHNIC, HELEN. "Aleksandr Solzhenitsyn," in her *Russian Writers,* pp. 432–50.

———. "*Cancer Ward:* Of Fate and Guilt," in *Aleksandr Solzhenitsyn: Critical Essays And Documentary Materials,* ed. John B. Dunlop, Richard Haugh, and Alexis Klimoff, pp. 277–94.

NIELSEN, NIELS C., Jr. *Solzhenitsyn's Religion,* pp. 72–79.

ROTHBERG, ABRAHAM. *Alexander Solzhenitsyn: The Major Novels,* pp. 134–90.

WEISSBORT, DANIEL. "Solzhenitsyn's 'Cancer Ward.' " *Survey: A Journal Of Soviet And East European Studies,* No.68 (1968), pp. 179–85.

WILLIAMS, C. E. "Not an Inn, But an Hospital. *The Magic Mountain* and *Cancer Ward.*" *Forum For Modern Language Studies,* 9 (1973), 311–32.

WILLIAMS, RAYMOND. "On Solzhenitsyn." *Triquarterly,* No.23/4 (1972), pp. 318–31.

Reviews

FRIEDBERG, MAURICE. "Gallery of Comrades Embattled Abed." *Saturday Review,* 9 November 1968, pp. 42–44.

———. "Gallery of Comrades Revisited." *Saturday Review,* 15 March 1969, p. 36.

McLAREN, JOHN. "Out of Suffering." *Overland,* No.43 (1969/70), pp. 54–55.

REES, DAVID. "The Way It Was." *Encounter,* 32, No.1 (1969), 83–85.

FIRST CIRCLE (V kruge pervom, 1968)

BÖLL, HEINRICH. "The Imprisoned World of Solzhenitsyn's *The First Circle,*" in *Aleksandr Solzhenitsyn: Critical Essays And Documentary Materials,* ed. John B. Dunlop, Richard Haugh, and Alexis Klimoff, pp. 219–30.

BROWN, DEMING. "*Cancer Ward* and *The First Circle.*" *Slavic Review,* 28 (1969), 304–13.

BROWN, EDWARD J. "Solžencyn's Cast of Characters." *Slavic And East European Journal,* 15 (1971), 153–66.

DES PRES, TERENCE. "The Heroism of Survival," in *Aleksandr Solzhenitsyn: Critical Essays And Documentary Materials,* ed. John B. Dunlop, Richard Haugh, and Alexis Klimoff, pp. 51–59.

DUNLOP, JOHN B. "The Odyssey of A Skeptic: Gleb Nerzhin," in *Aleksandr Solzhenitsyn: Critical Essays And Documentary Materials,* ed. John B. Dunlop, Richard Haugh, and Alexis Klimoff, pp. 241–59.

GARRARD, J. G. "The 'Inner Freedom' of Alexander Solzhenitsyn." *Books Abroad,* 45 (1971), 9–14.

HAFT, CYNTHIA J. "A Note on Captivity: Jorge Semprun, Arthur Adamov, Alexander Solzhenitsyn." *USF Language Quarterly,* 13, No.1/2 (1974), 42, 48.

HALPERIN, DAVID M. "The Role of the Lie in *The First Circle,*" in *Aleksandr Solzhenitsyn: Critical Essays And Documentary Materials,* ed. John B. Dunlop, Richard Haugh, and Alexis Klimoff, pp. 260–89.

JACOBSON, DAN. "The Example of Solzhenitsyn." *Commentary,* 47, No.5 (1969), 81–84.

KERN, GARY. "Solzhenitsyn's Portrait of Stalin." *Slavic Review,* 33 (1974), 1–22.

KORG, JACOB. "Solzhenitsyn's Metaphors." *Centennial Review,* 17 (1973), 70–80.

LAMONT, ROSETTE C. "Solzhenitsyn's Nationalism," in *Aleksandr Solzhenitsyn: Critical Essays And Documentary Materials,* ed. John B. Dunlop, Richard Haugh, and Alexis Klimoff, pp. 108–16.

LIAPUNOV, VADIM. "Limbo and the Sharashka," in *Aleksandr Solzhenitsyn: Critical Essays And Documentary Materials,* ed. John B. Dunlop, Richard Haugh, and Alexis Klimoff, pp. 231–40.

LUKÁCS, GEORG. *Solzhenitsyn,* pp. 49–65.

MOODY, CHRISTOPHER. *Solzhenitsyn,* rev. ed., pp. 98–134.

MUCHNIC, HELEN. "Aleksandr Solzhenitsyn," in her *Russian Writers,* pp. 409–32.

———. "Solzhenitsyn's 'The First Circle.' " *Russian Review,* 29 (1970), 154–66.

NIELSEN, NIELS C.,Jr. *Solzhenitsyn's Religion,* pp. 39–53.

ROTHBERG, ABRAHAM. *Alexander Solzhenitsyn: The Major Novels,* pp. 60–133.

UNBEGAUN, BORIS O. "The 'Language of Ultimate Clarity,' " in *Aleksandr Solzhenitsyn: Critical Essays And Documentary Materials,* ed. John B. Dunlop, Richard Haugh, and Alexis Klimoff, pp. 195–98.

Reviews
FITZLYON, KYRIL. *London Magazine,* NS 8, No.10 (1969), 97–101.

FRIEDBERG, MAURICE. "The Party Imposes Its Will." *Saturday Review,* 14 September 1968, pp. 36–37, 116.

MCLAREN, JOHN. "Out of Suffering." *Overland,* No.43 (1969/70), p. 55.

WEEKS, EDWARD. *Atlantic Monthly,* 222, No.4 (1968), 145–46.

ONE DAY IN THE LIFE OF IVAN DENISOVICH (Odin den Ivana Denisovicha, 1962)

AIZERMAN, L. S. "Contemporary Literature Through the Eyes of Upper-Grade Pupils." *Soviet Review,* 6, No.1 (1965), 34–39.

CLARDY, J. V. "Alexander Solzhenitsyn's Concept of the Artist's Relationship to Society." *Slavonic And East European Review,* 52 (1974), 1–9.

LAMONT, ROSETTE C. "Literature, the Exile's Agent of Survival: Alexander Solzhenitsyn and Charlotte Delbo." *Mosaic,* 9, No.1 (1975), 13–17.

LUKÁCS, GEORG. *Solzhenitsyn,* pp. 7–32.

LUPLOW, RICHARD. "Narrative Style and Structure in *One Day In The Life Of Ivan Denisovich." Russian Literature Triquarterly,* Nos. 1/2 (1971), 399–412.

MATTHEWS, IRENE J. "A. Solzhenitsyn's 'One Day in the Life of Ivan Denisovich:' Terseness and Restraint in Setting and Atmosphere?" *Humanities Association Bulletin,* 23, No. 2 (1972), 8–13.

MOODY, CHRISTOPHER. *Solzhenitsyn,* rev. ed., pp. 28–38.

NIELSEN, NIEL C., Jr. *Solzhenitsyn's Religion,* pp. 17–26.

RAHV, PHILIP. "Two Subversive Russians," in his *Literature And The Sixth Sense,* pp. 378–81.

ROTHBERG, ABRAHAM. *Aleksander Solzhenitsyn: The Major Novels,* pp. 19–59.

SOLZHENITSYN, ALEXANDER, ed. "How People Read 'Ivan Denisovich' (A Survey of Letters)." *Survey: A Journal Of Soviet And East European Studies,* No.74/5 (1970), 207–20.

SOREL, CHARLES (French, 1597–1674)

L'IIISTOIRE COMIQUE DE FRANCION (1622)

FROHOCK, W. M. "The 'Picaresque' in France before *Gil Blas." Yale French Studies,* no. 38 (1967), pp. 226–29.

GRIFFITHS, MICHAEL and WOLFGANG LEINER. "Some Thoughts on the Names of the Characters in Charles Sorel's *Histoire Comique De Francion." Romance Notes,* 15 (1974), 445–53.

GUTHRIE, J. RICHARD. "An Analysis of Style and Purpose in the First Episode of the *Histoire Comique De Francion." Romance Notes,* 15 (1973), 99–103.

RIDGELY, BEVERLY S. "The Cosmic Voyage in Charles Sorel's *Francion." Modern Philology,* 65 (1967), 1–8.

SOROMENHO, FERNANDO CASTRO (Portuguese–Angolan, 1910–1968)

A CHAGA (1970)

Reviews
MOSER, GERALD M. *Hispania,* 55 (1972), 974.

SŌSEKI, NATSUME see NATSUME SŌSEKI

SOTO, PEDRO JUAN (Puerto Rican, 1928–)

GENERAL

BORING, P. Z. "Escape from Reality in the Fiction of Pedro Juan Soto." *Papers On Language And Literature,* 8 (1972), 287–96.

EL FRANCOTIRADOR (1969)

MENTON, SEYMOUR. *Prose Fiction Of The Cuban Revolution,* pp. 260–62.

USMAÍL (1959)

BORING, PHYLLIS Z. "Usmail: The Puerto Rican Joe Christmas." *College Language Association Journal,* 16 (1973), 324–33.

SOUSTER, RAYMOND (Canadian, 1921–)

ON TARGET (1973)

Reviews
ORANGE, JOHN. "Near Miss." *Journal Of Canadian Fiction,* 3, No.2 (1974), 100–2.

SOYINKA, WOLE (Nigerian, 1934–)

GENERAL

GIBBS, JAMES. "Wole Soyinka: A Selected Bibliography." *Journal Of Commonwealth Literature,* 10, No.3 (1975), 33–45.

JONES, ELDRED D. "The Essential Soyinka," in *Introduction To Nigerian Literature,* ed. Bruce King, pp. 113–34.

———. "Progress and Civilization in the Work of Wole Soyinka," in *Perspectives On African Literature,* ed. Christopher Heywood, pp. 129–37.

KATAMBA, FRANCIS. "Death and Man in the Earlier Works of Wole Soyinka." *Journal Of Commonwealth Literature,* 9, No.3 (1975), 63–71.

LINDFORS, BERNTH. *Folklore In Nigerian Literature,* pp. 105–15.

THE INTERPRETERS (1965)

GORDIMER, NADINE. "Modern African Writing." *Michigan Quarterly Review,* 9 (1970), 226–27.

JONES, ELDRED. "The Essential Soyinka," in *Introduction To Nigerian Literature,* ed. Bruce King, pp. 129–32.

———. "Interpreting The Interpreters: A Note on Soyinka's Novel." *Association For African Literature In English Bulletin,* No.4 (1966), pp. 13–18.

———. "Wole Soyinka's *The Interpreters*—Reading Notes." *African Literature Today,* No. 2 (1969), pp. 42–50.

LARSON, CHARLES R. "The Novel of the Future: Wole Soyinka and Ayi Kwei Armah," in his *The Emergence Of African Fiction,* rev. ed., pp. 246–58.

LAURENCE, MARGARET. *Long Drums And Cannons*, pp. 64-74.

MOORE, GERALD. *The Chosen Tongue*, pp. 184-90.

―――. *Wole Soyinka*, pp. 78-88.

RAVENSCROFT, ARTHUR. "African Literature V: Novels of Disillusion." *Journal Of Commonwealth Literature*, No.6 (1969), 123-28; rpt. in *Readings In Commonwealth Literature*, ed. William Walsh, pp. 190-95.

Reviews
KING, BRUCE. *Black Orpheus*, No.19 (1966), p. 55.

SEASON OF ANOMY (1973)

SCHMIDT, NANCY J. "Wole Soyinka." *Conch Review Of Books*, 3, No.1 (1975), 269-70.

SPENCE, CATHERINE (1825-1910)

GENERAL

WALKER, R. B. "Catherine Helen Spence, Unitarian Utopian." *Australian Literary Studies*, 5 (1971), 31-41.

A WEEK IN THE FUTURE

WALKER, R. B. "Catherine Helen Spence, Unitarian Utopian." *Australian Literary Studies*, 5 (1971), 37-41.

SPENCE, RAYMOND

NOTHING BLACK BUT A CADILLAC

Reviews
HALL, W. F. "Making the Scene." *Canadian Literature*, No.12 (1969), pp. 101-2.

SPOTA, LUIS (Mexican, 1925-1985)

LA CARCAJADA DEL GATO

LANGFORD, WALTER M. *The Mexican Novel Comes Of Age*, pp. 116-20.

LO DE ANTES

LANGFORD, WALTER M. *The Mexican Novel Comes Of Age*, pp. 120-22.

LA PEQUEÑA EDAD

LANGFORD, WALTER M. *The Mexican Novel Comes Of Age*, pp. 114-16.

THE TIME OF WRATH (El tiempo de la ira)

LANGFORD, WALTER M. *The Mexican Novel Comes Of Age*, pp. 112-14.

SRIVASTAV, Dhanpat Rai see PREMCHAND

STAËL (-HOLSTEIN, ANNE LOUISE GERMAINE NECKER, BARONESS OF) CALLED MADAME DE (French, 1766-1817)

GENERAL

LIBHART, BYRON R. "Madame de Staël, Charles de Villers, and the Death of God in Jean Paul's *Songe*." *Comparative Literature Studies*, 9 (1972), 141-51.

LOMBARD, CHARLES M. "Mme de Staël's Image in American Romanticism." *College Language Association Journal*, 19 (1975), 57-64.

CORINNE; OU L'ITALIE (1807)

DAEMMRICH, INGRID G. "The Function of the Ruins Motif in Madame de Staël's *Corinne*." *Romance Notes*, 15 (1973), 255-58.

LEPSCHY, A. LAURA. "Madame de Staël's Views on Art in 'Corinne.' " *Studi Francesi*, 14 (1970), 481-89.

MOERS, ELLEN. "Mme de Staël and the Woman of Genius." *American Scholar*, 44 (1975), 225-41.

POSGATE, HELEN B. *Madame De Staël*, pp. 103-10.

DELPHINE (1802)

POSGATE, HELEN B. *Madame De Staël*, pp. 90-98.

STEAD, CHRISTIAN KARLSON (New Zealander, 1932-)

SMITH'S DREAM (1971)

ROBERTSON, R. T. "The Nightmare of Kiwi Joe: C. K. Stead's Double Novel." *Ariel: A Review Of International English Literature*, 6, No.2 (1975), 97-110.

STEAD, CHRISTINA (Australian, 1902-1983)

GENERAL

"Christina Stead: An Interview." *Australian Literary Studies*, 6 (1974), 230-48.

STEAD, CHRISTINA. "A Writer's Friends (Piece on 'a writer's life.')" *Southerly*, 28 (1968), 163-68.

COTTERS' ENGLAND see DARK PLACES OF THE HEART

DARK PLACES OF THE HEART

GEERING, R. G. "Christina Stead in the 1960s." *Southerly*, 28 (1968), 26-36.

Reviews
BAUMBACH, ELINOR. "A Talent for Tragedy." *Saturday Review*, 17 September 1966, pp. 43-44.

FOR LOVE ALONE (1944)

REID, IAN. " 'The Woman Problem' in Some Australian and New Zealand Novels." *Southern Review: Literary And Interdisciplinary Essays*, 7 (1974), 192-99.

WILDING, MICHAEL. "Christina Stead's Australian Novels." *Southerly*, 27 (1967), 20-23.

THE LITTLE HOTEL (1975)

Reviews
KOCH, STEPHEN. *Saturday Review*, 31 May 1975, p. 28.

THE MAN WHO LOVED CHILDREN (1940)

KATZ, ALFRED H. "Some Psychological Themes in a Novel by Christina Stead." *Literature And Psychology*, 15 (1965), 210-15.

Reviews
BARRETT, WILLIAM. *Atlantic Monthly*, 215, No.6 (1965), 142-43.

SEVEN POOR MEN OF SYDNEY (1934)

GREEN, DOROTHY. "Chaos, Or a Dancing Star? Christina Stead's 'Seven Poor Men of Sydney.' " *Meanjin*, 27 (1968), 150-61.

WILDING, MICHAEL. "Christina Stead's Australian Novels." *Southerly*, 27 (1967), 20-23.

STEINER, JÖRG (Swiss, 1930-)

GENERAL

WAIDSON, H. M. "Jörg Steiner: Lyrical Prose from the Swiss Jura." *Books Abroad*, 47 (1973), 71-73.

STENDHAL (French, 1783-1842) pseudonym of Marie-Henri Beyle

GENERAL

ATHERTON, JOHN. *Stendhal.*

BART, B. F. "Hypercreativity in Stendhal and Balzac." *Nineteenth-Century French Studies,* 3 (1974/5), 18–31.

BISHOP, MICHAEL. "Laughter and the Smile in Stendhal." *Modern Language Review,* 70 (1975), 50–70.

COE, RICHARD N. "From Correggio to Class Warfare: Notes on Stendhal's Ideal of 'La Grâce,' " in *Balzac And The Nineteenth Century,* pp. 239–54.

————. "Stendhal and the Art of Memory," in *Currents Of Thought In French Literature,* pp. 145–63.

COOK, ALBERT. "Stendhal and the Discovery of Ironic Interplay." *Novel,* 9 (1975), 40–54.

FOWLIE, WALLACE. "Stendhal the Writer." *Sewanee Review,* 78 (1970), 310–29.

GOODHEART, EUGENE. "The Aesthetic Morality of Stendhal," in his *The Cult Of The Ego,* pp. 36–60.

GUTWIRTH, MARCEL. *Stendhal.*

MAY, GITA. "Stendhal and the Age of Ideas," in *Literature And History In The Age Of Ideas,* ed. Charles G. S. Williams, pp. 343–57.

PORTER, DENNIS. "Stendhal and the Limits of Liberalism." *Modern Language Review,* 66 (1971), 542–53.

TALBOT, EMILE J. "Author and Audience: A Perspective on Stendhal's Concept of Literature." *Nineteenth-Century French Studies,* 2 (1974), 111–22.

TAYLOR, M. E. M. "After Stendhal," in his *The Arriviste,* pp. 150–55.

————. "Contemporary Influences upon the Stendhalian 'Arriviste,' " in his *The Arriviste,* pp. 109–19.

————. "The Influence of Other Writers upon the Stendhalian 'Arriviste,' " in his *The Arriviste,* pp. 98–108.

————. "The Influence of Stendhal's Reading of Rousseau upon his 'Arriviste,' " in his *The Arriviste,* pp. 36–48.

————. "The Influence of Stendhal's Reading of the Ideologists upon His 'Arriviste,' " in his *The Arriviste,* pp. 82–90.

————. "The Two H. B.'s: The Letters Link: How the Stendhalian 'Arriviste' Differs from the Balzacian 'Arriviste,' " in his *The Arriviste,* pp. 133–49.

ARMANCE (1827)

BROMBERT, VICTOR. *Stendhal: Fiction And The Themes Of Freedom,* pp. 27–60.

BROOKS, PETER. *The Novel Of Worldliness,* pp. 226–28.

FOWLIE, WALLACE. *Stendhal,* pp. 71–90.

————. "A Study of Stendhal's *Armance.*" *Novel,* 2 (1969), 230–40.

MICKEL, EMANUEL J., Jr. "Stendhal's Use of Irony in 'Armance.' " *South Atlantic Bulletin,* 35, No.4 (1970), 11–18.

RICHARDSON, JOANNA. *Stendhal,* pp. 203–5.

STRICKLAND, GEOFFREY. *Stendhal: The Education Of A Novelist,* pp. 131–33.

TILLETT, MARGARET. *Stendhal: The Background To The Novels,* pp. 83–96.

WOOD, MICHAEL. *Stendhal,* pp. 52–64.

THE CHARTERHOUSE OF PARMA (La chartreuse de Parme, 1839)

BERSANI, LEO. *Balzac To Beckett,* pp. 91–139.

BROMBERT, VICTOR. *Stendhal: Fiction And The Themes Of Freedom,* pp. 149–76.

BROOKS, PETER. *The Novel Of Worldliness,* pp. 266–77.

FOWLIE, WALLACE. *Stendhal,* pp. 159–204.

GOODHEART, EUGENE. "The Aesthetic Morality of Stendhal," in his *The Cult Of The Ego,* pp. 41–60.

————. "Aristocrats and Jacobins: 'The Happy Few' in the Charterhouse of Parma." *Yale Review,* 65 (1976), 370–91.

HAIG, STIRLING. "The Identities of Fabrice del Dongo." *French Studies,* 27 (1973), 170–76.

KOGAN, VIVIAN. "Signs and Signals in *La Chartreuse De Parme.*" *Nineteenth-Century French Studies,* 2 (1973/4), 29–38.

KRONENBERGER, LOUIS. "Stendhal's *Charterhouse.*" *Encounter,* 27, No.1 (1966), 32–38.

KRONENBERGER, LOUIS. "Stendhal's *Charterhouse:* Supreme Study of Worldliness." *Michigan Quarterly Review,* 5 (1966), 163–71.

MEYERS, JEFFREY. "The Influence of *La Chartreuse De Parme* on *Il Gattopardo.*" *Italica,* 44 (1967), 314–25.

MORRIS, HERBERT. *The Masked Citadel: The Significance Of The Title Of Stendhal's La Chartreuse De Parme.*

PURDY, STROTHER B. "Manzoni, Stendhal, and the Murder of Prina: A Counterpart of Literature and History." *Studies In Romanticism,* 7 (1968), 140–58.

RICHARDSON, JOANNA. *Stendhal,* pp. 267–75.

RUBIN, LOUIS D. "Don Quixote and Selected Progeny: Or, the Journey-man as Outsider." *Southern Review,* NS, 10 (1974), 43–47.

STRICKLAND, GEOFFREY. *Stendhal: The Education Of A Novelist,* pp. 223–54.

TALBOT, EMILE J. "Stendhal, the Artist, and Society." *Studies In Romanticism,* 13 (1974), 213–23.

————. "Style and the Self: Some Notes on *La Chartreuse De Parme.*" *Language & Style,* 5 (1972), 299–312.

TAYLOR, M. E. M. "Evidences of Ideological Inspiration of the Stendhalian 'Arriviste' and His 'Associate-Types,' " in his *The Arriviste,* pp. 95–97.

————. "Rousseauism in the Stendhalian 'Arriviste' and His Associate-Types," in his *The Arriviste,* pp. 73–78.

————. "The Two H. B.'s: The Letters Link: How the Stendhalian 'Arriviste' Differs from the Balzacian 'Arriviste,' " in his *The Arriviste,* pp. 133–41.

TILLETT, MARGARET. *Stendhal: The Background To The Novels,* pp. 124–42.

WOOD, MICHAEL. *Stendhal,* pp. 157–88.

LAMIEL

STRICKLAND, GEOFFREY. *Stendhal: The Education Of A Novelist,* pp. 254–58.

TAYLOR, M. E. M. "Rousseauism in the Stendhalian 'Arriviste' and His Associate-Types," in his *The Arriviste,* pp. 78–81.

LUCIEN LEUWEN

BROMBERT, VICTOR. *Stendhal: Fiction And The Themes Of Freedom,* pp. 101–27.

BROOKS, PETER. *The Novel Of Worldliness,* pp. 229–66.

FOWLIE, WALLACE. *Stendhal,* pp. 131–40.

RICHARDSON, JOANNA. *Stendhal,* pp. 252–56.

SMETHURST, COLIN. "Balzac and Stendhal: A Comparison of Electoral Scenes," in *Balzac And The Nineteenth Century,* pp. 111–21.

STRICKLAND, GEOFFREY. *Stendhal: The Education Of A Novelist,* pp. 171–212.

TAYLOR, M. E. M. "Rousseauism in the Stendhalian 'Arriviste' and His Associate-Types," in his *The Arriviste,* pp. 67–73.

WOOD, MICHAEL. *Stendhal,* pp. 115–41.

THE RED AND THE BLACK (Le rouge et le noir, 1830)

ADAMSON, DONALD. "Stendhal and Balzac as Connoisseurs of Italian Art," in *Balzac And The Nineteenth Century*," pp. 132-36.

ARTINIAN, ROBERT W. "Stendhal's *The Red And The Black.*" *Explicator*, 30 (1972), Item 74.

BORGERHOFF, E. B. O. "Hammer, Saw and Wheel in *Le Rouge Et Le Noir.*" *French Review*, 42 (1969), 518-23.

BROMBERT, VICTOR. *Stendhal: Fiction And The Themes Of Freedom*, pp. 61-99.

CAMERON, J. L. "Sons and Lovers in 'Le Rouge et le Noir.' " *AUMLA*, No. 36 (1971), pp. 206-9.

COOK, ALBERT. "Stendhal and the Discovery of Ironic Interplay." *Novel*, 9 (1975), 40-46.

DELUTRI, JOSEPH R. "Notes on the Chapter Titles and Content of *Le Rouge Et Le Noir.*" *Romance Notes*, 15 (1973), 64-67.

_____. "On an Episode of *Le Rouge Et Le Noir*, 'L'Ennui.' " *Nineteenth-Century French Studies*, 3 (1975), 192-99.

DENOMMÉ, ROBERT T. "Julian Sorel and the Modern Conscience." *Western Humanities Review*, 21 (1967), 227-34.

DIBON, ANNE-MARIE. "Form and Value in the French and English 19th-Century Novel." *MLN*, 87 (1972), 883-914.

DONNELLY, JEROME. "Stendhal and Thackeray: The Source of 'Henry Esmond.' " *Revue De Littérature Comparée*, 39 (1965), 372-81.

FELDMAN, BURTON. "Stendhal and Helvétius." *Symposium*, 23 (1969), 129-36.

FOWLIE, WALLACE. *Stendhal*, pp. 91-129.

FRIEDMAN, MELVIN J. "The Cracked Vase." *Romance Notes*, 7 (1966), 127.

GERHARDI, GERHARD C. "Psychological Time and Revolutionary Action in *Le Rouge Et Le Noir.*" *PMLA*, 88 (1973), 1115-26.

GUERARD, ALBERT J. "The Illuminating Distortion." *Novel*, 5 (1972), 108-9.

GUTWIRTH, MARCEL. "*Le Rouge Et Le Noir* as Comedy." *Romanic Review*, 56 (1965), 188-94.

JOHNSON, ROGER. " 'L'Âpre Vérité' and 'Le Style emphatique' in *Le Rouge Et Le Noir.*" *Texas Studies In Literature And Language*, 13 (1971), 475-80.

MITCHELL, JOHN. *Stendhal: Le Rouge Et Le Noir.*

MOSSOP, D. J. "Julien Sorel, the Vulgar Assassin." *French Studies*, 23 (1969), 138-44.

PALMER, WILLIAM J. "Abelard's Fate: Sexual Politics in Stendhal, Faulkner and Camus." *Mosaic*, 7, No.3 (1974), 29-41.

PARIS, BERNARD J. *A Psychological Approach To Fiction*, pp. 133-64.

PASCO, ALLAN H. "A Study of Allusion: Barbey's Stendhal in 'Le Rideau Cramoisi." *PMLA*, 88 (1973), 461-71.

PORTER, DENNIS. "Stendhal and the Limits of Liberalism." *Modern Language Review*, 66 (1971), 544-47.

REDFERN, W. D. "The Prisoners of Stendhal and Camus." *French Review*, 41 (1968), 649-59.

REXROTH, KENNETH. "Stendhal's 'The Red and the Black.' " *Saturday Review*, 11 June 1966, p. 28; rpt. in his *Classics Revisited*, pp. 233-38.

RICHARDSON, JOANNA. *Stendhal*, pp. 223-29.

RUBIN, LOUIS D. *The Teller In The Tale*, pp. 25-41.

SANDS, STEVEN. "The Narcissism of Stendhal and Julian Sorel." *Studies In Romanticism*, 14 (1975), 337-63.

STANFORD, RANEY. "The Romantic Hero and That Fatal Selfhood." *Centennial Review*, 12 (1968), 437-40.

STRICKLAND, GEOFFREY. *Stendhal: The Education Of A Novelist*, pp. 126-64.

TAYLOR, M. E. M. "Evidences of the Ideological Inspiration of the Stendhalian 'Arriviste' and His 'Associate-Types,' " in his *The Arriviste*, pp. 92-95.

_____. "Napoleon and the Stendhalian 'Arriviste,' " in his *The Arriviste*, pp. 31-33.

_____. "Rousseauism in the Stendhalian 'Arriviste' and His Associate-Types," in his *The Arriviste*, pp. 49-67.

_____. "The Stendhalian 'Arriviste': How He Differs from Other Romantic Heroes," in his *The Arriviste*, pp. 14-17.

_____. "Subjective Inspiration for the Stendhalian 'Arriviste,' " in his *The Arriviste*, pp. 125-32.

WHEELER, NANCY. "Stendhal's View of 'The System.' " *SubStance*, No.2 (1971/2), pp. 57-61.

WOOD, MICHAEL. *Stendhal*, pp. 65-93.

STIFTER, ADALBERT (Austrian, 1805-1868)

GENERAL

BROWNING, BARTON W. "Cooper's Influence on Stifter: Fact or Scholarly Myth?" *MLN*, 89 (1974), 821-28.

KLIENEBERGER, H. R. "A New Approach to Stifter?" *German Life And Letters*, 25 (1972), 231-36.

LO CICERO, DONALD. "Stifter and the Novelle: Some New Perspectives." *Modern Austrian Literature*, 1, No. 3 (1968), 18-30.

STERN, J. P. "Stifter's Fiction: '*Erhebung* Without Motion.' " *Novel*, 1 (1968), 239-50.

STILLMARK, A. "Stifter Contra Hebbel—An Examination of the Sources of Their Disagreement." *German Life And Letters*, 21 (1968), 93-102.

_____. "Stifter's Early Portraits of the Artist. Stages in the Growth of an Aesthetic." *Forum For Modern Language Studies*, 11 (1975), 142-64.

ABDIAS

GEORGE, E. F. "The Place of *Abdias* in Stifter's Thought and Work." *Forum For Modern Language Studies*, 3 (1967), 148-56.

GOODEN, CHRISTIAN. "Two Quests for Surety—A Comparative Interpretation of Stifter's *Abdias* and Kafka's *Der Bau.*" *Journal Of European Studies*, 5 (1975), 341-61.

GUMP, MARGARET. *Adalbert Stifter*, pp. 45-50.

DER BESCHRIEBENE TANNLING

GUMP, MARGARET. *Adalbert Stifter*, pp. 65-68.

STERN, J. P. "Stifter's Fiction: '*Erhebung* Without Motion.' " *Novel*, 1 (1968), 244-49.

DER HAGESTOLZ

GUMP, MARGARET. *Adalbert Stifter*, pp. 56-60.

DAS HAIDEDORF

GUMP, MARGARET. *Adalbert Stifter*, pp. 27-30.

DER HOCHWALD

GUMP, MARGARET. *Adalbert Stifter*, pp. 30-35.

LETZTE MAPPE

GUMP, MARGARET. *Adalbert Stifter*, pp. 141-45.

DIE MAPPE MEINES URGROSSVATERS

GUMP, MARGARET. *Adalbert Stifter*, pp. 40-44.

DER NACHSOMMER (1857)

BROWNING, BARTON W. "Stifter's *Nachsommer* and the Fourth Commandment." *Colloquia Germanica,* 1973, pp. 301–16.

BRUFORD, W. H. *The German Tradition Of Self-Cultivation,* pp. 128–46.

GUMP, MARGARET. *Adalbert Stifter,* pp. 92–117.

SJÖGREN, CHRISTINE OERTEL. "The *Cereus Peruvianus* in Stifter's *Nachsommer:* Illustration of a Gestalt." *German Quarterly,* 40 (1967), 664–72.

―――. "The Configuration of Ideal Love in Stifter's *Der Nachsommer.*" *Modern Austrian Literature,* 8, No. 3/4 (1975), 190–96.

―――. "The Equivocal Light of the *Marmorsaal:* Traces of Mysticism in Stifter's Novel, *Der Nachsommer.*" *Journal Of English And Germanic Philology,* 69 (1970), 108–17.

―――. "The Human *Gestalten* and the Fools in Adalbert Stifter's *Der Nachsommer.*" *Journal Of English And Germanic Philology,* 70 (1971), 86–101.

―――. "Isolation and Death in Stifter's *Nachsommer.*" *PMLA,* 80 (1965), 254–58.

―――. "Klotilde's Journey into the Depths: A Probe into a Psychological Landscape in Stifter's *Die Nachsommer.*" *Germanic Notes,* 2 (1971), 50–52.

―――. "Mathilde and the Roses in Stifter's *Nachsommer.*" *PMLA,* 81 (1966), 400–8.

―――. "The Monstrous Painting in Stifter's *Der Nachsommer.*" *Journal Of English And Germanic Philology,* 68 (1969), 92–99.

―――. "Stifter's Afirmation of Formlessness in *Nachsommer.*" *Modern Language Quarterly,* 29 (1968), 407–14.

STOWELL, J. D. "Some Archetypes in Stifter's *Der Nachsommer:* An Attempt at Restoring Fictional Interest." *Seminar,* 6 (1970), 31–47.

DIE NARRENBURG

GUMP, MARGARET. *Adalbert Stifter,* pp. 35–38.

WITIKO (1865–67)

GUMP, MARGARET. *Adalbert Stifter,* pp. 118–31.

ZWEI SCHWESTERN

GUMP, MARGARET. *Adalbert Stifter,* pp. 62–65.

STIGEN, TERJE

AN INTERRUPTED PASSAGE

Reviews

DAHLIE, HALLVARD. *Ariel: A Review Of International English Literature,* 6, No.2 (1975), 113–14.

FLATIN, KJETIL A. *American Scandinavian Review,* 62 (1974), 408–9.

STONE, LOUIS (1871–)

JONAH (1911)

GREEN, DOROTHY. "Louis Stone's *Jonah:* A Cinematic Novel." *Australian Literary Studies,* 2 (1965), 15–31; rpt. in *The Australian Nationalists,* ed. Chris Wallace-Crabbe, pp. 159–75.

STEPHENS, A. G. "Louis Stone's *Jonah,*" in *Twentieth Century Australian Literary Criticism,* ed. Clement Semmler, pp. 115–16.

STORM, THEODOR (German, 1817–1888)

GENERAL

MENHENNET, A. "The Time-Element in Storm's Later Novellen." *German Life And Letters,* 20 (1966), 43–52.

AQUIS SUBMERSUS (1877)

ALT, A. TILO. *Theodor Storm,* pp. 82–90.

DUROCHE, LEONARD L. "Like and Look Alike: Symmetry and Irony in Theodor Storm's *Aquis Submersus.*" *Seminar,* 7 (1971), 1–13.

ZUR CHRONIK VON GRIESHUUS

ALT, A. TILO. *Theodor Storm,* pp. 102–10.

EIN DOPPELGÄNGER (1887)

ALT, A. TILO. *Theodor Storm,* pp. 115–21.

DROUSSEN IM HEIDEDORF

BARRICK, RAYMOND E. "Ambivalence in Character Portrayal in Theodore Storm's Novelle *Draussen Im Heidedorf.*" *USF Language Quarterly,* 11, No.1/2 (1972), 29–34, 56.

EEKENHOF

ALT, A. TILO. *Theodor Storm,* pp. 90–94.

HANS UND HEINZ KIRCH

ALT, A. TILO. *Theodor Storm,* pp. 95–102.

IMMENSEE (1849)

ALT, A. TILO. *Theodor Storm,* pp. 75–82.

NOCH EIN LEMBECK

ALT, A. TILO. *Theodor Storm,* pp. 110–15.

THE RIDER ON THE WHITE HORSE (Der Schimmelreiter, 1888)

ALT, A. TILO. *Theodor Storm,* pp. 121–31.

ARTISS, DAVID S. "Bird Motif and Myth in Theodor Storm's *Schimmelreiter.*" *Seminar,* 4 (1968), 1–16.

ELLIS, J. M. "Narration in Storm's *Der Schimmelreiter.*" *Germanic Review,* 44 (1969), 21–30.

―――. *Narration In The German Novelle,* pp. 155–68.

FINDLAY, IAN. "Myth and Redemption in Theodor Storm's *Der Schimmelreiter.*" *Papers On Language And Literature,* 11 (1975), 397–403.

STOW, RANDOLPH (Australian, 1935–)

GENERAL

BESTON, JOHN B. "An Interview with Randolph Stow." *World Literature Written In English,* 14 (1975), 221–36.

DUTTON, GEOFFREY. "The Search for Permanence: The Novels of Randolph Stow." *Journal Of Commonwealth Literature,* No. 1 (1965), 135–48; rpt. in *Readings In Commonwealth Literature,* ed. William Walsh, pp. 377–91.

NEW, WILLIAM H. "Outsider Looking Out: The Novels of Randolph Stow." *Critique,* 9, No.1 (1966), 90–99.

OPPEN, ALICE. "Myth and Reality in Randolph Stow." *Southerly,* 27 (1967), 82–94.

WIGHTMAN, JENNIFER. "Waste Places, Dry Souls: The Novels of Randolph Stow." *Meanjin,* 28 (1969), 239–52.

A HAUNTED LAND (1956)

DUTTON, GEOFFREY. "The Search for Permanence: The Novels of Randolph Stow." *Journal Of Commonwealth Literature,* No.1 (1965), 137–40; rpt. in *Readings In Commonwealth Literature,* ed. William Walsh, pp. 380–83.

OPPEN, ALICE. "Myth and Reality in Randolph Stow." *Southerly,* 27 (1967), 82–85.

THE MERRY-GO-ROUND IN THE SEA (1965)

HASSALL, ANTHONY J. "Full Circle: Randolph Stow's 'The Merry-Go-Round in the Sea.' " *Meanjin,* 32 (1973), 58–64.

NEW, WILLIAM H. "Outsider Looking Out: The Novels of Randolph Stow." *Critique,* 9, No.1 (1966/7), 96–99.

WIGHTMAN, JENNIFER. "Waste Places, Dry Souls: The Novels of Randolph Stow." *Meanjin,* 28 (1969), 249–51.

Reviews
MCPHERSON, NEIL. "Writers for a 'No' Generation." *Westerly,* 2, No.1 (1966), 60–62.

TO THE ISLANDS (1958)

BESTON, JOHN B. "Heriot's Literary Allusions in Randolph Stow's *To The Islands.*" *Southerly,* 35 (1975), 168–77.

HERGENHAN, L. T. "Randolph Stow's *To The Islands.*" *Southerly,* 35 (1975), 234–47.

NEW, WILLIAM H. "Outsider Looking Out: The Novels of Randolph Stow." *Critique,* 9, No.1 (1966/7), 93–95.

OPPEN, ALICE. "Myth and Reality in Randolph Stow." *Southerly,* 27 (1967), 86–89.

TOURMALINE (1963)

OPPEN, ALICE. "Myth and Reality in Randolph Stow." *Southerly,* 27 (1967), 89–92.

WIGHTMAN, JENNIFER. "Waste Places, Dry Souls: The Novels of Randolph Stow." *Meanjin,* 28 (1969), 245–48.

STRINDBERG, AUGUST (Swedish, 1849–1912)

ALONE (Ensam, 1903)

JOHANNESSON, ERIC O. *The Novels Of August Strindberg: A Study In Theme And Structure,* pp. 210–26.

BY THE OPEN SEA (I havsbandet, 1890)

JOHANNESSON, ERIC O. *The Novels Of August Strindberg: A Study In Theme And Structure,* pp. 146–71.

THE CLOISTER

Reviews
SPECTOR, ROBERT D. *American Scandinavian Review,* 58 (1970), 311.

THE CONFESSION OF A FOOL (En dåres försvarstal, 1895)

JOHANNESSON, ERIC O. *The Novels Of August Strindberg: A Study In Theme And Structure,* pp. 91–108.

EN HÄXA

JOHANNESSON, ERIC O. *The Novels Of August Strindberg: A Study In Theme And Structure,* pp. 134–45.

THE INFERNO (1897)

JOHANNESSON, ERIC O. *The Novels Of August Strindberg: A Study In Theme And Structure,* pp. 172–209.

THE NATIVES OF HEMSÖ (Hemsöborna, 1887)

JOHANNESSON, ERIC O. *The Novels Of August Strindberg: A Study In Theme And Structure,* pp. 82–90.

Reviews
LUNDBERGH, HOLGER. *American Scandinavian Review,* 54 (1966), 195.

THE RED ROOM (Röda Rummet, 1879)

JOHANNESSON ERIC O. *The Novels Of August Strindberg: A Study In Theme And Structure,* pp. 25–45.

DEN ROMANTISKE KLOCKAREN

JOHANNESSON, ERIC O. *The Novels Of August Strindberg: A Study In Theme And Structure,* pp. 109–20.

THE SCAPEGOAT (Syndabocken, 1906)

JOHANNESSON, ERIC O. *The Novels Of August Strindberg: A Study In Theme And Structure,* pp. 267–94.

Reviews
POTOKER, EDWARD M. "Marked Man in Vicious Circles." *Saturday Review,* 29 July 1967, p. 30.

SPECTOR, ROBERT D. *American Scandanavian Review,* 57 (1969), 84–85.

THE SON OF A SERVANT (Tjänstekvinnans)

JOHANNESSON, ERIC O. *The Novels Of August Strindberg: A Study In Theme And Structure,* pp. 55–81.

SVARTA FANOR

JOHANNESSON, ERIC O. *The Novels Of August Strindberg: A Study In Theme And Structure,* pp. 227–45.

TAKLAGSÖL (1905)

JOHANNESSON, ERIC O. *The Novels Of August Strindberg: A Study In Theme And Structure,* pp. 246–66.

TSCHANDALA (1888)

JOHANNESSON, ERIC O. *The Novels Of August Strindberg: A Study In Theme And Structure,* pp. 121–33.

UTRECKLING

JOHANNESSON, ERIC O. *The Novels Of August Strindberg: A Study In Theme And Structure,* pp. 46–54.

STRITTMATTER, ERWIN (German, 1912–)

OLE BIENKOPP (1963)

Reviews
OSTERLE, HEINZ D. *Novel,* 1 (1967), 98–100.

STUART, DONALD

PRINCE OF MY COUNTRY

Reviews
EWERS, JOHN K. "The First of Six." *Overland,* No.60 (1975), 86–87.

SUAREZ Y ROMERO, ANSELMO (Cuban, 1818-1878)

GENERAL

TAYLOR, A. CAREY. "Balzac and the Latin-American Novel," in *Balzac And The Nineteenth Century,* pp. 181–82.

SUCH, PETER (Canadian)

FALLOUT (1969)

Reviews
SHARMAN, V. "A Junked-Up Landscape." *Canadian Literature,* No.44 (1970), pp. 92–93.

RIVERRUN

Reviews
BARBOUR, DOUGLAS. "Original People." *Canadian Literature,* No.61 (1974), p. 82.

PORTER, HELEN. "Death of a Race." *Journal Of Canadian Fiction,* 3, No.2 (1974), 93–94.

WRIGHT, MICHAEL WAYNE. *Dalhousie Review,* 53 (1973/4), 775–77.

SUE, EUGENE (French, 1804–1857)

MATHILDE (1841)

JONES, MALCOLM V. "An Aspect of Romanticism in Dostoevsky: 'Netochka Nezvanova' and Eugéne Sue's 'Mathilde.' " *Renaissance And Modern Studies,* 17 (1973), 38–61.

SUNDMAN, PER OLOF (Swedish, 1922–)

GENERAL

"An Interview with Per Olof Sundman." *Contemporary Literature,* 12 (1971), 267–75.

SJÖBERG, LEIF. "Per Olof Sundman and the Uses of Reality." *American Scandinavian Review,* 59 (1971), 145–54.

———. "Per Olof Sundman: The Writer as a Reasonably Unbiased Observer." *Books Abroad,* 47 (1973), 253–60.

THE EXPEDITION (Expeditionen, 1962)

Reviews
SMITH, A. M. SHERIDAN. *London Magazine,* NS 7, No.7 (1967), 103.

THE FLIGHT OF THE EAGLE (Ingenjör Andrée's luftfärd, 1967)

Reviews
FRIIS, ERIK J. *American Scandinavian Review,* 59 (1971), 84.

TWO DAYS, TWO NIGHTS (Två dagar, två nätter, 1965)

Reviews
SPECTOR, ROBERT D. *American Scandinavian Review,* 58 (1970), 86.

SUTHERLAND, RONALD (Canadian, 1933–)

LARK DES NIEGES (1971)

Reviews
DAVIS, FRANCES. *Dalhousie Review,* 52 (1972), 329–33.

ROITER, HOWARD. "Identity Crisis." *Journal Of Canadian Fiction,* 1, No.2 (1972), 91–92.

SHOHET, LINDA. "Lark Ascending." *Canadian Literature,* No.64 (1975), pp. 113–15.

SVEVO, ITALO (Italian, 1861–1928) pseudonym of Ettore Schmitz

GENERAL

BIASIN, GIAN-PAOLO. "Literary Diseases: From Pathology to Ontology." *MLN,* 82 (1967), 80–97.

BONDANELLA, PETER. "The Reception of Italo Svevo." *Italian Quarterly,* 12, No.47/48 (1969), 63–89.

BONDY, FRANÇOIS. "Italo Svevo and Ripe Old Age." *Hudson Review,* 20 (1967/8), 575–98.

CERNECCA, DOMENICO. "Dialectical Element and Linguistic Complex in Svevo." *Modern Fiction Studies,* 18 (1972), 81–89.

CHAMPAGNE, ROLAND A. "A Displacement of Plato's *Pharmakon:* A Study of Italo Svevo's Short Fiction." *Modern Fiction Studies,* 21 (1975/6), 564–72.

DE LAURETIS, TERESA. "Discourse and the Conquest of Desire in Svevo's Fiction." *Modern Fiction Studies,* 18 (1972), 91–103.

GALLI, LINA. "Svevo and Irredentism." *Modern Fiction Studies,* 18 (1972), 114–16.

MALONEY, BRIAN. *Italo Svevo: A Critical Introduction.*

———. "Svevo as a Jewish Writer." *Italian Studies,* 28 (1973), 52–63.

PACIFICI, SERGIO. *The Modern Italian Novel: From Manzoni To Svevo,* pp. 149–83.

ROCCO-BERGERA, NINY. "Italo Svevo and Trieste." *Modern Fiction Studies,* 18 (1972), 111–13.

ROCCO-BERGERA, NINY. "Joyce and Svevo: A Note." *Modern Fiction Studies,* 18 (1972), 116–17.

RUSSELL, CHARLES C. "Italo Svevo's Close Friend: Umberto Veruda." *Forum Italicum,* 9 (1975), 210–17.

STALEY, THOMAS F. "Italo Svevo and the Ambience of Trieste." *Modern Fiction Studies,* 18 (1972), 7–16.

AS A MAN GROWS OLDER (Senilità, 1898)

BIASIN, GIAN-PAOLO. "Literary Diseases: From Pathology to Ontology." *MLN,* 82 (1967), 81–85.

FURBANK, P. N. *Italo Svevo: The Man And The Writer,* pp. 162–73.

MARAMPON, LUCIO. "In Defense of the Title 'Senilità.' " *Italian Quarterly,* 17, No.65 (1973), 27–38.

PACIFICI, SERGIO. *The Modern Italian Novel: From Manzoni To Svevo,* pp. 167–74.

ROBISON, PAULA. "*Senilità:* The Secret of Svevo's Weeping Madonna." *Italian Quarterly,* 14, No.55 (1971), 61–84.

CONFESSIONS OF ZENO (La Coscienza di Zeno, 1923)

BIASIN, GIAN-PAOLO. "Literary Diseases: From Pathology to Ontology." *MLN,* 82 (1967), 85–97.

BIASIN, GIAN-PAOLO. "Zeno's Last Bomb." *Modern Fiction Studies,* 18 (1972), 17–32.

DAVIS, BARBARA A. "Zeno's Ontological Confessions." *Twentieth Century Literature,* 18 (1972), 45–56.

DE LAURETIS, TERESA. "Dreams as Metalanguage in Svevo's *Confessions Of Zeno.*" *Language And Style,* 4 (1971), 208–20.

FIFER, ELIZABETH. "The Confessions of Italo Svevo." *Contemporary Literature,* 14 (1973), 320–31.

FRECCERO, JOHN. "Italo Svevo: Zeno's Last Cigarette," in *From Verismo To Experimentalism,* ed. Sergio Pacifici, pp. 35–60.

FURBANK, P. N. *Italo Svevo: The Man And The Writer,* pp. 174–203, 205–8.

FURST, LILIAN R. "Italo Svevo's *La Conscienza Di Zeno* and Thomas Mann's *Der Zauberberg.*" *Contemporary Literature,* 9 (1968), 492–506.

GATT-RUTTER, JOHN. "Non-commitment in Italo Svevo." *Journal Of European Studies,* 3 (1973), 123–46.

GODT, CLAREECE. "Svevo and Coincidence." *MLN,* 89 (1974), 84–92.

JACOBS, LEE. "Zeno's Sickness Unto Death." *Italian Quarterly,* 11, No.44 (1968), 51–66.

LEBOWITZ, NAOMI. *Humanism And The Absurd In The Modern Novel,* pp. 110–17.

MOLONEY, BRIAN. "Italo Svevo and Thomas Mann's *Buddenbrooks,*" in *Essays In Honour Of John Humphreys Whitfield,* pp. 261–67.

———. "Psychoanalysis and Irony in 'La coscienza di Zeno.' " *Modern Language Review,* 67 (1972), 309–18.

———. "Svevo as a Jewish Writer." *Italian Studies,* 28 (1973), 60–63.

MARAMPON, LUCIO. "The Insight to Necessity of Zeno." *Italian Quarterly,* 18, No.71 (1975), 23–38.

MEYER, MARK. "Zeno: His Fictions and His Problems." *SubStance,* No.3 (1972), pp. 121–25.

PACIFICI, SERGIO. *The Modern Italian Novel: From Manzoni To Svevo,* pp. 174–83.

ROBISON, PAULA. "Svevo: Secrets of the Confessional." *Literature And Psychology,* 20 (1970), 101–5.

TREITEL, RENATA MINERBI. "Schopenhauer's Philosophy in Italo Svevo's *La Coscienza Di Zeno.*" *Modern Fiction Studies,* 18 (1972), 53–64.

———. "Zeno Cosini: The Meaning Behind the Name." *Italica,* 48 (1971), 234–45.

WAGNER, C. ROLAND. "Italo Svevo: The Vocation of Old Age." *Hartford Studies In Literature,* 2 (1970), 214–23.

WILDEN, ANTHONY. "Death, Desire, and Repetition in Svevo's *Zeno.*" *MLN,* 84 (1969), 98–119.

A LIFE (Una Vita, 1893)

FURBANK, P. N. *Italo Svevo: The Man And The Writer,* pp. 158–63.

MOLONEY, BRIAN. "Italo Svevo and Thomas Mann's *Buddenbrooks,*" in *Essays In Honour Of John Humphreys Whitfield,* pp. 251–61.

PACIFICI, SERGIO. *The Modern Italian Novel: From Manzoni To Svevo,* pp. 160–66.

ROBISON, PAULA. "*Una Vita* and the Family Romance." *Modern Fiction Studies,* 18 (1972), 33–44.

SYMONS, SCOTT (Canadian, 1933–)
PLACE D'ARMES (1967)

Reviews
SUTHERLAND, RONALD. "Brandy and Self-Abasement." *Canadian Literature,* No. 33 (1967), pp. 84–85.

T

TAGORE, RABINDRANATH (Indian, 1861-1941)

GENERAL

DHAR, BANSHI. "The Humanism of Rabindranath Tagore." *Indian Literature,* 16, Nos.1/2 (1973), 147–52.

RAO, A. V. KRISHNA. "The Novels of Rabindranath Tagore." *Triveni,* 33, No.2 (1964), 61–69.

SRINIVASA IYENGAR, K. R. *Indian Writing In English,* pp. 99–121.

GORA (1910)

RAO, A. V. KRISHNA. "The Novels of Rabindranath Tagore." *Triveni,* 33, No.2 (1964), 63–66.

TAHA HUSSEIN

GENERAL

SFEIR, GEORGE. "The Contemporary Arabic Novel." *Daedalus,* 95 (1966), 943–47.

ADIB

KILPATRICK, HILARY. *The Modern Egyptian Novel,* pp. 36–38, 203–4.

TAKEDA, TAIJUN

LUMINOUS MOSS

KIMBALL, ARTHUR G. *Crisis In Identity And Contemporary Japanese Novels,* pp. 36–42.

TAKEYAMA, MICHIO

HARP OF BURMA (Biruma no tategoto)

Reviews
PUTZAR, ED. *Arizona Quarterly,* 23 (1967), 82–83.

TAKTSIS, COSTAS (Greek, 1927–)

THE THIRD WEDDING (Tpito Stephani, 1963)

Reviews
MAURER, ROBERT. *Saturday Review,* 1 January 1972, p. 75.

TALE OF THE LADY OCHIKUBO (Ochikubo Monogatari)

Reviews
GHOSH, S. L. *Indian Horizons,* 21, No.2/3 (1972), 160.

TAMMUZ, BINYAMIN (Russian-born Israeli, 1919–)

HAPARDESS (1971)

Reviews
ARAD, MIRIAM. "New Novels." *Ariel: A Quarterly Review Of The Arts And Sciences In Israel,* No.31 (1972), p. 111.

TANIZAKI JUNICHIRŌ (Japanese, 1886–1965)

GENERAL

FALKE, WAYNE. "Tanizaki: Opponent of Naturalism." *Critique,* 8, No.3 (1966), 19–25.

HIBBETT, HOWARD. "Tradition and Trauma in the Contemporary Japanese Novel." *Daedalus,* 95 (1966), 928–36.

JONES, SUMIE. "How Tanizaki Disarms the Intellectual Reader." *Literature East And West,* 18 (1974), 321–29.

SEIDENSTICKER, EDWARD. "Tanizaki Jun-ichirō, 1886–1965." *Monumenta Nipponica,* 21 (1966), 249–65.

DIARY OF A MAD OLD MAN (Ruten Rojin Nikki, 1962)

GURR, ANDREW. "Engagement is not Marriage: Perspectives on Cultural Conflict in East Africa." *Mosaic,* 5, No.2 (1971/2), 68–70.

KIMBALL, ARTHUR G. *Crisis In Identity And Contemporary Japanese Novels,* pp. 109–14.

Reviews
FITZSIMMONS, THOMAS. "Rebellious Octogenarian." *Saturday Review,* 21 August 1965, pp. 26–27.

FYTTON, FRANCIS. "Delinquency and Desperation." *London Magazine,* NS 5, No.12 (1966), 100–1.

WRIGHT, HAROLD P. *Literature East And West,* 11 (1967), 465–66.

TARASHANKAR BANDYOPADHYAY

GENERAL

DEVI, MAHASVETA. "Tarashankar's World of Changes and the New Order." *Indian Literature,* 12, No.1 (1969), 71–79.

TARASSOFF, LEV see TROYAT, HENRI

TARSIS, VALERIY (Russian, 1906–1983)

THE PLEASURE FACTORY

Reviews
MAURER, ROBERT. "Soviet Playland." *Saturday Review,* 9 March 1968, p. 36.

WARD 7

Reviews

OBERBECK, S. K. "Underground Letters." *Reporter,* 33, No.7 (1965), 58.

TAWFIQ AL-HAKIM

AWDAT AL-RUH

MOOSA, MATTI I. "The Growth of Modern Arabic Fiction." *Critique,* 11, No.1 (1968/9), 14-15.

TAYLOR, KAMALA see MARKANDAYA, KAMALA

TEIRLINCK, HERMAN (Flemish, 1879-1967)

THE MAN IN THE MIRROR (Zelfportret of het glagemaal, 1955)

KORGES, JAMES. "Flemish Mirrors." *Critique,* 8, No.3 (1966), 85-92.

TEJERA, NIVARIA (Cuban, 1933-)

SONAMBULO DE SOL

MENTON, SEYMOUR. *Prose Fiction Of The Cuban Revolution,* pp. 74-76.

TENDRJAKOV, VLADIMIR (Russian, 1923-)

GENERAL

GARRAND, J. G. "Vladimir Tendrjakov." *Slavic And East European Journal,* 9 (1965), 1-18.

APOSTOL'SKAYA KOMANDIROVKA (1969)

HOSKING, GEOFFREY. "The Search for an Image of Man in Contemporary Soviet Fiction." *Forum For Modern Language Studies,* 11 (1975), 357-60.

TENNANT, KYLIE (Australian, 1912-) pseudonym of Kylie Tennant Rodd

GENERAL

MOORE, T. INGLIS. "The Tragi-Comedies of Kylie Tennant," in *Twentieth Century Australian Literary Criticism,* ed. Clement Semmler, pp. 324-33.

THE BATTLERS (1941)

PONS, XAVIER. "*The Battlers:* Kylie Tennant and the Australian Tradition." *Australian Literary Studies,* 6 (1974), 364-380.

TERTZ, ABRAHAM (Russian, 1925-) pseudonym of Abraham Sinyavsky

THE MAKEPEACE EXPERIMENT (Lubimow, 1963)

MUCHNIC, HELEN. "It Happened in Lyubimov: Tertz," in her *Russian Writers,* pp. 365-73.

Reviews

OBERBECK, S. K. "Underground Letters." *Reporter,* 33, No.7 (1965), 58-59.

VIERECK, PETER. "World Power Through Witchcraft." *Saturday Review,* 24 July 1965, pp. 45-46.

THE TRIAL BEGINS (Sud idët, 1959)

LEATHERBARROW, W. J. "The Sense of Purpose and Socialist Realism in Tertz's *The Trial Begins.*" *Forum For Modern Language Studies,* 11 (1975), 268-79.

RAHV, PHILIP. "Two Subversive Russians," in his *Literature And The Sixth Sense,* pp. 381-84.

TERZAKIS, ANGELOS (Greek, 1907-1979)

GENERAL

PROUSSIS, COSTAS M. "The Novels of Angelos Terzakis." *Daedalus,* 95 (1966), 1021-45.

THÉRAULT, YVES (French Canadian, 1915-)

GENERAL

HESSE, M. G. "The Significance of Death in the Works of Yves Therault." *Journal Of Canadian Fiction,* 2, No.1 (1973), 43-48.

AARON (1957)

SUTHERLAND, RONALD. "The Body-Odour of Race." *Canadian Literature,* No.37 (1968), pp. 60-62; rpt. in his *Second Image,* pp. 50-55.

THEROUX, PAUL

JUNGLE LOVERS

Reviews

RABAN, JONATHAN. "Rebels without Warning." *London Magazine,* NS 11, No.3 (1971), 152-56.

THIBAULT, Jacques-Anatole-Francois see FRANCE, Anatole

THOBY-MARCELIN, PHILIPPE (Haitian, 1904-1975) and MARCELIN, PIERRE (Haitian, 1908-)

ALL MEN ARE MAD (Tous les hommes sont fous, 1970)

Reviews

CLARK, JAMES ALAN. *America,* 25 July 1970; rpt. *Review,* No.3 (1971), pp. 70-71.

CONROY, JACK. *Chicago Daily News,* 23/24 May 1970; rpt. *Review,* No.3 (1971), pp. 71-72.

OBERBECK, S. K. *Newsweek,* 1 June 1970; rpt. *Review,* No.3 (1971), p. 73.

WILSON, EDMUND. *New York Review Of Books,* 26 March 1970; rpt. *Review,* No.3 (1971), pp. 73-76.

THOMAS, AUDREY (Canadian, 1935-)

BLOWN FIGURES (1974)

Reviews

BOWERING, GEORGE. "The Site of Blood." *Canadian Literature,* No.65 (1975), pp. 86-90.

JULIAN, MARILYN. *Tamarack Review,* No.66 (1975), pp. 109-10.

MRS. BLOOD (1970)

Reviews

COLDWELL, JOAN. "From the Inside." *Canadian Literature,* No.50 (1971), pp. 98-99.

THOMAS, HENRI (French, 1912-)

GENERAL

FROHOCK, W. M. "After the 'New Novel': Henri Thomas." *Southern Review,* NS 5 (1969), 1055-68.

THOMAS, JOHANN (German, 1624-1679)

DAMON UND LISILLE (1663)

WAGENER, HANS. *The German Baroque Novel,* pp. 21-23.

THOMPSON, KENT (Canadian, 1936–)
THE TENANTS WERE CORRIE AND TENNIE (1973)

Reviews
BAILEY, NANCY. "Semi-Detached." *Journal Of Canadian Fiction,* 2, No.4 (1973), 110–11.

MCCARTHY, RAE. *Dalhousie Review,* 53 (1973), 359–61.

THORDARSON, THORBERGUR (1889–)
IN SEARCH OF MY BELOVED

Reviews
MITCHELL, P. M. "Sweet Suffering in Iceland." *Saturday Review,* 11 November 1967, p. 58.

THE SWORD (Ef sverð pitterstutt, 1953)

Reviews
BESSASON, HARALDUR. *American Scandinavian Review,* 60 (1972), 83–84.

TIECK, LUDWIG (German, 1773–1853)
GENERAL

BELGARDT, RAIMUND. "Poetic Imagination and External Reality in Tieck: From Divergence to Convergence," in *Essays On German Literature In Honour Of G. Joyce Hallamore,* ed. Michael S. Batts and Marketa Goetz Stankiewicz, pp. 41–61.

GRIES, FRAUKE. "Two Critical Essays by Ludwig Tieck: On Literature and its Sociological Aspects." *Monatshefte,* 66 (1974), 157–65.

ZEYDEL, EDWIN H. "Edgar Allan Poe's Contacts with German as Seen in His Relations with Ludwig Tieck," in *Studies In German Literature Of The Nineteenth And Twentieth Centuries,* ed. Siegfried Mews, pp. 47–54.

DER BLONDE ECKBERT

BELGARDT, RAIMUND. "Poetic Imagination and External Reality in Tieck: From Divergence to Convergence," in *Essays On German Literature In Honour Of G. Joyce Hallamore,* ed. Michael S. Batts and Marketa Goetz Stankiewicz, pp. 43–49.

ELLIS, JOHN M. *Narration In The German Novelle,* pp. 77–93.

EWTON, RALPH W. "Childhood without End: Tieck's *Der Blonde Eckbert.*" *German Quarterly,* 46 (1973), 410–27.

HUBBS, V. C. "Tieck's Romantic Fairy Tales and Shakespeare." *Studies In Romanticism,* 8 (1969), 229–34.

KIMPEL, RICHARD W. "Nature, Quest, and Reality in Tieck's *Der Blonde Eckbert* and *Der Runnenberg.*" *Studies In Romanticism,* 9 (1970), 176–92.

LILLYMAN, W. J. "The Enigma of *Der Blonde Eckbert:* The Significance of the End." *Seminar,* 7 (1971), 144–55.

RIPPERE, VICTORIA L. "Ludwig Tieck's 'Der blonde Eckbert': A Psychological Reading." *PMLA,* 85 (1970), 473–86.

FRANZ STERNBALDS WANDERUNGEN

KAHN, ROBERT L. "Tieck's *Franz Sternbalds Wanderungen* and Novalis' *Heinrich Von Ofterdingen.*" *Studies In Romanticism,* 7 (1967), 40–64.

SAMMONS, JEFFREY L. "Tieck's *Franz Sternbald:* The Loss of Thematic Control." *Studies In Romanticism,* 5 (1965), 30–43.

DES LEBENS ÜBERFLUSS (1839)

BELGARDT, RAIMUND. "Poetic Imagination and External Reality in Tieck: From Divergence to Convergence," in *Essays On German Literature In Honour Of G. Joyce Hallamore,* ed. Michael S. Batts and Marketa Goetz Stankiewicz, pp. 54–58.

LILLYMAN, W. J. "Ludwig Tieck's *Des Lebens Überfluss:* The Crisis of a Conservative." *German Quarterly,* 46 (1973), 393–409.

DER RUNENBERG

BELGARDT, RAIMUND. "Poetic Imagination and External Reality in Tieck: From Divergence to Convergence," in *Essays On German Literature In Honour Of G. Joyce Hallamore,* ed. Michael S. Batts and Marketa Goetz Stankiewicz, pp. 49–54.

EWTON, RALPH W. "Life and Death of the Body in Tieck's *Der Runenberg.*" *Germanic Review,* 50 (1975), 19–33.

KIMPEL, RICHARD W. "Nature, Quest, and Reality in Tieck's *Der Blonde Eckbert* and *Der Runnenberg.*" *Studies In Romanticism,* 9 (1970), 176–92.

LILLYMAN, W. J. "Ludwig Tieck's 'Der Runenberg': The Dimensions of Reality." *Monatshefte,* 62 (1970), 231–44.

VREDEVELD, HARRY. "Ludwig Tieck's *Der Runnenberg:* An Archetypal Interpretation." *Germanic Review,* 49 (1974), 200–14.

VITTORIA ACCOROMBONA

LILLYMAN, W. J. "Ludwig Tieck's *Vittoria Accorombona.*" *Journal Of English And Germanic Philology,* 70 (1971), 468–87.

WILLIAM LOVELL

PROSKAUER, PAUL F. "Ludwig Tieck's *William Lovell* and Young Hugo von Hofmannsthal." *Modern Austrian Literature,* 3, No.3 (1970), 36–46.

TIEMPO, EDILBERTO
WATCH IN THE NIGHT (1953)

CASPER, LEONARD. *New Writing From The Philippines,* pp. 77–81.

TING LING (Chinese, 1904–) pseudonym of Chiang Ping-chih
GENERAL

HSIA, C. T. *A History Of Modern Chinese Fiction,* pp. 262–79.

THE SUN SHINES OVER THE SANGKAN RIVER (T'ai-yang chao tsai sang-kan, 1948)

HSIA, C. T. *A History Of Modern Chinese Fiction,* pp. 487–91.

HUANG, JOE C. *Heroes And Villains In Communist China,* pp. 183–95.

TOBINO, MARIO (Italian, 1910–)
THE UNDERGROUND (El clandestino, 1962)

ROSENGARTEN, FRANK. "The Italian Resistance Novel (1945-1962)," in *From Verismo To Experimentalism,* ed. Sergio Pacifici, pp. 234–36.

Reviews
MITGANG, HERBERT. "Medusa Was No Respecter of Politics." *Saturday Review,* 5 February 1966, p. 50.

TOLSTOY, ALEXEI (Russian, 1883–1945)
THE ROAD TO CALVARY (Syostry, 1922)

MATHEWSON, RUFUS. "Four Novels," in *Major Soviet Writers,* ed. Edward J. Brown, pp. 341–45.

TOLSTOY, LEO NIKOLAYEVICH (Russian, 1828–1910)
GENERAL

ALDANOV, MARK. "The Enigma of Tolstoy," in *Twentieth-Century Russian Literary Criticism,* ed. Victor Erlich, pp. 201–11.

ANZULOVIC, BRANIMIR. "Tolstoi and the Novel." *Genre,* 3 (1970), 1–16.

BARKSDALE, E. C. *The Dacha And The Duchess,* pp. 77-95.

BAUMGARTEN, MURRAY. "Irtenev, Olenin, Levin: Three Characters in Search of Nature." *Centennial Review,* 14 (1970), 188-200.

CURTIS, JAMES M. "Notes on Spatial Form in Tolstoy." *Sewanee Review,* 78 (1970), 517-30.

DYCK, J. W. "Aspects of Nihilism in German and Russian Literature: Nietzsche-Tolstoy." *Humanities Association Review,* 25 (1974), 187-96.

EIKHENBAUM, BORIS. "On Lev Tolstoy." Trans. Ray J. Parrott, jr. and Philip E. Frantz. *Russian Literature Triquarterly,* No. 10 (1974), pp. 198-200.

––––––. "On Tolstoy's Crises," in *Twentieth-Century Russian Literary Criticism,* ed. Victor Erlich, pp. 97-101.

FLOROVSKY, GEORGES. "Three Masters: The Quest for Religion in Nineteenth-Century Russian Literature." *Comparative Literature Studies,* 3 (1966), 133-36.

HEADINGS, PHILIP R. "The Question of Exclusive Art: Tolstoy and T. S. Eliot's *The Waste Land.*" *Revue Des Langues Vivantes,* 32 (1966), 82-95.

HEIER, EDMUND. "Tolstoj and the Evangelical Revival Among Russian Aristocracy." *Russian Literature,* No.1 (1971), pp. 28-48.

LEDNICKI, WACŁAW. "Tolstoy Between War and Peace." *California Slavic Studies,* 4 (1967), 73-91.

McLAUGHLIN, SIGRID. "Some Aspects of Tolstoy's Intellectual Development: Tolstoy and Shopenhauer." *California Slavic Studies,* 5 (1970), 187-245.

MATUAL, DAVID. "On the Poetics of Tolstoj's *Confession.*" *Slavic And East European Journal,* 19 (1975), 276-87.

MUCHNIC, HELEN. "About Tolstoy, Chekhov, Gorky," in her *Russian Writers,* pp. 194-99.

––––––. "Tolstoy the Great," in her *Russian Writers,* pp. 119-25.

OULIANOFF, NICHOLAS. "Tolstoy's Nationalism." *Review Of National Literatures,* 3, No.1 (1972), 101-24.

RAHV, PHILIP. "Tolstoy: The Green Twig and the Black Trunk," in his *Literature And The Sixth Sense,* pp. 134-39.

RALEIGH, JOHN HENRY. "Tolstoy and Sight: the Dual Nature of Reality." *Essays In Criticism,* 21 (1971), 170-79.

RUDY, PETER. "Lev Tolstoj's Apprenticeship to Laurence Sterne." *Slavic And East European Journal,* 15 (1971), 1-21.

SHIFMAN, A. "Tolstoy and Gandhi." *Indian Literature,* 12, No.1 (1969), 5-20.

SHKLOVSKIJ, VIKTOR. "Parallels in Tolstoy," in *Twentieth-Century Russian Literary Criticism,* ed. Victor Erlich, pp. 81-85.

ŠILBAJORIS, RIMVYDAS. "Lev Tolstoj: Esthetics and Art." *Russian Literature,* No.1 (1971), pp. 58-62.

SIMMONS, ERNEST J. "Tolstoy—'My Hero is Truth,'" in his *Introduction To Russian Realism,* pp. 135-80.

SOKOLSKY, ANATOLE A. "Leo N. Tolstoy: On the Occasion of the 140th Anniversary of His Birth in 1828." *USF Language Quarterly,* 7, No.3/4 (1969), 2-4.

SPEIRS, LOGAN. "Lawrence's Debt to Tolstoy in *The Rainbow,*" in his *Tolstoy And Chekhov,* pp. 227-37.

SPURDLE, SONIA. "Tolstoy and Martin Du Gard's *Les Thibault.*" *Comparative Literature,* 23 (1971), 325-45.

WESTON, BRUCE. "Leo Tolstoy and the Ascetic Tradition." *Russian Literature Triquarterly,* No.3 (1972), pp. 297-309.

WILLETT, MAURITA. "Tolstoy's Triunity: Truth, Simplicity, and Love." *Ball State University Forum,* 11, No.2 (1970), 53-59.

ANNA KARENINA (1877)

BENSON, RUTH C. *Women In Tolstoy,* pp. 75-110.

BLUMBERG, EDWINA JANNIE. "Tolstoy and the English Novel: A Note on *Middlemarch* and *Anna Karenina.*" *Slavic Review,* 30 (1971), 561-69.

BOYD, ALEXANDER F. *Aspects Of The Russian Novel,* pp. 87-108.

CALL, PAUL. "Anna Karenina's Crime and Punishment. The Impact of Historical Theory upon the Russian Novel." *Mosaic,* 1, No.1 (1967), 94-102.

CHRISTIAN, R. F. *Tolstoy: A Critical Introduction,* pp. 165-211.

DAVIES, RUTH. *The Great Books Of Russia,* pp. 276-92.

FREEBORN, R. H. "Realism in Russia, to the Death of Dostoevsky," in *The Age Of Realism,* ed. F. W. J. Hemmings, pp. 121-26.

GERSCHENKRON, ALEXANDER. "Time Horizon in Russian Literature." *Slavic Review,* 34 (1975), 711-12.

GREENWOOD, E. B. *Tolstoy: The Comprehensive Vision,* pp. 103-18.

GUNN, ELIZABETH. *A Daring Coiffeur,* pp. 91-146.

HEIER, EDMUND. "Tolstoj and the Evangelical Revival Among Russian Aristocracy." *Russian Literature,* No.1 (1971), pp. 32-37.

JONES, W. GARETH. "George Eliot's 'Adam Bede' and Tolstoy's Conception of 'Anna Karenina.'" *Modern Language Review,* 61 (1966), 473-81.

LEAVIS, F. R. "Anna Karenina: Thought and Significance in a Great Creative Work," in his *Anna Karenina And Other Essays,* pp. 9-32.

LEONTIEV, KONSTANTIN. "The Novels of Count L. N. Tolstoy: Analysis, Style, and Atmosphere—A Critical Study," in *Essays In Russian Literature,* ed. Spencer E. Roberts, pp. 225-356.

McLAUGHLIN, SIGRID. "Some Aspects of Tolstoy's Intellectual Development: Tolstoy and Shopenhauer." *California Slavic Studies,* 5 (1970), 207-16.

MUCHNIC, HELEN. "The Steeplechase in *Anna Karenina,*" in her *Russian Writers,* pp. 126-38.

PURSGLOV, MICHAEL. "The Smiles of *Anna Karenina.*" *Slavic And East European Journal,* 17 (1973), 42-48.

REEVE, F. D. *The Russian Novel,* pp. 236-73.

SCHULTZE, SYDNEY. "The Chapter in *Anna Karenina.*" *Russian Literature Triquarterly,* No. 10 (1974), pp. 351-59.

––––––. "Notes on Imagery and Motifs in *Anna Karenina.*" *Russian Literature Triquarterly,* No.1/2 (1971), 366-74.

SIMMONS, ERNEST J. *Introduction To Tolstoy's Writings,* pp. 83-93.

––––––. *Tolstoy,* pp. 93-102.

––––––. "Tolstoy—'My Hero is Truth,'" in his *Introduction To Russian Realism,* pp. 166-74.

SLADE, TONY. "*Anna Karenina* and the Family Ideal." *Southern Review: Literary And Interdisciplinary Essays,* 1, No.1 (1963), 85-90.

SPEIRS, LOGAN. "*Anna Karenina*—A Study in Structure." *Neophilologus,* 50 (1966), 3-27.

––––––. "The Structuring of *Anna Karenina,*" in his *Tolstoy And Chekhov,* pp. 84-116.

––––––. "Tolstoy's Morality in *Anna Karenina* and in *A Confession,*" in his *Tolstoy And Chekhov,* pp. 117-27.

SPENCE, G. W. *Tolstoy The Ascetic,* pp. 49-58.

STEVENS, MARTIN. "A Source for Frou-Frou in *Anna Karenina.*" *Comparative Literature,* 24 (1972), 63-71.

TROYAT, HENRI. *Tolstoy,* pp. 358-72.

CHILDHOOD, BOYHOOD, AND YOUTH (1852-1857)

BAUMGARTEN, MURRAY. "Irtenev, Olenin, Levin: Three Characters in Search of Nature." *Centennial Review,* 14 (1970), 188–93.

CHRISTIAN, R. F. *Tolstoy: A Critical Introduction,* pp. 20–38, 41–46.

GREENWOOD, E. B. *Tolstoy: The Comprehensive Vision,* pp. 22–28.

RUDY, PETER. "Lev Tolstoj's Apprenticeship to Laurence Sterne." *Slavic And East European Journal,* 15 (1971), 10–17.

THE COSSACKS (Kazaki, 1863)

BAUMGARTEN, MURRAY. "Irtenev, Olenin, Levin: Three Characters in Search of Nature." *Centennial Review,* 14 (1970), 193–98.

BENSON, RUTH C. *Women In Tolstoy,* pp. 16–22.

BONDANELLA, PETER F. "Rousseau, The Pastoral Genre, and Tolstoy's *The Cossacks.*" *Southern Humanities Review,* 3 (1969), 288–92.

CHRISTIAN, R. F. *Tolstoy: A Critical Introduction,* pp. 67–77.

GREENWOOD, E. B. *Tolstoy: The Comprehensive Vision,* pp. 43–46.

HAGAN, JOHN. "Ambivalence in Tolstoy's 'The Cossacks.'" *Novel,* 3 (1969), 28–47.

THE DEATH OF IVAN ILYCH (1886)

CATE, HOLLIS L. "*On Death And Dying* in Tolstoy's 'The Death of Ivan Ilych.'" *Hartford Studies In Literature,* 7 (1975), 195–205.

CHRISTIAN, R. F. *Tolstoy: A Critical Introduction,* pp. 236–38.

DAVIES, RUTH. *The Great Books Of Russia,* pp. 293–95.

DAYANANDA, Y. J. "*The Death Of Ivan Ilych:* A Psychological Study *On Death And Dying.*" *Literature And Psychology,* 22 (1972), 191–98.

GREENWOOD, E. B. *Tolstoy: The Comprehensive Vision,* pp. 121–24.

LEONTIEV, KONSTANTIN. "The Novels of Count L. N. Tolstoy: Analysis, Style, and Atmosphere—A Critical Study," in *Essays In Russian Literature,* ed. Spencer E. Roberts, pp. 274–78.

OLNEY, JAMES. "Experience, Metaphor, and Meaning: 'The Death of Ivan Ilych.'" *Journal Of Aesthetics And Art Criticism,* 31 (1972), 101–14.

RAHV, PHILIP. "The Death of Ivan Ilyich and Joseph K.," in his *Literature And The Sixth Sense,* pp. 38–54.

SIMONE, R. THOMAS. "The Mythos of 'The Sickness Unto Death': Kurosawa's *Ikiru* and Tolstoy's *The Death Of Ivan Ilych.*" *Literature/Film Quarterly,* 3 (1975), 2–12.

SOROKIN, BORIS. "Ivan Il'ich as Jonah: A Cruel Joke." *Canadian-American Slavic Studies,* 5 (1971), 487–507.

SPEIRS, LOGAN. "Chekhov and the Later Tolstoy: Studies in Death," in his *Tolstoy And Chekhov,* pp. 141–53.

SPENCE, G. W. *Tolstoy The Ascetic,* pp. 63–68.

TURNER, C. J. G. "The Language of Fiction: Word-Clusters in Tolstoy's 'The Death of Ivan Ilyich.'" *Modern Language Review,* 65 (1970), 116–21.

ZIMMERMAN, EUGENIA N. "Death and Transfiguration in Proust and Tolstoy." *Mosaic,* 6, No.2 (1973), 161–72.

FAMILY HAPPINESS (Semeinoe schaste, 1859)

BENSON, RUTH C. *Women In Tolstoy,* pp. 23–44.

GREENWOOD, E. B. *Tolstoy: The Comprehensive Vision,* pp. 47–50.

SPEIRS, LOGAN. "*Family Happiness:* A Prelude," in his *Tolstoy And Chekhov,* pp. 11–15.

HADJI MURAD (Khadzhi Murat, 1911)

CHRISTIAN, R. F. *Tolstoy: A Critical Introduction,* pp. 240–46.

DWORSKY, NANCY. "*Hadji Murad:* A Summary and a Vision." *Novel,* 8 (1975), 138–46.

SPEIRS, LOGAN. "*Resurrection* and *Hadji Murad,*" in his *Tolstoy And Chekhov,* pp. 132–34.

SPENCE, G. W. *Tolstoy The Ascetic,* pp. 74–77.

WOODWARD, JAMES B. "Tolstoy's 'Hadji Murat': The Evolution of its Theme and Structure." *Modern Language Review,* 68 (1973), 870–82.

THE KREUTZER SONATA (Kreitserova sonata, 1890)

BENSON, RUTH C. *Women In Tolstoy,* pp. 111–34.

CHRISTIAN, R. F. *Tolstoy: A Critical Introduction,* pp. 230–34.

ELLIS, KEITH. "Ambiguity and Point of View in Some Novelistic Representations of Jealousy." *MLN,* 86 (1971), 891–99.

GREENWOOD, E. B. *Tolstoy: The Comprehensive Vision,* pp. 137–40.

McLAUGHLIN, SIGRID. "Some Aspects of Tolstoy's Intellectual Development: Tolstoy and Shopenhauer." *California Slavic Studies,* 5 (1970), 233–38.

SIMMONS, ERNEST J. *Introduction To Tolstoy's Writings,* pp. 155–58.

TROYAT, HENRI. *Tolstoy,* pp. 465–85.

MASTER AND MAN (Khozyain i rabotnik, 1895)

DAVIES, RUTH. *The Great Books Of Russia,* pp. 296–97.

HAGAN, JOHN. "Detail and Meaning in Tolstoy's 'Master and Man.'" *Criticism,* 11 (1969), 31–58.

SPENCE, G. W. *Tolstoy The Ascetic,* pp. 71–74.

THE POWER OF DARKNESS

DONSKOV, ANDREW. "Tolstoj's Use of Proverbs in *The Power Of Darkness.*" *Russian Literature,* No.9 (1975), pp. 67–80.

RESURRECTION (Voskresenie, 1899)

CHRISTIAN, R. F. *Tolstoy: A Critical Introduction,* pp. 218–29.

DAVIES, RUTH. *The Great Books Of Russia,* pp. 297–306.

GREENWOOD, E. B. *Tolstoy: The Comprehensive Vision,* pp. 142–46.

HEIER, EDMUND. "Tolstoj and the Evangelical Revival Among Russian Aristocracy." *Russian Literature,* No.1 (1971), pp. 44–48.

SIMMONS, ERNEST J. *Introduction To Tolstoy's Writings,* pp. 187–98.

SPEIRS, LOGAN. "*Resurrection* and *Hadji Murad,*" in his *Tolstoy And Chekhov,* pp. 128–32.

SPENCE, G. W. *Tolstoy The Ascetic,* pp. 128–44.

TROYAT, HENRI. *Tolstoy,* pp. 535–56.

WAR AND PEACE (Voina i mir, 1869)

BENSON, RUTH C. *Women In Tolstoy,* pp. 45–74.

BIER, JESSE. "A Century of *War And Peace*—Gone, Gone With the Wind." *Genre,* 4 (1971), 107–41.

CAIN, TOM. "Tolstoy's Use of *David Copperfield.*" *Critical Quarterly,* 15 (1973), 237–46.

CHRISTIAN, R. F. *Tolstoy: A Critical Introduction,* pp. 97–164.

CURTIS, JAMES M. "The Function of Imagery in *War And Peace.*" *Slavic Review,* 29 (1970), 460–80.

DAVIES, RUTH. *The Great Books Of Russia,* pp. 259–75.

DEBRECZENY, PAUL. "Freedom and Necessity: A Reconsideration of *War And Peace.*" *Papers On Language And Literature,* 7 (1971), 185–98.

DUKAS, VYTAS and GLENN A. SANDSTROM. "Taoistic Patterns in *War And Peace.*" *Slavic And East European Journal,* 14 (1970), 182–93.

FEUER, KATHRYN B. "Alexis de Tocqueville and the Genesis of War and Peace." *California Slavic Studies,* 4 (1967), 92–118.

FREEBORN, R. H. "Realism in Russia, to the Death of Dostoevsky," in *The Age Of Realism,* ed. F. W. J. Hemmings, pp. 116-21.

———. *The Rise Of The Russian Novel,* pp. 208-66.

GREENSPAN, ELAINE. "Tolstoy: Colossus in the Classroom." *English Journal,* 57 (1968), 965-71.

GREENWOOD, E. B. *Tolstoy: The Comprehensive Vision,* pp. 65-102.

———. "Tolstoy's Poetic Realism in *War And Peace.*" *Critical Quarterly,* 11 (1969), 219-32.

GUNN, ELIZABETH. *A Daring Coiffeur,* pp. 3-87.

HAGAN, JOHN. "A Pattern of Character Development in Tolstoj's *War And Peace:* P'er Bezuxov." *Texas Studies In Literature And Language,* 11 (1969), 985-1011.

———. "A Pattern of Character Development in *War And Peace:* Prince Andrej." *Slavic And East European Journal,* 13 (1969), 164-90.

———. "Patterns of Character Development in Tolstoy's *War And Peace:* Nicholas, Natasha, and Mary." *PMLA,* 84 (1969), 235-44.

HARKINS, WILLIAM E. "A Note on the Use of Narrative and Dialogue in *War And Peace.*" *Slavic Review,* 29 (1970), 86-92.

JEPSEN, LAURA. "Prince Andrey as Epic Hero in Tolstoy's 'War and Peace.'" *South Atlantic Bulletin,* 34, No.4 (1969), 5-7.

LENGYEL, JÓZSEF. "Marginal Notes on Tolstoy's *War And Peace.*" *Mosaic,* 6, No.2 (1973), 85-102.

LEONTIEV, KONSTANTIN. "The Novels of Count L. N. Tolstoy: Analysis, Style, and Atmosphere—A Critical Study," in *Essays In Russian Literature,* ed. Spencer E. Roberts, pp. 225-356.

LYNGSTAD, ALEXANDRA H. "Tolstoj's Use of Parentheses in *War And Peace.*" *Slavic And East European Journal,* 16 (1972) 403-13.

McLAUGHLIN, SIGRID. "Some Aspects of Tolstoy's Intellectual Development: Tolstoy and Shopenhauer." *California Slavic Studies,* 5 (1970), 189-200.

RALEIGH, JOHN HENRY. "Tolstoy and the Ways of History." *Novel,* 2 (1968), 55-68.

REXROTH, KENNETH. "Classics Revisited—LIV: 'War and Peace.'" *Saturday Review,* 11 November 1967, pp. 10, 62; rpt. in his *Classics Revisited,* pp. 263-67.

RZHEVSKY, NICHOLAS. "The Shape of Chaos: Herzen and *War And Peace.*" *Russian Review,* 34 (1975), 367-81.

SILBAJORIS, RIMVYDAS. "Pasternak and Tolstoj: Some Comparisons." *Slavic And East European Journal,* 11 (1967), 23-34.

SIMMONS, ERNEST J. *Introduction To Tolstoy's Writings,* pp. 64-82.

———. *Tolstoy,* pp. 79-92.

———. "Tolstoy—'My Hero is Truth,'" in his *Introduction To Russian Realism,* pp. 149-66.

SPEIRS, LOGAN. "Introduction to a Study of *War And Peace,*" in his *Tolstoy And Chekhov,* pp. 16-22.

———. "The Pattern of *War And Peace,*" in his *Tolstoy And Chekhov,* pp. 23-63.

———. "Tolstoy's Thinking in *War And Peace.*" *Neophilologus,* 53 (1969), 423-39; rpt. in his *Tolstoy And Chekhov,* pp. 64-83.

SPENCE, G. W. *Tolstoy The Ascetic,* pp. 33-46.

STATES, BERT O. "The Hero and the World: Our Sense of Space in *War And Peace.*" *Modern Fiction Studies,* 11 (1965), 153-64.

STRAKHOV, NIKOLAI. "Tolstoy's *War And Peace,*" in *Literature And National Identity,* ed. Paul Debreczeny and Jesse Zeldin, pp. 119-67.

THALE, JEROME. "*War And Peace:* The Art of Incoherence." *Essays In Criticism,* 16 (1966), 398-415.

TOLSTOY, LEO. *War And Peace: The Maud Translation, Backgrounds And Sources, Essays In Criticism.* Ed. George Gibian.

TROYAT, HENRI. *Tolstoy,* pp. 299-315.

ZOLOTUSSKY, IGOR. "War and Peace: the Book and the Film: a Soviet View." *London Magazine,* NS 8, No. 12 (1969), 57-64.

TOMIZZA, FULVIO

L'ALBERO DE SOGNI (1969)

Reviews
BIASIN, GIAN-PAOLO. "The Tree of Life." *Forum Italicum,* 4 (1970), 101-3.

TORING, KNUT

GENERAL

ALEXIS, GERHARD T. "Vilhelm Moberg: You Can Go Home Again." *Scandanavian Studies,* 40 (1968), 225-32.

TORRENTE BALLESTER, GONZALO (Spanish, 1910-)

LA SAGA/FUGA DE J. B. (1972)

Reviews
RUGG, EVELYN. *Hispania,* 57 (1974), 603-4.

TORSVAN, TRISTAN see TRAVEN, B.

TŌSAN, SHIMAZAKI (Japanese, 1872-1943) pseudonym of Haruki Shimazaki

GENERAL

McCLELLAN, EDWIN. "The Impressionistic Tendency in Some Modern Japanese Writers." *Chicago Review,* 17, No.4 (1965), 52-56.

———. *Two Japanese Novelists: Sōseki And Tōson,* pp. 73-78.

BEFORE THE DAWN (Yoakemae, 1935)

McCLELLAN, EDWIN. *Two Japanese Novelists: Sōseki And Tōson,* pp. 137-63.

THE BROKEN COMMANDMENT (Hakai, 1906)

McCLELLAN, EDWIN. *Two Japanese Novelists: Sōseki And Tōson,* pp. 79-93.

Reviews
McCLELLAN, EDWIN. *Journal Of Japanese Studies,* 2 (1975), 169-71.

THE HOUSE (Ie)

McCLELLAN, EDWIN. *Two Japanese Novelists: Sōseki And Tōson,* pp. 101-23.

A NEW LIFE (Shinsei, 1919)

McCLELLAN, EDWIN. *Two Japanese Novelists: Sōseki And Tōson,* pp. 123-37.

SPRING (Haru, 1908)

McCLELLAN, EDWIN. *Two Japanese Novelists: Sōseki And Tōson,* pp. 93-101.

TOURNIER, MICHEL (French, 1924-)

THE OGRE (Le roi des aulnes, 1970)

WHITE, J. J. "Signs of Disturbance: The Semiological Import of Some Recent Fiction by Michel Tournier and Peter Handke." *Journal Of European Studies,* 4 (1974), 237-54.

TOZZI, FEDERIGO (Italian, 1883–1920)

GENERAL

PACIFICI, SERGIO. *The Modern Italian Novel: From Capuana To Tozzi,* pp. 136–64.

RIMANELLI, GIOSE. "Federigo Tozzi: Misfit and Master." *Italian Quarterly,* 14, No.56 (1971), 29–76.

DIARY OF A CLERK (Ricordi di un impiegato, 1927)

DEBENEDETTI, GIACOMO. "Federigo Tozzi: A Psychologial Interpretation," in *From Verismo To Experimentalism,* ed. Sergio Pacifici, pp. 106–10.

PACIFICI, SERGIO. *The Modern Italian Novel: From Capuana To Tozzi,* pp. 144–47.

THE FARM (Il podere, 1921)

PACIFICI, SERGIO. *The Modern Italian Novel: From Capuana To Tozzi,* pp. 151–56.

THREE CROSSES (Tre croci, 1920)

DEBENEDETTI, GIACOMO. "Federigo Tozzi: A Psychological Interpretation," in *From Verismo To Experimentalism,* ed. Sergio Pacifici, pp. 117–18.

PACIFICI, SERGIO. *The Modern Italian Novel: From Capuana To Tozzi,* pp. 156–62.

RIMANELLI, GIOSE. "Federigo Tozzi: Misfit and Master." *Italian Quarterly,* 14, No.56 (1971), 66–70.

WITH CLOSED EYES (Con gli occhi chiusi, 1919)

DEBENEDETTI, GIACOMO. "Federigo Tozzi: A Psychological Interpretation," in *From Verismo To Experimentalism,* ed. Sergio Pacifici, pp. 114–16.

PACIFICI, SERGIO. *The Modern Italian Novel: From Capuana To Tozzi,* pp. 147–51.

TRABA, MARTA

LOS LABERTINOS INSOLADOS

WALLER, CLAUDIA JOAN. "Light and Darkness in Marta Traba's *Los Labertinos Insolados.*" *Romance Notes,* 14 (1972), 262–68.

TRANQUILLI, Secondo see SILONE, Ignazio

TRAVEN, B. (Mexican, 1882?–)

GENERAL

BAUMANN, MICHAEL L. "Reflections on B. Traven's Language." *Modern Language Quarterly,* 36 (1975), 403–17.

MILLER, CHARLES H. "Our Great Neglected Wobbly." *Michigan Quarterly Review,* 6 (1967), 57–61.

THE COTTON-PICKERS (Die Baumwollpflücker, 1929)

MILLER, CHARLES H. "Our Great Neglected Wobbly." *Michigan Quarterly Review,* 6 (1967), 57–61.

Reviews
GELLER, STEPHEN. *Saturday Review,* 19 July 1969, p. 40.

THE DEATH SHIP: AN ESCAPE FANTASY (Das Totenschiff)

BRAYBROOKE, NEVILLE. "The Hero Without a Name." *Queen's Quarterly,* 76 (1969), 312–18.

CHANKIN, DONALD O. "Traven's *The Death Ship: An Escape Fantasy.*" *Texas Quarterly,* 18, No.2 (1975), 157–67.

FRASER, JOHN. "Rereading Traven's *The Death Ship.*" *Southern Review,* NS, 9 (1973), 69–92.

_____. "Splendour in Darkness: B. Traven's *The Death Ship.*" *Dalhousie Review,* 44 (1964), 35–43.

THE WOBBLY see THE COTTONPICKERS

TROFIMOV, NICOLAI

NA TIKHOM BEREGU

Reviews
HEIMAN, LEO. "Cloak-and-Dagger Literature Behind the Iron Curtain." *East Europe,* 14, No.1 (1965), 55–56.

TROYAT, HENRI (French, 1911–)

L'ARAIGNE (1938)

GEORGE, K. E. M. "The Rôle of the Suffix in Troyat's *L'araigne.*" *Modern Languages,* 50 (1969), 107–11.

AN EXTREME FRIENDSHIP (Une extreme amitie, 1963)

Reviews
LESAGE, LAURENT. "Tender Triangle." *Saturday Review,* 11 May 1968, p. 80.

LA NEIGE EN DEUIL (1952)

HARRISON, M. J. "The Imagery in Troyat's *La Neige En Deuil.*" *Modern Languages,* 52 (1971), 151–56.

LA PIERRE, LA FEUILLE ET LES CISEAUX (1972)

BOAK, DENNIS. "The Case of Henri Troyat." *International Fiction Review,* 1 (1974), 143–46.

TRUSS, JAN (Canadian, 1925–)

BIRD AT THE WINDOW (1974)

Reviews
PORTER, HELEN. "New Alberta Novelist No.1." *Journal Of Canadian Fiction,* 4, No.3 (1975), 180–82.

TS'AO CHAN (Chinese, 1715–1763)

THE DREAM OF THE RED CHAMBER (Hung-lou meng, 1792)

FU, JAMES S. "Liu Lao-and the Garden of Takuanyüan." *Literature East And West,* 17 (1973), 305–14.

HSIA, C. T. *The Classic Chinese Novel,* pp. 245–97.

REXROTH, KENNETH. "Classics Revisited—XXI: Dream of the Red Chamber." *Saturday Review,* 1 January 1966, p. 19; rpt. in his *Classics Revisited,* pp. 204–8.

WESTBROOK, FRANCIS A. "On Dreams, Saints, and Fallen Angels: Reality and Illusion in *Dream Of The Red Chamber* and *The Idiot.*" *Literature East And West,* 15 (1971), 371–91.

TS'AO HSUEH-CH'IN see TS'AO CHAN

TSUBOUCHI SHŌYŌ (Japanese, 1859–1935)
pseudonym of Tsubouchi Yūzō

IMOTOSE KAGAMI

RYAN, MARLEIGH GRAYER. *The Development Of Realism In The Fiction Of Tsubouchi Shōyō,* pp. 56–86.

MATSU NO UCHI

RYAN, MARLEIGH GRAYER. *The Development Of Realism In The Fiction Of Tsubouchi Shōyō,* pp. 87–101.

SAIKUN

RYAN, MARLEIGH GRAYER. *The Development Of Realism In The Fiction Of Tsubouchi Shōyō,* pp. 102–20.

TŌSEI SHOSEI KATAGI (1885)

RYAN, MARLEIGH GRAYER. *The Development Of Realism In The Fiction Of Tsubouchi Shōyō,* pp. 30–55.

TSUSHIMA, SHUJI see DESAI OSAMU

TUCKER, JAMES (Australian)
RALPH RASHLEIGH

ARGYLE, BARRY. *An Introduction To The Australian Novel, 1830-1930*, pp. 60-83.

_____. "Ralph Rashleigh." *Ariel: A Review Of International English Literature*, 2, No.1 (1971), 5-25.

BOEHM, HAROLD J. "The Date of Composition of *Ralph Rashleigh*." *Australian Literary Studies*, 6 (1973/4), 428-30.

HEALY, J. J. "The Convict and the Aborigine: The Quest for Freedom in *Ralph Rashleigh*." *Australian Literary Studies*, 3 (1968), 243-53.

TUN, MAO
MIDNIGHT

LAU, JOSEPH S. M. "Naturalism in Modern Chinese Fiction." *Literature East And West*, 12 (1968), 151-56.

TU PENG-CHENG
DEFENSE OF YENAN (Pao-wei Yen-an)

HUANG, JOE C. *Heroes And Villains In Communist China*, pp. 148-80.

TURGENEV, IVAN (Russian, 1818-1883)
GENERAL

CHAMBERLIN, WILLIAM HENRY. "Ivan Turgenev: Romantic Humanist." *Saturday Review*, 18 June 1966, pp. 24-25, 52.

DELANY, PAUL AND DOROTHY E. YOUNG. "Turgenev and the Genesis of 'A Painful Case.'" *Modern Fiction Studies*, 20 (1974), 217-21.

FREEBORN, RICHARD. "Turgenev at Ventnor." *Slavonic And East European Review*, 51 (1973), 387-412.

JACKSON, ROBERT LOUIS. "The Root and the Flower: Dostoevsky and Turgenev: A Comparative Esthetic." *Yale Review*, 63 (1973), 228-50.

KAPPLER, RICHARD GEORGES. "Ivan S. Turgenev As a Critic of French Literature." *Comparative Literature*, 20 (1968), 133-41.

MOSER, CHARLES A. "Turgenev: The Cosmopolitan Nationalist." *Review Of National Literatures*, 3, No.1 (1972), 56-88.

MUCHNIC, HELEN. "Turgenev: A Life," in her *Russian Writers*, pp. 185-87.

_____. "Turgenev: The Novelist's Novelist," in her *Russian Writers*, pp. 188-91.

TERRAS, VICTOR. "Turgenev's Aesthetic and Western Realism." *Comparative Literature*, 22 (1970), 19-35.

WADDINGTON, PATRICK. "Turgenev and Trollope: Brief Crossings of Paths." *AUMLA*, No. 42 (1974), pp. 199-201.

WOODWARD, JAMES B. "Typical Images in the Later Tales of Turgenev." *Slavic And East European Journal*, 17 (1973), 18-32.

DIARY OF A SUPERFLUOUS MAN

DUKAS, VYTAS AND RICHARD H. LAWSON. "*Werther* and *Diary Of A Superfluous Man*." *Contemporary Literature*, 21 (1969), 146-54.

FATHERS AND SONS (Otcy i Deti, 1862)

BACHMAN, CHARLES R. "Tragedy and Self-Deception in Turgenev's *Fathers And Sons*." *Revue Des Langues Vivantes*, 34 (1968), 269-76.

BLAIR, JOEL. "The Architecture of Turgenev's *Fathers And Sons*." *Modern Fiction Studies*, 19 (1973/4), 555-63.

BOYD, ALEXANDER. *Aspects Of The Russian Novel*, pp. 68-86.

BURNS, VIRGINIA M. "The Structure of the Plot in *Otcy I Deti*." *Russian Literature*, No.6 (1974), pp. 33-53.

CHAMBERLIN, VERNON A. and JACK WEINER. "Galdós' *Doña Perfecta* and Turgenev's *Fathers And Sons*: Two Interpretations of the Conflict between Generations." *PMLA*, 86 (1971), 19-24.

DAVIES, RUTH. *The Great Books Of Russia*, pp. 82-90.

FREEBORN, R. H. "Realism in Russia, to the Death of Dostoevsky," in *The Age Of Realism*, ed. F. W. J. Hemmings, pp. 110-12.

MAZLISH, BRUCE. "The Changing Face of Oedipus: Fathers and Sons in Modern Times." *Columbia Forum*, NS, 4, No.1 (1975), 21-23.

REEVE, F. D. *The Russian Novel*, pp. 119-58.

REXROTH, KENNETH. "Classics Reivisited—XXI." *Saturday Review*, 14 September 1968, p. 29.

HOME OF THE GENTRY (Dvorjanskoe gnezdo, 1859)

DAVIES, RUTH. *The Great Books Of Russia*, pp. 79-81.

GRIGOREV, APOLLON. "A Nest of the Gentry by Ivan Turgenev," in *Literature And National Identity*, ed. Paul Debreczeny and Jesse Zeldin, pp. 65-118.

RUDIN (1856)

DAVIES, RUTH. *The Great Books Of Russia*, pp. 75-79.

FREEBORN, R. H. "Realism in Russia, to the Death of Dostoevsky," in *The Age Of Realism*, ed. F. W. J. Hemmings, pp. 105-7.

SMITH, RAOUL N. "The Stylistic Use of Syntactic Features in Some Russian Novels." *Language And Style*, 6 (1973), 127-34.

SMOKE (Dym, 1867)

DAVIES, RUTH. *The Great Books Of Russia*, pp. 90-94.

VIRGIN SOIL (1877)

BRIGGS, ANTHONY D. "Someone Else's Sledge: Further Notes on Turgenev's *Virgin Soil* and Henry James's *The Princess Casamassima*." *Oxford Slavonic Papers*, NS 5 (1972), 52-60.

DAVIES, RUTH. *The Great Books Of Russia*, pp. 94-99.

DELBAERE-GARANT, JEANNE. "Henry James's Divergences from his Russian Model in *The Princess Casamassima*." *Revue Des Langues Vivantes*, 37 (1971), 535-44.

TUTUOLA, AMOS (Nigerian, 1922-)
GENERAL

COLLINS, HAROLD R. *Amos Tutuola*.

_____. "A Theory of Creative Mistakes and the Mistaking Style of Amos Tutuola." *World Literature Written In English*, 13 (1974), 155-71.

LINDFORS, BERNTH. "Amos Tutuola and D. O. Fagunwa." *Journal Of Commonwealth Literature*, No.9 (1970), pp. 57-65.

_____. "Amos Tutuola: Debts and Assets." *Cahiers D'Études Africaines*, 10, No.38 (1970), 306-34.

McDOWELL, ROBERT E. "Three Nigerian Storytellers: Okara, Tutuola, and Ekwensi." *Ball State University Forum*, 10, No.3 (1969), 69-73.

MOORE, GERALD. "Amos Tutuola: A Nigerian Visionary," in *Introduction To African Literature*, ed. Ulli Beier, pp. 179-87.

NEUMARKT, PAUL. "Amos Tutuola: Emerging African Literature." *American Imago*, 28 (1971), 129-45.

OBIECHINA, E. N. "Amos Tutuola and the Oral Tradition." *Presence Africaine*, No.65 (1968), pp. 85-106.

ROSCOE, ADRIAN A. *Mother Is Gold*, pp. 98-113.

TAKACS, SHERRYL. "Oral Tradition in the Works of A. Tutuola." *Books Abroad,* 44 (1970), 392-98.

BRAVE AFRICAN HUNTRESS (1958)

CARTEY, WILFRED. *Whispers From A Continent,* pp. 371-74.

FEATHER WOMAN OF THE JUNGLE (1962)

LAURENCE, MARGARET. *Long Drums And Cannons,* pp. 140-46.

MY LIFE IN THE BUSH OF GHOSTS (1954)

LAURENCE, MARGARET. *Long Drums And Cannons,* pp. 132-36.

LINDFORS, BERNTH. "Amos Tutuola's Television-handed Ghostess." *Ariel: A Review Of International English Literature,* 2, No.1 (1971), 68-77; rpt. in his *Folklore In Nigerian Literature,* pp. 61-72; rpt. in *Readings In Commonwealth Literature,* ed. William Walsh, pp. 142-51.

THE PALM-WINE DRINKARD AND HIS DEAD PALM-WINE TAPSTER IN THE DEAD'S TOWN (1952)

ANOZIE, S. O. "Structure and Utopia in Tutuola's *Palm Wine Drinkard.*" *Conch,* 2, No.2 (1970), 80-88.

ARMSTRONG, ROBERT P. "The Narrative and Intensive Continuity: *The Palm Wine Drinkard.*" *Research In African Literatures,* 1 (1970), 9-34.

ARNASON, DAVID. "Amos Tutuola's *The Palm Wine Drinkard:* The Nature of Tutuola's Achievement." *Journal Of Canadian Fiction,* 3, No.4 (1975), 56-59.

CARTEY, WILFRED. *Whispers From A Continent,* pp. 363-66.

DATHORNE, O. R. "Amos Tutuola: The Nightmare of the Tribe," in *Introduction To Nigerian Literature,* ed. Bruce King, pp. 64-76.

EDWARDS, PAUL. "The Farm and Wilderness in Tutuola's *The Palm-Wine Drinkard.*" *Journal Of Commonwealth Literature,* 9, No.1 (1974), 57-65.

FERGUSON, JOHN. "Nigerian Prose Literature in English." *English Studies In Africa,* 9 (1966), 43-46.

JONES, ELDRED. "Turning Back the Pages III: Amos Tutuola—The Palm Wine Drinkard: Fourteen Years On." *Association For African Literature In English Bulletin,* No. 4 (1966), pp. 24-30.

LARSON, CHARLES R. "Time, Space, and Description: The Tutuolan World," in his *The Emergence Of African Fiction,* rev. ed., pp. 93-112.

LAURENCE, MARGARET. *Long Drums And Cannons,* pp. 127-32.

LESLIE, OMOLARA. "*The Palm-Wine Drinkard:* A Reassessment of Amos Tutuola." *Journal Of Commonwealth Literature,* No.9 (1970), pp. 48-56.

LINDFORS, BERNTH. "Amos Tutuola's *The Palm-Wine Drinkard* and Oral Tradition." *Critique,* 11, No.1 (1968), 42-50.

————. *Folklore In Nigerian Literature,* pp. 32-40, 51-59.

————. "Oral Tradition and the Individual Literary Talent." *Studies In The Novel,* 4 (1972), 203-10.

MOORE, GERALD. *The Chosen Tongue,* pp. 163-66.

NEUMARKT, PAUL. "Amos Tutuola: Emerging African Literature." *American Imago,* 28 (1971), 136-39.

OGUNDIPE, MOLARA. "The Palm Wine Drinkard: A Reassessment of Amos Tutuola." *Presence Africaine,* No.71 (1969), pp. 99-108.

POVEY, JOHN. "The English Language of the Contemporary African Novel." *Critique,* 11, No.3 (1968/9), 85-86.

SIMBI AND THE SATYR OF THE DARK JUNGLE (1955)

CARTEY, WILFRED. *Whispers From A Continent,* pp. 367-71.

LAURENCE, MARGARET. *Long Drums And Cannons,* pp. 136-38.

TY-CASPER, LINDA (Philippine, 1931-)

THE PENINSULARS (1964)

CASPER, LEONARD. *New Writing From The Philippines,* pp. 134-37.

U

UNAMUNO, MIGUEL DE (Spanish, 1864–1936)

GENERAL

BARCIA, JOSÉ RUBIA. "Unamuno the Man," in *Unamuno: Creator And Creation*, ed. José Rubia Barcia and M. A. Zeitlin, pp. 4–25.

BASDEKIS, DEMETRIOS. "Cervantes in Unamuno: Toward a Clarification." *Romanic Review*, 60 (1969), 178–85.

———. *Unamuno And Spanish Literature*.

BATCHELOR, R. C. *Unamuno Novelist: A European Perspective*.

BLANCO-AGUINAGA, CARLOS. "'Authenticity' and the Image," in *Unamuno: Creator And Creation*, ed. José Rubia Barcia and M. A. Zeitlin, pp. 48–71.

BRAUN, LUCILLE V. "'Ver que me ves': Eyes and Looks in Unamuno's Works." *MLN*, 90 (1975), 212–30.

BUTT, J. W. "Unamuno's Idea of *Intrahistoria;* Its Origins and Significance," in *Studies In Modern Spanish Literature And Art*, ed. Nigel Glendinning, pp. 13–24.

CASTRO, AMÉRICO. "In Lieu of Prologue," in *Unamuno: Creator And Creation*, ed. José Rubia Barcia and M. A. Zeitlin, pp. 1–3.

CLOSE, A. J. "*Don Quixote* and Unamuno's Philosophy of Art," in *Studies In Modern Spanish Literature And Art*, ed. Nigel Glendinning, pp. 25–44.

CROWE, ELIZABETH P. "Miguel de Unamuno 1864–1936: A Restless Spirit." *Studies: An Irish Quarterly Review*, 55 (1966), 285–98.

DONOSO, ANTÓN. "Philosophy as Autobiography: A Study of the Person of Miguel de Unamuno." *Personalist*, 49 (1968), 183–96.

EARLE, PETER G. "Unamuno: *Historia* and *Intra-Historia*," in *Spanish Thought And Letters In The Twentieth Century*, ed. Germán Bleiberg and E. Inman Fox, pp. 179–86.

FOSTER, DAVID WILLIAM. "The 'Belle Dame Sans Merci' in the Fiction of Miguel de Unamuno." *Symposium*, 20 (1966), 321–28.

FOX, E. INMAN. "Maeztu and Unamuno: Notes on Two Spanish Intellectuals of 1898," in *Spanish Thought And Letters In The Twentieth Century*, ed. Germán Bleiberg and E. Inman Fox, pp. 207–17.

ILIE, PAUL. "Moral Psychology in Unamuno," in *Unamuno: Creator And Creation*, ed. José Rubia Barcia and M. A. Zeitlin, pp. 72–91.

LIVINGSTONE, LEON. "The Novel as Self-Creation," in *Unamuno: Creator And Creation*, ed. José Rubia Barcia and M. A. Zeitlin, pp. 92–115.

MEREGALLI, FRANCO. "Clarin and Unamuno: Parallels and Divergences," in *Unamuno: Creator And Creation*, ed. José Rubia Barcia and M. A. Zeitlin, pp. 156–70.

MORA, JOSÉ FERRATER. "Unamuno Today," in *Unamuno: Creator And Creation*, ed. José Rubia Barcia and M. A. Zeitlin, pp. 220–33.

NOZICK, MARTIN. "Unamuno and the Second Spanish Republic," in *Spanish Thought And Letters In The Twentieth Century*, ed. Germán Bleiberg and E. Inman Fox, pp. 379–93.

OTERO, C. P. "Unamuno and Cervantes," in *Unamuno: Creator And Creation*, ed. José Rubia Barcia and M. A. Zeitlin, pp. 171–87.

PAYNE, STANLEY. "Unamuno's Politics," in *Unamuno: Creator And Creation*, ed. José Rubia Barcia and M. A. Zeitlin, pp. 203–19.

SÁNCHEZ-REULET, ANÍBAL. "Unamuno's Other Spain," in *Unamuno: Creator And Creation*, ed. José Rubia Barcia and M. A. Zeitlin, pp. 188–202.

SCOTT, NINA M. "Unamuno and Painting." *Hispanofila*, 55 (1975), 57–66.

STERN, ALFRED. "Unamuno: Pioneer of Existentialism," in *Unamuno: Creator And Creation*, ed. José Rubia Barcia and M. A. Zeitlin, pp. 26–47.

UNGERER, GUSTAV. "Unamuno and Shakespeare," in *Spanish Thought And Letters In The Twentieth Century*, ed. Germán Bleiberg and E. Inman Fox, pp. 513–32.

VAREY, J. E. "*Maese Miguel:* Puppets as a Literary Theme in the Work of Unamuno," in *Spanish Thought And Letters In The Twentieth Century*, ed. Germán Bleiberg and E. Inman Fox, pp. 559–72.

ABEL SÁNCHEZ (Abel Sánchez, 1917)

BASDEKIS, DEMETRIOS. *Miguel De Unamuno*, pp. 28–31.

DOBSON, A. "Unamuno's *Abel Sánchez:* An Interpretation." *Modern Languages*, 54 (1973), 62–67.

KRONIK, JOHN W. "Unamuno's *Abel Sánchez* and Alas's *Benedictino:* A Thematic Parallel," in *Spanish Thought And Letters In The Twentieth Century*, ed. Germán Bleiberg and E. Inman Fox, pp. 287–97.

MARÍAS, JULIÁN. *Miguel De Unamuno*, pp. 94–101.

NOZICK, MARTIN. *Miguel De Unamuno*, pp. 150–52.

SLADE, CAROLE. "Unamuno's *Abel Sánchez:* 'L'Ombre Dolenti Nella Ghiaccia' (Inf. XXXII, 35)." *Symposium*, 28 (1974), 356–65.

TURNER, DAVID G. *Unamuno's Webs Of Fatality*, pp. 63–77.

AMOR Y PEDAGOGÍA (1902)

FRANZ, THOMAS R. "Ancient Rites and the Structure of Unamuno's *Amor Y Pedagogia*." *Romance Notes*, 13 (1971), 217–20.

MARÍAS, JULIÁN. *Miguel De Unamuno,* pp. 85–88.

NOZICK, MARTIN. *Miguel De Unamuno,* pp. 144–47.

OLSON, PAUL R. "The Novelistic Logos in Unamuno's *Amor Y Pedagogia.*" *MLN,* 84 (1969), 248–68.

TURNER, DAVID G. *Unamuno's Webs of Fatality,* pp. 27–43.

VAREY, J. E. "*Maese Miguel:* Puppets as a Literary Theme in the Work of Unamuno," in *Spanish Thought And Letters In The Twentieth Century,* ed. Germán Bleiberg and E. Inman Fox, pp. 563–69.

CÓMO SE HACE UNA NOVELA (1927)

NEWBERRY, WILMA. *The Pirandellian Mode In Spanish Literature From Cervantes To Sastre,* pp. 82–85.

NOZICK, MARTIN. *Miguel De Unamuno,* pp. 107–10.

TURNER, DAVID G. *Unamuno's Webs Of Fatality,* pp. 107–21.

UNA HISTORIA DE AMOR

TURNER, DAVID G. *Unamuno's Webs Of Fatality,* pp. 145–49.

MIST (Niebla, 1914)

ABRAMS, FRED. "Unamuno's Menendez y Pelayo Cryptogram in *Niebla.*" *Papers On Language And Literature,* 11 (1975), 203–5.

ALTER, ROBERT. *Partial Magic,* pp. 154–58.

BASDEKIS, DEMETRIOS. *Miguel De Unamuno,* pp. 24–28.

BERNS, GABRIEL. "Another Look Though Unamuno's *Niebla:* Augusto Pérez, 'Agonista-Lector.'" *Romance Notes,* 11 (1969), 26–29.

FRANZ, THOMAS R. "Menéndez y Pelayo as Antolin S. Paparrigopulos of Unamuno's *Niebla.*" *Papers On Language And Literature,* 9 (1973), 84–88.

MARÍAS, JULIÁN. *Miguel De Unamuno,* pp. 88–94.

NEWBERRY, WILMA. *The Pirandellian Mode In Spanish Literature From Cervantes To Sastre,* pp. 73–82.

NOZICK, MARTIN. *Miguel De Unamuno,* pp. 147–50.

PARKER, ALEXANDER A. "On the Interpretation of *Niebla,*" in *Unamuno: Creator And Creation,* ed. José Rubia Barcia and M. Z. Zeitlin, pp. 116–38.

RIBBANS, GEOFFREY. "The Structure of Unamuno's *Niebla,*" in *Spanish Thought And Letters Of The Twentieth Century,* ed. Germán Bleiberg and E. Inman Fox, pp. 395–406.

TULL, J. F., Jr. "Alienation, Psychological and Metaphysical, in Three 'Nivolas' of Unamuno." *Humanities Association Bulletin,* 21, No. 1 (1970), 28–29.

TURNER, DAVID G. *Unamuno's Webs Of Fatality,* pp. 44–62.

WEBER, FRANCES W. "Unamuno's *Niebla:* from Novel to Dream." *PMLA,* 88 (1973), 209–18.

NADA MENOS QUE TODO UN HOMBRE

JOHNSON, CARROLL B. "Unamuno and His Spanish Past: *Nada Menos Que Todo Un Hombre.*" *Kentucky Romance Quarterly,* 15 (1968), 319–40.

TULL, J. F., Jr. "Alienation, Psychological and Metaphysical, in Three 'Nivolas' of Unamuno." *Humanities Association Bulletin,* 21, No. 1 (1970), 29–31.

LA NOVELA DE DON SANDALIO, JUGADOR DE AJEDREZ

MARÍAS, JULIÁN. *Miguel De Unamuno,* pp. 101–04.

STEVENS, JAMES R. "Unamuno's *Don Sandalio:* Two Opposed Concepts of Fiction." *Romance Notes,* 11 (1969), 266–71.

TURNER, DAVID G. *Unamuno's Webs Of Fatality,* pp. 129–38.

OUR LORD DON QUIXOTE (Vida de Don Quijote y Sancho, 1905)

Reviews

WILSON, FRANCIS G. "The Magnificent Madmen." *Mundus Artium,* 12 (1968), 415–16.

PAZ EN LA GUERRA (1897)

MARÍAS, JULIÁN. *Miguel De Unamuno,* pp. 78–85.

NOZICK, MARTIN. *Miguel De Unamuno,* pp. 140–44.

TURNER, DAVID G. *Unamuno's Webs Of Fatality,* pp. 9–26.

UN POBRE HOMBRE RICO

TURNER, DAVID G. *Unamuno's Webs Of Fatality,* pp. 138–45.

SAINT EMMANUEL THE GOOD, MARTYR (San Manuel Bueno, Mártir, 1933)

MARÍAS, JULIÁN. *Miguel De Unamuno,* pp. 113–18.

NATELLA, ARTHUR A. "Saint Theresa and Unamuno's *San Manuel Bueno, Mártir.*" *Papers On Language And Literature,* 5 (1969), 458–64.

NOZICK, MARTIN. *Miguel De Unamuno,* pp. 160–67.

SHERGOLD, N. D. "Unamuno's Novelistic Technique in *San Manuel Bueno, Mártir,*" in *Studies In Modern Spanish Literature And Art,* ed. Nigel Glendinning, pp. 163–80.

TULL, J. F., Jr. "Alienation, Psychological and Metaphysical, in Three 'Nivolas' of Unamuno." *Humanities Association Bulletin,* 21, No. 1 (1970), 31–32.

TURNER, DAVID G. *Unamuno's Webs Of Fatality,* pp. 122–29.

VALDÉS, MARIO J. "Faith and Despair: A Comparative Study of Narrative Theme." *Hispania,* 49 (1966), 373–79.

LA TÍA TULA (1921)

MARÍAS, JULIÁN. *Miguel De Unamuno,* pp. 104–13.

NOZICK, MARTIN. *Miguel De Unamuno,* pp. 154–57.

TURNER, DAVID G. *Unamuno's Webs Of Fatality,* pp. 92–106.

DIE UNGLUCKLICHE FURSTIN AUS WEIN (Author Unknown)

HADLEY, MICHAEL. *The German Novel In 1790,* pp. 100–3.

UNSET, SIGRID (Norwegian, 1882–1949)

THE AXE

DUNN, MARGARET MARY. "*The Master Of Hestviken:* A New Reading." *Scandinavian Studies,* 38 (1966), 283–89.

THE BURNING BUSH (Den brennende busk, 1930)

BAYERSCHMIDT, CARL F. *Sigrid Undset,* pp. 128–37.

THE FAITHFUL WIFE (Den trofaste hustru, 1936)

BAYERSCHMIDT, CARL F. *Sigrid Undset,* pp. 143–47.

FRU MARTA OULIE (1907)

BAYERSCHMIDT, CARL F. *Sigrid Undset,* pp. 55–58.

GUNNAR'S DAUGHTER (Fortellingen om Viga-Ljot og Vigdis, 1909)

BAYERSCHMIDT, CARL F. *Sigrid Undset,* pp. 62–67.

GYMNADENIA (1929)

BAYERSCHMIDT, CARL F. *Sigrid Undset,* pp. 128–37.

IDA ELISABETH (1932)

BAYERSCHMIDT, CARL F. *Sigrid Undset,* pp. 137–43.

IN THE WILDERNESS

DUNN, MARGARET MARY. "*The Master Of Hestviken:* A New Reading, II." *Scandinavian Studies,* 40 (1968), 210–17.

JENNY (1911)

BAYERSCHMIDT, CARL F. *Sigrid Undset,* pp. 68–74.

KRISTIN LAVRANSDATTER (Kransen, 1920–22)

BAYERSCHMIDT, CARL F. *Sigrid Undset,* pp. 91–111.

DEN LYKKELIGE ALDER (1908)

BAYERSCHMIDT, CARL F. *Sigrid Undset,* pp. 58–62.

MADAME DOROTHEA (1938)

BAYERSCHMIDT, CARL F. *Sigrid Undset,* pp. 147–54.

THE MASTER OF HESTVIKEN (1925–27)

BAYERSCHMIDT, CARL F. *Sigrid Undset,* pp. 111–27.

DUNN, MARGARET MARY. "*The Master Of Hestviken:* A New Reading." *Scandinavian Studies,* 38 (1968), 281–94.

DUNN, MARGARET MARY. "*The Master Of Hestviken:* A New Reading, II." *Scandinavian Studies,* 40 (1968), 210–24.

THE SNAKE PIT

DUNN, MARGARET MARY. "*The Master Of Hestviken:* A New Reading." *Scandinavian Studies,* 38 (1966), 289–94.

THE SON AVENGER

DUNN, MARGARET MARY. "*The Master Of Hestviken:* A New Reading, II." *Scandinavian Studies,* 40 (1968), 217–23.

VAAREN

BAYERSCHMIDT, CARL F. *Sigrid Undset,* pp. 77–81.

UPADHYAY, VISHWAMBHAR

REECH (1967)

Reviews

SHIVPURI, JAGDISH. "The Heroic Plane: A Tragedy of Progress." *Indian Writing Today,* No.1 (1967), pp. 38–40.

URONDO, FRANCISCO

LOS PASOS PREVIOS

Reviews

TATUM, CHARLES M. *Chasqui,* 5, No.2 (1976), 89–93.

URZIDIL, JOHANNES (German, 1896–1970)

GENERAL

BERGER, DAVID. "Literature: A Conversation with Johannes Urzidil." *American-German Review,* 32, No.1 (1965), 23–24.

USIGLI, RODOLFO (Mexican, 1905–1979)

CROWN OF SHADOWS (Corona de sombra, 1943)

DAUSTER, FRANK. "Aristotle and Vargas Llosa: Literature, History and the Interpretation of Reality." *Hispania,* 53 (1970), 273.

USLAR PIETRI, ARTURO (Venezuelan, 1906–)

THE RED LANCES (Las lanzas coloradas, 1931)

BRUSHWOOD, JOHN S. *The Spanish American Novel,* pp. 89–91.

V

VACULÍK, LUDVÍK (Czechoslovak, 1926-)

THE AXE (Sekyra, 1966)

> EAGLE, HERBERT. "Ludvík Vaculík's *The Axe:* A Quest for Human Dignity." *Books Abroad,* 49 (1975), 7-12.

THE GUINEA PIGS (Morčata, 1977)

> **Reviews**
> OSERS, EWALD. *London Magazine,* NS 14, No.6 (1975), 137-39.

VAIČIULAITIS, ANTANAS (Lithuanian, 1906-)

GENERAL

> ŠILBAJORIS, RIMVYDAS. *Perfection Of Exile,* pp. 56-76.

VALENTINA (1936)

> ŠILBAJORIS, RIMVYDAS. *Perfection Of Exile,* pp. 58-66.

VAILLAND, ROGER (French, 1907-1965)

FETE (La Fête, 1960)

> FLOWER, J. E. *Roger Vailland: The Man And His Masks,* pp. 137-47.

THE LAW (La Loi, 1957)

> FLOWER, J. E. *Roger Vailland: The Man And His Masks,* pp. 119-31.

PLAYING FOR KEEPS (Drôle de jeu, 1946)

> FLOWER, J. E. *Roger Vailland: The Man And His Masks,* pp. 37-51.

THE SOVEREIGNS see FETE

325.000 FRANCS (1956)

> FLOWER, J. E. "Roger Vailland: *325.000 Francs.*" *Modern Languages,* 53 (1972), 63-71.

THE TROUT (La truite, 1964)

> FLOWER, J. E. *Roger Vailland: The Man And His Masks,* pp. 144-51.

> **Reviews**
> ROSE, MARILYN GADDIS. *French Review,* 40 (1966), 171-72.

TURN OF THE WHEEL (Les Mauvais Coups, 1959)

> FLOWER, J. E. *Roger Vailland: The Man And His Masks,* pp. 47-51.

VAITKUS, MYKOLAS

THE DELUGE

> **Reviews**
> MATULIS, ANATOLE C. "A Novel on Biblical Past." *Lituanus,* 12, No.3 (1966), 72-73.

VALDES, HERNAN

ZOOM (1971)

> **Reviews**
> MASSEY, KENNETH W. *Chasqui,* 2, No.3 (1973), 65-67.

VALERA (Y ALCALÁ GALIANO), JUAN (Spanish, 1824-1905)

GENERAL

> MARCUS, ROXANNE B. "Contemporary Life and Manners in the Novels of Juan Valera." *Hispania,* 58 (1975), 454-66.

> SMITH, PAUL. "Juan Valera and the Illegitimacy Motif." *Hispania,* 51 (1968), 804-11.

PEPITA JIMENEZ (1874)

> KNOWLTON, JOHN F. "The Hippolytus Myth in *Pepita Jiménez.*" *Romance Notes,* 11 (1969), 73-75.

> LOTT, ROBERT E. *Language And Psychology In <Pepita Jiménez.>*

> RUTHERFORD, J. D. and F. W. J. HEMMINGS. "Realism in Spain and Portugual," in *The Age Of Realism,* ed. F. W. J. Hemmings, pp. 280-82.

VALLE-INCLÁN, RAMÓN DE (Spanish, 1869-1936)

GENERAL

> BOUDREAU, HAROLD L. "Banditry and Valle-Inclan's *Ruedo Iberico.*" *Hispanic Review,* 35 (1967), 85-92.

> FLYNN, GERARD COX. "*Psiquismo:* The Principle of the *Sonata* of Don Ramón del Valle-Inclan," in *Spanish Thought And Letters Of The Twentieth Century,* ed. Germán Bleiberg and E. Inman Fox, pp. 201-6.

> LIMA, ROBERT. *Ramón Del Valle-Inclán.*

> RAMÍREZ, MANUEL D. "Valle-Inclan's Self-Plagiarism in Plot and Characterization." *Revista De Estudios Hispánicos.* 6 (1972), 71-83.

> TERRY, BARBARA A. "The Influence of Casanova and Barbey d'Aurevilly on the *Sonatas* of Valle-Inclan." *Revista De Estudios Hispánicos,* 1 (1967), 61-88.

BAZA DE ESPADAS

SMITH, VERITY. *Ramón Del Vallé-Inclán,* pp. 140-45.

CARTEL DE FERIAS

SINCLAIR, ALISON. "The First Fragment of *El Ruedo Ibérico?"* *Bulletin Of Hispanic Studies,* 49 (1972), 165-74.

LA CORTE DE LOS MILAGROS (1927)

BOUDREAU, HAROLD L. *"La Corte De Los Milagros:* The Title in the Work." *Romance Notes,* 10 (1969), 286-91.

LA CURA DE DIOS (1972)

Reviews
FRANZ, THOMAS R. *Hispania,* 57 (1974), 600.

FLOR DE SANTIDAD (1904)

SMITH, VERITY. *Ramón Del Vallé-Inclán,* pp. 118-22.

LIGHTS OF BOHEMIA (Luces de Bohemia, 1924)

WEBER, FRANCES WYERS. *"Luces De Bohemia* and the Impossibility of Art." *MLN,* 82 (1967), 575-89.

EL RUEDO IBÉRICO (1927-28)

BOUDREAU, HAROLD L. "The Circular Structure of Valle-Inclán's *Ruedo Ibérico."* *PMLA,* 82 (1967), 128-35.

SINCLAIR, ALISON. "The First Fragment of *El Ruedo Ibérico?"* *Bulletin Of Hispanic Studies,* 49 (1972), 165-74.

SINCLAIR, ALISON. "Nineteenth-Century Popular Literature as a Source of Linguistic Enrichment in Valle-Inclán's 'Ruedo Ibérico.' " *Modern Language Review,* 70 (1975), 84-96.

SONATA DE ESTÍO (1903)

SMITH, VERITY. *Ramón Del Vallé-Inclán,* pp. 111-14.

SONATA DE OTOÑO (1902)

GULSTAD, DANIEL E. "Parody in Valle Inclán's *Sonata De Otoño."* *Revista Hispanica Moderna,* 36 (1970/1), 21-31.

THE TYRANT (Tirano banderas, novela de tierra caliente, 1926)

LIMA, ROBERT. *Ramón Del Valle-Inclán,* pp. 20-23.

SMITH, VERITY. *Ramón Del Vallé-Inclán,* pp. 127-34.

————. *Valle-Inclán: Tirano Banderas.*

VALLEJO, Manuel Mejía see MEJÍA VALLEJO, Manuel

VALLÈS, JULES (French, 1832-1885)

GENERAL

EDMONDS, BARBARA P. "In Search of Jules Vallès." *French Review,* 40 (1967), 636-42.

KRANOWSKI, NATHAN. "The Undeserved Obscurity of Jules Vallès." *Romance Notes,* 14 (1973), 501-7.

REDFERN, W. D. "Vallès and the Existential Pun." *Mosaic,* 9, No.3 (1976), 27-39.

L'ENFANT (1879)

REDFERN, W. D. "Delinquent Parents: Jules Vallès and *L'Enfant." Mosaic,* 5, No.3 (1972), 167-77.

VALLIÈRES, PIERRE (Canadian)

WHITE NIGGERS OF AMERICA

KRAFT, JAMES. "Fiction as Autobiography in Québec: Notes on Pierre Vallières and Marie-Claire Blais." *Novel,* 6 (1972), 73-78.

VAN DER POST, LAURENS (South African, 1906-)

THE HUNTER AND THE WHALE (1967)

Reviews
HANDLIN, OSCAR. *Atlantic Monthly,* 220, No.4 (1967), 141.

VARGAS LLOSA, MARIO (Peruvian, 1936-)

GENERAL

DAUSTER, FRANK. "Vargas Llosa and the End of Chivalry." *Books Abroad,* 44 (1970), 41-45.

GALLAGHER, D. P. *Modern Latin American Literature,* pp. 122-43.

MCMURRAY, GEORGE R. "The Novels of Mario Vargas Llosa." *Modern Language Quarterly,* 29 (1968), 329-40.

OVIEDO, JOSE MIGUEL, Comp. "Chronology." Trans. Susan Jean Pels. *Review,* No.14 (1974), pp. 6-11.

CONVERSATION IN THE CATHEDRAL (Conversación en La Catedral, 1969)

BRUSHWOOD, JOHN S. *The Spanish American Novel,* pp. 326-30.

CHRIST, RONALD. "Novel Form, Novel Sense." *Review,* No.14 (1974), pp. 30-36.

EDWARDS, JORGE. "The Serpent of Remorse." Trans. Tom J. Lewis. *Review,* No.14 (1974), pp. 22-25.

LUCHTING, WOLFGANG A. "Masochism, Anyone?" *Review,* No.14 (1974), pp. 12-16.

RABASSA, GREGORY. "A Conversation with the Translator." *Review,* No.14 (1974), pp. 17 21.

TURNER, FERNANDO MORENO. "A Complex Space." Trans. Renata M. Treitel. *Review,* No.14 (1974), pp. 26-29.

Reviews
CRAIN, JANE LARKIN. *Saturday Review,* 11 January 1975, p. 26.

THE GREEN HOUSE (La casa verde, 1966)

HASSETT, JOHN J. "The Reader in Vargas Llosa's La Casa Verde." *Chasqui,* 1, No.2 (1972), 24-35.

KLARÉN, SARA CASTRO. "Fragmentation and Alienation in *La Casa Verde." MLN,* 87 (1972), 286-99.

JACQUES VINGTRAS

Reviews
BRUSHWOOD, JOHN S. *Kansas City Star,* 26 January 1969; rpt. *Review,* No.1 (1968), pp. 69-71.

COLEMAN, ALEXANDER. *New York Times Book Review,* 12 January 1969; rpt. *Review,* No.1 (1968), 68-69.

POORE, CHARLES. *New York Times,* 2 January 1969; rpt. *Review,* No.1 (1968), pp. 66-68.

THE TIME OF THE HERO (La ciudad y los perros, 1962)

BRUSHWOOD, JOHN S. *The Spanish American Novel,* pp. 253-56.

DAUSTER, FRANK. "Aristotle and Vargas Llosa: Literature, History and the Interpretation of Reality." *Hispania,* 53 (1970), 274-76.

HANCOCK, JOEL. "Animalization and Chiaroscuro Techniques: Descriptive Language in *La Ciudad Y Los Perros [The City And The Dogs]." Latin American Literary Review,* 4, No.7 (1975), 37-47.

MCMURRAY, GEORGE R. "Form and Content Relationships in Vargas Llosa's 'La ciudad y los perros.' " *Hispania,* 56 (1973), 579-86.

VASCONCELLOS, JORGE FERREIRA DE (Portuguese, ca. 1515-ca. 1563)

GENERAL

PIPER, ANSON C. "Courtly Love in the Works of Jorge Ferreira de Vasconcellos." *South Atlantic Bulletin,* 34, No.4 (1969), 7-9.

––––––. "Jorge Ferreira de Vasconcellos and the Spirit of Empire." *Hispania,* 50 (1967), 44-48.

––––––. "The Lisbon of Jorge Ferreira de Vasconcellos." *Luso-Brazilian Review,* 4, No.1 (1967), 17-25.

VASCONCELOS, José Mauro de see MAURO DE VASCONCELAS, José

VASIL'EV, ARKADI

BLUE MONDAY

EVENTOV, ISAAK S. "Laughter Is a Sign of Strength." *Soviet Studies In Literature,* 1, No.1 (1964/5), 10-14.

VASSILIKOS, VASSILIS (Greek, 1933-)

Z (Zeta, 1966)

Reviews
CLEMENTS, ROBERT J. "Prefiguring the Coup." *Saturday Review,* 16 November 1968, p. 51.

VATSYAYAN, S. H. see AGYEYA

VÁZQUEZ MONTALBÁN, MANUEL

RECORDANDO A DARDÉ (1969)

Reviews
BUTLER, C. W. *Hispania,* 54 (1971), 199-200.

VEDRÈS, NICOLE

GENERAL

SMITH, ANNETTE J. "Beyond Feminism: The Works of Nicole Vedrès." *Women's Studies,* 2 (1974), 79-89.

VEGA CARPIO, LOPE FELIX DE (Spanish, 1562-1635)

LA DOROTEA (1632)

ROTHBERG, IRVING P. "Two Similar Zeugmas in Cervantes and Lope." *Romance Notes,* 7 (1965), 51-53.

TRUEBLOOD, ALAN S. *Experience And Artistic Expression In Lope De Vega: The Making Of <La Dorotea.>*

LAS FORTUNAS DE DIANA

YUDIN, FLORENCE L. "The *Novela Corta* as *Comedia:* Lope's *Las Fortunas De Diana.*" *Bulletin Of Hispanic Studies,* 45 (1968), 181-88.

EL PEREGRINO EN SU PATRIA

Reviews
WILLIAMSEN, VERN G. *Hispania,* 56 (1973), 174-75.

VEIGU, JOSÉ J.

THE THREE TRIALS OF MANIREMA

Reviews
YATES, DONALD A. *Saturday Review,* 12 September 1970, pp. 33-34.

VELA, ARQUELES (Mexican, 1899-)

EL CAFE DE NADIE

BRUSHWOOD, JOHN S. *The Spanish American Novel,* pp. 52-55.

VERCORS (French, 1902-) pseudonym of Jean Bruller

QUOTA (1966)

Reviews
LESAGE, LAURENT. "Too Much and Maybe Too Late." *Saturday Review,* 12 March 1966, pp. 39, 152.

THE RAFT OF THE MEDUSA (Le radeau de la Méduse, 1969)

Reviews
BEAUCHAMP, WILLIAM. *Saturday Review,* 11 September 1971, p. 44.

YOU SHALL KNOW THEM (Les animaux dénaturés, 1952)

KOLBERT, J. "From Novel to Play: Vercor's Transformation of *Les Animaux Dénaturés* into *Zoo.*" *French Review,* 39 (1965), 398-409.

VERGA, GIOVANNI (Italian, 1840-1922)

GENERAL

BIASIN, GIAN-PAOLO. "The Sicily of Verga and Sciascia." *Italian Quarterly,* 9, No.34/5 (1965), 3-13.

DE VITO, ANTHONY J. "Disasters and Disease in the Work of Giovanni Verga." *Italica,* 46 (1969), 279-91.

––––––. "Politics and History in the Work of Giovanni Verga." *Forum Italicum,* 3 (1969), 386-403.

PACIFICI, SERGIO. *The Modern Italian Novel: From Manzoni To Svebo,* pp. 98-128.

––––––. "The Tragic World of Verga's Primitives," in *From Verismo To Experimentalism,* ed. Sergio Pacifici, pp. 3-34.

THE HOUSE BY THE MEDLAR TREE (I Malavoglia, 1881)

ALEXANDER, ALFRED. *Giovanni Verga: A Great Writer And His World,* pp. 82-86.

CARSANIGA, G. M. "Realism in Italy," in *The Age Of Realism,* ed. F. W. J. Hemmings, pp. 350-53.

CHANDLER, S. B. "The Primitive World of Giovanni Verga." *Mosaic,* 5, No.3 (1972), 117-28.

PACIFICI, SERGIO. *The Modern Italian Novel: From Manzoni To Svevo,* pp. 108-22.

––––––. "The Tragic World of Verga's Primitives," in *From Verismo To Experimentalism,* ed. Sergio Pacifici, pp. 16-29.

Reviews
CHANDLER, S. B. *Canadian Modern Language Review,* 29, No.4 (1973), 80-81.

MASTRO-DON GESUALDO (1889)

PACIFICI, SERGIO. *The Modern Italian Novel: From Manzoni To Svevo,* pp. 122-28.

––––––. "The Tragic World of Verga's Primitives," in *From Verismo To Experimentalism,* ed. Sergio Pacifici, pp. 29-34.

NEDDA (1874)

ALEXANDER, ALFRED. *Giovanni Verga: A Great Writer And His World,* pp. 71-74.

STORIA DI UNA CAPINERA (1871)

ALEXANDER, ALFRED. *Giovanni Verga: A Great Writer And His World,* pp. 53-56.

WILKIN, ANDREW. "Giovanni Verga's *Storia De Una Capinera*—100 Years On." *Modern Languages,* 52 (1971), 177-81.

SULLE LAGUNE (1863)

Reviews
PITT, RITA. *Italica,* 52 (1975), 291-94.

VERÍSSIMO, ÉRICO (Brazilian, 1905-1975)

GENERAL

MAZZARA, RICHARD A. "Structure and Verisimilitude in the Novels of Érico Veríssimo." *PMLA,* 80 (1965), 451-58.

HIS EXCELLENCY, THE AMBASSADOR (O senhor embaixador, 1967)

MAZZARA, RICHARD A. "Erico Verissimo's *O Senhor Embaixador.*" *Romance Notes,* 10 (1968), 41-44.

O TEMPO E O VENTO (1949-1962)

OLLIVIER, LOUIS L. "Universality of Yesterday: *O Tempo E O Vento.*" *Chasqui,* 4, No.1 (1974), 40-45.

VERNE, JULES (French, 1828-1905)

GENERAL

ANGENOT, MARC. "Jules Verne and French Literary Criticism." *Science-Fiction Studies,* 1 (1973), 33-37.

CHESNEAUX, JEAN. "Jules Verne's Image of the United States." *Yale French Studies,* No.43 (1969), pp. 111-27.

SERRES, MICHEL. "Jules Verne's Strange Journeys." *Yale French Studies,* No.52 (1975), pp. 174-88.

SUVIN, DARKO. "Communication in Quantified Space: The Utopian Liberalism of Jules Verne's Science Fiction." *Clio,* 4 (1974), 51-71.

WINANDY, ANDRE. "The Twilight Zone: Imagination and Reality in Jules Verne's *Strange Journeys.*" *Yale French Studies,* No.43 (1969), pp. 97-110.

AROUND THE WORLD IN EIGHTY DAYS (Le tour du monde en quatre-vingt jours, 1873)

EVANS, I. O. *Jules Verne And His Work,* pp. 69-72.

THE CLIPPER OF THE CLOUDS (Robur le conquérant, 1886)

EVANS, I. O. *Jules Verne And His Work,* pp. 93-95.

FIVE WEEKS IN A BALLOON (Cinq semaines en ballon, 1863)

EVANS, I. O. *Jules Verne And His Work,* pp. 38-42.

FROM THE EARTH TO THE MOON (De la terre à la lune, trajet direct en 97 heures, 1865-69)

EVANS, I. O. *Jules Verne And His Work,* pp. 47-49.

TWENTY THOUSAND LEAGUES UNDER THE SEA (Vingt mille lieues sous les mers, 1870)

EVANS, I. O. *Jules Verne And His Work,* pp. 59-66.

VESAAS, TARJEI (Norwegian, 1897-1970)

GENERAL

CHAPMAN, KENNETH. "Basic Themes and Motives in Vesaas' Earliest Writing." *Scandinavian Studies,* 41 (1969), 126-37.

DALE, JOHANNES A. "Tarjei Vesaas." *American Scandinavian Review,* 54 (1966), 369-74.

THE BIRDS (Fuglane, 1957)

CHAPMAN, KENNETH G. *Tarjei Vesaas,* pp. 132-38.

Reviews
NAESS, HARALD S. *Saturday Review,* 27 December 1969, p. 31.

SPECTOR, ROBERT D. *American Scandinavian Review,* 58 (1970), 199-200.

BLEIKEPLASSEN

CHAPMAN, KENNETH G. *Tarjei Vesaas,* pp. 75-80.

THE BOAT IN THE EVENING (Båten om kvelden, 1968)

Reviews

GATHORNE-HARDY, J. "Snow, Flak and Sunshine." *London Magazine,* NS 10, No.11 (1971), 96-97.

BRANNEN

CHAPMAN, KENNETH G. *Tarjei Vesaas,* pp. 139-45.

THE BRIDGES (Bruene, 1966)

CHAPMAN, KENNETH G. *Tarjei Vesaas,* pp. 153-61.

Reviews
SPECTOR, ROBERT D. *American Scandinavian Review,* 59 (1971), 80.

DEI UKJENDE MENNENE (1932)

CHAPMAN, KENNETH G. *Tarjei Vesaas,* pp. 46-51.

THE GREAT CYCLE (Det store spelet, 1934)

CHAPMAN, KENNETH G. *Tarjei Vesaas,* pp. 56-60.

STENDAHL, BRITA K. "Tarjei Vesaas, A Friend." *Books Abroad,* 42 (1968), 537-39.

Reviews
SPECTOR, ROBERT D. *American Scandinavian Review,* 57 (1969), 197.

HJARTA HÖYRER SINE HEIM LANDSTONAR (1938)

CHAPMAN, KENNETH G. *Tarjei Vesaas,* pp. 64-67.

THE HOUSE IN THE DARK (Huset i mörkret, 1945)

CHAPMAN, KENNETH G. *Tarjei Vesaas,* pp. 85-89.

HUSKULD THE HERALD

CHAPMAN, KENNETH. "Basic Themes and Motives in Vesaas' Earliest Writing." *Scandinavian Studies,* 41 (1969), 133-36.

———. *Tarjei Vesaas,* pp. 23-28, 34-37.

THE ICE PALACE (Is-slottet, 1963)

CHAPMAN, KENNETH G. *Tarjei Vesaas,* pp. 146-55.

LYKKA FOR FERDESMENN (1949)

CHAPMAN, KENNETH G. *Tarjei Vesaas,* pp. 102-8.

MENNESKEBONN (1923)

CHAPMAN, KENNETH G. *Tarjei Vesaas,* pp. 28-34.

SANDELTREET (1933)

CHAPMAN, KENNETH G. *Tarjei Vesaas,* pp. 52-56.

THE SEED (Kimen, 1940)

CHAPMAN, KENNETH G. *Tarjei Vesaas,* pp. 69-77.

Reviews
ARESTAD, SVERRE. *American Scandinavian Review,* 53 (1965), 314-16.

THE SIGNAL (1950)

CHAPMAN, KENNETH G. *Tarjei Vesaas,* pp. 91-94.

SPRING NIGHT (Vårnatt, 1954)

CHAPMAN, KENNETH G. *Tarjei Vesaas,* pp. 124-29.

Reviews
ARESTAD, SVERRE. *American Scandinavian Review,* 53 (1965), 314-16.

TÅRNET (1948)

CHAPMAN, KENNETH. *Tarjei Vesaas,* pp. 80-85.

VIAN, BORIS (French, 1920-1959)

GENERAL

CISMARU, ALFRED. "An Introduction to Boris Vian." *Critique,* 14, No.1 (1972), 17-26.

GERRARD, CHARLOTTE FRANKEL. "Anti-Militarism in Vian's Minor Texts." *French Review,* 45 (1972), 1117-24.

HEINEY, DONALD. "Boris Vian, The Marx Brothers, and Jean-Sol Partre." *Books Abroad,* 49 (1975), 66-69.

WALTERS, JENNIFER. "Death and Boris Vian." *Papers On Language And Literature,* 8 (1972), 97-109.

WALTERS, JENNIFER. "The Disquieting Worlds of Lewis Carroll and Boris Vian." *Revue De Littérature Comparée,* 46 (1972), 284-94.

L'AUTOMNE À PÉKIN (1947)

CISMARU, ALFRED. *Boris Vian,* pp. 42-51.

ELLES SE RENDENT PAS COMPTE (1950)

CISMARU, ALFRED. *Boris Vian,* pp. 69-73.

ET ON TUERA TOUS LES AFFREUX (1948)

CISMARU, ALFRED. *Boris Vian,* pp. 66-69.

FROTH ON THE DAYDREAM see MOOD INDIGO

THE HEART SNATCHER (L'Arrache-coeur, 1953)

CISMARU, ALFRED. *Boris Vian,* pp. 82-88.

LERNER, MICHAEL G. "Boris Vian's 'L'Arrache-Coeur': Some Comments on his Style." *Neophilologus,* 58 (1974), 195-98.

L'HERBE ROUGE (1950)

CISMARU, ALFRED. *Boris Vian,* pp. 73-82.

J'IRAI CRACKER SUR VOS TOMBES

CISMARU, ALFRED. *Boris Vian,* pp. 28-34.

MOOD INDIGO (L'écume des jours, 1947)

CISMARU, ALFRED. *Boris Vian,* pp. 54-66.

Reviews
BALAKIAN, ANNA. "Threnody in Blue." *Saturday Review,* 28 December 1968, p.34.

LES MORTS ONT TOUS LA MÊME PEAU (1947)

CISMARU, ALFRED. *Boris Vian,* pp. 51-54.

TROUBLE DANS LES ANDAINS (1966)

CISMARU, ALFRED. *Boris Vian,* pp. 88-91.

VERCOQUIN ET LE PLANCTON (1946)

CISMARU, ALFRED. *Boris Vian,* pp. 34-42.

VICAN, GEORGES (French, 1924-)

LES AVENTURES HUMAINES (1964)

Reviews
LOWE, ROBERT W. *French Review,* 40 (1967), 857.

VIETA, EZEQUIEL (Cuban, 1922-)

VIVIR EN CANDONGA

MENTON, SEYMOUR. *Prose Fiction Of The Cuban Revolution,* pp. 95-97.

VIGANÒ, RENATA

L'AGNESE VA A MORIRE

KLOPP, CHARLES D. "Nature and Human Nature in Renata Viga-

nò's *L'Agnese Va À Morire.*" *Italian Quarterly,* 19, No.73/4 (1975), 35-52.

VIGNY, ALFRED VICTOR, COMTE DE (French, 1797-1863)

CINQ-MARS (1847)

DOOLITTLE, JAMES. *Alfred De Vigny,* pp. 47-57.

VIGOUROUX, FRANÇOIS

LES NAINES BLANCHES (1972)

Reviews
GERRARD, CHARLOTTE FRANKEL. *French Review,* 47 (1974), 1025-26.

VIIRLAID, ARVED (Estonian, 1922-)

GRAVES WITHOUT CROSSES

Reviews
WOLFE, MORRIS. "The Strength to Rise." *Canadian Literature,* No.59 (1974), pp. 99-100.

VILAKAZI, BENEDICT WALLET (South African, 1906-1947)

NJE NEMPELA (1933)

NYEMBEZI, C. L. S. "The Use of Magic in Vilakazai's Novels." *African Studies,* 30 (1971), 331-39.

NOMA NINI (1935)

NYEMBEZI, C. L. S. "The Use of Magic in Vilakazai's Novels." *African Studies,* 30 (1971), 327-31.

UDINGISWAYO KAJOBE (1939)

NYEMBEZI, C. L. S. "The Use of Magic in Vilakazai's Novels." *African Studies,* 30 (1971), 315-27.

VILHJÁLMSSON, THOR (Icelandic, 1925-)

FLJOTT, FLJOTT SAGDI FUGLINN (1968)

HALLBERG, PETER. "The One Who Sees: The Icelandic Writer Thor Vilhjamsson." *Books Abroad,* 47 (1973), 54-59.

VILLASEÑOR, EDMUND

MACHO (1973)

Reviews
SANCHEZ, MARTA ESTER. *Latin American Literary Review,* 3, No.6 (1975), 99-100.

VILLEDIEU, CATHERINE DES JARDINS (French, 1640-1683)

NOUVELLES AFRIQUAINES

FROBE, EDWIN P. "The Source of Mme. de Villedieu's 'Nouvelles Afriquaines.'" *Romance Notes,* 8 (1966), 70-74.

VILLEGAS, ANTONIO DE (Spanish, ca. 1512-ca. 1551)

EL ABENCERRAJE Y DE LA HERMOSA JARIFA

GLENN, RICHARD F. "The Moral Implications of *El Abencerraje.*" *MLN,* 80 (1965), 202-9.

LA HISTORIA DE ABINDARRÁEZ Y LA HERMOSA JARIFA see EL ABENCERRAJE Y DE HERMOSA JARIFA

VIÑAS, DAVID (Argentinian, 1929-)

CAYO SOBRE SU ROSTRO (1955)

BRUSHWOOD, JOHN S. *The Spanish American Novel*, pp. 201-4.

VISALAKSHI, D.

GRAHANAM VIDICHINDI

Reviews
ANJANEYULU, D. *Indian Literature*, 11, No.3 (1968), 112-14.

VISCHER, FRIEDRICH THEODOR (German, 1807-1887)

AUCH EINER

BRUFORD, W. H. *The German Tradition Of Self-Cultivation*, pp. 147-63.

VITTORINI, ELIO (Italian, 1908-1966)

GENERAL

HEINEY, DONALD. *Three Italian Novelists*, pp. 147-63.

McCORMICK, C. A. "Elio Vittorini." *Italian Quarterly*, 10, No.39/40 (1967), 39-61.

POTTER, JOY HAMBUECHEN. "Vittorini's Literary Apprenticeship, 1926-1929." *Forum Italicum*, 3 (1969), 375-85.

CONVERSATION IN SICILY (Conversazione in Sicilia, 1941)

HEINEY, DONALD. "Elio Vittorini: The Operatic Novel," in *From Verismo To Experimentalism*, ed. Sergio Pacifici, pp. 162-82.

———. *Three Italian Novelists*, pp. 175-89.

MERRY, BRUCE. "Vittorini's Multiple Resources of Style: *Conversazione In Sicilia*." *Mosaic*, 5, No.3 (1972), 107-16.

POTTER, JOY HAMBUECHEN. "Patterns of Meaning in *Conversazione In Sicilia*." *Forum Italicum*, 9 (1975), 60-73.

SCHNEIDER, MARILYN. "Circularity as Mode and Meaning in *Conversazione In Sicilia*." *MLN*, 90 (1975), 93-108.

SHAPIRO, MARIANNE. "The *Gran Lombardo*: Vittorini and Dante." *Italica*, 52 (1975), 70-77.

ERICA (Erica e i suoi fratelli, 1956)

HEINEY, DONALD. *Three Italian Novelists*, pp. 169-75.

POTTER, JOY HAMBUECHEN. "The Poetic and Symbolic Function of Fable in *Erica*." *Italica*, 48 (1971), 51-70.

LA GARIBALDINA (1956)

HEINEY, DONALD. *Three Italian Novelists*, pp. 207-13.

MEN OR NOT (Uomini e no, 1945)

HEINEY, DONALD. *Three Italian Novelists*, pp. 189-94.

ROSENGARTEN, FRANK. "The Italian Resistance Novel (1945-1962)," in *From Verismo To Experimentalism*, ed. Sergio Pacifici, pp. 219-20.

VITTORINI, EDWINA. "Vittorini's *Uomini E No*: An Epic of the Resistance?" *Durham University Journal*, NS, 31 (1970), 65-78.

THE RED CARNATION (Il garofano rosso, 1948)

HEINEY, DONALD. *Three Italian Novelists*, pp. 163-69.

THE TWILIGHT OF THE ELEPHANT (Il Sempione strizza l'occhio al Fréjus, 1947)

HEINEY, DONALD. *Three Italian Novelists*, pp. 194-200.

WOMEN OF MESSINA (La Donne di Messina, 1949)

HEINEY, DONALD. *Three Italian Novelists*, pp. 200-6.

VIZINCZEY, STEPHEN (Canadian)

IN PRAISE OF OLDER WOMEN (1965)

Reviews
JONAS, GEORGE. "Experience and Innocence." *Canadian Literature*, No.28 (1966), pp. 57-61.

SAMSTAG, NICHOLAS. "A Seasoned Sensuality." *Saturday Review*, 23 April 1966, p. 48.

THE RULES OF CHAOS

Reviews
SPETTIGUE, D. O. "Where to Go?" *Canadian Literature*, No.45 (1970), pp. 75-76.

VLADIMOV, GEORGII (Russian, 1931-) pseudonym of G. N. Volosevich

TRI MINUTY MOLCHANIA

HOSKING, GEOFFREY. "The Search for an Image of Man in Contemporary Soviet Fiction." *Forum For Modern Language Studies*, 11 (1975), 351-54.

VOINOVICH, VLADIMIR (Russian, 1932-)

KHOCHU BYT' CHESTNYM (1963)

HOSKING, GEOFFREY. "The Search for an Image of Man in Contemporary Soviet Fiction." *Forum For Modern Language Studies*, 11 (1975), 354-57.

VOLOSEVICH, G. N. see VLADIMOV, Georgii

VOLPONI, PAOLO (Italian, 1924-)

THE WORLDWIDE MACHINE (La macchina mondiale, 1965)

Reviews
CLEMENTS, ROBERT J. "Departure from the Soil." *Saturday Review*, 9 December 1967, pp. 30-31.

VOLTAIRE, FRANÇOIS MARIE AROUET DE (French, 1694-1778)

GENERAL

AGES, ARNOLD. "Voltaire and the Rabbis: The Curious Allies." *Romanische Forschungen*, 79 (1967), 333-44.

BARBER, W. H. "Voltaire at Cirey: Art and Thought," in *Studies In Eighteenth-Century French Literature*, ed. J. H. Fox, M. H. Waddicor and D. A. Watts, pp. 1-13.

BESTERMAN, THEODORE. "The Real Voltaire Through His Letters," in *Voltaire: A Collection Of Critical Essays*, ed. William F. Bottiglia, pp. 31-63.

———. "Three Additions to Voltaire Bibliography," in *Studies In Eighteenth-Century French Literature*, ed. J. H. Fox, M. H. Waddicor, and D. A. Watts, pp. 29-30.

BRUMFITT, J. H. "The Present State of Voltaire Studies." *Forum For Modern Language Studies*, 1 (1965), 230-39.

———. "Voltaire Historian," in *Voltaire: A Collection Of Critical Essays*, ed. William F. Bottiglia, pp. 77-86.

GAY, PETER. "Voltaire's Politics: France and Consitutional Absolutism," in *Voltaire: A Collection Of Critical Essays*, ed. William F. Bottiglia, pp. 112-30.

GOSSMAN, LIONEL. "Voltaire's Heavenly City." *Eighteenth-Century Studies*, 3 (1969), 67-82.

LANSON, GUSTAVE. "The Voltairian Reformation of France," in *Voltaire: A Collection Of Critical Essays*, ed. William F. Bottiglia, pp. 131-39.

MASON, HAYDN T. "Voltaire and Camus." *Romanic Review,* 59 (1968), 198–212.

MONTY, JEANNE R. "Voltaire's Debt to the *Encyclopédie* in the *Opinion En Alphabet,*" in *Literature And History In The Age Of Ideas,* ed. Charles G. S. Williams, pp. 153–67.

NAVES, RAYMOND. "Voltaire's Wisdom," in *Voltaire: A Collection Of Critical Essays,* ed. William F. Bottiglia, pp. 150–65.

PERRY, NORMA. "French and English Merchants in the Eighteenth-Century: Voltaire Revisited," in *Studies In Eighteenth-Century French Literature,* ed. J. H. Fox, M. H. Waddicor and D. A. Watts, pp. 193–213.

POMEAU, RENÉ. "Voltaire's Religion," in *Voltaire: A Collection Of Critical Essays,* ed. William F. Bottiglia, pp. 140–49.

SENIOR, NANCY. "Voltaire and the Book of Job." *French Review,* 47 (1973), 340–47.

TATE, ROBERT S. "Voltaire and the Question of Law and Order in the Eighteenth Century: Locke against Hobbes," in *Studies In Eighteenth-Century French Literature,* ed. J. H. Fox, M. H. Waddicor, and D. A. Watts, pp. 269–85.

THOMAS, RUTH P. "The Theme of the Voyage in Voltaire's *Contes Philosophiques.*" *Kentucky Romance Quarterly,* 16 (1969), 383–95.

TORREY, NORMAN L. "Duplicity and Protective Lying," in *Voltaire: A Collection Of Critical Essays,* ed. William F. Bottiglia, pp. 18–30.

———. "Voltaire and the English Deists," in *Voltaire: A Collection Of Critical Essays,* ed. William F. Bottiglia, pp. 69–76.

VALENTI, Jack. "Voltaire's Timeless Eminence." *Saturday Review,* 11 March 1967, pp. 27, 138–39.

WADE, IRA O. "Voltaire and Madame du Châtelet," in *Voltaire: A Collection Of Critical Essays,* ed. William F. Bottiglia, pp. 64–68.

CANDIDE (1759)

BANKS, LOY OTIS. "Moral Perspective in *Gulliver's Travels* and *Candide.*" *Forum,* 4, No.7 (1965), 4–8.

BONHOMME, DENISE. *The Esoteric Substance Of Voltairian Thought,* pp. 226–342.

BOTTIGLIA, WILLIAM F. "Candide's Garden," in *Voltaire: A Collection Of Critical Essays,* ed. William F. Bottiglia, pp. 87–111.

BRADY, PATRICK. "Is *Candide* Really 'Rococo'?" *L'Esprit Créateur,* 7 (1967), 234–42.

CROCKER, LESTER G. "Professor Wolper's Interpretation of *Candide.*" *Eighteenth-Century Studies,* 5 (1971), 145–51.

DIECKMANN, HERBERT. "Philosophy and Literature in Eighteenth-Century France." *Comparative Literature Studies,* 8 (1971), 35–39.

FRAUTSHI, R. L. "Candide's Quarterings," in *Renaissance And Other Studies In Honor Of William Leon Wiley,* ed. George Bernard Daniel, pp. 93–106.

GROBE, EDWIN P. "Aspectual Parody in Voltaire's *Candide.*" *Symposium,* 21 (1967), 38–49.

GROBE, EDWIN P. "Discontinuous Aspect in Voltaire's *Candide.*" *MLN,* 82 (1967), 334–46.

GULLACE, GIOVANNI. "Voltaire's Idea of Progress and *Candide's* Conclusion." *Personalist,* 48 (1967), 167–86.

HAVENS, GEORGE R. "Some Notes on *Candide.*" *MLN,* 88 (1973), 841–47.

HENRY, PATRICK. "Candide as 'Etranger.'" *College Language Association Journal,* 19 (1976), 504–12.

JORY, D. H. "The Source of a Name in *Candide?*" *Romance Notes,* 13 (1971), 113–16.

LIEBERMAN, MARCIA R. "Moral Innocents: Ellison's *Invisible Man* and *Candide.*" *College Language Association Journal,* 15 (1971), 64–79.

McGREGOR, ROB ROY. "The Misunderstanding Over the Sabbath in *Candide.*" *Romance Notes,* 13 (1971), 288–91.

MARSLAND, AMY L. "Voltaire: Satire and Sedition." *Romanic Review,* 57 (1966), 35–40.

MASON, HAYDN. *Voltaire,* pp. 57–73.

RIDGWAY, R. S. *Voltaire And Sensibility,* pp. 239–42.

WOLPER, ROY S. "Candide, Gull in the Garden?" *Eighteenth-Century Studies,* 3 (1969), 265–77.

———. "Reply to Lester Crocker." *Eighteenth-Century Studies,* 5 (1971), 151–56.

CONTES PHILOSOPHIQUE

KEMPF, ROGER. "The Many Meals of Voltaire." *Triquarterly,* No.4 (1965), pp. 62–64.

MASON, H. T. "Voltaire's 'Contes': An 'État Présent.'" *Modern Language Review,* 65 (1970), 19–35.

HISTOIRE DU DOCTEUR AKAKIA

VARTANIAN, ARAM. "Voltaire's Quarrel with Maupertuis: Satire and Science." *L'Esprit Créateur,* 7 (1967), 252–58.

L'INGÉNU (1767)

BONHOMME, DENISE. *The Esoteric Substance Of Voltairian Thought,* pp. 343–471.

CLARK, PRISCILLA P. "'L'Ingénu': The Uses and Limitations of Naïveté." *French Studies,* 27 (1973), 278–86.

HAVENS, GEORGE R. "Voltaire's *L'Ingénu:* Composition and Publication." *Romanic Review,* 63 (1972), 261–71.

MASON, HAYDN. *Voltaire,* pp. 73–79.

RIDGWAY, R. S. *Voltaire And Sensibility,* pp. 242–47.

MICROMÉGAS (1752)

BONHOMME, DENISE. *The Esoteric Substance Of Voltairian Thought,* pp. 176–225.

HAVENS, GEORGE R. "Voltaire's *Micromégas* (1739–52): Composition and Publication." *Modern Language Quarterly,* 33 (1972), 113–18.

MASON, HAYDN. *Voltaire,* pp. 48–52.

SMITH, PETER LESTER. "New Light on the Publication of *Micromégas.*" *Modern Philology,* 73 (1975), 77–80.

LA TAUREAU BLANC (1774)

MASON, HAYDN. *Voltaire,* pp. 79–83.

ZADIG (1747)

BONHOMME, DENISE. *The Esoteric Substance Of Voltairian Thought,* pp. 25–175.

GREENE, E. J. H. "The Destiny of *Zadig.*" *L'Esprit Créateur,* 7 (1967), 243–51.

KRA, PAULINE. "Note on the Derivation of Names in Voltaire's *Zadig.*" *Romance Notes,* 16 (1975), 342–44.

MASON, HAYDN. *Voltaire,* pp. 52–57.

RIDGWAY, R. S. *Voltaire And Sensibility,* pp. 235–39.

SMITH, PETER LESTER. "A Note on the Publication of *Zadig:* Why Voltaire Cried Slander." *Romance Notes,* 16 (1975), 345–50.

WOLPER, ROY S. "*Zadig,* A Grim Comedy?" *Romanic Review,* 65 (1974), 237–48.

VYASAJI see JHA, Upendranath

W

WALIULLAH, SYED (Indian, 1922-)
TREE WITHOUT ROOTS (Lalshalu, 1949)

Reviews
BENNETT, CARL D. *Literature East And West,* 12 (1968), 315–16.

WALLACE, ELWYN
SYDNEY AND THE BUSH (1966)

Reviews
KEESING, NANCY. *Southerly,* 27 (1967), 141.

WALSER, MARTIN (German, 1927-)
GENERAL

PICKAR, GERTRUD B. "Martin Walser: The Hero of Accommodation." *Monatshefte,* 62 (1970), 357–66.

———. "Narrative Perspective in the Novels of Martin Walser." *German Quarterly,* 44 (1971), 48–57.

MARRIAGE IN PHLIPPSBURG (Die ehen in Philippsburg, 1957)

NELSON, DONALD F. "The Depersonalized World of Martin Walser." *German Quarterly,* 42 (1969), 205–11.

THOMAS, R. HINTON AND WILFRIED VAN DER WILL. *The German Novel And The Affluent Society,* pp. 86–90.

HALBZEIT (1960)

ANDREWS, R. C. "Comedy and Satire in Martin Walser's *Halbzeit.*" *Modern Languages,* 50 (1969), 6–10.

NELSON, DONALD F. "The Depersonalized World of Martin Walser." *German Quarterly,* 42 (1969), 211–15.

PARKES, K. S. "An All-German Dilemma: Some Notes on the Presentation of the Theme of the Individual and Society in Martin Walser's *Halbzeit* and Christa Wolf's *Nachdenken Über Christa T.*" *German Life And Letters,* 28 (1974), 58–61.

THOMAS, R. HINTON AND WILFRIED VAN DER WILL. *The German Novel And The Affluent Society,* pp. 90–104.

JAKOB VON GUTEN

Reviews
ZOHN, HARRY. *Saturday Review,* 20 June 1970, pp. 42–43.

THE UNICORN (Das einhorn, 1966)

THOMAS, R. HINTON AND WILFRIED VAN DER WILL. *The German Novel And The Affluent Society,* pp. 104–11.

WALTARI, MIKA (Finnish, 1908-)
THE ROMAN (Ihmiskunna viholliset, 1964)

Reviews
SPECTOR, ROBERT D. *American Scandinavian Review,* 57 (1969), 86.

WASTBERG, PER (Swedish, 1933-)
THE AIR CAGE (Luftburen, 1969)

Reviews
RABAN, JONATHAN. "On Losing the Rabbit: New Novels." *Encounter,* 40, No.5 (1973), 80–82.

WATEN, JUDAH (Russian-born Australian, 1911-)
GENERAL

WATEN, JUDAH. "My Two Literary Careers." *Southerly,* 31 (1971), 83–92.

SEASON OF YOUTH (1966)

Reviews
GEERING, R. G. *Southerly,* 27 (1967), 223–24.

SO FAR NO FURTHER (1971)

Reviews
MCCLAREN, JOHN. "New Novels." *Overland,* No.51 (1972), p. 53.

WATSON, SHEILA (Canadian, 1919-)
THE DOUBLE HOOK (1959)

CORBETT, NANCY J. "Closed Circle." *Canadian Literature,* No.61 (1974), pp. 46–53.

JONES, D. G. *Butterfly On Rock,* pp. 85–87.

LENNOX, JOHN WATT. "The Past: Themes and Symbols of Confrontation in The Double Hook and 'Le Torrent.' " *Journal Of Canadian Fiction,* 2, No.1 (1973), 70–72.

MITCHELL, BEVERLY. "Association and Allusion in The Double Hook." *Journal Of Canadian Fiction,* 2, No.1 (1973), 63–69.

MONKMAN, LESLIE. "Coyote as Trickster in The Double Hook." *Canadian Literature,* No.52 (1972), pp. 70–76.

MORRISS, MARGARET. "The Elements Transcended." *Canadian Literature,* No.42 (1969), pp. 56–71.

WEERTH, GEORG (German, 1822–1856)
FRAGMENT EINES ROMANS

RIDLEY, HUGH. "A Note on Georg Weerth's Unfinished Novel." *German Life And Letters,* 26 (1973), 275–78.

WEISE, CHRISTIAN (German, 1642–1708)
DIE DREI ARGSTEN ERZNARREN (1672)

WAGENER, HANS. *The German Baroque Novel,* pp. 86–96.

WEISS, PETER (German, 1916–)
GENERAL

MILFULL, JOHN. "From Kafka to Brecht: Peter Weiss's Development Towards Marxism." *German Life And Letters,* 20, No.1 (1966), 61–71.

NEUGROSCHEL, JOACHIM. "Peter Weiss' Search for Identity." *American-German Review,* 33, No.1 (1966), 34–36.

ROLOFF, MICHAEL. "An Interview with Peter Weiss." *Partisan Review,* 32 (1965), 220–32.

THE SHADOW OF THE COACHMAN'S BODY (Der schatten des körpers des kutschers, 1960)

CUNLIFFE, W. G. "*The Would-Be Novelist:* An Interpretation of Peter Weiss' *Der Schatten Des Korpers Des Kutschers.*" *MLN,* 86 (1971), 414–19.

PERRY, R. C. "Weiss's *Der Schatten Des Körpers De Kutschers:* A Forerunner of the Nouveau Roman?" *Germanic Review,* 47 (1972), 203–19.

WELLERSHOFF, DIETER (German, 1925–)
A BEAUTIFUL DAY (Ein schoner Tag, 1969)

Reviews
ZIOLKOWSKI, THEODORE. "Paradigms of the Recent German Novel." *Modern Language Journal,* 52 (1968), 30–31.

WENDT, ALBERT (West Samoan, 1939–)
SONS FOR THE RETURN HOME (1973)

ARVIDSON, K. O. "The Emergence of a Polynesian Literature." *World Literature Written In English,* 14 (1975), 104–8.

WERDER, HEINRICH
EDUARD ROSENHAIN ODER SCHWACHHEITEN UNSERS JAHRZEHENDS

HADLEY, MICHAEL. *The German Novel In 1790,* pp. 169–77.

WERFEL, FRANZ (Austrian, 1890–1945)
GENERAL

LEA, HENRY A. "Prodigal Sons in Werfel's Fiction." *Germanic Review,* 40 (1965), 41–54.

PACHMUSS, TEMIRA. "Dostoevsky, Werfel, and Virginia Woolf: Influences and Confluences." *Comparative Literature Studies,* 9 (1972), 416–28.

WILLIAMS, C. E. *The Broken Eagle,* pp. 60–90.

———. "The Theme of Political Activism in the Work of Franz Werfel." *German Life And Letters,* 24 (1970), 88–96.

CELLA ODER DIE UBERWINDER: VERSUCH EINES ROMANS

LEA, HENRY A. "Werfel's Unfinished Novel: Saga of the Marginal Jew." *Germanic Review,* 45 (1970), 105–14.

THE FORTY DAYS OF MUSA DAGH (Die vierzig tage des Musa Dagh, 1933)

WILLIAMS, CEDRIC E. *The Broken Eagle,* pp. 75–80.

THE PURE IN HEART (Barbara; oder, die Frömmigkeit, 1929)

WILLIAMS, C. E. *The Broken Eagle,* pp. 72–75.

———. "The Theme of Political Activism in the Work of Franz Werfel." *German Life And Letters,* 24 (1970), 88–91.

WERNER, ZACHARIAS (German, 1768–1824)
THE TWENTY-FOURTH OF FEBRUARY (Der 24. februar, 1809)

JENNINGS, LEE B. "The Freezing Flame: Zacharias Werner and the Twenty-Fourth of February." *Symposium,* 20 (1966), 24–42.

WEST, MORRIS L. (Australian, 1916–)
HARLEQUIN (1974)

Reviews
BENTLEY, ALLEN. *International Fiction Review,* 2 (1975), 87–88.

MOON IN MY POCKET (1945)

MCCALLUM, GERALD. "A Note on Morris West's First Novel." *Australian Literary Studies,* 6 (1974), 314–16.

THE TOWER OF BABEL (1967)

Reviews
WAKIN, EDWARD. "Spy in the Souks." *Saturday Review,* 24 February 1968, p. 43.

WHITE, PATRICK (Australian, 1912–)
GENERAL

BARNES, JOHN. "A Note on Patrick White's Novels," in *An Introduction To Australian Literature,* ed. C. D. Narasimhaiah, pp. 93–101.

BESTON, JOHN B. "A Brief Biography of Patrick White." *World Literature Written In English,* 12, No.2 (1973), 208–15.

———. "A Patrick White Bibliography." *World Literature Written In English,* 12, No.2 (1973), 215–29.

BESTON, ROSE MARIE. "Patrick White After the Nobel Prize." *World Literature Written In English,* 13 (1974), 91–92.

CROWCROFT, JEAN. "Patrick White: A Reply to Dorothy Green." *Overland,* No.59 (1974), pp. 49–53.

GREEN, DOROTHY. "Patrick White's Nobel Prize." *Overland,* No.57 (1973), pp. 23–25.

HELTAY, HILARY. "The Novels of Patrick White." *Southerly,* 33 (1973), 92–104.

———. "Patrick White in German." *Southerly,* 33 (1973), 421–27.

HERRING, THELMA AND G. A. WILKES. "A Conversation with Patrick White." *Southerly,* 33 (1973), 132–43.

LAWSON, ALAN. "Unmerciful Dingoes? The Critical Reception of Patrick White." *Meanjin,* 32 (1973), 379–92.

MACKENZIE, MANFRED. "Patrick White's Later Novels: A Generic Reading." *Southern Review: Literary And Interdisciplinary Essays,* 1, No.3 (1965), 5–17.

MCLAREN, JOHN. "The Image of Reality in Our Writing," in *Twentieth Century Australian Literary Criticism,* ed. Clement Semmler, pp. 235–44.

———. "Patrick White's Use of Imagery." *Australian Literary Studies,* 2 (1966), 217–20.

MCLEOD, A. L. "Patrick White: Nobel Prize for Literature 1973." *Books Abroad,* 48 (1974), 439–45.

MORLEY, PATRICIA. " 'An Honourably Failed Attempt to Convey the Ultimate': Patrick White's Fiction." *Journal Of Canadian Fiction,* 3, No.4 (1975), 60–63.

"PATRICK WHITE in *Southerly:* Some Earlier References." *Southerly,* 25 (1965), 45.

WALSH, WILLIAM. "Fiction as Metaphor: The Novels of Patrick White." *Sewanee Review,* 82 (1974), 197–211.

THE AUNT'S STORY (1958)

BESTON, JOHN and ROSE MARIE BESTON. "The Black Volcanic Hills of Meroë. Fire Imagery in Patrick White's 'The Aunt's Story.'" *Ariel: A Review Of International English Literature,* 3 (1972), 33-43.

_____. "The Several Lives of Theodora Goodman: The 'Jardin Exotique' Section of Patrick White's *The Aunt's Story.*" *Journal Of Commonwealth Literature,* 9, No.3 (1975), 1-13.

BURROWS, J. F. " 'Jardin Exotique:' The Central Phase of 'The Aunt's Story.' " *Southerly,* 26 (1966), 152-73.

HELTAY, HILARY. "The Novels of Patrick White." *Southerly,* 33 (1973), 96-99.

HERRING, THELMA. "Odyssey of a Spinster: A Study of 'The Aunt's Story.' " *Southerly,* 25 (1965), 6-22.

MACKENZIE, MANFRED. "Patrick White's Later Novels: A Generic Reading." *Southern Review: Literary And Interdisciplinary Essays,* 1, No.3 (1965), 5-17.

MORLEY, PATRICIA A. *The Mystery Of Unity: Theme And Technique In The Novels Of Patrick White,* pp. 63-84.

WALSH, WILLIAM. *A Manifold Voice,* pp. 89-98.

THE EYE OF THE STORM (1973)

BEATSON, P. R. "The Skiapod and the Eye: Patrick White's *The Eye Of The Storm.*" *Southerly,* 34 (1974), 219-32.

BESTON, ROSE MARIE. "A Self Centered Visionary: Patrick White's Latest Illuminate." *World Literature Written In English,* 13 (1974), 93-98.

CLANCY, PATRICIA. "The Actor's Dilemma: Patrick White and Henry de Montherlant." *Meanjin,* 33 (1974), 298-302.

DUTTON, GEOFFREY. "She Whipped You On." *Kansas Quarterly,* 7, No.4 (1975), 19-24.

MORLEY, PATRICIA. " 'The Road to Dover': Patrick White's *The Eye Of The Storm.*" *Humanities Association Review,* 26 (1975), 106-15.

REIMER, A. P. "The Eye of the Needle: Patrick White's Recent Novels." *Southerly,* 34 (1974), 248-66.

Reviews

BELLETTE, A. F. *Ariel: A Review Of International English Literature,* 5, No.3 (1974), 128-30.

LEMON, LEE T. "Static and Moving." *Prairie Schooner,* 48 (1974), 268-69.

McLAREN, JOHN. "The New White." *Overland,* No.57 (1973), pp. 59-60.

WEEKS, EDWARD. *Atlantic Monthly,* 233, No.2 (1974), 94-95.

HAPPY VALLEY (1939)

BESTON, JOHN B. "The Influence of John Steinbeck's *The Pastures Of Heaven* on Patrick White." *Australian Literary Studies,* 6 (1974), 317-19.

MORLEY, PATRICIA A. *The Mystery Of Unity: Theme And Technique In The Novels Of Patrick White,* pp. 33-47.

THE LIVING AND THE DEAD (1941)

MORLEY, PATRICIA A. *The Mystery Of Unity: Theme And Technique In The Novels Of Patrick White,* pp. 49-62.

WATSON, BETTY L. "Patrick White, Some Lines of Development: *The Living And The Dead* to *The Solid Mandala.*" *Australian Literary Studies,* 5 (1971), 158-67.

RIDERS IN THE CHARIOT (1961)

BURROWS, J. F. "Archetypes and Stereotypes: 'Riders in the Chariot.' " *Southerly,* 25 (1965), 46-68.

GZELL, SYLVIA. "Themes and Imagery in *Voss* and *Riders In The Chariot,*" in *Twentieth Century Australian Literary Criticism,* ed. Clement Semmler, pp. 252-67.

McLAREN, JOHN. "Patrick White's Use of Imagery," in *Twentieth Century Australian Literary Criticism,* ed. Clement Semmler, pp. 268-72.

MOORE, SUSAN. "The Quest for Wholeness in *Riders In The Chariot.*" *Southerly,* 35 (1975), 50-67.

MORLEY, PATRICIA A. *The Mystery Of Unity: Theme And Technique In The Novels Of Patrick White,* pp. 153-83.

WALSH, WILLIAM. *A Manifold Voice,* pp. 112-17.

THE SOLID MANDALA (1966)

HERRING, THELMA. "Self and Shadow: The Quest for Totality in 'The Solid Mandala.' " *Southerly,* 26 (1966), 180-89.

_____. "*The Solid Mandala:* Two Notes." *Southerly,* 28 (1968), 216-22.

MACKENZIE, MANFRED. "The Consciousness of 'Twin Consciousness': Patrick White's *The Solid Mandala.*" *Novel,* 2 (1969), 241-54.

MORLEY, PATRICIA A. *The Mystery Of Unity: Theme And Technique In The Novels Of Patrick White,* pp. 185-207.

PHILLIPS, A. A. " 'The Solid Mandala': Patrick White's New Novel." *Meanjin,* 25 (1966), 31-33.

WALSH, WILLIAM. *A Manifold Voice,* pp. 117-23.

_____. "Patrick White's Vision of Human Incompleteness: *The Solid Mandala* and *The Vivisector,*" in *Readings In Commonwealth Literature,* ed. William Walsh, pp. 420-25.

WATSON, BETTY L. "Patrick White, Some Lines of Development: *The Living And The Dead* to *The Solid Mandala.*" *Australian Literary Studies,* 5 (1971), 158-67.

WILKES, G. A. "An Approach to White's *The Solid Mandala.*" *Southerly,* 29 (1969), 97-110.

Reviews

BYATT, A. S. "The Battle Between Real People and Images." *Encounter,* 28, No.2 (1967), 71-78.

McCABE, BERNARD. *Saturday Review,* 12 February 1966, p. 36.

McLAREN, JOHN. "Recent Novels." *Overland,* No. 34 (1966), pp. 49-50.

TANNER, TONY. *London Magazine,* NS 6, No.3 (1966), 112-17.

WALSH, WILLIAM. "Patrick White's Vision of Human Incompleteness." *Journal Of Commonwealth Literature,* No.7 (1969), pp. 127-32.

THE TREE OF MAN (1956)

BARDEN, GARRETT. "Patrick White's *The Tree Of Man.*" *Studies: An Irish Quarterly Review,* 57 (1968), 78-85.

BESTON, JOHN B. "Dreams and Visions in *The Tree Of Man.*" *Australian Literary Studies,* 6 (1973/4), 152-66.

_____. "The Influence of *Madame Bovary* on *The Tree Of Man.*" *Revue De Littérature Comparée,* 46 (1972), 555-68.

BURROWS, J. F. "Stan Parker's *Tree Of Man.*" *Southerly,* 29 (1969), 257-79.

MACKENZIE, MANFRED. "Apocalypse in Patrick White's 'The Tree of Man.' " *Meanjin,* 25 (1966), 405-16.

MORLEY, PATRICIA A. *The Mystery Of Unity: Theme And Technique In The Novels Of Patrick White,* pp. 97-115.

RIEMER, A. P. "Visions of the Mandala in 'The Tree of Man.' " *Southerly,* 27 (1967), 3-19.

THOMSON, A. K. "Patrick White's *The Tree Of Man.*" *Meanjin,* 25 (1966), 21-30.

WALSH, WILLIAM. *A Manifold Voice,* pp. 98-106.

WILKES, G. A. "Patrick White's 'The Tree of Man.' " *Southerly,* 25 (1965), 23-33.

THE VIVISECTOR (1970)

BESTON, JOHN B. "Patrick White's *The Vivisector:* The Artist in

Relation to His Art." *Australian Literary Studies,* 5 (1971), 168–75.

BRADY, VERONICA. "The Artist and the Savage God: Patrick White's 'The Vivisector.'" *Meanjin,* 33 (1974), 136–45.

COE, RICHARD N. "The Artist and the Grocer: Patrick White's 'The Vivisector.'" *Meanjin,* 29 (1970), 526–29.

DOCKER, JOHN. "Patrick White and Romanticism: *The Vivisector.*" *Southerly,* 33 (1973), 44–61.

HERRING, THELMA. "Patrick White's *The Vivisector.*" *Southerly,* 31 (1971), 3–16.

MORLEY, PATRICIA A. "Doppelganger's Dilemma Artist and Man: 'The Vivisector.'" *Queen's Quarterly,* 78 (1971), 407–20.

————. *The Mystery Of Unity: Theme And Technique In The Novels Of Patrick White,* pp. 209–32.

RIEMER, A. P. "The Eye of the Needle: Patrick White's Recent Novels." *Southerly,* 34 (1974), 248–66.

SMITH, TERRY. "A Portrait of the Artist in Patrick White's 'The Vivisector.'" *Meanjin,* 31 (1972), 167–77.

TURNER, GEORGE. "A Hurtle Duffield Retrospective." *Overland,* No.50 (1972), 93–95.

WALSH, WILLIAM. "Patrick White's Vision of Human Incompleteness: *The Solid Mandala* and *The Vivisector,*" in *Readings In Commonwealth Literature,* ed. William Walsh, pp. 425–26.

Reviews

MCLAREN, JOHN. "Search for Truth." *Overland,* No.46 (1970/1), pp. 37–38.

OSBORNE, CHARLES. "The Artist's Life." *London Magazine,* NS 10, No.10 (1971), 98–101.

VOSS (1957)

BEATSON, ROBERT. "The Three Stages: Mysticism in Patrick White's *Voss.*" *Southerly,* 30 (1970), 111–21.

BESTON, JOHN B. "Alienation and Humanization, Damnation and Salvation in 'Voss.'" *Meanjin,* 30 (1971), 208–16.

———— AND ROSE MARIE BESTON. "The Theme of Spiritual Progression in Voss." *Ariel: A Review Of International English Literature,* 5, No.3 (1974), 99–114.

BRADY, VERONICA. "In My End is My Beginning: Laura as Heroine of *Voss.*" *Southerly,* 35 (1975), 16–32.

BURROWS, J. F. "'Voss' and the Explorers." *AUMLA,* No. 26 (1966), pp. 234–40.

DAY, MARTIN S. "Australian Fiction Scrutinizes National Life." *Forum,* 9, No.3 (1972), 4–5.

GZELL, SYLVIA. "Themes and Imagery in *Voss* and *Riders In The Chariot,*" in *Twentieth Century Australian Literary Criticism,* ed. Clement Semmler, pp. 252–67.

LAIDLAW, R. P. "The Complexity of *Voss.*" *Southern Review: Literary And Interdisciplinary Essays,* 4 (1970), 3–14.

MCAULEY, JAMES. "The Gothic Splendours: Patrick White's 'Voss.'" *Southerly,* 25 (1965), 34–44.

MCLAREN, JOHN. "Patrick White's Use of Imagery," in *Twentieth Century Australian Literary Criticism,* ed. Clement Semmler, pp. 268–72.

MORLEY, PATRICIA A. *The Mystery Of Unity: Theme And Technique In The Novels Of Patrick White,* pp. 117–52.

WALSH, WILLIAM. *A Manifold Voice,* pp. 105–12.

WILKES, G. A. "A Reading of Patrick White's 'Voss.'" *Southerly,* 27 (1967), 159–73.

WIEBE, RUDY (Canadian, 1934–)

THE BLUE MOUNTAINS OF CHINA (1970)

TIESSEN, HILDEGARD. "A Mighty Inner River: 'Peace' in the Fic-

tion of Rudy Wiebe." *Journal Of Canadian Fiction,* 2, No.4 (1973), 71–76.

FIRST AND VITAL CANDLE (1966)

Reviews

READ, S. E. "Maverick Novelist." *Canadian Literature,* No.31 (1967), pp. 76–77.

PEACE SHALL DESTROY MANY (1962)

TIESSEN, HILDEGARD. "A Mighty Inner River: 'Peace' in the Fiction of Rudy Wiebe." *Journal Of Canadian Fiction,* 2, No.4 (1973), 71–76.

THE TEMPTATIONS OF BIG BEAR (1973)

WIEBE, RUDY. "On the Trail of Big Bear." *Journal Of Canadian Fiction,* 3, No.2 (1974), 45–48.

Reviews

BARBOUR, DOUGLAS. "Original People." *Canadian Literature,* No.61 (1974), pp. 82–84.

BEVAN, ALLAN. *Dalhousie Review,* 54 (1974), 377–79.

DUECK, ALLAN. "A Sense of the Past." *Journal Of Canadian Fiction,* 2, No.4 (1973), 88–91.

ROEMER, KENNETH M. *World Literature Written In English,* 13 (1974), 263–64.

WIECHERT, ERNST (German, 1887–1950)

GENERAL

MATULIS, ANATOLE. "Lithuanian Folksong as a Philosophical 'Leitmotif' in German Literature: Ernst Wiechert." *Lituanus,* 12, No.4 (1966), 49–55.

WEGENER, ADOLPH. "Ernst Wiechert's Mater Dolorosa." *Germanic Notes,* 3 (1972), 26–28.

WIELAND, CHRISTOPH MARTIN (German, 1733–1813)

DIE GESCHICHTE DER ABDERITEN (1774)

YUILL, W. E. "Abderitis and Abderitism: Some Reflections on a Novel by Wieland," in *Essays In German Literature*—I, ed. F. Norman, pp. 72–91.

THE GOLDEN MIRROR (Der goldene spiegel, 1772)

MEYER, HERMANN. *The Poetics Of Quotation In The European Novel,* pp. 97–104.

THE TALE OF THE WISE DANISCHMEND (1775)

MEYER, HERMANN. *The Poetics Of Quotation In The European Novel,* pp. 104–24.

WIESEL, ELIE (Romanian, 1928–)

GENERAL

ALTER, ROBERT. "Elie Wiesel: Between Hangman and Victim," in his *After The Tradition,* pp. 151–60.

CARGAS, HARRY JAMES. "After Auschwitz: 'A Certain Script:' An Interview with Elie Wiesel." *Christian Century,* 17 September 1975, pp. 791–92.

FRIEDMAN, MAURICE. "Elie Wiesel—The Modern Job." *Commonweal,* 85 (1966), 48–52.

JOSELOFF, SAMUEL H. "Link and Promise: The Works of Elie Wiesel." *Southern Humanities Review,* 8 (1974), 163–70.

KNOPP, JOSEPHINE. "Wiesel and the Absurd." *Contemporary Literature,* 15 (1974), 212–20.

LEVIANT, CURT. "Elie Wiesel: A Soul on Fire." *Saturday Review,* 31 January 1970, pp. 25–28.

A BEGGAR IN JERUSALEM (Le Mendicant de Jérusalem, 1968)

Reviews

KOLBERT, JACK. *French Review,* 44 (1970), 189–90.

THE GATES OF THE FOREST (Les Portes de la forêt, 1964)

IDINOPULOS, THOMAS A. "The Holocaust in the Stories of Elie Wiesel." *Soundings,* 55 (1972), 200–15.

Reviews

CAPOUYA, EMILE. "The Cry of the Forsaken." *Saturday Review,* 28 May 1966, pp. 32–33.

DAICHES, DAVID. "'After Such Knowledge . . .'" *Commentary,* 40, No.6 (1965), 105–10.

HANDLIN, OSCAR. *Atlantic Monthly,* 217, No.6 (1966), 135–36.

KAHN, LOTHAR. "Books: The Jewish Novel." *Catholic World,* 204 (1967), 242–44.

NIGHT (La Nuit, 1958)

LANGER, LAWRENCE L. *The Holocaust And The Literary Imagination,* pp. 75–89.

THE OATH (Le Serment de kolvillag, 1973)

Reviews

LEVIANT, CURT. "Wrestling With Demons." *Saturday Review,* 12 January 1974, pp. 49–50.

MALIN, IRVING. "Worlds Within Worlds." *Midstream Magazine,* 20, No.2 (1974), 79–82.

WIESELTIER, LEON. "History as Myth." *Commentary,* 57, No.1 (1974), 66–67.

WILKINSON, Iris Guiver see HYDE, Robin

WILLIAMS, DENIS (Guyanese, 1923–)

OTHER LEOPARDS (1963)

JAMES, LOUIS. "Introduction," in *The Islands In Between,* ed. Louis James, pp. 7–10.

MOORE, GERALD. *The Chosen Tongue,* pp. 119–25.

———. "The Revenants," in *Readings In Commonwealth Literature,* ed. William Walsh, pp. 342–48.

WILSON, ETHEL (Canadian, 1888–1980)

GENERAL

BIRBALSINGH, FRANK. "Ethel Wilson: Innocent Traveller." *Canadian Literature,* No.49 (1971), pp. 35–46.

DAHLIE, HALLVARD. "Self-Conscious Canadians." *Canadian Literature,* No.62 (1974), pp. 10–11.

HINCHCLIFFE, P. M. "'To Keep the Memory of So Worthy a Friend': Ethel Wilson as an Elegist." *Journal Of Canadian Fiction,* 2, No.2 (1973), 62–67.

NEW, WILLIAM H. "The 'Genius' of Place and Time: The Fiction of Ethel Wilson." *Journal Of Canadian Studies,* 3, No.4 (1968), 39–48; rpt. in his *Articulating West,* pp. 68–82.

PACEY, DESMOND. "The Innocent Eye—The Art of Ethel Wilson," in his *Essays In Canadian Literature, 1938–1968,* pp. 90–100.

SONTHOFF, H. W. "The Novels of Ethel Wilson." *Canadian Literature,* No.26 (1965), pp. 33–42.

URBAS, JEANETTE. "Equations and Flutes." *Journal Of Canadian Fiction,* 1, No.2 (1972), 69–73.

———. "The Perquisites of Love." *Canadian Literature,* No.59 (1974), pp. 6–15.

HETTY DORVAL (1947)

MACDONALD, R. D. "Serious Whimsy." *Canadian Literature,* No.63 (1975), pp. 40–51.

PACEY, DESMOND. "Ethel Wilson's First Novel." *Canadian Literature,* No.29 (1966), pp. 43–55.

THE INNOCENT TRAVELLER (1949)

NEW, WILLIAM H. "The Irony of Order: Ethel Wilson's *The Innocent Traveller,*" in his *Articulating West,* pp. 83–92.

WISEMAN, ADELE (Canadian, 1928–)

CRACKPOT

Reviews

ENGEL, MARIAN. *Tamarack Review,* No.65 (1975), pp. 91–93.

ROSENTHAL, HELENE. "Comedy of Survival." *Canadian Literature,* No.64 (1975), pp. 115–18.

THE SACRIFICE (1956)

JONES, D. G. *Butterfly On Rock,* pp. 147–53.

STEPHENS, DONALD. "Lilacs out of the Mosaic Land: Aspects of the Sacrificial Theme in Canadian Fiction." *Dalhousie Review,* 48 (1968/9), 505–9.

SUTHERLAND, RONALD. "Cornerstone for a New Morality," in his *Second Image,* pp. 145–48.

WITKIEWICZ, STANISLAW IGNACY (Polish, 1885–1939)

GENERAL

MILOSZ, CZESLAW. "Stanislaw Ignacy Witkiewicz: A Polish Writer for Today." *Triquarterly,* No.9 (1967), pp. 143–54.

WITTIG, MONIQUE (French, 1935–)

LES GUÉRILLÈRES (1969)

DURAND, LAURA G. "Heroic Feminism as Art." *Novel,* 8 (1974), 71–77.

OSTROVSKY, ERIKA. "A Cosmogony of O: Wittig's *Les Guerillères,*" in *Twentieth Century French Fiction,* pp. 241–51.

THE OPOPANAX (L'Opoponox, 1964)

MCCARTHY, MARY. "Everybody's Childhood," in her *The Writing On The Wall And Other Literary Essays,* pp. 102–11.

Reviews

BALAKIAN, ANNA. "Child's World Without Wonder." *Saturday Review,* 2 July 1966, p. 33.

SONNENFELD, ALBERT. *Novel,* 2 (1969), 185–86.

WOHMANN, GABRIELE (German, 1932–)

GENERAL

WAIDSON, H. M. "The Short Stories and Novels of Gabriele Wohmann." *German Life And Letters,* 26 (1973), 214–27.

WOLF, CHRISTA (German, 1929–)

DIVIDED HEAVEN (Der geteilte himmel, 1963)

JENKINSON, D. E. "Three East German Novels." *Modern Languages,* 53 (1972), 119–21.

SCHLANT, ERNESTINE. "Fiction in the German Democratic Republic During the Past Decade." *Modern Fiction Studies,* 21 (1975), 151.

THE QUEST FOR CHRISTA T. (Nachdenken über Christa T., 1969)

PARKES, K. S. "An All-German Dilemma: Some Notes on the Presentation of the Theme of the Individual and Society in Martin Walser's *Halbzeit* and Christa Wolf's *Nachdenken Über Christa T.*" *German Life And Letters,* 28 (1974), 61–64.

SCHLANT, ERNESTINE. "Fiction in the German Democratic Republic During the Past Decade." *Modern Fiction Studies,* 21 (1975), 151–52.

ZIPES, JACK D. "Growing Pains in the Contemporary German Novel—East and West." *Mosaic,* 5, No.3 (1971/2), 13–14.

Reviews

MOSCOSO-GÓNGORA, PETER. *Saturday Review,* 8 May 1971, pp. 31–32.

WEYR, THOMAS. "Nachdenken über Christa T." *American-German Review,* 35, No.6 (1969), 27–28.

WOLKERS, JAN (Dutch, 1925–)

A ROSE OF FLESH

WOLF, MANFRED. "Our Daily Gall and Wormwood." *Saturday Review,* 15 April 1967, p. 37.

WRIGHT, BRUCE S. (Canadian, 1912–1975)

BLACK DUCK SPRING (1966)

Reviews

ERSKINE, J. S. *Dalhousie Review,* 46 (1966), 419–21.

WRIGHT, RICHARD B. (Canadian, 1937–)

IN THE MIDDLE OF A LIFE (1973)

Reviews

PARR, JOHN. "What Wright Hath Wrought." *Journal Of Canadian Fiction,* 3, No.1 (1974), 114–15.

WU CH'ENG-EN (Chinese, 1500–1582)

JOURNEY TO THE WEST (Hsi yu chi)

HSIA, C. T. *The Classic Chinese Novel,* pp. 115–64.

WU CHIANG (Chinese, 1910–)

RED SUN (Hung jih, 1958)

HUANG, JOE C. *Heroes And Villains In Communist China,* pp. 148–80.

WU CHING-TZU (Chinese, 1701–1754)

THE SCHOLARS (Ju-lin Wai-shih, 1768–1777)

HSIA, C. T. *The Classic Chinese Novel,* pp. 203–44.

WUNDERLICHEN NACBARSKINDER (Author Unknown)

MILFULL, JOHN. "The Function of the Novelle 'Die wunderlichen Nachbarskinder' in Goethe's *Die Wahlverwandtschaften.*" *German Life And Letters,* 25 (1971/2), 1–5.

Y

YACINE, KATEB (Algerian, 1929–)

NEDJMA (1956)

MORTIMER, MILDRED P. "Kateb Yacine in Search of Algeria: A Study of *Nedjma* and *Le Polygone Étoilé.*" *L'Esprit Créateur,* 12 (1972), 276–84.

LE POLYGONE ÉTOILÉ (1966)

MORTIMER, MILDRED P. "Kateb Yacine in Search of Algeria: A Study of *Nedjma* and *Le Polygone Étoilé.*" *L'Esprit Créateur,* 12 (1972), 284–88.

YAN YI-YEN See Lo Kuang-pin

YÁÑEZ, AGUSTÍN (Mexican, 1904–1980)

GENERAL

WALKER, JOHN L. "Timelessness through Memory in the Novels of Agustin Yáñez." *Hispania,* 57 (1974), 445–51.

THE EDGE OF THE STORM (Al filo del agua, 1947)

BRUSHWOOD, JOHN S. *The Spanish American Novel,* pp. 163–67.

DOUDOROFF, MICHAEL J. "Tensions and Triangles in 'Al filo del agua.'" *Hispania,* 57 (1974), 1–12.

DURAND, FRANK. "The Apocalyptic Vision of *Al Filo Del Agua.*" *Symposium,* 25 (1971), 333–46.

LANGFORD, WALTER M. *The Mexican Novel Comes Of Age,* pp. 71–72, 75–82.

O'NEILL, SAMUEL J. "Interior Monologue in 'Al Filo del Agua.'" *Hispania,* 51 (1968), 447–56.

SOMMERS, JOSEPH. *After The Storm,* pp. 37–68.

WALKER, JOHN L. "Subjective Time and Images in *Al Filo Del Agua.*" *Latin American Literary Review,* 1, No.2 (1973), 51–57.

THE LEAN LANDS (Las tierras flacas, 1962)

Reviews
CLEMENTS, ROBERT J. *Saturday Review,* 21 June 1969, pp. 60–61.

YANG MO (Chinese, 1915–)

THE SONG OF YOUTH (Ch'ing-ch'un chih ko, 1958)

HUANG, JOE C. *Heroes And Villains In Communist China,* pp. 56–73.

YASHPAL

GENERAL

MADHURESH. "The Social Purpose of Yashpal." *Indian Literature,* 11, No.3 (1968), 61–68.

AMITA

Reviews
KING, CHRISTOPHER R. *Literature East And West,* 19 (1975), 260–61.

YEHOSHUA, AVRAHAM B. (Israeli, 1936–)

GENERAL

ALTER, ROBERT B. "New Israeli Fiction." *Commentary,* 47, No.6 (1969), 59–66.

YIZHAR, S.

THE DAYS OF ZIKLAG

ALTER, ROBERT. "*The Days Of Ziklag*—In Search of a Cultural Past," in his *After The Tradition,* pp. 210–25.

YOSHITSUNE

Reviews
MINER, EARL. "Lucky in Love but Not in Life." *Saturday Review,* 11 June 1966, p. 58.

YOURCENAR, MARGUERITE

A COIN IN NINE HAND (Denier du rêve, 1934)

Reviews
BUCKNALL, BARBARA J. *French Review,* 45 (1972), 905–6.

Z

ZAMIATIN, EUGENE (Russian, 1884–1937)

GENERAL

EHRE, MILTON. "Zamyatin's Aesthetics." *Slavic And East European Journal,* 19 (1975), 288–96.

LAYTON, SUSAN. "Zamjatin and Literary Modernism." *Slavic And East European Journal,* 17 (1973), 279–87.

MUCHNIC, HELEN. "The Literature of Nightmare," in her *Russian Writers,* pp. 383–92.

SHANE, ALEX M. "Zamjatin's Prose Fiction." *Slavic And East European Journal,* 12 (1968), 14–26.

VORONSKY, A. K. "Evgeny Zamyatin." Trans. Paul Mitchell. *Russian Literature Triquarterly,* No.2 (1972), pp. 153–75.

WE (My, 1927)

BEAUCHAMP, GORMAN. "Future Words: Language and the Dystopian Novel." *Style,* 8 (1974), 462–76.

———. "Of Man's Last Disobedience: Zamiatin's *We* and Orwell's *1984.*" *Comparative Literature Studies,* 10 (1973), 285–93.

COLLINS, CHRISTOPHER. "Zamyatin, Wells and the Utopian Literary Tradition." *Slavonic And East European Review,* 44 (1966), 351–60.

———. "Zamjatin's *We* as Myth." *Slavic and East European Journal,* 10 (1966), 125–33.

GREGG, RICHARD A. "Two Adams and Eve in the Crystal Palace: Dostoevsky, the Bible, and *We.*" *Slavic Review,* 24 (1965), 680–87; rpt. in *Major Soviet Writers,* ed. Edward J. Brown, pp. 202–8.

LEWIS, KATHLEEN AND HARRY WEBER. "Zamyatin's *We,* The Proletarian Poets, and Bogdanov's *Red Star.*" *Russian Literature Triquarterly,* No.12 (1975), 253–78.

PARRINDER, PATRICK. "Imagining the Future: Zamyatin and Wells." *Science-Fiction Studies,* 1 (1973), 17–26.

RUSSELL, ROBERT. "Literature and Revolution in Zamyatin's *My.*" *Slavonic And East European Review,* 51 (1973), 36–46.

ULPH, OWEN. "I-330: Reconsiderations on the Sex of Satan." *Russian Literature Triquarterly,* No.9 (1974), pp. 262–75.

WHITE, JOHN J. "Mathematical Imagery in Musil's *Young Törless* and Zamyatin's *We.*" *Comparative Literature,* 18 (1966), 71–78.

Reviews

FITZLYON, KYRIL. *London Magazine,* NS 10, No.1 (1970), 103–6.

MIHAILOVICH, VASA D. *Saturday Review,* 6 May 1972, p. 88.

ZATZIKHOVEN, ULRICH VON

LANZELET

JACKSON, W. H. "Ulrich von Zatzikhoven's *Lanzelet* and the Theme of Resistance to Royal Power." *German Life And Letters,* 28 (1975), 285–97.

ZEMAN, Kamil see OLBRACHT, Ivan

ZESEN, PHILIPP VON (German, 1619–1689)

DIE ADRIATISCHE ROSEMUND (1645)

WAGENER, HANS. *The German Baroque Novel,* pp. 24–34.

ASSENAT (1670)

WAGENER, HANS. *The German Baroque Novel,* pp. 142–50.

ZIGLER UND KLIPHAUSEN, HEINRICH ANSELM VON (German, 1663–1696)

DIE ASIATISCHE BANISE (1689)

WAGENER, HANS. *The German Baroque Novel,* pp. 126–34.

ZOLA, ÉMILE ÉDUARD CHARLES ANTOINE (French, 1840–1902)

GENERAL

ALCORN, CLAYTON. "The Domestic Servant in Zola's Novels." *L'Esprit Créateur,* 11, No.4 (1971), 21–35.

BRAUDY, LEO. "Zola on Film: the Ambiguities of Naturalism." *Yale French Studies,* No.42 (1969), pp. 68–88.

BUTLER, R. "Zola between Taine and Sainte-Beuve: 1863–1869." *Modern Language Review,* 69 (1974), 279–89.

———. "Zola's Art Criticism (1865–1868)." *Forum For Modern Language Studies,* 10 (1974), 334–47.

DUNCAN, PHILLIP A. "Echoes of Zola's Experimental Novel in Russia." *Slavic And East European Journal,* 18 (1974), 11–19.

HEMMINGS, F. W. J. "Fire in Zola's Fiction: Variations on an Elemental Theme." *Yale French Studies,* No.42 (1969), pp. 26–37.

LERNER, MICHAEL G. "Edouard Rod and Emile Zola, II: From 'La Course à la Mort' to Dreyfus." *Nottingham French Studies,* 8 (1969), 28–39.

MAURIN, MARIO. "Zola's Labyrinths." *Yale French Studies,* No.42 (1969), pp. 89–104.

NEWTON, JOY. "Émile Zola and the French Impressionist Novel." *L'Esprit Créateur,* 13 (1973), 320–28.

SHOR, IRA NEIL. "The Novel in History: Lukács and Zola." *Clio,* 2 (1972), 19–41.

———. "Zola and *La Nouvelle Critique.*" *L'Esprit Créateur,* 11, No.4 (1971), 11–20.

TANCOCK, LEONARD. "On Translating Zola," in *Balzac And The Nineteenth Century,* pp. 377–89.

WALKER, PHILIP. "The Mirror, The Window, and the Eye in Zola's Fiction." *Yale French Studies,* No.42 (1969), pp. 52–67.

WALKER, PHILIP. "*The Octopus* and Zola: A New Look." *Symposium,* 21 (1967), 155–65.

———. "The Survival of Romantic Pantheism in Zola's Religious Thought." *Symposium,* 23 (1969), 354–65.

———. "Zola, Myth, and the Birth of the Modern World." *Symposium,* 25 (1971), 204–20.

———. "Zola: Poet of an Age of Transition." *L'Esprit Créateur,* 11, No.4 (1971), 3–10.

WEINBERG, HENRY H. "Some Observations on the Early Development of Zola's Style." *Romanic Review,* 62 (1971), 283–88.

L'ARGENT

GRANT, ELLIOTT M. *Émile Zola,* pp. 151–53.

HEMMINGS, F. W. J. *Emile Zola,* pp. 249–52.

L'ASSOMMOIR see GERVAISE

AU BONHEUR DES DAMES

GRANT, ELLIOTT M. *Émile Zola,* pp. 108–10.

CLAUDE'S CONFESSION (La Confession de Claude, 1865)

HEMMINGS, F. W. J. *Emile Zola,* pp. 16–19.

LA CURÉE

GRANT, ELLIOTT M. *Émile Zola,* pp. 64–67.

HEMMINGS, F. W. J. *Emile Zola,* pp. 91–97.

PETREY, SANDY. "Stylistics and Society in *La Curée.*" *MLN,* 89 (1974), 626–40.

LA DÉBÂCLE (1892)

GRANT, ELLIOTT M. *Émile Zola,* pp. 153–62.

HEMMINGS, F. W. J. *Emile Zola,* pp. 252–56.

SHOR, IRA NEIL. "The Novel in History: Lukács and Zola." *Clio,* 2 (1972), 33–36.

THE DEVIL'S COMPACT (Thérèse Raquin, 1867)

FURST, LILIAN R. "Zola's *Thérèse Raquin:* A Re-Evaluation." *Mosaic,* 5, No.3 (1972), 189–202.

GRANT, ELLIOTT M. *Émile Zola,* pp. 34–37.

HEMMINGS, F. W. J. *Emile Zola,* pp. 34–42.

LE DOCTEUR PASCAL (1893)

BUTOR, MICHEL. "Zola's Blue Flame." *Yale French Studies,* No.42 (1969), pp. 9–25.

HEMMINGS, F. W. J. *Emile Zola,* pp. 256–59.

LA FAUTE DE L'ABBÉ MOURET

BUTOR, MICHEL. "Zola's Blue Flame." *Yale French Studies,* No.42 (1969), pp. 15–16.

GRANT, ELLIOTT M. *Émile Zola,* pp. 74–78.

HEMMINGS, F. W. J. *Emile Zola,* pp. 105–9.

MUSEMECI, ANTONINO. "Tasso, Zola and the Vicissitudes of Pastoralism." *Nineteenth Century French Studies,* 4 (1976), 344–60.

FÉCONDITÉ

HEMMINGS, F. W. J. *Emile Zola,* pp. 290–96.

LA FORTUNE DES ROUGON

GERHARDI, GERHARD C. "Zola's Biological Vision of Politics: Revolutionary Figures in *La Fortune Des Rougon* and *Le Ventre De Paris.*" *Nineteenth Century French Studies,* 2 (1974), 164–77.

GRANT, ELLIOTT M. *Émile Zola,* pp. 59–64.

HEMMINGS, F. W. J. *Emile Zola,* pp. 76–80.

KANES, MARTIN. "*La Fortune Des Rougon* and the Thirty-Third Cousin." *L'Esprit Créateur,* 11, No.4 (1971), 36–44.

SCHOR, NAOMI. "Zola: From Window to Window." *Yale French Studies,* No.42 (1969), pp. 38–51.

GERMINAL (1885)

BAGULEY, DAVID. "The Function of Zola's Souvarine." *Modern Language Review,* 66 (1971), 786–97.

BERG, WILLIAM. "A Note on Imagery as Ideology in Zola's Germinal." *Clio,* 2 (1972), 43–45.

GOLDBERG, M. A. "Zola and Social Revolution: A Study of *Germinal.*" *Antioch Review,* 27 (1967/8), 491–507.

GRANT, ELLIOTT M. "A Correction in the Manuscript of *Germinal.*" *French Review,* 39 (1966), 521–22.

———. *Émile Zola,* pp. 113–31.

HAYMAN, DAVID. "The Broken Cranium—Headwounds in Zola, Rilke, Céline: A Study in Contrasting Modes." *Comparative Literature Studies,* 9 (1972), 207–15.

HEMMINGS, F. W. J. *Emile Zola,* pp. 186–211.

HOWE, IRVING. "Zola: The Genius of 'Germinal.'" *Encounter,* 34, No.4 (1970), 53–61.

MITTERAND, HENRI. "The Calvary of Catherine Maheu: The Description of a Page in *Germinal.*" *Yale French Studies,* No.42 (1969), pp. 115–25.

NEWTON, JOY. "Zola and Eisenstein." *French Review,* 44, Special Issue No.2 (1971), 106–16.

PASCO, ALLAN H. "Myth, Metaphor, and Meaning in *Germinal.*" *French Review,* 46 (1973), 739–49.

PETRY, D. SANDY. "The Revolutionary Setting of *Germinal.*" *French Review,* 43 (1969), 54–63.

ROSENBERG, RACHELLE A. "The Slaying of the Dragon: An Archetypal Study of Zola's *Germinal.*" *Symposium,* 26 (1972), 347–62.

SHOR, IRA NEIL. "The Novel in History: Lukács and Zola." *Clio,* 2 (1972), 26–33.

SMETHURST, COLIN. *Émile Zola: Germinal.*

TOPAZIO, VIRGIL W. "A Study of Motion in *Germinal.*" *Kentucky Foreign Language Quarterly,* 13, suppl. (1967), 60–70.

WALKER, PHILIP. "The *Ébauche* of *Germinal.*" *PMLA,* 80 (1965), 571–83.

GERVAISE (L'Assommoir, 1877)

BAGULEY, DAVID. "Event and Structure: The Plot of Zola's *L'Assommoir.*" *PMLA,* 90 (1975), 823–33.

BLOCK, HASKELL M. *Naturalistic Triptych,* pp. 16–31.

GRANT, ELLIOTT M. *Émile Zola,* pp. 83–97.

GROBE, EDWIN P. "Narrative Technique in *L'Assommoir.*" *L'Esprit Créateur,* 11, No.4 (1971), 56–66.

HEMMINGS, F. W. J. *Emile Zola,* pp. 110–27.

LAFRANCE, MARSTON. "Crane, Zola and the Hot Ploughshares." *English Language Notes,* 7 (1970), 285–87.

MICHOT-DIETRICK, HELA. "Blindness to :Goodness': The Critics' Chauvanism? An Analysis of Four Novels by Zola and the Goncourts." *Modern Fiction Studies,* 21 (1975), 216–18.

NIESS, ROBERT J. "Remarks on the *Style Indirect Libre* in *L'As-*

sommoir." *Nineteenth Century French Studies,* 3 (1975), 124–35.

PLACE, DAVID. "Zola and the Working Class: The Meaning of *L'Assommoir.*" *French Studies,* 28 (1974), 39–49.

THE HUMAN BEAST (La bête humaine, 1890)

GRANT, ELLIOTT M. *Émile Zola,* pp. 147–51.

HEMMINGS, F. W. J. *Émile Zola,* pp. 239–44.

———. "The Realist and Naturalist Movements in France," in *The Age Of Realism,* ed. F. W. J. Hemmings, p. 192.

LA JOIE DE VIVRE

HEMMINGS, F. W. J. *Émile Zola,* pp. 178–86.

LOURDES

HEMMINGS, F. W. J. *Émile Zola,* pp. 262–69.

MADELEINE FÉRAT (1868)

GRANT, ELLIOTT. *Émile Zola,* pp. 38–40.

HEMMINGS, F. W. J. *Émile Zola,* pp. 42–50.

LAFRANCE, MARSTON. "Crane, Zola, and the Hot Ploughshares." *English Language Notes,* 7 (1969/70), 285–87.

MICHOT-DIETRICH, HELA. "Blindness to 'Goodness': The Critics' Chauvinism? An Analysis of Four Novels by Zola and the Goncourts." *Modern Fiction Studies,* 21 (1975), 216–18.

THE GIN PALACE see GERVAISE

THE MASTERPIECE (L'Oeuvre)

BRADY, PATRICK. "Symbolic Structures of Mediation and Conflict in Zola's Fiction: From *Un Farce* to *Madam Sourdis* to *L'Oeuvre.*" *Sub-Stance,* No.2 (1971/2), pp. 85–92.

GRANT, ELLIOTT M. *Émile Zola,* pp. 132–37.

HEMMINGS, F. W. J. *Émile Zola,* pp. 211–25.

NIESS, ROBERT J. "George Moore and Émile Zola Again." *Symposium,* 20 (1966), 43–49.

———. *Zola, Cézanne, And Manet: A Study of <L'Oeuvre.>*

PASCO, ALLAN H. "The Failure of *L'Oeuvre.*" *L'Esprit Créateur,* 11, No.4 (1971), 45–55.

ZAMPARELLI, THOMAS. "Zola and the Quest for the Absolute in Art." *Yale French Studies,* No.42 (1969), pp. 143–58.

NANA (1880)

GRANT, ELLIOTT M. *Émile Zola,* pp. 101–7.

HEMMINGS, F. W. J. *Émile Zola,* pp. 133–41.

LAPP, JOHN C. "The Jealous Window-Watcher in Zola and Proust." *French Studies,* 29 (1975), 165–76.

MICHOT-DIETRICH, HELA. "Blindness to 'Goodness': The Critics' Chauvinism? An Analysis of Four Novels by Zola and the Goncourts." *Modern Fiction Studies,* 21 (1975), 219–21.

L'OEUVRE see THE MASTERPIECE

UN PAGE D'AMOUR

HEMMINGS, F. W. J. *Émile Zola,* pp. 129–33.

PARIS

GRANT, ELLIOTT M. "Zola and the Sacré-Coeur." *French Studies,* 20 (1966), 243–52.

HEMMINGS, F. W. J. *Émile Zola,* pp. 277–80.

NIESS, ROBERT J. "Zola's *Paris* and the Novels of the *Rougon-Macquart* Series." *Nineteenth Century French Studies,* 4 (1975/6), 89–104.

POT-BOUILLE (1882)

HEMMINGS, F. W. J. *Émile Zola,* pp. 141–46.

LES QUATRE ÉVANGILES

GRANT, ELLIOTT M. *Émile Zola,* pp. 174–77.

ROME

HEMMINGS, F. W. J. *Émile Zola,* pp. 269–74.

ROUGON-MACQUART

ALCORN, CLAYTON R. "The Child and his Milieu in the *Rougon-Macquart.*" *Yale French Studies,* No.42 (1969), pp. 105–14.

HEMMINGS, F. W. J. "The Elaboration of Character in the *Ébauches* of Zola's *Rougon-Macquart* Novels." *PMLA,* 81 (1966), 286–96.

———. "The Realist and Naturalist Movements in France," in *The Age Of Realism,* ed. F. W. J. Hemmings, pp. 184–87.

KAMM, LEWIS. "People and Things in Zola's *Rougon-Macquart*: Reification Re-humanized." *Philological Quarterly,* 53 (1974), 100–9.

———. "The Structural and Functional Manifestation of Space in Zola's *Rougon-Macquart.*" *Nineteenth Century French Studies,* 3 (1975), 224–36.

———. "Time and Zola's Characters in the *Rougon-Macquart.*" *Romance Notes,* 16 (1974), 83–86.

PETREY, SANDY. "Sociocriticism and *Les Rougon-Macquart.*" *L'Esprit Créateur,* 14 (1974), 219–35.

SON EXCELLENCE EUGÈNE ROUGON

GRANT, ELLIOTT M. *Émile Zola,* pp. 78–81.

HEMMINGS, F. W. J. *Émile Zola,* pp. 82–85.

LA TERRE (1887)

GRANT, ELLIOTT M. *Émile Zola,* pp. 137–45.

HEMMINGS, F. W. J. *Émile Zola,* pp. 225–36.

THÉRÈSE RAQUIN see THE DEVIL'S COMPACT

LES TROIS VILLES

GRANT, ELLIOTT M. *Émile Zola,* pp. 169–72.

TRUTH (Vérité, 1902)

HEMMINGS, F. W. J. *Émile Zola,* pp. 299–302.

ROSS, PETER. "Émile Zola, the Teachers and the Dreyfus Affair." *Nottingham French Studies,* 14 (1975), 77–85.

SHOR, IRA NEIL. "The Novel in History: Lukács and Zola." *Clio,* 2 (1972), 36–39.

LA VENTRE DE PARIS

GERHARDI, GERHARD C. "Zola's Biological Vision of Politics: Revolutionary Figures in *La Fortune Des Rougon* and *Le Ventre De Paris.*" *Nineteenth Century French Studies,* 2 (1974), 164–80.

GRANT, ELLIOTT M. *Émile Zola,* pp. 67–71.

HEMMINGS, F. W. J. *Émile Zola,* pp. 97–103.

ZOŠČENKO, MIXAIL (Russian, 1895–1958)

GENERAL

TITUNIK, I. R. "Mixail Zoščenko and the Problem of *Skaz.*" *California Slavic Studies,* 6 (1971), 83–96.

BEFORE SUNRISE (Pered voskhodom solntsa, 1937–43)

McLEAN, HUGH. "Zoschenko's Unfinished Novel: *Before Sunrise,*" in *Major Soviet Writers,* ed. Edward J. Brown, pp. 310–32.

BELATED SUNRISE

McLEAN, HUGH. "Belated Sunrise: A Review Article." *Slavic And East European Journal,* 18 (1974), 406–10.

ZUMTHOR, PAUL

LE PUITS DE BABEL (1969)

Reviews
ROSE, MARILYN GADDIS. *French Review,* 44 (1970), 190–91.

ZUNZUNEGUI, JUAN ANTONIO DE (Spanish, 1901-)

GENERAL

GUARDIOLA, CONRADO and ALFRED RODRÍGUEZ. "Some Aspects of the Character and Function of Poetry in the Novels of Zunzunegui." *Romance Notes,* 11 (1970), 487–91.

LA VIDA COMO ES

WINECOFF, JANET. "The Twentieth-Century Picaresque Novel and Zunzunegui's *La Vida Como Es.*" *Romance Notes,* 7 (1966), 108–12.

ZWEIG, STEFAN (Austrian, 1881–1942)

THE ROYAL GAME (Schachnovelle, 1942)

DAVIAU, DONALD G. and HARVEY I. DUNKLE. "Stefan Zweig's 'Schachnovelle.'" *Monatshefte,* 65 (1973), 370–84.

BIBLIOGRAPHY

The Achievement Of Isaac Bashevis Singer. Ed. Marcia Allentuck. Carbondale: Southern Illinois University Press, 1969.

ADAMS, M. IAN. *Three Authors Of Alienation: Bombal, Onetti, Carpentier.* Austin: University of Texas Press, 1975.

ADAMSON, DONALD. *The Genesis Of Le Cousin Pons.* Oxford University Press, 1966.

ADERETH, M. *Commitment In Modern French Literature: Politics And Society In Péguy, Aragon, And Sartre.* New York: Shocken Books, 1968.

Affinities: Essays In German And English Literature. Ed. R. W. Last. London: Oswald Wolff, 1971.

African Literature And The Universities. Ed. Gerald Moore. Ibadan: Ibadan University Press, 1965.

AFFRON, CHARLES. *Patterns Of Failure In La Comédie Humaine.* New Haven: Yale University Press, 1966.

The Age Of Realism. Ed. F. W. J. Hemings. Harmondsworth, Eng.: Penguin Books, 1974.

ALBÉRÈS, R. M. AND PIERRE DE BOISDEFFRE. *Kafka: The Torment Of Man.* New York: Philosophical Library, 1968.

Aleksandr Solzhenitsyn: Critical Essays And Documentary Materials. Ed. John B. Dunlop, Richard Haugh, and Alexis Klimoff. Belmont, Mass.: Nordland Publishing Co., 1973.

ALEXANDER, ALFRED. *Giovanni Verga: A Great Writer And His World.* London: Grant & Cutler, 1972.

ALT, A. TILO. *Theodor Storm.* New York: Twayne Publishers, 1973.

ALTER, ROBERT. *After The Tradition: Essays On Modern Jewish Writing.* New York: Dutton, 1969.

——— . *Partial Magic: The Novel As A Self-Conscious Genre.* Berkeley: University of California Press, 1975.

AMUR, G. S. *Manohar Malgonkar.* London: Arnold-Heinemann India, 1973.

ANDERSON, DONALD. *The Genesis Of Le Cousin Pons.* Oxford University Press, 1966.

APPIGNANESI, LISA. *Femininity & The Creative Imagination: A Study Of Henry James, Robert Musil & Marcel Proust.* London: Vision Press, 1973.

Approaches To The Twentieth-Century Novel. Ed. John Unterecker. New York: Thomas Y. Crowell Company, 1965.

ARGYLE, BARRY. *An Introduction To The Australian Novel, 1830-1930.* Oxford: Clarendon Press, 1972.

ARNOLD, ARMIN. *Friedrich Dürrenmatt.* New York: Ungar, 1972.

ATHERTON, JOHN. *Stendhal.* New York: Hilary House Publishers, 1965.

The Australian Nationalists: Modern Critical Essays. Ed. Chris Wallace-Crabbe. Melbourne: Oxford University Press, 1971.

BAKHTIN, M. M. *Rabelais And His World.* Trans. Helene Iswolsky. Cambridge, Mass.: M. I. T. Press, 1968.

BALES, RICHARD. *Proust And The Middle Ages.* Geneva: Librairie Droz, 1975.

Balzac And The Nineteenth Century: Studies In French Literature Presented To Herbert J. Hunt By Pupils, Colleagues And Friends. Ed. D. G. Charlton, J. Gaudon and Anthony R. Pugh.

Leicester: Leicester University Press, 1972.

BAND, ARNOLD J. *Nostalgia And Nightmare: A Study In The Fiction Of S. Y. Agnon.* Berkeley: University of California Press, 1968.

BARKSDALE, E. C. *The Dacha And The Duchess: An Application Of Levi-Strauss's Theory Of Myth In Human Creativity To Works Of Nineteenth-Century Russian Novelists.* New York: Philosophical Library, 1974.

BARNES, H. G. *Goethe's <Die Wahlverwandtschaften:> A Literary Interpretation.* Oxford: Clarendon Press, 1967.

BARNES, HAZEL E. *Sartre.* Philadelphia: J. B. Lippincott Company, 1973.

BARNES, JOHN. *Henry Kingsley And Colonial Fiction.* Australian Writers and Their Work. Melbourne: Oxford University Press, 1971.

BARROW, LEO L. *Negation In Baroja: A Key To His Novelistic Creativity.* Tucson: University of Arizona Press, 1971.

BART, B. F. *Madame Bovary And The Critics: A Collection Of Essays.* New York: New York University Press, 1966.

BASDEKIS, DEMITRIOS. *Miguel De Unamuno.* New York: Columbia University Press, 1969.

——— . *Unamuno And Spanish Literature.* University of California Publication in Modern Philology, vol. 85. Berkeley: University of California Press, 1967.

BATCHELOR, R. E. *Unamuno Novelist: A European Perspective.* Oxford: Dolphin Book Co., 1972.

BAUER, GEORGE HOWARD. *Sartre And The Artist.* Chicago: University of Chicago Press, 1969.

BAUMER, FRANZ. *Franz Kafka.* New York: Ungar, 1971.

——— . *Hermann Hesse.* New York: Ungar, 1970.

BAYERSCHMIDT, CARL F. *Sigrid Undset.* New York: Twayne Publishers, 1970

BAYLEY, JOHN. *Pushkin: A Comparative Commentary.* Cambridge: Cambridge University Press, 1971.

BEAUJOUR, ELIZABETH KLOSTY. *The Invisible Land: A Study Of The Artistic Imagination Of Iurii Olesha.* New York: Columbia University Press, 1970.

BECK, EVELYN TORTON. *Kafka And The Yiddish Theater, Its Impact On His Work.* Madison: University of Wisconsin Press, 1971.

BECKER, LUCILLE F. *Henry De Montherlant: A Critical Biography.* Carbondale: Southern Illinois University Press, 1970.

——— . *Louis Aragon.* New York: Twayne, 1971.

BELKNAP, ROBERT L. *The Structure Of The Brothers Karamazov.* The Hague: Mouton, 1967.

BENSON, RUTH C. *Women In Tolstoy: The Ideal And The Erotic.* Urbana: University of Illinois, 1973.

BERRY, MARGARET. *Mulk Raj Anand: The Man And The Novelist.* Amsterdam: Oriental Press, 1971.

BERSANI, LEO. *Balzac To Beckett: Center And Circumference In French Fiction.* New York: Oxford University Press, 1970.

——— . *Marcel Proust: The Fictions Of Life And Of Art.* New York: Oxford University Press, 1965.

BETTINSON, CHRISTOPHER D. *Gide: Les Caves Du Vatican.* London:

Edward Arnold, 1972.

BIASIN, GIAN-PAOLO. *The Smile Of The Gods: A Thematic Study Of Cesare Pavese's Works.* Ithaca, N.Y.: Cornell University Press, 1968.

BIEN, PETER. *Kazantzakis And The Linguistic Revolution In Greek Literature.* Princeton, N.J.: Princeton University Press, 1972.

_____. *Nikos Kazantzakis.* New York: Columbia University Press, 1972.

Black Africa. Ed. Albert S. Gerard. Jamaica, N.Y.: St. John's Press, 1972.

BLOCK, HASKELL M. *Naturalistic Triptych: The Fictive And The Real In Zola, Mann, And Dreiser.* New York: Random House, 1970.

BOAK, DENIS. *André Malraux.* Oxford: Clarendon Press, 1968.

BONHOMME, DENISE. *The Esoteric Substance Of Voltairian Thought.* New York: Philosophical Library, 1974.

BOULBY, MARK. *Hermann Hesse: His Mind And Art.* Ithaca, N.Y.: Cornell University Press, 1967.

_____. *Uwe Johnson.* New York: Ungar, 1974.

BOWEN, BARBARA C. *The Age Of Bluff: Paradox & Ambiguity In Rabelais & Montaigne.* Urbana: University of Illinois Press, 1972.

BOYD, ALEXANDER F. *Aspects Of The Russian Novel.* London: Chatto and Windus, 1972.

BRADBROOK, M. C. *Malcolm Lowry: His Art And Early Life.* London: Cambridge University Press, 1974.

BRAUN, LEV. *Witness Of Decline; Albert Camus: Moralist Of The Absurd.* Rutherford: Fairleigh Dickinson University Press, 1974.

BRÉE, GERMAINE. *Camus.* Revised edition. New Brunswick, N.J.: Rutgers University Press, 1972.

_____. *Marcel Proust And Deliverance From Time.* Trans. C. J. Richards and A. D. Truitt. Second edition. New Brunswick, N.J.: Rutgers University Press, 1969.

BRENCH, A. C. *The Novelists' Inheritance In French Africa: Writers From Senegal To Cameroon.* London: Oxford University Press, 1967.

BRESKY, DUSHAN. *The Art Of Anatole France.* The Hague: Mouton, 1969.

BRIDGWATER, PATRICK. *Kafka And Nietzsche.* Bonn: Bouvier Verlag Herbert Grundmann, 1974.

BRISSENDEN, ALAN. *Rolf Boldrewood.* Australian Writers and Their Work. Melbourne: Oxford University Press, 1972.

BROMBERT, VICTOR. *Stendhal: Fiction And The Themes Of Freedom.* New York: Random House, 1968.

BRØNNER, HEDIN. *Three Faroese Novelists.* New York: Twayne Publishers, 1973.

BROOKS, PETER. *The Novel Of Worldliness: Crebillon, Marivaux, Laclos, Stendhal.* Princeton, N.J.: Princeton University Press, 1969.

The Brothers Karamazov. Dutch Studies in Russian Literature, No.2. The Hague: Mouton, 1971.

BRUFORD, W. H. *The German Tradition Of Self-Cultivation: 'Bildung' From Humboldt To Thomas Mann.* London: Cambridge University Press, 1975.

BRUSHWOOD, JOHN S. *The Spanish American Novel: A Twentieth Century Survey.* Austin: University of Texas Press, 1975.

BUCK, STRATTON. *Gustave Flaubert.* New York: Twayne, 1972.

BUCKNALL, BARBARA J. *The Religion Of Art In Proust.* Illinois Studies in Language and Literature, No.60. Urbana: University of Illinois Press, 1969.

BÜDEL, OSCAR. *Pirandello.* New York: Hillary House, 1966.

BURG, DAVID and GEORGE FEIFER. *Solzhenitsyn.* New York: Stein and Day, 1972.

BURNE, GLENN S. *Julian Green.* New York: Twayne, 1972.

CALLAN, EDWARD. *Alan Paton.* New York: Twayne Publishers, 1968.

CAMUS, ALBERT. *Lyrical And Critical Essays.* Ed. Philip Thody. Trans. Ellen Conroy Kennedy. New York: A. Knopf, 1968.

CARDEN, PATRICIA. *The Art Of Isaac Babel.* Ithaca: Cornell University Press, 1972.

CARROLL, DAVID. *Chinua Achebe.* New York: Twayne, 1970.

CARTEY, WILFRED. *Whispers From A Continent: The Literature Of Contemporary Black Africa.* New York: Random House, 1969.

CASPER, LEONARD. *New Writing From The Philippines: A Critique And Anthology.* Syracuse, N.Y.: Syracuse University Press, 1966.

CATSORIS, JOHN A. *Azorin And The Eighteenth Century.* Madrid: Playor, 1973.

CATTAUI, GEORGES. *Marcel Proust.* Trans. Ruth Hall. New York: Funk & Wagnalls, 1967.

CHAPMAN, KENNETH G. *Tarjei Vesaas.* New York: Twayne Publishers, 1970.

A Choice Of Critics: Selections From Canadian Literature. Ed. George Woodcock. Toronto: Oxford University Press, 1966.

CHRISTIAN, R. F. *Tolstoy: A Critical Introduction.* Cambridge: Cambridge University Press, 1969.

CIHOLAS, KARIN NORDENHAUS. *Gide's Art Of The Fugue: A Thematic Study Of 'Les Faux-Monnayeurs.'* Chapel Hill: University of North Carolina Press, 1974.

CISMARU, ALFRED. *Boris Vian.* New York: Twayne Publishers, 1974.

_____. *Marguerite Duras.* New York: Twayne Publishers, 1971.

CITATI, PIETRO. *Goethe.* New York: Dial Press, 1974.

COE, RICHARD N. *The Vision Of Jean Genet.* London: Peter Owen, 1968.

COLEMAN, DOROTHY GABE. *Rabelais: A Critical Study In Prose Fiction.* Cambridge: University Press, 1971.

COLLINS, HAROLD R. *Amos Tutuola.* New York: Twayne Publishers, 1969.

The Contemporary Novel In German: A Symposium. Ed. Robert R. Heitner. Austin: University of Texas Press, 1967.

COOK, MERCER and STEPHEN E. HENDERSON. *The Militant Black Writer In Africa And The United States.* Madison: University of Wisconsin, 1969.

CORDLE, THOMAS. *Andre Gide.* New York: Twayne Publishers, 1969.

CORNGOLD, STANLEY. *The Commentators' Despair: The Interpretation Of Kafka's <Metamorphosis.>* Port Washington, N. Y.: Kennikat Press, 1973.

CORTLAND, PETER. *A Reader's Guide To Flaubert.* New York: Helios Books, 1968.

_____. *Sentiment In Flaubert's <Education Sentimentale.>* Muncie, Ind.: Ball State University Press, 1966.

_____. *The Sentimental Adventure: An Examination Of Flaubert's <Education Sentimentale.>* The Hague: Mouton, 1967.

COSTA, RICHARD HAUER. *Malcolm Lowry.* New York: Twayne Publishers, 1972.

COTTRELL, JANE E. *Alberto Moravia.* New York: Frederick Ungar Publishing Co., 1974.

COTTRELL, ROBERT D. *Simone De Beauvoir.* New York: Frederick Ungar Publishing Co., 1975.

COX, ROGER L. *Between Earth And Heaven: Shakespeare, Dostoevsky, And The Meaning Of Christian Tragedy.* New York: Holt, Rinehart and Winston, 1969.

CROSS, RICHARD K. *Flaubert And Joyce: The Rite Of Fiction.* Princeton, N.J.: Princeton University Press, 1971.

_____. *Malcolm Lowry: A Preface To His Fiction.* Chicago: University of Chicago Press, 1974.

Currents Of Thought In French Literature: Essays In Memory Of G. T. Clapton. New York: Barnes & Noble, 1966.

DAVEY, FRANK. *Earle Birney.* Copp Clark, 1971.

DAVIES, ROBERTSON. *Stephen Leacock.* Toronto: McClelland and Stewart, 1970.

DAVIES, RUTH. *The Great Books Of Russia.* Norman: University of Oklahoma Press, 1968.

DAVISON, NED. *Eduardo Barrios.* New York: Twayne Publishers, 1970.

DAY, DOUGLAS. *Malcolm Lowry: A Biography.* New York: Oxford University Press, 1973.

DE JONGE, ALEX. *Dostoevsky And The Age Of Intensity.* London: Secker & Warburg, 1975.

DELEUZE, GILLES. *Proust And Signs.* Trans. Richard Howard. New York: George Braziller, 1972.

DEYERMOND, A. D. *<Lazarillo De Tormes:> A Critical Guide.* London: Grant & Cutler, 1975.

DIAMOND, MARIE J. *Flaubert: The Problem Of Aesthetic Discontinuity.* Port Washington, N. Y.: Kennikat Press, 1975.

DÍAZ, JANET. *Ana María Matute.* New York: Twayne Publishers, 1971.

DILLER, EDWARD. *A Mythic Journey: Günter Grass's Tin Drum.* University Press of Kentucky, 1974.

The Discontinuous Tradition: Studies In German Literature In Honour Of Ernest Ludwig Stahl. Ed. P. F. Ganz. Oxford: Clarendon Press, 1971.

DOBRÉE, BONAMY. *Milton To Ouida: A Collection Of Essays.* London: Frank Cass and Co. Ltd., 1970.

DOOLITTLE, JAMES. *Alfred De Vigny.* New York: Twayne Publishers, 1967.

Doris Lessing: Critical Studies. Ed. Annis Pratt and L. S. Dembo. Madison: University of Wisconsin Press, 1974.

DRIVER, TOM F. *Jean Genet.* New York: Columbia University Press, 1966.

DUBRUCK, ALFRED. *Gérard De Nerval And The German Heritage.* London: Mouton Publishers, 1965.

DUGAN, JOHN RAYMOND. *Illusion And Reality: A Study Of Descriptive Techniques In The Works Of Guy De Maupassant.* The Hague: Mouton, 1973.

DYCK, J. W. *Boris Pasternak.* New York: Twayne, 1972.

EARLE, PETER G. *Prophet In The Wilderness: The Works Of Ezequiel Martínez Estrada.* Austin: University of Texas Press, 1971.

EBEL, HENRY. *After Dionysus: An Essay On Where We Are Now.* Rutherford: Fairleigh Dickinson University Press, 1972.

EDWARDS, SAMUEL. *Victor Hugo: A Tumultuous Life.* New York: David McKay, 1971.

EHRE, MILTON. *Oblomov And His Creator: The Life And Art Of Ivan Goncharov.* Princeton, N. J.: Princeton University Press, 1973.

ELDRIDGE, PAUL. *François Rabelais: The Great Story Teller.* South Brunswick: A. S. Barnes and Company, 1971.

ELLIS, J. M. *Kleist's 'Prinz Friedrich Von Homburg': A Critical Study.* University of California Publications in Modern Philology, vol. 97. Berkeley: University of California Press, 1970.

ELLIS, JOHN M. *Narration In The German Novelle: Theory And Interpretation.* Cambridge: Cambridge University Press, 1974.

EPSTEIN, PERLE S. *The Private Labyrinth Of Malcolm Lowry: Under The Volcano And The Cabbala.* New York: Holt, Rinehart and Winston, 1969.

ERLICH, VICTOR. *Gogol.* New Haven: Yale University Press, 1969.

Essays In German And Dutch Literature. Ed. W. D. Robson-Scott. London: University of London, 1973.

Essays In German Literature. Ed. F. Norman. London: London University Institute of Germanic Studies, 1965.

Essays In Honour Of John Humphreys Whitfield: Presented To Him On His Retirement From The Serena Chair Of Italian At The University Of Birmingham. Ed. H. C. Davis, D. G. Rees, J. M. Hatwell, and G. W. Slowey. London: St. George's Press, 1975.

Essays In Russian Literature: The Conservative View: Leontiev, Rozanov, Shestov. Ed. Spencer E. Roberts. Athens: Ohio University Press, 1968.

Essays on European Literature: In Honor Of Liselotte Dieckmann. Ed. Peter Uwe Hohendahl, Herbert Lindenberger, and Egon Schwarz. St. Louis: Washington University Press, 1972.

Essays On German Literature In Honour Of G. Joyce Hallamore. Ed. Michael S. Batts and Marketa Goetz Stankiewicz. Toronto: University of Toronto, 1968.

EVANS, I. O. *Jules Verne And His Work.* New York: Twayne Publishers, 1966.

F. M. Dostoevsky: 1821-1881. Ed. Nicholas Arseniev and Constantine Belousow. New York: Association of Russian-American Scholars, 1971.

FALK, EUGENE H. *Types Of Thematic Structure: The Nature And Function Of Motifs In Gide, Camus, And Sartre.* Chicago: University of Chicago Press, 1967.

FANGER, DONALD. *Dostoevsky And Romantic Realism: A Study Of Dostoevsky In Relation To Balzac, Dickens, And Gogol.* Cambridge: Harvard University Press, 1965.

FARRELLY, DANIEL J. *Goethe And Inner Harmony: A Study Of The 'Schöne Seele' In The <Apprenticeship Of Wilhelm Meister.>* Shannon, Ireland: Irish University Press, 1973.

FEUERLICHT, IGNACE. *Thomas Mann.* New York: Twayne Publishers, 1968.

FIELD, GEORGE W. *Hermann Hesse.* New York: Twayne Publishers, 1970.

FISCHER, G. K. *In Search Of Jerusalem: Religion And Ethics In The Writings Of A. M. Klein.* Montreal: McGill-Queen's University Press, 1975.

FLETCHER, JOHN. *A Critical Commentary On Flaubert's 'Trois Contes.'* London: Macmillan, 1968.

FLOWER, J. E. *Intention And Achievement: An Essay On The Novels Of François Mauriac.* Oxford: Clarendon Press, 1969.

———. *Roger Vailland: The Man And His Masks.* London: Hodder and Stoughton, 1975.

FLOWER, JOHN. *A Critical Commentary On Mauriac's 'Le Noeud De Vipères.'* London: Macmillan, 1969.

FOLEJEWSKI, ZBIGNIEW. *Maria Dabrowska.* New York: Twayne, 1967.

FORCIONE, ALBAN K. *Cervantes, Aristotle, And The Persiles.* Princeton, N. J.: Princeton University Press, 1970.

———. *Cervantes' Christian Romance: A Study Of <Persiles And Sigismunda.>* Princeton, N. J.: Princeton University Press, 1972.

FOSTER, DAVID WILLIAM. *Currents In The Contemporary Argentine Novel: Arlt, Mallea, Sabato, And Cortazar.* Columbia, Mo.: University of Missouri Press, 1975.

FOWLER, DOUGLAS. *Reading Nabokov.* Ithaca: Cornell University Press, 1974.

FOWLIE, WALLACE. *André Gide: His Life And Work.* New York: Macmillan, 1965.

———. *A Reading Of Proust.* Second Edition. Chicago: University of Chicago Press, 1975.

———. *Stendhal.* London: Macmillan Company, 1969.

Franz Kafka: A Collection Of Criticism. Ed. Eugene Ehrlich and Daniel Murphy. New York: McGraw-Hill, 1974.

FREEBORN, RICHARD. *The Rise Of The Russian Novel: Studies In The Russian Novel From Eugene Onegin To War And Peace.* Cambridge: Cambridge University Press, 1973.

The French Renaissance And Its Heritage: Essays Presented To Alan M. Bouse By Colleagues, Pupils And Friends. Ed. D. R. Haggis, Et. Al. London: Methuen, 1968.

FRIEDMAN, NORMAN. *Form And Meaning In Fiction.* Athens: University of Georgia, 1975.

FROHOCK, W. M. *Style And Temper: Studies In French Fiction, 1925-1960.* Cambridge: Harvard University Press, 1967.

From Verismo To Experimentalism: Essays On The Modern Italian Novel. Ed. Sergio Pacifici. Bloomington: Indiana University Press, 1969.

FURBANK, P. N. *Italo Svevo: The Man And The Writer.* Berkeley: University of California Press, 1966.

GALLAGHER, D. P. *Modern Latin American Literature.* London: Oxford University Press, 1973.

GARFIELD, EVELYN PICON. *Julio Cortázar.* New York: Ungar, 1975.

GARZILLI, ENRICO. *Circles Without Center: Paths To The Discovery And Creation Of Self In Modern Literature.* Cambridge: Harvard University Press, 1972.

GEAREY, JOHN. *Heinrich Von Kleist: A Study In Tragedy And Anxiety.* Philadelphia: University of Pennsylvania Press, 1968.

GIBSON, A. BOYLE. *The Religion Of Dostoevsky.* London: SCM Press, 1973.

GIBSON, ROBERT. *The Land Without A Name: Alain-Fournier And His World.* London: Paul Elek, 1975.

Gide: A Collection Of Critical Essays. Ed. David Littlejohn. Englewood Cliffs, N. J.: Prentice-Hall, 1970.

GIERGIELEWICZ, MIECZYSLAW. *Henryk Sienkiewicz.* New York: Twayne, 1968.

GILMAN, STEVE. *The Spain Of Fernando De Rojas: The Intellectual And Social Landscape Of <La Celestina.>* Princeton, N. J.: Princeton University Press, 1972.

GLEASON, JUDITH ILLSLEY. *This Africa: Novels By West Africans In English And French.* Evanston: Northwestern University Press, 1965.

GLENN, KATHLEEN M. *The Novelistic Technique Of Azorin.* Madrid: Playor, 1973.

Goethe: A Collection Of Critical Essays. Ed. Victor Lange. Englewood Cliffs: N. J.: Prentice-Hall, 1968.

Gogol From The Twentieth Century: Eleven Essays. Ed. Robert A. Maguire. Princeton, N. J.: Princeton University Press, 1974.

GOODHEART, EUGENE. *The Cult Of The Ego: The Self In Modern Literature.* Chicago: University of Chicago Press, 1968.

GRAHAM, VICTOR E. *The Imagery Of Proust.* Barnes & Noble, 1966.

The Grand Inquisitor. Ed. Jerry S. Wasserman. Columbus, Ohio: C. E. Merrill, 1970.

GRANT, ELLIOTT M. *Émile Zola.* New York: Twayne Publishers, 1966.

GRANT, RICHARD B. *The Goncourt Brothers.* New York: Twayne, Publishers, 1972.

———. *The Perilous Quest: Image, Myth, And Prophecy In The Narratives Of Victor Hugo.* Durham, N. C.: Duke University Press, 1968.

———. *Théophile Gautier.* Boston: Twayne Publishers, 1975.

GRAY, RONALD. *Franz Kafka.* Cambridge: Cambridge University Press, 1973.

———. *The German Tradition In Literature: 1871-1945.* Cambridge: Cambridge University Press, 1965.

———. *Goethe: A Critical Introduction.* London: Cambridge University Press, 1967.

GREENBERG, MARTIN. *The Terror Of Art: Kafka And Modern Literature.* New York: Basic Books, 1965.

GREENE, THOMAS M. *Rabelais: A Study In Comic Courage.* Englewood Cliffs, N. J.: Prentice-Hall, 1970.

GREENLEE, JAMES W. *Malraux's Heroes And History.* Dekalb: Northern Illinois University Press, 1975.

GROSSMAN, LEONID. *Dostoevsky: A Biography.* Indianapolis: Bobbs-Merrill, 1975.

GROSSVOGEL, DAVID I. *Limits Of The Novel: Evolutions Of A Form From Chaucer To Robbe-Grillet.* Ithaca, New York: Cornell University Press, 1968.

GULLACE, GIOVANNI. *Gabriele D'Annunzio In France: A Study In Cultural Relations.* Syracuse, N. Y.: Syracuse University Press, 1966.

GUMP, MARGARET. *Adalbert Stifter.* New York: Twayne Publishers, 1974.

GUNN, ELIZABETH. *A Daring Coiffeur: Reflections On <War And Peace> And <Anna Karenina.>* Totowa, N. J.: Rowman and Littlefield, 1971.

A Günter Grass Symposium. Ed. A. Leslie Willson. Austin: University of Texas Press, 1971.

GUTWIRTH, MARCEL. *Stendhal.* New York: Twayne Publishers, 1971.

GUZMAN, DANIEL DE. *Carlos Fuentes.* New York: Twayne, 1972.

HAAC, OSCAR A. *Marivaux.* New York: Twayne Publishers, 1973.

HADLEY, MICHAEL. *The German Novel In 1790: A Descriptive Account And Critical Bibliography.* Bern: Herbert Lang, 1973.

HAIG, STIRLING. *Madame De Lafayette.* New York: Twayne, 1970.

HALL, CALVIN S. and RICHARD E. LIND. *Dreams, Life, And Literature: A Study Of Franz Kafka.* Chapel Hill: University of North Carolina Press, 1970.

HALLBERG, PETER. *Halldór Laxness.* New York: Twayne, 1971.

HARRISON, ROBERT. *Samuel Beckett's Murphy: A Critical Excursion.* Athens: University of Georgia Press, 1968.

HATFIELD, HENRY. *Crisis And Continuity In Modern German Fiction: Ten Essays.* Ithaca: Cornell University Press, 1969.

HAYDEN, ROSE LEE. *An Existential Focus On Some Novels Of The River Plate.* East Lansing: Michigan State University Press, 1973.

HEATH, STEPHEN. *The Nouveau Roman: A Study In The Practice Of Writing.* London: Elek, 1972.

HEBBLETHWAITE, PETER. *Bernanos: An Introduction.* London: Bowes and Bowes, 1965.

HEINEY, DONALD. *Three Italian Novelists: Moravia, Pavese, Vittorini.* Ann Arbor: University of Michigan Press, 1968.

HELBLING, ROBERT E. *The Major Works Of Heinrich Von Kleist.* New York: New Directions, 1975.

HELLER, ERICH. *Franz Kafka.* New York: Viking Press, 1974.

HELLER, PETER. *Dialectics And Nihilsim: Essays On Lessing, Nietzsche, Mann And Kafka.* University of Massachusetts Press, 1966.

HEMMINGS, F. W. J. *Balzac: An Interpretation Of La Comedie Humaine.* New York: Random House, 1967.

———. *Emile Zola.* Second edition. Oxford: Clarendon Press, 1966.

HENDRICK, GEORGE. *Mazo De La Roche.* New York: Twayne Publishers, 1970.

HESELTINE, HARRY. *Vance Palmer.* St. Lucia: University of Queensland Press, 1970.

Hesse: A Collection Of Critical Essays. Ed. Theodore Ziolkowski. Englewood Cliffs, N. J.: Prentice-Hall, 1973.

HEWITT, JAMES ROBERT. *Marcel Proust.* New York: Frederick Ungar Publishing Co., 1975.

HIBBERD, JOHN. *Kafka In Context.* London: Studio Vista, 1975.

HIND-SMITH, JOAN. *Three Voices: The Lives Of Margaret Laurence, Gabrielle Roy, Frederick Philip Grove.* Toronto: Clarke, Irwin, 1975.

Hispanic Studies In Honour Of Joseph Manson. Ed. Dorothy M. Atkinson and Anthony H. Clarke. Oxford: Dolphin Book Co., 1972.

HOCHMAN, BARUCH. *The Fiction Of S. Y. Agnon.* Ithaca, N. Y.: Cornell University Press, 1970.

HOLDHEIM, W. WOLFGANG. *Theory And Practice Of The Novel: A Study On André Gide.* Geneve: Librairie Droz, 1968.

HOLLINGDALE, R. J. *Thomas Mann: A Critical Study.* London: Rupert Hart-Davis, 1971.

HORVATH, VIOLET M. *Andre Malraux: <The Human Adventure.>* New York: New York University Press, 1969.

HSIA, C. T. *The Classic Chinese Novel: A Critical Introduction.* New York: Columbia University Press, 1968.

———. *A History Of Modern Chinese Fiction.* Second edition. New Haven: Yale University Press, 1971.

HUANG, JOE C. *Heroes And Villains In Communist China: The Contemporary Chinese Novel As A Reflection Of Life.* New York: Pica Press, 1973.

Image And Theme: Studies In Modern French Fiction: Bernanos, Malraux, Sarraute, Gide, Martin Du Gard. Ed. W. M. Frohock. Cambridge: Harvard University Press, 1969.

Introduction To African Literature: An Anthology Of Critical Writing From 'Black Orpheus.' Ed. Ulli Beier. Evanston: Northwestern University Press, 1967.

An Introduction To Australian Literature. Ed. C. D. Narasimhaiah. Brisbane: Jacaranda Press, 1965.

Introduction To Nigerian Literature. Ed. Bruce King. New York: Africana Publishing Company, 1971.

IRELAND, G. W. *André Gide: A Study Of His Creative Writings.* Oxford: Clarendon Press, 1970.

ISER, WOLFGANG. *The Implied Reader: Patterns Of Communication In Prose Fiction From Bunyan To Beckett.* Baltimore: John Hopkins University Press, 1974.

The Islands In Between: Essays On West Indian Literature. London: Oxford University Press, 1968.

JAFFE, ADRIAN. *The Process Of Kafka's <Trial.>* East Lansing: Michigan State University Press, 1967.

JENKINS, CECIL. *André Malraux.* New York: Twayne Publishers, 1972.

———. *Mauriac.* New York: Barnes & Noble, 1965.

JEPHCOTT, E. F. N. *Proust And Rilke: The Literature Of Expanded Consciousness.* New York: Barnes & Noble, 1972.

JOHANNESSON, ERIC O. *The Novels Of August Strindberg: A Study In Theme And Structure.* Berkeley: University of California Press, 1968.

JOHNSON, ROBERT B. *Henry De Montherlant.* New York: Twayne Publishers, 1968.

JONES, D. G. *Butterfly On Rock: A Study Of Themes And Images In Canadian Literature.* Toronto: University of Toronto Press, 1970.

JONES, MARGARET E. W. *The Literary World Of Ana María Matute.* Lexington: University Press of Kentucky, 1970.

JOSEPHS, HERBERT. *Diderot's Dialogue Of Language And Gesture: Le Neveu De Rameau.* Columbus: Ohio State University Press, 1969.

JULLIAN, PHILIPE. *D'Annunzio.* New York: Viking Press, 1973.

KAHLER, ERICH. *The Inward Turn Of Narrative.* Trans. Richard and Clara Winston. Bolingen Series LXXXIII. Princeton: N. J.: Princeton University Press, 1973.

KAHLER, HAROLD. *The Passive Voice.* Athens: Ohio University Press, 1966.

KAHN, LOTHAR. *Insight And Action: The Life And Work Of Lion Feuchtwanger.* Rutherford: Fairleigh Dickinson University Press, 1975.

KANES, MARTIN. *Balzac's Comedy Of Words.* Princeton, N. J.: Princeton University Press, 1975.

KAPS, HELEN KAREN. *Moral Perspective In La Princesse De Clèves.* Eugene. University of Oregon Press, 1968.

KEATING, L. CLARK. *Critic Of Civilization: Georges Duhamel And His Writings.* University of Kentucky Press, 1965.

KENNER, HUGH. *A Reader's Guide To Samuel Beckett.* New York: Farrar, Straus and Giroux, 1973.

KENT, LEONARD J. *The Subconscious In Gogol And Dostoevskij And Its Antecedents.* Slavistic Printings and Reprintings. Ed. C. H. Van Schooneveld. The Hague: Mouton, 1969.

KILLAM, G. D. *The Novels Of Chinua Achebe.* New York: Africana, 1969.

KILPATRICK, HILARY. *The Modern Egyptian Novel: A Study In Social Criticism.* London: Ithaca Press, 1974.

KIMBALL, ARTHUR G. *Crisis In Identity And Contemporary Japanese Novels.* Rutland, Vt.: Charles E. Tuttle Co., 1973.

KIRK, IRINA. *Dostoevskij And Camus: The Themes Of Consciousness, Isolation, Freedom And Love.* Munchen: Wilhelm Fink, 1974.

KLIBBE, LAWRENCE H. *Jose Maria De Pereda.* Boston: Twayne Publishers, 1975.

KNAPP, BETTINA L. *Jean Genet.* New York: Twayne, 1968.

Knaves And Swindlers: Essays On The Picaresque Novel In Europe. Ed. Christine J. Whitbourn. London: Oxford University Press, 1974.

KOPP, RICHARD L. *Marcel Proust As A Social Critic.* Rutherford: Fairleigh Dickinson University Press, 1971.

KOSTIS, NICHOLAS. *The Exorcism Of Sex And Death In Julien Green's Novels.* The Hague: Mouton, 1973.

KRZYANOWSKI, JERZY R. *Wladyslaw Stanislaw Reymont.* New York: Twayne, 1972.

KUNA, FRANZ. *Kafka: Literature As Corrective Punishment.* Bloomington: Indiana University Press, 1974.

KURZ, PAUL KONRAD. *On Modern German Literature.* Trans. Mary Frances McCarthy. 4 vols. University, Alabama: University of Alabama Press, 1970-1977.

LANG, OLGA. *Pa Chin And His Writings: Chinese Youth Between The Two Revolutions.* Cambridge: Harvard University Press, 1967.

LANGENBRUCH, THEODORE. *Dialectical Humor In Hermann Kant's Novel 'Die Aula.'* Bonn: Bouvier, 1975.

LANGER, LAWRENCE L. *The Holocaust And The Literary Imagination.* New Haven: Yale University Press, 1975.

LANGFORD, WALTER M. *The Mexican Novel Comes Of Age.* Notre Dame: University of Notre Dame Press, 1971.

LARSON, CHARLES R. *The Emergence Of African Fiction.* Revised ed. Bloomington: Indiana University Press, 1972.

LARY, N. M. *Dostoevsky And Dickens: A Study Of Literary Influence.* London: Routledge and Kegan Paul, 1973.

LAST, REX W. *German Dadaist Literature: Kurt Schwitters, Hugo Ball, Hans Arp.* New York: Twayne Publishers, 1973.

LAURENCE, MARGARET. *Long Drums And Cannons: Nigerian Dramatists And Novelists.* New York: Frederick A. Praeger, 1968.

LAZERE, DONALD. *The Unique Creation Of Albert Camus.* New Haven: Yale University Press, 1973.

LEAL, LUIS. *Mariano Azuela.* New York: Twayne, 1971.

LEAVIS, F. R. *'Anna Karenina' And Other Essays.* London: Chatto & Windus, 1967.

LEBOWITZ, NAOMI. *Humanism And The Absurd In The Modern Novel.* Evanston, Ill.: Northwestern University Press, 1971.

LEGATE, DAVID M. *Stephen Leacock: A Biography.* Toronto: Doubleday Canada, 1970.

LEMAITRE, GEORGES. *Jean Giraudoux: The Writer And His Work.* New York: Ungar, 1971.

LENNIG, WALTER. *Portrait Of De Sade: An Illustrated Biography.* Trans. Sarah Twohig. New York: Herder and Herder, 1971.

LERNER, MICHAEL G. *Maupassant.* London: George Allen & Unwin Ltd., 1975.

LIMA, ROBERT. *Ramón Del Valle-Inclán.* New York: Columbia University Press, 1972.

LINDFORS, BERNTH. *Folklore In Nigerian Literature.* New York: Africana Publishing Company, 1973.

LINDSAY, J. M. *Gottfried Keller: Life And Works.* London: Wolff, 1968.

LINN, ROLF N. *Heinrich Mann.* New York: Twayne Publishers, 1967.

Lion Feuchtwanger: The Man, His Ideas, His Work. Ed. John M. Spalek. Los Angeles: Hennessey & Ingalls, 1972.

Literature And History In The Age Of Ideas: Essays On The French Enlightenment Presented To George R. Havens. Ed. Charles G. S. Williams. Columbus: Ohio State University Press, 1975.

Literature And National Identity: Nineteenth-Century Russian Critical Essays. Trans. and ed. Paul Debreczeny and Jesse Zeldin. Lincoln: University of Nebraska Press, 1970.

LOTT, ROBERT E. *Language And Psychology In <Pepita Jiménez.>* Urbana: University of Illinois Press, 1970.

LOWRIE, JOYCE O. *The Violent Mystique: Thematics Of Retribution And Expiation In Balzac, Barbey D'Aurevilly, Bloy And Huysmans.* Geneve: Librairie Droz, 1974.

LUKÁCS, GEORG. *Goethe And His Age.* Trans. Robert Anchor. New York: Grosset & Dunlap, 1968.

———. *Solzhenitsyn.* Trans. William David Graf. Cambridge: MIT Press, 1969.

LYNGSTAD, ALEXANDRA AND SVERRE LYNGSTAD. *Ivan Goncharov.* New York: Twayne, 1971.

McCARTHY, MARY. *The Writing On The Wall And Other Literary Essays.* New York: Harcourt, Brace & World, 1970.

McCLELLAN, EDWIN. *Two Japanese Novelists: Sōseki And Tōson.* Chicago: University of Chicago Press, 1969.

McGRADY, DONALD. *Mateo Alemán.* New York: Twayne, 1968.

Major Soviet Writers: Essays In Criticism. Ed. Edward J. Brown. London: Oxford University Press, 1973.

MAKOUTA-MBOUKOU, J. P. *Black African Literature: An Introduction.* Washington, D. C.: Black Orpheus, 1973.

Malcolm Lowry: The Man And His Work. Ed. George Woodcock. Vancouver: University of British Columbia Press, 1971.

MALONEY, BRIAN. *Italo Svevo: A Critical Introduction.* Edinburgh: Edinburgh University Press, 1974.

Marcel Proust: A Critical Panorama. Ed. Larkin B. Price. Urbana: University of Illinois Press, 1973.

MARE, MARGARET. *Annette Von Droste-Hülshoff.* Lincoln: University of Nebraska Press, 1965.

MARIAS, JULIÁN. *Miguel De Unamuno.* Trans. Frances M. López-Morillas. Cambridge, Mass.: Harvard University Press, 1966.

MARTIN, JUNE HALL. *Love's Fools: Aucassin, Troilus, Calisto And The Parody Of The Courtly Lover.* London: Tamesis Books Limited, 1972.

MASON, ANN L. *The Skeptical Muse: A Study Of Günter Grass' Conception Of The Artist.* Bern: Herbert Lang, 1974.

MASON, HAYDN. *Voltaire.* London: Hutchinson, 1975.

MASTERS, BRIAN. *Camus: A Study.* London: Heinemann, 1974.

———. *Sartre: A Study.* London: Heinemann, 1974.

———. *A Student's Guide To Sartre.* London: Heinemann Educational Books, 1970.

MASTERS, G. MALLARY. *Rabelaisian Dialect And The Platonic-Hermetic Tradition.* Albany: State University of New York Press, 1969.

MATTHEWS, J. H. *Surrealism And The Novel.* Ann Arbor: University of Michigan Press, 1966.

MAYER, HANS. *Steppenwolf And Everyman.* Trans. Jack Zipes. New York: Thomas Y. Crowell Co., 1971.

MEIN, MARGARET. *A Foretaste Of Proust: A Study Of Proust And His Precursors.* Westmead, Farnborough, Hants, England: Saxon House, 1974.

MENTON, SEYMOUR. *Prose Fiction Of The Cuban Revolution.* Austin: University of Texas Press, 1975.

MERCIER, VIVIAN. *The New Novel From Queneau To Pinget.* New York: Farrar, Straus, and Giroux, 1971.

MERTON, THOMAS. *Albert Camus' The Plague: Introduction And Commentary.* New York: Seabury Press, 1968.

MEYER, HERMANN. *The Poetics Of Quotation In The European Novel.* Trans. Theodore and Yetta Ziolkowski. Princeton: Princeton University Press, 1968.

MEYERS, JEFFREY. *Painting And The Novel.* Manchester: Manchester University Press, 1975.

MILES, DAVID H. *Hofmannsthal's Novel Andreas: Memory And Self.* Princeton, N. J.: Princeton University Press, 1972.

MILES, KEITH. *Günter Grass.* London: Vision Press, 1975.

MINOGUE, VALERIE. *Proust: Du Côté De Chez Swann.* London: Edward Arnold, 1973.

MITCHELL, JOHN. *Stendhal: Le Rouge Et Le Noir*. London: Edward Arnold, 1975.

MIYOSHI, MASAO. *Accomplices Of Silence: The Modern Japanese Novel*. Berkeley: University of California Press, 1974.

MOCHULSKY, KONSTANTIN. *Dostoevsky: His Life And Work*. Princeton, N. J.: Princeton University Press, 1967.

MODDY, CHRISTOPHER. *Solzhenitsyn*. New York: Harper & Row, 1973.

_____ . *Solzhenitsyn*. Rev. ed. New York: Harper & Row, 1975.

MOORE, GERALD. *The Chosen Tongue: English Writing In The Tropical World*. London: Longmans, 1969.

_____ . *Wole Soyinka*. Ibadan, Nigeria: Evans Brothers Limited, 1971.

MORLEY, PATRICIA A. *The Immoral Moralists: Hugh MacLennan And Leonard Cohen*. Toronto: Clarke, Irwin & Company, 1972.

_____ . *The Mystery Of Unity: Theme And Technique In The Novels Of Patrick White*. Montreal: McGill-Queen's University Press, 1972.

MORRIS, HERBERT. *The Masked Citadel: The Significance Of The Title Of Stendhal's La Chartreuse De Parme*. University of California Publications in Modern Philology, vol. 93. Berkeley: University of California Press, 1968.

MORRISETTE, BRUCE. *The Novels Of Robbe-Grillet*. Ithaca: Cornell University Press, 1975.

MORTON, DONALD E. *Vladimir Nabokov*. New York: Frederick Ungar Publishing Co., 1974.

MOSER, CHARLES A. *Pisemsky: A Provincial Realist*. Cambridge, Mass.: Harvard University Press, 1969.

MUCHNIC, HELEN. *Russian Writers: Notes And Essays*. New York: Random House, 1971.

MUIR, EDWIN. *Essays On Literature And Society*. Rev. ed. Cambridge: Harvard University Press, 1965.

MULHAUSER, RUTH E. *Sainte-Beauve And Greco-Roman Antiquity*. Cleveland: Press of Case Western Reserve University, 1969.

MYLNE, VIVIENNE. *The Eighteenth-Century French Novel: Techniques Of Illusion*. Manchester, Eng.: Manchester University Press, 1965.

_____ . *Prévost: Manon Lescaut*. London: Edward Arnold, 1972.

Nabokov: Criticism, Reminiscences, Translations And Tributes. Ed. Alfred Appel Jr. and Charles Newman. Evanston: Northwestern University Press, 1970.

Nabokov: The Man And His Work. Ed. L. S. Dembo. Madison: University of Wisconsin Press, 1967.

NADEAU, MAURICE. *The Greatness Of Flaubert*. New York: Library Press, 1972.

NEVILLE, DANIEL E. *Henry De Montherlant: A Contemporary Master*. Lawrence, Kansas, 1966.

NEW, WILLIAM H. *Articulating West: Essays On Purpose And Form In Modern Canadian Literature*. Toronto: New Press, 1972.

NEWBERRY, WILMA. *The Pirandellian Mode In Spanish Literature From Cervantes To Sastre*. Albany: State University of New York Press, 1973.

NEWCOMBE, JOSEPHINE M. *Leonid Andreyev*. New York: Frederick Ungar Publishing Co., 1973.

NIALL, BRENDA. *Martin Boyd*. Australian Writers and Their Work. Melbourne: Oxford University Press, 1974.

NIELSON, NIELS C., JR. *Solzhenitsyn's Religion*. Nashville: Thomas Nelson, 1975.

NIESS, ROBERT J. *Zola, Cézanne, And Manet: A Study Of <L'Oeuvre.>* Ann Arbor: University of Michigan Press, 1968.

NIMETZ, MICHAEL. *Humor In Galdós: A Study Of The Novelas Contemporáneas*. New Haven: Yale University Press, 1968.

NORTON, ROGER C. *Hermann Hesse's Futuristic Idealism: The Glass Bead Game And Its Predecessors*. Bern: Herbert Lang, 1973.

NOZICK, MARTON. *Miguel De Unamuno*. New York: Twayne Publishers, 1971.

NUTTALL, A. D. *A Common Sky: Philosophy And The Literary Imagination*. London: Chatto & Windus, 1974.

OBERHELMAN, HARLEY D. *Ernesto Sábato*. New York: Twayne Publishers, 1970.

O'BRIEN, JAMES A. *Dazai Osamu*. Boston: Twayne, 1975.

O'BRIEN, JUSTIN. *Contemporary French Literature: Essays*. Ed. Leon S. Roudiez. New Brunswick, N. J.: Rutgers University Press, 1971.

O'GORMAN, DONALD. *Diderot The Satirist*. Toronto: University of Toronto Press, 1971.

O'NAN, MARTHA. *The Role Of Mind in Hugo, Faulkner, Beckett And Grass*. New York: Philosophical Library, 1969.

OUSTON, PHILIP. *The Imagination Of Maurice Barrès*. Toronto: University of Toronto Press, 1974.

PACEY, DESMOND. *Essays In Canadian Criticism, 1938-1968*. Toronto: Ryerson Press, 1969.

PACIFICI, SERGIO. *The Modern Italian Novel: From Capuana To Tozzi*. Carbondale: Southern Illinois University Press, 1973.

_____ . *The Modern Italian Novel: From Manzoni To Svevo*. Carbondale: Southern Illinois University Press, 1967.

PALACHE, JOHN GARBER. *Four Novelists Of The Old Regime: Crebillon, Laclos, Diderot, Restif De La Bretonne*. New York: Haskell House Publishers, 1972.

PALMER, EUSTACE. *An Introduction To The African Novel: A Critical Study Of Twelve Books By Chinua Achebe, James Ngugi, Camara Laye, Elechi Amadi, Ayi Kwei Armah, Mongo Beti, And Gabriel Okara*. New York: Africana Publishing Corp., 1972.

PARIS, BERNARD J. *A Psychological Approach To Fiction: Studies In Thackery, Stendhal, George Eliot, Dostoevsky, And Conrad*. Bloomington: Indiana University Press, 1974.

Pasternak: Modern Judgements. Ed. Donald Davie and Angela Livingstone. Nashville: Aurora Publishers, 1970.

PATT, BEATRICE P. *Pío Baroja*. New York: Twayne Publishers, 1971.

PATTISON, WALTER THOMAS. *Benito Pérez Galdós*. Boston: Twayne Publishers, 1975.

PAYNE, ROBERT. *A Portrait Of André Malraux*. Englewood Cliffs, N. J.: Prentice-Hall, 1970.

PEACE, RICHARD. *Dostoevsky: An Examination Of The Major Novels*. Cambridge, Eng.: Cambridge University Press, 1971.

PEARCE, RICHARD. *Stages Of The Clown: Perspectives On Modern Fiction From Dostoevsky To Beckett*. Carbondale: Southern Illinois University Press, 1970.

PENUEL, ARNOLD M. *Charity In The Novels Of Galdós*. Athens: University of Georgia Press, 1972.

PERRY, BEN EDWIN. *The Ancient Romances: A Literary-Historical Account Of Their Origins*. Berkeley: University of California Press, 1967.

PERRY, KENNETH I. *The Religious Symbolism Of André Gide*. The Hague: Mouton, 1969.

Perspectives On African Literature: Selections From The Proceedings Of The Conference On African Literature Held At The University Of Ife 1968. Ed. Christopher Heywood. New York: Africana, 1971.

Perspectives On Fiction. Ed. James L. Calderwood and Harold E. Toliver. New York: Oxford University Press, 1968.

PETERSON, CAROL. *Max Frisch*. New York: Ungar, 1972.

PEYRE, HENRI. *Marcel Proust*. Columbia Essays on Modern Writers, 48. New York: Columbia University Press, 1970.

Pirandello: A Collection Of Critical Essays. Ed. Glauco Cambon. Englewood Cliffs, N. J.: Prentice-Hall, 1967.

POSGATE, HELEN B. *Madame De Staël*. New York: Twayne Publishers, 1968.

PREDMORE, RICHARD L. *Cervantes*. London: Thames & Hudson, 1973.

_____ . *The World Of Don Quixote*. Cambridge, Mass.: Harvard University Press, 1967.

PRITCHETT, V. S. *Balzac*. London: Chatto & Windus, 1973.

_____ . *The Working Novelist*. London: Chatto & Windus, 1965.

PROFFER, CARL R. *The Simile And Gogol's <Dead Souls.>* The Hague: Mouton, 1967.

Protest And Conflict In African Literature. Ed. Cosmo Pieterse and Donald Munro. New York: Africana, 1969.

QUILLIOT, ROGER. *The Sea And Prisons: A Commentary On The Life And Thought Of Albert Camus*. Trans. Emmett Parker. University of Alabama Press, 1970.

Rabelais. Ed. August Buck, Darmstadt. Wissenschaftliche Buchgesellschaft, 1973.

RABINOVICH, ISAIAH. *Major Trends In Modern Hebrew Fiction*. Trans. M. Roston. Chicago: University of Chicago Press, 1968.

RAGUSA, OLGA. *Luigi Pirandello.* Columbia Essays on Modern Writers, 37. New York: Columbia University Press, 1968.

RAHV, BETTY T. *From Sartre To The New Novel.* Port Washington, N. Y.: Kennikat Press, 1974.

RAHV, PHILIP. *Literature And The Sixth Sense.* Boston: Houghton Mifflin, 1969.

RAITT, A. W. *Prosper Mérimée.* London: Eyre & Spottiswoode, 1970.

RAITT, JANET. *Madame De Lafayette And 'La Princesse De Clèves'.* London: George G. Harrap, 1971.

RAMSCHAND, KENNETH. *The West Indian Novel And Its Background.* New York: Barnes & Noble, 1970.

RAND, MARGUERITE C. *Ramón Pérez De Ayala.* New York: Twayne Publishers, 1971.

RANDALL, FRANCES B. *N. G. Chernyshevskii.* New York: Twayne Publishers, 1967.

RASER, GEORGE B. *The Heart Of Balzac's Paris.* Choisy-le-Roi: Imprimerie de France, 1970.

RAVENSCROFT, ARTHUR. *Chinua Achebe.* London: Longmans, Green, 1969.

RAYMOND, JOHN. *Simenon In Court.* London: Hamish Hamilton, 1968.

REBAY, LUCIANO. *Alberto Moravia.* Columbia Essays on Modern Writers, 52. New York: Columbia University Press, 1970.

RECK, RIMA DRELL. *Literature And Responsibility: The French Novelist In The Twentieth Century.* Baton Rouge: Louisiana State University Press, 1969.

REDDICK, JOHN. *The 'Danzig Trilogy' Of Gunter Grass.* London: Secker & Warburg, 1975.

REDFERN, W. D. *The Private World Of Jean Giono.* Durham, N. C.: Duke University Press, 1967.

Rediscoveries: Informal Essays In Which Well-Known Novelists Rediscover Neglected Works Of Fiction By One Of Their Favorite Authors. Ed. David Madden. New York: Crown Publishers, 1971.

REEVE, F. D. *The Russian Novel.* New York: McGraw-Hill, 1966.

REICHERT, HERBERT W. *Friedrich Nietzsche's Impact On Modern German Literature: Five Essays.* University of North Carolina Studies in the German Languages and Literatures, No.84. Chapel Hill: University of North Carolina Studies in the German Languages and Literatures, No.84. Chapel Hill: University of North Carolina Press, 1975.

REIGSTAD, PAUL. *Rölvaag: His Life And Art.* Lincoln: University of Nebraska Press, 1972.

REINHARDT, KURT F. *The Theological Novel Of Modern Europe: An Analysis Of Masterpieces By Eight Authors.* New York: Frederick Ungar, 1969.

REISS, HANS. *Goethe's Novels.* Coral Gables, Fla.: University of Miami Press, 1969.

Renaissance And Other Studies In Honor Of William Leon Wiley. Ed. George Bernard Daniel. University of North Carolina Studies in Romance Languages and Literatures, No.72. Chapel Hill: University of North Carolina Press, 1968.

REVEL, JEAN FRANÇOIS. *On Proust.* Trans. Martin Turnell. New York: The Library Press, 1972.

REXROTH, KENNETH. *Classics Revisited.* Chicago: Quadrangle Books, 1968.

RICHARDSON, JOANNA. *Stendhal.* London: Victor Gollancz, 1974.

RICOU, LAURENCE. *Vertical Man/Horizontal World: Man And Landscape In Canadian Prairie Fiction.* Vancouver: University of British Columbia Press, 1973.

RIDGE, GEORGE R. *Joris-Karl Huysman.* New York: Twayne, 1968.

RIDGEWAY, R. S. *Voltaire And Sensibility.* Montreal: McGill-Queen's University Press, 1973.

ROBERTS, DAVID. *Artistic Consciousness And Political Conscience: The Novels Of Heinrich Mann, 1900-1938.* Berne: Herbert Lang & Co., 1971.

ROBINSON, MICHAEL. *The Long Sonata Of The Dead: A Study Of Samuel Beckett.* London: Rupert Hart-Davis, 1969.

RODINI, ROBERT J. *Antonfrancesco Grazzini: Poet, Dramatist, And Novelist, 1503-1584.* Madison: University of Wisconsin Press, 1970.

RODRÍGUEZ, ALFRED. *An Introduction To The Episodios Nacionales Of Galdós.* New York: Las Americas Publishing Co., 1967.

ROGERS, B. G. *Proust's Narrative Techniques.* Geneva: Librairie Droz, 1965.

ROGERS, ROBERT. *A Psychoanalytic Study Of The Double In Literature.* Detroit: Wayne State University Press, 1970.

ROLLESTON, JAMES. *Kafka's Narrative Theater.* University Park: Pennsylvania State University Press, 1974.

RORABACKER, LOUISE E. *Marjorie Barnard And M. Barnard Eldershaw.* New York: Twayne Publishers, 1973.

ROSBOTTOM, RONALD C. *Marivaux's Novels: Theme And Function In Early Eighteenth-Century Narrative.* Rutherford: Fairleigh Dickinson University Press, 1974.

ROSCOE, ADRIAN A. *Mother Is Gold: A Study In West African Literature.* Cambridge: Cambridge University Press, 1971.

ROSE, MARILYN GADDIS. *Julian Green: Gallic-American Novelist.* Berne: Herbert Lang, 1971.

ROSENGARTEN, FRANK. *Vasco Pratolini: The Development Of A Social Novelist.* Carbondale: Southern Illinois University Press, 1965.

ROSS, JOAN and DONALD FREED. *The Existentialism Of Alberto Moravia.* Carbondale: Southern Illinois University Press, 1972.

ROSS, STEPHEN D. *Literature & Philosophy: An Analysis Of The Philosophical Novel.* New York: Appleton-Century-Crofts, 1969.

ROSSI, VINIO. *André Gide: The Evolution Of An Aesthetic.* New Brunswick, N. J.: Rutgers University Press, 1967.

ROTHBERG, ABRAHAM. *Alexander Solzhenitsyn: The Major Novels.* Ithaca, N. Y.: Cornell University Press, 1971.

ROWE, WILLIAM W. *Dostoevsky: Child And Man In His Works.* New York: New York University Press, 1968.

ROWLAND, MARY F. AND PAUL ROWLAND. *Pasternak's 'Doctor Zhivago.'* Carbondale: Southern Illinois University Press, 1967.

ROZANOV, VASILY. *Dostoevsky And The Legend Of The Grand Inquisitor.* Trans. Spencer E. Roberts. Ithaca, N. Y.: Cornell University Press, 1972.

RUBIN, LOUIS D. *The Teller In The Tale.* Seattle: University of Washington Press, 1967.

RUTHERFORD, JOHN. *Leopoldo Alas: La Regenta.* London: Grant & Cutler, 1974.

RYAN, MARLEIGH GRAYER. *The Development Of Realism In The Fiction Of Tsubouchi Shōyō.* Seattle: University of Washington Press, 1975.

RYSTEN, FELIX S. A. *False Prophets In The Fiction Of Camus, Dostoevsky, Melville, And Others.* Coral Gables, Fla.: University of Miami Press, 1972.

SACHS, MURRAY. *The Career Of Alphonse Daudet.* Cambridge, Mass.: Harvard University Press, 1965.

SAMMONS, JEFFREY L. *Six Essays On The Young German Novel.* University of North Carolina Studies in the Germanic Languages and Literatures. Chapel Hill: University of North Carolina Press, 1972.

Samuel Beckett Now. Ed. Melvin J. Friedman. Chicago: University of Chicago Press, 1970.

SANDOZ, ELLIS. *Political Apocalypse: A Study Of Dostoevsky's Grand Inquisitor.* Baton Rouge: Louisiana State University Press, 1971.

SANSOM, WILLIAM. *Proust And His World.* London: Thames and Hudson, 1973.

SANTALÓ, JOAQUÍN. *The Tragic Import In The Novels Of Pérez Galdós.* Madrid: Playor, 1973.

SAVAGE, CATHARINE. *Malraux, Sartre, And Aragon As Political Novelists.* Gainesville: University of Florida Press, 1965.

Scandanavian Studies: Essays Presented To Dr. Henry Goddard Leach On The Occasion Of His Eighty-Fifth Birthday. Ed. Carl F. Bayerschmidt and Erik J. Friis. Seattle: University of Washington Press, 1965.

SCHEUERLE, WILLIAM H. *The Neglected Brother: A Study Of Henry Kingsley.* Tallahassee: Florida State University Press, 1971.

SCHILLING, BERNARD N. *The Comic Spirit: Boccaccio To Thomas Mann.* Detroit: Wayne State University Press, 1965.

————. *The Hero As Failure: Balzac And The Rubempré Cycle.* Chicago: University of Chicago Press, 1968.

SCHLUETER, PAUL. *The Novels Of Doris Lessing.* Carbondale: Southern Illinois University Press, 1973.

SCHÜTZ, HERBERT. *Hermann Kasack: The Role Of The Critical Intellect In The Creative Writer's Work. Bern: Herbert Lang, 1972.

SCHWARTZ, KESSEL. Juan Goytisolo. New York: Twayne, 1970.

SCHWARTZ, RONALD. José María Gironella. New York: Twayne, 1972.

SCOBIE, ALEXANDER. More Essays On The Ancient Romance And Its Heritage. Beltrage zur Klassischen Philologie, Band 46. Ernst Heitsch, Reinhold Merkelbach, and Clemens Zintzen. Meisenheim am Glan: Verlag Anton Hain, 1973.

SCOTT, NATHAN A. Craters Of The Spirit: Studies In The Modern Novel. Washington: Corpus Books, 1968.

SCOTT STOKES, HENRY. The Life And Death Of Yukio Mishima. London: Peter Owen, 1975.

SEDURO, VLADIMIR. Dostoevski's Image In Russia Today. Belmont, Mass.: Nordland, 1975.

SELTZER, ALVIN J. Chaos In The Novel: The Novel In Chaos. New York: Schocken, 1974.

SERRANO-PLAJA, ARTURO. 'Magic' Realism In Cervantes: Don Quixote As Seen Through Tom Sawyer And The Idiot. Berkeley: University of California Press, 1970.

SETCHKAREV, VSEVOLOD. Ivan Goncharov: His Life And His Works. Würzburg: Jal-Verlag, 1974.

The Shaken Realist: Essays In Modern Literature In Honor Of Frederick J. Hoffman. Ed. Melvin Friedman and John B. Vickery. Baton Rouge: Louisiana State University Press, 1970.

SHATTUCK, ROGER. Marcel Proust. New York: Viking Press, 1974.

SHEPPARD, RICHARD. On Kafka's Castle: A Study. London: Croom Helm, 1973.

SHERRINGTON, R. J. Three Novels By Flaubert: A Study Of Techniques. Oxford: Clarendon Press, 1970.

ŠILBAJORIS, RIMVYDAS. Perfection Of Exile: Fourteen Contemporary Lithuanian Writers. Norman: University of Oklahoma Press, 1970.

SIMMONS, ERNEST J. Feodor Dostoevsky. New York: Columbia University Press, 1969.

_____ . Introduction To Russian Realism. Bloomington: Indiana University Press, 1965.

_____ . Introduction To Tolstoy's Writings. Chicago: University of Chicago Press, 1968.

_____ . Tolstoy. London: Routledge & Kegan Paul, 1973.

SINHA, KRISHNA NANDAN. Mulk Raj Anand. New York: Twayne, 1972.

SINYAVSKY, ANDREI. For Freedom Of Imagination. New York: Holt, Rinehart and Winston, 1971.

SMETHURST, COLIN. Emile Zola: Germinal. Studies in French Literature No. 29. London: Edward Arnold, 1974.

SMITH, ALBERT B. Ideal And Reality In The Fictional Narratives Of Theophile Gautier. Gainesville: University of Florida Press, 1969.

SMITH, MAXWELL A. François Mauriac. New York: Twayne Publishers, 1970.

_____ . Jean Giono. New York: Twayne, 1966.

SMITH, VERITY. Ramón Del Valle-Inclán. New York: Twayne Publishers, 1973.

_____ . Valle-Inclán: Tirano Banderas. London: Grant & Cutler, 1971.

SOKEL, WALTER H. Franz Kafka. New York: Columbia University Press, 1966.

SOMMERS, JOSEPH. After The Storm: Landmarks Of The Modern Mexican Novel. Albuquerque: University of New Mexico Press, 1968.

SORELL, WALTER. Hermann Hesse: The Man Who Sought And Found Himself. London: Wolff, 1974.

SOUCY, ROBERT. Fascism In France: The Case Of Maurice Barrès. Berkeley: University of California Press, 1972.

SPAHR, BLAKE LEE. Anton Ulrich And Aramena: The Genesis And Development Of A Baroque Novel. Berkeley: University of California Press, 1966.

Spanish Thought And Letters In The Twentieth Century: An International Symposium Held At Vanderbilt University To Commemorate The Centenary Of The Birth Of Miguel De Unamuno, 1864-1964. Nashville: Vanderbilt University Press, 1966.

SPECTOR, ROBERT D. Pär Lagerkvist. New York: Twayne, 1973.

SPEAIGHT, ROBERT. Georges Bernanos: A Study Of The Man And Writer. New York: Liveright, 1974.

SPEIRS, LOGAN. Tolstoy And Chekhov. Cambridge: Cambridge University Press, 1971.

SPENCE, G. W. Tolstoy The Ascetic. Edinburgh: Oliver and Boyd, 1967.

SPRINGER, MARY DOYLE. Forms Of The Modern Novella. Chicago: University of Chicago Press, 1975.

SRINIVASA IYENGAR, K. R. Indian Writing In English. Second edition. New York: Asia Publishing House, 1973.

STACK, OSWALD. Pasolini On Pasolini: Interviews With Oswald Stack. London: British Thames and Hudson, 1969.

STAMBOLIAN, GEORGE. Marcel Proust And The Creative Encounter. Chicago: University of Chicago Press, 1972.

STARKIE, ENID. Flaubert The Master: A Critical And Biographical Study (1856-1880). London: Weidenfeld and Nicholson, 1971.

_____ . Flaubert: The Making Of The Master. New York: Atheneum, 1967.

STARKIE, WALTER. Luigi Pirandello: 1867-1936. Berkeley: University of California Press, 1965.

STEEL, ERIC M. Diderot's Imagery: A Study Of A Literary Personality. New York: Haskell House, 1966.

STEGNER, PAGE. Escape Into Aesthetics: The Art Of Vladimir Nabokov. New York: Dial Press, 1966.

STEINER, GEORGE. Literature And Silence: Essays On Language, Literature, And The Inhuman. New York: Atheneum, 1967.

STEWART, D. H. Mikhail Sholokov: A Critical Introduction. Ann Arbor: University of Michigan Press, 1967.

STOBIE, MARGARET R. Frederick Philip Grove. New York: Twayne, 1973.

STOLZFUS, BEN. Gide's Eagles. Carbondale: Southern Illinois University Press, 1969.

STOMECKY, O. The How Of Gogol: A Study Of The Methods And Sources Of Gogol. Huntsville: UAH Press, 1975.

STONE, DONALD. From Tales To Truths: Essays On French Fiction In The Sixteenth Century. Analecta Romanica Heft 34. Frankfurt am Main: Vittorio Klostermann, 1973.

STRICKLAND, GEOFFREY. Stendhal: The Education Of A Novelist. London: Cambridge University Press, 1974.

Studies In Eighteenth-Century French Literature. Ed. J. H. Fox, M. H. Waddicor and D. A. Watts. University of Exeter, 1975.

Studies In German Literature Of The Nineteenth And Twentieth Centuries: Festschrift For Frederic E. Coenen. Ed. Siegfied Mews. University of North Carolina Studies in Germanic Languages and Literatures, No.67. Chapel Hill: University of North Carolina Press, 1970.

Studies In Modern Spanish Literature And Art Presented To Helen F. Grant. Ed. Nigel Glendinning. London: Tamesis Books, 1972.

Studies In Spanish Literature Of The Golden Age Presented To Edward M. Wilson. Ed. R. O. Jones. London: Tamesis, 1973.

STURROCK, JOHN. The French New Novel: Claude Simon, Michel Butor, Alain Robbe-Grillet. London: Oxford University Press, 1969.

SUTHERLAND, RONALD. Frederick Philip Grove. Toronto: McClelland and Stewart, 1969.

_____ . Second Image: Comparative Studies In Quebec/ Canadian Literature. Toronto: New Press, 1971.

SWAIN, JAMES O. Juan Marín—Chilean: The Man And His Writings. Cleveland, Tenn.: Pathway Press, 1971.

TANK, KURT L. Günter Grass. New York: F. Ungar, 1969.

TAUBER, HERBERT. Franz Kafka: An Interpretation Of His Works. New York: Haskell House, 1967.

TAYLOR, M. E. M. The Arriviste: The Origins And Evolution Of The 'Arriviste' In The 19th Century French Novel With Particular Reference To Stendhal And Balzac. Bala, New Wales: Dragon Books, 1975.

TENNANT, P. E. Théophile Gautier. London: Athlone Press, 1975.

TETEL, MARCEL. Rabelais. New York: Twayne Publishers, 1967.

THEROUX, PAUL. V. S. Naipaul: An Introduction To His Work. New York: Africana Publishing Corp., 1972.

THODY, PHILIP. Jean Genet: A Study Of His Novels And Plays. New York: Stein and Day, 1968.

_____ . Laclos: Les Liaisons Dangereuses. London: Edward Arnold, 1970.

THOMAS, R. HINTON and WILFRIED VAN DER WILL. The German Novel

And The Affluent Society. Toronto: University of Toronto Press, 1968.

THORLBY, ANTHONY. *Kafka: A Study*. Totowa, N. J.: Rowman and Littlefield, 1972.

TILLETT, MARGARET. *Stendhal: The Background To The Novels*. London: Oxford University Press, 1971.

TOLSTOY, LEO. *War And Peace: The Maud Translation, Backgrounds And Sources, Essays In Criticism*. Ed. George Gibian. New York: W. W. Norton Company, 1966.

Tradition And Renewal: Essays On Twentieth-Century Latin American Literature And Culture. Ed. Merlin H. Forster. Urbana: University of Illinois Press, 1975.

TROYAT, HENRI. *Divided Soul: The Life Of Gogol*. Trans. Nancy Amphoux. Garden City, N. Y.: Doubleday, 1973.

———. *Tolstoy*. Trans. Nancy Amphoux. Garden City, N. Y.: Doubleday, 1967.

TRUEBLOOD, ALAN S. *Experience And Artistic Expression In Lope De Vega: The Making Of <La Dorotea.>* Cambridge, Mass.: Harvard University Press, 1974.

TURNER, DAVID. *Roles And Relationships In Otto Ludwig's Narrative Fiction*. University of Hull, 1975.

———. *Unamuno's Webs Of Fatality*. London: Tamesis Books, 1974.

Twentieth Century Australian Literary Criticism. Ed. Clement Semmler. Melbourne: Oxford University Press, 1967.

Twentieth Century French Fiction: Essays For Germaine Bree. Ed. George Stambolian. New Brunswick, N. J.: Rutgers University Press, 1975.

Twentieth Century Interpretations Of Crime And Punishment. Ed. Robert L. Jackson. Englewood Cliffs, N. J.: Prentice-Hall, 1974.

Twentieth Century Interpretations Of Molloy, Malone Dies, The Unnamable: A Collection Of Critical Essays. Ed. J. D. O'Hara. Englewood Cliffs, N. J.: Prentice-Hall, 1970.

Twentieth Century Interpretations Of <The Castle>: A Collection Of Critical Essays. Ed. Peter F. Neumeyer. Englewood Cliffs, N. J.: Prentice-Hall, 1969.

Twentieth-Century Russian Literary Criticism. Ed. Victor Erlich. New Haven: Yale University Press, 1975.

Unamuno: Creator And Creation. Ed. José Rubia Barcia and M. A. Zeitlin. Berkeley: University of California Press, 1967.

University Of British Columbia Hispanic Studies. Ed. Harold Livermore. London: Tamesis, 1974.

URZIDIL, JOHANNES. *There Goes Kafka*. Detroit: Wayne State University Press, 1968.

VALENZUELA, VICTOR M. *Contemporary Latin American Writers*. Long Island City, N. Y.: Las Americas, 1971.

VAN ABBÉ, DEREK. *Goethe: New Perspectives On A Writer And His Time*. London: Allen and Unwin, 1972.

VAREY, J. E. *Perez Galdos: Dona Perfecta*. London: Grant & Cutler, 1971.

VICKERY, WALTER N. *Alexander Pushkin*. New York: Twayne Publishers, 1970.

VIRTANEN, REINO. *Anatole France*. New York: Twayne Publishers, 1968.

Voltaire: A Collection Of Critical Essays. Ed. William F. Bottiglia. Englewood Cliffs, N. J.: Prentice-Hall, 1968.

WAGENER, HANS. *The German Baroque Novel*. New York: Twayne Publishers, 1973.

WAIDSON, H. M. *The Modern German Novel, 1945-1965*. Second ed. London: Oxford University Press, 1971.

WAIN, JOHN. *A House For The Truth: Critical Essays*. London: Macmillan, 1972.

WALLACE, A. H. *Guy De Maupassant*. New York: Twayne Publishers, 1973.

WALSH, P. G. *The Roman Novel: The 'Satyricon' Of Petronius And The 'Metamorphoses' Of Apuleius*. Cambridge: University Press, 1970.

WALSH, WILLIAM. *A Manifold Voice: Studies In Commonwealth Literature*. London: Chatto & Windus, 1970.

WARD, PATRICIA A. *The Medievalism Of Victor Hugo*. University Park: Pennsylvania State University Press, 1975.

WATSON-WILLIAMS, HELEN. *André Gide And The Greek Myth*. Oxford: Clarendon Press, 1967.

WEATHERS, WINSTON. *Par Lagerkvist: A Critical Essay*. Grand Rapids, Mich.: William B. Eerdmans, 1968.

WEINBERG, FLORENCE M. *The Wine & The Will: Rabelais's Bacchic Christianity*. Detroit: Wayne State University Press, 1972.

WEINBERG, KURT. *On Gide's <Prométhée:> Private Myth And Public Mystification*. Princeton, N. J.: Princeton University Press, 1972.

WEINSTEIN, ARNOLD L. *Vision And Response In Modern Fiction*. Ithaca, N. Y.: Cornell University Press, 1974.

WEISSTEIN, ULRICH. *Max Frisch*. New York: Twayne, 1967.

WHITE, JOHN J. *Mythology In The Modern Novel: A Study Of Prefigurative Techniques*. Princeton, N. J.: Princeton University Press, 1971.

WILLIAMS, CEDRIC E. *The Broken Eagle: The Politics Of Austrian Literature From Empire To Anschluss*. London: Paul Elek, 1974.

WILLIAMS, D. A. *Psychological Determinism In <Madame Bovary.>* Hull: University of Hull, 1973.

WILSON, ARTHUR M. DIDEROT. New York: Oxford University Press, 1972.

WOLITZ, SETH L. *The Proustian Community*. New York: New York University Press, 1971.

WOOD, MICHAEL. *Stendhal*. London: Elek, 1971.

WOODHOUSE, J. R. *Italo Calvino: A Reappraisal And An Appreciation Of The Trilogy*. University of Hull, 1968.

WOODWARD, JAMES. *Leonid Andreyev: A Study*. Oxford: Clarendon Press, 1969.

YARMOLINSKY, AVRAHAM. *Dostoevsky: Works And Days*. New York: Funk & Wagnalls, 1971.

YATES, NORRIS W. *Günter Grass: A Critical Essay*. Grand Rapids, Mich.: William B. Eerdmans, 1967.

YATES, W. E. *Grillparzer: A Critical Introduction*. Cambridge: University Press, 1972.

YOUNG, MICHAEL T. *Saint-Exupéry: Vol De Nuit*. London: Edward Arnold, 1971.

YU, BEONGCHEON. *Natsume Soseki*. New York: Twayne Publishers, 1969.

ZELLER, BERNHARD. *Portrait Of Hesse: An Illustrated Biography*. New York: Herder and Herder, 1971.

ZIOLKOWSKI, THEODORE. *Dimensions Of The Modern Novel: German Texts And European Contexts*. Princeton: Princeton University Press, 1969.

———. *The Novels Of Hermann Hesse: A Study In Theme And Structure*. Princeton, N. J.: Princeton University Press, 1965.

ZOLBROD, LEON M. *Takizawa Bakin*. New York: Twayne Publishers, 1967.

JOURNAL LIST

AUMLA: Journal of the Australasian University Language and
   Literature Association
African Literature Today
African Studies
African Studies Bulletin
African Studies Review
American Book Collector
American-German Review
American Imago: A Psychoanalytic Journal for Culture, Science
   & the Arts
American Quarterly
American Scandinavian Review
American Scholar
Anglia: Zeitschrift fur Englische Philologie
Approach: A Literary Quarterly
The Antioch Review
Ariel: A Quarterly Review of the Arts and Sciences in Israel
Ariel: A Review of International English Literature
Arizona Quarterly
Arlington Quarterly
Association for African Literature in English. Bulletin
Atlantic Monthly
Australian Letters
Australian Literary Studies

Ball State University Forum
Bibliothèque d'Humanisme et Renaissance
Black Images: A Critical Quarterly on Black Arts and Culture
Black Orpheus: Journal of African and Afro-American Literature
Books Abroad
Boundary 2: A Journal of Postmodern Literature
Bucknell Review: A Scholarly Journal of Letters, Arts, and
   Science
Bulletin Hispanique
Bulletin of Hispanic Studies

California Slavic Studies
Canadian-American Slavic Studies
Canadian Journal of African Studies/ Revue Canadienne des
   Etudes Africaines
Canadian Literature
Canadian Modern Language Review/ La Revue Canadienne des
   Langues Vivantes
Canadian Review of Comparative Literature/ Revue Canadienne
   de Littérature Comparée
Canadian Slavic Studies
Catholic World
Centennial Review
Chasqui: Revista de Literatura Latinoamericana
Chicago Review
Christian Century
Christian Scholar

Classical Journal
Clio: A Journal of Literature, History, and the Philosophy of
   History
College English
College Language Association Journal
College Literature
Colloquia Germanica: Internationale Zeitschrift fur Germanische
   Sprach-und Literaturwissenschaft
Colorado Quarterly
Columbia Forum
Columbia University Forum
Commentary
Commonweal
Comparative Literature
Comparative Literature Studies
Conch Review of Books: A Literary Supplement on Africa
Contemporary Literature
Contemporary Review
Cornhill
Critical Inquiry
Critical Quarterly
Critical Survey
Criticism: A Review of Literature and the Arts
Critique: Studies in Modern Fiction

Daedalus: Journal of the American Academy of Arts and Sciences
Dalhousie Review
Delta (Amsterdam)
Delta: The Cambridge Literary Magazine
Deutsche Vierteljahresschrift fur Literaturwissenschaft und
   Geistegeschichte
Diacritics: A Review of Contemporary Criticism
Dublin Review
Durham University Journal

East Europe
The Eighteenth Century: Theory and Interpretation
Eighteenth-Century Studies
Eire-Ireland: A Journal of Irish Studies
Emory University Quarterly
Encounter
English Journal
English Studies: A Journal of English Language and Literature
English Studies in Africa
English Studies in Canada
Essays in Criticism: A Quarterly Journal of Literary Criticism
Essays in Literature
L'Esprit Créateur
Explicator
Extrapolation

Forum (Houston)

Forum for Modern Language Studies
Forum Italicum
French Historical Studies
French Review: Journal of the American Association of Teachers
    of French
French Studies: A Quarterly Review

Genre
The Georgia Review
German Life and Letters
German Quarterly
Germanic Notes
Germanic Review

Harvard Journal of Asiatic Studies
Hibbert Journal
Hispania: A Journal Devoted to the Interests of the Teaching of
    Spanish and Portuguese
Hispanic Review
Hispanofila
Hudson Review
Humanities Association Review/ La Revue de l'Association des
    Humanities

Indian Horizons
Indian Literature
Indian Writing Today
International Fiction Review
Italian Quarterly
Italian Studies
Italianistica: Revista di Letterature Italiana
Italica

Journal of Aesthetics and Art Criticism
Journal of Arabic Literature
Journal of Asian Studies
Journal of Canadian Fiction
Journal of Canadian Studies
The Journal of Commonwealth Literature
Journal of English and Germanic Philology
Journal of European Studies
The Journal of Indian Writing in English
Journal of Japanese Studies
Journal of Modern African Studies
Journal of Modern Literature
Journal of Near Eastern Studies
Journal of South Asian Literature
Journal of Southeast Asian Studies
Journal of Spanish Studies: Twentieth Century
Journal of the American Oriental Society
Journal of the History of Ideas
Journal of the New African Literature and the Arts

Kansas Magazine
Kansas Quarterly
Kentucky Foreign Language Quarterly
Kentucky Romance Quarterly

Language and Style: An International Journal
Latin American Literary Forum
Literary Review: An International Journal of Contemporary Writing
Literature and Psychology
Literature/ Film Quarterly
Lituanus: Baltic States Quarterly of Arts and Culture
London Magazine
London Quarterly Review
Luso-Brazilian Review

MLN
Mary Wollstonecraft Journal
Massachusetts Review: A Quarterly of Literature, the Arts and
    Public Affairs
Meanjin

Medium AEvum
Michigan Quarterly Review
Midstream Magazine: A Monthly Jewish Review
Midwest Quarterly: A Journal of Contemporary Thought
Minnesota Review
Mnemosyne: Bibliotheca Classica Batava
Modern Age: A Quarterly Review
Modern Austrian Literature
Modern Fiction Studies
Modern Hebrew Literature
Modern Language Journal
Modern Language Quarterly
Modern Language Review
Modern Languages: Journal of the Modern Language Association
Modern Philology: A Journal Devoted to Research in Medieval
    and Modern Literature
Monatshefte: Für Deutschen Unterricht. Deutsche Sprache und
    Literatur
The Month
Mosaic: A Journal for the Interdisciplinary Study of Literature
Monumenta Nipponica
Mundus Artium: A Journal of International Literature and the
    Arts

Neophilologus
Neuphilologische Mitteilungen: Bulletin de la Societe Neophilolo-
    gique/ Bulletin of the Modern Language Society
New Catholic World
The New England Quarterly: A Historical Review of New
    England Life and Letters
New Orleans Review
Nineteenth-Century Fiction
Nineteenth-Century French Studies
Nottingham French Studies
Novel: A Forum on Fiction

Obsidian: Black Literature in Review
The Ohio Review
Ohio University Review
Overland

PMLA: Publications of the Modern Language Association of
    America
Papers on Language and Literature: A Journal for Scholars and
    Critics of Language and Literature
Partisan Review
The Personalist
Perspectives on Contemporary Literature
Philological Quarterly
Prairie Schooner
Presence Africaine: Revue Culturelle du Monde Noir/ Cultural
    Review of the Negro World
Psychoanalytic Review

Quarterly Review of Literature
Queen's Quarterly

Renaissance and Modern Studies
Renaissance News
Renaissance Quarterly
Renascence: Essays on Value in Literature
Reporter
Research in African Literatures
Review (Center for Inter-American Relations)
Review of National Literatures
Revista de Estudios Hispanicos
Revista Hispanica Moderna: Columbia University Hispanic
    Studies
Revue de Littérature Comparée
Revue des Langues Vivantes
Revue du Pacifique
Revue d'Histoire Litteraire de la France
Romance Notes

Romance Philology
Romanic Reivew
Romanische Forschungen
Rundschau: American-German Review
Russian Literature
Russian Literature Triquarterly
Russian Review: An American Quarterly Devoted to Russia Past
    and Present

Saturday Review
Scandinavian Review
Scandinavian Studies
Scandinavica: An International Journal of Scandinavian Studies
Science-Fiction Studies
Seminar: A Journal of Germanic Studies
Sewanee Review
Shenandoah
Slavic and East European Journal
Slavic Review: American Quarterly of Soviet and East European
    Studies
Slavonic and East European Review
Soundings: An Interdisciplinary Journal
South Atlantic Bulletin
Southerly: A Review of Australian Literature
Southern Humanities Reivew
Southern Review
Southern Review: Literary and Interdisciplinary Essays
Southwest Review
Soviet Review: A Journal of Translations
Soviet Studies in Literature
Studi Francesi
Studies: An Irish Quarterly Reivew
Studies in Black Literature
Studies in Burke and His Time
Studies in Contemporary Satire: A Creative and Critical Journal
Studies in Philology
Studies in Romanticism
Studies in Short Fiction

Studies in the Humanities
Studies in the Literary Imagination
Studies in the Novel
Studies in the Renaissance
Studies in Twentieth Century Literature
Style
Sub-Stance: A Review of Theory and Literary Criticism
Survey: A Journal of East & West Studies
Survey: A Journal of Soviet and East European Studies
Symposium

Texas Quarterly
Texas Studies in Literature and Language: A Journal of the
    Humanities
Thought: A Review of Culture and Idea
TriQuarterly
Triveni: Journal of Indian Renaissance
Twentieth Century
Twentieth Century Literature: A Scholarly and Critical Journal

THE USF Language Quarterly
University of Toronto Quarterly: A Canadian Journal of the
    Humanities

Virginia Quarterly Review: A National Journal of Literature and
    Discussion

Western Humanities Review
Wisconsin Studies in Contemporary Literature
Women & Literature
Women's Studies: An Interdisciplinary Journal
World Literature Written in English

Xavier University Studies: A Journal of Critical and Creative
    Scholarship

Yale French Studies
Yale Review: A National Quarterly

A Note about the Author

Harriet Semmes Alexander is Reference Librarian and Assistant Professor at Memphis State University.